Voyages
Childhood and Adolescence

Spencer A. Rathus
New York University

THOMSON
WADSWORTH

Australia • Canada • Mexico • Singapore • Spain • United Kingdom • United States

THOMSON

WADSWORTH

Psychology Publisher: Edith Beard Brady
Development Editor: Sherry Symington
Editorial Assistant: Maritess A. Tse
Technology Project Manager: Michelle Vardeman
Executive Marketing Manager: Caroline Croley
Marketing Assistant: Laurel Anderson
Advertising Project Manager: Tami Strang
Project Manager, Editorial Production: Lisa Weber
Print/Media Buyer: Karen Hunt
Permissions Editor: Robert Kauser

Production: Mary Douglas, Rogue Valley Publications
Text Designer: Roy Neuhaus
Photo Researcher: Myrna Engler
Copy Editor: Joan Pendleton
Illustrator: Precision Graphics
Cover Designers: Roy Neuhaus and Stephen Rapley
Cover Image: Richard Simpson/FPG
Cover Printer: Phoenix Color Corp.
Compositor: New England Typographic Service
Printer: Quebecor/World, Versailles

Printed in the United States of America
1 2 3 4 5 6 7 06 05 04 03 02

For more information about our products, contact us at:
Thomson Learning Academic Resource Center
1-800-423-0563

For permission to use material from this text, contact us by:
Phone: 1-800-730-2214 **Fax:** 1-800-730-2215
Web: http://www.thomsonrights.com

Library of Congress Control Number: 2002107777

Student Edition with InfoTrac College Edition ISBN 0-534-52785-X

Student Edition without InfoTrac College Edition ISBN 0-534-52802-3

Instructor's Edition ISBN 0-534-52795-7

Wadsworth/Thomson Learning
10 Davis Drive
Belmont, CA 94002-3098
USA

Asia
Thomson Learning
60 Albert Street, #15-01
Albert Complex
Singapore 189969

Australia
Nelson Thomson Learning
102 Dodds Street
South Melbourne, Victoria 3205
Australia

Canada
Nelson Thomson Learning
1120 Birchmount Road
Toronto, Ontario M1K 5G4
Canada

Europe/Middle East/Africa
Thomson Learning
Berkshire House
168-173 High Holborn
London WC1V 7AA
United Kingdom

Latin America
Thomson Learning
Seneca, 53
Colonia Polanco
11560 Mexico D.F.
Mexico

Spain
Paraninfo Thomson Learning
Calle/Magallanes, 25
28015 Madrid, Spain

To whom would I dedicate **Voyages: Childhood and Adolescence** *if not to my own children? In addition to providing me with love and focus in life, they have demonstrated how different children can be in temperament and in specific talents, even when the environmental backgrounds are similar. One, Jill, has become a psychologist. The lives of the others—Allyn, Jordan, and Taylor—revolve around the performing and visual arts, yet they each have their unique strengths. All are a continual pleasure. I thank them for the inspiration and the education they have given me.*

About the Author

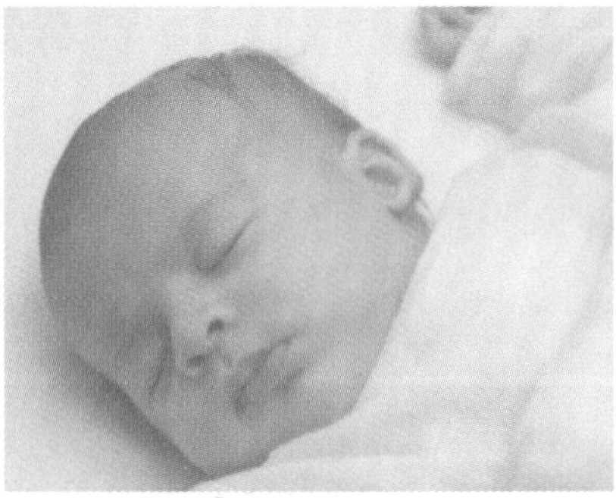

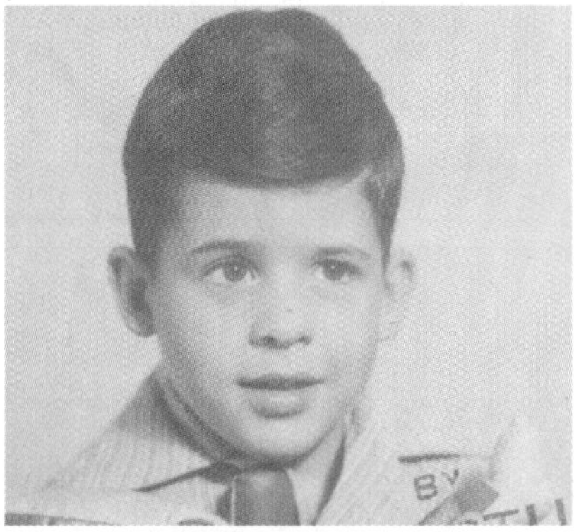

Numerous personal experiences enter into Rathus's textbooks. For example, he was the first member of his family to go to college. He found college textbooks to be cold and intimidating, and when his opportunity came to write college textbooks, he wanted them to be different—warm and encouraging, especially to students who were also the first generation in their families to be entering college.

Rathus's first professional experience was in teaching high school English. Part of the task of the high school teacher is to motivate students, and so motivating students, humor, and personal stories became part of his textbook approach. Rathus wrote poetry and novels while he was an English teacher—and some of the poetry was published in poetry journals. The novels never saw the light of day (which is just as well, Rathus admits).

Rathus earned his Ph.D. in psychology more years ago than he would like to admit, and he entered clinical practice and teaching. Still interested in writing, he co-authored a Doubleday nonfiction book—*BT: Behavior Therapy Strategies for Solving Problems in Living.*

Rathus went on to publish more than twenty research articles in journals such as *Adolescence, Behavior Therapy, Journal of Clinical Psychology, Behaviour Research and Therapy, Journal of Behavior Therapy and Experimental Psychiatry,* and *Criminology*. His research interests lie in the areas of human growth and development, psychological disorders, methods of therapy, and psychological assessment. Foremost among his research publications was that of the Rathus Assertiveness Schedule. The "RAS" remains widely used in research and clinical practice and has been referenced often enough to become a "citation classic."

Rathus has since poured his energies into his textbooks, while teaching at Northeastern University, St. John's University, and currently at New York University. His introductory psychology textbook, *Psychology in the New Millennium*, is in its eighth edition.

Rathus is proud of his family. His wife chairs her department. Two of his daughters attend New York University's Tisch School of the Arts, one as a musical theatre major and the other in film/video production. The youngest, a fifth-grader, can dance the pants off of both of them. The oldest daughter has become a psychologist (a case of profession-envy) and teaches at C. W. Post College of Long Island University.

The author at various stages of development

I (S.R.) was asked to submit a more recent photo, but believed that the above were more appropriate because they cover the periods of development in this text and because I still wear blue jeans and sneakers whenever possible.

Brief Contents

Contents

Part I ■ What Is Child Development?

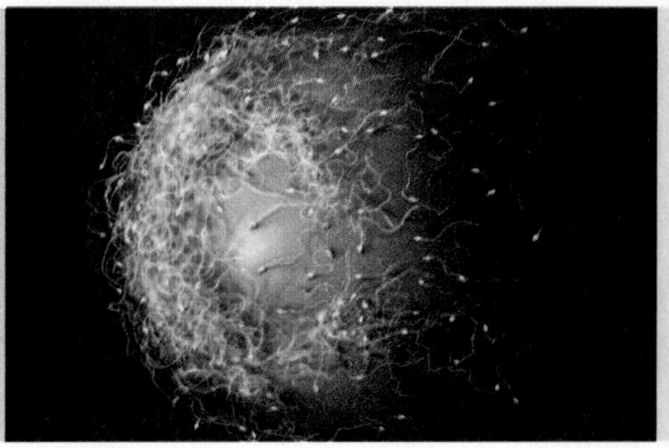

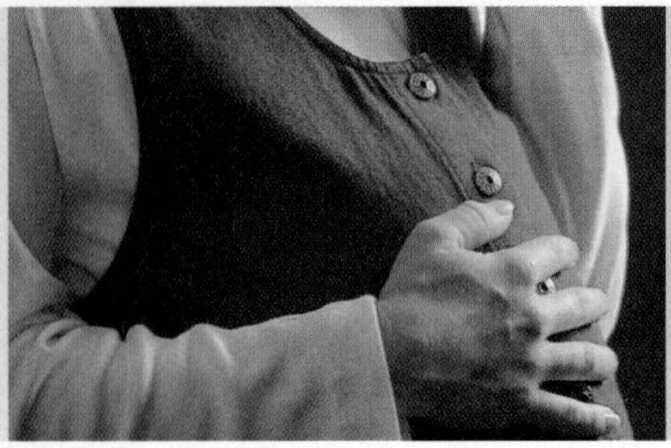
© American Cancer Society

© Elizabeth Crews

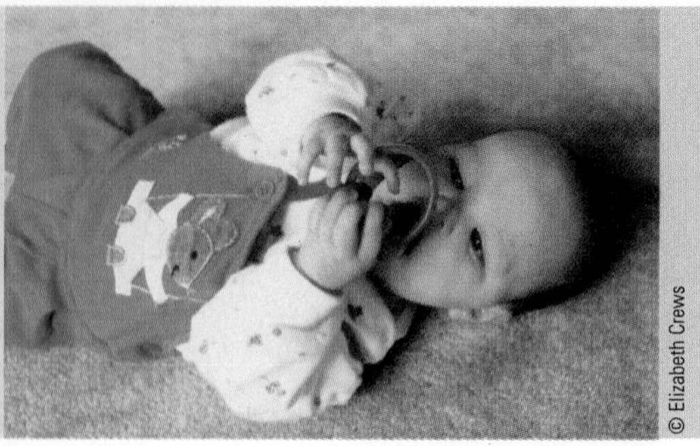
© Elizabeth Crews

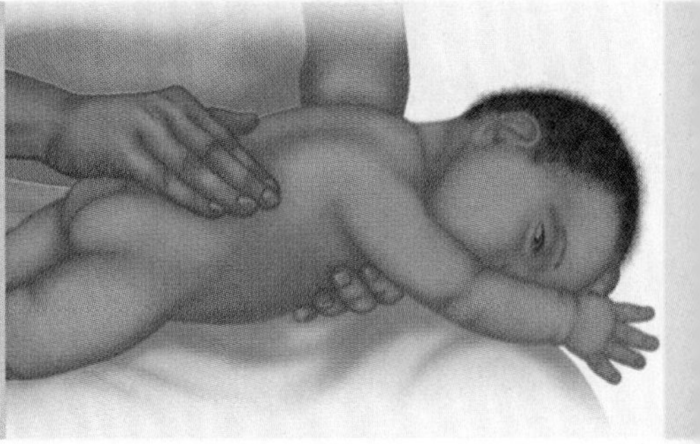

Part III ■ Infancy

5 Infancy: Physical Development 170

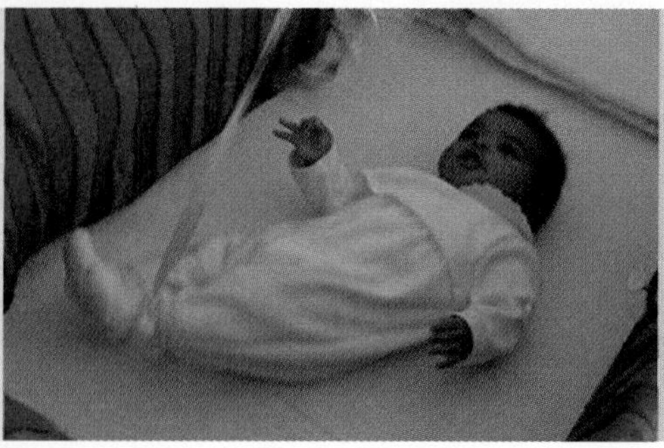
Courtesy of Prof. Carolyn Rovee-Collier

© Elizabeth Crews

© Elizabeth Crews

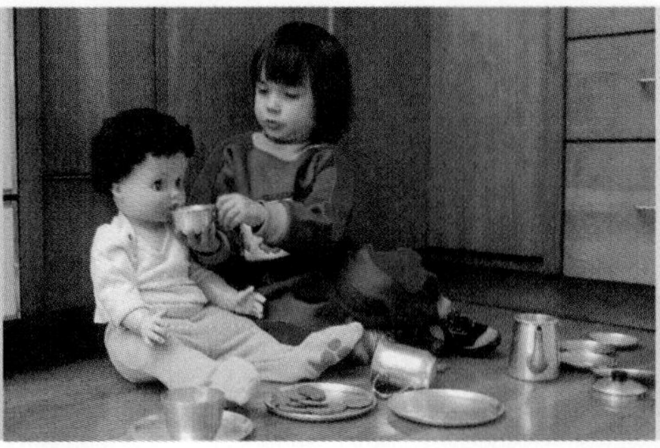

© Elizabeth Crews

Part IV ■ Early Childhood

8 Early Childhood: Physical Development 284

© Elizabeth Crews

10 Early Childhood: Social and Personality Development 350

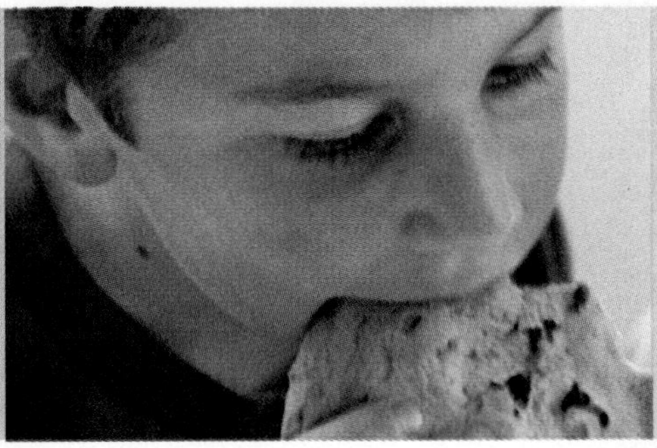
© Nicole Katano/Brand X Pictures/PictureQuest

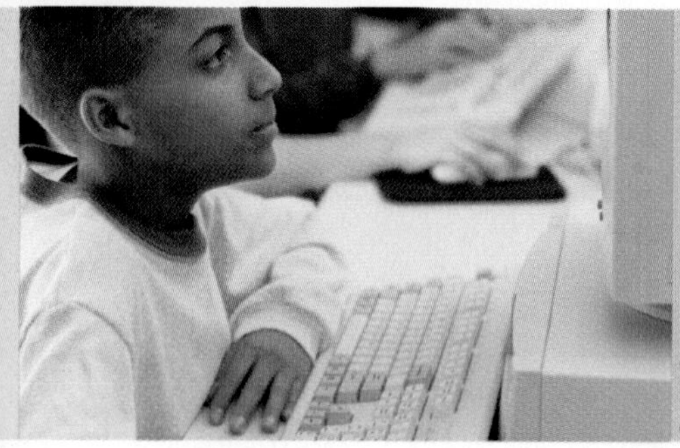

12 Middle Childhood: Cognitive Development 420

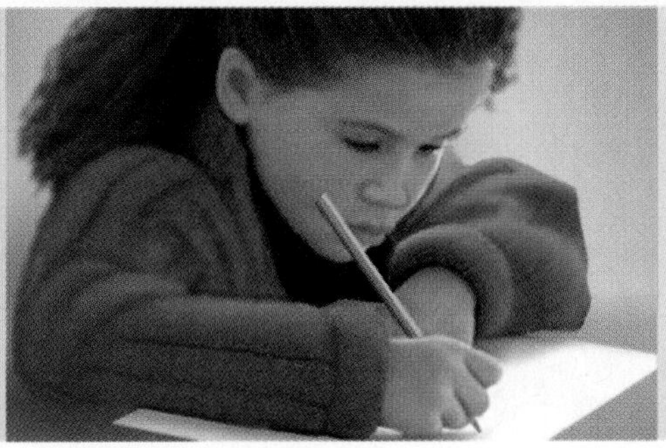

© Joel Gordon

15 Adolescence: Cognitive Development 550

16 Adolescence: Social and Emotional Development 584

Hi!
My name is Chuck.
What's your's?

Boxed Features

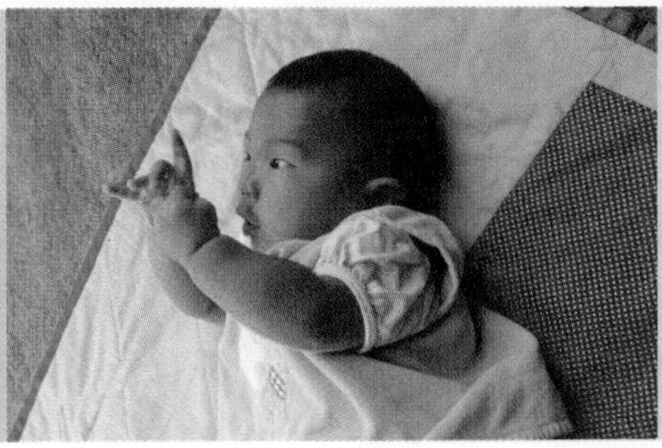

Developing in the New Millennium

Developing in a World of Diversity

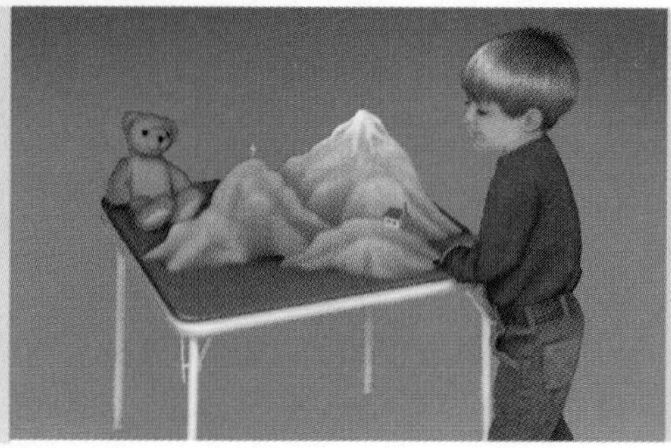

A Closer Look

© Elyse Lewin/Brand X Pictures/PictureQuest

Preface

These are our children.

These are our selves.

In children, we have the making of ourselves. In children, we also have the most impetuous, comical, ingratiating, delightful, and—at times—frustrating versions of ourselves. Will the little babies we hold in our hands at birth someday be larger and stronger, more talented, and more insightful than we? It almost seems impossible, yet it has happened many billions of times.

Portraying the Fascination of Children

Children are endlessly fascinating. Yet too often textbooks portray these captivating children without any sense of their allure. How often textbooks of child and adolescent development manage to transform the excitement of development into the drab grays of academic discourse. Not this book.

One of my goals has been to capture the fun of child and adolescent development, even as—at the same time—I portray the field of development as the rigorous science it is. My approach not only motivates students but also is in keeping with the joy of observing children and adolescents. How can one hope to convey a true sense of development if one is blind to its marvels?

Personal and Scientific

All in all, we must admit that there is a certain madness to human development. But to paraphrase the poet Michael Drayton, it is often a "fine madness." And as Shakespeare said through Hamlet, "Though this be madness, yet there is method in it."

In this text, I shall decipher much of the "method" in this madness. I shall also report the methods used by researchers to learn what leads to what, how it all unfolds, how it is influenced by the context in which children and adolescents develop. And that which we cannot yet fully explain we can at least appreciate and enjoy.

Voyages: Childhood and Adolescence develops from my scientific interest and research in human growth and development and also from my experiences with my own developing family. This book is an extremely personal textbook because we were all children, and many of us wish we could retain more of the child in our adult lives.

Cutting-Edge Topic Coverage

Yet the book also presents cutting-edge topic coverage, emphasizing the latest findings and research in key areas. This coverage is summarized on pages xxxi and xxxii, which give details on where to find material in the following three areas:

- Biology and Development—Evolution, Heredity, Neuroscience, and Endocrinology
- Gender and Development
- Culture, Ethnicity, and Development

Coverage of Biology and Development: *Evolution, Heredity, Neuroscience, and Endocrinology*

Coverage of Gender and Development

(continued)

Coverage of Culture, Ethnicity and Development

This is an exciting time to be studying child and adolescent development: Every day new research and new insights help us to better understand the mysteries and marvels of many aspects of development, including the development of the brain in infants, changing conceptions of adolescence, the origins of risky behavior, the intricacies of the genetic code, the effects of day care, even some parents' efforts to create "superkids."

The book covers what is happening today and how we arrived here: It covers issues such as the effects of the Internet and the selection of the sex of one's children, and it also takes a close look at the historical contributions of thinkers ranging from Lev Vygotsky to John Locke and Jean-Jacques Rousseau.

I have not stepped back from controversies in the field and try to present opposing views as clearly and fairly as possible on such issues as using stem cells, using and abusing methylphenidate, and providing adolescents with contraceptives.

In addition, I would hope that students come away after reading this book with a much deeper understanding of the nature of human diversity and how it affects the development of the child. We address the most challenging issues as to how children and adolescents are influenced by their ethnic backgrounds and gender in areas ranging from intellectual development to substance abuse. We find that in many cases, cultural and ethnic factors affect the very survival of the child.

Chronological Approach

The material is organized in chronological sequence that takes students from the micro world of genetics and neuroscience to the macro world of a child's growth from infancy through adolescence.

Part I, "What Is Child Development?" introduces the history of the field of child development as well as the theories and methods of researchers in Chapter 1. This chapter also sets the stage for a continuing theme throughout the text—that centuries of tradition and folklore do not necessarily point people in the right direction as parents and educators.

Part II, "Beginnings," includes three chapters that take us back before the conception of the child to matters of heredity and bring us forward in time to the child's entry into life outside the womb. Throughout these chapters, the issues of "nature" versus "nurture" are touched on in the light of new scientific findings and controversies.

Parts III, IV, V, and VI discuss infancy (the ages of approximately birth to 2), early childhood (2 to 5 or 6), middle childhood (6 to 12 or 13), and adolescence (puberty to emerging adulthood). Each of these four parts discusses three aspects of development: physical development, cognitive development, and social and emotional development.

The Pedagogical Approach: PQ4R

A good part of the book's philosophy is reflected in its pedagogical package. That is, one major issue considered by adopters is "how much" subject matter one finds in the book—and there is much. But the book's pedagogy is also designed to satisfy students and instructors with the amount of knowledge students *take away* from the book. *Voyages: Childhood and Adolescence* fully integrates the PQ4R method in a most stimulating embodiment to help students learn and retain the subject matter.

PQ4R discourages students from believing that they are sponges. After all, sponges need merely passively sit in a pool of water to soak it up. The PQ4R method stimulates students to *actively* engage the subject matter. Students are encouraged to become *proactive* rather than *reactive*. *PQ4R* is the acronym for Preview, Question, Read, Reflect, Review, and Recite, a method that is related to the work of educational psychologist Francis P. Robinson.

PowerPreview™

Previewing the material helps shape students' expectations. It enables them to create mental templates or "advance organizers" into which they categorize the subject matter. Each chapter of *Voyages* previews the subject matter with the author's trademarked PowerPreview™ feature. PowerPreviews outline the sections in each chapter, but also do much more. They are made up of provocative statements and questions that give students a sense of what each section covers, often in an entertaining manner. They also speak directly to students in personal ways. For example:

Samples of PowerPreview™ Chapter Openers

Chapter 2, Heredity and Conception: "Something Old, Something New"

- Where does conception normally occur?
- What is a "test-tube baby"?
- Developing embryos can be transferred from the uterus of one woman to the uterus of another.
- Can you select the gender of your child? (Would you want to?)

Chapter 5, Infancy: Physical Development

- Does feeding infants skim milk help prevent obesity later in life?
- Is breast milk the perfect fast food?
- Which infants sit, walk, and run at earlier ages—African Americans or European Americans?

Chapter 13, Middle Childhood: Social and Emotional Development

- Should parents who are in conflict stay together "for the sake of the children," or do children fare better when fighting parents separate?
- Did you know that teachers are more likely to accept calling out from boys than from girls? Why?
- What is meant by the term "conduct disorder"? (Is bad behavior a mental illness?)

Question

Devising questions about the subject matter, before reading it in detail, is another feature of the PQ4R method. Writing questions gives students goals: They attend class or read the text *in order to answer the questions.* Questions are placed in all primary sections of the text to help students use the PQ4R method most effectively. They are printed in ***blue.*** When students see a question, they can read the material that follows in order to answer that question. If they wish, they can also write the questions and answers in their notebooks, as recommended by Robinson.

Read

Reading is the first R in the PQ4R method. Although students will have to read for themselves, they are not alone. The text helps them by providing the lively and motivating PowerPreview™ that helps them organize the material and by presenting the subject matter in clear, stimulating prose. A running glossary defines key terms in the margin of the text, near the sentences where the terms appear in the text. Concepts are developed in an orderly fashion and built one upon the other.

The writing style is "personal" in that it speaks directly to the student and employs humor and personal anecdotes as ways of motivating and stimulating students. All in all, *Voyages* defies the time-honored tradition of presenting scientific material in a boring, deadening fashion. It is as alive as the young people it talks about, and it is intended to leave the reader interested and refreshed.

Reflect

Students learn more effectively when they *reflect* (the second R in PQ4R is for "Reflect") on what they are learning. Psychologists who study learning and memory refer to reflection on subject matter as *elaborative rehearsal.* One way for students to reflect on a subject is to relate it to something they already know about, whether it be academic material or events in their own lives.[1] Reflecting makes the material meaningful and easier to remember.[2] It also makes it more likely that students will be able to *apply* the information to their own lives.[3] Through effective reflection, students can embed material firmly in their memory so that rote repetition is unnecessary.

[1]Willoughby, T., Wood, E., & Khan, M. (1994). Isolating variables that impact on or detract from the effectiveness of elaboration strategies. *Journal of Educational Research, 86,* 279–289.

[2]Woloshyn, V. E., Paivio, A., & Pressley, M. (1994). Use of elaborative interrogation to help students acquire information consistent with prior knowledge and information inconsistent with prior knowledge. *Journal of Educational Psychology, 86,* 79–89.

[3]Kintsch, W. (1994). Text comprehension, memory, and learning. *American Psychologist, 49,* 294–303.

Because of the value of reflection, Reflect features are placed within or adjacent to the text. Some of them ask students to compare what they are reading with the ideas they had before they took the course.

Review

Review sections follow major sections in the text. They include two types of items that foster active learning and retention. The first type of item is in a fill-in-the-blank format. Students are asked to *produce,* not simply recognize, the answer. For example, the following is part of the first review in Chapter 5, "Infancy: Physical Development":

(1) Cephalocaudal development describes the processes by which development proceeds from the __________ to the lower parts of the body. (2) The head __________ in length between birth and maturity, but the torso triples in length. (3) The __________ principle means that development proceeds from the trunk outward. (4) The tendency of responses to become more specific is termed __________. (5) Infants usually double their birthweight in about __________ months and triple it by the first birthday. (5) Non-organic failure to __________ (NOFTT) seems to have psychological and/or social roots.

The second part of the Review, *Pulling It Together,* includes questions that encourage students to think critically about the subject matter and relate it to the bigger picture. For example, the following is from Chapter 5, "Infancy: Physical Development":

Pulling It Together: How can the principle of canalization be used to mitigate the effects of early malnutrition?

Recite

The PQ4R method recommends that students regularly recite the answers to the questions aloud. Reciting answers aloud helps students remember them by means of repetition, by stimulating students to produce concepts and ideas they have learned, and by associating them with spoken words and gestures.

Recite sections are found at the end of each chapter. They help students summarize the material, but they are active summaries. They are written in question-and-answer format. To provide a sense of closure, the summaries repeat the questions found within the chapters, and are again printed in *blue.* The answers are concise but include most of the key terms found in the text.

The Recite sections are designed in two columns so that students can cover the second column (the answers) as they read the questions. They can recite the answers as they remember or reconstruct them and then check what they have recited against the answers they had covered. Students should not feel that they are incorrect if they have not exactly produced the answer written in the second column; their individual approach might be slightly different, even more inclusive. The answers provided in the second column are intended to be a guide, to provide a check on students' learning. They are not carved in stone.

Features

In addition to the PQ4R pedagogical method, *Voyages* contains three kinds of features that provide in-depth looks at certain topics and provide students with advice that they can apply in their own lives—and in the lives of the children in their lives. These include "A Closer Look," "Developing in a World of Diversity," and "Developing in the New Millennium."

"Developing in the New Millennium" Features

As the times change, science, technology, and medicine all advance; local tradition comes into conflict with "globalization." Parents and educators, children and adolescents all grapple with these changes. The "Developing in the New Millennium" features highlight some aspects of life in the new millennium and how they affect the development of children and adolescents. (For a complete list of "Developing in the New Millennium" features, see p. xxvii.) Sample features include

- Web Sites on Child Development
- The Promise of Embryonic Stem Cells: "Infant Cells That Have Not Yet Chosen a Profession"
- Preventing One's Baby From Being Infected With HIV
- The Quest for a Superkid
- Back to School—With Methylphenidate
- Keeping Teenagers in Line Online

"Developing in a World of Diversity" Features

This textbook is inclusive. It includes relevant information on the links between diversity—ethnicity, gender, sexual orientation, and so on—and the development of children and adolescents. This coverage helps students understand why parents of different backgrounds and genders rear their children and adolescents in certain ways, why children and adolescents from various backgrounds behave and think in different ways, and how the study of child and adolescent development is enriched by addressing those differences. (For a complete list of "Developing in a World of Diversity" features, see p. xxvii.) Sample features include

- Down Syndrome, Race, and Mortality
- Where Are the Missing Girls?
- A Racial Gap in Infant Deaths and a Search for Reasons
- Gender Differences in Motor Activity
- Cross-Cultural Differences in Sleeping Arrangements
- Stereotype Vulnerability and IQ
- Bilingual Education

"A Closer Look" Features

The "A Closer Look" features provide in-depth looks at interesting and useful topics in the study of child and adolescent development. Think of them as "highlights," many of which are written to be entertaining as well as edifying. The "A Closer Look" features serve many purposes:

Some give in-depth looks at research methods such as "Studying Visual Acuity in Neonates: How Do You Get Babies to Tell You How Well They Can See?" or describe valuable studies such as "How Child Abuse May Set the Stage for Psychological Disorders in Adulthood."

Others provide advice on issues in child and adolescent development such as "Ten Things You Need to Know About Immunizations" and "What Parents Can Do About Bed-Wetting." Still others highlight important issues in child and adolescent development, such as "Children's Eyewitness Testimony" and "The Controversy Over *The Bell Curve*." (For a complete list, see p. xxviii.)

The Package

Voyages: Childhood and Adolescence is accompanied by a wide array of supplements prepared for both the instructor and student.

For the Instructor

Instructor's Manual Written by Anne C. Watson of Illinois Wesleyan University, this manual contains chapter-specific lecture outlines; a list of print, video, and online resources; and student learning objectives. The manual has a special emphasis on active learning with suggested student activities and projects for each chapter.

Test Bank Written by Randall Osborne of Southwest Texas State University, the test bank consists of 120 multiple-choice questions, 20 matching questions, 15 true-false questions, and 5 essay questions with model answers for each chapter, all with page references. Each multiple-choice item is labeled with question type (factual, application, or conceptual) and level of difficulty.

ExamView® Computerized Testing Create, deliver, and customize printed and online tests and study guides in minutes with this easy-to-use assessment and tutorial system. ExamView includes a Quick Test Wizard and an Online Test Wizard to guide instructors step by step through the process of creating tests. The test appears on screen exactly as it will print or display online. Using ExamView's complete word-processing capabilities, instructors can enter an unlimited number of new questions or edit questions included with ExamView.

Classroom Presentation Tools for the Instructor

Multimedia Manager for Developmental Psychology 2003: A Microsoft® PowerPoint® Link Tool With this one-stop digital library and presentation tool, instructors can assemble, edit, and present custom lectures with ease. The Multimedia Manager contains a selection of digital media from Wadsworth's latest titles in developmental psychology, including figures and tables. Also included are animations, CNN video clips, and preassembled Microsoft PowerPoint lecture slides based on each specific text. Instructors can use the material or add their own material for a truly customized lecture presentation.

Transparency Acetates 100 four-color acetates featuring figures from the text selected by the author to enhance lecture presentations.

CNN® Today Developmental Psychology Video Series, Volumes 1–3. Lifespan Development Video Series, Volumes 1–2 Illustrate the relevance of developmental psychology to everyday life with this exclusive series of videos for the child and adolescent course. Jointly created by Wadsworth and CNN, each video consists of approximately 45 minutes of footage originally broadcast on CNN and specifically selected to illustrate important developmental psychology concepts. The videos are divided into short two- to seven-minute segments, perfect for use as lecture launchers or as illustrations of key developmental psychology concepts. Special adoption conditions apply.

Wadsworth Developmental Psychology Video Library Bring developmental psychology concepts to life with videos from Wadsworth's Developmental Psychology Video Library, which includes thought-provoking offerings from Films for Humanities, as well as other excellent educational video sources. This extensive collection illustrates important developmental psychology concepts covered in many life-span courses. Certain adoption conditions apply.

For the Student

Study Guide Written by Randall Osborne and Shirley Ogletree of Southwest Texas State University, the Study Guide is designed to promote active learning through a guided review of the important principles and concepts in the text. The study materials for each chapter include a chapter summary, a comprehensive multiple-choice self-test, as well as critical thinking, Internet, and InfoTrac® College Edition exercises that challenge students to think about and to apply what they have learned.

Practice Tests This booklet is designed to help students test their knowledge of the chapter concepts in *Voyages: Childhood and Adolescence, First Edition.* It contains a practice multiple-choice test for each chapter of the text.

Child and Adolescent Development CD-ROM This interactive CD-ROM stimulates students to learn about key theories and important concepts through the use of narrative, video, animations, quizzes, and Web links. The material is organized into three major areas: Physical Development; Cognition, Language, and Learning; and Personality, Social-Emotional, and Moral Development. Coverage of the theorists includes:

- Brief biography
- Brief description of theory
- Video segments with audio introduction and written script guiding user to key components to observe
- Multiple-choice quiz to help students test their knowledge
- Embedded applications that present a scenario followed by questions that stimulate students to think critically
- Research Online: link to book's Web site

Coverage of broader concepts includes narrative, accompanied by video, challenge questions, quizzes, applications, and links to the book's Web site.

Internet-Based Supplements

WebTutor™ Advantage on WebCT and Blackboard This Web-based software for students and instructors takes a course beyond the classroom to an anywhere, anytime environment. Students gain access to a full array of study tools, including chapter outlines, chapter-specific quizzing material, interactive games, and videos. With WebTutor Advantage, instructors can provide virtual office hours, post syllabi, track student progress with the quizzing material, and even customize content to meet their needs. Instructors can also use the communication tools to set up threaded discussions and conduct "real-time" chats. "Out of the box" or customized, WebTutor Advantage provides a powerful tool for instructors and students alike.

InfoTrac College Edition With InfoTrac College Edition, instructors can stimulate discussions and supplement lectures with the latest developments in developmental psychology. Available as a free option with newly purchased texts, InfoTrac College Edition gives instructors and students four months of free access to an extensive database of reliable, full-length articles (not just abstracts) from hundreds of top academic journals and popular periodicals. In-text exercises suggest search terms to make the most of this resource.

Wadsworth Psychology Resource Center at http://www.wadsworth.com/psychology_d. This Web site provides instructors and students with a wealth of *free* information and resources, such as

- Journals
- Associations
- Conference Listings
- Psych-in-the-news
- Hot topics
- Book-specific Student Resources

Additional instructor resources include:

- Research and Teaching Showcase
- Resources for Instructors Archives
- Book-Specific Instructor Resources

Acknowledgments

This book is about human development. This section is about the development of this book. The book may have a single author, but its existence reflects the input and aid of a significant cast of characters.

First among these are my professional academic colleagues—the people who teach the course, the people who conduct the research. They know better than anyone else what's going on "out there"—out there in the world of children and adolescents, out there in the classroom. The book you hold in your hands would not be what it is without their valuable insights and suggestions. They include: Jackie L. Adamson, California State University–Fresno; Frank R. Asbury, Valdosta State University; Daniel R. Bellack, Trident Technical College; Pearl Susan Berman, Indiana University of Pennsylvania; Elizabeth Cauffman, Stanford Center on Adolescence; Margaret Sutton Edmands, University of Massachusetts–Boston; JoAnn Farver, University of Southern California; William Franklin, California State University–Los Angeles; Hulda Goddy Goodson, Palomar College; Tresmaine R. Grimes, Iona College; Jane Hovland, University of Minnesota, Duluth; Charles LaBounty, Hamline University; Richard Langford, California State University–Humboldt; Dennis A. Lichty, Wayne State College; Rebecca K. Loehrer, Blinn College; Patricia M. Martin, Onondaga Community College; Laura Massey, Montana State University–Bozeman; John Prange, Irvine Valley College; Mary Ann Ringquist, University of Massachusetts–Boston; Lee B. Ross, Frostburg State University; Julia Rux, Georgia Perimeter College; Alice A. Scharf-Matlick, Iona College; Debra Grote Schwiesow, Creighton University; and Linda Sperry, Indiana State University.

I said that the book you hold in your hands would not be what it is without the insights and suggestions of my academic colleagues. I must also say that this book simply would not be without the fine editorial and production team at Wadsworth and assembled by Wadsworth. They include Eve Howard, vice president/editor in chief, social sciences; Edith Beard Brady, publisher; Sherry Symington, development editor; Lisa Weber, production project manager; Mary Douglas of Rogue Valley Publications, production services; Michelle Vardeman, technology project manager; Rebecca Heider, assistant editor; Maritess Tse, editorial assistant; Robert Kauser, permissions editor; Joan Pendleton, copy editor; Myrna Engler, photo researcher; Roy Neuhaus, designer; Stephen Rapley, creative director; Precision Graphics, art studio; Nancy Ball, indexer; Susan Gall, proofreader; and New England Typographic Service, compositor.

Finally, I must acknowledge the loving assistance of my family. My wife, Lois Fichner-Rathus, continues in her supportive role of author's widow and (somewhat less supportive) role of critical reviewer. As shown in experiments with the visual cliff, infants will not usually go off the deep end. As a textbook author herself, and as an academic, Lois often prevents me from going off the deep end. My children I thank as the sources of stories—and stories and more stories. But mostly I thank them for being what they are: sources of delight and fancy, occasional annoyances, and perpetual goads. They are in the world as it is now, and they keep me in the world as it is now. I need them all more than they will know.

1 History, Theories, and Methods

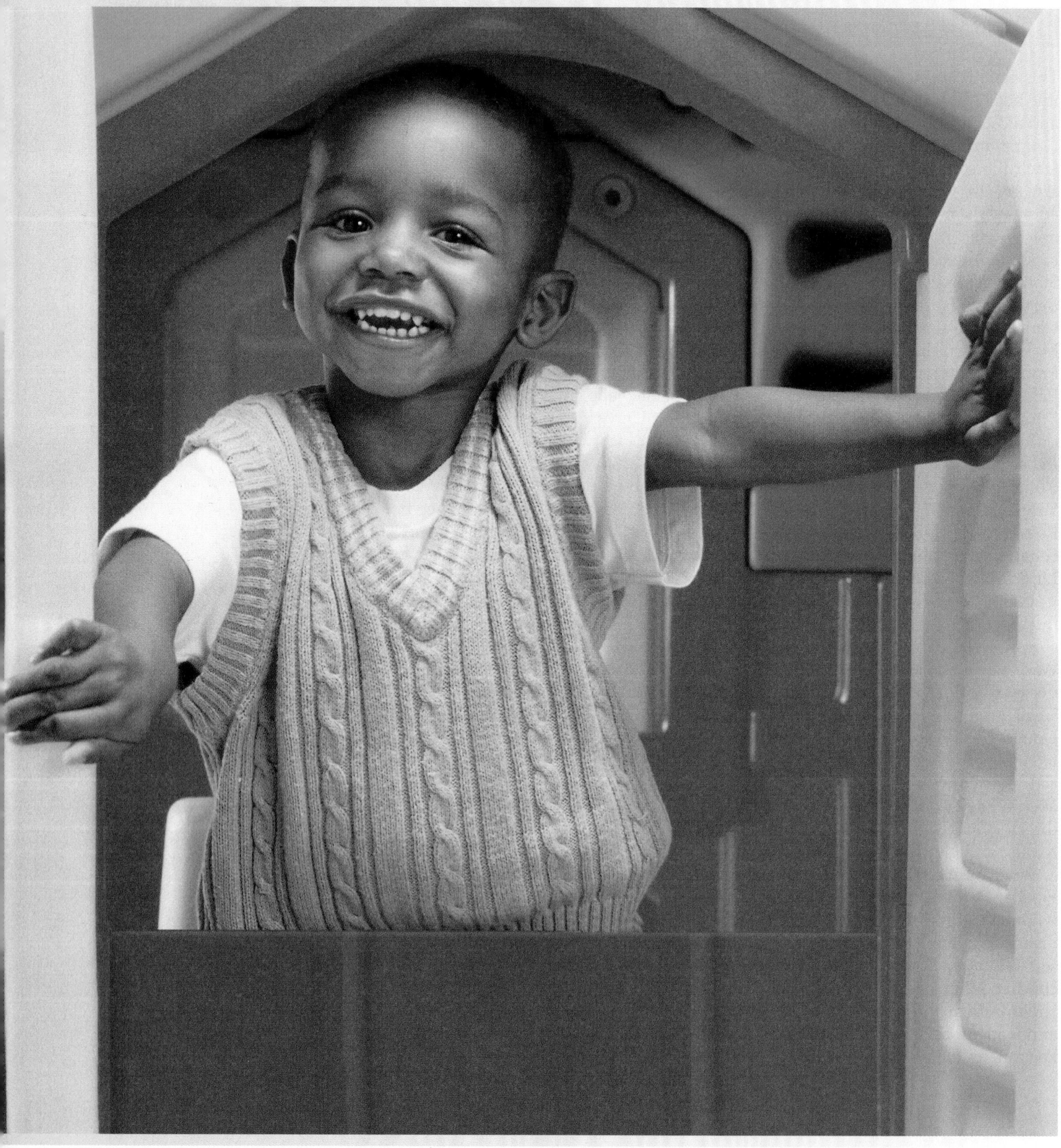

PowerPreview™

What Is Child Development?—Coming to Terms with Terms

- **Do you know** what a child is? (This is not a trick question.)

Why Do We Study Child Development?

- **Sure, it's fun, but** what are some of the other reasons that scientists are interested in studying the development of children?

History of Child Development

- **During the Middle Ages,** children were often treated as miniature adults.
- **Are children the** property of their parents?

Theories of Child Development

- **How long do** the effects of childhood events linger?
- **Does punishment work?** What are the risks in punishing children?
- **Piaget believed that** children are budding scientists who actively intend to learn about and take charge of their worlds.
- **How do biological processes** influence development and behavior?
- **Newborn babies influence** their parents to treat them in certain ways. How do they do it?
- **Did you know that** before 1833 no college in the United States admitted women?

Controversies in Child Development

- **Which exerts the greater influence** on children—their genetic heritage or their environments?
- **Does development occur gradually** or in sudden leaps called "stages"?
- **Are children sponges** who soak up their environments, or do they seek to understand and act on their environments?

How Do We Study Child Development?

- **Research with rhesus monkeys** has helped psychologists understand the formation of attachment in humans.
- **Researchers have followed** some participants in developmental research for more than 50 years.

This book has a story to tell. An important story. A remarkable story. It is your story. It is about the remarkable journey you have already taken through childhood and adolescence. It is about the unfolding of your adult life. Billions have made this journey before. You have much in common with them. Yet you are unique and things will happen to you, and because of you, that have never happened before.

The development of children and adolescents is what this book is about, but in our children we see mirrors of ourselves. In a very real sense, we cannot hope to understand ourselves as adults—we cannot catch a glimpse of the remarkable journeys we have taken—unless we understand children.

Let's embark on our search for ourselves by considering a basic question: ***Question: What is child development?*** Then we shall explore some of the reasons for studying child development. After that we take a brief tour of the history of child development. It may surprise you to learn that until relatively recent times, people were not particularly sensitive to the many ways in which children differ from adults. Next we examine some controversies in child development, such as whether there are distinct stages of development. We see how theories help illuminate our observations and help point the way toward new observations. Then we consider methods for the study of child development. We shall see that scientists have devised sophisticated methods for studying children and that ethics help determine the types of research that are deemed proper and improper.

What Is Child Development?—Coming to Terms With Terms

You have heard the word *child* all your life, so why bother to define it? We do so because words in common usage are frequently used in inexact ways. A **child** is a person undergoing the period of development from *infancy* to *puberty*—two more familiar words that are frequently used inexactly. The term **infancy** derives from Latin roots meaning "not speaking," and infancy is usually defined as the first 2 years of life, or the period of life prior to the development of complex speech. We stress the word *complex* because many children have a large vocabulary and use simple sentences well before their second birthday. **Puberty** refers to the period of development during which people gain reproductive capacity. Puberty signals the beginning of **adolescence,** a transitional period between childhood and adulthood in most industrial societies.

Researchers commonly speak of two other periods of development that lie between infancy and adolescence: early childhood and middle childhood. Early childhood encompasses the ages from 2 to 5 years. These are the years before the child starts school, and so early childhood is sometimes referred to as the preschool period. Middle childhood generally is defined as the years from 6 to 12. The beginning of this period usually is marked by the child's entry into first grade. We discuss these periods of life yet go back farther. We describe the origin of sperm and ova (egg cells), the process of **conception,** and the **prenatal period.** Yet this is not far enough to satisfy scientists. We also describe the mechanisms of heredity that give rise to traits, in both humans and other animals.

Development is the orderly appearance, over time, of physical structures, psychological traits, behaviors, and ways of adapting to the demands of life. The changes brought on by development are both *qualitative* and *quantitative.* Qualitative changes are changes in type or kind. Consider **motor development.** As we develop, we gain the capacities to lift our heads, sit up, creep, stand, and walk. These changes are qualitative. However, within each of these qualitative changes are quantitative developments. Quantitative changes are changes in amount. Once babies begin to lift their heads, they lift them higher and higher.

child A person undergoing the period of development from infancy through puberty.

infancy The period of very early childhood, characterized by lack of complex speech; the first 2 years after birth.

puberty (PEW-burr-tee) The stage of development characterized by changes that lead to reproductive capacity.

adolescence The stage bounded by the advent of puberty at the lower end and the taking on of adult responsibilities at the upper end. Puberty is a biological concept, while adolescence is a psychological concept.

conception The process of becoming pregnant; the process by which a sperm cell joins with an ovum to begin a new life.

prenatal period The period of development from conception to birth (from roots meaning "prior to birth").

development The processes by which organisms unfold features and traits, grow, and become more complex and specialized in structure and function.

motor development The development of the capacity for movement, particularly that made possible by changes in the nervous system and the muscles.

Soon after children walk, they also begin to run. And, as their running advances, they gain the capacity to go faster and faster.

Development occurs across many dimensions at once—physiological, cognitive, social, emotional, and behavioral. Development is spurred on by internal factors, such as the genetic code, and it is shaped by external factors, such as nutrition and culture.

The terms *growth* and *development* are not synonymous, although many people use them interchangeably. **Growth** is usually used to refer to changes in size or quantity, whereas development also refers to changes in quality. During the early days following conception, the fertilized egg cell develops rapidly. It divides repeatedly, and cells begin to take on specialized forms. However, it does not "grow" in the sense that there is no gain in mass. Why? It has not yet become implanted in the uterus and therefore is without any external source of nourishment. Language development refers to the process by which the child's use of language becomes progressively more sophisticated and complex during the first few years of life. Vocabulary growth, by contrast, refers to the simple accumulation of knowledge of new words and their meanings.

Child development, then, is a field of inquiry that attempts to understand the processes that govern the appearance and growth of children's physical structures, psychological traits, behavior patterns, understanding, and ways of adapting to the demands of life. To test your knowledge of child development, see the nearby "A Closer Look" feature.

Professionals from many fields are interested in child development. They include psychologists, educators, anthropologists, sociologists, nurses, medical researchers, and many others. Each brings his or her own brand of expertise to the quest for knowledge. Intellectual cross-fertilization enhances the skills of developmentalists and enriches the lives of children.

Question: Why do researchers study child development?

Motor Development

Development refers to orderly changes in physical and psychological traits and abilities that occur over time. This infant has just mastered the ability to pull herself to a standing position. Soon she will be able to stand alone and then begin to walk.

Review

(1) A child is a person undergoing the period of development from *infancy* to __________. (2) __________ is the orderly appearance, over time, of structures, traits, and behaviors. (3) The term __________ is usually used to refer to changes in size or quantity.

Pulling It Together: How do we define *child development?*

Why Do We Study Child Development?

An important motive for studying child development is curiosity—the desire to learn about children. Curiosity may be driven by the desire to answer questions about development that remain unresolved. It may also be driven by the desire to have fun. (Yes, I admit that children and the study of child development can be fun.)

To Gain Insight Into Human Nature

For centuries, philosophers, theologians, natural scientists, psychologists, and educators have held different perspectives on development and argued about the basic nature of children. They have argued over whether children are basically antisocial and aggressive or prosocial and loving. They have argued over whether children are conscious and self-aware. They have disputed whether children have a natural curiosity that demands to unravel the mysteries of the universe or whether children are merely mechanical reactors to environmental stimulation.

Reflect

What are your reasons for studying child development this term? How will your reasons affect what you gain from your study?

growth The processes by which organisms increase in size, weight, strength, and other traits as they develop.

If their arguments had remained theoretical—limited to discussion in the seminar—they might have gained little notice. But their perspectives on child development have led to very different suggestions for child rearing and education. They have an important impact on the daily lives of children, parents, educators, and others who interact with children.

To Gain Insight Into the Origins of Adult Behavior

> The child is father of the man.
>
> —William Wordsworth

How do we explain the origins of empathy in adults? Of antisocial behavior? How do we explain the assumption of "feminine" and "masculine" behavior patterns? The origins of special talents in writing, music, athletics, and math? Many investigators agree with Wordsworth that the child is frequently "the father" of the adult, and they look to childhood events to explain adult traits, abilities, and behavior.

Consider **gender roles,** which are cultural expectations of how females and males should behave. How do gender roles develop? Is the process a natural unfolding of inborn tendencies? Or do boys and girls choose gender-related behavior patterns once they become aware of cultural expectations? Is the learning process more mechanical? Are "masculine" and "feminine" behavior patterns "stamped in" by rewards from parents, other adults, and peers? We will see that the research in child development suggests that the answer might be "all of the above" and more.

gender roles Complex clusters of behavior that are considered stereotypical of females and males.

A Closer Look

How Much Do You Know About Child Development?

So, you think, what is there to learn about child development? After all, you were a child yourself. Having been one, you should be something of an expert, right?

Perhaps you are. Perhaps you aren't. If you are, I will admit that you are far ahead of where I was as a student.

To test your knowledge of child development, indicate whether you think each of the following items is true or false by circling the T or the F. Then compare your answers with the key at the end of the chapter.

1. T F Conception takes place in the uterus.
2. T F Pregnant women can have one or two drinks a day without being concerned about their effects on the embryo.
3. T F Parents must spend the first few hours after birth with their newborn babies if adequate bonding is to take place.
4. T F Newborn babies sleep about 16 hours a day.
5. T F Newborn babies usually cannot see for several hours.
6. T F Nine-month-old babies will usually crawl off the edges of beds, couches, and tables if not prevented from doing so.
7. T F Although it may be difficult to measure intelligence in newborn babies, a child's IQ remains fixed from birth.
8. T F Nine-month-old babies who fear strangers are likely to become anxious adults.
9. T F Babies placed in day care grow less attached to their mothers than babies reared by their mothers in the home.
10. T F It is better for parents in conflict to stay together for the sake of the children than to get a divorce.
11. T F More attractive children are usually more popular with peers.
12 T F Boys are usually more aggressive than girls.
13. T F Boys usually have greater verbal skills than girls.
14. T F TV violence contributes to aggressive behavior in children who watch it.
15. T F Most children who wet their beds simply outgrow the problem.
16. T F Marijuana is the drug most frequently abused by adolescents.

To Gain Insight Into the Origins, Prevention, and Treatment of Developmental Problems

Fetal alcohol syndrome, **PKU, SIDS,** Down syndrome, autism, hyperactivity, dyslexia, child abuse—these are but a handful of the buzzwords that stir fear in parents and parents-to-be. A major focus in child development research is the search for the causes of such problems so that they can be prevented and, when possible, treated.

To Optimize the Conditions of Development for All Children

Most children, fortunately, do not encounter such developmental problems. Yet we wish to optimize the conditions of their development in order to foster positive traits. At the most basic level, most parents want their infants to survive. They want to provide the best in nutrition and medical care so their children will develop strong and healthy bodies. Parents want their infants to feel secure with them. They want to assure that major transitions, such as the transition from the home to the school, will be as stress-free as possible.

Consider some of the issues that have been studied in recent years in an effort to optimize the conditions of development:

- The effects of various foods and agents on the development of the embryo and the fetus
- The effects of intense parent–infant interaction immediately following birth on bonds of attachment
- The effects of bottle-feeding versus breast-feeding on mother–infant attachment and on babies' health
- The effects of day-care programs on parent–child bonds of attachment and on children's social and intellectual development
- The effects of different patterns of child rearing on the fostering of independence, competence, and social adjustment

We treat each of these issues in depth in the following chapters.

PKU Phenylketonuria. A genetic abnormality in which a child cannot metabolize phenylalanine, an amino acid, which consequently builds up in the body and causes mental retardation. If treated with a special diet, retardation is prevented.

SIDS Sudden infant death syndrome (discussed in Chapter 5).

Review

(4) Researchers study child development to gain insight into the origins of __________ behavior. (5) Another motive is to gain insight into the origins, prevention, and treatment of developmental __________.

Pulling It Together: How can studying children provide insight into human nature?

History of Child Development

Child development as a field of scientific inquiry has existed for little more than a century. ***Question: What views of children do we find throughout history?***

In ancient times and in the Middle Ages, children often were viewed as innately evil, and discipline was harsh. Legally, medieval children were treated as property and servants. They enjoyed no civil rights. They could be sent to the monastery, married without consultation, or convicted of crimes. Children were nurtured until they were 7, which was considered the "age of reason."[1] Then they were expected to work alongside adults in the home and in the field (Aries, 1962). They ate, drank, and dressed as miniature adults. For much of the Middle Ages, artists depicted children as small adults.

Reflect

Are children "wild"? Must children be "tamed"? Do you see dangers (to children) in answering yes to either question?

[1] When we consider Piaget's cognitive-developmental theory, we shall see that the reasoning of the 7-year-old is concrete, at best.

Developing in the New Millennium

Web Sites on Child Development

In the new millennium, information and contacts concerning child development are just clicks away. It may not all be at your electronic fingertips, but you will find more than you could possibly assimilate in a lifetime. The following Web sites have been selected because they are responsible and of broad interest. When you search for topics related to child development, you will find thousands (thousands!) of others.

One general word of caution: URLs (universal resource locators) with a .com at the end of the address are commercial Web sites. They intend to sell you something or at least are funded by organizations with this goal in mind. Some of them are excellent, but never forget this caveat.

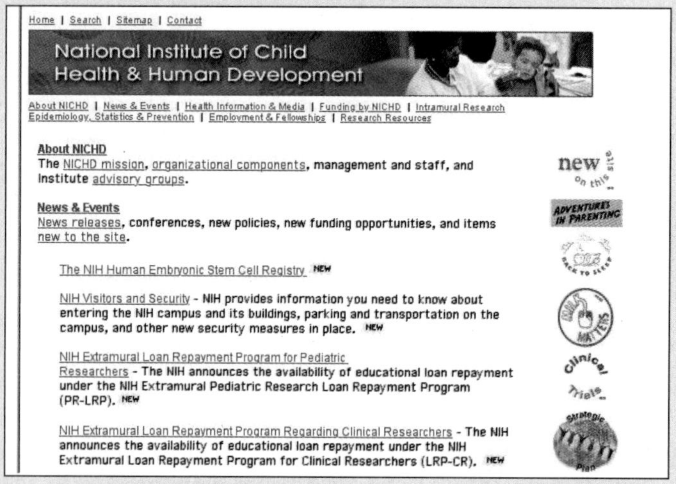

The Web site of the National Institute of Child Health and Human Development.

Sample helpful Web sites:

http://www.nichd.nih.gov/ The Web site of the National Institute of Child Health and Human Development. NICHD conducts and supports research "to advance knowledge of pregnancy, fetal development, and birth; to develop strategies to prevent infant and child mortality; to identify and promote the prerequisites of optimal physical, mental, and behavioral growth and development through infancy, childhood, and adolescence; and to contribute to the prevention and amelioration of mental retardation and developmental disabilities."

http://www.srcd.org/ The Web site of the Society for Research in Child Development. The Society for Research in Child Development, housed at the University of Michigan, publishes the journal *Child Development.* The Society promotes research in human development, facilitates exchange of information among professionals, and encourages applications of research findings. SRCD also publishes the *Monographs of the Society for Research in Child Development, Child Development Abstracts and Bibliography,* the *Social Policy Report,* and the *SRCD Newsletter.*

http://www.nbcdi.org/ The Web site of The National Black Child Development Institute. NBCDI aims to improve and protect the quality of life of African American children and their families: "We have worked to improve child welfare services, make universal early care and education a reality, build family support services, press for educational reform and provide vital information on children's health. As we are now into the new millennium, it is critical that we continue to dedicate ourselves to giving every child a chance."

http://www.childcare-experts.org/ The Web site of the Child Care Experts National Network. CCENN aims to help parents and employers access information about child development, child care, early education, family support systems, and resources for care from knowledgeable people across the country. It seeks to help families balance the demands of family and work, obtain and disseminate information with parents and child-care providers, support programs that care for children, and help create additional resources for child care.

http://www.w-cpc.org/fetal.html A Web site provided by the University of Pennsylvania that provides an overview of prenatal development. The site includes color photos and a QuickTime movie of events of prenatal development.

http://www.who.int/chd/ The World Health Organization Web site on child health and development. The site focuses on the identification and amelioration of children's health problems around the world.

http://www.apa.org/journals/dev.html The Web site of *Developmental Psychology,* a bimonthly journal of the American Psychological Association. Abstracts and some key articles are available without charge.

Search Online With InfoTrac® College Edition

For additional information, explore InfoTrac Edition, your online library. Go to **http://www.infotrac-college.com** and use the passcode from the InfoTrac card that came with your book. Try these search terms: web sites and child development, child development, child development and information services.

A View of Children as Perceived in the 1600s

Centuries ago, children were viewed as miniature adults. In this 17th-century painting, notice how the body proportions of the young princess (in the middle) are similar to those of her adult attendants. (Painting by Diego Velazquez, Las Meninas, *1656, oil on canvas, 10′5″ × 9′1″, Musea del Prado, Madrid)*

The transition to modern times is marked by the thinking of philosophers such as John Locke and Jean-Jacques Rousseau. The Englishman John Locke (1632–1704) believed that the child came into the world as a *tabula rasa*—a "blank tablet" or clean slate—that was written upon by experience. Locke did not believe that inborn predispositions toward good or evil played an important role in the conduct of the child. Instead, he focused on the role of the environment or of experience. Social approval and disapproval, he believed, are powerful shapers of behavior. Jean-Jacques Rousseau (1712–1778), a Swiss-French philosopher, reversed the stance of the Middle Ages. Rousseau argued that children are inherently good and that, if allowed to express their natural impulses, they will develop into generous and moral individuals.

During the Industrial Revolution, family life came to be defined in terms of the nuclear unit of mother, father, and children, rather than the extended family. Children became more visible, fostering awareness of childhood as a special time of life. Still, girls and boys often labored in factories from dawn to dusk through the early years of the 20th century.

In the 20th century, laws were passed to protect children from strenuous labor, to require that they attend school until a certain age, and to prevent them from getting married or being sexually exploited. Whereas children were once considered the property of parents to do with as they wished, laws now protect children from the abuse and neglect of parents and other caretakers. Juvenile courts see that children who break the law receive fair and appropriate treatment in the criminal justice system.

Pioneers in the Study of Child Development

Various thoughts about child development coalesced into a field of scientific study in the 19th and early 20th centuries. Many individuals, including Charles Darwin, G. Stanley Hall, and Alfred Binet, made important contributions to the emerging field.

Best known as the originator of the modern theory of evolution, the Englishman Charles Darwin (1809–1882) also was one of the first observers to keep a *baby biography,* in which he described his infant son's behaviors in great detail. G. Stanley Hall (1844–1924) is credited with founding child development as an academic discipline. He adapted the new questionnaire method for use with large groups of

Young Child Laborers

Children often worked long days in factories up through the early years of the 20th century. There remain a number of cultures in the world in which child labor is used today. Is some cultures, sad to say, children are even used as soldiers.

children so that he could study the "contents of children's minds." After Hall published his major two-volume work, *Adolescence,* in 1904, adolescence was recognized as a separate stage of life. The Frenchman Alfred Binet (1857–1911), along with Theodore Simon, developed the first standardized intelligence test near the turn of the 20th century. Binet's purpose was twofold: to assess individual differences in intellectual functioning and to identify public schoolchildren who might profit from special education. By the beginning of the 20th century, child development had emerged as a scientific field of study. Within a short time, major theoretical views of the developing child had begun to emerge, proposed by such developmentalists as Arnold Gesell, Sigmund Freud, John B. Watson, and Jean Piaget. We describe their theories of child development, and those of others, next.

Review

(6) In ancient times, children were often viewed as innately __________. (7) John __________ believed that the child came into the world as a *tabula rasa.* (8) Jean-Jacques __________ argued that children are inherently good. (9) Charles __________ was one of the first observers to keep a baby biography. (10) G. Stanley __________ founded child development as an academic discipline. (11) Alfred __________ developed the first standardized intelligence test.

Pulling It Together: How did Rousseau reverse long-held views of children?

Reflect

What is your view of human nature? For example, do you see people as basically antisocial and aggressive or as prosocial and loving? How can the study of child development inform an answer?

Theories of Child Development

"Give me a dozen healthy infants, well-formed, and my own specified world to bring them up in, and I'll guarantee to train them to become any type of specialist I might suggest—doctor, lawyer, merchant, chief, and, yes, even beggar and thief, regardless of their talents, penchants, tendencies, abilities, vocations, and the race of their ancestors" (adapted from Watson, 1924, p. 82).

John B. Watson, the founder of American **behaviorism,** was speaking from a perspective that sees development in terms of learning. It is consistent with Locke's idea that children come into the world as a *tabula rasa* and that their ideas,

behaviorism John B. Watson's view that a science or theory of development must study observable behavior only and investigate relationships between stimuli and responses.

preferences, and skills are shaped by experience. There has been a long-standing nature–nurture controversy in the study of children. In his theoretical approach to understanding children, Watson emphasized the role of nurture, or of the physical and social environments—the role, for example, of parental training and approval.

Click *Select Theorist* in the Child and Adolescent CD-ROM for more on Watson and the behavioral perspective.

Watson's view turned upside down the history of approaches to understanding children. Nature—the inherited, genetic characteristics of the child—had long been the more popular explanation of how children get to be what they are. Just 4 years after Watson sounded his clarion call for the behavioral view, Arnold Gesell expressed the idea that biological **maturation** was the main principle of development: "All things considered, the inevitability and surety of maturation are the most impressive characteristics of early development. It is the hereditary ballast which conserves and stabilizes growth of each individual infant" (Gesell, 1928, p. 378).

Watson was talking largely about the behavior patterns children develop, while Gesell was perhaps focusing mainly on physical aspects of growth and development. Still, the behavioral and maturational perspectives lie at opposite ends of the continuum of theories of development. Many scientists fall into the trap of overemphasizing the importance of either nature or nurture at the risk of overlooking the ways in which nature and nurture interact. Just as a child's environments and experiences influence the development of his or her biological endowment, children often place themselves in environments that are harmonious with their personal characteristics. Children, for example, are influenced by teachers and by other students. Nevertheless, because of the psychological traits they bring to school with them, some children may choose to socialize as much as possible with other children, while other children may prefer the company of teachers. Still other children may prefer to remain by themselves as much as they can.

What Are Theories of Child Development? Why Do We Have Them?

Child development is a scientific enterprise. Like other scientists, developmentalists seek to describe, explain, predict, and influence the events they study.

Developmentalists attempt to describe and explain behavior in terms of concepts such as heredity, perception, language, learning, cognition, emotion, socialization, and gender roles. For example, we may describe learning as a process in which behavior changes as a result of experience. We can be more specific and describe instances of learning in which children memorize the alphabet through repetition or acquire gymnastic skills through practice in which their performance gradually approximates desired behavior. We may explain how learning occurs in terms of rules or principles that govern learning. Thus we might explain the trainer's use of words such as "fine" and "good" as "reinforcers" that provide the gymnast with "feedback."

Questions: What are theories? Why do we have them? **Theories** are related sets of statements about events. When possible, descriptive terms and concepts are interwoven into theories. Theories are based on certain assumptions about behavior, such as Watson's assumption that training outweighs talents and abilities or Gesell's assumption that the unfolding of maturational tendencies is inevitable. Theories allow us to derive explanations and predictions. Many developmental theories combine statements about psychological concepts (such as learning and motivation), behavior (such as reading or problem solving), and anatomical structures or biological processes (such as maturation of the nervous system). For instance, a child's ability to learn to read is influenced by her or his motivation, attention span, level of perceptual development—and also by the integrity of processes that are based in the occipital and temporal lobes of the brain.

A satisfactory theory must allow us to make predictions. For instance, a theory concerning the development of gender roles should allow us to predict the circumstances under which children will acquire stereotypical feminine or

maturation The unfolding of genetically determined traits, structures, and functions.

theory A formulation of relationships underlying observed events. A theory involves assumptions and logically derived explanations and predictions.

masculine gender-typed behavior patterns. A broadly satisfying, comprehensive theory should have a wide range of applicability. A broad theory of the development of gender roles might apply to children from different cultural and racial backgrounds and, perhaps, to children with gay male and lesbian sexual orientations as well as children with a heterosexual orientation. If observations cannot be explained by or predicted from a theory, we may need to revise or replace it.

Many theories have been found incapable of explaining or predicting new observations. As a result, they have been revised extensively. For example, Sigmund Freud's psychoanalytic view that assertive career women are suffering from unconscious "penis envy" has met with criticism from his followers (such as Karen Horney) and his antagonists alike. Most modern-day, or "neo-," Freudians have developed different views concerning assertive behavior in girls and women.

Useful theories enable researchers to influence events. This does not mean that developmentalists seek to make children do their bidding—as if they were puppets on strings. Instead, it means that useful theories help developmental professionals consult with parents, teachers, nurses, and children themselves to promote the welfare of children. Psychologists, for example, may summarize and interpret theory and research on the effects of day care to help day-care workers provide an optimal child-care environment. Teachers may use learning theory to help children learn to read and write. In each case, the professional is influencing children, but with the benefit of the children in mind and also, ultimately, with the understanding and approval of parents. Let us consider various theoretical approaches to child development.

Sigmund Freud

Freud is the originator of psychoanalytic theory. He proposed five stages of psychosexual development and emphasized the importance of biological factors in the development of personality. He believed that too little—or too much—gratification during any stage of development could lead to fixation in that stage and to the development of traits that are characteristic of that stage. For example, too little gratification during the oral stage could lead to dependence on others and feelings of depression.

stage theory A theory of development characterized by hypothesizing the existence of distinct periods of life. Stages follow one another in an orderly sequence.

The Psychoanalytic Perspective

According to the psychoanalytic perspective, much—much!—goes on beneath the surface. There are a number of theories within the psychoanalytic perspective. ***Question: What are psychoanalytic theories of child development?*** Each psychoanalytic theory owes its origin to Sigmund Freud. Each psychoanalytic theory sees children—and adults—as caught in conflict. Early in development the conflict is between the child and the world outside. The expression of basic drives such as sex and aggression conflict with parental expectations, social rules, moral codes, even laws. However, the external limits—parental demands and social rules—are brought inside. That is, they are *internalized.* Once this happens, the conflict actually takes place between opposing *inner* forces. The behavior you then observe in the child, even the child's innermost thoughts and emotions, all reflect the results of these hidden battles.

In this section, we explore Freud's theory of psychosexual development and Erik Erikson's theory of psychosocial development. Each is a **stage theory.** That is, each theory sees children as developing through distinct periods of life. Each suggests that the child's experiences during early stages affect the child's emotional balance and social adjustment.

Sigmund Freud's Theory of Psychosexual Development

Sigmund Freud (1856–1939) was a mass of contradictions. He has been lauded as the greatest thinker of the 20th century, the most profound of psychologists. He has been criticized as overrated, even a "false and faithless prophet." He preached liberal views on sexuality but was himself a model of sexual restraint. He invented a popular form of psychotherapy but experienced lifelong psychologically related problems such as migraine headaches, bowel irregularities, fainting under stress, hatred of the telephone, and an addiction to cigars. He smoked 20 cigars a day and could not or would not break the habit even after he developed cancer of the jaw. Despite his personal shortcomings, we can note that few people have shaped our thinking about human nature as deeply as the compassionate physician from Vienna.

Freud formulated the psychoanalytic theory of development and the form of psychotherapy called *psychoanalysis.* He focused on the emotional and social development of children and on the origins of psychological traits such as dependence, obsessive neatness, and vanity. Let's dive into Freud's theory. *Diving* is a good metaphor because Freud believed that most of the human mind lay beneath consciousness, like an iceberg.

Click *Select Theorist* for more on Freud and the psychoanalytic perspective.

The child you are observing is doing and saying many things—crying, crawling, running, talking, building, playing, but all this is the tip of the iceberg. Remember that the tip of an iceberg—even the tip of the giant iceberg that struck the *Titanic*—is only the smaller part of the iceberg. Its greater mass lies below, where it darkens the deep. Freud theorized that people, because of their childhood experiences, are only vaguely aware of the ideas and impulses that actually occupy the greater depths of their minds. Even in children, their deepest thoughts and fears, their most basic urges, remain in the deep waters beneath the surface of awareness, where little light can be shed on them.

Yes, some of the iceberg is visible. Some part of the mind surfaces into consciousness—into the light of awareness. Freud recognized this region as the conscious part of the human mind. He labeled those parts that lie beneath the surface of conscious awareness the preconscious and unconscious parts of the mind. The **preconscious** mind is near the surface. It contains ideas and feelings that are presently beyond awareness, but children and adults can become aware or conscious of them simply by focusing attention on them. An example might be a teacher's name. The **unconscious** mind contains genetic instincts and urges such as hunger, thirst, sexuality, and aggression that we only partially perceive. Some unconscious urges cannot be experienced consciously, because mental images and words cannot portray them in all their color and fury.

This is where our analogy to the iceberg comes to an end. An iceberg is unified and cold, devoid of feeling. The parts of the human personality are intense and often at war with one another; these parts—the id, ego, and superego—all stake claims to our experience and our behavior. Each wishes to prevail. To be sure, we cannot see the id, ego, and superego, which is why Freud referred to them as *psychic structures* rather than *physical structures.* However, Freud inferred their presence from the behavior of the adults he saw in therapy. The only psychic structure present at birth is the **id.** The id is unconscious and represents the biological drives within the infant. The id demands instant gratification of these drives. It cares nothing for parental preferences, moral codes, social rules, or even the law. The seething id is not alone for long. The second psychic structure begins to develop within the first few months: the **ego.** It develops when an infant experiences delays prior to receiving gratification. It blossoms as children learn to obtain gratification for themselves, without screaming or crying. The ego provides rational ways of coping with frustration. The ego curbs the appetites of the id and makes plans that are in keeping with social convention so that a person can find gratification yet avoid the disapproval of others. The id lets children know that they are hungry. The ego creates the idea of walking to the refrigerator, warming up some chicken and broccoli (one can hope, can't one?), and pouring a glass of milk. The **superego** develops over the first few years. It brings inward the wishes and morals of the child's caregivers and other members of the community that are experienced by the child. Throughout the remainder of the child's life, the superego will monitor the intentions and behavior of the ego and send down judgments of right and wrong. If the child misbehaves, it is the superego that will flood him or her with guilt and shame.

Freud was no stranger to conflict himself. The medical establishment of his day was outraged by his view that sexual impulses and their gratification are central factors in children's development. Freud taught that children's instinctive behavior patterns, even those as basic as sucking, urinating, and moving their bowels, involved sexual feelings and that these feelings are centered in different parts of the body during the stages of **psychosexual development.** Freud labeled these the oral, anal, phallic, latency, and genital stages.

The **oral stage** comprises the first year of life. Why "oral"? Give a 5-month-old infant a new toy and watch—it will find its way into the child's mouth. Freud believed that so-called oral activities such as sucking and biting do more than

preconscious In psychoanalytic theory, refers to a state where something is not in awareness but capable of being brought into awareness by focusing of attention.

unconscious In psychoanalytic theory, refers to a state where something is not available to awareness by simple focusing of attention.

id An element of personality that is present at birth, represents physiological drives, and is fully unconscious (a Latin word meaning "it").

ego (EE-go) The second element of personality to develop, characterized by self-awareness, planning, and the delay of gratification (a Latin word meaning "I").

superego The third element of personality, which functions as a moral guardian and sets forth high standards for behavior.

psychosexual development In psychoanalytic theory, the process by which libidinal energy is expressed through different erogenous zones during different stages of development.

oral stage The first stage of psychosexual development, during which gratification is attained primarily through oral activities such as sucking and biting.

nourish the child; they also bring sexual gratification. Freud believed that children encounter conflicts during each stage of psychosexual development. During the oral stage, conflict centers on the nature and extent of oral gratification. Early weaning can lead to frustration. Excessive gratification, on the other hand, can lead an infant to expect that it routinely will be handed everything in life. Too little or too much gratification in a stage of psychosexual development can lead to **fixation** in that stage. Such fixations are made evident by the development of characteristic traits. Among the oral traits we find dependency, gullibility, and optimism—or, the other side of the coin, pessimism. Thus adults with oral fixations might be overly dependent, gullible, and, if pessimistic, depressed. Such adults may also develop exaggerated dependence on "oral activities" such as smoking, eating (that is, *over*eating), alcohol abuse, and nail biting. Even a "biting wit" can be seen as deriving from an oral fixation.

The **anal stage** begins in the second year. During this stage, sexual gratification is derived from contraction and relaxation of the sphincter muscles that control elimination of waste products. During the first year, elimination is reflexive. As the infant matures, it comes increasingly under voluntary muscular control. During toilet training, parents encourage their children to delay the gratification of instant elimination. The increasing demand for self-control can become a source of parent–child conflict, especially when "friends" and relatives tell the parents that *their* child was toilet trained at 18 months! Two kinds of anal fixations may develop. *Anal-retentive* traits like perfectionism, neatness, and cleanliness employ extreme self-control. *Anal-expulsive* traits, on the other hand, tend to let it all hang out; they include traits like carelessness and sloppiness.

Reflect

If you were fixated in a stage of psychosexual development, what stage would it be? Why?

The **phallic stage** begins during the third year of life. Parent–child conflict may develop over masturbation, which many parents treat with punishment and threats. It is normal for children to develop strong sexual attachments to the parent of the other sex during the phallic stage. It is also considered normal for them to begin to view the parent of the same sex as a rival. Girls in this stage may express the wish to marry their fathers when they grow up. Boys are likely to have similar designs on their mothers. At the same time, children notice that girls do not have a penis. The girl becomes envious of the boy's penis ("penis envy") and blames mother for not giving her one. The boy fears that father will castrate him ("castration anxiety") and that he, too, will lose his penis. Freud labeled this conflict in boys the **Oedipus complex.** In the Greek play, *Oedipus Rex,* we find that a Greek king, Oedipus, has unknowingly killed his father and married his mother. Freud labeled similar feelings in girls the **Electra complex.** According to another Greek myth, Electra's father was King Agamemnon. He was killed by her mother and her mother's lover, and Electra seeks revenge. Remember that within Freudian theory, these complexes are normal. Freud believed them to be universal. The complexes normally come to an end by about the ages of 5 or 6. Children resolve them by repressing their hostilities toward the parent of the same sex and identifying with (trying to become like) that parent.

Enough is enough. By the age of 5 or 6, Freud believed, children have experienced more than enough Oedipal conflict. They are motivated to repress their sexual urges, and they enter a **latency stage.** Latency means hidden, and during this period, sexual feelings remain unconscious. During the latency stage, children turn to schoolwork and typically prefer playmates of their own gender. The final stage of psychosexual development, the **genital stage,** begins at puberty. Adolescents in the genital stage prefer to seek sexual gratification through intercourse with a member of the other sex. Freud believed that interest in oral or anal stimulation, masturbation, and male–male or female–female sexual activity are immature forms of sexual conduct that reflect fixations at earlier stages of psychosexual development. Adolescents are again interested in people like their parents of the other sex, but now they normally transfer, or displace, that interest onto other adolescents or adults of the other sex.

Freud's ideas have influenced many areas that affect children, including child-rearing practices, education, and therapy. For example, Freud's views about the

fixation In psychoanalytic theory, arrested development; attachment to objects of an earlier stage.

anal stage The second stage of psychosexual development, when gratification is attained through anal activities such as eliminating wastes.

phallic stage The third stage of psychosexual development, characterized by a shift of libido to the phallic region (from the Greek phallos, meaning "image of the penis").

oedipus complex (ED-uh-puss) A conflict of the phallic stage in which the boy wishes to possess his mother sexually and perceives his father as a rival in love.

electra complex A conflict of the phallic stage in which the girl longs for her father and resents her mother.

latency stage The fourth stage of psychosexual development, characterized by repression of sexual impulses.

genital stage The mature stage of psychosexual development, in which gratification is attained through intercourse with an adult of the other gender.

anal stage have influenced pediatricians and other child-care experts to recommend that toilet training not be started too early nor handled in a punitive manner. Freud's emphasis on the emotional needs of children has influenced educators to be more sensitive to the possible emotional reasons behind a child's misbehavior. He also was an early advocate of sex education in the schools. Freudian theory has had an impact on techniques of child psychotherapy as well.

Reflect

Some developmentalists argue that Freud's theory has been discredited and should not even appear in a scientific work such as a textbook. Others argue that it should be mentioned, briefly, and that it should be clearly stated that Freud's theory is mentioned for historic purposes only. Still others believe that Freud's views remain essential in the understanding of child development. What do you think?

Evaluation Freud's theory has had tremendous appeal and was a major contribution to 20th century thought. It is one of the richest theories of development, explaining the childhood origins of many behaviors and traits and stimulating research on attachment, development of gender roles, moral development, and identification. But despite its richness, Freud's work has been criticized on many grounds. For one thing, Freud developed his theory on the basis of contacts with patients (mostly women) who were experiencing emotional problems (Hergenhahn, 2000). He also concluded that most of his patients' problems originated in childhood conflicts. It is possible that he might have found less evidence of childhood conflict if his sample had consisted of less-troubled individuals. He was also dealing with recollections of his patients' pasts rather than observing children directly. Such recollections are subject to errors in memory, and it may also be that Freud subtly guided his patients into expressing ideas consistent with his own theoretical views.

Some of Freud's own disciples, including Erik Erikson and Karen Horney, believe that Freud placed too much emphasis on basic instincts, unconscious motives, and the like. They argue that people are governed not only by drives such as sex and aggression but also by learning experiences and social relationships. They argue that people are also motivated by conscious desires to achieve, to have aesthetic experiences, and to help others, as well as by the primitive id.

Renate Horney

Karen Horney

Horney, a follower of Freud, argued that he placed too much emphasis on sexual and biological determinants of behavior while neglecting the importance of social factors.

Nor has Freud's theory of psychosexual development escaped criticism. Children may begin to masturbate as early as the first year of life, rather than in the phallic stage. As parents can testify from observing their children play doctor, sexuality in the "latency stage" is not as latent as Freud believed. Freud's view of female development and gender-role behavior reflects the ignorance and male-centered prejudice of his times. The assumption that girls suffer from penis envy has been attacked strongly by modern-day psychoanalysts and others. Karen Horney (1967), for example, contended that little girls do not feel inferior to little boys and that the penis-envy hypothesis is not supported by observations of children. Horney argued that Freud's views reflected a Western cultural prejudice, not good psychological theory.

There has been a historic prejudice against self-assertive, competent women (Worell, 1990; Worell et al., 1999). Many people believe that women should remain passive and submissive, emotional, and dependent on men. In Freud's day these prejudices were more extreme. Psychoanalytic theory, in its original form, reflected the belief that motherhood and family life were the only proper avenues of fulfillment for women.

Once we have catalogued our criticisms of Freud's views, what of merit is left? A number of things. Freud pointed out that behavior is determined and not arbitrary. He pointed out that childhood experiences can have far-reaching effects. He noted that we have defensive ways of looking at the world, that our cognitive processes can be distorted by our efforts to defend ourselves against anxiety and guilt. If these ideas no longer impress us as unique or innovative, it is largely because they have been so widely accepted since Freud gave voice to them.

Erik Erikson's Theory of Psychosocial Development

Question: How does Erikson's theory differ from Freud's? Erikson modified and expanded Freud's theory. Throughout his early childhood in Germany, Erikson did not know that his biological father had left his mother before he was born in 1902 (Erikson, 1975). Erikson's mother and his stepfather, Theodor

Harvard University Archives

■ **Erik Erikson**

Erikson proposed eight stages of psychosocial development extending through the life span. Whereas Freud focused on the expression of primitive drives such as sex and aggression, Erikson focused on social relationships. Whereas Freud believed that personality development involved unconscious conflict and distortion of reality, Erikson believed that we play conscious roles in the development of our own personality and are capable of seeing other people—and ourselves—as we are.

Click *Select Theorist* for more on Erikson and the psychosocial perspective.

identity crisis According to Erikson, a period of inner conflict during which one examines one's values and makes decisions about one's life roles.

life crisis An internal conflict that attends each stage of psychosocial development. Positive resolution of early life crises sets the stage for positive resolution of subsequent life crises.

psychosocial development Erikson's theory, which emphasizes the importance of social relationships and conscious choice throughout the eight stages of development.

trust versus mistrust The first of Erikson's stages of psychosocial development, during which the child comes to (or comes not to) develop a basic sense of trust in others.

Homburger, a pediatrician, reared the boy. Yet Erikson did not look like them. Erikson's blond hair and his blue eyes looked like those of his biological father. His mother and his adoptive father were Jewish and they took young Erikson to the synagogue, but the congregation noted that the youngster looked like a Dane. He felt out of place. He also felt out of place among his classmates, to whom he was Jewish. Many children fantasize that they have been adopted and wonder who their real parents are. So did young Erik, who did not quite fit in either with his family or his peers. He become obsessed with the question "Who am I?". It was the beginning of his quest for self-identity.

As the years went on, Erikson faced another issue that had to do with his identity, a question that is faced by millions of children and adolescents: "What am I to do in life?" Unlike children born into caste systems where they automatically adopt the pathways of their families, Erikson had choices. His stepfather, the physician, encouraged young Erikson to follow in his footsteps, but Erikson forged his own directions in the search for identity. He traveled throughout Europe and studied art. He was painfully aware of a period of serious self-questioning and soulsearching that the older Erikson labeled an **identity crisis.**

He came to realize that he was no Michelangelo, no Monet. The turmoil of his personal quest for identity oriented Erikson toward his life's work: psychotherapy. He met Sigmund Freud and other psychoanalysts in Vienna and plunged into psychoanalytic training under the tutelage of Anna Freud, a distinguished psychoanalyst and the daughter of Sigmund. After his graduation from the Vienna Psychoanalytic Institute in 1933, he came to the United States.

Erikson's psychoanalytic theory, like Freud's, focuses on the development of the emotional life and psychological traits—on social adjustment. But Erikson also focuses on the development of self-identity. Out of the chaos of his own identity problems, Erikson forged a personally meaningful life pattern, and his theory of development differs dramatically from that of his intellectual forebear, Sigmund Freud. To Erikson, development is not the outcome of environmental forces and intrapsychic conflict. Erikson's social relationships had been more crucial than sexual or aggressive instinct as determinants of his development. Therefore, Erikson speaks of *psychosocial development* rather than *psychosexual development.* Furthermore, it seemed to Erikson that he had developed his own personality through a series of conscious and purposeful acts. Consequently, he places greater emphasis on the ego and on one's ability to actively deal with life's conflicts than Freud did.

Erikson (1963) extended Freud's five developmental stages to eight in order to include the developing concerns of the seasons of adulthood. Rather than label his stages after parts of the body, Erikson labeled stages after the **life crises** that the child (and, later, the adult) might develop and experience during that stage. Erikson's stages are outlined in Table 1.1.

Erikson proposed that our social relationships, as well as our levels of physical maturation, give each stage its character. For example, the parent–child relationship and the infant's utter dependence and helplessness are responsible for the nature of the earliest stages of development. The 6-year-old's capacity to profit from the school setting reflects the cognitive capacities to learn to read and to understand the rudiments of mathematics and the physical/perceptual capacities to sit relatively still and focus on schoolwork.

According to Erikson, early experiences exert a continued influence on future development. With proper parental support during the early years, most children resolve early life crises productively. Successful resolution of each crisis bolsters their sense of identity—of who they are and what they stand for—and their expectation of future success.

Stages of Psychosocial Development Each stage in Erikson's theory of **psychosocial development** carries a specific developmental task. Successful completion of this task depends heavily on the nature of the child's social relationships at each stage.

The first stage of psychosocial development is labeled **trust versus mistrust.** The developmental task of this stage is to develop a sense of trust in one's care-

TABLE 1.1 *Comparison of Freud's Stages of Psychosexual Development and Erikson's Stages of Psychosocial Development*

Age	Freud's Stages of Psychosexual Development	Erikson's Stages of Psychosocial Development
Birth to 1 year	**Oral Stage.** Gratification derives from oral activities such as sucking. Fixation leads to development of oral traits such as dependence, depression, gullibility.	**Basic Trust versus Mistrust.** The developmental task is to come to trust the key caregivers, primarily the mother, and the environment. It is desirable for the infant to connect its environment with inner feelings of satisfaction and contentment.
About 1 to 3 years	**Anal Stage.** Gratification derives from anal activities involving elimination. Fixation leads to development of anal-retentive (e.g., excessive neatness) or anal-expulsive traits (e.g., sloppiness).	**Autonomy versus Shame and Doubt.** The developmental task is to develop the desire to make choices and the self-control to regulate one's behavior so that choices can be actualized.
About 3 to 6 years	**Phallic Stage.** Gratification derives from stimulation of the genital region. Oedipal and Electra complexes emerge and are resolved. Fixation leads to development of phallic traits, such as vanity.	**Initiative versus Guilt.** The developmental task is to add initiative—planning and attacking—to choice. The preschooler is on the move and becomes proactive.
About 6 to 12 years	**Latency Stage.** Sexual impulses are suppressed, allowing child to focus on development of social and technological skills.	**Industry versus Inferiority.** The developmental task is to become absorbed in the development and implementation of skills, to master the basics of technology, to become productive.
Adolescence	**Genital Stage.** Reappearance of sexual impulses, with gratification sought through sexual relations with an adult of the other gender.	**Ego Identity versus Role Diffusion.** The developmental task is to associate one's social skills with the development of career goals. More broadly, the development of identity refers to a sense of who one is and what one believes in.
Young Adulthood		**Intimacy versus Isolation.** The developmental task is to commit oneself to another person, to engage in a mature sexual love.
Middle Adulthood		**Generativity versus Stagnation.** The developmental task is to appreciate the opportunity to "give back." Generative people are not only creative; they also give encouragement and guidance to the younger generation, which may include their own children.
Late Adulthood		**Ego Integrity versus Despair.** The developmental task is to achieve wisdom and dignity in the face of declining physical abilities. Ego integrity also means accepting the time and place of one's own life cycle.

Note: Freud believed that development involved the movement of libido (sexual energy) from one erogenous zone to another. He hypothesized that childhood and adolescence can be described in terms of five stages of psychosexual development. Erikson focused more on social relationships, and so he speaks of psychosocial rather than psychosexual development. Erikson added three stages to include development through various stages of adulthood.

givers that will foster feelings of attachment and pave the way for the development of future intimate relationships. A warm, loving relationship with caregivers during infancy leads to a basic sense of trust in people and the world. A cold, nongratifying relationship with caregivers, however, may lead to a pervasive sense of mistrust.

The second stage, **autonomy versus shame and doubt,** occurs during the second and third years. The central tasks are to develop and exercise self-control and independence. Toilet training is one of the challenges faced during the second year. During this year, children also become mobile and inquisitive. Warmly encouraging parents can provide guidance yet teach their children to be proud of

autonomy versus shame and doubt Erikson's second stage of psychosocial development, during which the child develops (or does not develop) the capacity to exercise self-control and independence.

their newly developing autonomy. But parents who demand too much too soon at this stage or who are arbitrarily restrictive can lead a child to perceive self-control as an unattainable goal. A lifelong pattern of self-doubt can follow.

The third stage, **initiative versus guilt,** takes place during the fourth and fifth years. The central tasks are to test new language, motor, and social skills; initiate behavior; and become more independent from one's parents. If the child is supported and encouraged in these efforts, a sense of initiative develops. If, however, the child's initiatives are punished, feelings of guilt may develop.

The fourth stage, **industry versus inferiority,** occurs during the elementary school years, from about ages 6 to 12. The major developmental task is to acquire the basic academic and cultural skills that will enable one to achieve. A sense of industry will contribute to achievement motivation. A sense of inferiority may turn the child away from attempts to acquire skills and compete with peers.

During the elementary school years, children learn to evaluate their competence by comparing their performance to that of peers. If schoolchildren do well in their studies, in sports, and in their social activities, they are likely to develop a sense of industry and become productive. Fine performance in, say, math may compensate for poor or average athletic performance and vice versa. But if children fail consistently in most areas, they are likely to develop feelings of inferiority and withdraw from the arenas of competition.

The fifth stage, **identity versus identity diffusion,** takes place during the teenage years. The central developmental task is for adolescents to develop identity—that is, a sense of who they are and what they stand for. Adolescents may simply adopt the expectations others have for them, or they may examine expectations in the light of their own understanding of the world around them. One aspect of attaining identity is learning "how to connect the roles and skills cultivated earlier with the occupational prototypes of the day" (Erikson, 1963, p. 261)—that is, with jobs. But identity also extends to sexual, political, and religious beliefs and commitments.

If the life crisis of identity versus diffusion is resolved properly, adolescents develop a firm sense of who they are and what they stand for. Identity can then carry them through difficult times and color their achievements with meaning. But if they do not resolve this life crisis properly, they may experience identity diffusion. In this case, they spread themselves thin, running down one blind alley after another and placing themselves at the mercy of leaders who promise to give them the sense of identity they cannot mold for themselves. Erikson's final three stages of development concern adult development rather than child development.

Erikson's views, like Freud's, have influenced child rearing, early childhood education, and therapy with children. For example, Erikson's views about an adolescent identity crisis have entered the popular culture and affected the way many parents and teachers deal with teenagers. Some schools help students master the crisis by means of life-adjustment courses and study units on self-understanding in social studies and literature classes.

Evaluation Erikson's views have received much praise and much criticism. They are appealing in that they emphasize the importance of human consciousness and choice and minimize the role—and the threat—of dark, poorly perceived urges. They are also appealing in that they paint us as prosocial and giving, whereas Freud portrayed us as selfish and needing to be forced into adherence to social norms. Erikson has been praised as well for presenting a unified view of development throughout the life span.

There is also some empirical support for the Eriksonian view that positive resolutions of early life crises lead to more positive behavior later on. For example, infants and toddlers who are securely attached to their mothers—children who appear to have a sense of basic trust in their mothers—are more sociable with their peers than are insecure children (Thompson, 1991a). Trust in the mother seems to develop into willingness to relate to others.

initiative versus guilt Erikson's third stage of psychosocial development, during which the child initiates new activities. Punishment of the child's activities may produce feelings of guilt.

industry versus inferiority Erikson's fourth stage of psychosocial development, in which the child masters (or fails to master) many skills during the elementary school years.

identity versus identity diffusion Erikson's fifth stage of psychosocial development, during which adolescents develop (or fail to develop) a sense of who they are and what they stand for.

The Learning Perspective

During the 1930s, psychologists derived from the learning perspective an ingenious method for helping 5- and 6-year-old children overcome bed-wetting. Most children at this age wake up and go to the bathroom when their bladders are full. But bed wetters sleep through bladder tension and reflexively urinate in bed. The psychologists' objective was to teach sleeping children with full bladders to wake up rather than wet their beds.

The psychologists placed a special pad beneath the sleeping child. When the pad was wet, an electrical circuit was closed, causing a bell to ring and the sleeping child to waken. After several repetitions, most children learned to wake up before they wet the pad. How? Through a technique called classical conditioning, which we explain in this section.

The so-called bell-and-pad method for bed-wetting is an exotic example of the application of learning theory in child development. However, the great majority of applications of learning theory to development are found in everyday events. For example, children are not born knowing what the letters *A* and *B* sound like or how to tie their shoes. They learn these things. They are not born knowing how to do gymnastics. Nor are they born understanding the meanings of abstract concepts such as big, blue, decency, and justice. All these skills and knowledge are learned.

In this section, we discuss learning theories and see how they are involved in child development. We shall see that children are capable of mechanical learning by association (as in the bell-and-pad method), but we shall also see that children are capable of intentional learning. Children purposefully engage in rote learning and trial-and-error learning. Children purposefully observe and imitate the behavior of other people. We shall also see how the principles of learning have been used in **behavior modification** to help children overcome behavior disorders or cope with adjustment problems. Let's begin with John B. Watson's theory of behaviorism.

Behaviorism

Question: What is the theory of behaviorism? John Watson argued that scientists must address observable behavior only. Therefore, a scientific approach to development must focus on the observable behavior of humans and not on thoughts, plans, fantasies, and other mental images.

Let's see how two types of learning—classical and operant conditioning—have contributed to behaviorism and the understanding of development. Then we shall consider a more recently developed theory of learning that deals with children's cognitive processes as well as their overt behavior—social cognitive theory.

Classical conditioning is a simple form of learning in which an originally neutral **stimulus** comes to bring forth, or elicit, the response usually brought forth by a second stimulus as a result of being paired repeatedly with the second stimulus.

Like many other important scientific discoveries, classical conditioning was discovered by accident. Russian physiologist Ivan Pavlov (1849–1936) was doing research on the salivary reflex in dogs. He discovered that reflexes can be learned, or conditioned, through association. Pavlov's dogs began salivating in response to clinking food trays, because clinking had been paired repeatedly with the arrival of food. Pavlov then carried out experiments in which he conditioned his dogs to salivate to the sound of a bell, which had been paired with food.

In the bell-and-pad method for bed-wetting, psychologists repeatedly pair tension in the children's bladders with a stimulus that wakes them up (the bell). The children learn to respond to the bladder tension as if it were a bell—that is, they wake up (see Figure 1.1).

The bell is an unlearned or **unconditioned stimulus** (UCS). Waking up in response to the bell is an unlearned or **unconditioned response** (UCR). Bladder tension is at first a meaningless, or neutral, stimulus (see Figure 1.1). Then, through repeated association with the bell, bladder tension becomes a learned or **conditioned stimulus** (CS) for waking up. Waking up in response to bladder tension (the CS) is a learned or **conditioned response** (CR).

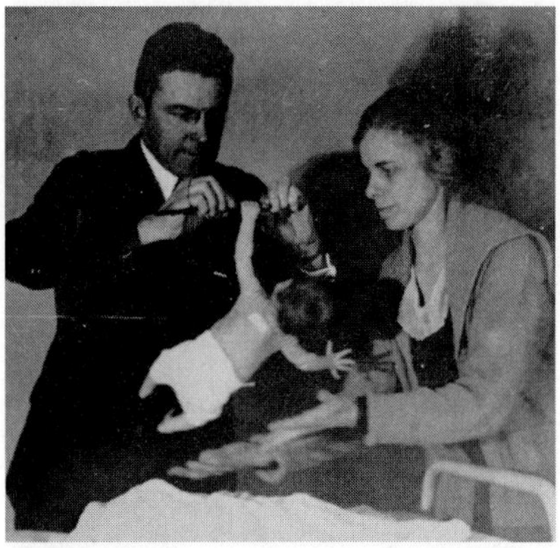

Ferdinand Hamburger, Jr. Archives of The Johns Hopkins University

John B. Watson

Watson is shown here testing the grasping reflex of an infant. As a behaviorist, he believed that the environment is all-important in shaping development.

Click *Select Theorist* for more on Pavlov and classical conditioning.

Reflect

Do you agree or disagree with Watson that any child can be trained to be a "doctor, lawyer, merchant, chief, and, yes, even beggar and thief"? Explain.

behavior modification The systematic application of principles of learning to change problem behaviors or encourage desired behaviors.

classical conditioning A simple form of learning in which one stimulus comes to bring forth the response usually brought forth by a second stimulus by being paired repeatedly with the second stimulus.

stimulus A change in the environment that leads to a change in behavior.

unconditioned stimulus (UCS) A stimulus that elicits a response from an organism without learning.

unconditioned response (UCR) An unlearned response. A response to an unconditioned stimulus.

conditioned stimulus (CS) A previously neutral stimulus that elicits a response, because it has been paired repeatedly with a stimulus that already elicited that response.

conditioned response (CR) A learned response to a previously neutral stimulus.

AP/Wide World Photos

B. F. Skinner

*Skinner, a behaviorist, developed principles of operant conditioning and focused on the role of reinforcement of behavior. He was always interested in writing and spent some time in New York's Greenwich Village, attempting to write fiction. In later years, a successful novel—*Walden II*—described Skinner's view that society shapes children into* wanting *to engage in behavior that is considered socially appropriate within a given cultural setting. Skinner was also the originator of programmed learning.*

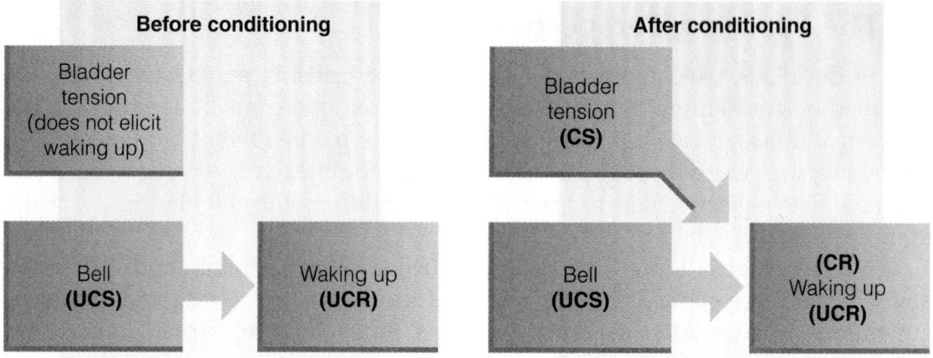

Figure 1.1
A Schematic Representation of Classical Conditioning

Prior to conditioning, the bell elicits waking up. Bladder tension, a neutral stimulus, does not elicit waking up. During conditioning, bladder tension always precedes urination, which in turn causes the bell to ring. After conditioning, bladder tension has become a conditional stimulus (CS) that elicits waking up, which is the conditioned response (CR).

Click *Select Theorist* for more on Skinner and operant conditioning.

operant conditioning A simple form of learning in which an organism learns to engage in behavior that is reinforced.

reinforcement The process of providing stimuli following a response, which has the effect of increasing the frequency of the response.

positive reinforcer A reinforcer that, when applied, increases the frequency of a response.

negative reinforcer A reinforcer that, when removed, increases the frequency of a response.

extinction The cessation of a response that is performed in the absence of reinforcement.

Behaviorists argue that a good deal of emotional learning is acquired through classical conditioning. For example, touching a hot stove is painful, and one or two incidents may elicit a fear response when a child looks at a stove or considers touching it again.

In classical conditioning, children learn to associate stimuli so that a response made to one is then made in response to the other. But in **operant conditioning,** children learn to operate on the environment, or to engage in certain behavior, because of the effects of that behavior.

B. F. Skinner introduced one of the central concepts of operant conditioning—the concept of **reinforcement.** Reinforcers are stimuli that increase the frequency of the behavior they follow. Most children learn to conform their behavior to social codes and rules to earn reinforcers such as the attention and approval of their parents and teachers. Other children, ironically, may learn to misbehave, since misbehavior also draws attention.

In operant conditioning, it matters little how the first desired response is made. The child can happen upon it by chance, as in random behavior, or the child can be physically or verbally guided. A 2-year-old child may be shown how to turn the crank on a music box to play a tune by an adult placing his or her hand over the child's and doing the turning. The child is reinforced by the sound of music, and after training she or he will be able to turn the crank alone.

Various behaviors—such as vocalizing, smiling, and looking at objects—have been conditioned in infants (Gewirtz & Pelaez-Nogueras, 1992). For one example, see the nearby "A Closer Look" feature.

How do we know whether a stimulus is a reinforcer? Any stimulus that increases the frequency of the responses preceding it serves as a reinforcer. Most of the time, food, social approval, and attention serve as reinforcers.

Skinner distinguished between positive and negative reinforcers. **Positive reinforcers** increase the frequency of behaviors when they are *applied.* Food and approval usually serve as positive reinforcers. **Negative reinforcers** increase the frequency of behaviors when they are *removed.* Children often learn to plan ahead so that they need not fear that things will go wrong. Fear acts as a negative reinforcer in that its removal increases the frequency of the behaviors preceding it; for example, fear of failure is removed when students study for a quiz. Figure 1.2 compares positive and negative reinforcers.

Extinction results from repeated performance of operant behavior without reinforcement. After a number of trials, the operant behavior is no longer shown. In many cases children's temper tantrums and crying at bedtime have been

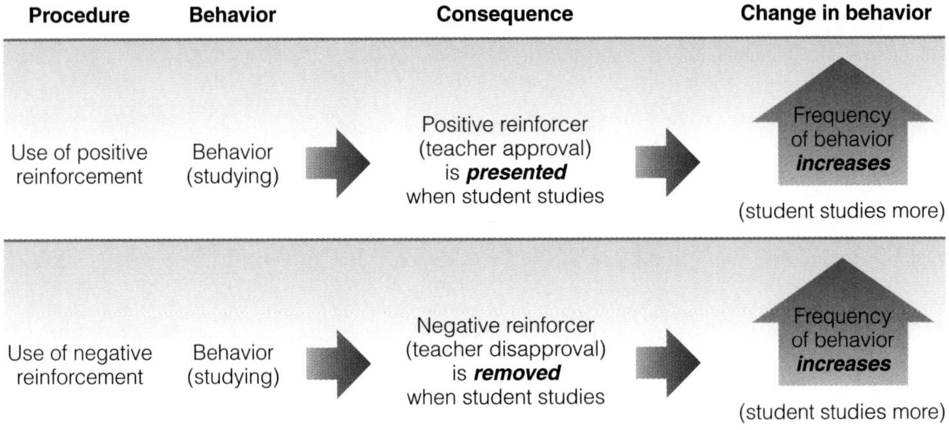
Procedure
Behavior
Consequence
Change in behavior
Use of positive reinforcement
Behavior (studying)
Positive reinforcer (teacher approval) is **presented** when student studies
Frequency of behavior **increases**
(student studies more)
Use of negative reinforcement
Behavior (studying)
Negative reinforcer (teacher disapproval) is **removed** when student studies
Frequency of behavior **increases**
(student studies more)

Figure 1.2
Positive versus Negative Reinforcers

All reinforcers increase *the frequency of behavior. However, negative reinforcers are aversive stimuli that increase the frequency of behavior when they are* removed. *In these examples, teacher approval functions as a positive reinforcer when students study harder because of it. Teacher* disapproval *functions as a negative reinforcer when its* removal *increases the frequency of studying. Can you think of situations in which teacher approval might function as a negative reinforcer?*

extinguished within a few days by simply having parents remain out of the bedroom after the children have been put to bed. Previously, parental attention and company had reinforced the tantrums and crying. When the reinforcement of the problem behavior was removed, the behavior was eliminated.

Punishments are aversive stimuli that *decrease* the frequency of behavior. Negative reinforcers, by contrast, are defined in terms of increasing behavior. (Figure 1.3 compares negative reinforcers with punishments.) Punishing events may be physical (such as spanking), verbal (for example, scolding or criticizing),

punishment An unpleasant stimulus that suppresses behavior.

A Closer Look

Operant Conditioning of Vocalizations in Infants

A classic study by psychologist Harriet Rheingold and her colleagues (Rheingold, Gewirtz, & Ross, 1959) demonstrates how reinforcement and extinction can influence the behavior of infants—in this case, vocalization. A female researcher first observed the subjects, 3-month-old infants, for about half an hour to record baseline (preexperimental) measures of the frequency of their vocalizing. Infants averaged about 13–15 vocalizations each. During the conditioning phase of the study, the researcher reinforced the vocalizations with social stimuli, such as encouraging sounds, smiles, and gentle touches. There was a significant increase in the frequency of vocalizing throughout this phase. By the end of an hour of conditioning spread over a two-day period, the average incidence of vocalizations had nearly doubled to about 24–25 within a half hour. During the extinction phase, as during the baseline period, the researcher passively observed each infant, no longer reinforcing vocalization. After two half-hour extinction periods, average vocalizing had returned to near baseline, about 13–16 per half hour.

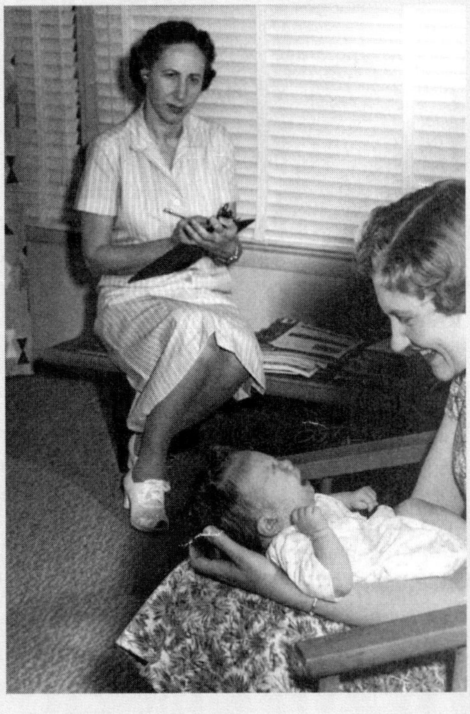

Courtesy of Dr. Arnold Rheingold

Conditioning Verbalizations in Infants

Infants make sounds without being prompted to do so, but research has shown that adults can increase the frequency of infants' verbalizations through use of reinforcement. In this historic photo, Harriet Rheingold observes as a mother attempts to condition verbalizing in her infant.

Figure 1.3
Negative Reinforcers versus Punishments

Negative reinforcers and punishments both tend to be aversive stimuli. However, reinforcers increase *the frequency of behavior. Punishments* decrease *the frequency of behavior. Negative reinforcers increase the frequency of behavior when they are* removed. *Punishments decrease or suppress the frequency of behavior when they are* applied. *Can you think of situations in which punishing students might have effects other than those desired by the teacher?*

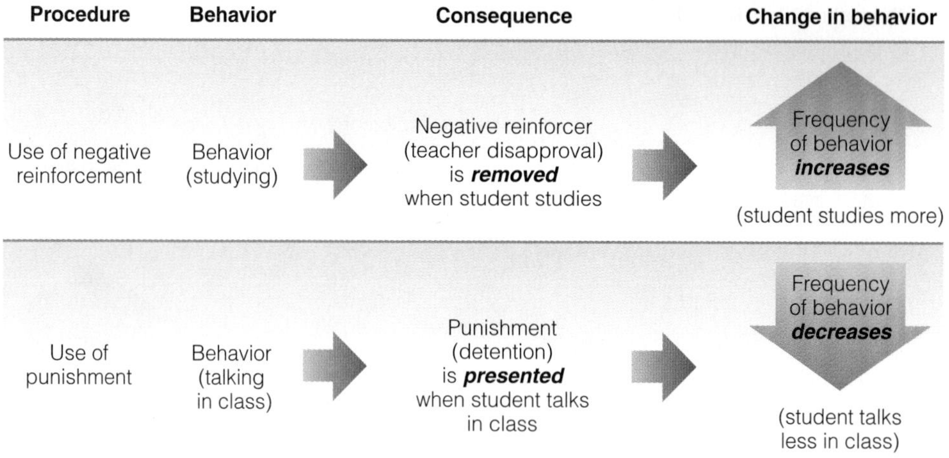
Procedure
Behavior
Consequence
Change in behavior
Use of negative reinforcement
Behavior (studying)
Negative reinforcer (teacher disapproval) is removed when student studies
Frequency of behavior increases
(student studies more)
Use of punishment
Behavior (talking in class)
Punishment (detention) is presented when student talks in class
Frequency of behavior decreases
(student talks less in class)

or may involve removal of privileges. Punishments, like rewards, can influence the probability that behavior will be shown. Strong punishments can rapidly suppress unacceptable behavior. For this reason, punishment may be appropriate in emergencies, as when a child is trying to hit another child with a pointed toy. But many learning theorists prefer to avoid using punishment in rearing children, whenever possible, for reasons such as the following:

- Although punishment suppresses unwanted behavior, it does not in itself suggest alternative, more desirable forms of behavior.
- Punishment tends to be very specific. Although it may suppress unwanted behavior when it is guaranteed, it may not extend to similar situations. It is not unusual for schoolchildren to discover that they can "get away" with almost anything with one teacher but not another. Children may also try to "split" parents—that is, go to the other parent for help or understanding when one parent punishes them.
- Punished children may withdraw from the situation. Severely punished children may run away, cut class, or drop out of school.
- Punishment can create anger and hostility. After being spanked by their parents, children may hit smaller siblings or destroy objects in the home.
- Punishment may generalize too far. The child who is punished severely for bad table manners may stop eating altogether. Overgeneralization is more likely to occur when children do not know exactly why they are being punished and when they have not been shown acceptable alternative behaviors.
- Ironically, children may learn to imitate punishment as a way of dealing with others who fall short of expectations. Children learn by observation, and observing parents use punishment may not only teach them *how* to punish but also lead them to believe that punishment—including physical punishment—is an appropriate form of discipline. It turns out that many child abusers and abusers of intimate partners were harshly punished by their own parents (Ertem Leventhal, & Dobbs, 2000; Swinford et al., 2000).

For all these reasons, many psychologists recommend that it is preferable to reward children for desirable behavior than to punish them for unwanted behavior. By ignoring their misbehavior, or by using **time out** from positive reinforcement, we can consistently avoid reinforcing children for misbehavior.

We can teach children complex behaviors by **shaping,** or at first reinforcing small steps toward the behavioral goals. If a child is being taught to use the potty, the parent may first generously reinforce the learner simply for sitting on the potty for a while, even if the child insists on wearing a diaper at the time. As training proceeds, the parent can demand more before dispensing reinforcement. In teaching a 2-year-old child to put on her own coat, it helps first to praise her for trying to stick her arm into a sleeve on a couple of occasions. Then praise her for actually getting her arm into the sleeve and so on.

time out A behavior-modification technique in which a child who misbehaves is temporarily placed in a drab, restrictive environment in which reinforcement is unavailable.

shaping A procedure for teaching complex behavior patterns by means of reinforcing small steps toward the target behavior.

Operant conditioning is used every day in the **socialization** of young children. For example, as we shall see in Chapter 10, parents and peers influence children to acquire gender-appropriate behaviors through the elaborate use of rewards and punishments. Thus, boys may ignore other boys when they play with dolls and housekeeping toys but play with boys when they use transportation toys.

Many studies have found that when teachers praise and attend to appropriate behavior and ignore misbehavior, study behavior and classroom performance improve, whereas disruptive and aggressive behaviors decrease (Greenwood et al., 1992).

Teachers also frequently use time out from positive reinforcement to discourage misbehavior. In this method, children are placed in drab, restrictive environments for a specified time period, usually about 10 minutes, when they behave disruptively. When isolated, they cannot earn the attention of peers or teachers, and no reinforcing activities are present.

It may strike you that these techniques are not new. Perhaps we all know parents who have ignored their children's misbehavior and have heard of teachers making children sit facing the corner. What is novel is the focus on (1) avoiding punishment and (2) being consistent so that undesirable behavior is not reinforced.

Social Cognitive Theory

Behaviorists tend to limit their discussions of human learning to the classical and operant conditioning of observable behaviors. They theorize that learning in children can be fully explained as the cumulative effect of numerous instances of the association of stimuli (classical conditioning) or the reinforcement of operant behavior (operant conditioning). ***Question: How does social cognitive theory differ from behaviorism?***

Adherents of **social cognitive theory,** such as Albert Bandura (1989, 1991), have shown that much of children's learning also occurs by observing parents, teachers, other children, even characters on TV.[2] Children may need some practice to

[2] The name of this theory remains somewhat in flux. It was originally termed social-learning theory. More recently, it has been referred to as social cognitive theory and sometimes as cognitive social theory. Since a major proponent of this view, Albert Bandura, refers to it as social cognitive theory in recent writings, we shall refer to it in the same way.

socialization The systematic exposure of children to rewards and punishments and to role models who guide them into socially acceptable behavior patterns.

social cognitive theory A cognitively oriented learning theory that emphasizes observational learning in the determining of behavior.

A Closer Look

Using Conditioning to Save an Infant's Life

Methods of conditioning can be used with children who are too young or distressed to respond to verbal forms of therapy. In a classic case study reported by Lang and Melamed (1969), a 9-month-old infant vomited regularly within 10–15 minutes of eating. Diagnostic workups had found no medical basis for the problem, and medical treatments were to no avail. When the case was brought to the attention of Lang and Melamed, the infant weighed only 9 pounds and was in critical condition, being fed by a pump.

The psychologists monitored the infant for the local muscle tension that indicated that vomiting was about to occur. When the child tensed prior to vomiting, a tone was sounded, followed by painful but harmless electric shock. After two 1-hour treatment sessions, the infant's muscle tensions ceased in response to the tone alone, and vomiting soon ceased altogether. At a 1-year follow-up, the infant was still not vomiting and had caught up in weight.

This remarkable procedure included classical and operant conditioning. Through repeated pairings, the tone (CS) came to elicit expectation of electric shock (UCS), so that the psychologists could use the shock sparingly. The shock and, after classical conditioning, the tone served as punishments. The infant soon learned to suppress the behaviors (muscle tensions) that were followed by punishments. By so doing, punishment was avoided. This learning occurred at an age long before verbal intervention was useful, and it apparently saved the infant's life.

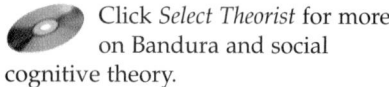

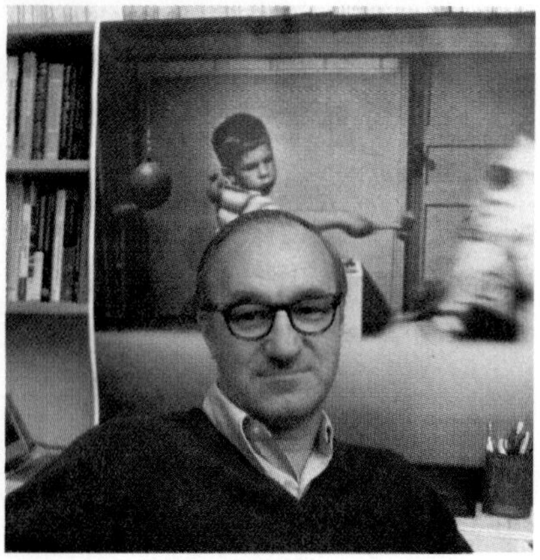

Jon Brenneis/TimePix

■ **Albert Bandura**

Bandura and other social cognitive theorists have shown that one way children learn is by observing others. Whereas behaviorists like John Watson and B. F. Skinner portrayed children as reactive to environmental stimuli, social cognitive theorists depict children as active learners who are capable of fashioning new environments.

Click *Select Theorist* for more on Bandura and social cognitive theory.

Reflect

What kinds of things have you learned by observation? (Is your list long enough?)

reciprocal determinism Mutual interplay of the child's behavior, cognitive characteristics, and environment.

observational learning The acquisition of expectations and skills by means of observing others. In observational learning, skills can be acquired without being emitted and reinforced.

refine their skills, but they can acquire basic know-how through observation. Children may also let these skills *lie latent.* For example, children (and adults) are not likely to imitate aggressive behavior unless they are provoked and believe they are more likely to be rewarded than punished for aggressive behavior (Hall, Herzberger, & Skowronski, 1998).

In the view of the behaviorists, learning occurs by means of mechanical conditioning. There is no reference to thought processes that may occur as a result of conditioning and prior to the performance of responses. There is no role for cognition. In social cognitive theory, by contrast, cognition plays a central role. In fact, Bandura (1991, 2000) now labels the theory social cognitive theory. For social cognitive theorists, learning alters children's mental representation of the environment and influences their belief in their ability to act effectively on the environment. Children choose whether or not to show the new behaviors they have learned. In social cognitive theory, children acquire behaviors without necessarily being directly reinforced. Children's values and expectations of reinforcement also influence the likelihood that they will attempt to imitate the behavior they observe.

Social cognitive theorists see children as active. They intentionally seek out or create environments in which reinforcers are available. As an example of how a child's behavior and characteristics create a reinforcing environment, consider the child who has artistic ability. The child may develop this skill by taking art lessons and by modeling the behaviors of her art teacher. In doing so, she creates an environment of social reinforcement in the form of praise from others. This reinforcement, in turn, influences the child's view of herself as a good artist. This mutual interplay of the child's behavior, cognitive characteristics, and environment is known as **reciprocal determinism** (Bandura, 1989).

Observational Learning **Observational learning,** which is of most interest to social cognitive theorists, may account for most of human learning. It occurs when children observe how parents cook, clean, or repair a broken appliance. It takes place when children watch teachers solve problems on the blackboard or hear them speak in a foreign language. Observational learning does not occur because of direct reinforcement. Children can learn without engaging in overt responses at all. Learning will occur as long as children pay attention to the behavior of others.

Identification, a term derived from Freud's psychoanalytic theory, refers to children's attempts to internalize the traits of other people. However, from the perspective of social cognitive theory, identification may be viewed as a broad process of imitation through which children acquire behavior patterns that are similar to those of other people. Once children are a few years old, observational learning becomes intentional, and children appear to select models for imitation who show certain positive characteristics.

In social cognitive theory, the people after whom children pattern their own behavior are termed *models.* Traits that encourage children to identify with models include warmth, competence, social dominance, and social status. Traits such as these appear to give models access to the tangible rewards and social success to which children themselves aspire. Children are also likely to imitate models they perceive to be similar to themselves.

Evaluation of Learning Theories

Learning theories have done a fine job of allowing us to describe, explain, predict, and influence many aspects of children's behavior. Psychologists and educators have developed many innovative applications of conditioning and social cognitive theory. The use of the bell-and-pad method for bed-wetting is an example of behavior modification that probably would not have been derived from any other theoretical approach. Behavior modification has been used in innovative ways to deal with autistic children, self-injurious children, and children showing temper tantrums and conduct disorders. Many of the teaching approaches used in educational TV shows are based on learning theory.

Despite the demonstrated effectiveness of behavior-modification procedures, learning-theory approaches to child development have been criticized in several ways. First, there is the theoretical question as to whether the conditioning process in children is mechanical or whether it changes the ways in which children mentally represent the environment. In addition, learning theorists may have exaggerated the role of learning in development by underestimating the role of biological-maturational factors (Horowitz, 1992). Social cognitive theorists seem to be working on these issues. For example, social cognitive theorists place more value on cognition and view children as being active, not as merely reacting mechanically to stimuli. Now let us turn to theories that place cognition at the heart of development.

The Cognitive Perspective

Psychologists with a cognitive perspective focus on children's mental processes. They investigate the ways in which children perceive and mentally represent the world, how they develop thought and logic, how they develop the ability to solve problems. Cognitive psychologists, in short, attempt to study all those things we refer to as the *mind.*

Click *Select Theorist* for more on Piaget and cognitive-developmental theory.

The cognitive perspective has many faces. One is the **cognitive-developmental theory** advanced by the Swiss biologist Jean Piaget (1896–1980). Another is information-processing theory.

Jean Piaget's Cognitive-Developmental Theory

Jean Piaget was born and reared in Switzerland. His first intellectual love was biology, and he published his first scientific article at the age of 10. He became a laboratory assistant to the director of a museum of natural history and engaged in research on mollusks (oysters, clams, snails, and such). The director soon died, and Piaget published the findings himself. On the basis of these papers, he was offered a curatorship at a museum in Geneva, but had to turn it down. After all, he was only 11.

During adolescence Piaget studied philosophy, logic, and mathematics, but took his Ph.D. in biology. In 1920, Piaget obtained a job at the Binet Institute in Paris, where work on intelligence tests was being conducted. His initial task was to adapt a number of verbal reasoning items that had originated in England for use with French children. To do so, Piaget had to try out the items on children in various age groups and see whether they could arrive at correct answers. The task was becoming boring until Piaget became intrigued by the children's incorrect answers. Another investigator might have shrugged them off and forgotten them, but young Piaget realized that there were methods to his children's madness. The wrong answers seemed to reflect consistent, if illogical, cognitive processes. Piaget investigated these "wrong" answers by probing for the underlying patterns of thought that had led to them. He began to publish a series of articles on children's thought processes.

Reflect

When you get an item wrong on a test, do you sometimes wish that the professor would pay more attention to how you arrived at the answer than the fact that it is wrong? Why did Piaget do precisely that with children?

Piaget wrote dozens of books and scores of articles, but his work was almost unknown in English-speaking countries until the mid-1950s. For one thing, Piaget's writing is difficult to understand, even to native speakers of French. (One of Piaget's favorite jokes was that he had the advantage of *not* having to read Piaget.) For another, it took him years to formulate his ideas. Piaget's views were also very different from those of other developmentalists. Psychology in England and the United States was dominated by behaviorism and psychoanalysis, and Piaget's writings had a biological-cognitive flavor. They didn't fit the mold. Today the world of child development has been turned topsy-turvy, with many English-speaking developmentalists trying to fit their views to Piaget's.

Various theorists have attempted to explain different types of events and have had very different views of the basic nature of children. Behaviorists such as John B. Watson have focused on the acquisition of overt behavior. They see children as blank slates that are written upon by experience—as reactors to environmental stimulation, not as actors. Freud's psychoanalytic theory focuses on personality

cognitive-developmental theory The stage theory that holds that the child's abilities to mentally represent the world and solve problems unfold as a result of the interaction of experience and the maturation of neurological structures.

Jean Piaget

Piaget's cognitive-developmental theory is a stage theory that focuses on the ways children adapt to the environment by mentally representing the world and solving problems. Piaget's early training as a biologist led him to view children as mentally assimilating, and accommodating to, aspects of their environment.

and emotional development. It portrays children as largely irrational and at the mercy of instinctive impulses—as driven creatures caught between sexual and aggressive urges and the stifling codes of parents and society.

Question: What are Jean Piaget's views on development? Piaget was concerned with how children form concepts or mental representations of the world and how they manipulate their concepts in order to plan changes in the external world. Freud believed that conscious thought represents only a small portion of what occurs in the mind and an illusory portion at that. Piaget, by contrast, believed that thought processes are at the heart of what it is to be human. But Piaget, like the behaviorists, recognized that thoughts cannot be measured directly, and so he tried to link his views on children's mental processes to observable behavior.

Piaget regarded maturing children as natural physicists who actively intend to learn about and take intellectual charge of their worlds. In the Piagetian view, children who squish their food and laugh enthusiastically are often acting as budding scientists. In addition to enjoying a response from parents, they are studying the texture and consistency of their food. (Parents, of course, often prefer that their children practice these experiments in the laboratory, not the dining room.)

Piaget's Basic Concepts Researchers tie concepts together in theoretical packages. Psychoanalysts integrate concepts such as *ego* and *anal traits* into principles that govern personality development. Behaviorists tie concepts such as *stimulus* and *reinforcement* together into principles that govern processes of learning. Piaget tied concepts such as *schemes, adaptation, assimilation, accommodation,* and *equilibration* together to describe and explain cognitive development.

Piaget defines the **scheme** as a pattern of action or a mental structure that is involved in acquiring or organizing knowledge. According to Piaget, acting on the environment and acquiring knowledge occur simultaneously. As action patterns, schemes tend to be repeated and to occur in certain types of situations.

Among older children and adults, a scheme may be the inclusion of an object in a class. For example, the mammal class, or concept, includes a group of animals that are warm-blooded and nurse their young. The inclusion of cats, apes, buffalo, whales, and people in the mammal class involves a series of schemes that expand the child's knowledge of the natural world.

But schemes need not involve words. Babies, for example, are said to have sucking schemes, grasping schemes, and looking schemes. Newborn babies tend to suck things that are placed in their mouths, to grasp objects placed in their hands, and to visually track moving objects. Piaget would say that infants' schemes give meaning to the objects around them. Even in the first months of life, infants are responding to objects as "things I can suck" versus "things I can't suck," and as "things I can grasp" versus "things I can't grasp."

Sucking and grasping are reflexes, but Piaget called them schemes because the concept of the reflex implies that children behave mechanically—that they do not act until they are stimulated. While newborns do respond mechanically to certain stimuli, they also show some flexibility in their behavior. Piaget described behavior as becoming active, intentional, and purposeful even within the first few weeks. Piaget drew a connection between the wordless schemes of infants and the complex mental structures of older children and adults, because both transform experience into knowing. Both reflect an active and organized quest for knowledge.

Adaptation refers to the interaction between the organism and the environment. This term reflects Piaget's early interest in biology. According to Piaget, all organisms adapt to their environment; it is a biological tendency. Adaptation consists of two complementary processes, assimilation and accommodation, that occur throughout life.

The concept of **assimilation** also has its roots in biology. In biology, assimilation is the process by which food is digested and converted into the tissues that compose an animal. Cognitive assimilation refers to the process by which someone responds to new objects or events according to existing schemes or ways of organizing knowledge. Infants, for example, usually try to place new objects in their

scheme According to Piaget, an action pattern or mental structure that is involved in the acquisition and organization of knowledge.

adaptation According to Piaget, the interaction between the organism and the environment. It consists of two processes: assimilation and accommodation.

assimilation According to Piaget, the incorporation of new events or knowledge into existing schemes.

mouths to suck, feel, or explore them. Piaget would say that the child is assimilating (fitting) a new toy or object into the sucking-an-object activity or scheme. Similarly, 2-year-olds who refer to sheep and cows as "doggies" or "bow-wows" can be said to be assimilating these new animals into the doggy (or bow-wow) scheme. As they develop, children adapt by acquiring more precise schemes for assimilating these animals. Their cognitive organization will blossom into a hierarchical structure in which dogs and sheep are assimilated as mammals and mammals are further assimilated as animals.

Sometimes, a novel object or event cannot be made to fit (that is, cannot be assimilated into an existing scheme). In that case, the scheme may be changed or a new scheme created in order to incorporate the new event. This process is called **accommodation.** Accommodation is also a biological term, meaning a change in structure that permits an organism to adjust or adapt to a novel object or event, to a new source of stimulation.

Reflect

How do Piaget's views on cognitive development reflect his background as a biologist?

Consider the sucking reflex. Within the first month of life, infants modify sucking behavior as a result of experience sucking various objects. The nipple on the bottle is sucked one way; the thumb in a different way. Infants accommodate further by rejecting objects that are too large, that taste bad, or that are of the wrong texture or temperature. They learn that certain things are not to be sucked and may experiment with new ways to relate to them.

Two-year-olds may at first try to assimilate cats and other animals into the "doggy" scheme. However, children accommodate to parental correction and the desire to be understood by creating new mental structures, such as classes or categories for cats, cows, sheep, and other animals.

Piaget theorized that when children can assimilate new events to existing schemes, they are in a state of cognitive harmony, or equilibrium. When something that does not fit happens along, their state of equilibrium is disturbed and they may try to accommodate to it. The process of restoring equilibrium is termed **equilibration.** Piaget believed that the attempt to restore equilibrium is the source of intellectual motivation and lies at the heart of the natural curiosity of the child.

Piaget's Stages of Cognitive Development Piaget (1963) hypothesized that children's cognitive processes develop in an orderly sequence, or series, of stages. As with motor development, some children may be more advanced than others at particular ages, but the development sequence is normally invariant. Piaget identified four major stages of cognitive development: *sensorimotor, preoperational, concrete operational,* and *formal operational.* These stages are described in Table 1.2 and will be discussed in detail in Chapters 6, 9, 12, and 15.

Piaget believed that the cognitive developments of each stage, and of the substages within them, are universal. One reason for this is that cognitive development largely depends on the maturation of the brain; and, assuming minimal nourishment, the course of brain maturation will be similar from child to child. Second, cognitive developments are based on children's interactions with their environments. While no two children share exactly the same environment, the broad realities are compelling enough that practically all children must learn to cope with them. For example, gravity affects us all, so all children have the opportunity to learn that dropped objects move downward. Children from different cultures may reach for different objects, but all normally learn that reaching for things enables them to touch or grasp them.

Piaget also believed that the cognitive developments of one stage, or one substage, are made possible by the cognitive achievements of the preceding stage. In Chapter 6, we shall see how stage develops from stage and how substage grows out of substage.

Because Piaget's theory focuses on cognitive development, its applications are primarily in educational settings. Teachers following Piaget's views would engage the child actively in solving problems. They would gear instruction to the child's developmental level and offer activities that challenge the child to advance to the next level. For example, 5-year-olds learn primarily through play and direct

accommodation According to Piaget, the modification of existing schemes to permit the incorporation of new events or knowledge.

equilibration The creation of an equilibrium, or balance, between assimilation and accommodation as a way of incorporating new events or knowledge.

TABLE 1.2 *Jean Piaget's Stages of Cognitive Development*

Stage	Approximate Age	About . . .
Sensorimotor	Birth–2 years	At first, the child lacks language and does not use symbols or mental representations of objects. In time, reflexive responding ends, and intentional behavior—as in making interesting stimulation last—begins. The child develops the object concept and acquires the basics of language.
Preoperational	2–7 years	The child begins to represent the world mentally, but thought is egocentric. The child does not focus on two aspects of a situation at once and therefore lacks conservation. The child shows animism, artificialism, and objective responsibility for wrongdoing.
Concrete operational	7–12 years	Logical mental actions—called operations—begin. The child develops conservation concepts, can adopt the viewpoint of others, can classify objects in series, and shows comprehension of basic relational concepts (such as one object being larger or heavier than another).
Formal operational	12 years and above	Mature, adult thought emerges. Thinking is characterized by deductive logic, consideration of various possibilities (mental trial and error), abstract thought, and the formation and testing of hypotheses.

sensory contact with the environment. Early formal instruction using workbooks and paper may be less effective in this age group (Crain, 2000).

Evaluation Many researchers, using a variety of methods, have found that Piaget may have underestimated the ages when children are capable of doing certain things. It also appears that cognitive skills may develop more gradually than Piaget thought and not in discrete stages. Here let it suffice to note that Piaget presented us with a view of children very different from the psychoanalytic and behaviorist views, along with a strong theoretical foundation for researchers concerned with sequences in children's cognitive development.

Information-Processing Theory

Click *Cognition* for more on information-processing theory.

Another face of the cognitive perspective is information processing (Klahr, 1992; Flavell, Miller, & Miller, 2002). ***Question: What is information-processing theory?*** Psychological thought has long been influenced by the status of the physical sciences of the day. For example, Freud's psychoanalytic theory was related to the development of thermodynamics in the 19th century. Many of today's cognitive psychologists are influenced by concepts of computer science. Computers process information to solve problems. Information is encoded so that it can be accepted as input and then fed ("inputted") into the computer. Then it is placed in working memory (RAM) while it is manipulated. The information can be stored more permanently on a storage device such as a hard drive or a CD. Many psychologists speak of people as having working or short-term memory (corresponding to RAM) and a more permanent long-term memory (corresponding to storage). If information has been placed in long-term memory, it must be retrieved before we can work on it again. To retrieve information from computer storage, we must know the code or name for the data file and the rules for retrieving data files. Similarly, note psychologists, we must have appropriate cues to retrieve information from our own long-term memories, or the information is lost to us.

Thus, many cognitive psychologists focus on information processing in people—the processes by which information is encoded (input), stored (in long-term memory), retrieved (placed in short-term memory), and manipulated to solve problems (output). Our strategies for solving problems are sometimes referred to as our "mental programs" or "software." In this computer metaphor, our brains are the "hardware" that runs our mental programs. Our brains—consisting of billions of neurons that may be combined in multiple ways—become the most "personal" computers.

Reflect

Think of your own brain as a computer. Where is your "hard drive"? How do you keep information in "memory"? What academic discipline tries to answer these questions?

When psychologists who study information processing contemplate the cognitive development of children, they are likely to talk in terms of the size of the child's short-term memory at a given age and of the number of programs a child can run simultaneously. Research suggests that these are indeed useful ways of talking about children (see Chapter 12).

The most obvious applications of information processing occur in teaching. For example, information-processing models alert teachers to the sequence of steps by which children acquire information, commit it to memory, and retrieve it to solve problems. By understanding this sequence, teachers can provide experiences that give students practice with each stage. The information-processing model is also a useful guide in diagnosing and treating children's learning difficulties. Each "component" in the information-processing "system" can be assessed when the trouble spot has been identified, and methods for correcting the problem can be applied.

Now that we have established that the brain can be thought of as a biological computer, let us see what other aspects of biology can be theoretically connected with child development.

The Biological Perspective

The biological perspective pertains to aspects of physical development. ***Question: What is the scope of the biological perspective?*** The biological perspective refers to gains in height and weight, development of the nervous system, developments that are connected with hormones, and heredity. The key role of the biological perspective threads its way through this book, from the discussion of heredity to the ways in which sperm and ova are formed, the dramatic multiplication of cells during the embryonic stage of prenatal development, and ways in which hormones stoke the changes of puberty. But the psychological and social developments of the child and adolescent are also rooted in biological structures and processes. Here we consider two biologically oriented theories of development: *maturational theory* and *ethology.*

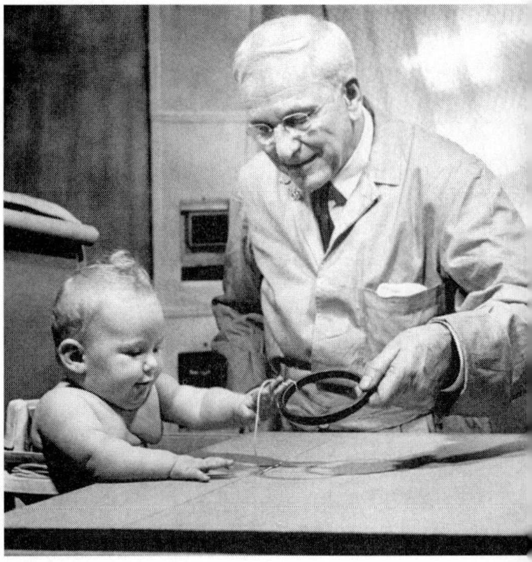

Herbert Gehr/TimePix

Arnold Gesell

Gesell was a major proponent of the maturational theory of child development. This theory focuses largely on the unfolding of genetically determined developmental sequences.

Maturational Theory—Development as Unfolding

Question: What is maturational theory? **Maturational theory** focuses on the unfolding of genetically determined developmental sequences. The theory of Sigmund Freud assumes that biological maturation provides the foundation for changes in personality and emotional development. However, maturational theory, as propounded by Arnold Gesell (1880–1961), argues that all areas of development are self-regulated by the unfolding of natural plans and processes. Few contemporary students of child development would agree that maturation is the central factor in all areas of development. However, very few would dispute that maturation plays the major role in areas such as motor development.

Maturational processes tend to follow invariant sequences. In the case of motor development, children sit up before they stand, and they stand before they walk. It appears that these motor skills are made possible by the progressive maturation of certain parts of the nervous system. Numerous investigators have also wondered whether learning experiences have an important influence on motor development—whether, for example, training can accelerate children's progress through this sequence. Early training only slightly accelerates motor development (see Chapter 5). No amount of training, moreover, can teach these skills to children whose levels of maturation are not sufficiently advanced. In maturational terms, children must be "ready" to acquire new behavior patterns. The unfolding of natural processes creates the foundation on which experiences can build.

Click *Physical Development* for more on the biological perspective.

A few studies have focused on the effects of purposefully preventing infants from practicing certain motor skills during the early months. When children who are deprived of experience in this way are again permitted to move about freely at more advanced ages, they tend to acquire these motor skills almost literally overnight. When we are ready to learn, we tend to learn quickly. When we are not

maturational theory Arnold Gesell's view that development is self-regulated by the unfolding of natural plans (that is, heredity) and processes.

ready, learning proceeds tediously, if it occurs at all. Educators are understandably concerned with knowing when children are ready to acquire academic skills.

The work of maturational theorists has provided standards in many areas of development against which children may be compared to see if they are developing normally (Thelen & Adolph, 1992). Parents (especially first-time parents) frequently consult child-rearing books to check whether the age when their child first sits up, walks, talks, and so forth is typical for its age.

Reflect

What aspects of your own development have mainly involved "maturation"? How do you know your views are accurate?

Evaluation Most psychologists acknowledge that maturation—the unfolding of the genetic code—plays a key role in the child's development. But they also note how children's environments interact with inherited and maturational tendencies in directing their development. For example, although children cannot throw a ball or play the piano before reaching a certain level of neurological and physical maturation, they also acquire these behaviors through the learning process (Crain, 2000).

Click *Select Theorist* for more on Bowlby and ethology.

Ethology—"Doing What Comes Naturally"

Ethology is another biologically oriented theory, and it points to the evolution of humans within the animal kingdom. It was heavily influenced by the 19th-century work of Charles Darwin and by the work of the 20th-century European ethologists Konrad Lorenz and Niko Tinbergen.

Question: What is ethology? The core of ethology involves instinctive, or inborn, behavior patterns. There is no question that physical traits are inborn, but the notion of "inheriting" behavior has been more controversial. Yet it would appear that animals tend to be neurally "prewired"—that is, born with preprogrammed tendencies—to respond to specific situations in specific ways. For example, birds that are reared in isolation from other birds will build nests during the mating season—even if they have never seen another bird building a nest or, for that matter, a nest itself. Similarly, male Siamese fighting fish that are reared in isolation will assume stereotypical threatening stances and attack other males that are introduced into their tanks.

Reflect

Do you believe that any aspects of human behavior are instinctive? Explain.

These behaviors could not have been learned. They are "built in," or instinctive. They are also referred to as inborn **fixed-action patterns (FAPs).** Why are male Siamese fighting fish more aggressive than females? It is known that during prenatal development, genes and sex hormones are responsible for the physical development of female and male sex organs. Most theorists also believe that in many species, including humans, sex hormones can "masculinize" or "feminize" the embryonic brain by creating tendencies to behave in stereotypical masculine or feminine ways (Bailey, Dunne, & Martin, 2000). Testosterone, the male sex hormone, seems to be connected with feelings of self-confidence, high activity levels, and—the negative side—aggressiveness (Pope, Kouri, & Hudson, 2000; Sullivan, 2000).

The FAP of attachment, like other FAPs, is theorized to occur in the presence of a species-specific **releasing stimulus.** Questions arise as to how much, if any, behavior is instinctive in humans. According to John Bowlby (Bowlby, 1988; Ainsworth & Bowlby, 1991), babies instinctively smile in response to a human face, stimulating caretaking behavior, and the formation of bonds of attachment.

Ethologists theorize that many FAPs, including those involved in attachment, occur during a **critical period** of life. Young animals become attached to their mothers or parents if releasing stimuli are present during such a period (see Chapter 7). Ducks and geese, for example, become attached to the first moving object they encounter during the critical period (Lorenz, 1962, 1981). If that object is human, so be it—"Mommy" is then a person and not a duck or goose.

Most theorists with an ethological perspective do not maintain that the process of forming attachments is so mechanical with humans. Moreover, they tend to assume that instinctive behaviors can be modified through learning.

It has been generally believed that the higher we go in the animal kingdom, the less the animal is driven by instinct. In the case of humans, it has generally been assumed that learning and culture are more important than instinct as determi-

ethology The study of behavior patterns that are characteristic of various species.

fixed-action pattern An instinct; abbreviated FAP.

releasing stimulus In ethology, a stimulus that elicits an instinctive response.

critical period A period of time when an instinctive response can be elicited by a particular stimulus.

nants of behavior. Research into the ethological perspective suggests, however, that instinct continues to play a role in human behavior. The questions research seeks to answer are, What areas of behavior and development involve instinct? How vital a role does instinct play? What are the ways in which instinct manifests itself among humans?

The Ecological Perspective

Ecology is the branch of biology that deals with the relationships between living organisms and their environment. ***Question: What is the ecological systems theory of child development?*** The **ecological systems theory** of child development addresses aspects of psychological, social, and emotional development, as well as biological development. Ecological theorists explain child development in terms of the interaction between children and the settings in which they live (Bronfenbrenner, 1989; Bronfenbrenner & Evans, 2000).

According to Urie Bronfenbrenner, the first proposition of ecological theory is that the traditional, unidirectional approach to understanding child–environment relationships is insufficient. The ecological approach argues that the developmental process cannot be completely understood unless we focus on the *reciprocal interactions* between the child and the parents, not just maturational forces (nature) or parental child-rearing approaches (nurture).

Consider the example of the ways in which parents interact with infants. Some parents may choose to feed newborns on demand, whereas others may decide to adhere to a schedule in which feedings occur 4 hours apart. Certainly, parental feeding plans will affect the child. But the basic (apparently inborn) temperaments of children differ (see Chapter 7), and some children are more likely than others to accept their parents' feeding patterns. Some children, that is, are basically "easy." Easy children readily develop regular cycles of eating and sleeping and are likely to conform to a rigid feeding schedule. Other children are basically "difficult." Difficult children are slow to develop regular cycles of eating and sleeping. They may not readily adapt to a rigid feeding schedule, and the parents' wishes may have to be modified if the peace is to be kept.

The point is this: Parents are part of the child's environment, and while parents have a major influence on the child, the influence is not a one-way street.

Bronfenbrenner (1979, 1989) suggests that we can view the setting or contexts of human development as consisting of four systems. Each of these systems is embedded within the next larger context. From narrowest to widest, these systems consist of the microsystem, the mesosystem, the exosystem, and the macrosystem (see Figure 1.4).

The Microsystem

The **microsystem** involves the interactions of the child and other people in the immediate setting, such as the home, the school, or the peer group. Initially, the microsystem is small, involving care-giving interactions with the parents or others, usually at home. As children get older, they do more, with more people, in more places (Garbarino, 1982).

The Mesosystem

The **mesosystem** involves the interactions of the various settings within the microsystem. For instance, the home and the school interact during parent–teacher conferences. The school and the larger community interact when children are taken on field trips. The ecological approach addresses the joint impact of two or more settings on the child. The Harmonium Project teaches school counselors how to investigate the patterns that affect a child's life so that problems at home, school, or in the community can be treated within the relational context of the family and the community (Laveman, 2000).

Reflect

What people and institutions make up the microsystem, mesosystem, exosystem, and macrosystem in which you are functioning today? How has the makeup of these systems changed as you have developed?

ecology The branch of biology that deals with the relationships between living organisms and their environment.

ecological systems theory The view that explains child development in terms of the reciprocal influences between children and the settings that make up their environment.

microsystem The immediate settings with which the child interacts, such as the home, the school, and one's peers (from the Greek *mikros,* meaning "small").

mesosystem The interlocking settings that influence the child, such as the interaction of the school and the larger community when children are taken on field trips (from the Greek *mesos,* meaning "middle").

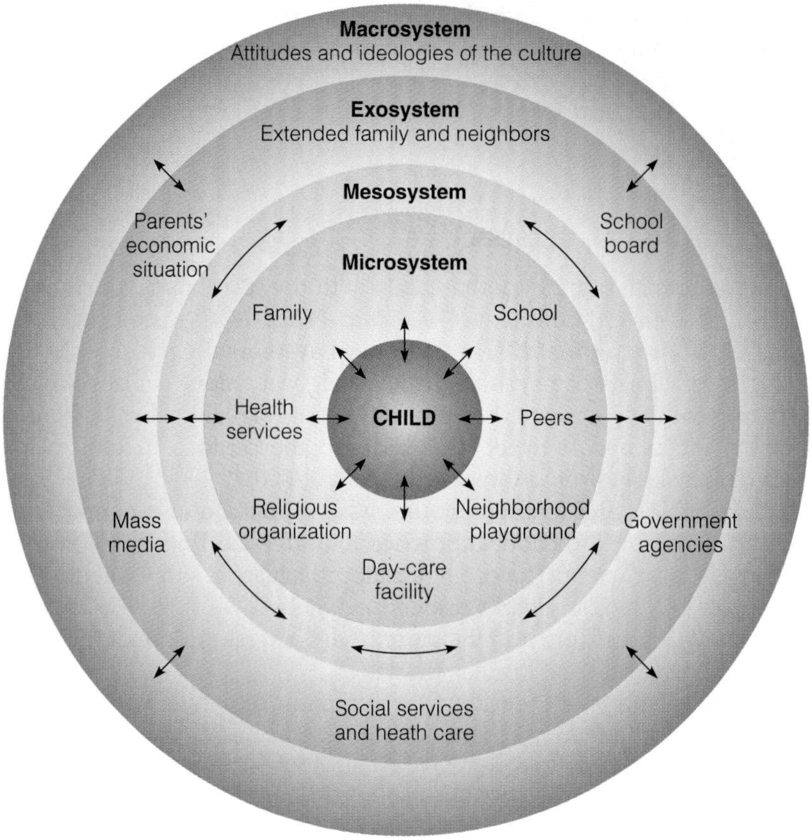

Figure 1.4
The Contexts of Human Development

According to ecological theory, the systems within which children develop are embedded within larger systems. Children and these systems reciprocally influence each other.
Source: *Garbarino, 1982.*

The Exosystem

The **exosystem** involves the institutions in which the child does not directly participate, but which exert an indirect influence on the child. For example, the school board is part of the child's exosystem because board members construct curricula for the child's education, determine what books will be in the school library, and so forth. In similar fashion, the parents' workplaces and economic situations determine the hours during which they will be available to the child, help determine what mood they will be in when they interact with the child, and so on. Poverty and unemployment cause psychological distress in parents, which in turn decreases their capacity for supportive, consistent, and involved parenting (Corcoran, 2001; Stockhammer et al., 2001). Their children, as a result, may experience adjustment problems both at home and in school (Brunswick, 1999). Studies that address the effects of housing, health care, TV programs, church attendance, government agencies, or even the presence or absence of a telephone on children all examine the interactions of the exosystem with the child.

The Macrosystem

The **macrosystem** involves the interaction of children with the beliefs, values, expectations, and lifestyles of their cultural settings. Cross-cultural studies examine children's interactions with their macrosystem in different cultures. Macrosystems exist within a particular culture as well. For example, within the United States, the two-wage-earner family, the low-income single-parent household, and the more traditional family with father as sole breadwinner constitute three different macrosystems. Each exhibits its own characteristic lifestyle, set of values, and expectations (Bronfenbrenner, 1989). One issue affecting children in the United States today is multiculturalism. A study with 258 Mexican American 8th- to 11th-graders in various school districts found that those who perceived their environment to be multicultural found school to be easier, obtained relatively higher grades, and said that they were likely to stay in school (Tan, 1999).

exosystem Community institutions and settings that indirectly influence the child, such as the school board and the parents' workplaces (from the Greek *exo-*, meaning "outside").

macrosystem The basic institutions and ideologies that influence the child, such as the American ideals of freedom of expression and equality under the law (from the Greek *makros*, meaning "long" or "enlarged").

The ecological ("multisystemic") approach broadens the strategies for intervention in problems such as prevention of teenage pregnancy (Corcoran, 2000, 2001), child abuse (Stockhammer et al., 2001), and juvenile offending, including substance abuse (Brunswick, 1999).

Evaluation

Ecological theory may be most valuable in helping researchers become aware of the systems with which children interact. Much research at the level of the mesosystem focuses on the shifts in setting that children encounter as they develop. For example, the health of the child requires interlocking relationships between parents and the health system, just as the education of the child requires the interaction of parents and school personnel. At the level of the exosystem, researchers look into the effects of parents' work lives, welfare agencies, transportation systems, shopping facilities, and so on. At the level of the macrosystem, we may compare child-rearing practices in the United States with those in other countries. We will learn more about the role of culture in our discussion of the sociocultural perspective.

The Sociocultural Perspective

According to the sociocultural perspective, children (and adults) are social beings who are greatly influenced by the cultures in which they live. Yes, we may all have a certain genetic heritage. There is no question that we are affected by biochemical forces such as neurotransmitters and hormones. We may be biologically "prewired" to form attachments and engage in other behaviors. Perhaps there are psychological tendencies to learn in certain ways or ways in which the psychological past affects the present. But, as noted within the ecological perspective, we are also affected by the customs, traditions, languages, and heritages of the societies in which we live. ***Question: What is meant by the sociocultural perspective?*** The sociocultural perspective overlaps with other perspectives on child development; however, developmentalists are likely to use the term *sociocultural* in a couple of different ways. One refers quite specifically to the *sociocultural theory* of the Russian psychologist Lev Semenovich Vygotsky (1896–1934). The

Developing in a World of Diversity

© 2002 David Hanover/Stone/Getty Images

Influence of the Macrosystem on the Development of Independence

Cross-cultural studies provide interesting insights into the way children interact with their macrosystems. Consider the development of independence. Among the !Kung (Ju/'hoansi) people of Namibia, babies are kept in close contact with their mothers during the first year (Konner, 1977). !Kung infants are frequently carried in slings across their mothers' hips that allow them to nurse at will—literally all day long. The !Kung seem to follow the commandment, The infant shall not go hungry—not even for 5 seconds. In every way, !Kung mothers try to respond at once to their babies' cries and whims. By Western standards, !Kung babies are "spoiled." However, overindulgence does not appear to make !Kung babies overly dependent on their mothers. By the time they are capable of walking, they do. They do not cling to their mothers. In comparison to Western children of the same age, !Kung children spend less time with their mothers and more time with their peers.

Also compare Urie Bronfenbrenner's (1973) observations of child rearing in the United States and Russia. Russian babies, as a group, are more likely than U.S. babies to be cuddled, kissed, and hugged. Russian mothers are not quite so solicitous as their !Kung counterparts, but they are highly protective as compared with U.S. mothers. However, Russian children are taught to take care of themselves at younger ages than U.S. children. By 18 months of age, Russian children are usually learning to dress themselves and are largely toilet trained.

Lev Semenovich Vygotsky

The Russian psychologist is said to have possessed the genius of a Mozart, but to have lived in a time and place that was deaf to genius. In his youth he was interested in literature and philosophy. He enrolled in medical school at Moscow University, switched to law school, then returned to literature, and later became interested in psychology. After his death from tuberculosis in 1934, the Soviet Union repudiated his ideas, but they have since been revived. Vygotsky is known for showing how social speech becomes inner speech and how "scaffolding" by others assists children in developing the cognitive skills to succeed.

Reflect

How have your ethnic background and your gender influenced your development? Consider factors such as race, country of origin, language, nutrition, values, and the dominant culture's reaction to people of your background.

zone of proximal development (ZPD) Vygotsky's term for the situation in which a child carries out tasks with the help of someone who is more skilled, frequently an adult who represents the culture in which the child develops.

scaffolding Vygotsky's term for temporary cognitive structures or methods of solving problems that help the child as he or she learns to function independently.

other broadly addresses the impact on children of human diversity, including factors such as ethnicity and gender.

Lev Vygotsky's Sociocultural Theory

Whereas genetics is concerned with the biological transmission of traits from generation to generation, Vygotsky's (1978) theory is vitally concerned with the transmission of information and cognitive skills from generation to generation. The transmission of skills involves teaching and learning, but Vygotsky is no behaviorist. He does not view learning as a mechanical process that can be described in terms of the conditioning of units of behavior. Rather, he focuses more generally on how the child's social interaction with adults, largely in the home, organizes a child's learning experiences in such a way that the child can obtain cognitive skills—such as computation or reading skills—and use them to acquire information. Like Piaget, Vygotsky sees the child's functioning as adaptive (Piaget & Smith, 2000), and the child adapts to his or her social and cultural interactions.

Question: What are the key concepts of Vygotsky's sociocultural theory? Key concepts in Vygotsky's theory include the *zone of proximal development* and *scaffolding*. The word *proximal* means "nearby" or "close," as in the words *approximate* and *proximity*. The **zone of proximal development (ZPD)** refers to a range of tasks that a child can carry out with the help of someone who is more skilled (Haenen, 2001). It is similar to the context of an apprenticeship. Many developmentalists find that observing how a child learns when working with others provides more information about that child's cognitive abilities than does a simple inventory of knowledge (Meijer & Elshout, 2001). When learning with other people, the child tends to internalize—or bring inward—the conversations and explanations that help him or her gain the necessary skills (Prior & Welling, 2001; Vygotsky, 1962; Yang, 2000). Children in other words, not only learn the meanings of words from teachers, but also learn ways of talking to themselves about solving problems within a cultural context (DeVries, 2000). Outer speech becomes inner speech. What was the teacher's becomes the child's. What was a social and cultural context becomes embedded within the child (Moro & Rodriguez, 2000).

A *scaffold* is a temporary skeletal structure that enables workers to fabricate a building, bridge, or other, more permanent, structure. In Vygotsky's theory, teachers and parents provide children with problem-solving methods that serve as cognitive **scaffolding** while the child gains the ability to function independently. For example, a child's instructors may offer advice on sounding out letters and words that provide a temporary support until reading "clicks" and the child no longer needs the device. Children may be offered scaffolding that enables them to use their fingers or their toes to do simple calculations. Eventually, the scaffolding is removed, and the cognitive structures stand alone. A Puerto Rican study found that students also use scaffolding when they are explaining to one another how they can improve school projects, such as essay assignments (De Guerrero & Villamil, 2000). Children at first even view the value of education in terms of their parents' verbalizations about school success (Bigelow, 2001). Vygotsky's theory points out that children's attitudes toward schooling are embedded within the parent–child relationship.

The Sociocultural Perspective and Human Diversity

The field of child development focuses mainly on individuals and is committed to the dignity of the individual child. ***Question: What is the connection between the sociocultural perspective and human diversity?*** The sociocultural perspective recognizes that we cannot understand individual children without an awareness of the richness of their diversity (Basic Behavioral Science Task Force, 1996). Two of the ways in which children diverge or differ from one another are in their ethnicity and their gender.

Until recently, much of the research on child development was confined to middle-class European American children (Greenfield & Cocking, 1994; R. M. Lerner, 1991). But we live in a nation and a world of diverse cultures. There is a growing recognition among developmentalists that the cultural context in which the child grows up must be taken into account to better understand children's development and behavior.

One kind of cultural diversity involves children's **ethnic groups,** which tend to unite them according to features such as their cultural heritage, their race, their language, and their common history. One reason for studying ethnic diversity is the changing ethnic makeup of the United States.

Click *Select Theorist* for more on Vygotsky and the sociocultural perspective.

Figures 1.5 and 1.6 highlight the population shifts under way in the United States due to reproductive patterns and immigration. The numbers of African Americans and Latino and Latina Americans (who may be White, Black, or Native American in racial origin) are growing more rapidly than those of European Americans. The cultural heritages, languages, and histories of ethnic minority groups are thus likely to have increasing impact on the cultural life of the United States. Yet it turns out that the dominant culture of the United States has often disparaged the traditions and languages of people from ethnic minority groups. The achievements of members of these groups have often been judged by inappropriate yardsticks and deemed inferior (Betancourt & Lopez, 1993; J. Jones, 1991; McAdoo, 1993; Sue, 1991). For example, the type of English spoken by many children in African American communities—called *Ebonics*—has been considered inferior to standard English, even though it allows for the expression of equally complex concepts. It has even been considered harmful to rear children bilingually, although research suggests that bilingualism broadens children (see Chapter 12). Thus, we cannot understand the development of children without reference to their cultural heritages and how these heritages have been viewed by the dominant culture.

Studying diversity is also important so that children have appropriate educational experiences. Educators need to understand children's family values and cultural expectations in order to teach them and guide their learning.

Many professionals—psychologists, teachers, social workers, psychiatrists, and others—are called upon to help children and families who are having problems in

ethnic groups Groups of people distinguished by cultural heritage, race, language, and common history.

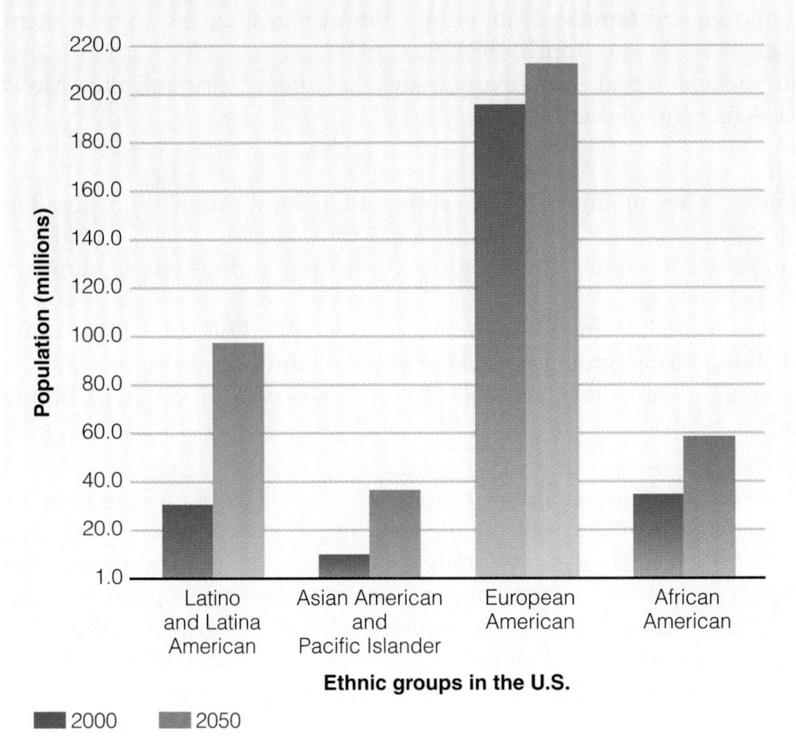

Figure 1.5
Numbers of Various Ethnic Groups in the United States, Year 2000 versus Year 2050 (in millions)

The numbers of each of the various ethnic groups in the United States will grow over the next half century, with the numbers of Latino and Latina Americans and Asian Americans and Pacific Islanders growing most rapidly. Source: *U.S. Bureau of the Census, 2000.*

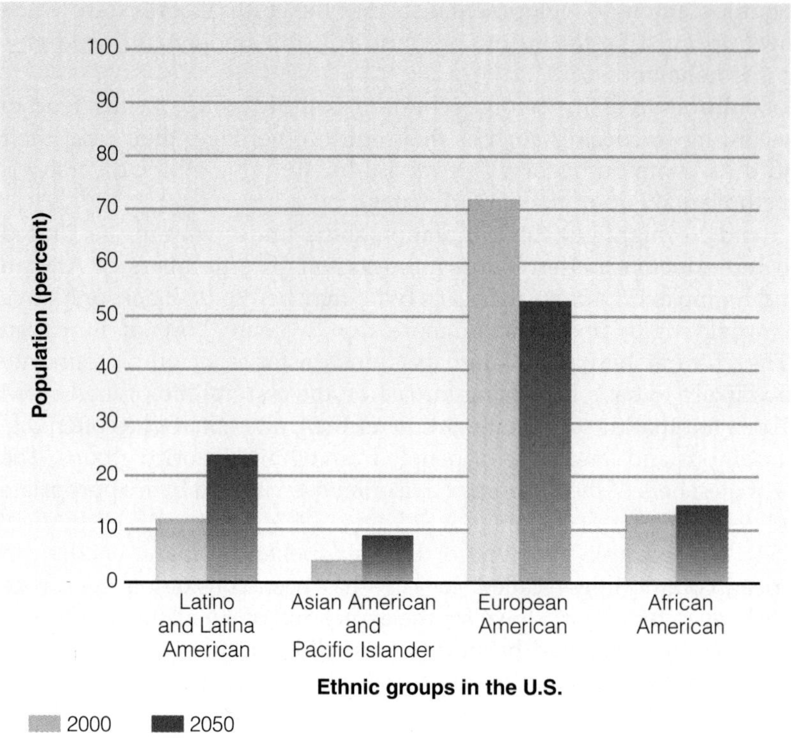

■ **Figure 1.6**
Percentages of Various Ethnic Groups in the United States, Year 2000 versus Year 2050

Although European Americans are projected to remain the most populous ethnic group within the United States in the year 2050, the group's percentage of the population will diminish from about 72% to about 53%. But because of general population growth, there will still be more European Americans in the United States in 2050 than there are today. Source: *U.S. Census Bureau, 2000.*

school or in the community. In many cases, these are individual problems, and professionals may be sensitive to their nature and know how to intervene. But in many other cases, individual problems are intertwined with cultural issues such as prejudice and discrimination. Helping professionals are then handicapped in their efforts unless they are familiar with the ethnic group's history of interaction with dominant culture. Professionals may need special training to identify the problems of children and families from ethnic minority groups and to treat them in culturally sensitive ways (J. Jones, 1991; Sue, 1991).

Throughout the text, we consider many issues that affect children from various ethnic groups. A handful of them include

- Bilingualism
- Ethnic differences in intelligence test scores—their implications and possible origins
- Alcohol and substance abuse among adolescents from various ethnic minority groups
- The prevalence of suicide among members of different ethnic minority groups
- Patterns of child rearing among parents of various ethnic minority groups
- Development of identity and self-esteem in adolescents of different ethnic backgrounds

Gender is another crucial aspect of human diversity. Gender is the state of being male or being female. The French have a saying, *Vive la difference* ("Long live the difference!"), which celebrates the difference between females and males. The French expression exudes the excitement people may feel when they are interacting with individuals of the other sex, but, unfortunately, it also alludes to the problem that females and males are often polarized by cultural expectations. That is, the differences may be exaggerated, as in the case of intellectual abilities, and too often females are seen as inferior. Put it this way; males may very well differ from females in some respects, but history has created more burdens for women than

gender The state of being female or male.

men as a result. Gender-role expectations affect children's self-esteem and limit their hopes and dreams for the future. Dare a girl yet dream she will grow up to be president? Or the CEO of a Fortune 500 company? Or a ground-breaking mathematician or architect?

Girls have been traditionally discouraged from careers in the sciences, politics, and business. Not until recent times have there even been large numbers of women in the arts.

Women today are making inroads into academic and vocational spheres—such as medicine, law, engineering, and the military—that have been traditionally male preserves. Today the numbers of women in medical and law schools have risen to equal the numbers of men entering these professions (Glater, 2001). But in other professional fields, particularly math, science, and engineering, the gap has not narrowed as much. Still, it is no longer widely expected—at least in the United States and other developed nations—that girls will have to remain in the domestic arena.

Today the majority of college students in the United States are female, but it is worth noting that girls were not considered qualified for education until recent times. How many gifted and talented girls and women have been lost to history because of prejudice? How many have lived lives of quiet frustration? Who, for example, is Lucinda Foote? She was a brilliant young woman who is known to us only because of her rejection letter from Yale University in 1792, which confirmed that she was qualified for Yale in every way—*except* for her gender (G. Lerner, 1993). It many surprise you to learn that women were not admitted to college in the United States until 1833, the year that Oberlin College opened its doors to women. Yet there remain many—many!—parts of the world in which women are not permitted to obtain an education. As this book goes to press, many readers will still be aware of the tragedy of women in Afghanistan under Taliban rule—denied the privileges of education and choice of clothing, denied the very privilege of leaving their homes unless in the company of a male.

Opportunities for women are crucial to the development of girls. Children learn early about gender roles and gender-role stereotypes. Cultural opportunities for, and limitations on, adults give children their own sense of what is possible for them and what is not. Just as many children from ethnic minority groups wonder whether they can experience the rewards and opportunities they see in the dominant culture, so do girls wonder whether the career and social roles they admire are available to them. I was astonished to learn that my daughters had assumed that the presidency of the United States was open only to men. The effects of cultural expectations on girls' self-concepts, motivation, and behavior are clear and compelling.

This book's focus on human diversity extends beyond ethnicity and gender to include children and adolescents with various sexual orientations and a number of disabilities. Our approach broadens our understanding of all children as they experience the developmental changes brought about by quite different influences of heredity and experience. Yes, the presentation of human diversity complicates matters, but that is only because matters are complex. If we simplify, we fail reality.

Table 1.3 summarizes some of the important similarities and differences among the various perspectives on child development.

Review

(12) __________ are related sets of statements about events. (13) Satisfactory theories allow us to explain, __________, and influence events. (14) Freud's theory of __________ development is psychoanalytic. (15) Freud hypothesized five stages of development: oral, __________, phallic, latency, and genital. (16) Erikson's psychoanalytic theory focuses on __________ development. (17) Erikson named stages after life __________. (18) John B. __________ is the founder of behaviorism. (19) Behaviorism sees children's learning as mechanical and relies on classical and __________ conditioning. (20) B. F. __________ introduced the concept of

TABLE 1.3 *Comparison of Perspectives on Child Development*

Perspective or Theory	Core Concepts	Is Nature or Nurture More Important?	Is Development Viewed as Being Continuous or Discontinuous?	Is the Child Viewed as Being Active or Passive?
The Psychoanalytic Perspective				
Theory of psychosexual development (Sigmund Freud)	Instinctive impulses are channeled via social codes, but conflict develops as a result. Much of the mind is unconscious.	Interaction of nature and nurture: Biological maturation sets the stage for reaction to social influences.	Discontinuous: There are five stages of development, each of which involves the expression of sexual impulses.	Passive: Child is largely at the mercy of older people and cultural modes of conduct.
Theory of psychosocial development (Erik Erikson)	Child (and adult) experiences life crises based largely on social relationships, opportunities, and expectations.	Interaction of nature and nurture: Biological maturation sets the stage for reaction to social influences and opportunities.	Discontinuous. There are eight stages of development, each of which involves a particular kind of life crisis.	Active: Child (and adult) makes conscious decisions about formation of his/her own personality and behavior.
The Learning Perspective				
Behaviorism (John B. Watson, Ivan Pavlov, B. F. Skinner)	Behavior is learned by association; two key types of learning are classical and operant conditioning.	Nurture: Children are seen almost as blank tablets.	Continuous: Behavior reflects the summation of conditioned responses.	Passive: Responses are learned by association, and behavior is maintained due to its effects.
Social cognitive theory (Albert Bandura and others)	Conditioning occurs, but children also learn purposefully by observing others, and they choose whether to display learned responses.	Emphasizes nurture but allows for expression of natural tendencies	Continuous	Active: Principle of reciprocal determinism states that children influence the environment even as the environment influences them.
The Cognitive Perspective				
Cognitive-developmental theory (Jean Piaget)	Children adapt to the environment via processes of assimilation to existing mental structures (schemes) or by changing these structures (accommodation).	Emphasizes nature but allows for influences of experience	Discontinuous: Cognitive development follows an invariant sequence of four stages.	Active: Children are budding scientists who seek to understand and manipulate their worlds.
Information-processing theory (numerous theorists)	Children's cognitive functioning is compared to that of computers, involving the inputting, manipulating, storage, and output of information.	Interaction of nature and nurture	Continuous: Development facilitates the child's storage capacity and ability to run multiple "programs" simultaneously; cognitive skills are cumulative.	Active: Children seek to obtain and manipulate information.

TABLE 1.3 *(continued)*

Perspective or Theory	Core Concepts	Is Nature or Nurture More Important?	Is Development Viewed as Being Continuous or Discontinuous?	Is the Child Viewed as Being Active or Passive?
		The Biological Perspective		
Maturational theory (Arnold Gesell)	Development involves the unfolding of genetically determined processes. Children do not do certain things until they are biologically *ready*.	Nature is emphasized although environmental support (e.g., nutrition) is needed for maturation to occur.	Discontinuous: Development occurs in sequences of discrete events, as in crawling preceding walking.	Not specifically indicated, although children are portrayed as being responsive to unfolding biological processes.
Ethology (Charles Darwin, Konrad Lorenz, Niko Tinbergen)	Organisms are biologically "prewired" to show inborn fixed-action patterns (FAPS) in response to species-specific releasing stimuli.	Emphasizes nature but experience is also critical; for example, imprinting occurs at a given point in development, but *what* an organism is imprinted on is determined by experience.	Discontinuous: Certain kinds of learning, for example, are said to occur during *critical periods,* which are biologically determined.	Not specifically indicated, although organisms are depicted as responding automatically (passively) to FAPs.
		The Ecological Perspective		
Ecological systems theory (Urie Bronfenbrenner)	Children's development occurs within interlocking systems. Development is enhanced by intervening at the levels of various systems.	Interaction of nature and nurture: Children's personalities and skills contribute to their development.	Not specifically indicated	Active: Influences are bidirectional: Systems influence the child and vice versa.
		The Sociocultural Perspective		
The sociocultural perspective and human diversity (numerous theorists)	Focuses on the influences of sociocultural factors such as ethnic background and gender on development.	Nurture	Not specifically indicated	Not specifically indicated
Sociocultural theory (Lev Vygotsky)	Addresses the ways in which children internalize sociocultural dialogues as ways of guiding their own behavior and developing problem-solving skills.	Interaction of nature and nurture; nurture is discussed in social and cultural terms.	Continuous: Learning in the presence of experienced members of a culture enables the child to accumulate knowledge and skills.	Both: Children seek to develop problem-solving abilities by internalizing cultural dialogues, but the dialogues originate within society, not within the individual.

reinforcement. (21) Social __________ theorists like Albert Bandura have shown that much of children's learning is intentional and occurs by observation. (22) Social cognitive theorists believe in __________ determinism—that is, that children and the environment influence one another. (23) Jean Piaget's cognitive-__________ theory is a stage theory that sees children as budding scientists who seek to understand and manipulate their worlds. (24) According to Piaget, children assimilate new events to existing schemes or else __________ their schemes to incorporate novel events. (25) Information-__________ theory focuses on the processes by which information is encoded, stored, retrieved, and manipulated. (26) Information-processing theorists talk in terms of the number of __________ a child can run simultaneously. (27) The __________ perspective refers to gains in height and weight, development of the nervous system, and heredity. (28) __________ theory focuses on the unfolding of genetically determined developmental sequences. (29) Ethologists speak of the importance of inborn __________ action patterns (FAPs). (30) The __________ systems theory explains child development in terms of the interaction between children and the settings in which they live. (31) These systems consist of the microsystem, the mesosystem, the exosystem, and the __________. (32). Vygotsky's __________ theory is concerned with the transmission of information and cognitive skills from generation to generation. (33) The zone of __________ development (ZPD) refers to a range of tasks that a child can carry out with the help of someone who is more skilled.

Pulling It Together: What role does human diversity play in various theories of child development?

Controversies in Child Development

The discussion of theories of development reveals that developmentalists can see things in very different ways. Let's consider how they react to three of the most important debates in the field.

The Nature–Nurture Controversy

Question: Which exerts the greater influence on children: nature or nurture? Think about your friends for a moment. Some may be tall and lanky; others, short and stocky. Some are outgoing and sociable; others are more reserved and quiet. One may be a good athlete; another a fine musician. What made them this way? How much does inheritance have to do with it, and how much does the environment play a role?

Researchers are continually trying to sort out the extent to which human behavior is the result of **nature** (heredity) and of **nurture** (environmental influences). What aspects of behavior originate in our **genes** and are biologically programmed to unfold in the child as time goes on, so long as minimal nutrition and social experience are provided? What aspects of behavior can be traced largely to such environmental influences as nutrition and learning?

Scientists seek the natural causes of development in children's genetic heritage, the functioning of the nervous system, and in the process of maturation. Scientists seek the environmental causes of development in children's nutrition, cultural and family backgrounds, and opportunities to learn about the world, including cognitive stimulation during early childhood and formal education.

Some theorists lean heavily toward natural explanations of development (e.g., cognitive-developmental and biological theorists), whereas others lean more heavily toward environmental explanations (e.g., learning theorists). But today nearly all researchers would agree that, broadly speaking, nature and nurture

nature The processes within an organism that guide that organism to develop according to its genetic code.

nurture The processes external to an organism that nourish it as it develops according to its genetic code or cause it to swerve from its genetically programmed course. Environmental factors that influence development.

genes The basic building blocks of heredity.

Which Aspects of Development Are Continuous and Which Are Discontinuous?

The adolescent growth spurt is an example of discontinuity in development. Developmentalists debate whether other aspects of development—such as cognitive development—are most accurately described as continuous or discontinuous.

each play important roles in virtually every area of child development. Consider the development of language. Language is based in structures found in certain areas of the brain. Thus, biology (nature) plays an indispensable role in language development. But children also come to speak the languages spoken by their caretakers. Parent–child similarities in accent and vocabulary provide additional evidence for an indispensable role for learning (nurture) in language development.

The Continuity–Discontinuity Controversy

Question: Is development continuous or discontinuous? Do developmental changes occur gradually (continuously), the way a seedling becomes a tree? Or do changes occur in major qualitative leaps (discontinuously) that dramatically alter our bodies and behavior, the way a caterpillar turns into a butterfly?

Some developmentalists have viewed human development as a continuous process in which the effects of learning mount gradually, with no major sudden qualitative changes. Other theorists, in contrast, believe there are a number of rapid qualitative changes that usher in new stages of development. Maturational theorists point out that the environment, even when enriched, profits us little until we are ready, or mature enough, to develop in a certain direction. For example, newborn babies will not imitate their parents' speech, even when parents speak clearly and deliberately. Nor does aided practice in "walking" during the first few months after birth significantly accelerate the emergence of independent walking.

Stage theorists such as Sigmund Freud and Jean Piaget saw development as being discontinuous. Both theorists saw biological changes as providing the potential for psychological changes. Freud focused on the ways in which physical sexual developments might provide the basis for personality development. Piaget emphasized the ways in which maturation of the nervous system permitted cognitive advances. Stage theorists see the sequences of development as being invariant (occurring in the same order), although they allow for individual differences in timing.

Certain aspects of physical development do appear to occur in stages. For example, from the age of 2 to the onset of puberty, children gradually grow larger. Then the adolescent growth spurt occurs, ushered in by hormones and characterized by rapid biological changes in structure and function (as in the development of the sex organs) as well as in size. A new stage of life has begun. Psychologists disagree more strongly on whether aspects of development such as cognition, attachment, and assumption of gender roles occur in stages.

The Active–Passive Controversy

In the broad sense, all living organisms are active. However, in the field of child development, the question has a more specific meaning. ***Questions: Are children "prewired" to try to act on and take charge of the world (active)? Or are children shaped by experience so that they will fit within almost any behavioral or cultural mold (passive)?***

Historical views of children as willful and unruly suggest that people have generally seen children as active—even if mischievous (at best) or evil (at worst). John Locke introduced a view of children as passive beings (blank tablets) upon whom external experience writes features of personality and moral virtue.

At one extreme, educators who view children as passive may assume that they must be motivated to learn by their instructors. Such educators are likely to provide a traditional curriculum with rigorous exercises in spelling, music, and math to promote absorption of the subject matter. They are also likely to apply a powerful system of rewards and punishments to keep children on the straight and narrow.

At the other extreme, educators who view children as active may assume that they have a natural love of learning. Such educators are likely to espouse open education and encourage children to explore an environment rich with learning materials. Rather than attempting to coerce children into specific academic activities, such educators are likely to listen to the children to learn about their unique likes and talents and then support children as they pursue their inclinations.

These are extremes. Most educators would probably agree that children show major individual differences and that some children require more guidance and external motivation than others. In addition, children can be active in some subjects and passive in others. Whether children who do not actively seek to master certain subjects are coerced tends to depend on how important the subject is to functioning in today's society, the age of the child, the attitudes of the parents, and many other factors.

Urie Bronfenbrenner (1977) argues that we miss the point when we assume that children are either entirely active or passive. Children are influenced by the environment, but children also influence the environment. The challenge is to observe the many ways in which children interact with their settings. Social cognitive theorist Albert Bandura agrees. He refers to the mutual influences of people and the environment as *reciprocal determinism.*

These debates are theoretical. Scientists value theory for its ability to tie together observations and suggest new areas of investigation, but they also follow an **empirical** approach. That is, they engage in research methods, such as those described in the following section, to find evidence for or against various theoretical positions.

empirical Based on observation and experimentation.

Review

(34) Researchers in child development try to sort out the effects of ________ (heredity) and nurture (environmental influences). (35) Learning theorists tend to see development as continuous, whereas stage theorists see development as ________. (36) According to Urie ________, children are influenced by the environment (passive), but children also influence the environment (active).

Pulling It Together: What does the concept of reciprocal determinism suggest about the controversies in child development?

How Do We Study Child Development?

What is the relationship between intelligence and achievement? What are the effects of aspirin and alcohol on the fetus? How can you rear children to become competent and independent? What are the effects of divorce on children?

Many of us have expressed opinions on questions such as these at one time or another. But scientists insist that such questions be answered by research. Strong arguments, reference to authority figures, even tightly knit theories, are not considered adequate as scientific evidence. Scientific evidence is obtained by the scientific method. ***Question: What is the scientific method?***

The Scientific Method

The scientific method is a way of formulating and answering research questions that makes (some) scientists more qualified to study children than parents and grandparents. There are five basic steps to the scientific method:

Step 1: *Formulating a Research Question* Our daily experiences, developmental theory, and even folklore help generate questions for research. Daily experience in using day-care centers may motivate us to conduct research to find out whether day care influences children's intellectual or social development or the bonds of attachment between children and their parents. Social cognitive principles of observational learning may prompt research into the effects of TV violence.

Step 2: *Developing a Hypothesis* A **hypothesis** is a specific statement about behavior that is tested through research.

One hypothesis about day care might be that preschool children placed in day care will acquire greater social skills in relating to peers than will preschool children who are cared for in the home. A hypothesis about TV violence might be that elementary school children who watch more violent TV shows tend to behave more aggressively toward their peers.

Step 3: *Testing the Hypothesis* Psychologists test the hypothesis through carefully controlled information-gathering techniques and research methods, such as naturalistic observation, the case study, the correlational method, and the experiment.

For example, we could introduce day-care and non-day-care children to a new child in a college child-research center and observe how each group acts toward the new acquaintance. Concerning the effects of TV violence, we could have parents help us tally which TV shows their children watch and rate the shows for violent content. Each child could receive a total score for exposure to TV violence. Teachers could report on how aggressively the children act toward their peers. Then we could determine whether more aggressive children also watch more violence on TV. We describe research methods such as these later in the chapter.

Step 4: *Drawing Conclusions About the Hypothesis* Psychologists draw conclusions about the accuracy of their hypothesis on the basis of the results of their research findings. When research does not bear out their hypotheses, the researchers may modify the theories from which the hypotheses were derived. Research findings often suggest new hypotheses and new studies.

In our research on the effects of day care, we would probably find that day-care children show somewhat greater social skills than children cared for in the home (see Chapter 7). We would probably also find that more aggressive children spend more time watching TV violence (see Chapter 10). But we shall also see in the following pages that it might be wrong to conclude from this kind of evidence that TV violence *causes* aggressive behavior.

Step 5: *Publishing Findings* Scientists publish their research findings in professional journals and make their data available to scientists and the public at large

hypothesis (high-POTH-uh-sis) A Greek word meaning "groundwork" or "foundation" that has come to mean a specific statement about behavior that is tested by research.

for scrutiny. Thus they grant their peers the opportunity to review their data and conclusions to help determine their accuracy.

Now let's consider the information-gathering techniques and the research methods used by developmentalists. Then we discuss ethical issues concerning research in child development.

Reflect

How have you gathered information about the behavior of children over the years? Which of the methods described in this section come closest to your own?

Gathering Information

Developmentalists use various methods for gathering information. For example, they may ask children to keep diaries of their behavior, ask teachers or parents to report on the behavior of their children, or use interviews or questionnaires with children themselves. They also directly observe children in the laboratory or in the natural setting. Let's expand on the naturalistic-observation method and the case-study method.

Naturalistic Observation

Question: What is naturalistic observation? **Naturalistic observation** studies of children are conducted in "the field"—that is, in the natural, or real-life, settings in which they happen. In field studies, investigators observe the natural behavior of children in settings such as homes, playgrounds, and classrooms and try not to interfere with it. Interference could influence or bias the results so that researchers would be observing child–investigator interactions and not genuine behavior. Thus, researchers may try to blend in with the woodwork by sitting quietly in the back of a classroom or by observing the class through a one-way mirror (see the nearby "A Closer Look" feature).

Naturalistic observation is frequently the first type of study carried out in new areas of investigation. Through careful observation, scientists gather an initial impression of what happens in certain situations. In their interpretation of the data, they may use the mathematical correlational method, described later in this chapter, to refine their observations of how strongly different **variables** are related. For example, they may explore whether the rate of vocabulary growth is related to gender or to cultural background. Afterward, they may attempt to investigate cause and effect through experimental research.

A number of important naturalistic-observation studies have been done with children of different cultures. For example, researchers have observed the motor behavior of Native American Hopi children who are strapped to cradleboards during the first year. They have observed language development in the United States, Mexico, Turkey, Kenya, and China—seeking universals that might suggest a major role for maturation in the acquisition of language skills. They have also observed the ways in which children are socialized in Russia, Israel, Japan, and other nations in an effort to determine what patterns of child rearing are associated with development of behaviors such as attachment and independence.

The Case Study

Another way of gathering information about children is the case-study method. ***Question: What is the case study?*** The **case study** is a carefully drawn account or biography of the behavior of an individual child. Parents who keep diaries of their children's activities are involved in informal case studies. Case studies themselves often use a number of different kinds of information about children. In addition to direct observation, case studies may include questionnaires, **standardized tests,** and interviews with the child and his or her parents, teachers, and friends. Information gleaned from school and other records may be included. Scientists who use the case-study method take great pains to record all the relevant factors in a child's behavior, and they are very cautious in drawing conclusions about what leads to what.

naturalistic observation A method of scientific observation in which children (and others) are observed in their natural environments.

variable Quantity that can vary from child to child, or from occasion to occasion, such as height, weight, intelligence, and attention span.

case study A carefully drawn biography of the life of an individual.

standardized test A test of some ability or trait in which an individual's score is compared to the scores of a group of similar individuals.

Jean Piaget used the case-study method in carefully observing and recording the behavior of children, including his own (see Chapter 6). Sigmund Freud developed his psychoanalytic theory largely on the basis of case studies. Freud studied his patients in great depth and followed some of them for many years.

Some of the most fascinating case studies of children are found in baby biographies. Baby biographies are careful observations of children that frequently begin just after birth. As was the case with Piaget's and Charles Darwin's accounts of their own children, baby biographies often include accounts of a parent or observer touching the child or serving as a model for the child and then recording the child's responses.

In many instances, case studies, like naturalistic observation, form the basis for sophisticated correlational and experimental studies that follow. The early case

A Closer Look

How Do You Ease Your Child Into Nursery School or Day Care? A Field Study by Tiffany Field

The big moment has arrived. It's Allison's first day at the day-care center. Although you've done everything to prepare her—lengthy explanations and gradually longer stays in the care of babysitters—she's clutching and crying and begging you not to go. How do parents take leave of their children in such situations? How do the children adjust? A naturalistic observation study by Tiffany Field and her colleagues (1984) provides some clues. They observed leave-takings for infants (ages 3–17 months), toddlers (ages 18–29 months), and preschoolers (ages 30–69 months) at the beginning of the fall semester and again 6 months later.

Various relationships (correlations) were observed between children's gender, age, and behavior. For example, girls were more likely than boys to approach their teachers, and boys were more likely to immediately get involved in play activities. Preschoolers were most likely to kiss and hug their parents, and toddlers were most likely to cry, complain, and cling to their parents. The parents of the toddlers—the group of children for whom adjustment was most difficult—were most likely to try to distract their children by getting them involved in activities in the schoolroom and then quietly slipping out.

Observations made 6 months later showed that children of all age groups spent less time relating to their departing parents. There was less crying, less protesting. The children had generally adjusted to nursery school. Interestingly, children whose parents left abruptly showed less distress than children whose parents stayed for several minutes, attempting to distract them.

But a note of caution: This field study uses the correlational method, and it can be misleading to try to ferret out cause and effect from correlational studies. You cannot conclude that parental lingering and distraction *caused* child distress. It could be that child distress caused the parents to linger and try to sneak out. Or perhaps causal effects were reciprocal or bidirectional. That is, the children and parents may have influenced each other's behavior.

In any event, a comforting thought may be drawn from this study. Most children do adjust reasonably quickly to nursery school and day care, regardless of the distress they may show at first.

© Michael Newman/PhotoEdit

How Do Children (and Their Parents!) Adjust to Nursery School?

Toddlers are likely to cry at first, whereas preschoolers—a bit older—are likely to kiss and hug their parents. Parents typically try to get the children involved in activities so that they can depart without a fuss. No, we're not sure exactly how long parents continue to sneak looks through the windows or doors before leaving.

© Bob Daemmrich/Stock, Boston

How Do We Describe the Relationship Between Intelligence and Achievement?

Correlations between intelligence test scores and academic achievement—as measured by school grades and achievement tests—tend to be positive and strong. Does the correlational method allow us to say that intelligence causes or is responsible for academic achievement? Why or why not?

studies of Freud and Piaget have led to countless experiments that have attempted to find evidence to support or disconfirm their theories.

The Correlational Method

Question: What is the correlational method? The **correlational method** is a mathematical method that researchers use to determine whether one behavior or trait being studied is related to, or correlated with, another. Consider, for example, the variables of intelligence and achievement. These variables are assigned numbers such as intelligence test scores and academic grade averages. Then the numbers or scores are mathematically related and expressed as a correlation coefficient. A **correlation coefficient** is a number that varies between +1.00 and –1.00.

Reflect

No surprise: There is a correlation between time spent studying and grades. Can you think of different ways to explain the connection?

Numerous studies report **positive correlations** between intelligence and achievement. Generally speaking, the higher children score on intelligence tests, the better their academic performance is likely to be. The scores attained on intelligence tests are positively correlated (about +0.60 to +0.70) with overall academic achievement.[3]

There is a **negative correlation** between teenagers' working after school and their academic performance. As we shall see in Chapter 15, the more hours teenagers are employed, the lower are their school grades. Figure 1.7 illustrates positive and negative correlations.

Naturalistic observation studies may also use the correlational method. Consider the study by Tiffany Field and her colleagues (1984) described in the "A Closer Look" feature. There were numerous correlations in this study—including correlations between children's ages and their behavior at leave-taking and correlations between parental behavior at leave-taking and level of distress shown by the child.

correlational method A method in which researchers determine whether one behavior or trait being studied is related to, or correlated with, another.

correlation coefficient A number ranging from +1.00 to –1.00 that expresses the direction (positive or negative) and strength of the relationship between two variables.

positive correlation A relationship between two variables in which one variable increases as the other variable increases.

negative correlation A relationship between two variables in which one variable increases as the other variable decreases.

Limitations of Correlational Research

Correlational studies can reveal relationships between variables, but they do not show cause and effect. For example, studies have found that children who watch TV shows with a lot of violence are more likely to show aggressive behavior at home and in school. It may seem logical to assume that exposure to TV violence

[3] Of course +0.60 is the same as +.60. We insert the zeroes to help prevent the decimal points from getting lost.

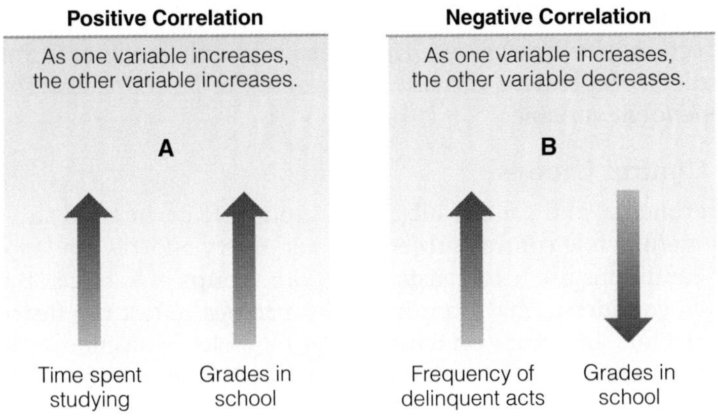
Positive Correlation
As one variable increases, the other variable increases.
A
Time spent studying
Grades in school
Negative Correlation
As one variable increases, the other variable decreases.
B
Frequency of delinquent acts
Grades in school

Figure 1.7
Examples of Positive and Negative Correlations
When two variables are correlated positively, *one increases as the other increases. There is a positive correlation between the amount of time spent studying and grades, as shown in Part A. By and large, the more time students spend studying, the better their grades are likely to be. When two variables are correlated* negatively, *one increases as the other decreases. There is a negative correlation between the frequency of an individual's delinquent acts and his and her grades, as shown in Part B. As one's number of delinquent acts per year increases, one's grade point average tends to decline. Correlational research may suggest but does not prove cause and effect. Can you think of two possible explanations for* each *of the correlations shown in this figure? (After Wayne Weiten,* Psychology Themes & Variations, 5/E, *p. 54. © 2001, Wadsworth.)*

makes children more aggressive. But it may be that children who are more aggressive to begin with prefer TV shows that contain a good deal of violence. The relationship between watching violence and engaging in aggressive behavior may not be as simple as it originally seems.

Similarly, studies that relate divorce to behavior and adjustment report that children (especially boys) in divorced families sometimes show more problems than do children in intact families (Hetherington et al., 1992). However, these studies do not show that divorce causes these adjustment problems. It could be that the factors that led to divorce (such as parental disorganization or conflict) also led to adjustment problems among the children (Clarke-Stewart et al., 2000). Or having a child with problems might put a strain on the parents' marriage and ultimately be a factor contributing to divorce.

In the studies on patterns of child rearing, we must also ask why parents choose to raise their children in certain ways. It is possible the same factors that lead them to make these choices also influence the behavior of their children.

Thus, correlational research does not allow us to place clear "cause" and "effect" labels on variables. To investigate cause and effect, researchers turn to the experimental method.

The Experimental Method

Most psychologists would agree that the preferred method for investigating questions of cause and effect is the *experiment.* ***Question: What is an experiment?*** An **experiment** is a research method in which a group of participants (also called subjects) receives a **treatment** while another group does not. The subjects are then observed to determine whether the treatment makes a difference in their behavior.

Experiments are used whenever possible because they allow researchers to directly control the experiences of children and other subjects in order to determine the outcomes of a treatment. Experiments, like other research methods, are usually undertaken to test a hypothesis. For example, a social cognitive theorist might hypothesize that TV violence will cause aggressive behavior in children because of principles of observational learning. To test this hypothesis, she might devise an experiment in which some children are purposely exposed to TV violence while others are not. Remember that it is not enough to demonstrate that children who choose to watch more violent shows behave more aggressively; such evidence is only correlational. We review this research—correlational and experimental—in Chapter 10.

experiment A method of scientific investigation that seeks to discover cause-and-effect relationships by introducing independent variables and observing their effects on dependent variables.

Independent and Dependent Variables

In an experiment to determine whether TV violence causes aggressive behavior, experimental subjects would be shown a TV program containing violence, and its effects on behavior would be measured. TV violence would be considered an

treatment In an experiment, a condition received by participants so that its effects may be observed.

independent variable, a variable whose presence is manipulated by the experimenters so that its effects may be determined. The measured result, in this case the child's behavior, is called a **dependent variable.** Its presence or level presumably depends on the independent variables.

Experimental and Control Groups

Experiments use experimental and control subjects or groups. **Experimental subjects** receive the treatment, while **control subjects** do not. Every effort is made to ensure that all other conditions are held constant for both groups of subjects. By doing so, we can have confidence that experimental outcomes reflect the treatments and not chance factors. In a study on the effects of TV violence on children's behavior, children in the experimental group would be shown TV programs containing violence, and children in the control group would be shown programs that did not contain violence.

Random Assignment

Subjects should be assigned to experimental or control groups on a chance or random basis. We could not conclude much from an experiment on the effects of TV violence if the children were allowed to choose whether they would be in a group that watched a lot of TV violence or in a group that watched TV shows without violence. This is because children who choose to watch TV violence might have more aggressive tendencies to begin with. Therefore, if children who watched violent TV programs wound up showing more aggression, we could not attribute this difference to the TV viewing itself. It might, instead, reflect the children's greater initial aggressiveness.

In an experiment on the effects of TV violence, we would therefore have to assign children randomly to view shows with or without violence, regardless of their personal preferences. As you can imagine, this would be difficult, if not impossible, to do in the child's own home. But such studies can be performed in laboratory settings, as we will see in Chapter 10.

Ethical and practical considerations also prevent researchers from doing experiments on the effects of many significant life circumstances such as divorce or different patterns of child rearing. We cannot randomly assign some families to divorce or to conflict, and other families to perpetual harmony. Nor can we randomly assign parents with an authoritarian bent to raising their children in a permissive manner, or vice versa. In some areas of investigation, we must be relatively satisfied with correlational evidence.

When experiments cannot ethically be performed on humans, researchers sometimes have carried out experiments with animals and then generalized the findings to humans. For example, no researcher would wish to separate human infants from their parents to study the effects of isolation on development. But experimenters have deprived rhesus monkeys of early social experience. Such research has helped psychologists investigate the formation of parent–child bonds of attachment (see Chapter 7).

independent variable A condition in a scientific study that is manipulated (changed) so that its effects may be observed.

dependent variable A measure of an assumed effect of an independent variable.

experimental subjects Participants who receive a treatment in an experiment.

control subjects Participants in an experiment who do not receive the treatment but for whom all other conditions are held comparable to those of experimental subjects.

longitudinal research The study of developmental processes by taking repeated measures of the same group of children at various stages of development.

cross-sectional research The study of developmental processes by taking measures of children of different age groups at the same time.

Studying Development Over Time

The processes of development occur over time, and researchers have evolved different strategies for comparing children of one age to children (or adults) of other ages. ***Question: How do researchers study development over time?*** In **longitudinal research,** the same children are observed repeatedly over time, and changes in development, such as gains in height or changes in approach to problem solving, are recorded. In **cross-sectional research,** children of different ages are observed and compared. It is assumed that when large numbers of children are chosen at random, the differences found in the older age groups are a reflection of how the younger children will develop, given time. Table 1.4 summarizes the major features of cross-sectional and longitudinal research.

TABLE 1.4 *Comparison of Cross-Sectional and Longitudinal Research*

	Cross-Sectional	Longitudinal
Description	• Studies children of different ages at the same point in time	• Studies the same children repeatedly over time
Advantages	• Inexpensive • Can be completed in short period of time • No drop-out or practice effects	• Allows researchers to follow development over time • Studies the relationships between behavior at earlier and later ages
Disadvantages	• Does not study development across time • Cannot study relationship between behavior displayed at earlier and later ages • Is prey to cohort effect (subjects from different age groups may not be comparable)	• Expensive • Takes a long time to complete • Subjects drop out • Subjects who drop out may differ systematically from those who remain in study • Practice effects may occur

Longitudinal Studies

Some ambitious longitudinal studies have followed the development of children and adults for more than half a century. One, the Fels Longitudinal Study, began in 1929. Children were observed twice a year in their homes and twice a year in the Fels Institute nursery school. From time to time, various investigators have dipped into the Fels pool of subjects, further testing, interviewing, and observing these individuals as they have grown into adults. In this way, researchers have been able to observe, for example, the development of intelligence and of patterns of independence and dependence.

The Terman Studies of Genius, also begun in the 1920s, tracked children with high IQ scores. The men in this study, but not the women, went on to high achievements in the professional world (see Chapter 12). Why is this? Contemporary studies of women show that those with high intelligence generally match the achievements of men and suggest that women of the earlier era were held back by traditional gender-role expectations.

Most longitudinal studies span months or a few years, not decades. In Chapter 13, for example, we shall see that briefer longitudinal studies have found that the children of divorced parents undergo the most severe adjustment problems within a few months of the divorce. By 2 or 3 years afterward, many children have regained their equilibrium, as indicated by improved academic performance, social behavior, and other measures (Hetherington et al., 1992).

Longitudinal studies have drawbacks. For example, it can be difficult to enlist volunteers to participate in a study that will last a lifetime. Many participants fall out of touch as the years pass; others die. Furthermore, those who remain in the study tend to be brighter and more motivated than those who drop out. The researchers, of course, must be very patient. To compare 3-year-olds with 6-year-olds, they must wait 3 years. And in the early stages of such a study, the idea of comparing 3-year-olds with 21-year-olds remains a distant dream. When the researchers themselves are middle-aged or older, they must hope that the candle of yearning for knowledge will be kept lit by a new generation of researchers.

Reflect

How are the experiences of children who are being born today likely to differ from your own?

Cross-Sectional Studies

Because of the drawbacks of longitudinal studies, most research that compares children of different ages is cross-sectional. Most investigators, in other words, gather data on what the "typical" 6-month-old is doing by finding children who are 6 months old today. When they expand their research to the behavior of typical 12-month-olds, they seek another group of children and so on.

Is Surfing the Internet an Activity That Illustrates the Cohort Effect?

Children and adults of different ages experience cultural and other events unique to their age group. This is known as the cohort effect. For example, today's children—unlike their parents—are growing up taking video games, the Internet, and rap stars for granted. They have no experience of the Cold War, but the threat of terrorism in the United States may become part of their world.

A major drawback to cross-sectional research is the **cohort effect.** A cohort is a group of people born at about the same time. As a result, they experience cultural and other events unique to their age group. In other words, children and adults of different ages are not likely to have shared similar cultural backgrounds. People who are 70 years old today, for example, grew up without TV. (It could happen.) People who are 50 years old today grew up before the era of space travel. When they were children, no explorers had yet left Earth. Today's 40-year-olds did not spend their earliest years with *Sesame Street,* a TV program that has greatly influenced millions of a somewhat younger cohort of children and young adults. And today's children are growing up taking video games and the Internet for granted. In fact, for today's children, Britney Spears is an older woman.

Children of past generations also grew up with very different expectations about gender roles and appropriate social behavior. Remember that women in the Terman study generally chose motherhood over careers. Today's girls are growing up with female role models who are astronauts, high government officials, and powerful athletes. Moreover, today more than 60 percent of mothers are in the workforce, and their attitudes about women's roles have changed.

In other words, today's 25-year-olds are not today's 5-year-olds as seen 20 years later. And today's 10-year-olds may not even be today's 5-year-olds as seen 5 years later. The times change, and their influence on children changes also. In longitudinal studies, we know that we have the same individuals as they have developed over 5, 10, and 20 years. In cross-sectional research, we can only hope they will be comparable.

Cross-Sequential Research

Cross-sequential research combines the longitudinal and cross-sectional methods in such a way that many of their individual drawbacks are overcome. In the cross-sequential study, the full span of the ideal longitudinal study is first broken up into convenient segments (see Figure 1.8). For example, let us assume we wish to follow the gender-role attitudes of children from the age of 4 through the age of 12. The typical longitudinal study would take 8 years. However, we can divide this 8-year span in half by attaining two samples of children (a cross-section) instead of one: 4-year-olds and 8-year-olds. We would then interview, test, and observe each group at the beginning of the study (2003) and 4 years later (2007). By the time of the second observation period, the 4-year-olds would have become 8 years old, and the 8-year-olds would have become 12.

cohort effect Similarities in behavior among a group of peers that stem from the fact that group members are approximately of the same age (a possible source of misleading information in cross-sectional research).

cross-sequential research An approach that combines the longitudinal and cross-sectional methods by following individuals of different ages for abbreviated periods of time.

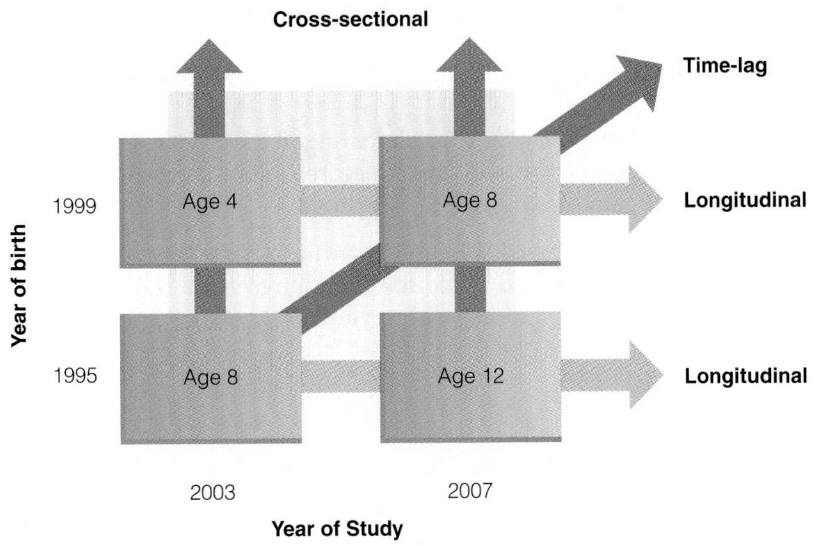

Figure 1.8
An Example of Cross-Sequential Research

Cross-sequential research combines three methods: cross-sectional, longitudinal, and time lag. The child's age at time of testing appears in the boxes. Vertical columns represent cross-sectional comparisons. Horizontal rows represent longitudinal comparisons. Diagonals represent time-lag comparisons.

An obvious advantage to this collapsed method is that the study is completed in 4 rather than 8 years. Still, the testing and retesting of samples provides some of the continuity of the longitudinal study. By observing both samples at the age of 8 (this is called a **time-lag** comparison), we can also determine whether they are, in fact, comparable or whether the 4 years' difference in their birthdate is associated with cultural and other environmental changes that lead to different attitudes. The fact that both groups of children overlap in age at one point (8 years old), when the younger group is tested for the second time and the older group for the first time, may also provide insight as to whether the process of testing itself makes a difference in future performance. That is, differences between samples tested at the same age may reflect the experience of having been tested before, as well as other environmental differences.

This combined method may include more than two samples and briefer time spans. For example, it is possible to recruit five groups of children, not two. If these children are 2, 4, 6, 8, and 10 years old at the outset of the study, they can be followed for 2 years, until their ages overlap, and then be retested. In this way, 10 years of "longitudinal" data can be acquired in 2. Eight years are saved, and some of the objections to longitudinal research are overcome. Quite a bargain.

Ethical Considerations

Psychologists adhere to a number of ethical standards that are intended to promote the dignity of the individual, foster human welfare, and maintain scientific integrity (McGovern et al., 1991). These standards also ensure that psychologists do not undertake research methods or treatments that are harmful to research participants (American Psychological Association, 1992). ***Question: What ethical guidelines are involved in research in child development?***

Various professional groups—such as the American Psychological Association and the Society for Research in Child Development—and government review boards have proposed guidelines for research with children. The overriding purpose of these guidelines is to protect children from harm. These guidelines include the following:

- Researchers are not to use treatments or methods of measurement that may do physical or psychological harm.
- Children and their parents must be informed of the purposes of the research and about the research methods.
- Children and their parents must provide voluntary consent to participate in the study.

time lag The study of developmental processes by taking measures of children of the same age group at different times.

Reflect

Why is it important to keep the identities of children who have participated in research studies confidential?

- Children and their parents may withdraw from the study at any time, for any reason.
- Children and their parents should be offered information about the results of the study.
- The identities of the children participating in a study are to remain confidential.
- Researchers should present their research plans to a committee of their colleagues and gain the committee's approval before proceeding.

These guidelines present researchers with a number of hurdles to overcome before proceeding with and while conducting research. But since they protect the welfare of children, the guidelines are valuable.

Review

(37) The five steps of the scientific method include formulating a research question, developing a hypothesis, testing the ________, drawing conclusions, and publishing results. (38) Naturalistic observation studies of children are conducted in "the field"—that is, in the real-life setting. (39) The ________ study is a carefully drawn account or biography of the behavior of an individual child. (40) A ________ coefficient is a number that shows the relationship between variables and varies between +1.00 and –1.00. (41) In an experiment, an experimental group of participants receives a ________, while a control group does not. (42) ________ research observes the same children repeatedly over time. (43) In cross-________ research, children of different ages are observed and compared. (44) Cross-sequential research combines the ________ and cross-sectional methods to overcome their individual drawbacks. (45) The purpose of ________ guidelines is to protect children from harm.

Pulling It Together: Why is the experiment considered the best way to show cause and effect?

Recite Recite Recite Recite

1. What is child development?

The field of child development attempts to advance knowledge of the processes that govern the development of children's physical structures, traits, behavior, cognition, and ways of adapting to the demands of life. *Growth* usually refers to changes in size or quantity, whereas *development* also refers to changes in quality.

2. Why do researchers study child development?

Researchers study child development out of curiosity and to gain insight into human nature; the origins of adult behavior; the origins, prevention, and treatment of developmental problems; and ways of optimizing the development of all children.

3. What views of children do we find throughout history?

In ancient times and in the Middle Ages, children often were viewed as innately evil, and discipline was harsh. Children were treated as property and servants. John Locke did not believe that children were "born" good or evil, and he focused on the role of the environment or experience. Jean-Jacques Rousseau argued that children are good by nature; and if allowed to express their natural impulses, they would develop into moral and giving people. In the 20th century, laws were passed to protect children from arduous labor and to require that they attend school until a certain age. Charles Darwin originated the modern theory of evolution and was one of the first observers to keep a baby biography. G. Stanley Hall founded child development as an academic discipline. Alfred Binet developed the first modern standardized intelligence test.

Recite Recite Recite Recite

4. What are theories? Why do we have them?

Theories are related sets of statements about events. Theories of development help us describe, explain, and predict development. Useful theories also enable us to influence development in a positive way.

5. What are psychoanalytic theories of child development?

Psychoanalytic theories are stage theories that owe their origin to Freud. They view children as caught in conflict. Freud argued that the unconscious mind contains sexual and aggressive instincts and urges that we only partly perceive. Freud labeled the clashing forces of personality the *id, ego,* and *superego.* He believed that sexual feelings were expressed via different parts of the body during different stages of psychosexual development: *oral, anal, phallic, latency,* and *genital.* Too little or too much gratification in a stage could lead to fixation. The Oedipus and Electra complexes are key conflicts of the phallic period.

6. How does Erikson's theory differ from Freud's?

Erikson's psychoanalytic theory sees social relationships as more important than sexual or aggressive impulses and therefore addresses psycho*social* rather than psycho*sexual* development. Erikson extended Freud's five developmental stages to eight to include adulthood and labeled stages after life crises. Those of childhood and adolescence include *trust versus mistrust, autonomy versus shame and doubt, initiative versus guilt, industry versus inferiority,* and *identity versus identity diffusion.*

7. What is the theory of behaviorism?

Watson argued that scientists must address observable behavior only, not mental activity. Behaviorism relies on two types of learning: classical and operant conditioning. In classical conditioning, one stimulus (the CS) comes to signal another (the UCS) by being paired repeatedly with the other stimulus. In operant conditioning, children learn to engage in behavior because of its effects. Reinforcement *increases* the frequency of behavior. Extinction of behavior results from repeated performance without reinforcement. Punishments are aversive events that *decrease* the frequency of behavior. Children can be taught complex behaviors by shaping, or reinforcing, small steps toward goals.

8. How does social cognitive theory differ from behaviorism?

Social cognitive theorists, such as Bandura, argue that much learning occurs by observing models and that the relationship between children and the environment is one of reciprocal determinism. Learning influences children's belief in their ability to manipulate the environment. Children choose whether or not to display behaviors they have learned.

9. What are Jean Piaget's views on development?

Piaget saw children as actors on the environment, not reactors. He studied how children form mental representations of the world and manipulate them. Piaget's theory uses the concepts of *schemes, adaptation, assimilation, accommodation,* and *equilibration.* He hypothesized that children's cognitive processes develop in an invariant series of stages: *sensorimotor, preoperational, concrete operational,* and *formal operational.*

10. What is information-processing theory?

Information-processing theory deals with the ways in which children encode information, transfer it to working memory (short-term memory), manipulate it, place information in storage (long-term memory), and retrieve it from storage. Information-processing theorists talk about the size of the child's short-term memory at a given age and about the number of "programs" a child can run simultaneously.

11. What is the scope of the biological perspective?

The biological perspective refers to heredity and to developments such as formation of sperm and ova, gains in height and weight, maturation of the nervous system, and the way hormones spur the changes of puberty.

12. What is maturational theory?

Gesell's maturational theory asserts that development is self-regulated by the unfolding of natural plans and processes. Maturational processes follow invariant sequences. Children cannot learn new things until they are *ready* to learn them.

Recite Recite Recite Recite

13. What is ethology?

Ethology involves instinctive, or inborn, behavior patterns termed *fixed-action patterns (FAPs)*. FAPs occur in the presence of species-specific *releasing stimuli*. Many FAPs, such as those involved in attachment, occur during a *critical period* of life.

14. What is the ecological systems theory of child development?

Bronfenbrenner's ecological theory explains development in terms of the *reciprocal interaction* between children and the settings in which it occurs—not just maturational forces (nature) or child-rearing practices and experiences (nurture). The settings of human development include four systems: the *microsystem, mesosystem, exosystem,* and *macrosystem.*

15. What is meant by the sociocultural perspective?

The sociocultural perspective emphasizes that children are social beings who are influenced by their cultural backgrounds.

16. What are the key concepts of Vygotsky's sociocultural theory?

Vygotsky's key concepts include the *zone of proximal development (ZPD)* and *scaffolding.* When learning with other people, the children tend to internalize conversations and explanations that help them gain skills. Children learn ways of thinking about solving problems within a cultural context.

17. What is the connection between the sociocultural perspective and human diversity?

The sociocultural perspective addresses the richness of children's diversity, as in their ethnicity and gender. Understanding of the cultural heritages and historical problems of children from various ethnic groups is necessary for education and psychological intervention. Children learn early about gender roles and gender-role stereotypes. Cultural limitations on women give girls a sense of what is possible for them.

18. Which exerts the greater influence on children: nature or nurture?

Development would appear to reflect the interaction of nature (genetics) and nurture (nutrition, cultural and family backgrounds, and opportunities to learn about the world).

19. Is development continuous or discontinuous?

Maturational theorists, psychoanalytic theorists, and Piaget saw development as being discontinuous (occurring in stages). Aspects of physical development, such as the adolescent growth spurt, do occur in stages. Learning theorists tend to see development as more continuous.

20. Are children active ("prewired" to act on world) or are they passive (shaped by experience)?

Bronfenbrenner and Bandura do not see children as either entirely active or entirely passive. They believe that children are influenced by the environment, but that the influence is reciprocal; that is, children also influence the environment.

21. What is the scientific method?

The scientific method is a systematic way of formulating and answering research questions that includes formulating a research question, developing a hypothesis, testing the hypothesis, drawing conclusions, and publishing results.

22. What is naturalistic observation?

Naturalistic observation is conducted in "the field"—that is, in the real-life settings in which children develop. Investigators try not to interfere with the behavior they are observing.

23. What is the case study?

The case study is a carefully drawn account or biography of the behavior of an individual child. Information may be derived from diaries, observation, questionnaires, standardized tests, interviews, and public records.

24. What is the correlational method?

The correlational method enables researchers to determine whether one behavior or trait is related to another. A correlation coefficient can vary between +1.00 and –1.00. Correlations can be positive or negative. Correlational studies reveal relationships between variables but not cause and effect.

Recite Recite Recite Recite

25. What is an experiment?

In an experiment, an experimental group receives a treatment (independent variable), whereas another group (a control group) does not. Participants are observed to determine whether the treatment has an effect (on dependent variables). Participants are assigned at random to experimental or control groups.

26. How do researchers study development over time?

Longitudinal research studies the same children repeatedly over time. Cross-sectional research observes and compares children of different ages. A drawback to cross-sectional research is the cohort effect. Cross-sequential research combines the longitudinal and cross-sectional methods by breaking down the full span of the ideal longitudinal study into convenient segments.

27. What ethical guidelines are involved in research in child development?

Ethical standards promote the dignity of the individual, foster human welfare, and maintain scientific integrity. Researchers are not to use treatments that may do harm, and children and parents must participate voluntarily.

On the Web

Search Online With InfoTrac® College Edition

For additional information, explore InfoTrac College Edition, your online library. Go to http://www.infotrac-college.com and use the passcode from the InfoTrac card that came with your book. Try these search terms: child development study and teaching, constructivism, ecological perspective and child development, social learning, Sigmund Freud, Jean Piaget, longitudinal method.

Visit Our Web Site

Go to http://www.wadsworth.com/psychology where you will find online resources directly linked to your book.

Child Development CD-ROM

Go to the Wadsworth Child Development CD-ROM for further study of the concepts in this chapter. The CD-ROM also includes quizzes and additional activities to expand your learning experience.

Answer Key to A Closer Look: "How Much Do You Know About Child Development?" page 4

1. F	5. F	9. F	13. F
2. F	6. F	10. F	14. T
3. F	7. F	11. T	15. T
4. T	8. F	12. T	16. F

2 Heredity and Conception—"Something Old, Something New"

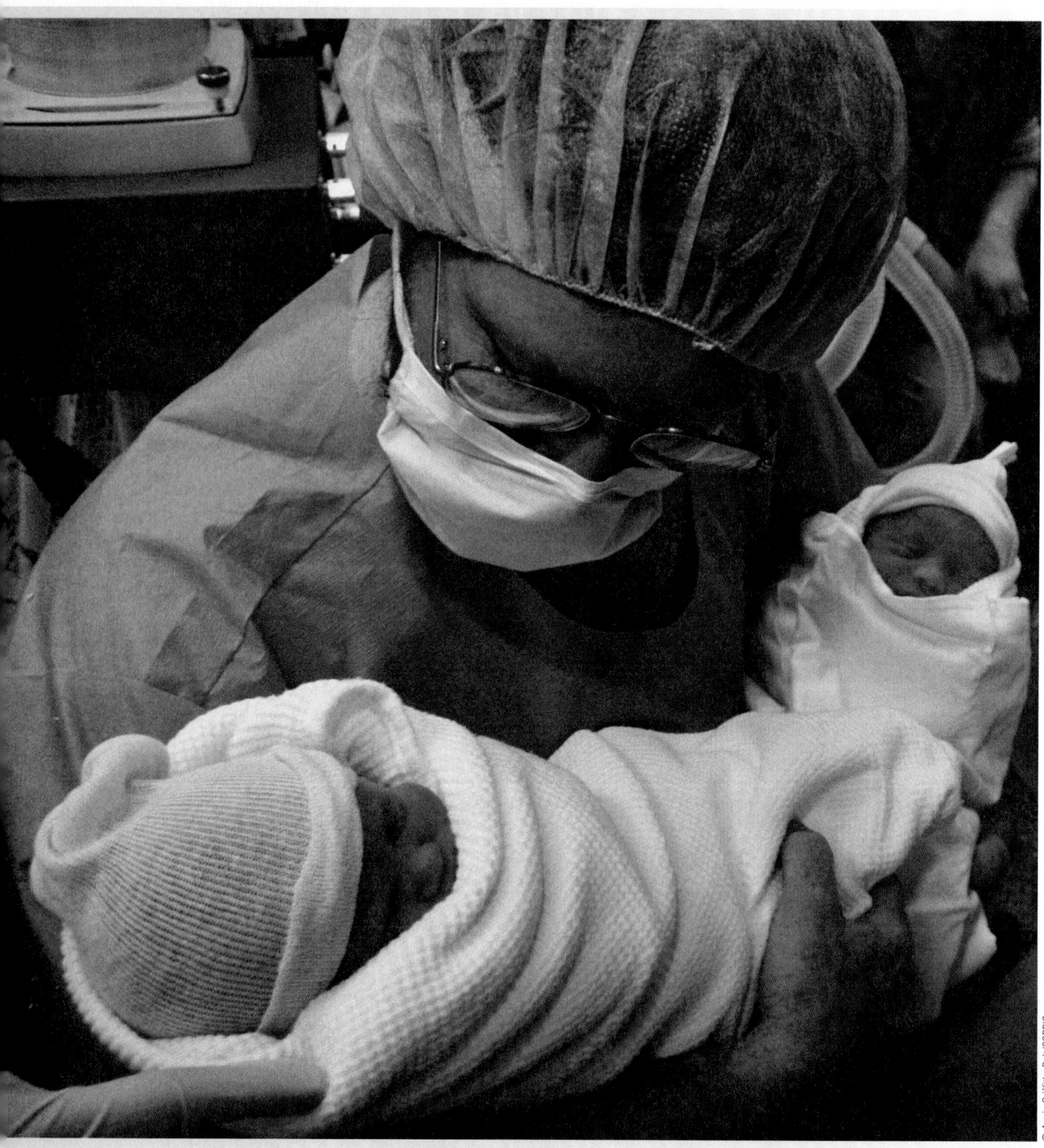

PowerPreview™

The Influence of Heredity on Development

- **What is a** gene? What is a chromosome?
- **How are** sperm and egg cells formed?
- **Why are couples** who delay childbearing more likely to have twins?

Heredity and the Environment

- **Identical twins are more likely** than fraternal twins to share disorders such as schizophrenia and vulnerability to alcoholism.
- **If adopted children are more like** their biological parents than their adoptive parents on a trait—such as eye color or sociability—then heredity is likely to play a key role in the development of that trait.

Conception: Against All Odds

- **Where does** conception normally occur?
- **Did you know** that for every "successful" sperm cell, there are literally hundreds of millions of "failures"?
- **What is a** "test-tube baby"?
- **Developing embryos can be** transferred from the uterus of one woman to the uterus of another.
- **Can you select** the gender of your child? (Would you want to?)

She went for the girl. Kathy des Jardins had three boys—a pair of 10-year-old twins and a 5-year-old—and decided, "Enough is enough." How delightful it would be to have a little girl. Though she was in her early 40s and had some fertility problems, she didn't want to think of herself as "out of the baby business." So she would try. But was she going to leave the sex of her baby up to chance? You might think that after having three boys, the odds were now in her favor. But that's not the way it works. The more boys you have already, the more likely it is you'll have another boy if you try again. (That's because there may be something systematic—even if unknown—about the way the couple determine the sex of their child.)

So Kathy placed her (sex-selection) fate in the hands of a company that touted a 90% success rate in helping couples have girls rather than boys (and a lower success rate in selecting boys). How does the company do it? By sorting sperm according to whether they bear Y sex chromosomes (which combine with ova to develop into boys) or X sex chromosomes (which make girls). Kathy and her husband spent thousands of dollars, chemically induced her reluctant **ovaries** to produce **ova,** underwent artificial insemination to maximize the chances of conception, and—as we see later in the chapter—she didn't get pregnant.

Click *Physical Development* in the Child and Adolescent CD-ROM for more on prenatal development.

But each year, millions upon millions of other women do. In this chapter, we explore heredity and **prenatal** development. We could say that development begins long before conception in the sense that it also involves the origins of the genetic structures which determine that human embryos will grow arms rather than wings, a mouth rather than gills, and hair rather than scales. Our discussion thus begins with an examination of the building blocks of heredity: genes and chromosomes. Then we describe the process of conception and find that the odds against any one sperm uniting with an ovum are, as Kathy des Jardins found, quite literally astronomical.

The Influence of Heredity on Development

Consider some of the facts of life:

- People cannot breathe underwater (without special equipment).
- People cannot fly (without special equipment).
- Fish cannot learn to speak French or dance an Irish jig, even if they are raised in enriched environments and sent to finishing school.

We cannot breathe underwater or fly, because we have not inherited gills or wings. Fish are similarly limited by their **heredity.** ***Question: What is meant by heredity?*** Heredity defines one's nature—which is based on the biological transmission of traits and characteristics from one generation to another. Because of their heredity, fish cannot speak French or do a jig.

Heredity plays a momentous role in the determination of human traits. The structures we inherit both make our behaviors possible and place limits on them. The field within the science of biology that studies heredity is called **genetics.**

Genetic (inherited) influences are fundamental in the transmission of physical traits, such as height, hair texture, and eye color. Genetics also appear to be a factor in intelligence and in the origins of personality traits such as activity level, sociability, shyness, fearfulness, **neuroticism, empathy,** effectiveness as a parent, happiness, and even interest in arts and crafts (Carey & DiLalla, 1994; Loehlin, 1992; Lykken et al., 1992; Lykken & Tellegen, 1996). Genetic influences are also implicated in psychological problems and disorders such as schizophrenia; anxiety and depression; dependence on nicotine, alcohol, and other substances; and criminal behavior (Kendler et al., 2000; Kendler, Myers, & Neale, 2000; Nurnberger et al., 2001; Plomin, 2000; Sullivan, Neale, & Kendler, 2000). Even so, most behavior patterns also reflect life experiences and, once people come to understand their situations and their own abilities, personal choice (Sullivan et al., 2000).

ovary A female reproductive organ, located in the abdomen, that produces female reproductive cells (ova).

ovum A female reproductive cell.

prenatal Refers to period before birth.

heredity The transmission of traits and characteristics from parent to child by means of genes.

genetics The branch of biology that studies heredity.

neuroticism A personality trait characterized by anxiety and emotional instability.

empathy The ability to share another person's feelings or emotions.

Chromosomes and Genes

Heredity is made possible by microscopic structures called chromosomes and genes. ***Question: What are chromosomes and genes?*** **Chromosomes** are rod-shaped structures found in the nuclei of the body's cells. A normal human cell contains 46 chromosomes organized into 23 pairs. Each chromosome contains thousands of segments called genes. **Genes** are the biochemical materials that regulate the development of traits. Some traits, such as blood type, appear to be transmitted by a single pair of genes—one of which is derived from each parent. Other traits, referred to as **polygenic,** are determined by combinations of pairs of genes. Most human behaviors are believed to be affected by combinations of genes (McGuffin, Riley, & Plomin, 2001).

We have about 30,000 to 40,000 genes in every cell in our bodies (International Human Genome Sequencing Consortium, 2001). Genes are segments of large strands of **deoxyribonucleic acid (DNA).** In the 1950s James Watson and Francis Crick (1958) discovered that DNA takes the form of a double spiral, or helix, similar in appearance to a twisting ladder (see Figure 2.1). In all living things, from one-celled animals to fish to people, the sides of the "ladder" consist of alternating segments of phosphate (P) and simple sugar (S). The "rungs" of the ladder are attached to the sugars and consist of one of two pairs of bases, either adenine with thymine (A with T) or cytosine with guanine (C with G). The sequence of the "rungs" is the genetic code that will cause the developing organism to grow arms or wings, skin or scales.

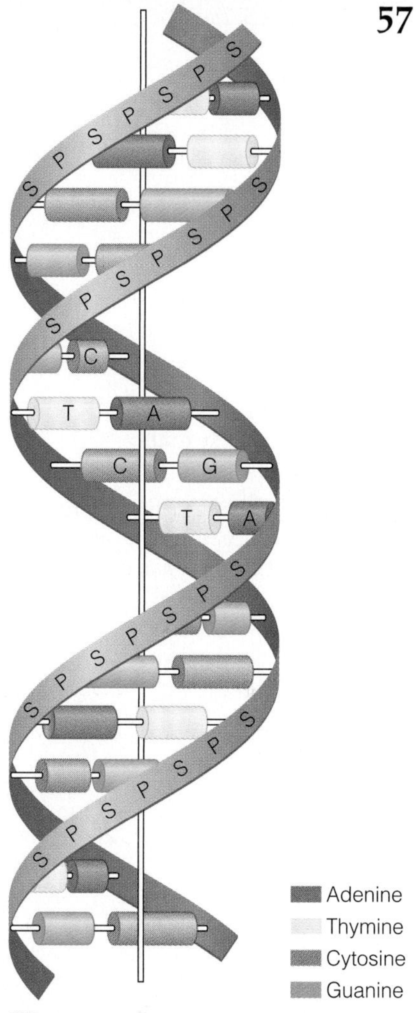

Figure 2.1
The Double Helix of DNA

DNA consists of phosphate, sugar, and a number of bases. It takes the form of a double spiral, or helix.

Mitosis and Meiosis

We begin life as a single cell, or zygote, that divides again and again. ***Question: How do cells divide?*** There are two types of cell division: *mitosis* and *meiosis*. **Mitosis** is the cell-division process by which growth occurs and tissues are replaced. Through mitosis, the identical genetic code is carried into each new cell in the body. To accomplish this, the strands of DNA break apart, or "unzip" (see Figure 2.2). The double helix is then rebuilt in the cell. Each incomplete rung combines with the appropriate "partner" element (that is, G combines with C, A with T, and so on) to form a complete ladder. The two resulting identical copies of the DNA strand move apart when the cell divides, each

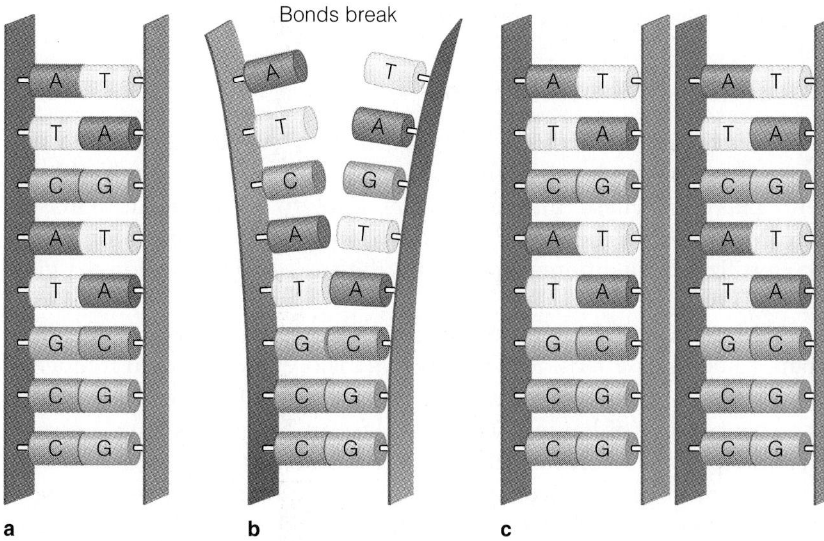

Figure 2.2
Mitosis

*(**a**) A segment of a strand of DNA before mitosis. (**b**) During mitosis, chromosomal strands of DNA "unzip." (**c**) The double helix is rebuilt in the cell as each incomplete "rung" combines with appropriate molecules. The resulting identical copies of the DNA strand move apart when the cell divides, each joining one of the new cells.*

chromosomes Rod-shaped structures, composed of genes, that are found within the nuclei of cells.

gene The basic unit of heredity. Genes are composed of deoxyribonucleic acid (DNA).

polygenic Refers to characteristic that results from many genes.

deoxyribonucleic acid (DNA) Genetic material that takes the form of a double helix composed of phosphates, sugars, and bases.

mitosis The form of cell division in which each chromosome splits lengthwise to double in number. Half of each chromosome combines with chemicals to retake its original form and then moves to the new cell.

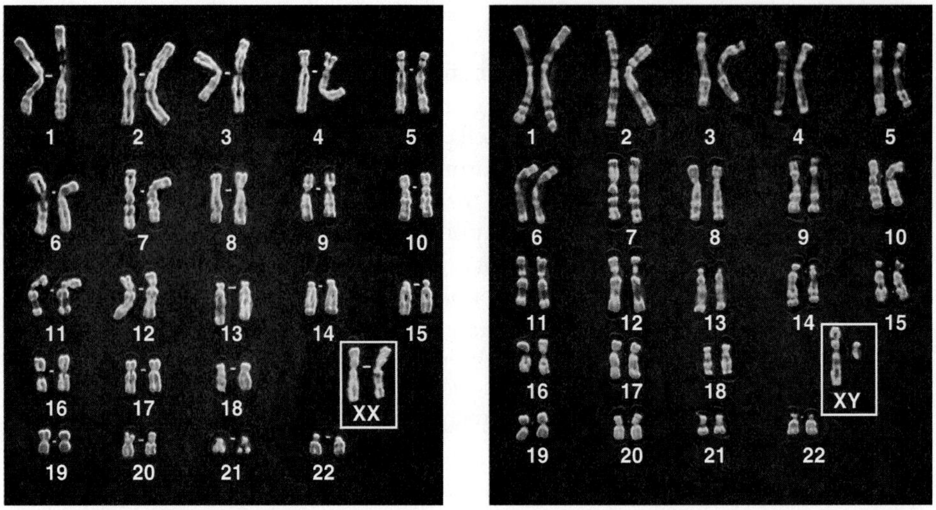

Figure 2.3
The 23 Pairs of Human Chromosomes

People normally have 23 pairs of chromosomes. Females have two X chromosomes, whereas males have an X and a Y sex chromosome.

becoming a member of one of the newly formed cells. As a consequence, the genetic code is identical in every cell of the body unless **mutations** occur through radiation or other environmental influences. On rare occasions, mutations may occur by chance.

Sperm and ova are produced through **meiosis,** or *reduction division.* In meiosis, the 46 chromosomes within the cell nucleus first line up into 23 pairs. When the cell divides, one member of each pair goes to each newly formed cell. As a consequence, each new cell nucleus contains only 23 chromosomes, not 46. And so a cell that results from meiosis has half the genetic material of one that results from mitosis.

Through reduction division, or meiosis, we receive 23 chromosomes from our father's sperm cell and 23 from our mother's ovum. When a sperm cell fertilizes an ovum, the chromosomes form 23 pairs (Figure 2.3). Twenty-two of the pairs are **autosomes**—that is, chromosomes that are matched pairs and possess genetic information concerning the same set of traits. The 23rd pair consists of **sex chromosomes** that look different and determine our gender. We all receive an X sex chromosome (so called because of its X shape) from our mothers. If we receive another X sex chromosome from our fathers, we develop into females. If we receive a Y sex chromosome (named after its Y shape) from our fathers, we develop into males.

Identical and Fraternal Twins

Question: How are twins formed? Now and then, a **zygote** divides into two cells that separate so that each subsequently develops into an individual with the same genetic makeup. These individuals are known as identical twins, or **monozygotic (MZ) twins.** If the woman produces two ova in the same month, and they are each fertilized by a different sperm cell, they develop into fraternal twins, or **dizygotic (DZ) twins.**

MZ twins are rarer than DZ twins, occurring once in about every 300 pregnancies (Behrman, Kliegman, & Jenson, 2000). MZ twins occur with equal frequency in all ethnic groups, but the incidence of DZ twins varies. European Americans have about 1 chance in 90 of having DZ twins. African Americans have 1 chance in 70. Asian Americans have only about 1 chance in 150 (Behrman et al., 2000).

DZ twins run in families. If a woman's mother was a twin, chances are one in eight that she will bear twins. If a woman has previously borne twins, the chances similarly rise to one in eight that she will bear twins in subsequent pregnancies. Similarly, women who have borne several children have an increased likelihood of twins in subsequent pregnancies.

As women reach the end of their childbearing years, **ovulation** becomes less regular, resulting in a number of months when more than one ovum is released. Thus the chances of twins increase with parental age (Raschka, 2000). Fertility

mutation A sudden variation in an inheritable characteristic, as by an accident that affects the composition of genes.

meiosis The form of cell division in which each pair of chromosomes splits, so that one member of each pair moves to the new cell. As a result, each new cell has 23 chromosomes.

autosome Either member of a pair of chromosomes (with the exception of sex chromosomes).

sex chromosome A chromosome in the shape of a Y (male) or X (female) that determines the sex of the child.

zygote A fertilized ovum.

monozygotic (MZ) twins Twins that derive from a single zygote that has split into two; identical twins. Each MZ twin carries the same genetic code.

dizygotic (DZ) twins Twins that derive from two zygotes; fraternal twins.

ovulation The release of an ovum from an ovary.

drugs also enhance the chances of multiple births by causing more than one ovum to ripen and be released during any particular cycle (Division of Reproductive Health, 2000).

Dominant and Recessive Traits

Question: How do genes determine traits? Traits are determined by pairs of genes. Each member of a pair of genes is referred to as an **allele.** When both of the alleles for a trait, such as hair color, are the same, the person is said to be **homozygous** for that trait. (*Homo,* in this usage, derives from the Greek root meaning "same," not the Latin root meaning "man.") When the alleles for a trait differ, the person is **heterozygous** for that trait.

Gregor Mendel (1822–1884), an Austrian monk, established a number of laws of heredity through his work with plants. Mendel realized that some traits may result from an "averaging" of the genetic instructions carried by the parents. When the effects of both alleles are shown, there is said to be incomplete dominance or codominance.

Mendel also discovered the "law of dominance." For example, the offspring from the crossing of purebred tall peas and purebred dwarf peas were tall, suggesting that tallness is dominant over dwarfism. We now know that many genes determine **dominant traits** or **recessive traits.** When a dominant allele is paired with a recessive allele, the trait determined by the dominant allele appears in the individual.

Brown eyes, for instance, are dominant over blue eyes. If one parent carried genes for only brown eyes, and the other for only blue eyes, the children would invariably have brown eyes. But brown-eyed parents may also carry recessive genes for blue eyes, as shown in Figure 2.4. Similarly, the offspring of Mendel's crossing of purebred tall and purebred dwarf peas were not pure. They carried recessive genes for dwarfism.

Reflect

What dominant and recessive traits do you have? What dominant and recessive traits do you share with your parents or your siblings?

allele A member of a pair of genes.

homozygous Having two identical alleles.

heterozygous Having two different alleles.

dominant trait A trait that is expressed.

recessive trait A trait that is not expressed when the gene or genes involved have been paired with dominant genes. Recessive traits are transmitted to future generations and expressed if they are paired with other recessive genes.

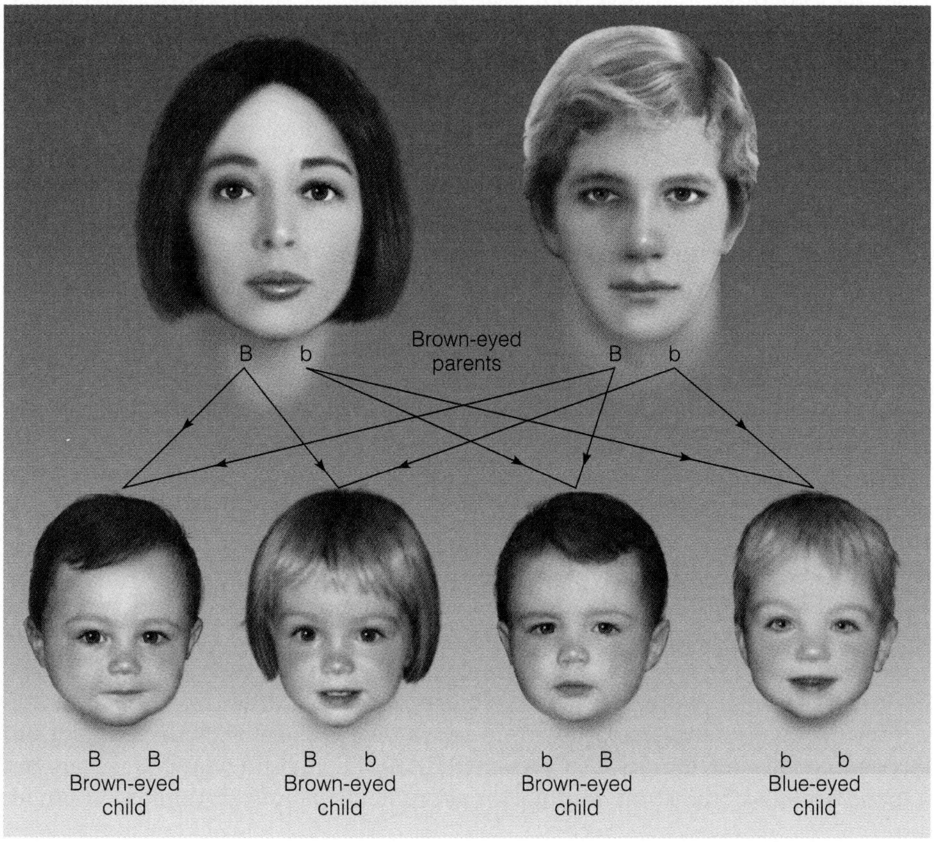

Figure 2.4
The Transmission of Dominant and Recessive Traits

Two brown-eyed parents each carry a gene for blue eyes. Their children have an equal opportunity of receiving genes for brown eyes and blue eyes. In such cases, 25% of the children show the recessive trait—blue eyes. The other 75% show the dominant trait—brown eyes. But two of three who have brown eyes carry the recessive trait for transmittal to future generations.

TABLE 2.1 *Examples of Dominant and Recessive Traits*

Dominant Trait	Recessive Trait
Dark hair	Blond hair
Dark hair	Red hair
Curly hair	Straight hair
Normal color vision	Red-green color blindness
Normal vision	Myopia (nearsightedness)
Farsightedness	Normal vision
Normal pigmentation	Deficiency of pigmentation in skin, hair, and retina (albinism)
Normal sensitivity to touch	Extremely fragile skin (i.e., epidermolysis bullosa, as in "butterfly children")
Normal hearing	Some forms of deafness (i.e., keratitis ichthyosis deafness [KID] syndrome)
Dimples	Lack of dimpling
Rh-positive blood	Rh-negative blood
Type A blood	Type O blood
Type B blood	Type O blood
Tolerance of lactose	Lactose intolerance

If the recessive gene from one parent should combine with the recessive gene from the other, the recessive trait will be shown. As suggested by Figure 2.4, approximately 25% of the offspring of brown-eyed parents who carry recessive blue eye color will have blue eyes. Mendel found that 25% of the offspring of parent peas that carried recessive dwarfism would be dwarfs. Table 2.1 shows a number of dominant and recessive traits in humans.

Our discussion of eye color has been simplified. The percentages are not always perfect, because other genes may alter the expression of the genes for brown and blue eyes, producing hazel, or greenish, eyes. Some genes also switch other genes "on" or "off" at various times during development. For example, we normally reach reproductive capacity in the teens and not earlier, and men who go bald usually do so during adulthood. Similarly, the heart and the limbs develop at different times in the embryo, again because of the switching on or off of certain genes by other genes.

People who bear one dominant gene and one recessive gene for a trait are said to be **carriers** of the recessive gene. In the cases of recessive genes that give rise to serious illnesses, carriers of those genes are fortunate to have dominant genes that cancel their effects. Unfortunately, carriers can still transmit their recessive genes to their children.

A number of health problems can result from chromosomal or genetic abnormalities. Some chromosomal disorders reflect abnormalities in the autosomes (such as Down syndrome), while others reflect abnormalities in the sex chromosomes (as in XYY syndrome). Some genetic abnormalities, such as cystic fibrosis, are caused by a single pair of genes, while others are caused by complex combinations of genes. **Multifactorial problems** reflect a genetic predisposition and environmental contributors. Diabetes mellitus, epilepsy, and peptic ulcers are but a few examples of the many multifactorial problems people encounter. A number

carrier A person who carries and transmits characteristics but does not exhibit them.

multifactorial problems Problems that stem from the interaction of heredity and environmental factors.

of chromosomal and genetic abnormalities are discussed in the following sections and summarized in Table 2.2.

Chromosomal Abnormalities

Normally speaking, people have 46 chromosomes. When children have more or fewer chromosomes, they usually experience health problems or behavioral abnormalities. The risk of chromosomal abnormalities rises with the age of the parents (Behrman et al., 2000). ***Question: What kinds of disorders are caused by chromosomal abnormalities?***

Down Syndrome

Down syndrome is usually caused by an extra chromosome on the 21st pair, resulting in 47 chromosomes. The probability of having a child with Down syndrome varies positively with the age of the parents: Older parents are more likely to bear children with the syndrome. The chances of parents in their early 20s bearing children with Down syndrome are fewer than 1 in 1,000. However, in the mid-30s, a women has 1 chance in 300–400 of bearing a child with the syndrome, and by the mid-40s, her chances rise to about 1 in 30–40 (K. B. Roberts, 2000).

Children with the syndrome have characteristic facial features that include a rounded face, a protruding tongue, a broad, flat nose, and a sloping fold of skin over the inner corners of the eyes that has in the past given rise to the racially biased term *mongolism* (Figure 2.5). Children with Down syndrome usually die from cardiovascular problems by middle age, although modern medicine has extended life appreciably. The children show deficits in cognitive development, including language development, and in motor development (Berglund, Eriksson, & Johansson, 2001; Capone, 2001). They also encounter frequent disorders of the ear, nose, and throat, which contribute to academic problems (Shott, 2000).

As you can imagine, children with Down syndrome have adjustment problems in school and in the community at large (King et al., 2000). Other children are not always sensitive to their needs and feelings and may poke fun at them. Children with Down syndrome and other problems also tend to need more attention from

Reflect

Do you know anyone with Down syndrome? Was he or she place in special education or "mainstreamed" in regular classes? How did other children react to him or her? How did he or she adjust?

Down syndrome A chromosomal abnormality characterized by mental retardation and caused by an extra chromosome in the 21st pair.

Developing in a World of Diversity

Down Syndrome, Race, and Mortality

Down syndrome is caused by an extra chromosome on the 21st pair and characterized by a cluster of facial features, mental retardation, and a variety of physical health problems, including heart defects. By and large, people with Down syndrome do not live past middle age.

Researchers for the Centers for Disease Control and Prevention (2001b) are currently analyzing 34,000 death records from 1968 to 1997 of people with Down syndrome, and some numbers are beginning to be published. The analysis shows that people with Down syndrome are now living longer in part because, in the 1970s, surgeons began to correct a common congenital heart defect.

This area is one where significant disparities based on ethnicity come into play. Although surgeons started to do the operation in the 1970s, European American children were first to benefit from it. Surgeons did not begin to correct the same defect in large numbers among African Americans until the 1980s. This may be one of the reasons that the average age of death among European Americans with Down syndrome is now about 50, as compared with an average age at death of only 25 among African Americans with the disorder.

Investigators are studying the reasons for the discrepancy, but it seems clear that access to medical care is a key cause. You can keep abreast of recent developments in this research by going to **http://www.cdc.gov**, clicking on "Search," and entering the phrase "down syndrome."

■ **Figure 2.5**
Down Syndrome
How children with Down syndrome develop and adjust relates to their acceptance by their families. Children with Down syndrome reared at home develop more rapidly and achieve higher levels of functioning than do those reared in institutions.

their parents. Parental response is variable. Some parents are overwhelmed and a few are abusive, but many parents report that the special needs of their children have contributed to their own self-esteem and self-worth (King et al., 2000). The adjustment of the siblings of children with Down syndrome also varies, but siblings in families that communicate well and work together on problems appear to do quite well (Van Riper, 2000). We can make the generalization that parents who *want* their children usually do a better job of parenting, and this same principle applies when their children have special needs.

Sex-Linked Chromosomal Abnormalities

A number of disorders stem from abnormal numbers of sex chromosomes and are therefore said to be sex-linked chromosomal abnormalities. Most individuals with an abnormal number of sex chromosomes are infertile. Beyond that common finding, there are many differences, some of them associated with "maleness" or "femaleness." But there are also many myths and misunderstandings about these chromosomal abnormalities, even among health professionals (Biesecker, 2001).

Approximately 1 male in 700–1,000 has an extra Y chromosome. The Y chromosome is associated with maleness, and the extra Y sex chromosome apparently heightens male secondary sex characteristics. For example, XYY males are somewhat taller than average and develop heavier beards. For these kinds of reasons, males with XYY sex chromosomal structure were once referred to as "supermales." But the prefix *super* often implies superior, and it turns out that XYY males tend to have more problems than XY males. For example, they are often mildly retarded, particularly in language development. As part of their "excessive maleness," it was once thought that XYY males were given to aggressive, criminal behavior. When we examine prison populations, we find the numbers of XYY males to be "overrepresented" relative to their numbers in the population. However, it may be that the number of XYY males in prisons reflects their levels of intelligence rather than aggressiveness. Most XYY males in prison have committed crimes against property (such as stealing) rather than crimes against persons (such as assault and battery). And when we examine XYY individuals in the general population, the great majority do not have records of aggressive, criminal behavior (Goetz, Johnstone, & Ratcliffe, 1999; Ike, 2000).

Klinefelter's syndrome A chromosomal disorder found among males that is caused by an extra X sex chromosome and characterized by infertility and mild mental retardation.

About 1 male in 500–900 has **Klinefelter's syndrome,** which is caused by an extra X sex chromosome (an XXY sex chromosomal pattern) (Smyth & Bremner, 1998). XXY males produce less of the male sex hormone—*testosterone*—than normal males. As a result, male primary and secondary sex characteristics, such as the testes, deepening of the voice, musculature, and the male pattern of bodily hair, do not develop properly. XXY males usually have enlarged breasts (*gynecomastia*) and are usually mildly mentally retarded, particularly in language skills. XXY males are typically treated with testosterone replacement therapy, which can foster growth of sex characteristics and elevate the mood, but does not reverse infertility.

About 1 girl in 2,500–8,000 has a single X sex chromosome and as a result develops what is called **Turner's syndrome.** The external genitals of girls with Turner's syndrome are normal, but their ovaries are poorly developed, and they produce little of the female sex hormone *estrogen*. Girls with this problem are shorter than average and infertile. Because of low estrogen production, they do not develop breasts or menstruate. Researchers have connected a specific pattern of cognitive deficits with low estrogen levels: problems in visual-spatial skills, mathematics, and nonverbal memory (Buchanan, Pavlovic, & Rovet, 1998; Ross, Zinn, & McCauley, 2000). They have also found these problems to be somewhat reversible with estrogen therapy (Ross, Roeltgen, Feuillan, Kushman, & Cutler, 2000). Other researchers find that girls with Turner's syndrome have some motor impairment (Nijhuis-van der Sanden, Smits-Engelsman, & Eling, 2000). Such motor impairment may be connected with their having higher verbal scores than performance scores on intelligence tests (O'Connor, Fitzgerald, & Hoey, 2000).

About 1 girl in 1,000 has XXX sex chromosomal structure. These girls are normal in appearance. However, they tend to show lower-than-average language skills and poorer memory for recent events, suggestive of mild mental retardation (Rovet, 1993).

Genetic Abnormalities

A number of disorders have been attributed to defective genes (Grodin & Laurie, 2000). ***Question: What kinds of disorders are caused by genetic abnormalities?***

PKU

The enzyme disorder **phenylketonuria (PKU)** is transmitted by a recessive gene and affects about 1 child in 8,000. Therefore, if both parents possess the gene, PKU will be transmitted to one child in four (as in Figure 2.4). Two children in four will possess the gene but not develop the disorder. These two, like their parents, will be carriers of the disease. One child in four will not receive the recessive gene. Therefore, he or she will not be a carrier.

Children with PKU cannot metabolize an amino acid called phenylalanine. As a consequence, it builds up in their bodies and impairs the functioning of the central nervous system. The results are serious: mental retardation and psychological disorders. We have no cure for PKU, but PKU can be detected in newborn children through analysis of the blood or urine (Pharoah, 2001). Children with PKU who are placed on diets low in phenylalanine within 3 to 6 weeks after birth develop normally. The diet prohibits all meat, poultry, fish, dairy products, beans, and nuts. Fruits, vegetables, and some starchy foods are allowed. Pediatricians recommend staying on the diet at least until adolescence, and some encourage staying on it for life (Hunt & Berry, 1993).

Huntington's Disease

The disease that afflicted folksinger Woody Guthrie, **Huntington's disease** is a fatal progressive degenerative disorder and is a dominant trait (Pharoah, 2001). Physical symptoms include uncontrollable muscle movements. Psychological symptoms include loss of intellectual functioning and personality change. Because its onset is delayed until middle adulthood, many individuals with the defect have borne children only to discover years later that they, and possibly half

Turner's syndrome A chromosomal disorder found among females that is caused by having a single X sex chromosome and characterized by infertility.

phenylketonuria (PKU) (fee-nill-key-tone-NEW-ree-uh) A genetic abnormality in which phenylalanine builds up and causes mental retardation.

Huntington's disease A fatal genetic neurologic disorder with onset in middle age.

TABLE 2.2 *Chromosomal and Genetic Disorders*

Health Problem	Incidence	About ...	Treatment
		Chromosomal Disorders	
Down syndrome	1 birth in 700–800 overall; risk increases with parental age	A condition characterized by a 3rd chromosome on the 21st pair. The child with Down syndrome has a characteristic fold of skin over the eye and mental retardation.	No treatment, but educational programs are effective; usually fatal due to complications by middle age
Klinefelter's syndrome	1 male in 500–900	A disorder affecting males that is characterized by an extra X sex chromosome and connected with underdeveloped male secondary sex characteristics, gynecomastia, and mild mental retardation, particularly in language skills	Hormone (testosterone) replacement therapy; special education
Turner's syndrome	1 girl in 2,500–8,000	A disorder that affects females, characterized by single X-sex-chromosomal structure and associated with infertility, poorly developed ovaries, underdevelopment of female secondary sex characteristics, and problems in visual-spatial skills	Hormone (estrogen) replacement therapy; special education
XXX syndrome	1 girl in 1,000	A sex-chromosomal disorder that affects females and is connected with mild mental retardation	Special education
XYY syndrome	1 male in 700–1,000	A sex-chromosomal disorder that affects males—sometimes referred to as "supermale syndrome," connected with heavy beards, tallness, and mild mental retardation, particularly in language development	None
		Genetic Disorders	
Cystic fibrosis	1 birth in 2,000 among European Americans; 1 birth in 16,000 among African Americans	A genetic disease caused by a recessive gene in which the pancreas and lungs become clogged with mucus, impairing the processes of respiration and digestion	Physical therapy to loosen mucus and prompt bronchial drainage; antibiotics for infections of respiratory tract; management of diet
Duchenne muscular dystrophy	1 male birth in 3,000–5,000	A fatal sex-linked degenerative muscle disease caused by a recessive gene, usually found in males and characterized by loss of ability to walk during middle childhood or early adolescence	None; usually fatal by adolescence due to respiratory infection of cardiovascular damage

of their offspring, will inevitably develop it. Fortunately, the disorder is rare—affecting about 1 American in 18,000.

Sickle-Cell Anemia

A recessive gene causes **sickle-cell anemia** (Pharoah, 2001). It is most common among African Americans but also occurs in people from Central and South America, the Caribbean, Mediterranean countries, and the Middle East. Nearly one African American in 10 and 1 Latino or Latina American in 20 is a carrier. In sickle-cell anemia, red blood cells take on the shape of a sickle and clump together, obstructing small blood vessels and decreasing the oxygen supply. The reduced oxygen supply can impair academic performance (Schatz et al., 2001) and performance on tests of verbal skills, attention, and memory (Noll et al., 2001).

sickle-cell anemia A genetic disorder that decreases the blood's capacity to carry oxygen.

TABLE 2.2 *(continued)*

Health Problem	Incidence	About . . .	Treatment
		Genetic Disorders ***(continued)***	
Hemophilia	1 male in 4,000–10,000	A sex-linked disorder in which blood does not clot properly	Transfusion of blood to introduce clotting factors; proactive avoidance of injury
Huntington's disease	1 birth in 18,000	A fatal neurological disorder caused by a dominant gene; the onset occurs in middle adulthood	None; usually fatal within 20 years of onset of symptoms
Neural-tube defects	1 birth in 1,000	Disorders of the brain or spine, such as *anencephaly,* in which part of the brain is missing, and *spina bifida,* in which part of the spine is exposed or missing. Some individuals with spina bifida survive for years, albeit with handicaps.	None for anencephaly, which is fatal; surgery to close spinal canal in spina bifida
Phenylketonuria (PKU)	1 birth in 8,000–10,000	A disorder caused by a recessive gene in which children cannot metabolize the amino acid phenylalanine, which builds up in the form of phenylpyruvic acid and causes mental retardation. PKU is diagnosable at birth.	Controlled by special diet, which can prevent mental retardation
Sickle-cell anemia	1 African American in 500	A blood disorder caused by a recessive gene that mostly afflicts African Americans; deformed blood cells obstruct small blood vessels, decreasing their capacity to carry oxygen and heightening the risk of occasionally fatal infections	Transfusions to treat anemia and prevent strokes; antibiotics for infections; anesthetics; fatal to about half of those with disorder prior to adulthood
Tay-Sachs disease	1 in 3,000–3,600 among Jewish Americans of Eastern European origin	A fatal neurological disorder caused by a recessive gene that primarily afflicts Jews of European origin	None; usually fatal by ages 3–4
Thalassemia (Cooley's anemia)	1 birth in 400–500 among Mediterranean American children	A disorder caused by a recessive gene that primarily afflicts people of Mediterranean origin and causes weakness and susceptibility to infections; usually fatal in adolescence or young adulthood	Frequent blood transfusions; usually fatal by adolescence

Problems can also include painful and swollen joints, jaundice, and potentially fatal conditions such as pneumonia, stroke, and heart and kidney failure. Some children with sickle-cell anemia are being taught to cope with the pain it causes through techniques such as relaxation training and focusing on pleasant imagery (Gil et al., 2001).

Tay-Sachs Disease

Tay-Sachs disease is also caused by a recessive gene. It causes the central nervous system to degenerate, resulting in death. The disorder is most commonly found among children in Jewish families of an Eastern European background. About 1 in 30 Jewish Americans of this background carries the recessive gene for Tay-Sachs. Victims of the disorder progressively lose control over their muscles. They

Tay-Sachs disease A fatal genetic neurological disorder.

experience visual and auditory sensory losses, develop mental retardation, become paralyzed, and die toward the end of early childhood, by about the age of 5.

Cystic Fibrosis

Also caused by a recessive gene, **cystic fibrosis** is the most common fatal hereditary disease among European Americans. About 30,000 Americans have the disorder, but another 10 million (1 in every 31 people) are carriers (Cystic Fibrosis Foundation, 2001). Children with the disease suffer from excessive production of thick mucus that clogs the pancreas and lungs. Most victims die of respiratory infections in their 20s.

Sex-Linked Genetic Abnormalities

Some genetic defects, such as hemophilia, are carried on only the X sex chromosome. For this reason, they are referred to as **sex-linked genetic abnormalities.** Those defects also involve recessive genes. Females, who have two X sex chromosomes, are less likely than males to show sex-linked disorders, since the genes that cause the disorder would have to be present on both of a female's sex chromosomes for the disorder to be expressed. Sex-linked diseases are more likely to afflict sons of female carriers, since they have only one X sex chromosome, which they inherit from their mothers. Queen Victoria was a carrier of **hemophilia** and transmitted the blood disorder to many of her children, who, in turn, carried it into a number of the ruling houses of Europe. For this reason, hemophilia has been referred to as the "royal disease."

One form of **muscular dystrophy,** Duchenne muscular dystrophy, is sex-linked. Muscular dystrophy is characterized by a weakening of the muscles that can lead to wasting away, inability to walk, and sometimes death. Other sex-linked abnormalities include diabetes, color blindness, and some types of night blindness.

Genetic Counseling and Prenatal Testing

It is now possible to detect the genetic abnormalities that are responsible for hundreds of diseases. ***Questions: What is genetic counseling? How do health professionals determine whether children will have genetic or chromosomal abnormalities?***

In an effort to help parents avert these predictable tragedies, **genetic counseling** is becoming widely used. Genetic counselors compile information about a couple's genetic heritage to explore whether their children might develop genetic abnormalities. Couples who face a high risk of passing along genetic defects to their children sometimes elect to adopt children rather than conceive their own.

There are also many methods that indicate whether the embryo or fetus carry genetic abnormalities. These include amniocentesis, chorionic villus sampling, ultrasound, a number of blood tests, and fetoscopy.

Amniocentesis

Amniocentesis is usually performed on the mother at about 14–16 weeks after conception, although many physicians now perform the procedure earlier ("earlier amniocentesis"). In this method, the health professional uses a syringe (needle) to withdraw fluid from the amniotic sac (also called the "bag of waters") (Figure 2.6). The fluid contains cells that are sloughed off by the fetus. The cells are separated from the amniotic fluid, grown in a culture, and then examined microscopically for genetic and chromosomal abnormalities.

Amniocentesis has become routine among American women who become pregnant past the age of 35, because the chances of Down syndrome increase dramatically as women approach or pass the age of 40. But women carrying the children of aging fathers may also wish to have amniocentesis. Amniocentesis can detect the presence of well over 100 chromosomal and genetic abnormalities, including sickle-cell anemia, Tay-Sachs disease, **spina bifida,** muscular dystrophy,

cystic fibrosis A fatal genetic disorder in which mucus obstructs the lungs and pancreas.

sex-linked genetic abnormalities Abnormalities due to genes that are found on the X sex chromosome. They are more likely to be shown by male offspring (who do not have an opposing gene from a second X chromosome) than by female offspring.

hemophilia A genetic disorder in which blood does not clot properly.

muscular dystrophy (DISS-tro-fee) A chronic disease characterized by a progressive wasting away of the muscles.

genetic counseling Advice concerning the probabilities that a couple's children will show genetic abnormalities.

amniocentesis (AM-nee-oh-sen-TEE-sis) A procedure for drawing and examining fetal cells sloughed off into amniotic fluid to determine the presence of various disorders.

spina bifida A neural-tube defect that causes abnormalities of the brain and spine.

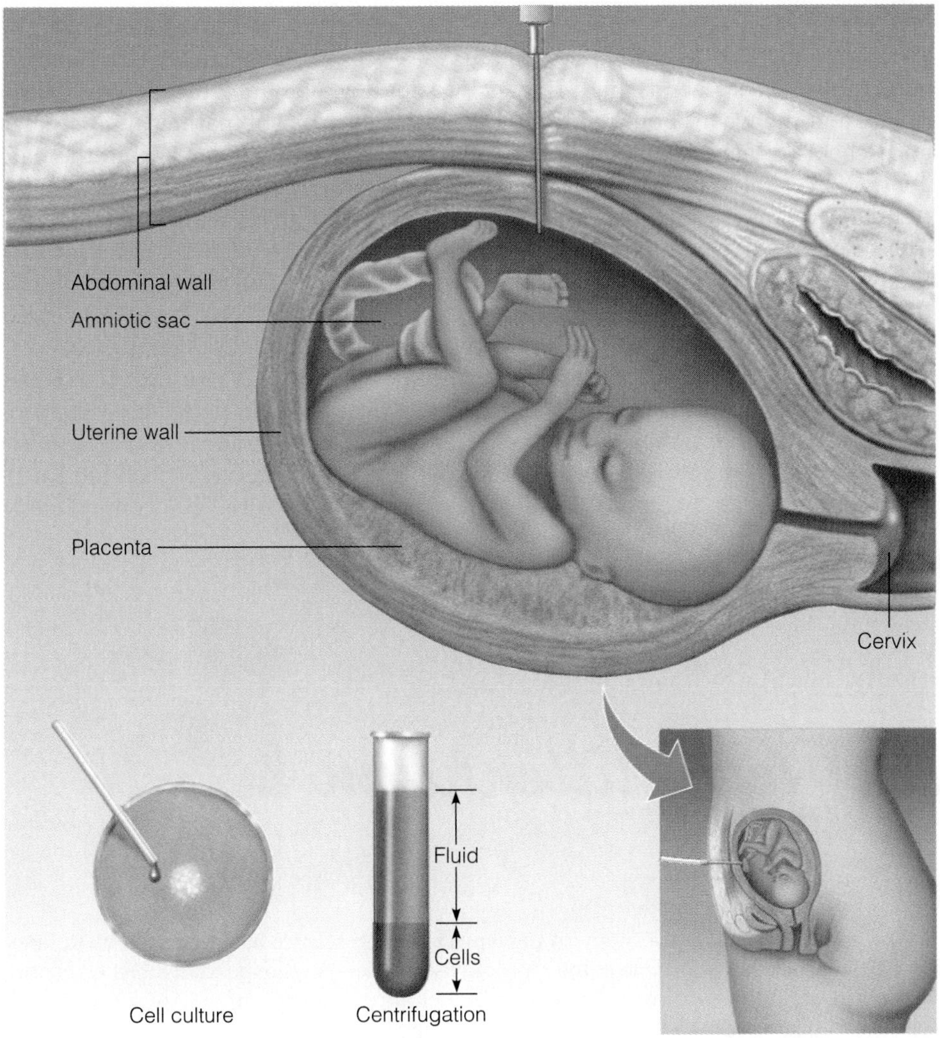

■ **Figure 2.6**
Amniocentesis

Amniocentesis allows prenatal identification of certain genetic and chromosomal disorders by examining genetic material sloughed off by the fetus into amniotic fluid. Amniocentesis also allows parents to learn the sex of their unborn child. Would you want to know?

and Rh incompatibility in the fetus. If a woman or her partner carries or has a family history of any of these disorders, she is advised to have amniocentesis performed. If the test reveals the presence of a serious disorder, the parents may decide to abort the fetus. Or they may decide to continue the pregnancy and prepare themselves to raise a child who has special needs.

Amniocentesis also permits parents to learn the gender of their unborn child through examination of the sex chromosomes. But because the test carries some risk of **spontaneous abortion,** or miscarriage (in about 1 in 100 who undergo the procedure), it is considered unwise to have amniocentesis done for this purpose.

Reflect

If you were having amniocentesis, would you want to know the gender of your child, or would you prefer to wait? Explain.

CVS

Chorionic villus sampling (CVS) is similar to amniocentesis but offers the advantage of diagnosing fetal abnormalities much earlier in pregnancy. CVS is carried out during the 9th or 10th week of pregnancy. A small syringe is inserted through the vagina into the **uterus.** The syringe gently sucks out a few of the threadlike projections (villi) from the outer membrane that envelops the amniotic sac and fetus. Results are available within days of the procedure. CVS has not been used as frequently as amniocentesis, because many studies have shown that CVS carries a slightly greater risk of spontaneous abortion. However, recent research suggests that the risks of the procedures may be equivalent (J. L. Simpson, 2000). Since CVS yields results earlier, we might expect to see it used more often—unless these research results are overturned or the "habits" of medical practice rule the day.

spontaneous abortion Unplanned, accidental abortion (*miscarriage* is the popular term).

chorionic villus sampling (CORE-ee-ON-ick Vill-iss) A method for the prenatal detection of genetic abnormalities that samples the membrane enveloping the amniotic sac and fetus.

uterus The hollow organ within females in which the embryo and fetus develop.

Ultrasound

Click *Physical Development* for more on the ultrasound technique.

For more than half a century, the military has been using sonar to locate enemy submarines. Sonar sends high-frequency sound waves into the depths of the ocean, and the waves bounce back from objects such as submarines (and whales and schools of fish and the ocean floor) to reveal their presence. Within the past generation, health professionals have also innovated the use of (very!) high-frequency sound waves to obtain information about the fetus (Carlson, 2001). These sound waves, called **ultrasound,** are too high in frequency to be heard by the human ear. However, they are reflected by the fetus, and a computer can use the information to generate a picture (visual) of the fetus. The picture is referred to as a **sonogram,** from roots meaning "written with sound" (see Figure 2.7).

ultrasound Sound waves too high in pitch to be sensed by the human ear.

sonogram A procedure for using ultrasonic sound waves to create a picture of an embryo or fetus.

Ultrasound is used as an adjunct to amniocentesis or CVS in order to better determine the position of the fetus. In this way the physician performing the procedure can make sure the needle enters the sac surrounding the fetus and not the fetus itself. Ultrasound is also employed to locate fetal structures when intrauterine transfusions are necessary for the survival of a fetus with Rh incompatibility (see Chapter 3).

Developing in the New Millennium

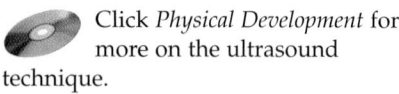

Gene Therapy

Someday, gene therapy may provide couples whose embryos are genetically abnormal the possibility of correcting the problem in the uterus. In gene therapy, the genetic structures of organisms are changed by direct manipulation of their cells (Carter & Schuchman, 2001). Even as you read these words, patents are pending on new life forms—mostly microscopic—that biologists and corporations hope will be marketable.

Innovations in genetic engineering have already given us screening methods for fatal hereditary diseases such as Huntington's disease and cystic fibrosis. The following are in development:

New vaccines for diseases such as hepatitis and herpes.

Ways to detect predispositions for disorders such as cancer or bipolar disorder by studying a newborn's (or fetus's) genetic code.

Modification of the genetic codes of fetuses or children to prevent or cure disease (Carter & Schuchman, 2001). For example, a 4-year-old girl was the first to get new genes in an effort to cure a severe inherited immune deficiency disorder. Prior to treatment, the girl and her family rarely left home for fear of bringing back even a minor infection, which could have been life-threatening. Within a year after receiving gene therapy, the child's immune system responded so well that she could swim, take dancing lessons, and even go to school (B. S. Greenough, 1993).

Insertion of foreign genes into human lymphocytes (white blood cells) to enhance the cells' ability to combat cancer and other diseases.

Creation of wonder drugs from DNA.

Many of the ways in which science has permitted us to intervene in the reproductive process have engendered heated controversy. Some people, including a number of religious leaders, fear that we are converting natural biological processes into a calamity that will have profound moral consequences and change the face of our species (and others) in ways that we cannot foresee. Other people fear the invention of various kinds of biological monsters or disease agents—most of them microscopic—that we may not be able to control.

What is there to conclude? Ugly scenarios are indeed possible, but so are splendid, health-enhancing outcomes. As scientists, we believe there is no such thing as bad knowledge—only bad use of knowledge. As citizens, it is our duty to keep abreast of technical innovations and to ensure that their applications are beneficial.

Search Online With InfoTrac College Edition

For additional information, explore InfoTrac College Edition, your online library. Go to http://www.infotrac-college.com and use the passcode from the InfoTrac card that came with your book. Try these search terms: human genetic engineering, gene therapy, DNA vaccines.

Ultrasound also is used to track the growth of the fetus, to determine fetal age and gender, and to detect multiple pregnancies and structural abnormalities. While ultrasound is beneficial for pregnant women whose fetuses are at risk of serious medical problems, it may not improve birth outcomes for women with low-risk pregnancies. Multiple usage may increase the risk of having a child who is low in birthweight (Newnham et al., 1993).

Blood Tests

Parental blood tests can reveal the presence of recessive genes for a variety of disorders, such as sickle-cell anemia, Tay-Sachs disease, and cystic fibrosis. When both parents carry genes for these disorders, the disorders can be detected in the fetus by means of amniocentesis or CVS.

Another kind of blood test, the **alpha-fetoprotein (AFP) assay,** is used to detect neural-tube defects such as spina bifida and certain chromosomal abnormalities. Neural-tube defects cause an elevation in the AFP level in the mother's blood. Elevated AFP levels also are associated with increased risk of fetal death. However, the mother's AFP level also varies with other factors. For this reason, a presumed diagnosis of neural-tube defect is confirmed by other methods of observation, such as amniocentesis, ultrasound, or fetoscopy.

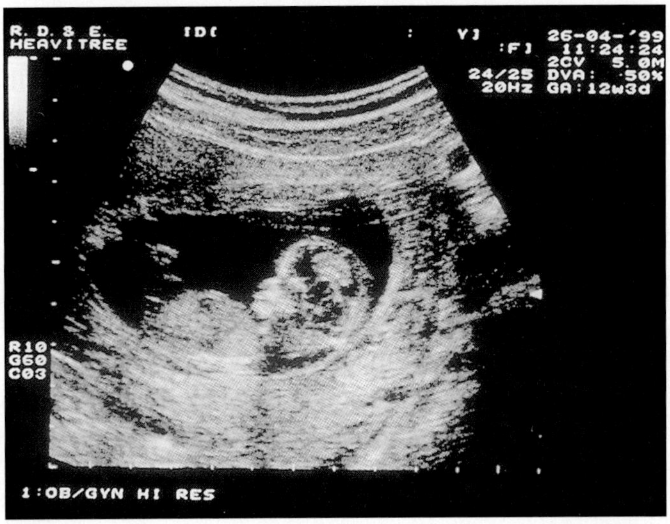

Figure 2.7
Sonogram of a 5-Month-Old Fetus
In the ultrasound technique, sound waves are bounced off the fetus and provide a picture called a sonogram that enables professionals to detect various abnormalities.

Fetoscopy

In **fetoscopy,** a narrow tube is surgically inserted through the abdomen into the uterus to allow examination of the fetus during the second and third trimesters of pregnancy. A small lens and a light can be attached to the fetoscope, permitting visual examination. A small needle may also be attached, which enables the direct withdrawal of a blood sample from the fetus. Fetoscopy is riskier than amniocentesis, and its use is more limited.

In the future, we may be able to modify problem genes while babies are developing within the uterus. Researchers now are able to identify genetic defects such as cystic fibrosis in embryos only a few days old. In one landmark study, embryos obtained by in vitro fertilization were examined for cystic fibrosis. Both parents were carriers of the disease. Only healthy embryos were implanted in the mother's uterus, and a healthy child was born (Handyside et al., 1992). But this technique is still in the experimental stage. For the time being, families whose unborn children face serious genetic disorders can only choose whether or not to have an abortion, which raises painful personal dilemmas for most couples.

In the following section, we see that our development is affected not only by genes, but also by environmental influences. ***Question: What is the difference between our* genotypes *and our* phenotypes?**

Review

(1) The field of biology that studies heredity is called ________. (2) A normal human cell contains 46 ________, which are organized into 23 pairs. (3) Each chromosome contains thousands of segments called ________, which are the

alpha-fetoprotein (AFP) assay A blood test that assesses the mother's blood level of alpha-fetoprotein, a substance that is linked with fetal neural-tube defects.

fetoscopy (fee-TOSS-co-pea) Surgical insertion of a narrow tube into the uterus in order to examine the fetus.

biochemical materials that regulate the development of traits. (4) Genes are segments of strands of _________ (DNA), which takes the form of a twisting ladder. (5) _________ is the cell-division process by which growth occurs and tissues are replaced. (6) Sperm and ova are produced through _________. (7) After meiosis, each new cell nucleus contains _________ chromosomes. (8) When a zygote divides into two cells that separate so that each develops into an individual, we have _________ (MZ) twins. (9) If two ova are fertilized by different sperm cells, they develop into _________ (DZ) twins. (10) Fertility drugs (decrease or increase?) the chances of multiple births. (11) (Brown or blue?) eyes are dominant. (12) People who bear one dominant gene and one recessive gene for a trait are said to be _________ of the recessive gene.

(13) In _________ syndrome, the 21st pair of chromosomes has an extra, or third, chromosome. (14) Chromosomal abnormalities are more likely to occur among the children of (younger or older?) parents. (15) Males with an extra _________ sex chromosome are somewhat taller than average and develop heavier beards. (16) Girls with a single _________ sex chromosome produce less-than-normal amounts of estrogen. (17) Phenylketonuria (PKU) is an enzyme disorder that is transmitted by a (dominant or recessive?) gene. (18) _________ disease is a fatal progressive degenerative disorder that is characterized by uncontrollable muscle movements. (19) _________-cell anemia is caused by a recessive gene and is most common among African Americans. (20) Tay-_________ disease is a fatal degenerative disease of the central nervous system that is most common in Jewish families of Eastern European origin. (21) Cystic _________ is caused by a recessive gene and is characterized by excessive production of mucus that clogs the pancreas and lungs. (22) Hemophilia is carried on only the _________ sex chromosome and is referred to as a sex-linked genetic abnormality.

(23) In the prenatal testing method of _________, fetal cells found in amniotic fluid are examined for genetic abnormalities. (24) The use of _________ can form a picture ("sonogram") of the fetus. (25) Parental _________ tests can reveal the presence of recessive genes for disorders such as sickle-cell anemia, Tay-Sachs disease, cystic fibrosis, and neural-tube defects.

Pulling It Together: How have advances in genetic counseling and prenatal testing created moral and ethical issues?

Heredity and the Environment

The sets of traits that we inherit from our parents are referred to as our **genotypes.** But none of us is the result of heredity, or genotype, alone. Heredity provides the biological basis for a **reaction range** in the expression of traits. Our inherited traits can vary in expression, depending on environmental conditions. In addition to inheritance, the expression of our traits is also influenced by nutrition, learning, exercise, and—unfortunately—accident and illness. A potential Shakespeare who is reared in an impoverished neighborhood and never taught to read or write is unlikely to create a Hamlet. Thus, behavior appears to represent the interaction between heredity and environment. Our actual sets of characteristics or behaviors at any point in time are referred to as our **phenotypes.** Phenotypes are the product of genetic and environmental influences.

Researchers have developed a number of strategies to help determine the relative effects of heredity and the environment on development. ***Question: What kinds of research strategies do researchers use to sort out the effects of genetics and environmental influences on development?***

genotype The genetic form or constitution of a person as determined by heredity.

reaction range The variability in the expression of inherited traits as they are influenced by environmental factors.

phenotype The actual form or constitution of a person as determined by heredity and environmental factors.

Kinship Studies

Researchers study the distribution of a particular behavior pattern among relatives who differ in degree of genetic closeness. The more closely people are related, the more genes they have in common. Parents and children have a 50% overlap in their genetic endowments, and so do siblings (brothers and sisters), on average. Aunts and uncles have a 25% overlap with nieces and nephews, and so do grandparents with their grandchildren. First cousins share 12.5% of their genetic endowment. So if genes are implicated in a physical trait or behavior pattern, people who are more closely related should be more likely to share the pattern.

Twin Studies

Monozygotic (MZ) twins share 100% of their genes, whereas dizygotic (DZ) twins have a 50% overlap, just as other siblings do. If MZ twins show greater similarity on some trait or behavior than DZ twins, a genetic basis for the trait or behavior is indicated.

MZ twins resemble each other more closely than DZ twins on a number of physical and psychological traits. MZ twins are more likely to look alike and to be similar in height, even to have more similar cholesterol levels than DZ twins (D. A. Heller et al., 1993). This finding holds even when the identical twins are reared apart and the fraternal twins are reared together (Stunkard et al., 1990). Other physical similarities between pairs of MZ twins may be more subtle, but they are also strong. For example, research shows that MZ twin sisters begin to menstruate about 1 to 2 months apart, whereas DZ twins begin to menstruate about a year apart. MZ twins are more alike than DZ twins in their blood pressure, brain wave patterns, and even in their speech patterns, gestures, and mannerisms (Lykken et al., 1992).

MZ twins resemble one another more strongly than DZ twins in intelligence and in personality traits such as sociability, anxiety, friendliness, conformity, and even happiness (McCourt et al., 1999; McCrae et al., 2000). David Lykken and Auke Tellegen (1996) suggest that we inherit a tendency toward a certain level of happiness. Despite the ups and downs of life, we tend to drift back to our usual levels of cheerfulness or irritability. It seems that our bank accounts, our levels of education, and our marital status are less influential than genes as contributors to happiness. Heredity is also a key contributor to psychological developmental factors such as cognitive functioning, **autism,** and early signs of attachment like smiling, cuddling, and expressing fear of strangers (DiLalla et al., 1996; Scarr & Kidd, 1983).

MZ twins are more likely than DZ twins to share psychological disorders such as autism, depression, schizophrenia, and even vulnerability to alcoholism (Plomin, 2000; McGue, Pickens, & Svikis, 1992). In one study on autism, the **concordance** rate for MZ twins was 96%. The concordance rate for DZ twins was only 24% (Ritvo et al., 1985).

Of course, twin studies are not perfect. MZ twins may resemble each other more closely than DZ twins partly because they are treated more similarly. MZ twins frequently are dressed identically, and parents sometimes have difficulty telling them apart (Vandell, 1990).

One way to get around this difficulty is to find and compare MZ twins who were reared in different homes. Any similarities between MZ twins reared apart cannot be explained by a shared home environment and would appear to be largely a result of heredity. In the fascinating Minnesota Study of Twins Reared Apart (T. J. Bouchard et al., 1990; DiLalla et al., 1999; Lykken et al., 1992), researchers have been measuring the physiological and psychological characteristics of 56 sets of MZ adult twins who were separated in infancy and reared in

Reflect

Do you know sets of twins? Are they monozygotic or dizygotic? How are they alike? How do they differ?

Reflect

It is clear that there is an inherited component in psychological disorders. Does this fact mean that it is useless to try to prevent or treat them? Explain.

autism A developmental disorder characterized by failure to relate to others, communication problems, intolerance of change, and ritualistic behavior (see Chapter 6).

concordance Agreement.

different homes. The MZ twins reared apart are about as similar as MZ twins reared together on a variety of measures of intelligence, personality, temperament, occupational and leisure-time interests, and social attitudes. These traits thus would appear to have a genetic underpinning.

Adoption Studies

Adoption studies in which children are separated from their natural parents at an early age and reared by adoptive parents provide special opportunities for sorting out nature and nurture. As we shall see in discussions of the origins of intelligence (Chapter 11) and of various problem behaviors (Chapters 10 and 13), psychologists look for the relative similarities between children and their adoptive and natural parents. When children who are reared by adoptive parents are nonetheless more similar to their natural parents in a trait, a powerful argument is made for a genetic role in the appearance of that trait.

Review

(26) The sets of traits that we inherit are referred to as our (genotypes or phenotypes?). (27) Our actual traits are our (genotypes or phenotypes?), which are the product of genetic and environmental influences. (28) Parents and children have a ________% overlap in their genetic endowments. (29)________ twins share 100% of their genes, whereas dizygotic (DZ) twins have a 50% overlap, as do other siblings. (30) MZ twins resemble each other (less or more?) closely than DZ twins on physical and psychological traits.

Pulling It Together: Why are developmentalists so interested in conducting research with twins who have been reared apart and with adopted children?

Conception: Against All Odds

Traits are determined by pairs of genes. One member of each pair comes from each parent. The genetic codes of the parents are the "something old" in the title of the chapter. Let's move on to something new: ***Question: What process brings together the genes from each parent?*** That process is called *conception.* Let's talk about the birds and the bees and the microscope to understand how it works.

Conception is the union of an ovum and a sperm cell. Conception, from one perspective, is the beginning of a new human life. But conception is also the end of a fantastic voyage in which one of several hundred thousand ova produced by the woman unites with one of hundreds of millions of sperm produced by the man in the average ejaculate.

Ova

At birth a women's ovaries already contain their 400,000 or so ova. However, they are immature in form. The ovaries also produce the female hormones estrogen and progesterone. At puberty, in response to hormonal command, some ova begin to mature (Figure 2.8). Each month, one egg (occasionally more than one) is released from its ovarian follicle about midway during the menstrual cycle and enters a nearby **Fallopian tube.** It might take 3 to 4 days for an egg to be propelled the few inches to the uterus by small, hairlike structures called cilia and, perhaps, by contractions in the wall of the tube. Unlike sperm, eggs do not propel themselves.

conception The union of a sperm cell and an ovum, which occurs when the chromosomes of each of these cells combine to form 23 new pairs.

Fallopian tube A tube through which ova travel from an ovary to the uterus.

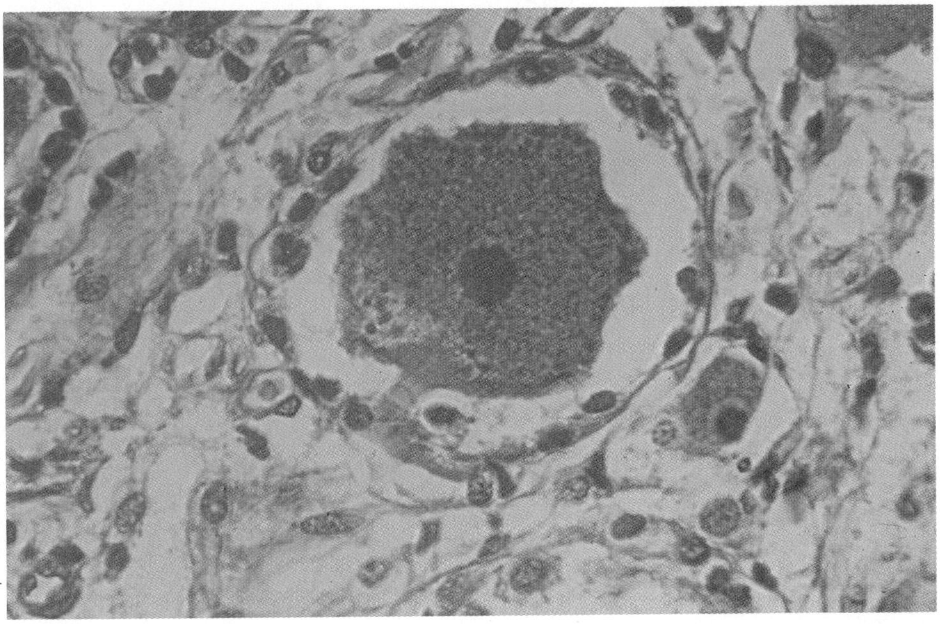

Figure 2.8
A Ripening Ovum in an Ovarian Follicle

At puberty, some ova begin to mature. Each month one egg (occasionally more than one) is released from its ovarian follicle and enters a Fallopian tube.

If the egg is not fertilized, it is discharged through the uterus and the vagina—sloughed off, along with the **endometrium** that had formed to support an embryo, in the menstrual flow. During a woman's reproductive years, only about 400 ova (that is, 1 in 1,000) will ripen and be released. How these ova are selected is a mystery.

In an early stage of development, egg cells contain 46 chromosomes. Each developing egg cell contains two X sex chromosomes. After meiosis, each ovum contains 23 chromosomes, one of which is an X sex chromosome.

Ova are much larger than sperm. (The chicken egg and the 6-inch ostrich egg are each just one cell.) Human ova are barely visible to the eye, but their bulk is still thousands of times larger than that of sperm cells.

Sperm Cells

Sperm cells develop through several stages. In one early stage, like ova, they each contain 46 chromosomes, including one X and one Y sex chromosome. After meiosis, each sperm has 23 chromosomes. Half have X sex chromosomes, and the other half have Y sex chromosomes. Each sperm cell is about $^{1}/_{500}$ inch long, one of the smallest types of cells in the body. Sperm with Y sex chromosomes appear to swim faster than sperm with X sex chromosomes. This is one reason why between 120 and 150 boys are conceived for every 100 girls. Male fetuses suffer a higher rate of spontaneous abortion than females, however, often during the first month of pregnancy. At birth, boys outnumber girls by a ratio of only 106 to 100. Boys also have a higher incidence of infant mortality, which further equalizes the numbers of girls and boys in a population by the time they show an interest in pairing off.

The 200 to 400 million sperm in the ejaculate may seem a wasteful investment since only one can fertilize an ovum. But only 1 in 1,000 will ever arrive in the vicinity of an ovum. Millions deposited in the vagina simply flow out of the woman's body because of gravity, unless she remains prone for quite some time. Normal vaginal acidity kills many more. Many surviving sperm swim against the current of fluid coming from the cervix (see Figure 2.9).

Sperm who survive these initial obstacles may reach the Fallopian tubes 60–90 minutes after ejaculation. About half the sperm enter the wrong tube—that is, the tube without the egg. Perhaps 2,000 enter the "correct" tube. Fewer still manage to swim the final 2 inches against the currents generated by the cilia that

endometrium The inner lining of the uterus.

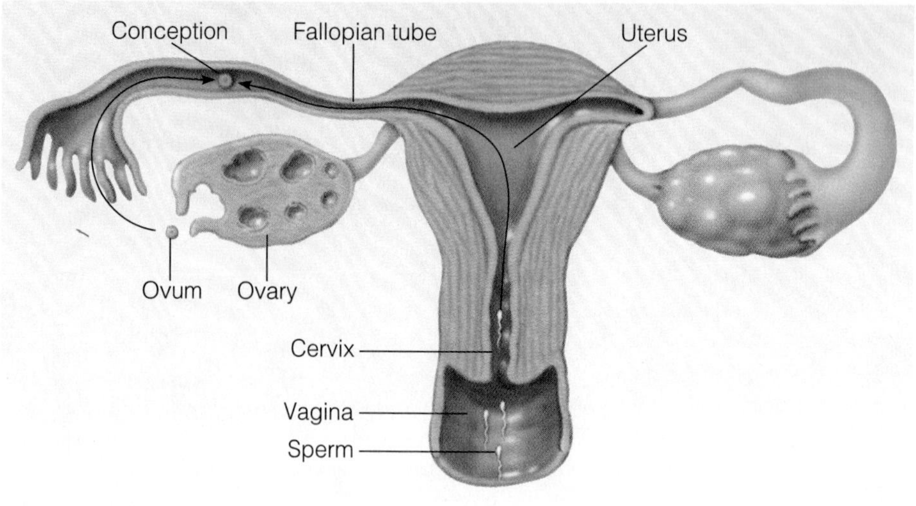

Figure 2.9
Female Reproductive Organs

Conception is something of an obstacle course. Sperm must survive the pull of gravity and vaginal acidity, risk winding up in the wrong Fallopian tube, and surmount other hurdles before they reach the ovum.

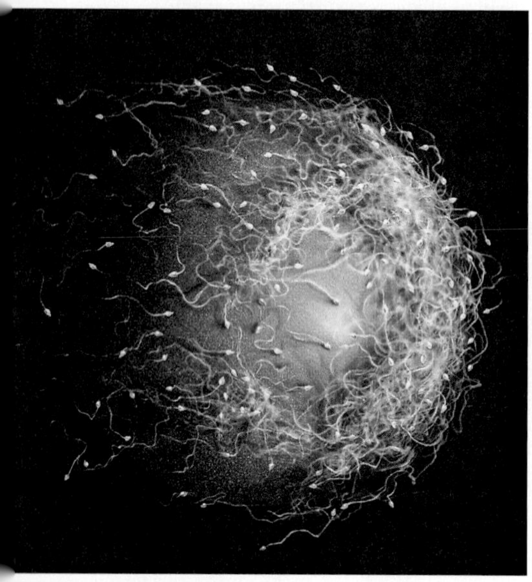

© Francis Leroy, Biocosmos/SPL/Photo Researchers

Figure 2.10
Human Sperm Swarming Around an Ovum in a Fallopian Tube

Fertilization normally occurs in a Fallopian tube, not in the uterus. Thousands of sperm may wind up in the vicinity of an ovum, but only one fertilizes it. How this sperm cell is "selected" remains one of the mysteries of nature.

zona pellucida A gelatinous layer that surrounds an ovum (from roots referring to a "zone through which light can shine").

hyaluronidase An enzyme that briefly thins the zona pellucida, enabling a single sperm cell to penetrate (from roots referring to a "substance that breaks down a glasslike fluid").

line the tube. Sperm cells appear to be attracted by a compound secreted by the ovum.

Of all the sperm swarming around the egg, only one enters (see Figure 2.10). Ova are surrounded by a gelatinous layer called the **zona pellucida.** This is the layer that must be penetrated if fertilization is to occur. Multiple sperm that have completed their journey to the ovum secrete an enzyme called **hyaluronidase.** The group bombardment of hyaluronidase briefly thins the zona pellucida, but it enables only one sperm to penetrate. Once a sperm cell has entered, the zona pellucida thickens, locking other sperm out. How this one sperm cell is "selected" is another biological mystery. Nevertheless, other sperm are unable to enter.

The chromosomes from the sperm cell line up across from the corresponding chromosomes in the egg cell. Conception finally occurs as the chromosomes combine to form 23 new pairs with a unique set of genetic instructions. The new being is the "something new" in the title of this chapter—something quite new, an individual.

For couples who want children, few problems are more frustrating than inability to conceive. Physicians often recommend that couples try to conceive on their own for 6 months before seeking medical assistance. The term *infertility* usually is not applied until the couple has failed to conceive for a year. We consider the problem of infertility next.

Infertility and Other Ways of Becoming Parents

About one American couple in six or seven has fertility problems (Howards, 1995). Infertility was once viewed as a problem of the woman, but it turns out that the problem lies with the man in about 40% of cases. ***Questions: What are the causes of infertility? How are couples helped to have children?***

Causes of Infertility

Five major fertility problems are found among men. These include (1) too few sperm (officially, "a low sperm count"), (2) deformed sperm, (3) poor ability of the sperm to swim to the ovum (officially, "low sperm motility"), (4) infectious diseases, and (5) direct trauma to the testes (Hatcher et al., 1998; Howards, 1995). A low sperm count—or complete lack of sperm—is the most common infertility problem found among men. Men's fertility problems have a variety of causes. Among these are genetic factors, poisons found in the environment, diabetes, sexually transmitted infections (STIs), overheating of the testes (which happens now and then among athletes, such as long-distance runners), pressure (which can be caused by certain bicycle seats—have your doctor recommend a more comfortable and less harmful seat), aging, and the use of certain prescription and illicit drugs (te Velde & Cohlen, 1999; Velez de la Calle, 2001). Sometimes the sperm count is adequate, but other factors such as prostate or hormonal problems deform sperm or deprive them of their **motility.** Motility can also be impaired by the scar tissue from infections, such as sexually transmitted infections.

Women encounter the following four major fertility problems: (1) failure to ovulate, (2) various infections, (3) inflammation of the tissue that is sloughed off during menstruation (officially, "endometriosis"), and (4) barriers or disorders in the passageways through which the ovum must pass (Hatcher et al., 1998). The most common problem in women is irregular ovulation or complete lack of ovulation. This problem can have many causes, including irregularities among the hormones that govern ovulation, stress, and malnutrition (te Velde & Cohlen, 1999). So-called fertility drugs are made up of hormones that cause women to ovulate, such as clomiphene and pergonal. These drugs often cause multiple births by stimulating more than one ovum to ripen during a month.

Infections may scar the Fallopian tubes and other organs, impeding the passage of sperm or ova. Such infections include **pelvic inflammatory disease (PID).** PID can result from any of a number of bacterial or viral infections, but infertility can be irreversible if the infection goes without treatment for too long.

Endometriosis can obstruct the Fallopian tubes, where conception normally takes place. This problem is clear enough. But endometriosis is also believed to somehow dampen the "climate" for conception; the mechanisms involved in this effect are not as well understood. Endometriosis has become a fairly frequent cause of infertility today, because so many women are delaying childbearing to further their educations and to establish their careers. What apparently happens is this: Each month tissue develops to line the uterus in case the woman conceives. This tissue, called the endometrium, is then normally sloughed off during menstruation. However, some of it backs up into the abdomen through the same Fallopian tubes that would provide a duct for an ovum. Endometrial tissue then collects in the abdomen, where it can cause a good deal of abdominal pain and also somehow impede the chances of conception. Physicians may treat endometriosis with hormone treatments that temporarily prevent menstruation or with surgery. These treatments are often successful, but they are certainly not reliable.

Let's now consider some of the methods that have been developed in recent years to help infertile couples bear children.

Artificial Insemination

Multiple ejaculations of men with low sperm counts can be collected and quick-frozen. The sperm can then be injected into the woman's uterus at the time of ovulation. This is one **artificial insemination** procedure. Sperm from a man with low sperm motility can also be injected into his partner's uterus, so that the sperm can begin their journey closer to the Fallopian tubes. When a man is completely infertile or has an extremely low sperm count, his partner can be artificially inseminated with the sperm of a donor who resembles the man in physical traits. The child then bears the genes of one of the parents, the mother.

In Vitro Fertilization

Have you heard the expression "test-tube baby"? Does it sound as though a baby develops in a test tube? Not so. Does it sound as though a baby is conceived in a test tube? Not so—but close. In this method, which is more technically known as **in vitro fertilization (IVF),** ripened ova are removed surgically from the mother and placed in a laboratory dish. The father's sperm are also placed in the dish. One or more ova are fertilized and then injected into the mother's uterus to become implanted. In vitro fertilization may be used when the Fallopian tubes are blocked, because with this method the ova need not travel through them. If the father's sperm are low in motility, they are sometimes injected directly into the ovum (Meschede et al., 2000).

motility Self-propulsion.

pelvic inflammatory disease (PID) An infection of the abdominal region that may have various causes and impair fertility.

endometriosis Inflammation of endometrial tissue sloughed off into the abdominal cavity rather than out of the body during menstruation and characterized by abdominal pain and, sometimes, infertility.

artificial insemination Injection of sperm into the uterus to fertilize an ovum.

in vitro fertilization (VEE-tro) Fertilization of an ovum in a laboratory dish.

It can take several tries to achieve a pregnancy, since only a minority of attempts lead to births. Often several embryos are injected into the uterus at once, heightening the odds. In vitro fertilization remains costly but has become rather routine.

Embryonic Transplant

The method of **embryonic transplant** transfers the embryo into a host uterus. This procedure is used when a woman cannot produce ova. Another woman can be artificially inseminated with sperm from the infertile woman's husband. After a few days, the embryo can be removed from the woman who conceived and transferred to the wife's uterus.

Sometimes a woman can produce ova but cannot carry a pregnancy to term. In this case, her ova can be fertilized by her husband's sperm by means of the IVF procedure. The fertilized egg is then implanted in the uterus of another woman, who carries the baby to term. This was the procedure followed in the publicized case of 53-year-old Geraldine Wesolowski, who gave birth to her own grandson. She agreed to carry the child for her daughter-in-law, whose uterus had been surgically removed (Gruson, 1993).

Donor IVF

A 50-year-old California therapist explains to her 5-year-old daughter how she became pregnant: "I tell her Mommy was having trouble with, I call them ovums, not eggs, . . . I say that I needed these to have a baby, and there was this wonderful woman and she was willing to give me some, and that was how she helped us. I want to be honest that we got pregnant in a special way" (cited in Stolberg, 1998, p. 1).

The therapist became a mother by means of **donor IVF.** This method is used when a woman does not produce ova of her own, but when her uterus is apparently capable of providing an adequate environment to bring a baby to term. An ovum is harvested from another woman—the donor. It is fertilized in vitro—often by sperm from the husband of the recipient. Then, as in other cases of in vitro fertilization, it is directly implanted into the uterus of the recipient. The embryo becomes implanted and undergoes the remainder of prenatal development in the recipient's uterus. This method of overcoming infertility has become quite popular over the past ten years or so (Stolbert, 1998).

Surrogate Mothers

In recent years, stories about **surrogate mothers** have filled the headlines. Surrogate mothers bring newly conceived babies to term for other women who are infertile. (The word *surrogate* means "substitute.") Surrogate mothers may be artificially inseminated by the husbands of infertile women, in which case the baby thus carries the genes of the father. But sometimes—as with 53-year-old singer-songwriter James Taylor and his 47-year-old wife—ova are surgically extracted from the biological mother, fertilized in vitro by the biological father, and then implanted in another woman's uterus, where the baby is brought to term (Byrd, 2001). Surrogate mothers are usually paid fees ranging from $10,000 to $20,000 and sign agreements to surrender the baby. (These contracts have been annulled in some states, however, so that surrogate mothers cannot be forced to hand over their babies.) In the case of Taylor and his wife, the surrogate mother was a friend of the family, and she delivered twins in 2001.

Ethical and legal dilemmas revolve around the fact that artificially inseminated surrogate mothers have a genetic link to their babies. If they change their minds and do not want to hand the babies over to the contractual parents, there can be legal struggles (Kanefield, 1999).

Just as new technologies are enhancing the chances for infertile couples to become parents, new methods seem to be leading to the day when we can preselect the gender of our children.

embryonic transplant The transfer of an embryo from the uterus of one woman to that of another.

donor IVF The transfer of a donor's ovum, fertilized in a laboratory dish, to the uterus of another woman.

surrogate mother A woman who is artificially inseminated and carries to term a child who is then given to another woman, typically the spouse of the sperm donor.

Selecting the Sex of Your Child: Fantasy or Reality?

What would happen if we could select the sex of our children? In many cultures, one sex—usually male—has been preferred over the other. Would Americans predominantly select boys or girls? Would it all balance out in the end? Then, too, there are sex-linked diseases that show up only in sons. In such cases would-be parents might feel more secure if they could choose to have daughters (Bennett, 1998).

Reflect

Would you prefer to determine the gender of your children or leave it up to chance? Explain.

Question: Just how do people attempt to select the sex of their children? Folklore is replete with methods. Some cultures have advised having sexual intercourse under the full moon as a way of begetting boys. The Greek philosopher Aristotle—who was a genius in so many other ways—suggested making love during a north wind to conceive sons. A south wind would lead to the conception of daughters. Sour foods were once suggested for parents desirous of having boys. Those who wanted girls were advised to consume sweets. In more recent times, men who desired to father boys might be advised to wear their boots to bed. At one time people believed that the right testicle was responsible for siring boys. Noblemen in 18th-century France were thus advised to have their left testicles removed if they wanted sons. (One wonders what they did to the prescribing physician when the method failed.) In any event, need we point out that none of these methods worked?

Methods after conception, such as selective abortion and infanticide, have also been used to obtain children of the desired sex. Such practices are especially widespread in developing nations like China and India (see the nearby "Developing in a World of Diversity" feature).

Let's consider the methods that are being suggested for conceiving boys or girls today.

Developing in a World of Diversity

Where Are the Missing Girls?

In India, "the boy is like the lamp of the family," reports a women's health worker in India (cited in Dugger, 2001b). Chinese scientists note that the preference for boys is jeopardizing China's family-planning goal of one child per family (Dugger, 2001b). These preferences stem to some degree from the belief that sons can work harder in the fields and from the tradition that sons provide for aging parents. Thus, it is considered a misfortune for a family to be without a male child. Many nations other than China and India have traditionally valued sons more than daughters; these include nations ranging from Pakistan and Bangladesh to Egypt and Nepal. Even in Western Europe and the United States we find some preference for sons.

A form of "family planning" *after birth* may be taking place in China and other developing nations (Dugger, 2001a, 2001b). Given the usual birth ratio of about 106 boys for every 100 girls, censuses taken in 2000 and 2001 (Dugger, 2001b) show that millions of girls in these countries are "missing." In some cases, infant girls are killed at birth by midwives on the orders of parents who desire sons. In other cases, girls have been abandoned or given up for adoption. In some rural areas of China, newborn girls may be drowned by midwives who keep a bucket by the mother's side for this purpose. The prevalence of infanticide in developing nations is unknown, but in many cases baby girls may die at a young age from neglect. For example, an infant daughter with diarrhea may be ignored, whereas the same problem in a boy is viewed as a crisis that requires medical help. When food is scarce in a poor family, boys may receive more than their fair share.

In recent years, technology has provided parents with yet another gender selection option: the use of amniocentesis or ultrasound. In many parts of India and China, these tests are widely used to determine the sex of the child. If it is a female, it is frequently aborted. The government of India has banned the use of these technologies for purposes of determining the gender of the fetus, yet they remain widespread in parts of the country (Dugger, 2001a, 2001b; Agence France-Presse, 2001). In China, the year 2000 census found that 117 boys were born for every 100 girls, up from a ratio of 114 to 100 in 1990. Where are the missing girls?

Shettles's Approach

Landrum Shettles (1982) noted that sperm bearing the Y sex chromosome are smaller than those bearing the X sex chromosome and are faster swimmers. But sperm with the X sex chromosome are more durable. From these assumptions, Shettles and other researchers derive a number of strategies for selecting the sex of one's children.

To increase the chances of having a girl: (1) the couple should engage in sexual intercourse two days (or slightly more) before ovulation; (2) the woman should make the vagina less hospitable to Y-bearing sperm by douching with 2 tablespoons of vinegar per quart of warm water to raise vaginal acidity before intercourse; (3) the woman should avoid orgasm on the (debatable) assumption that orgasm facilitates the journey of sperm; and (d) the man should ejaculate with shallow penetration.

Developing in the New Millennium

Going for the Girl

Can you choose your baby's gender? Should you? After three sons, Kathy des Jardins tried it the high-tech way, as she reports in her own words:

As the mother of three boys, I admit I occasionally drift away from the cacophony—my 5-year-old burping his ABC's and my 10-year-old twins competing to see who can make the most body parts sound like a whoopee cushion—and wistfully think, Wouldn't it be nice to have a little girl?

I happened upon a story in my local newspaper that inspired me to try to do just that. Under the headline "Sorting Lets Couple Pick Baby's Sex," I read about a fertility clinic in Fairfax, Virginia, that was conducting clinical trials with a sperm-sorting procedure reported to have had amazing results producing female babies. The clinic was the MicroSort division of Genetics & IVF Institute (GIVF), a facility that, besides providing infertility treatment and genetic services, is the only place in the world where couples can avail themselves of this patented procedure. (GIVF has the exclusive license on the patent.) When I called, I was told that since I was married, had already had at least one child, and was selecting for the less-represented gender in my family, I qualified for the study. I also discovered that "research study" doesn't mean "free science." Spinning the wheel of fortune would cost $3,200—with no guarantees. However, the company reported that it had achieved a total of 259 pregnancies, with 148 births and "many more" due to deliver. Of the pregnancies in which the gender of the fetus was known, plus the births that have already taken place, the clinic claims just over 90% success in choosing girls and about 72% success in selecting boys, leaving plenty of would-be parents eager to pay the price for a chance at a prize in pink or blue. I certainly was, and not just because I was living a *Malcolm in the Middle* life.

Motherless, sisterless, and down a few aunts, I hoped to infuse some more femininity into my life by stirring the genetic pot one last time. My mother had been just 47 when she died after a long illness. Might my daughter have her eyes, her laugh, or her green thumb?

And although I was in my early 40s, because I had lost a child from a first marriage in a house fire—a little boy who was only 5—I was more reluctant than many women to consider myself out of the baby business. I wanted to be pregnant one last time, and a girl would be nice after having had four boys. To that end, sperm sorting seemed the best way to go.

From Calves to Kids

The technology involves staining sperm with a fluorescent dye, and then sending them single file past an ultraviolet laser, which gauges how much genetic material each possesses by how brightly it glows: Sperm with Y chromosomes (female) are larger and therefore brighter. The machine then sorts the X's from the Y's. Called flow cytometric sperm separation, this procedure was developed by a scientist with the Department of Agriculture for use in cattle breeding. It has successfully helped select the sex of several generations of farm animals. In the early 1990s, geneticists at GIVF began adapting the process for use in humans. The first patients were women seeking to avoid the approximately 350 so-called X-linked genetic diseases, including Duchenne muscular dystrophy and hemophilia, which almost exclusively strike boys. A clinical trial included couples seeking a child of a specific sex. Currently, MicroSort claims to produce enriched sperm specimens that make it either approximately nine times more likely to have a female or two to three times more likely to have a male. Both numbers beat nature's odds, which are about 50–50.

The Egg Hunt

I was 5 months shy of my 42nd birthday when I finally talked my husband, Ron, into giving MicroSort a try. The clinic's materials suggest two to five attempts may be required to conceive (the preferred-gender sperm are inserted directly into the uterus at ovulation), and disclaimers abound as to the many factors affect-

Source: Adapted from Kathy des Jardins, "Going for the Girl," *Parenting Magazine*, May 2001.

To increase the chances of having a boy: (1) the man should not ejaculate for several days preceding his partner's expected time of ovulation; (2) the couple should engage in sexual intercourse on the day of ovulation; (3) the man should penetrate deeply at the moment of ejaculation; and (4) the woman should make the vagina more hospitable to Y-bearing sperm by douching with 2 tablespoons of baking soda per quart of warm water before intercourse. This will lower vaginal acidity.

According to Shettles, a combination of these methods results in the conception of a child of the desired sex in about 80% of cases. However, researchers other than Shettles have not found these methods to be reliable (Rawlins, 1998; Wilcox et al., 1995).

Sperm-Separation Procedures

Several sperm-separation procedures are in use. One is based on the swimming rates of X- and Y-bearing sperm. Another reflects the finding that the two types of

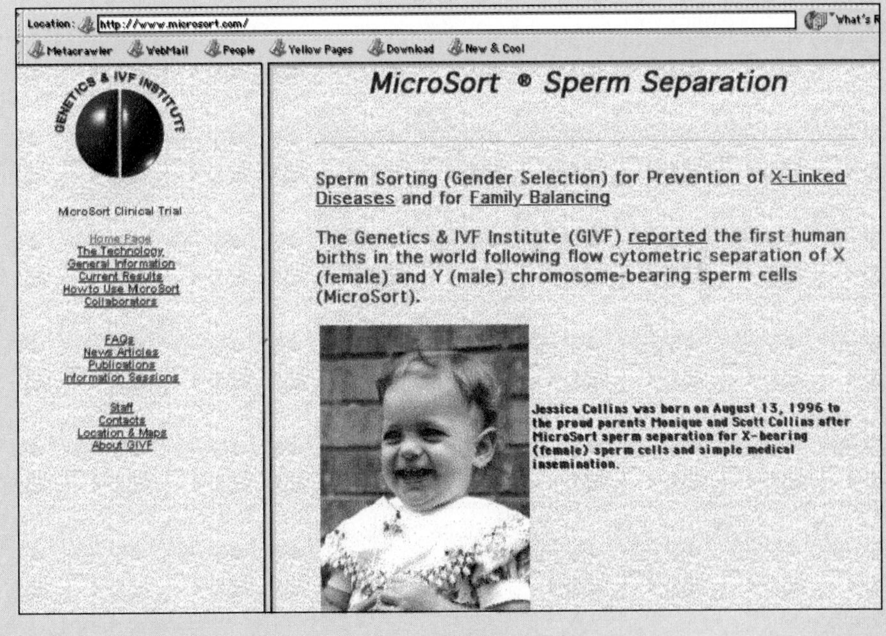

Selecting the Sex of Your Child

Sperm-separation procedures now give couples more than a 50–50 chance at selecting the sex of their children. Does allowing couples to do so pose any problems for society at large?

ing anyone trying to get pregnant. But given my age and reproductive history, I figured I stood about a 23% chance of conceiving, and if God wanted me to have a girl—or another boy, which would have been fine too—one shot with those odds was good enough. The number swept me from my suburban Atlanta home and onto a Washington, DC–bound jet, with Ron set to join me four nights later, leaving the boys with family and friends.

When I arrived at the clinic, I was struck by how small and empty it was. There were no baby pictures posted on the walls; the waiting room wasn't filled with anxious clients. Two nurses set about conducting my initial vaginal ultrasound, in search of all-important egg-bearing follicles. (I had been taking Clomid to stimulate egg production.) When several minutes passed with nothing more than a lava-lamplike ooze filling the screen, they called in their supervisor, Rekha Matken.

Matken took up the search for a follicle. Without at least one, the trip would have been in vain. (I realized too late that this phase of monitoring could have been performed at a clinic near my home.) Not only was she unable to see a follicle, but she also couldn't see my left ovary clearly. I was told to come back in the morning for another ultrasound and blood test that might confirm that an egg was indeed maturing.

The next day, I was sent to GIVF's somber infertility unit, where a sonographer finally located the elusive left ovary. On it sat that month's lone follicle. (Drugs that enhance fertility typically stimulate one to three follicles per cycle.) The follicle didn't seem to be growing, however, and so for the next 3 days it was entirely possible that the cycle could be canceled at any point. I needed to return the next morning to have the follicle measured and blood drawn, after which I had a chance to ponder the sperm carry different electrical charges. A more recent method relies on the fact that sperm carrying the Y sex chromosome have a bit less (about 2.8% less) genetic material (DNA) than sperm carrying the X sex chromosome (Kolata, 1998c). Fugger (1998) and his colleagues have managed to pass the hundreds of millions of sperm cells in an ejaculation through a "DNA detector" and separate them on this basis. Mothers have then been artificially inseminated with the chosen sperm. Still, there remains the question of reliability. The method seems to create female babies on about 85% of attempts, and male babies on about 65% of attempts (Kolata, 1998c).

Moral and Ethical Questions

Such methods raise momentous moral and ethical questions. Many people wonder whether people have the "right" to select the sex of their children. For some people, the word *right* has a religious meaning. That is, they think that only God should determine the sex of a child. Others may consider the word *right* in terms of balancing the numbers of females and males within a culture. Since males tend

Developing in the New Millennium (continued)

myriad mysteries of reproduction, wait for Ron, and commiserate with two other patients I had met, Mary Carter, 33, and Louise Reynolds, 34. (Both names have been changed.) Together we'd experience just about every end result possible with MicroSort: success, disappointment, and something in between.

Three Women and Hope for a Baby

Mary and her husband, John, had come from Colorado with their 2-year-old, Michael. Louise, the mother of 3- and 5-year-old sons, had arrived from another Washington, DC, suburb.

Mary and I had both lost children. Hers was a 4-month-old fetus, Michael's fraternal twin, conceived after a year and a half of infertility treatments. The twin, gender undetermined, had been in Mary's left Fallopian tube, which she also lost during the harrowing emergency surgery that saved her life and Michael's. So Mary, formerly infertile and not far removed from a difficult pregnancy, assumed there could be just one more. And with males by far the predominant sex in her husband's densely populated family, she was also fairly certain what the gender would be.

"There's been one girl born on my husband's side in about a hundred years," she said. "So we just wanted to up our chances."

Several days later, Louise Reynolds sat one seat away, waiting for her second procedure in two months. She and her husband had decided that spending $9,600 for three attempts at a girl would be more cost-effective than continuing to have children until they conceived one on their own.

Though our motivations differed, we had similar misgivings. As much as we each wanted daughters, we were well aware of the host of arguments—ethical, moral, and religious—against this use of science.

The Carters were so sensitive about possible repercussions that they hadn't even told their families. "They wouldn't understand. They would think we were trying to play God," Mary said. "We don't feel that way—we feel children are gifts from God, but if you've got to go through medical procedures to get a child, that's the reason we have medical advances today."

Louise was more concerned about the "decadent" commercial impression that ordering up a daughter gives, the act of trying to control all aspects of life: "Your decor, what you get for lunch, and the arrangement you want for your family."

Their worries didn't even take into consideration broader ethical issues inherent in the idea of choosing a child's sex. These range from the very basic objection about the idea of messing around with Mother Nature to futuristic fears that the technology will evolve to the point that couples are able to "pick out" such characteristics as eye color, athletic excellence, or intelligence. Some experts have voiced concerns that if sperm sorting were to become available in Asia, where the desire for male offspring is so intense that female fetuses are routinely aborted, few baby girls would be born in those countries.

So, having come to terms with our own personal feelings about what we were attempting and why, there the three of us were, in a low-tech office, hoping for high-tech daughters. As the veteran among us, Louise admitted that she was completely cynical. The first time had seemed so promising; she'd had a great follicle but hadn't gotten pregnant. This time, like me, she had a problem follicle and wound up in GIVF's infertility division for monitoring, where she was chastened by "the weariness, the kind of fatigue and hopelessness that I felt in there."

Mary's mood was markedly different. Despite the long plane trip with a 2-year-old, she radiated hopeful joy, because after four months of ultrasounds in Colorado to determine whether her eggs were forming on the side with her one remaining Fallopian tube, she finally had two "beautiful" follicles. And after hearing their fertility doctor's suggestions for optimizing their chances of success, both Mary and John had taken vitamins, tweaked their diets, and forsaken caffeine.

My own stint was basically an exercise in diminishing expectations. Although with Clomid I thought I stood a 23% chance of conceiving at all—let alone conceiving a girl—Rekha Matken later explained that because miscarriage and other complications are more common in older mothers, the "take-home rate" for someone my age really wasn't so great after all.

to be preferred, sex selection can lead quickly to an overabundance of males within a society, as it may do in India (Dugger, 2001a, 2001b). Some, like the Ethics Committee of the American Society of Reproductive Medicine (2000), consider sex selection for nonmedical reasons to be sexist. Yet many people believe that selecting the sex of one's children is a personal and not a social matter: "By what authority," they challenge, "do some decide whether the rest of us have acceptable reasons for selecting the sex of our children?" (Holmes-Farley, 1998). You may consult articles such as the following if you want to join in the debate more deeply: Benagiano and Bianchi (1999), Savulescu and Dahl (2000), Simpson and Carson (1999), and Sureau (1999). As the new millennium brings more efficient and affordable methods for the sex selection of babies, we will be dealing with such moral and ethical questions on a grand scale.

But most of the next chapter deals with issues on a smaller scale—beginning with the division of the single cell formed by union of sperm cell and ovum into two, then four, and so on.

When pressed, one nurse could remember only one 41-year-old who eventually conceived a daughter with MicroSort. It took her five cycles. I knew I wouldn't spend $16,000 on what I now felt was a high-stakes, low-hope crapshoot for a girl.

Uneven Results

On my 5th and final day, my single follicle had rallied enough that we could proceed and I was inseminated with sperm Ron had provided earlier that morning. The sample had yielded 149,000 sperm, less than one cc ($^{1}/_{5}$ teaspoon of an enriched sperm specimen).*

Ever the ovulatory optimist, I entertained myself on the return flight to Georgia by harkening back to my teen years and the tales of girls getting pregnant by sitting on toilet seats. I figured less than $^{1}/_{5}$ teaspoon of semen deposited directly into my uterus via a catheter was still almost equivalent to a full night of passion. Sure enough, within a couple of days, I was queasy, my breasts were tender, and I was absolutely certain I was expecting.

Back in Colorado, Mary was also having early-pregnancy symptoms. Always on schedule, her period didn't come on time.

Outside Washington, DC, Louise wasn't feeling pregnant at all. In fact, she felt premenstrual—and frustrated by busy MicroSort's inability to schedule active patients consecutively. Her period didn't arrive either. Mine, however, did. And several days later, so did Mary's. Louise, though, was pregnant.

"It just shows that you can't necessarily rely on your instincts, particularly if you have drugs messing with your system," she said. Months later, 27 weeks into her pregnancy, an ultrasound determined the baby was "probably" a girl. Still, Louise has told only her closest confidants about how she got pregnant. "I have good reasons for doing it, and I think a lot of people would understand." Nevertheless, she is afraid that her choice would "eclipse all the other nuances" about her character and she'd just be known for having done "that crazy sex-selection thing."

*Remember that the typical normal ejaculation contains hundreds of millions of sperm.

Back in Colorado, Mary and John carried on with their plans to give the procedure three more shots. But the next month, all of Mary's eggs were on the side without the Fallopian tube. A doctor at the clinic suggested she try combining the technology with in vitro fertilization, or IVF (the egg and sperm are fertilized in a test tube and the resulting embryo is placed directly in the uterus, in hopes that it will implant and thrive). In some women, IVF is more likely to produce a successful pregnancy than artificial insemination, but at more than $9,000 it's much more expensive. Even so, the Carters signed on—with a twist.

Their Colorado doctor would work with their eggs; MicroSort would sort the sperm. In May John traveled back to the Fairfax clinic, where a sperm sample was sorted, frozen, and shipped to the fertility doctor. To cover the $15,000—the cost of the combined procedures—the Carters remortgaged their home, a move that paid off in June, when Mary discovered she was pregnant with twins. Still, she remained less than pleased with the MicroSort process. "It was more cumbersome than I'd been led to believe," she said. "But if we really get a girl—or two—then I think it will have all been worth it."

At press time, Mary's healthy twin girls were just a few weeks old and Louise's daughter was 4 months old. As for me, Ron decided a few weeks after our trip to Fairfax that I needed a puppy.

And we'll all be fine.

Search Online With InfoTrac College Edition

For additional information, explore InfoTrac College Edition, your online library. Go to **http://www.infotrac-college.com** and use the passcode from the InfoTrac card that came with your book. Try these search terms: sex pre-selection, designer babies, sex ratio, sex disrimination.

Review

(31) The union of an ovum and a sperm cell is called ________. (32) The ovaries produce ova and the female sex hormones, estrogen and ________. (33) Each month, an ovum is released from its follicle and enters a nearby ________ tube. (34) More (girls or boys?) are conceived. (35) Low ________ count is the most common infertility problem in the male. (36) Failure to ________ is the most frequent infertility problem in women. (37) Infections such as pelvic ________ disease (PID) may also scar the Fallopian tubes and other organs, impeding the passage of sperm or ova. (38) ________ is a common cause of infertility among women who postpone childbearing. (39) It seems that various sperm-________ procedures provide couples with better-than-chance ability to select the sex of their child.

Pulling It Together: How do various procedures for treating infertility get around the obstacles experienced by infertile couples?

Recite Recite Recite Recite

1. What is meant by heredity?

Heredity defines one's nature as determined by the biological transmission of traits and characteristics from one generation to another. The field of biology that studies heredity is called genetics. Genetic influences are fundamental in the transmission of physical traits and are also involved in psychological traits, including psychological disorders.

2. What are chromosomes and genes?

Chromosomes are rod-shaped structures found in cell nuclei. People normally have 46 chromosomes organized into 23 pairs. Each chromosome contains thousands of genes—the biochemical materials that regulate the development of traits. Genes are segments of strands of deoxyribonucleic acid (DNA), which takes the form of a helix. The series of compounds—e.g., G, C, T, A—determines traits.

3. How do cells divide?

Cells divide by means of mitosis and meiosis. In mitosis, strands of DNA break apart and are rebuilt in the new cell. Sperm and ova are produced by meiosis—or reduction division—and have 23 rather than 46 chromosomes. The 23rd pair of chromosomes determines gender (XX for female, XY for male).

4. How are twins formed?

If a zygote divides into two cells that separate and each develops into an individual, we obtain monozygotic (MZ) twins, which are identical. If two ova are each fertilized by a different sperm cell, they develop into dizygotic (DZ) twins, which are fraternal. DZ twins run in families. Irregular ovulation and fertility drugs enhance the chances of multiple births.

5. How do genes determine traits?

Traits are determined by pairs of genes. Mendel established laws of heredity and realized that some traits result from an "averaging" of the genetic instructions carried by the parents. However, genes may also be dominant (as in the case of brown eyes) or recessive (blue eyes). When recessive genes from both parents combine, the recessive trait is shown. People who bear one dominant gene and one recessive gene for a trait are carriers of the recessive gene. Some genetic abnormalities, like cystic fibrosis, are caused by a single pair of genes; others are polygenic—caused by combinations of genes.

6. What kinds of disorders are caused by chromosomal abnormalities?

Chromosomal abnormalities become more likely as parents age. Mental retardation is common in many such disorders. Down syndrome is caused by an extra chromosome on the 21st pair. Children with Down syndrome have characteristic facial features, including a downward-sloping fold of skin at the inner corners of the eyes and various physical health problems. Disorders that arise from abnormal numbers of sex chromosomes are called sex-linked chromosomal abnormalities. XYY males have heightened male secondary sex characteristics, such as heavy beards. XXY males produce less-than-normal amounts of testosterone, resulting in inadequate development of sex characteristics. Girls with a single X sex chromosome have less-than-normal amounts of estrogen and poorly developed ovaries.

7. What kinds of disorders are caused by genetic abnormalities?

The enzyme disorder phenylketonuria (PKU) is transmitted by a recessive gene and prevents children from metabolizing phenylalanine. PKU is controlled by diet. Huntington's disease is a fatal progressive degenerative disorder and a dominant trait. Sickle-cell anemia is caused by a recessive gene and is most common among African Americans. Tay-Sachs disease is a fatal disease of the nervous system that is caused by a recessive gene and is most common among children in Jewish families of Eastern European origin. Cystic fibrosis is caused by a recessive gene and is the most common fatal hereditary disease among European Americans. Sex-linked genetic abnormalities are carried only on the X sex chromosome and include hemophilia, Duchenne muscular dystrophy, diabetes, and color blindness.

Recite Recite Recite Recite

8. What is genetic counseling? How do health professionals determine whether children will have genetic or chromosomal abnormalities?

Genetic counseling compiles information about a couple's genetic background to determine the possibility that their children may develop genetic abnormalities. The procedure called amniocentesis cultures fetal cells found in amniotic fluid at 14–16 weeks after conception to detect genetic abnormalities. Amniocentesis also permits parents to learn the sex of the baby. Chorionic villus sampling (CVS) is similar to amniocentesis but conducted earlier. Ultrasound can be used to form a picture of the fetus. Ultrasound is used as a guide in amniocentesis or CVS and can also be used to track the growth of the fetus and find structural abnormalities. Parental blood tests can reveal the presence of recessive genes for disorders such as sickle-cell anemia, Tay-Sachs disease, cystic fibrosis, and neural-tube defects. In fetoscopy, a narrow tube is surgically inserted through the abdomen into the uterus to allow visual examination of the fetus.

9. What is the difference between our genotypes and our phenotypes?

Our genotypes are the sets of traits that we inherit. However, inherited traits vary in expression, depending on environmental conditions. One's actual sets of traits at a given point in time is one's phenotype.

10. What kinds of research strategies do researchers use to sort out the effects of genetics and environmental influences on development?

Researchers can study the distribution of a trait among relatives who differ in degree of genetic closeness. Parents and children have a 50% overlap in genes, as do brothers and sisters, with the exception of MZ twins, who have 100% overlap. MZ twins resemble each other more closely than DZ twins on physical and psychological traits. Finding and comparing MZ twins who are reared apart enables researchers to learn how much traits can vary because of environmental factors. If adopted children are closer to their natural than their adoptive parents on a physical or psychological trait, that trait is likely to have a strong genetic basis.

11. What process brings together the genes from each parent?

The process is the union of a sperm and an ovum—conception. Women at birth already have their 400,000 or so ova, but they are immature. Female sex hormones cause some ova to mature on a monthly basis. Fertilization normally occurs in a Fallopian tube. If the egg is not fertilized, it is discharged. Ova are much larger than sperm. Men typically ejaculate hundreds of millions of sperm. Between 120 and 150 boys are conceived for every 100 girls, but male fetuses have a higher rate of spontaneous abortion (miscarriage). Only one sperm cell can enter an ovum. Chromosomes from the sperm cell align with chromosomes in the egg cell, combining to form 23 new pairs.

12. What are the causes of infertility? How are couples helped to have children?

Male fertility problems include low sperm count (the most common problem) and motility, infections, and trauma to the testes. Female fertility problems include failure to ovulate (the most common problem), infections (such as PID), endometriosis, and obstructions or malfunctions in the reproductive tract. Fertility drugs help regulate ovulation. Artificial insemination may be done with the sperm resulting from multiple ejaculations of a man with a low sperm count or with that of a donor. In vitro fertilization (IVF) may be used when the Fallopian tubes are blocked. Embryonic transplant is a method that transfers an embryo into the mother's uterus when she cannot produce ova.

13. How do people attempt to select the sex of their children?

Methods have been developed for sorting male (Y) and female (X) sperm cells. Shettles suggested methods based on the swimming rates and other characteristics of X- and Y-bearing sperm cells, but these methods have not been shown to be reliable. Others have developed methods based on the electrical charges of sperm cells and on the bulk of their genetic material. These methods may be more reliable than Shettles's. Use of these methods raises profound ethical questions.

On the Web

Search Online With InfoTrac College Edition

For additional information, explore InfoTrac College Edition, your online library. Go to **http://www.infotrac-college.com** and use the passcode from the Infotrac card that came with your book. Try these search terms: genes and intelligence, genetic screening, nature and nurture, conception, twins, genetic disorders.

Visit Our Web Site

Go to **http://www.wadsworth.com/psychology** where you will find online resources directly linked to your book.

Child Development CD-ROM

Go to the Wadsworth *Child Development* CD-ROM for further study of the concepts in this chapter. The CD-ROM also includes quizzes and additional activities to expand your learning experience.

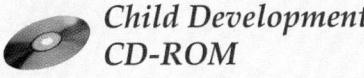

3 Prenatal Development

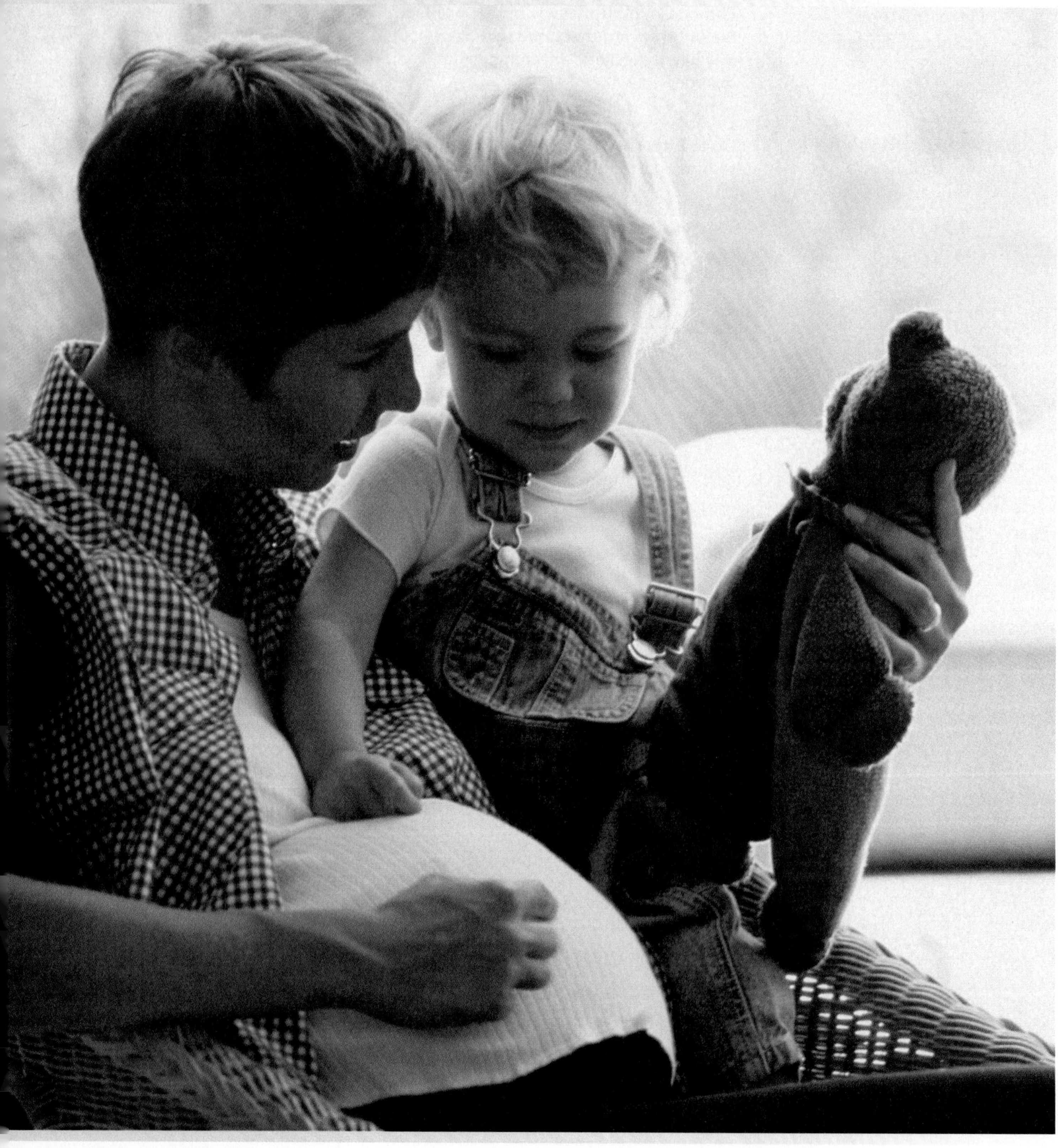

PowerPreview™

The Germinal Stage—Wanderings

- **The most dramatic changes** in development are out of sight—that is, they occur prior to birth.
- **Newly fertilized egg cells** survive without any nourishment from the mother for more than a week.

The Embryonic Stage

- **Your heart started beating** when you were only one-quarter of an inch long and weighed but a fraction of an ounce.
- **Was Eve born from a rib** of Adam, or do "Adams" develop from "Eves"?

The Fetal Stage

- **Fetuses suck their thumbs and hiccough,** and—as pregnant women know!—the hiccoughing can last for hours on end.
- **Why do some parents** play classical music and point the speakers toward their abdomens during pregnancy?

Environmental Influences on Prenatal Development

- **Is it true that embryos** and fetuses take what they need from their mothers? Do pregnant women need to be concerned about their diets?
- **What disease-causing germs** can cross the placental barrier and infect the embryo and fetus? How about HIV (the virus that causes AIDS)?
- **Is it safe for a pregnant woman** to have a couple of glasses of wine in the evening? Does it matter if she smokes?
- **What is the ideal age** for carrying and bearing a child?

Back in 1938, when rapping was still something that hurt the knuckles, L. W. Sontag and T. W. Richards reported the results of a study in fetal behavior. They stimulated pregnant woman in various ways and measured the results on the heart rate of the fetus, as assessed by an instrument placed on the mother's abdomen. Many of the mothers smoked cigarettes, and the researchers assessed the effects of smoking on the fetal heart rate. They also got the mother and fetus all shook up by applying a vibrator to the mother's abdomen.

Sontag and Richards learned that powerful vibrations usually induced faster heart rates in the fetus (big surprise?), but maternal smoking had less predictable effects on the fetus. Cigarette smoke contains nicotine, which is a stimulant; but smoke also reduces the supply of oxygen in the bloodstream, and oxygen is needed to fuel bursts of activity. How could the researchers spend their time assessing the effects of maternal smoking rather than warning the mothers that their smoking was placing their fetuses at risk for low birthweight, prematurity, short attention span, academic problems, or hyperactivity? This was 1938, and little was known of the harmful effects of smoking.

In any event, Sontag and Richards also discovered that fetuses are sensitive to sound waves during the latter months of pregnancy, which has led to a wave of more recent research—including research into whether **neonates** are "loyal" and prefer their mothers' voices to those of strangers and whether listening to classi-

neonate A newborn baby.

TABLE 3.1 *Highlights of Prenatal Development*

	First Trimester
Period of the Ovum	
First 2 weeks	At first the dividing cluster of cells moves into and around the uterus, living off the yolk of the egg cell. It becomes implanted in the uterine wall, possibly accompanied by implantation bleeding.
Embryonic Stage	
3 weeks	The head and blood vessels form. The brain begins to develop.
4 weeks	Heart begins to beat and pump blood. Arm buds and leg buds appear. Eyes, ears, nose, and mouth form. Nerves begin to develop. The umbilical cord is functional. The embryo weighs a fraction of an ounce and is $^1/_2$ inch long.
5–8 weeks	Hands and feet develop; webbed fingers and toes form. Undifferentiated sex organs appear. Teeth buds develop. The kidneys are filtering uric acid from the blood, and the liver is producing blood cells. Bone cells appear. The head is half the length of the entire body. The embryo now weighs about $^1/_{13}$ ounce and is 1 inch long.
Fetal Stage	
9–12 weeks	All major organ systems are formed. Fingers and toes are fully formed. Eyes can be clearly distinguished. The sex of the fetus can be determined visually (e.g., by ultrasound). The mouth opens and closes, and the fetus swallows. The fetus responds to external stimulation. The fetus weighs 1 ounce and is 3 inches long.

cal music during pregnancy rather than heavy metal has noticeable effects (on the brain as well as the heart rate). Stay tuned . . .

Researchers are finding that the most rapid and dramatic human developments are literally "out of sight"—they take place in the uterus. Within 9 months a child develops from a nearly microscopic cell to a neonate about 20 inches long. Its weight increases by a billionfold.

We can date pregnancy from the onset of the last menstrual period before conception, which makes the normal gestation period 280 days. We can also date pregnancy from the assumed date of fertilization, which normally occurs 2 weeks after the beginning of the woman's last menstrual cycle. With this accounting method, the gestation period is 266 days.

Soon after conception, the single cell formed by the union of sperm and egg begins to multiply—becoming two cells, then four, then eight, and so on. During the weeks and months that follow, tissues, organs, and structures begin to form, and the fetus gradually takes on the unmistakable shape of a human being. By the time a fetus is born, it consists of hundreds of billions of cells—more cells than there are stars in the Milky Way galaxy. Prenatal development is divided into three periods: the germinal stage (approximately the first 2 weeks), the embryonic stage (the 3rd through the 8th weeks), and the fetal stage (the 3rd month through birth). Health professionals also commonly speak of prenatal development in terms of three trimesters of 3 months each. Highlights of prenatal development are summarized in Table 3.1. Let us begin by asking, ***Question: What happens during the germinal stage of prenatal development?***

TABLE 3.1 *Highlights of Prenatal Development (continued)*

Second Trimester	
13–16 weeks	Mother detects fetal movement. Many reflexes are present. Fingernails and toenails form. The head is now about one fourth the length of the body.
17–20 weeks	Hair develops on head. Fine, downy hair (lanugo) covers body. The fetus sucks its thumb and hiccoughs. The heartbeat can be heard when the listener presses his or her head against the mother's abdomen.
21–24 weeks	Eyes open and shut. Light and sounds are perceived. The fetus alternates between periods of wakefulness and sleep. The skin looks ruddy because blood vessels show through the surface. Survival rate is low if fetus is born. Fetus now weighs about 2 pounds and is 14 inches long; the growth rate is slowing down.
Third Trimester	
25–28 weeks	Organ systems continue to mature. Fatty layer begins to develop beneath the skin. Fetus turns head down in the uterus. The fetus cries, swallows, and sucks its thumb. The chances of survival are good if born. The fetus now weighs about 3–4 pounds and is 16 inches long.
29–36/38 weeks	Organ systems function well. Fatty layer continues to develop. The fetus's activity level decreases in the weeks before birth due to crowding. Weight increases to an average of about 7–7$^1/_2$ pounds, with boys being about half a pound heavier than girls; length increases to about 20 inches.

The Germinal Stage—Wanderings

Click *Physical Development* in the Child and Adolescent CD-ROM for more on the germinal stage.

germinal stage The period of development between conception and the implantation of the embryo in the uterine wall.

blastocyst A stage within the germinal period of prenatal development in which the zygote has the form of a sphere of cells surrounding a cavity of fluid.

embryonic disk The platelike inner part of the blastocyst that differentiates into the ectoderm, mesoderm, and endoderm of the embryo.

trophoblast The outer part of the blastocyst, from which the amniotic sac, placenta, and umbilical cord develop.

umbilical cord A tube that connects the fetus to the placenta.

placenta (pluh-SENT-uh) An organ connected to the uterine wall and to the fetus by the umbilical cord. The placenta serves as a relay station between mother and fetus for exchange of nutrients and wastes.

Within 36 hours after conception, the zygote divides into two cells. It then divides repeatedly as it proceeds on its journey to the uterus. Within another 36 hours, it has become 32 cells. It takes the zygote 3 to 4 days to reach the uterus. The mass of dividing cells wanders about the uterus for another 3 to 4 days before it begins to become implanted in the uterine wall. Implantation takes another week or so. The period from conception to implantation is called the **germinal stage** (see Figure 3.1).

A few days into the germinal stage, the dividing cell mass takes the form of a fluid-filled ball of cells called a **blastocyst.** A blastocyst already shows cell differentiation. Cells begin to separate into groups that will eventually become different structures. Two distinct inner layers of cells are forming within a thickened mass of cells called the **embryonic disk.** These cells will become the embryo and eventually the fetus.

The outer part of the blastocyst, or **trophoblast,** at first consists of a single layer of cells. But it rapidly differentiates into four membranes that will protect and nourish the embryo. One membrane produces blood cells until the embryo's liver develops and takes over this function. Then the membrane disappears. Another membrane develops into the **umbilical cord** and the blood vessels of the **placenta.** A third develops into the amniotic sac, and the fourth becomes the chorion, which will line the placenta. ***Question: If the dividing mass of cells is moving through a Fallopian tube and then "wandering" through the uterus for another few days, how does it obtain any nourishment?***

Without Visible Means of Support . . .

I will make one of this book's more controversial statements: People are not chickens. Nevertheless, the dividing cluster of cells that will become the embryo and then the fetus is at first nourished only by the yoke of the egg cell, as is a chick developing in an egg. Therefore, it makes no gains in mass. The blastocyst gains mass only when it receives nourishment from the outside. For that to happen, it must be implanted in the wall of the uterus.

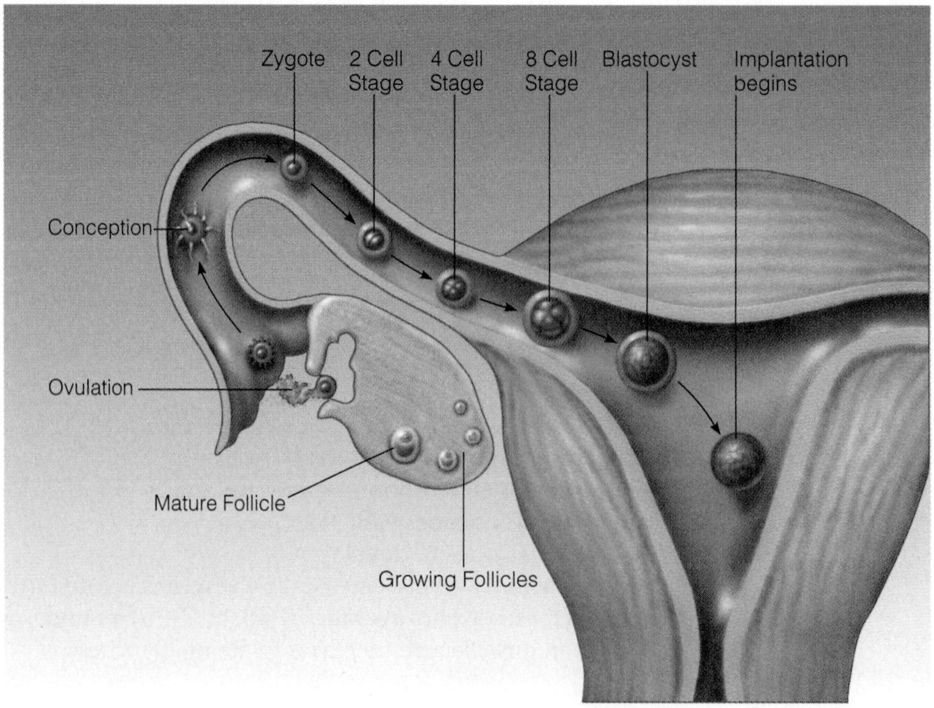

Figure 3.1
The Ovarian Cycle, Conception, and the Early Days of the Germinal Stage

The zygote first divides about 36 hours after conception. Continuing division creates the hollow sphere of cells termed the blastocyst. The blastocyst normally becomes implanted in the wall of the uterus.

Implantation may be accompanied by some bleeding, which is usually normal enough and results from the rupturing of small blood vessels that line the uterus. But bleeding can also be a sign of miscarriage (which is also called spontaneous abortion). Miscarriage usually stems from abnormalities in the developmental process. Many women miscarry early in pregnancy, but their menstrual flows appear nearly on schedule, so that they may not even realize they had conceived. Nearly a third of all pregnancies result in miscarriage, the majority of them occurring in the first 3 months (Sciarra et al., 2000). However, most women who experience implantation bleeding do not miscarry but go on to have normal pregnancies and normal babies.

Review

(1) If we date pregnancy from the assumed date of fertilization, the gestation period is ________ days. (2) Prenatal development is divided into three periods: the ________ stage, the embryonic stage, and the fetal stage. (3) A few days into the germinal stage, the dividing cell mass becomes a fluid-filled ball of cells that is called a ________. (4) The outer part of the blastocyst—called the

stem cells Cells that have the ability to divide for indefinite periods in culture and to give rise to specialized cells.

totipotent stem cells Stem cells that have total potential, or unlimited capability. Totipotent stem cells have the capacity to specialize into the embryo and supportive tissues and organs, such as the placenta.

pluripotent stem cells Stem cells that are capable of giving rise to most tissues of an organism, but not the placenta. Thus they cannot form an embryo.

multipotent stem cells More specialized stem cells, capable of giving rise to a specific group of cells, such as blood cells or skin cells.

Developing in the New Millennium

The Promise of Embryonic Stem Cells: "Infant Cells That Have Not Yet Chosen a Profession"

> Embryonic stem cells . . . are infant cells that have not yet chosen a profession.
>
> David J. Anderson, Biology Professor, California Institute of Technology in *New York Times,* July 15, 2001

> Locked into the tiny specks of embryonic stem cells is the ability to grow into the hundreds of types of tissue that make up the body. This means they could be coaxed to become new, healthy cells to rejuvenate, restore and repair ailing hearts, livers, brains and other organs.
>
> Paul Recer, AP science writer in *Los Angeles Times,* August 9, 2001

Stem cells are created during the germinal stage of prenatal development. The isolation and successful culturing of human stem cell lines have generated great excitement and brought biomedical research to the edge of a new frontier. Because of the promise of this research, the National Institutes of Health have written a primer on stem cells—what they are, how they are used, and the controversies concerning their use—to help educate the public.

What Are Stem Cells?

Stem cells have the ability to divide for indefinite periods in cultures and to give rise to specialized cells. Human development begins when a sperm fertilizes an egg and creates a single cell that has the potential to form an entire organism. This fertilized egg is **totipotent,** meaning that its potential is total. In the first hours after fertilization, this cell divides into identical totipotent cells (see Figure 3.2). This means that either one of these cells, if placed into a woman's uterus, has the potential to develop into a fetus. In fact, identical twins develop when two totipotent cells separate and develop into two individual, genetically identical human beings. Approximately four days after fertilization and after several cycles of cell division, these totipotent cells begin to specialize, forming a hollow sphere of cells, called a blastocyst. The blastocyst has an outer layer of cells and inside the hollow sphere, there is a cluster of cells called the inner cell mass.

The outer layer of cells will go on to form the placenta and other supporting tissues needed for fetal development in the uterus. The cells of the inner cell mass cells will go on to form virtually all of the tissues of the human body. Although these cells can form virtually every type of cell found in the human body, they cannot form an organism because they are unable to give rise to the placenta and supporting tissues necessary for development in the human uterus. These cells of the inner cell mass are said to be **pluripotent.** This means that they can give rise to many types of cells but not all types of cells necessary for fetal development. Because their potential is not total, they are not totipotent and they are not embryos. In other words, if one of these cells were placed into a woman's uterus, it would not develop into a fetus.

The pluripotent stem cells undergo further specialization into **multipotent** stem cells, which give rise to cells that have a

Note: This feature is adapted from National Institutes of Health. (2000, May). Stem Cells: A primer. Retrieved from **http://www.nih.gov/news/stemcell/primer.htm**

_________ —differentiates into membranes that will protect and nourish the embryo. (5) Prior to _________, the dividing cluster of cells is nourished by the yolk of the original egg cell.

Pulling It Together: Since the conceived baby makes no gains in mass during the germinal stage, how can it be said to develop?

The Embryonic Stage

embryonic stage The stage of prenatal development that lasts from implantation through the 8th week and is characterized by the development of the major organ systems.

cephalocaudal From head to tail.

proximodistal From the inner part (or axis) of the body outward.

The **embryonic stage** begins with implantation and covers the period during which the major organ systems differentiate, which comprises the first two months of development. ***Question: What happens during the embryonic stage of prenatal development?*** Development follows two general trends—**cephalocaudal** (Latin for "head to tail") and **proximodistal** (Latin for "near to far"). The apparently oversized heads of embryos and fetuses at various stages of prenatal development show that growth of the head takes precedence over the growth of the lower parts of the body (see Figure 3.3). You can also think of the body as containing a central axis that coincides with the spinal cord. The growth of the organ systems close to this axis (that is, in close *proximity* to the axis) occurs earlier than the

Developing in the New Millennium (continued)

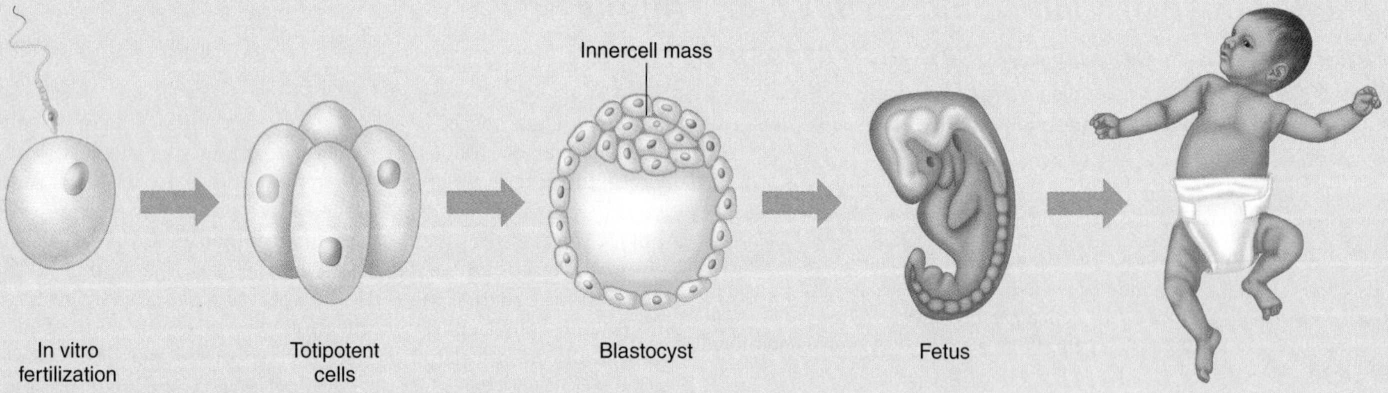

Figure 3.2
From Fertilization to Totipotent Cells to Fetus

Human development begins when a sperm cell fertilizes an ovum, creating a single cell that is totipotent, *meaning that it has the potential to form a complete organism. Within a few hours, the zygote divides into identical totipotent cells. Either one of them can develop into a fetus, which is what happens in the case of identical twins, who are two individual but genetically identical human beings. About four days after fertilization and after several cycles of cell division, the totipotent cells begin to specialize, forming a blastocyst. The blastocyst then develops into a fetus.*

particular function. Examples include blood stem cells, which give rise to red blood cells, white blood cells, and platelets, and skin stem cells, which give rise to the various types of skin cells.

Multipotent stem cells are also found in children and adults. One of the best understood stem cells is the blood stem cell. Blood stem cells reside in the bone marrow of every child and adult. They can also be found in very small numbers circulating in the bloodstream. Blood stem cells perform the critical role of continually replenishing our supply of blood cells—red blood cells, white blood cells, and platelets—throughout life.

Stem Cells From Embryos and Fetuses

Most controversy over the use of stem cells concerns the use of cells derived from embryos and fetuses.

growth of the extremities, which are farther away (that is, *distant* from the axis). Relatively early maturation of the brain and organ systems that lie near the central axis allows these organs to play important roles in the further development of the embryo and fetus.

During the embryonic stage, the outer layer of cells of the embryonic disk, or **ectoderm,** develops into the nervous system, sensory organs, nails, hair, teeth, and the outer layer of skin. At about 21 days, two ridges appear in the embryo and fold to compose the **neural tube,** from which the nervous system will develop. The inner layer, or **endoderm,** forms the digestive and respiratory systems, the liver, and the pancreas. A bit later during the embryonic stage, the mesoderm, a middle layer of cells, becomes differentiated. The **mesoderm** develops into the excretory, reproductive, and circulatory systems; the muscles; the skeleton; and the inner layer of the skin.

Click *Physical Development* for more on the embryonic stage.

During the third week after conception, the head and blood vessels begin to form. ***Question: When does the heart begin to beat?*** During the fourth week, a primitive heart begins to beat and pump blood—in an organism that is only $\frac{1}{4}$ of an inch in length and that weighs a fraction of an ounce. The heart will continue to beat without rest every minute of every day for perhaps 80 or 90 years. Arm buds and leg buds begin to appear toward the end of the first month. Eyes, ears, nose, and mouth begin to take shape. By this time, the nervous system, including the brain, has also begun to develop.

In accord with the principle of proximodistal development, the upper arms and legs develop before the forearms and lower legs. Next come hands and feet, followed at 6 to 8 weeks by webbed fingers and toes. By the end of the second month,

ectoderm The outermost cell layer of the newly formed embryo, from which the skin and nervous system develop.

neural tube A hollowed-out area in the blastocyst from which the nervous system develops.

endoderm The inner layer of the embryo, from which the lungs and digestive system develop.

mesoderm The central layer of the embryo, from which the bones and muscles develop.

How Are Pluripotent Stem Cells Derived?

At present, human pluripotent cell lines have been developed from two sources.

- One method isolates pluripotent stem cells directly from the inner cell mass of human embryos at the blastocyst stage. Embryos from IVF (in vitro fertilization) clinics are used. These embryos are in excess of the clinical need for infertility treatment. The embryos were made for purposes of reproduction, not research. Informed consent is obtained from the donor couples. The inner cell mass is isolated and cultured, producing a pluripotent stem cell line. (Although this usage of embryonic tissue is seen by some as the destruction of human life, in 2001, President Bush decided to provide federal funding for research with stem cell lines obtained in this fashion.)
- Another method isolates pluripotent stem cells from fetal tissue obtained from terminated pregnancies. Informed consent is obtained from the donors after they have independently made the decision to terminate their pregnancy. (This usage of aborted embryos and fetuses strikes some as ghoulish and as supporting abortion.)

Somatic cell nuclear transfer (SCNT) may be another way to isolate pluripotent stem cells. In studies with animals using SCNT, researchers take a normal animal egg cell and remove the nucleus (the cell structure containing the chromosomes). The material left behind in the egg cell contains nutrients and other energy-producing materials that are essential for embryonic development. Then a somatic cell—any cell other than an egg or a sperm cell—is placed next to the egg from which the nucleus has been removed, and the two are fused. The resulting fused cell, and its immediate descendants, are believed to have the full potential to develop into an entire animal and hence are totipotent.* These totipotent cells will soon form a blastocyst. Cells from the inner cell mass of this blastocyst could, in theory, be used to develop pluripotent stem cell lines.

Potential Applications of Pluripotent Stem Cells

There are several important reasons why the isolation of human pluripotent stem cells is important to science and to advances in health care. At the most fundamental level, pluripotent stem cells could help us to understand the complex events that occur during human development. Some of our most serious medical conditions, such as cancer and birth defects, are due to abnormal cell specialization and cell division. A better understanding of normal cell processes will allow us to further delineate the fundamental errors that cause these often deadly illnesses.

Perhaps the most far-reaching potential application of human pluripotent stem cells is the generation of cells and tissue that could be used for so-called "cell therapies." Many diseases and disorders result from disruption of cellular function or destruction of tissues of the body. Today, donated organs and tissues are often used to replace ailing or destroyed tissue. Unfortunately, the number of people with these disorders far outstrips the number of organs available for transplantation. Pluripotent stem cells, stimulated to develop into specialized cells, offer the possibility of a renewable source of replacement cells and tissue to treat many diseases, conditions, and disabilities, including Parkinson's and Alzheimer's diseases, spinal cord injury, stroke, burns, heart disease, diabetes, osteoarthritis, and rheumatoid arthritis. Note some details of two of these examples:

- Transplant of healthy heart muscle cells could provide new hope for patients with chronic heart disease whose hearts can

*This method is also termed *cloning*.

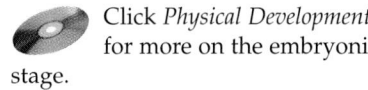

the limbs are elongating and separated. The webbing is gone. By this time the embryo is looking quite human. The head has the lovely round shape of your own and the facial features have become quite distinct. Bear in mind that all this detail is inscribed on an embryo that is only about 1 inch long and weighing in at only about $\frac{1}{30}$th of an ounce. During the second month of embryonic development, the cells in the nervous system begin to "fire"—that is, to send messages among themselves. This is most likely random firing; the "content" of such "messages" is anybody's guess. (No, the embryo isn't contemplating Shakespeare or Confucius.) By the end of the embryonic period, the embryo's teeth buds have formed, its kidneys are filtering acid from the blood, and its liver is producing red blood cells.

Sexual Differentiation: How Some "Eves" Become "Adams"

According to the Bible, Adam arrived first in Paradise, and Eve was born from one of his ribs. According to biological science, it would appear more accurate to think of Adam(s) as developing from Eve(s).

By 5 to 6 weeks, the embryo is only a $\frac{1}{4}$ to $\frac{1}{2}$ inch long. Nevertheless, nondescript sex organs will already have formed, including the internal and external genital organs shown in Figures 3.4 and 3.5. Both female and male embryos possess a pair of sexually undifferentiated gonads, and two sets of primitive duct structures, the so-called Müllerian (female) ducts and the Wolffian (male) ducts.

Developing in the New Millennium *(continued)*

no longer pump adequately. Scientists hope to develop heart muscle cells from human pluripotent stem cells and transplant them into the failing heart muscle in order to augment the function of the failing heart. Preliminary work in mice and other animals has demonstrated that healthy heart muscle cells transplanted into the heart successfully repopulate the heart tissue and work together with the host cells. These experiments show that this type of transplantation is feasible.

- In the many individuals who suffer from type 1 diabetes, the production of insulin by specialized pancreatic cells, called islet cells, is disrupted. There is evidence that transplantation of either the entire pancreas or isolated islet cells could mitigate the need for insulin injections. Islet cell lines derived from human pluripotent stem cells could be used for diabetes research and, ultimately, for transplantation.

Stem Cells From Adults

Multipotent stem cells can be found in some types of adult tissue. In fact, stem cells are needed to replenish the supply of cells in our body that normally wear out, as in the case of the blood stem cell. Multipotent stem cells have not been found for all types of adult tissue, but discoveries in this area of research are increasing. For example, in recent years, neuronal stem cells have been isolated from the nervous systems of rats and mice.

Do Adult Stem Cells Have the Same Potential as Pluripotent Stem Cells?

Researchers have shown that in mice, some adult stem cells previously thought to be committed to the development of one line of specialized cells are able to develop into other types of specialized cells. For example, recent experiments in mice suggest that when neural stem cells were placed into the bone marrow, they appeared to produce a variety of blood cell types. In addition, studies with rats have indicated that stem cells found in the bone marrow were able to produce liver cells. These exciting findings suggest that even after a stem cell has begun to specialize, the stem cell may, under certain conditions, be more flexible than first thought.

Why Not Just Pursue Research With Adult Stem Cells?

The use of adult stem cells for cell therapies would certainly reduce or even avoid the practice of using stem cells derived from human embryos or human fetal tissue, sources that trouble many people on ethical grounds.

While adult stem cells hold promise, there are limitations to what we may be able to accomplish with them. First of all, stem cells from adults have not been isolated for all tissues of the body. Secondly, adult stem cells are often present in only minute quantities; they are difficult to isolate and purify, and their numbers may decrease with age. In addition, there is no clear evidence that stem cells from adults, human or animal, are pluripotent. Thus, at least for the time being, research with embryonic stem cells holds more potential.

Search Online With InfoTrac College Edition

For additional information, explore InfoTrac College Edition, your online library. Go to **http://www.infotrac-college.com** and use the passcode from the InfoTrac card that came with your book. Try these search terms: human embryo usage, human embryo research, embryonic stem cell.

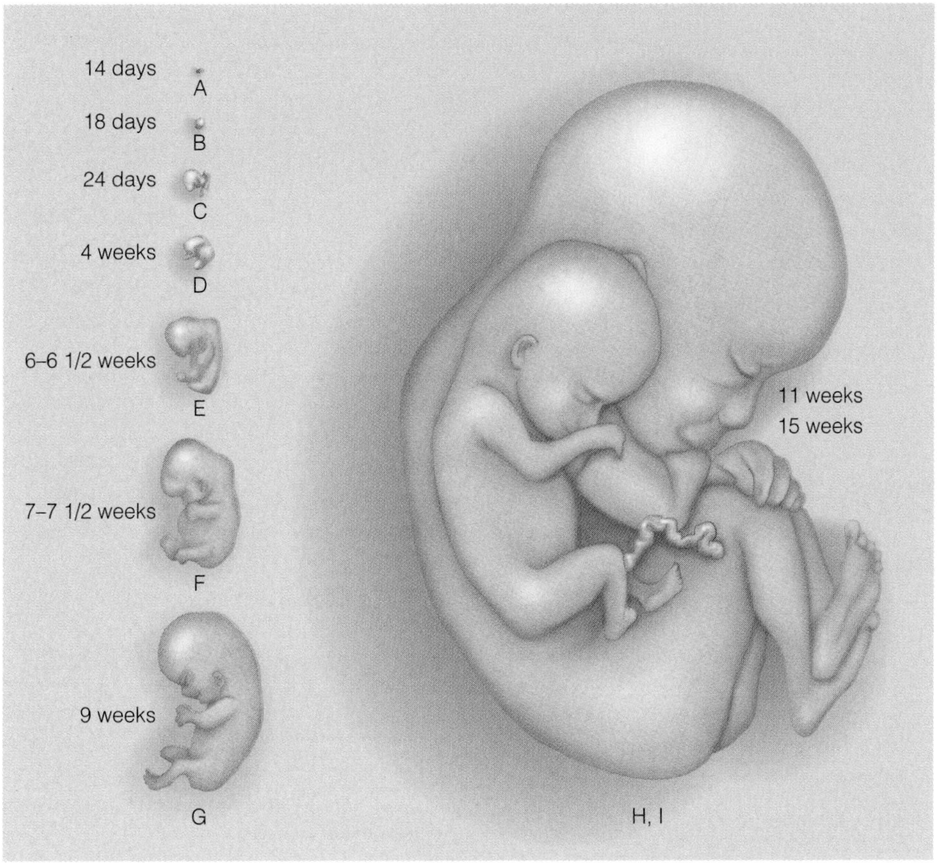

Figure 3.3
Human Embryos and Fetuses at Various Stages of Development

Development proceeds in cephalocaudal and proximodistal directions. Development of the head takes precedence over development of the lower parts of the body, enabling the brain to be involved in subsequent developments. Development of organs near the central axis of the body precedes development of the extremities. The embryo and fetus make use of organs such as the heart and kidneys before they make use of arms and legs.

Why do we speak of Adams as developing from Eves? The first reason is that at this stage of development, the internal and external genitals both resemble primitive female structures.

By about the 7th week, the genetic code (XY or XX) begins to assert itself, causing sex organs to differentiate. Genetic activity on the Y sex chromosome causes the testes to begin to differentiate (National Center for Biotechnology Information, 2000). Ovaries begin to differentiate if the Y chromosome is absent. By about four months after conception, males and females show distinct external genital structures.

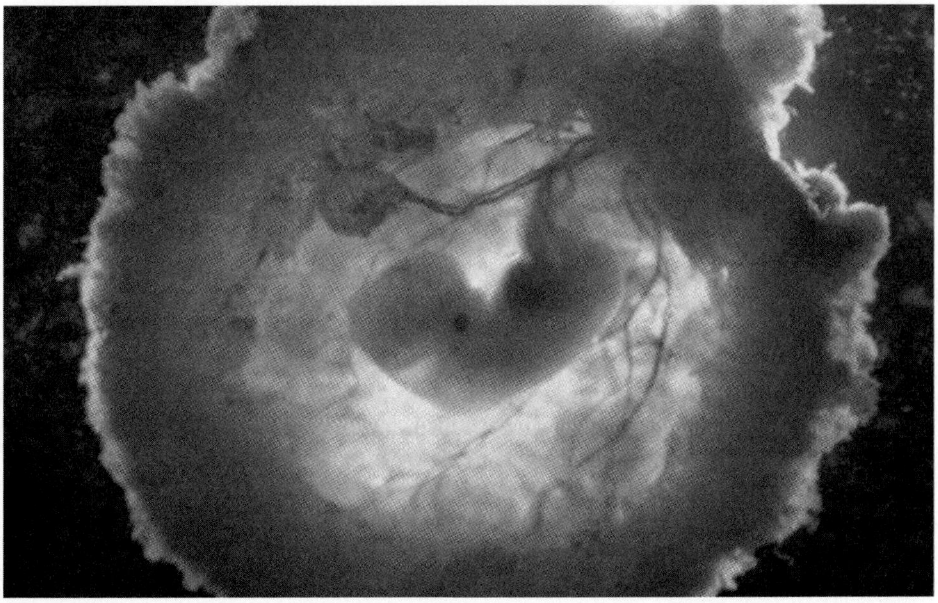

A Human Embryo at 7 Weeks

At this late part of the embryonic stage, the major organ systems have already become differentiated, except for the sex organs.

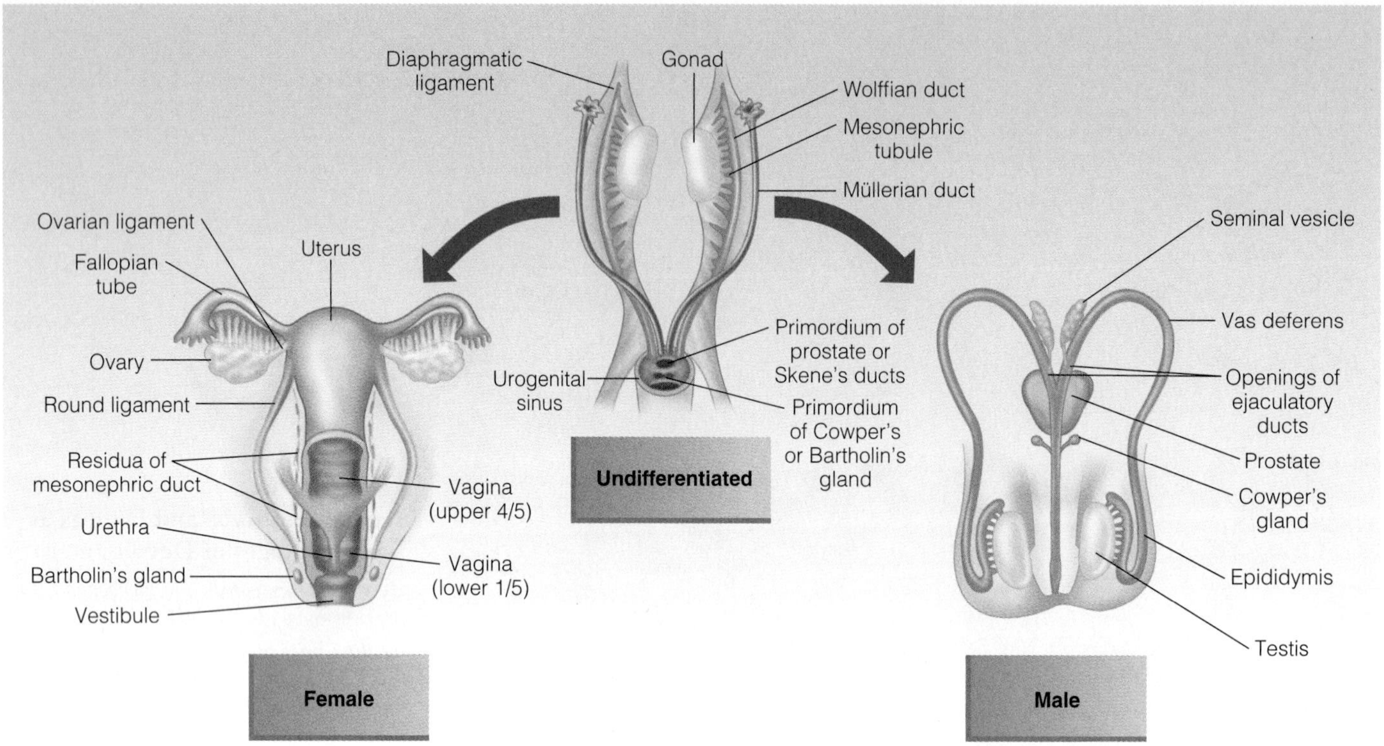

Figure 3.4 Development of the Internal Genital Organs From an Age of 5–6 Weeks Following Conception

Is that it? X and Y sex chromosomes? What is happening on the genetic level to determine the baby's sex? Check the nearby "A Closer Look" feature and you will learn all about the SRY gene, which is connected with developing into a male physically and—apparently—psychologically, at least to some degree.

Sex Hormones and Sexual Differentiation

Prenatal sexual differentiation requires hormonal influences as well as genetic influences. Male sex hormones—**androgens**—are critical in the development of male genital organs. Without them, we would all—whether genetically female or male—develop into females in terms of anatomic structure, although such "females" would be infertile. This is the second reason that we speak of Adams as developing from Eves: The basic blueprint for the development of genital organs is female. Androgens are required to "deviate" from that pattern.

Once the genetic code has done its work and testes have developed in the embryo, they begin to produce androgens. The most important of these is **testosterone.** Testosterone spurs the differentiation of the male (Wolffian) duct system (see Figure 3.4) and remains involved in sexual development and activity for a lifetime. Each Wolffian duct develops into a complex maze of ducts and storage facilities for sperm. At about the 8th week of prenatal development, another androgen, *dihydrotestosterone* (DHT), spurs the formation of the external male genital organs, including the penis. Yet another testicular hormone, secreted somewhat later, prevents the Müllerian ducts from developing into the female duct system. That hormone is appropriately labeled the Müllerian inhibiting substance (MIS).

Female embryos and fetuses do produce small amounts of androgens, but not normally enough to cause sexual differentiation along male lines. However, they do play important roles in the development of some secondary sexual characteristics, as we will see in our discussion of adolescence. These androgens are also—perhaps ironically—important in the sex drive of females, for a lifetime. But in female embryo and fetus, the low levels of androgens are connected with degeneration of the Wolffian ducts and further development of female sexual organs.

androgens Male sex hormones (from roots meaning "giving birth to men").

testosterone A male sex hormone—a steroid—that is produced by the testes and promotes growth of male sexual characteristics and sperm.

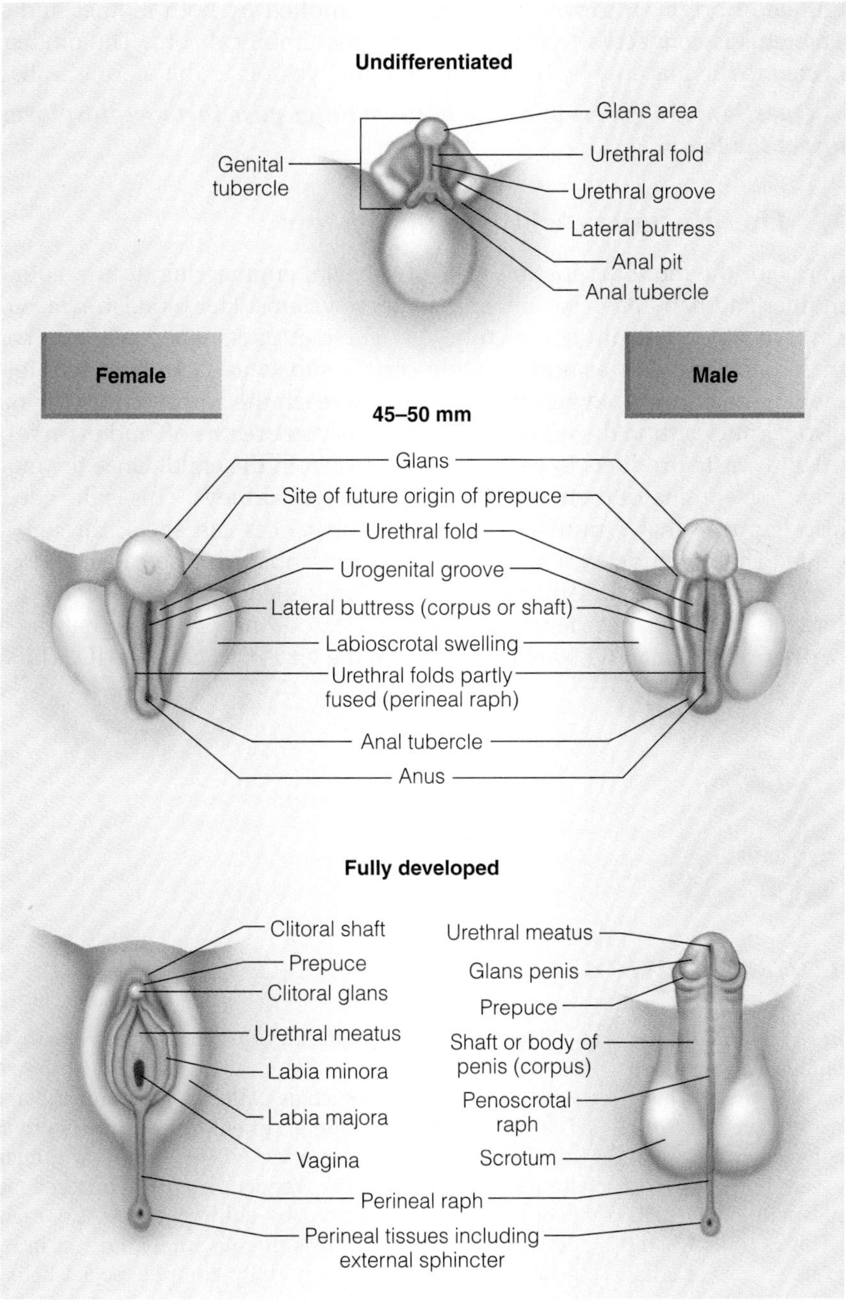

Figure 3.5 Development of the External Genital Organs From an Undifferentiated Stage at 5–6 Weeks Following Conception

The Müllerian ducts develop into Fallopian tubes, the uterus, and the inner part of the vagina. Female sex hormones need not be present for these developments to occur, although they will become crucial in puberty.

The Amniotic Sac

The embryo and fetus develop suspended within a protective **amniotic sac** in the uterus. The sac is surrounded by a clear membrane and contains **amniotic fluid.** The fluid serves as a kind of natural air bag, allowing the embryo and fetus to move around without injury. It also helps maintain an even temperature.

Questions: How does the embryo get nourishment from its mother? How does it eliminate waste products? The answers involve the placenta and the umbilical cord. The placenta is a mass of tissue that permits the embryo (and, later on, the fetus) to exchange nutrients and wastes with the mother. The placenta is

amniotic sac The sac containing the fetus.

amniotic fluid Fluid within the amniotic sac that suspends and protects the fetus.

unique in origin. It grows from material supplied by both mother and embryo. The fetus is connected to the placenta by the umbilical cord. The mother is connected to the placenta by the system of blood vessels in the uterine wall.

Question: Do germs or drugs in the mother pass through the placenta and affect the baby?

The Placenta: A Filtration System

In one of the more fascinating feats of prenatal engineering, it turns our that the mother and baby have separate circulatory systems. Her bloodstream is hers; the embryo's bloodstream is the embryo's. The pancake-shaped placenta contains a membrane that acts as a filter: Only certain substances can pass through it. The membrane permits oxygen and nutrients to reach the embryo from the mother. It also permits carbon dioxide (which is the gas you breathe off and plants "breathe" in) and waste products to pass to the mother from the child. Once the mother has them she eliminates them through her lungs and kidneys. This is the good part. It also happens that a number of harmful substances can sneak through the placenta. They include various "germs" (microscopic disease-causing organisms), such as those that cause syphilis (a bacterium called *treponema pallidum*), German measles, and, to some degree, AIDS. But the good news here is that the majority of pregnant women who are infected with the virus that causes AIDS (HIV) do *not*

A Closer Look

Genetic Factors in Sexual Differentiation

Question: How do some babies develop into girls and others develop into boys? For decades, developmentalists have known that the quick answer is "genes," but in recent years we have learned much about exactly which genes are involved and the ways in which they affect sexual differentiation—and behavior (Vilain, 2000).

Consider crustaceans, for example—animals with bony shells like lobsters, crabs, and shrimp. (Why not? This is college, isn't it?) The interaction of a number of genes in one species of crustacean has led to the development of three different types of males and rather complicated mating strategies (Shuster & Sassaman, 1997). (You'll have to check the source for the intriguing details.) And then consider the female fruit fly. A sex-determining gene referred to as "transformer" (tra) is needed in their development. Chromosomal (XX) female fruit flies with inactive tra attempt to mate with other females, yet they remain attractive to males because they still emit female chemical attractants (Arthur et al., 1998). Fruit fly experts have concluded that sexual determination (whether an organism becomes female or male), sexual orientation (whether it seeks to mate with females or males), and sexual behavior patterns are all determined by the interactions of genes (O'Dell & Kaiser, 1997). Think, then, about mice. In an article that might have been titled "The Mouse That Roared," researcher Stephen Maxson (1998) reported that a group of genes is involved in determining maleness in mice. The same genes, including SRY (which stands for sex-determining region Y gene), also appear to be connected with aggressive behavior.

These studies suggest that genes may do more than determine sexual differentiation in humans. They may also be connected with social behaviors such as patterns of mating and aggression. The studies with mice are pertinent because the National Center for Biotechnology Information (2000) finds that human SRY is similar to the SRY of mice. Yet people are not mice, of course, and people are also influenced by culture, values, experiences, and personal choice. In humans there is rarely a direct link between genetics and behavior, especially complex social behavior patterns like those involved in sexual and aggressive behaviors.

SRY, as noted, is one of the molecules involved in the sexual determination of humans (National Center for Biotechnology Information, 2000; Nordqvist & Lovell-Badge, 1994; Vilain, 2000). It binds to DNA and distorts it out of shape. The distortion changes the DNA and alters the expression of a number of other genes, leading to the development of testes.* Another gene involved in sexual determination has also been researched in mice: Sox 9. It seems that Sox 9 regulates the expression of SRY (Overbeek, 1999). The XX sex chromosomal structure characteristic of females typically suppresses the action of Sox 9, which in turn prevents the action of SRY. However, when XX mice are chemically prevented from switching off Sox 9, they develop as males—even though they are sterile males.

*The author's spouse notes that this scientific finding would appear to support the widely observed phenomenon that males are bent out of shape.

transmit it to the baby through the placenta. We will see that HIV is more likely to be transmitted through childbirth. But some drugs—aspirin, narcotics, alcohol, tranquilizers, and others—also cross the placenta and can affect the baby in one way or another.

The placenta also secretes hormones that preserve the pregnancy, prepare the breasts for nursing, and stimulate the uterine contractions that prompt childbirth. Ultimately, the placenta passes from the woman's body after the child is delivered. For this reason, it is also called the afterbirth.

Review

(6) The embryo and fetus develop within the __________ sac, which functions as a sort of shock absorber. (7) During the __________ stage, the major organ systems differentiate. (8) Development follows two general trends: cephalocaudal and __________. (9) The (inner or outer?) layer of cells of the ectoderm develops into the nervous system, sensory organs, and the outer layer of skin. (10) The __________ forms the digestive and respiratory systems, liver, and pancreas. (11) The __________ develops into the excretory, reproductive, and circulatory systems; muscles; skeleton; and inner layer of skin. (12) The __________ gene, which is involved in sexual differentiation, binds to DNA and distorts it. (13) At 5 to 6 weeks, genital organs are sexually (differentiated or undifferentiated?). (14) Without sex hormones, all embryos would develop into (males or females?). (15) The __________ permits the embryo to exchange nutrients and wastes with the mother. (16) The embryo and fetus are connected to the placenta by the __________ cord. (17) Some drugs, such as aspirin, narcotics, and alcohol, (can or cannot?) cross the placenta.

Pulling It Together: Provide examples of the ways in which prenatal development is cephalocaudal and proximodistal.

Developing in the New Millennium

Preventing One's Baby From Being Infected With HIV

Pregnant women who have or fear they have HIV/AIDS or other sexually transmitted infections (STIs) should discuss them with their physicians. Measures can be taken that will help protect their children. For example, pregnant women who are infected with HIV and use zidovudine (AZT) reduce the rate of infection by HIV in their neonates by two thirds (Connor et al., 1994). Zidovudine works by reducing the amount of the virus in the mother's bloodstream. In one study, only 8% of the babies born to the zidovudine-treated women became infected with HIV, as compared to 25% of babies whose mothers were untreated (Connor et al., 1994).

For up-to-date information on HIV/AIDS, call the National AIDS Hotline at 1-800-342-AIDS. If you want to receive information in Spanish, call 1-800-344-SIDA. You can also log on to the Web site of the Centers for Disease Control and Prevention: **http://www.cdc.gov.** Once you're there, you can click on "Health Topics A–Z" and then on "AIDS/HIV."

Search Online With InfoTrac College Edition

For additional information, explore InfoTrac College Edition, your online library. Go to **http://www.infotrac-college.com** and use the passcode from the InfoTrac card that came with your book. Try these search terms: HIV infants, HIV infection and pregnancy, HIV pregnancy.

The Fetal Stage

The **fetal stage** lasts from the beginning of the third month until birth. ***Question: What happens during the fetal stage of prenatal development?*** The fetus begins to turn and respond to external stimulation at about the 9th or 10th week. By the end of the first trimester, all the major organ systems have been formed. The fingers and toes are fully formed. The eyes can be clearly distinguished, and the sex of the fetus can be determined visually.

Click *Physical Development* for more on the fetal stage.

The second trimester is characterized by further maturation of fetal organ systems and dramatic gains in size. The brain continues to mature, contributing to the fetus's ability to regulate its own basic body functions. During the second trimester, the fetus advances from 1 ounce to 2 pounds in weight and grows four to five times in length, from about 3 inches to 14 inches. Soft, downy hair grows above the eyes and on the scalp. The skin turns ruddy because of blood vessels that show through the surface. (During the third trimester, fatty layers will give the skin a pinkish hue.)

By the end of the second trimester, the fetus opens and shuts its eyes, sucks its thumb, alternates between periods of wakefulness and sleep, and perceives light and sounds. Sharp spasms of the diaphragm, or fetal hiccoughs, may last for hours. Only about 4 babies in 10 who are born at 22–25 weeks of gestation will survive (Allen, Donahue, & Dusman, 1993).

During the third trimester, the organ systems of the fetus continue to mature. The heart and lungs become increasingly capable of sustaining independent life. The fetus gains about 5 $\frac{1}{2}$ pounds and doubles in length. Newborn boys average about 7 $\frac{1}{2}$ pounds and newborn girls about 7 pounds.

During the seventh month, the fetus normally turns upside down in the uterus so that delivery will be headfirst. By the end of the seventh month, the fetus will have almost doubled in weight, gaining another 1 pound 12 ounces, and will have increased another 2 inches in length. If born now, chances of survival are nearly 90%. If born at the end of the eighth month, the odds are overwhelmingly in favor of survival.

fetal stage The stage of development that lasts from the beginning of the 9th week of pregnancy through birth and is characterized by gains in size and weight and maturation of the organ systems.

Question: Why did my Aunt Margaret play classical music (and put the speakers near her abdomen) when she was seven months pregnant?

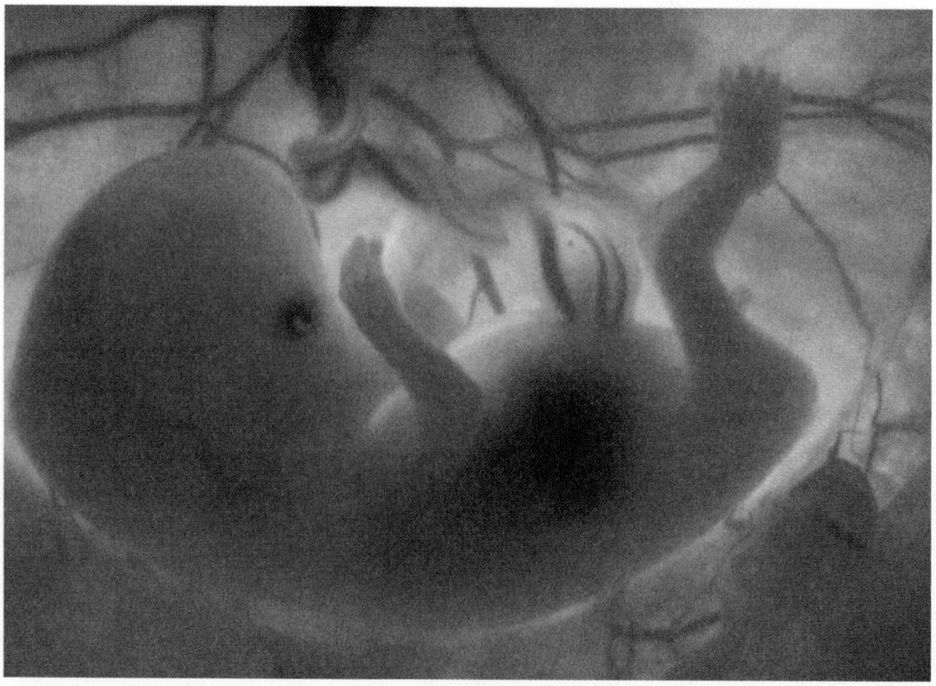

A Human Fetus at 12 Weeks

By the end of the first trimester, formation of all the major organ systems is complete. Fingers and toes are fully formed, and the sex of the fetus can be determined visually.

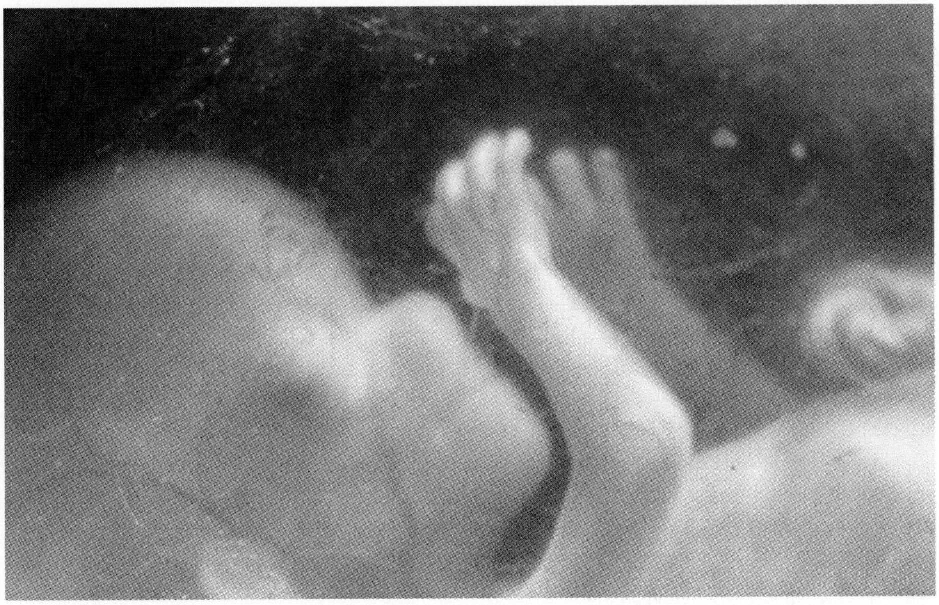

A Human Fetus at $4\frac{1}{2}$ Months

At this midway point between conception and birth, the fetus is covered with fine, downy hair called lanugo.

Fetal Perception: Bach at Breakfast and Beethoven at Brunch?

I never met your Aunt Margaret, so I can't be sure about this, but I'll share something with you: When I was a beginning graduate student and thought I knew everything, I was astounded by what I thought was the naivete of parents-to-be who listened to Bach or Beethoven or who read Shakespeare aloud to promote the cultural development of their fetuses. But in more recent years, I admit that my wife and I have made more of an effort to expose our fetuses to good music as well.

Why? Classic research shows that by the 13th week of pregnancy, the fetus responds to sound waves. In research cited at the beginning of the chapter—but repeated here so that you cannot complain I sent you searching—Sontag and Richards (1938) rang a bell near the mother. The fetus responded with movements similar to those of the startle reflex shown after birth. During the third trimester, fetuses respond to sounds of different frequencies through a variety of movements and changes in heart rate, suggesting that by this time they can discriminate pitch (Lecanuet et al., 2000).

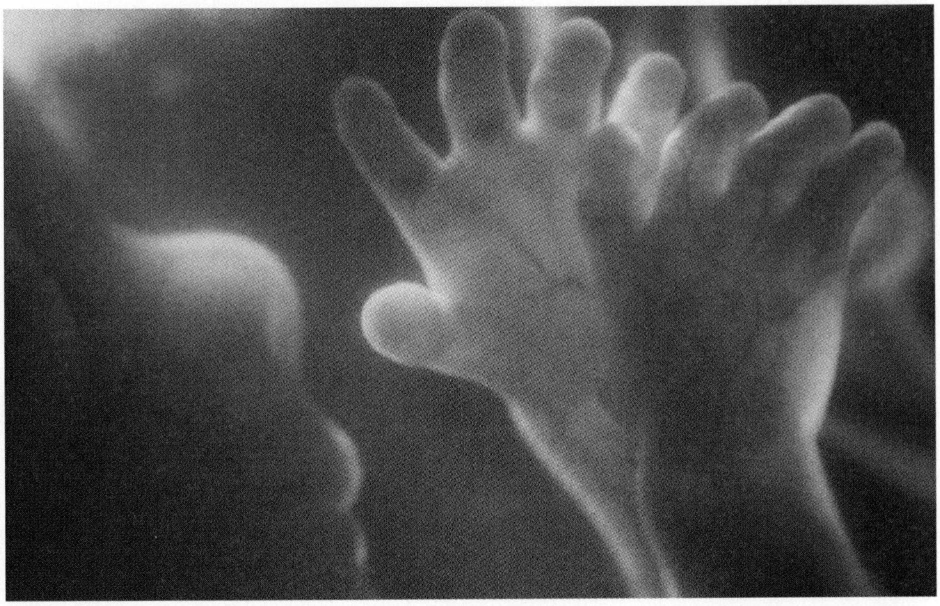

The Hands of a Human Fetus at 5 Months

By 5 months of age, the hands have been fully formed for a month or so. At this age, the fetus may occasionally suck its thumb.

An experiment by DeCasper and Fifer (1980) is even more intriguing. In this study, women read the Dr. Seuss book *The Cat in the Hat* out loud twice daily during the final month and a half of pregnancy. After birth, their babies were given special pacifiers: sucking on them in one way would activate recordings of their mothers reading *The Cat in the Hat.* Sucking on them in another way would activate their mothers' readings of another book—*The King, the Mice, and the Cheese*—which was written in very different cadences. The newborns chose to hear *The Cat in the Hat.* Using similar research methods, DeCasper and his colleagues also found that newborns prefer the mother's voice to that of their father or an unfamiliar woman (DeCasper & Prescott, 1984; DeCasper & Spence, 1986, 1991). Presumably, preference for the mother's voice is established through prenatal exposure.

Is it possible that Bach at breakfast and Beethoven at brunch may not be a bad idea during the later days of pregnancy? Perhaps. It just may do more than help the food go down.

So the fetus can hear toward the end of the pregnancy. But when does the mother get her kicks? That is, ***Question: When does the mother begin to detect fetal movements?***

Reflect

During the fourth month, when the baby's movements can be detected, many women have the feeling that their babies are "alive." What is your view on when the baby is alive? What standard or standards are you using to form your opinion?

Fetal Movements

In the middle of the fourth month, the mother usually detects the first fetal movements (Eaton & Saudino, 1992). By the end of the second trimester, the fetus moves its limbs so vigorously that the mother may complain of being kicked—often at 4 A.M. The fetus also turns somersaults, which are clearly felt by the mother. Fortunately, the umbilical cord will not break or become dangerously wrapped around the fetus, no matter how many acrobatic feats the fetus performs.

Fetuses show different patterns of prenatal activity (Sontag, 1966). Slow squirming movements begin at about 5 or 6 months. Sharp jabbing or kicking movements begin at about the same time and increase in intensity until shortly prior to birth. As the fetus grows it becomes cramped in the uterus, and movement is constricted. Many women become concerned that their fetuses are markedly less active during the ninth month than previously, but most of the time this change is normal.

Different fetuses show different levels of activity. Moreover, prenatal activity predicts activity levels after birth. For instance, highly active fetuses show more advanced motor development 6 months after birth than do their more lethargic counterparts (Richards & Nelson, 1938).

Review

(18) The fetal stage is characterized by __________ of organ systems and gains in size and weight. (19) Research shows that fetuses respond to sound waves by about the __________ week of pregnancy. (20) Mothers usually detect fetal movements during the __________ month.

Pulling It Together: What prenatal events may be connected with a parent's perception that the baby is "alive"? If you were observing prenatal events, what developments would make the baby appear to be "human"?

Environmental Influences on Prenatal Development

Yes, the fetus develops in a protective "bubble"—the amniotic sac. Nevertheless, the developing fetus is subject to many environmental hazards. Scientific advances have made us keenly aware of the types of things that can go wrong and what we can do to prevent these problems. In this section, we consider some of the environmental factors that have an impact on prenatal development. ***Question: How does the mother's nutrition affect prenatal development?***

Nutrition

Reflect

Have you heard that fetuses take what they need from their mothers, even at the expense of their mothers' own nutritional needs? If this were true, mothers would not have to be overly concerned about what they eat. But what does the research evidence show?

We quickly bring nutrition inside, but nutrition originates outside. Therefore, it is one environmental factor in prenatal (and subsequent) development.

It is a common misconception that fetuses take what they need from their mothers. If this were true, pregnant women would not have to be highly concerned about their diets. But malnutrition in the mother, especially during the last trimester when the fetus should be making rapid gains in weight, has been linked to low birthweight, prematurity, stunted growth, retardation of brain development, cognitive deficiencies, and behavioral problems (Bauerfeld & Lachenmeyer, 1992).

As if a pregnant woman did not have enough to be concerned about, there are risks in her being too slender or being obese. Women who are overly slender risk preterm deliveries and having babies who are low in birthweight (Cnattingius et al., 1998). However, maternal *obesity* is linked with a higher risk of stillbirth (Cnattingius et al., 1998).

Maternal malnutrition can lead to long-term behavioral effects. Studies done in Mexico, Guatemala, and South America indicate that children whose mothers were malnourished during their pregnancies show deficits in motor and cognitive skills and general intelligence (Schultz, 1990). Fortunately, the effects of fetal malnutrition may be overcome by a supportive, care-giving environment. By and large, randomized, controlled experiments on the kinds of interventions that help children who had suffered from fetal malnutrition show that enriched day-care programs enhance intellectual and social skills at 5 years of age (Ramey et al., 1992; Ramey, Campbell, & Ramey, 1999).

When pregnant women who might otherwise be deficient in their intake of calories and protein receive dietary supplementation, modest positive effects can be seen in the motor development of their infants. In one study, 8-month-old children of Taiwanese women who had received prenatal calorie and protein supplements showed more advanced motor development than did controls, as measured by crawling and sitting, pulling themselves to a standing position, and making stepping movements (Joos et al., 1983).

Pregnant women require the following food elements to maintain themselves and to give birth to healthy babies: protein, most heavily concentrated in meat, fish, poultry, eggs, beans, milk, and cheese; vitamin A, found in milk and vegetables; vitamin B, found in wheat germ, whole-grain breads, and liver; vitamin C, found in citrus fruits; vitamin D, derived from sunshine, fish-liver oil, and vitamin-D-fortified milk; vitamin E, found in whole grains, some vegetables, eggs, and peanuts; iron, concentrated heavily in meat—especially liver—egg yolks, fish, and raisins; the trace minerals zinc and cobalt, found in seafood; calcium, found in dairy products; and, yes, calories (Schultz, 1990). Research also demonstrates the importance of consuming folic acid, which is found in leafy green vegetables. Pregnant women who take extra folic acid greatly reduce the risk of giving birth to babies with neural-tube defects, which can cause paralysis and death (Balluz et al., 2000; Hendricks et al., 2000; Honein et al., 2001; Thorpe et al., 2000).

Obesity during pregnancy increases the likelihood of neural-tube defects. Consider two studies reported in the April 10, 1996, issue of the *Journal of the American Medical Association.* Women who weighed 176 to 195 pounds before pregnancy were about twice as likely as women who weighed 100 to 130 pounds to bear children with neural-tube defects ("Obesity Is Linked," 1996). Women who weighed 242 pounds or more were four times as likely to have children with neural-tube defects. Note that these findings were for obese women only. Very tall women will normally weigh more than shorter women, so the studies' findings must be considered in terms of women's desirable weights for a given height. In these studies, folic acid supplements did not appear to prevent neural-tube defects in the babies of women who weighed more than 154 pounds.

Women who eat a well-rounded diet do not require food supplements. On the other hand, to be on the safe side, most doctors recommend vitamin and mineral supplements (Balluz et al., 2000).

Women can expect to gain quite a bit of weight during pregnancy because of the growth of the placenta, amniotic fluid, and the fetus itself. Women who do not restrict their diet during pregnancy normally will gain 25 to 35 pounds. Overweight women may gain less, and slender women may gain more. Regular weight gains are most desirable, about $\frac{1}{2}$ pound per week during the first half of pregnancy, and 1 pound per week during the second half. Sudden large gains or losses in weight should be discussed with the doctor.

Over the years, the pendulum has swung back and forth between views of ideal weight gains during pregnancy. Early in this century, it was believed that greater weight gains would assure proper nutrition for mother and fetus. During the 1960s and part of the 1970s, pregnant women were advised to watch their weight. It was felt that excess weight posed risks for the mother and might be hard to take off following pregnancy—concerns with some basis in fact. But the pendulum has swung again. It is now known that inadequate weight gain in pregnancy increases the chances of having a premature or low-birth-weight baby (Scholl et al., 1991). Women who gain 25 to 35 pounds during pregnancy are more likely to have healthy babies than those who gain less (Ekvall, 1993b). But a woman in the seventh or eighth month who finds herself overshooting a weight-gain target of, say, 25–30 pounds, should avoid a crash diet—especially during the period when the fetus is making its most dramatic gains in weight.

Teratogens and Health Problems of the Mother

Click *Physical Development* for more on teratogens.

Most of what the mother does for the embryo is not only remarkable, it is also healthful. But there are exceptions. Consider the case of teratogens. **Teratogens** (the word derives from frightening roots meaning "giving birth to monsters") are environmental agents that can harm the embryo or fetus. Teratogens include drugs that the mother ingests, such as thalidomide (connected with birth deformities) and alcohol, and substances that the mother's body produces, such as Rh-positive antibodies. Other kinds of teratogens are the heavy metals such as lead and mercury, which are toxic to the embryo. Hormones are healthful in countless ways, including the fact that they help maintain pregnancy; however, excessive quantities of hormones are harmful to the embryo. If the mother is exposed to radiation, that radiation can harm the embryo. Then of course, disease-causing organisms—also called *pathogens*—such as bacteria and viruses are also teratogens. In the case of pathogens, bigger is better for the embryo. That is, larger pathogens are less likely to pass through the placenta and affect the embryo. But smaller ones sneak through, including those that cause mumps, syphilis, measles, and chicken pox. Some disorders such as toxemia are not transmitted to the embryo or fetus but adversely affect the environment within which it develops. ***Question: Does it matter when, during pregnancy, a woman is exposed to a teratogen?***

Critical Periods of Vulnerability

Exposure to particular teratogens is most harmful during certain critical periods. These **critical periods** correspond to the times during which certain organs are developing. For example, the heart develops rapidly during the 3rd to 5th weeks after conception. As you can see in Figure 3.6, the heart is most vulnerable to certain teratogens at this time. The arms and legs, which develop later, are most vulnerable during the 4th through 8th weeks. Since the major organ systems differentiate during the embryonic stage, the embryo is generally more vulnerable to teratogens than the fetus. But many teratogens are harmful throughout the entire course of prenatal development.

teratogens Environmental influences or agents that can damage the embryo or fetus (from the Greek *teras,* meaning "monster").

critical period In this usage, a period during which an embryo is particularly vulnerable to a certain teratogen.

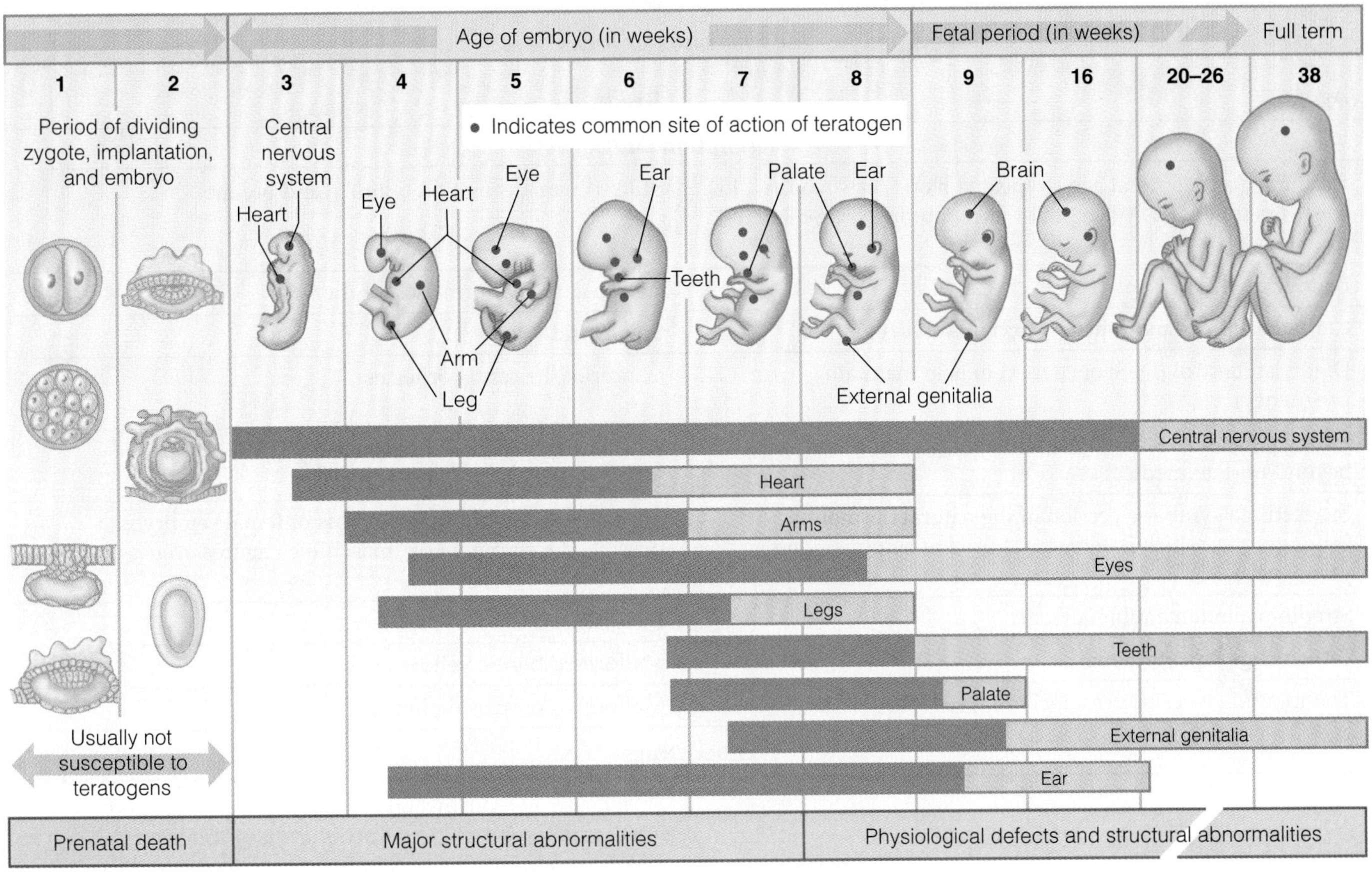

Figure 3.6
Critical Periods in Prenatal Development

Knowledge of the sequences of prenatal development allows one to understand why specific teratogens are most harmful during certain periods of prenatal development. Major structural abnormalities are most likely to occur when teratogens strike during the embryonic period.

Question: What are the effects of specific maternal health problems? We begin our discussion with rubella, discuss a number of teratogens that give rise to sexually transmitted infections (STIs), and consider the effects of some other health problems of the mother. Many of these effects are summarized in Table 3.2.

Rubella

What is commonly called German measles—**rubella**—is a viral infection. Women who contract rubella during the first month or two of pregnancy, when the major organ systems are undergoing rapid differentiation, may bear children who suffer from deafness, mental retardation, heart disease, or cataracts. Risk of these disorders declines as the pregnancy progresses.

Many adult women had rubella as children and acquired immunity in this way. Women who are uncertain as to whether they have had rubella may be tested. If they are not immune, they can be vaccinated prior to pregnancy. Inoculation during pregnancy is risky because the vaccine gives the mother a mild case of the disease, which can affect the unborn child.

Increased awareness of the dangers of rubella during pregnancy and of the protective effects of inoculation has led to a dramatic decline in the number of children born in the United States with defects caused by rubella, from about 20,000 cases in 1964–1965 to 28 in year 2000 (Centers for Disease Control and Prevention [CDC], 2001a).

rubella A viral infection that can cause retardation and heart disease in the embryo. Also called *German measles*.

TABLE 3.2 *Risks of Certain Agents to the Embryo and Fetus*

Agent	Risks
Prescription Drugs*	
Accutane (used to treat acne; repeated blood tests required to show that one is not pregnant or encountering drug-related problems)	Stillbirth, malformation of limbs and organs
Bendectin	Cleft palate, malformation of the heart
Carbamazepine (and other anticonvulsant drugs)	Spina bifida
Diethylstilbestrol (DES; once used to help maintain pregnancy)	Cancer of the cervix or testes
Strong general anesthesia during labor (sedation that goes beyond normal medical practice)	Anoxia, asphyxiation, brain damage
Progestin (a synthetic version of the natural hormone progesterone, which is sometimes used to help maintain pregnancy)	Masculinization of the sex organs of female embryos, possible development of "masculine" aggressiveness
Streptomycin (an antibiotic)	Deafness
Tetracycline (an antibiotic)	Malformed bones, yellow teeth
Thalidomide (several uses, including sedation)	Malformed or missing limbs
Other Drugs	
Alcohol	Fetal death, low birthweight, addiction, academic and intellectual problems, hyperactivity, distractibility, fetal alcohol syndrome (FAS, including characteristic facial features)
Aspirin (high doses)	Bleeding, respiratory problems
Caffeine (the stimulant found in coffee, tea, colas, chocolate)	Stimulates fetus (not necessarily a problem in itself), miscarriage, low birthweight
Cigarette smoke (carbon monoxide and the stimulant nicotine are transmitted through the placenta)	Stimulates fetus (not necessarily a problem in itself), premature birth, low birthweight, fetal death, academic problems, hyperactivity, short attention span
Opiates—heroin, morphine, others	Low birthweight, premature birth, addiction, toxemia
Marijuana	Tremors, startling, premature birth, birth defects, neurological problems

Syphilis

Caused by the *Treponema pallidum* bacterium, **syphilis** is an STI that can lead to miscarriage, **stillbirth,** or **congenital** syphilis. Routine blood tests early in pregnancy can diagnose syphilis and other problems.

The good news is that *Treponema pallidum* is vulnerable to antibiotics. Thus rates of syphilis are at an all-time low. Also, *Treponema pallidum* does not readily cross the placental membrane during the first months of pregnancy. Therefore, the fetus will probably not contract syphilis if an infected mother is treated successfully with antibiotics before the fourth month of pregnancy. The bad news is that a woman who is infected still has about a 40% chance of having a child who is stillborn or who dies shortly after birth (CDC, 1999). Although women can be effectively treated for syphilis during pregnancy, a baby who is born to a mother with untreated syphilis has a 40% to 70% chance of being infected with syphilis in utero (that is, of developing congenital syphilis). Infected babies may show no symptoms of syphilis when they are born, but they may develop them within a few weeks, if they are not treated promptly.

syphilis A sexually transmitted infection (STI) that, in advanced stages, can attack major organ systems.

stillbirth The birth of a dead fetus.

congenital Present at birth; resulting from the prenatal environment.

TABLE 3.2 *Risks of Certain Agents to the Embryo and Fetus (continued)*

Agent	Risks
	Vitamins†
Vitamin A (high doses)	Cleft palate, damage to the eyes
Vitamin D (high doses)	Mental retardation
	Pathogens (Disease-causing agents)
HIV	The virus that causes AIDS; physical deformity, mental retardation
Rubella (German measles)	Neurological impairment involving sensation and perception (vision, hearing), mental retardation, heart problems, cataracts
Syphilis (a sexually transmitted infection caused by the *Treponema pallidum* bacterium)	Infant mortality, seizures, mental retardation, sensory impairment (vision, hearing), liver damage, malformation of bones and teeth
	Environmental Hazards
Heavy metals (lead, mercury, zinc)	Mental retardation, hyperactivity, stillbirth, problems in memory formation
Paint fumes (heavy exposure)	Mental retardation
PCBs (polychlorinated biphenyls), dioxin, other insecticides and herbicides	Stillbirth, low birthweight, cognitive impairment, motor impairment
X-rays	Deformation of organs
	Biochemical Incompatibility with Mother
Rh antibodies	Infant mortality, brain damage

*Normally healthful even life-saving drugs can be harmful to the embryo and fetus. Women should inform their physicians when they are pregnant, may be pregnant, or are planning to become pregnant.

†Adequate intake of vitamins is essential to the well-being of the mother and the embryo and fetus. Most obstetricians advise pregnant women to take vitamin supplements. However, too much of a good thing can be harmful. In brief, don't do "megavitamins." And when in doubt, ask your obstetrician.

The symptoms of congenital syphilis include skin sores, a runny nose, which is sometimes bloody (and infectious), slimy patches in the mouth, inflamed bones in the arms and legs, swollen liver, jaundice, anemia, or a small head. Congenital syphilis can impair vision and hearing, damage the liver, or deform the bones and teeth. Untreated babies may develop mental retardation or have seizures. About 12% of babies with congenital syphilis die from the disease. Other maternal STIs that affect the fetus include chlamydia, genital herpes, and HIV/AIDS.

HIV/AIDS

The relatively new STI known as HIV/AIDS (human immunodeficiency virus/acquired immune deficiency syndrome) disables the body's immune system, leaving victims prey to a wide variety of fatal illnesses, including respiratory disorders and certain types of cancer. Current data indicate that nearly all individuals who are infected by HIV, the virus that causes **AIDS,** will develop the syndrome, which is almost always lethal unless treated with a combination of antiviral drugs (Carpenter et al., 2000). Yet the drugs do not work for everyone, and even when they have an effect, the eventual outcome remains in doubt (Rathus, Nevid, & Fichner-Rathus, 2002).

AIDS Acronym for *acquired immune deficiency syndrome.* A fatal, usually sexually transmitted infection (STI) that is caused by a virus (HIV) and cripples the body's immune system, making the person vulnerable to opportunistic diseases.

HIV can be transmitted by sexual relations, blood transfusions, sharing hypodermic needles while injecting drugs, and breast-feeding. Studies show that 14% to 32% of babies born to mothers who are infected with HIV end up infected themselves. Research suggests that about half of these infected infants are infected while in the uterus, and half are infected during childbirth (Mofenson, 2000; E. Wood et al., 2000). During childbirth, blood vessels in the mother and baby rupture, providing an opportunity for an exchange of blood and transmission of the virus. The virus also can be transmitted in breast milk. An African study followed mothers infected with HIV and their babies for 2 years. It found that the probability of transmission of HIV via breast milk was about 1 in 6 (16.2%) (Nduati et al., 2000). Children have also been infected with HIV through blood transfusions, but the proportion of children who contract HIV in this manner has decreased dramatically due to better blood testing (H. G. Klein, 2000).

Children from ethnic minority groups are disproportionately infected with HIV. African Americans account for more than half of the pediatric cases of HIV/AIDS, and Latino and Latina Americans account for almost one quarter of them (CDC, 2000a). Inner city neighborhoods, where there is widespread intravenous drug use, have been especially hard hit (CDC, 2000a). Death rates due to AIDS are much higher among African American and Latino and Latina American children (especially Latino and Latina children of Puerto Rican origin) than among European American children (CDC, 2000a), apparently because African Americans and Latino and Latina Americans have less access to high-quality health care.

Toxemia

Characterized by high blood pressure, **toxemia** is a life-threatening disease that may afflict women late in the second or early in the third trimester. The first stage of toxemia, preeclampsia, is characterized by protein in the urine, swelling from fluid retention, and high blood pressure and may be relatively mild. As preeclampsia worsens, the mother may have headaches and visual problems from the heightened blood pressure, along with abdominal pain. Eclampsia, the final stage, may bring convulsions, coma, and death of the mother or fetus. Women with toxemia often have **premature** or undersized babies. Preeclampsia and

toxemia A life-threatening disease that can afflict pregnant women and is characterized by high blood pressure.

premature Born before the full term of gestation (also referred to as *preterm*).

A Closer Look

Spacing Children the Goldilocks Way: What Is "Just Right"?

No, this feature is not about spacing children apart in the back seat to prevent them from slaughtering each other. It refers to the length of time it is advisable for a woman to wait between pregnancies. Some considerations are psychological: For example, is it desirable to have children close together so that they can be close companions and share experiences as they develop? Is it advisable to space them several years apart? By doing so, each might receive more parental attention during the early years of childhood. What about having them while you (the parent) are as young as possible so that you have more time for yourself during middle adulthood, when you can still enjoy it?

What of the health issues? Is it more healthful to have children back to back? To space them several years apart? If one is too hot and the other too cold, how do we define "just right"?

In a South American study, Conde-Agudelo and Belizán (2000) studied the health records of more than 450,000 Uruguayan women. They compared health outcomes for women who had spaced their children at short intervals (becoming pregnant within 5 months of bearing the earlier child) and at long intervals (5 years or more after bearing the earlier child). They compared these groups to women who had spaced their children at $1\frac{1}{2}$ to 2 years (18–23 months).

It turned out that having children back to back was riskiest in terms of maternal death, bleeding during the third trimester, premature rupture of membranes, and anemia. But women who spaced their children at 5 years or more also had health problems: significantly greater risks of preeclampsia and eclampsia.

In terms of maternal health, the spacing of $1\frac{1}{2}$ to 2 years may be "just right."

eclampsia are leading causes of pregnancy-related maternal deaths (MacKay, Berg, & Atrash, 2001).

Toxemia appears to be linked to malnutrition, but the causes are unclear. Ironically, undernourished women may gain weight rapidly through fluid retention, but their swollen appearance may then discourage eating. Pregnant women who gain weight rapidly but have not increased their food intake should consult their obstetricians.

Women who do not receive prenatal care are more than seven times as likely to die from preeclampsia and eclampsia as women who receive prenatal care (MacKay et al., 2001). African American women are more than three times as likely as European American women to die from preeclampsia or eclampsia. Both African American and European American women who receive prenatal care have a lower risk of death, but the reduction in risk of death is far greater for European American women than for African American women. It may thus be that the quality of prenatal care also plays a key role in the risk of death from preeclampsia and eclampsia (American College of Obstetricians and Gynecologists, 2001).

Rh Incompatibility

In **Rh incompatibility,** antibodies produced by the mother are transmitted to a fetus or newborn infant and cause brain damage or death. Rh is a blood protein that is found in the red blood cells of some individuals. Rh incompatibility occurs when a woman who does not have this factor, and is thus Rh negative, is carrying an Rh-positive fetus, which may happen if the father is Rh positive. This negative-positive combination occurs in about 10% of marriages in the United States but becomes a problem only in a minority of the resulting pregnancies. Rh incompatibility does not usually adversely affect a first child because women will typically not have formed antibodies to the Rh factor.

Since mother and fetus have separate circulatory systems, it is unlikely that Rh-positive fetal red blood cells will enter the mother's body. But the chances of an exchange of blood increase during childbirth, especially when the placenta detaches from the uterine wall. If an exchange of blood occurs, the mother produces Rh-positive antibodies to the baby's Rh-positive blood. These antibodies may enter the fetal bloodstream during subsequent pregnancies or deliveries and attack the red blood cells, causing anemia, mental deficiency, or death to the fetus.

If an Rh-negative mother is injected with a substance called Rh immune globulin within 72 hours after delivery of an Rh-positive baby, she will not develop the dangerous antibodies. A fetus or newborn child at risk of Rh disease may also receive a preventive blood transfusion, which removes the mother's antibodies from its blood.

Drugs Taken by the Parents

Rh antibodies can be lethal to children, and many other substances can have harmful effects. ***Question: What are the effects of drugs taken by the mother on prenatal development?*** In this section, we discuss the effects of various drugs on the unborn child—prescription drugs, over-the-counter drugs, and illegal drugs. Even commonly used medications, such as aspirin, may be harmful to the fetus. If a woman is pregnant or thinks she may be, it is advisable for her to consult her obstetrician before taking any drugs, not just prescription medications. A physician usually can recommend a safe and effective substitute for a drug that could potentially harm a developing fetus.

Thalidomide

The drug **thalidomide** was marketed in the early 1960s as a safe treatment for insomnia and nausea. It was available in Germany and England without prescription. Within a few years, over 10,000 babies with missing or stunted limbs had been born in these countries and elsewhere because their mothers had taken thalidomide during pregnancy (Gillio, 1999; National Library of Medicine, 1997).

Rh incompatibility A condition in which antibodies produced by the mother are transmitted to the child and may cause brain damage or death.

thalidomide A sedative used in the 1960s that has been linked to birth defects, especially deformed or absent limbs.

Thalidomide is still in use to treat problems ranging from dermatological conditions to Kaposi's sarcoma, a form of cancer that tends to affect people with HIV/AIDS (Dezube, 2000; Lipper et al., 2000).

Thalidomide provides a dramatic and tragic example of the critical periods of vulnerability to various teratogens. The extremities undergo rapid development during the last 4 weeks of the embryonic stage (see Figure 3.6). Thalidomide taken during this period of development almost invariably causes limb deformities. The Food and Drug Administration (1997) has issued extremely strict guidelines for the use of thalidomide, which are designed to ensure that people who use the drug are not pregnant or impregnating women.

Antibiotics

Several antibiotics may be harmful to the fetus. Tetracycline, which is frequently prescribed for bacterial infections, may lead to yellowed teeth and bone abnormalities. Other antibiotics have been implicated in hearing loss.

Hormones

Women at risk for miscarriages have been prescribed hormones such as progestin and DES to help maintain their pregnancies.

Progestin is similar in chemical composition to male sex hormones. When taken at about the time that male sex organs begin to differentiate in the embryo, progestin can masculinize the external sex organs of embryos with a female (XX sex chromosome) genotype. Progestin taken during pregnancy also has been linked to increased levels of aggressive behavior during childhood and to masculine play patterns in girls (Hines, 1990; Reinisch, Ziemba-Davis, & Sanders, 1991).

DES (short for diethylstilbestrol), a powerful estrogen, was given to many women during the 1940s and 1950s to help prevent miscarriage. As many as 3 million women took DES (Hatch et al., 1998). DES appears to have caused cervical and testicular cancer in some children of women who used it to maintain their pregnancies. Among daughters of DES users, about 1 in 1,000 will develop cancer in the reproductive tract. Daughters of DES users also are more likely to have babies who are premature or of low birthweight (Linn et al., 1988). However, it has not been shown that these women are more likely to develop cancers in other parts of the body (Hatch et al., 1998). Both daughters and sons whose mothers took DES have higher-than-average rates of infertility and immune system disorders.

Vitamins

While pregnant women are often prescribed daily multivitamins to maintain their own health and to promote the development of their fetuses, too much of a good thing can be dangerous. High doses of vitamins A and D have been associated with central nervous system damage, small head size, and heart defects.

Heroin and Methadone

Maternal addiction to heroin or methadone is linked to low birthweight, prematurity, and toxemia. Narcotics such as heroin and methadone readily cross the placental membrane. These drugs are highly addictive, and the fetuses of women who use them regularly during pregnancy can become addicted to them.

The addicted newborns may be given the narcotic shortly after birth so they will not suffer withdrawal symptoms such as muscle tremors, fever, intestinal problems, difficulty in breathing, and, in severe cases, convulsions and death. The neonates are then usually withdrawn gradually from the drug. Still, infant mortality, usually from respiratory problems, is more likely to occur among the children of mothers addicted to heroin or methadone. Behavioral effects still are apparent years later. For example, infants whose mothers were on methadone maintenance programs throughout pregnancy are slower in motor and language development at the age of 2 years (Hans, Henson, & Jeremy, 1992). During the elementary school years, methadone-exposed children exhibit more anxiety and aggression than do non-exposed children (deCubas & Field, 1993).

progestin A hormone used to maintain pregnancy that can cause masculinization of the fetus.

DES Abbreviation for *diethylstilbestrol,* a powerful estrogen that has been linked to cancer in the reproductive organs of children whose mothers used the hormone when pregnant.

Marijuana (Cannabis)

Using marijuana during pregnancy apparently poses a number of risks for the fetus. For example, babies of women who regularly used marijuana have been found to show increased tremors and startling and failure to **habituate** to a stimulus, possibly indicating immature development of the central nervous system (Dahl et al., 1995).

Research into the cognitive effects of the mother's using marijuana during pregnancy suggests that there may be no impairment in global intellectual functioning per se (Fried & Smith, 2001). However, problem solving and decision making do appear to be impacted. Ability to pay attention and visual analysis/hypothesis testing are particularly affected in children assessed beyond the toddler stage.

One study (Goldschmidt, Day, & Richardson, 2000) assessed the behavioral problems of 10-year-olds whose mothers had used marijuana while pregnant. All in all, this prospective study included the children of 635 mothers aged 18–42. The study found that prenatal use of marijuana was significantly related to increased hyperactivity, impulsivity, and problems in paying attention as measured by the Swanson, Noland, and Pelham checklist; increased delinquency as measured by the Child Behavior Checklist; and increased delinquency and aggressive behavior as measured by teacher report, using the Teacher's Report Form. In seeking the connection between maternal marijuana use and delinquency, the researchers found that marijuana exposure affected the ability to pay attention, thus impairing ability to profit from the classroom experience and studying, and reducing capacity to conform to social rules and norms. This is a pathway to delinquency.

Reflect

Do you believe that the information presented in this text about the effects of drugs used by pregnant women consists of "phony horror stories," or do you believe it is as up to date and accurate as possible? Explain.

Researchers have also found that maternal use of marijuana predisposes offspring to dependence on opiates (narcotics derived from the opium poppy). The fetal brain, like the adult brain, has cannabinoid receptors—called CB-1 receptors—and other structures that are altered by exposure to marijuana. The alterations make the individual more sensitive to the reinforcing properties of opiates, even in adulthood (Navarro & Rodriguez de Fonseca, 1998). Research with laboratory rats suggests that daughters may be more vulnerable than sons to this effect of exposure to marijuana in utero (Ambrosio et al., 1999).

Cocaine

Most studies suggest that prenatal exposure to cocaine can have harmful effects on the child. Abuse of cocaine by women during pregnancy increases the risk of stillbirth, low birthweight, and birth defects (Coles et al., 1992; Woods et al., 1993). The infants are often excitable, irritable, easily overstimulated, or lethargic. The more heavily exposed to cocaine they are in utero, the more problems they have with jitteriness and concentration (Singer et al., 2000). As they get older, they are more likely to show learning and behavioral disabilities such as hyperactivity, disorganization, delayed language and cognitive development, and problems relating to others.

One study matched 56 infants aged 12–28 months who were exposed prenatally to cocaine with 56 infants who were not (Chapman, 2000a). The infants were matched according to sex, marital status of the mother, present residence, and ethnic background. All infants were administered the Mullen Scales of Early Learning, the Bayley Scales of Infant Development–II (BSID–II), and the Behavior Rating Scale of the BSID–II. The results showed that the infants and toddlers who were prenatally exposed to cocaine obtained significantly lower scores in the areas of receptive language development (that is, understanding language) and expressive language development (producing language). The investigator found that the differences in language development persisted at the ages of 48–64 months (Chapman, 2000b). Yet another study examined 458 children who were 6 years old (Delaney-Black et al., 2000). Of this group, 204 had been exposed to cocaine in utero. Children who had been exposed to cocaine were 2.4 times as likely to lag in their expressive language development as children who had not been exposed to cocaine.

Another study examined the cognitive functioning of 236 infants at the ages of 8 and 18 months (Alessandri, Bendersky, & Lewis, 1998). Of these infants, 37 were heavily exposed to cocaine in utero, 30 were lightly exposed, and the remaining

habituate To pay less attention to a repeated stimulus.

169 were not exposed at all. As in the Chapman (2000a) study, the Bayley Scales of Infant Development–II were used to assess cognitive functioning. The infants who had been exposed to cocaine in utero were found to be at greater risk for health problems. On the other hand, the groups did not differ in their motor development. Infant groups did not differ at 8 months on cognitive measures; but by 18 months, the cognitive development scores of infants who were heavily exposed to cocaine in utero decreased when compared with the scores of infants who were not exposed to cocaine in utero.

Many studies have found that prenatal exposure to cocaine is connected with problems in arousal and behavioral regulation in infants. That is, the infants become overly aroused by stressors and do not recover as rapidly as infants who were not exposed to cocaine in utero. In one such study, 8-week-old infants who had been exposed to cocaine did not recover their normal heart rates as rapidly as controls did after they were exposed to a stressor (Bard et al., 2000). This finding fits with research that shows infants exposed to cocaine to be more "jittery" (Singer et al., 2000).

Reflect

What is your personal reaction to the kinds of treatments to which the rats in the experiments by Huber, Campbell, and Overstreet were exposed? Why do researchers conduct such experiments when correlational evidence with humans is available? In your view, are such experiments justified by the information they provide?

Numerous experiments have been conducted with laboratory rodents to help determine the effects of prenatal exposure to cocaine. In one study, pregnant rats were given cocaine during days 12–21 of gestation, whereas controls received no cocaine (Huber et al., 2001). The rat pups were then exposed to stressors such as cold-water swimming and tail-flicks. The pups exposed to cocaine showed less tolerance of the stressors—as measured by behaviors such as tail twitches and convulsions—than controls. Another study found that such group differences in response to stressors endure into rat adulthood, that is, 90–120 days of age (Campbell et al., 2000). A third study found that even as adults (120 days old), rats who had been exposed to cocaine in utero were less capable than nonexposed rats of coping with a forced swim (as shown by immobility) (Overstreet et al., 2000). The cocaine-exposed rats were also more startled by sudden noises and less likely to seek social interaction (social comfort?) with other rats.

In another study, rabbit embryos were exposed to cocaine during various periods of prenatal brain development (Stanwood, Washington, & Levitt, 2001). The researchers found that a structure in the brain called the anterior cingulate cortex (ACC) showed long-term changes in development. The ACC is involved in the functions of attention and self-control.

Some of the developmental problems of children exposed to cocaine during fetal life may not be due directly to the drug itself. Cocaine-abusing parents often do not nurture or supervise their children adequately (Alessandri et al., 1998; Finch, Vega, & Kolody, 2001). This pattern of parental neglect and rejection may help explain why many children of cocaine abusers are insecurely attached to their parents (Rodning, Beckwith, & Howard, 1991). Studies find that children exposed to cocaine-abusing parents at home had more serious behavior problems than those exposed to cocaine during prenatal life (Finch et al., 2001; Youngstrom, 1991). So it appears that inadequate parenting can compound the effects of early drug exposure. By the same token, good parenting can help counteract the effects of early exposure to drugs. Research shows that if babies who have been exposed to drugs in the uterus are raised in a relatively warm, stable, and caring home environment, the long-term developmental outcome may be positive (Youngstrom, 1991; Zuckerman & Frank, 1992).

Having noted this body of research, let me point out that a review of the literature published in the prestigious *Journal of the American Medical Association* argued that carefully conducted studies do *not* prove that prenatal exposure to cocaine is harmful (Frank et al., 2001). The review pointed out the weaknesses of much of this research with humans, such as the confounding factors of maternal cocaine abuse with polydrug abuse and general neglect of health during pregnancy. The review also pointed to inconsistent clinical observations (sometimes this, sometimes that). I will agree that the total body of research on the effects of prenatal exposure to cocaine has been inconsistent and, all in all, less than perfect. However, as noted in a letter to the editor, the review seemed to ignore reports of subtle but consistent deficits in cognitive functioning and attention among children in early and middle childhood (Stanwood et al., 2001). The review also tended to avoid the carefully conducted studies with rats and other animals that reveal developmental changes that are similar to those reported in children.

I would summarize this literature by saying that there is ample reason to be concerned about the effects of prenatal exposure to cocaine. Unless experimental research findings with rodents and other animals are found to be inconsistent or, simply, wrong, I will believe that it is foolish to rule out prenatal exposure to cocaine as a health hazard for children.

Alcohol

What is there to say about alcohol—the social lubricant, the ubiquitous tranquilizer, the socially acceptable drug (when taken in moderation)? Actually, quite a bit. Drinking by a pregnant woman poses some risks for the embryo and fetus. Heavy drinking may actually be lethal to the fetus and neonate. It is also connected with deficiencies and deformities in growth. Some children of heavy drinkers develop **fetal alcohol syndrome,** or FAS (Barr & Streissguth, 2001; Olofsson, 200). Babies with FAS are often smaller than normal, and so are their brains. They have a distinct pattern of facial features, characterized by widely spaced eyes, an underdeveloped upper jaw, and a flat-looking nose. Children with FAS have been known to have malformation of the limbs, poor coordination, and cardiovascular problems. A number of psychological characteristics are connected with FAS and appear to reflect dysfunction of the brain: mental retardation, hyperactivity, distractibility, lessened verbal fluency, and learning disabilities (Astley & Clarren, 2001; Schonfeld et al., 2001). A cluster of cognitive motor problems includes deficits in speech and hearing, practical reasoning, and visual-motor coordination (Adnams et al., 2001).

The characteristic facial deformities of FAS diminish as the child moves into adolescence and most such children catch up in height and weight (Spohr, Willms, & Steinhaussen, 1993). But the intellectual, academic, and behavioral deficits of individuals with FAS persist into adolescence and adulthood (Autti-Raemoe, 2000). Academic and intellectual problems relative to peers range from verbal difficulties to deficiency in spatial memory (Kaemingk & Halverson, 2000; Timler & Olswang, 2001). Studies by Ann Streissguth and her colleagues (1991; Olson et al., 1992) found that the average academic functioning of adolescents and young adults with FAS was at the second- to fourth-grade level. Maladaptive behaviors such as poor judgment, distractibility, and difficulty perceiving social cues were common.

Certain ethnic groups appear to be more vulnerable to the effects of alcohol than others, perhaps because of genetic factors. African American women are seven times more likely to have children affected by alcohol intake during pregnancy than are European American women with similar drinking habits. And FAS is 30 times more common among Native Americans than European Americans (Rosenthal, 1990b).

What about the effects of what is commonly called "social drinking"? Many physicians allow their pregnant patients a glass of wine with dinner. However, research has found that even moderate drinkers place their offspring at increased risk for a somewhat less severe set of effects known as **fetal alcohol effect (FAE).** For example, one study of nearly 32,000 women reported that pregnant women who had as few as one or two drinks a day were more likely to miscarry and to have growth-retarded babies than were women who did not drink at all (Mills et al., 1984). By the age of 4, children whose mothers had only three to five drinks a week during midpregnancy show deficits that may predict academic difficulties. They show longer reaction time and attention deficits, lower intelligence, and poorer motor functioning than 4-year-olds whose mothers did not drink during pregnancy (Barr et al., 1990; Streissguth, Barr, & Sampson., 1992).

The reported effects of maternal drinking during prenatal development are based on correlational evidence. No researcher would attempt to randomly assign some pregnant women to drinking and others to abstention. However, researchers have done so in experiments with animals, and the evidence gained in this manner supports the correlational evidence with humans. For example, research with animals finds that exposure to alcohol during gestation is connected with retarded growth, the facial malformations characteristic of FAS,

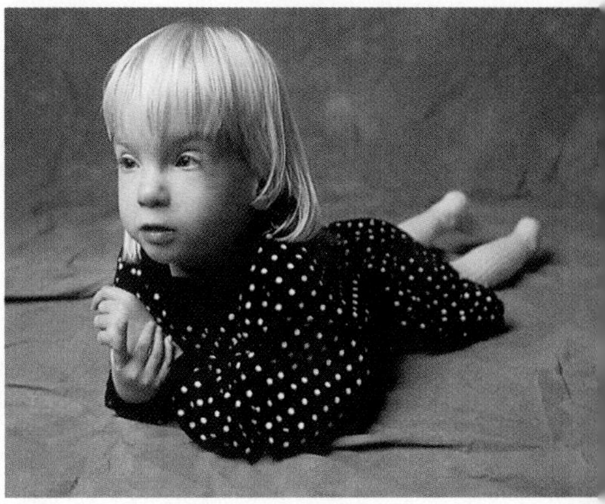

Fetal Alcohol Syndrome (FAS)

The children of many mothers who drink alcohol during pregnancy exhibit FAS. This syndrome is characterized by developmental lags and such facial features as an underdeveloped upper jaw, a flattened nose, and widely spaced eyes.

fetal alcohol syndrome (FAS) A cluster of symptoms shown by children of women who drink heavily during pregnancy, including characteristic facial features and mental retardation.

fetal alcohol effect (FAE) A cluster of symptoms less severe than those of FAS shown by children of women who drink moderately during pregnancy.

deficiencies in the functioning of the immune system, and structural and chemical differences in the development of the central nervous system (Ponnappa & Rubin, 2000).

The safest course for a pregnant woman is to abstain from alcohol. If she does drink, small amounts of alcohol may be less risky than larger amounts, *but there is no guaranteed safe minimum*. It also makes sense for women who are trying to become pregnant—or who are not taking precautions against becoming pregnant—to assume that they may conceive a child any month and to modify their drinking habits accordingly.

And what of the father's drinking habits? The father's alcohol consumption just before conception may create risks. In one study, for example, newborns whose fathers regularly drank at least two glasses of wine or two bottles of beer per day prior to conception weighed less than babies whose fathers drank only occasionally (Merewood, 1991).

Caffeine

Many pregnant women consume caffeine in the form of coffee, tea, soft drinks, chocolate, and nonprescription drugs. Until recently, research into caffeine's effects on the developing fetus had shown inconsistent findings. Some studies reported no adverse findings (Mills et al., 1993; McDonald, Armstrong, & Sloan, 1992a). But others found that pregnant women who take in a good deal of caffeine are more likely than non-users to have a miscarriage or a low-birthweight baby (Klebanoff et al., 1999; McDonald, Armstrong, & Sloan, 1992b; Parazzini et al., 1998).

A Swedish study suggests that intake of caffeine during pregnancy may well be a risky business. Sven Cnattingius and his colleagues (2000) performed a population-based study of early miscarriage in Uppsala County, Sweden. They compared 562 women who had had a miscarriage at 6 to 12 weeks of gestation with 953 women who had not. They obtained information on caffeine intake by means of personal interviews. They also obtained information on the smoking habits of the women. Among nonsmokers, it turned out that the more caffeine the women ingested, the more likely they were to have a miscarriage, with the heaviest users of caffeine (those likely to have the equivalent of several cups of coffee a day) more than twice as likely as non-users to have a miscarriage. (These findings are inconsistent with those of the study by Mark Klebanoff and his colleagues [1999], who found that low to moderate caffeine intake did not increase the risk of miscarriage.) Ironically, intake of caffeine in the Cnattingius study did not increase the chances of miscarriage among women who smoked. But do not think of smoking as protecting the embryo and fetus; as amply documented in the following pages, smoking is connected with multiple risks for the baby, including stillbirth.

The Cnattingius study (like the Klebanoff and Parazzini studies) was correlational and not experimental. Pregnant women were *not* assigned at random to use or not to use caffeine. (Consider the ethical problems in attempting to use such a method.) Thus it could be that other factors, such as stress or fatigue, contributed both to caffeine intake and the probability of miscarriage. Put it this way: If you're going to drink coffee, tea, or colas while you are pregnant, it may be wisest to select decaffeinated beverages. It may be that a little caffeine won't hurt, but we cannot be certain of that.

Cigarettes

Cigarette smoke contains many ingredients, including the stimulant nicotine, the gas carbon monoxide, and hydrocarbons ("tars"), which are carcinogens. Fortunately, only the first two of these, the nicotine and the carbon monoxide, are known to pass through the placenta and reach the fetus. That's the end of the fortunate news. Nicotine stimulates the fetus, but its long-term effects are uncertain. Carbon monoxide is toxic in that it decreases the amount of oxygen available to the fetus. Oxygen deprivation is connected with cognitive and behavioral problems, including impaired motor development. The cognitive difficulties include academic delays, learning disabilities, and mental retardation. Not all children of smokers will develop these problems, but many will clearly not function as well cognitively as they would have if they had not been exposed to cigarette smoke.

Pregnant women who smoke are likely to deliver smaller babies than nonsmokers (Haslam & Draper, 2001; McDonald et al., 1992b). In addition, their babies are more likely to be stillborn or die soon after birth (McDonald et al., 1992b; Tizabi et al., 2000).

Maternal smoking may also have long-term negative effects on development. Children whose mothers smoked during pregnancy are more likely to show short attention spans, hyperactivity, lower cognitive and language scores, and relatively poor school performance (Fried, O'Connell, & Watkinson, 1992). In one study, women who smoked during pregnancy were 50% more likely than women who did not to have children whose intelligence test scores placed them in the mentally retarded range (scores under 70) when the children were 10 years old (Drews et al., 1996). Women who smoked at least a pack a day were 85% more likely to have mentally retarded children.

Okay—smoking during pregnancy poses significant threats to the fetus. So why do pregnant women do it? Are they ignorant of the risks to their children? Perhaps. In fact, we can assert that despite decades of public education efforts, some women remain unaware that smoking will hurt the fetus. But the majority of American women who smoke are aware of the threat. Yet they say they can't quit, or they can't suspend smoking until the baby is born. Why? They offer many reasons: Some claim that they are under too much stress to stop smoking, although cigarette smoking actually contributes to stress; it's not a one-way ticket to relaxation. Others smoke to fight feelings of depression (nicotine is an upper and depression is a downer), because "everybody" around them smokes (often, "everybody" translates into the husband), or they just don't have the willpower (or perhaps I should say, the "won't-power") to deal with the withdrawal symptoms of quitting (Haslam & Draper, 2001; Ludman et al., 2000; Rodriguez, Bohlin, & Lindmark, 2000). Some parents simply deny that their smoking is likely to harm their children, despite knowledge to the contrary (Haslam & Draper, 2001). That kind of reasoning also goes something like this: Why worry about quitting smoking? I could be run over by a truck tomorrow. (Yes, one can be run over by a truck, but one can also look both ways before crossing the street, and one can choose to act as if one is in control of one's life.[1])

A father's smoking may also hold dangers. Men who smoke are more likely than nonsmokers to produce abnormal sperm. Babies of fathers who smoke have higher rates of birth defects and infant mortality and lower birthweights. Fathers who smoke around the time of conception increase their child's risk of later developing cancer (Merewood, 1991).

Smoking after the baby is born also is harmful. Children of smokers are more likely to develop respiratory infections, asthma, and certain kinds of cancer. They also score lower on tests of reasoning ability and vocabulary and show more behavior problems than children of nonsmokers (Chilmonczyk et al., 1993; Martinez , Cline, & Burrows, 1992; U.S. Environmental Protection Agency, 1993; Weitzman, Gortmaker, & Sóbol, 1992).

Why Start a New Life Under a Cloud?

This American Cancer Society poster dramatizes the risks posed by maternal smoking during pregnancy.

Environmental Hazards

Mothers know when they are ingesting drugs, but there are many (many!) other substances in the environment that they may take in unknowingly. We are all exposed to these environmental hazards, which are collectively termed pollution. ***Question: What are the effects of environmental hazards during pregnancy?***

Prenatal exposure to heavy metals such as lead, mercury, and zinc threatens the development of children. In one longitudinal study, newborns who had even

[1] About the sermonizing—you're reading a book written by a psychologist. Don't expect recipes for soup.

mildly elevated levels of lead in their umbilical cord blood showed slower mental development at 1 and 2 years of age (Bellinger et al., 1987). By age 6, the cognitive functioning of these children had improved if they no longer were exposed to elevated lead levels in the home. But those children who continued to be exposed to higher lead levels still showed cognitive deficits (Bellinger et al., 1991).

One study of the effects of prenatal exposure to lead recruited 442 children in Yugoslavia (Wasserman et al., 2000). Some of the children lived in a town with a smelter; the others did not. The children received intelligence testing at the ages of 3, 4, 5, and 7, using Wechsler and other scales. The researchers found that the children from the town with the smelter obtained somewhat lower intelligence test scores. It is conceivable, of course, that people who choose to live in a town without a smelter differ from those who are willing to cozy up to one.

Experiments with rodents support the correlational findings with humans. For example, mice exposed to lead in utero do not form memories as well as those who are free of prenatal exposure to lead (de Oliveira et al., 2001). Research with rats finds that prenatal exposure to lead decreases the levels of neurotransmitters (the chemical messengers of the brain) in all areas of the brain, but especially in the hippocampus. The hippocampus is highly involved in the formation of memories.

Prenatal exposure to lead is connected with more than cognitive deficits. One study, for example, found that exposure to lead was connected with higher scores on the delinquency scale of a psychological test, among children aged 4 and 5 (Wasserman et al., 2001). However, delinquency is also associated with cognitive deficits, so it remains difficult in such correlational studies to tease out cause and effect.

Reflect

Are you aware of the presence of heavy metals and other environmental hazards in the area in which you live and attend school? If not, why not?

The devastating effects of mercury on the developing fetus were first recognized among the Japanese who lived around Minimata Bay. Industrial waste containing mercury was dumped into the bay and accumulated in the fish that were a major food source for local residents. Children born to women who had eaten the fish during pregnancy often were profoundly retarded and neurologically damaged (Vorhees & Mollnow, 1987). Prenatal exposure to even small amounts of mercury and other heavy metals such as cadmium and chromium can produce subtle deficits in cognitive functioning and physical health (Lewis et al., 1992).

Experimental research with rats finds that prenatal exposure to mercury leads to degeneration of cells in the amygdala and hippocampus (Kakita et al., 2000). The hippocampus, as noted earlier, is involved in the formation of memories (maintenance of learning). The amygdala is involved in emotional responses, especially rage and fear, learning, and memory. It helps individuals focus attention, and paying attention is vital to learning. (So read this book carefully.) Thus there is every reason to think that prenatal exposure to mercury, like lead, can cause problems in learning and memory.

Polychlorinated biphenyls (PCBs) are chemicals used in many industrial products. Like mercury, they accumulate in fish that feed in polluted waters. Newborns whose mothers had consumed PCB-contaminated fish from Lake Michigan were smaller and showed poorer motor functioning and less responsiveness than newborns whose mothers had not eaten these fish. Furthermore, even those PCB-exposed infants who appeared normal at birth showed deficits in memory at 7 months and at 4 years of age (Jacobson & Jacobson, 1990; Jacobson et al., 1992).

An unfortunate natural experiment in the effects of prenatal exposure to PCBs took place in Taiwan during the late 1970s, when a group of people accidentally ingested contaminated rice oil. Children born to mothers who ate the rice had characteristic signs of PCB poisoning, including hyperpigmented skin. The researchers (Lai et al., 2001). had the opportunity to compare the cognitive development of 118 children born to exposed mothers with that of other children in the community. The children were all followed through the age of 12 and tested with instruments including the Bayley Scale for Infant Development, the Chinese version of the Stanford-Binet IQ test, and two nonverbal intelligence tests. The children of mothers who ate the contaminated rice scored lower than the control children on each of these methods of measurement throughout the observation period. It appears that prenatal exposure to PCBs has long-term harmful effects on cognitive development.

Fetal exposure to radiation in high doses can cause defects in a number of organs, including the eyes, central nervous system, and skeleton (Michel, 1989). Pregnant women who were exposed to atomic radiation during the bombing of Hiroshima and Nagasaki in World War II gave birth to babies who were more likely to be mentally retarded in addition to being physically deformed (Yamazaki & Schull, 1990). The effects of exposure to low levels of radiation remain unclear. The best advice for a pregnant woman is to avoid any unnecessary exposure to X-rays.

Until recently, studies of the effects of environmental hazards on the fetus focused on the pregnant woman's exposure to these dangers. Research suggests that men exposed to such substances as lead and nuclear radiation also may produce children with serious abnormalities (Merewood, 1991; Purvis, 1990). For example, children of fathers employed in jobs with high exposure to lead had three times more kidney tumors than children whose fathers were not exposed (Davis, 1991). Another study found a higher incidence of leukemia among children whose fathers worked in nuclear plants where they were exposed to high levels of radiation prior to the children's conception ("British Study Finds," 1990).

Maternal Stress

Although pregnancy can be a time of immense gratification for women, it can also be a time of stress. The baby might be unplanned and unwanted. Parents might not have the financial resources or the room for the child. The mother might be experiencing physical discomforts because of the pregnancy. She might also fear the birth process itself or be concerned as to whether the baby will be normal. ***Question: What, then are the apparent effects of maternal stress on the child?***

But how does a mother's emotional state influence her unborn child? Although emotions are psychological feeling states, they also have physiological components. For example, they are linked to the secretion of hormones such as **adrenaline.** Adrenaline stimulates the mother's heart rate, respiratory rate, and many other bodily functions. Hormones pass through the placenta and also have a physiological influence on the unborn child.

The effects of maternal stress on the fetus are open to question. Some reports indicate that anxious, stressed mothers are more likely to have pregnancy and labor complications and premature or low-birthweight babies (Lobel, Dunkel-Schetter, & Scrimshaw, 1992). Other studies show that the infants of emotionally anxious or distressed women have high activity levels both before and after birth. These babies have also been described as irritable, poor sleepers, and prone to gastrointestinal problems (Van den Bergh, 1990).

There are also confounding factors in the research on the effects of maternal stress. For example, pregnant women who are under stress may be more likely to consume alcohol or smoke cigarettes. The apparent effects of prenatal stress might actually be due to exposure to these harmful substances.

While some reports on the effects of maternal stress have been alarming, other evidence on the issue is less convincing. It makes sense for pregnant women to regulate the stresses affecting them, just as it makes sense for all of us to be aware of and regulate the stresses to which we are exposed. But it may be that the effects of maternal stress upon the fetus are mostly temporary.

The Mother's Age

What, then, of the mother's age? ***Question: Is the mother's age connected with the outcome of pregnancy?***

The mother's age matters. From a biological vantage point, the 20s may be the ideal age for women to bear children. Teenage mothers have a higher incidence of

adrenaline A hormone that generally arouses the body, increasing the heart and respiration rates.

infant mortality and children with low birthweight. Early teenagers who become pregnant may place a burden on bodies that have not adequately matured to facilitate pregnancy and childbirth. Teenage mothers also are less educated and less likely to seek prenatal care. All of these factors are associated with a greater likelihood of high-risk pregnancy (Rossetti, 1990).

What about women over the age of 30? Women's fertility declines gradually until the mid-30s, after which it declines more rapidly. Women beyond their middle 30s may have passed the point at which their reproductive systems function most efficiently. As noted, women possess all their ova in immature form at birth. Over 30 years, these cells are exposed to the slings and arrows of an outrageous environment of toxic wastes, chemical pollutants, and radiation, thus increasing the risk of chromosomal abnormalities such as Down syndrome (Behrman et al., 2000). Women who wait until their 30s or 40s to have children also increase the likelihood of having stillborn or preterm babies (Cnattingius et al., 1992). But with adequate prenatal care, the risk of bearing a premature or unhealthy baby still is relatively small even for older first-time mothers (Berkowitz et al., 1990). This news should be encouraging for women who have delayed, or plan to delay, bearing children until their 30s or 40s.

Whatever the age of the mother, the events of childbirth provide some of the most memorable moments in the lives of parents. In Chapter 4, we examine the process of birth and the characteristics of the newborn child.

Review

(21) Women who are too slender risk preterm deliveries and babies who are low in _________. (22) Mothers who ingest folic acid reduce the risk of giving birth to babies with _________ tube defects. (23) _________ are environmental agents that can harm the developing embryo or fetus. (24) Women who contract _________ during the embryonic period may bear children who suffer from deafness, mental retardation, heart disease, or cataracts. (25) Women (can or cannot?) be successfully treated for syphilis during pregnancy. (26) Treatment with the drug _________ reduces the risk that a mother will transmit HIV to her baby during childbirth. (27) Toxemia is mainly characterized by high _________ pressure. (28) In _________ incompatibility, antibodies produced by the mother are transmitted to a fetus or newborn infant and cause brain damage or death. (29) The drug _________, a treatment for insomnia and nausea, causes missing or stunted limbs in babies. (30) The antibiotic _________ may cause yellowed teeth and bone abnormalities in the baby. (31) _________ was prescribed to help women maintain their pregnancies, but caused cervical and testicular cancer in some of their children. (32) The babies of women who regularly used _________ during pregnancy have been found to show increased tremors and startling and failure to habituate to a stimulus. (33) Maternal use of cocaine during pregnancy can result in stillbirth, (high or low?) birthweight, and irritable infants. (34) Heavy maternal use of alcohol is linked to _________ alcohol syndrome (FAS). (35) Infants with FAS are often undersized and show distinct facial features, including (narrowly or widely?) spaced eyes. (36) A Swedish study suggests that the heaviest users of caffeine are more than twice as likely as non-users to have a _________. (37) Women who smoke during pregnancy deprive their fetuses of _________, sometimes resulting in stillbirth and persistent academic problems. (38) Fetal exposure to the heavy metals lead and mercury can (slow or accelerate?) mental development.

Pulling It Together: How does knowledge of critical periods of prenatal development allow us to predict—and possibly prevent—the effects of various agents on the embryo?

Recite Recite Recite Recite

1. What happens during the germinal stage of prenatal development?

During the germinal stage, the single cell formed by the union of sperm and egg divides repeatedly but does not gain in mass. It travels through a Fallopian tube to the uterus and then travels within the uterus prior to implantation. The dividing cell mass takes the form of a fluid-filled ball of cells called a blastocyst. Distinct inner layers of cells form within the embryonic disk. The outer part of the blastocyst, the trophoblast, differentiates into membranes that will protect and nourish the embryo.

2. How does the dividing mass of cells obtain nourishment during the germinal stage?

Prior to implantation, the dividing cluster of cells is nourished by the yolk of the original egg cell. Once implanted in the uterine wall, it obtains nourishment from the mother. Many women miscarry in the germinal stage, often without realizing they had conceived.

3. What happens during the embryonic stage of prenatal development?

The embryonic stage lasts from implantation until about the 8th week of development, a time during which the major body organ systems differentiate. Development follows cephalocaudal and proximodistal trends. The outer layer of the embryonic disk, or ectoderm, develops into the nervous system, sensory organs, nails, hair, teeth, and skin. Two ridges form the neural tube, from which the nervous system will develop. The inner layer, or endoderm, forms the digestive and respiratory systems, the liver, and the pancreas. The mesoderm, or middle layer, becomes excretory, reproductive, and circulatory systems; the muscles; the skeleton; and the inner layer of the skin.

4. When does the heart begin to beat?

The heart begins to beat during the 4th week. Toward the end of the first month, arm and leg buds appear and the face takes shape. The nervous system has also begun to develop. By the end of the second month, the limbs are elongating, the facial features are becoming distinct, teeth buds have formed, the kidneys are working, and the liver is producing red blood cells.

5. How do some babies develop into girls and others develop into boys?

By 5 to 6 weeks, the embryo has undifferentiated sex organs that resemble female structures. A group of genes, including SRY (sex-determining region Y) causes male sexual differentiation and may be connected with patterns of mating and aggression. SRY binds to and distorts DNA, altering the expression of other genes, leading to the development of testes. Testes produce male sex hormones called androgens that spur development of male genital organs. Testosterone spurs the differentiation of the male duct system. Toward the end of the embryonic stage, dihydrotestosterone (DHT) spurs the formation of the external male genital organs.

6. How does the embryo get nourishment from its mother?

How does it eliminate waste products? The embryo and fetus exchange nutrients and wastes with the mother through a mass of tissue called the placenta. The umbilical cord connects the fetus to the placenta.

7. Do germs or drugs in the mother pass through the placenta and affect the baby?

Many do, including the germs that cause syphilis and rubella. Some drugs also pass through, including aspirin, narcotics, alcohol, and tranquilizers.

8. What happens during the fetal stage of prenatal development?

The fetal stage lasts from the end of the embryonic stage until birth. The fetus begins to turn at the 9th or 10th week. By the end of the first trimester, the major organ systems have been formed. The second trimester is characterized by maturation of organs and gains in size. During the second trimester, the fetus advances from 1 ounce to 2 pounds, and from about 3 inches to 14 inches. By the end of the second trimester, the fetus opens and shuts its eyes, sucks its thumb, alternates between periods of wakefulness and sleep, and responds to light and sounds. During the third trimester, the heart and lungs become increasingly capable of sustaining independent life. The fetus gains about $5\frac{1}{2}$ pounds and doubles in length.

Recite Recite Recite Recite

9. Why did my Aunt Margaret play classical music when she was seven months' pregnant?

We can't speak for your Aunt Margaret, but the fetus responds to sound waves by the 13th week of pregnancy. Newborn babies prefer their mother's voice to that of other women, apparently because of prenatal exposure to it.

10. When does the mother begin to detect fetal movements?

The mother usually detects fetal movements during the fourth month. By the end of the second trimester, the fetus turns somersaults.

11. How does the mother's nutrition affect prenatal development?

Malnutrition in the mother, especially during the last trimester, has been linked to low birthweight, prematurity, stunted growth, retardation of brain development, cognitive deficiencies, and behavioral problems. Obesity during pregnancy increases the likelihood of neural-tube defects. Pregnant women who take folic acid reduce the risk of neural-tube defects in their babies. Women normally gain 25–35 pounds during pregnancy.

12. Does it matter when, during pregnancy, a woman is exposed to a teratogen?

Often, it does. Teratogens are environmental agents that can harm the developing embryo or fetus. Exposure to particular teratogens is most harmful during critical periods—that is, the times during which certain organs are developing. The embryo is generally more vulnerable to teratogens than the fetus because the major organ systems differentiate during the embryonic stage.

13. What are the effects of specific maternal health problems?

Women who contract rubella during the embryonic stage may bear children who suffer from deafness, mental retardation, heart disease, or cataracts. Syphilis, a sexually transmitted infection, can cause miscarriage, stillbirth, or congenital syphilis. Congenital syphilis can be lethal; it can also impair vision and hearing, damage the liver, and deform the bones. One in 3 to 1 in 7 babies born to mothers who are infected with HIV (the AIDS virus) end up infected themselves. Babies can be infected in utero, during childbirth, or—after birth—by breast-feeding. African American and Latino and Latina American children are disproportionately infected with HIV. Toxemia is a life-threatening disease, characterized by high blood pressure, that may afflict pregnant women and is connected with having preterm or undersized babies. In Rh incompatibility, antibodies produced by the mother are transmitted to a fetus or newborn infant and cause brain damage or death.

14. What are the effects of drugs taken by the mother on prenatal development?

Thalidomide, used in the 1960s as a treatment for insomnia and nausea, causes missing or stunted limbs in babies. The antibiotic tetracycline can cause yellowed teeth and bone abnormalities in children. The children of women who used the hormonal preparation DES to help maintain their pregnancies have a high risk of developing cervical and testicular cancer. High doses of vitamins A and D have been associated with nervous system damage, small head size, and heart defects. Maternal addiction to heroin or methadone is linked to low birthweight, prematurity, and toxemia; and the fetuses of women who use them regularly can become addicted to them. Using marijuana during pregnancy may cause greater-than-normal tremors and startling in babies. Maternal use of cocaine during pregnancy increases the risk of stillbirth, low birthweight, and birth defects. The infants are often excitable and less tolerant of stress. Heavy maternal use of alcohol is linked to death of the fetus and neonate, malformations, growth deficiencies, and fetal alcohol syndrome (FAS). Pregnant women who take in much caffeine are more likely than non-users to have a miscarriage or a low-birthweight baby. Maternal cigarette smoking deprives the fetus of oxygen and is linked with low birthweight, stillbirth, mental retardation, learning disorders, and behavioral problems. Babies of fathers who smoke have higher rates of birth defects and infant mortality and lower birthweights.

Recite Recite Recite Recite

15. What are the effects of environmental hazards during pregnancy?

Prenatal exposure to heavy metals threatens the cognitive development of children. Mice exposed to lead in utero do not form memories as well as mice who are not, possibly because of lowered levels of neurotransmitters in the hippocampus. A Japanese disaster showed that prenatal exposure to mercury is connected with mental retardation and neurological damage. Children with prenatal exposure to polychlorinated biphenyls (PCBs) are smaller, less responsive than normal, and more likely to develop cognitive deficits. Fetal exposure to radiation can cause problems in the nervous system and skeleton and is also connected with mental retardation.

16. What are the apparent effects of maternal stress on the child?

Strong maternal emotions are linked to the secretion of hormones such as adrenaline that pass through the placenta and affect the baby. It may be that maternal stress is connected with complications during pregnancy and labor, preterm or low-birthweight babies, and irritable babies.

17. Is the mother's age connected with the outcome of pregnancy?

Yes. Teenage mothers—especially early teenage mothers—have a higher incidence of infant mortality and children with low birthweight. Women over the age of 30 run increasing risk of chromosomal abnormalities and of having stillborn or preterm babies.

On the Web

Search Online With InfoTrac College Edition

For additional information, explore InfoTrac College Edition, your online library. Go to http://www.infotrac-college.com and use the passcode from the InfoTrac card that came with your book. Try these search terms: prenatal influences, prenatal diagnosis, human embryo, fetal development, teratogenic agents.

Visit Our Web Site

Go to http://www.wadsworth.com/psychology where you will find online resources directly linked to your book.

Child Development CD-ROM

Go to the Wadsworth Child Development CD-ROM for further study of the concepts in this chapter. The CD-ROM also includes quizzes and additional activities to expand your learning experience.

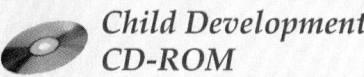

4 Birth and the Newborn Baby: In the New World

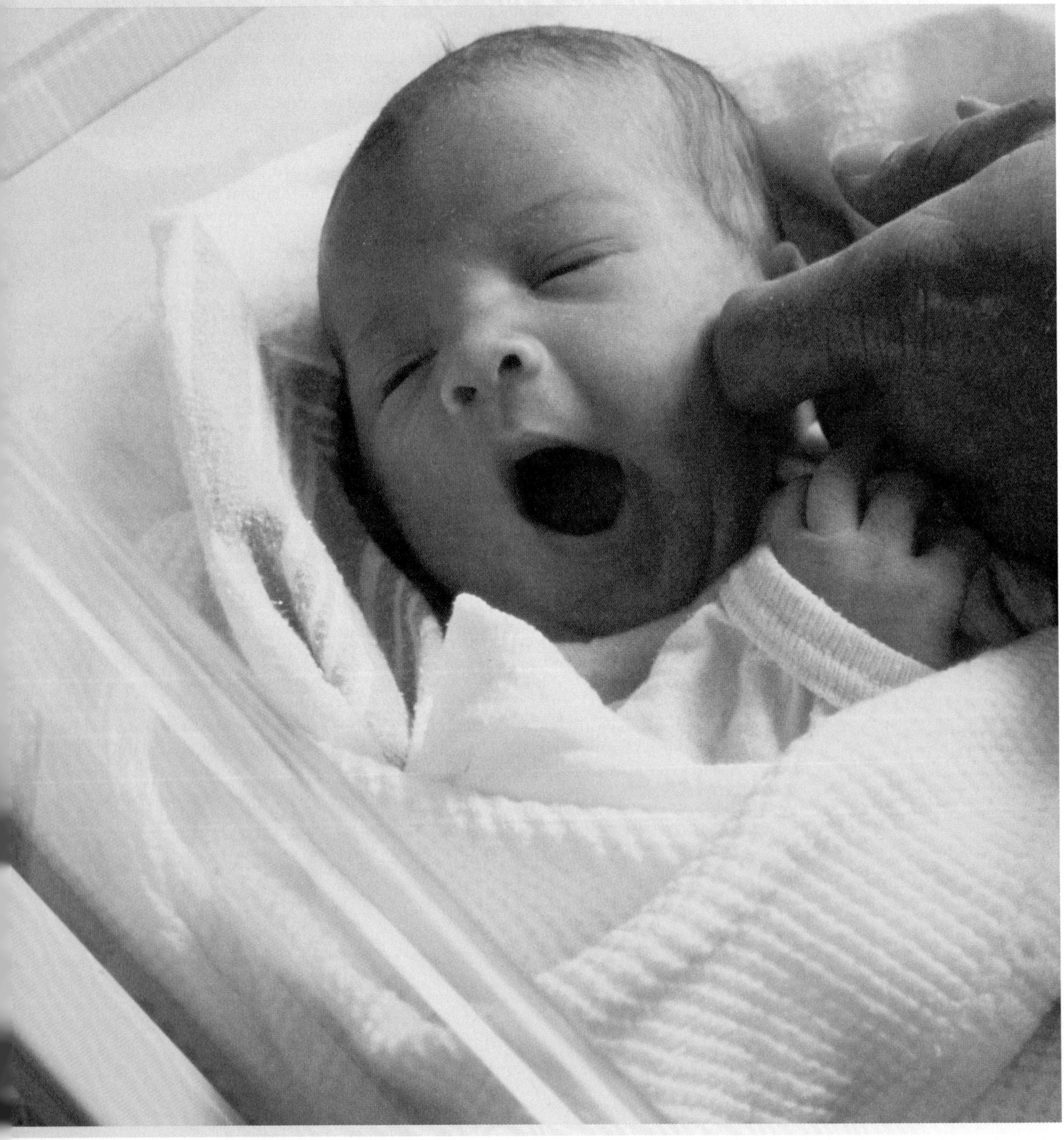

© Tom Stewart/Corbis Stock Market

PowerPreview™

Countdown . . .

- **The fetus apparently signals** its mother when it is ready to be born. (Really.)

The Stages of Childbirth

- **Yes, an episiotomy** can be a pain. Should it be done routinely anyhow?
- **Guess what:** After birth, babies are no longer slapped on the buttocks to stimulate independent breathing. Instead, mucus is removed from their mouths by suction.
- **Is your "belly button"** an "inny" or an "outy"? How did it get to be an inny or an outy?

Methods of Childbirth

- **What are the pluses** and minuses of using anesthetics during childbirth?
- **Women who give birth** according to the Lamaze method may still experience pain, but they become active participants in the birth process rather than victims or medical patients.
- **How many women deliver** their babies by C-section? Does delivering a baby by C-section make a difference?
- **Is it safe for a woman** to give birth at home?

Birth Problems

- **What is prenatal anoxia?** How does it happen? What are its effects?
- **Should we handle preterm** babies extensively or try to leave them undisturbed?

The Postpartum Period

- **How many women** experience depression after childbirth? Why?
- **Must parents have extended** early contact with their newborn children if adequate bonding is to take place?

Characteristics of Neonates

- **Did you know that** if you place a newborn baby face down in comfortably warm water, it will attempt to swim?
- **How well do newborn** babies see? How well do they hear? (Probably a lot better than you think!)
- **More children die from** sudden infant death syndrome (SIDS) than die from cancer, heart disease, pneumonia, child abuse, AIDS, cystic fibrosis, and muscular dystrophy combined.
- **How much sleep does** a newborn baby need? (And how much sleep does it allow its parents to get?)

Oops, she did it again. Michele stirred and discovered that she still had not learned. She had tried to sit up in bed. "Fat chance," she thought. "Not *fat!*" she corrected herself, "just pregged out."

She had fantasies of borrowing a crane that she had watched hoisting steel I-beams to the fiftieth floor of a skyscraper to help her get out of bed. "Well, maybe it's not that bad," she thought. Okay. She rolled over onto her side and almost—but not quite!—onto her tummy and sort of backed or sidled out of bed. "This is dignified," she thought.

"I've had it!" she said to the room at large. "Huh?" Matt muttered, still mostly asleep. "Oh, shut up!" she said.

"What did I do?"

"Nothing, absolutely nothing."

During the last few weeks before she gave birth, Michele later explained, "I couldn't get my mind off the pregnancy—what it was going to be like when I finally delivered Lisa. I'd had the amniocentesis, so I knew it was a girl. I'd had the ultrasounds, so all her fingers and toes had been counted, but I was still hoping and praying that everything would turn out all right. To be honest, I was also worried about the delivery. I had always been an A student, and I guess I wanted to earn an A in childbirth as well. Matt was understanding, and he was even helpful. But, you know, it wasn't him.

"My obstetrician was bending over backwards (*she* could bend—I couldn't) being politically correct and kept on talking about how *we* had gotten pregnant and about how we were going to have the baby. Toward the end there, I would have been thrilled if it had really been *we*. Or I would even have allowed Matt to do it all by himself. But the fact is it was *me*. And I was worrying about how I could even reach the steering wheel of the car in those days, much less deliver a perfect healthy child. On TV, of course, they do it without even disturbing their mascara, but I was living in the real world. And waiting, waiting, waiting. And, oh yes, did I mention waiting?"

Nearly all first-time mothers struggle through the last weeks of pregnancy and worry about the mechanics of delivery. Childbirth is a natural function, of course, but so many of them have gone to classes to learn how to do what comes naturally! They worry about whether they'll get to the hospital or birthing center on time ("Is there gas in the car?" "Is it snowing?"). They worry about whether the baby will start breathing on its own properly. They may wonder if they'll do it on their own or need a C-section. And they may worry about whether it will hurt and how much, and when they should ask for anesthetics, and, well, how to earn that A.

Close to full **term,** Michele and other women are big—as in big—and they feel bent out of shape. Guess what: They are. The weight of the fetus may also be causing backaches. Will they deliver the baby, or will the baby—by being born—deliver them? "Hanging in and bearing Lisa was a wonderful experience," Michele said. "I think Matt should have had it."

Countdown . . .

Question: What events occur just prior to the beginning of childbirth? Early in the last month of pregnancy, the head of the fetus settles in the pelvis. This is called dropping or lightening. Since lightening decreases pressure in the diaphragm, the mother may, in fact, feel lighter.

The first uterine contractions are called **Braxton-Hicks contractions,** or false labor contractions. They are relatively painless and may be experienced as early as the sixth month of pregnancy. They tend to increase in frequency as the pregnancy progresses and may serve to tone the muscles that will be used in delivery. Although they may be confused with actual labor contractions, real labor contractions are more painful and regular and are also usually intensified by walking.

term A set period of time.

Braxton-Hicks contractions The first, usually painless, contractions of childbirth.

A day or so before labor begins, increased pelvic pressure from the fetus may rupture superficial blood vessels in the birth canal so that blood appears in vaginal secretions. The mucus tissue that had plugged the cervix and protected the uterus from infection becomes dislodged. At about this time, 1 woman in 10 has a rush of warm liquid from the vagina. This liquid is amniotic fluid, and its discharge means that the amniotic sac has burst; in most cases, however, the amniotic sac usually does not burst until the end of the first stage of childbirth. Indigestion, diarrhea, an ache in the small of the back, and abdominal cramps are also common signs that labor is beginning.

Believe it or not, the fetus may normally signal the mother when it is "ready" to be born—that is, when it is mature enough to sustain life outside the uterus. The adrenal and pituitary glands of the fetus may trigger labor by secreting hormones. The fetal hormones would stimulate the placenta (which is a gland as well as a relay station) and the uterus to secrete **prostaglandins.** Prostaglandins are the main culprits when women experience uncomfortable cramping prior to or during menstruation; they also serve the function of exciting the muscles of the uterus to engage in labor contractions. As labor progresses, the pituitary gland releases **oxytocin,** another hormone. Oxytocin stimulates contractions that are powerful enough to expel the fetus—although now, of course, we call it a baby.

In this chapter, we discuss the events of childbirth and the characteristics of the **neonate.** Arriving in the new world may be a bit more complex than you had thought, and it may also be that neonates can do a bit more than you had imagined.

The Stages of Childbirth

Regular uterine contractions signal the beginning of childbirth. Developmentalists speak of childbirth as occurring in three stages.

The First Stage

Question: What happens during the first stage of childbirth? In the first stage of childbirth, uterine contractions **efface** and **dilate** the cervix. This passageways need to widen to about 4 inches (10 cm) to allow the baby to pass. The dilation of the cervix is responsible for most of the pain that is experienced during childbirth. In cases in which the cervix dilates rapidly and easily, there may be little or no discomfort.

The first stage is the long stage. Among women undergoing their first deliveries, it may last from a few hours to more than a day. Half a day to a day is about average, but for some women, the first stage is much briefer and for others, it lasts up to a couple of days. Subsequent pregnancies take less time and may be surprisingly rapid—sometimes between one hour and two hours. The first contractions are not usually all that painful[1] and are spaced 10 to 20 minutes apart. They may last from 20 to 40 seconds each.

As the process continues, the contractions become more powerful, frequent, and regular. Women are usually advised to go to the hospital or birthing center when contractions are spaced 4 to 5 minutes apart. Until the end of the first stage of labor, the mother is frequently in a labor room with the father or another companion.

If the woman is to be "prepped"—that is, if her pubic hair is to be shaved—it takes place during the first stage. The prep is intended to lower the chances of infection during delivery and to facilitate the performance of an **episiotomy** (see "The Second Stage"). A woman may also be given an enema to prevent an involuntary bowel movement during contractions of labor. However, many women find prepping and enemas degrading and seek obstetricians who do not perform

[1]Easy for a man to write, notes the author's wife.

prostaglandins (pross-tuh-GLAND-ins) Hormones that stimulate uterine contractions.

oxytocin (ox-see-TOE-sin) A pituitary hormone that stimulates labor contractions (from the Greek *oxys,* meaning "quick," and *tokos,* meaning "birth").

neonate A newborn child (from the Greek *neos,* meaning "new," and the Latin *natus,* meaning "born").

efface To rub out or wipe out; to become thin.

dilate To make wider or larger.

episiotomy (ep-pee-zee-OTT-to-me) A surgical incision in the perineum that widens the vaginal opening, preventing random tearing during childbirth.

them routinely. The medical necessity of these procedures has been questioned (Scott et al., 1999).

During the first stage of childbirth, **fetal monitoring** may be used. One kind of monitoring is an electronic sensing device strapped around the woman's abdomen. It can measure the fetal heart rate as well as the frequency, strength, and duration of the mother's contractions. Another type of fetal monitor has electrodes that are attached directly to the scalp of the baby. An abnormal heart rate alerts the medical staff to possible fetal distress so that appropriate steps can be taken, such as speeding up the delivery with **forceps** or the **vacuum extraction tube.** The forceps is a curved instrument that fits around the baby's head and allows the baby to be pulled out of the mother's body. The vacuum extraction tube relies on suction to pull the baby through the birth canal.

When the cervix is nearly fully dilated, the head of the fetus begins to move into the vagina, or birth canal. This process is called **transition.** During transition, which lasts about 30 minutes or less, contractions usually are frequent and strong.

The Second Stage

The second stage of childbirth follows transition. ***Question: What occurs during the second stage of childbirth?*** This stage begins when the baby appears at the opening of the vagina (which is now technically referred to as the birth canal; see Figure 4.1). The second stage is briefer than the first stage. It may last minutes or a few hours, and it culminates in the birth of the baby. The woman may be taken to a delivery room for the second stage of childbirth.

The contractions of the second stage stretch the skin surrounding the birth canal farther and propel the baby farther along. The baby's head is said to have crowned when it begins to emerge from the birth canal. Once crowning has occurred, the baby usually emerges completely within minutes.

The physician, nurse, or midwife may perform an episiotomy once crowning takes place. The purpose of the episiotomy is to prevent random tearing when the **perineum** becomes severely effaced. Women are unlikely to feel the incision because the pressure of the crowning head tends to numb the region between the vagina and the anus. The episiotomy, like prepping and the enema, is controversial and is not practiced in Europe. The incision may cause itching and discomfort as it heals. The discomfort may make sexual relations impossible for months following the delivery. An article that appeared in *Obstetrics & Gynecology* argued that "Episiotomy should no longer be routine" (Eason & Feldman, 2000). Some practitioners apparently exaggerate the problem of "random tearing." Others suggest that prenatal massage of the perineum may avert excessive tearing (Eason et al., 2000; Johanson, 2000). I do not take a stand on this issue, because there is too much individual variation among women to make generalizations. But I will note that health professionals are in general agreement that an episiotomy is warranted when the baby's shoulders are quite wide or if the baby's heart rate declines for a long period of time (Eason & Feldman, 2000). Having noted all this complicated reasoning, let us also report that the strongest predictor of whether a practitioner will choose to use episiotomy is not the condition of the mother or the baby, but rather whether he or she normally uses episiotomy (Robinson et al., 2000).

Whether or not an episiotomy is performed, the passageway into the world outside is a tight fit, and the baby squeezes through. Mothers may be alarmed at the visual results of the tight fit. Sometimes the baby's head and facial features are quite bent out of shape. The baby's head can be elongated, its nose can be flattened or pushed to the side, and its ears can be contorted—as though this little thing[2] had gotten caught up in a vicious prizefight. My wife and I sometimes joke that our second child was born with her nose apparently coming out the side of her cheek. (And listeners yawn every time, notes the author's wife.) Parents

[2]"This little thing?" asks the editor. "My, such technically challenging language."

fetal monitoring The use of instruments to track the heart rate and oxygen levels of the fetus during childbirth.

forceps A curved instrument that fits around the head of the baby and permits it to be pulled through the birth canal.

vacuum extraction tube An instrument that uses suction to pull the baby through the birth canal.

transition The initial movement of the head of the fetus into the birth canal.

perineum The area between the female's genital region and the anus.

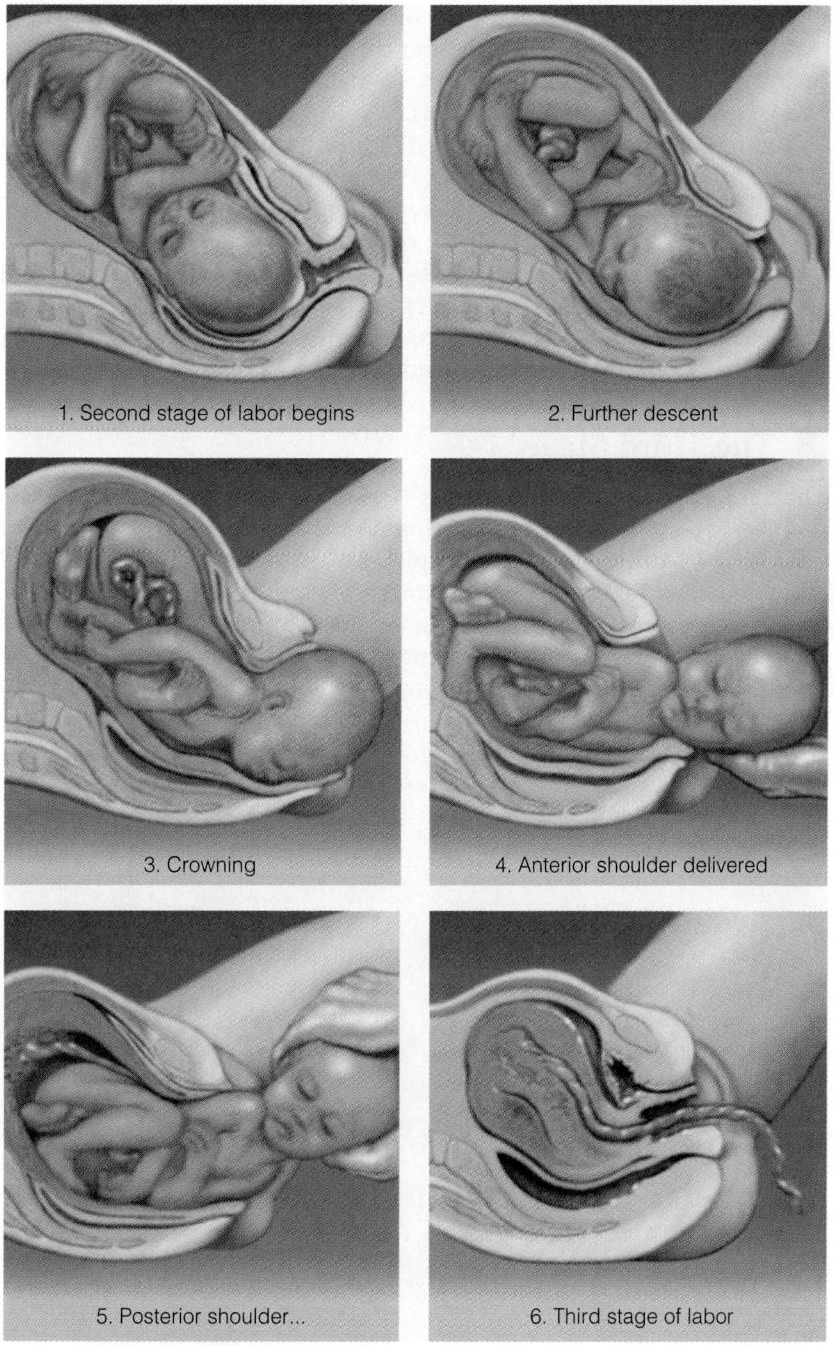

Figure 4.1
The Stages of Childbirth
In the first stage, uterine contractions efface and dilate the cervix to about 4 inches so that the baby may pass. The second stage begins with movement of the baby into the birth canal and ends with birth of the baby. During the third stage, the placenta separates from the uterine wall and is expelled through the birth canal.

understandably wonder whether their baby's features will "pop up" properly or return to a more normal shape. Usually they need not worry. (At least they need not worry about that.)

Don't wait for the baby to be held upside down and slapped on the buttocks to spur breathing on its own. That happens in old movies but not in today's hospitals and birthing centers. Today, mucus is suctioned from the baby's mouth as soon as the head emerges from the birth canal, to clear the passageway for breathing from any obstructions. The procedure may be repeated when the baby has fully emerged.

When the baby is breathing adequately on its own, the umbilical cord is clamped and severed about 3 inches from the baby's body (Figure 4.2). At about 266 days after conception, mother and infant have finally become separate beings. The stump of the umbilical cord will dry and fall off on its own in about 7 to 10 days. There are exceptions. My daughter Allyn, nearly 2 at the time, yanked off the umbilical cord of her newborn sister Jordan, causing a crisis. (The only crisis was in the author's head, which is not an unusual event, notes the author's wife.) In any event, your belly-button status—that is, whether you have an "outy" or an "inny"—is unrelated to the methods of your obstetrician.

You might think that it would be nice for mother and baby to hang out for a while at this juncture, but the baby is frequently whisked away by a nurse who will perform various procedures—for example, she or he footprints the baby and gives the baby a plastic ID bracelet, puts an antibiotic ointment (erythromycin) or drops of silver nitrate into the baby's eyes to prevent bacterial infections, and gives the baby a Vitamin K injection to help its blood clot properly if it bleeds (newborn babies do not manufacture their own Vitamin K). While this goes on, the mother is in the third stage of labor.

The Third Stage

The third stage of labor is also referred to as the placental stage. It lasts from a few minutes to an hour or more. ***Question: What happens during the third stage of childbirth?*** During this stage, the placenta separates from the wall of the uterus and is expelled through the birth canal along with fetal membranes. Some bleeding is normal at this time. The uterus begins to contract, although it will take some time for it to approximate its pre-pregnancy size. The obstetrician now sews the episiotomy—if one has been performed—and any lacerations in the perineum.

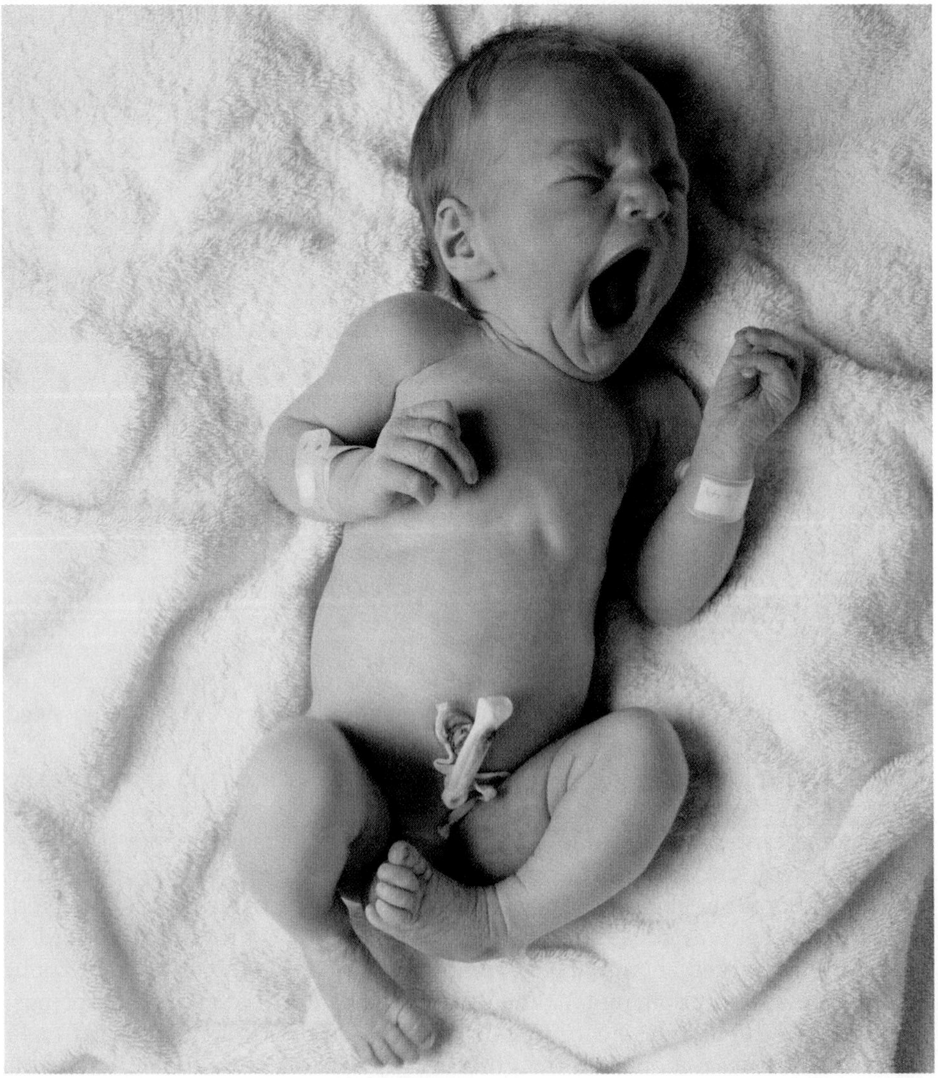

Figure 4.2
A Clamped and Severed Umbilical Cord

The stump of the cord dries and falls off in about 10 days.

Review

(1) The first uterine contractions are "false," and are called _________ -Hicks contractions. (2) A day or so before delivery about 1 woman in 10 has a rush of _________ fluid from the vagina. (3) In the first stage of childbirth, uterine contractions cause the cervix to become effaced and _________. (4) Fetal _________ measures the fetal heart rate as well as the frequency, strength, and duration of the mother's contractions. (5) The _________ is a curved instrument that fits around the baby's head and allows the baby to be pulled out of the birth canal. (6) _________ occurs when the cervix is nearly fully dilated and the head of the fetus begins to move into the birth canal. (7) The second stage of childbirth is (longer or shorter?) than the first stage and ends with the birth of the baby. (8) An episiotomy may be performed to prevent random tearing of the _________. (9) When the baby is breathing adequately, the _________ cord is clamped and severed. (10) During the third stage, the _________ separates from the uterine wall and is expelled.

Pulling It Together: What is the role of hormones in childbirth?

Methods of Childbirth

Think of those old Western movies in which a woman is giving birth in her home on the prairie, and a neighbor emerges heralding the good news to the anxious father and members of the community. Perhaps prairies have not hosted the majority of childbirths over the millennia, but there certainly was a time when childbirth was a more intimate procedure—one that usually took place in the woman's home and involved her, perhaps a **midwife,** family members, friends, and neighbors. How different things are in the United States today. Contemporary American childbirths usually take place in hospitals where they are overseen by physicians who use sophisticated instruments and **anesthetics** to protect mother and child from complications and discomfort. There is no question that modern medicine has saved lives, millions of them. However, childbearing has also become more impersonal. Some argue that modern methods wrest control over their own bodies from women. They even argue that anesthetics have denied many women the experience of giving birth—an experience that the author's wife admits she appreciated having "muted."

In this section, we consider a number of contemporary methods for facilitating childbirth.

Use of Anesthesia: Or How Not to "Bring Forth Children" in Too Much "Sorrow"

In sorrow thou shalt bring forth children.
—Genesis 3:16

As noted in this excerpt from the Bible, painful childbirth has historically been seen the standard for women. But during the past two centuries, the development of modern medicine and effective anesthetics has led many people to believe that women need not experience discomfort during childbirth. In the United States, at least some anesthesia is used in most deliveries. ***Questions: How is anesthesia used in childbirth? What are its effects on the baby?***

General anesthesia was popularized in England when Queen Victoria delivered her eighth child under chloroform anesthesia in 1853. General anesthesia, like the chloroform of old, achieves its anesthetic effect by putting the woman to sleep. The barbiturate Pentothal sodium produces general anesthesia and is

midwife An individual who helps women in childbirth (from Old English roots meaning "with woman").

anesthetics Agents that produce partial or total loss of the sense of pain (from Greek roots meaning "without feeling").

general anesthesia The process of eliminating pain by putting the person to sleep.

usually injected into a vein in the hand or arm. Other drugs in common use are **tranquilizers** such as Valium, oral barbiturates such as Seconal, and narcotics such as Demerol. These drugs are not anesthetics per se, but they may be used to reduce anxiety and the perception of pain without inducing sleep.

All these drugs—general anesthetics and tranquilizers—lessen the strength of uterine contractions during delivery, increase the duration of the second stage of labor, and, by crossing the placental membrane, lower the overall physiological and behavioral responsiveness of the neonate (Sepkoski et al., 1992, 1994; Walker & O'Brien, 1999). Negative effects include abnormal patterns of sleep and wakefulness and decreased attention and social responsiveness for at least the first 6 weeks of life (Sepkoski et al., 1992, 1994). The higher the dosage, the greater the impact.

A major question is whether these anesthetics have long-term effects on the child. The evidence is mixed (Brazelton, 1990a). Some studies show no long-term effects. Others, however, suggest that children whose mothers received heavy doses of anesthetics during delivery lag in their motor development and cognitive functioning at least through 7 years of age (Brackbill, McManus, & Woodward, 1985).

Regional or **local anesthetics** deaden the pain in certain areas of the body without generally decreasing the mother's alertness or putting her to sleep. Physicians have hoped that they would also have less impact on the neonate. In the pudendal block, the mother's external genitals are numbed by local injection. In an epidural block, anesthesia is injected into the spinal canal, temporarily numbing the body below the waist. Anesthesia is injected directly into the spinal cord in the spinal block, which also numbs the body from the waist down.

It appears, however, that local anesthesia does decrease the strength and lower the activity levels of neonates, at least during the first 8 hours following birth (Sepkoski et al., 1992, 1994). Even low doses of local anesthesia make the baby less alert.

Some researchers have also found that medicated childbirth negatively influences parent-baby interactions during the month after birth (Hollenbeck et al., 1984). Why should this be so?

Medicated babies are less responsive after birth, and it is possible that their relationships with their mothers get off on the wrong foot. Perhaps the mothers' first impressions of lower responsiveness persist even after their babies' responsiveness levels have risen to normal. Note also that most studies in this area are "natural experiments." Mothers are not randomly assigned to medication or no-medication groups. Some mothers ask for medication; others do not. Thus, it might be that the same factors that influence some mothers to refuse medication also influence them to appreciate their children more. Given that questions remain about the effects of medicated delivery on the child, one such factor could be greater concern about the welfare of their babies. It could also be that the mothers who do not ask for medication are better prepared for childbirth—and child rearing.

Natural Childbirth

Question: What is meant by the term* natural childbirth*? After all, isn't childbirth by definition a "natural event"? Childbirth may be a natural occurrence, but English obstetrician Grantly Dick-Read became concerned that the use of anesthetics and other medical procedures was denying women the opportunity to experience **natural childbirth.**[3] In any event, Dick-Read wrote about his concerns in his 1944 book *Childbirth Without Fear*. He argued that women's labor pains are heightened by their fear of the unknown and the resultant muscle tensions. He argued further against the use of medication during childbirth. Instead, he helped shape modern childbirth practices by educating women about the biological aspects of reproduction and delivery, encouraging physical fitness, and teaching relaxation and breathing exercises. As we will see, however, these techniques use medication along with the methods suggested by Dick-Read.

[3]Leave it to a man to voice that concern "for" women, notes the author's wife.

tranquilizer A drug that reduces feelings of anxiety and tension.

local anesthetic A method that reduces pain in an area of the body.

natural childbirth A method of childbirth in which women use no anesthesia and are educated about childbirth and strategies for coping with discomfort.

An Exercise Class for Pregnant Women

Years ago, the rule of thumb was that pregnant women were not to exert themselves. Today, it is recognized that exercise is healthful for pregnant women, because it promotes cardiovascular fitness and increases muscle strength. Fitness and strength are assets during childbirth—and at other times.

Prepared Childbirth: The Lamaze Method

Most women who are pregnant for the first time expect pain and discomfort during childbirth. Certainly the popular media image of childbirth is one in which the woman sweats profusely and screams and thrashes in pain. The French obstetrician Fernand Lamaze shared this impression until he visited the Soviet Union in 1951. ***Question: What is the Lamaze method?***

The Lamaze method is based on Lamaze's discovery that many Russian women bore babies without anesthetics or pain. (He may well have exaggerated the Russian woman's ease of delivery.) He studied their techniques and brought them to Western Europe. In the 1950s, they crossed the Atlantic to the United States, where they became known as the **Lamaze method,** or *prepared childbirth.* Lamaze acknowledged his debt to the conditioning concepts of Ivan Pavlov that are described in Chapter 1. Lamaze (1981) contended that women made childbirth more painful and fearful than it had to be because they had associated the prospect of childbirth with cultural expectations of pain and the threat of medical complications. He believed that women could learn to *dissociate* uterine contractions from pain and fear by associating them with *competing* responses, such as the creation of pleasant mental images. For example, women could be taught to envision a park, a beach, or (pleasant!) family scenes during delivery, and they could engage in breathing and relaxation exercises that would further lessen fear and pain by giving them something to do and distracting them from discomfort.

In the Lamaze method, women do not go it alone.[4] The mother-to-be attends Lamaze classes with a "coach—most often, the father-to-be—who will aid her in the delivery room by doing things like massaging her, timing the contractions, offering social support, and coaching her in patterns of breathing and relaxation. The woman is taught to breathe in a specific way during contractions. She is taught how to contract specific muscles in her body while remaining generally relaxed. The idea is that she will be able to transfer this training to the process of childbirth by remaining generally at ease while her uterine muscles contract. The Lamaze procedure tones muscles that will be helpful in childbirth, such as leg muscles, and it enables her to minimize tension, conserve energy, and experience less anxiety.

The woman is also educated about the process of childbirth. The father-to-be or another "coach" is integrated into the process. The woman receives more social support as a result. Women apparently also report less pain and ask for less

Reflect

If you were delivering a child, would you want to use anesthetic medication? Would you use the Lamaze method? Why or why not?

Lamaze method A childbirth method in which women are educated about childbirth, learn to relax and breathe in patterns that conserve energy and lessen pain, and have a coach (usually the father) present during childbirth. Also termed *prepared childbirth.*

[4]At least in theory, notes the author's wife.

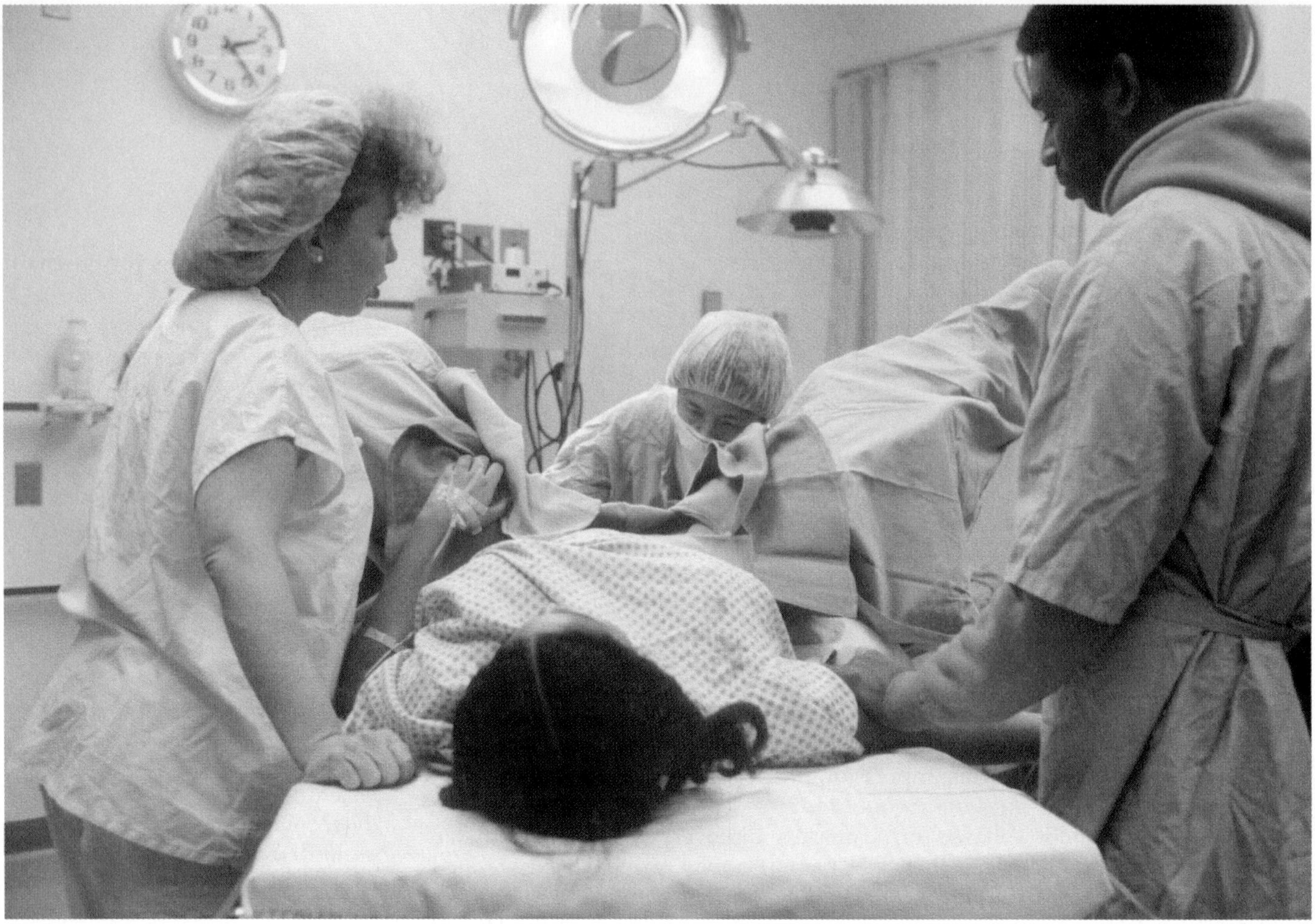

Father in the Delivery Room

Today, the father is usually integrated into the process of childbirth. The father and mother take pride in "their" accomplishment of childbirth.

medication when their husbands are present (Leventhal et al., 1989; Mackey, 1995). (If she can put up with *one* pain, she can put up with another!)

Lamaze's goal was for women to be able to use psychological techniques—today we would refer to them as cognitive-behavioral techniques—to deliver children with less pain and discomfort. Yet women who use the Lamaze method generally experience enough discomfort to encourage them to request anesthesia. Most Lamaze instructors are perfectly comfortable with what we can call partial success. We should also note that many women find the Lamaze method—plus a bit of anesthesia—to be quite helpful. Why? To begin with, the education about childbirth removes much of the mystery. Most, though not all, people can cope better with stress when they know what to expect. The method also gives women the feeling that they are taking charge of delivery and thus enhances their self-efficacy expectancies. They see themselves as the central actors in the process, not as victims who mentally sit on the sidelines while the doctor does it all (Mackey, 1990, 1995). The breathing and relaxation exercises may not eliminate discomfort, but they re-deploy the woman's attention by providing coping strategies and something to think about other than fear and discomfort.

Social support during labor may be provided by individuals other than the father. A woman's mother, sister, or friend also may serve as a labor coach. Studies in three countries have demonstrated the positive impact of continuous emotional support during labor by an experienced female companion known as a "doula"

(Kennell & McGrath, 1993; Kennell et al., 1991). Women in an American hospital who had a doula randomly assigned to them during labor had fewer cesarean deliveries ("C-sections"), less anesthesia, and shorter labors than women without a doula. In a similar South African study, doula-supported women reported less pain and anxiety during labor. Six weeks after childbirth, they were less likely to experience postpartum depression. Two studies in Guatemala found that women who were randomly assigned the support of a doula showed more affectionate interactions with their babies after delivery. Emotional support during labor clearly has beneficial effects for both mothers and infants.

Cesarean Section

There are many controversies about the cesarean section. The first that comes to my mind is the proper spelling. Years ago the term was spelled *Caesarean* section, after the Roman emperor Julius Caesar, who was thought to have been delivered in this manner. Health professionals question whether medical methods would have been sophisticated enough to allow delivery in this manner so long ago, but the term had staying power. Now, however, the more common spelling, *cesarean*, seems to have been divorced from this historic route. In any event, the term is usually abbreviated as *C-section*.

Reflect

Do you know someone who has had a C-section? What were the reasons for it? How did she react to the experience?

Questions: What is the C-section? Why is it so common? In a **cesarean section** (C-section) the physician delivers the baby by means of abdominal surgery. She or he cuts through the abdomen and the uterus and physically removes the baby. The incisions are then sewn up. Most health professionals encourage the mother to get up and walk around on the same day as the surgery but, make no mistake about it, doing so is usually painful. When the C-section first came into common practice, it left visible scars in the abdomen. Physicians usually perform C-sections today so that the incision is more or less hidden by the upper edge of the woman's pubic hair. This method is commonly referred to as the "bikini cut," referring to the shape of the brief swimsuit.

Physicians prefer C-sections to vaginal delivery when they believe that normal delivery may threaten the mother or child, or simply be more difficult than desired. Typical indications of the C-section are a small pelvis in the mother, maternal weakness or fatigue (for example, if labor has been prolonged), or a baby that is too large or in apparent distress. C-sections are also performed when the physician wants to prevent the circulatory systems of the mother and baby from mixing, as might occur when there is bleeding during vaginal delivery. C-sections in such cases may prevent the transmission of genital herpes or HIV (the AIDS virus). The physician may also perform a C-section when it appears that the baby is facing in the wrong direction. It is normal, and safest, for babies to be head first. A C-section is indicated if the baby is going to be born sideways or "backward"—that is, feet first.

Return to the matter of the transmission of HIV. The results of the European Mode of Delivery Collaboration Trial compared the use of C-section versus vaginal delivery as a means of decreasing the risk of maternal transmission of HIV to the baby (Ricci, Parazzini, & Pardi, 2000). The study enlisted about 400 infected mothers. All of the women received zidovudine (AZT) during pregnancy. Half of the mothers were then randomly assigned to deliver vaginally, and the other half by C-section. The rate of HIV infection rate among the babies was 10.6% for those delivered vaginally as compared with 1.7% for those delivered by C-section. Thus the combination of AZT and C-section cuts the chance that an HIV-infected mother will transmit HIV to her baby to about 1 in 50.

The use of the C-section has grown rapidly over the past generation. In the United States today, C-sections account for one out of every four or five births—about 22% (Nano, 2001). This figure is actually down a bit from the peak year of 1988, when C-sections accounted for 25% of births. To gain some perspective, note that C-sections accounted for only one in twenty births (5%) in 1965. Why the upsurge? Some of the increase in C-sections is due to advances in medicine. For

cesarean section A method of childbirth in which the neonate is delivered through a surgical incision in the abdomen. (Also spelled *Caesarean.*)

example, fetal monitors now allow physicians to more readily detect fetal distress. But other factors are not quite—shall we say—"medical." Physicians also perform C-sections because they make more money (sorry, idealists), because they are concerned about the possibility of malpractice suits if something goes wrong during a vaginal delivery, and also, frankly, because so many physicians are being trained to perform them whenever they suspect that there *might* be a reason for them (DiMatteo et al., 1996). But women also ask for C-sections. Some mothers want to avoid the pain of vaginal delivery, or they want to control exactly when the baby will be born. So how many C-sections are "necessary"? The U.S. Department of Health and Human Services suggests that 15%, not 22%, might be an appropriate figure for the benefit of the mother or the baby (Paul, 1996). The argument for maintaining the higher rate of C-sections is that performing one should be a medical decision and not a political or financial decision. In other words, let's not endanger the mother or the baby because someone is touting a theoretical figure (Nano, 2001; J. M. Roberts, 2000). Sounds reasonable—idealistic in fact, but one of the more common reasons for performing C-sections remains "doctors' habits" ("After years of decline," 2000). When shopping around for an obstetrician, it's kosher to ask how many C-sections the doctor performs, and why.

Some women who have C-sections are less than happy with them. An analysis of a large number of studies on the issue found that women who have C-sections tend to be less satisfied with the birth than women who deliver vaginally. They are less likely to breast-feed their babies and somewhat less likely to interact with them (DiMatteo et al., 1996). Some studies suggest that women who undergo planned C-sections fare better than women who have them "at the last minute" (Durik, Hyde, & Clark, 2000). Fore-warned is fore-armed? But let us admit that C-sections have *not* been connected with meaningful and prolonged physical or emotional problems in mothers, children, or mother–child relationships.

Obstetricians used to believe something like this: "Once you have a C-section, you must always have a C-section." That is, women who had C-sections, for whatever reason, would need to deliver subsequent babies by C-section as well. If they attempted vaginal delivery, uterine scars might rupture and result in dire consequences such as excessive bleeding (possibly causing the death of the mother or the need for blood transfusions) and brain damage in, or loss of, the baby. With such concerns in mind, only 60% of women in the United States who have previously had a C-section attempt labor in subsequent pregnancies (Lydon-Rochelle et al., 2001). Research is mixed on the likelihood of uterine rupture, however. One study found that only about three women in one thousand (10 of 3,249) who attempted vaginal delivery after a C-section experienced rupture of the uterus (McMahon et al., 1996). (Even so, this low percentage is about twice as high as uterine rupture among women who have had a cesarean experience during or following a subsequent cesarean [Lydon-Rochelle et al., 2001].) Moreover, there were no maternal deaths.

A study by Mona Lydon-Rochelle and her colleagues (2001) of 20,095 women in Washington State has heightened concern, especially for women who have induced labor. The researchers compared the risk of uterine rupture for deliveries by repeated cesarean with the risk for those following a cesarean with spontaneous onset of labor, labor induced by prostaglandins, and labor induced by other methods. They found that uterine rupture occurred at a rate of 0.16% among women who underwent repeated cesarean delivery without labor. About 0.52% of women who attempted vaginal delivery when they naturally went into labor experienced uterine rupture (a higher percentage than that reported in the McMahon study). The risks of uterine rupture were significantly higher for labors induced by prostaglandins (2.5%) and other methods (0.77%). "By no means does our study suggest that no woman should have a vaginal birth after a Caesarean. What it says is there are risks of doing that that we didn't fully appreciate," one of the researchers, Thomas Easterling, said in an interview (Nano, 2001).

The debate as to the safety of vaginal delivery—and what kind of vaginal delivery—following a cesarean section continues. Women are advised to consult with their obstetricians for the most recent statistics and recommendations.

Laboring Through the Birthing Options: Where Should a Child Be Born?

Question: We have considered some of the kinds of childbirth available today. Now let us ask, Where should a woman deliver her child? (And why?) Women have never had so many choices in childbirth.[5] They have the option to labor in a pool of warm water or at home in bed, in a cozy hospital "birthing suite" or in a traditional labor room. They can choose between an obstetrician or midwife—or both. How about some aromatherapy or acupuncture, yoga or Yanni to help ease the pain and discomfort? Whatever your desire, those in the baby-delivery business want to make sure your "birth experience" is all it can be.

"I think women definitely have a strong interest in getting back to natural, less-invasive childbirth," says Dr. Amy VanBlaricom, an obstetrician at the University of Washington in Seattle. She points to the increasing demand in many parts of the country for nurse-midwives—trained professionals, usually women, who stay with a woman throughout her labor, supporting her and working with techniques like massage to avoid surgery, forceps, and other interventions. There's also growing interest in doulas, lay women with minimal training who don't perform deliveries but offer support during childbirth.

More and more women also want a family atmosphere for their deliveries, often inviting their mothers or sisters, friends, and sometimes their other children to witness the blessed event. And unhappy with the days when obstetricians dictated every step, today's mothers-to-be want control, many working through every detail of their "birth plan" with their providers.

The industry is eager to please. Hospitals or birthing centers with satisfied customers stand to gain much more than a one-time payment. Women who are happy with their care are likely to return to that institution for future deliveries or other medical services. And because women are the main health-care decision makers in the family, they are also likely to bring in their kids, their husbands, and their aging parents or grandparents. Women who feel as though the hospital somehow dampened one of life's greatest experiences may simply opt to take their future business elsewhere.

Reflect

Where would you like to deliver your child? In the hospital? In a "birthing suite"? At home? In a pool? Doctor, midwife, or doula? Aromatherapy or yoga? There are so many choices. How will you determine which is the right one for you?

State-of-the-Art Birthing

A few years ago, hospital administrators at Duke University Medical Center in Durham, North Carolina, recognized that their obstetric facilities, while offering high-quality care, weren't as cushy as competing hospitals in the area. Officials consulted with other medical institutions nationwide, conducted focus groups with area women, and began planning a new state-of-the-art birthing center.

"We realized that changes needed to be made if we were going to survive," says Dr. William Herbert, medical director of obstetrics at the hospital. "Our rooms were far inferior in terms of the amenities and expectations that people have now."

Herbert says women desire something more than the traditional, sterile hospital room. "They want a very home-like atmosphere that's family friendly, to celebrate delivery."

Duke opened its new birthing center within the hospital. Twenty-one private rooms serve as LDRPs—labor, delivery, recovery, and postpartum, all in one. Traditionally, labor and delivery take place in separate rooms or in the same room, after which a woman may be transferred to a recovery room and then a hospital room for the duration of her stay. Herbert says the LDRP concept is aimed at reducing the hassle for the mother as well as the medical staff.

"From the time the patient gets there until the time she leaves, she's in the same room," Herbert says. However, he notes that if a woman needs a cesarean section, she would be transferred to a nearby surgical operating room for the procedure, as would any woman with complications.

[5]This section is adapted from Jacqueline Stenson. (2000). Laboring through the birthing options. MSNBC online: **http://www.msnbc.com**

A View of an LDRP

Duke University has a birthing center within its hospital, which includes LDRPs—labor, delivery, recovery, and postpartum rooms, all in one. Traditionally speaking, labor and delivery take place in separate rooms or in the same room, but then the woman may be transferred to a recovery room and, finally, a hospital room for the duration of her stay. The LDRP provides a homelike room that also reduces the hassle for the mother and the medical staff.

The rooms resemble high-class hotel suites more than drab hospital rooms. They're decorated in soft pastels, with hardwood floors, track lighting, armoires, televisions, refrigerators, and private bathrooms with makeup mirrors and whirlpools (where women can labor to ease the pain). A daybed folds out for dads or other overnight guests. Artwork from area talent adorns the walls, and windows overlook a courtyard below. Bassinets allow the babies to stay in the same room with the new parents.

At the same time, the LDRPs are fully equipped with all the medical necessities for an uncomplicated birth, explains Herbert. Much of it is tucked into closets or behind wall hangings, yet all is within easy reach of the doctors and nurses. "We've merged safety, top-notch medical care, and a family atmosphere," Herbert says.

There are no hard data on whether such amenities actually translate into improved birth outcomes, he notes, but they seem to make mothers feel more comfortable and perhaps reduce stress. And while Duke's emergency facilities are just down the hall, some doctors worry about the safety of delivering babies at free-standing birthing centers, where there are no surgical facilities should complications arise and a woman need to be transferred elsewhere.

"Birthing centers outside a hospital are a big problem for me," says Dr. Yvonne Thornton, a clinical professor of obstetrics and gynecology at the University of Medicine and Dentistry of New Jersey in Newark. Even if the nearest hospital is just a 10-minute drive away, Thornton says, too much time could pass while the woman is transferred onto the gurney and into the ambulance, and then the ambulance fights traffic to get to the emergency room.

The Home Birth Debate

The same goes for home births, she adds, where there are even fewer resources.

"People don't understand that women die, babies die. People keep forgetting that," she says. "Why are we going back to the dark ages? You don't have the necessary equipment should something go wrong."

[In the United States, there are about 10 maternal deaths per every 100,000 live births. In developing countries, where medical resources are scarce, there are as many as 480 deaths per 100,000 births. However, the nearby feature, "Developing in a World of Diversity," reveals that there are "nations with the nation" in the

United States, when it comes to the risk of maternal death due to pregnancy-related causes.] Common causes of death are hemorrhage, pregnancy-induced hypertension, and infection.

Thornton says the dramatically reduced death rate in the United States points to the fact that most women here have access to quality care. The overwhelming majority give birth in hospitals. But even in America, African American women die during childbirth at twice the rate of European Americans, she says, because many are poor and lack access to quality care.

VanBlaricom agrees that births outside of hospitals present a threat, particularly for women at high risk of complications. "Home births are not something I would recommend," she says. "The main reason is that the labor and delivery process is so unpredictable." Birthing at home probably poses less of a threat for women who've had uncomplicated pregnancies in the past, she notes, but there still is more risk than giving birth in a hospital. "With childbirth, you just never know ahead of time if there is going to be a problem," she adds.

But Marion McCartney, director of professional services at the American College of Nurse–Midwives in Washington, DC, who has delivered babies in the home, says it can be done safely. "Our policy is that women have a right to choose where they give birth," McCartney says, adding that a certified nurse–midwife will carefully assess a woman's risk for complications and her proximity to emergency medical care before agreeing to assist with a home birth. "You'd like the woman to be able to have a C-section within 30 minutes," should the need arise, she says. But most nurse–midwives (who differ from lay midwives in terms of advanced training) practice in hospitals alongside obstetricians. The nurse–midwives typically handle the lower-risk births, with an obstetrician on hand should a problem arise.

Some studies show that midwife-assisted, low-risk births involve fewer C-sections, episiotomies, anesthesia, forceps, and other interventions than do those with an obstetrician. McCartney points to the extra support offered by midwives, who stay with the woman during the entire process, encouraging her to relax, try different positions and techniques such as acupuncture or yoga to ease pain, and to just take things slowly. Midwives appeal to many women because of this openness to alternative techniques.

Developing in a World of Diversity

Pregnancy-Related Deaths Among Women From Different Ethnic Backgrounds

In considering where a child is to be born, parents need to consider the fact that not only the baby, but also the mother is at risk of injury or death. A survey by the Centers for Disease Control and Prevention reveals a number of factors that affect the risk to the mother: her ethnic background, whether she was born in the United States or elsewhere, and her age (Division of Reproductive Health, 2001).

The CDC found that women from ethnic minority groups in the United States have markedly greater mortality rates from complications during pregnancy than European American women. Table 4.1 reveals that African American women are most likely to die from pregnancy-related causes, and European American women are least likely to die. The CDC notes that the findings underscore the need for targeted interventions that address the maternal health needs of women from ethnic minority groups.

TABLE 4.1 *Ethnic Background of Mother and Risk of Death Due to Complications of Pregnancy (per 100,000 live births)*

Ethnicity of Mother	Risk of Pregnancy-Related Death
African American	30.0
Asian American	11.3
European American	7.3
Latina American	10.3
Native American	12.2

Delivering With a Doula

Research also suggests that doulas can be a big help. "They're wonderful patient advocates, and they can be especially good for people who don't have a partner who can help," VanBlaricom says.

Another option that's popular in Europe, but much less so in America, is water birth. Although most U.S. experts say laboring in water is safe as long as the tub has been thoroughly disinfected, they're skeptical about underwater deliveries. "That's on the fringe of what we consider safe," VanBlaricom says. Thornton says she knows of two cases in which the infants drowned. "I don't encourage water births," she says. "Why are we taking a chance here?"

With all the options available, experts encourage women to be fully informed of the risks and benefits of each before making a decision. "There's always something that someone can offer, but the bottom line is that you want a healthy baby," says Dr. Ruth Fretts, an assistant professor of obstetrics and gynecology at Beth Israel Deaconess Medical Center in Boston. "Make sure you don't miss the point."

Review

(11) ________ anesthesia achieves its anesthetic effect during childbirth by putting the woman to sleep. (12) General anesthetics (increase or decrease?) the overall responsiveness of the neonate. (13) ________ anesthetics deaden the pain in areas of the body without decreasing the mother's alertness or putting her to sleep. (14) In an ________ block, anesthesia is injected into the spinal canal, numbing the body below the waist. (15) In his book *Childbirth Without* ________, Dick-Read argued that women's labor pains are heightened by their fear of the unknown and resultant muscle tensions. (16) ________ argued that women can learn to dissociate uterine contractions from pain and fear by associating responses such as pleasant imagery with contractions. (17) In the Lamaze method, a person called a ________ helps the mother by timing contractions, offering moral support, and coaching her in patterns of breathing and relaxation. (18) The continuous emotional support during labor by an experienced female

Developing in a World of Diversity (continued)

The CDC also found differences in mortality rates from complications during pregnancy between women who were born in the United States and women who had immigrated to the United States. For example, there were 8 maternal deaths per 100,000 live births among Latina Americans born in the United States, as opposed to 11.8 deaths per 100,000 among Latina Americans who were born elsewhere. Also, there were 6.1 maternal deaths per 100,000 for Asian American women born in the United States, as compared with twice as many—12.7 deaths—for foreign-born Asian American women. Therefore, the CDC also notes the desirability of attempting to provide foreign-born women with prenatal care.

Finally, the CDC found that older women experienced a higher mortality rate due to pregnancy-related complications than younger women. As you can see in Table 4.2, the mortality rate increases sharply during the mid- and late thirties and is highest for women older than 39. Does this mean that when it comes to pregnancy and delivery, we should declare "the younger the better"? Not necessarily. Teenagers in the United States may not have established relationships and sources of income that will enable them to support children emotionally and financially. And for women of any age, high-quality prenatal health care is connected with healthier outcomes—for mother and child.

TABLE 4.2 *Age of Mother and Risk of Death Due to Complications of Pregnancy (per 100,000 live births)*

Age of Mother	Risk of Pregnancy-Related Death
<20	8.5
20–29	9.3
30–34	11.9
35–39	21.1
>39	44.3

companion known as a ________ apparently enables mothers to deliver with less anesthesia and shorter labor. (19) Herpes and HIV infections in the birth canal can be bypassed by a surgical procedure called the ________ section. (20) ________ center rooms resemble high-class hotel suites more than drab hospital rooms. (21) ________ American women run the highest risk of a pregnancy-related death.

Pulling It Together: What are the advantages and risks of delivering a child at home?

Developing in the New Millennium

Clicking Around for Advice on Pregnancy and Childbirth

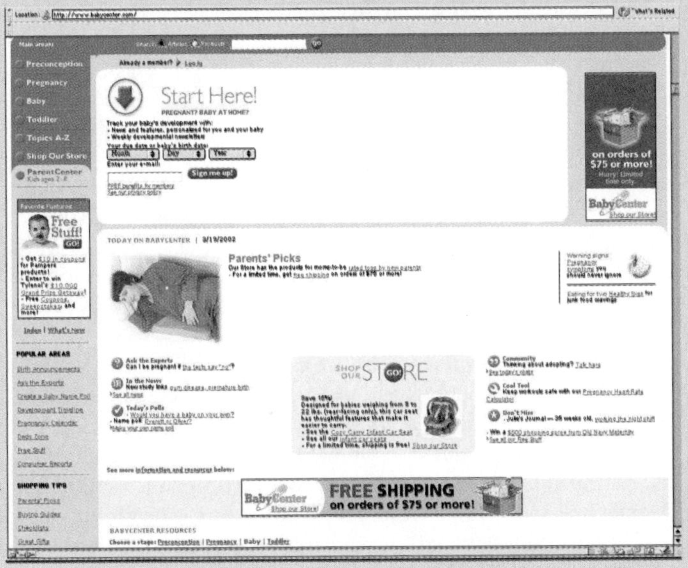

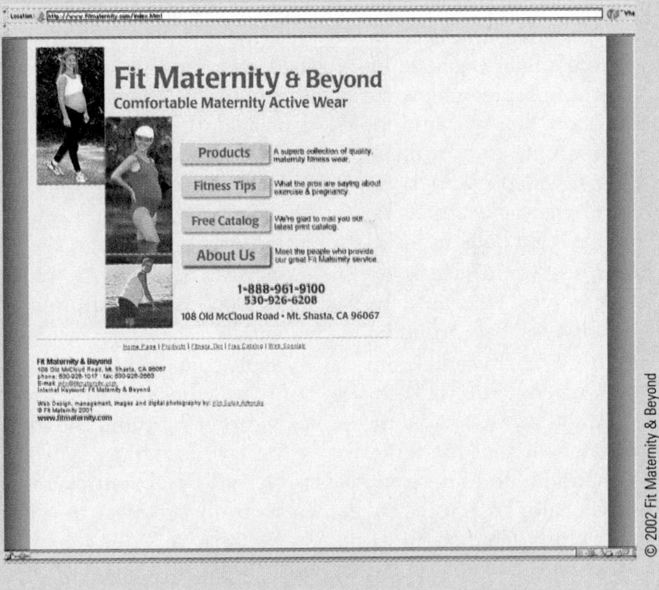

Oh, no. It's 2 o'clock in the morning. It's snowing. You're huge—in fact, reaching the steering wheel of the car has become a major life challenge—but you're not due for another month. And you've got some stuff going on that feels like contractions just where you don't want to have contractions—yet. So what do you do? Do you call the doctor? She's probably asleep. Do you run over to the E.R.? Not so fast; you're not running anywhere. You can wake up Henry, of course, but he's not of much use during the afternoon let alone in the wee hours of the morning. Nor do you want to risk "crying wolf"; Henry may be less likely to jump when you've "really" got to get to the hospital. But you might need to go . . . Where to go?

One possibility in the new millennium is to go shopping for information online. There are more birth-related Web sites than you can . . . click a mouse at. If you know where to go online, you may not need to go anywhere by car—at least not tonight. The Internet has all the info you could ever hope for on gynecological issues, pregnancy and childbirth, doulas and moulah (doulas don't work for free), birthing centers, doctors who belong to all the right professional organizations, Lamaze classes, anesthetics (why should birth be as much of a pain as Henry?), vitamins and minerals (some of which you might actually need), maternity wear, and chat rooms where you can share your concerns with health professionals and other pregnant women ("Hey, that's just what happened to me, and . . .").

Just one catch. If you search "birth" or "childbirth," you may find thousands upon thousands of Web sites. I just searched "birth" on Google (there was no "goo-goo" search engine). The search took 0.17 seconds and yielded 13,200,000 Web sites plus or minus one or two. So you have to separate the wheat from the chaff, and the more useful wheat from the less useful wheat. What you want are Web sites that are reputable, trustworthy, and have the information you need. You could ask your obstetrician for advice on the matter, but

Birth Problems

Although the great majority of deliveries are unremarkable from a medical standpoint, perhaps every delivery is most remarkable from the parents' point of view. Still, there are a number of problems that can and do occur. In this section, we discuss the effects of oxygen deprivation and the problems of preterm and low-birth-weight neonates.

Oxygen Deprivation

anoxia A condition characterized by lack of oxygen.

hypoxia A condition characterized by less oxygen than is required.

Question: What are the effects of oxygen deprivation at birth? Researchers use two terms to discuss oxygen deprivation: *anoxia* and *hypoxia*. **Anoxia** derives from roots meaning "without oxygen." **Hypoxia** derives from roots meaning "under" and "oxygen"—the point again being that the baby does not receive enough oxygen to

Developing in the New Millennium (continued)

you might be more Net-savvy than she is. So here goes with some ideas for reliable, useful Web sites on childbirth:

http://www.acog.org/ The American College of Obstetricians and Gynecologists. This Web site, maintained by a respected professional organization, focuses on women's health issues, including pregnancy and childbirth. In the "Women's Issues" section, you will find topics such as adolescent care, smoking cessation, and violence against women. Under "News Releases" on January 14, 2002, I found interesting question-and-answer features on "Postpartum Depression" and on "Having a Baby in the 21st Century."

http://www.midwife.org/ The American College of Nurse-Midwives. Find out who's around. Don't be hesitant to check midwives' background and credentials.

http://www.babycenter.com/ Babycenter.com. Babycenter.com is also a commercial Web site, but it provides expert information on a variety of topics. Click your way around the menu. Many sections are written by experts whose biographies are included, and site content is reviewed by obstetricians and gynecologists. You can get answers to practical questions such as "What should I take to the hospital? or "When is it too late to change obstetricians?" (Carroll, 2000). The site includes discussions about the various types of childbirth classes and an interactive survey designed to help you figure out which kind of class would best fit your needs. For specific information about contractions and what they might mean you can check out "false labor" under the "birth and labor" section.

http://www.childbirth.org/ Childbirth.org. This Web site is run by a doula and is oriented toward "natural childbirth" (use of little or no anesthesia). If you keep the bias in mind, you will find some useful information.

http://www.dona.com/ Doulas of North America. As with midwives, find out who's around, and don't hesitate to ask about doulas' background and credentials.

http://www.drugstore.com/ Drugstore.com. They deliver. If you call early enough, they deliver before you do. Enter "pregnancy" in the Web site's search engine and click go. You can order diapers, vitamins, beauty and spa products, and the like.

http://www.fitmaternity.com/index.html Fitness Wear for Pregnant Women. Shop till the baby drops (that is, until the head of the fetus settles in the pelvis during the final month of pregnancy). Yes, I hear you: Why stop then? Good point. The site also contains information on exercise during pregnancy, in accord with recommendations of the American College of Obstetricians and Gynecologists. Check out "Fitness Tips."

http://www.intelihealth.com/ Intelihealth. This Web site, maintained by Johns Hopkins Medical Institutions and Aetna Insurance Company, offers links to reputable sources of information, including its own experts on pregnancy and childbirth. Check out "Ask the Expert" under Home, or "Women's Health" under Your Health.

http://www.parentsplace.com/pregnancy/ iVillage.com. The site has an excellent question-and-answer section. Check out their "Morning Sickness Survival Guide."

http://www.obgyn.net/ Obgyn.net. This site contains chat rooms and forums that focus on topics such as pregnancy, childbirth, and breast-feeding. You can chat about everything from swollen ankles to getting the milk flowing (and keeping it flowing) and also link to experts.

If none of these is of any help, you can always wake Henry. Why should he sleep if you're awake?

Search Online With InfoTrac College Edition

For additional information, explore Info Trac College Edition, your online library. Go to **http://www.infotrac-college.com** and use the passcode from the Info Trac card that came with your book. Try these search terms: childbirth, infant care, childbirth and psychological aspects, childbirth and technique, labor (obstetrics).

develop properly. Prenatal oxygen deprivation can impair the development of the central nervous system, leading to a host of problems, including cognitive and motor problems and even psychological disorders (Stevens, Raz, & Sander, 1999). Much research has focused on the effects of oxygen deprivation on the hippocampus, a brain structure that is vital in memory formation. Children who were deprived of oxygen at birth often show the predicted problems in learning and memory, but their cognitive problems tend to be much broader, including problems in spatial relations (Caine & Watson, 2000; Myers et al., 2000) and motor development (Raz et al., 1998). Prolonged cutoff of the baby's oxygen supply during delivery can also cause a variety of psychological and physical health problems, such as early-onset **schizophrenia** and cerebral palsy (Rosso et al., 2000). Schizophrenia is now considered by most researchers to be a disease of the brain, and oxygen deprivation is believed to impair the development of neural connections in the brain (Rosso et al., 2000). And, of course, severe, prolonged oxygen deprivation is lethal.

schizophrenia A severe psychological disorder that is characterized by disturbances in thought and language, perception and attention, motor activity, and mood and by withdrawal and absorption in daydreams or fantasy.

Oxygen deprivation can be caused by maternal disorders, such as diabetes, by immaturity of the baby's respiratory system, and by accidents, some of which involve pressure against the umbilical cord during birth (Caine & Watson, 2000; C. A. Nelson et al., 2000). The fetus and emerging baby receive oxygen through the umbilical cord. Passage through the birth canal is tight, and the umbilical cord is usually squeezed during the process. If the squeezing is temporary, the effect is like holding one's breath for a moment, and no problems are likely to ensue. (In fact, slight oxygen deprivation at birth is not unusual because the transition from receiving oxygen through the umbilical cord to breathing on its own may not take place immediately after the baby is born.) But if constriction of the umbilical cord is prolonged, developmental problems can result. Prolonged constriction is more likely during a breech presentation, when the baby's body may press the umbilical cord against the birth canal.

Fetal monitoring can help detect anoxia before it causes damage. A C-section can be performed if the fetus seems to be in distress.

Preterm and Low-Birthweight Infants

Since the fetus makes dramatic gains in weight during the last weeks of pregnancy, prematurity and low birthweight usually go hand in hand. ***Question: What is meant by the terms* prematurity *and* low birthweight?** A baby is considered premature or **preterm** when birth occurs at or before 37 weeks of gestation, as compared with the normal 40 weeks. A baby is considered to have a low birthweight when it weighs less than 5½ pounds (about 2,500 grams). When a baby is low in birthweight, even though it is born at full term, it is referred to as being **small for dates.** Mothers who smoke, use other drugs, or fail to receive proper nutrition place their babies at risk of being small for dates (Ahluwalia et al., 2001). Small-for-dates babies tend to remain shorter and lighter than their age-mates (Barros et al., 1992; Niedbala & Tsang, 1993). Preterm babies who survive are more likely than small-for-dates babies to achieve normal heights and weights.

About 7% of children are born preterm or low in birthweight, although the incidence varies in different racial and ethnic groups (Singh & Yu, 1995). However, among multiple births, even twins, the risk of having a preterm child rises to at least 50% (Kogan et al., 2000).

Question: What risks are connected with being born prematurely or low in birthweight?

Risks Associated With Prematurity and Low Birthweight

Neonates weighing between 3¼ and 5½ pounds (1,500–2,500 grams) are 7 times more likely to die than infants of normal birthweight, while those weighing less than 3½ pounds are nearly 100 times more likely to die (Overpeck, Hoffman, & Prager, 1992). But physical survival is only one issue connected with prematurity and low birthweight.

By and large, the lower a child's birthweight, the more poorly he or she fares on measures of neurological development and cognitive functioning throughout

preterm Born at or prior to completion of 37 weeks of gestation.

small for dates Descriptive of neonates who are unusually small for their age.

most of the school years (Wood et al., 2000). A study by H. Gerry Taylor and colleagues (2000) found that children whose birthweight was less than 750 grams fared generally less well at middle school age than children whose birthweight was 750–1,499 grams. Both low-birthweight groups performed more poorly than children whose birthweight was in the normal range. There seem to be gender differences. The cognitive functioning and school achievement of girls with low birthweight seem to improve more rapidly than that of boys with low birthweight (Hindmarsh et al., 2000).

There are also risks for motor development. One study compared 96 very-low-birthweight children with normal-term children at 6, 9, 12, and 18 months, correcting for age according to the expected date of delivery (Jeng, et al., 2000). The median age at which the full-term infants began walking was 12 months as compared with 14 months for the very-low-birthweight infants. By 18 months of age, all full-term infants were walking, whereas 11% of the very-low-birthweight infants had not yet begun to walk.

The neurological problems of very-low-birthweight children—like those of children who are deprived of oxygen prenatally—also apparently make them vulnerable to schizophrenia. One study found that children born prematurely are at greater risk of perinatal brain damage and subsequent neurodevelopmental problems, such as schizophrenia (Kunugi, Nanko, & Murray, 2001). A longitudinal study of people in Finland, begun in 1966, found that the combination of low birthweight, premature birth, oxygen deprivation or other problems during birth, and viral infections of the central nervous system during infancy contributed to the likelihood of developing schizophrenia (Veijola et al., 2000–2001). Another factor in the Finnish study was whether the pregnancy was wanted. Women who did not want to become pregnant apparently obtained poorer prenatal care. However, schizophrenia affects only about 1% of the population overall and also a small percentage of low-birthweight children.

Developing in a World of Diversity

A Racial Gap in Infant Deaths and a Search for Reasons

Ethelyn Bowers had a master's degree, an executive-level job, and a husband who was a doctor. But her accomplishments and connections seemed to make little difference when she endured the premature births and subsequent deaths of three babies, two of whom were in a set of triplets.

A competitive businesswoman who is immersed in her career and the hectic schedule of her surviving children, now 9 and 11, Ms. Bowers is candid about her losses but does not dwell on their possible causes. "I just chalked it up to bad luck, mainly," said Ms. Bowers, a sales director for Lucent Technologies who lives with her family in Livingston, New Jersey.

But her husband is haunted by the notion that somehow, in a way experts have yet to fully grasp, the fact that he and his wife are African American was a factor in their children's deaths.

"At the time of the death, you don't really dissect out the reasons; all you really think about is the tremendous sorrow," said her husband, Dr. Charles H. Bowers, chief of obstetrics and gynecology at Kings County Hospital Center in Brooklyn. "In retrospect, I think you need to look at psychosocial causes—the euphemism I use for racism. If in fact my counterpart, a [European American] physician making six figures, had a wife the same age and her likelihood of losing their child was less than half of my wife's chances of losing my child, why should that be?"

It is a mystery that consumes not only Dr. Bowers but also a growing field of researchers struggling to explain a persistent racial gap in American infant mortality rates. For years, the number of babies who die before their first birthday has been a source of shame for public health advocates; in international comparisons of infant mortality, the World Health Organization has ranked the United States 25th, below Japan, Israel, and Western Europe. But even as infant mortality rates improve—to a record low national average of 7.2 deaths per 1,000 live births—the disparity between African Americans and European Americans has grown, from 2 to nearly 2.4 times the number of infant deaths.

Especially troubling is evidence that this is not simply because of poverty (Foster et al., 2000). Though college-educated African

The outcomes for low-birthweight children are variable. One research group followed a group of 1,338 Dutch individuals who were born in 1983 with either a gestational age of less than 32 weeks or a birthweight of less than 1,500 grams (Walther, den Ouden, & Verloove-Vanhorick, et al., 2000). The children were assessed at the age of 2 by their pediatricians and at the ages of 5 and 9–14 by teams of investigators, including teachers and parents. All in all, only 10% of the group could be characterized as having a severe disability at ages 9–14. However, many more children appeared to have mild to moderate problems in learning or behavior.

Another study compared 39 individuals born prior to 35 weeks of completed gestation with 23 people born at full term. The comparisons took place at the ages of 4, 9, and 19 (Tideman, 2000). Psychological tests found the cognitive development of the preterm individuals to be inferior to that of the full-term individuals at the age of 4, but within normal limits. The difference was no longer evident by the ages of 9 and 19. Why do the findings of this study differ from those of the Dutch study? One reason may be that the premature individuals in this study were less premature, by about 3 weeks.

Preschool experience appears to foster the cognitive and social development of very-low-birthweight (VLBW) children. A study by Hoy and McClure (2000) compared a group of VLBW children who attended preschool with a group who did not and also with a group of normal-birthweight children of the same age. The VLBW children who attended preschool outperformed the VLBW children who did not on measures of cognitive functioning and teacher ratings. They earned higher grades, worked harder, were more likely to participate in social interactions, and were more likely to be rated as "learns a lot." However, their performance on all measures was still exceeded somewhat by the normal-birthweight children.

Signs of Prematurity

Preterm babies show characteristic signs of immaturity. They are relatively thin, because they have not yet formed the layer of fat that gives so many full-term children their round, robust appearance. They often have fine, downy hair referred to as **lanugo,** and an oily, white substance on the skin known as **vernix.** Lanugo and vernix disappear within a few days or weeks. If they are born 6 weeks or more prior to full term, their nipples will not yet have emerged. The testicles of boys

lanugo (lan-OO-go) Fine, downy hair that covers much of the body of the neonate, especially preterm babies.

vernix An oily, white substance that coats the skin of the neonate, especially preterm babies.

American women do better than impoverished women, they are still twice as likely to bury their babies as European American women. And immigrants have better pregnancy outcomes than assimilated minorities. What happens to their health once they move here? Why haven't education, better jobs, and health care made a bigger difference in closing the infant mortality gap?

"There's no single answer," said Dr. Solomon Iyasu, an epidemiologist at the Centers for Disease Control and Prevention in Atlanta. "Infant mortality is such a complex issue because it's driven both by medical issues as well as by social issues."

Because premature deliveries and low birthweights account for two-thirds of infant deaths, much recent research has focused on the causes of early labor. Medical complications from diabetes and high blood pressure, more prevalent illnesses in African Americans, can be blamed for some of the cases but do not account for the huge disparity. So researchers have begun exploring more subtle factors, like crime, pollution, and family support. Another hypothesis is that chronic stress caused by racial discrimination can elevate the hormones that set off premature labor.

"We're starting to think it's something about lifelong minority status," said Dr. James W. Collins, Jr., a neonatologist in Chicago who teaches pediatrics at Northwestern University Medical School.

Dr. Collins has compared the newborns of African Americans born in the United States with those of mothers who came directly from Africa and found that the immigrants' babies were bigger, with birthweights more comparable with European Americans than African Americans. Another study involving interracial couples indicated that the mother's race was crucial; babies born to African American mothers and European American fathers had higher rates of low birthweight.

The intergenerational effects of poverty and discrimination are also being explored amid concerns that a woman's health and personal experiences—even before she becomes pregnant—can affect her children's health.

"It's not clear that if you have a woman who's first-generation college-educated that she's still not carrying the risks of generations of poverty," said Dr. Marie McCormick, a pediatrician and professor of child and maternal health at the Harvard School of Public Health. "There is also increasing evidence that having been born with a low birthweight yourself, you're more likely to have a low-birthweight child."

Source: Reprinted with permission from Leslie Berger. (2000, June 25). A racial gap in inant deaths, and a search for reasons. *New York Times,* p. WH13.

born this early will not yet have descended into the scrotum. However, the nipples develop further and the testes descend after birth.

The muscles of preterm babies are immature. As a result, the babies' vital sucking and breathing reflexes are weak. The muscles of preterm babies may not be mature enough to sustain independent breathing. Also, the walls of the tiny air sacs within their lungs may tend to stick together because they do not yet secrete **surfactants,** substances that lubricate the walls of the sacs. As a result, babies born more than a month prior to full term may breathe irregularly or suddenly stop breathing, evidence of a cluster of problems known as **respiratory distress syndrome.** About one baby in seven born one month early shows the syndrome. It is found more frequently among infants born still earlier (Behrman et al., 2000). Respiratory distress syndrome causes a large percentage of neonatal deaths in the United States. Preterm infants with severe respiratory stress syndrome show poorer development in cognitive, language, and motor skills, and more persistent neurological abnormalities over the first 2 years of development than do infants with less severe respiratory distress and full-term infants (Smith et al., 1999).

Major strides have been made in helping low-birthweight children survive. Still, low-birthweight children who do survive often have problems, including below-average verbal ability and academic achievement and various physical, motor, perceptual, neurological, and behavioral impairments (Byrne et al., 1993; Goldson, 1992; Hoy & McClure, 2000).

Preterm infants with very low birthweights (under 1,500 grams) are likely to show the greatest cognitive deficits and developmental delays (Hack, Breslau, & Aram, 1992; Rose, Feldman, & Rose, 1992; Roussounis, Hubley, & Dear, 1993). Still, medical advances in recent years have reduced the severity and incidence of handicaps among babies with very low birthweights. A review of 111 studies that followed the development of very low birthweight babies into the preschool years and beyond reported that 75% had no disabilities (Escobar, Littenberg, & Petitti, 1991).

But let's not jump too far ahead. ***Question: How are preterm infants treated following birth?***

Reflect

If you had a preterm infant, do you think you would want to handle the baby as much as possible or tend to leave him or her alone? Explain.

Treatment of Preterm Babies

Because of their physical frailty, preterm infants usually remain in the hospital and are placed in **incubators** that maintain a temperature-controlled environment and afford some protection from disease. They may be given oxygen, although excessive oxygen can cause permanent eye injury or a form of blindness referred to as **retrolental fibroplasia.**

A generation ago, preterm babies were left as undisturbed as possible. For one thing, concern was aroused by the prospect of handling such a tiny, frail creature. For another, preterm babies would not normally experience interpersonal contact or other sources of external stimulation until full term. However, experiments carried out over the past two decades have suggested that preterm infants profit from early stimulation just as do full-term babies. One type of approach attempts to compensate somewhat for early removal from the uterus by exposing preterm infants to treatments that provide features of the intrauterine environment. These treatments include recordings of maternal heartbeats as they might be heard from within the uterus and placement in incubator waterbeds and **womb simulators** whose movements presumably capture some of the sensations of floating within the amniotic sac (Thoman, 1993).

Another approach is to provide preterm infants with the types of experiences that full-term babies receive. The babies may be cuddled, rocked, talked and sung to, and exposed to recordings of their mothers' voices; they may have mobiles placed within view. One study combined mechanical rocking with a recorded heartbeat for several 15-minute periods on a daily basis (Barnard & Bee, 1983). Immediately following the treatment, the infants showed increased activity levels. At a 2-year follow-up, their intellectual functioning was significantly ahead of preterm babies not given this treatment. Other recent innovations in stimulating

surfactants Substances that lubricate the walls of the air sacs in the lungs.

respiratory distress syndrome A cluster of breathing problems, including weak and irregular breathing, to which preterm babies are particularly prone.

incubator A heated, protective container in which premature infants are kept.

retrolental fibroplasia A form of blindness that stems from excessive oxygen, such as may be found in an incubator.

womb simulator An artificial environment that mimics some of the features of the womb, particularly temperature, sounds, and rocking movements.

premature babies include massage (Field, 1992) and "kangaroo care," in which the baby spends several hours a day lying skin to skin, chest to chest, with one of its parents (Dombrowski et al., 2000). By and large, preterm infants exposed to stimulation tend to gain weight more rapidly, show fewer respiratory problems, and make greater advances in motor, intellectual, and neurological development than do controls (Caulfield, 2000; Dombrowski et al., 2000; see Figure 4.3).

Parents and Preterm Neonates

One might assume that parents would be more concerned about preterm babies than babies who have gone to full term and thus treat them better. Ironically, this is not the case. Parents often do not treat preterm neonates as well as they treat full-term neonates. For one thing, preterm neonates are less attractive than full-term babies. Preterm infants usually do not have the robust, appealing appearance of many full-term babies. Their cries are more high-pitched and grating (Frodi & Senchak, 1990). Their behavior is more irritable (Eckerman et al., 1999). Fear of hurting preterm babies can further discourage parents from handling them, even when the hospital encourages it. Preterm children are also more likely to be abused by their parents in later years (Korner, 1987).

Mothers of preterm babies frequently report that they feel alienated from them and harbor feelings of failure, guilt, and low self-esteem. They respond less sensitively to their infants' behavior than mothers of full-term babies (Pederson & Moran, 1993). Mothers of preterm infants also touch and talk to their infants less and hold them at a greater distance during feeding (Eckerman & Oehler, 1992).

Once they come home from the hospital, preterm infants remain more passive and less sociable than full-term infants (Crnic et al., 1983; Garcia-Coll et al., 1992), so they demand less interaction with parents. However, when their parents do interact with them during the first year, they are more likely to poke at preterm babies, caress them, and talk to them, apparently in an effort to prod them out of their passivity. Yet, this high level of parental activity is not necessarily all positive in nature. Parents and preterm babies smile at one another less frequently during the first year than do parents and full-term babies (Field, 1980; Garner & Landry, 1992). Preterm babies also show less positive emotional tone in their vocalizations (Crnic et al., 1983). Mothers of preterm babies report feeling overprotective toward them. This may explain why 1-year-old preterm infants explore less and stay closer to their mothers than do full-term babies of the same age (Macey, Harmon, & Easterbrooks, 1987).

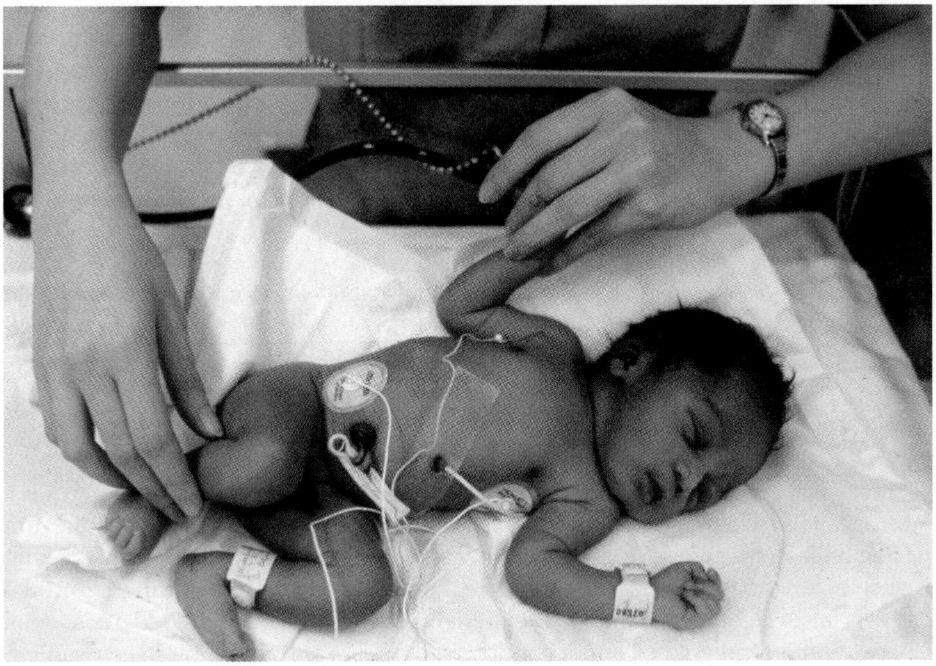

Figure 4.3
Stimulating a Preterm Infant

It was once believed that preterm infants should be left as undisturbed as possible. Today, however, it is recognized that preterm infants usually profit from various kinds of stimulation.

Preterm infants fare better when they have responsive and caring parents. Longitudinal research shows that preterm children who are reared in attentive and responsive environments attain higher intelligence test scores, have higher self-esteem, show more positive social skills, and have fewer behavioral and emotional problems in childhood than do preterm children reared in less responsive homes (Kirsh, Crnic, & Greenberg, 1995).

Intervention Programs

Intervention programs aimed at helping parents adjust to the birth and care of a low-birthweight infant can be beneficial to both the parents and the baby (Parker et al., 1992; Zahr, Parker, & Cole, 1992). In one such program, a specially trained nurse provided mothers with information, practical experience handling the infant, and emotional support. At the completion of the program, the mothers reported greater self-confidence and satisfaction with mothering and more favorable perceptions of their infants' temperament than did mothers who were not in the program (Rauh et al., 1988). At 3, 7, and 9 years of age, children of participating mothers showed more advanced intellectual development than did control children (Achenbach et al., 1990, 1993).

In another intervention program, the Infant Health and Development Program, parents of preterm babies in eight different locations were visited by child development specialists during their children's first 3 years. Parents were taught what to expect from their baby and how to respond to foster the child's development. Between the ages of 1 and 3, the children attended a day-care program that focused on language, social, and motor skills. At age 3, the children showed more advanced intellectual functioning and fewer behavior problems than preterm babies who were not in the program (Brooks-Gunn et al., 1993; Ramey et al., 1992).

Review

(22) Prenatal ________ deprivation can impair the development of the central nervous system, leading to cognitive and motor problems, even psychological disorders. (23) Oxygen deprivation can be caused by maternal disorders and by pressure against the ________ cord during birth. (24) A baby is considered to be ________ when birth occurs at or before 37 weeks of gestation, as compared with the normal 40 weeks. (25) A baby has a low ________ when it weighs less than 5½ pounds (about 2,500 grams). (26) The (higher or lower?) a child's birthweight, the more poorly he or she does on measures of cognitive functioning during most of the school years. (27) Preterm babies often have fine, downy hair referred to as ________ and an oily white substance on the skin known as vernix. (28) The walls of the air sacs in preterm babies' lungs may stick together because they do not yet secrete ________. (29) Preterm infants usually remain in the hospital and are placed in ________ to maintain a temperature-controlled environment. (30) Research suggests that it is (helpful or harmful?) to stimulate preterm infants.

Pulling It Together: What are the reasons that babies are born preterm or low in birthweight?

The Postpartum Period

postpartum period The period that immediately follows childbirth.

Postpartum derives from roots meaning "after" and "birth." The **postpartum period** refers to the weeks following delivery, but there is no specific limit. "Parting is such sweet sorrow," Shakespeare has Juliet tell Romeo. The "parting" from the baby is also frequently a happy experience. The family's long wait is over. Concerns about pregnancy and labor are over, fingers and toes have been counted, and despite some local discomfort, the mother finds her "load" to be lightened—most literally. However, according to the American Psychiatric Association (2000), about 70% of new mothers have periods of tearfulness, sadness, and irritability that the association refers to as "baby blues." In this section, we discuss two issues of the postpartum period: maternal depression and bonding.

Maternal Depression

Question: What kinds of problems in mood do women experience during the postpartum period? These problems include the baby blues and more serious mood disorders ("postpartum-onset mood episodes"), which occasionally include "psychotic features" (American Psychiatric Association, 2000). These problems are not limited to the United States, nor even to developed nations. They are far-flung, and researchers find them in China, Turkey, Guyana, Australia, and South Africa—occurring with similar frequency (Affonso et al., 2000; Cooper et al., 1999; Guelseren, 1999; Lee et al., 2001).

Baby blues affect the majority of women in the weeks after delivery (American Psychiatric Association, 2000). Researchers believe that the reason they are so common is that they are caused by the hormonal changes that attend and continue following delivery (Guelseren, 1999; Morris, 2000). They last for about ten days and are not severe enough to impair the mother's functioning. Don't misunderstand; the baby blues are seriously discomforting and not to be ignored as in "Oh, you're just experiencing what most women experience." The point is that most women can get by with them even though they're pretty awful at times, partly because they know that they are transient. Baby blues may be worsened—if not caused—by the multitude of changes that are taking place in the mother's daily life. Perhaps she had imagined that her greatest chores would involve taking care of the baby. She finds that she must also take care of herself. A word to fathers, partners, and other helpers: Mother may need your support (in terms of emotional support and doing things) as much as the baby does.

Reflect

Baby blues and postpartum mood episodes are found around the world. What does that fact suggest about their origins?

A minority of women, but perhaps as many as one in five to ten, encounter the more serious mood disorder that is frequently referred to as **postpartum depression (PPD).** PPD begins within four weeks after the delivery and may linger for weeks, even months. PPD is technically referred to as a major depressive disorder with postpartum onset. Like other major depressive disorders, it is symptomized by serious sadness, feelings of hopelessness and helplessness, feelings of worthlessness, difficulty concentrating, and major changes in appetite (usually loss of appetite) and sleep patterns (frequently insomnia). There can also be severe fluctuations in mood, with women sometimes feeling elated. Some women show obsessive concern with the well-being of their babies at this time.

Many researchers suggest that PPD is caused by the interactions of physiological (mainly hormonal) and psychological factors, including a precipitous decline in estrogen (Johnstone et al., 2001). Feelings of depression prior to getting pregnant or during pregnancy are a major risk factor for PPD (Ritter et al., 2000). It is possible that PPD, like baby blues, is worsened by concerns about all the life changes that motherhood creates and about whether one will be a good mother (Grazioli & Terry, 2000; Ritter et al., 2000). There is also little question that marital problems and having a sick or unwanted baby heighten the likelihood and severity of PPD (Terry, Mayocchi, & Hynes, 1996; Zelkowitz & Milet, 1996). But the focus today is on the physiological, because there are major changes in body chemistry during and after pregnancy, and because women around the world seem to experience similar disturbances in mood, even when their life experiences and support systems are radically different from those we find in the United States.

Researchers also suggest that infants with "difficult" temperaments can contribute to PPD. Some infants cry almost incessantly and do not settle into regular eating and sleeping routines. Infants like these not only create more stress for the parents, but they also challenge their parents' sense of self-efficacy. Yet, let's not place the blame on the baby; it's too common for babies like these to be abused.

postpartum depression (PPD) More severe, prolonged depression that afflicts 10–20% of women after delivery and is characterized by sadness, apathy, and feelings of worthlessness.

According to the American Psychiatric Association (2000), postpartum mood episodes are accompanied by "psychotic features" in one woman in five hundred to one thousand. A psychotic feature may mean a break with reality. Mothers with these features may have delusional thoughts about the infant that place the infant at risk of injury of death. Some women experience delusions that the infant is possessed by the Devil or "command hallucinations" to kill the infant. That is, they experience a command to kill the infant as though it is coming from the outside—perhaps from a commanding person or some kind of divine or evil spirit—even though the idea originates from within. But they may not be able to tell the difference, and the infant may be in serious jeopardy. But remember that these psychotic features are rather rare and that when they occur, they need not always place the baby at risk.

Women who experience PPD usually profit from social support and a general history of high self-esteem (Grazioli & Terry, 2000; Ritter et al., 2000). They may profit from psychotherapy, even if therapy does little more than explain that many women encounter PPD and get over it. Drugs that increase estrogen levels or act as antidepressants may be of help. Most women will get over PPD on their own, but with greater personal cost. At the very least, they should know that the problem is not unusual and does not necessarily mean that there is something seriously wrong with them or that they are failing to live up to their obligations. The majority of new mothers experience baby blues, and a sizable minority encounter PPD. It's mainly biological, and women almost always get over it. But they need

A Closer Look

Beginning and End

This is what happens, once the placenta is expelled: estrogen, that lubricating elixir, plummets in the minutes, the hours, after birth. Progesterone, too, takes a tumble while the anterior pituitary gland, responsible for lactation, swells to twice its normal size. Meanwhile, of course, you are lying in your hospital bed, babe to the breast, your caesarean scar still fresh, your episiotomy not yet beginning to burn. Or maybe you've gone "natural"; no matter. How you had the baby is not at issue, only that you had the baby, and in expelling it, expelled the royal purple parachute that floated you and yours through the nine months. Suddenly it's gone. And you come crashing down.

Eighty percent of all new mothers experience the baby blues; one in 10 new mothers develop from this a full-blown clinical depression, and one in 1,000 develop psychosis, which is 16 times more common during the postpartum period than at any other point. Andrea Yates was very likely suffering from a postpartum psychosis when she drowned her five children [in June 2001].

The story, frankly, did not surprise me. I am a psychologist and have seen in my female patients the dramatic effects hormones have on the mind. I once treated a woman with no prior psychiatric history who had had her ovaries removed because of a cancerous condition. Post-surgery, this woman developed a debilitating set of obsessions and compulsions that included the bizarre need to eat only Cheerios, only in sets of three. Prozac? No. Hormone replacement therapy, yes, and her symptoms almost immediately disappeared. During my own difficult pregnancy, I

Source: Reprinted from Lauren Slater. (2001, July 8). Beginning and end. New York Times Magazine, *pp. 11–12.*

© CORBIS SYGMA

Andrea Yates

Andrea Yates, the Texas mother shown here, drowned her children. It appears that she may have been experiencing postpartum psychosis at the time. Are women who commit crimes while they are suffering from postpartum psychosis to be held criminally responsible for their actions? The Texas court in which she was tried believed that Yates was indeed responsible for her crime. She was found guilty and sentenced to life in prison.

support not criticism when they encounter these problems. They certainly don't need to hear that they're just undergoing "another woman problem."

Bonding

Bonding—the formation of bonds of attachment between parents and their children—is essential to the physical survival and psychological well-being of children. How does bonding take place? Does bonding involve instinct, learning, or both? We address many of these issues in Chapter 7. Here let's focus on this question: ***Question: How critical is parental interaction with neonates in the formation of bonds of attachment?***

Click *Social-Emotional Development* in the Child and Adolescent CD-ROM for more on bonding and attachment.

Actually, parents may begin to form feelings of attachment to their babies before they are born. They feel them moving inside the mother and begin to fantasize about what it will be like to have them "on the outside." Babies may also begin to develop a "relationship" with their mothers prior to birth, at least in the sense that they can hear their mother's voices and seem to prefer their voices to those of strangers after birth. But one question of interest to developmentalists has been whether the first hours postpartum provide a special opportunity—or a necessary opportunity—for bonding between parents and neonates. A controversial study on this issue was carried out by Marshall Klaus and John Kennell (1976). They asserted that the first few hours after birth present a "maternal-sensitive" period during which the mother is particularly disposed, largely because of hormone levels, to form a bond with the neonate.

In their study, one group of mothers was randomly assigned to standard hospital procedure in which their babies were whisked away to the nursery shortly after birth. Throughout the remainder of the hospital stay, the babies visited with

bonding The process of forming bonds of attachment between parent and child.

experienced a persistent paranoia, strange voices, and the smell of orange peels and burning rubber in the air.

So why is it that despite 40 years of feminism and an overwhelming amount of evidence, we still refuse to release our notions of what motherhood means? Believing that childbirth is miraculous should not mean denying that it can be bad for a woman's health—and lethal for the little one. In hunter-gatherer tribes like the !Kung of the Kalahari Desert, estimates for infanticide are about one in 100 births.

Hormones are a biological reality, but they intersect with culture at every point. Postpartum depression occurs less frequently in other regions, like China, Jamaica, and some parts of Africa—where, not coincidentally, well-entrenched social rituals or government support cast a kind of protective balm over the raw days following birth. In Nigeria, new mothers rest for 40 days, while grandmothers, aunts, and sisters bring spiced tea, jasmine-scented water, and plates heaped with food, and so the mother is mothered. Contrast this to our own culture, where our naive notions of maternity intersect with the unforgiving schedule of managed care. A woman is released from the hospital 24 hours after a vaginal birth, 72 hours if her viscera have been split. If she is incredibly lucky (or if, as in my case, her doctors are "a little worried" about her), her health insurance may pay for a visiting nurse: a once-a-week 15-minute visit by a woman in a white hat, carrying a baby scale. If she wants to hire her own nighttime help, the cost is $100 for a 10 P.M.-to-6 A.M. stretch of sleep.

But it's all too easy, especially in the aftermath of Andrea Yates's tale, to imagine the pendulum swinging too far in the other direction—until all new mothers' normal mood variations are seen as sickness and women return to their Victorian status as womb-based beings of ooze and grease biologically incapable of reason. Testosterone, its levels fluctuating hour by hour, remains a far more lethal brew than estrogen or progesterone. More to the point, postpartum depression may be a hormone-related syndrome, but a syndrome is not just a "chemical imbalance." A syndrome is a complex cascade of biological events that have a recursive relationship to the individual and the culture in which these events are made manifest.

Perhaps the solution to our lack of support for mothers and children will come from one of those other cultures, those pockets of relative maternal sanguineness. Perhaps we will offer longer maternity leave or programs to help fathers share in parental responsibility as well as in parental passion, a phenomenon every bit as hormonal in men as in women. In male gerbils the level of prolactin, a hormone that spurs bonding, rises prior to the birth of the first litter; male prairie voles, injected with oxytocin, snuffle and lick their young pups. In the postpartum period, a man's testosterone levels often fall, perhaps enabling him to focus on his child.

In the meantime, my own child, Clara, has just turned 2, and I feel lucky to be past the treacherous time of just-born, more lucky still to have the financial resources that allow me to type these words while another woman watches her and her father stirs soup on the stove. Two is the age when language comes, and Clara has a love of language. We have bought her magnetic letters, which my husband uses to spell out cryptic messages to me on the refrigerator. How odd, to come downstairs each morning and see these mystery missives spelled out in primary colors and puerile shapes; beneath the bright stripes and simple sweetness of motherhood there are myriad, multiple swerves. Anything can happen. 4 QUARTz PONIES IN A diSh, my husband writes on the freezer door. GrAVity wouNds me TOO. And, the day Andrea Yates's mind did its final fizz, I came downstairs to find this magnetic message in a rainbow of color: SaDNESs wItHOUT RemeDY.

their mothers for half-hour periods at feeding time. The other group of mothers spent a half-hour with their neonates within 3 hours after birth, and they spent 5 hours a day with their infants for the remainder of the stay. The hospital staff encouraged and reassured the group of mothers who had extended contact.

Follow-ups over a 2-year period suggested that extended contact benefited both the mothers and children (Klaus & Kennell, 1978). For example, extended-contact mothers were more likely than controls to cuddle their babies, pick them up and soothe them when they cried, and interact with them. Some later studies also suggested that extended early contact may lead to better parent–child relationships, at least on a short-term basis (Fleming, 1989; Goldberg, 1983; Thomson & Kramer, 1984).

Critics note that these studies of bonding are fraught with methodological problems, however (Goldberg, 1983; Thomson & Kramer, 1984). Perhaps the most telling criticism is that it is impossible to determine if the benefits resulted from the extended contact or from parents' knowledge that they were in a special group. For example, not only did mothers in the Klaus and Kennell study receive extra time with their babies, but the hospital staff also gave them encouragement and support. Did their infants fare better because of superior bonding or because the hospital staff taught them that their relationships with their children were special and instructed them how to play with their babies and care for them? In short, research is not compelling that the hours after birth are critical or that failure to "form bonds" during this time will result in a second-rate parent–child relationship (Eyer, 1993). There are millions of fine parent–child relationships in which the parents were denied these early hours with their children (Rutter, 1981). Even Kennell and Klaus (1984) have toned down their views in their more recent writings. They now view the hours after birth as just one element in a complex and prolonged bonding process.

Review

(31) The weeks following delivery are called the ________ period. (32) Research suggests that the (majority or minority?) of new mothers experience periods of "postpartum blues." (32) The most serious form of postpartum blues is postpartum ________. (33) Research (does or does not?) show that early parental interaction with neonates is critical in the formation of bonds of attachment.

Pulling It Together: Cite evidence that hormonal imbalances following childbirth are involved in postpartum blues.

Characteristics of Neonates

Many neonates come into the world looking a bit fuzzy, because the lanugo has not yet disappeared, although full-term babies show less of this downy substance than preterm babies do. Full-term babies also show something of the protective oily coating, or vernix, shown by preterm babies. It dries up within a few days. Neonates tend to be pale, regardless of race. Their skin is thin, and the blood flowing through surface capillaries creates a pinkish cast.

In this section, we discuss several aspects of the behavior of neonates. Neonates may be utterly dependent on others; but they are probably more aware of their surroundings than you had imagined, and they make rapid adaptations to the world around them.

Assessing the Health of Neonates

Apgar scale A measure of a newborn's health that assesses appearance, pulse, grimace, activity level, and respiratory effort.

Question: How do health professionals assess the health of neonates? The neonate's overall level of health is usually evaluated at birth according to the **Apgar scale,** developed by Virginia Apgar in 1953. Apgar scores are based on five

TABLE 4.3 *The Apgar Scale*

	Points		
Sign	**0**	**1**	**2**
Appearance			
Color	Blue, pale	Body pink, extremities blue	Entirely pink
Pulse			
Heart rate	Absent (not detectable)	Slow—below 100 beats/minute	Rapid—100–140 beats/minute
Grimace			
Reflex irritability	No response	Grimace	Crying, coughing, sneezing
Activity level			
Muscle tone	Completely flaccid, limp	Weak, inactive	Flexed arms and legs; resists extension
Respiratory effort			
Breathing	Absent (infant is apneic)	Shallow, irregular, slow	Regular breathing; lusty crying

signs of health, as shown in Table 4.3. The neonate can receive a score of 0, 1, or 2 on each sign. The total Apgar score can, therefore, vary from 0 to 10. A score of 7 or above usually indicates that the baby is not in danger. A score below 4 suggests that the baby is in critical condition and requires medical attention. By 1 minute after birth, most normal babies attain scores of 8 to 10 (Bornstein & Lamb, 1992).

An acronym using the name APGAR is commonly used to aid in remembering the five criteria:

A: the general appearance or color of the neonate
P: the pulse or heart rate
G: grimace (the 1-point indicator of reflex irritability)
A: general activity level or muscle tone
R: respiratory effort, or rate of breathing

The **Brazelton Neonatal Behavioral Assessment Scale,** developed by pediatrician T. Berry Brazelton, measures neonates' reflexes and other behavior patterns (Brazelton, Nugent, & Lester, 1987; Brazelton, 1990b). The test screens neonates for behavioral and neurological problems by assessing four areas of behavior—motor behavior, including muscle tone and most **reflexes;** response to stress, as shown, for example, by the startle reflex; adaptive behavior, such as orientation to the examiner and responsiveness to cuddling; and control over physiological state, as shown by quieting oneself after being disturbed.

Reflexes

If soon after birth you had been held gently for a few moments with your face down in comfortably warm water, you would not have drowned. Instead of breathing the water in, you would have exhaled slowly through the mouth and engaged in swimming motions. (We urge readers not to test babies for this reflex. The hazards are obvious.) This swimming response is "prewired"—innate or inborn—and it is just one of the many reflexes shown by neonates. ***Questions: What are reflexes? What kinds of reflexes are shown by neonates?*** Reflexes are simple, unlearned, stereotypical responses that are elicited by certain types of stimulation. They do not

Brazelton Neonatal Behavioral Assessment Scale A measure of a newborn's motor behavior, response to stress, adaptive behavior, and control over physiological state.

reflex An unlearned, stereotypical response to a stimulus.

require higher brain functions; they occur automatically, without thinking. Reflexes are the most complicated motor activities displayed by neonates. Neonates cannot roll over, sit up, reach for an object that they see, or raise their heads.

Click *Physical Development* for more on reflexes.

Let's return to our early venture into the water. If you had been placed into the water not a few moments but several months after birth, the results might have been very different and disastrous. After a few months, the swimming reflex, like many others, ceases to exist. However, at 6 to 12 months of age infants can learn how to swim **voluntarily.** In fact, the transition from reflexive swimming to learned swimming can be reasonably smooth with careful guided practice.

Many reflexes have survival value. Adults and neonates, for example, will reflexively close their eyes when assaulted with a puff of air or sudden bright light. Other reflexes seem to reflect interesting facets of the evolution of the nervous system. The swimming reflex seems to suggest that there was a time when our ancestors profited from being born able to swim.

Pediatricians learn a good deal about the adequacy of neonates' **neural** functioning by testing their reflexes. The absence or weakness of a reflex may indicate immaturity (as in prematurity); slowed responsiveness, which can result from anesthetics used during childbirth; brain injury; or retardation. Let's examine some of the reflexes shown by neonates.

The rooting and sucking reflexes are basic to survival. In the **rooting reflex,** the baby turns the head and mouth toward a stimulus that strokes the cheek, chin, or corner of the mouth (Figure 4.4). The rooting reflex helps a newborn find the mother's nipple in preparation for sucking. Babies will suck almost any object that touches the lips. The sucking reflex grows stronger during the first days after birth and can be lost if not stimulated (Figure 4.5). As the months go on, reflexive sucking becomes replaced by voluntary sucking.

In the startle or **Moro reflex,** the back arches and the legs and arms are flung out and then brought back toward the chest, with the arms in a hugging motion (Figure 4.6). The Moro reflex occurs when a baby's position is suddenly changed or support for the head and neck is suddenly lost. It can also be elicited by loud

voluntarily Intentionally.

neural Referring to the nervous system.

rooting reflex A reflex in which infants turn their mouths and heads in the direction of a stroking of the cheek or the corner of the mouth.

Moro reflex A reflex in which infants arch their back, fling out their arms and legs, and draw them back toward the chest in response to a sudden change in position.

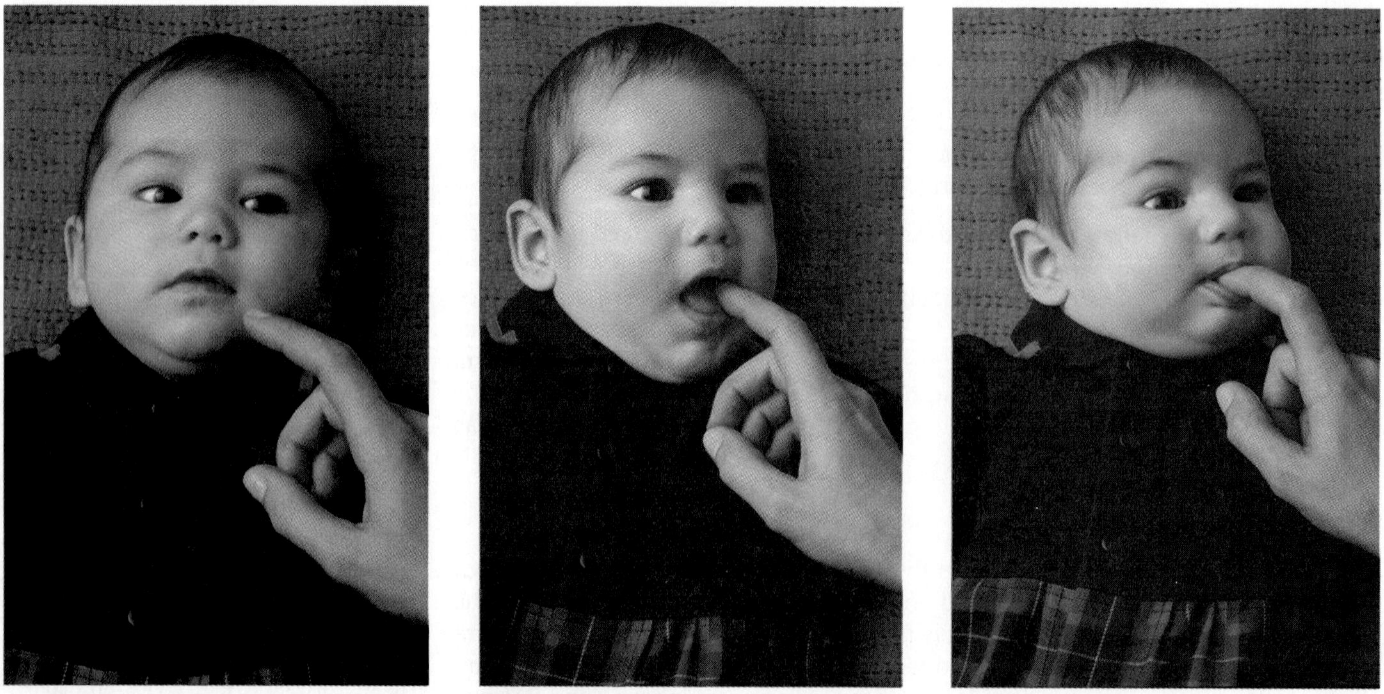

Figure 4.4
The Rooting Reflex
Tactile stimulation of the corner of the mouth elicits turning of the head toward the stimulus.

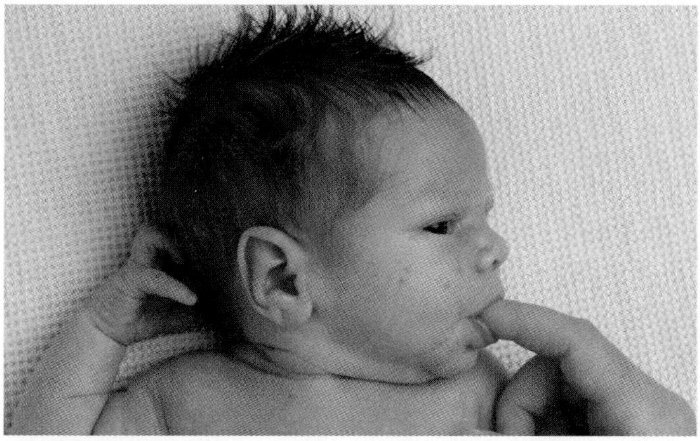

Figure 4.5
Testing the Sucking Reflex

The sucking reflex grows stronger during the days after birth. After several months, reflexive sucking is replaced by voluntary sucking.

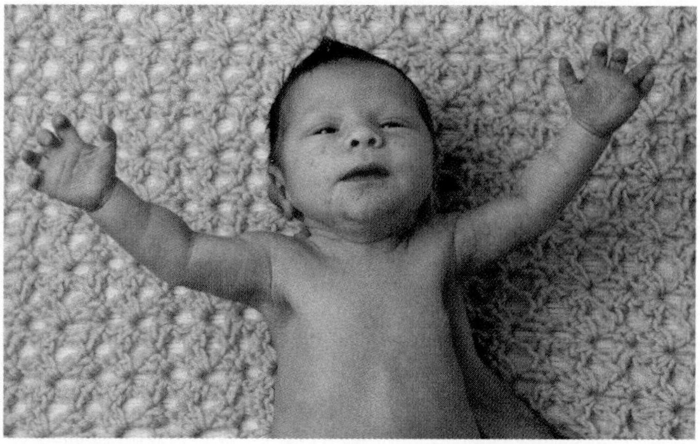

Figure 4.6
The Moro Reflex

The startle, or Moro, reflex is elicited by sudden changes such as loud noises or loss of support of the head and neck.

noises, by bumping the baby's crib, or by jerking the baby's blanket. The Moro reflex is usually lost by 6 to 7 months after birth, although similar movements can be found in adults who suddenly lose support. Absence of the Moro reflex can indicate immaturity or brain damage.

During the first few weeks following birth, babies show an increasing tendency to reflexively grasp fingers or other objects pressed against the palms of their hands (Figure 4.7). In this **grasping reflex,** or palmar reflex, they use four fingers only (the thumbs are not included). The grasping reflex is stronger when babies are simultaneously startled. Most babies can support their own weight in this way. They can be literally lifted into the air as they reflexively cling with two hands. Some babies can actually support their weight with just one hand. (Please do not try this, however!) Absence of the grasping reflex may indicate depressed activity of the nervous system, which can stem from use of anesthetics during childbirth. The grasping reflex is usually lost by 3 to 4 months of age, and babies generally

grasping reflex A reflex in which infants grasp objects that cause pressure against the palms.

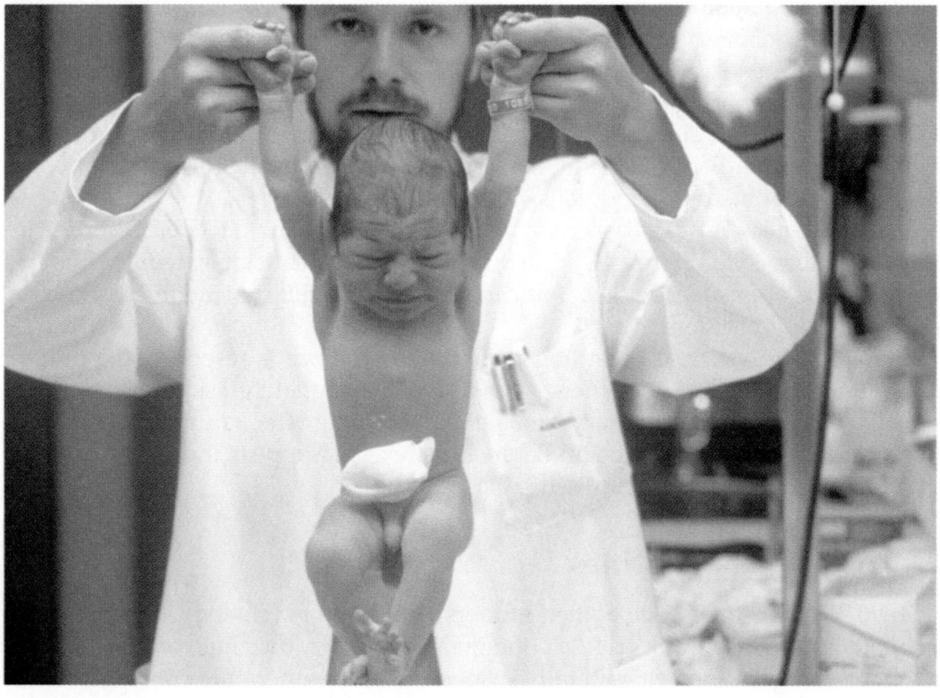

Figure 4.7
The Grasping Reflex

Neonates reflexively grasp objects pressed against the palms of their hands. By 3 to 4 months, the grasping reflex is lost and is gradually replaced by voluntary grasping.

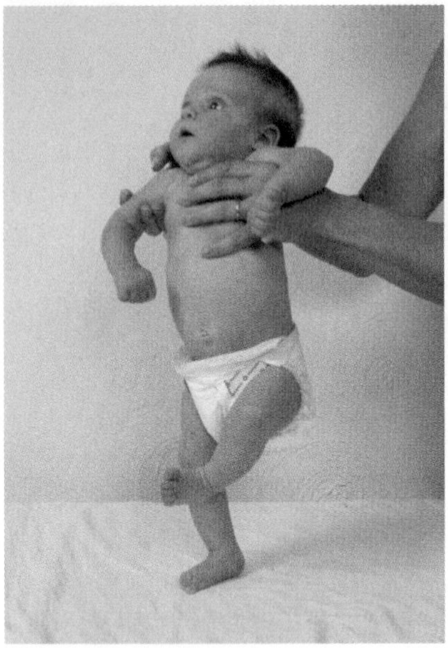

© Clarke & Priest/SPL/CMSP

Figure 4.8
The Stepping Reflex

The stepping reflex mimics walking. It is elicited by tilting the baby forward so that its feet press against a solid surface. True walking does not appear until the beginning of the second year.

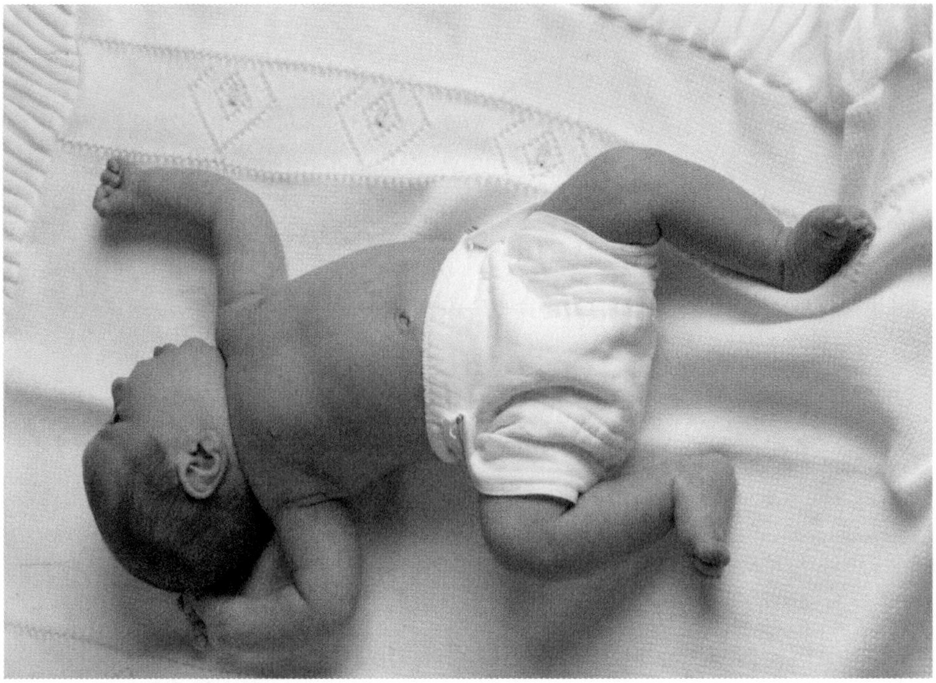

© D. Weinstein & Assoc/CMSP

Figure 4.9
The Tonic-Neck Reflex

The tonic-neck reflex, or "fencing position," is observed when the baby is on its back and turns its head to one side. The arm and leg on that side extend, while the limbs on the other side flex.

show voluntary grasping by 5 to 6 months. The Moro and grasping reflexes, like the swimming reflex, may suggest something about our evolutionary history. For example, the startle and grasping reflexes could work together to allow baby monkeys to cling to their mothers (Field, 1990).

One or 2 days after birth, babies show a reflex that mimics walking. When held under the arms and tilted forward so that the feet press against a solid surface, a baby will show a **stepping reflex** in which the feet advance one after the other (Figure 4.8). A full-term baby "walks" heel to toe, whereas a preterm infant is more likely to remain on tiptoe. The stepping reflex usually disappears by about 3 or 4 months of age.

In the **Babinski reflex,** the neonate fans or spreads the toes in response to stroking of the foot from heel to toes. The Babinski reflex normally disappears toward the end of the first year, to be replaced by curling downward of the toes. Persistence of the Babinski reflex may suggest defects of the lower spinal cord, lagging development of nerve cells, or other disorders.

The **tonic-neck reflex** is observed when the baby is lying on its back and turns its head to one side (Figure 4.9). The arm and leg on that side extend, while the limbs on the opposite side flex. You can see why this reflex sometimes is known as the "fencing position."

Some reflexes, such as breathing and blinking the eye in response to a puff of air, remain with us for life. Others, such as the sucking and grasping reflexes, are gradually replaced by voluntary sucking and grasping after a number of months. Still others, such as the Moro and Babinski reflexes, disappear, indicating that the nervous system is maturing on schedule.

stepping reflex A reflex in which infants take steps when held under the arms and leaned forward so that the feet press against the ground.

Babinski reflex A reflex in which infants fan their toes when the undersides of their feet are stroked.

tonic-neck reflex A reflex in which infants turn their head to one side, extend the arm and leg on that side, and flex the limbs on the opposite side. Also known as the "fencing position."

Sensory Capabilities

In 1890, William James, one of the founders of modern psychology, wrote that the neonate must sense the world "as one great blooming, buzzing confusion." The neonate emerges from being literally suspended in a temperature-controlled environment to being—again, in James's words—"assailed by eyes, ears, nose, skin, and entrails at once." ***Question: Just how well do neonates see, hear, and so on?*** In this section, we describe the sensory capabilities of neonates, and we see that James, for all his eloquence, probably exaggerated their disorganization.

Vision

Neonates can see, but they do not possess great sharpness of vision, or **visual acuity.** Visual acuity is expressed in numbers such as 20/20 or 20/200. Think for a moment of the big E on the Snellen chart (Figure 4.10), which you have probably seen during many eye examinations. If you were to stand 20 feet from the Snellen chart and could see only the E, we would say that your vision is 20/200. This would mean that you can see from a distance of 20 feet what a person with normal vision can discriminate from a distance of 200 feet. In such a case, you would be quite nearsighted. You would have to be unusually close to an object to discriminate its details.

Expressed in these terms, investigators have arrived at various approximations of the visual acuity of neonates, with the best estimates in the neighborhood of 20/600 (Banks & Salapatek, 1983). Neonates can best see objects that are about 7 to 9 inches away from their eyes. Neonates also see best through the centers of their eyes. They do not have the peripheral vision of older children. To learn how psychologists measure the visual acuity of infants, check the nearby "A Closer Look" feature.

Neonates can visually detect movement, and many neonates can **track** movement the first day after birth. In fact, they appear to prefer (that is, they spend more time looking at) moving objects to stationary objects (Kellman & von Hofsten, 1992). In one study (Haith, 1966), for example, 1- to 4-day-old neonates were exposed to moving or nonmoving lights while sucking on a pacifier. The frequency of their sucking decreased significantly when moving lights were presented, suggesting that they preferred this visual stimulus.

Visual accommodation refers to the self-adjustments made by the lens of the eye to bring objects into focus. If you hold your finger at arm's length and bring it gradually nearer, you will feel tension in your eyes as your lenses automatically foreshorten and thicken in an effort to maintain the image in focus. When you move the finger away, the lens accommodates by lengthening and flattening to keep the finger in focus. Neonates show little or no visual accommodation; they see as through a fixed-focus camera. Objects placed about 7–9 inches away are in clearest focus for most neonates, although this range can be somewhat expanded when lighting conditions are very bright. Interestingly, this is about the distance of the face of an adult who is cradling a neonate in the arms. It has been speculated that this sensory capacity for gazing into others' eyes may promote attachment between neonates and caregivers. Visual accommodation improves dramatically within the first 2 months (Hainline & Abramov, 1992).

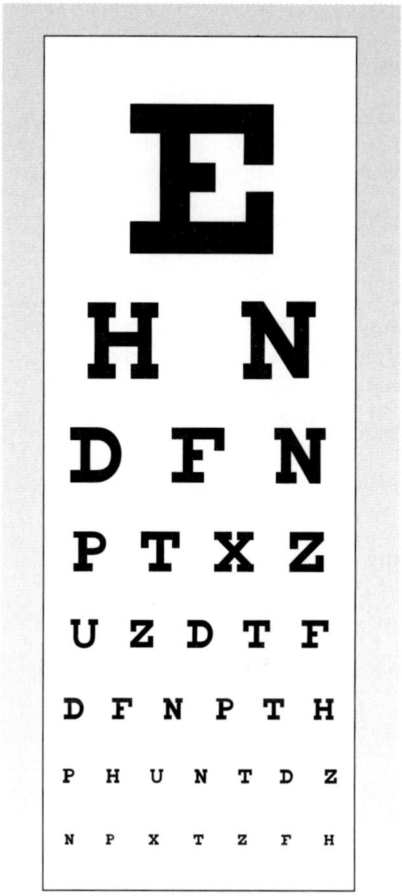

Figure 4.10
The Snellen Chart
The Snellen chart is used in eye examinations to provide an approximate measure of visual acuity.

Click *Physical Development* for more on vision and visual acuity.

visual acuity Keenness or sharpness of vision.

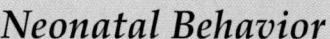

Developing in a World of Diversity

Neonatal Behavior

Neonates from different ethnic groups show some differences in their behavior. For example, compared with European American neonates, Chinese American, Japanese American, and Navajo infants are less likely to fret or cry, are calmed more readily when upset, are less excitable, and **habituate** faster to repeated presentation of stimuli (Chisholm, 1983; Kagan, 1992). These differences are thought to reflect a variety of factors including genetic endowment, the prenatal environment, and the mother's reproductive history (Garcia-Coll, 1990). Cultural differences in the way parents respond to their babies may strengthen early biologically based differences in emotional reactivity. For example, Japanese mothers are much more likely than American mothers to carry their infants and to sleep with them. Japanese mothers also are more apt to try to minimize their infant's crying and to emotionally indulge them (Camras et al., 1992). These maternal behaviors may contribute to the lower emotional reactivity of Japanese infants.

track To follow.

visual accommodation The automatic adjustments made by the lenses of the eyes to bring objects into focus.

habituate To show a decline in interest as a repeated stimulus becomes familiar.

convergence The inward movement of the eyes as they focus on an object that is drawing nearer.

intensity Brightness.

saturation Richness or purity of a color.

hue Color.

Now bring your finger toward your eyes trying to maintain a single image of the approaching finger. If you do so, it is because your eyes turn inward, or converge on the finger, resulting in a crossed-eyes look and feelings of tension in the eye muscles (see Figure 4.12). **Convergence** is made possible by the coordination of the eye muscles. Neonates do not have the muscular control to converge their eyes on an object that is very close to them. For this reason, one eye may be staring off to the side, while the other fixates on an object straight ahead. Convergence does not occur until 7 or 8 weeks of age for near objects. Neonates do show some convergence for objects that are at intermediate viewing distances (Aslin, 1987).

The degree to which neonates perceive color remains an open question. The research problem is that colors vary in **intensity** (that is, brightness) and **saturation** (richness), as well as in **hue.** For this reason, when babies appear to show preference for one color over another, we cannot be certain that they are responding to the hue. They may also be responding to the difference in brightness or saturation. So, you say, simply change hues and keep intensity and saturation constant. A marvelous idea—but easier said than done, unfortunately.

Physiological observations also cast doubt on the capacity of neonates to have highly developed color vision. There are two types of cells in the retina of the eye

A Closer Look

Studying Visual Acuity in Neonates: How Do You Get Babies to Tell You How Well They Can See?

How do psychologists determine the visual acuity of neonates? Naturally, they can't ask babies to report how well they see, but psychologists can determine what babies are looking at and draw conclusions from this information.

One method of observing what a baby is looking at is by using a "looking chamber" of the sort used in research by Robert Fantz and his colleagues (1975) (see Figure 4.11). In this chamber, the baby lies on its back, with two panels above. Each panel contains a visual stimulus. The researcher observes the baby's eye movements and records how much time is spent looking at each panel. A similar strategy can be carried out in the baby's natural environment. Filtered lights and a movie or TV camera can be trained on the baby's eyes. Reflections from objects in the environment can then be recorded to show what the baby is looking at.

Neonates will stare at almost any nearby object for minutes—golf balls, wheels, checkerboards, bull's-eyes, circles, triangles, even lines (Maurer & Maurer, 1976). But babies have their preferences, as measured by the amount of time they spend fixating on (looking at) certain objects. For example, they will spend more time looking at black and white stripes than at gray blobs. This fact suggests one strategy for measuring visual acuity in the neonate. As black and white stripes become narrower, they eventually take on the appearance of that dull gray blob. And, as they are progressively narrowed, we can assume that babies continue to discriminate them as stripes only so long as they spend more time looking at them than at blobs.

Studies such as these suggest that neonates are very nearsighted. But we should remember that they, unlike adults or older children, are not motivated to "perform" in such experiments. If they were, they might show somewhat greater acuity.

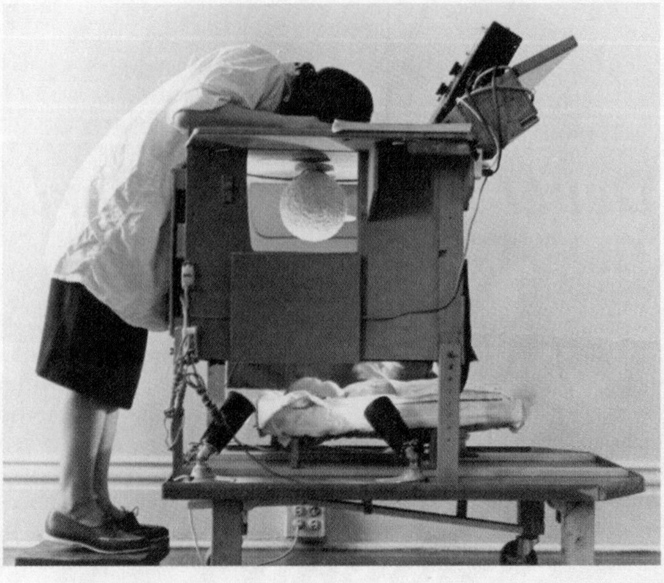

David H. Linton, courtesy of Ann Linton

■ **Figure 4.11**
The Looking Chamber

This chamber makes it easier for the researcher to observe the baby's eye movements and record how much time is spent looking at a visual stimulus.

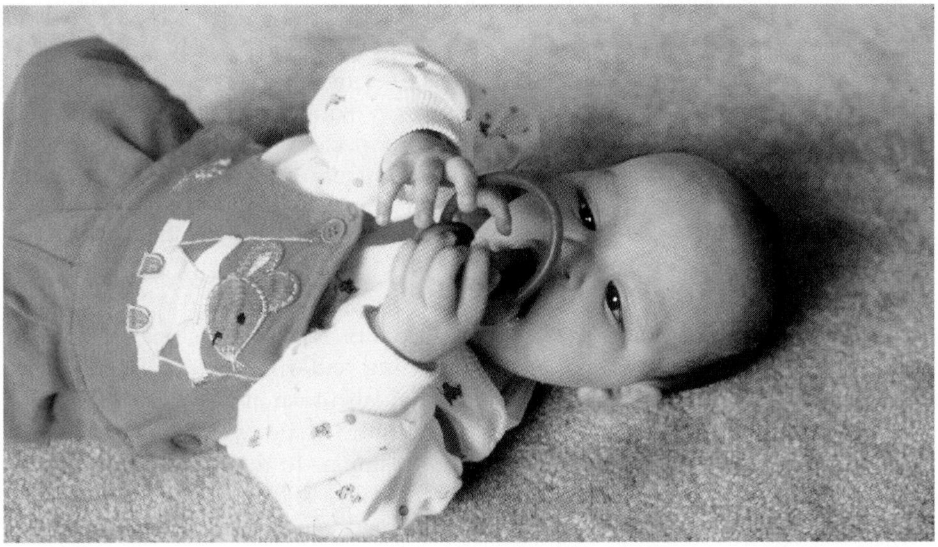

Figure 4.12
Convergence of the Eyes

Neonates do not have the muscular control to converge their eyes on an object that is very close to them. However, they do show some convergence for objects at intermediate viewing distances.

that are sensitive to light: rods and cones. **Rods** transmit sensations of light and dark. **Cones** transmit sensations of color. At birth, the cones are less well-developed than rods in structure.

Infants under 1 month of age do not show the ability to discriminate stimuli that differ in color. Two-month-olds can do so, but require large color differences. By 3 months, infants can see most, if not all, the colors of the visible spectrum (Banks & Shannon, 1993; Brown, 1990; Teller & Lindsey, 1993).

Even at birth, babies do not just passively respond to visual stimuli. For example, babies placed in absolute darkness open their eyes wide and actively search the visual field, moving their eyes two to three times a second (Haith, 1986).

Click *Physical Development* for more on methods of studying sensory and perceptual development in infancy.

Hearing

Fetuses respond to sound months before they are born. Although myelination of the auditory pathways is not complete prior to birth, fetuses' middle and inner ears normally reach their mature shapes and sizes before they are born (Aslin, Pisoni, & Juscyk, 1983). Normal neonates can also hear remarkably well, unless their middle ears are clogged with amniotic fluid. In fact, most neonates will turn their heads toward unusual sounds, such as that of a shaking rattle.

Neonates have the capacity to respond to sounds of different **amplitude** and to **pitch.** They are more likely to respond to high-pitched sounds than to low-pitched sounds (Bergeson & Trehub, 1999; Morrongiello & Clifton, 1984; Werner & Gillenwater, 1990). By contrast, speaking or singing to infants softly, in a relatively low-pitched voice, can have a soothing effect (Papousek, Papousek, & Symmes, 1991). This may explain the widespread practice in many cultures of singing lullabies to infants to promote sleep (Trehub, Trainor, & Unyk, 1993).

Click *Physical Development* for more on hearing.

It may well be that the sense of hearing plays a role in the formation of affectional bonds between neonates and their mothers that goes well beyond the soothing potential of the mothers' voices. Research indicates that neonates prefer their mothers' voices to those of other women, but do not show similar preferences for the voices of their fathers (DeCasper & Prescott, 1984; Freeman, Spence, & Oliphant, 1993). It may seem tempting to conclude that the human nervous system is "prewired" to respond positively to the voice of one's biological mother. However, neonates have already had several months of experience in the uterus; and, for a good part of this time, they have been capable of sensing sounds. Since they are predominantly exposed to prenatal sounds produced by their mothers, learning appears to play a role in neonatal preferences.

There is fascinating evidence that neonates are particularly responsive to the sounds and rhythms of speech, although they do not show preferences for specific languages. Condon and Sander (1974) filmed the bodily responses of 12-hour- to

rods Rod-shaped receptors of light that are sensitive to intensity only. Rods permit black-and-white vision.

cones Cone-shaped receptors of light that transmit sensations of color.

amplitude Height. The higher the amplitude of sound waves, the louder they are.

pitch The highness or lowness of a sound, as determined by the frequency of sound waves.

2-week-old infants to human speech (English or Chinese), disconnected vowel sounds, and tapping. The babies—most of whom were under 2 days old—tended to synchronize the movements of their heads, arms, and legs to the pattern of speech. They were equally adept at "dancing" to the sounds of English and Chinese, but showed little synchronization with the disconnected vowels or the tapping. It has also been shown that neonates can discriminate between different speech sounds (Molfese et al., 1991). And they can discriminate between new sounds of speech and those that they have heard before (Brody, Zelazo, & Chaika, 1984).

Smell: The Nose Knows, and Early

Neonates can definitely discriminate distinct odors, such as those of onions and anise (licorice). They show more rapid breathing patterns and increased bodily movement in response to powerful odors. They also turn away from unpleasant odors, such as ammonia and vinegar, as early as the first day after birth.

The nasal preferences of neonates are quite similar to those of older children and adults (Steiner, 1979; Ganchrow, Steiner, & Daher, 1983). When a cotton swab saturated with the odor of rotten eggs was passed beneath their noses, neonate infants spat, stuck out their tongues, wrinkled their noses, and blinked their eyes. However, they showed smiles and licking motions when presented with the odors of chocolate, strawberry, vanilla, butter, bananas, and honey. (It would be interesting to run a longitudinal study to determine whether neonates who show relatively less response to the aromas of chocolate, butter, and honey are more slender during later childhood and adulthood.)

Click *Physical Development* for more on smell, taste, and the sense of touch.

Research by Aidan Macfarlane (1975, 1977) and others suggests that the sense of smell, like hearing, may provide a vehicle for mother–infant recognition and attachment. Macfarlane suspected that neonates may be sensitive to the smell of milk, because, when held by the mother, they tend to turn toward her nipple before they have had a chance to see or touch it. In one experiment, Macfarlane placed nursing pads above and to the sides of neonates' heads. One pad had absorbed milk from the mother, and the other was clean. Neonates less than a week old spent more time turning to look at their mothers' pads than at the new pads.

In the second phase of this research, Macfarlane suspended pads with milk from the neonates' mothers and strangers to the sides of the babies' heads. For the first few days following birth, the infants showed no preference for the pads. However, by the time they were 1 week old, they spent more time looking at their mothers' pads than at the strangers'. It appears that they learned to respond positively to the odor of their mothers' milk during the first few days. Afterward, a source of this odor received preferential treatment even when the infants were not nursing.

Breast-fed 15-day-old infants also prefer their mother's axillary (underarm) odor to odors produced by other lactating women and by nonlactating women. Bottle-fed infants do not show this preference (Cernoch & Porter, 1985; Porter et al., 1992). The authors explain this difference by suggesting that breast-fed infants may be more likely than bottle-fed infants to be exposed to their mother's axillary odor. That is, mothers of bottle-fed infants usually remain clothed. Axillary odor, along with odors from breast secretions, might contribute to the early development of recognition and attachment.

Taste

Neonates are sensitive to different tastes. Research shows that neonates form facial expressions similar to those of adults in response to various kinds of fluids. Neonates swallow without showing any facial expression suggestive of a positive or negative response when distilled water is placed on their tongues (Steiner, 1979). Sweet solutions are met with smiles, licking, and eager sucking, as in Figure 4.13 (Rosenstein & Oster, 1988). Neonates apparently do discriminate among solutions with salty, sour, and bitter tastes, as suggested by different reactions in the lower part of the face (Rosenstein & Oster, 1988). Sour fluids frequently elicit pursing of the lips, nose wrinkling, and eye blinking. Bitter solutions stimulate spitting, gagging, and sticking out of the tongue.

Sweet solutions have a calming effect on neonates (Blass & Smith, 1992; Rosenstein & Oster, 1988; Smith, Fillion, & Blass, 1990). One study found that sweeter solutions increase the heart rates of neonates, suggesting heightened arousal, but also slow down their rates of sucking (Crook & Lipsitt, 1976). The researchers interpret this finding as an effort to savor the sweeter solution—to make the flavor last. Although we don't know why infants ingest sweet foods more slowly, this difference could be adaptive in the sense of preventing overeating. Sweet foods tend to be high in calories; eating them slowly gives infants' brains more time to respond to bodily signals that they have eaten enough and thus to stop eating. Ah, to have the wisdom of a neonate!

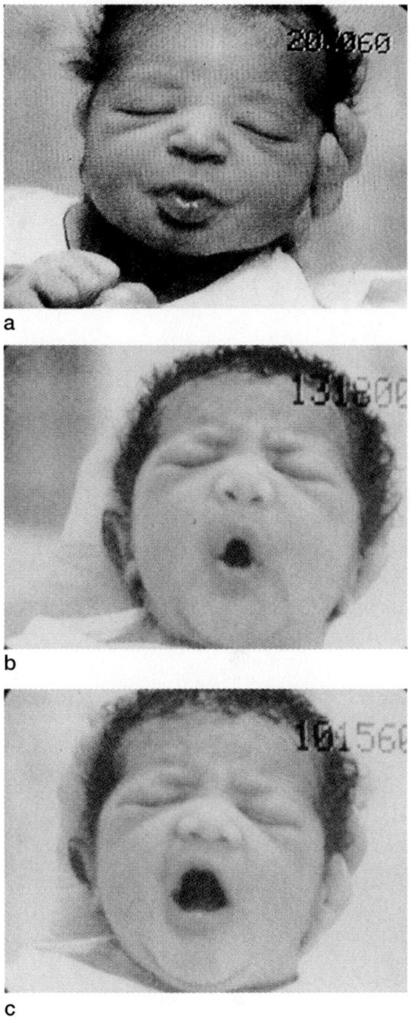

Figure 4.13
Facial Expressions Elicited by Sweet, Sour, and Bitter Solutions

Neonates are sensitive to different tastes, as shown by their facial expressions when tasting (a) sweet, (b) sour, and (c) bitter solutions.

Touch and Pain

The sense of touch is an extremely important avenue of learning and communication for babies. Not only do the skin senses provide information about the external world, but the sensations of skin against skin also appear to provide feelings of comfort and security that may be major factors in the formation of bonds of attachment between infants and their caregivers, as we shall see in Chapter 7.

Neonates are sensitive to touch. As noted earlier in the chapter, many reflexes—including the rooting, sucking, Babinski, and grasping reflexes, to name a few—are activated by pressure against the skin. However, neonates do not seem as sensitive to pain as slightly older babies are (Reisman, 1987). Considering the squeezing that takes place during childbirth, relative insensitivity to pain seems to be adaptive.

Learning—On *Really* Early Childhood "Education"

Question: Can neonates learn? The somewhat limited sensory capabilities of neonates suggest that they may not learn as rapidly as older children do. After all, we must sense clearly those things we are to learn about. However, neonates seem capable of at least two basic forms of learning: classical and operant conditioning.

Classical Conditioning of Neonates

In classical conditioning of neonates, involuntary responses are conditioned to new stimuli. In a typical study (Lipsitt, 1990b), neonates were taught to blink in response to a tone. Blinking (UCR) was elicited by a puff of air directed toward the infant's eye (UCS). A tone was sounded (CS) as the puff of air was delivered. After repeated pairings, sounding the tone (CS) gained the capacity to elicit blinking (CR).

Classical conditioning takes longer in neonates than in older infants. By the end of the first month, babies already have improved their ability to show classical conditioning and to retain what they have learned (Little, Lipsitt, & Rovee-Collier, 1984). But even neonates are equipped to learn that events peculiar to their own environments (touches or other conditioned stimuli) may mean that a meal is at hand—or, more accurately, at mouth. One neonate may learn that a light switched on overhead precedes a meal. Another may learn that feeding is preceded by the rustling of a carpet of thatched leaves. The conditioned stimuli are culture-specific; the capacity to learn is universal.

Operant Conditioning of Neonate

Operant conditioning, like classical conditioning, can take place in neonates. In Chapter 3 we described an experiment in which neonates learned to suck on a pacifier in such a way as to activate a recording of their mothers reading *The Cat in the Hat* (DeCasper & Fifer, 1980; DeCasper & Spence, 1991; Figure 4.14). The mothers had read this story aloud during the final weeks of pregnancy. In this example, the infants' sucking reflexes were modified through the reinforcement of hearing their mothers read a familiar story.

The younger the child, the more important it is that reinforcers be administered rapidly. Among neonates, it seems that reinforcers must be administered within a second after the desired behavior is performed if learning is to occur (Millar,

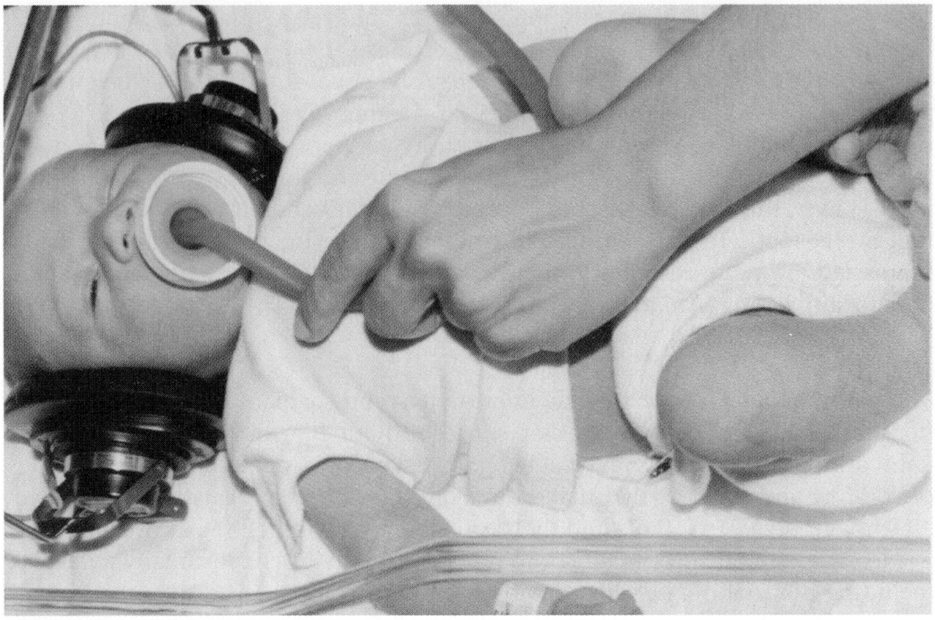

Figure 4.14
A Neonate Sucking to Hear Its Mother's Voice
Neonates learned to suck on a pacifier in a certain way to activate a recording of their mothers reading The Cat in the Hat. *Their mothers had read the story aloud during the final weeks of pregnancy.*

1972). Infants aged 6–8 months can learn if the reinforcer is delayed by 2 seconds, but if the delay is 3 seconds or more, learning does not take place (Millar, 1990).

There are large individual differences in conditionability among neonates. Some can be conditioned with relatively few trials, while others apparently cannot be conditioned at all (Fitzgerald & Brackbill, 1976). However, it would be premature to attribute differences in conditionability to differences in intelligence. Although intelligence is often loosely thought of as learning ability, conditionability is not comparable with the complex cognitive tasks that define intellectual performance in older children. Measures of intelligence in infants do not correlate very well with measures of intelligence that are taken at later ages.

Sleeping and Waking

Reflect

Have you or a family member had to adjust to the waking and sleeping patterns of a baby? Do you think that it is normal to occasionally resent being awakened repeatedly through the night? Explain.

As adults, we spend about one third of our time sleeping. ***Question: What patterns of sleep are found among neonates?*** Neonates greatly outdo us, spending two thirds of their time, or about 16 hours per day, in sleep. And in one of life's basic challenges to parents, neonates do not sleep their 16 hours consecutively.

A number of different states of sleep and wakefulness have been identified in neonates and infants, as shown in Table 4.4 (Berg & Berg, 1987; Colombo, Moss, & Horowitz, 1989; Wulff & Siegmund, 2001). Although individual babies differ in the amount of time they spend in each of these states, sleep clearly predominates over wakefulness in the early days and weeks of life.

Different infants require different amounts of sleep and follow different patterns of sleep, but virtually all infants distribute their sleeping throughout the day and night through a series of naps. The typical infant has about six cycles of waking and sleeping in a 24-hour period (Bamford et al., 1990). The longest nap typically approaches 4½ hours, and the neonate is usually awake for a little more than 1 hour during each cycle.

This pattern of waking and sleeping changes rapidly and dramatically over the course of the years (Berg & Berg, 1987; Lowrey, 1986). Even after a month or so, the infant has fewer but longer sleep periods and will usually take longer naps during the night. Parents whose babies do not know the difference between night and day usually teach them the difference by playing with them during daytime hours, once feeding and caretaking chores have been carried out, and by putting them back to sleep as soon as possible when they awaken hungry during the night. Most parents do not require professional instruction in this method. At 3:00 A.M., parents are not likely to feel playful.

By the ages of about 6 months to a year, many infants begin to sleep through the night. Some infants start sleeping through the night even earlier (Anders, Halpern, & Hua, 1992). A number of infants begin to sleep through the night for a week or so and then revert to their wakeful ways again for a while.

REM and NREM Sleep

Sleep itself is not a consistent state. It can be divided into **rapid-eye-movement (REM) sleep** and **non-rapid-eye-movement (NREM) sleep** (Figure 4.15). Studies with the **electroencephalograph (EEG)** show that we can subdivide NREM sleep into four additional stages, each with its characteristic brain waves, but our discussion will be limited to REM and NREM sleep. REM sleep is characterized by rapid eye movements that can be observed beneath closed lids. The EEG patterns produced during REM sleep resemble those of the waking state. For this reason, REM sleep is also called paradoxical sleep. However, it's difficult to awaken someone who is in REM sleep. Adults who are roused during REM sleep report that they have been dreaming about 80% of the time. Adults report dreaming only about 20% of the time when they are awakened during NREM sleep. The reasons for dreaming remain a mystery, although the content of dreams most often parallels the experiences of the waking day.

Note from Figure 4.15 that neonates spend about half their time sleeping in REM sleep. By 6 months or so, REM sleep accounts for only about 30% of the baby's sleep, and by 2 to 3 years, REM sleep drops off to about 20–25% (Coons & Guilleminault, 1982). There is a dramatic falling off in the total number of hours spent in sleep as we develop. Figure 4.15 shows that the major portion of the drop-off can be attributed to less REM sleep.

Why does the amount of REM sleep decline? According to **autostimulation theory,** the brain requires a certain amount of neural activity to develop properly (Roffwarg, Muzio, & Dement, 1966). This activity can be stimulated from internal or external sources. In older children and adults, external sources of stimulation are provided by activity, a vast and shifting array of sensory impressions, and, perhaps, thought processes during the waking state. The neonate, however, spends its brief waking periods largely isolated from the kaleidoscope of events of the world outside and is not likely to be lost in deep thought. Thus, in the waking state, the brain may not be provided with the needed stimulation. As a compensatory measure, the neonate spends relatively more time in REM sleep, which most closely parallels the waking state in terms of brain waves. While infants are in REM sleep, internal physiological stimulation spurs the brain on to appropriate development. Preterm babies spend even greater proportions of their time in REM sleep than full-term babies, perhaps—goes the argument—because they might require relatively greater stimulation of the brain.

rapid-eye-movement (REM) sleep A period of sleep during which we are likely to dream, as indicated by rapid eye movements.

non-rapid-eye-movement (NREM) sleep Periods of sleep during which we are unlikely to dream.

electroencephalograph (EEG) An instrument that measures electrical activity of the brain.

autostimulation theory The view that REM sleep in infants fosters the development of the brain by stimulating neural activity.

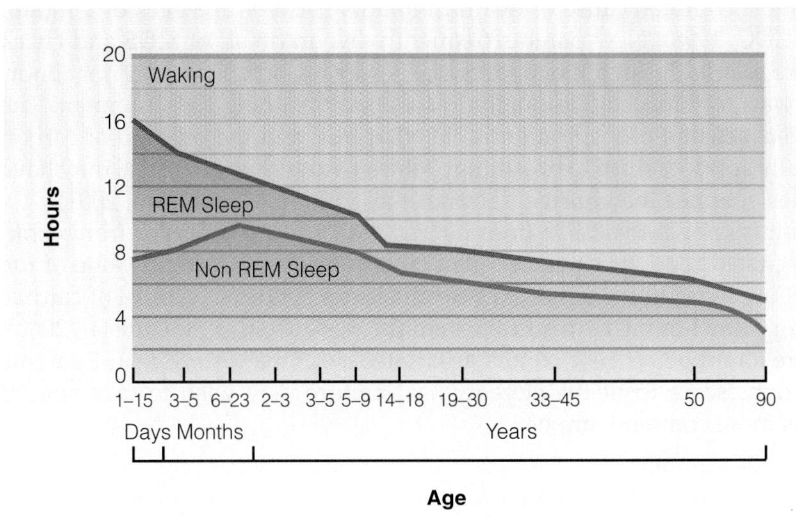

Figure 4.15
REM Sleep and NREM Sleep

Neonates spend nearly 50% of their time sleeping in rapid-eye movement (REM) sleep. The percentage of time spent in REM sleep drops off to 20–25% for 2- to 3-year-olds. As we mature, we sleep fewer hours, and most of the drop-off can be attributed to decline in REM sleep. Source: Roffwarg et al., 1966.

TABLE 4.4 *States of Sleep and Wakefulness in Infancy*

State	About . . .
Quiet sleep (NREM)	Regular breathing, eyes closed, no movement
Active sleep (REM)	Irregular breathing, eyes closed, rapid eye movement, muscle twitches
Drowsiness	Regular or irregular breathing, eyes open or closed, little movement
Alert inactivity	Regular breathing, eyes open, looking around, little body movement
Alert activity	Irregular breathing, eyes open, active body movement
Crying	Irregular breathing, eyes open or closed, thrashing of arms and legs, crying

In support of autostimulation theory, one study found that circumcised neonates spent less time in REM sleep than did neonates who were not circumcised (Emde et al., 1971). The process of circumcision is highly stimulating to neonates, and perhaps this external experience decreases the amount of internal stimulation or autostimulation they require. Another study found that infants who spent a good deal of time fixating on visual stimuli while awake showed temporary decreases in REM sleep (Boismier, 1977). Again, external stimulation might have reduced the need for internal stimulation.

A different view is that protein synthesis plays an important role in REM sleep. Protein concentrations in the brain increase during REM and decrease during REM deprivation (McGinty & Drucker-Colin, 1982). The large amount of time infants spend in REM sleep may indicate increased levels of protein synthesis during this period of rapid development (Berg & Berg, 1987).

Sudden Infant Death Syndrome

More children die from **sudden infant death syndrome (SIDS)** than die from cancer, heart disease, pneumonia, child abuse, AIDS, cystic fibrosis, and muscular dystrophy combined (SIDS Network, 2001). ***Questions: What is SIDS? What are the risk factors for SIDS?***

SIDS—also known as crib death—is a disorder of infancy that apparently strikes while the baby is sleeping. In the typical case, a baby goes to sleep, apparently in perfect health, and is found dead the next morning. There is no sign that the baby struggled or was in pain. The incidence of SIDS has been declining, but each year in the United States 2,000–3,000 infants in their first year die of SIDS (CDC, 1998). SIDS is the most common cause of death in infants between the ages of 1 month and 1 year (CDC, 1998). New parents frequently live in dread of SIDS and check their babies regularly through the night to see if they are breathing. It is not abnormal, by the way, for babies occasionally to suspend breathing for a moment. The intermittent suspension of respiration is called **apnea,** and the buildup of carbon dioxide usually spurs a return to breathing. Babies who succumb to SIDS may have more episodes of apnea than normal (Horne et al., 2001; J. M. Simpson, 2001).

Although it is known that SIDS does not result from suffocation or from choking on regurgitated food, its causes remain largely obscure. Currently, one of the most compelling hypotheses is that SIDS results from abnormal control of cardiac and respiratory functioning by the brain stem (Browne, Colditz, & Dunster, 2000). Still, there are a number of **risk factors** associated with the disorder, and parents whose situations seem to fit the stereotypical picture may wish to take special heed. SIDS is more common among

- babies aged 2–4 months
- babies who are put to sleep in the prone position (on their stomachs)

sudden infant death syndrome (SIDS) The death, while sleeping, of apparently healthy babies who stop breathing for unknown medical reasons. Also called *crib death.*

apnea (AP-knee-uh) Temporary suspension of breathing (from the Greek *a-*, meaning "without," and *pnoie,* meaning "wind").

risk factors Variables such as ethnicity and social class that are associated with the likelihood of problems but do not directly cause problems.

- premature and low-birthweight infants
- male infants
- families of lower socioeconomic status
- African American families (adjusting for their numbers in the population, more than twice as many African American babies as European American babies die of SIDS)
- babies of teenage mothers
- babies whose mothers smoked during or after pregnancy or used narcotics during pregnancy

Studies also have found a higher risk of SIDS among babies who sleep on their stomachs (CDC, 1998; Myers et al., 1998). These findings led the American Academy of Pediatrics in 1992 to recommend putting babies down to sleep on their sides or back. In 1994 a national "back to sleep" campaign was launched to encourage parents to put their babies to sleep in a supine position (on their backs rather than on their stomachs). In 1996, the American Academy of Pediatrics adjusted its recommendation to suggest that babies be put to sleep on their backs only (CDC, 1998). A recent national survey revealed that prior to the campaign, 43% of infants were usually placed to sleep in the prone position (on their stomachs), and 27% in the supine position. By 1998, however, only 17% were still placed in the prone position, and 56% were placed in the supine position (Willinger et al., 2000).

Home monitoring systems have been developed to alert parents to episodes of apnea and to give them time to intervene—as by artificial respiration. However, use of home monitors can be stressful for the families (SIDS Network, 2001). Moreover, there is little evidence that SIDS rates have been reduced as a result of using monitors (SIDS Network, 2001).

What should you do about SIDS? Bear in mind that the prevention of SIDS begins during pregnancy. Smoking and using other drugs during pregnancy increases the risk of SIDS. Obtain adequate nutrition and health care during pregnancy. Place your baby to sleep in the supine position (on its back). Keep current with research data on SIDS: Check with your pediatrician and check Web sites such as that of the Centers for Disease Control and Prevention (http://www.cdc.gov/) and that of the SIDS Network (http://www.sids-network.org/).

Crying

No discussion of the sleeping and waking states of the neonate would be complete without mentioning crying—a comment that parents will view as an understatement. I have known first-time parents who have attempted to follow an imaginary 11th commandment: "The baby shall not cry." ***Question: Why do babies cry?***

The main reason that babies cry seems to be simple enough: Repeated experiments with heel sticks (pardon my yuck) and other "stimuli" suggest that a one-word answer often suffices: pain (Gormally et al., 2001; Isik et al., 2000).

Some parents have entered into conflict with hospital nurses who tell them not to worry when their babies are crying on the other side of the nursery's glass partition. Nurses often tell the parents that their babies must cry because crying helps clear their respiratory systems of fluids that linger from the amniotic sac and also stimulates the circulatory system.

Whether crying is healthful and necessary remains an open question, but at least some crying among babies seems to be universal. Some scholars have thought of crying as a sort of primitive language, but it is not. Languages contain units and groupings of sounds that symbolize objects and events. Crying does not. Still, crying appears to be both expressive and functional. Crying, that is, serves as an infant's expressive response to aversive stimulation and also stimulates caretakers to do something to help. Crying thus communicates something, even though it is not a form of language. Crying may also communicate the identity of the crier across distance. Cries, that is, have multiple markers of individuality, and they may signal parents and other caretakers as to the location of their infant in a group (Gustafson, Green, & Cleland, 1994).

There are different types of cries (Gustafson & Harris, 1990). Schaffer (1971) suggests the existence of three distinct causes and patterns of crying: crying that stems from (1) hunger, (2) anger, and (3) pain. A sudden, loud, insistent cry associated with flexing and kicking of the legs may indicate colic (pain due to gas or other sources of distress in the digestive tract). The baby may seem to hold its breath for a few moments, and then gasp and begin to cry again. Crying from colic can be severe and persistent—lasting for hours, although cries generally seem to settle into a pattern after a while (Barr et al., 1992; Lester et al., 1992). Much to the relief of parents, colic tends to disappear by the 3rd to 6th month, as a baby's digestive system matures.

Prior to parenthood, many people wonder whether they will be able to recognize the meaning of their babies' cries, but it usually does not take them long. Parents are also somewhat better than other people at interpreting the cries of unfamiliar babies, probably because of their greater experience with infant cries and caregiving (Green et al., 1987; Gustafson & Harris, 1990).

Parents and other people, including children, have similar physiological responses to infant crying—increases in heart rate, blood pressure, and sweating (Frodi, 1985). Infant crying makes them feel irritated and anxious and motivates them to run to the baby to try to relieve the distress. The pitch of an infant's cries appears to provide information (Dessureau et al., 1998). Adults perceive high-pitched crying to be more urgent, distressing, and sick-sounding than low-pitched crying (Crowe & Zeskind, 1992; Lester et al., 1992).

Certain high-pitched cries, when prolonged, may signify health problems. For example, the cries of chronically distressed infants differ from those of normal infants in both rhythm and pitch. Patterns of crying may be indicative of such problems as chromosomal abnormalities, infections, fetal malnutrition, and exposure to narcotics (Huntington, Hans, & Zeskind, 1990; Sepkoski et al., 1993). A striking example of the link between crying and a health problem is the syndrome called *cri du chat,* French for "cry of the cat." This is a genetic disorder that produces abnormalities in the brain, atypical facial features, and a high-pitched, squeaky cry.

There are certain patterns of crying. For example, peaks of crying appear to be concentrated in the late afternoon and early evening (McGlaughlin & Grayson, 2001). While some cries may seem extreme and random at first, they tend to settle into a pattern that is recognizable to most parents (Green, Gustafson, & McGhie, 1998; Gustafson & Harris, 1990). Infants seem to produce about the same number of crying bouts during the first 9 months or so, but the *duration* of the bouts grows briefer, by half, during this period (Van Ijzendoorn & Hubbard, 2000). The response of the mother apparently influences infants' crying. It turns out that the more frequently mothers ignore their infants' crying bouts in the first 9 weeks, the less frequently their infants cry in the following 9-week period (Van Ijzendoorn & Hubbard, 2000). Please do *not* interpret this finding to mean that infant crying is best ignored. At least at first, crying communicates pain and hunger, and these are conditions that it is advisable to correct. Persistent crying can strain the mother–infant relationship (Papousek & von Hofacker, 1998).

Question: Now that I'm an expert on the causes and patterns of crying, what can I do to stop an infant from crying?

Soothing

How can a crying baby be soothed? For one thing, sucking seems to function as a built-in tranquilizer. Sucking on a **pacifier** decreases crying and agitated movement in neonates who have not yet had the opportunity to feed (Kessen, Leutzendoff, & Stoutsenberger, 1967). Therefore, the soothing function of sucking need not be learned through experience. However, sucking (drinking) a sweet solution also appears to have a soothing effect (Gormally et al., 2001; Isik et al., 2000). (Can it be that even babies will eat in order to cope with negative emotions?)

Parents find many other ways to soothe infants—picking them up; patting, caressing, and rocking them; and speaking to them in a low voice (Acebo & Thomas, 1992; Gustafson & Harris, 1990). Parents then usually try to find the specific cause of the distress by offering a bottle or pacifier or checking the diaper.

pacifier An artificial nipple, teething ring, or similar device that soothes babies.

Soothing
How can a crying baby be soothed? Picking the baby up, talking to it quietly, patting, stroking, and rocking all seem to have calming effects.

These responses to a crying infant are shown by parents in cultures as diverse as those of the United States, France, and Japan (Bornstein et al., 1992b).

Learning occurs quickly during the soothing process. Parents learn by trial and error what types of embraces and movements are likely to soothe their infants. And infants learn quickly that crying is followed by being picked up or other forms of intervention. Parents sometimes worry that if they pick up the crying baby quickly, they are reinforcing the baby for crying. In this way, they believe, the child may become spoiled and find it progressively more difficult to engage in self-soothing to get to sleep.

Fortunately, as infants mature and learn, crying tends to become replaced by less upsetting verbal requests for intervention. Among adults, of course, soothing techniques take very different forms—a bouquet of flowers or admission that one started the argument.[6]

Review

(34) In the United States today, the neonate's overall level of health is usually evaluated at birth according to the ________ scale. (35) In the ________ reflex, the baby turns the head and mouth toward a stimulus that strokes the cheek, chin, or corner of the mouth. (36) The startle reflex is also known as the ________ reflex. (37) Neonates are rather (nearsighted or farsighted?). (38) Neonates are more likely to respond to (high- or low-?) pitched sounds. (39) Neonates (do or do not?) prefer their mothers' voices to those of other women. (40) The nasal preferences of neonates are (similar to or different from?) those of older children and adults. (41). In terms of taste, ________ solutions have a soothing effect on neonates. (42) Neonates seem to be capable of two basic forms of learning: classical and ________ conditioning. (43) Neonates spend about ________ hours per day sleeping. (44) As babies mature, they spend (less or more?) time sleeping in REM sleep. (45) ________ is the most common cause of death in infants between the ages of 1 month and 1 year. (46) Parents are advised to put their babies to sleep in the (prone or supine?) position. (47) (High- or low-?) pitched cries, when prolonged, may signify health problems in infants.

Pulling It Together: Agree or disagree with William James's statement that the neonate must perceive the world "as one great blooming, buzzing confusion." Support your answer.

[6]"Perhaps that used to work," notes the author's wife. "Not any more."

Recite Recite Recite Recite

1. What events occur just prior to the beginning of childbirth?

Early in the last month of pregnancy, the head of the fetus settles in the pelvis. This is called dropping or lightening. The first uterine contractions are called Braxton-Hicks contractions, or false labor contractions. They are relatively painless. A day or so before labor begins, increased pelvic pressure from the fetus may rupture superficial blood vessels in the birth canal so that blood appears in vaginal secretions. At about this time, 1 woman in 10 has a rush of amniotic fluid from the vagina, and its discharge means that the amniotic sac has burst. The initiation of labor may be triggered by the secretion of hormones by the adrenal and pituitary glands of the fetus. The fetal hormones stimulate the placenta and the uterus to secrete prostaglandins, which cause labor contractions by exciting the muscles of the uterus. Later during labor, the pituitary gland releases oxytocin, a hormone that stimulates contractions strong enough to expel the baby.

2. What happens during the first stage of childbirth?

Childbirth begins with the onset of regular contractions of the uterus, which cause the cervix to become effaced and dilated. Most of the pain of childbirth is caused by stretching the cervix. The first stage may last from a few hours to more than a day. The medical necessity of prepping and enemas has been questioned. Fetal monitoring may be used to measure the fetal heart rate. During transition, the cervix is nearly fully dilated and the head of the fetus begins to move into the birth canal.

3. What occurs during the second stage of childbirth?

The second stage begins when the baby appears at the opening of the birth canal. It lasts from a few minutes to a few hours and ends with the birth of the baby. When the baby's head is crowned, an episiotomy may be performed to prevent random tearing of the perineum. The episiotomy, like prepping and the enema, is controversial. Once the baby's head emerges from the mother's body, mucus is removed from its mouth by suction so that the passageway for breathing will not be obstructed. When the baby is breathing on its own, the umbilical cord is clamped and severed. Most states require that drops of silver nitrate or an antibiotic ointment be put into the baby's eyes to prevent bacterial infections. The neonate may also receive an injection of vitamin K to ensure that the baby's blood will clot normally in the event of bleeding.

4. What happens during the third stage of childbirth?

During this stage, the placenta separates from the uterine wall and is expelled along with fetal membranes.

5. How is anesthesia used in childbirth? What are its effects on the baby?

General anesthesia achieves its effects by putting the woman to sleep, but it decreases the strength of uterine contractions and lowers the responsiveness of the neonate. Evidence is mixed as to whether it has long-term effects. Regional or local anesthetics—such as pudendal and epidural blocks—deaden pain in areas of the body without putting the mother to sleep. Local anesthesia also appears to decrease the responsiveness of neonates, but not seriously.

6. What is meant by the term *natural childbirth?*

Dick-Read became concerned that the use of anesthetics and other medical procedures was denying women the opportunity to experience natural childbirth and argued that women's labor pains are heightened by fear of the unknown and resultant muscle tensions. He encouraged educating women about reproduction and delivery, encouraging physical fitness, and teaching relaxation and breathing exercises.

7. What is the Lamaze method?

The Lamaze method—"prepared childbirth"—teaches women to dissociate uterine contractions from pain and fear by associating other responses, such as pleasant imagery, with contractions. It uses breathing and relaxation exercises, along with a "coach" who aids the mother in the delivery room. Women say they experience less pain, and they ask for less medication when their husbands are present during delivery. The Lamaze method, as practiced today, does permit the woman to request anesthetics, but women become actors, not victims.

Recite Recite Recite Recite

8. What is the C-section? Why is it so common?

A cesarean section delivers a baby surgically rather than through the vagina. C-sections are most likely to be advised if the baby is large or in distress or if the mother's pelvis is small or she is tired or weak. Herpes and HIV infections in the birth canal can be bypassed by C-section. More than 1 of every 5 births in the United States today are by C-section. Critics claim that many C-sections are unnecessary. Research suggests that it may be safe for women who have had a C-section to deliver subsequent babies vaginally.

9. Where should a woman deliver her child? (And why?)

Women have choices in childbirth—for example, home delivery, birthing suite, traditional labor room, use of a doula. Birthing suites—like the Duke University LDRPs—provide homelike surroundings with immediate hospital backup available. Birthing centers outside of a hospital may not have medical backup available as rapidly. In the United States, there are about 10 maternal deaths per every 100,000 live births, with hemorrhage and pregnancy-induced hypertension and infection being common causes of death.

10. What are the effects of oxygen deprivation at birth?

Researchers use two terms to discuss oxygen deprivation: *anoxia* and *hypoxia.* Prenatal oxygen deprivation can be fatal if prolonged; it can also impair the development of the nervous system, leading to cognitive and motor problems, even to psychological and physical disorders such as early-onset schizophrenia and cerebral palsy. Oxygen deprivation can be caused by maternal disorders, immaturity of the baby's respiratory system, and pressure against the umbilical cord during birth. Fetal monitoring may detect anoxia before it is damaging.

11. What is meant by the terms *prematurity* and *low birthweight?*

A baby is preterm when birth occurs at or before 37 weeks of gestation. It has a low birthweight when it weighs less than 5½ pounds (about 2,500 grams). A baby who is low in birthweight but born at full term is said to be small for dates. Maternal smoking, use of drugs, or malnutrition places babies at risk of being small for dates. About 7% of children are preterm or low in birthweight, and the risk rises among multiple births.

12. What risks are connected with being born prematurely or low in birthweight?

Risks include infant mortality. Delayed neurological and motor development and cognitive functioning are common, even when infants' ages are adjusted according to apparent date of conception. Very-low-birthweight (VLBW) children also appear to be especially vulnerable to schizophrenia. Outcomes for low-birthweight children are variable. Preschool experience appears to enhance the cognitive and social development of VLBW children. Preterm babies are relatively thin and often have vernix on the skin and lanugo. Sucking and breathing reflexes may be weak. The walls of air sacs in the lungs may stick together because they do not yet secrete surfactants. They may thus encounter respiratory distress syndrome.

13. How are preterm infants treated following birth?

Preterm babies usually remain in the hospital in incubators. Research finds that preterm infants profit from early stimulation just as full-term babies do. Forms of stimulation may include recordings of maternal heartbeats or womb simulators. Others involve cuddling, rocking, talking, and singing to them. "Kangaroo care" may be used. Parents often do not treat preterm neonates as well as they treat full-term neonates, perhaps because they are less attractive than full-term babies and have irritating, high-pitched cries. Research shows that preterm children who are reared in responsive environments attain higher intelligence test scores and have higher self-esteem and more social skills.

14. What kinds of problems in mood do women experience during the postpartum period?

Women may encounter maternity blues, postpartum depression, and postpartum psychosis. These problems are found around the world and probably reflect hormonal changes following birth, although stress can play a role. A history of depression also places a woman in a high-risk category for postpartum depression. High self-esteem and social support help women get through these adjustment problems.

Recite Recite Recite Recite

15. How critical is parental interaction with neonates in the formation of bonds of attachment?

Research by Klaus and Kennell suggested that the first few hours after birth present a "maternal-sensitive" period during which women's hormone levels particularly dispose them to "bond" with their neonates. However, the study confounded the effects of extra time with their babies with special attention from health professionals. Even Klaus and Kennell have come to view the hours after birth as just one element in a complex and prolonged bonding process.

16. How do health professionals assess the health of neonates?

The neonate's overall level of health is usually evaluated according to the Apgar scale, which considers the general appearance of the neonate, the heart rate, reflex irritability, general activity level, and respiratory effort. The Brazelton Neonatal Behavioral Assessment Scale screens neonates for behavioral and neurological problems by assessing motor behavior, response to stress, adaptive behavior, and control over physiological state.

17. What are reflexes? What kinds of reflexes are shown by neonates?

Reflexes are simple, unlearned, stereotypical responses that are elicited by specific stimuli. Pediatricians learn about the neonates' neural functioning by testing their reflexes. The rooting and sucking reflexes are basic to survival. Other key reflexes include the startle or Moro reflex, the grasping or palmar reflex, the stepping reflex, the Babinski reflex, and the tonic-neck reflex. These reflexes disappear or are replaced by voluntary behavior within months.

18. How well do neonates see, hear, and so on?

Neonates can see, but they are nearsighted. Neonates visually detect movement, and many track movement. Neonates show little or no visual accommodation. It is unclear how well neonates perceive color. Fetuses respond to sound months before they are born. Neonates are more likely to respond to high-pitched sounds than to low-pitched sounds. Neonates are particularly responsive to the sounds and rhythms of speech. The nasal preferences of neonates are similar to those of older children and adults. The senses of hearing and smell may provide vehicles for mother–infant recognition and attachment. Neonates prefer sweet solutions and find them soothing. The sensations of skin against skin are also soothing and apparently contribute to formation of bonds of attachment.

19. Can neonates learn?

Yes. Neonates seem capable of classical and operant conditioning. For example, they can be conditioned to blink their eyes in response to a tone. They will also learn to suck on a pacifier in such a way as to activate a preferred stimulus, such as a recording of their mothers reading *The Cat in the Hat.* (No comment.)

20. What patterns of sleep are found among neonates?

Neonates spend two thirds of their time in sleep. Virtually all neonates distribute sleeping through a series of naps. But even after a month, the infant has fewer but longer sleep periods. Neonates spend about half their time sleeping in REM sleep; but as time goes on, REM sleep accounts for less and less of their sleep. Perhaps the neonatal tendency to spend more time in REM sleep is connected with development of the brain.

21. What is SIDS? What are the risk factors for SIDS?

Sudden infant death syndrome is a disorder of infancy that apparently strikes while the baby is sleeping. SIDS is the most common cause of death in infants between the ages of 1 month and 1 year. Babies who succumb to SIDS may have more episodes of apnea than normal. SIDS is more common among babies who are put to sleep in the prone position, preterm and low-birthweight infants, male infants, and infants whose mothers smoked during or after pregnancy or used narcotics during pregnancy.

22. Why do babies cry?

Babies mainly cry because of pain and discomfort. Crying is an infant's expressive response to aversive stimulation and also stimulates caretakers to do something to

Recite Recite Recite Recite

help. Crying may also communicate the identity of the crier across distance, as well as hunger, anger, pain, and the presence of health problems. Parents usually learn to recognize the meaning of their babies' cries. Peaks of crying appear to be concentrated in the late afternoon and early evening.

23. What can I do to stop an infant from crying?

Many parents use pacifiers because sucking seems to be soothing. Parents also try picking babies up, patting, caressing and rocking them, speaking to them in a low voice, and feeding them a sweet solution.

On the Web

Search Online With InfoTrac College Edition

For additional information, explore Info Trac College Edition, your online library. Go to **http://www.infotrac-college.com** and use the passcode from the InfoTrac card that came with your book. Try these search terms: childbirth, low birth weight, sudden infant death syndrome, infants and sleep, infants (newborn), infants perception.

Visit Our Web Site

Go to **http://www.wadsworth.com/psychology** where you will find online resources directly linked to your book.

Child Development CD-ROM

Go to the Wadsworth Child Development CD-ROM for further study of the concepts in this chapter. The CD-ROM also includes quizzes and additional activities to expand your learning experience.

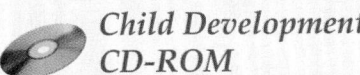

5 Infancy: Physical Development

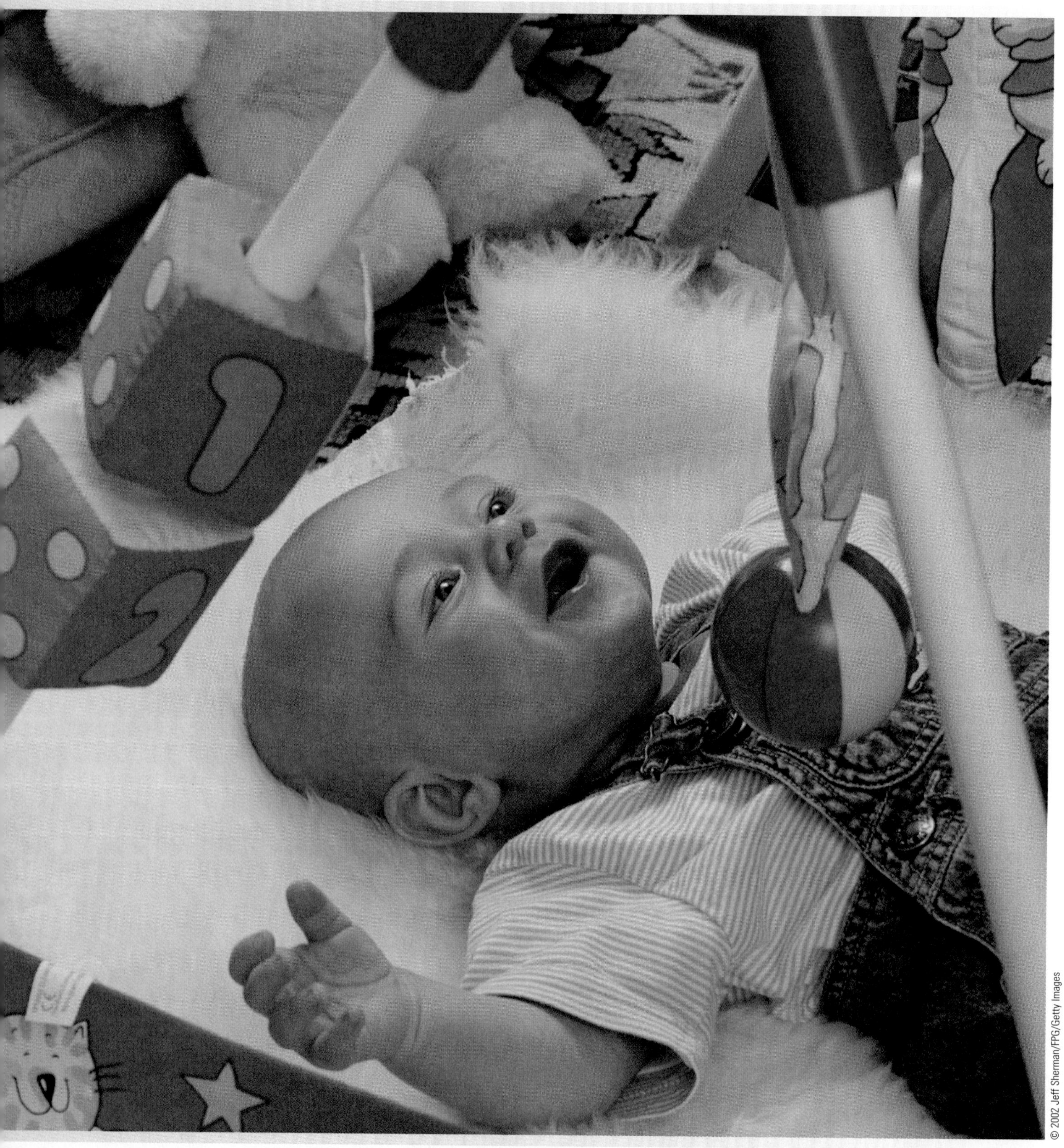

PowerPreview™

Physical Growth and Development

- **The head of** the newborn child (neonate) doubles in length by adulthood, but the legs increase in length by about five times.
- **Infants triple** their birthweight within a year.
- **Does feeding** infants skim milk help prevent obesity later in life?
- **Is breast milk** the perfect fast food?

Development of the Brain and Nervous System

- **A child's brain** reaches nearly 70% of its adult weight by the age of 1 year.

Motor Development

- **Which infants** sit, walk, and run at earlier ages—African Americans or European Americans?
- **Native American Hopi** infants spend the first year of life strapped to a board, yet they begin to walk at about the same time as children who are reared in other cultures.

Sensory and Perceptual Development

- **Neonates** are nearsighted.
- **Two-month-old infants** prefer to look at human faces rather than at brightly colored objects.
- **Do infants need** to have experience crawling before they develop fear of heights?
- **What happens** to neonatal kittens that are raised with a patch over one eye?

I am a keen observer of children—of my own, that is. From my experiences, I have derived the following basic principles of physical development:

- Just when you think your child has finally begun to make regular gains in weight, she or he will begin to lose weight or go for months without gaining an ounce.
- No matter how early your child sits up or starts to walk, your neighbor's child will do it earlier.
- Children first roll over when one parent is watching but will steadfastly refuse to repeat it when the other parent is called in.
- Children begin to get into everything before you get childproof latches on the cabinets.
- Every advance in locomotor ability provides your child with new ways in which to get hurt.
- Children will display their most exciting developmental milestones when there is no film in the camera.

More seriously, in this chapter we discuss various aspects of physical development during infancy. We examine changes in physical growth, the development of the brain and the nervous system, motor development, and the devel-opment and coordination of sensory and perceptual capabilities such as vision and hearing.

Physical Growth and Development

Click *Physical Development* in the Child and Adolescent CD-ROM for more on sequences of physical development.

During the first 2 years after birth, children make enormous strides in their physical growth and development. In this section, we explore sequences of physical development, changes in height and weight, and nutrition. ***Question: What are the sequences of physical development?***

Sequences of Physical Development

Three key sequences of physical development include *cephalocaudal development, proximodistal development,* and *differentiation.*

cephalocaudal (SEFF-uh-low-CAW-d'l) From top to bottom; from head to tail.

Cephalocaudal Development

The word **cephalocaudal** derives from the Greek *kephale,* meaning "head" or "skull," and from the Latin *cauda,* meaning "tail." It refers to the fact that development proceeds from the upper part of the head to the lower parts of the body.

When we consider the central role of the brain, which is contained within the skull, the cephalocaudal sequence appears quite logical. The brain regulates essential functions, such as heartbeat. Through the secretion of hormones, the brain also regulates the growth and development of the body and influences basic drives, such as hunger and thirst.

The head develops more rapidly than the rest of the body during the embryonic stage. By 8 weeks after conception, the head constitutes half of the entire length of the embryo. The brain develops more rapidly than the spinal cord. Arm buds form before leg buds. Most neonates have a strong, well-defined sucking reflex, although their legs are spindly and their limbs move back and forth only in diffuse excitement or agitation. Infants can hold up their heads before they gain control over their arms, their torsos, and, finally, their legs. They can sit up before they can crawl and walk. When they first walk, they use their hands to hold on to a person or object for support.

Cephalocaudal Development
Babies gain control over their head and upper body before they gain control over their lower body.

The lower parts of the body, because they get off to a later start, must do more growing to reach adult size. For example, the head doubles in length between birth and maturity, but the torso triples in length. The arms increase their length about four times, but the legs and feet do so by about five times.

© Sue Klemens/Stock, Boston

Proximodistal Development

Babies can grab large objects before picking up tiny things with their fingers.

Proximodistal Development

The **proximodistal** principle means that growth and development proceed from the trunk outward—from the body's central axis toward the periphery. This principle, too, makes a good deal of sense. The brain and spinal cord follow a central axis down through the body, and it is essential that the nerves be in place before the infant can gain control over the arms and legs. Also, the life functions of the neonate (the newborn baby)—heartbeat, respiration, digestion, and elimination of wastes—are all carried out by organ systems close to the central axis. These must be in operation or ready to operate when the child is born.

In terms of motor development, infants gain control over their trunks and their shoulders before they can control their arms, hands, and fingers. They make clumsy swipes at objects with their arms before they can voluntarily grasp them with their hands. Infants can grab large objects before picking up tiny things with their fingers. Similarly, infants gain control over their hips and upper legs before they can direct their lower legs, feet, and toes.

Reflect

Check yourself out in the mirror. Where are the "control systems" of your body? Does their location fit with the principles of cephalocaudal and proximodistal development?

Differentiation

As children mature, their physical reactions become less global and more specific. The tendency of behavior to become more specific and distinct is called **differentiation.** If a neonate's finger is pricked or burned, he or she may withdraw the finger, but will also thrash about, cry, and show general signs of distress. Toddlers are also likely to cry and show distress, but are more likely to withdraw the finger and less likely to thrash about. An older child or adult is also likely to withdraw the finger, but less likely to wail (sometimes) and show general distress.

Growth Patterns in Height and Weight

The most dramatic gains in height and weight occur during prenatal development. Within a span of 9 months, children develop from a zygote about $^1/_{175}$ inch long to a neonate about 20 inches in length. Weight increases by a factor of billions.

Question: What patterns of growth occur in infancy? During the first year after birth, gains in height and weight are also dramatic, although not by the standards of prenatal gains. Infants usually double their birthweight in about 5 months and triple it by the first birthday (Kuczmarski et al., 2000). Their height increases by about 50% in the first year, so that a child whose length at birth was 20 inches is likely to be about 30 inches tall at 12 months.

Growth in infancy has long been viewed as a slow and steady process. Growth charts in pediatricians' offices resemble the smooth, continuous curves shown in Figure 5.1. But research suggests that infants actually grow in spurts. About 90–95% of the time they are not growing at all. One study measured the height of infants throughout their first 21 months (Lampl, Veldhuis, & Johnson, 1992). The researchers found that the infants would remain the same size for 2 to 63 days and then would shoot up in length from a fifth of an inch (0.5 centimeters) to a full inch (2.5 centimeters) in less than 24 hours. Parents who swear that their infants sometimes consume enormous amounts of food and grow overnight may not be exaggerating all that much.

Infants grow another 4 to 6 inches during the second year and gain another 4 to 7 pounds. Boys generally reach half of their adult height by the second

Reflect

How closely did your parents pay attention to your height and weight? Did they chart it? When did you begin to think that you were average or above or below average in height and weight? What effect did your size have on your self-concept and self-esteem?

Click *Physical Development* for more on growth patterns.

proximodistal From near to far; from the central axis of the body outward to the periphery.

differentiation The processes by which behaviors and physical structures become more specialized.

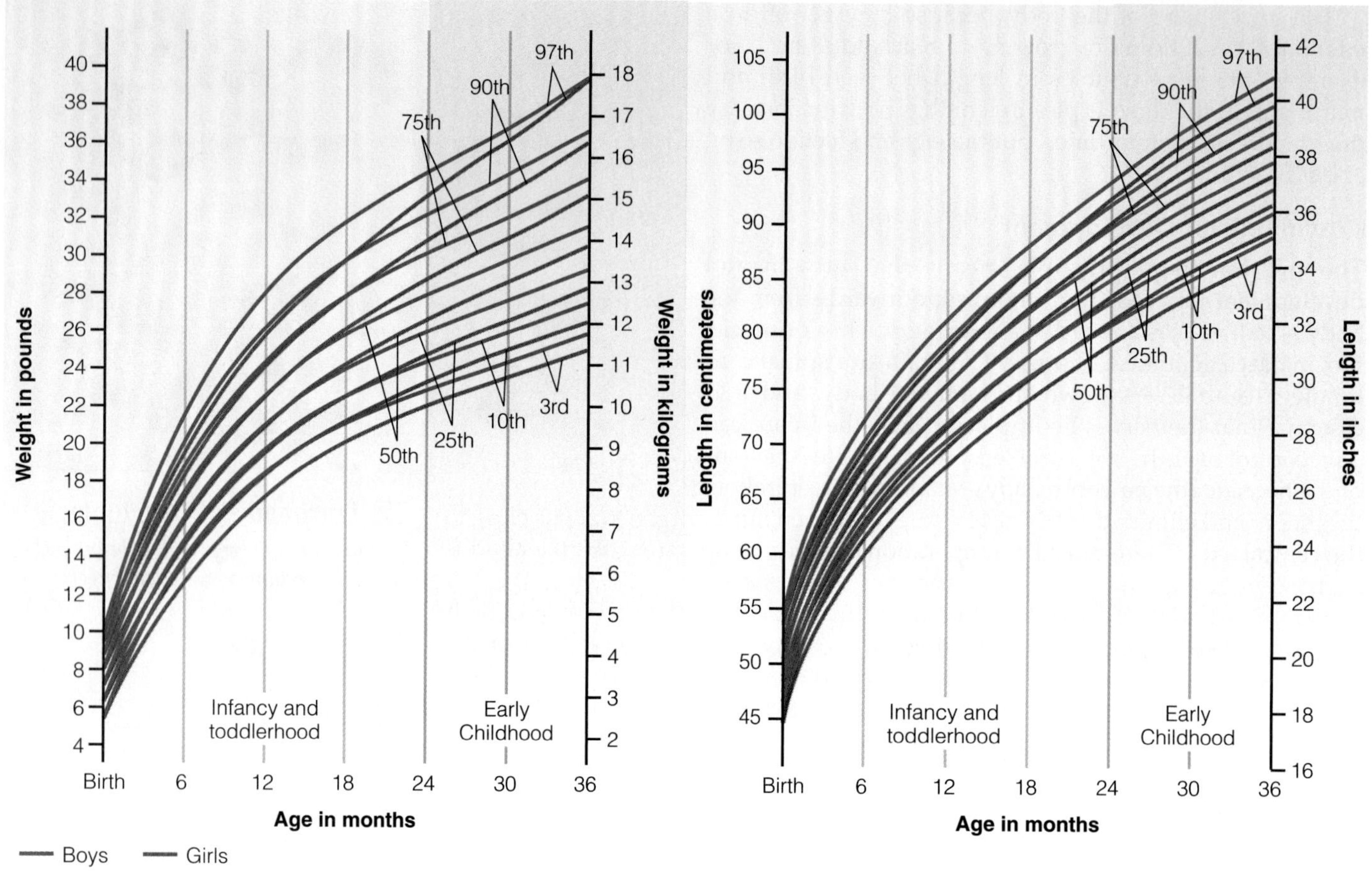

■ **Figure 5.1**
Growth Curves for Weight and Height (Length) From Birth to Age 3 Years

The curves indicate the percentiles for weight and length at different ages. Lines labeled 97th show the height and weight of children who are taller and heavier than 97% of children of a particular age. Lines marked 50th indicate the height and weight of the average child of a given age. Half of their age-mates are shorter and lighter, and half are heavier and taller. Lines labeled 10th designate children who are taller and heavier than only 10% of children their age, and so on.

Source: Figures 1–4, R. J. Kuczmarski et al. (2000, December 4). CDC Growth charts: United States. Advance Data From Vital and Health Statistics, *no. 314. Hyattsville, MD: National Center for Health Statistics.*

birthday. Girls, however, mature more quickly than boys and are likely to reach half of their adult height at the age of 18 months (Tanner, 1989). Taller-than-average infants, as a group, tend to slow down in their growth rates. Shorter-than-average infants, as a group, tend to speed up. This is not to suggest that there is no relationship between infant and adult heights or that we all wind up in an average range. Tall infants, as a group, wind up taller than short infants, but in most cases not by as much as seemed likely during infancy.

Reflect

Measure the length of your head and compute it as a fraction of your total height. Is your result something like 12%? Now look at a baby or some baby pictures. What would the baby look like if its head were only 12% of its total length?

Changes in Body Proportions

In rendering the human form, Greek classical sculptors followed the rule of the "Golden Section": The length of the head must equal one eighth of the height of the body (including the head). The ideal of human beauty may be so, but the reality is that, among adults, the length of the head actually varies from about one eighth to one tenth of the entire body. Among children, the head is proportionately larger (see Figure 5.2).

Development proceeds in a cephalocaudal manner. A few weeks after conception, an embryo is almost all head. When entering the fetal stage, the head is about half the length of the unborn child. In the neonate, it is about one quarter of the

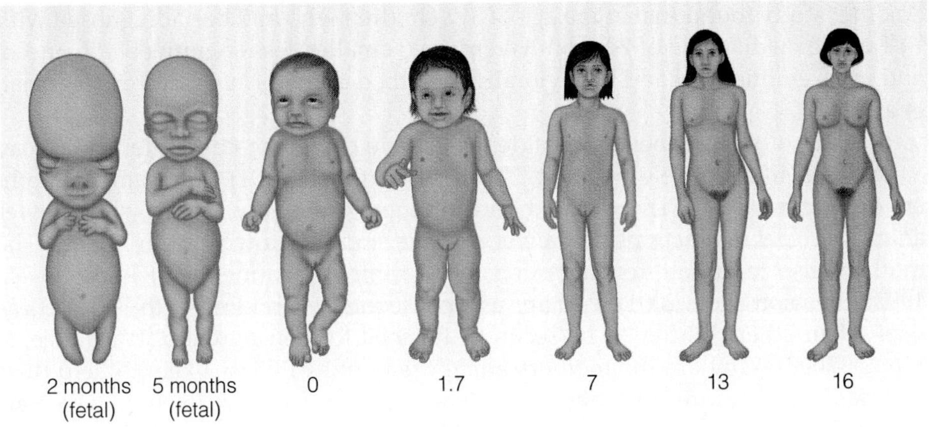

Figure 5.2
Changes in the Proportions of the Body

Development proceeds in a cephalocaudal direction. The head is proportionately larger among younger children.

length of the body. The head gradually diminishes in proportion to the rest of the body, even though it doubles in size by adulthood.

Among adults, the arms are nearly three times the length of the head. The legs are about four times as long—nearly half the length of the body. Among neonates, the arms and legs are about equal in length. Each is only about $1\frac{1}{2}$ times the length of the head. By the first birthday, the neck has begun to lengthen visibly, as have the arms and legs. The arms grow more rapidly than the legs do at first (an example of the cephalocaudal trend), and by the second birthday, the arms are actually longer than the legs. The legs then grow more rapidly, soon catching up with and surpassing the arms in length.

We have described typical growth patterns. Most infants follow these patterns and thrive. Some do not. ***Question: What is failure to thrive?***

Failure to Thrive

Haley is 4 months old. Her mother is breast-feeding her, and, as she puts it, "all the time," because Haley "refuses" to gain weight. Yes, Haley has been "stuck" for a few weeks at the same weight. Not gaining weight for a while is normal enough, but Haley is also irritable, and she feeds "fitfully," sometimes refusing the breast entirely. Her pediatrician is evaluating her for a syndrome called **failure to thrive (FTT).**

We live in one of the world's most bountiful nations. Very few have difficulty finding access to food. Nevertheless, a number of infants, like Haley, show FTT, which is a serious disorder that impairs growth in infancy and early childhood (Gardner et al., 1995; Polan & Ward, 1994). FTT is sometimes a fuzzy diagnosis. Historically, researchers have spoken of organically based (or organic) FTT versus non–organically based (non-organic) FTT. The idea is that in organic FTT, there is a specific underlying health problem that accounts for the failure to obtain, or make use of, adequate nutrition. So-called non-organic FTT (abbreviated as NOFTT in the research literature) apparently has psychological and/or social roots. In either case, the infant does not make normal gains in weight and size. In many cases, FTT is spoken of more generally, as a condition that has possible biological and psychosocial causes (Gardner et al., 1995; Robinson, Drotar, & Boutry, 2001).

Regardless of the cause or causes, feeding problems are certainly central to FTT. Research has shown that infants with FTT tend to be introduced to solid and finger foods later than other children. Like Haley, they are more likely to be described as variable eaters, and they are less often described as being hungry (Wright & Birks, 2000). FTT is linked not only to slow physical growth, but also to behavioral and emotional problems (Boddy, Skuse, & Andrews, 2000; Robinson et al., 2001). For example, at the ages of 2–12 months, infants with FTT display more problem behaviors during play; they express more negative feelings, vocalize less, refuse more often to make eye contact with adults (Stewart, 2001).

failure to thrive (FTT) A disorder of impaired growth in infancy and early childhood, characterized by failure to gain weight within normal limits.

Another study found that at the age of 8½, children who had been diagnosed with FTT at the median age of 20 months remained smaller, less cognitively advanced, and more emotionally and behaviorally disturbed than normal children (Dykman et al., 2001).

Many investigators believe that deficiencies in caregiver–child interaction play a major role in the development of FTT (Robinson et al., 2001). For example, mothers of infants with FTT, compared with mothers of healthy infants, show fewer adaptive social interactions and fewer positive emotions toward their infants. The mothers also terminate feedings in a more arbitrary manner (Hutcheson et al., 1997; Robinson et al., 2001). Perhaps as a consequence, children with FTT are less likely than other children to be securely attached to their mothers (Ward, Lee, & Lipper, 2000). Why are the mothers of children with FTT less likely to help their children to feel secure? One answer may be that they are more likely to have various psychological and personality disorders than mothers of healthier children (Polan et al., 1991).

Since FTT often results from a combination of factors, treatment may not be easy. Children with FTT need both nutritional support and attention to possible psychosocial problems (Gardner et al., 1995; Hutcheson et al., 1997; Robinson et al., 2001). It turns out that Haley's parents will profit from both personal counseling and advice on relating to Haley.

Catch-Up Growth

A child's growth can be slowed from its genetically predetermined course by many organic factors, including illness and dietary deficiency. However, once the problem is alleviated, the child's rate of growth frequently accelerates and returns to approximate its normal, deflected course. The tendency to return to one's genetically determined pattern of growth is referred to as **canalization.**

Reflect

Have you heard of the "food pyramid"? What elements from the pyramid should be in the diet of an infant? (And what about your own diet?)

Nutrition

The overall nutritional status of infants and children in the United States is fairly good compared with that of children in many other countries. The nutritional status of poor children has improved considerably in recent years, helped by various federal programs such as the Food Stamp Program, the Supplemental Food Program for Women, Infants and Children (WIC), the Child and Adult Care Food Program, and the National School Breakfast and Lunch programs. Even so, infants and young children from low-income families are more likely than other children to display signs of poor nutrition such as retarded growth and anemia (National Center for Children in Poverty, 2001). For more information on children in poverty, go to http://cpmcnet.columbia.edu/dept/nccp/. ***Question: Just what are the nutritional needs of infants?***

From the time of birth, infants should be fed either breast milk or an iron-fortified infant formula. The introduction of solid foods is not recommended until the infant is able to indicate hunger by leaning forward and indicate fullness by turning away from food. This stage normally occurs at 4 to 6 months of age, although the American Academy of Pediatrics recommends that infants be fed breast milk throughout the first year and longer if possible (AAP Media Alert, 1999). For more information, visit the American Academy of Pediatrics at http://www.aap.org. The first solid food is usually iron-enriched cereal, followed by strained fruits, then vegetables, and finally meats, poultry, and fish. Whole cow's milk is normally delayed until the infant is 9 to 12 months old. Finger foods such as teething biscuits are introduced in the latter part of the first year.

Here are some useful guidelines for infant nutrition (U.S. Department of Agriculture, 2000):

- Build up to a variety of foods. Introduce new foods one at a time, if possible, to determine whether they make a difference in the infant's behavior. (The infant

canalization The tendency of growth rates to return to genetically determined patterns after undergoing environmentally induced change.

may be allergic to a new food, and introducing foods one at a time helps isolate their possible effects on the infant.)

- Generally speaking, pay attention to the infant's appetite to help avoid overfeeding or underfeeding. (If the infant seems to have a very poor appetite, discuss it with the pediatrician.)
- Don't restrict fat and cholesterol too much. (For example, don't substitute skim milk for whole milk.) Infants need calories and some fat.
- Don't overdo high-fiber foods.
- Generally avoid items with added sugar and salt.
- Encourage high-iron foods; infants need more iron, pound for pound, than adults.

When in doubt, check with your pediatrician. Keep in mind that what is good for you—a late adolescent or an adult—is not necessarily good for an infant. If you are on a low-fat, high-fiber diet in an effort to ward off cardiovascular problems, cancer, and other health problems, good for you. But check with your pediatrician before assuming that the diet will benefit your infant.

Breast-Feeding and Bottle-Feeding: Pros and Cons, Biological and Political

The issues surrounding breast-feeding sometimes make one want to throw her or his hands up into the air and exclaim, "What will they politicize next?" No one can argue as to whether breast-feeding is the "natural" way to nourish a baby. Of course it is. Even aristocratic women in Europe's past who balked at the idea of breast-feeding themselves would arrange for "wet nurses"—women who earned an income by breast-feeding babies—to do the job. Breast-feeding was the standard American way of feeding infants until the early 1930s, when infant formulas were developed. Over the next three decades, breast-feeding declined dramatically for various reasons. More women were entering the workforce, breast-feeding was not seen as "scientific," and the women's movement of the 1960s and 1970s encouraged women to become liberated from traditional roles (Reiger, 2000). Breast-feeding thus has its political and social aspects as well as nutritional aspects (Law, 2000). A survey of the literature on breast-feeding finds that much of it has to do with domestic and occupational arrangements, day care, the ridicule or support of friends, reactions of public breast-feeding, issues of mother–infant bonding, and—as in the abortion debate—the extent to which the woman is in control over her own body (Guttman & Zimmerman, 2000).

Reflect

Do you "believe in" bottle-feeding or breast-feeding? Why? Have you ever thought about bottle-feeding versus breast-feeding? If not, why not?

A survey of 35 African American and Latina American mothers or pregnant adolescents (aged 12–19 years) found that those who recognized the benefits of breast-feeding were more likely to engage in the practice (Hannon et al., 2000). They reported benefits such as promoting mother–infant bonding and the infant's health. Barriers to breast-feeding included fear of pain, embarrassment due to public exposure, and unease with the act itself. This survey and others (e.g., by Mahoney & James, 2000) find that an influential person—such as the infant's father or the woman's mother—can often successfully encourage the mother to breast-feed. Better-educated women are more likely to breast-feed, even among low-income women (Hannon et al., 2000).

In any event, breast-feeding has become more popular during the past generation, largely because of increased knowledge of its health benefits, even among women at the lower end of the socioeconomic spectrum (Hannon et al., 2000). The majority of mothers in the United States today—about three in five—breast-feed their children (American Academy of Pediatrics, 2002). However, only about one woman in five continues to breast-feed after six months, and the American Academy of Pediatrics (2002) recommends that women breast-feed for a year or more.

Question: Why do women bottle-feed or breast-feed their children? Many women bottle-feed because they return to the workforce soon after childbirth and they are simply unavailable for regular breast-feeding. Their partners, extended families, nannies, or child care workers give their children bottles during the day. Some mothers pump their own milk and bottle it for their children for the hours when they are away, but pumping has its own problems. Some parents bottle-feed because it permits both parents to share equally in feeding their children—around the clock. The father may not be equipped to breast-feed, but he can bottle-feed. Even though bottle-feeding requires obtaining and preparing formulas, many women find it to be less troublesome overall.

Is Breast Milk the Perfect Fast Food?

These are the times for fast food. People rush out to class, to work, even to relaxation exercises at the psychologist's office. In this welter of activity, nutritionists note that it could be that the best fast food has been with us since the beginning of our species. This may be one case in which development in the new millennium and development in the ancient cave are one and the same.

As more and more plaudits come in, mother's milk is also referred to as the perfect health food. ***Question: What are the advantages and disadvantages of breast milk?*** Let's begin with the positive (American Academy of Pediatrics, 2002; Kramer et al., 2001; Lawrence et al., 2001):

- Breast milk conforms to human digestion processes (that is, it is unlikely to "upset the stomach" and cause babies to vomit).
- Breast milk possesses the nutrients that babies require (even though most physicians prescribe supplementary vitamins and, sometimes, minerals).
- As the infant matures, the composition of breast milk changes to help meet its changing needs.
- Breast milk contains the mother's antibodies; when they are transmitted to the infant, they help can prevent problems ranging from ear infections *(otitis media),* pneumonia, wheezing, bronchiolitis, and tetanus to chicken pox, bacterial meningitis, and typhoid.
- Breast milk helps protect against the form of cancer known as childhood lymphoma (a cancer of the lymph glands).
- Diarrhea can be a persistent and deadly disease for millions of infants in developing countries, and breast milk decreases the likelihood of developing serious and lingering cases of diarrhea.
- Infants who are nourished by breast milk are less likely to develop allergic responses and constipation than infants who are bottle-fed.
- Infants who are nourished by breast milk are less likely to develop obesity later in life.
- Breast-feeding also has health benefits for the mother: It reduces the risk of early breast cancer and ovarian cancer and builds bone strength, which can reduce the likelihood of the hip fractures that result from osteoporosis following menopause.

But it's not all good news. There is a downside to breast-feeding. For example, one of the bodily fluids that transmits the virus that causes AIDS (HIV) is breast milk. The United Nations estimates that as many as one third of the world's infants who have HIV/AIDS were infected in this manner (United Nations Special Session on AIDS, 2001). Alcohol, many drugs taken by the mother, and environmental hazards such as PCBs can also be transmitted to infants through breast milk. Therefore, breast milk may not always be as pure as it seems. Moreover, for breast milk to contain the necessary nutrients, the mother must be adequately nourished herself. In many cases, mothers in developing countries do not eat sufficiently well to pass along proper nutrition to their infants (Crossette, 2000).

Other negatives in breast-feeding include the mother's assumptions of the sole responsibility for nighttime feedings. She also encounters the physical demands of producing and expelling milk, tendency for soreness in the breasts, and the inconvenience of being continually available to meet the infant's feeding needs.

Hormones produced by the pituitary gland, prolactin and oxytocin, are involved in breast-feeding. Think of *prolactin* as meaning *pro* (in favor of) *lactation* (the process of producing milk); within a few days of delivery, prolactin stimulates the mammary glands to produce milk. Oxytocin is secreted in response to suckling and stimulates the breasts to eject milk. Following weaning (cessation of nursing), prolactin and oxytocin are no longer secreted, and lactation ceases.

Some final bits of information from the American Academy of Pediatrics (2002): The uterine contractions that occur during breast-feeding help return the uterus to its regular size. Breast-feeding also inhibits the resumption of normal menstrual cycles, thus interfering with the likelihood of conception. Nevertheless, breast-feeding is not a very reliable birth-control "device." But women who are nursing are advised not to use birth-control pills, since the hormonal contents of the pills are transmitted to the infant via the milk.

Developing in the New Millennium

Getting Help on Breast-feeding

Many women romanticize breast-feeding during pregnancy. They assume that this natural function will be pleasant and trouble-free. Breastfeeding is clearly "natural," but many women encounter problems ranging from local irritation to difficulty maintaining the flow of milk. As noted by lactation consultant Corky Harvey (2000), breast-feeding can be painful, inconvenient, and stressful, especially at first.

Harvey suggests that women who are having problems breast-feeding call the hospital where they delivered and ask whether it has a lactation consultant or can refer them to one. Or they can call the pediatrician or obstetrician or a friend or relative who has successfully breast-fed. There is also (800) TELLYOU, the hotline of Medela, a supplier of lactation equipment. Medela can provide a list of nearby lactation centers that rent equipment and offer support. Another resource is a La Leche League chapter.

The Internet can also be of help: **http://www.BreastfeedingTaskForLA.org** is the Web site of the Breastfeeding Task Force of Greater Los Angeles. Other Web sites of use:

http://www.breastfeeding.org
http://www.breastfeeding.com
http://www.lalecheleague.org
http://www.ILCA.org, the site for the International Lactation Consultants Association.

Search Online With InfoTrac College Edition

For additional information, explore InfoTrac College Edition, your online library. Go to **http://www.infotrac-college.com** and use the passcode from the InfoTrac card that came with your book. Try these search terms: breast feeding and health aspects, breast feeding and nutritional aspects, breast feeding and research, breast feeding and technique.

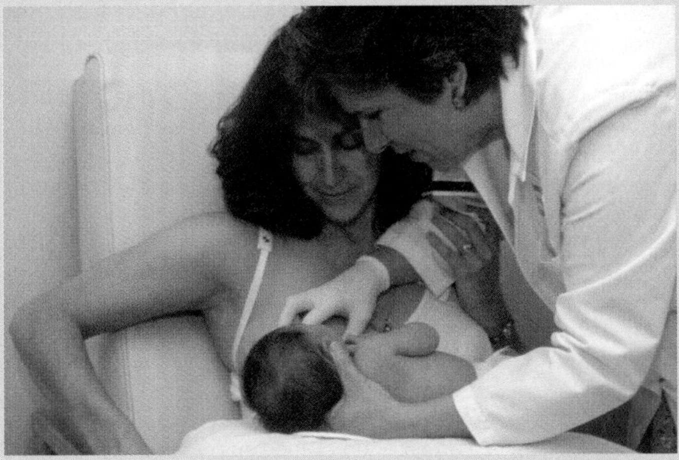

Michael Newman/PhotoEdit

A Lactation Consultant Advises a Woman on Breast-feeding

Yes, breast-feeding is a natural process. Yes, billions of mothers have successfully breast-fed their infants over the millennia without benefit of medical advice or "lactation consultants." However, many women experience problems ranging from local irritation to difficulty maintaining the flow of milk. Breast-feeding can be painful, inconvenient, and stressful, especially in the first days and weeks.

Review

(1) Cephalocaudal development describes the processes by which development proceeds from the ________ to the lower parts of the body. (2) The head ________ in length between birth and maturity, but the torso triples in length. (3) The ________ principle means that development proceeds from the trunk outward. (4) The tendency of responses to become more specific is termed ________. (5) Infants usually double their birthweight in about ________ months and triple it by the first birthday. Non-organic failure to ________ (NOFTT) seems to have psychological and/or social roots. (6) Mothers of infants with failure to thrive, as compared to mothers of healthy infants, show fewer (positive or negative?) feelings toward their infants. (7) After illness or dietary deficiency, children show ________, which is a tendency to return to their genetically determined pattern of growth. (8) The American Academy of ________ recommends that infants be fed breast milk throughout the first year. (9) Breast milk contains ________ that can prevent problems such as ear infections, meningitis, tetanus, and chicken pox. (10) HIV (can or cannot?) be transmitted to infants by breast milk. (11) An estimated ________ percent of children around the world suffer from malnutrition.

Pulling It Together: How can the principle of canalization be used to mitigate the effects of early malnutrition?

Developing in the New Millennium

Malnutrition in the United States and Elsewhere

An estimated 40–60% of children around the world suffer from malnutrition. The many reasons for malnutrition in developing countries incllude famine, war, and poverty (Cutts et al., 1998; Brentlinger et al., 1999). Another contributing factor is the decline of breast-feeding. Ironically, much malnutrition occurs in areas where the overall food is adequate, including the United States. American parents with less access to health care are likely to know less about nutrition and are thus less likely to provide their children with an adequate diet (Carvalho, 2001; Cutts, Pheley, & Geppert, 1998). Poor health care is also connected with frequent illness, which, in turn, reduces the child's appetite and lowers food intake, causing malnutrition (Grant, 1994). The combination of frequent illness and malnutrition leads to stunted physical and cognitive development, impaired attention span, low activity level, and reduced social responsiveness (Drewett et al., 2001; Ricciuti, 1993).

The long-term effects of severe malnutrition are illustrated by a longitudinal study conducted in Barbados by Janina Galler and her colleagues (Galler, 1989; Galler et al., 1990). They compared children who had experienced severe protein malnutrition during the first year of life with children who had received adequate nutrition. By age 11, the undernourished children had caught up in physical growth, but they continued to show cognitive and behavioral deficits such as impaired attention, poor school performance, and distractibility. These problems continued through age 18.

Even mild to moderate malnutrition adversely affects the physical, cognitive, and motor development of children. A series of studies in Kenya and Egypt compared infants and children who suffered mild to moderate malnutrition with children who were well-nourished (Espinosa et al., 1992; Sigman & Sena, 1993; Wachs, 1993). The children with less adequate diets were shorter and weighed less. They were less active, showed less advanced forms of play, and appeared more anxious. They also had lower scores on tests of verbal skills and other cognitive abilities. As adolescents and young adults, they remained behind their peers in reading, vocabulary, and general knowledge (Pollitt et al., 1993).

The good news is that the effects of malnutrition early in life can be reversed to some extent. Malnourished Guatemalan children who received food supplements during the first years of life became more socially involved, more interested in the environment, and more active (Barrett, Radke-Yarrow, & Klein, 1982). In another study (Super, Herrena, & Mora, 1990), Colombian infants at risk of malnutrition were assigned randomly to one of four groups. One group received food supplements for the entire family from the middle of the mother's pregnancy until the child was 3 years old. In another group, home visitors tutored mothers in how to stimulate their children's cognitive and social development. A third group received both food supplements and visits, and the fourth group received neither. At 3 years of age, children who had received food supplements were taller and heavier than those who had not. This effect remained when the children reached age 6. The combination of food supplements plus home visits had an even stronger effect on children's growth.

Development of the Brain and Nervous System

The nervous system is a system of **nerves** involved in heartbeat, visual-motor coordination, thought and language, and so on. The human nervous system is more complex than that of lower animals. Although elephants and whales have heavier brains, our brains constitute a larger proportion of our body weight.

Development of Neurons

Questions: What are neurons? How do they develop? The basic units of the nervous system are **neurons.** Neurons are cells that are specialized to receive and transmit messages from one part of the body to another. The messages transmitted by neurons account for phenomena as varied as reflexes, the perception of an itch from a mosquito bite, the visual-motor coordination of a skier, the composition of a concerto, and the solution of a math problem.

People are born with about 100 billion neurons, most of which are in the brain. Neurons vary according to their functions and locations in the body. Some neurons in the brain are only a fraction of an inch in length, while neurons in the leg grow to be several feet long. Each neuron possesses a cell body, **dendrites,** and an **axon** (see Figure 5.3). The dendrites are short fibers that extend from the cell body and receive incoming messages from up to 1,000 adjoining neurons. The axon extends trunklike from

Reflect

We are born with 100,000,000,000 neurons, give or take a few. How much is 100 billion? What can you compare that number with?

nerves Bundles of axons from many neurons.

neurons Nerve cells; cells found in the nervous system that transmit messages.

dendrite A rootlike part of a neuron that receives impulses from other neurons (from the Greek *dendron,* meaning "tree," and referring to the branching appearance of dendrites).

axon A long, thin part of a neuron that transmits impulses to other neurons through small branching structures called axon terminals.

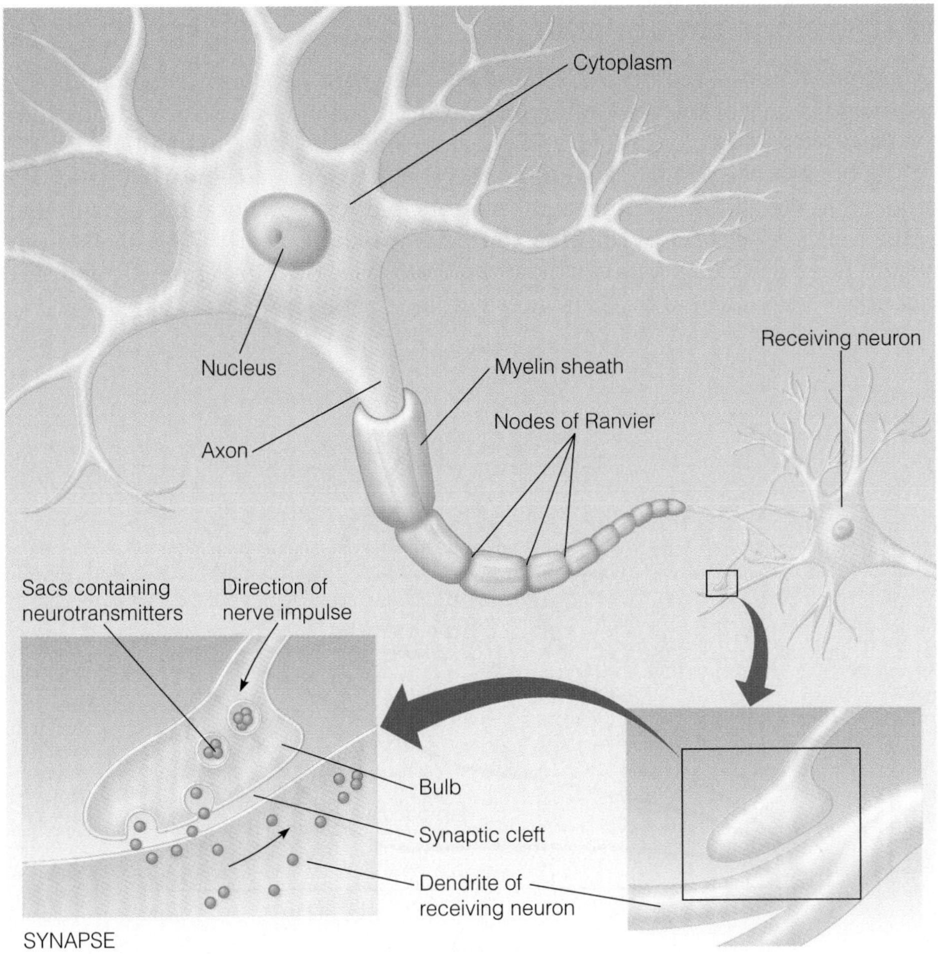

Figure 5.3
The Anatomy of a Neuron

"Messages" enter neurons through dendrites, are transmitted along the axon, and then are sent through axon terminals to muscles, glands, and other neurons. Neurons develop via proliferation of dendrites and axon terminals and through myelination.

the cell body and accounts for much of the difference in length in neurons, ranging up to several feet in length if it is carrying messages from the toes upward. Messages are released from axon terminals in the form of chemicals called **neurotransmitters.** These messages are then received by the dendrites of adjoining neurons, muscles, or glands. As the child matures, the axons of neurons grow in length, and the dendrites and axon terminals proliferate, creating vast interconnected networks for the transmission of complex messages.

Myelin

Click *Physical Development* for more on the development of the brain and nervous system.

Many neurons are tightly wrapped with white, fatty **myelin sheaths** that give them the appearance of a string of white sausages. The high fat content of the myelin sheath insulates the neuron from electrically charged atoms in the fluids that encase the nervous system. In this way, leakage of the electric current being carried along the axon is minimized, and messages are conducted more efficiently.

The term **myelination** refers to the process by which axons are coated with myelin. Myelination is not complete at birth, but rather is part of the maturation process that leads to the abilities to crawl and walk during the first year after birth. Incomplete myelination accounts for some of the helplessness of neonates. Myelination of the prefrontal matter of the brain continues into the second decade of life and is connected with advances in the capacity of working memory (Klingberg et al., 1999).

In the disease **multiple sclerosis,** myelin is replaced by a hard, fibrous tissue that disrupts the timing of neural transmission and in this way interferes with muscle control. The disorder phenylketonuria (PKU) leads to mental retardation by inhibiting the formation of myelin in the brain (Dyer, 1999). Congenital infection with HIV (the virus that causes AIDS) was shown to be connected with abnormalities in the formation of myelin and with cognitive and motor impairment, as measured by the Bayley Scales of Infant Development (Blanchette et al., 2001).

neurotransmitter A chemical substance that enables the transmission of neural impulses from one neuron to another.

myelin sheath (MY-uh-lin) A fatty, whitish substance that encases and insulates neurons, permitting more rapid transmission of neural impulses.

myelination The process by which axons are coated with myelin.

multiple sclerosis A disorder in which myelin is replaced by hard fibrous tissue that impedes neural transmission.

Development of the Brain

Question: What is the brain? How does the brain develop? The brain is the command center of the developing organism. It contains neurons and provides the basis for physical, cognitive, and personal and social development.

The brain of the neonate weighs a little less than a pound—nearly one-fourth of its adult weight. In keeping with the principles of cephalocaudal growth, the brain triples in weight by the first birthday, reaching nearly 70% of its adult weight (see Figure 5.4). Let us look at the brain, as shown in Figure 5.5, and discuss the development of the structures within.

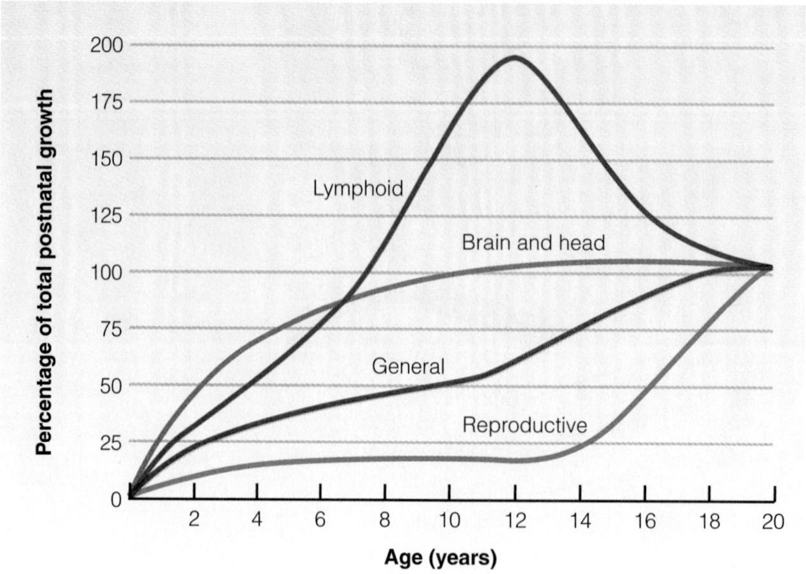

Figure 5.4
Growth of Body Systems as a Percentage of Total Postnatal Growth

The brain of the neonate weighs about one fourth its adult weight. In keeping with the principle of cephalocaudal growth, it will triple in weight by the first birthday, reaching nearly 70% of its adult weight.

Structures of the Brain

Many nerves that connect the spinal cord to higher levels of the brain pass through the **medulla.** The medulla is vital in the control of basic functions such as heartbeat and respiration. The medulla is part of an area called the brain stem, which may be implicated in Sudden Infant Death Syndrome (SIDS; see Chapter 4).

Above the medulla lies the **cerebellum,** which is Latin for "little brain." The cerebellum helps the child maintain balance, control motor behavior, and coordinate eye movements with bodily sensations.

The **cerebrum** is the crowning glory of the brain. It makes possible the breadth and depth of human learning, thought, memory, and language. Only in human beings does the cerebrum constitute such a large proportion of the brain. The surface of the cerebrum consists of two hemispheres—left and right—that become increasingly wrinkled, or convoluted, as the child develops, coming to show ridges and valleys called fissures. This surface is the cerebral cortex. The convolutions allow a great deal of surface area to be packed into the brain.

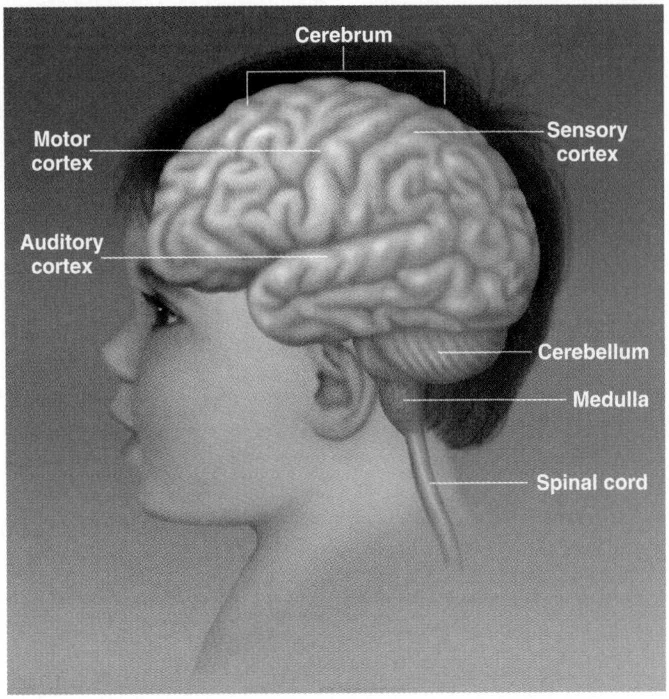

Figure 5.5
Structures of the Brain

The convolutions of the cortex increase its surface area and, apparently, its intellectual capacity. (In this case, wrinkles are good.) The medulla is involved in vital functions such as respiration and heartbeat; the cerebellum is involved in balance and coordination.

Growth Spurts of the Brain

The brain makes gains in size and weight in different ways. One is in the formation of neurons, a process complete by birth. The first major growth spurt of the brain occurs during the 4th and 5th months of prenatal development, when neurons proliferate. A second growth spurt in the brain occurs between the 25th week of prenatal development and the end of the 2nd year after birth. Whereas the first growth spurt of the brain was due to the formation of neurons, the second growth spurt is due primarily to the proliferation of dendrites and axon terminals (see Figure 5.6).

Brain Development in Infancy

There is a clear link between what infants can do and the myelination of areas within the brain. At birth, the parts of the brain involved in heartbeat and respiration, sleeping and arousal, and reflex activity are fairly well myelinated and functional.

Myelination of motor pathways allows neonates to show stereotyped reflexes, but otherwise their motor activity tends to be random and diffuse. Myelination of the motor area of the cerebral cortex begins at about the 4th month of prenatal development. Myelin develops rapidly along the major motor pathways from the cerebral cortex during the last month of pregnancy and continues after birth. The development of voluntary motor activity coincides with myelination, and so the diffuse movements of the neonate come under increasing control. Myelination of

Reflect

Did you know that the cerebral cortex—the structure that is vital to human thought and reason—is only $^1/_8$ inch thick?

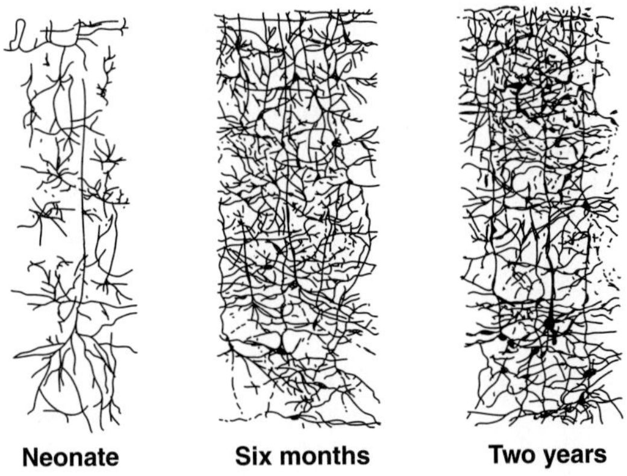

Figure 5.6
Increase in Neural Connections in the Brain

A major growth spurt in the brain occurs between the 25th week of prenatal development and the end of the 2nd year after birth. This growth spurt is due primarily to the proliferation of dendrites and axon terminals.
Source: Conel, 1959.

medulla (meh-DULL-ah) An oblong-shaped area of the hindbrain involved in heartbeat and respiration.

cerebellum (sera-BELL-um) The part of the hindbrain involved in muscle coordination and balance.

cerebrum (sir-REE-brum) The large mass of the forebrain, which consists of two hemispheres.

the motor pathways is largely developed by the age of 2, although research using magnetic resonance imaging (MRI) suggests that myelination continues to some degree into adolescence (Paus et al., 1999).

Although neonates respond to touch and can see and hear quite well, the areas of the cortex that are involved in vision, hearing, and the skin senses are less well myelinated at birth. As myelination progresses and the interconnections between the various areas of the cortex thicken, children become increasingly capable of complex and integrated sensorimotor activities (Tanner, 1989).

Neonates whose mothers read *The Cat in the Hat* aloud during the last few weeks of pregnancy show a preference for this story (see Chapter 3). It turns out that myelination of the neurons involved in the sense of hearing begins at about the sixth month of pregnancy—coinciding with the period in which fetuses begin to respond to sound. Myelination of these pathways is developing rapidly at term and continues until about the age of 4.

Although the fetus shows some response to light during the third trimester, it is hard to imagine what use the fetus could have for vision. It turns out that the neurons involved in vision begin to myelinate only shortly before full term, but then they complete the process of myelination rapidly. Within a short 5 to 6 months after birth, vision has become the dominant sense. ***Question: How do nature and nurture affect the development of the brain?***

Nature and Nurture in the Development of the Brain

Development of the sensory and motor areas of the brain starts on course as a result of maturation, but sensory stimulation and motor activity during early infancy may also contribute to their development (Jones & Greenough, 1996; Jones et al., 1997). Experience seems to fine-tune the unfolding of the genetic code (Gottlieb, 1991).

Reflect

Are you surprised that there is such a close connection between experience and development of the brain? How does the information presented in this section fit with the adage "Use it or lose it"?

Research with animals shows how the flood of sensory stimulation that neonates experience apparently spurs growth of the cortex. Researchers have created rat "amusement parks" to demonstrate the effects of enriched environments on neural development. Rats have been given toys such as ladders, platforms, and boxes. They have been provided with exploratory sessions in mazes and in fields with barriers. In these studies, the "enriched" rats invariably develop heavier brains than control animals. The weight differences in part reflect greater numbers of dendrites and axon terminals (Jones et al., 1997; Werry, 1991). On the other hand, animals raised in darkness show shrinkage of the visual cortex and impaired visual behavior (Greenough, Black & Wallace, 1987; Klintsova & Greenough, 1999).

Human brains also are affected by experience. Infants actually have more connections among their neurons than adults do (Rakic, 1991). Those connections that are activated by experience survive; the others do not (Casaer, 1993; Greenough, 1991; Tsuneishi & Casaer, 2000).

The great adaptability of the brain appears to be a double-edged sword. Adaptability allows us to develop different patterns of neural connections to meet the demands of our different environments. However, lack of stimulation—especially during critical early periods of development (as we shall see later)—can apparently impair our adaptability.

The nourishment the brain receives, like early experience, plays a role in its achieving the upper limits of the reaction range permitted by the child's genes. Inadequate nutrition in the fetus, especially during the prenatal growth spurt of the brain, has several negative effects. These include smallness in the overall size of the brain, the formation of fewer neurons, and less myelination (Bauerfeld & Lachenmeyer, 1992; Lukas & Campbell, 2000).

Review

(12) ________ are the basic units of the nervous system. (13) Each neuron possesses a cell body, dendrites, and an ________. (14) Axon terminals release "messages" in the form of chemicals called ________. (15) The brain reaches

nearly _________% of its adult weight by the first birthday. (16) The part of the brain called the _________ enables the child to maintain balance and control motor behavior. (17) The brain grows (in spurts or continuously?). (18) Sensory stimulation (does or does not?) spur growth of the cortex among infants.

Pulling It Together: What is the role of myelination in child development?

Motor Development

"Allyn couldn't walk yet at 10 months, but she zoomed after me in her walker, giggling her head off." "Anthony was walking forward and backward by the age of 13 months."

These are some of the types of comments parents make about their children's motor development. ***Question: What is motor development?*** How does it occur? Motor development involves the activity of muscles, leading to changes in posture, movement, and coordination of movement with the infant's developing sensory apparatus. Motor development provides some of the most fascinating changes in infants, in part because so much seems to happen so quickly—and so much of it during the first year.

Reflect

"When did your baby first sit up?" "When did he walk?" Why are people so concerned about when *infants do* what?

Motor development, like physical development, follows patterns of cephalocaudal and proximodistal development, and differentiation. As noted earlier in this chapter, for example, infants gain control of their heads and upper torsos before they can effectively use their arms. This trend illustrates cephalocaudal development. Infants also can control their trunks and shoulders before they can use their hands and fingers, demonstrating the proximodistal trend in development.

Lifting and Holding the Torso and Head: Heads Up

Click *Physical Development* for more on motor development.

Neonates can move their heads slightly to the side. This ability permits them to avoid suffocation if they are lying face down and their noses or mouths are obstructed by the bedding. At about 1 month, infants raise their heads. By about 2 months, they can also lift their chests while prone.

When neonates are held, their heads must be supported. But by 3 to 6 months of age, infants generally manage to hold their heads quite well, so that supporting the head is no longer necessary. Unfortunately, infants who can normally support their heads cannot do so when they are lifted or moved about in a jerky manner, and infants who are not handled carefully can develop neck injuries.

Control of the Hands: Getting a Grip on Things

The development of hand skills is a clear example of the process of proximodistal development. Infants will track (follow) slowly moving objects with their eyes from shortly after birth, but generally will not reach for them. They show a grasp reflex, but they do not reliably reach for the objects that appear to interest them. Voluntary reaching and grasping require visual-motor coordination. By about 3 months of age, infants will make clumsy swipes at objects, failing in efforts to grasp them, because their aim is poor or they close their hands too soon or too late.

Between 4 and 6 months, infants become increasingly successful at grasping objects (Santos, Gabbard, & Goncalves, 2000). However, they may not know how to let go of an object and may hold on to it indefinitely, until their attention is diverted and the hand opens accidentally. Four to 6 months is a good age for giving children rattles, large plastic spoons, mobiles, and other brightly colored hanging toys that are harmless when they wind up in the mouth.

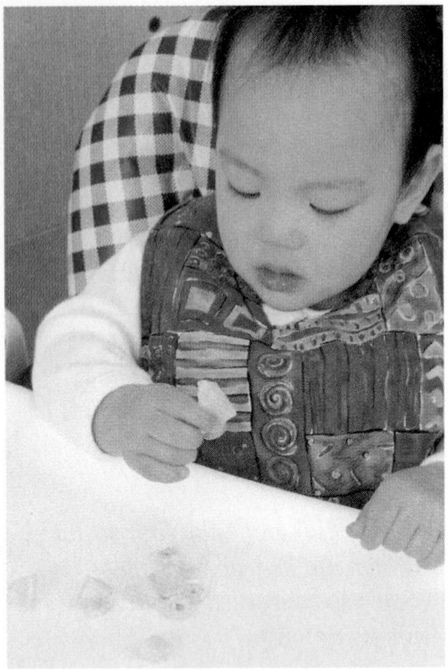

Pincer Grasp

Infants first hold objects between their fingers and palm. Once the oppositional thumb comes into play at about 9 to 12 months of age, infants are able to pick up tiny objects using what is termed a pincer grasp.

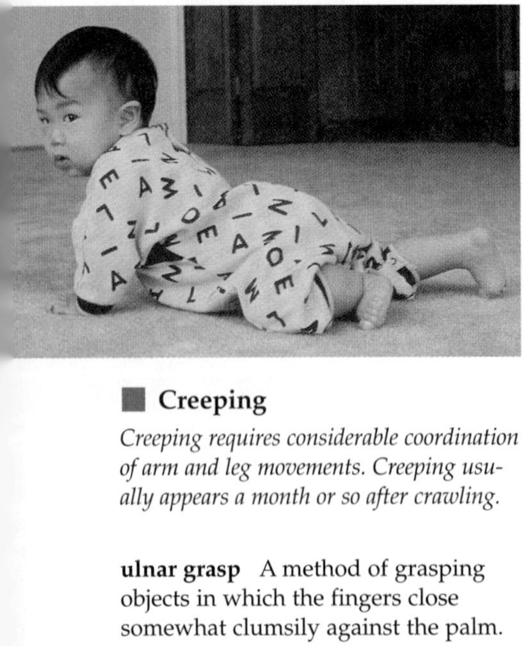

Creeping

Creeping requires considerable coordination of arm and leg movements. Creeping usually appears a month or so after crawling.

ulnar grasp A method of grasping objects in which the fingers close somewhat clumsily against the palm.

pincer grasp The use of the opposing thumb to grasp objects between the thumb and other fingers.

locomotion Movement from one place to another.

toddler A child who walks with short, uncertain steps. Toddlerhood lasts from about 18 to 30 months of age, thereby bridging infancy and early childhood.

Grasping is reflexive at first. As voluntary grasping (holding) replaces reflexive grasping by 3–4 months, infants initially use an **ulnar grasp** in which they hold objects somewhat clumsily between their fingers and their palm (Butterworth, Verweij, & Hopkins, 1997). By 4–6 months, they are capable of transferring objects back and forth from one hand to the other. The oppositional thumb does not come into play until 9 to 12 months or so. Use of the thumb gives infants the ability to pick up tiny objects in what is called a **pincer grasp.** By about 11 months, infants can hold objects in each hand and inspect them in turn.

Between the ages of 5 and 11 months infants develop anticipatory adjustment of hand alignment to capture moving targets. They also glean information from the objects' patterns of spinning and oscillating to predict their future location and capture them (Wentworth, Benson, & Haith, 2000). Think of the complex concepts it requires to explain this behavior and how well infants perform it—without any explanation at all! Of course, I am not suggesting that infants solve problems in geometry and physics to grasp moving objects; that interpretation, as developmental psychologist Marshall M. Haith (1998) would describe it, would put a "cog in infant cognition."

The research by Wentworth and colleagues (2000) shows developing visual-motor coordination. Another aspect of visual-motor coordination is the ability to stack blocks. On average, children can stack two blocks at the age of 15 months, three blocks at 18 months, and five blocks at 24 months. At about 24 months, children also can copy horizontal and vertical lines.

Locomotion: Getting a Move On

Locomotion is movement from one place to another. Children gain the capacity to move their bodies about through a sequence of activities that includes rolling over, sitting up, crawling, creeping, walking, and running (see Figure 5.7). There is a great deal of variation in the ages at which infants first engage in these activities, but the sequence remains generally invariant. A number of children will skip a step, however. For example, an infant may creep without ever having crawled.

Most infants can roll over, from back to stomach and stomach to back, by about 6 months. They are also capable of sitting (and holding their upper bodies, necks, and heads) for extended periods if they are supported by a person or placed in a seat with a strap, such as a high chair. By about 7 months, infants usually begin to sit up by themselves.

At about 8 to 9 months, most infants begin to crawl, a motor activity in which they lie prone and use their arms to pull themselves along, dragging their bellies and feet behind. Creeping, a more sophisticated form of locomotion in which infants move themselves along up on their hands and knees, requires a good deal more coordination and usually appears a month or so after crawling.

There are fascinating alternatives to creeping. Some infants travel from one place to another by rolling over and over. Some lift themselves and swing their arms while in a sitting position, in effect dragging along on their buttocks. Still others do a "bear walk" in which they move on their hands and feet, without allowing their elbows and knees to touch the floor. And some, as noted, just crawl until they are ready to stand and walk from place to place while holding on to chairs, other objects, and people.

Standing overlaps with crawling and creeping. Most infants can remain in a standing position if holding on to something by about 8 or 9 months. At this age they may also be able to walk a bit when supported by adults. This walking is voluntary and does not have the stereotyped appearance of the walking reflex described in Chapter 4. About 2 months later, they can pull themselves to a standing position by holding on to the sides of their cribs or other objects and can also stand briefly without holding on. Shortly afterward, they walk about unsteadily while holding on. By 12 to 15 months or so, they walk by themselves, earning them the name **toddler.** Attempts at mastering each of these new motor skills often are accompanied by signs of pleasure such as smiling, laughing, and babbling (Mayes & Zigler, 1992).

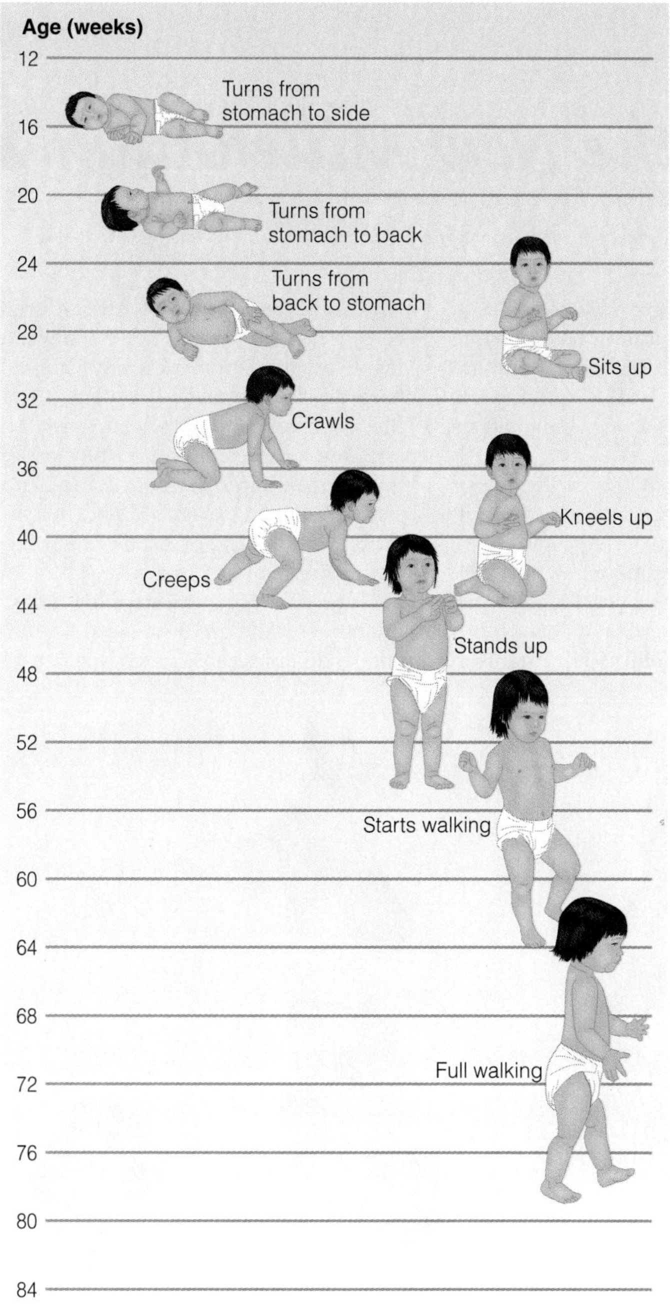

Figure 5.7
Motor Development in Infancy

Motor development proceeds in an orderly sequence, but there is considerable variation in the timing of the marker events shown in this figure. An infant who is a bit behind will most likely develop without problems, and a precocious infant will not necessarily become a rocket scientist (or gymnast).

Toddlers soon run about in a bowlegged fashion, supporting their relatively heavy heads and torsos by spreading their legs. Because they are top-heavy and inexperienced, they fall frequently. Some toddlers require a good deal of consoling when they fall. Others spring right up and run on again with barely an interruption. Many toddlers are quite skillful at navigating safely down steep and shallow slopes (Weiner & Adolph, 1993). They walk down shallow slopes but prudently elect to slide or crawl down steep ones.

Click *Physical Development* for more on locomotion.

The ability to move about on the legs provides children with new freedom. It allows them to get about rapidly and grasp objects that were formerly out of reach. Give toddlers a large ball to toss and run after; it is about the least expensive and most enjoyable toy they can be given.

As children mature, their muscle strength, the density of their bones, and their balance and coordination all improve. By 2 years of age, they can climb steps one at a time, placing both feet on each step. They can run well, walk backward, kick a large ball, and jump several inches.

Developing in the New Millennium

Formal Handling and Motor Development

Black African and African American infants generally reach such motor milestones as sitting, walking, and running before White infants do. This finding has been obtained for both premature and full-term infants (Allen & Alexander, 1990; Capute et al., 1985) and in Third World countries as well as in the United States (Garcia-Coll, 1990).

While genetic factors may be involved in the earlier motor development of Black African and African American infants, environmental factors also appear to play a role (see Figure 5.8). African infants excel in areas of motor development in which they have received considerable stimulation and practice. For example, African infants sit and walk earlier than American infants do, but they do not crawl any sooner (Rogoff & Morelli, 1989). Parents in Africa and in cultures of African origin, such as Jamaica, place considerable importance on the development of sitting and walking. Crawling is not culturally valued because it is seen as being hazardous and apelike (Hopkins, 1991; Hopkins & Westra, 1990). Black African and Jamaican parents provide experiences from birth onward that stimulate the development of sitting and walking in their infants. These activities, known as *formal handling*, consist of stretching exercises and massages that start shortly after birth. From the 2nd or 3rd months, other activities are added, such as propping infants in a sitting position, bouncing them on their feet, and exercising the stepping reflex. But African and Jamaican infants typically are not placed on the ground on their stomachs and so do not receive much practice in crawling.

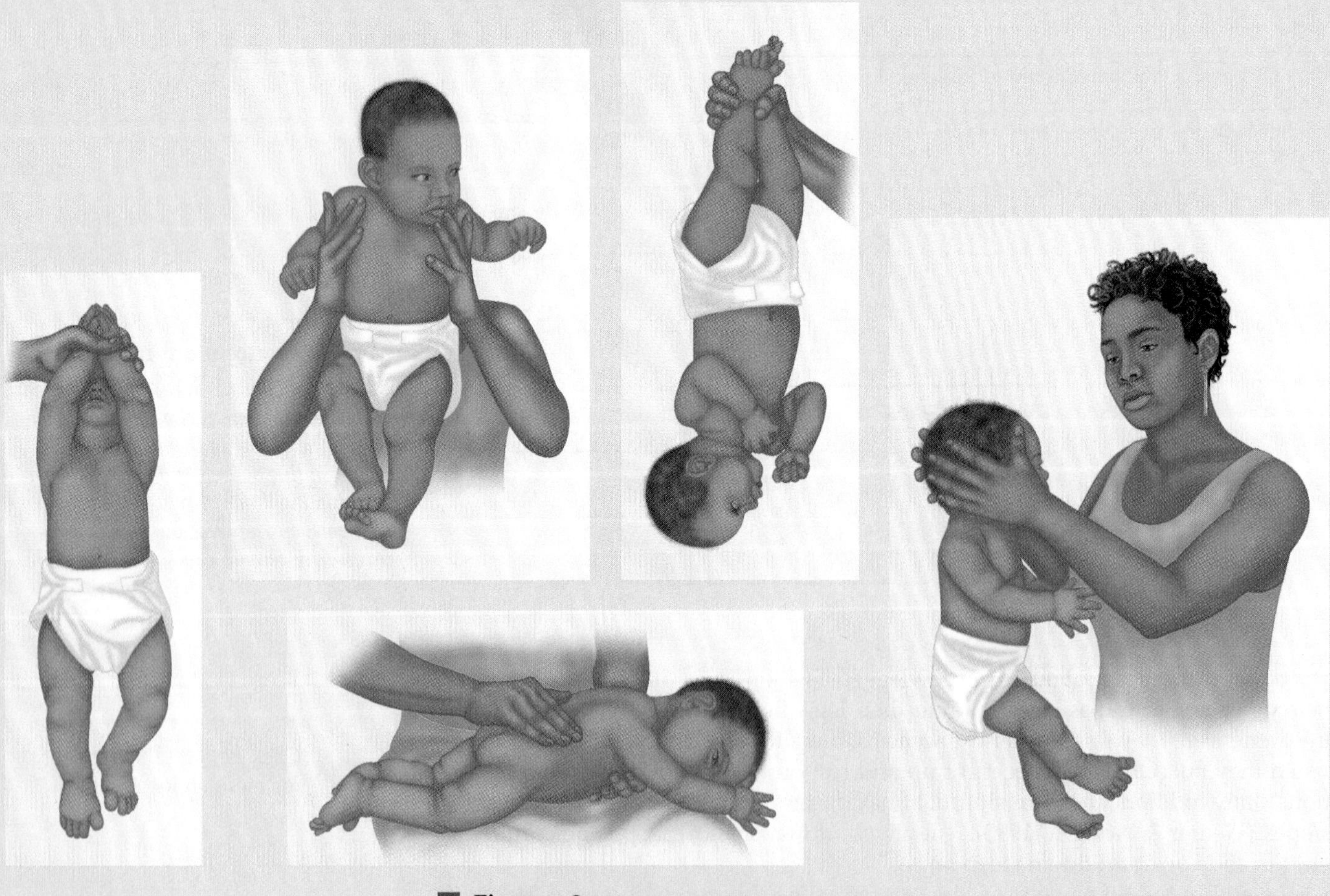

Figure 5.8
The Jamaican Formal-Handling Routine

Parents in Africa and in cultures of African origin, such as Jamaica, provide experience from birth onward that stimulates the development of sitting and walking in their infants. These activities, known as formal handling, include stretching exercises and massage (as shown here), as well as propping infants in a sitting position, bouncing them on their feet, and exercising the stepping reflex.

Source: Hopkins, 1991.

Nature and Nurture in Motor Development

Question: What are the roles of nature and nurture in motor development? Research with humans and other species leaves little doubt that maturation (nature) and experience (nurture) both play indispensable roles in motor development (Muir, 2000; Pryce et al., 2001; Roncesvalles, Woollacott, & Jensen, 2001). Certain types of voluntary motor activities do not seem possible until the brain has matured in terms of myelination and the differentiation of the motor areas of the cortex. While it is true that the neonate shows stepping and swimming reflexes, these behaviors are controlled by more primitive areas of the brain. They disappear when cortical development inhibits some of the functions of the lower areas of the brain; and when they reappear, their quality is quite different.

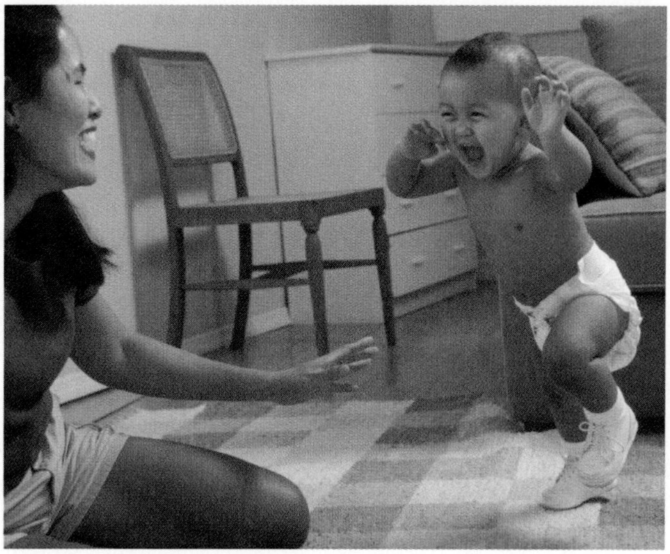

Walking

By 12 to 15 months or so, babies walk by themselves, earning them the name toddler.

Infants also need some opportunity for motor experimentation before they can engage in milestones such as sitting up and walking. But although it may take them several months to sit up and, as described earlier, more months to take their first steps, most of this time can apparently be attributed to maturation. In a classic study, Wayne and Marsena Dennis (1940) reported on the motor development of Native American Hopi children who spent their first year strapped to a cradleboard. Although denied a full year of experience in locomotion, the Hopi infants gained the capacity to walk early in their second year, at about the same time as children reared in other cultures. A more recent cross-cultural study (Hindley et al., 1966) reported that infants in five European cities began to walk at about the same time (generally, between 12 and 15 months), despite cultural differences in encouragement to walk.

Reflect

Does it "matter" if parents teach their infants to sit up or walk before they would have done so on their own?

On the other hand, evidence is mixed as to whether specific training can accelerate the appearance of motor skills. For example, in a classic study with identical twins, Arnold Gesell (1929) gave one twin extensive training in hand coordination, block building, and stair climbing from early infancy. The other was allowed to develop on his own. But as time passed, the untrained twin became as skilled in these activities as the other.

More recent research indicates that the appearance and development of motor skills can be accelerated by training (Zelazo et al., 1993; Zelazo, 1998). Yet this effect generally remains slight; guided practice in the absence of neural maturation apparently has limited results. There is also little evidence that this sort of training leads to eventual superior motor skills or other advantages.

A Native American Hopi Infant Strapped to a Cradleboard

Researchers have studied Hopi children who are strapped to cradleboards during the first year to see if their motor development is delayed significantly. Once released from their boards, Hopi children make rapid advances in motor development, suggesting the importance of maturation in motor development.

Although being strapped to a cradleboard did not permanently prevent the motor development of Hopi infants, Wayne Dennis (1960) reported that infants in an Iranian orphanage were significantly retarded in their motor development. In contrast to the Hopi infants, the institutionalized infants were exposed to extreme social and physical deprivation. Under these conditions, they grew apathetic, and all aspects of development suffered. But there is also a bright side to this tale of deprivation. The motor development of infants in a Lebanese orphanage accelerated dramatically in response to such minimal intervention as being propped up in their cribs and being given a few colorful toys (Dennis & Sayegh, 1965).

Nature, as noted, provides the reaction range for the expression of inherited traits. Nurture determines whether the child will develop skills in accord with the upper limits of the inherited range. Research by Esther Thelen and her colleagues indicates that even a fundamental skill such as locomotion is determined by a complex interplay of both maturational and environmental factors (Thelen, 1990, 2000; Thelen & Ulrich, 1991). There may be little purpose in trying to train children to enhance their motor skills before they are ready. Once they are ready, however, teaching and practice do make a difference. One does not become an Olympic athlete without "good genes." But one also usually does not become an Olympic athlete without high-quality training. And since motor skills are important to the self-concepts of children, good teaching is all the more important.

Review

(19) Infants first gain control over their (heads or arms?). (20) Infants can first raise their heads at about the age of __________ month(s). (21) Infants at first use a(n) __________ grasp for holding objects. (22) Developmentalists assess infants' ability to stack blocks as a measure of their __________-motor coordination. (23) Infants (sit up or crawl?) before they (sit up or crawl?). (24) Toddlers run around bowlegged, supporting their heads and torsos by __________ their legs. (25) As children mature, their bones (increase or decrease?) in density. (26) Black infants generally reach the motor milestones of walking and running (after or before?) White infants do. (27) Many Black parents provide their infants with exercises referred to as formal __________. (28) Research reveals that maturation and __________ both play indispensable roles in motor development. (29) Wayne and Marsena Dennis engaged in classic research with Hopi infants who were strapped to a __________. (30) Arnold Gesell (did or did not?) find that extensive training in hand coordination, block building, and stair climbing gave infants enduring advantages over untrained infants in these skills.

Pulling It Together: How does motor development follow cephalocaudal and proximodistal trends?

Sensory and Perceptual Development

Click *Physical Development* for more on sensory and perceptual development.

What a world we live in—green hills and reddish skies; rumbling trucks, murmuring brooks, and voices; the sweet and the sour; the acrid and the perfumed; the metallic and the fuzzy. What an ever-changing display of sights, sounds, tastes, smells, and touches.

The pleasures of the world, and its miseries, are known to us through sensory impressions and the organization of these impressions into personal inner maps of reality. Our eyes, our ears, the sensory receptors in our noses and our mouths, our skin senses—these are our tickets of admission to the world.

Chapter 4 examined the sensory capabilities of the neonate. ***Question: How do sensation and perception develop in the infant?*** In this section, we follow infants to learn how they develop their abilities to integrate disjointed sensory impressions into meaningful patterns of events known as perceptions. We see what sorts of things capture the attention of infants, and we see how young children develop into purposeful seekers of information—selecting the sensory impressions they will choose to capture and weeding out the sensory chaff. We will focus on the development of vision and hearing, since most of the research on sensory and perceptual development after the neonatal period has been done in these areas.

We shall see that many things that are obvious to us are not obvious to young infants. You may know that a coffee cup is the same whether you see it from above or from the side, but make no such assumptions about the infant. You may know that an infant's mother is the same size whether she is standing next to the infant or approaching from two blocks away, but do not assume that the infant agrees with you.

We cannot ask infants to explain why they look at some things and not at others. Nor can we ask them if their mother appears to be the same size whether she is standing close to them or far away. But investigators of childhood sensation and perception have devised clever methods to answer these questions and so provide us with fascinating insights into the perceptual processes of even the neonate. These methods reveal that many basic perceptual competencies are present early in life (Pick, 1991).

Development of Vision: The Better to See You With

Development of Visual Acuity and Peripheral Vision

Neonates are quite nearsighted. The most dramatic gains in visual acuity are made between birth and 6 months of age, with acuity reaching about 20/50 (Haith, 1990). Gains in visual acuity then become more gradual, approximating adult levels (20/20) by about 3 to 5 years of age (Fielder et al., 1992).

Neonates also have poor peripheral vision (Courage & Adams, 1993). Adults can perceive objects that are nearly 90 degrees off to the side (that is, directly to the left or right), although objects at these extremes are unclear. Neonates cannot perceive visual stimuli that are off to the side by an angle of more than 30 degrees, but their peripheral vision expands to an angle of about 45 degrees by the age of 7 weeks (Macfarlane, Harris, & Barnes, 1976). By 6 months of age, their peripheral vision is about equal to that of an adult (Cohen, DeLoache, & Strauss, 1979).

Click *Physical Development* for more on the development of vision.

Let's now consider the development of visual perception. In so doing we shall see that infants frequently prefer the strange to the familiar and will avoid going off the deep end—sometimes.

Visual Preferences: How Do You Capture an Infant's Attention?

Questions: What captures the attention of infants? How do visual preferences develop? Neonates look at stripes longer than at blobs. This finding has been used in much of the research on visual acuity. By 8 to 12 weeks, most infants also show distinct preferences for curved lines over straight ones (Fantz, Fagan, & Miranda, 1975).

Robert Fantz (1961) also wondered whether there was something intrinsically interesting about the human face that drew the attention of infants. To investigate this question, he showed 2-month-old infants the six disks illustrated in Figure 5.9. One contained a caricature of human features, another newsprint, and still another a bull's-eye. The remaining three were featureless but colored red, white, and yellow. In this study, the infants fixated significantly longer on the human face.

Subsequent studies have suggested that the infants in the Fantz (1961) study may not have preferred the human face so much because it was a face as because it had a complex, intriguing pattern of dots (eyes) within an outline. In some of these studies, infants have been shown drawings that resemble a face and other drawings that contain the same elements of a face (such as eyes, nose, and mouth) but in scrambled order. Neonates pay about an equal amount of attention to both types of drawings (Easterbrook, Kisilevsky, Muir, & LaPlante, 1999). But by 2 months of age, they begin to prefer the "real" face to the scrambled one (Johnson et al., 1992; Morton & Johnson, 1991).

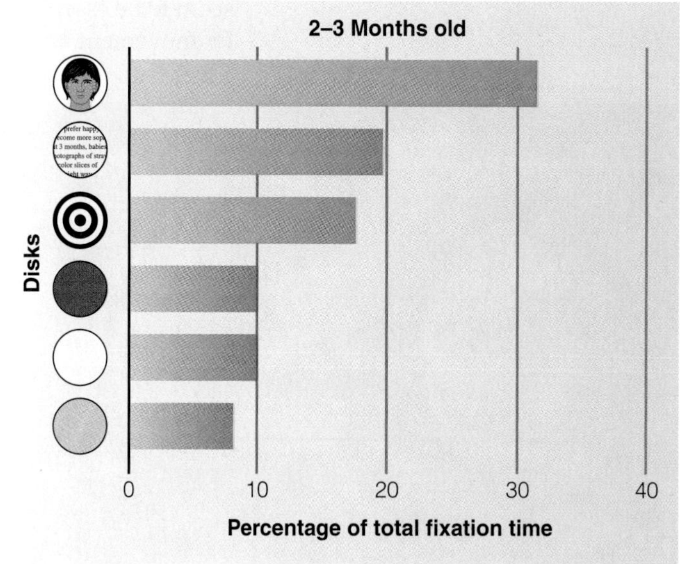

Figure 5.9
Preferences for Visual Stimuli in 2-Month-Olds

Infants appear to prefer complex to simple visual stimuli. By the time they are 2 months old, they also tend to show preference for the human face. Researchers continue to debate whether the face draws attention because of its content (that is, being a face) or because of its stimulus characteristics (complexity, arrangement, etc.).

Reflect

What do you think it would it mean if infants came into the world "prewired" to prefer the human face to other, equally complex visual stimulation?

Researchers continue to be vitally interested in infants' preferences for the human face. The preference raises fascinating questions as to whether humans come into the world "prewired" to prefer human stimuli to other, equally complex stimuli, and—if so—just what it is about human stimuli that draws attention (Easterbrook, Kisilevsky, Hains, & Muir, 1999). Therefore, studies along these lines continue. Some researchers argue that neonates do not "prefer" faces because they are faces per se, but because of the structure of their immature visual systems (Simion, Cassia, Turate, & Valenza, 2001). A supportive study of 34 neonates found that the longer fixations on facelike stimuli resulted from a larger number of brief fixations (looks) rather than a few prolonged fixations (Cassia, Simion, & Umilta, 2001). The infants' gaze, then, was sort of bouncing around from feature to feature rather than "staring" at the face in general. The researchers interpret the finding to show that the stimulus properties of the visual object are more important than the fact that it represents a human face. Even so, of course, the "immature visual system" would be providing some "prewired" basis for attending to the face.

Neonates can discriminate their mother's face from a stranger's after 8 hours of mother–infant contact spread over 4 days (Bushnell, 2001). By 3 to 5 months of age, infants respond differently to happy, surprised, and sad faces (Muir & Hains, 1993; Nelson & Ludemann, 1989). Moreover, infants as young as 2 months of age prefer attractive faces to unattractive faces (Langlois et al., 1990, 1991). This preference is more deeply ingrained by 6 months of age (Rubenstein, Kalakansis, & Langlois, 1999). Do standards of attractiveness have an inborn component, or are they learned very (very!) early?

Neonates appear to direct their attention to the edges of objects. This pattern persists for the first several weeks (Bronson, 1991). When they are given the opportunity to look at human faces, 1-month-old infants tend to pay most attention to the "edges"—that is, the chin, an ear, or the hairline. Two-month-old infants move in from the edge, as shown in Figure 5.10. They focus particularly on the eyes, though they also inspect other inner features, such as the mouth and nose (Nelson & Ludemann, 1989).

Some researchers (Haith, 1979) explain infants' tendencies to scan from the edges of objects inward by noting that for the first several weeks of life, infants seem to be essentially concerned with *where* things are. Their attention is captured by movement and sharp contrasts in brightness and shape, such as those that are found where the edges of objects stand out against their backgrounds. But by about 2 months, infants tend to focus on the *what* of things. They may locate objects by looking at their edges, but now they scan systematically within the boundaries of objects (Bronson, 1990, 1997).

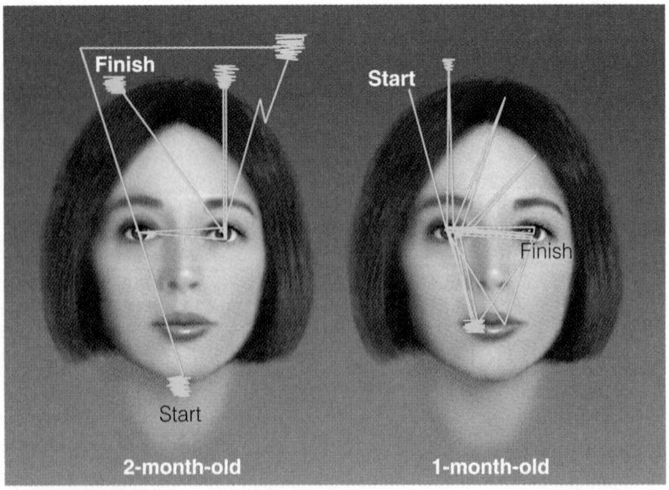

Figure 5.10
Eye Movements of 1- and 2-Month-Olds

One-month-olds direct their attention to the edges of objects. Two-month-olds "move in from the edge." When looking at a face, for example, they focus on the eyes and other inner features. How do researchers explain this change?

Source: Salapatek, 1975.

Development of Depth Perception: On *Not* Going Off the Deep End

Infants generally respond to cues for depth by the time they are able to crawl about (6 to 8 months of age or so), and most have the good sense to avoid "going off the deep end"—that is crawling off ledges and tabletops into open space (Campos et al., 1978). ***Question: How do researchers determine whether infants will "go off the deep end"?***

In a classic study on depth perception, Eleanor Gibson and Richard Walk (1960) placed infants of various ages on a fabric-covered runway that ran across the center of a clever device called a visual cliff (see Figure 5.11). The visual cliff consists of a sheet of Plexiglas that covers a cloth with a high-contrast checkerboard pattern. On one side the cloth is placed immediately beneath the plexiglass, and on the other, it is dropped about 4 feet below. Since the Plexiglas alone would easily support the infant, this is a visual cliff rather than an actual cliff. In the Gibson and Walk study, 8 out of 10 infants who had begun to crawl refused to venture onto the seemingly unsupported surface, even when their mothers beckoned encouragingly from the other side.

Psychologists can assess infants' emotional responses to the visual cliff long before they can crawl. For example, Joseph Campos and his colleagues (1970) found that 1-month-old infants showed no change in heart rate when placed face down on the visual cliff. Apparently, they did not perceive the depth of the cliff. At 2 months of age, the infants showed decreases in heart rate when so placed, which psychologists interpret as a sign of interest. The heart rates of 9-month-olds accelerated when they were placed on the cliff, which is interpreted as a fear response. The study appears to suggest that infants may need to have some experience crawling about (and, perhaps, accumulating some bumps) before they develop fear of heights. The 9-month-olds but not the 2-month-olds had had such experience. Other studies support the view that infants usually do not develop fear of heights until they can move around (Bertenthal & Campos, 1990).

Figure 5.11
The Visual Cliff

This young explorer has the good sense not to crawl out onto an apparently unsupported surface, even when mother beckons from the other side. Do infants have to experience some of life's "bumps" before they avoid "going off the deep end"?

More recent research suggests that infants' tendencies to avoid falling off a "cliff" are connected with their bodily positions at the time (Adolph, 2000). Infants generally sit before they crawl, and by 9 months of age, we can think of most of them as somewhat experienced sitters. Crawling enters the picture at about 9 months. Karen Adolph examined the behavior of nineteen 9-month-old infants who were on the edge of crawling as well as the edge of a visual cliff. The infants were placed in a sitting or crawling position and enticed to reach for an object out over the cliff. The infants were more likely to avoid the cliff when they were in a sitting position, suggesting that each postural development involves a different control system and that infants' adaptive avoidance of the cliff is based on information about their postural stability relative to the size of a visually perceived gap. Adolph's findings bring into question the conclusions of some other researchers that avoidance of the cliff depends on general knowledge such as fear of heights, or associations between perceived depth and falling—or even awareness that the body cannot be supported in empty space.

Reflect

Does it make sense from an evolutionary perspective for infants to develop fear of falling off an edge before they can crawl? Explain.

Development of Perceptual Constancies

Questions: What are perceptual constancies? How do they develop?

It may not astonish you that a 12-inch ruler is the same length whether it is 2 feet or 6 feet away. Or that a door across the room is a rectangle whether closed or ajar. Awareness of these facts depends not on sensation alone, but on the development of perceptual constancies. **Perceptual constancy** is the tendency to perceive an object to be the same, even though the sensations produced by the object may differ under various conditions.

Consider again the example of the ruler. When it is 2 feet away, its image, as focused on the retina, is a certain length. This length is the image's "retinal size." From 6 feet away, the 12-inch ruler is only one-third as long in terms of retinal size, but we perceive it as being the same size because of size constancy. **Size constancy** is the tendency to perceive the same objects as being of the same size even though their retinal sizes vary as a function of their distance. From 6 feet away, a 36-inch yardstick casts an image equal in retinal size to the 12-inch ruler at 2 feet, but—if recognized as a yardstick—it is perceived as longer, again because of size constancy.

perceptual constancy The tendency to perceive objects as the same although sensations produced by them may differ when, for example, they differ in position or distance.

size constancy The tendency to perceive objects as being the same size although the sizes of their retinal images may differ as a result of distance.

In a classic study of the development of size constancy, Thomas Bower (1974) conditioned infants $2\frac{1}{2}$ – 3 months old to turn their heads to the left when shown a 12-inch cube from a distance of 3 feet. He then presented them with three experimental stimuli: (1) a 12-inch cube 9 feet away, whose retinal size was smaller than that of the original cube; (2) a 36-inch cube 3 feet away, whose retinal size was larger than that of the original cube; and (3) a 36-inch cube 9 feet away, whose retinal size was the same as that of the original cube. The infants turned their heads most frequently in response to the first experimental cube, although its retinal image was only one-third the length of that to which they had been conditioned, suggesting that they had achieved size constancy. Later studies have confirmed Bower's finding that size constancy is present in early infancy. Some research suggests that even neonates possess rudimentary size constancy (Granrud, 1987; Slater, Mattock, & Brown, 1990).

Shape constancy is the tendency to perceive an object as having the same shape even though, when perceived from another angle, the shape projected onto the retina may change dramatically. When the top of a cup or a glass is seen from above, the visual sensations are in the shape of a circle. When seen from a slight angle, the sensations are elliptical, and when seen from the side, the retinal image is the same as that of a straight line. However, we still perceive the rim of the cup or glass as being a circle, because of our familiarity with the object. In the first few months after birth, infants see the features of their mothers, of bottles, of cribs, and of toys from all different angles, so that by the time they are 4 or 5 months old, a broad grasp of shape constancy seems to be established, at least under certain conditions (Aslin, 1987; Dodwell, Humphrey, & Muir, 1987). Strategies for studying the development of shape constancy are described in the nearby "A Closer Look" feature.

shape constancy The tendency to perceive objects as being the same shape although the shapes of their retinal images may differ when the objects are viewed from different positions.

A Closer Look

Strategies for Studying the Development of Shape Constancy

People are said to show shape constancy when they perceive an object as having the same shape even though, when viewed from another angle, the shape projected onto the retina may be very different. We can determine whether infants have developed shape constancy through the process of habituation, which, as you may recall from Chapter 3, involves paying less attention to a repeated stimulus.

Neonates tend to show a preference for familiar objects (Barrile, Armstrong, & Bower, 1999). But once they are a few months old, infants show a preference for novel objects. They have become habituated to familiar objects, and—if we can take the liberty of describing their responses in adult terms—they are apparently bored by them. Certain bodily responses indicate interest in an object, including a slower heart rate (as with 2-month-old infants placed face-down on a visual cliff) and concentrated gazing. Therefore, when infants have become habituated to an object, their heart rates speed up moderately, and they no longer show concentrated gazing.

Here, then, is the research strategy. Show an infant stimulus A for a prolonged period of time. At first the heart rate will slow, and the infant will focus on the object. But as time goes on, the heart rate will again rise to prestimulated levels, and the infant's gaze will wander. Now show the infant stimulus B. If the heart rate again slows, and the gaze again becomes concentrated, we can infer that stimulus B is perceived as a novel (different) object. But if the heart rate and pattern of gazing does not change, we can infer that the infant does not perceive a difference between stimuli A and B.

Here is the 64-day-old question: If stimuli A and B are actually the same object, but are seen from different angles, what does it mean when the infant's heart rate and pattern of gazing do not change? We can assume that lack of change means that the infant perceives stimuli A and B to be the same—in this case, the same object. Therefore, we can conclude that the infant has developed shape constancy.

Using a strategy similar to that above, Caron and his colleagues (1979) first habituated 3-month-old infants to a square shown at different angles. The infants then were presented with one of two test stimuli: (1) the identical square, shown at an entirely new angle or (2) a novel figure (a trapezoid) shown at the new angle. The two test stimuli projected identical trapezoidal images on the retina, even though their real shapes were different. Infants who were shown the square at the new angle showed little change in response. However, infants shown the trapezoid did show different responses. Therefore, it seems that infants perceived the trapezoid as novel, even though it cast the same retinal image as the square. But the infants were able to recognize the "real" shape of the square despite the fact that it cast a trapezoidal image on the retina. In other words, they showed shape constancy.

Development of Hearing: The Better to Hear You With

Question: How does the sense of hearing develop in infancy? Neonates can crudely orient their heads in the direction of a sound (Aslin, 1987). By 18 months, the accuracy of sound-localizing ability approaches that of adults (Morrongiello, Fenwick, & Chance, 1990). Sensitivity to sounds increases in the first few months of life (Trehub et al., 1991; Werner & Bargones, 1992). As infants mature, the range of the pitch of the sounds they can sense gradually expands to include the adult 20–20,000 cycles per second. The ability to detect differences in the pitch and loudness of sounds improves considerably throughout the preschool years (Jensen & Neff, 1993). Auditory acuity also improves gradually over the first several years (Aslin, 1987), although the hearing of infants can be so fine that many parents complain their napping infants will awaken at the slightest sound. Some do, especially if parents have been overprotective in attempting to keep their rooms as silent as possible. Infants who are normally exposed to a backdrop of moderate noise levels become habituated to them and are not likely to awaken unless there is a sudden, sharp noise.

Click *Physical Development* for more on the development of hearing.

By the age of 1 month, infants perceive differences between speech sounds that are highly similar. In a classic study relying on the **habituation** method, infants of this age could activate a recording of "bah" by sucking on a nipple (Eimas et al., 1971). As time went on, habituation occurred, as shown by decreased sucking in order to hear the "bah" sound. Then the researchers switched from "bah" to "pah." If the sounds had seemed the same to the infants, their lethargic sucking patterns would have continued. But they immediately sucked harder, suggesting that they perceived the difference. Other researchers have found that within another month or two, infants reliably discriminate three-syllable words such as *marana* and *malana* (Kehl, 1987).

Reflect

What do you think it might mean that infants reared in English-speaking homes can discriminate sounds heard in Hindi and Salish prior to 6 months of age but lose this ability by the ages of 10–12 months?

Infants can discriminate the sounds of their parents' voices by 3½ months of age. In one study, infants of this age were oriented toward their parents as they reclined in infant seats. The researchers (Spelke & Owsley, 1979) played recordings of the mother's or father's voice, while the parents themselves remained inactive. The infants reliably looked at the parent whose voice was being played.

habituation A process in which one becomes used to and therefore pays less attention to a repeated stimulus.

Young infants are capable of perceiving most of the speech sounds present in the world's languages. But after exposure to one's native language, infants gradually lose the capacity to discriminate those sounds that are not found in the native language. Prior to 6 months of age, for example, infants reared in an English-speaking environment could discriminate sounds found in Hindi (a language of India) and Salish (a Native American language). But by 10 to 12 months of age, they had lost the ability to do so, as shown in Figure 5.12 (Werker, 1989).

Infants also learn at an early age to ignore small, meaningless variations in the sounds of their native language. Adults do this routinely. For example, if someone speaking your language has a head cold or a slight accent, you ignore the minor variations in the person's pronunciation and hear these variations as the same sound. But when you hear slight variations in the sounds of a foreign language, you might assume that each variation carries a different meaning and so you hear the sounds as different.

Infants show this ability to screen out meaningless sounds as early as 6 months of age.

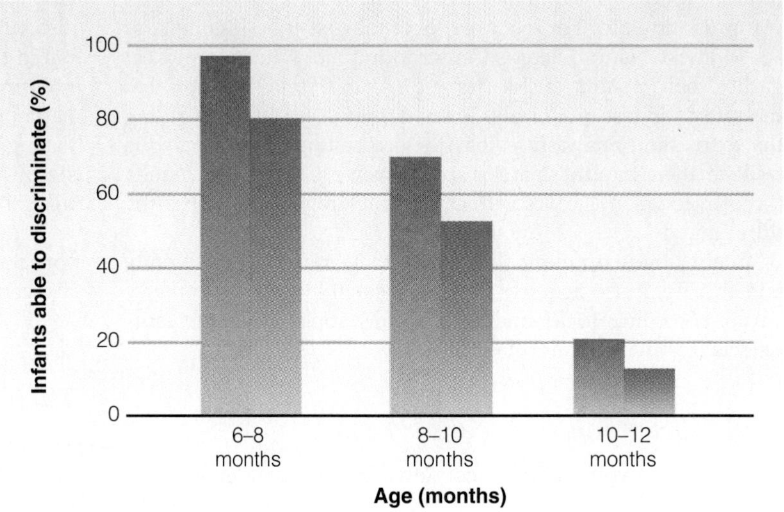

Figure 5.12
Declining Ability to Discriminate the Sounds of Foreign Languages

Infants show a decline in the ability to discriminate sounds not found in their native language. Before 6 months of age, infants from English-speaking families could discriminate sounds found in Hindi (red bars) and Salish, a Native American language (blue bars). By 10 to 12 months of age, they could no longer do so.
Source: Werker, 1989.

Patricia Kehl and her colleagues (1992) presented American and Swedish infants with pairs of sounds in either their own language or the other language. The infants were trained to look over their shoulder when they heard a difference in the sounds and to ignore sound pairs that seemed to be the same. The infants routinely ignored variations in sounds that were part of their language, because they apparently perceived them as being the same sound. But they noticed slight variations in the sounds of the other language. A later study demonstrated this same ability in infants as young as 2 months of age (Marean, Werner, & Kuhl, 1992).

By the first birthday, many infants understand many words, and some may even say a word or two of their own. During infancy the auditory apparatus for language learning is well in place.

Development of Coordination of the Senses: If I See It, Can I Touch It?

Neonates crudely orient their heads toward sounds and pleasant odors. In this way, they increase the probability that the sources of the sounds and odors will also be sensed through visual scanning. Young infants also have the ability to recognize that an object experienced in one sensory modality is the same as an identical object experienced in a different modality. This ability, known as cross-modal

A Closer Look

Effects of Early Exposure to Garlic, Alcohol, and—Gulp—Veggies

New research shows that infants begin to learn about the flavors found within their cultures through breast milk, possibly even via amniotic fluid. For example, psychologist Julie Mennella of the Monell Chemical Senses Center found that when women eat garlic, their infants suckle longer (Azar, 1998). It's not that the infants ingest more milk. Instead, they seem to be spending the extra time analyzing what they're tasting. They keep the milk in their mouths, pause, and perceive the flavors. Vanilla flavoring has a similar effect on suckling—enhancing the duration.

Infants ingest amniotic fluid while they are still in the womb, and this fluid also acquires a distinct smell after a woman eats garlic, according to Mennella. It would appear that the fetus detects this change in its environment.

No Direct Road to Alcohol Abuse

We know that you made the cognitive leap to wonder whether exposure to alcohol in the breast milk of mothers who drink creates a disposition toward alcohol abuse in the infant. That was an excellent thought, but Mennella's research suggests that the truth may lie in the opposite direction. First of all, infants appear not to like the taste of alcohol in breast milk. Mennella (2001) found that infants aged about 2–5 months drink less breast milk when the mother has recently ingested alcohol. In fact, they ingest more breast milk once the alcohol has been metabolized out of the mother's system, apparently to compensate for the reduced calorie intake at the previous feeding.

A related study by Mennella and a colleague, Pamela Garcia (2000), showed that early exposure to the odor of alcohol may also be something of a turn-off to infants. In this study, they compared the preferences of children who had been exposed to alcohol around the house during infancy with other children who had not. All the children were aged about 4–6 years at the time of testing. Children who had been exposed to alcohol early were significantly more likely than the other children (the "controls") to dislike the odor of a bottle containing alcohol.

I am not suggesting that parents drink alcohol in order to discourage their children from drinking it later on. But the findings do seem to contradict what one might have expected.

And What About Encouraging Children to Eat Their Veggies Through Early Exposure?

Many parents in the United States understand the benefits of eating vegetables and bring out the jars of vegetable baby food when they are feeding their infants. Does early exposure to these foods encourage the infants to eat them or discourage them from doing so?

Early exposure generally seems to have a positive effect on children's appetites for vegetables. Consider a study of infants 4 to 7 months old by Leann Birch and her colleagues (1998). The investigators repeatedly exposed infants to vegetables like peas and green beans in the form of baby food to see whether they would subsequently eat more or less of them. Thirty-nine infants were fed the target foods once a day for 10 consecutive days.

transfer, has been demonstrated in infants as young as 1 month of age (Bushnell, 1993; Rose & Ruff, 1987). One experiment demonstrating **cross-modal transfer** in 12-month-olds takes advantage of the fact that children of this age prefer novel to familiar sources of stimulation. Susan Rose and Esther Orlian (1991) allowed the infants to handle, but not see, an object (for example, a plastic triangle). This object and a novel object (for example, a plastic cross) then were shown to the infants, but they were not allowed to touch them. The children spent more time looking at the novel object. This indicates that they recognized the handled object, even though they were now experiencing it visually.

Do Children Play an Active or Passive Role in Perceptual Development?

Question: Do children play an active or passive role in perceptual development? Neonates may have more sophisticated sensory capabilities than you expected. Still, their ways of perceiving the world are largely mechanical, or passive. The description of a stimulus capturing an infant's attention seems quite appropriate. Neonates seem to be generally at the mercy of external stimuli. When a bright light strikes, they attend to it. If the light moves slowly across the plane of their vision, they track it.

cross-modal transfer The ability to recognize that an object experienced in one sensory modality is the same as an identical object experienced in a different modality.

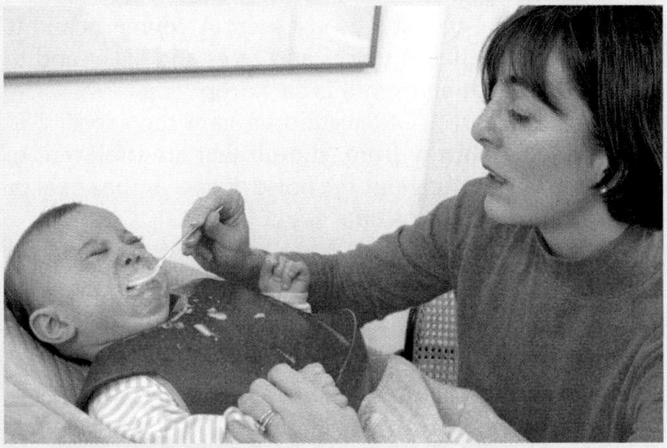

© Laura Dwight/PhotoEdit

How Do You Encourage Children To Eat Their—Ugh!—Veggies?

Do you want to talk about cruel experimental treatments that skirt the edges of the ethical limits of the researchers? Try this one on for size. Leann Birch and her colleagues repeatedly exposed 4–7-month-old infants to baby food consisting of vegetables. *Actually, the "treatment" apparently had the effect of teaching the infants to like vegetables. In terms of what the experimenters measured, they found that the infants exposed to vegetables ate more of them during test trials. Of course, an alternative interpretation is that early exposure to vegetables damaged the infants' brains so that they could not make judgments as to what they were eating later on.*[1]

[1] I encouraged Dr. Rathus to delete this last sentence from the caption, but he refused, insisting that students would understand that it is a joke. Nevertheless, I am appalled.

—The Editor

During that period, their consumption of the vegetables doubled from an average of 35 grams to an average of 72 grams. Moreover, the infants became more likely to eat similar foods—that is, other vegetables. Julie Mennella and her colleagues have also found that the infants of mothers who eat more diverse diets are more willing to eat a variety of foods (Azar, 1998). Moreover, studies of rodents, pigs, and sheep show that once they are weaned, young animals prefer the flavors to which they were exposed through their mothers' milk. Early exposure to the foods that are traditional within a culture may be a key to shaping an infant's preferences in food.

Reflect

When it comes to feeding infants vegetables like peas and green beans, would you agree that "Familiarity leads to contempt" or that "Familiarity leads to contentment"? Explain.

As time passes, broad changes occur in the perceptual processes of children, and the child's role in perception appears to become decidedly more active. Developmental psychologist Eleanor Gibson (1969, 1991) notes a number of these changes:

1. Intentional action replaces "capture." As infants mature and gain experience, purposeful scanning and exploration of the environment take the place of mechanical movements and passive responses to potent stimulation.

   Consider the scanning "strategies" of neonates. In a lighted room, neonates move their eyes mostly from left to right and back again. Mechanically, they sweep a horizontal plane. If they encounter an object that contrasts sharply with the background, their eye movements bounce back and forth against the edges. However, even when neonates awaken in a dark room, they show the stereotypical horizontal scanning pattern, with about two eye movements per second (Haith, 1990).

   The stereotypical quality of these initial scanning movements suggests that they are inborn. They provide strong evidence that the neonate is neurologically prewired to gather and seek visual information. They do not reflect what we would consider a purposeful, or intentional, effort to learn about the environment.
2. Systematic search replaces unsystematic search. Over the first few years of life, children become more active as they develop systematic ways of exploring the environment. They come to pay progressively more attention to details of objects and people and to make finer and finer discriminations.
3. Attention becomes selective. Older children become capable of selecting the information they need from the welter of confusion in the environment. For example, when older children are separated from their parents in a department store, they have the capacity to systematically scan for people of their parents' height, hair color, vocal characteristics, and so on. They are also more capable of discriminating the spot where the parent was last seen. A younger child is more likely to be confused by the welter of voices and faces and aisles and to be unable to extract essential information from this backdrop.
4. Irrelevant information becomes ignored. Older children gain the capacity to screen out, or deploy their attention away from, stimuli that are irrelevant to the task at hand. This might mean shutting out the noise of cars in the street or radios in the neighborhood in order to focus on a book.

Children, in short, develop from passive, mechanical reactors to the world about them into active, purposeful seekers and organizers of sensory information. They develop from beings whose attention is diffuse and "captured" into people who make decisions as to what they will attend to. This is a process that, like so many others, appears to depend on both maturation and experience.

Let us now screen out distractions and turn our attention to consideration of the importance of maturation and experience in perceptual development.

Nativism and Empiricism in Perceptual Development

Question: What is meant by the nativist and empiricist views of perceptual development? The nature–nurture issue is found in perceptual development, just as it is in other dimensions of development. In the area of perception, the issue can be traced to the philosophers of the 17th and 18th centuries. René Descartes and Immanuel Kant took the **nativist** view that children are born with predispositions to perceive the world in certain ways. Kant, for example, believed that our innate makeup causes us to sense and organize the objects of the world according to certain "categories." We perceive some things and are oblivious to others because of our inborn ways of organizing the world outside.

nativism The view that children are born with predispositions to perceive the world in certain ways.

empiricism The view that experience determines the ways in which children perceive the world.

George Berkeley and John Locke took the **empiricist** view that experience determines our ways of perceiving the world. Locke, for example, argued that mental representations reflect the impact of the world on the sense organs. There is no particular inborn way of organizing sensations of the world. The world, instead, impresses the mind with its own stamp. ***Question: What is the evidence for the nativist and empiricist views?***

Evidence for the Nativist View

There is compelling evidence that our inborn sensory capacities play a crucial role in our perceptual development. For one thing, neonates have already come into the world with a good number of perceptual skills. They can see nearby objects quite well, and their hearing is usually fine. They are also born with tendencies to track moving objects, to systematically scan the horizon, and to prefer certain kinds of stimuli to others. Preferences for different kinds of visual stimuli appear to unfold on schedule as the first months wear on. Sensory changes, like the motor changes discussed earlier in this chapter, appear to be linked to maturation of the nervous system.

For these reasons, it seems clear that we do have certain inborn ways of responding to sensory input—certain "categories" and built-in limits—that allow us to perceive certain aspects of the world of physical reality.

Evidence for the Empiricist View

Evidence that experience plays a crucial role in perceptual development is also compelling. We could use any of hundreds of studies with children and other species to make the point, but, for the sake of convenience, let us limit our discussion to a couple of examples of research with kittens and human infants.

Numerous studies have shown that there are critical periods in the perceptual development of children and lower animals. Failure to receive adequate sensory stimulation during these critical periods can result in permanent sensory deficits (Greenough et al., 1987). For example, neonatal kittens raised with a patch over one eye wind up with few or no cells in the visual area of the cerebral cortex that would normally be activated by sensations of light that enter that eye. In effect, that eye becomes blind, even though sensory receptors in the eye itself may fire in response to light. On the other hand, if the eye of an adult cat is patched for the same amount of time, the animal will not lose vision in that eye. The critical period apparently will have passed. Similarly, if medical problems require that a child's eye must be patched for an extensive period of time during the first year, the child's visual acuity in that eye may be impaired.

Consider a study of visual acuity among 28 human infants who had been deprived of all patterned visual input by cataracts in one or both eyes until they were treated at 1 week to 9 months of age (Maurer et al., 1999). Immediately following treatment, their visual acuity was no better than that of normal neonates, suggesting that their lack of visual experience had impaired their visual development. However, their visual acuity improved rapidly over the month following treatment. They showed some improvement as little as one hour following adequate visual input.

And so, with perceptual development, as with other dimensions of development, nature and nurture play indispensable roles. Today, few developmentalists would subscribe to either the nativist or empiricist extreme. Most would agree that nature (the nativist view) and nurture (the empiricist view) *interact* to give shape to perceptual development. Nature continues to guide the unfolding of the child's physical systems. Yet nurture continues to interact with nature in the development of these systems. We know that inborn physical structures, such as the nature of the cortex of the brain, place limits on our abilities to respond to the world. But we also know that experience continues to help shape our most basic physical structures. For example, sensorimotor experiences thicken the cortex of the brain. Sensory experiences are linked to the very development of neurons in the cortex, causing dendrites to proliferate and affecting myelination.

In the next chapter, we will see how nature and nurture influence the development of thought and language in infants.

Review

(31) Neonates are (nearsighted or farsighted?). (32) Robert Fantz presented infants with drawings of various objects, including newsprint, a bull's-eye, a face, and colored orbs and found that they fixated longest on the __________. (33) By 2 months of age, infants tend to fixate longer on a (scrambled or real?) face. (34) After less than a week of contact, neonates (can or cannot?) discriminate their mother's face from that of a stranger. (35) Neonates direct their attention to the (center or edges?) of objects. (36) Infants generally respond to visual cues for depth by the time they are able to __________. (37) In classic research, Eleanor Gibson and Richard Walk used a device called the visual __________ to assess depth perception in infants. (38) Karen Adolph's research suggests that infants' tendencies to avoid falling off a cliff are connected with their __________. (39) Thomas Bower found that __________ constancy is present in early infancy. (40) By the age of __________ months, infants can locate sounds about as well as adults can. (41) As infants mature, they have (greater or lesser?) ability to discriminate sounds used in foreign languages. (42) According to Eleanor Gibson, as infants mature and gain experience, intentional action replaces __________.

Pulling It Together: Review evidence for the nativist and empiricist views in perceptual development.

Recite Recite Recite Recite

1. What are the sequences of physical development?

Three key sequences of physical development include cephalocaudal development, proximodistal development, and differentiation. Cephalocaudal development refers to the fact that development proceeds from the upper part of the head to the lower parts of the body, enabling the brain to participate in the development of other parts of the body. Proximodistal development means that development proceeds from the central axis of the body outward. Differentiation refers to the tendency of behavior to become more specific and distinct.

2. What patterns of growth occur in infancy?

Infants usually double their birthweight in 5 months and triple it by the first birthday. Height increases by about half in the first year. Infants apparently grow in spurts, so that most of the time they are not growing at all. Infants grow another 4 to 6 inches the second year and gain another 4 to 7 pounds. The head gradually diminishes in proportion to the rest of the body, even though it doubles in size by adulthood.

3. What is failure to thrive?

Failure to thrive (FTT) is a serious disorder that impairs growth in infancy and early childhood. FTT can have organic causes or nonorganic causes. Feeding problems are central. Infants with FTT are likely to be described as variable eaters, not often hungry. FTT is linked to slow growth and behavioral and emotional problems. Deficiencies in caregiver–child interaction may play a major role in FTT.

4. What are the nutritional needs of infants?

Infants require breast milk or an iron-fortified infant formula. Introduction of solid foods is recommended at 4–6 months. Caregivers are advised to build up to a variety of foods, avoid overfeeding or underfeeding, avoid items with added sugar and salt, and encourage high-iron foods.

5. Why do women bottle-feed or breast-feed their children?

The likelihood of breast-feeding is connected with factors such as the mother's availability (most women are in the workforce), the women's movement, parental knowledge of the advantages of breast-feeding, availability of high-quality alternatives to breast milk, and ideas about marital roles.

6. What are the advantages and disadvantages of breast milk?

Breast milk has been dubbed the "ultimate fast food" because it is tailored to human digestion, contains all essential nutrients, contains antibodies that can prevent health problems in infants, helps protect against infant diarrhea, and is less likely than formula to give rise to allergies.

7. What are neurons? How do they develop?

Neurons are cells that receive and transmit messages in the form of chemicals called neurotransmitters. Most neurons are in the brain. Neurons have cell bodies, dendrites, and axons. As the child matures, axons grow in length, dendrites and axon terminals proliferate, and many neurons become wrapped in myelin that insulates them from the fluid encasing the nervous system. The symptoms of multiple sclerosis and PKU are caused by their effects on myelin.

8. What is the brain? How does the brain develop?

The brain is the command center of the developing organism. The brain triples in weight by the first birthday, reaching nearly 70% of its adult weight. The brain stem may be implicated in sudden infant death syndrome (SIDS). The formation of neurons is complete by birth. There are two major prenatal growth spurts; neurons proliferate during the first, and the second is due mainly to the proliferation of dendrites and axon terminals. Myelination during infancy enables infants to control movements and integrate sensory-motor activities (e.g., reach for what they see).

9. How do nature and nurture affect the development of the brain?

The sensory and motor areas of the brain begin to develop as a result of maturation, but sensory stimulation and motor activity also spur growth of the cortex. Rats raised in enriched environments develop heavier brains than control animals due in part to

Recite Recite Recite Recite

greater numbers of dendrites and axon terminals. Infants have more connections among neurons than adults do. Connections that are activated by experience survive; others do not. Malnutrition is connected with smallness in size of the brain, formation of fewer neurons, and less myelination.

10. What is motor development? How does it occur?

Motor development refers to developments in the activity of muscles and is connected with changes in posture, movement, and sensorimotor coordination. Motor development also follows patterns of cephalocaudal and proximodistal development, and differentiation. At about 1 month, infants can raise their heads. By 3–6 months, they usually hold their heads well. By about 3 months of age, infants make clumsy swipes at objects. Later they develop an ulnar grasp, and by 9–12 months, a pincer grasp. Between 5 and 11 months infants adjust their hands to capture moving targets. Infants can stack more blocks as they develop. Children gain the ability to move their bodies through a sequence of activities that includes rolling over, sitting up, crawling, creeping, walking, and running. The sequence remains generally invariant, but some children skip a step.

11. What are the roles of nature and nurture in motor development?

Maturation (nature) and experience (nurture) both play indispensable roles in motor development. Infants need some opportunity for experimentation before they can engage in milestones such as sitting up and walking. Development of motor skills can be accelerated by training, but the effect generally remains slight. There may be little purpose in trying to train children to enhance their motor skills before they are mature enough.

12. How do sensation and perception develop in the infant?

Neonates are nearsighted and have poor peripheral vision. Acuity and peripheral vision approximate adult levels by the age of 6 months.

13. What captures the attention of infants? How do visual preferences develop?

Neonates attend longer to stripes than blobs, and by 8–12 weeks show preference for curved lines over straight ones. Fantz found that 2-month-old infants fixate longer on the human face than on other stimuli. Some researchers argue that neonates do not "prefer" faces because they are faces per se, but because of the structure of their immature visual systems. They argue that the stimulus properties of the visual object are more important than whether it represents a face. Infants can discriminate their mother's face from a stranger's after about 8 hours of mother–infant contact. Neonates direct their attention to the edges of objects, but 2-month-olds scan from the edges inward.

14. How do researchers determine whether infants will "go off the deep end"?

Many use the classic visual cliff apparatus. Most infants refuse to venture out over the visual cliff by the time they can crawl. Researchers have speculated that infants may need some experience crawling before they develop fear of heights.

15. What are perceptual constancies? How do they develop?

A perceptual constancy is a tendency to perceive an object to be the same, even though the sensations it produces differ under various conditions. Size constancy appears to be present as early as 2½ to 3 months of age. Infants appear to have established shape constancy by 4–5 months.

16. How does the sense of hearing develop in infancy?

Neonates reflexively orient their heads toward a sound. By 18 months, infants locate sounds about as well as adults. Ability to detect differences in pitch develops throughout infancy and even throughout the preschool years. Auditory acuity also improves gradually over the first few years. By the age of 1 month, infants perceive differences between similar sounds of speech, such as "bah" and "pah." Infants discriminate their caregivers' voices by 3½ months of age. Early infants can perceive most of the speech

Recite Recite Recite Recite

sounds throughout the languages of the world, but by 10–12 months of age, this ability diminishes dramatically. Infants can screen out meaningless sounds as early as 6 months of age.

17. Do children play an active or passive role in perceptual development?

Neonates seem to be at the mercy of external stimuli. For example, they track a light that moves slowly across the plane of their vision. But infants develop from passive reactors to purposeful seekers and organizers of information: Intentional action replaces "capture" by stimuli, systematic search replaces unsystematic search, attention becomes selective, and irrelevant information becomes ignored.

18. What is meant by the nativist and empiricist views of perceptual development?

The nativist view holds that children are born with predispositions to perceive the world in certain ways. The empiricist view is that experience determines children's ways of perceiving the world.

19. What is the evidence for the nativist and empiricist views?

There is compelling evidence that inborn sensory capacities play a crucial role in perceptual development. Infants are born with many perceptual skills. There is no question that sensory changes are linked to maturation of the nervous system. Yet experience also plays a crucial role in perceptual development. For one thing, there are critical periods in the perceptual development of children and lower animals, such that sensory experience is required to optimize—or maintain—sensory capacities.

On the Web

Search Online With InfoTrac College Edition

For additional information, explore InfoTrac College Edition, your online library. Go to http://www.infotrac-college.com and use the passcode from the InfoTrac card that came with your book. Try these search terms: infants and weight, failure to thrive, neonatal jaundice, infants physiological aspects, MRI and brain development.

Visit Our Web Site

Go to http://www.wadsworth.com/psychology where you will find online resources directly linked to your book.

Child Development CD-ROM

Go to the Wadsworth Child Development CD-ROM for further study of the concepts in this chapter. The CD-ROM also includes quizzes and additional activities to expand your learning experience.

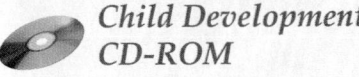

6 Infancy: Cognitive Development

Richard Hutchings/PhotoEdit

PowerPreview™

Cognitive Development: Jean Piaget

- **What kinds** of cognitive developments occur prior to the use of language? How do researchers assess them?
- **For 2-month-old** infants, "out of sight" is also apparently "out of mind." When toys are placed behind a screen, they act as if they no longer exist.

Information Processing

- **Why did** Carolyn Rovee-Collier and her colleagues tie one end of a ribbon to an infant's ankle and the other end to a brightly colored mobile?
- **A 1-hour-old** infant may imitate an adult who sticks out his or her tongue. (Really.)

Individual Differences in Intelligence Among Infants

- **Yes, your own** infant may be brilliant, but at how early an age can researchers begin to measure intelligence? (What signs of intelligence do you look for in an infant?)

Language Development: "Of Shoes and Ships and Sealing Wax, . . . and Whether Pigs Have Wings"

- **Infants cry.** (And cry some more.) Is crying a primitive form of language?
- **Do deaf children** babble?
- **Do you advance** children's language development by correcting their errors?
- **Don't waste** your time making threats: House plants won't talk.
- **Children are** "prewired"' to listen to language in such a way that they come to understand rules of grammar.

> Laurent . . . resumes his experiments of the day before. He grabs in succession a celluloid swan, a box, etc., stretches out his arm and lets them fall. He distinctly varies the position of the fall. Sometimes he stretches out his arm vertically, sometimes he holds it obliquely, in front of or behind his eyes, etc. When the object falls in a new position, he lets it fall two or three times more on the same place, as though to study the spatial relation; then he modifies the situation.

Is this the description of a scientist at work? In a way, it is. Although Swiss psychologist Jean Piaget (1936/1963) was describing his 11-month-old son, Laurent, children of this age frequently act like scientists, performing what Piaget called "experiments in order to see."

This chapter chronicles the developing thought processes of infants and toddlers—that is, their cognitive development. We focus on the sensorimotor stage of cognitive development hypothesized by Piaget. Then we examine infant memory and imitation. We next explore individual differences in infant intelligence. Finally, we turn our attention to a remarkable aspect of cognitive development: language.

Cognitive Development: Jean Piaget

Reflect

Piaget studied the mental, or cognitive, development of children. As you are reading through his "experiments," ask yourself what Piaget is actually observing in his subjects. That is, does he directly observe cognitive processes, or does he make inferences about them? Why do some psychologists—such as behaviorists—object to making any effort to study mental or cognitive processes?

Cognitive development focuses on the development of children's ways of perceiving and mentally representing the world. Piaget labeled children's concepts of the world **schemes.** He hypothesized that children attempt to **assimilate** new events into existing schemes; and when assimilation does not allow the child to make sense of novel events, children try to **accommodate** by modifying existing schemes.

Piaget (1936/1963) hypothesized that children's cognitive processes develop in an orderly sequence, or series of stages. As is the case with motor and perceptual development, some children may be more advanced than others at particular ages, but the developmental sequence does not normally vary (Thomas, 1992). Piaget identified four major stages of cognitive development: sensorimotor, preoperational (see Chapter 9), concrete operational (see Chapter 12), and formal operational (see Chapter 15). In this chapter, we discuss the sensorimotor stage.

The Sensorimotor Stage

Click *Cognition* in the Child and Adolescent CD-ROM for more on the sensorimotor stage.

Question: What is the sensorimotor stage of cognitive development? Piaget's sensorimotor stage refers to the first 2 years of cognitive development, a time when these developments are demonstrated by means of sensory and motor activity. Although it may be difficult for us to imagine how we can develop and use cognitive processes in the absence of language, children do so in many ways.

During the sensorimotor stage, infants progress from responding to events with reflexes, or ready-made schemes, to goal-oriented behavior that involves awareness of past events. During this stage, they come to form mental representations of objects and events, to hold complex pictures of past events in mind, and to solve problems by mental trial and error (Yates, 1991).

Question: What are the parts or* substages *of the stage of sensorimotor development? Piaget divided the sensorimotor stage into six substages, each of which is characterized by more complex behavior than the preceding substage. But there is also continuity from substage to substage. Each could be characterized as a variation on a theme in which earlier forms of behavior are repeated, varied, and coordinated. The approximate time periods of the substages and some characteristics of each are summarized in Table 6.1.

Simple Reflexes

The first substage covers the first month after birth. It is dominated by the assimilation of sources of stimulation into inborn reflexes such as grasping, visual tracking, crying, sucking, and crudely turning the head toward a sound.

scheme According to Piaget, an action pattern (such as a reflex) or mental structure that is involved in the acquisition or organization of knowledge.

assimilation According to Piaget, the incorporation of new events or knowledge into existing schemes.

accommodation According to Piaget, the modification of existing schemes in order to incorporate new events or knowledge.

At birth, reflexes may have a stereotypical, inflexible quality. But even within the first few hours, neonates begin to modify reflexes as a result of experience. For example, infants will adapt (accommodate) patterns of sucking to the shape of the nipple and the rate of flow of fluid.

During the first month or so, infants apparently make no connection between stimulation perceived through different sensory modalities. They make no effort to grasp objects that they visually track. Crude turning toward sources of auditory and olfactory stimulation has a ready-made look about it that cannot be considered purposeful searching.

Primary Circular Reactions

The second substage, primary circular reactions, lasts from about 1 to 4 months of age and is characterized by the beginnings of the ability to coordinate various sensorimotor schemes. In this substage, infants tend to repeat stimulating actions that first occurred by chance. A circular reaction is a behavior that is repeated. **Primary circular reactions** focus on the infant's own body rather than on the external environment. Piaget noticed the following primary circular reaction in his son Laurent:

> At 2 months 4 days, Laurent by chance discovers his right index finger and looks at it briefly. At 2 months 11 days, he inspects for a moment his open right hand, perceived by chance. At 2 months 17 days, he follows its spontaneous movement for a moment, then examines it several times while it searches for his nose or rubs his eye.
>
> At 2 months 21 days, he holds his two fists in the air and looks at the left one, after which he slowly brings it toward his face and rubs his nose with it, then his eye. A moment later the left hand again approaches his face; he looks at it and touches his nose. He recommences and laughs five or six times in succession while moving the left hand to his face. He seems to laugh before the hand moves, but looking has no influence on its movement. He laughs beforehand but begins to smile again on seeing the hand. Then he rubs his nose. At a given moment he turns his head to the left, but looking has no effect on the direction. The next day, same reaction. At 2 months 23 days, he looks at his right hand, then at his clasped hands (at length). At 2 months 24 days, at last it may be stated that looking acts on the orientation of the hands which tend to remain in the visual field (Piaget, 1936/1963, pp. 96–97).

Laurent, early in the 3rd month, thus visually tracks the behavior of his hand, but his visual observations do not seem to influence their movement. At about 2 months 21 days, Laurent can apparently exert some control over his hands, because he seems to know when a hand is about to move (and entertain him). But the link between looking at and moving the hands remains weak. A few days later, however, his looking "acts" on the hands, causing them to remain in his field of vision. Sensorimotor coordination has been achieved. An action is repeated because it stimulates the infant.

In terms of assimilation and accommodation, the child is attempting to assimilate the motor scheme (moving the hand) into the sensory scheme (looking at it). But the schemes do not automatically fit. Several days of apparent trial and error pass during which the infant seems to be trying to make accommodations so that they will fit.

Goal-directed behavior makes significant advances during the second substage. During the month after birth, infants visually track objects that contrast with their backgrounds, especially moving objects. But this ready-made behavior is largely automatic, so that the infant is "looking and seeing." But by the 3rd month, infants may examine objects repeatedly and intensely, as Laurent did. It seems clear that the infant is no longer simply looking and seeing, but is now "looking in order to see." And by the end of the 3rd month, Laurent seems to be moving his hands in order to look at them.

Since Laurent (and other infants) will repeat actions that allow them to see, cognitive-developmental psychologists consider sensorimotor coordination self-reinforcing. Laurent does not seem to be looking or moving his hands because

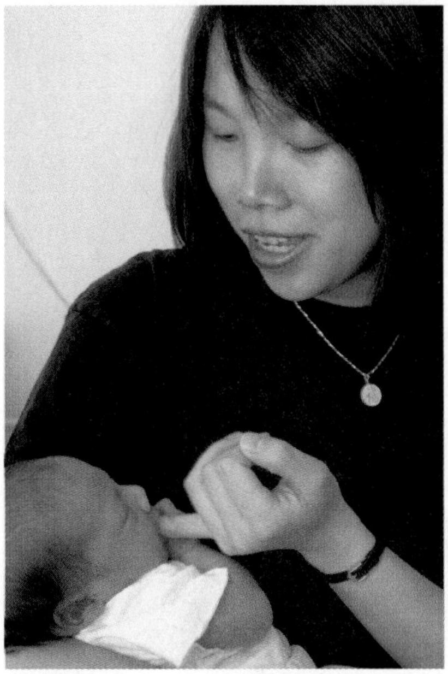

Laura Dwight/PhotoEdit

Simple Reflexes

At birth, neonates assimilate objects into reflexive responses. But even within hours after birth, neonates begin to modify reflexes as a result of experience. For example, they adapt sucking patterns to the shape of the nipple. (But don't be too impressed; porpoises are born swimming and "know" to rise to the surface of the ocean to breathe. Why did I decide to bring up porpoises? Because they need to be brought up to the surface to breathe.) Editor's comment: Are there no limits to the nonsense in this book? Author's reply: If I can't be childish in this book, where can I be?

Reflect

Here we speak of Laurent as being about to move his hand so that his hand movement will "entertain" him. Are we justified in speaking of what an infant might find to be entertaining, or should we find more scientific language? How would you phrase this paragraph?

primary circular reactions The repetition of actions that first occurred by chance and that focus on the infant's own body.

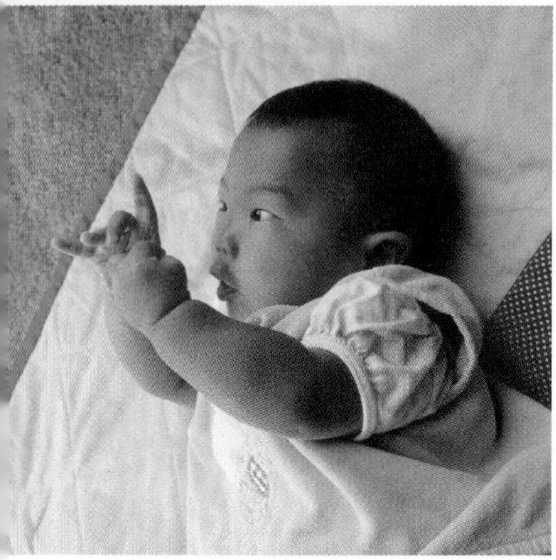

Primary Circular Reactions

In the substage of primary circular reactions, infants repeat actions that involve their bodies. The 3-month-old in this picture is also beginning to coordinate visual and sensorimotor schemes—that is, looking at the hand is becoming coordinated with holding it in the field of vision.

these acts allow him to satisfy a more basic drive such as hunger or thirst. The desire to prolong stimulation may be just as basic.

Secondary Circular Reactions

The third substage lasts from about 4 to 8 months and is characterized by **secondary circular reactions,** in which patterns of activity are repeated because of their effect on the environment. In the second substage (primary circular reactions), infants are focused on their own bodies. In the third substage (secondary circular reactions), the focus shifts to objects and environmental events. Infants may now learn to pull strings in order to make a plastic face appear or to shake an object in order to hear it rattle.

Although infants in this substage track the trajectory of moving objects, they abandon their searches when the objects disappear from view. As we shall see later in this chapter, the object concepts of infants are quite limited at these ages, especially the age at which the third substage begins.

Coordination of Secondary Schemes

In the fourth substage, infants no longer act simply to prolong interesting occurrences. Now they can coordinate schemes to attain specific goals. Infants begin to show intentional, goal-directed behavior in which they differentiate between the means of achieving a goal and the goal or end itself. For example, they may lift a piece of cloth in order to reach a toy that they had seen a parent place under the cloth earlier. In this example, the scheme of picking up the cloth (the means) is coordinated with the scheme of reaching for the toy (the goal or end).

Reflect

Were you surprised to learn that Piaget breaks down the events of the first two years into six substages? Were you surprised that he—and other researchers—track the developments of infants so closely? What might be the researchers' motives for doing so?

secondary circular reactions The repetition of actions that produce an effect on the environment.

This example indicates that the infant has mentally represented the toy placed under the cloth. Consider another example. At the age of 5 months, one of Piaget's

TABLE 6.1 *Piaget's Sensorimotor Stage: Six Substages*

Substage	About . . .
1. Simple reflexes (0–1 month)	Assimilation of new objects into reflexive responses. Infants "look and see." Inborn reflexes can be modified by experience.
2. Primary circular reactions (1–4 months)	Repetition of actions that may have initially occurred by chance but that have satisfying or interesting results. Infants "look in order to see." The focus is on the infant's body. Infants do not yet distinguish between themselves and the external world.
3. Secondary circular reactions (4–8 months)	Repetition of schemes that have interesting effects on the environment. The focus shifts to external objects and events. There is initial cognitive awareness that schemes influence the external world.
4. Coordination of secondary schemes (8–12 months)	Coordination of secondary schemes, such as looking and grasping to attain specific goals. There is the beginning of intentionality and means–end differentiation. We find imitation of actions not already in infants' repertoires.
5. Tertiary circular reactions (12–18 months)	Purposeful adaptation of established schemes to specific situations. Behavior takes on an experimental quality. There is overt trial and error in problem solving.
6. Invention of new means through mental combinations (18–24 months)	Mental trial and error in problem solving. Infants take "mental detours" based on cognitive maps. Infants engage in deferred imitation and symbolic play. Infants' cognitive advances are made possible by mental representations of objects and events and the beginnings of symbolic thought.

daughters, Lucienne, was reaching across her crib for a toy. As she did so, Piaget obscured the toy with his hand. Lucienne pushed her father's hand aside but, in doing so, became distracted and began to play with the hand. A few months later, Lucienne did not allow her father's hand to distract her from the goal of reaching the toy. She moved the hand firmly to the side and then grabbed the toy. The mental representation of the object appears to have become more persistent. The intention of reaching the object was also maintained, and so the hand was perceived as a barrier and not as another interesting stimulus.

During the fourth substage, infants also gain the capacity to copy actions that are not in their own repertoires. Infants can now imitate many gestures and sounds they had previously ignored. The imitation of a new facial gesture implies that infants have mentally represented their own faces and can tell what parts of their faces they are moving through feedback from facial muscles. For example, when a girl imitates her mother sticking out her tongue, it would appear that she has coordinated moving her own tongue with feedback from muscles in the tongue and mouth. In this way, imitation suggests a great deal about the child's emerging self-concept.

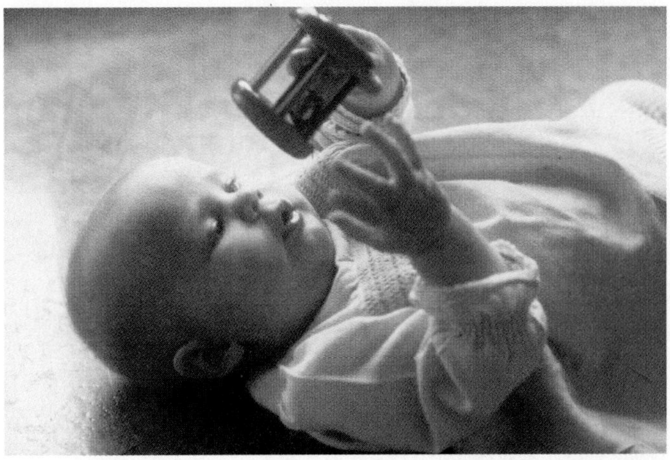

© Sandra Lousada/Woodfin Camp & Associates

Secondary Circular Reactions

In the substage of secondary circular reactions, patterns of activity are repeated because of their effect on the environment. This infant shakes a rattle to produce an interesting sound.

Tertiary Circular Reactions

In the fifth substage, which lasts from about the ages of 12 to 18 months, Piaget looked upon the behavior of infants as characteristic of budding scientists. Infants now engage in **tertiary circular reactions,** or purposeful adaptations of established schemes to specific situations. Behavior takes on a new experimental quality, and infants may vary their actions dozens of times in a deliberate trial-and-error fashion in order to learn how things work. Piaget's description of Laurent's behavior at the beginning of this chapter is a good example of tertiary circular reactions.

Piaget reported another example of tertiary circular reactions by his daughter Jacqueline. The episode was an experiment in which Piaget placed a stick outside of Jacqueline's playpen, which had wooden bars (Piaget, 1936/1963). At first, Jacqueline grasped the stick and tried to pull it sideways into the playpen. The stick was too long and could not fit through the bars. Over a number of days of trial and error, however, Jacqueline discovered that she could bring the stick between the bars by turning it upright. In future presentations, she would immediately turn the stick upright and bring it in.

Jacqueline's eventual success with the stick was the result of overt trial and error. In the sixth substage, described next, the solution to problems is often more sudden, suggesting that children have manipulated the elements of the problems in their minds and engaged in mental trial and error before displaying the correct overt response.

© Elizabeth Crews

Coordination of Secondary Schemes

During this substage, infants coordinate their behaviors to attain specific goals. This infant lifts a piece of cloth to retrieve a toy that has been placed under the cloth.

Invention of New Means Through Mental Combinations

The sixth substage lasts from about 18 to 24 months of age. It serves as a transition between sensorimotor development and the symbolic thought that characterizes the preoperational stage. External exploration is replaced by mental exploration.

Recall Jacqueline's trials (in more ways than one) with the stick. Piaget cleverly waited until his other children, Lucienne and Laurent, were 18 months old, and then he presented them with the playpen and stick problem. By waiting until 18 months, he could attribute differences in their performance to advanced age instead of a possible warm-up effect from earlier tests. Rather than engage in overt trial and error, the 18-month-old children sat and studied the situation for a few moments. Then they grasped the stick, turned it upright, and brought it into the playpen with little overt effort.

Reflect

How do we know that infants are engaging in "mental" trial and error?

tertiary circular reactions The purposeful adaptation of established schemes to new situations.

© Elizabeth Crews

Tertiary Circular Reactions

In this substage, infants vary their actions in a trial-and-error fashion to learn how things work. This infant is fascinated by what happens when you pull tissues out of a box.

Jacqueline had at first failed with the stick. She then turned it every which way, happening upon a solution almost by chance. Lucienne and Laurent solved the problem fairly rapidly, suggesting that they mentally represented the stick and the bars of the playpen and perceived that the stick would not fit through as it was. They must then have rotated the mental image of the stick until they perceived a position that would allow the stick to pass between the bars.

At around 18 months old, children may also use imitation to symbolize or stand for a plan of action. Consider how Lucienne goes about retrieving a watch chain her father placed in a matchbox. It seems that symbolic imitation serves her as a way of thinking out loud.

> I put the chain back into the box and reduce the opening. [Lucienne] is not aware of [how to open and close] the match box. [She] possesses two preceding schemes: turning the box over in order to empty it of its contents, and sliding her fingers into the slit to make the chain come out. [She] puts her finger inside and gropes to reach the chain, but fails. A pause follows during which Lucienne manifests a very curious reaction. . . .
>
> She looks at the slit with great attention. Then, several times in succession, she opens and shuts her mouth, at first slightly, then wider and wider! Apparently Lucienne understands the existence of a cavity . . . and wishes to enlarge that cavity. The attempt at representation which she thus furnishes is expressed plastically. That is to say, due to inability to think out the situation in words or clear visual images, she uses a simple motor indication as "signifier" or symbol. [Lucienne then] puts her finger in the slit, and, instead of trying as before to reach the chain, she pulls so as to enlarge the opening. She succeeds and grasps the chain (Piaget, 1936/1963, pp. 337–338).

In Chapter 9, we will see that children at this age also begin to use symbolic (or "pretend") play. For example, an 18–24-month-old child who is scolded by parents for throwing food may later return the scolding through play with dolls or even imaginary figures.

Development of Object Permanence

One important aspect of the development of cognitive processes is the appearance of **object permanence.** ***Questions: What is object permanence? How does it develop?*** Object permanence is the recognition that an object or person continues to exist when out of sight. Your child development textbook continues to exist when you accidentally leave it in the library after studying for the big test, and an infant's mother continues to exist even when she is in another room. Your realization that your book exists, although out of view, is an example of object permanence. If an infant acts as if its mother no longer exists when she is out of sight, the infant does not have the concept of object permanence.

According to Jean Piaget and other theorists, various facets of object permanence develop during infancy and correspond to the sequences of the child's general cognitive development (Flavell et al., 2002). The development of object permanence is tied into infants' general tendency to form mental representations of sensory impressions and then reason about them (Aguiar & Baillargeon, 1998, 1999; Hespos & Baillargeon, 2001a, 2001b).

Neonates show no tendency to respond to objects that are not within their immediate sensory grasp. By 2 months, infants may show some surprise if an object (such as a toy duck) is placed behind a screen and then taken away so that when the screen is lifted, it is absent. However, they make no effort to search for the missing object. Through the first 6 months or so, when the screen is placed between the object and the infant, the infant behaves as though the object is no longer there (see Figure 6.1).

Reflect

When your car (or boyfriend or girlfriend) is out of sight, does it, he, or she continue to exist? How do you know? (You're allowed to get philosophical; this is college.)

Click *Cognition* for more on object permanence.

object permanence Recognition that objects continue to exist even when they are not seen.

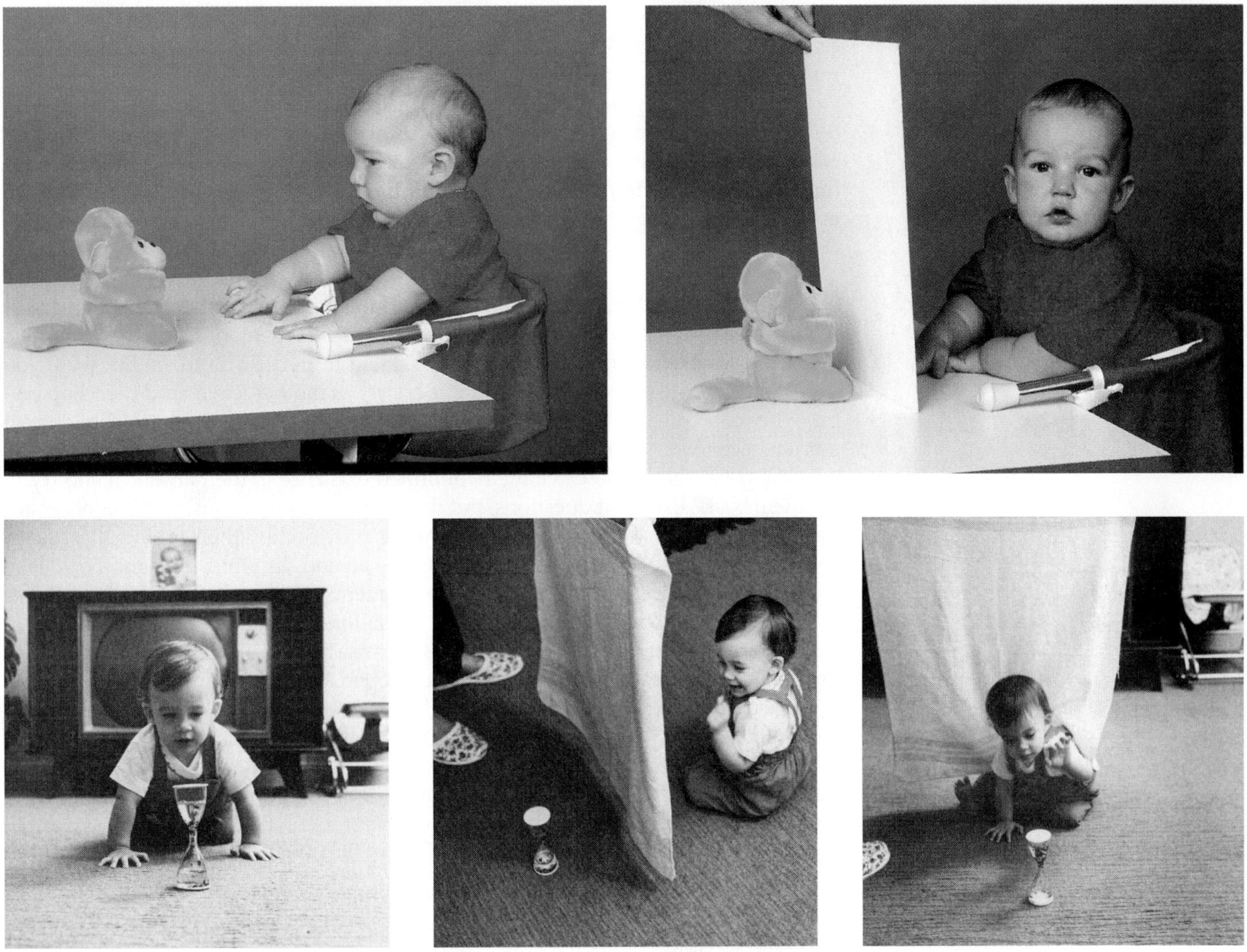

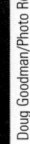

Figure 6.1
Development of Object Permanence

To this infant, who is in the early part of the sensorimotor stage, out of sight is truly out of mind. Once a sheet of paper is placed between the infant and the toy monkey, the infant loses all interest in the toy. From evidence of this sort, Piaget concluded that the toy is not mentally represented. The bottom series of photos shows a child in a later part of the sensorimotor stage. This child does mentally represent objects and pushes through a towel to reach an object that has been screened from sight.

There are some interesting advances in the development of the object concept by about the 6th month (Piaget's substage 3). For example, an infant at this age will tend to look for an object that has been dropped, behavior that suggests some form of object permanence. By this age, there is also reason to believe that the infant perceives a mental representation (image) of an object, such as a favorite toy, in response to sensory impressions of part of the object. This is shown by the infant's reaching for a preferred object when it has been partially hidden by a cloth.

By the ages of 8 to 12 months (Piaget's substage 4), infants will seek to retrieve objects that have been completely hidden behind screens. But in observing his own children, Piaget (1936/1963) noted an interesting error known as the *A not B* error. Piaget repeatedly hid a toy behind a screen (A), and each time his infant removed the screen and retrieved the toy. Then, as the infant watched, Piaget hid the toy behind another screen (B) in a different place. Still, the infant tried to recover the toy by pushing aside the first screen (A). It is as though the child had learned that a certain motor activity would reinstate the missing toy. The child's concept of the object did not, at this age, extend to recognition that objects usually remain in the place where they have been most recently mentally represented.

More recent research, however, indicates that under certain conditions, 8–12-month-olds do not show the *A not B* error (Harris, 1987; Small, 1990). For example, if infants are allowed to search for the object immediately after seeing it hidden, the error often does not occur. But if they are forced to wait 5 or more seconds before looking, they are likely to commit the *A not B* error (Wellman, Cross, & Bartsch, 1986).

In the next chapter, we see that most children have developed some notion of object permanence before they develop emotional bonds to specific caregivers. It seems logical that infants must have permanent representations of their mothers before they will show distress at being separated from their mothers. But wait, you say? Won't even 3- or 4-month-old infants cry when mother leaves and then stop crying when she comes and picks them up? Doesn't this behavior pattern show object permanence in very young infants? Don't these infants "miss" their mothers when they are gone (that is, perceive their continued existence in their absence) and try to get them back? Excellent questions, but the scientific answer must be "Not necessarily." Infants appear to appreciate the comforts provided by their mothers' presence and to express displeasure when they come to an end (as when their mothers leave the room). The expression of displeasure frequently results in the reinstatement of pleasure (being held, fed, and spoken to). Therefore, infants may learn to engage in these protests when their mothers leave because of the positive consequences of protesting—and not because they have developed object permanence.

Nevertheless, studies by Renee Baillargeon and her colleagues (Aguiar & Baillargeon, 1999; Baillargeon et al., 1990) show that some rudimentary knowledge of object permanence may be present as early as $2\frac{1}{2}$–$3\frac{1}{2}$ months of age. In one clever study, Baillargeon (1987) first showed $3\frac{1}{2}$- and $4\frac{1}{2}$-month-olds the event illustrated in the top part of Figure 6.2. A screen rotated back and forth through a 180-degree arc like a drawbridge. After several trials, the infants showed habituation; that

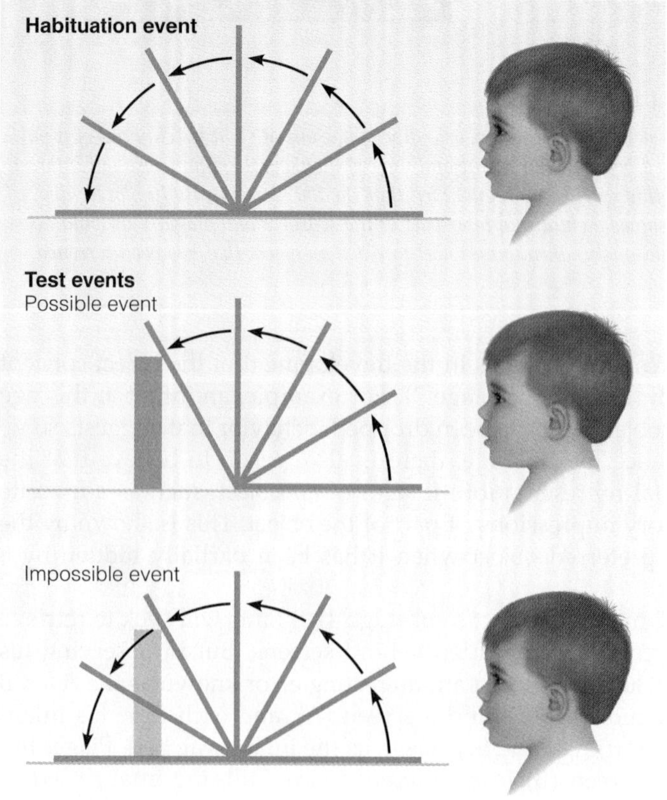

Figure 6.2
Object Permanence Before 4 Months of Age?

Renee Baillargeon (1987) used the technique shown here to demonstrate that knowledge of object permanence may exist prior to 4 months of age. She first showed infants a screen rotated back and forth like a drawbridge (top drawing). After infants showed habituation, a box was placed in the path of the screen. The middle drawing shows a possible event—the screen stops when it reaches the box. The bottom drawing shows an impossible event—the screen rotates through a full 180-degree arc as though the box were no longer behind it. (The experimenter had removed it, unknown to the infant.) Infants looked longer at the impossible event, indicating they realized the box still existed even when hidden behind the screen.
Source: Baillargeon, 1987.

is, they spent less and less time looking at the screen. Next, a box was placed in the path of the screen, as shown in the middle drawing of Figure 6.2. The infant could see the box at the beginning of each trial, but could no longer see it when the screen reached the box. In one condition, labeled the "possible event," the screen stopped when it reached the box. In another condition, labeled the "impossible event," the screen rotated through a full 180-degree arc, as though the box were no longer behind it. (How could this happen? Unknown to the infant, a trapdoor was released, causing the box to drop out of the way.) The infants looked longer at the "impossible event" than at the "possible" one. Infants tend to look longer at unexpected events. So their behavior indicates they were surprised that the screen did not stop when it reached the box. This reaction indicates that children as young as $3\frac{1}{2}$ months of age realized that the box continued to exist even when it was hidden behind the screen (Baillargeon, 1991). But why then do infants not actively look for hidden objects until about 8 months of age? It may be that Piaget was correct in stating that coordination of acts (such as removing a barrier in order to reach a toy) does not occur until this later age (Baillargeon et al., 1990).

Evaluation of Piaget's Theory

Question: What are the strengths and limitations of Piaget's theory? Piaget's theory remains a most comprehensive model of infant cognition. Many of his observations of his own three infants have been confirmed by others. The pattern and sequence of events he described have been observed among American, European, African, and Asian infants (Werner, 1988). Still, recent research has raised questions about the validity of many of Piaget's claims (Flavell et al., 2002).

For one thing, most cognitive researchers now agree that cognitive development is not as tied to discrete stages as Piaget believed (Flavell et al., 2002). The heart of the stage-theory approach is that changes are discontinuous. In the case of Piaget's theory, children's responses to the world, as governed by their cognitive processes, would have to change relatively suddenly. While later cognitive acquisitions do appear to build on earlier ones, the process appears to be more gradual than discontinuous.

A second criticism of Piaget's theory is that he appears to have underestimated the young infant's competence (Flavell et al., 2002). For example, as we saw earlier in this chapter, infants display object permanence at a much earlier age than Piaget believed.

Another example of early infant competence is provided by studies on **deferred imitation,** which is imitation of an action that may have occurred hours,

Reflect

Which is a more important criticism of Piaget's theory: That the stages of development are more continuous than he believed or that he underestimated the timing of the development of cognitive milestones? Explain.

deferred imitation The imitation of people and events that occurred hours, days, or weeks in the past.

A Closer Look

On Orangutans, Chimps, Magpies, and Object Permanence

Let's not limit our discussion of the development of object permanence to humans. Comparative psychologists have also studied the development of object permanence in nonhuman species, including dogs, cats, primates, and even magpies. Animal boosters will be quite intrigued by the findings reported in an article titled "Object Permanence in Orangutans (*Pongo pygmaeus*), Chimpanzees (*Pan troglodytes*), and Children (*Homo sapiens*)." Despite the conclusion of most researchers that primates such as chimpanzees and gorillas do not make use of language—even sign language—in the sophisticated way that humans do, Josep Call (2001), the author of the article, found that the three species—orangutan, chimp, and human—performed at the same intellectual level in tasks used to assess object permanence. The key caveat is that orangutans and chimpanzees mature more rapidly than humans, and Call was comparing juvenile and adult orangutans with 19–26-month-old human infants. (Go, *Homo sapiens!*).

Now what about the magpies? Magpies are notorious thieves in the bird world, and they also hide their food to keep it safe from other animals—especially other magpies. Bettina Pollock and her colleagues (2000) found that magpies develop object permanence before they begin to hide food. Think about it: Magpies would not profit from secreting away their food if out of sight meant the same thing as "out of existence."

days, or even weeks earlier. A young child may do an excellent imitation of Mommy mowing the lawn or Daddy changing the infant (by using a doll). The presence of deferred imitation suggests that children have mentally represented complex behavior patterns and actions. Piaget believed that deferred imitation appears at about 18 months, but more recent findings indicate that infants can show deferred imitation as early as 9 months of age (Meltzoff, 1988). In Meltzoff's study, 9-month-old infants watched an adult perform a series of novel actions, such as pushing a button on a box to produce a beeping sound. When given a chance to play with the same objects 24 hours later, many of the infants reproduced the actions they had seen the adult perform.

A Closer Look

Counting in the Crib? Findings From a "Mickey Mouse Experiment"

Infants as young as 5 months of age may have some ability to "add" and "subtract," according to research by Karen Wynn (1992a). Wynn's method was based on the fact that infants look longer at unexpected (novel) events than at expected (familiar) events. (Baillargeon's studies of object permanence in young infants were also based on this fact.) If infants are able to engage in some form of rudimentary addition and subtraction, they should look longer at a "wrong answer"—that is, an unexpected answer—than at an expected "correct answer."

In her research, Wynn showed infants 4-inch Mickey Mouse dolls. (Yes, this was a "Mickey Mouse experiment," literally speaking.) One group of infants saw a single doll. Then a screen was raised, blocking the infants' view. Some behind-the-scenes manipulation occurred so that when the screen was removed, the infants were presented with either two dolls (the expected or "right answer") or only one doll (the unexpected or "wrong answer"). Another group of infants was initially shown two dolls. The screen was raised and the infants observed while one doll was removed. But some manipulation took place behind the scenes again, so that when the screen was removed, the infants were shown either one doll (the right answer) or two dolls (the wrong answer). The infants consistently looked longer at the two dolls—that is, the wrong answer.

These results suggest that infants were responsive to some change in quantity—perhaps they showed some rudimentary sense of "more" or "less." But how do we know that the infants were aware of a difference in the *number* of objects? Can infants somehow calculate the change in number that was produced in the experiment?

To gain some insight into infants' abilities to "count," Wynn first presented a third group of infants with a single doll. She raised the screen and added one doll as the infants observed. Again, some behind-the-scenes manipulation took place so that when the screen was removed, the infants would be presented with either two Mickeys (the right answer) or three Mickeys (the wrong answer; see Figure 6.3). In this phase of the research, the infants stared longer at the three Mickeys than the two, suggesting that they might have somehow calculated the number of Mickeys that should have resulted from the researcher's manipulations. But again, we cannot say that the infants are adding per se. Other researchers suggest that the infants are more likely to be sensitive to simpler concepts of "more" and "less" (Gao et al., 2000).

So where was Minnie?

Reflect

Why do you think that it makes sense—from an evolutionary perspective—that infants would gaze longer at novel stimuli than at familiar stimuli?

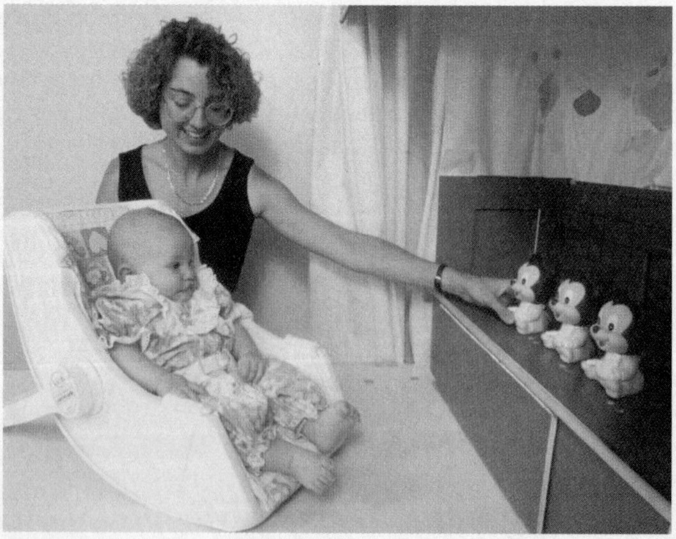

Photo by David Sanders, The Arizona Daily Star

Figure 6.3
Counting in the Crib?

Research by Karen Wynn suggests that 5-month-old infants may know when simple computations—or demonstrations involving concepts of more *and* less*—are done correctly. The research is made possible by the fact that infants stare longer at unexpected stimuli—in this case, at a "wrong answer." Wynn conducted her research by exposing infants to Mickey Mouse dolls. She then added or removed one or more dolls behind a screen as the infant watched her, removed the screen, and observed how long the infants gazed at "right" or "wrong" answers.*

A final example of infant competence that occurs much earlier than Piaget predicted comes from recent research that suggests that 5-month-old infants may be able to grasp some basic computational concepts—*more* and *less* (see the nearby "A Closer Look" feature). In Piaget's view, this ability does not emerge until the preoperational stage, which begins at approximately 2 years of age.

Psychologists Andrew Meltzoff and M. Keith Moore (1998) assert bluntly that "the sensorimotor theory of infancy has been overthrown," but they admit that "there is little consensus on a replacement." Other researchers agree about the replacement possibilities (Parent, Normandeau, & Larivee, 2000). In an interview with a staff writer for the *Monitor* of the American Psychological Association, Meltzoff remarked that "Piaget's theories were critical for getting the field of [cognitive development] off the ground, . . . but it's time to move on" (1997, p. 9). But to move on to exactly what? Again, there is no consensus. Piaget is not so readily replaced.

Review

(1) Piaget labeled children's concepts of the world __________. (2) Children try to __________ new events into existing schemes. (3) Piaget's __________ stage spans the first 2 years of cognitive development. (4) The first substage is dominated by the assimilation of stimulation into __________ such as grasping and sucking. (5) Primary __________ reactions are characterized by repeating stimulating actions that occur by chance. (6) In __________ circular reactions, activity is repeated because of its effect on the environment. (7) In the __________ substage, infants coordinate schemes to attain specific goals. (8) __________ circular reactions are purposeful adaptations of established schemes to specific situations. (9) The sixth substage is a transition between sensorimotor development and __________ thought. (10) Object __________ is recognition that an object or person continues to exist when out of sight. (11) Research into Piaget's theory (supports or disconfirms?) the pattern and sequence of events he described. (12) Current research suggests that cognitive development is more (gradual or discontinuous?) than Piaget believed.

Pulling It Together: How do Piaget's substages of the sensorimotor stage portray cognitive developments as growing out of other cognitive developments?

Information Processing

The information-processing approach to cognitive development focuses on how children manipulate or process information coming in from the environment or already stored in the mind (Flavell et al., 2002). ***Question: What are infants' tools for processing information?*** One is memory. Another is imitation.

Infants' Memory

Many of the cognitive capabilities of infants—recognizing the faces of familiar people, developing object permanence, and, in fact, learning in any form—depend on one critical aspect of cognitive development: memory (Lipsitt, 1990a; Pascual-Leone, 2000b).

Even neonates demonstrate memory for stimuli to which they have been exposed previously. Neonates adjust their rate of sucking to hear a recording of their mother reading a story she had read aloud during the last weeks of pregnancy (DeCasper & Fifer, 1980; DeCasper & Spence, 1991). Remember, too, that neonates who are breast-fed are able to remember and show recognition of their mother's unique odor (Cernoch & Porter, 1985).

Reflect

Why is memory a critical component of the learning process?

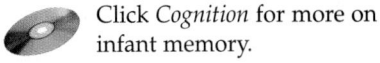

Click *Cognition* for more on infant memory.

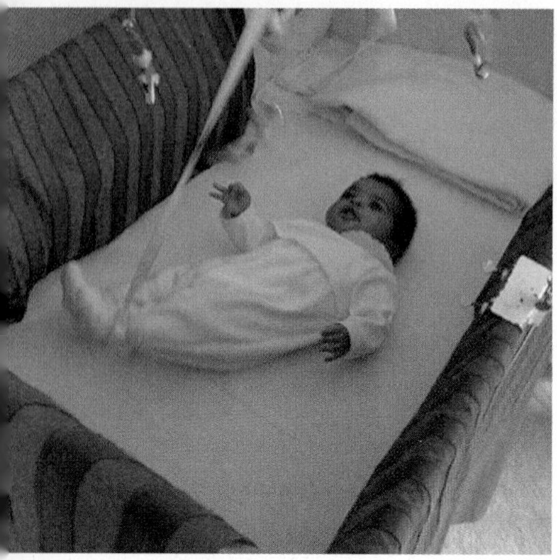

■ **Figure 6.4**
Investigating Infant Memory

In this technique, developed by Carolyn Rovee-Collier, the infant's ankle is connected to a mobile by a ribbon. Infants quickly learn to kick to make the mobile move. Two- and 3-month-olds remember how to perform this feat after a delay of a few days. If given a reminder of simply viewing the mobile, their memory lasts for 2 to 4 weeks.

Memory improves dramatically between 2 and 6 months of age and then again by 12 months (Rose, Feldman, & Jankowski, 2001). The improvement may indicate that older infants are more capable than younger ones of encoding (that is, storing) information, retrieving information already stored, or both (Kail, 1990).

A fascinating series of studies by Carolyn Rovee-Collier and her colleagues (Rovee-Collier, 1993) illustrates some of these developmental changes in infant memory (see Figure 6.4). One end of a ribbon was tied to a brightly colored mobile suspended above the infant's crib. The other end was tied to the infant's ankle, so that when the infant kicked, the mobile moved. Infants quickly learned to increase their rate of kicking. To measure memory, the infant's ankle was again fastened to the mobile after a period of one or more days had elapsed. In one study, 2-month-olds remembered how to make the mobile move after delays of up to 3 days, and 3-month-olds remembered for more than a week (Greco et al., 1986).

Infant memory can be improved if infants receive a reminder before they are given the memory test (Rovee-Collier & Shyi, 1992). In one study that used this reminder procedure, infants were shown the moving mobile on the day prior to the memory test, but they were not allowed to activate it. Under these conditions, 3-month-olds remembered how to move the mobile after a 28-day delay (Rovee-Collier, 1993).

■ Imitation: Infant See, Infant Do?

Imitation is the basis for much of human learning. Deferred imitation—that is, the imitation of actions after a time delay—occurs as early as 9 months of age. To help them remember the imitated act, infants are usually permitted to practice it when they learn it. But in one study, 12-month-old infants were prevented from practicing the behavior they imitated. Yet they were able to demonstrate it 4 weeks later, suggesting that they had mentally represented the act (Klein & Meltzoff, 1999).

But infants have the capacity to imitate certain actions at a much earlier age. Neonates only 0.7 to 71 hours old have been found to imitate adults who open their mouths or stick out their tongues (Anisfeld, 1991; Meltzoff, 1990; Meltzoff & Moore, 1992) (see Figure 6.5).

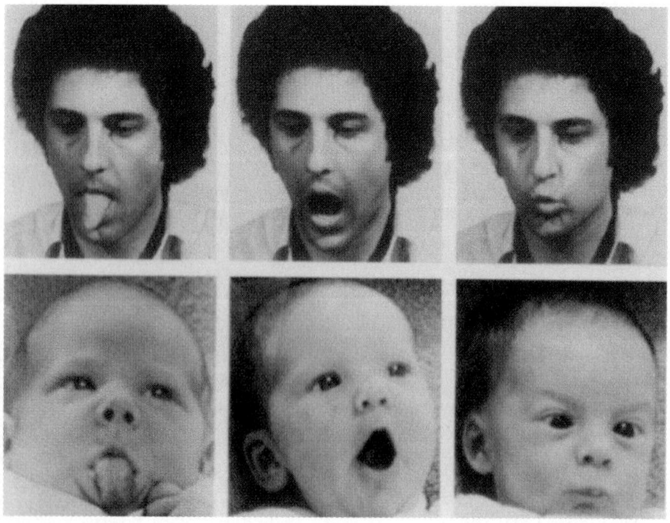

■ **Figure 6.5**
Imitation in Infants

These 2–3-week-old infants are imitating the facial gestures of an adult experimenter. How are we to interpret these findings? Shall we say that the infants "knew" what the experimenter was doing and "chose" to imitate the behavior, or is there an alternate explanation?

Before you become too impressed with this early imitative ability of neonates, you should know that some studies have not found imitation in early infancy (Abravanel & DeYong, 1991). Furthermore, 6-week-old infants stick out their tongues when nonhuman stimuli, such as small balls or felt-tipped pens, are moved toward their mouths (Jacobson, 1979). This cannot be considered imitative behavior because it did not occur in response to another person's engaging in the same (or highly similar) behavior.

One key factor may be the infants' age. The studies that find imitation generally have been done with very young infants—up to 2 weeks old—while the studies that do not find imitation have tended to use older infants (Reissland, 1988). So the imitation of neonates is likely to be reflexive. Thus it might disappear at the time reflexes are "dropping out" and reemerge when it has a firmer cognitive footing (Anisfeld, 1991; Reissland, 1988).

We reported some rather harsh commentaries on the status of Piaget's theory in the new millennium. Many researchers and theorists seek to replace—or augment—Piaget's views by way of information-processing theory. Some of this research is termed neo-Piagetan (new-Piagetan) and some is sort of anti-Piagetan. There is no doubt that information-processing theory has given rise to key research in cognitive development. On the other hand, as of today, information-processing theorists have not created a grand cognitive developmental theory on the order of Piaget's (Parent et al., 2000; Pascual-Leone, 2000a, 2000b). This does not mean that we should ignore the chinks in the armor of

Piaget's theory. It simply means that the struggle for knowledge continues—which is a good thing, considering the alternative. (Sermon over.)

Reflect

Why do adolescents and adults stick their tongues out at infants? (Why not ask a few—a few adolescents and adults, that is?)

Review

(13) The __________-processing approach to cognitive development focuses on how children manipulate or process information. (14) __________ improves dramatically between 2 and 6 months. (15) In her studies of infant memory, Rovee-Collier tied one end of a ribbon to a mobile and the other to the infant's __________. (16) The imitation of actions after a time delay is called __________ imitation. (17) The imitation of neonates appears to be __________.

Pulling It Together: How do memory and imitation help enable the infant to process information?

Individual Differences in Intelligence Among Infants

Cognitive development does not proceed in the same way or at the same pace for all infants (Rose et al., 2001). ***Question: What are the individual differences in the development of cognitive functioning?*** Efforts to understand the development of infant differences in cognitive development have relied on so-called scales of infant development or infant intelligence.

Reflect

When you have observed infants, what kinds of behaviors have led you to think that one is "brilliant" or another one "dull"? How do your "methods" correspond to those used by researchers who attempt to assess intellectual functioning among infants?

Measuring cognition or intelligence in infants is very different from measuring it in adults. Infants cannot, of course, be assessed by asking them to explain the meanings of words, the similarity between concepts, or the rationales for social rules. One of the most important tests of intellectual development among infants contains very different kinds of items: the Bayley Scales of Infant Development, constructed in 1933 by psychologist Nancy Bayley and revised most recently in 1993.

The Bayley test currently consists of 178 mental-scale items and 111 motor-scale items. The mental scale assesses verbal communication, perceptual skills, learning and memory, and problem-solving skills. The motor scale assesses gross motor skills, as in standing, walking, and climbing, and fine motor skills, as shown by ability to manipulate the hands and fingers. A behavior rating scale based on examiner observation of the child during the test is also used. The behavior rating scale assesses attention span, goal-directedness, persistence, and aspects of social and emotional development. Table 6.2 contains sample items from the mental and motor scales and shows the ages at which 50% of the infants taking the test passed the items.

The Bayley Scales of Infant Development

The Bayley Scales measure the infant's mental and motor development.

Testing Infants—Why, and With What?

As you can imagine, it is no easy matter to test an infant. The items must be administered on a one-to-one basis by a patient tester, and it can be difficult to judge whether the infant is showing the targeted response. Why, then, do we test infants?

One reason is to screen infants for handicaps. A highly trained tester may be able to detect early signs of sensory or neurological problems. In addition to the Bayley Scales, a number of tests have been developed to screen infants for such difficulties: these include the Brazelton Neonatal Behavioral Assessment Scale (see Chapter 4) and the Denver Developmental Screening Test (Frankenburg, 1992; Mayes, 1991).

A second use of infant scales is to make developmental predictions. Here the scales do not fare so well.

The Instability of Intelligence Scores Attained in Infancy

Question: How well do infant scales predict later intellectual performance? The answer is somewhat less than clear. Certain items on the Bayley Scales have been found to predict specific intellectual skills later in childhood. For example, Linda Siegel found that Bayley items measuring infant motor skills predicted subsequent fine-motor and visual-spatial skills at 6 to 8 years of age. Bayley language items also predicted language skills at the same age (Siegel, 1992).

But overall or global scores on the Bayley and other infant scales do not predict school grades or later IQ scores very well (Colombo, 1993; Storfer, 1990). Why do infant tests fail to do a good job of predicting IQ scores among preschoolers and school-aged children? First of all, cognitive functioning seems to change so quickly during infancy that reliable measurement may be impossible. Second, the sensorimotor test items used during infancy may not be strongly related to the verbal and symbolic items used at later ages (Colombo, 1993; Seefeldt, 1990; Thompson, Fagan, & Fulker, 1991).

TABLE 6.2 *Items From the Bayley Scales of Infant Development (BSID-II)*

Age	Mental-Scale Items	Motor-Scale Items
1 month	The infant quiets when picked up.	The infant makes a postural adjustment when put to examiner's shoulder.
2 months	When examiner presents two objects (bell and rattle) above the infant in a crib, she or he glances back and forth from one to the other.	The infant holds his or her head steady when being carried about in a vertical position.
5 months	The infant is observed to transfer an object from one hand to the other during play.	When seated at a feeding-type table and presented with a sugar pill that is out of reach, the infant attempts to pick it up.
8 months	When an object (toy) in plain view of the infant (that is, on a table) is covered by a cup, the infant removes the cup in order to retrieve the object.	The infant raises herself or himself into a sitting position.
12 months	The infant imitates words that are spoken by the examiner.	When requested by the examiner, the infant stands up from a position in which she or he had been lying on her or his back on the floor.
14–16 months	The infant builds a tower with two cubes (blocks) after the examiner demonstrates the behavior.	The infant walks alone with good coordination.

Use of Visual Recognition Memory: An Effort to Enhance Predictability

In a continuing effort to find aspects of intelligence and cognition that might remain consistent from infancy through later childhood, a number of researchers have recently focused on **visual recognition memory.** ***Questions: What is visual recognition memory? How is it used?*** Visual recognition memory refers to an infant's ability to discriminate previously seen objects from novel objects. How is it used? This procedure is based on habituation, as are many of the methods for assessing perceptual development (see Chapter 5).

Let's consider longitudinal studies of this type. Susan Rose and her colleagues (Rose, Feldman, & Wallace, 1992) showed 7-month-old infants pictures of two identical faces. After 20 seconds, the pictures were replaced with one picture of a new face and a second picture of the familiar face. The amount of time the infants

visual recognition memory The kind of memory shown in an infant's ability to discriminate previously seen objects from novel objects.

Developing in the New Millennium

The Quest for a Superkid

At the dawn of the 21st century, a curious—and unsettling—transformation has come over American kids. The marvelously anarchic institution of childhood has been slowly turning into little more than an apprentice adulthood. Toddlers who once would have been years away from starting their formal education are being hothoused in nursery schools. Preschoolers who would have spent their time learning simply to play and share are being bombarded with flash cards, educational CD-ROMs, and other gadgets designed to teach reading, writing, and even second languages. Grade-schoolers are spending longer hours at school, still longer ones sweating over homework, and filling what time they have left with a buffet line of outside activities that may or may not build character but definitely build résumés. Kids who once had childhoods now have curriculums; kids who ought to move with the lunatic energy of youth now move with the high purpose of the worker bee.

The engine behind this early striving is, often, the parents, who are increasingly consumed by the idea that if they can't perfect their children, they must at least get them as close to that ideal as possible. And who can blame them? Birth rates, while short of baby-boom levels, are nonetheless robust, tightening the competition for spots in the best schools. At the same time, almost all those schools have democratized their admissions policies, meaning it's no longer just the elite who can attend. With competition getting ever keener, kids have to do ever more to distinguish themselves.

Parents are also driven by old-fashioned guilt. Even as men take on more responsibility for rearing children, the lion's share of baby care is still handled by mothers. But in an era in which it often takes two incomes to meet the monthly nut, increasing numbers of moms can't spend nearly as much time with their kids as they'd like. Into this anxious mix have stepped hucksters and marketers who see worried parents as the most promising pigeons. Store shelves groan with new products purported to stimulate babies' brains in ways harried parents don't have time for. There are baby Mozart tapes said to enhance spatial reason-

How to Make a Superkid?

There was a time when young people might have competed in athletics or college admissions. But nowadays, many parents are struggling to enroll their infants in challenging pre-nursery-school programs to prepare them for challenging nursery schools to prepare them for challenging kindergartens to prepare them for . . . you get the idea. In the quest to rear superkids, toddlers and preschoolers who might once have spent their days at play are being bombarded with flash cards, educational CD-ROMs, and other gadgets designed to teach reading, writing, and even second languages. Many children who once had childhoods now have curriculums.

Source: Adapted from Jeffrey Kluger (with Alice Park). (2001, April 30). The quest for a superkid. Time, *pp. 48–55. ©2001 Time, Inc. Reprinted by permission.*

spent looking at each of the faces in the second set of pictures was recorded. Some infants spent more time looking at the new face than the older face, suggesting that they had better memory for visual stimulation. The children were given standard IQ tests yearly from ages 1 through 6. It was found that the children with greater visual recognition memory later attained higher IQ scores.

Rose and her colleagues (2001) have also shown that there is some stability from age to age in individual differences in capacity for visual recognition memory. This finding is important because intelligence—the quality that many researchers seek to predict from visual recognition memory—is also theorized to be a reasonably stable trait. Similarly, items on intelligence tests are age-graded; that is, older children perform better than younger children, even as developing intelligence remains constant. So, too, with visual recognition memory. Capacity for visual recognition memory increases over the 1st year after birth (Rose et al., 2001).

Developing in the New Millennium (continued)

ing and perhaps musical and artistic abilities too. There are black, white, and red picture books, said to sharpen visual acuity. There are bilingual products said to train baby brains so they will be more receptive to multiple languages. Parents who don't avail themselves of these products do so at their children's peril: The brain, they are told, has very limited windows for learning certain skills. Let them close, and kids may be set back forever.

But is any of this true? Is it possible to turn an ordinary kid into an exceptional kid? Even if it is, is it worth it to try? Is it better to steer children gently through childhood, letting them make some mistakes and take some scrapes and accept the fact that some of them may not be marked for excellence? Or is it better to strive for a family of superkids, knowing that they are getting the most out of their potential if not out of their youth? Clearly, many parents are caught up in that quest, even if they quietly harbor doubts about its merits. "Parents have, to a large extent, lost confidence in themselves and in their own good judgment," says Peter Gorski, a committee chair of the American Academy of Pediatrics.

The phenomenon of the driven child has been coming for a while, but it was in 1994 that the new breed was truly born. That was the year the Carnegie Corporation published a 134-page report describing a "quiet crisis" among U.S. children, who, it argued, were being ill served by their twin-career parents and their often failing school systems. The report's findings were worrisome enough, but buried in its pages were two disturbing paragraphs warning that schoolkids might not be the only ones suffering; babies could be too. Young brains are extremely sensitive to early influences, the report cautioned, and the right—or wrong—stimuli could have a significant impact on later development.

"Every parent began to worry," says John Bruer, president of the McDonnell Foundation and author of the book *The Myth of the First Three Years.* "They thought, 'If I don't have the latest Mozart CD, my child is going to jail rather than Yale?'"

In order to make up for their feared lapses, parents indeed started buying the approved kinds of music—and a whole lot more. A study conducted by Zero to Three, a nonprofit research group, found that almost 80% of parents with a high school education or less were assiduously using flash cards, television, and computer games to try to keep their babies' minds engaged.

Child development experts, however, consider these sterile tools inferior to more social and emotional activities such as talking with or reading to children. These specialists agree that the only thing shown to optimize children's intellectual potential is a secure, trusting relationship with their parents. Time spent cuddling, gazing, and playing establishes a bond of security, trust, and respect on which the entire child development pyramid is based. "We have given social and emotional development a back seat," says UCLA's Tyler, "and that's doing a great disservice to kids and to our society."

Baby Brains

It is true, as the marketers say, that a baby's brain is a fast-changing thing. Far from passively sponging up information, it is busy from birth laying complex webs of neurons that help it grow more sophisticated each day. It takes anywhere from 1 year to 5 years, depending on the part of the brain, for this initial explosion of connections to be made, after which many of them shut down and wither away, as the brain decides which it will keep, which new ones it will need, and which it can do without. During this period, it's important that babies get the right kinds of stimulation so their brains can make the right decisions. The right kinds of stimulation, however, may not be the ones people think they are.

Asked in a recent study what skills children need in order to be prepared for school, parents of kindergartners routinely cited definable achievements such as knowing numbers, letters, colors, and shapes. Teachers, however, disagree. Far more important, they say, are social skills, such as sharing, interacting with others, and following instructions. Kids who come to school with a mastery of these less showy abilities stand a better chance of knocking off not only reading and writing when they are eventually presented but everything else that comes along as well. "Intelligence is based on emotional adequacy," says child development expert T. Berry Brazelton.

It may not even be possible to prod children's intellectual growth. As babies' brains weave their neuronal connections,

A number of other studies have examined the relationship between either infant visual recognition memory or preference for novel stimulation (which is a related measure) and later IQ scores (Colombo, 1993; Fagan & Detterman, 1992; McCall & Carriger, 1993). The average correlation between the earlier and later measures is about +0.45. These moderate correlations are stronger than the correlations attained using more traditional assessment techniques. Perhaps infants' tendencies to scan stimuli and retain images will yield even more precise measures in future years.

In sum, scales of infant development may provide useful data as screening devices, as research instruments, or simply as a way to describe the things that infants do and do not do. However, their predictive power as intelligence tests has so far been disappointing. Tests of visual recognition hold better promise as predictors of later intelligence.

Now let us turn our attention to a fascinating aspect of cognitive development, the development of language.

parents may be able to stimulate, say, the visual or musical ones by exposing kids to picture books or CDs, but it is doubtful that these fortify the brain in any meaningful way. "It's a myth that we can accelerate a child's developmental milestones," says Alan Woolf, a pediatrician at Children's Hospital. "Children are kind of preprogrammed to reach those points."

How Much Attention Is Enough?

Studies indicate that children raised without sufficient nurturing often suffer from cognitive deficiencies. However, no evidence indicates that a lot of attention, in the form of early and constant stimulation, enhances a child's intellectual growth. According to the current scientific literature, the type and amount of stimulation needed for proper childhood development is already built into the normal life of an average baby. No whizbang tricks are necessary.

Parents might find it easier to believe all this if it weren't for the increasingly fashionable theory of windows of opportunity for learning—the idea that there are comparatively narrow periods when various parts of the brain can be taught various types of skills. What gives the theory special weight is that there is, in fact, a little truth to it—but only very little. When it comes to language—perhaps the most nuanced skill a person can master—the brain does appear to have fertile and less fertile periods. At birth, babies have the potential to learn any language with equal ease, but by six months, they have begun to focus on the one tongue they hear spoken most frequently. Parents can take advantage of this brain plasticity by introducing a second or even third language, but only if they intend to speak them all with equal frequency until the child is fluent. Merely buying the occasional bilingual toy or videotape will teach kids little, and it certainly will not make it easier for children to learn for real when they get to school.

When it comes to other skills, such as math or music, there is virtually no evidence for learning windows at all. Children grasp things at different rates, and parents whose child can read by age 3 may thus conclude that they somehow threaded the teaching needle perfectly, introducing letters and words at just the right time. But the reality is often that they simply got lucky and had a kid who took a shine early on to a particular skill.

Putting Down the Brain Toys?

So if parents should be putting down the brain toys, what should they be picking up? For one thing, the kids themselves. If interpersonal skills are the true predictors of how well a child will do in school, parents are the best tutors. Experiments reveal that by the time babies are 2 months old, they are already fluent in the complex language of their parents' faces and count on them for their sense of well-being. "Think about the human face," says Sparrow, "the wrinkles, the expressions in the eyes—and think about the infant brain being stimulated by that." To believe that even the best video game or toy could replace this kind of learning, Sparrow thinks, misses the point of just what it is babies are truly hungering to know.

Does this mean educational toys are useless? No. Babies are as engaged by pictures as adults are, and exposing them to books or flash cards early—especially black, white, and red ones, which are indeed easier for them to perceive—helps them develop their ability to focus and follow, undeniably a form of learning. Babies are as soothed by music as their parents are, and a little Mozart may indeed hold their attention better than something less rich. Beyond that, however, there's a limit to what the products can do—and parents who follow their children's cues quickly learn that. "When our son was little, all he wanted to do was play with us," says Sharon Chantiles, a casting director and the mother of a 4-year-old. "I decided to walk away from the fancy toys and invest in him as a child."

Search Online With InfoTrac College Edition

For additional information, explore InfoTrac College Edition, your online library. Go to **http://www.infotrac-college.com** and use the passcode from the InfoTrac card that came with your book. Try these search terms: education, preschool curricula, preschool children, early childhood education.

Review

(18) Cognitive development (does or does not?) proceed at the same pace for all infants. (19) The Bayley Scales of Infant Development contains mental-scale items and __________-scale items. (20) The __________ Neonatal Behavioral Assessment Scale is used to screen for sensory or neurological problems. (21) Overall scores on the Bayley (do or do not?) predict later IQ scores very well. (22) __________ recognition memory refers to an infant's ability to discriminate previously seen objects from novel objects. (23) Rose found that infants with greater visual recognition memory later attain (higher or lower?) IQ scores.

Pulling It Together: What are the problems in assessing intelligence among infants, and how do researchers attempt to overcome them?

Language Development: "Of Shoes and Ships and Sealing Wax, . . . and Whether Pigs Have Wings"

"The time has come," the Walrus said,
  "To talk of many things
Of shoes—and ships—and sealing wax—
  Of cabbages—and kings—
And why the sea is boiling hot—
  And whether pigs have wings."

—Lewis Carroll, *Through the Looking-Glass*

No, in his well-known children's book, Lewis Carroll wasn't quite telling the truth. The sea is not boiling hot—at least in most places and at most times. Nor do walruses speak. At the risk of alienating walrus afficionados, I will assert, and boldly, that walruses neither speak nor use other forms of language to communicate.

But children do. Children come "to talk of many things," perhaps only rarely of sealing wax and cabbages, but certainly about the things more closely connected with their environments and their needs. Children may be unlikely to debate "whether pigs have wings," unless they are reared on an unusual farm, but they do develop the language skills that will eventually enable them to do just that. Lewis Carroll enjoyed playing with language, and we will see that children also join in that game. In physical development, the most dramatic developments come early—fast and furious—long before the child is born. Language doesn't come quite so early, and its development may not seem quite so fast and furious. Nevertheless, during the years of infancy, most children develop from creatures without language to little people who understand nearly all of the things that are said to them and who are relentlessly sputtering words and simple sentences for all the world to hear. If much of the world might think that they do not yet have much of value to say, most parents find their utterances to be just priceless.

In this section, we trace language development from early crying and cooing through the production of two-word sentences. We then consider theoretical views of language development.

TABLE 6.3 *Milestones in Language Development in Infancy*

Approximate Age	Vocalization and Language
Birth	The infant cries.
12 weeks	There is markedly less crying than at 8 weeks. The infant smiles when talked to and nodded at, then engages in squealing-gurgling sounds (*cooing*) that are vowel-like in nature and modulated according to pitch (high or low). The infant sustains cooing for 15–20 seconds.
16 weeks	The infant responds to human sounds more definitely. He or she turns his or her head. His or her eyes seem to search for the speaker. She or he occasionally makes some chuckling sounds.
20 weeks	The sounds of vowel-like cooing begin to be interspersed with more consonant-like sounds. Acoustically speaking, the infant's vocalizations differ from the sounds of the mature language spoken in the infant's environment.
6 months	Cooing changes into babbling that has the sound of single-syllable utterances. Neither vowels nor consonants have a fixed pattern of recurrence. The most common utterances sound somewhat like *ma, mu, da,* or *di.*
8 months	"Reduplication"—that is, one or more continuous repetitions—becomes a frequent feature of babbling. The patterns of intonation become distinct. The infant's utterances can signal emphasis and emotion.
10 months	Vocalizations are mixed with sound-play such as gurgling sounds or bubble blowing. The infant appears to wish to imitate the sounds of older people, but the imitations are not fully successful.
12 months	Identical sequences of sounds are replicated with higher frequency. Words (e.g, *mamma* or *dadda*) are emerging. There are definite signs of understanding some words and simple commands ("Show me your eyes").
18 months	The infant has a repertoire of 3–50 words. Explosive vocabulary growth begins. Babbling remains, but now consists of several syllables with intricate intonation. There is usually no attempt to communicate information, and the infant usually does not appear to be frustrated when he or she is not understood. Vocabulary may include pat phrases like *thank you* and *come here,* but there is little ability to join words into spontaneous two-word utterances. The infant understands nearly everything that is said.
24 months	Vocabulary has grown to more than 50 words. Some children appear able to name everything in their environment. The infant begins to spontaneously join vocabulary words into two-word phrases. All phrases seem to be created originals, even if they repeat what others have said. There is clear increase in efforts to communicate and general interest in language.

Note: The ages in this table are approximations. Parents are advised not to assume that their children will have language problems if they are somewhat behind. Albert Einstein did not talk until the age of 3. Source: Table items adapted from Lenneberg, 1967, pages 128–130.

Early Vocalizations

Children develop language according to an invariant sequence of steps, or stages, as outlined in Table 6.3. We begin with the **prelinguistic** vocalizations. ***Question: What are prelinguistic vocalizations?*** True words are symbols of objects and events. Prelinguistic vocalizations do not represent objects or events. In this section we discuss the prelinguistic vocalizations of crying, cooing, and babbling.

Newborn children, as parents are well aware, have an unlearned but highly effective form of verbal expression: crying and more crying. Crying is accomplished by blowing air through the vocal tract. There are no distinct, well-formed sounds. Crying is about the only sound that infants make during the first month.

During the second month, infants begin **cooing.** Infants use their tongues when they coo. For this reason, coos are more articulated than cries. Coos are often vowel-like and may resemble extended "oohs" and "ahs." Cooing appears linked to feelings of pleasure or positive excitement. Infants tend not to coo when they are hungry, tired, or in pain.

Cries and coos are innate but can be modified by experience. When parents respond positively to cooing by talking to their infants, smiling at them, and imitating them, cooing increases. Early parent–child "conversations," in which parents respond to coos and then pause as the infant coos, may foster early infant awareness of turn-taking as a way of verbally relating to other people.

Click *Language* for more on the development of language in infancy.

prelinguistic Referring to vocalizations made by the infant prior to the development of language. (In language, words symbolize objects and events.)

cooing Prelinguistic, articulated vowel-like sounds that appear to reflect feelings of positive excitement.

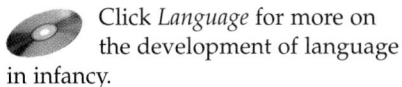

By about 8 months of age, cooing decreases markedly. Somewhere between 6 and 9 months, children begin to babble. **Babbling** is the first vocalizing that sounds like human speech. In babbling, infants frequently combine consonants and vowels, as in *ba, ga,* and, sometimes, the much valued *dada* (Mitchell & Kent, 1990). At first, "dada" is purely coincidental (sorry, you Dads), despite the family's jubilation over its appearance.

In verbal interactions between infants and adults, the adults frequently repeat the syllables produced by their infants. They are likely to say "dadada" or "bababa" instead of simply "da" or "ba." Such redundancy apparently helps infants discriminate these sounds from others and further encourages them to imitate their parents (Goodsitt et al., 1984).

After infants have been babbling for a few months, parents often believe that their children are having conversations with themselves. At 10 to 12 months, infants tend to repeat syllables, showing what linguists refer to as **echolalia.** Parents overhear them going on and on, repeating consonant-vowel combinations ("ah-bah-bah-bah-bah"), pausing, and then switching to other combinations.

Toward the end of the first year, infants are also using patterns of rising and falling **intonation** that resemble the sounds of adult speech. It may sound as if the infant is trying to speak the parents' language. In fact, parents may think that their children are babbling in English or in whatever tongue is spoken in the home (Bates, O'Connell, & Shore, 1987).

Reflect

Why are parents concerned with exactly when their children learn to talk?

Development of Vocabulary

Question: How does vocabulary develop? *Vocabulary development* refers to the child's learning the meanings of words. Generally speaking, children's **receptive vocabulary** development outpaces their **expressive vocabulary** development (Baker & Cantwell, 1991; Lickliter, 2001). This means that at any given time, they can understand more words than they can use. One study, for example, found that 12-month-olds could speak an average of 13 words but could comprehend the meaning of 84 words (Thal & Bates, 1990). In fact, infants usually understand much of what others are saying well before they themselves utter any words at all.

babbling The child's first vocalizations that have the sounds of speech.

echolalia The automatic repetition of sounds or words.

intonation The use of pitches of varying levels to help communicate meaning.

receptive vocabulary The sum total of the words whose meanings one understands.

expressive vocabulary The sum total of the words that one can use in the production of language.

The Child's First Words

Ah, that long-awaited first word! What a milestone! Sad to say, many parents miss it. They are not quite sure when their infants utter their first word, often because the first word is not pronounced clearly or because pronunciation varies from usage to usage.

Developing in a World of Diversity

Babbling Here, There, and Everywhere

Babbling, like crying and cooing, appears inborn. Children from different cultures, where languages sound very different, all seem to babble the same sounds, including many they could not have heard (Oller, 1981). Babbling also occurs in deaf infants, although its onset is delayed (Oller & Eilers, 1988). Deaf infants of deaf parents babble with their hands as well, using repetitive gestures that resemble the vocal babbling of hearing infants (Petittio & Marentette, 1991).

Despite the fact that it is innate, babbling is readily modified by the child's language environment. One study followed infants growing up in French-, Chinese-, and Arabic-speaking households (de Boysson-Bardies et al., 1989). At 4 to 7 months of age, the infants began to use more of the sounds in their language environment; foreign phonemes began to drop out. The role that experience plays in language development is further indicated by the fact that the babbling of deaf infants never begins to approximate the sounds of the parents' language. Deaf children tend to lapse into silence by the end of the first year.

The first word typically is spoken between 11 and 13 months, but a range of 8 to 18 months is considered normal (Baker & Cantwell, 1991; Bates, Thal, & Janowsky, 1992). First words tend to be brief, consisting of one or two syllables. Each syllable is likely to consist of a consonant followed by a vowel. Vocabulary acquisition is slow at first. It may take children 3 or 4 months to achieve a vocabulary of 10 to 30 words after the first word is spoken (deVilliers & deVilliers, 1992).

By about 18 months, children may be producing up to about 50 words. Many of them are quite familiar, such as *no, cookie, mama, hi,* and *eat*. Others, such as *allgone* and *bye-bye,* may not be found in the dictionary, but they function as words. That is, they are used consistently to symbolize the same meaning.

More than half (65%) of children's first words comprise what Katherine Nelson (1973) refers to as "general nominals" and "specific nominals." General nominals are like nouns in that they include the names of classes of objects (*car, ball, doggy*), animals (*doggy, poo-cat*), and people (*boy*). But they also include both personal and relative pronouns (she and that). Specific nominals are proper nouns, such as *Daddy* (used as the father's name, not the category of men to which he belongs) and *Rover*. The attention of infants seems to be captured by movement. Words expressing movement are frequently found in early speech (Stockman & Vaughn-Cooke, 1992). Nelson (1973, 1981) found that of children's first 50 words, the most common words were names for people, animals, and objects that move (*Mommy, car, doggy*) or that can be moved (*dolly, milky*); action words (*bye-bye*); a number of modifiers (*big, hot*); and expressive words (*no, hi, oh*). Reading to children increases their vocabulary, so parents do well to stock up on storybooks (Arnold et al., 1994; Robbins & Ehri, 1994).

Nelson found a surprising diversity in the nominals used by these children, reflecting the objects that surrounded them and what was important to their parents. Some children, for example, may number words as exotic as "ohgi" (*yogurt*) and "bay" (*bagel*) among their first 50 or so, whereas others accumulate more traditional nominals such as *baby, ball,* and *juice* (Bloom, 1993). These first words that children produce tend to be words their parents frequently use when talking to them (Barrett, Harris, & Chasin, 1991; Hart, 1991).

At about 18 to 22 months of age, there is a rapid burst in the number of new words learned (Reznick & Goldfield, 1992). The child's vocabulary may increase from 50 to more than 300 words in just a few months (Bates et al., 1992). This vocabulary spurt could also be called a "naming explosion," since almost 75 percent of the words added during this time are nouns (Goldfield & Reznick, 1990). The rapid pace of vocabulary growth continues through the preschool years, with children acquiring an average of nine new words per day (Rice, 1989).

Referential and Expressive Styles in Language Development

Nelson (1981) also found that some children prefer a referential approach in their language development, whereas others take a more expressive approach.

Children who show the **referential language style** use language primarily to label objects in their environments. Their early vocabularies consist mainly of nominals. Children who use an **expressive language style** use language primarily as a means for engaging in social interactions. Children with an expressive style use more pronouns and many words involved in social routines, such as *stop, more,* and *all gone*. More children use an expressive style than a referential style (Hampson, 1989), but most use a combination of the styles.

Why do some children prefer a referential style and others an expressive style? It may be that some children are naturally oriented toward objects, whereas others are primarily interested in social relationships. Nelson also found that the mother's ways of teaching her children play a role. Some mothers focus on labeling objects for their children as soon as they notice their vocabularies expanding in the second year. Other mothers are more oriented toward social interactions themselves, teaching their children to say "hi," "please," and "thank you."

referential language style Use of language primarily as a means for labeling objects.

expressive language style Use of language primarily as a means for engaging in social interaction.

Fostering Language Development

Language growth in young children is enhanced when parents and caregivers engage the infant "in conversation" about activities and objects in the environment.

Reflect

Can you think of examples of overextension in your own experience?

Overextension

Young children try to talk about more objects than they have words for (not so surprising—so too, now and then, do we). To accomplish their linguistic feats, children often extend the meaning of one word to refer to things and actions for which they do not have words. This process is called **overextension.** Eve Clark (1973, 1975) studied diaries of infants' language development and found that overextensions generally are based on perceived similarities in function or form between the original object or action and the new one to which the first word is being extended. She provides the example of the word "mooi," which one child originally used to designate the moon. Then "mooi" became overextended to designate all round objects, including the letter o and cookies and cakes.

Clark (1973) also found that overextensions gradually pull back to their proper references as the child's vocabulary and ability to classify objects develop. Consider the example of a child who first refers to a dog as a "bow-wow." The word *bow-wow* then becomes overextended to also refer to horses, cats, and cows. In effect, *bow-wow* comes to mean something akin to "familiar animal." Next the child learns to use the word *moo* to refer to cows. But *bow-wow* still remains extended to horses and cats. As the child's vocabulary develops, she acquires the word *doggy*. So dogs and cats may now be referred to either with *bow-wow* or *doggy*. Eventually, each animal has one or more correct names.

Development of Sentences: Telegraphic Speech

Question: How do infants create sentences? The infant's first sentences are typically one-word utterances, but these utterances appear to express complete ideas and therefore can be thought of as sentences. Roger Brown (1973) calls brief expressions that have the meanings of sentences **telegraphic speech.** Telegrams have always relied on principles of syntax to cut out all the unnecessary words. "Home Tuesday" might stand for "I expect to be home on Tuesday." Similarly, only the essential words are used in children's telegraphic speech—in particular, nouns, verbs, and some modifiers.

overextension Use of words in situations in which their meanings become extended, or inappropriate.

telegraphic speech Type of speech in which only the essential words are used, as in a telegram.

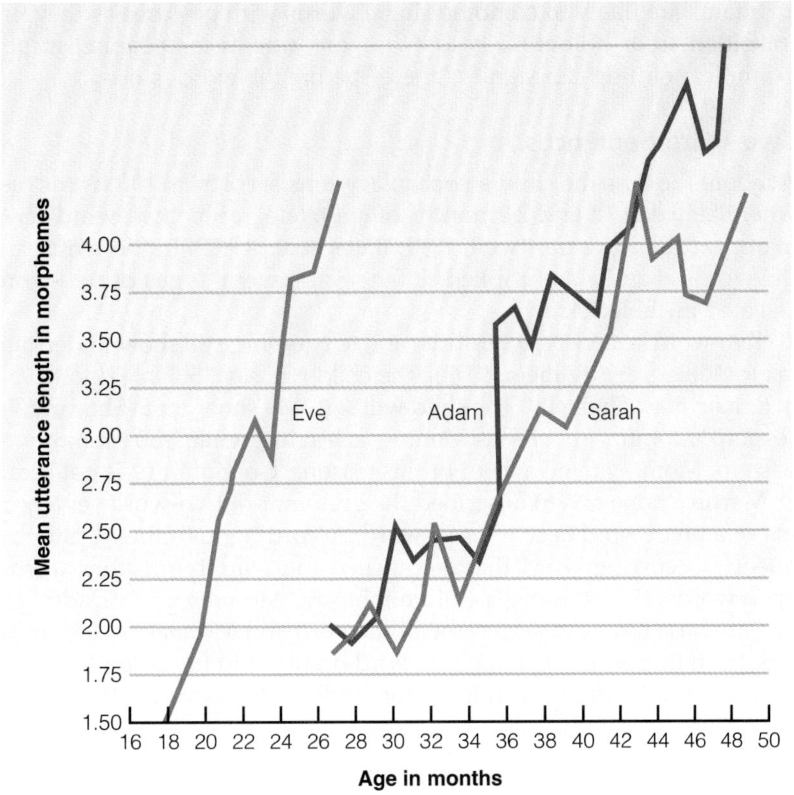

Figure 6.6
Mean Length of Utterance for Three Children

Some children begin speaking earlier than others. However, the mean length of utterance (MLU) increases rapidly once speech begins.

Mean Length of Utterance

To students who think of "bad" or "abusive" when they hear the word *mean*, the phrase "mean length of utterance" might sound like a complaint about speakers who go on and on. However, the term actually refers to Roger Brown's (1973, 1977) methodology for studying telegraphic speech in children. He describes telegraphic speech in terms of an average (the *mean*)—therefore, **mean length of utterance (MLU).** The MLU is defined as the average number of **morphemes** children use in their sentences. Morphemes are the smallest units of meaning in a language. A morpheme may be a whole word or part of a word, such as a prefix or suffix. For example, the word *walked* consists of two morphemes: the verb *walk* and the suffix *ed,* which changes the verb to the past tense. In Figure 6.6, we see the relationship between chronological age and MLU for three children tracked by Brown: Eve, Adam, and Sarah.

The patterns of growth in MLU are similar for each child, showing swift upward movement, broken by intermittent and brief regressions. Figure 6.6 also shows us something about individual differences. Eve was precocious compared to Adam and Sarah, extending her MLU at much earlier ages. However, as suggested earlier, the receptive language of all three children would have exceeded their expressive language at any given time. Also, Eve's earlier extension of MLU does not guarantee that she will show more complex expressive language than Adam and Sarah at maturity. Let us now consider the features of two types of telegraphic speech: the holophrase and two-word utterances.

Holophrases

Holophrases are single words that are used to express complex meanings. For example, *Mama* may be used by the child to signify meanings as varied as "There goes Mama," "Come here, Mama," and "You are Mama." Most children readily teach their parents what they intend by augmenting their holophrases with gestures, intonations, and reinforcers. That is, they act delighted when parents do as requested and howl when they do not.

mean length of utterance (MLU) The average number of morphemes used in an utterance.

morpheme The smallest unit of meaning in a language.

holophrase A single word that is used to express complex meanings.

Infants are likely to combine single words with gestures as they undertake the transition from holophrases to two-word utterances (Capirci et al., 1996). For example, pointing can signify "there" before the word is used.

Two-Word Sentences

At about the time the child's vocabulary consists of 50 to 100 words (usually somewhere between 18 and 24 months of age), telegraphic two-word sentences begin to appear (Baker & Cantwell, 1991; Bates et al., 1992). In the sentence "That ball," the words *is* and *a* are implied. Infants use several types of two-word sentences, as listed in Table 6.4.

Two-word sentences, while brief and telegraphic, still show understanding of **syntax** (deVilliers & deVilliers, 1992). The child will say "Sit chair" to tell a parent to sit in a chair, not "Chair sit." The child will say "My shoe," not "Shoe my," to show possession. "Mommy go" means Mommy is leaving, while "Go Mommy" expresses the wish for Mommy to go away. For this reason, "Go Mommy" is not heard frequently.

Martin Braine (1976) described the grammar of two-word sentences as consisting of a pivot word and an open word. According to Braine, a pivot word is a frequently occurring word that is attached to a variety of other words, known as open words. For example, a child might say "Mommy go," "Daddy go," and "Car go." In these utterances, *go* is the pivot word and *Mommy, Daddy,* and *car* are open words. In this example, the pivot word occurred in the second position. but it can also occur in the first position ("More milk," "More read," "More swing").

Theories of Language Development

> Since all normal humans talk but no house pets or house plants do, no matter how pampered, heredity must be involved in language. But since a child growing up in Japan speaks Japanese whereas the same child brought up in California would speak English, the environment is also crucial. Thus, there is no question about whether heredity or environment is involved in language, or even whether one or the other is "more important." Instead, . . . our best hope [might be] finding out how they interact.
>
> —Steven Pinker

Countless billions of children have learned the languages spoken by their parents and have passed them down, with minor changes, from generation to generation. But how do they do so? In discussing this question—and so many others—we refer to the possible roles of nature and nurture. Learning theorists have come down on the side of nurture, and those who point to a basic role for nature are said to hold a *nativist* view.

syntax The rules in a language for placing words in proper order to form meaningful sentences (from the Latin *syntaxis,* meaning "joining together").

Developing in a World of Diversity

Two-Word Sentences Here, There, and . . .

Two-word sentences appear at about the same time in the development of all languages (Slobin, 1973). Also, the sequence of emergence of the types of two-word utterances (for example, first, agent-action, then action-object, location, and possession) is the same in languages as diverse as English, Luo (an African tongue), German, Russian, and Turkish (Slobin, 1983). This is an example of the point that language develops in a series of steps that appear to be invariant. The lack of wide cultural differences in the developmental sequence can be seen as supporting the view that the human tendency to develop language according to universal processes is innate (Slobin, 1988).

TABLE 6.4 *Some Uses of Children's Two-Word Sentences*

Type of Utterance	Examples	Types of Knowledge Suggested by Utterance
Naming, locating	That ball. Car there.	Objects exist, and they have names.
Negating	Milk allgone. No eat.	Objects may become used up or leave. People may choose not to do things.
Demanding, expressing desire	Want Mommy. More milk.	Objects can be reinstated. Quantities can be increased.
Agent–action	Mommy go. Doggy bark.	People, animals, and objects can act or move.
Action–object	Hit you.	Actions can have objects (*direct* objects of the action).
Agent–object	Daddy car.	People do things to objects (although, in this particular utterance, the action is not stated).
Action–location	Sit chair.	A person (unstated) is engaging in an act in a place.
Action–recipient	Give Mama.	An object (unstated) is being moved in relation to a person (the *indirect* object of the action).
Action–instrument	Cut knife.	An instrument is being used for an act.
Attribution	Pretty Mommy. Big glass.	People or objects have traits or qualities.
Possession	Mommy cup. My shoe.	People possess objects.
Question	Where Mommy? Where milk?	People can provide information when they are prompted to do so.

Note. The sequence of emergence of the types of two-word utterances appears to be the same in languages as different as English, Luo, German, Russian, and Turkish. How are we to interpret the observation that all languages appear to develop in a series of invariant steps? Source: Adapted from Slobin, 1972.

Learning-Theory Views

Question: How do learning theorists account for language development? Learning plays an obvious role in language development. Children who are reared in English-speaking homes learn English, not Japanese or Russian. Learning theorists usually explain language development in terms of imitation and reinforcement.

The Role of Imitation From a social cognitive perspective, parents serve as **models.** Children learn language, at least in part, by observation and imitation. It seems likely that many vocabulary words, especially nouns and verbs (including irregular verbs), are learned by imitation.

But imitative learning does not explain why children spontaneously utter phrases and sentences that they have not observed (J. Harris, 1990). Parents, for example, are unlikely to model utterances such as "bye-bye sock" and "allgone Daddy," but children do say them.

And children sometimes steadfastly avoid imitating certain language forms suggested by adults, even when the adults are insistent. Note the following exchange between 2-year-old Ben and a (very frustrated) adult:

Ben: I like these candy. I like they.
Adult: You like them?
Ben: Yes, I like they.
Adult: Say them.

models In learning theory, those whose behaviors are imitated by others.

Ben: Them.
Adult: Say "I like them."
Ben: I like them.
Adult: Good.
Ben: I'm good. These candy good too.
Adult: Are they good?
Ben: Yes. I like they. You like they? (Kuczaj, 1982, p. 48).

Ben is not resisting the adult because of obstinacy. He does repeat "I like them" when asked to do so. But when given the opportunity, afterward, to construct the object "them," he reverts to using the subjective form, "they." Ben is likely at this period in his development to use his (erroneous) understanding of syntax spontaneously to actively produce his own language, rather than just imitate a model.

Click *Language* for more on the role of learning in language development.

The Role of Reinforcement In his classic book, *Verbal Behavior,* B. F. Skinner outlined his view of the role of reinforcement in language development: "A child acquires verbal behavior when relatively unpatterned vocalizations, selectively reinforced, assume forms which produce appropriate consequences in a given verbal community" (Skinner, 1957, p. 31).

Skinner allows that prelinguistic vocalizations such as cooing and babbling may be inborn. But parents reinforce children for babbling that approximates the form of real words, such as "da," which, in English, resembles "dog" or "daddy." Children, in fact, do increase their babbling when it results in adults smiling at them, stroking them, and talking back to them. We have seen that as the first year progresses, children babble the sounds of their native tongues with increasing frequency; foreign sounds tend to drop out. The behaviorist explains this pattern of changing frequencies in terms of reinforcement (of the sounds of the adults' language) and **extinction** (of foreign sounds). An alternate (nonbehavioral) explanation is that children actively attend to the sounds in their linguistic environments and are intrinsically motivated to utter them.

From Skinner's (1957, 1983) perspective, children acquire their early vocabularies through **shaping.** That is, parents require that children's utterances be progressively closer to actual words before they are reinforced. In support of Skinner's position, more recent research shows that reinforcement accelerates the growth of vocabulary in young children (Whitehurst & Valdez-Menchaca, 1988). Skinner viewed multiword utterances as complex stimulus–response chains that are also taught by shaping. As children's utterances increase in length, parents foster correct word order by uttering sentences to their children and reinforcing imitation. As with Ben, when children make grammatical errors, parents recast their utterances correctly. They reinforce the children for repeating them.

But recall Ben's refusal to be shaped into correct syntax. If the reinforcement explanation of language development were sufficient, parents' reinforcement would facilitate children's learning of syntax and pronunciation. We do not have such evidence. For one thing, parents are more likely to reinforce their children for the accuracy, or "truth value," of their utterances than for their grammatical correctness (Brown, 1973). Parents, in other words, generally accept the syntax of their children's vocal efforts. The child who points down and says "The grass is purple" is not likely to be reinforced, despite correct syntax. But the enthusiastic child who shows her empty plate and blurts out "I eated it all up" is likely to be reinforced, despite the grammatical incorrectness of "eated." Research confirms that while parents do expand and rephrase their children's ungrammatical utterances more than their grammatically correct ones, they do not overtly correct their children's language mistakes (Bohannon & Stanowicz, 1988; Coley, 1993; Penner, 1987).

Also, selective reinforcement of children's pronunciation can actually backfire. Children whose parents reward proper pronunciation but correct poor pronunciation develop vocabulary more slowly than children whose parents are more tolerant about pronunciation (Nelson, 1973).

extinction The decrease and eventual disappearance of a response in the absence of reinforcement.

shaping In learning theory, the gradual building of complex behavior patterns through reinforcement of successive approximations of the target behavior.

Learning theory also cannot account for the invariant sequences of language development and for children's spurts in acquisition. Even the types of two-word utterances emerge in a consistent pattern in diverse cultures. Although timing differs from child to child, the types of questions used, passive versus active sentences, and so on all emerge in the same order. It is unlikely that parents around the world teach language skills in the same sequence.

On the other hand, there is ample evidence that aspects of the child's language environment influence the development of language. Much of the research in this area has focused on the ways in which adults—especially mothers—interact with their children.

Studies show that language growth in young children is enhanced when mothers and other adults do the following things:

- Use a simplified form of speech known as "Motherese." (See the nearby "A Closer Look" feature.)
- Use questions that engage the child in conversation (Hoff-Ginsberg, 1986, 1990).
- Respond to the child's expressive language efforts in a way that is "attuned"; for example, they relate their speech to the child's utterance by saying "Yes, your doll is pretty" in response to the child's statement "My doll" (Hoff-Ginsberg, 1991, 1998; Nicely, Tamis-LeMonda, & Bornstein, 1999; Tamis-LeMonda, Bornstein, & Baumwell, 2001).
- Join the child in paying attention to a particular activity or toy (Akhtar, Dunham, & Dunham, 1991; Tamis-LeMonda & Bornstein, 1991; Oram & Oshima-Takane, 1993).
- Gesture to help the child understand what they are saying (Gogate, Bahrick, & Watson, 2000; Iverson et al., 1999).
- Describe aspects of the environment occupying the infant's current focus of attention (Dunham & Dunham, 1992).
- Read to the child (Hale & Windecker, 1993; Hoff-Ginsberg, 1998; Scarborough, 1993; Whitehurst et al., 1993).
- Talk to the child a great deal (Hoff-Ginsberg, 1998; Huttenlocher et al., 1991).

Developing in a World of Diversity

Talking to Infants

Mothers in different cultures show certain similarities in the way they talk to their infants, but cultural variations in their speech patterns exist as well. One study analyzed how Argentinian, French, Japanese, and American mothers spoke to their 5- and 13-month-old infants (Bornstein et al., 1992a). Mothers in all four cultures spoke more to older infants. When the infants were 5 months old, mothers' speech was more heavily laced with expressive statements such as greetings, songs, nonsense sounds, and endearing terms. As children got older, mothers in all groups provided more information in their speech. They made statements; gave reports about the infant, mother, or environment; and asked the child questions.

But there were also variations in the speech of mothers in the four cultures that appeared to reflect cultural values and beliefs. Japanese mothers used expressive speech more often than Western mothers did, consistent with the Japanese mothers' child-rearing emphasis on social and emotional closeness and interdependence. Mothers from the three Western cultures favored speech containing information. This may reflect American and European traditions of encouraging interpersonal independence and interest in the environment (Barratt, Negayama, & Minami, 1993; Tamis-LeMonda et al., 1992).

Even within the three Western cultures, there were differences in the types of information mothers provided to their infants. Argentinian mothers used more direct statements, perhaps reflecting their more directive view of child rearing. American mothers asked the most questions, possibly indicating an emphasis on the child as an active learner. French mothers conveyed less information in their speech than other Western mothers. French mothers placed less emphasis on stimulating achievement and more on emotional support (Bornstein et al., 1992a).

Do these variations in maternal speech affect the infant's behavior? The answer seems to be yes. For example, at 13 months of age, American infants are more advanced than Japanese infants in vocabulary development, possibly reflecting the more information-oriented speech of American mothers (Tamis-LeMonda et al., 1992).

The Nativist View

Question: What is the nativist view of language development? The nativist view holds that innate or inborn factors cause children to attend to and acquire language in certain ways. From this perspective, children bring an inborn tendency in the form of neurological "prewiring" to language learning (Newport, 1998; Pinker, 1994).

Click *Language* for more on Chomsky and the nativist view of language development.

psycholinguistic theory The view that language learning involves an interaction between environmental influences and an inborn tendency to acquire language. The emphasis is on the inborn tendency.

language acquisition device (LAD) In psycholinguistic theory, neural "prewiring" that facilitates the child's learning of grammar.

surface structure The superficial grammatical construction of a sentence.

deep structure The underlying meaning of a sentence.

aphasia A disruption in the ability to understand or produce language.

Psycholinguistic Theory According to **psycholinguistic theory,** language acquisition involves an interaction between environmental influences—such as exposure to parental speech and reinforcement—and an inborn tendency to acquire language, which Chomsky (1988, 1990) and some others refer to as a **language acquisition device (LAD).** Evidence for an inborn tendency is found in the universality of human language abilities; in the regularity of the early production of sounds, even among deaf children; and in the invariant sequences of language development, regardless of which language the child is learning.

The inborn tendency primes the nervous system to learn grammar. On the surface, languages differ a great deal in their vocabulary and grammar. Chomsky refers to these elements as the **surface structure** of language. However, the LAD serves children all over the world because languages share what Chomsky refers to as a "universal grammar"—an underlying **deep structure,** or set of rules for transforming ideas into sentences. From Chomsky's perspective, children are predisposed to attend to language and to deduce the transformational rules. Consider an analogy with computers: According to psycholinguistic theory, the universal grammar that resides in the LAD is the basic operating system of the computer, whereas the particular language that a child learns to use is the word-processing program.

Brain Structures Involved in Language ***Question: What parts of the brain are involved in language development?*** Research shows that many parts of the brain are involved in language development and that each person may have a unique pattern of organization for language ability (Rosen et al., 2000; Schwartz et al., 2000). However, some of the key biological structures that may provide the basis for the functions of the LAD appear to be based in the left hemisphere of the cerebral cortex for nearly all right-handed people and for two out of three left-handed people (Pinker, 1994).

Even at birth, the sounds of speech elicit greater electrical activity in the left hemisphere than in the right, as indicated by the activity of brain waves. This pattern does not hold for non-speech-related sounds. Music tends to elicit greater electrical activity in the right hemispheres of infants (Young & Gagnon, 1990).

Within the left hemisphere of the cortex, the two areas most involved in speech are Broca's area and Wernicke's area (see Figure 6.7). Even in the human fetus, Wernicke's area is usually larger in the left hemisphere than the right. Damage to either area is likely to cause an **aphasia**—that is, a disruption in the ability to understand or produce language.

Broca's area is located near the section of the motor cortex that controls the muscles of the tongue and throat and other areas of the face that are used when speaking. When Broca's

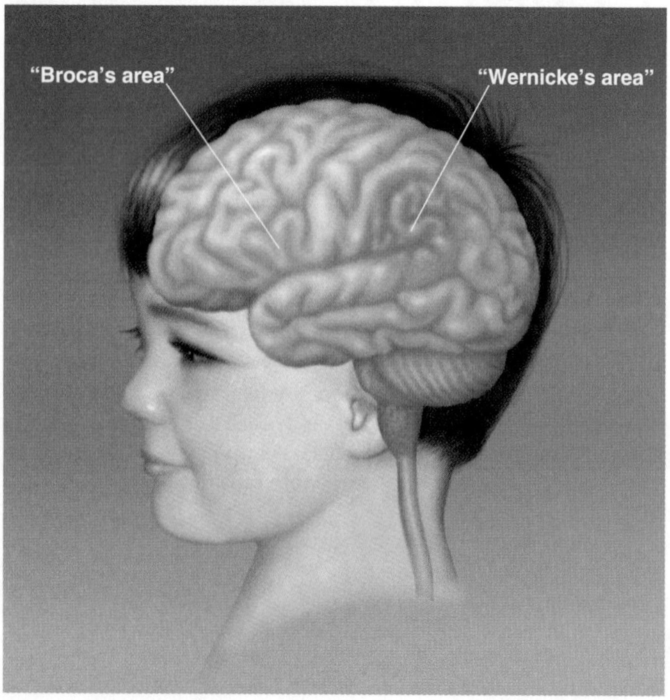

Figure 6.7
Broca's and Wernicke's Areas of the Cerebral Cortex
Broca's area and Wernicke's area of the (usually left) hemisphere are most involved in speech. Damage to either area can produce an aphasia—an impairment in the ability to understand or produce language.

area is damaged, people speak slowly and laboriously, with simple sentences—a pattern known as **Broca's aphasia.** Their ability to understand the speech of others is relatively unaffected, however. Wernicke's area lies near the auditory cortex and is connected to Broca's area by nerve fibers. People with damage to Wernicke's area may show **Wernicke's aphasia.** Although they usually speak freely and with proper syntax, their abilities to comprehend other people's speech and to think of the words to express their own thoughts are impaired. Thus, Wernicke's area seems to be essential to understanding the relationships between words and their meanings.

A part of the brain called the *angular gyrus* lies between the visual cortex and Wernicke's area. The angular gyrus "translates" visual information, such as written words, into auditory information (sounds) and sends it on to Wernicke's area. It appears that problems in the angular gyrus can give rise to *dyslexia,* or serious impairment in reading, because it becomes difficult for the reader to segment words into sounds (Pugh et al., 2000).

The Sensitive Period Lenneberg (1967) proposes that there is a **sensitive period** for learning language that begins at about 18 to 24 months and lasts until puberty. ***Question: What is meant by a* sensitive period *for language development?*** During the sensitive period, neural development (as in the differentiating of brain structures) provides a degree of plasticity that facilitates language learning.

Evidence for a sensitive period is found in recovery from brain injuries in some people. Injuries to the hemisphere that controls language (usually the left) can impair or destroy the ability to speak. But prior to puberty, children suffering left-hemisphere injuries frequently recover a good deal of speaking ability. Lenneberg (1967) suggests that in very young children, left-hemisphere damage may encourage the development of language functions in the right hemisphere. But adaptation ability wanes in adolescence, when brain tissue has reached adult levels of differentiation.

The best way to determine whether people are capable of acquiring language once they have passed puberty would be to run an experiment in which one or more children were reared in such severe isolation that they were not exposed to language until puberty. Of course, such an experiment could not be run because of ethical and legal barriers.

However, the disturbing case history of Genie offers insights into the issue of whether there is a sensitive period for language development (Curtiss, 1977; Rymer, 1993). Genie's father locked her in a small room at the age of 20 months and kept her there until she was 13. Her social contacts during this period were limited to her mother, who entered the room only to feed Genie, and to beatings by her father. When Genie was rescued, she weighed only about 60 pounds, did not speak, was not toilet-trained, and could barely stand. Genie was placed in a foster home, where she was exposed to English for the first time in nearly 12 years. Her language development followed the normal sequence of much younger children in a number of ways, but she never acquired the proficiency of children reared under normal circumstances. Five years after her liberation, Genie's language remained largely telegraphic. She still showed significant problems with syntax—failing, for example, to reverse subjects and verbs to phrase spontaneous questions. She showed confusion concerning the use of the past tense (adding *ed* to words) and had difficulty using negative helping verbs such as isn't and haven't.

Genie's language development provides some support for the sensitive-period hypothesis, although it is possible that her language problems can also be attributed to her long years of malnutrition and abuse. It is also possible that she was retarded to begin with. Her efforts to acquire English after puberty were clearly laborious, and the results were substandard when compared even to the language of many 2- and 3-year-olds.

Further evidence for the sensitive-period hypothesis is provided by a study of a 9-year-old deaf boy named Simon (Newport, 1992). Researchers who studied Simon from the time he was $2\frac{1}{2}$ years old reported that he signed in **American**

Broca's aphasia A form of aphasia caused by damage to Broca's area and characterized by slow, laborious speech.

Wernicke's aphasia A form of aphasia caused by damage to Wernicke's area and characterized by impaired comprehension of speech and difficulty in attempting to produce the right word.

sensitive period In linguistic theory, the period from about 18 months to puberty when the brain is thought to be especially capable of learning language because of plasticity of the brain.

Sign Language (ASL) using correct grammar, even though he had been exposed only to grammatically incorrect ASL by his parents and their friends, who also were deaf. Simon's parents and their friends had not learned to sign until they were teenagers. At that age, people often learn languages imperfectly. But Simon showed early mastery of grammatical rules that his parents used incorrectly or not at all. Simon's deduction of these rules on his own supports the view that the tendency to acquire language is inborn and also provides evidence that such learning occurs most readily during a sensitive period early in life.

In sum, the development of language in infancy represents the interaction of environmental and biological factors. The child brings a built-in readiness to the task of language acquisition—while houseplants and other organisms do not. At the same time, the child must also have the opportunity to hear spoken language and to interact verbally with others (deVilliers & deVilliers, 1992). In the next chapter, we see how interaction with others affects the social development of the infant.

American Sign Language (ASL) The communication of meaning through the use of symbols that are formed by moving the hands and arms. The language used by some deaf people.

Review

(24) Children develop language according to a(n) (variable or invariant?) sequence of steps. (25) Crying, cooing, and babbling are _________ vocalizations. (26) _________ is the first vocalizing that sounds like human speech. (27) The first

A Closer Look

"Motherese"

One fascinating way adults influence the language development of young children is through the use of baby talk, or "Motherese." But "Motherese" is a limiting term, because fathers, siblings, and unrelated people, including older children, also use varieties of Motherese when talking to infants (Fernald, 1991; Shute & Wheldall, 1999; Trehub et al., 1993). Motherese occurs in languages as different as Arabic, English, Comanche, Italian, French, German, Xhosa (an African language), Japanese, and Mandarin Chinese (Fernald & Morikawa, 1993; Masataka, 1998; Papousek et al., 1991).

Reflect

Do you find it entertaining or annoying when you hear someone talking to an infant in Motherese? Explain.

Researchers have found that Motherese has a number of characteristics (Fernald & Mazzie, 1991; Gogate et al., 2000; Mumme, Fernald, & Herrera, 1996; Trehub et al., 1993):

1. Motherese is spoken more slowly than speech addressed to adults. Motherese is spoken at a higher pitch, and there are distinct pauses between ideas.
2. Sentences are brief, and adults make the effort to speak in a grammatically correct manner.

For Better or For Worse® **by Lynn Johnston**

"Motherese"

Adults and older children use a simplified form of language known as "Motherese" when they talk to infants. Motherese is spoken slowly, at a higher pitch than is used with adults, using brief sentences that are simple in syntax.

word is typically spoken at about _________ months. (28) More than half of children's first words are made up of what Nelson terms _________. (29) Children with a(n) _________ language style use language mainly to label objects. (30) Children try to talk about more objects than they have words for, often resulting in _________ of the meanings of words. (31) Brown refers to brief expressions that have the meanings of sentences as _________ speech. (32) Brown's methodology for studying telegraphic speech assesses the mean _________ of utterance (MLU). (33) _________ are single words that are used to express complex meanings. (34) The sequence of emergence of types of two-word utterances is (the same or different?) in diverse languages. (35) _________ theorists explain language development in terms of imitation and reinforcement. (36) The _________ view holds that children are prewired to attend to and acquire language in certain ways. (37) According to _________ theory, language acquisition involves an interaction between environmental influences and an inborn tendency to acquire language. (38) Chomsky refers to this inborn tendency as a language _________ device (LAD). (39) Key biological structures that provide a basis for language are based in the (left or right?) hemisphere of the cerebral cortex for most people. (40) The brain areas most involved in speech are Broca's area and _________ area. (41) Lenneberg proposes that plasticity of the brain makes possible a _________ period for learning language. (42) _________ is a simplified form of language used to speak to infants that is characterized by high pitch, brief sentences, and repetition.

Pulling It Together: How are we to interpret the research finding that children in diverse cultures initially babble the same sounds, but as they develop, they babble more of the sounds found in their own linguistic environments?

A Closer Look *(continued)*

3. Sentences are simple in syntax. The focus is on nouns, verbs, and just a few modifiers.
4. Key words are put at the ends of sentences and are spoken in a higher and louder voice.
5. The diminutive morpheme "y" is frequently added to nouns. "Dad" becomes "Daddy" and "horse" becomes "horsey."
6. Motherese is repetitive. Adults repeat sentences several times, sometimes using minor variations, as in "Show me your nose." "Where is your nose?" "Can you touch your nose?" Adults also repeat children's utterances, often rephrasing them in an effort to expand children's awareness of their expressive opportunities. If the child says, "Baby shoe," the mother may reply, "Yes, that's your shoe. Shall Mommy put the shoe on baby's foot?"
7. Motherese includes a type of repetition called reduplication. "Yummy" becomes "yummy-yummy." "Daddy" may alternate with "Da-da."
8. Vocabulary is concrete, referring, when possible, to objects that are in the immediate environment. For example, stuffed lions may be referred to as "kitties." Purposeful overextension is intended to avoid confusing the child by adding too many new labels.
9. Objects may be overdescribed by being given compound labels. Rabbits may become "bunny rabbits," and cats may become "kitty cats." In this way parents may try to be sure that they are connecting with the child by using at least one label that the child will recognize.
10. Parents speak for the children, as in "Is baby tired?" "Oh, we're so tired." "We want to take our nap now, don't we?" This parent is pretending to have a two-way conversation with the child. In this way, parents seem to be trying to help their children express themselves by offering children models of sentences they can use later on.
11. Users of Motherese stay a step ahead of the child. As children's vocabularies grow and their syntax develops, adults step up their own language levels—remaining just ahead of the child. In this way, adults seem to be encouraging the child to continue to play catch-up.

And so, adults and older children use a variety of strategies to communicate with young children and to draw them out. Does it work? Does Motherese foster language development?

Research on the effects of Motherese is supportive of its use. Infants as young as 2 days old prefer baby talk over adult talk (Cooper & Aslin, 1990). The short, simple sentences and high pitch used in Motherese are more likely to produce a response from the child and to enhance vocabulary development than are complex sentences and those spoken in a lower pitch (Fernald, 1992; Murray, Johnson, & Peters, 1990). Children who hear their utterances repeated and recast do seem to learn from the adults who are modeling the new expressions (Nicely et al., 1999; Tamis-LeMonda et al., 2001). Repetition of children's vocalizations also appears to be one method of reinforcing vocalizing. In sum, Motherese may be of significant help in fostering children's language development.

Recite Recite Recite Recite

1. What is the sensorimotor stage of cognitive development?

Piaget's sensorimotor stage refers to the first 2 years of cognitive development, during which changes are shown by means of sensory and motor activity. Infants progress from responding to events with ready-made schemes to goal-oriented behavior that involves awareness of past events.

2. What are the parts, or substages, of the stage of sensorimotor development?

The first substage is dominated by the assimilation of stimulation into reflexes. The second substage, primary circular reactions, is characterized by the beginnings of the coordination of sensorimotor schemes. Infants repeat stimulating actions that occur by chance. The third substage is characterized by secondary circular reactions, in which patterns of activity are repeated because of their effects. In the fourth substage, infants intentionally coordinate schemes to attain goals. In the fifth substage, infants engage in tertiary circular reactions, or purposeful adaptations of established schemes to specific situations. The sixth substage is a transition between sensorimotor development and symbolic thought in which external exploration is replaced by mental exploration.

3. What is object permanence? How does it develop?

Object permanence is recognition that an object or person continues to exist when out of sight. The development of object permanence is tied into infants' tendency to form mental representations of sensory impressions. Through the first 6 months or so, when a screen is placed between the object and the infant, the infant behaves as if the object is no longer there. By 8–12 months, infants will seek to retrieve objects that have been hidden behind screens. But infants at this age often make the *A not B* error.

4. What are the strengths and limitations of Piaget's theory of sensorimotor development?

Evidence supports the pattern and sequence of events described by Piaget. However, cognitive development may not be tied to discrete stages as Piaget believed. Piaget also appears to have been incorrect about the ages at which infants develop various concepts.

5. What are infants' tools for processing information?

These include memory and imitation. Memory improves dramatically during the first year. Studies by Rovee-Collier and others suggest that older infants are more capable of encoding and retrieving information. Neonates reflexively imitate certain behaviors, such as sticking out the tongue. Infants later show capacity for deferred imitation, suggesting that they have mentally represented actions.

6. What are the individual differences in the development of cognitive functioning?

The Bayley Scales of Infant Development consist of mental-scale and motor-scale items. A tester may be able to detect early signs of sensory or neurological problems. The BSID and other tests show that some infants develop more rapidly than others.

7. How well do infant scales predict later intellectual performance?

Certain BSID items predict intellectual skills later in childhood, but overall scores on such scales do not predict school grades or later IQ scores very accurately.

8. What is visual recognition memory? How is it used?

Visual recognition memory is the ability to discriminate previously seen objects from novel objects. Its use is based on habituation—the fact that infants gaze longer at new faces than familiar faces. Infants with greater visual recognition memory generally attain higher IQ scores in later childhood; the average correlation is about +0.45.

9. What are prelinguistic vocalizations?

Prelinguistic vocalizations do not represent objects or events and include crying, cooing, and babbling. Coos are often vowel-like, resembling "oohs" and "ahs," and are linked to positive feelings. By about 8 months of age, cooing decreases and babbling begins. Babbling may combine consonants and vowels and sounds more like speech. Toward the end of the first year, infants use intonation that resembles the sounds of speech. Children from different cultures babble the same sounds, as do deaf infants. As time passes, babbling sounds more like the sounds spoken in the infant's environment.

10. How does vocabulary develop?

Infants' receptive vocabulary development outpaces their expressive vocabulary. The first word typically is spoken between 11 and 13 months and is brief, consisting of one or two

Recite Recite Recite Recite

syllables. It may take children 3 or 4 months to achieve a vocabulary of 10 to 30 words after the first word is spoken, but by about 18 months, children may produce nearly 50 words. Most of children's first words are nominals. From about 18 to 22 months, vocabulary may increase from 50 to more than 300 words. Children with a referential language style use language mainly to label objects. Those with an expressive language style mainly seek to engage in social interactions. Infants often use overextension; that is, they extend the meaning of one word to refer to things and actions for which they do not have words.

11. How do infants create sentences?

Infants' early sentences are telegraphic. First come holophrases, then two-word utterances. Roger Brown studied telegraphic speech in infants in terms of their mean length of utterance (MLU). Two-word sentences show understanding of syntax, and the kinds of two-word sentences are the same among children from diverse linguistic environments.

12. How do learning theorists account for language development?

Learning theorists explain language development in terms of imitation and reinforcement. However, children resist imitating sentences that do not fit with their awareness of grammar. Skinner believed that children acquire their early vocabularies through shaping.

13. What is the nativist view of language development?

The nativist view holds that innate or inborn "prewiring" causes children to attend to and acquire language in certain ways. Psycholinguistic theory considers that language acquisition involves the interaction between environmental influences and such prewiring, which Chomsky terms the language acquisition device (LAD). Chomsky argues that all languages share a "universal grammar" that children are prewired to perceive and use in their own language production.

14. What parts of the brain are involved in language development?

Many parts of the brain are involved in language development, but key biological structures are based in the left hemisphere for most people: Broca's area and Wernicke's area. Damage to either area may cause a characteristic aphasia. In Broca's aphasia, children continue to understand the speech of others but speak laboriously. In Wernicke's aphasia, children may speak with proper syntax, but their ability to comprehend speech is compromised.

15. What is meant by a *sensitive period* for language development?

Lenneberg proposes that plasticity of the brain provides a sensitive period for learning language that begins at about 18 to 24 months and lasts until puberty. The case history of "Genie" offers some support for the sensitive-period hypothesis.

On the Web

Search Online With InfoTrac College Edition

For additional information, explore InfoTrac College Edition, your online library. Go to **http://www.inftrac-college.com** and use the passcode from the InfoTrac card that came with your book. Try these search terms: language acquisition—parent participation, speech development, language awareness, memory in infants.

Visit Our Web Site

Go to **http://www.wadsworth.com/psychology** where you will find online resources directly linked to your book.

Child Development CD-ROM

Go to the Wadsworth Child Development CD-ROM for further study of the concepts in this chapter. The CD-ROM also includes quizzes and additional activities to expand your learning experience.

7 Infancy: Social and Emotional Development

PowerPreview™

Attachment: Bonds That Endure

- **An infant's willingness** to leave the mother in order to explore the environment is a sign of secure attachment.
- **You can predict** how strongly infants are attached to their fathers if you know how many diapers per week the father changes.
- **Does the path** to an infant's heart lie through its stomach?
- **Must children become** attached to their parents before a critical period elapses if bonds of attachment are to form properly?

When Attachment Fails

- **Child abusers have frequently** been the victims of child abuse themselves. Why?
- **Autistic children are alone,** even when they are surrounded by people who are doing their best to get through to them.

Day Care

- **Children placed in day care** are more aggressive than children who are cared for in the home. Should the kids be kept at home?

Emotional Development

- **Is fear of strangers** normal among infants? (And just what do we mean by "normal"?)
- **Do you check out** what other people do when you are faced with a novel situation? So do infants—at least, they do so once they reach the halfway point of the first year.

Personality Development

- **When did you first realize** that you exist? (Don't worry if your answer is "Not sure"; it applies to everyone.)
- **All children are temperamental.** (That is, they have "temperaments," some of which are easy-going, despite the use of the term *temperament*.)
- **As early as 12 to 18 months** of age, girls prefer dolls and toy animals, while boys prefer toy trucks and sports equipment (you know, like "gear").

At the age of 2, my daughter Allyn almost succeeded at preventing publication of a book I was writing. When I locked myself into my study, she positioned herself outside the door and called, "Daddy, oh Daddy." At other times she would bang on the door or cry. When I would give in (several times a day) and open the door, she would run in and say, "I want you to pick up me," and hold out her arms or climb into my lap. How would I ever finish the book?

Being a psychologist, I easily saw solutions. For example, I could write outside the home. But this solution had the drawback of distancing me from my family. Another solution was to ignore my daughter and let her cry. If I refused to reinforce crying, crying would become extinguished. (And research does suggest that ignoring crying discourages it [Van IJzendoorn & Hubbard, 2000].) There was only one problem with this solution. I didn't *want* to extinguish her efforts to get to me. **Attachment,** you see, is a two-way street.

Attachment is one of the key issues in the social and personality development of the infant. If this chapter had been written by the poet John Donne, it might have begun, "No children are islands unto themselves." Children come into this world fully dependent on others for their survival and well-being.

This chapter is about some of the consequences of that absolute dependency. It is about the social relationships between infants and caregivers and about the development of the bonds of attachment that usually—but not always—bind them. It is about the ways infant behavior prompts social and emotional responses from adults and the way adult behavior prompts social and emotional responses from infants. It is also about the unique and different ways infants react socially and emotionally.

Let's first consider the issue of attachment and the factors that contribute to its development. Then we shall examine some circumstances that interfere with the development of attachment: social deprivation, child abuse, and autism. We turn next to a discussion of day care. Finally, we look at the development of emotions and personality in infancy, including the self-concept, temperament, and gender differences.

Attachment: Bonds That Endure

Question: Just what is meant by "attachment"? Attachment is what most people refer to as affection or love. Mary Ainsworth (1989), one of the preeminent researchers in attachment, defines attachment as an emotional tie that is formed between one animal or person and another specific individual. Attachment keeps organisms together and tends to endure. John Bowlby (1988; Ainsworth & Bowlby, 1991) believes that attachment is essential to the very survival of the infant. He argues that babies are born with behaviors—crying, smiling, clinging—that elicit protective caregiving responses from parents.

Babies and children try to maintain contact with caregivers to whom they are attached. They engage in eye contact, pull and tug at them, and ask to be picked up. When they cannot maintain contact, infants show behaviors suggestive of **separation anxiety.** They may thrash about, fuss, cry or screech, or whine. Parents who are seeking a few minutes to attend to their own legitimate needs sometimes see these behaviors as manipulative and, in a sense, they are. That is, children learn that the behaviors achieve desired ends. But what is wrong with "manipulating" a loved one to end one's distress?

attachment An affectional bond between individuals characterized by a seeking of closeness or contact and a show of distress upon separation.

separation anxiety Fear of being separated from a target of attachment—usually a primary caregiver.

The Strange Situation Method

One of Mary Ainsworth's major contributions to the study of child development is the innovation of the Strange Situation method of measuring attachment. In this method, an infant is exposed to a series of separations and reunions with a caregiver (usually the mother) and a stranger who is a confederate of the researchers.

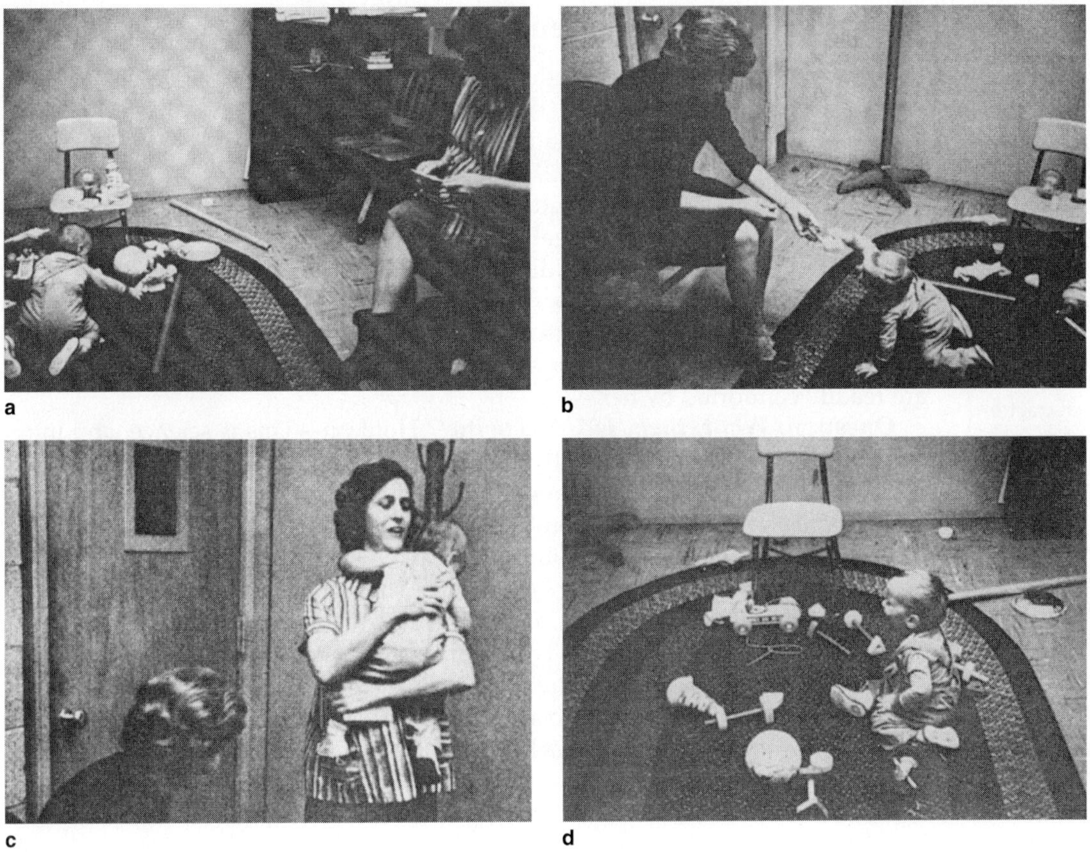

Figure 7.1
The Strange Situation

These historic photos show a 12-month-old child in the Strange Situation. In (a), the child plays with toys, glancing occasionally at mother. In (b), the stranger approaches with a toy. While the child is distracted, mother leaves the room. In (c), mother returns after a brief absence. The child crawls to her quickly and clings to her when picked up. In (d), the child cries when mother again leaves the room. What pattern of attachment is this child showing?

Children are led through eight episodes (Ainsworth et al., 1978).

1. The mother carries the infant into the laboratory room.
2. The mother puts the infant down and then sits quietly in a chair. She does not interact with the infant unless the infant seeks her attention.
3. A stranger enters the room and converses with the mother. The stranger then gradually approaches the infant with a toy. The mother leaves the room.
4. If the infant is involved in active play, the stranger observes unobtrusively. If the infant is passive, the stranger tries to interest him or her in a toy. If the infant shows distress (as by crying), the stranger tries to comfort him or her.
5. The mother returns and the stranger leaves. After the infant has again begun to play, the mother also departs.
6. The infant is left alone briefly.
7. The stranger reenters the room and behaves as described in number 4.
8. The mother returns and the stranger leaves.

Although the Strange Situation method has been the most widely used method of assessing patterns of attachment, it is not the only one. Other methods such as the California Attachment Procedure have been developed, and it may be that one or more of these will prove to be more reliable and useful (Clarke-Stewart, Goossens, & Allhusen, 2001).

secure attachment A type of attachment characterized by mild distress at leave-takings, seeking nearness to an attachment figure, and being readily soothed by the figure.

avoidant attachment A type of insecure attachment characterized by apparent indifference to the leave-takings of, and reunions with, an attachment figure.

ambivalent/resistant attachment A type of insecure attachment characterized by severe distress at the leave-takings of, and ambivalent behavior at reunions with, an attachment figure.

disorganized–disoriented attachment A type of insecure attachment characterized by dazed and contradictory behaviors toward an attachment figure.

Patterns of Attachment

Reflect

What does it mean for a child to be secure? Were you "secure" as a child? How do you know?

Using the Strange Situation method, Mary Ainsworth and her colleagues (1978) have identified various patterns of attachment. Broadly speaking, babies have either **secure attachment** or insecure attachment. Ainsworth and other investigators have found that about 65–70% of middle-class babies in the United States are securely attached. ***Question: What does it mean for a child to be "secure"?*** Think of security in terms of what infants *do.* In the Strange Situation, securely attached infants mildly protest the mother's departure, seek interaction upon reunion, and are readily comforted by her.

Question: What, then, is "insecurity"? Hold on—This is science, and in the science of development we speak of insecurity as "insecure attachment." The two major types of insecure attachment identified by Ainsworth and her colleagues are **avoidant attachment** and **ambivalent/resistant attachment.** Approximately 20–25% of babies in the United States show avoidant attachment. These babies are least distressed by their mothers' departure. They play without fuss when alone and ignore their mothers upon reunion. Ambivalent/resistant babies make up another 10–15% of the samples. These babies are the most emotional. They show severe signs of distress when their mothers leave and show ambivalence upon reunion by alternately clinging to and pushing away their mothers. More recently, a third category of insecure attachment, **disorganized–disoriented attachment,**

Developing in a World of Diversity

Cross-Cultural Patterns of Attachment

How widespread are the patterns of attachment we discuss in this chapter? Studies using the Strange Situation in seven European and Asian countries have found that secure attachments predominate, just as in the United States. Avoidant attachments are more common in some European countries, especially Germany, than in the United States. While avoidant attachment is more common than ambivalent/resistant attachment in most countries, the opposite pattern has been found for Japan and Israel (van IJzendoorn & Kroonenberg, 1988; van IJzendoorn et al., 1992; Sagi, Van IJzendoorn, & Koren-Karie, 1991). See Table 7.1.

Different child-rearing practices and attitudes may account for these differences in attachment patterns. For example, German parents encourage independence in the child at an early age. Compared with American parents, they are less likely to pick up a crying baby and more likely to leave the baby alone in bed (Grossmann & Grossmann, 1991). This pattern may be more likely to foster avoidant attachment in the child. Japanese mothers, on the other hand, emphasize close and continuous contact with their babies and rarely leave them with other caretakers (Barratt et al., 1993; Takahashi, 1990). These infants are not used to being alone or with strangers, which may account for their distressed behavior in the Strange Situation.

The Israeli studies have involved children raised in a collective farm community known as a *kibbutz.* Parents visit and play with

© Karen Kasmauski/Woodfin Camp and Associates

Child-Rearing Practices and Attachment

Japanese mothers emphasize close, continuous contact with their babies and rarely leave them with other caretakers. Might this account for the distress shown by Japanese babies in the Strange Situation?

has been proposed (Main & Hesse, 1990). Babies showing this pattern appear dazed, confused, or disoriented. They may show contradictory behaviors, such as moving toward the mother while looking away from her.

Consequences of Patterns of Attachment

Question: Is it better for an infant to be securely attached to its caregivers? Sure it is. Securely attached infants and toddlers are happier, more sociable with unfamiliar adults, more cooperative with parents, and get along better with peers than do insecurely attached children (Belsky, Steinberg, & Draper, 1991a; Thompson, 1991a). They use the mother as a secure base from which to venture out and explore the environment (Ainsworth & Bowlby, 1991). Research suggests that secure attachment encourages positive emotions toward neutral stimuli in children, encouraging them to explore (Mikulincer et al., 2001). The other side of the coin is that children who are securely attached also experience fewer negative emotions toward members of outgroups (Mikulincer & Shaver, 2001). Security thus encourages children to explore interactions with unfamiliar people, broadening their horizons.

Reflect

Which child is securely attached to its mother? The one who clings to his or her mother when a stranger approaches or the one who is willing to interact with the stranger?

Securely attached toddlers also have longer attention spans, are less impulsive, and are better at solving problems (Frankel & Bates, 1990; Granot & Mayseless, 2001; Lederberg & Mobley, 1990; Olson, Bates, & Bayles, 1990). At ages 5 and 6, securely attached children are better liked by peers and teachers, are more competent, are less aggressive, and have fewer behavior problems than insecurely attached children (Lyons-Ruth, Alpern, & Repacholi, 1993; Suess, Grossmann, & Sroufe, 1992; Youngblade & Belsky, 1992). We must keep in mind that these positive developmental outcomes may be caused not only by secure infant attachments but also by the continuation of good parent–child relationships throughout childhood (Lamb, 1987).

Yet some research questions whether infant attachment as measured by means of the Strange Situation predicts adjustment later on. For example, Michael Lewis (1997) located 84 high school seniors who had been evaluated by the Strange

their children frequently during the day and evening. The children's primary care and training, however, is entrusted to a child-rearing specialist called a *metapelet*, who also spends the night with the children. Despite the reduced parent–child contact, kibbutz life does not seem to impair parent–child bonds of attachment (Maccoby & Feldman, 1972). Babies, however, appear to become equally attached to their metapelet (Van IJzendoorn et al., 1992).

How can we explain the finding that kibbutz-reared children show a higher incidence of ambivalent/resistant attachment than avoidant attachment? Like the Japanese child, the kibbutz-reared child has close, continuous contact with its primary caretakers but little contact with strangers. For both these groups of children, then, the Strange Situation may produce intense distress.

TABLE 7.1 *Some Patterns of Insecure Attachment and Child-Rearing Practices Found in Other Countries*

Country	Predominant Patterns of Insecure Attachment	Child-Rearing Practices and Attitudes (compared with other European and Asian Countries, and with the United States)
Germany	Avoidant	• Parents are less likely to pick up a crying infant. • Parents are more likely to leave the infant alone in bed.
Japan	Ambivalent/Resistant	• Parents are less likely to leave an infant with strangers. • Parents are more likely to emphasize continuous, close contact with the mother.
Israel	Ambivalent/Resistant	• Parents are less likely to leave an infant with strangers. • Parents are more likely to emphasize continuous, close contact with primary caregivers.

Situation method at the age of 1. Extensive interviews showed that of the 49 who had been considered securely attached at the age of 1, 43% were currently maladjusted. Of the 35 who had been considered insecurely attached in infancy, only 26% were rated as currently maladjusted. Lewis (1998) suggests that childhood events such as accidents, parental divorce, and illness can be more powerful influences on adolescents' security than is the quality of parenting during the first year. But most developmental psychologists continue to endorse the Strange Situation as a predictor of adjustment later in life (Blakeslee, 1998). For example, Alan Sroufe (1998) found that insecure attachment at the age of 1 year predicted psychological disorders at the age of 17.

Question: What are the roles of the parents in the formation of bonds of attachment?

The Role of the Mother in Attachment

Reflect

Do you believe that women are "natural mothers"? Do women have instincts that influence them to love and become attached to their children? Explain.

Attachment is one measure of the quality of care that infants receive (Rosen & Rothbaum, 1993). The mothers of securely attached babies are more likely to be affectionate, cooperative, reliable, and predictable in their caregiving. They respond more sensitively to their babies' smiles, cries, and other social behaviors (Cox et al., 1992; Isabella, 1993; Rosen & Rothbaum, 1993).

A Japanese study found evidence for the "intergenerational transmission of attachment" from mother to child (Kazui et al., 2000). For example, the children of secure mothers showed the most secure patterns of attachment themselves, as assessed by various means. The children of secure mothers interacted positively with both their mothers and strangers, so their pattern of attachment provided a secure base for exploration.

Providing economically stressed mothers with support services can enhance their involvement with their infants and increase secure attachment. In one study, low-income women received child-care information and social support from home visitors during pregnancy and for a year following childbirth (Jacobson & Frye, 1991). In another study, low-income women suffering from depression received similar support services until their child was 18 months old (Lyons-Ruth et al., 1990). In both instances, children whose mothers received support services showed more secure attachment than control children whose mothers had not. Even something as simple as increasing the amount of physical contact between mothers and their infants appears to promote greater maternal responsiveness and more secure attachment between infant and mother (Anisfeld et al., 1990).

Insecure attachment is found more frequently among babies whose mothers are mentally ill or who abuse them (Teti, Gelfand, Messinger, 1992; van IJzendoorn, Sagi, & Lambermon, 1992). It is found more often among babies whose mothers are slow to meet their needs or who meet them in a cold manner (DeMulder & Radke-Yarrow, 1991; Izard et al., 1991).

Research by Marinus van IJzendoorn and colleagues (2000), published in the journal *Child Development,* suggests that siblings tend to develop similar attachment relationships with their mother. Girls and boys growing up in the same family are likely to relate in similar ways to their parents. The study pooled data on sibling attachment from research groups in the United States, the Netherlands, and Canada to form 138 pairs of siblings. The security of attachment of each child was assessed with the Strange Situation procedure 12–14 months after birth. Maternal sensitivity to infants' needs was observed with the same rating scale. Sibling attachment relationships with the mother were found to be significantly alike when classified broadly as secure/insecure, but not when further efforts were made to subcategorize the type of security. Maternal insensitivity to infants was found to strongly predict insecurity in both siblings in a given pair. On the other hand, what's sauce for the goose may not be sauce for the gander. Siblings of the same gender are more likely to form similar attachment relationships with their mother than are girl-and-boy pairs. Mothers, that is, may interact quite differently with daughters and sons.

Although it's tempting to seek the origins of secure and insecure attachment in the mother's behavior, that's not the whole story. Security of attachment seems to depend on the baby's temperament as well as on the mother's behavior and personality (Fagot & Kavanagh, 1993; Mangelsdorf et al., 1990). Babies who are more active and irritable and who display more negative emotion are more likely to develop insecure attachment (Fox, 1992; Vaughn et al., 1992). Such babies may elicit parental behaviors that are not conducive to the development of secure attachment. For example, mothers of "difficult" children are less responsive to their children and report that they feel less emotionally close to them (Sheeber & Johnson, 1992; Spangler, 1990). Caregivers respond to babies' behavior, just as the babies respond to caregivers' behavior. The processes of attachment are a two-way street.

And the father also plays a role. Let's not forget him.

The Role of the Father in Attachment

Yes, you can predict how well babies are attached to their fathers if you know how many diapers the fathers change each week. Gail Ross and her colleagues (1975) found that the more diapers the father changed, the stronger the attachment. No, there is no magical connection between diapers and love. (No comment.) Rather, the number of diapers the father changes roughly reflects his involvement in child rearing. Sometimes, very roughly.

Reflect

To which parent are you more attached? Why?

Until recently, fathers had been largely left out of the theory and research concerning attachment. (My wife is standing behind me and editorializing, "And with good reason.") A major reason was the traditional division of labor in most societies. The father was the breadwinner and the mother the primary caregiver to the children. Traditionally, mothers have been given the responsible roles of feeder, changer, and comforter of children. Fathers have more or less been expected to play with, enjoy, and, perhaps, discipline them (Draper, 1990).

Involvement of Fathers

How involved is the average father with his children? Fathers are just as capable as mothers of acting competently and sensitively toward their infants (Lamb & Oppenheim, 1989; Parke & Tinsley, 1987). But studies of parents in the United States show that father–child interactions differ qualitatively and quantitatively from mother–child interactions (Lamb & Oppenheim, 1989). Mothers engage in far more interactions with their infants (Belsky, Rovine, & Fish, 1989). Most fathers spend much less time on basic child-care tasks, such as feeding and diaper changing, than mothers do. Fathers are more likely to play with their children than to feed or clean them (Cowan, 1992; Lamb, Sternberg, & Ketterlinus, 1992). Fathers more often than mothers engage in physical, rough-and-tumble play, such as tossing their babies into the air and poking them. Mothers are more likely to play games like pat-a-cake and peekaboo and to play games involving toys (Bretherton, Golby, & Halvorsen, 1993; Carson, Burks, & Parke, 1993).

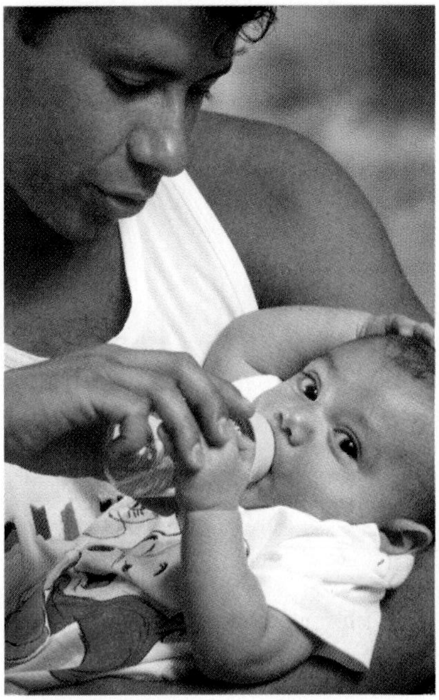

Fathers and Attachment

The number of diapers a father changes reflects his involvement in child rearing. Children develop strong attachments to fathers as well as mothers, especially if the father interacts positively and affectionately with the child.

Factors Influencing Involvement of Fathers

Which fathers are most likely to be involved with their infants? Fathers who are more actively involved believe that the father plays an important role in the child's development (Palkovitz, 1984). Fathers also are more involved with their infants when they have positive attitudes toward parenting and their marriage (Belsky et al., 1989; Cox et al., 1992; Noppe, Noppe, & Hughes, 1991). Involved fathers are more likely to believe that infants are socially and cognitively competent (and thus perhaps more interesting to interact with!) (Ninio & Rinotti, 1988).

Attachment to Fathers

How strongly, then, do infants become attached to their fathers? The answer seems to depend on the quality of the time the father spends with the baby (Easterbrook & Goldberg, 1984). The more positive and physically affectionate the interaction between the father and his infant, the stronger the attachment of the child (Cox et al., 1992). Infants under stress still seek out mothers more than fathers (Lamb, Steinberg, & Prodromidis, 1992). But when observed at their natural activities in the home and other familiar settings, they seek proximity and contact with their fathers about as often as with their mothers (Lamb, 1981).

It appears that babies develop attachments for both parents at about the same time (Lamb, Steinberg, & Prodromidis). This is interesting for two reasons. First, it flies in the face of Freudian theory, which argues that babies become more attached to their mothers—who are the more common providers of "oral gratification"—during the first year. Second, most mothers provide a markedly greater amount of caregiving than fathers do during the first few months.

Babies who are securely attached to one parent are likely to be securely attached to the other (Fox, Kimmerly, & Schafer, 1991; Fox, 1992). But infants who are securely attached to only one parent are as likely to be attached to the father as to the mother (Main & Weston, 1981).

Stability of Attachment

Individual patterns of attachment tend to persist when caregiving conditions remain consistent (Main & Cassidy, 1988). Attachment patterns can change, however, when conditions of child care change appreciably (Thompson, 1991a). Egeland and Sroufe (1981) followed a number of infants who were severely neglected and others who received high-quality care from 12 to 18 months of age. Attachment patterns remained stable (secure) for infants receiving fine care. However, many neglected infants changed from insecurely to securely attached over the 6-month period, sometimes because of a relationship with a supportive family member, sometimes because home life grew less tense. Other studies show that children can become less securely attached to caregivers when the quality of home life deteriorates (Egeland & Farber, 1984; Thompson, Lamb, & Estes, 1982).

Even when children are adopted as late as the age of 4, they can become securely attached to their adoptive parents (Hodges & Tizard, 1989). Young children show resilience in their social and emotional development. Early insecurities apparently can be overcome.

Developing in a World of Diversity

Parents' Involvement With Their Infants, Here and There

Studies have examined variations in parents' interactions with their babies in cultures in Africa, Asia, and Western Europe (Nugent, Lester, & Brazelton, 1991), as well as within the United States (Hossain & Roopnarine, 1994). One consistent finding in both Western and Eastern societies is that mothers are usually more involved and affectionate with their children than fathers are (Berndt et al., 1993; Hossain et al., 1997). Some patterns of parenting, however, vary across cultures.

For example, in studies carried out in New Delhi, India, and the United States, mothers were more likely than fathers to pick up, hold, feed, comfort, and show affection to their 1-year-old infants (Hossain et al., 1997; Hossain & Roopnarine, 1993; Roopnarine et al., 1990). Fathers in India and the United States engaged in more rough play than mothers, and mothers were more likely to play peekaboo. The families studied within the United States included African Americans and Latino and Latina Americans. Researchers found that African American and Latino American fathers were as involved with their children as European American fathers. The researchers (Hossain et al., 1997) discuss this finding in relation to the preconceived notion that low-income, minority fathers are "uninvolved."

There were some differences between the Indian and American parents. When Indian parents held their babies, they were more likely to display affection than to comfort or play with them. This is the reverse of the American pattern. Rough physical play also was much less frequent among the Indian parents. The researchers suggest that Indian cultural values emphasizing tranquility and nonaggressiveness may account for these differences.

Stages of Attachment

Several important cross-cultural studies have led to a theory of stages of attachment. In one study, Ainsworth (1967) tracked the attachment behaviors of Ugandan infants. Over a 9-month period, she noted their efforts to maintain contact with the mother, their protests when separated, and their use of the mother as a base for exploring the environment. ***Question: What did Ainsworth learn about the stages of attachment?*** At first the Ugandan infants showed **indiscriminate attachment.** That is, they showed no particular preferences for the mother or another familiar caregiver. Specific attachment to the mother, as evidenced by separation anxiety and other behaviors, began to develop at about 4 months and grew intensely by about 7 months. Fear of strangers developed 1 or 2 months later.

In another study (see Figure 7.2), Scottish infants showed indiscriminate attachment during the first 6 months or so after birth (Schaffer & Emerson, 1964). Then indiscriminate attachment waned. Specific attachments to the mother and other familiar caregivers intensified, as demonstrated by the appearance of separation anxiety, and remained at high levels through the age of 18 months. Fear of strangers occurred a month or so after the intensity of specific attachments began to mushroom. Thus, in both this and the Ugandan study, fear of strangers followed separation anxiety and the development of specific attachments by a number of weeks. Other cross-cultural studies have found that the onset of separation anxiety occurs earliest in cultures in which mothers care for their infants almost exclusively and are in close physical contact with them for extended periods (Crowell & Waters, 1990).

From studies such as these, Ainsworth and her colleagues (1978) identified the following three phases of attachment:

1. **The initial-preattachment phase,** which lasts from birth to about 3 months and is characterized by indiscriminate attachment
2. **The attachment-in-the-making phase,** which occurs at about 3 or 4 months and is characterized by preference for familiar figures
3. **The clear-cut-attachment phase,** which occurs at about 6 or 7 months and is characterized by intensified dependence on the primary caregiver—usually the mother

Most infants have more than one adult caregiver, however, and are likely to form multiple attachments—to the father, day-care providers, grandparents, and other caregivers, as well as to the mother. In most cultures, single attachments are the exception, not the rule (Howes & Matheson, 1992a).

indiscriminate attachment The display of attachment behaviors toward any person.

initial-preattachment phase The first phase in the formation of bonds of attachment, lasting from birth to about 3 months of age and characterized by indiscriminate attachment.

attachment-in-the-making phase The second phase in the development of attachment, occurring at 3 or 4 months of age and characterized by preference for familiar figures.

clear-cut-attachment phase The third phase in the development of attachment, occurring at 6 or 7 months of age and characterized by intensified dependence on the primary caregiver.

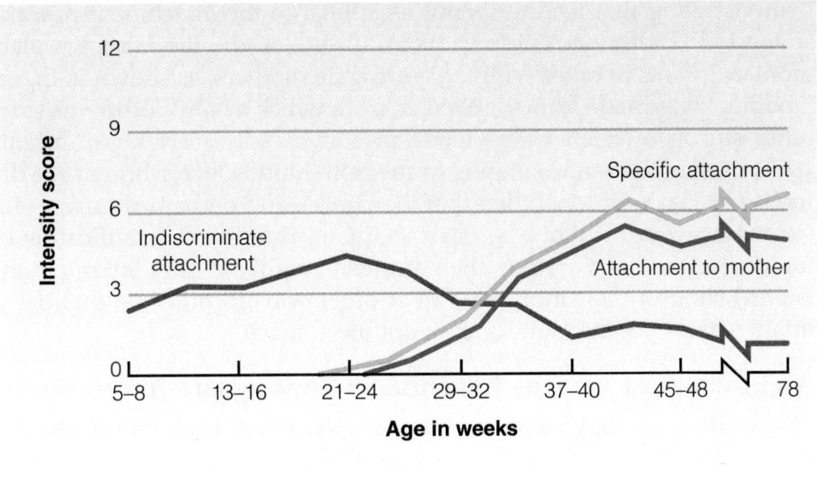

Figure 7.2
The Development of Attachment
During the first 6 months, infants tend to show indiscriminate attachment. Indiscriminate attachment then wanes while specific attachments grow intense and remain at high levels. Fear of strangers develops a month or so after the intensity of specific attachments begins to blossom.

Theories of Attachment

Attachment, like so many other behavior patterns, seems to develop as a result of the interaction of nature and nurture. ***Question: How do different theorists emphasize nature or nurture in their explanation of the development of attachment?***

A Cognitive View of Attachment

The cognitive view focuses on the contention that an infant must have developed some concept of object permanence before specific attachment becomes possible. In other words, if caregivers are to be missed when absent, the infant must perceive that they continue to exist. We have seen that infants tend to develop specific attachments at about 6 to 7 months. In support of the cognitive view, recall that rudimentary object permanence concerning physical objects develops somewhat earlier (Chapter 6).

A Behavioral View of Attachment: Caregiver as Reinforcer

Early in the century, behaviorists argued that attachment behaviors are learned through conditioning. Caregivers feed their infants and tend to their other physiological needs. Thus, infants associate their caregivers with gratification and learn to approach them to meet their needs. From this perspective, a caregiver becomes a conditioned reinforcer.

The feelings of gratification that are associated with meeting specific needs generalize into feelings of security when the caregiver is present.

Psychoanalytic Views of Attachment: Caregiver as Love Object

Psychoanalytic theorists view the development of attachment somewhat differently from behaviorists. The caregiver, usually the mother, becomes not just a "reinforcer" but also a love object who forms the basis for all later attachments.

In both the psychoanalytic and behaviorist views, however, the caregiver's role in gratifying the child's needs is of paramount importance. Sigmund Freud emphasized the importance of oral activities such as eating in the first year of life. Freud believed that the infant becomes emotionally attached to the mother during this time, because she is the primary satisfier of the infant's needs for food and sucking.

Erik Erikson also believed the first year to be critical for developing a sense of trust in the mother. This sense of trust fosters feelings of attachment. Erikson stressed that the mother's sensitivity to all the child's needs, and not just the need for food, is essential for the child to develop trust and attachment.

The Harlows' View of Attachment: Caregiver as a Source of Contact Comfort

Harry and Margaret Harlow conducted an ingenious series of experiments demonstrating that feeding is not as critical to the attachment process as Freud suggested (Harlow & Harlow, 1966). In one study, the Harlows placed rhesus monkey infants in cages with two surrogate mothers, as shown in Figure 7.3. One "mother" was made from wire mesh, from which a baby bottle was extended. The other surrogate mother was made of soft, cuddly terry cloth. Infant monkeys spent most of their time clinging to the cloth mother, even though she did not offer food. The Harlows concluded that monkeys—and perhaps humans—have a need for **contact comfort** that is as basic as the need for food. Gratification of the need for contact comfort, rather than hunger, might be why infant monkeys (and babies) cling to their mothers. Put another way, it might be that the path to an infant's heart lies through its skin, not its stomach.

contact comfort The pleasure derived from physical contact with another; a hypothesized need or drive for physical contact with another.

ethologist A scientist who studies the behavior patterns that are characteristic of various species.

fixed action pattern (FAP) Instinct; a stereotyped behavior pattern that is characteristic of a species and is triggered by a releasing stimulus.

releasing stimulus A stimulus that elicits a fixed action pattern (FAP).

An Ethological View of Attachment: Smiling and Imprinting

Ethologists note that for many animals, attachment is an inborn **fixed action pattern (FAP).** The FAP of attachment, like other FAPs, is theorized to occur in the presence of a species-specific **releasing stimulus.** According to John Bowlby (1988;

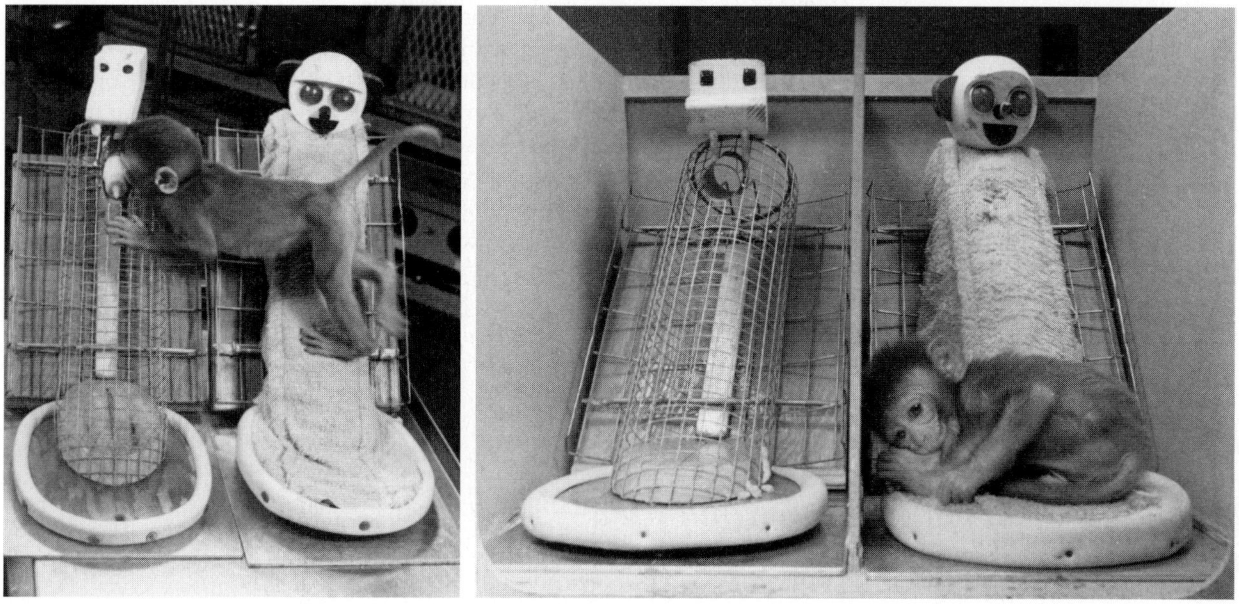

Harlow Primate Laboratory, University of Wisconsin

Figure 7.3
Attachment in Infant Monkeys

As shown in this classic series of photos, although this rhesus monkey infant is fed by the "wire mother," it spends most of its time clinging to a soft, cuddly "terry-cloth mother." It knows where to get a meal, but contact comfort is apparently more central to attachment than feeding in infant monkeys (and infant humans?).

Ainsworth & Bowlby, 1991), one component of the FAP of attachment in humans, and its releasing stimulus, is a baby's smile in response to a human voice or face. Bowlby proposes that the baby's smile helps ensure survival by eliciting affection in its caregivers. By 2 to 3 months of age, the human face begins to elicit a **social smile** (Emde, Gaensbauer, & Harmon, 1976). The development of smiling seems to follow the same sequence in many cultures. Smiling responses increase dramatically between 2 to 4 months of age in Native American infants; infants reared in Israeli middle-class homes and on the kibbutz; infants of Bedouin Arabs, African hunter-gatherers, and agriculturists; and infants in metropolitan Japan (Werner, 1988).

The FAP of attachment is also theorized to occur during a **critical period** of life. If it does not, it may never occur. During this period, young animals are capable of forming an instinctive attachment to their mothers or parents if the releasing stimuli are present. Waterfowl become attached during the critical period to the first moving object they encounter. It's as if the image of the moving object becomes "imprinted" upon the young animal, so the formation of an attachment in this manner is called **imprinting.**

Ethologist Konrad Lorenz (1962, 1981) became well known when pictures of his "family" of goslings were made public (see Figure 7.4). How did Lorenz acquire his "family"? He was present when the goslings hatched and during their critical periods, and he allowed them to follow him. The critical period for geese and ducks begins when they first engage in locomotion and ends when they develop fear of strangers. The goslings followed Lorenz persistently, ran to him when frightened, honked with distress at his departure, and tried to overcome barriers placed between them and him. If you substitute crying for honking, it all sounds rather human.

If imprinting occurs with children, it does not follow the mechanics that apply to waterfowl. As shown by the 4-year-old adoptees who formed strong attachments to their adoptive parents (Tizard, Philips, & Plewis, 1976), there is apparently no critical period for the development of attachment in humans. Klaus and Kennell (1978) suggested that there might be a weaker "maternal-sensitive"

social smile A smile that occurs in response to a human voice or face.

critical period A period of development during which a releasing stimulus can elicit a fixed action pattern (FAP).

imprinting The process by which some animals exhibit the fixed action pattern (FAP) of attachment in response to a releasing stimulus. The FAP occurs during a critical period and is difficult to modify.

Nina Leen/TimePix

Figure 7.4
Imprinting

Quite a following? Konrad Lorenz may not look like Mommy to you, but these goslings became attached to him because he was the first moving object they perceived and followed. This type of attachment process is referred to as imprinting.

period, governed by hormones, for becoming attached to a newborn. But the evidence for even this watered-down sensitive period is questionable.

In sum, attachment in humans is a complex process that continues for months or years. Certainly, it includes learning in the broad sense of the term—as opposed to a limited, mechanistic-behaviorist sense. Attachment involves infant perceptual and cognitive processes, and the type of attachment that develops is related to the quality of the caregiver–infant relationship. The caregiving itself and infant responsiveness, such as infant smiling, appear to spur the development of attachment.

A Closer Look

Hormones and Attachment: Of Mice and Men—and Women and Infants

The pituitary gland lies below the hypothalamus in the brain (see Figure 7.5). Although it's only a pea-sized structure, it is so central to the body's functioning that it has been referred to as the "master gland." The pituitary secretes a variety of hormones, and a number of them are involved in reproduction and nurturing of young. For example, the hormone prolactin largely regulates maternal behavior in lower mammals such as rats, and it also stimulates the production of milk in women. Antidiuretic hormone—also termed vasopressin—enables the body to conserve water by inhibiting urine production when fluid levels are low. Yet vasopressin is also connected with stereotypical paternal behavior patterns in some mammals. For example, male prairie voles—a kind of tailless mouse*—form pair-bonds with female prairie voles after mating with them (Liu, Curtis, & Wang, 2001). Mating stimulates the secretion of vasopressin, and vasopressin causes the previously roaming male to sing "I only have eyes for you." Or put it this way: When it comes to the new HBO series, "Sex and the Prairie," we have sex first, vasopressin second, and relationships third.

Vasopressin is also connected with attachment between fathers and their young among meadow voles. It transforms an unconcerned male meadow vole (a mouselike rodent) into an affectionate and protective mate and father (Parker & Lee, 2001).

Vasopressin has not yet been shown to be so tightly connected with the formation of bonds between men and women, and men and children, however. So women readers may be premature in stopping by the pharmacy to search out the vasopressin spray mist.

Oxytocin is the pituitary hormone that stimulates labor in pregnant women and is also connected with maternal behavior (cuddling and caring for young) in some mammals (Insel, 2000; Taylor et al., 2000). Obstetricians may induce labor by injecting pregnant women with oxytocin. During nursing, stimulation of nerve endings in and around the nipples sends messages to the brain that cause oxytocin to be secreted. Oxytocin then causes the breasts to eject milk. This is mechanical stuff. The thought that oxytocin may also be even slightly connected with maternal–infant attachment in humans raises interesting psychological issues, such as whether changes in levels of oxytocin are linked to changes in women's perceptions of their infants.

*In fact, one could say, "Thereby hangs *not* a tail." I won't say that, but one could.

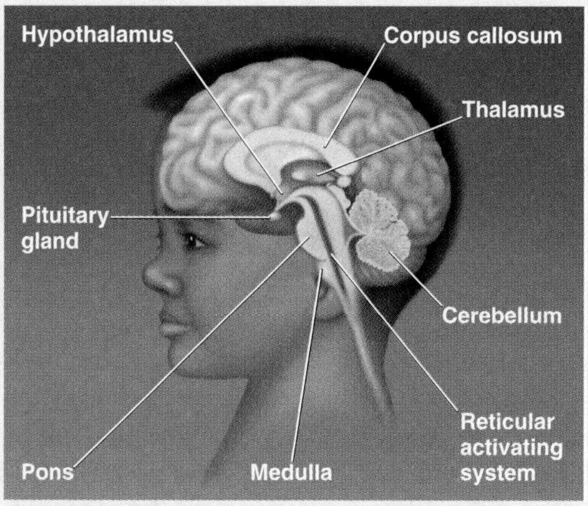

Figure 7.5
The Pituitary Gland

This pea-sized structure is gigantic in its effects. For example, it secretes the hormones oxytocin and vasopressin, which regulate important aspects of reproductive behavior in humans and lower animals. The hypothalamus secretes a number of releasing hormones or factors that regulate the pituitary gland.

Pituitary Hormones and Autism: Is There a Connection?

Autism is a poorly understood developmental disorder that is symptomized by social impairment, communication problems, and compulsive behavior. Deficiency in formation of bonds of attachment is a most striking feature of autism. Researcher Thomas Insel and his colleagues (1999) reviewed the evidence that shows that oxytocin and vasopressin influence attachment and various kinds of social and communicative behaviors among rodents. They hypothesize that an abnormality in the transmission or utilization of oxytocin or vasopressin might account for several symptoms of autism. Because autism appears to be a genetic disorder, researchers might seek out mutations in the response of the brain to these hormones. It could eventually be that modifying the receptivity of the individual to these hormones might have a positive effect on their behavior.

Review

(1) Ainsworth defines attachment as an _________ tie that is formed between one animal or person and another specific individual. (2) When infants cannot maintain contact with people to whom they are attached, they show _________ anxiety. (3) One of Ainsworth's contributions to the field of child development is the innovation of the _________ Situation method of measuring attachment. (4) Broadly speaking, infants have either secure attachment or _________ attachment. (5) The two major types of insecure attachment are _________ attachment and ambivalent/resistant attachment. (6) Securely attached infants use the mother as a secure base from which to _________ the environment. (7) The mothers of _________ attached babies respond sensitively to their babies' smiles, cries, and other social behaviors. (8) Siblings tend to develop (similar or dissimilar?) attachment relationships with their mother. (9) Ainsworth's study of Ugandan infants found that they at first show _________ attachment. (10) The clear-cut-attachment phase occurs at about _________ months. (11) From the _________ perspective, a caregiver becomes a conditioned reinforcer. (12) Psychoanalysts view the caregiver as a _________ object who forms the basis for subsequent attachments. (13) The Harlows' research with monkeys suggests that _________ comfort is a key source of attachment. (14) Ethologists believe that attachment is an inborn _________ action pattern (FAP). (15) The FAP of attachment is theorized to occur during a _________ period.

Pulling It Together: What are the consequences later in life of secure or insecure attachment in infancy?

When Attachment Fails

We have considered effects of rearing children in a group setting (the kibbutz) on attachment (see "Developing in a World of Diversity," earlier in this chapter). But children in the kibbutz continue to have contact with their parents. What happens when children are reared in group settings such as some orphanages where they have no contact with parents and little contact with other caregivers? What happens when parents neglect or abuse their children? In both cases, children's attachments may be impaired. Some children also fail to develop attachments as a result of a disorder called autism. In this section, we consider the effect of social deprivation, child abuse, and autism on the development of attachment.

Social Deprivation

Studies of children reared in institutions where they receive little social stimulation from caregivers are limited in that they are correlational. In other words, family factors that led to the children's placement in institutions may also have contributed to their developmental problems. Ethical considerations prevent us from conducting experiments in which we randomly assign children to social deprivation. However, experiments of this kind have been undertaken with rhesus monkeys, and their results are consistent with those of the correlational studies of children. Let us first examine these animal experiments and then turn to the correlational research involving children.

Reflect

Why would it be unethical to run experiments on the effects of social deprivation with human infants?

Experiments With Monkeys

The Harlows and their colleagues conducted studies of rhesus monkeys who were "reared by" wire-mesh and terry-cloth surrogate mothers. In later studies, rhesus monkeys were reared without even this questionable "social" support. They were reared without seeing any other animal, whether monkey or human.

Question: What are the findings of the Harlows' studies on the effects of social deprivation with monkeys? The Harlows (Harlow, Harlow, & Suomi, 1971) found that rhesus infants reared in this most solitary confinement later avoided contact with other monkeys. They did not engage in the characteristic playful chasing and romping. Instead, they cowered in the presence of others and failed to respond to them. Nor did they make any effort to fend off attacks by other monkeys. Rather, they sat in the corner, clutching themselves and rocking back and forth. Females who later had children of their own tended to ignore or abuse them (Higley, Lande, & Suomi, 1989).

Can the damage done by social deprivation be overcome? When monkeys deprived for 6 months or more are placed with younger, 3- to 4-month-old females for a couple of hours a day, the younger monkeys make efforts to initiate social interaction with their deprived elders (see Figure 7.6). Many of the deprived monkeys begin to play with the youngsters after a few weeks and many of them eventually expand their social contacts to other rhesus monkeys of various ages (Suomi, Harlow, & McKinney, 1972). Perhaps of greater interest is the related finding that socially withdrawn 4- and 5-year-old children make gains in their social and emotional development when they are provided with younger playmates (Furman, Rahe, & Hartup, 1979).

Question: What are the findings of correlational research into the effects of social deprivation with humans?

Studies With Children

Institutionalized children whose material needs are met but who receive little social stimulation from caregivers encounter problems in their physical, intellectual, social, and emotional development (Grusec & Lytton, 1988; Provence & Lipton, 1962; Spitz, 1965). Spitz (1965) noted that many institutionalized children appear to develop a syndrome characterized by withdrawal and depression. They show progressively less interest in their world and become progressively inactive. Some of them die.

Consider a report of life in one institution (Provence & Lipton, 1962). Infants were maintained in separate cubicles for most of their first year to ward off infectious diseases. Adults tended to them only to feed and change their diapers. As a rule, baby bottles were propped up in the infants' cribs. Attendants rarely responded to the babies' cries, and the infants were rarely played with or spoken to. By the age of 4 months, the infants in this institution showed little interest in adults. They rarely tried to gain their attention, even when in distress. A few months later, some of them sat withdrawn in their cribs and rocked back and forth, almost like the Harlows' monkeys. Language deficiencies were striking. As the first year progressed, little babbling was heard within the infants' cubicles. None was speaking even one word at 12 months.

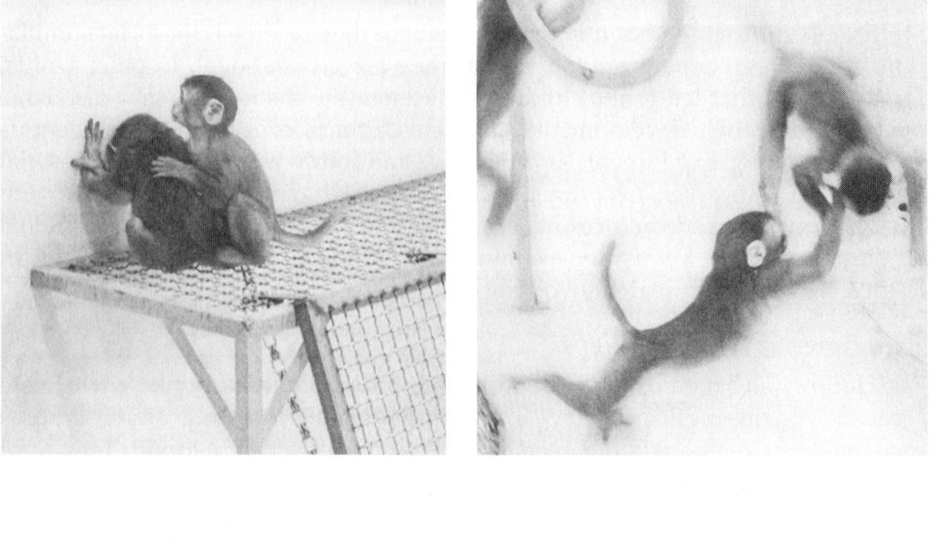

Figure 7.6
Monkey Therapists

In the left photo, a 3–4-month-old rhesus monkey "therapist" tries to soothe a monkey who was reared in social isolation. The deprived monkey remains withdrawn. She clutches herself into a ball and rocks back and forth. The right photo was taken several weeks later and shows that deprived monkeys given young "therapists" can learn to play and adjust to community life. Socially withdrawn preschoolers have similarly profited from exposure to younger peers.

Why do children whose material needs are met show such dramatic deficiencies? Is it because they do not receive the love and affection of a mother or stable surrogate mother? Or is it that they do not receive adequate sensory or social stimulation?

The answer may, in part, depend on the age of the child. Studies by Leon Yarrow and his colleagues (1971; Yarrow & Goodwin, 1973) suggest that deficiencies in sensory stimulation and social interaction may cause more problems than lack of love in infants who are too young to have developed specific attachments. However, once infants have developed specific attachments, separation from their primary caregivers can lead to major problems.

In the first study, the development of 53 adopted children was followed over a 10-year period (Yarrow et al., 1971). The researchers compared the development of three subgroups: (1) children who were transferred to their permanent adoptive homes almost immediately after birth; (2) children who were given temporary foster mothers and then transferred to permanent adoptive homes before they were 6 months old; and (3) children who were transferred from temporary foster mothers to their permanent adoptive homes after they were 6 months old. At the age of 10, children in the first two groups showed no differences in social and emotional development. However, children in the third group showed significantly less ability to relate to other people. Perhaps their deficits resulted from being separated from their initial foster mothers, after they had become attached to them.

In the second study, Yarrow and Goodwin (1973) followed the development of 70 adopted children who were separated from temporary foster parents between birth and the age of 16 months. The researchers found strong correlations between the age at which the children were separated and feeding and sleeping problems, decreased social responsiveness, and extremes in attachment behaviors (see Figure 7.7). Disturbed attachment behaviors included excessive clinging to the new mother and violent rejection of her. None of the children who were separated from the initial foster mothers prior to the age of 3 months showed moderate or severe disturbances. All of the children who were separated at 9 months or older did show such disturbances. From 40% to 90% of the children separated between the ages of 3 and 9 months showed moderate to severe disturbances. The incidence of problems increased as the age advanced.

The Yarrow studies suggest that babies in institutions, at least up to the age of 3 months or so, may require general sensory and social stimulation more than a specific relationship with a primary caregiver. After the age of 3 months, some disturbance is likely if there is instability in the caregiving staff. By the ages of 6 to 9 months, disturbance seems to be guaranteed if there is instability in the position of primary caregiver. Fortunately, there is also evidence that children show some capacity to recover from early social deprivation.

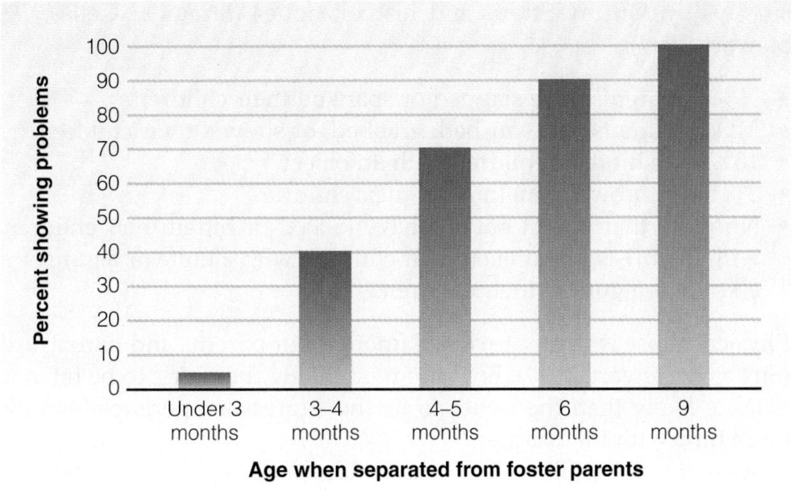

Figure 7.7
The Development of Adopted Children Separated From Temporary Foster Parents

The older the child at time of separation, the more likely it is that behavioral disturbances will occur.

Source: Yarrow & Goodwin, 1973.

The Capacity to Recover From Social Deprivation

Studies with animals and children show that early social deprivation is linked to developmental deficits. However, other studies suggest that infants also have powerful capacities to recover from deprivation.

Kagan and Klein (1973) report that many children may be able to recover fully from 13 or 14 months of deprivation. The natives in an isolated Guatemalan village believe that fresh air and sunshine will make children ill. Children are thus kept in windowless huts until they can walk. They are also played with infrequently. During their isolation, the infants behave apathetically, and they are physically and socially retarded when they start to walk. However, by 11 years of age, they are alert, active, and as intellectually competent as American children of the same age.

A longitudinal study of orphanage children also provides dramatic evidence of the ability of children to recover from social deprivation (Skeels, 1966). In this study, a group of 19-month-old apparently retarded children was placed in the care of older institutionalized girls who spent a great deal of time playing with, talking to, and generally nurturing them. This placement occurred many months past the age at which specific attachments develop. However, 4 years after being placed with the girls, the "retarded" children made dramatic gains in intelligence-test scores, whereas children remaining in the orphanage showed declines in IQ scores.

The children placed in the care of the older girls also appeared to be generally well adjusted. By the time Skeels reported on their progress in 1966, most were married and were rearing children of their own who showed no intellectual or social deficits. Unfortunately, many of the children who had been left in the orphanage were still in some type of institutional setting. Few of them showed normal social and emotional development. Few were functioning as independent adults.

The good news from this and other studies is that many children who have been exposed to early social deprivation can catch up in their social and emotional development and lead normal adult lives if they receive individual attention and environmental stimulation (Landesman, 1990). The bad news is that society has not yet allocated the resources to give all children the opportunity to do so.

Child Abuse and Neglect

We have considered the results of rearing children in settings in which contact with parents is reduced or absent. But living with one's parents does not guarantee that a child will receive tender loving care. Sadly, there's no place like home—for violence, that is. ***Questions: What is the incidence of child abuse and neglect? What are their effects?*** Consider the following statistics from national surveys by Murray Straus and his colleagues (Straus & Gelles, 1990; Straus & Stewart, 1999):

- 55% of parents have slapped or spanked their children.
- 31% of parents have pushed, grabbed, or shoved their children.
- 10% have hit their children with an object.
- 3% have thrown something at their children.
- No more than 1% of parents have kicked or bitten their children or hit them with their fists; threatened their children with a knife or a gun; or actually used a knife or a gun on their children.

Physical abuse is more prevalent among poor parents and parents from the South (Straus & Stewart, 1999). Boys are more likely than girls to be hit, and the mother is more likely than the father to be the aggressor—perhaps because she spends more time with the children.

As many as 3 million American children are neglected or abused each year by their parents or caregivers (Herman-Giddens et al., 1999). About one in six of these experiences serious injury. Thousands of them die. More than 150,000 of the 3 million are sexually abused (Trickett & Putnam, 1993). However, researchers believe that many cases of child abuse and neglect go unreported, so that the actual incidences are much higher.

The U.S. Department of Health and Human Services recognizes six types of maltreatment of children:

- Physical abuse: actions causing pain and physical injury
- Sexual abuse: sexual molestation, exploitation, and intercourse
- Emotional abuse: actions impairing the child's emotional, social, or intellectual functioning
- Physical neglect: failure to provide adequate food, shelter, clothing, or medical care
- Emotional neglect: failure to provide adequate nurturance and emotional support
- Educational neglect: permitting or forcing the child to be truant

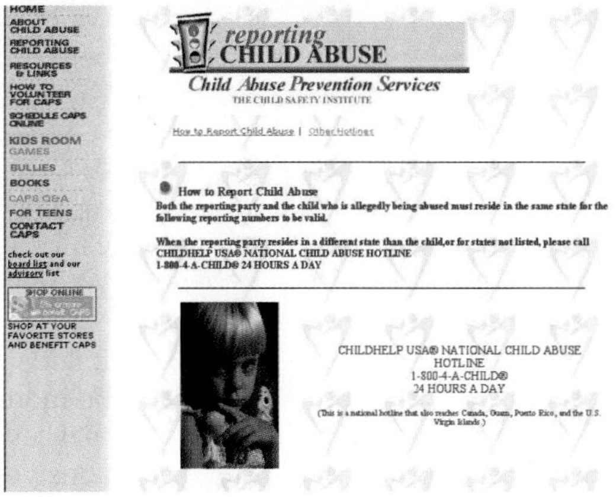

Courtesy CHILDHELP USA © National Child Abuse Hotline

Child Abuse

Nearly 3 million children in the United States are neglected or abused each year. More than half a million suffer serious injuries, more than 150,000 are sexually abused, and thousands die.

Physical neglect is more common than active physical abuse (Sondik, 2001). Although blatant abuse is more horrifying, more injuries, illnesses, and deaths result from neglect (Finkelhor & Dziuba-Leatherman, 1994; Sondik, 2001).

Sexual Abuse of Children

About 150,000 children are victims of sexual abuse each year. The sexual abuse of children can be difficult to detect or define (Haugaard, 2000), because adults interact with children in many ways that involve touching, and, sometimes, touching of the genital organs. For example, adults touch and rub children's bodies, including their genital organs, when they are bathing or changing them. They may (literally) sleep with their children and wander around in the nude near them. Most of these behavior patterns are innocent enough, but some adults fondle children's genital organs, kiss children in sexual ways, or actually have sexual intercourse with them. These behaviors clearly fit the definition of child sexual abuse.

Effects of Child Abuse

Abused children show a high incidence of personal and social problems and psychological disorders (Toth, Manly, & Cicchetti, 1992; Wagner, 1997). In general, abused children are less securely attached to their parents. They are less intimate with their peers, more aggressive, angry, and noncompliant than other children (DeAngelis, 1997; Parker & Herrera, 1996; Rothbart & Ahadi, 1994; Shields, Ryan, & Cicchetti, 2001). They rarely express positive emotions, have lower self-esteem, and show impaired cognitive functioning, leading to poorer performance in school (Shonk & Cicchetti, 2001). When they reach adulthood, they are more likely to act aggressively toward their intimate partners—their dates and their spouses (Malinosky-Rummell & Hansen, 1993). As they mature, maltreated children are also at greater risk for delinquency, academic failure, and substance abuse (Eckenrode, Laird, & Doris, 1993; Kendall-Tackett, Williams, & Finkelhor, 1993; Trickett & Putnam, 1993; Watkins & Bentovim, 1992).

There is no single concrete identifiable syndrome—cluster of symptoms—that indicates a history of physical abuse or neglect or sexual abuse (Saywitz et al., 2000). More generally speaking, however, there seems to be little doubt that victims of child sexual abuse develop a higher incidence of psychological and physical health problems than other children (Saywitz et al., 2000). Child sexual abuse, like physical abuse, also appears to have lingering effects on one's relationships in adulthood. For one thing, sexually abused children are more likely to engage in risky sexual behavior later in life (Noll, Trickett, & Putnam, 2000). Abusive experiences at the hands of adults also color children's expectation of other adults.

Causes of Child Abuse

A number of factors contribute to the probability that parents will abuse their children. They include situational stress, a history of child abuse in at least one of the parents' families of origin, lack of adequate coping and problem-solving skills, deficiency in child-rearing skills, unrealistic expectations of what a child should be able to do at a given developmental level, and substance abuse (Famularo, Kinscherff, & Fenton, 1992; Kaplan, 1991).

Stress has many sources, including such life changes as parental conflict and divorce or separation, the loss of a job, moving, and the birth of a new family member. Unemployment seems to be a particularly predisposing life change. Child abuse increases among the unemployed (Price, 1992; Straus & Smith, 1990; Wolfner & Gelles, 1993).

Stress is created by crying infants themselves (Green et al., 1987). Ironically, infants who are already in pain of some kind and relatively difficult to soothe may be more likely to be abused (Frodi, 1985). Abusive parents may find the cries of their infants to be particularly aversive, and so the infants' crying may precipitate abusive behavior (Crowe & Zeskind, 1992; Zeskind & Shingler, 1991). Children who act disobediently, inappropriately, or unresponsively also are at greater risk of abuse (Bugental, Blue, & Lewis, 1990; Trickett & Kuczynski, 1986). Why? Parents tend to become frustrated and irritated when their children show prolonged signs of distress or misbehavior. Abusive mothers are more likely than nonabusive mothers to assume that their children's misbehavior is intentional, even when it is not (Bauer & Twentyman, 1985). Within our culture, intentional misconduct is seen as more deserving of punishment than incidental misconduct. Abusive mothers also tend to believe that they have little control over their child's misbehavior (Bugental et al., 1989). Parents who abuse often have high standards of achievement for the child, but at the same time, they are dissatisfied with the child and don't enjoy parenting very much (Trickett et al., 1991).

A Closer Look

How Child Abuse May Set the Stage for Psychological Disorders in Adulthood

There is a significant correlation between child abuse and psychological disorders in adulthood. However, the causal connections remain somewhat clouded. But a study reported in the *Journal of the American Medical Association* suggests that two bodily systems pave the route from child abuse to psychological disorders in adulthood. The first is the endocrine system, which consists of ductless glands that release hormones directly into the bloodstream. We have seen how the sex hormones estrogen and testosterone stoke the development of the sexual organs and how estrogen and progesterone regulate the menstrual cycle. We have also seen how the pituitary hormones oxytocin and prolactin are involved in childbirth and breast-feeding. Other hormones—so-called stress hormones—are released when the body is under stress. And child abuse is a most prominent stressor. The second is the autonomic nervous system (ANS), which is of great interest to psychologists because it is intimately involved in stress reactions and negative emotions such as anxiety and fear.

Researchers assess the individual's responses to stress by means of the quantities of stress hormones in bodily fluids, such as blood or saliva. One such hormone is the pituitary hormone ACTH, which, in a sort of domino effect, stimulates the cortex (outer layer) of the adrenal glands to release corticosteroids such as cortisol. Corticosteroids increase resistance to stress in ways such as promoting muscle development and causing the liver to release stored sugar, which makes more energy available in emergencies. The sympathetic division of the ANS goes into overdrive under stress, as can be measured by the heart rate, the blood pressure, muscle tension, and sweating.

This particular study, conducted by Christine Heim and her colleagues (2000), recruited 49 women whose average age was 35. The sample was specifically selected to have high numbers of women who had suffered child abuse and who were currently depressed. In interviews, 27 of the recruits reported that they had experienced physical and/or sexual abuse in childhood, whereas the other 22 had not. And 23 of the group members were experiencing major depressive episodes at the time of the study, as compared with 26 who were not. All of the participants in the experiment were exposed to a stressor that other studies have shown to stimulate reactions of the endocrine system and ANS. The women were given the task of making a speech in front of strangers; moreover the speech would entail doing mental arithmetic. The women's levels of stress hormones and heart rates were measured while the women anticipated and made the speeches.

Results of the experiment are shown in Table 7.2, which reports the participants' blood levels of ACTH and cortisol and their heart rates. When we consider women who did not experience child abuse (Groups A and B), the presence of depression did not make a significant difference. Now consider the two groups of women who had been abused as children (Groups C

What of the role of failure of attachment in abuse? The parents of preterm children have more difficulty becoming attached to them (see Chapter 4). One reason may be that the early parent–infant relationship is interrupted by hospital procedures. Preterm children are more likely than their full-term counterparts to be abused (Crittenden & Ainsworth, 1989). With prematurity, of course, we are dealing with more than possible failures in attachment. Preterm children are also more likely to develop illnesses and other problems. As a consequence, they may cry more frequently and generally make more demands on their parents.

Abusive parenting tends to run in families (Ertem et al., 2000). Yet most individuals who were abused as children do not abuse their own children (Kaufman & Zigler, 1992). This fact is extremely important because many adults who were victims of child abuse are (unjustifiably) concerned that they are destined to abuse their own children. One study found that abused mothers who were able to break the cycle of abuse were more likely to have received emotional support from a nonabusive adult during childhood, to have participated in therapy at some point in their lives, and to have had a nonabusive and supportive mate (Egeland, Jacobovitz, & Sroufe, 1988).

Question: Why does child abuse run in families? There are a number of reasons (Belsky, 1993). Parents serve as role models for their children, of course. As noted by Murray Straus (1995), "Spanking teaches kids that when someone is doing something you don't like and they won't stop doing it, you hit them." If children grow up observing their parents using violence as a means of coping with stress and feelings of anger, they are less likely to learn to diffuse anger through techniques such as humor, verbal expression of feelings, reasoning, or even counting to 10 to let the anger pass.

Exposure to violence in their own homes may lead some children to accept family violence as a norm when they become adults. They may see little or nothing wrong in it. Certainly, there are any number of "justifications" they can find for

and D). When they were subjected to the stressor, they were significantly more likely to show high blood levels of ACTH and cortisol than women who had not been abused as children (women in groups A and B). The women in Group D showed the greatest hormonal and cardiac responses to the stressor, and these were women who (1) had been abused as children and (2) were undergoing a major depressive episode. The researchers conclude that child abuse leads to more reactive endocrine and autonomic nervous systems and that a combination of abuse and depression makes the body most reactive to stress.

These stress reactions have the effect of exhausting the body. Women who were abused as children are apparently carrying a historic burden that makes current burdens all the more unbearable.

TABLE 7.2 *Responses of Women With or Without a History of Child Abuse to a Stressor*

	Women Who Are Not Experiencing a Major Depressive Episode	Women Who Are Experiencing a Major Depressive Episode
Women With No History of Child Abuse	**GROUP A—12 WOMEN** **Endocrine System:** ACTH peak: 4.7 parts/liter Cortisol peak: 339 parts/liter **Autonomic Nervous System:** Heart rate: 78.4/minute	**GROUP B—10 WOMEN** **Endocrine System:** ACTH peak: 5.3 parts/liter Cortisol peak: 337 parts/liter **Autonomic Nervous System:** Heart rate: 83.8/minute
Women With a History of Child Abuse	**GROUP C—14 WOMEN** **Endocrine System:** ACTH peak: 9.3 parts/liter Cortisol peak: 359 parts/liter **Autonomic Nervous System:** Heart rate: 82.2/minute	**GROUP D—13 WOMEN** **Endocrine System:** ACTH peak: 12.1 parts/liter Cortisol peak: 527 parts/liter **Autonomic Nervous System:** Heart rate: 89.7/minute

violence—if they are seeking them. One is the age-old adage, "Spare the rod, spoil the child." Another is the belief that they are hurting their children "for their own good"—to discourage behavior that is likely to get them into trouble.

Still another "justification" of child abuse is the sometimes cloudy distinction between the occasional swat on the rear end and spanking or other types of repeated hitting. Child abusers may argue that all parents hit their children (which is not true), and they may claim not to understand why outsiders are making such a fuss about their private family behavior. Child abusers who come from families in which they were subjected to abuse also may be more likely to have the (incorrect) perspective that "everyone does it."

The patterns of attachment of the perpetrators of child abuse have also been studied. One study, for example, found that nonfamilial perpetrators of sexual child abuse were significantly less likely to have a secure attachment style in their relationships (Jamieson & Marshall, 2000).

In any event, child abuse must be conceptualized and dealt with as a crime of violence. Whether or not child abusers happen to be victims of abuse themselves, child abusers are criminals and their children must be protected from them.

A Closer Look

What to Do if You Think a Child You Know Has Been the Victim of Sexual Abuse

What can you do if you suspect that a child has been victimized by sexual abuse? The American Psychological Association (APA) suggests the following guidelines:

- Give the child a safe environment in which to talk to you or another trusted adult. Encourage the child to talk about what he or she has experienced, but be careful to not suggest events to him or her that may not have happened. Guard against displaying emotions that would influence the child's telling of the information.
- Reassure the child that he or she did nothing wrong.
- Seek mental health assistance for the child.
- Arrange for a medical examination for the child. Select a medical provider who has experience in examining children and identifying sexual and physical trauma. It may be necessary to explain to the child the difference between a medical examination and the abuse incident.
- Be aware that many states have laws requiring that persons who know or have a reason to suspect that a child has been sexually abused must report that abuse to either local law enforcement officials or child protection officials. In all 50 states, medical personnel, mental health professionals, teachers, and law enforcement personnel are required by law to report suspected abuse.

The APA also lists the following resources as places to go to for help:

American Professional Society on the Abuse of Children
407 South Dearborn
Suite 1300
Chicago, IL 60605
(312) 554-0166
http://www.apsac.org/

National Center for Missing and Exploited Children
Charles B. Wang International Children's Building
699 Prince Street
Alexandria, VA 22314-3175
24-hour hotline: 1-800-THE-LOST
http://www.missingkids.com/

Child Help USA
15757 North 78th Street
Scottsdale, AZ 85260
1-800-4-A-CHILD
http://www.childhelpusa.org/

National Clearinghouse on Child Abuse and Neglect Information
U.S. Department of Health and Human Services
P.O. Box 1182
Washington, DC 20013
1-800-FYI-3366
http://www.calib.com/nccanch/

Prevent Child Abuse America
332 S. Michigan Avenue
Suite 1600
Chicago, IL 60604-4357
1-800-CHILDREN
http://www.childabuse.org/

Source: Guidelines from Office of Public Communications, American Psychological Association, 750 First Street, NE, Washington, DC 20002-4242. (202) 336-5700. **http://www.apa.org/releases/sexabuse/todo.html**

What to Do

Dealing with child abuse is a frustrating task. Social agencies and the courts can find it as difficult to distinguish between spanking and abuse as many abusers do. Because of the belief in this country that parents have the right to rear their children as they wish, police and the courts have also historically tried to avoid involvement in domestic quarrels and family disputes. However, the alarming incidence of child abuse has spawned new efforts at detection and prevention. Many states require helping professionals such as psychologists and physicians to report any suspicion of child abuse. Many states legally require anyone who suspects child abuse to report it to authorities.

A number of techniques have been developed to help prevent child abuse. One approach focuses on strengthening parenting skills among the general population (Altepeter & Walker, 1992). Parent-education classes in high school are an example of this approach.

Another approach targets groups at high risk for abuse, such as poor, single teen mothers (Kaufman & Zigler, 1992; Roberts et al., 1991). In some programs, for example, home visitors help the new mother develop skills in parenting and home management.

A third technique focuses on presenting information about abuse and providing support to families. For instance, many locales have child-abuse hotlines. Private citizens who suspect child abuse may call for advice. Parents who are having difficulty controlling aggressive impulses toward their children are encouraged to call. Some hotlines are serviced by groups such as Parents Anonymous, whose members have had similar difficulties and may help callers diffuse feelings of anger in less harmful ways.

Another helpful measure is increased publicity on the dimensions of the child-abuse problem. The public may also need more education about where an occasional swat on the behind ends and child abuse begins. Perhaps the format for such education could be something like, "If you are doing such and such, make no mistake about it—you are abusing your child."

Reflect

What would you do if you learned that the child of a neighbor was being abused? What would you do if you were a teacher and learned that a child in your class was being abused?

Autism—Alone Among the Crowd

> Peter nursed eagerly, sat and walked at the expected ages. Yet some of his behavior made us vaguely uneasy. He never put anything in his mouth. Not his fingers nor his toys—nothing. . . .
>
> More troubling was the fact that Peter didn't look at us, or smile, and wouldn't play the games that seemed as much a part of babyhood as diapers. He rarely laughed, and when he did, it was at things that didn't seem funny to us. He didn't cuddle, but sat upright in my lap, even when I rocked him. But children differ and we were content to let Peter be himself. We thought it hilarious when my brother, visiting us when Peter was 8 months old, observed "That kid has no social instincts, whatsoever." Although Peter was a first child, he was not isolated. I frequently put him in his playpen in front of the house, where the schoolchildren stopped to play with him as they passed. He ignored them, too.
>
> It was Kitty, a personality kid, born two years later, whose responsiveness emphasized the degree of Peter's difference. When I went into her room for the late feeding, her little head bobbed up and she greeted me with a smile that reached from her head to her toes. And the realization of that difference chilled me more than the wintry bedroom.
>
> Peter's babbling had not turned into speech by the time he was 3. His play was solitary and repetitious. He tore paper into long thin strips, bushel baskets of it every day. He spun the lids from my canning jars and became upset if we tried to divert him. Only rarely could I catch his eye, and then saw his focus change from me to the reflection in my glasses. . . .
>
> [Peter's] adventures into our suburban neighborhood had been unhappy. He had disregarded the universal rule that sand is to be kept in sandboxes, and the children themselves had punished him. He walked around a sad and solitary figure, always carrying a toy airplane, a toy he never played with. At that time, I had not heard the

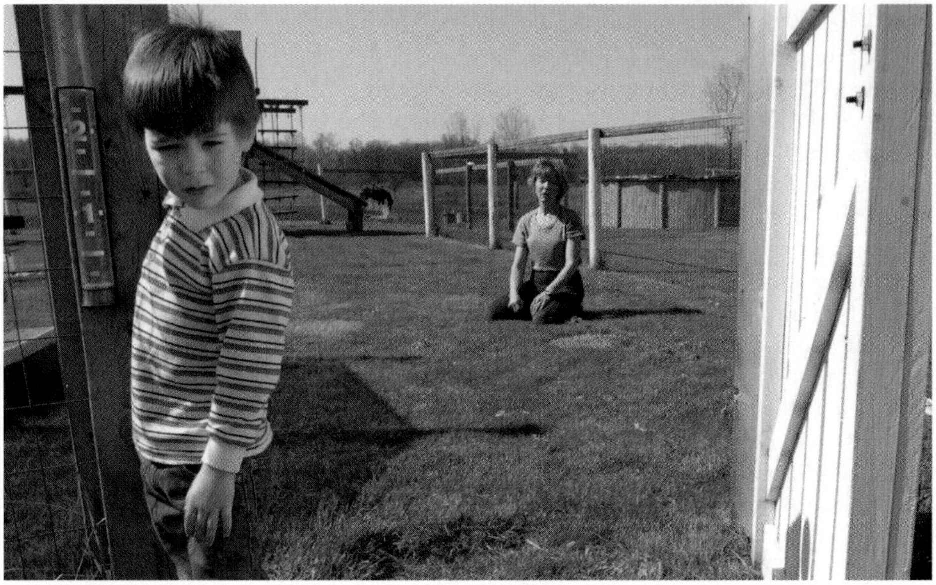

Lori Furton, China Township, Mich. Photo, Melissa Wawzysko/Times Herald-Port Huron, Mich.

■ **Autism**

The most poignant feature of autism is the child's utter aloneness. Autism is rather rare, but more common in boys than girls. Symptoms include communication problems, intolerance of any change, and ritualistic or stereotypical behavior.

word that was to dominate our lives, to hover over every conversation, to sit through every meal beside us. That word was autism.

—Adapted from Eberhardy, 1967

Some children fail to develop attachments to others. A number of them, like Peter, experience a psychological disorder known as autism. ***Question: What is autism?*** The word autism derives from the Greek *autos,* meaning "self." (An *automobile* is a self-driven method of moving from place to place.) **Autism,** or *autistic disorder,* strikes 4 to 5 children in 10,000 and usually becomes evident between the ages of 18 and 30 months (American Psychiatric Association, 2000; Rapin, 1997). It is four to five times more common among boys than girls. Perhaps the most poignant feature of autistic disorder is the child's utter aloneness. Autistic children do not show interest in social interaction, and their attachment to others is weak or absent. They may avoid all eye contact.

Other features of autism include communication problems, intolerance of change, and ritualistic or stereotypical behavior (see Table 7.3). Parents of autistic children frequently report that they were "good babies." This usually means that they made few demands. However, as autistic children develop, they tend to shun affectionate contacts such as hugging, cuddling, and kissing (Borden & Ollendick, 1992).

Development of speech lags. There is little babbling and communicative gesturing during the first year. Autistic children may show **mutism, echolalia,** and pronoun reversal, referring to themselves as "you" or "he." About half of autistic children use some form of language by middle childhood, but their use of speech in social interactions is unusual and troubled (Stone & Caro-Martinez, 1990; Volden & Lord, 1991).

Autistic children become bound by ritual in their demands on others and in their own behavior. Even slight changes in routines or in physical aspects of the environment may cause extreme distress. This feature of autistic disorder is termed "preservation of sameness." When familiar objects are moved even slightly from their usual places, children with autism may throw tantrums or cry until they are restored. They may insist on eating the same food every day. Autistic children also show deficits in peer play, imaginative play, imitation skills, and emotional expression (Stone & Lemanek, 1990; Yirmiya et al., 1992).

Some children with autistic disorder mutilate themselves, even as they cry out in pain. They may bang their heads, slap their faces, bite their hands and shoulders, or pull out their hair.

Question: What are the origins of autism?

Reflect

Have you known an autistic child? How did his or her behavior compare to that described in this text?

autism A developmental disorder characterized by extreme aloneness, communication problems, intolerance of change, and ritualistic behavior. Also called autistic disorder.

mutism Inability or refusal to speak.

echolalia The automatic repetition of sounds or words.

TABLE 7.3 *Features of Autistic Disorder*

A. An autistic child displays a combination of features from the following groups:

(1) Impaired social interaction	1. Shows impairment in the nonverbal behaviors such as facial expressiveness, posture, gestures, and eye contact that normally regulate social interaction 2. Does not develop age-appropriate peer relationships 3. Fails to express pleasure in the happiness of other people 4. Does not show social or emotional reciprocity (give-and-take)
(2) Impaired communication	1. Shows delay in development of spoken language and in use of gestures 2. Lacks ability to initiate or sustain conversation even when speech is adequate 3. Shows abnormalities in form or content of speech (e.g., stereotyped or repetitive speech, as in echolalia; idiosyncratic use of words; speaking about the self in the second or third person—using "you" or "he" to mean "I") 4. Does not show spontaneous social or imaginative (make-believe) play
(3) Restricted, repetitive, and stereotyped behavior	1. Shows restricted range of interests 2. Insists on routines (e.g., always uses same route to go from one place to another) 3. Shows stereotyped movements (e.g., hand flicking, head banging, rocking, spinning) 4. Shows preoccupation with parts of objects (e.g., repetitive spinning of wheels of toy car) or unusual attachments to objects (e.g., carrying a piece of string)

B. Onset occurs prior to the age of 3 through display of abnormal functioning in at least one of the following: social behavior, communication, or imaginative play.

Source: Adapted from the DSM–IV–TR (American Psychiatric Association, 2000).

Causes of Autism

Psychoanalytic and learning theorists have argued that children become autistic in response to rejection by, or lack of adequate reinforcement from, their parents. From this perspective, autistic behavior patterns shut out the cold outside world. But research evidence makes it abundantly clear that deviant child-rearing practices do not account for autism. The parents of autistic children do not exhibit specific deficits in child-rearing practices, nor do they show unusual personality traits (Volkmar, 1991; Borden & Ollendick, 1992).

Various lines of evidence suggest a key role for biological factors in autism (Insel, O'Brien, & Leckman, 1999). A role for genetic mechanisms is suggested by kinship studies (Gutknecht, 2001; Pickles et al., 2000; Piven, 1999; Plomin, 2001b). For example, the concordance (agreement) rates for autistic disorder are about 60% among pairs of identical (MZ) twins, who fully share their genetic heritage, as compared with about 10% for pairs of fraternal (DZ) twins, whose genetic codes only overlap by 50% (Plomin, Owen, & McGuffin, 1994). Researchers also suspect that multiple genes are involved in autistic disorder and interact with other factors, environmental and/or biological.

Researchers are also investigating possible patterns of neurological involvement in autistic disorder. For one thing, many autistic children have abnormal brain wave patterns or seizures. Brain scans show structural differences in the brains of children and adults with autistic disorder, including enlarged ventricles that suggest a loss of brain cells (Haznedar et al., 1997; Piven et al., 1995, 1997). Other researchers find that, compared to others, children and adults with autistic disorder show fewer receptors in the brain for neurotransmitters such as acetylcholine (Perry et al., 2001); unusual patterns of activation in the motor region of the cerebral cortex (Mueller et al., 2001); less activity in various areas of the brain—including the frontal and temporal lobes and the anterior cingulate gyrus (Ohnishi et al., 2000; Shu, Jia, & Zhang, 2001). Yet other researchers suggest that some children with autism may have brain damage, whereas others do not, and the origins of the disorder are different in each case (e.g., DeLong, 1999).

Question: What can be done to help autistic children?

Treatment

Treatment for autism today is mainly based on principles of learning, although investigation of biological approaches is also under way.

Operant conditioning methods (that is, the systematic use of reinforcements and punishments) have been used to increase the child's ability to attend to others, to play with other children, and to discourage self-mutilation. Techniques like extinction (withholding reinforcement following a response) are sometimes effective for behaviors like head-banging, but observers may have to ignore more than a thousand incidents to eliminate the response. Repetitive behavior patterns like rocking and self-injurious behaviors may be maintained by internal reinforcers such as increased stimulation. Therefore, the withdrawal of social reinforcement may have little if any effect.

Use of aversive stimulation such as spanking and electric shock is more effective than extinction. Brief bursts of mild but painful electric shock rapidly eliminate self-mutilation (Lovaas, 1977). The use of electric shock raises serious moral, ethical, and legal concerns, but Lovaas has countered that failure to eliminate self-injurious behavior places the child at yet greater risk and denies the child the opportunity to participate in other kinds of therapy.

Reflect

When I was discussing Lovaas's methods for treating autistic children—slapping them to gain their attention and shocking them to prevent them from mutilating themselves—one student commented, "There's nothing new about child abuse." Do Lovaas's methods strike you as forms of child abuse? Explain.

Because autistic children show behavioral deficits, behavior modification is used to help them develop new behavior. New behaviors are maintained by reinforcements, so autistic children, who often respond to people as they would to a piece of furniture, need to be taught to accept people as reinforcers (Drasgow, Halle, & Phillips, 2001). People can be established as reinforcers by pairing praise (social reinforcement) with primary reinforcers like food. Then praise can be used to shape toileting behaviors, speech, and social play.

Some learning-based treatment programs have yielded promising results. The most effective programs focus a great deal of individualized instruction on behavioral, educational, and communication deficits (Rapin, 1997). In a classic study conducted by O. Ivar Lovaas at UCLA (Lovaas, Smith, & McEachin, 1989), autistic children received more than 40 hours of one-to-one behavior modification each week for at least 2 years. Significant intellectual and educational gains were reported for 9 of the 19 children (47%) in the program. The children who improved achieved normal scores on intelligence tests and succeeded in the first grade. Only 2% of an untreated control group achieved similar gains. Treatment gains were maintained at a follow-up at the age of 11 (McEachin, Smith, & Lovaas, 1993).

Biological approaches for the treatment of autism are under study. One line of research has shown that drugs that enhance serotonin activity (such as those usually used to treat depression) can help prevent self-injury, aggressive outbursts, depression and anxiety, and repetitive thoughts and behavior (Aman, Arnold, & Armstrong, 1999; Hellings, 1999). Other research has focused on drugs normally used to treat schizophrenia—the "major tranquilizers"—which block the utilization of the neurotransmitter dopamine (Volkmar, 2001). Despite these drugs' ability to help with active symptoms of autism—for example, repetitive motor behavior (such as rocking), aggression, hyperactivity, and self-injury—it has not been shown that they lead to consistent relief of the cognitive and language problems we find in children with autism.

Autistic behavior generally continues into adulthood to one degree or another. Yet some autistic children go on to achieve college degrees and function independently (Rapin, 1997). Others need continuous treatment, which may include institutionalized care. Even the highest-functioning autistic adults remain deficient in their social and communication skills and show a limited range of interests and activities (American Psychiatric Association, 2000).

We have been examining the development of attachment and some of the circumstances that may interfere with its development. In recent years, a lively debate has sprung up concerning the effects of day care on children's attachment, as well as on their social and cognitive development. Let us turn now to a consideration of these issues.

Review

(16) The Harlows found that rhesus infants reared in isolation later (sought or avoided?) contact with other monkeys. (17) Spitz noted that many institutionalized children appear to develop a syndrome characterized by _________ and depression. (18) Studies by Yarrow and his colleagues suggest that deficiencies in (sensory stimulation or love?) are mainly responsible for the problems of institutionalized children. (19) The (minority or majority?) of parents in the United States have slapped or spanked their children. (20) Relatively more deaths occur from (physical abuse or neglect?). (21) The study by Heim and her colleagues suggests that child abuse sets the stage for problems later in life by raising levels of _________ hormones. (22) Children with _________ do not show interest in social interaction, have communication problems, are intolerant of change, and display repetitive behavior. (23) There (is or is not?) evidence for a role for heredity in autism.

Pulling It Together: What are some of the various hypotheses as to why child abuse tends to run in families?

Day Care

Looking for a phrase that can strike fear in the hearts of millions of Americans? Try "day care." Only a relatively small percentage of American families still fits the conventional model that places the husband at the head of the table as the breadwinner and the wife as the, well, "housewife." We may no longer use the oppressive term *housewife*, but we do speak of full-time *homemakers*. Nowadays the great majority of mothers, including the majority of mothers of infants, are in the workforce (Erel, Oberman, & Yirmiya, 2000; U.S. Bureau of the Census, 2000). As a result, millions of American parents are obsessed with trying to find proper day care.

When both parents spend the day on the job, the children must be taken care of by others, although many older children take care of themselves after school until their parents come home. Studies of children at least 9 years of age who care for themselves after school have found no significant problems on several measures of psychological, social, and intellectual functioning (Berman et al., 1992; Diamond, Kataria, & Messer, 1989; Galambos & Maggs, 1991; Vandell & Ramanan, 1991; Woodard & Fine, 1991).

But what of younger children whose care is entrusted to others while their parents are at work? ***Questions: Does day care affect children's bonds of attachment with their parents? Does it affect their social and cognitive development?*** In this section, we examine different types of day-care arrangements and then consider the effects of day care on the child's development.

What Is Day Care Like?

There are four major types of day care: group day care, family day care, in-home care, and care by relatives outside the immediate family. In group day care, children receive care in a nursery school or day-care center that may be private but is frequently affiliated with a university, church, housing project, or community agency. Family day care is provided by parents who take the children of others into their homes. In a number of states, people who offer family day care must be licensed. In-home care (baby-sitting) is care in the child's home by a nonrelative. Finally, relatives may look after the child either in their own home or the child's home.

Even when the mother is employed, the most common arrangement for infants and toddlers is to be cared for by one of their parents. The parents may work alternate shifts in order to share child-care responsibilities. Family day care is the second most common arrangement for infants and toddlers. Group day care is the most popular form of child care for older preschoolers.

Children's experiences in day care vary. Some children are placed in centers or day-care homes for a few hours a week, and others for the entire day, 5 days a week. Some day-care centers or homes have an adult caregiver for every three children, and others place as many as 12 children in the care of one adult. Infants require more care than older children. Thus, a caregiver in a day-care center typically is assigned no more than 4 or 5 infants under 18 months of age, but might be given responsibility for 10 or 11 children who are 3 years old. The purposes and

A Closer Look

Finding Child Care You (and Your Child) Can Live With

It's normal to be anxious. You are thinking about selecting a day-care center or a private home for your precious child, and there are risks. So be a little anxious, but it may not be necessary to be overwhelmed. You can go about the task with a checklist that can guide your considerations. Above all: Don't be afraid to open your mouth and ask questions, even pointed, challenging questions. If the day-care provider doesn't like questions, or if the provider does not answer them satisfactorily, *you want your child someplace else.* So much for the preamble. Here's the checklist.

Reflect

What would be the most important factor in your selection of a day-care center? Why?

1. Does the day-care center have a license? Who issued the license? What did the day-care center have to do to acquire the license? (You can also call the licensing agency to obtain the answer to the last question.)
2. How many children are cared for by the center? How many caregivers are there? Remember this nursery rhyme:

   There was an old woman who lived in a shoe.

   She had so many children she didn't know what to do.

   All right, the rhyme is sexist and ageist and maybe even shoe-ist. But it suggests that it is important for caregivers not to be overburdened by too many children, especially infants. It is desirable to have at least one caregiver for every four infants, although fewer workers are required for older children.
3. How were the caregivers hired? How were they trained? Did the center check references? What were the minimum educational credentials? Did the center check them out? Do the caregivers have any education or training in the behavior and

personnel of day-care settings also vary. Some programs are intended to provide early cognitive stimulation to prepare children for entry into elementary school. Others focus on custodial care and entertainment. Some have college-educated personnel. Others have caregivers who function on the basis of life experience or specific training. Standards for the licensing of day-care centers and homes vary from locale to locale. Parents, therefore, need to determine the adequacy of the day-care setting they are considering for their children.

Most parents want day-care centers and homes to provide more than the basics of food, warmth, and security. They want the caregivers in these settings to stimulate their children intellectually, to provide a variety of toys and games, and to provide successful peer interactions and experience in relating to adults other than family members.

What should parents look for when they are in the process of selecting a day-care center or family day-care home for their child? Some suggestions are offered in the nearby "A Closer Look" feature.

How Does Day Care Affect Bonds of Attachment?

Many parents wonder whether day care will affect their children's attachment to them. After all, at a tender age, the child will be spending more hours away from them than with them. During these periods, their child's needs will be met by outsiders. Parents also have mixed feelings about day care. If they had the time and money, most parents would prefer to care for their children personally. And so parents often feel some guilt about placing their children in day care.

Are such concerns valid? The issue has been hotly debated. Some studies have found that infants who are in day care full-time (more than 20 hours a week) are somewhat more likely than children without day-care experience to show insecure attachment in the Strange Situation (Baydar & Brooks-Gunn, 1991; Belsky & Rovine, 1988). Some psychologists have concluded from these studies that a mother who works full-time puts her infant at risk for developing emotional insecurity (Belsky, 1990a, 1990b). Others feel that these results may be interpreted quite differently (Clarke-Stewart 1989; Lamb, Sternberg, & Ketterlinus, 1992; Thompson, 1991b).

needs of children? Do the caregivers seem to be proactive and attempt to engage the children in activities and educational experiences? Or are they inactive unless a child cries or screams? Sometimes it is impossible to find qualified day-care workers, because they tend to be paid poorly—often the minimum wage, and sometimes less.

4. Is the environment child-proofed and secure? Can children stick their fingers in electric sockets? Are toys and outdoor equipment in good condition? Are sharp objects within children's reach? Can anybody walk in off the street? What is the history of children being injured or otherwise victimized in this day-care center? Is the day-care provider hesitant about answering any of these questions?
5. When are meals served? Snacks? What do they consist of? Will your child find it appetizing or go hungry? Some babies are placed in day care at 6 months or younger, and parents will need to know what formulas are used.
6. Is it possible for you to meet the caregivers who will be taking care of your child? If not, why not?
7. With what children will your child interact and play?
8. Does the center seem to have an enriching environment? Do you see books, toys, games, and educational objects strewn about?
9. Are there facilities and objects like swings and tricycles that will enhance your child's physical and motor development? Are children supervised when they play with these things or are they pretty much left on their own?
10. Does the center's schedule coincide with your needs?
11. Is the center located conveniently for you? Does it appear to be in a safe location or else to have adequate security arrangements? (Let me emphasize that you have a right to ask whether neighborhood or other people can walk in unannounced to where the children are. It's a fair question. You can also ask what they would do if a stranger broke into the place.)
12. Are parents permitted to visit unannounced?
13. Do you like the overall environment and feel of the center or home? Listen to your "gut."

One key factor is that the Strange Situation may be less stressful for children of employed mothers than for those with unemployed mothers and, therefore, may be a less valid indicator of attachment for them. Infants whose mothers work encounter daily separation from and reunions with their mothers. Young children adapt to repeated separations from their mothers (Field, 1991c). Therefore, infants whose mothers work may be less distressed by her departure in the Strange Situation and less likely to seek her out when she returns. A second point to keep in mind is that the likelihood of insecure attachment is not much greater in infants placed in day care than in those cared for in the home; in fact, most infants in both groups are securely attached (Clarke-Stewart, 1989; Lamb, Sternberg, & Prodromidis, 1992).

How Does Day Care Influence Social and Cognitive Development?

Day care has mixed effects on children's social and cognitive development. Infants with day-care experience are more peer-oriented and play at higher developmental levels than do home-reared babies. Day-care children are also more likely to share their toys. They are more independent, self-confident, outgoing, and affectionate as well as more helpful and cooperative with peers and adults (Clarke-Stewart, 1991; Field, 1991b). Participation in day care also is associated with better school performance during the elementary school years, especially for children from low-income families (Andersson, 1992; Caughy, DiPietro, & Strobino, 1994; Vandell & Ramanan, 1992).

Consider a study funded by the National Institute on Child Health and Human Development. It compared the development of children in "high-quality" day care with that of children in low-quality day care and that of children reared in the home by their mothers. The quality of the day care was defined in terms of the richness of the learning environment (availability of toys, books, and other materials), the ratio of caregivers to children (high quality meant more caregivers), the amount of individual attention received by the child (more was better), and the extent to which caregivers talked to the children and asked them questions (again, more was considered better). The researchers found high-quality day care resulted in scores on tests of language and cognitive skills that rivaled those of the children reared in the home by their mothers (Azar, 1997). A study carried out in Sweden found that children placed in high-quality day care actually fared better on tests of language skills and math than children who were reared in the home by their mothers (Broberg et al., 1997). It may thus be that we cannot come to any overall conclusions about the effects of day care on social and cognitive development. It appears that high-quality day care enhances the development of social and cognitive skills, whereas low-quality day care may be problematic.

Yet some studies find that children placed in day care are less cooperative and more aggressive toward peers and adults than children who are reared in the home by their mothers. For example, Jay Belsky and his colleagues (2001) found that once children are in school, about 17% of those who had spent more than 30 hours per week in day care were rated by teachers, caregivers, and mothers as being aggressive toward other children. This compares with 6% of the children who had spent less than 10 hours per week in day care. The Belsky group found that children with extensive experience in day care are also more likely to be cruel, explosive, and argumentative. The researchers followed more than 1,300 children from 10 cities for 10 years.

Allison Clarke-Stewart (1989, 1990) suggests that "aggression" and "noncompliance" are sometimes indicative of independence and not of maladjustment. Put another way, children with day-care experience may be more likely to think for themselves and want their own way.

There is yet another possibility. Studies of children in full-time day care or home care involve children whose parents had already chosen whether or not to use day care. It could be that preexisting personality differences in the children played a role in influencing parents to place them, or not to place them, in day care. Perhaps parents with more aggressive and less cooperative children are more highly motivated to use day care. Remember that the studies on day care have been correlational and not experimental. Infants have not been assigned at random to day care or home care. And so one must consider the possibility that any group differences preexisted and were not the result of day care.

Even if day care sometimes fosters aggressiveness and lower compliance, these outcomes are by no means inevitable. The research also finds that children who attend better-quality day-care centers and homes are more socially competent (for example, more considerate and friendly) than children who attend lower-quality day-care centers or who are cared for in homes (Howes, Phillips, & Whitebook, 1992; Kontos, 1993; Zaslow, Rabinovich, & Suwalsky, 1991).

Developing in the New Millennium

The Child Care H-Bomb of 2001

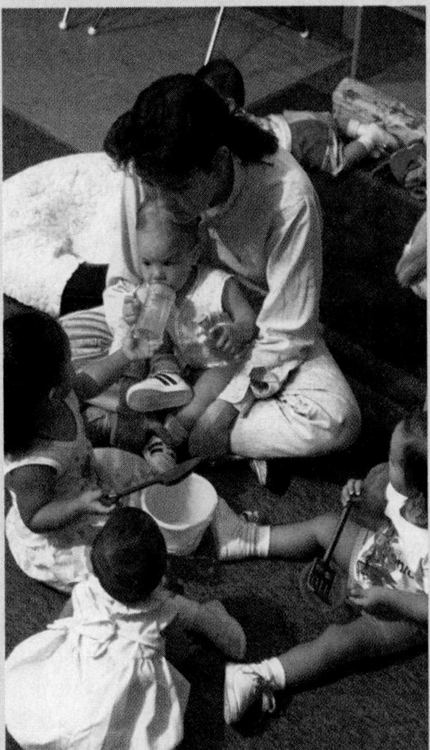

© Bob Daemmrich/Stock, Boston/PictureQuest

Children in Day Care

Day care often has a positive influence on children's social and cognitive development. Children with day-care experience are more helpful and cooperative with other children and adults, and they are more likely to share their toys. On the other hand, research also suggests that children in day care are more likely to be aggressive than children cared for in the home. For many millions of American families, day care is a necessity and not an option. The question then becomes, How can parents and child-care workers obtain the positive benefits of day care for children and mitigate—or eliminate—the negative?

This is the new millennium, and mothers are nearly as likely as fathers to work. The great majority of mothers are in the workforce, including more than half of those with infants under 1 year of age. Day care is no luxury; it's a necessity. Most families can't get by on one income.

For decades parents have had to put their trust in some form of child care or day care, and most have been told repeatedly that their children would get by just fine and might even benefit from "high-quality" day care. So imagine the waves of anxiety and guilt that hit parents when they learned, in 2001, of the results of the largest and most authoritative long-term study of child care in the United States that had been done until that time (Belsky et al., 2001). One of the findings of the study from the National Institute of Child Health and Human Development was that the more time preschoolers spent in child care, the more likely they were to display behavioral problems in kindergarten. The more time spent away from their mothers, the more likely the children were to be rated as defiant, aggressive, and disobedient once they got to kindergarten. Seventeen percent of children who were in child care for more than 30 hours a week received higher scores on rating items like "gets in lots of fight," "cruelty," "talking too much," "explosive behavior," "argues a lot," and "demands a lot of attention." Only 6% of children who were in child care for less than 10 hours a week had these problems. The finding held regardless of the background of the child or the quality or type of child care the children received. It held for African American and European American children, for boys and for girls, for children whose parents were affluent or poor. Children who were cared for in traditional day-care settings, by a grandmother, by a nanny, even by their fathers received the troublesome ratings. It appeared that Mom was the only answer.

Good News, Too

The research findings sent shudders through millions of American homes. Nevertheless, the study also held good news for working parents. For example, it found that children who are enrolled in

Review

(24) The (minority or majority?) of mothers in the United States work outside the home. (25) Most infants placed in day care are (securely or insecurely?) attached to their mothers. (26) Infants with day-care experience play at (higher or lower?) developmental levels than do home-reared babies. (27) Children whose day-care providers spend time talking to them and asking them questions achieve (low or high?) scores on tests of cognitive and language ability. (28) Belsky and his colleagues found that once children are in school, those who had spent more time in day care were rated by teachers, caregivers, and mothers as being (more or less?) aggressive toward other children.

Pulling It Together: What are some different ways of interpreting the finding that children who spend more time in day care tend to be more aggressive than other children?

Developing in the New Millennium *(continued)*

high-quality child care show cognitive benefits as compared with children who are in lower-quality day care or who spend more time in the home with their mothers. For example, they perform better on tests of memory, language, and knowledge.

Although the study found a positive correlation between time spent away from mothers and aggression, disobedience, and defiance in kindergarten, the reasons for the behavioral problems were not clear. For example, was it actually the time spent away from mothers that brought on the problems, or did the problems stem from other factors such as the stresses encountered by families who need to get by on two incomes? The researchers also had to admit that they did not know whether the problem behavior would continue as the children moved into higher grades. Most of them cautioned against reading too much into the study, not in the least because most of the children's behavior fell within the normal range; even most of the aggressive behavior was not out of bounds.

The government-sponsored research project, widely considered the most massive and authoritative of its kind in the nation, started in 1991. The researchers went from room to room along hospital corridors, asking new mothers to participate in a study of child development. More than 1,000 of the original mothers in 10 cities remain in the study, and the researchers have closely followed the children ever since. Most of the them were in fourth grade when the "hydrogen bomb" was dropped. The investigators collect data by visiting with the children's parents, having them complete personality tests and checklists. They also observe the children in day-care centers and in the classroom. They interview their day-care providers and their teachers. And, of course, they apply complex statistical analyses to the data they obtain, trying to figure out what is related to what, and what leads to what.

Despite the rigor of the research, it still evoked an animated and sometimes outraged reaction from some women's advocates. California State Senator Jackie Speier, an advocate of increased funding for day care, remarked: "It's like just yank every woman out of the job and tell her to get back in her house and take care of her kids. We are living in the 21st century. Everyone's got to get over that."

On the other hand, more conservative observers, like John Fugatt of the Christian Coalition of California, said "It is better in the early years for kids to have a mom at home if at all possible. Why would you want to pay someone who doesn't care as much about your child as you do? You know what your child's needs are and can focus on those needs rather than someone who is watching eight to 10 kids and doesn't give them individual attention."

Some researchers, like Virginia Allhusen of the University of California at Irvine, suggested that observers avoid overreacting in either direction: "We can't tell parents, 'Oh, don't worry, you can wash your hands of the responsibility of looking at where your kids spend their days.' But at the same time, it's not such a cause for alarm that we need to tell parents 'Quit your job immediately and stay home with your kids.'"

Researchers Can Disagree, Too

At various conferences, the researchers themselves argued back and forth about the data and the interpretation. Jay Belsky of the University of London, the lead researcher, made the politically incorrect recommendation that families decrease the amount of time that their children spend in child care. It should be noted that women's advocates have blasted Belsky over the years for his critical views on child care.

But another investigator, Sarah Friedman, a psychologist at the National Institute of Child Health and Human Development, disagreed. She pointed out that parents who work fewer hours and spend more time with their children bring in less money. Low family income is a source of stress that diminishes the quality of family life and also hurts children. Moreover, having women surrender their jobs and remain in the home also deprives them of the intellectual and social rewards of work, which may depress them—another outcome that is bad for the children. "You may solve one problem by cutting hours in child care, but create other problems that are not good for children," she said. She noted that alternate solutions include training caregivers to foster children's social skills and help prevent behavioral problems.

California State Senator Liz Figueroa, who has worked to support and train teachers in government-supported child-care programs, remarked: "Most of us know that our children are going to do better if they stay home with a parent. But that isn't the reality.

Emotional Development

Emotions color our lives. We are green with envy, red with anger, blue with sorrow. Positive emotions such as love can fill our days with pleasure. Negative emotions such as fear, depression, and anger can fill us with dread and make each day a chore.

Question: What are emotions? An **emotion** is a state of feeling that has physiological, situational, and cognitive components. Physiologically, when emotions are strong, our hearts may beat more rapidly, and our muscles may tense. Situationally, we may feel fear in the presence of a threat and joy or relief in the presence of a loved one. Cognitively, fear is accompanied by the idea that we are in danger.

Reflect

Do you consider yourself to be an "emotional" person? Why or why not?

Theories of the Development of Emotions

Question: How do emotions develop? There are a number of theories concerning the development of emotions. Basically they break down into two camps. The first, proposed originally by Katherine Bridges (1932), holds that we are born with

emotion A state of feeling that has physiological, situational, and cognitive components.

Parents have to work." In fact, the national welfare reform policy of 1996 forced low-income women into the workforce, and they had to scramble to find whatever child care they could afford.

More Findings, More Rifts

At news conferences and by telephone interview, several researchers involved in the study called its conclusion overstated and said that other important findings, which were less sensational, had not received the same attention. Margaret Burchinal, the lead statistician in the study, placed some of the blame on the researchers themselves: "I feel we have been extremely irresponsible, and I'm very sorry the results have been presented in this way. I'm afraid we have scared parents, especially since most parents in this country [have to work]."

The attacks on Belsky continue. Several of those in the research project accuse him of having an anti-child-care agenda that leads him to downplay the positive findings. But Belsky retorts that his colleagues are "running from this data like a nuclear bomb went off" because—for political reasons—they are committed to freeing women by approving child care. "I sometimes feel I'm in the old Soviet Union, where only certain facts are allowed to be facts, and only certain news is allowed to be news," he said. "I've yet to hear a compelling argument that's evenhandedly applied to all our data."

This high-profile, academic altercation illustrates to the public how difficult it is to separate ideology from objective research findings, particularly on topics as volatile as child care. (Another issue in which ideology affects interpretation of research findings would be on the psychological effects of abortion on women [Rathus et al., 2002].) The findings of the study by the National Institute of Child Health and Human Development sent many parents into a tizzy. Many working mothers worried about their choices or emotionally defended them, while stay-at-home mothers seized on the findings as vindication. But a number of the researchers on the team said that if other information yielded by the study—or *not* yielded by the study—had been emphasized to the public, the reaction might have been different. Note the following:

- Although 17% of kindergartners who had been in child care acted more assertively and aggressively, that percentage is actually the norm for the general population of children. (And it remains true that 9% of the children who spent most of their time with their mothers were also rated by teachers as showing the more troubling behaviors.)
- The nature of family–child interactions had a greater impact on children's behavior than the number of hours spent in child care.
- Cruelty is never acceptable, but some other aspects of aggressiveness—and the fact that infants in day care may demand more attention as kindergartners—may in many ways be adaptive social responses to being placed in a situation in which multiple children may be competing for limited physical and human resources.
- In addition, the researchers admitted that the statistics are very modest: Yes, 17% acted aggressively and assertively, but only a few of them exhibited above-average behavior problems. Moreover, the problems were not that serious.

Belsky continues to suggest that parents consider cutting back on the number of hours of child care to which they subject their children. He argued that his colleagues are "so busy trying to protect mothers from feeling guilty, they've lost track of the science." He continues to believe that the link between child care and aggression is as significant as the finding that high-quality child care is connected with greater cognitive development, but "One set of findings gets emblazoned, and the other gets censored."

Search Online With InfoTrac College Edition

For additional information, explore InfoTrac College Edition, your online library. Go to **http://www.infotrac-college.com** and use the passcode from the InfoTrac card that came with your book. Try these search terms: child care evaluation, day care social aspects, aggressiveness in children, children of working mothers.

Source: Quotations in this feature are derived from Jessica Garrison, (2001, April 19; April 26). Toddlers' time in child care linked to behavior problems; Researchers in child-care study clash over findings. The Los Angeles Times Online.

Reflect

What emotion or emotions is a baby born with? What is the evidence for your point of view?

a single emotion and that other emotions become differentiated as time passes. The second, proposed by Carroll Izard (1991, 1992), holds that all emotions are present and adequately differentiated at birth. However, they are not shown all at once. Instead, they emerge in response to the child's developing needs and maturational sequences.

Bridges's and Sroufe's Theory

On the basis of her observations of babies, Bridges proposed that newborns experience one emotion—diffuse excitement. By 3 months, two other emotions have differentiated from this general state of excitement—a negative emotion, distress, and a positive emotion, delight. By 6 months, fear, disgust, and anger will have developed from distress. By 12 months, elation and affection will have differentiated from delight. Jealousy develops from distress, and joy develops from delight—both during the 2nd year.

Alan Sroufe (1979) has advanced Bridges's theory, focusing on the ways in which cognitive development may provide the basis for emotional development. Jealousy, for example, could not become differentiated without some understanding of object permanence (the continuing existence of people and objects) and possession.

Sroufe also links development of fear of strangers to the perceptual cognitive capacity to discriminate the faces of familiar people from those of unfamiliar people. Infants usually show distress at the mother's departure after they have developed a rudimentary concept of object permanence.

Izard's Theory

Carroll Izard (1991, 1992) proposes that infants are born with discrete emotional states. However, the timing of their appearance is linked to the child's cognitive development and social experiences. For example, Izard and his colleagues (1987) reported that 2-month-old babies receiving inoculations showed distress, whereas older infants showed anger.

Izard's view may sound very similar to Sroufe's. Both suggest an orderly unfolding of emotions such that they become more specific as time passes. However, in keeping with Izard's view, researchers have found that a number of different emotions appear to be shown by infants at ages earlier than those suggested by Bridges and Sroufe. In one study of emotions shown by babies during the first 3 months, 99% of the mothers interviewed reported that their babies showed the emotion of interest. Ninety-five percent of mothers reported joy; 84%, anger; 74%, surprise; and 58%, fear (Johnson et al., 1982). These figures are based on mothers' reports, and it is possible that the infants were actually showing more diffuse emotions (Murphy, 1983). Perhaps the mothers were reading specific emotions into the babies' behavior based on their own knowledge of appropriate (adult) emotional reactions to the infants' situations. This problem extends to Izard's interpretations of infants' facial expressions.

Izard (1983) claims to have found many discrete emotions at the age of 1 month by using his Maximally Discriminative Facial Movement Scoring System. Figure 7.8 shows some infant facial expressions that Izard believes are associated with the basic emotions of anger–rage, enjoyment–joy, fear–terror, and interest–excitement. Izard and his colleagues report that facial expressions indicating interest, disgust, and pain are present at birth. They and others have observed expressions of anger and sadness at 2 months of age, expressions of surprise at 4 months, and expressions of fear at 7 months (Izard & Malatesta, 1987). However, some researchers have suggested that this type of research is fraught with problems. First, observers cannot always accurately identify the emotions shown in slides or drawings of infant facial expressions (Oster, Hegley, & Nagel, 1992). Second, we cannot know the exact relationship between a facial expression and an infant's inner feelings, which, of course, are private events (Camras, Sullivan, & Michel, 1993). In other words, even if the drawings accurately represent young infants' facial expressions, we cannot be certain they express the specific emotions they would suggest if they were exhibited by older children and adults.

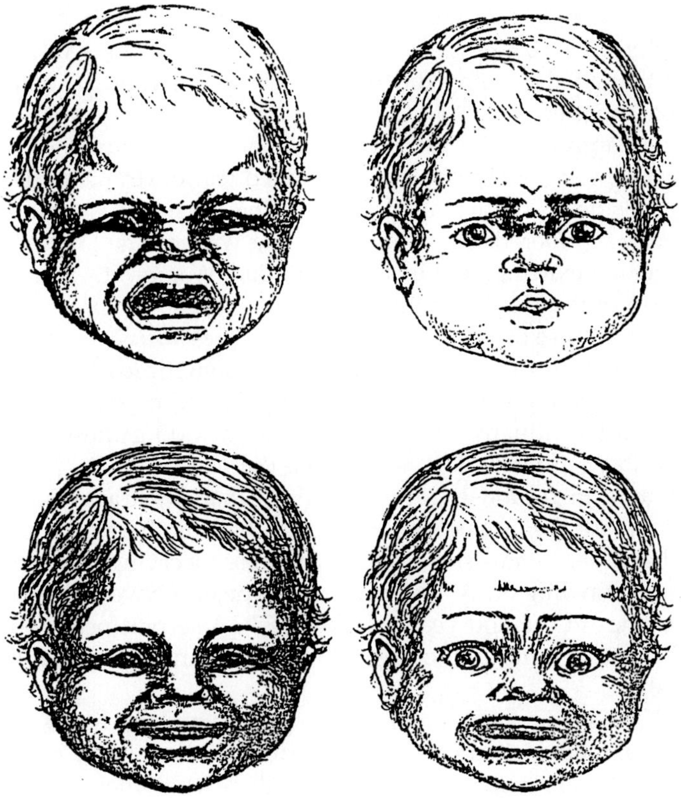

Figure 7.8
Illustrations from Izard's Maximally Discriminative Facial Movement Scoring System

What emotion do you think is being experienced by each of these infants?
Source: Izard, 1983.

In sum, researchers agree that a handful of emotions are shown by infants during the first few months. They agree that other emotions develop in an orderly manner. They agree that emotional development is linked to cognitive development and social experience. They do not agree as to exactly when specific emotions are first shown or whether discrete emotions are present at birth.

Emotional Development and Patterns of Attachment

Research by Grazyna Kochanska (2001) links emotional development with various histories of attachment. Kochanska studied the development of fear, anger, and joy in 112 children longitudinally: at 9, 14, 22, and 33 months in laboratory situations designed to evoke these emotions. Patterns of attachment were assessed in the Strange Situation. Differences in emotional development could first be related to attachment at the age of 14 months. Resistant children were most fearful and least joyful. Fear was their most powerful emotion. They frequently responded with distress even in episodes designed to evoke joy. When they were assessed repeatedly over time, it became apparent that securely attached children were becoming significantly less angry. By contrast, the negative emotions of insecurely attached children rose: Avoidant children grew more fearful, and resistant children became less joyful. At 33 months, securely attached children were less likely to show fear and anger, even when they were exposed to situations designed to elicit these emotions.

Enough disagreement. Let us focus in on an emotion that we'll all agree is very little fun: fear. We will focus on a common fear of infants, the fear of strangers.

Fear of Strangers

When Jordan was 1 year old, her mother and I decided we had to get a nanny for a few hours a day so that we could teach, write, breathe, and engage in certain other discretionary life activities. We hired a graduate student in social work who had rosy cheeks and a mild, engaging way about her. She nurtured Jordan and played with her for about 4 months, during which time Jordan came to somewhat grudgingly accept her—most of the time. Still, Jordan was never completely comfortable with her and frequently let out a yowl as if buildings were collapsing around her, although the nanny did nothing except attempt to soothe her in a calm, consistent manner.

Jordan had a nanny and she had fear of strangers. Unfortunately, she met the nanny during the period when she had developed fear of strangers. The fear was eventually to subside, as these fears do, but during her entire encounter with the nanny, the nanny wondered what she was doing wrong. The answer, of course, was simple: she was existing, within sight of Jordan. Worse yet, when her parents were not there to protect Jordan from this vicious foe.

Was Jordan's response to her nanny "normal"? ***Question: Is fear of strangers normal?*** Development of fear of strangers—sometimes termed **stranger anxiety**—is normal enough. Most infants develop it. Stranger anxiety appears at about 6 to 9 months in many different cultures, including those of the United States, Great Britain, Guatemala, and Zambia (Smith, 1979). By 4 or 5 months, infants smile more in response to their mothers than to strangers. At this age, infants may compare the faces of strangers and their mothers, looking back and forth. Somewhat older infants show marked distress by crying, whimpering, gazing fearfully, and crawling away. Fear of strangers peaks between 9 and 12 months of age and declines in the 2nd year (Marks, 1987). A second peak of fearfulness often occurs between 18 and 24 months, with a decline in the 3rd year (Thompson & Limber, 1990).

Children who have developed fear of strangers show less distress in response to strangers when their mothers are present. Babies are less likely to show fear of strangers when they are held by their mothers than when they are placed a few feet away (Thompson & Limber, 1990). Children also are less likely to show fear of strangers when they are in familiar surroundings, such as their homes, than when they are in the laboratory (Sroufe, Waters, & Matas, 1974).

In terms of proximity, the fear response to strangers is the mirror image of attachment. Children attempt to remain near people to whom they are attached. However, the closer they are to strangers, the greater their signs of distress (Boccia & Campos, 1989). They are most distressed when the strangers touch them. For this reason, if you find yourself in a situation in which you are trying to comfort an infant who does not know you, it may be more effective to talk in a friendly and soothing manner from a distance. Reconsider rushing in and picking up the child. Your behavior with an unfamiliar child also can make a difference. Studies

stranger anxiety A fear of unfamiliar people that emerges between 6 and 9 months of age. Also called *fear of strangers.*

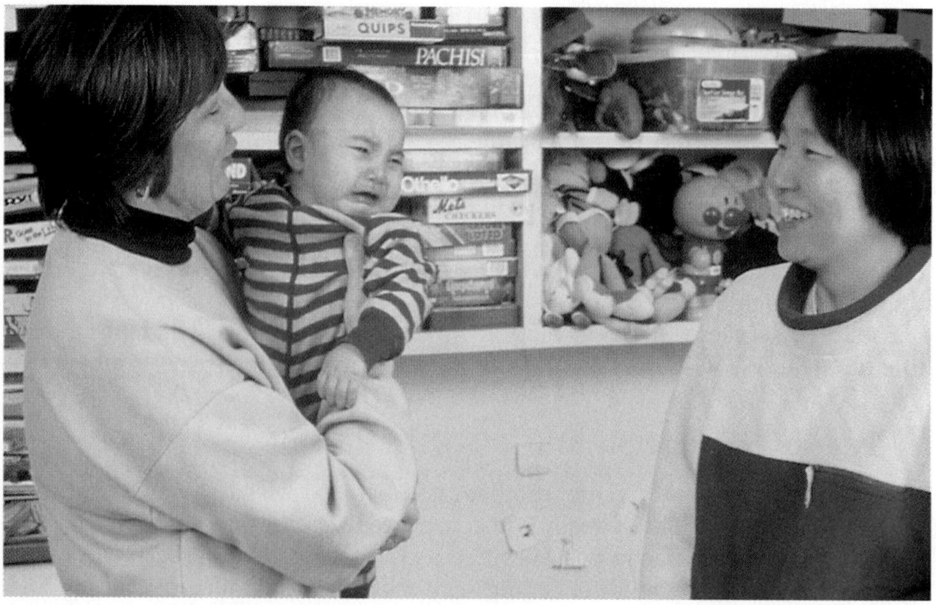

Stranger Anxiety

Infants in many cultures develop a fear of strangers, known as stranger anxiety, at about 6 to 9 months of age. This infant shows clear signs of distress when held by a stranger, even though mother is close by. How would you behave around an infant who does not know you to minimize its stranger anxiety?

have found that adults who are active and friendly—who gesture, smile, and offer toys—receive more positive response from 6–18-month-olds than do strangers who are quiet and passive (Bretherton, Stolberg, & Kreye, 1981; Mangelsdorf, 1992).

Social Referencing: What Should I Do Now?

Social referencing is the seeking out of another person's perception of a situation to help us form our own view of it (Feinman & Lewis, 1983; Rosen, Adamson, & Bakeman, 1992). In novel situations, we as adolescents and adults frequently observe how others behave and pattern our own behavior after them. So do children. For example, observing people who are not afraid may help children reduce their fears. Essentially, the models provide information about how to act in a frightening situation.

Question: When does social referencing develop? Infants display social referencing as early as 6 months of age, using their caregiver's facial expressions or tone of voice to provide clues on how to respond (Walden & Baxter, 1989). In one study, for example, 8-month-old infants were friendlier to a stranger when their mothers exhibited a friendly facial expression in the stranger's presence than when she displayed a worried expression (Boccia & Campos, 1989).

Infants also use their mother's facial expression to help them interpret ambiguous situations. Do you recall our discussion of the visual cliff in Chapter 6? Most infants are reluctant to cross over to the deep side of the cliff. James Sorce and his colleagues (Sorce et al., 1985) adjusted the deep side of a visual cliff so that it was neither very deep nor very shallow. In this situation, 1-year-old babies initially hesitated and looked back and forth at the drop-off and at their mother's face. If the mother's facial expression exhibited joy or interest, most infants crossed the deep side. But if the mother looked fearful or angry, few infants crossed.

Infants will use emotional signals from their fathers as often as those from their mothers (Dickstein & Parke, 1988; Hirshberg & Svejda, 1990). They also are influenced by the emotional expressions of a familiar day-care worker (Camras & Sachs, 1991) and even of a friendly adult whom they have just met (Klinnert, Emde, & Butterfield, 1986).

Reflect

Have you ever been in a novel situation and uncertain as to what to do? How about when you entered adolescence or began your first college class? Did you observe other people's reactions to the situation in an effort to determine what to do? This behavior is termed social referencing. *At what age do humans begin to use social referencing?*

Emotional Regulation: Keeping on an Even Keel

Infants use emotional signals from an adult to help them cope with uncertainty. Another important feature of early emotional development is *emotional regulation* (Kopp, 1992; Thompson, 1990). ***Question: What is emotional regulation?*** **Emotional regulation** refers to the ways in which young children control their own emotions. Even very young infants display certain behaviors to control unpleasant emotional states. They may look away from a disturbing event or suck their thumbs (Rothbart, Ziaie, & O'Boyle, 1992; Tronick, 1989). Caregivers play an important role in helping infants learn to regulate their emotions. Early in life, a two-way communication system develops in which the infant signals the caregiver that help is needed and the caregiver responds. Claire Kopp (1989, p. 347) gives an example of how this system works:

> A 13-month-old, playing with a large plastic bottle, attempted to unscrew the cover, but could not. Fretting for a short time, she initiated eye contact with her mother and held out the jar. As her mother took it to unscrew the cover, the infant ceased fretting.

Evidence from a Japanese study suggests that the children of secure mothers are not only likely to be securely attached themselves, but also likely to regulate their own emotions in a positive manner (Kazui et al., 2000). A German longitudinal study (Zimmermann et al., 2001) related emotional regulation in adolescence with patterns of attachment during infancy, as assessed via the Strange Situation. Forty-one adolescents aged 16 and 17 were placed in complex problem-solving situations with friends. It turned out that those adolescents who were

social referencing Using another person's reaction to a situation to form one's own assessment of it.

emotional regulation Techniques for controlling one's emotional states.

secure as infants were most capable of regulating their emotions to interact cooperatively with their friends. Yet another study (Volling, 2001) addressed the relationship between attachment in infancy and emotional regulation in an interaction with a distressed sibling at the age of 4. Of 45 preschoolers in the study, those who had an insecure-resistant infant–mother attachment at the age of 1 year engaged in more conflict with their siblings and showed greater hostility at the age of 4.

Review

(29) __________ proposed that we are born with a single emotion and that other emotions become differentiated as time passes. (30) __________ holds that all emotions are present and differentiated at birth, but we do not show them all at once. (31) According to Bridges, neonates experience one emotion: __________ excitement. (32) Sroufe also links development of fear of strangers to the capacity to __________ the faces of familiar people from those of unfamiliar people. (33) The (majority or minority?) of infants develop fear of strangers. (34) Social __________ is the seeking out of another person's perception of a situation to help us form our own view of it.

Pulling It Together: What are some of the roles of attachment in social referencing and emotional regulation?

Personality Development

An individual's **personality** refers to his or her distinctive ways of responding to people and events. In this section, we examine important aspects of personality development in the infant years. First, we look at the emergence of the self-concept. We then turn to a discussion of temperament. Finally, we consider gender differences in behavior.

Reflect

Think of a friend who is single. If you were trying to fix him or her up on a date and you were asked what kind of "personality" he or she had, what would you answer? What features do you imagine enter into the "personality" of an infant?

The Self-Concept

At birth, we may find the world to be a confusing blur of sights, sounds, and inner sensations. Yet, the "we" may be missing, at least for a while. When our hands first come into view, there is little evidence we realize that that hand "belongs" to us and that we are somehow separate and distinct from the world outside.

Questions: What is the self-concept? How does it develop? The **self-concept** is the sense of self. It appears to emerge gradually during infancy. At some point, infants understand the hand they are moving in and out of sight is "their" hand. At some point, they understand that their own bodies extend only so far and that at a certain point, external objects and the bodies of others begin.

Reflect

Do infants know that they exist? Can you think of a way of determining whether or not they do?

Development of the Self-Concept

Psychologists have devised ingenious methods to assess the development of the self-concept among infants. One of these is the mirror technique. This technique involves the use of a mirror and a dot of rouge. Before the experiment begins, the researcher observes the infant for baseline data on how frequently the infant touches his or her nose. Then the mother places rouge on the infant's nose, and the infant is placed before a mirror. Not until about the age of 18 months do infants begin to touch their own noses upon looking in the mirror (Butterworth, 1990; Schneider-Rosen & Cicchetti, 1991).

Nose touching suggests that children recognize themselves and that they have a mental picture of themselves that allows them to perceive that the dot of rouge

personality An individual's distinctive ways of responding to people and events.

self-concept One's impression of oneself; self-awareness.

is an abnormality. By 30 months, most infants also can point to pictures of themselves, and they begin to use their own name spontaneously (Bullock & Lutkenhaus, 1990; Stipek, Gralinski, & Kopp, 1990).

Self-awareness has a powerful impact on social and emotional development (Asendorpf & Baudonniere, 1993; M. Lewis, 1991). Knowledge of the self permits the child to develop notions of sharing and cooperation. In one study, for example, 2-year-olds who had a better-developed sense of self were more likely to cooperate with other children (Brownell & Carriger, 1990).

Self-awareness also makes possible the development of "self-conscious" emotions such as embarrassment, envy, empathy, pride, guilt, and shame (M. Lewis, 1990). One illustration of the development of these "self-conscious" emotions comes from a recent study by Deborah Stipek and her colleagues (1992). They found that children over the age of 21 months often seek their mother's attention and approval when they have successfully completed a task, whereas younger toddlers do not.

Self-Awareness

In the middle of the 2nd year, infants begin to develop self-awareness, which has a powerful impact on social and emotional development.

Psychoanalytic Views of the Self-Concept

Margaret Mahler (Mahler, Pine, & Bergman, 1975), a psychoanalyst, has proposed that development of self-concept comes about through a process of **separation–individuation** that lasts from about 5 months until 3 years of age. Separation involves the child's growing perception that her mother is separate from herself. Individuation refers to the child's increasing sense of independence and autonomy.

The word *autonomy* may remind you of a similar view proposed by Erik Erikson that was discussed in Chapter 1. Erikson states that the major developmental task of the child from ages 2 to 3 is acquiring a sense of autonomy and independence from parents. Remember that Freud, too, believed that children of this age are gaining greater independence and control. His focus, however, was primarily on such bodily functions as toileting behavior.

One of the ways toddlers demonstrate their growing autonomy, much to the dismay of their parents, is by refusing to comply with parental requests or commands. Studies of toddlers and preschoolers between the ages of $1^1/_2$ and 5 years have found that as children grow older, they adopt more skillful ways of expressing resistance to parental requests (Klimes-Dougan, 1993; Kuczynski & Kochanska, 1990). For example, young toddlers are more likely to ignore a parent's request or defy it ("No, I won't," accompanied by foot stamping). Older toddlers and preschoolers are more likely to make excuses ("I'm not hungry") or engage in negotiations ("Can I just eat some of my vegetables?").

Temperament: Easy, Difficult, or Slow to Warm Up?

Question: What is meant by the temperament of a child? Each child has a characteristic way of reacting and adapting to the world. The term **temperament** refers to stable individual differences in styles of reaction that are present very early in life. Some researchers believe that temperament forms the basic core of personality.

The child's temperament includes many aspects of behavior. Alexander Thomas and Stella Chess, in their well-known New York Longitudinal Study, followed the development of temperament in 133 girls and boys from birth to young adulthood (Chess & Thomas, 1991; Thomas & Chess, 1989). They identified the following nine characteristics of temperament:

1. Activity level: How active is the child?
2. Regularity: How regular are the child's biological functions, such as eating and sleeping?
3. Approach or withdrawal: Does the child respond positively or negatively to new situations and people?
4. Adaptability: How easily does the child adapt to new situations?
5. Response threshold: How sensitive is the child to sensory stimulation?
6. Response intensity: How intensely does the child respond?

separation–individuation The child's increasing sense of becoming separate from and independent of the mother.

temperament Individual differences in styles of reaction that are present very early in life.

7. Mood quality: Is the child's mood usually cheerful or unpleasant?
8. Distractibility: How easily is the child distracted?
9. Attention span and persistence: How long does the child stay with a particular activity?

A child's temperament includes many characteristics. ***Questions: What types of temperament do we find among children? How do they develop?***

Types of Temperament

Thomas and Chess found that from the first days of life, many of the children in their study could be classified into one of three types of temperament: "easy" (40% of their sample), "difficult" (10%), and "slow to warm up" (15%). Some of the differences among these three types of children are shown in Table 7.4. As you can see, the easy child has regular sleep and feeding schedules, approaches new situations (such as a new food, a new school, or a stranger) with enthusiasm and adapts easily to them, and is generally cheerful. It's obvious why such a child would be relatively easy for parents to raise.

The difficult child, on the other hand, has irregular sleep and feeding schedules, is slow to accept new people and situations, takes a long time to adjust to new routines, and responds to frustrations with tantrums and loud crying. Parents find this type of child more difficult to deal with (Chess & Thomas, 1991). The slow-to-warm-up child falls somewhere between the other two. These children have somewhat irregular feeding and sleeping patterns and do not react as strongly as difficult children. They initially respond negatively to new experiences and adapt slowly only after repeated exposure (Chess & Thomas, 1984).

Only 65% of the children studied by Chess and Thomas fit into one of the three types of temperament. Some children are more inconsistent and show a mixture of temperament traits. For example, a toddler may have a pleasant disposition but be frightened of new situations.

Reflect

Think of some infants you have known. How would you classify their temperaments according to the categories of easy-going, difficult, or slow-to-warm-up?

Stability of Temperament

How stable is temperament? Evidence indicates at least moderate consistency from infancy into childhood, adolescence, and young adulthood (Asendorpf, 1993; Broberg, 1993; Kochanska & Radke-Yarrow, 1992). The infant who is highly active and cries frequently in unfamiliar situations often becomes a fearful toddler (Kagan & Snidman, 1991). An anxious, unhappy toddler tends to become an anx-

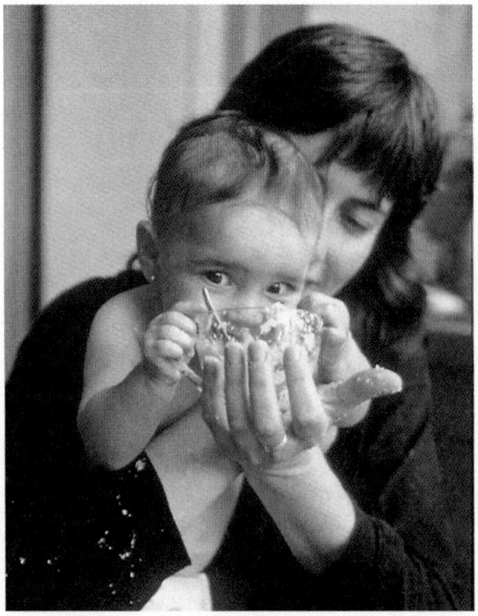

© Elizabeth Crews

© Elizabeth Crews

Differences in Temperament

Differences in temperament emerge in early infancy. The photo on the left shows the positive reactions of a 5-month-old girl being fed a new food for the first time. The photo on the right shows the very different response of another girl of about the same age when introduced to a new food.

TABLE 7.4 *Types of Temperament*

Temperament Categories	Easy	Difficult	Slow to Warm Up
Regularity of biological functioning	Regular	Irregular	Somewhat irregular
Response to new stimuli	Positive approach	Negative withdrawal	Negative withdrawal
Adaptability to new situations	Adapts readily	Adapts slowly or not at all	Adapts slowly
Intensity of reaction	Mild or moderate	Intense	Mild
Quality of mood	Positive	Negative	Initially negative; gradually more positive

Sources: Chess & Thomas, 1991; Thomas & Chess, 1989.

ious, unhappy adolescent (Lerner et al., 1988). The child who refuses to accept new foods during infancy may scream when getting the first haircut, refuse to leave mother's side during the first day of kindergarten, and have difficulty adjusting to college as a young adult. Difficult children in general are at greater risk for developing psychological disorders and adjustment problems later in life (Coon et al., 1992; Mehregany, 1991; Tubman et al., 1992). A longitudinal study tracked the progress of infants with a difficult temperament from $1\frac{1}{2}$ through 12 years of age (Guerin, Gottfried, & Thomas, 1997). Temperament during infancy was assessed by the mother. Behavior patterns were assessed by both parents during the 3rd year through the age of 12, and by teachers from the ages of 6 to 11. A difficult temperament correlated significantly with parental reports of behavioral problems from 3 to 12, including problems with attention span and aggression. Teachers concurred that children who had shown difficult temperaments during infancy were more likely to be aggressive later on and have shorter attention spans.

Many researchers believe that such consistency indicates that temperament is influenced by genetic factors (Braungart et al., 1992). Indeed, studies suggest that many aspects of temperament—such as activity level, shyness, fearfulness, sociability, and emotionality—are influenced by heredity (Emde et al., 1992; Kagan, Snidman, & Arcus, 1993; Plomin, 2000). Another intriguing bit of evidence that temperament has an innate component is that infants and young children with different temperaments have different patterns of electrical activity in the left and right sides of their brain's cortex. A series of studies by Nathan Fox and his colleagues has found that less cheerful infants, children, and adults show greater right-brain activity, whereas happier individuals demonstrate greater left-brain activity (Adler, 1993a; N. A. Fox, 1991).

Goodness of Fit: The Role of Environment

The environment also affects the development of temperament. An initial biological predisposition toward a certain temperament may be strengthened or weakened by the parents' reaction to the child. Consider the following: Parents may react to a difficult child by becoming less available and less responsive (Spangler, 1990). They may insist on imposing rigid caregiving schedules, which in turn can cause the child to become even more difficult to handle (Power, Gershenhorn, &

Stafford, 1990). This example illustrates a discrepancy, or poor fit, between the child's behavior style and the parents' expectations and behaviors.

On the other hand, parents may respond in such a way as to modify a child's initial temperament in a more positive direction. Take the case of Carl, who in early life was one of the most difficult children in the New York Longitudinal Study:

> Whether it was the first solid foods in infancy, the beginning of nursery and elementary school, first birthday parties, or the first shopping trip, each experience evoked stormy responses, with loud crying and struggling to get away. However, his parents learned to anticipate Carl's reactions, knew that if they were patient, presented only one or a few new situations at a time, and gave him the opportunity for repeated exposure, Carl would finally adapt positively. Furthermore, once he adapted, his intensity of responses gave him a zestful enthusiastic involvement, just as it gave his initial negative reactions a loud and stormy character. His parents became fully aware that the difficulties in raising Carl were due to his temperament and not to their being "bad parents." The father even looked on his son's shrieking and turmoil as a sign of lustiness. As a result of this positive parent–child interaction, Carl never became a behavior problem. (Chess & Thomas, 1984, p. 263)

Developing in a World of Diversity

Goodness of Fit

In middle-class Western society, the difficult child often has difficulty meeting cultural demands for task mastery at home, in school, and with peers (Chess & Thomas, 1991). But children with difficult temperament may have an easier time in cultural settings that have different value systems or different expectations.

For example, Super and Harkness (1981) compared infants in suburban Boston and rural Kenya. Temperamentally irregular infants who awoke at night caused considerable stress for American parents, who needed their sleep to be alert for their scheduled daytime activities. But rural Kenyan parents did not consider night waking stressful (see Table 7.5).

In other research, the children from the New York Longitudinal Study, who were predominantly from middle-class backgrounds, were compared with children from Puerto Rican working-class families (Chess & Thomas, 1984). The middle-class preschool children with difficult temperament were more likely to show adjustment problems than difficult preschool children from working-class families. The researchers believe that this finding is a result of differences in parental child-care attitudes and practices. The middle-class parents made more demands on their children for regular sleeping and feeding schedules, for early self-feeding and self-dressing behaviors, and for quick adaptation to new people and situations. These demands, as we have seen, are stressful for children with difficult temperament.

TABLE 7.5 *Some Parental Expectations and Behavioral Outcomes in Kenya, Boston, and New York*

Cultural Setting	Parental Expectations	Outcomes
Rural Kenya	Infants may or may not sleep through the night.	The family does not experience stress if the infant awakens during the night.
Suburban, European American Boston	Infants *should* sleep through the night.	The family experiences stress if the infant awakens during the night.
Puerto Rican, working class, U.S.A.	Infants need not become self-reliant very quickly.	Children are less likely to experience adjustment problems as preschoolers.
Middle Class, predominantly European American, U.S.A.	Infants *should* become self-reliant relatively quickly.	Children are more likely to experience adjustment problems as preschoolers.

Sources: Kenya and Boston: Super & Harkness, 1981; Working class and middle class: Chess & Thomas, 1984.

This example demonstrates **goodness of fit** between the behaviors of child and parent. A key factor is the parents' realization that their youngster's behavior does not mean that the child is weak or deliberately disobedient, nor that they are bad parents. This realization helps parents modify their attitudes and behaviors toward the child, whose behavior may in turn change in the desired direction (Chess & Thomas, 1984, 1991).

Gender Differences

All cultures make a distinction between females and males and have beliefs and expectations about how they ought to behave. For this reason, a child's gender is a key factor in shaping its personality and other aspects of development. ***Questions: Just how different are girls and boys in their social, emotional, and other behaviors? How early in life do gender differences arise?***

Behaviors of Infant Girls and Boys

Girls are more advanced in their motor development: they sit, crawl, and walk earlier than boys do (Hutt, 1978; Matlin, 1999). Girl and boy babies are quite similar in their responses to sights, sounds, tastes, smells, and touch. While a few studies have found that infant boys are more active and irritable than girls, others have not (Cossette, Malcuit, & Pomerleau, 1991; Matlin, 1999). Girls and boys also are similar in their social behaviors. They are equally likely to smile at people's faces, for example, and do not differ in their dependency on adults (Maccoby & Jacklin, 1974; Matlin, 1999). One area in which girls and boys begin to differ early in life is their preference for certain toys and play activities. By 12 to 18 months of age, girls prefer to play with dolls, doll furniture, dishes, and toy animals, while boys prefer transportation toys (trucks, cars, airplanes, and the like), tools, and sports equipment (Caldera, Huston, & O'Brien, 1989; Etaugh, 1983; Hanna, 1993).

Adults' Behaviors Toward Infant Girls and Boys

One reason for these early gender differences in play preferences seems to be that adults respond differently to girls and boys. In some studies, for example, adults are presented with an unfamiliar infant who is dressed in boy's clothes and has a boy's name, while other adults are introduced to a baby with a girl's name and dressed in girl's clothing. (In reality, it is the same baby who simply is given different names and clothing.) When adults believe they are playing with a girl, they are more likely to offer "her" a doll; when they think the child is a boy, they are more likely to offer a football or a hammer. "Boys" also are encouraged to engage in more physical activity than are "girls" (Stern & Karraker, 1989). And perhaps it is no wonder, for infants labeled as "girls" are perceived as littler and softer (as well as nicer and more beautiful) than infants labeled as "boys" (Vogel et al., 1991).

Parents' Behaviors Toward Sons and Daughters

How do parents behave toward their own infants? Like the adults with the unfamiliar babies, parents are more likely to encourage rough-and-tumble physical activity in their sons than in their daughters. Fathers are especially likely to do this (Siegel, 1987). On the other hand, parents talk more to their infant daughters than to their infant sons (Matlin, 1999). They also smile more at their daughters, are more emotionally expressive toward them, and focus more on emotions when talking to them (Fivush, 1993; Malatesta et al., 1989).

Perhaps the most obvious way in which parents treat their baby girls and boys differently is in their choice of clothing, room furnishings, and toys. Even very young infant girls are likely to be decked out in a pink or perhaps yellow dress, embellished with ruffles and lace, whereas infant boys wear blue or red (Pomerleau et al., 1990; Shakin, Shakin, & Sternglanz, 1985). Parents also provide their baby girls and boys with different bedroom decorations and toys. For example, examination of the rooms of children from 5 months to 6 years of age found that boys' rooms were often decorated with animal themes and with blue bedding

goodness of fit Agreement between the parents' expectations of or demands on the child and the child's temperamental characteristics.

Adults Treat Infant Girls and Boys Differently

Perhaps the most obvious way in which parents treat their baby girls and boys differently is in their choice of clothing, toys, and room furnishings. If you were to meet this child, would you have any doubt as to her gender?

and curtains. Girls' rooms featured flowers, lace, ruffles, and pastel colors (Pomerleau et al., 1990; Rheingold & Cook, 1975). Girls owned more dolls, while boys had more vehicles, military toys, and sports equipment.

Other studies find that parents react favorably when their preschool daughters play with "toys for girls" toys and their sons play with "toys for boys" toys. Parents and other adults show more negative reactions when girls play with toys for boys and boys play with toys for girls (Caldera et al., 1989; Etaugh, 1983; Martin, 1990). Fathers are more concerned than mothers that their children engage in activities viewed as "appropriate" for their gender (Bradley & Gobbart, 1989; Lytton & Romney, 1991).

Parents thus begin to shape their children's behavior during infancy and help lay the foundation for development in early childhood. It is to that period of life that we turn next.

Review

(35) The self-__________ is the sense of self. (36) Psychologists have devised the __________ technique to assess development of the self-concept. (37) Mahler proposed that development of self-concept comes about through a process of __________–individuation that lasts from about 5 months until 3 years of age. (38) The child's __________ refers to the stable individual differences in styles of reaction that are present very early in life. (39) The three basic types of temperament are easy, difficult, and __________ to warm up. (40) Children's temperaments tend to be (consistent or inconsistent?) from infancy through young adulthood. (41) Studies suggest that many aspects of temperament—such as activity level, shyness, fearfulness, sociability, and emotionality—are influenced by __________. (42) Infant (boys or girls?) are more advanced in their motor development. (43) By __________ girls prefer to play with dolls, while boys prefer transportation toys.

Pulling It Together: How might nature and nurture interact in the development of temperament?

Recite Recite Recite Recite

1. **What is meant by "attachment"?**

An attachment is an enduring emotional tie between one animal or person and another specific individual. Children try to maintain contact with caregivers to whom they are attached, and when they cannot, they show separation anxiety. Ainsworth innovated the Strange Situation to assess attachment.

2. **What does it mean for a child to be "secure"?**

About two thirds of middle-class infants in the United States are securely attached. In the Strange Situation, securely attached infants mildly protest mother's departure and are readily comforted by her.

3. **What, then, is "insecurity"?**

The two major types of insecure attachment are avoidant attachment and ambivalent/resistant attachment. One in 4 or 5 infants shows avoidant attachment, and these infants are least distressed by their mothers' departure. About one infant in 7 or 8 is ambivalent/resistant, and these show severe signs of distress when their mothers leave, but are ambivalent upon reunion—alternately clinging to and pushing away their mothers.

4. **Is it better for an infant to be securely attached to its caregivers?**

Yes, securely attached infants are happier, more sociable, and more cooperative. They use the mother as a secure base from which to explore the environment. At 5 and 6, securely attached children are preferred by peers and teachers, more competent, and less aggressive.

Recite Recite Recite Recite

5. What are the roles of the parents in the formation of bonds of attachment?

Children who receive higher-quality care are more likely to be securely attached. The mothers of securely attached infants are more likely to be affectionate and sensitive to their children's needs. Japanese research finds that the children of secure mothers are most secure themselves. Siblings of the same gender are more likely to form similar attachment relationships with their mother than are girl-and-boy pairs. Security of attachment seems to depend on the baby's temperament as well as the mother's behavior. Fathers are as capable as mothers of acting competently and sensitively toward their infants, but in the United States, mothers engage in more interactions with their infants. Fathers are more likely to play with their children than to feed or clean them. Fathers who are more actively involved in child rearing believe that the father plays an important role in the child's development. As with the mother, the more positive and physically affectionate the interaction between the father and his infant, the stronger the attachment of the child.

6. What did Ainsworth learn about the stages of attachment?

The initial-preattachment phase lasts from birth to about 3 months and is characterized by indiscriminate attachment. The attachment-in-the-making phase occurs at about 3 or 4 months and is characterized by preference for familiar figures. The clear-cut-attachment phase occurs at about 6 or 7 months and is characterized by intensified dependence on the primary caregiver.

7. How do different theorists emphasize nature or nurture in their explanation of the development of attachment?

The cognitive view suggests that an infant must have developed a concept of object permanence before specific attachment becomes possible. According to the behavioral perspective, infants become attached to caregivers because the caregivers meet their physiological needs. According to psychoanalytic theory, the primary caregiver becomes a love object who forms the basis for subsequent attachments. The Harlows' experiments with monkeys suggest that contact comfort is a key source of formation of bonds of attachment. Ethologists view attachment as an inborn fixed action pattern (FAP) which occurs during a critical period in the presence of a species-specific releasing stimulus. One component of the FAP of attachment in humans is a baby's smile. Hormones including oxytocin and vasopressin are connected with nurturant parental behavior in some lower animals.

8. What are the findings of the Harlows' studies on the effects of social deprivation with monkeys?

The Harlows found that rhesus infants reared in isolation confinement later avoided contact with other monkeys. Females who later had offspring tended to ignore or abuse them. Socially isolated monkeys were placed with younger females and many began to play with the youngsters after a few weeks.

9. What are the findings of correlational research into the effects of social deprivation with humans?

Institutionalized children who receive little social stimulation encounter problems in all areas of development. Many develop a syndrome characterized by withdrawal and depression. Deficiencies in sensory stimulation and social interaction may cause more problems than lack of love per se. Yet infants have much capacity to recover from deprivation.

10. What is the incidence of child abuse and neglect? What are their effects?

More than half of parents have slapped or spanked their children, and about one third have pushed, grabbed, or shoved them. Nearly 3 million American children are neglected or abused each year, and neglect results in more serious harm than abuse. About 150,000 children are sexually abused each year. Abuse leads to a high incidence of adjustment problems and psychological disorders. Psychological disorders may be connected with elevated levels of stress hormones (ACTH and cortisol). Maltreated children are less intimate with peers and more aggressive, angry, and noncompliant than other children. School performance suffers. Contributors to child abuse include stress, lack of adequate coping skills, deficiency in child-rearing skills, unrealistic expectations of children, and substance abuse. Yet stress is created by crying infants themselves.

Recite Recite Recite Recite

11. Why does child abuse run in families?

There are several reasons. Abusive parents serve as role models. Exposure to violence in the home may lead children to accept family violence as the norm. Some parents rationalize they are hurting their children "for their own good"—to discourage problematic behavior. There is sometimes an unclear distinction between the occasional swat on the rear end and spanking or repeated hitting.

12. What is autism?

The most striking feature of autistic disorder is the child's utter aloneness. Other features include communication problems, intolerance of change, ritualistic or stereotypical behavior, mutism, echolalia, and self-injurious behavior.

13. What are the origins of autism?

Evidence suggests a role for biological factors in autism. Genetic studies find higher concordance rates for autism among identical than fraternal twins. Researchers also find possible patterns of neurological involvement, For example, many autistic children have abnormal brain wave patterns or seizures. Brain scans show structural differences in the brains of children and adults with autistic disorder or less activity in various parts of the brain.

14. What can be done to help autistic children?

Operant conditioning methods have been used to increase the child's attention to others and social play with other children and to decrease self-mutilation. Aversive stimulation has been used to curtail self-injury. Intense learning-based programs with much individual attention have led to improvement in many autistic children. Researchers are also investigating the use of drugs that enhance serotonin activity and "major tranquilizers."

15. Does day care affect children's bonds of attachment with their parents? Does it affect their social and cognitive development?

Some studies find that infants who are in full-time day care are somewhat more likely than children without day-care experience to show insecure attachment in the Strange Situation. Does day care place infants at risk of developing emotional insecurity, or do infants in day care simply become less dependent on the mother? Infants with day-care experience are more independent, self-confident, outgoing, and affectionate as well as more helpful and cooperative with peers and adults. A Swedish study found that children in high-quality day care outperformed children who remained in the home on tests of math and language skills. Yet some studies find that children in day care are less compliant and more aggressive toward peers and adults than other children. However, Clarke-Stewart suggests that greater aggression and noncompliance are sometimes indicative of greater independence rather than social maladjustment.

16. What are emotions?

Emotions are states of feeling that have physiological, situational, and cognitive components.

17. How do emotions develop?

Bridges proposed that we are born with a single emotion—diffuse excitement—and that other emotions become differentiated over time. Sroufe advanced Bridges' theory by focusing on the ways in which cognitive development may provide the basis for emotional development. Izard proposes that infants are born with several discrete emotional states, but that the timing of their appearance is linked to cognitive development and social experiences. Research by Kochanska links emotional development with the infant's history of attachment.

18. Is fear of strangers normal?

Fear of strangers is normal in that most infants develop it at about 6 to 9 months. It peaks between 9 and 12 months of age and declines in the second year.

19. When does social referencing develop?

Infants display social referencing as early as 6 months of age, when they use caregivers' facial expressions or tones of voice for information as to how to respond in novel or ambiguous situations.

Recite Recite Recite Recite

20. What is emotional regulation?

Emotional regulation refers to the ways in which children, including infants, control unpleasant emotional states. Caregivers help infants learn to regulate their emotions. The children of secure mothers are likely to regulate their own emotions in a positive manner.

21. What is the self-concept? How does it develop?

The self-concept is the sense of self. Findings using the mirror technique suggest that the self-concept develops by about 18 months. Self-awareness enables the child to develop concepts of sharing and cooperation and "self-conscious" emotions such as embarrassment, envy, empathy, pride, guilt, and shame. Mahler proposed that development of self-concept comes about through a process of separation–individuation that lasts from about 5 months until 3 years. One of the ways toddlers demonstrate autonomy is by refusing to comply with parental requests or commands.

22. What is meant by the temperament of a child?

The term *temperament* refers to stable individual differences in styles of reaction to the world that are present very early in life. These include activity level, regularity, approach or withdrawal, adaptability, response threshold, response intensity, quality of mood, distractibility, attention span, and persistence.

23. What types of temperament do we find among children? How do they develop?

Thomas and Chess found that most infants can be classified as having easy, difficult, or slow-to-warm-up temperaments. Temperament remains at least moderately consistent from infancy through young adulthood. Temperament is apparently influenced by genetic factors. However, an initial predisposition toward a certain temperament may be strengthened or weakened by the parents' reaction to the child.

24. How different are girls and boys in their social, emotional, and other behaviors? How early in life do gender differences arise?

Female infants sit, crawl, and walk earlier than boys do. Their sensory responses are similar. Female and male infants are similar in social behavior. But by 12 to 18 months, girls prefer to play with dolls and similar toys, whereas boys prefer transportation toys and gear. One reason for early gender differences in play preferences seems to be that adults respond differently to girls and boys.

On the Web

Search Online With InfoTrac College Edition

For additional information, explore InfoTrac College Edition, your online library. Go to http://www.infotrac-college.com and use the passcode from the InfoTrac card that came with your book. Try these search terms: attachment behavior in children, bonding (psychology), emotions in infants, temperament, personality in children, autistic children.

Visit Our Web Site

Go to http://www.wadsworth.com/psychology where you will find online resources directly linked to your book.

Child Development CD-ROM

Go to the Wadsworth Child Development CD-ROM for further study of the concepts in this chapter. The CD-ROM also includes quizzes and additional activities to expand your learning experience.

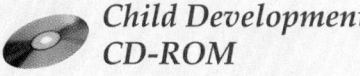

8 Early Childhood: Physical Development

© Ariel Skelley/Corbis Stock Market

PowerPreview™

Growth Patterns

- **During early childhood,** the brain develops more quickly than any other organ.

Motor Development

- **Do girls or boys** show better balance and precision of movement throughout early childhood?
- **Do children's levels** of motor activity increase or decrease during the preschool years? (And does it matter?)
- **Are sedentary parents** more likely to have "couch potatoes" for children?
- **What do Michelangelo,** Leonardo da Vinci, and Oprah have in common? (Hint: They don't all have book clubs.)
- **A disproportionately high percentage** of math whizzes are left-handed.

Nutrition

- **Is it a good idea** to bribe children to eat their veggies?

Health and Illness

- **What are the "normal"** childhood diseases?
- **What is the most common cause** of death among children in the United States?

Sleep Patterns and Sleep Disorders

- **Is it harmful for children** to sleep with their parents?
- **Is it dangerous to awaken** a sleepwalker? That is, do sleepwalkers become violently agitated if they are awakened during an episode?

Elimination Disorders

- **It is normal for children** who have gained bladder control to continue to have bed-wetting accidents at night for a year or more.
- **Are boys or girls more likely** to wet their beds?

Mark is a 2-year-old boy having lunch in his high chair. He is not without ambition. He begins by shoving fistfuls of hamburger into his mouth. He picks up his cup with both hands and drinks milk. Then he starts banging his spoon on his tray and his cup. He kicks his feet against the chair. He throws hamburger on the floor.

Compare Mark's behavior with that of Larry, age $3^{1}/_{2}$, who is getting ready for bed. Larry carefully pulls his plastic train track apart and places each piece in the box. Then he walks to the bathroom, takes his stool over to the sink, and stands on it. He takes down his toothbrush and toothpaste, opens the cap, squeezes toothpaste on the brush, and begins to brush his teeth (Rowen, 1973).

During the preschool years, physical and motor development proceeds, literally, by leaps and bounds. While toddlers like Mark are occupied by grasping, banging, and throwing things, 3-year-olds like Larry are busy manipulating objects and exercising their newly developing fine motor skills. In this chapter, we explore these and other aspects of physical and motor development in the early years.

Reflect

Have you ever compared the growth of a child to the norms on a growth chart? What were you looking for? What were your concerns?

Growth Patterns

Question: What changes occur in height and weight during early childhood?

Height and Weight

Click *Physical Development* in the Child and Adolescent CD-ROM for more on growth patterns.

Following the dramatic gains in height of the first 2 years, the rate of growth slows down during the preschool years (Kuczmarski et al., 2000). Girls and boys tend to gain about 2 to 3 inches in height per year throughout early childhood. Weight gains also remain fairly even at about 4 to 6 pounds per year (see Figure 8.1). Children become increasingly slender during early childhood, as they gain in height and lose some of their "baby fat." Boys as a group are only slightly taller and heavier than girls in early childhood (Figure 8.1). Noticeable variations in growth patterns also occur from child to child.

Development of the Brain

Question: How does the brain develop during early childhood? The brain develops more quickly than any other organ in early childhood. At 2 years of age, for example, the brain already has attained 75% of its adult weight. And by the age of 5, the brain has reached 90% of its adult weight, even though the total body weight of the 5-year-old is barely one third of what it will be as an adult (Tanner, 1989).

The increase in brain size is due in part to the continuing process of myelination of nerve fibers (see Chapter 5). Completion of the myelination of the neural pathways that link the cerebellum to the cerebral cortex facilitates the development of fine motor skills (Paus et al., 1999). The cerebellum is involved in balance as well as coordination, and the young child's balancing abilities increase dramatically as myelination of these pathways nears completion.

Brain Development and Visual Skills

The development of the brain also is linked to improvements in children's ability to attend to and process visual information (Yamada et al., 2000). These skills are critical in learning to read (Bornstein, 1992). The parts of the brain that enable the child to sustain attention and screen out distractions become increasingly myelinated between the ages of about 4 and 7 (Higgins & Turnure, 1984). As a consequence, most children are ready to focus on schoolwork at some time between these ages.

Click *Physical Development* for more on brain development.

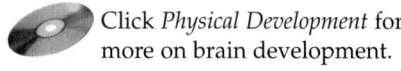

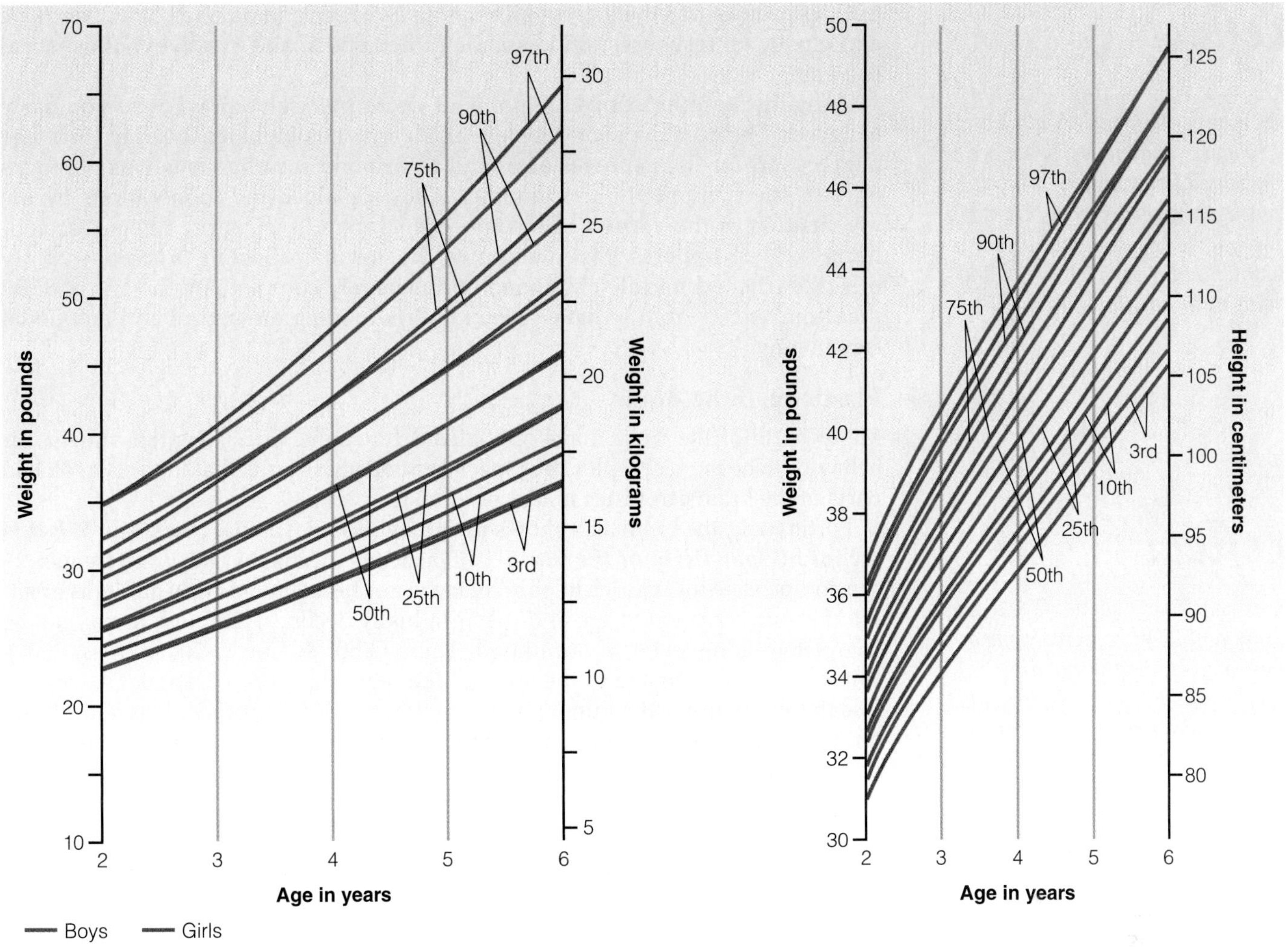

■ **Figure 8.1**
Growth Curves for Height and Weight, Ages 2 to 6 Years

The numbers on the curves indicate the percentiles for height and weight at different ages. The growth rate slows down during early childhood. As in infancy, boys are only slightly taller and heavier than girls. Variations in growth patterns from child to child are evident.

Source: Figures 9–12, Kuczmarski, R. J., et al. (2000, December 4). CDC Growth charts: United States. Advance data from vital and health statistics, *no. 314. Hyattsville, MD: National Center for Health Statistics.*

The speed with which children process visual information improves throughout childhood, reaching adult levels at the beginning of adolescence (Paus et al., 1999; Wilson, Nettelbeck, Turnbull, & Young, 1992). The child's ability to systematically scan visual material also improves in early childhood. For example, one classic study presented children with pairs of pictures of similar-looking houses and asked the children whether or not the houses were identical (Vurpillot, 1968). Four-year-olds almost never showed thorough, systematic visual scanning of the features of the houses, whereas 9-year-olds frequently did so.

Right Brain/Left Brain?

It has become popular to speak of people as being "right-brained" or "left-brained." We have even heard it said that some instructional methods are aimed at the right brain (they are presented in an emotionally laden, aesthetic way), while others are aimed at the left brain (they are presented in a logical and straightforward manner).

Question: What does it mean to be left-brained or right-brained? The notion is that the hemispheres of the brain are involved in different kinds of intellectual and emotional functions and responses. Research does suggest that in right-handed individuals, the left hemisphere is relatively more involved in intellectual undertakings that require logical analysis and problem solving, language, and mathematical computation (Gazzaniga, 1995). The other hemisphere (usually the right hemisphere) is usually superior in visual-spatial functions (it's better at

Reflect

Are some people left-brained and others right-brained? What aspects of behavior and mental processes are considered left-brained? Which are considered right-brained? Does research evidence support a sharp distinction between left-brain and right-brain functions?

putting puzzles together), recognition of faces, discrimination of colors, aesthetic and emotional responses, understanding metaphors, and creative mathematical reasoning.

Actually, these functions are not split up so precisely as has been popularly believed. The functions of the left and right hemispheres overlap to some degree, and the hemispheres also tend to respond simultaneously as we focus our attention on one thing or another. They are aided in "cooperation" by the myelination of the **corpus callosum**—a thick bundle of nerve fibers that connects the hemispheres. Myelination of the corpus callosum proceeds rapidly during early and middle childhood and is largely complete by the age of 8. By that time, we apparently have greater ability to integrate logical and emotional functioning.

Plasticity of the Brain

Many parts of the brain have specialized functions. Specialization allows our behavior to be more complex. But specialization also means that injuries to certain parts of the brain can result in loss of these functions.

Fortunately, the brain also shows **plasticity** (Bouma, 2001). ***Question: What is meant by "plasticity of the brain"?*** "Plasticity" means that the brain frequently can compensate for injuries to particular areas. This compensatory ability is greatest at about 1–2 years of age and then gradually declines, although it may not be completely gone, even in adulthood (Kolb, Gibb, & Gorny, 2001; Stiles, 2001). When we suffer damage to the areas of the brain that control language, we may lose the ability to speak or understand language. However, other areas of the brain may assume these functions in young children who suffer such damage. As a result, they sometimes dramatically regain the ability to speak or comprehend language (Booth & Burman, 2001). In adolescence and adulthood, regaining such functions is much more difficult and may be all but impossible.

At least two factors are involved in the brain's plasticity. The first is "sprouting," or the growth of new dendrites. To some degree new dendrites can allow for the rearrangement of neural circuits. The second is the redundancy of certain neural connections. In some cases, similar functions are found in two or more locations within the brain, although they are developed to different degrees. If one location is damaged, the other one, in time, may be able to develop greater proficiency in performing the function.

Reflect

Have you known an adult who had a stroke and then recovered some or most of his or her functioning? What was the "stroke"? How and why did recovery occur? What does this have to do with "plasticity" of the brain?

Review

(1) Children gain about __________ inches in height per year throughout early childhood. (2) Weight gains are about __________ pounds per year. (3) The __________ develops more rapidly than any other organ in early childhood. (4) Completion of __________ of the neural pathways that link the cerebellum to the cerebral cortex facilitates the development of fine motor skills. (5) The __________ is involved in balance and coordination. (6) Research suggests that in __________-handed individuals, the left hemisphere is relatively more involved in logical analysis and problem solving, language, and mathematical computation. (7) The __________ hemisphere is usually superior in visual-spatial functions and emotional responses. (8) The brain can often compensate for injuries to particular areas because of its __________.

Pulling It Together: How does myelination of the brain contribute to the processing of visual information?

corpus callosum The thick bundle of nerve fibers that connects the left and right hemispheres of the brain.

plasticity The tendency of new parts of the brain to take up the functions of injured parts.

Motor Development

The preschool years witness an explosion of motor skills, as children's nervous systems mature and their movements become more precise and coordinated. ***Question: How do motor skills develop in early childhood?***

© Elizabeth Zuckerman/PhotoEdit

Gross Motor Skills

During the preschool years, children make great strides in the development of gross motor skills. By 4 or 5, they can pedal a tricycle quite skillfully.

Gross Motor Skills

During the preschool years, children make great strides in the development of **gross motor skills,** which involve the large muscles used in locomotion (see Table 8.1). At about the age of 3, children can balance on one foot. By 3 or 4, they can walk up stairs as adults do, by placing a foot on each step. By 4 or 5, they can skip and pedal a tricycle (McDevitt & Ormrod, 2002). Older preschoolers are better able to coordinate two tasks, such as singing and running at the same time, than are younger preschoolers (Whitall, 1991). In general, preschool children appear to acquire motor skills by teaching themselves and observing the behavior of other children. The opportunity to play with other children seems more important than adult instruction at this age.

Throughout early childhood, girls and boys are not far apart in their motor skills. Girls are somewhat better in tasks requiring balance and precision of movement. Boys, on the other hand, show some advantage in throwing and kicking (McDevitt & Ormrod, 2002).

Individual differences are more impressive than gender differences throughout early and middle childhood. Some children develop motor skills earlier than others. Some are genetically predisposed toward developing better coordination or more strength than others. Motivation and practice also are extremely important in children's acquisition of motor skills. Motor experiences in infancy may affect the development of motor skills in early childhood. For example, children with early crawling experience perform better than noncrawlers on tests of motor skills in the preschool years (McEwan, Dihoff, & Brosvic, 1991).

Click *Physical Development* for more on motor development.

Physical Activity

Preschool children spend quite a bit of time engaging in physical activity. One recent study, for example, found that preschoolers spent an average of more than 25 hours a week in large muscle activity (Poest et al., 1989). Younger preschoolers are even more likely than older preschoolers to engage in physically oriented play such as grasping, banging, and mouthing objects (Fromberg, 1990). Consequently, they need more space and less furniture in a preschool or day-care setting. Contrary to what you might expect, children who are the most physically active tend to show less-well-developed motor skills (Eaton & Yu, 1989).

Motor activity level begins to decline after 2 or 3 years of age. Children become less restless and are able to sit still for longer periods of time (Eaton & Yu, 1989; Eaton, McKeen, & Campbell, 2001). Between the ages of 2 and 4, children show an increase in sustained, focused attention during free play (Ruff & Lawson, 1990).

Rough-and-Tumble Play

One form of physical and social activity often observed in young children is known as **rough-and-tumble play.** Rough-and-tumble play consists of running, chasing, fleeing, wrestling, hitting with an open hand, laughing, and making faces (Garvey, 1990). Rough-and-tumble play should not be confused with aggressive behavior (S. L. Kagan, 1990). Aggression involves hitting with fists, pushing, taking, grabbing,

Reflect

How do gender differences in the development of motor skills fit with traditional gender-role stereotypes?

Reflect

Have you ever heard a male preschooler described as "having his motor running"? What does the expression mean? How do we explain the behavior that gives rise to the saying?

gross motor skills Skills employing the large muscles used in locomotion.

rough-and-tumble play Play-fighting and chasing.

TABLE 8.1 *Development of Gross Motor Skills in Early Childhood*

2 Years (24–35 months)	3 Years (36–47 months)	4 Years (48–59 months)	5 Years (60–71 months)
Runs well straight ahead	Goes around obstacles while running	Turns sharp corners while running	Runs lightly on toes
Walks up stairs, two feet to a step	Walks up stairs, one foot to a step	Walks down stairs, one foot to a step	
Kicks a large ball	Kicks a large ball easily		
Jumps a distance of 4–14 inches	Jumps from the bottom step	Jumps from a height of 12 inches	Jumps a distance of 3 feet
Throws a small ball without falling	Catches a bounced ball, using torso and arms to form a basket	Throws a ball overhand	Catches a small ball, using hands only
Pushes and pulls large toys	Goes around obstacles while pushing and pulling toys	Turns sharp corners while pushing and pulling toys	
Hops on one foot, two or more hops	Hops on one foot, up to three hops	Hops on one foot, four to six hops	Hops 2 to 3 yards forward on each foot
Tries to stand on one foot	Stands on one foot	Stands on one foot for 3–8 seconds	Stands on one foot for 8–10 seconds
Climbs on furniture to look out of window	Climbs nursery-school apparatus	Climbs ladders	Climbs actively and skillfully
		Skips on one foot	Skips on alternate feet
		Rides a tricycle well	Rides a bicycle with training wheels

Note: The ages presented are averages; there are wide individual variations.

and angry looks. Unlike aggression, rough-and-tumble play helps develop both physical and social skills in children (Pellegrini & Perlmutter, 1988).

Play-fighting and chasing activities are found among young children in societies around the world (Whiting & Edwards, 1988). But the particular form that rough-and-tumble play takes is influenced by culture and environment. For example, rough-and-tumble play among girls is quite common among the Pilaga Indians and the !Kung of Botswana but less common among girls in the United States. In the United States, rough-and-tumble play usually occurs in groups made up of the same gender. However, the !Kung girls and boys engage in rough-and-tumble play together. And among the Pilaga, girls often are matched off against the boys (Garvey, 1990).

Reflect

What is suggested by the fact that play-fighting and chasing activities are found in young children around the globe? Cross-cultural findings are interesting in themselves, of course, but what does this finding suggest about human nature in general?

Rough-and-Tumble Play

Play-fighting and chasing activities—known as rough-and-tumble play—are found among young children in societies around the world.

Individual Differences in Activity Level

Children differ widely in their activity levels. Some children are much more active than others. Children who are physically active are more likely to have physically active parents (Poest et al., 1989). In one recent study of 4–7-year-olds (L. L. Moore et al., 1991), children of active mothers were twice as likely to be active as children of inactive mothers. Children of active fathers were 3.5 times as likely to be active as children of inactive fathers. A number of possible mechanisms may account for this relationship. First, active parents may serve as role models for activity. Second, sharing of activities by family members may be responsible. Parents who are avid tennis players may involve their children in games of tennis from an early age. By the same token, "couch potato" parents who prefer to view tennis on television rather than play it may be more likely to share this sedentary activity with their children. A third factor is that active parents may encourage and support their child's participation in physical activity. Finally, a tendency to be active or inactive may be transmitted genetically. Results from twin studies (see Chapter 2) show evidence of genetic influences on activity level (Saudino & Eaton, 1993; Stevenson, 1992). Most likely, both genetic and environmental factors are involved in determining a child's activity level.

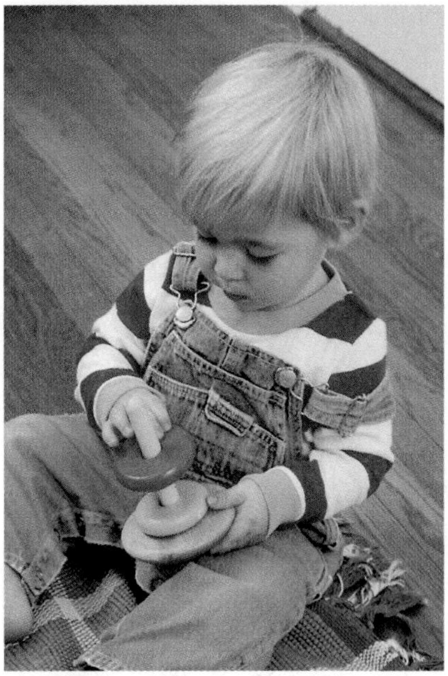

Fine Motor Skills

Control over the wrists and fingers enables children to hold a pencil, play musical instruments, and, as shown in this photograph, play with stack toys.

Fine Motor Skills

Fine motor skills develop gradually and lag behind gross motor skills. This is yet another example of the proximodistal trend in development (see Chapters 3 and 5). Fine motor skills involve the small muscles used in manipulation and coordination. Control over the wrists and fingers enables children to hold a pencil properly, dress themselves, and stack blocks (see Table 8.2). Preschoolers can labor endlessly in attempting to tie their shoelaces and get their jackets zipped. There are terribly frustrating (as well as funny) scenes of children alternating between steadfastly refusing to allow a parent to intervene and requesting the parent's help.

Reflect

Does it make sense in terms of the child's survival that gross motor skills develop before fine motor skills do? Explain.

Children's Drawings

The development of drawing in young children is closely linked to the development of both motor and cognitive skills. Children first begin to scribble during the 2nd year of life. Initially, they seem to enjoy making marks for the sheer enjoyment of it (Eisner, 1990).

fine motor skills Skills employing the small muscles used in manipulation, such as those in the fingers.

Developing in a World of Diversity

Gender Differences in Motor Activity

Question: Do girls and boys differ in their activity levels during early childhood? During early childhood, boys tend to be more active than girls, at least in some settings (Campbell & Eaton, 1999; Danner et al., 1991). Boys spend more time than girls in large muscle activities (Poest et al., 1989). One study found that preschool boys were more active than girls during indoor play but that girls and boys were equally active outdoors (Maccoby & Jacklin, 1987). Boys tend to be more fidgety and distractible than girls and to spend less time focusing on tasks (McGuinness, 1990).

Why are boys more active and restless than girls? One theory is that boys of a given age are less mature physically than girls of the same age. Children tend to become less active as they develop. Therefore, the gender difference in activity level may really be a maturational difference (Eaton & Yu, 1989). While maturation does appear to account for some of the gender difference in activity level, it may not be the whole story. Other factors such as parental encouragement and reward of motor activity in boys and discouragement of such behavior in girls probably are involved as well.

Boys also are more likely than girls to engage in rough-and-tumble play (Moller, Hymel, & Rubin, 1992; Pellegrini, 1990). What might account for this gender difference? Some psychologists suggest that the reasons might be based partly in biology (Maccoby, 1990a, 1991b). Others argue that the socializing influences of the family and culture at large promote play differences among girls and boys (Caplan & Larkin, 1991; Meyer et al., 1991).

Reflect

The relationships between physical abilities and social expectations can be said to be "circular." What does that mean?

TABLE 8.2 *Development of Fine Motor Skills in Early Childhood*

2 Years (24–35 months)	3 Years (36–47 months)	4 Years (48–59 months)	5 Years (60–71 months)
Builds tower of 6 cubes	Builds tower of 9 cubes	Builds tower of 10 or more cubes	Builds 3 steps from 6 blocks, using a model
Copies vertical and horizontal lines	Copies circle and cross	Copies square	Copies triangle and star
	Copies letters	Prints simple words	Prints first name and numbers
Imitates folding of paper		Imitates folding paper 3 times	Imitates folding of piece of square paper into a triangle
Prints on easel with a brush	Holds crayons with fingers, not fist	Uses pencil with correct hand grip	Traces around a diamond drawn on paper
Places simple shapes in correct holes	Strings 4 beads using a large needle	Strings 10 beads	Laces shoes

Note: The ages presented are averages; there are wide individual variations.

Figure 8.2
The Twenty Basic Scribbles (Really)

By the age of 2, children can scribble. Rhoda Kellogg has identified these 20 basic scribbles as the building blocks of the young child's drawings.
Source: Kellogg, 1970.

Question: Are children's scribbles the result of random motor activity? Rhoda Kellogg (1970) has studied more than a million drawings made by children. Her conclusion is that a meaningful pattern can be found in children's scribbles. She identifies 20 basic scribbles that she considers the building blocks of all art: vertical, horizontal, diagonal, circular, curving, waving or zigzagging lines, and dots (see Figure 8.2).

Children go through four stages as they progress from making scribbles to drawing pictures. These are the **placement, shape, design,** and **pictorial stages** (see Figure 8.3). Two-year-olds place their scribbles in various locations on the page (for instance, in the middle of the page or near one of the borders). By age 3, children are starting to draw basic shapes: circles, squares, triangles, crosses, X's, and odd shapes. As soon as they can draw shapes, children begin to combine them in the design stage. Between 4 and 5, the child reaches the pictorial stage, in which designs begin to resemble recognizable objects.

Children's early drawings tend to be symbolic of a broad category rather than very specific. For example, a child might draw the same simple building whether she is asked to draw a school or a house (Tallandini & Valentini, 1991). Children between 3 and 5 years old usually do not start out to draw a particular thing. They are more likely to first see what they have drawn and then name it (Winner, 1989). As motor and cognitive skills continue to improve after the age of 5, children become able to purposely draw something they have in mind (Matthews, 1990). They also become better at copying simple and complex figures (Karapetsas & Kantas, 1991; Pemberton, 1990).

placement stage An early stage in drawing, usually found among 2-year-olds, in which children place their scribbles in various locations on the page (such as in the middle or near a border).

shape stage A stage in drawing, attained by age 3, in which children draw basic shapes such as circles, squares, triangles, crosses, X's, and odd shapes.

design stage A stage in drawing in which children begin to combine shapes.

pictorial stage A stage in drawing attained between ages 4 and 5 in which designs begin to resemble recognizable objects.

Handedness

What do Michelangelo, Leonardo da Vinci, and Oprah have in common? No, they are not all artists. One is an African American female talk-show host. The commonality is that they are all left-handed. Some other well-known lefties are shown in Figure 8.4. ***Questions: When does handedness emerge? How many children are left-handed?***

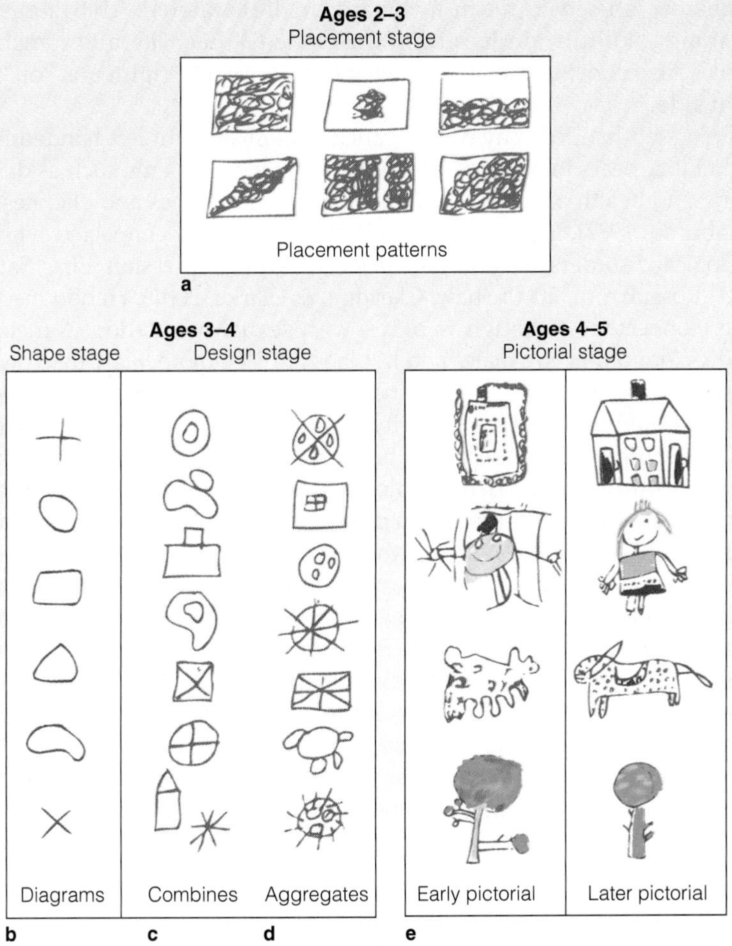

Figure 8.3
Four Stages in Children's Drawings

Children go through four stages in drawing pictures. (a) They first place their scribbles in various locations on the page. They then (b) draw basic shapes, and (c, d) combine shapes into designs. Finally, (e) they draw recognizable objects.
Source: Kellogg, 1970.

Handedness emerges during infancy. By 2 to 3 months, a rattle placed in the infant's hand is held longer with the right hand than with the left if a child will be right-handed (Fitzgerald et al., 1991). By 6 months, the majority of infants show a clear-cut right-hand preference in reaching and grasping things (Shucard & Shucard, 1990). Handedness becomes even more strongly established during the early childhood years (McManus et al., 1988).

The great majority of people are right-handed, although studies vary as to how many are left-handed. Overall, perhaps 7–10% of us are lefties (Gan, 1998; Rosenbaum, 2000), although the prevalence of left-handedness was found to be lower (3–4%) in a study conducted in India (Singh, Manjary, & Dellatolas, 2001). Most studies find that left-handedness is more common in boys than girls (Oeztuerk et al., 1999; Rosenbaum, 2000; Singh et al., 2001). We are usually labeled right-handed or left-handed on the basis of our handwriting preferences, yet some people write with one hand and pass a football with the other or write with one hand and hold a toothbrush with the other (Peters, 1990). Some people swing a tennis racket and pitch a baseball with different hands. President Ronald Reagan wrote and ate with his right hand, but shot pistols and waved with his left hand (Rosenbaum, 2000).

Reflect

Think of left-handed people you know (perhaps including yourself). Do they seem to be awkward in any activities? Explain.

Left-Handedness: Is It Gauche to Be Left-Handed? Myths and Realities

Question: Are there problems connected with being left-handed? Being a "lefty" is often regarded as a deficiency. The language swarms with slurs on lefties. We speak of "left-handed compliments," of having "two left feet," of strange events as "coming out of left field." The word *sinister* means "left-hand or unlucky side" in Latin. *Gauche* is a French word that literally means "left," though in

handedness The tendency to prefer using the left or right hand in writing and other activities.

English it is used to mean awkward or ill-mannered. The English word *adroit*, meaning "skillful," derives from the French *à droit*, literally translated as "to the right." Also consider positive usages such as "being righteous" or "being on one's right side."

Being left-handed may not be gauche or sinister, but left-handedness may matter in that it appears to be connected with language problems such as dyslexia and stuttering and health problems such as migraine headaches and allergies (Geschwind & Galaburda, 1987). Left-handedness is also apparently connected with a host of psychological disorders, including schizophrenia and depression (Elias, Saucier, & Guylee, 2001; Rosenbaum, 2000; Shaw, Claridge, & Clarke, 2001). Handedness is also apparently connected—although weakly—with sexual orientation. A meta-analysis of 20 studies found that gay males and lesbians are 39% more likely than people with a heterosexual orientation to be left-handed (Lalumière, Blanchard, & Zucker, 2000). Even so, we should note that the majority of gay males and lesbians are right-handed.

On the other hand, there may be advantages to being left-handed. According to a British study, left-handed people are twice as likely as right-handed people to be numbered among the ranks of artists, musicians, and mathematicians (Kilshaw & Annett, 1983). Figure 8.4 shows that some of the greatest artists were lefties.

Because of the negative stereotypes associated with left-handedness, for many years left-handed children were encouraged to switch to writing with their right hands (Hoosain, 1991; Porac & Buller, 1990). This "encouragement" sometimes was quite unpleasant. Even today, social pressure against using the left hand for writing persists in many parts of the world, including Italy, Germany, Russia, Japan, China, Singapore, and many African nations (L. J. Harris, 1991; Gan, 1998). However, research strongly suggests that the negative stereotypes of the left-handed child may be exaggerated.

Reflect

Do you know anyone who was "changed" from a lefty to a righty? Why was the change made? How was it done? Was it successful? Explain.

From Napoleon to Oprah—Famous Lefties

© Bettmann/CORBIS

Napoleon Bonaparte—Soldier, Emperor, and Leftie

Historical Figures: Alexander the Great, Charlemagne, Julius Caesar, Napoleon Bonaparte, Dr. Albert Schweitzer

AP/Wide World Photos

Oprah Winfrey—Talk Show Host, Actor, Author, and Leftie

Entertainers (present): Oprah Winfrey, Whoopi Goldberg, Jay Leno, Jerry Seinfeld, Robert Redford

People in the News: Gen. Colin L. Powell, Gen. H. Norman Schwarzkopf, Fidel Castro, Steve Forbes, Ross Perot

Entertainers (past): Marilyn Monroe, Greta Garbo, Judy Garland, W. C. Fields, Charlie Chaplin

Authors: Mark Twain, Lewis Carroll, Eudora Welty, James Baldwin, Peter Benchley

Athletes: Ben Hogan (golf), Mark Spitz (swimming), Pelé (soccer), Bill Russell (basketball), Bruce Jenner (track)

Artists: Leonardo da Vinci, Michelangelo, Raphael, Albrecht Dürer

Music: Ludwig van Beethoven, Ringo Starr, Paul McCartney, Cole Porter, Jimi Hendrix

Law: Justice Ruth Bader Ginsberg, Justice Anthony M. Kennedy, Marcia Clark, Clarence Darrow, F. Lee Bailey

Criminals: John Dillinger, Billy the Kid, Boston Strangler, Jack-the-Ripper, John Wesley Hardin

Figure 8.4
Some Well-Known Left-Handed People

Being left-handed is connected with language problems such as dyslexia and stuttering, physical health problems such as migraine headaches and allergies, and psychological disorders like schizophrenia. However, left-handed people are also twice as likely as right-handed people to be artists, musicians, and mathematicians.

Source: Rosenbaum, D. E. (2000, May 16). On left-handedness, its causes and costs. New York Times, *p. F6.*

In one study, Peters (1990) compared the performance of left-handed and right-handed individuals on a number of tests of motor skill and coordination. The left-handers performed as well as the right-handers on all the tasks. In another recent series of studies, Camilla Benbow (O'Boyle & Benbow, 1990) related handedness and other factors to scores on the math part of the Scholastic Aptitude Test (SAT) among 12- and 13-year-olds. (The SAT is designed to assess older adolescents applying for college admission.) Twenty percent of the highest-scoring group was left-handed. Only 10% of the general population is left-handed, so it appears that left-handed children are more than adequately represented among the most academically gifted.

Left-handedness (or use of both hands) also has been associated with success in athletic activities such as fencing, boxing, basketball, and baseball (Coren, 1992; L. J. Harris, 1990). Higher frequencies of left-handedness also are found among musicians, architects, and artists (Natsopoulos et al., 1992; O'Boyle & Benbow, 1990). It bears repeating that three of the greatest artists in history—Leonardo da Vinci, Michelangelo, and Pablo Picasso—were left-handed.

How can it be that left-handedness is associated with both talent and giftedness on the one hand (excuse the pun!) and with problems and deficits on the other? ***Question: What are the origins of handedness?***

Theories of Handedness

The origins of handedness are likely to have a genetic component (Geschwind, 2000). Left-handedness runs in families. In the English royal family, the Queen Mother, Queen Elizabeth II, and Princes Charles and William are all left-handed (Rosenbaum, 2000). If both of your parents are right-handed, your chances of being right-handed are about 92%. If one of your parents is left-handed, your chances of being right-handed drop to about 80%. And if both of your parents are left-handed, your chances of also being left-handed are about 1 in 2 (Rosenbaum, 2000).

Handedness also develops early. A study employing ultrasound found that about 95% of fetuses suck their right thumbs rather than their left (Hepper, Shahidullah, & White, 1990). Geneticist Amar J. S. Klar believes that about 80% of people have a dominant gene that makes them right-handed. The other 20% lack this gene and have a 50-50 chance of becoming right-handed or left-handed. This view explains why somewhere between 7% and 10% of us are left-handed and why about 18% of identical twins have different handedness (Rosenbaum, 2000).

It should be noted that handedness is found in many species other than humans, including chimpanzees and parrots (yes, parrots). It appears that hand preferences in chimpanzees are heritable, as they are in humans, but that environmental factors can modify inborn preferences—in the chimps as in humans (Hopkins, Dahl, & Pilcher, 2001).

Norman Geschwind has expanded on this view by arguing that certain prenatal influences act to diminish the genetic predisposition toward right-handedness. Specifically, he proposes that exposure to excessive amounts of the hormone testosterone in prenatal life slows development of the left hemisphere, causing an increase both in left-handedness and in problems such as learning disorders and immunological and allergic diseases (Bakan, 1990; Habib, Touze, & Galaburda, 1990; McManus & Bryden, 1991). Related research suggests that higher levels of prenatal testosterone promote lateralization—or specialization—of the cerebral hemispheres. Gina Grimshaw and her colleagues (1995) found that girls with relatively higher prenatal testosterone levels, as measured via hormonal concentrations in amniotic fluid, were more strongly right-handed and had stronger left-hemisphere speech representation at the age of 10. Boys with relatively higher prenatal testosterone levels appear to have had stronger right-hemisphere specialization for the recognition of emotion at 10 years of age.

A related theory is that various pregnancy and birth complications may increase both left-handedness and some of the problems just mentioned (Coren & Searleman, 1990). Both of these views propose that at least some cases of left-handedness are due to damage or delayed development in the left hemisphere. But the same prenatal hormones that slow left-hemisphere development could speed up the development of the right hemisphere (O'Boyle & Benbow, 1990). The right hemisphere is highly involved in control of mathematical reasoning and spatial abilities (Gazzaniga, 1995). Thus right-hemisphere development could account for a combination of left-handedness and ability in math, as well as in art and architecture.

In sum, there is no convincing evidence that left-handed children are clumsier than right-handed children. They are somewhat more prone toward developing allergies. Academically speaking, left-handedness is associated with positive as well as negative academic performance. Since handedness may reflect the differential development of the hemispheres of the cortex, it is doubtful that struggling to write with the nondominant hand would correct any academic shortcoming that may exist in some left-handed children—any more than training right-handed children to write with their left hands would increase their math ability.

Review

(9) At about the age of _________, children can balance on one foot. (10) Preschoolers generally acquire motor skills by teaching themselves and _________ the behavior of other children. (11) (Girls or Boys?) are somewhat better in tasks requiring balance and precision of movement. (12) (Girls or Boys?) show some advantage in throwing and kicking. (13) Preschoolers spend an average of more than _________ hours a week in large muscle activity. (14) Motor activity level begins to (increase or decrease?) after 2 or 3 years of age. (15) Rough-and-tumble play (is or is not?) the same thing as aggressive behavior. (16) Active children are (more or less?) likely to have active parents. (17) During early childhood, (girls or boys?) tend to be more active. (18) Kellogg identifies _________ basic "scribbles" that she considers the building blocks of art. (19) By _________ months, most infants show clear hand preference in reaching and grasping. (20) Most studies find that left-handedness is more common in (boys or girls?). (21) Left-handed people have a (higher or lower?) incidence of language problems and psychological disorders, when compared with right-handed people. (22) Left-handed people are (more or less?) likely than right-handed people to be artists, musicians, and mathematicians. (23) Left-handedness (does or does not?) run in families.

Pulling It Together: Why are psychologists and educators interested in whether children are right-handed or left-handed?

Nutrition

Nutrition affects both physical and behavioral development. ***Question: What are children's nutritional needs and their eating behavior like in early childhood?***

Nutritional Needs

As children move from infancy into the preschool years, their nutritional needs change. True, they still need to consume the basic foodstuffs: proteins, fats, carbohydrates, minerals, and vitamins. But more calories are required as children get older. For example, the average 4–6-year-old needs 1,800 calories compared with only 1,300 for the average 1–3-year-old (Ekvall, 1993b). However, preschoolers grow at a slower rate than infants. This means that preschoolers need fewer calories per pound of body weight.

"He just learned in school that potato chips are vegetables."

Food Aversions

Strong preferences for—and aversions to—certain foods may develop in early childhood.

Eating Behaviors

During the 2nd and 3rd years, a child's appetite typically decreases and becomes erratic, often causing parents great worry. But it must be remembered that the child is growing more slowly now and needs fewer calories. Also, young children who eat less at one meal typically compensate by eating more at another (Shea, Stein, Basch, Contento, & Zybert, 1992). Strong (and strange) preferences for particular foods may develop (Lucas, 1991). At one time during her 3rd year, my daughter Allyn wanted to eat nothing but Spaghetti-Os.

Many children (and adults) consume excessive amounts of sugar and salt, which can be harmful to their health. Infants seem to be born liking the taste of sugar, although they are fairly indifferent to salty tastes. But preference for both sweet and salty foods increases if children are repeatedly exposed to them during childhood (Sullivan & Birch, 1990). The message to parents is clear: Give your child food in the way you want the child to accept it in the future.

Parents also serve as role models in the development of food preferences. If a parent displays an obvious dislike for vegetables, children may develop a similar dislike (Rozin, 1990). Parents need to be careful not to be too rigid in trying to control their children's eating at mealtimes. Research finds that excessive parental demands in this area are associated with problems of weight control and difficulty in controlling food intake at college age (Birch, 1990).

What, then, is the best way to get children to eat their green peas or spinach or other disliked food? (Notice that it is rarely dessert that the child refuses to eat.) According to Leann Birch, bribing or rewarding a child to eat a new food does not help and may even backfire. She recommends instead that adults encourage the child to taste tiny amounts of the food 8 or 10 times within a period of a few weeks so that it becomes more familiar (Kutner, 1993b).

Reflect

Did you ever try to convince a 2- or 3-year-old to eat something? What did you do? What were the consequences?

Review

(24) (More or Fewer?) calories are required as children get older. (25) During the 2nd and 3rd years, a child's appetite typically (increases or decreases?).

Pulling It Together: How do parents serve as role models for the nutritional preferences of children?

Health and Illness

Questions: How healthy are children in the United States and in other countries? What are some of the illnesses and environmental hazards encountered during early childhood?

Minor Illnesses

The incidence of minor illness in childhood is high. We are referring to respiratory infections such as colds and to gastrointestinal upsets such as nausea, vomiting, and diarrhea. These illnesses typically last only a few days and are not life-threatening (Parmelee, 1986). Although diarrheal illness in the United States is usually mild, it is one of the leading killers of children in developing countries (World Health Organization, 2001).

American children between the ages of 1 and 3 generally average eight to nine minor illnesses a year. Between the ages of 4 and 10, this drops to about four to six

A Closer Look

Ten Things You Need to Know About Immunizations

1. *Why should my child be immunized?* Children need immunizations (shots) to protect them from dangerous childhood diseases. These diseases can have serious complications and even kill children.
2. *What diseases do childhood vaccines prevent?*
   - Measles
   - Mumps
   - Polio
   - Rubella (German measles)
   - Hepatitis B
   - Pertussis (whooping cough)
   - Diphtheria
   - Tetanus (lockjaw)
   - Varicella (chicken pox)
   - *Haemophilus influenzae* type b (Hib disease—a major cause of bacterial meningitis)
   - Pneumococcal disease (causes bacterial meningitis and blood infections)
3. *How many shots does my child need?* The following vaccinations are recommended by age 2 and can be given over five visits to a doctor or clinic:
   4 doses of diphtheria, tetanus, and pertussis vaccine (DtaP)
   4 doses of Hib vaccine
   3 doses of polio vaccine
   3 doses of hepatitis B vaccine
   3 doses of pneumococcal vaccine
   1 dose of measles, mumps, and rubella vaccine (MMR)
   1 dose of varicella vaccine
4. *Do these vaccines have any side effects?* Side effects can occur with any medicine, including vaccines. Depending on the vaccine, these can include: slight fever, rash, or soreness at the site of injection. Slight discomfort is normal and should not be a cause for alarm. Your health-care provider can give you additional information.
5. *Can they cause serious reactions?* Yes, but serious reactions to vaccines are extremely rare. The risks of serious disease from not vaccinating are far greater than the risks of serious reaction to a vaccination.
6. *What do I do if my child has a serious reaction?* If you think your child is experiencing a persistent or severe reaction, call your doctor or get the child to a doctor right away. Write down what happened and the date and time it happened. Ask your doctor, nurse, or health department to file a Vaccine Adverse Event Report form or call 1-800-338-2382 to file this form yourself.
7. *Why can't I wait until school to have my child immunized?* Children under 5 are especially susceptible to disease because their immune systems have not built up the necessary defenses to fight infection. By immunizing on time (by age 2), you can protect your child from disease and also protect others at school or day care.
8. *Why is a vaccination health record important?* A vaccination health record helps you and your health-care provider keep your child's vaccinations on schedule. If you move or change providers, having an accurate record might prevent your child from repeating vaccinations he or she has already had. A shot record should be started when your child receives his or her first vaccination and updated with each vaccination visit.
9. *Where can I get free vaccines?* A federal program called Vaccines for Children provides free vaccines to eligible children, including those without health insurance coverage, all those who are enrolled in Medicaid, American Indians, and Alaskan Natives.
10. *Where can I get more information?* You can call the National Immunization Information Hotline at 1-800-232-2522 (English) or 1-800-232-0233 (Spanish).

Source: Reprinted from Centers for Disease Control and Prevention. (2001). 10 Things you need to know about immunizations.
http://www.cdc.gov/nip/publications/fs/gen/shouldknow.htm

illnesses a year. You may be surprised to learn that being ill can actually have beneficial effects on a child's development. Illnesses provide opportunities for children to learn more about themselves and their feelings. Children also gain a better understanding of caring behavior as their parents and other caregivers help them cope with their illness (Parmelee, 1986).

Major Illnesses

Advances in immunization, along with the development of antibiotics and other medications, have dramatically reduced the incidence of serious and potentially fatal childhood diseases in the United States. Because the great majority of preschoolers and schoolchildren have been inoculated against major childhood illnesses such as rubella (German measles), measles, tetanus, mumps, whooping cough (pertussis), diphtheria, and polio, these diseases no longer pose the threat they once did. Still, immunization is far from universal. The recommended immunization schedule of the American Academy of Pediatrics is shown in Figure 8.5.

Nearly one third of the children in the United States under 18 years of age—about 20 million children—suffer from some type of chronic illness (Newacheck & Taylor, 1992). These include such major disorders as arthritis, diabetes, cerebral palsy, and cystic fibrosis. Other chronic medical problems such as asthma and migraine headaches are less serious but still require extensive health supervision.

While many of the major childhood diseases have been largely eradicated in the United States and other industrialized nations, they remain fearsome killers of

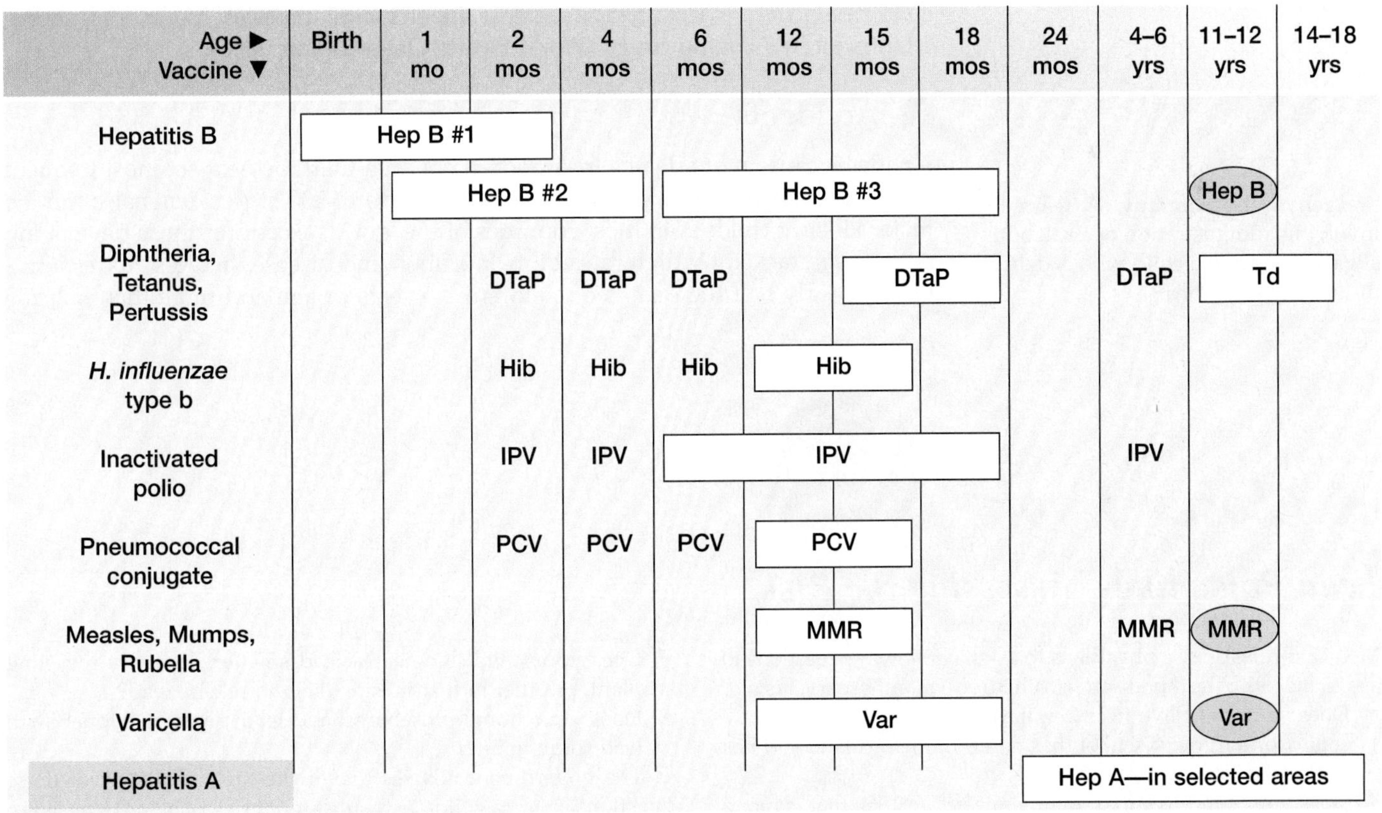

Figure 8.5
Recommended Childhood Immunization Schedule, United States, 2001

Vaccines are listed under routinely recommended ages. Bars [Bars] *indicate range of recommended ages for immunization. Ovals* (Ovals) *indicate vaccines to be given if previously recommended doses were missed or given earlier than the recommended minimum age. For more information, go to the National Immunization Program home page at* http://www.cdc.gov/nip *or call the National Immunization Hotline at 800-232-2522 (English) or 800-232-0233 (Spanish).*

Source: Centers for Disease Control and Prevention.

Reflect

What pollutants in your area are harmful to children? What are you doing about them? (End of speech.)

children in developing countries. Around the world, more than 13 million children die each year. Two thirds of these children die of just six diseases: pneumonia, diarrhea, measles, tetanus, whooping cough, and tuberculosis (World Health Organization, 2001). Air pollution from the combustion of fossil fuels for heating and cooking gives rise to many respiratory infections, which are responsible for nearly one death in five among children who are younger than 5 years of age (World Health Organization, 2001). Diarrhea kills nearly 2 million children under the age of 5 around the world. Diarrheal diseases are almost completely related to unsafe drinking water and a general lack of sanitation and hygiene. Children's immune systems and detoxification mechanisms are not as strong as those of adults, and they are thus more vulnerable to chemical, physical, and biological hazards in the water, soil, and air (World Health Organization, 2001).

Lead is a particularly harmful pollutant. Many are exposed to lead in early childhood, often by eating chips of lead paint from their homes or by breathing in dust from the paint. Infants fed formula made with tap water also are at risk of lead poisoning, since the pipes that carry water into homes often contain lead. Lead causes neurological damage and may result in lowered cognitive functioning and other developmental delays in early childhood (Mendelsohn et al., 1999; Nation & Gleaves, 2001; Needleman & Bellinger, 2001). To help you assess the risk of lead poisoning in children under 6 years of age, see the nearby "A Closer Look" feature.

Low-cost measures such as vaccines, antibiotics, and a technique called **oral rehydration therapy** could prevent most of these deaths. Oral rehydration therapy involves giving a simple salt and sugar solution to a child who is dehydrated from diarrhea. One promising step is that the great majority of children in developing countries now are immunized against tuberculosis, measles, polio, diphtheria, tetanus, and whooping cough (World Health Organization, 2001).

Accidents

oral rehydration therapy A treatment involving administration of a salt and sugar solution to a child who is dehydrated from diarrhea.

Accidents cause more deaths in American children than the next six most frequent causes combined (National Institute of Child Health, 2001). Accidents also are the major killer of children in most countries of the world, except for those developing nations still racked by high rates of malnutrition and disease. Injuries are responsible for nearly half the deaths of children 1–4 years of age and more than half the

A Closer Look

Lead Poisoning—Assessing the Risk

Medicaid rules advise physicians to ask the following questions to assess the risk of lead poisoning in children 6 months to 6 years old:

- Does your child live in or regularly visit a house, a day-care center, or a nursery school that was built before 1960 and has peeling or chipping paint?
- Does your child live in a home built before 1960 that is being remodeled or renovated?
- Does your child live near a heavily traveled major highway where soil and dust may be contaminated with lead?
- Have any of your children or their playmates had lead poisoning?
- Does your child often come in contact with an adult who works with lead—in construction, welding, plumbing, pottery, or other trades?
- Does your child live near a lead smelter, a battery-recycling plant, or other industrial site likely to release lead?
- Does your home plumbing have lead pipes or copper with lead solder joints?

The government advises that if the answer to any of these questions is yes, a child has a substantial risk of being exposed to lead and should receive a blood lead test. If the answers to all questions are negative, the child is said to have a low risk, but should nevertheless be tested for lead poisoning at 12 months of age and again, if possible, at 24 months, federal officials say.

Source: Pear, 1993.

deaths of children 5–14 years old. Motor vehicle accidents are the most common cause of death in young children in the United States, followed by drowning and fires (National Institute of Child Health, 2001). Boys are more likely than girls to incur accidental injuries at all ages and in all socioeconomic groups.

Accidental injuries occur more often among low-income children than among others. For example, poor children are five times as likely to die from fires and more than twice as likely to die in motor vehicle accidents (National Center for Children in Poverty, 2001). The high accident rate of low-income children probably results partly from living in dangerous housing and neighborhoods. Poor parents also are less likely than higher-income parents to take such preventive measures as using infant safety seats, fastening children's seat belts, installing smoke detectors, or having the telephone number of a poison control center. The families of children who are injured frequently may be more disorganized and under more stress than other families. The injuries often occur when family members are distracted and children may be under minimal supervision.

Developing in a World of Diversity

Ethnicity, Level of Income, and Immunization—USA

The likelihood that children will be immunized is related to their ethnic background and family level of income (Centers for Disease Control, 2000b). Table 8.3 summarizes data collected by the National Immunization Survey for a recent year. Immunization rates generally increased through much of the 1990s, to some degree as a result of a federal government program established in 1993 that provides free immunizations for poor or uninsured children. Still, as you can see, differences remain. European Americans and Asian Americans are more likely than African Americans, Native Americans, and Latino and Latina Americans to obtain vaccinations for diphtheria, tetanus, pertussis, polio, the flu, *Haemophilus influenzae* type B, and measles. Efforts to immunize children who live below the poverty level have apparently been particularly successful in the cases of polio and measles, where the difference according to family income level is only 2–3%. However, as we scan the table, we can note that African Americans, Latino and Latina Americans, and children living below the poverty level are least likely to get all their oral vaccinations or "shots." The income levels of these two groups are lower than those for European Americans and Asian Americans, so the overlap between ethnicity and income level in terms of vaccinations is not surprising. Note, however, that vaccination is far from universal among any group in the United States, regardless of ethnicity, regardless of level of family income.

TABLE 8.3 *Percentage of Children in the United States Who Have Received Vaccinations, According to Ethnicity and Family Level of Income*

		Ethnicity					Family Income	
Vaccination	All	European American	African American	Native American	Asian American	Latino/ Latina American	Below poverty level	At or above poverty level
Combined series (4:3:1:3)*	79	82	73	78	79	75	74	82
DTP†	84	87	77	83	89 p	81	80	86
Polio (3 or more doses)	91	92	88	85	93	89	90	92
Measles‡	92	93	89	91	92	91	90	93

Adapted from Health, United States, 2000. *Centers for Disease Control and Prevention, National Center for Health Statistics and National Immunization Program. Data from the National Immunization Survey.*

**The 4:3:1:3 combined series contains 4 doses of DTP vaccine, 3 doses of polio vaccine, 1 dose of a measles-containing vaccine, and 3 doses of Haemophilus influenzae type B (Hib) vaccine.*

†Diphtheria-tetanus-pertussis vaccine.

‡Measles-containing or MMR (measles-mumps-rubella) vaccines.

© Mitch Diamond/Index Stock Imagery

■ **Automobile Safety**

Automobile accidents are the most common cause of death in young children in the United States. All 50 states now require child-restraint seats in automobiles. These laws have contributed to a reduction in child deaths and injuries.

Prevention of Accidental Injury

Legislation has helped reduce certain injuries in children. For example, all 50 states now require child safety seats in automobiles. These laws have contributed to a decrease in child deaths due to automobile injuries (Osberg & DiScala, 1992). Most large cities in the United States also now have laws mandating the installation of window guards on all high-rise residential buildings. Window guards have sharply reduced the number of children killed by falling out of windows in New York City (National Institute of Child Health, 2001). And in a number of countries, the risks of injury to children have been substantially reduced as a result of legislation requiring manufacturers to meet certain safety standards for such items as toys and flammable clothing (Havard, 1991).

But remember that young children are active and curious creatures. Legislation cannot substitute for the parents' and caregivers' responsibility for monitoring the child's behavior and environment (Garling & Garling, 1993; Glik, Greaves, Kronenfeld, & Jackson, 1993). Unfortunately, some parents neglect to engage in good safety practices. A 1992 U.S. Department of Transportation Survey, for example, found that 16% of parents didn't use a child safety seat. And of the parents who did use a seat, 36% did not use it correctly ("Child Safety Seats," 1992).

In addition to legislation, other approaches to injury control include providing health education to parents (Peterson & Roberts, 1992). Expectant parents seem particularly receptive to such messages. Another injury-control strategy involves directly rewarding parents and children for engaging in good safety behaviors such

Developing in the New Millennium

Children in War Zones—New York, California, South Africa, the Middle East

On the afternoon of September 11, 2001, my family began to play host to a 10-year-old girl who lived across West Street from the World Trade Center. She was in the local school, a couple of blocks away, when the airplanes struck the towers and they exploded in flames and black and gray debris. She witnessed people jumping to their death from the towers before the flames caught them. Her mother grabbed her out of school and joined the crowds walking north, escaping the area before the towers collapsed. When they arrived here, she was crying about the dog and cat they had left in their apartment.

War Zone, New York

That morning we were frantic about our adolescent Allyn—once the 2-year-old who had knocked on my door when I was trying to write, saying "Pencer, Pencer, let me in." An NYU student, she called by cell phone from lower Manhattan when the first tower went up in flames and told us to turn on our TV sets. We watched in amazement as the second tower was struck and it became clear that terrorism was at work. She was not far from the towers and we tried to maintain contact with her to tell her to get out, but the sound became all chopped up. After several minutes we managed to catch her long enough to tell her to walk north and avoid the Empire State Building and Times Square—other landmarks. Then we lost contact again. Soon we saw the lower part of Manhattan covered with flames, black smoke, and ashen debris as the first tower collapsed; our stomachs felt empty. A half hour later Allyn called to say that a taxi driver had given her a lift uptown and refused to take a penny. My wife and I became conscious of breathing again.

War Zone, California

Another girl lives in another war zone. She is only 6 years old, but her most important family responsibility is to find her 2-year-old sister and hide with her in the bathtub whenever she sees someone with a gun or hears shooting. She has had to do this only twice so far but it is always on her mind—showing up in nightmares, nervousness, and a constant vigilance.

She does not live in Kosovo, Northern Ireland, Rwanda, or Israel. She lives in a housing project in northern California. Research suggests that 30% of inner-city children have seen someone killed before they reach the age of 15, and more than 70% have witnessed a beating (Goleman, 1992b). One survey of African American eighth-graders living in a violent low-income neighborhood in Chicago found that 55% of the boys and 45% of the girls had seen someone shot (Shakoor & Chalmers, 1991). Another survey of elementary school children in New Orleans reported that 90% had witnessed violence, 70% had seen a weapon used, and 40% had seen a dead body (Groves et al., 1993). A study of Latino and Latina American children found that 32% had witnessed violence (Eiden, 1999).

Researchers have studied children around the world who have experienced war-torn conditions. They find that many of these children exhibit symptoms of **post-traumatic stress disorder (PTSD),** such as nightmares, insomnia, anxiety, extreme vigilance, and reduced expectations for the future (Garbarino et al., 1991; Garbarino, 1992; Laor et al., 2001). Symptoms of PTSD often are shown by children who have experienced natural disasters, wit-as wearing seat belts. These techniques have met with some success (Christophersen, 1989; Frank et al., 1992).

Review

(26) _________ illness in the United States is usually mild, but it is a leading killer of children in developing countries. (27) Children need _________ to protect them from dangerous childhood diseases. (28) Of those children around the world who die from disease, two thirds die of just six: _________, diarrhea, measles, tetanus, whooping cough, and tuberculosis. (29) Many children are exposed to _________ by eating chips of paint. (30) European Americans and Asian Americans are (more or less?) likely than African Americans, Native Americans, and Latino and Latina Americans to obtain vaccinations for most diseases. (31) The most common cause of death among children in the United States is _________.

Pulling It Together: What obstacles must be overcome in order to prevent illnesses and accidents during early childhood?

Sleep Patterns and Sleep Disorders

Question: How much sleep is needed during early childhood? Children in the early years do not need as much sleep as infants. Most 2- and 3-year-olds sleep about 10 hours at night and also have one nap during the day (Handford, Mattison, &

post-traumatic stress disorder (PTSD) A disorder that follows a psychologically distressing event that is outside the range of normal human experience. It is characterized by symptoms such as intense fear, avoidance of stimuli associated with the event, and reliving of the event.

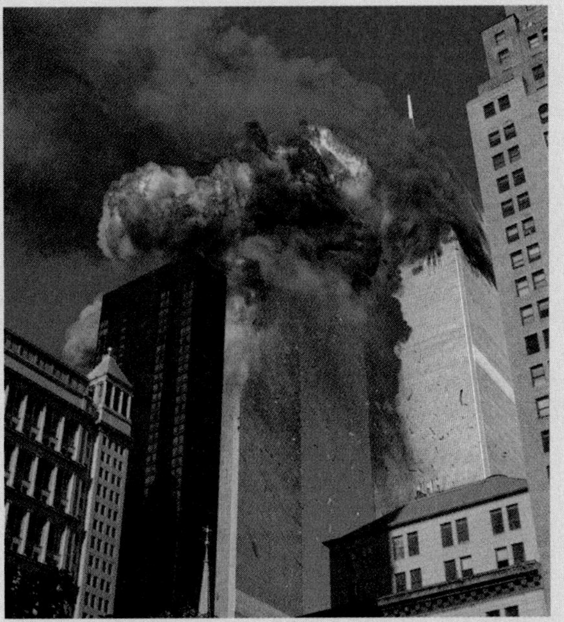

AP Wide World Photo/Chao Soi Cheong

War Zone, New York City

Everything changed in the United States on September 11, 2001, when the World Trade Center in New York and the Pentagon in Washington, DC, were attacked by terrorists. Children in the United States have been living in a war zone ever since, along with many others around the world.

nessed extreme violence, or been victims of sexual and physical abuse (Barbarin, Richter, & deWet, 2001; Eiden, 1999).

A study of 625 South African 6-year-olds suggests that the problems experienced by children who witness violence are similar to those of children who were the actual victims (Barbarin et al., 2001). Garbarino (2001) speaks of the witnesses as experiencing a "philosophical wound" rather than a physical wound. We also find the term *covictimization* in the literature, which is another way of saying that witnesses are also victims of violence (Kuther, 1999).

Research shows that support from adults in the children's lives can help them cope with violence (Al-Krenawi et al., 2001; Laor et al., 2001). Israeli and South African studies suggest that when mothers cope successfully with their surroundings, the children fare better (Barbarin et al., 2001; Laor et al., 2001). Violence makes children anxious, but solid family support helps mitigate the feelings of anxiety (Al-Krenawi et al., 2001; White et al., 1998).

Search Online With InfoTrac College Edition

For additional information, explore InfoTrac College Edition, your online library. Go to **http:www.inftrac-college.com** and use the passcode from the InfoTrac card that came with your book. Try these search terms: children and war, post-traumatic stress disorder, trauma children, violence in children.

Kales, 1991). In the United States, the young child's bedtime routine typically includes putting on pajamas, brushing teeth, and being read a story. Many young children also take a favorite object—such as a blanket or stuffed animal—to bed with them. These so-called **transitional objects** are seen as helping children make the transition to greater independence and separation from their parents.

Sleep Disorders

Question: What kinds of problems or disorders disrupt sleep during early childhood? In this section we shall discuss sleep terrors, nightmares, and sleepwalking.

transitional object A soft, cuddly object often carried to bed by a child to ease the separation from parents.

sleep terrors Frightening, dreamlike experiences that occur during the deepest stage of NREM sleep, shortly after the child has gone to sleep.

nightmares Frightening dreams that occur during REM sleep, often in the morning hours.

Sleep Terrors and Nightmares

Sleep terrors are much more severe than the anxiety dreams we refer to as nightmares. For one thing, sleep terrors usually occur during deep (stages 3 and 4) sleep. **Nightmares** take place during rapid-eye-movement (REM) sleep, when about 80% of normal dreams occur. Sleep terrors tend to occur early during the night, nightmares in the morning hours (Barabas, 1990).

Sleep terrors usually begin in childhood or early adolescence and are outgrown by late adolescence (Handford et al., 1991). Children who encounter sleep terrors

Developing in a World of Diversity

Cross-Cultural Differences in Sleeping Arrangements

The commonly accepted practice in middle-class American families is for infants and children to sleep in separate beds and usually in separate rooms from their parents. Child-care experts in the United States have generally endorsed this practice. Sleeping in the same room, they warn, can lead to problems such as the development of overdependence, the difficulty of breaking the habit when the child gets older, even sexual stimulation of the child.

Yet, in many other cultures, children sleep with their mothers for the first few years of life, often in the same bed (Barratt et al., 1993; Whiting & Edwards, 1988). This practice, known as co-sleeping, occurs in cultures that are technologically advanced as well as in those that are less technologically sophisticated. Children in Japanese cities, for example, often sleep with a parent or other adult family member into the adolescent years (Takahashi, 1990).

In the United States, mothers who are college-educated are less likely to sleep with or near their babies than mothers with a high school education (Wolf & Lozoff, 1989). In parts of rural eastern Kentucky, the majority of infants and toddlers sleep in the same bed or same room as their parents (Abbott, 1992).

Resistance to going to bed occurs regularly in 20–40% of American infants and preschoolers (C. M. Johnson, 1991), but it seldom occurs in cultures that practice co-sleeping. Some psychologists believe that the resistance shown by some young American children at bedtime is caused by the stress of separating from their parents and going off to bed by themselves. This view is supported by the finding that young children who sleep with or near their parents are less likely to use transitional objects or to suck their thumbs at night than are children who sleep alone (Wolf & Lozoff, 1989).

When my daughter Allyn wanted to sleep in the same room with us, my wife wondered whether it was "healthy" for her. I was not an expert on such matters, but I was also unaware of any empirical evidence that sleeping in the same bed or the same room with parents was harmful to children. It also occurred to me that among mammals, the rule seems to be for the young to sleep (and crawl) all over their mother, each other, and sometimes both parents. Allyn is now a normal college student (well, as normal as she can be, given that she is my daughter), and her sleeping preferences in infancy and early childhood do not seem to have affected her current independence. In fact, she's too independent, if you ask me. (Usually, nobody asks me.) Jordan, her younger sister, never wanted to sleep anywhere near anyone else. She found being in contact with us to be uncomfortable. (No comment.) Jordan, now a high school senior, is also normal enough. (At least as normal as one can be who is also a member of my family.) Our third daughter, Taylor, is simply easygoing. She generally accepted any choices we made for her, including sleeping in her own room. (I hope she's not reading this.)

Getting Their Z's
In the United States, most parents believe that it is harmful, or at least inappropriate, for parents to sleep with their children. Parents in many other cultures are more relaxed about sleeping arrangements.

wake up suddenly with a surge in heart and respiration rates, talk incoherently, and thrash about wildly. They sometimes scream piercingly. Children are not completely awake during sleep terrors and may fall back into more restful sleep as suddenly as they awake. It can be difficult to awaken them during sleep terrors. Once awakened, children may be disoriented and difficult to soothe. Memories of sleep terrors are not very vivid and usually cannot be recalled at all. Fortunately, the incidence of sleep terrors wanes dramatically as children develop and spend progressively less time in deep sleep. They are all but absent among adults.

Children are easier to awaken during nightmares, and they tend to recall nightmares more vividly than sleep terrors. When children are having nightmares, their heart and respiration rates show less arousal than when they are experiencing sleep terrors. About one third of all preschool children have had at least one nightmare (Hawkins & Williams, 1992). Children are more likely to experience nightmares when they are undergoing situational stress, such as moving to a new neighborhood, attending school for the first time, or adjusting to a parental divorce (Barabas, 1990).

Children who have frequent nightmares or sleep terrors may come to fear going to sleep. They may show distress at bedtime, refuse to get into their pajamas, and insist that the lights be kept on during the night. As a result, they can develop **insomnia.** Children with frequent nightmares or sleep terrors need their parents' understanding and affection. Yelling at them over their "immature" refusal to have the lights out and return to sleep will not alleviate their anxieties.

Sleepwalking

Sleepwalking, or **somnambulism,** is much more common among children than adults. Like sleep terrors, sleepwalking tends to occur during deep (stages 3 and 4) sleep (Barabas, 1990; Handford et al., 1991). Onset is usually between the ages of 3 and 8.

During medieval times, people believed sleepwalking to be a sign of possession by evil spirits. Psychoanalytic theory suggests that sleepwalking allows people the chance to express feelings and impulses they would inhibit while awake. But children who sleepwalk have not been shown to have any more trouble controlling impulses than other children do. Moreover, what children do when they sleepwalk is usually too boring to suggest exotic motivation. They may rearrange toys, go to the bathroom, go to the refrigerator and have a glass of milk. Then they return to their rooms and go back to bed. Their lack of recall in the morning is consistent with sleep terrors, which also occur during deep sleep. Sleepwalking episodes may be very brief; most tend to last no longer than half an hour.

There are some myths about sleepwalking—for example, that sleepwalkers' eyes are closed, that they will avoid harm, and that they will become violently agitated if they are awakened during an episode. All of these are false. Sleepwalkers' eyes are usually open, although they may respond to onlooking parents as furniture to be walked around and not as people. Children may incur injury when sleepwalking, just as they may when awake. And, finally, children may be difficult to rouse when they are sleepwalking, just as during sleep terrors. But if they are awakened, they are more likely to show confusion and disorientation (again, as during sleep terrors) than violence.

Today, sleepwalking among children is assumed to reflect immaturity of the nervous system and not the acting out of dreams or of psychological conflicts. As in the case of sleep terrors, the incidence of sleepwalking drops dramatically as children develop. When sleep terrors or sleepwalking are persistent, it may be wise to discuss them with the pediatrician.

Review

(32) Most 2–3-year-olds sleep about _________ hours at night and also have one nap during the day. (33) Most child-care experts in the United States recommend that children sleep (with their parents or in separate rooms?). (34) The anxiety

insomnia One or more of a number of sleep problems—difficulty falling asleep, difficulty remaining asleep during the night, and waking early.

somnambulism Sleepwalking (from the Latin *somnus,* meaning "sleep," and *ambulare,* meaning "to walk").

dreams we refer to as __________ take place during rapid-eye-movement (REM) sleep. (35) Sleep __________ usually occur during deep (stages 3 and 4) sleep. (36) It is usually (easy or difficult?) to awaken children during sleep terrors. (37) __________ is also referred to as somnambulism. (38) Sleepwalking tends to occur during (light or deep?) sleep. (39) Sleepwalkers' eyes are usually (open or closed?).

Pulling It Together: Which sleeping problems are likely to reflect immaturity of the nervous system?

Elimination Disorders

The elimination of waste products occurs reflexively in neonates. As children develop, their task is to learn to inhibit the reflexes that govern urination and bowel movements. The process by which parents teach their children to inhibit these reflexes is referred to as toilet training. The inhibition of eliminatory reflexes makes polite conversation possible. ***Questions: When are children considered to be gaining control over elimination too slowly? What can be done to help them gain control?***

Most children in the United States are reasonably well toilet trained between the ages of 3 and 4 (Liebert & Fischel, 1990). They continue to have accidents at night for about another year.

In toilet training, as in so many other areas of physical growth and development, maturation plays a crucial role. During the 1st year, only an exceptional child can be toilet trained, even when parents devote a great deal of time and energy to the task. If parents wait until the 3rd year to begin toilet training, the process usually runs smoothly.

An end to diaper changing is not the only reason parents are motivated to toilet train their children. Parents often experience pressure from grandparents, other relatives, and friends who point out that so and so's children were all toilet trained before the age of __________. (You fill it in. Choose a number that will make most of us feel like inadequate parents.) Parents, in turn, may pressure their children to become toilet trained. And so toilet training can become a major arena for parent–child conflict. Children who do not become toilet trained within reasonable time frames are said to have either enuresis, encopresis, or both.

Enuresis

Give it a name like **enuresis** (en-you-REE-sis), and suddenly it looms like a serious medical problem rather than a bit of an annoyance. Enuresis is the failure to control the bladder (urination) once the "normal" age for achieving control of the bladder has been reached. Conceptions as to the normal age vary. The American Psychiatric Association (2000) is reasonably lenient on the issue and places the cutoff age at 5 years. The frequency of "accidents" is also an issue. The American Psychiatric Association does not consider such accidents enuresis unless the incidents occur at least twice a month for 5- and 6-year-olds or once a month for children who are older.

Reflect

Why do you think that so many parents become so upset when their children are a bit behind in toilet training? Do you think it is terrible to get a little behind in toilet training?

enuresis (en-you-REE-sis) Failure to control the bladder (urination) once the normal age for control has been reached.

bed-wetting Failure to control the bladder during the night. (Frequently used interchangeably with *enuresis,* although bed-wetting refers to the behavior itself and *enuresis* is a diagnostic category, related to the age of the child.)

A nighttime accident is referred to as **bed-wetting.** Nighttime control is more difficult to achieve than daytime control. At night, children must first wake up when their bladders are full. Only then can they go to the bathroom.

Bed-wetting is more common among boys than girls. In the United States, nearly 12% of boys and 8% of girls in the early elementary school years still wet their beds at night (Liebert & Fischel, 1990). The incidence drops to about 5% for children 10 to 15 years old (Leary, 1992). A study of 3,344 Chinese children found that these children appeared to attain control a bit earlier: 7.7% obtained nocturnal urinary control by the age of 2, 53% by the age of 3, and 93% by the age of 5 (Liu et al., 2000). As with American studies, girls achieved control somewhat earlier than boys.

© Piotr Powietrzynski/Index Stock Imagery

Toilet Training

If parents wait until the 3rd year to begin toilet training, the process usually goes relatively rapidly and smoothly.

Causes of Enuresis

Enuresis can have organic causes, such as infections of the urinary tract or kidney problems. Numerous psychological explanations of enuresis have also been advanced (Mikkelsen, 1991). Psychoanalytic theory suggests that enuresis is a way of expressing hostility toward parents (because of their harshness in toilet training) or a form of symbolic masturbation. These views are largely unsubstantiated. Learning theorists point out that enuresis is most common among children whose parents attempted to train them early. Early failures might have conditioned anxiety to attempts over control the bladder. Conditioned anxiety, then, prompts, rather than inhibits, urination.

Situational stresses seem to play a role. Children are more likely to wet their beds when they are entering school for the first time, when a sibling is born, or when they are ill. There may also be a genetic component, in that the concordance rate for enuresis is higher among MZ twins than among DZ twins (Barabas, 1990).

It has also been noted that bed-wetting tends to occur during the deepest stage of sleep. This is also the stage when sleep terrors and sleepwalking take place. For this reason, bed-wetting could be considered a sleep disorder. Like sleepwalking, bed-wetting could reflect immaturity of certain parts of the nervous system. Just as children outgrow sleep terrors and sleepwalking, they tend to outgrow bed-wetting. In most cases bed-wetting resolves itself by adolescence, and usually by the age of 8.

Treatment

When parents (and children) feel that they cannot wait for bed-wetting to resolve itself, they may turn to behavioral methods that condition the child to awaken when their bladders are full. One reasonably reliable method for conditioning is the bell-and-pad method, originated by O. Hobart Mowrer (see Chapter 2). Numerous studies have shown that variants of Mowrer's method, in which nocturnal bed-wetting triggers an alarm and awakens the child, are effective with most children (Alcazar, Rodriguez, & Sanchez Meca, 1999; Mellon & McGrath, 2000).

Bed-wetting alarms are small electrical devices that awaken children as soon as they begin to pass urine. One kind of alarm uses an audible buzzer. Another vibrates like a cell phone or a pager, which has the advantage of allowing other members of the family to remain asleep. However, if the bed-wetter is a deep sleeper, the alarm may not be sufficient. When this happens, the parents or other caregivers need to get up when they hear the buzzer to awaken the child.

The mechanism is simple enough. Small metal strips touch the child's underwear or pajamas. When the cloth becomes wet, a small electric current—too small to cause a shock; in fact, too little for the child to detect—flows between the strips and triggers the buzzer or vibrator.

Mellon and McGrath (2000) recommend combining an alarm system with the antidiuretic medication *desmopressin. Diuretics* (pronounced die-you-RET-ticks) prevent the body from retaining water and cause frequent urination. *Antidiuretics* have the opposite effect: They encourage people—including children—to hold their water. Tricyclic antidepressants like Tofranil also have an antidiuretic effect (Toren et al., 2001). The fact that they may work does not mean that the children with enuresis had underlying depression. Drugs are chemicals that may have a variety of effects. Despite the fact that tricyclics help with enuresis, they are most often used for depression. Newer antidepressants—the selective serotonin reuptake inhibitors (SSRIs)—are also sometimes used with enuresis because of an antidiuretic effect. However, reviews of the effectiveness of the SSRIs are mixed (Kano & Arisaka, 2000; Toren et al., 2001).

Often, all that is needed is reassurance that neither parents nor children are necessarily to blame for bed-wetting and that most children will outgrow it. A study of 55 individuals who had been enuretic in early childhood found that they did not differ from the general population in terms of psychological health 13 years later (Brieger et al., 2001).

Encopresis

Soiling, or **encopresis,** is lack of control over the bowels. Soiling, like enuresis, is more common among boys. However, the overall incidence of soiling is lower than that of enuresis. About 1–2% of children at the ages of 7 and 8 have continuing problems controlling their bowels (Liebert & Fischel, 1990).

Soiling, in contrast to enuresis, is more likely to occur during the day. Thus it can be acutely embarrassing to the child. Classmates may avoid or poke fun at the soiler. Since bowel movements have a powerful odor, teachers may find it difficult to function as though nothing of importance has occurred. Parents, too, eventually become aggravated by persistent soiling and may heighten their demands for self-control, using powerful punishments for failure. As a result of all this, children with encopresis may begin to hide soiled underwear (Mikkelsen, 1991). They may perceive themselves as less competent than other children (Johnson & Moely, 1993). They may isolate themselves from schoolmates, pretending to be sick in the

encopresis Failure to control the bowels once the normal age for bowel control has been reached. Also called *soiling*.

A Closer Look

What Parents Can Do About Bed-Wetting

Parents are understandably disturbed when their children continue to wet their beds long after most children are dry through the night. Cleaning up is a hassle, and parents also often wonder what their child's bed-wetting "means"—what it means about the child, and what it means about their own adequacy as parents.

Bed-wetting may only "mean" that the child is slower than most children to keep his or her bed dry through the night. Bed-wetting may mean nothing at all about the child's intelligence or personality or about the parents' capabilities.

Certainly there are a number of devices (alarms) that can be used to teach the child to awaken in response to bladder pressure. There are also medications that can be used to help the child retain fluids through the night. Before turning to these methods, however, methods such as the following may do the trick (Needlman, 2000):

- *Limit fluid intake late in the day.* Less pressure on the bladder makes it easier to control urinating, but do not risk depriving the child of liquids. On the other hand, it makes sense to limit fluid intake in the evening, especially at bedtime. Drinks with caffeine, such as colas, coffee, and tea, act as diuretics, making it more difficult to control urination. So it's helpful to cut down on them after lunch.
- *Wake the child during the night.* Waking the child at midnight or 1:00 in the morning may make it possible for him or her to go to the bathroom and urinate. Children may complain and say that they don't have to, but often they will. Praise the child for making the effort.
- *Try a night light.* Many children fear getting up in the dark and trying to find their way to the bathroom. A night light can make the difference. If the bathroom is far from the child's bedroom, it may be helpful to place a chamber pot in the bedroom. The child can empty the pot in the morning.
- *Maintain a consistent schedule so that the child can form helpful bedtime and nighttime habits.* Having a regular bedtime not only helps ensure that your child gets enough sleep but also enables the child to get into a routine of urinating before going to bed and keeps the child's internal clock in sync with the clock on the wall. Habits can be made to work for the child rather than against the child.
- *Use a "sandwich" bed.* A sandwich bed? This is simply a plastic sheet, covered with a cloth sheet, covered with yet another plastic sheet, and then still another cloth sheet. If the child wets his or her bed, the top wet sheet and plastic sheet can be pulled off, and the child can get back into a comfortable dry bed. In this way, the child develops the habit of sleeping in a dry bed. Moreover, the child learns how to handle his or her "own mess" by removing the wet sheets.
- *Have the child help clean up.* The child can throw the sheets into the wash and, perhaps, operate the washing machine. The child can make the bed, or at least participate. These behaviors are not punishments; they help connect the child to the reality of what is going on and what needs to be done to clean things up.
- *Reward the child's successes.* Parents risk becoming overly punitive when they pay attention only to the child's failures. Ignoring successes also allows them to go unreinforced. When the child has a dry night, or half of a dry night, make a note of it. Track successes on a calendar. Connect them with small treats, such as more TV time or time with you. Make a "fuss"—that is, a positive fuss. Also consider rewarding partial successes, such as the child's getting up after beginning to urinate so that there is less urine in the bed.
- *Have a positive attitude.* ("Accentuate the positive.") Talk with your child about "staying dry" rather than "not wetting." Communicate the idea that you have confidence that things will get better. (They almost always do.)

morning to stay at home. Their anxiety level increases. And since anxiety prompts bowel movements, control can become increasingly elusive.

Causes of Encopresis

Encopresis stems from both physical causes, such as chronic constipation, and psychological factors (Cox et al., 1998; McGrath, Mellon, & Murphy, 2000; Needlman, 2001). Soiling may follow harsh punishment of toileting accidents, especially in children who are already anxious or under stress. Punishment may cause the child to tense up on the toilet, when moving one's bowels requires that one relax the anal sphincter muscles. Harsh punishment also focuses the child's attention on soiling. The child then begins to ruminate about soiling, so that soiling, punishment, and worrying about future soiling become a vicious cycle.

Treatment: Toilet Training in a Day?

Operant conditioning methods are usually helpful in dealing with soiling. Parents reward (through praise and other means) incidents of self-control, that they would normally take for granted. Parents mildly punish continued soiling for example, by gently reminding the child to pay more attention to bowel sensations and having the child clean the soiled underwear (Stark et al., 1991).

Richard Foxx and Nathan Azrin (1973) trained normal children ranging in age from 20 to 36 months to control their bladders and bowels through a single day of intense operant conditioning. They shaped self-control by reinforcing the children for engaging in each of the steps involved in using the potty—approaching the potty, taking down their pants, sitting, eliminating, wiping themselves, and so on. Reinforcers included praise, embraces, and special treats. Following treatment, the children had an average of one accident a week, as compared with a pretreatment average of six a day. Parents have learned to use this method, with about a 90% success rate, although it usually takes them about 6 weeks rather than a day (Liebert & Fischel, 1990). The method has been used in a variety of settings and—with some modifications—to help deficient adults (Cox et al., 1998; Didden et al., 2001).

As with enuresis, some professionals bring medications into the treatment of encopresis (McGrath et al., 2000). Some evidence indicates that selective serotonin reuptake inhibitors may be useful with encopresis (Kano & Arisaka, 2000). The use of laxatives has helped children overcome constipation and relieve themselves voluntarily (Needlman, 2001).

The various treatments of encopresis—some emphasizing learning, others emphasizing medication—remind us once again of the close ties that exist among the areas of physical, cognitive, and social development. We now leave our exploration of physical development in early childhood and begin an examination of cognitive development.

Review

(40) Most children in the United States are reasonably well toilet trained by the age of __________. (41) In toilet training, maturation (does or does not?) play a crucial role. (42) __________ is failure to control the bladder once the "normal" age for achieving bladder control has been reached. Bed-wetting is more common among (girls or boys?). (43) Stress (does or does not?) play a role in enuresis. (44) Mowrer originated the __________-and-pad method for treating enuresis. (45) __________ drugs are also used to treat enuresis. (46) Lack of control over bowel movements is called soiling, or __________. (47) A common physical cause of encopresis is __________. (48) Treatment of encopresis has involved __________ conditioning methods and use of laxatives.

Pulling It Together: Why are so many parents concerned about when their children are successfully toilet trained?

Recite Recite Recite Recite

1. What changes occur in height and weight during early childhood?

Children gain about 2 to 3 inches in height and 4 to 6 pounds in weight per year in early childhood. Boys are slightly larger than girls.

2. How does the brain develop during early childhood?

The brain develops more quickly than any other organ in early childhood, due in part to continuing myelination. Development of the brain enhances children's ability to attend to and process visual information, enabling them to read and to screen out distractions.

3. What does it mean to be left-brained or right-brained?

The left hemisphere is relatively more involved in logical analysis and problem solving, language, and mathematical computation. The right hemisphere is usually superior in visual-spatial functions, aesthetic and emotional responses, and creative mathematical reasoning. Nevertheless, the functions of the left and right hemispheres "cooperate" by the myelination of the corpus callosum.

4. What is meant by "plasticity of the brain"?

"Plasticity" means that the brain compensates for injuries to particular areas. Two factors involved in the brain's plasticity are the growth of new dendrites and the redundancy of neural connections.

5. How do motor skills develop in early childhood?

In the preschool years, children make great strides in the development of gross motor skills, which involve the large muscles used in locomotion. Girls are somewhat better in tasks requiring balance and precision, and boys have some advantage in throwing and kicking. Fine motor skills develop gradually and lag behind gross motor skills. Preschoolers spend much of their time in physical activity. The most active children generally show less-well-developed motor skills. After 2 or 3 years of age, children become less restless and are more able to sustain attention during play. Rough-and-tumble play is found among young children around the world. Genetic and environmental factors apparently interact to determine a child's activity level.

6. Do girls and boys differ in their activity levels during early childhood?

Boys tend to be more active than girls in large muscle activities. Boys are more fidgety and distractible, perhaps because they are less mature physically than girls of the same age. But parents are also more likely to encourage motor activity in boys.

7. Are children's scribbles the result of random motor activity?

Apparently not. Kellogg identifies 20 scribbles that she considers the building blocks of all art. She also theorizes that children undergo four stages of progressing from scribbles to drawing pictures: the placement, shape, design, and pictorial stages.

8. When does handedness emerge? How many children are left-handed?

By 6 months, most infants show clear-cut hand preferences, which become still more established during early childhood. More than 90% of children are right-handed.

9. Are there problems connected with being left-handed?

Left-handedness may be connected with language problems and some physical health problems (migraine headaches and allergies) and psychological health problems (schizophrenia and depression). On the other hand, a disproportionately large number of artists, musicians, and mathematicians are left-handed.

10. What are the origins of handedness?

The origins of handedness apparently have a genetic component. An ultrasound study found that about 95% of fetuses suck their right thumbs. Perhaps most people have a dominant gene that makes them right-handed, and other people have an even chance of becoming right-handed or left-handed. It may be that prenatal exposure to excessive testosterone slows development of the left hemisphere, leading to an increase in left-handedness and in problems such as learning disorders and certain health problems.

11. What are children's nutritional needs and their eating behavior like in early childhood?

The typical 4–6-year-old needs 1,800 calories a day as compared with only 1,300 for the average 1–3-year-old. During the 2nd and 3rd years, children's appetites typically wane and grow erratic. Many children eat too much sugar and salt, which can be harmful to their health. Parents serve as role models in the development of food preferences.

Recite Recite Recite Recite

12. How healthy are children in the United States and in other countries? What are some of the illnesses and environmental hazards encountered during early childhood?

The incidence of minor illnesses like colds, nausea and vomiting, and diarrhea is high. Although diarrheal illness is usually mild in the United States, it is a leading killer of children in developing countries. American children generally average eight to nine minor illnesses a year at ages 1–3, dropping to four to six between the ages of 4 and 10. Immunization and antibiotics have reduced the incidence of serious childhood diseases in the United States. Millions of children in other nations die each year from pneumonia, diarrhea, measles, tetanus, whooping cough, and tuberculosis. Air pollution contributes to respiratory infections. Diarrheal diseases are almost completely related to unsafe drinking water and lack of sanitation. Lead poisoning causes neurological damage. Accidents are the major cause of death in American children during early childhood.

13. How much sleep is needed during early childhood?

Most 2- and 3-year-olds sleep about 10 hours at night and have a nap during the day.

14. What kinds of problems or disorders disrupt sleep during early childhood?

Sleep terrors are more severe than nightmares. Sleep terrors usually occur during deep sleep. They begin in childhood and are "outgrown" by late adolescence. Children who have frequent nightmares or sleep terrors may fear going to sleep, show distress at bedtime, insist that the lights be kept on during the night, and develop insomnia. Sleepwalking (somnambulism) also occurs during deep sleep. Sleepwalkers' eyes are usually open; and if they are awakened, they may show confusion and disorientation but are unlikely to be violent. Sleepwalking probably reflects immaturity of the nervous system.

15. When are children considered to be gaining control over elimination too slowly? What can be done to help them gain control?

Most American children are toilet trained by about 3 or 4 but continue to have "accidents" at night for another year or so. Enuresis is the failure to control the bladder once a child has reached the "normal" age for doing so—placed at 5 years by the American Psychiatric Association. Encopresis (soiling) is lack of control over the bowels. Enuresis and encopresis are both more common among boys. Enuresis is likely to occur at night ("bed-wetting"), and encopresis is more likely to occur during the day. Enuresis is apparently connected with physical immaturity and stress. Encopresis can stem from physical causes, such as constipation, and psychological factors. Children almost invariably "outgrow" these problems, but they can also be treated by conditioning and by drugs (e.g., antidiuretics for enuresis and laxatives for encopresis).

On the Web

Search Online With InfoTrac College Edition

For additional information, explore InfoTrac College Edition, your online library. Go to **http://www.infotrac-college.com** and use the passcode from the InfoTrac card that came with your book. Try these search terms: child growth, children dietary requirements, sleep disorders in children, left- and right-handedness, enuresis.

Visit Our Web Site

Go to **http://www.wadsworth.com/psychology** where you will find online resources directly linked to your book.

Child Development CD-ROM

Go to the Wadsworth Child Development CD-ROM for further study of the concepts in this chapter. The CD-ROM also includes quizzes and additional activities to expand your learning experience.

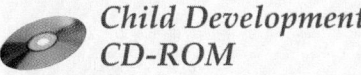

9 Early Childhood: Cognitive Development

PowerPreview™

Jean Piaget's Preoperational Stage

- **ARE IMAGINARY PLAYMATES** signs of loneliness or psychological problems?
- **ANY RESEMBLANCE BETWEEN** the logic of a preschooler and your own may be purely coincidental.
- **TWO-YEAR-OLDS TEND TO ASSUME** that their parents are aware of everything that is happening to them, even when their parents are not present.
- **THREE-YEAR-OLD CHILDREN MAY BELIEVE** that it gets dark outside so that they can go to sleep.
- **"BECAUSE MOMMY WANTS ME TO"** can be a perfectly good explanation—for a 3-year-old.
- **ARE DREAMS REAL?** A typical 4-year-old child may believe that they are.

Theory of Mind: What Is the Mind? How Does It Work?

- **MANY PRESCHOOL CHILDREN** cannot separate their beliefs from those of another person. They assume that if they believe something, everyone else believes it too. (As adults, do we sometimes fall into the same trap?)

Development of Memory: Creating Files and Retrieving Them

- **EVEN 1- AND 2-YEAR-OLDS** can remember past events.
- **THREE-YEAR-OLD CHILDREN** often use rehearsal (spoken or mental repetition) to help them remember things, without having been specifically taught how to do so.

Factors in Cognitive Development: Much of It Is in the HOME

- **CHILDREN'S LEVELS OF INTELLIGENCE**—not just their knowledge—are influenced by early learning experiences.
- **A HIGHLY ACADEMIC PRESCHOOL EDUCATION** provides children with advantages in school later on.
- **PRESCHOOLERS OFTEN CANNOT** differentiate between commercials and the TV programs themselves.

Language Development: Why "Daddy Goed Away"

- **DURING HER 3RD YEAR,** a girl explained that she and her mother had finished singing a song by saying, "We singed it all up."
- **THREE-YEAR-OLDS USUALLY SAY** "Daddy goed away" instead of "Daddy went away" because they *do* understand rules of grammar.

I was confused when my daughter Allyn, at the age of $2\frac{1}{2}$, insisted that I continue to play "Billy Joel" on the stereo. Put aside the question of her taste in music. My problem stemmed from the fact that when Allyn asked for Billy Joel, the name of the singer, she could be satisfied only by my playing the first song of the album, "Moving Out." When "Moving Out" had ended and the next song, "The Stranger," had begun to play, she would insist that I play "Billy Joel" again. "That is Billy Joel," I would protest. "No, no," she would insist, "I want Billy Joel!"

Finally, it dawned on me that "Billy Joel," for her, symbolized the song "Moving Out," not the name of the singer. Of course my insistence that the second song was also "Billy Joel" could not satisfy her! She was conceptualizing Billy Joel as a property of a particular song, not as the name of a person who could sing many songs.

Children between 2 and 4 tend to show confusion between symbols and the objects they represent. At their level of cognitive development, they do not recognize that words are arbitrary symbols for objects and events and that people could get together and decide to use different words for things. Instead, children of this age tend to think of words as inherent properties of objects and events.

This chapter discusses cognitive development during early childhood. First we examine the preoperational stage of cognitive development proposed by Swiss psychologist Jean Piaget. Then we consider other aspects of cognitive development, such as how children acquire a "theory of mind" and develop memory. We shall look at the influence of parents, preschool education, and television on cognitive development. Finally, we continue our exploration of language development.

Jean Piaget's Preoperational Stage

Click *Cognition* in the Child and Adolescent CD-ROM for more on the preoperational stage and symbolic thought.

According to Piaget, the **preoperational stage** of cognitive development lasts from about age 2 to about age 7. ***Question: How do children in the preoperational stage think and behave?***

Symbolic Thought

Reflect

Is it possible for you to think about something without using words? Why not give it a try?

Preoperational thought is characterized by the use of symbols to represent objects and the relationships among them. Perhaps the most important kind of symbolic activity of young children is language. Language takes on greater importance in this stage of cognitive development, as children become increasingly verbal. But we shall see that children's early use of language leaves something to be desired in the realm of logic.

Children begin to scribble and draw pictures in the early years. These drawings are symbols of objects, people, and events in children's lives. Another example of symbolism that emerges during these years is symbolic play, also known as pretend play. ***Question: So what is "child's play" like in early childhood?***

Symbolic or Pretend Play: "Make Believe"

Children's **symbolic play**—the "let's pretend" type of play—may seem immature to busy adults meeting the realistic demands of the business world, but it requires cognitive sophistication (Doyle et al., 1991; Nichols & Stich, 2000; Nielsen & Dissanayake, 2000).

According to Piaget (1946/1962), pretend play usually begins in the 2nd year, when the child begins to symbolize objects. Piaget argued that the ability to engage in pretend play is based on the use and recollection of symbols—that is, on mental representations of things children have encountered or heard about. At 19 months, Allyn picked up a pine cone and looked it over. Her babysitter Jill said,

preoperational stage The second stage in Piaget's scheme, characterized by inflexible and irreversible mental manipulation of symbols.

symbolic play Play in which children make believe that objects and toys are other than what they are. Also termed *pretend play.*

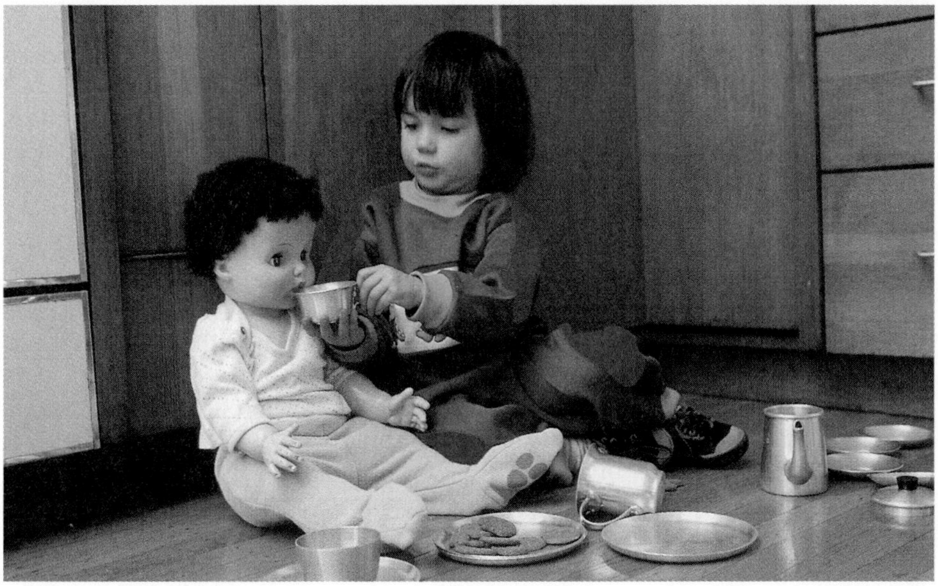

© Elizabeth Crews

Symbolic Play

Symbolic play—also called pretend play*—usually begins in the 2nd year, when the child begins to form mental representations of objects. Pretend play increases in frequency and becomes more complex throughout the preschool years. This $2^1/_2$-year-old may engage in a sequence of play acts such as making a doll sit down at the table and offering it a make-believe cup of tea.*

"That's a pine cone." Allyn started pretending to lick it, as if it were an ice cream cone.

Children first engage in pretend play at about 12 or 13 months. They make believe they are performing familiar activities such as sleeping or feeding themselves. By 15 to 20 months, they can shift their focus from themselves to others. A child at this age may pretend to feed her doll instead of herself. By 30 months of age, she or he can make believe that the other object takes an active role. For example, the child may pretend that the doll is feeding itself (Campbell, 1990; McCune, 1993).

Pretend play increases in frequency during the preschool years and becomes more complex (Nichols & Stich, 2000; Stagnitti, Unsworth, & Rodger, 2000). Pretend play takes on longer, coordinated sequences (Harris & Kavanaugh, 1993). For example, a 2-year-old might simply comb a doll's hair. An older preschooler is more likely to comb the doll's hair, put clothes on the doll, make it sit down at a table, pretend to make tea, and offer some to the doll.

The quality of preschoolers' pretend play has implications for development in later years. Research suggests that preschoolers who engage in more violent pretend play are less empathic, less likely to help other children, and more likely to engage in antisocial behavior later on (Dunn & Hughes, 2001). Preschoolers who engage in more elaborate pretend play are also more likely to do well in school later on (Stagnitti et al., 2000). The quality of pretend play is also connected with preschoolers' creativity and their ability to relate to their peers, both in the United States and in Korea (Farver, Kim, & Lee-Shin, 2000).

Joanne Curran (1999) observed the pretend play of 3-, 4-, and 5-year-olds and found that a number of rules of pretend play emerged and solidified over time. For example, one child—the "director"—suggests engaging plot ideas. The children in the play group are all encouraged to participate and take specific roles in the emerging scenario. Children also tend to be willing to redirect their play as participants make proposals for altering or embellishing the plot.

Shaun Nichols and Stephen Stich (2000) theorize that preschoolers keep their mental play representations in a cognitive "Possible World Box." However, children operate on the false beliefs in this "box" with the same logic (or lack of logic) they apply to actual events. They find "updating" mechanisms that allow contents within the box to change as play evolves. Moreover, children attempt to keep playful behavior consistent with the contents of the possible world box.

Reflect

Do adults use symbolic play or pretend play? How? How does it differ from symbolic play in early childhood?

Reflect

Did you ever have an imaginary friend? What do you remember about it? For students with children: Do any of your children have imaginary friends? What are the friends "like"?

Imaginary Friends: "Wouldn't It Be . . . Loveliness?"

Imaginary friends are one example of pretend play. At age 2, Allyn acquired an imaginary playmate named "Loveliness." He told Allyn to do lots of things—move things from here to there, get food for him, and so on. At times, Allyn was overheard talking to Loveliness in her room. As many as 65% of preschoolers have such friends, and they are more common among first-born and only children (Gleason, Sebanc, & Hartup, 2000). Many mothers report that their preschoolers' relationships with their imaginary playmates are sociable and friendly and that they may be fulfilling the need for a relationship (Gleason et al., 2000). Yet having an imaginary playmate does not mean that the child is having difficulty maintaining contact with reality. In fact, children with imaginary companions are less aggressive, more cooperative, and more creative. They have more real friends, show a greater ability to concentrate, and are more advanced in their language development (Meador, 1992; Singer, 1998; Taylor, Cartwright, & Carlson, 1993).

Since we are talking about play, let's note that some toys are called "Transformers." In the following section, we see that the mental processes of children are also "transformers." (Do you believe that transition from one section to another?)

Operations: The "Transformers" of the Mind

Any resemblance between the logic of children ages 2 to 7 and your own may be purely coincidental. ***Question: How do we characterize the logic of the preoperational child?***

The peculiar nature of young children's logic reflects the fact that they are generally not capable of performing what Piaget refers to as operations. Or, if they can perform some operations, the circumstances under which they can perform them are limited.

Operations are mental acts (or schemes) in which objects are changed or transformed and can then be returned to their original states. Mental operations are flexible and reversible.

Consider the example of planning a move in checkers or chess. A move in either game requires knowledge of the rules of the game. The child who plays the game well (as opposed to just making moves) is able to picture the results of the move—how, in its new position, the piece will support or be threatened by other pieces and how other pieces might be left undefended by the move. Playing checkers or chess well requires that the child be able to picture, or focus on, different parts of the board and on relationships between pieces at the same time. By considering several moves, the child shows flexibility. By picturing the board as it would be after a move, and then as it is, the child shows reversibility.

Having said all this, let us return to the fact that this section is about preoperational children—children who cannot yet engage in flexible and reversible mental operations. The preoperational stage of cognitive development is characterized by many features, including egocentrism, immature notions about causality in the physical world, confusion between mental and physical events, and ability to focus on only one dimension at a time.

Click *Cognition* for more on egocentrism.

operations Flexible, reversible mental manipulations of objects, in which objects can be mentally transformed and then returned to their original states.

egocentrism Putting oneself at the center of things such that one is unable to perceive the world from another person's point of view. Egocentrism is normal in early childhood but a matter of choice, and rather intolerable, in adults. (Okay, I sneaked an editorial comment into a definition. So did Dr. Samuel Johnson.)

Egocentrism: It's All About . . . Me

Sometimes the attitude "It's all about me" is a sign of early childhood, not of selfishness. One consequence of one-dimensional thinking is **egocentrism.** Preoperational children cannot understand that other people do not see things as they do. When I asked Allyn—still at the age of $2\frac{1}{2}$—to tell me about a trip to the store with her mother, she answered "You tell me." It did not occur to her that I could not see the world through her eyes.

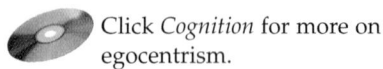

Question: What is egocentrism? Egocentrism, in Piaget's use of the term, does not mean that preoperational children are selfish (although, of course, they may be). It means that they have not yet developed a complete understanding that other people may have different perspectives on the world. They often view the world as a stage that has been erected to meet their needs and amuse them.

Piaget used the so-called three-mountains test (see Figure 9.1) to show that egocentrism means that young children literally cannot take the viewpoints of others. In this demonstration, the child sits at a table before a model of three mountains. The mountains differ in color. One also has a house on it, and another a cross at the summit.

Piaget then places a doll elsewhere around the table and asks the child what the doll sees. The language abilities of very young children do not permit them to provide verbal descriptions of what can be seen from where the doll is situated, so they can answer in one of two ways. They can either select a photograph taken from the proper vantage point, or they can construct another model of the mountains, as they would be seen by the doll. The results of an experiment with the three-mountains test suggest that 4-year-olds frequently do not understand the problem and that 5- and 6-year-olds usually select photos or build models that correspond to their own viewpoints (Laurendeau & Pinard, 1970).

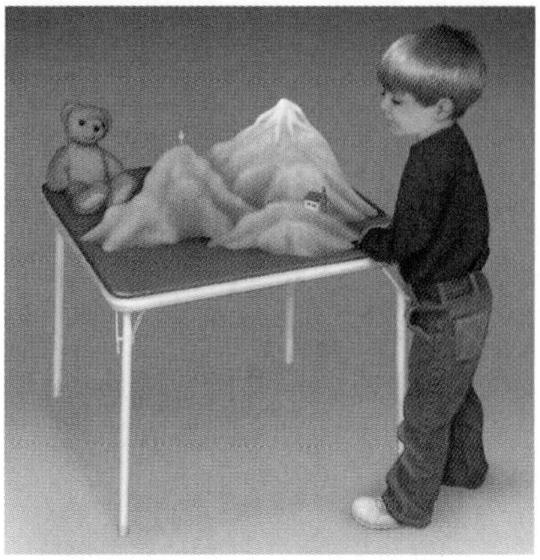

Figure 9.1
The Three-Mountains Test

Piaget used the "three-mountains test" to learn whether children at certain ages are egocentric or can take the viewpoints of others. Researchers have developed many other methods for assessing egocentrism.
Source: Piaget & Inhelder, 1969.

Causality: Why? Because

Preoperational children's responses to questions such as "Why does the sun shine?" may show some other facets of egocentrism. At the age of 2 or so, they may simply answer that they do not know or change the subject. But children a year or two older may report themselves as doing things because they want to do them, or, perhaps, "Because Mommy wants me to." In egocentric fashion, this explanation of behavior is extended to inanimate objects. And so, the sun may be thought of as shining because it wants to shine or because someone (or something) else wants it to shine.

A preoperational child might also respond that the sun shines "to keep me warm." In this case, the sun's behavior is thought of as being caused by will—perhaps the sun's voluntary wish to bathe the child in its rays or the child's wish to remain warm. In either case, such an answer places the child at the center of the conceptual universe. The sun itself becomes as much an instrument as a lightbulb.

Piaget considers this type of structuring of cause and effect **precausal.** ***Question: What is precausal thinking?*** Preoperational children believe that things happen for reasons and not by accident. However, unless preoperational children are quite familiar with the natural causes of an event, their reasons are likely to have an egocentric, psychological flavor and not be based on physical causes or natural law.

Preoperational children are likely to offer mechanical explanations for familiar events (R. Gelman, 1978; Hickling, 2001), such as how food gets onto a dish ("Mommy put it there") or why a tower of blocks falls ("It's too tall"). But consider the question "Why does it get dark outside?" The preoperational child usually does not have knowledge of the earth's rotation and is likely to answer something like "So I can go to sleep."

Another example of precausal thinking is **transductive reasoning.** In transductive reasoning, children reason by going from one specific isolated event to another. For example, a 3-year-old may argue that she should go on her swings in the backyard *because* it is light outside, or that she should not go to sleep *because* it is light outside. That is, separate specific events, daylight and going on the swings (or being awake) are thought of as having cause-and-effect relationships.

By contrast, older children and adults usually show inductive reasoning and deductive reasoning. In inductive reasoning, we go from the specific to the general, as in, "I get tired when I jog; therefore, exercise must be fatiguing." (A good reason to avoid jogging.) In deductive reasoning, we go from the general to the specific, as in "Exercise is fatiguing; therefore, if I jog, I'll get tired." (Another good reason to avoid jogging.)

Reflect

Would you label any of the people you know as "egocentric"? How does their egocentricity differ from the egocentricity of early childhood?

Reflect

Can you think of examples of "transductive reasoning" in your own life? (Are these really instances of transductive reasoning, or are they simply conventions of speech?)

precausal A type of thought in which natural cause-and-effect relationships are attributed to will and other preoperational concepts. (For example, the sun sets because it's tired.)

transductive reasoning Reasoning from the specific to the specific. (In deductive reasoning, one reasons from the general to the specific; in inductive reasoning, one reasons from the specific to the general.)

Click *Cognition* for more on animism.

Preoperational children also show **animism** and **artificialism** in their attributions of causality. In animistic thinking, they attribute life and intentions to inanimate objects, such as the sun and the moon. ("Why is the moon gone during the day?" "It is afraid of the sun.") Artificialism is the belief that environmental features such as rain and thunder have been designed and constructed by people. In *Six Psychological Studies,* Piaget (1964/1967) wrote that "Mountains 'grow' because stones have been manufactured and then planted. Lakes have been hollowed out, and for a long time the child believes that cities are built [prior to] the lakes adjacent to them" (p. 28). Other examples of egocentrism, animism, and artificialism are shown in Table 9.1.

Reflect

Do you recall ever believing that a dream must be real? What was the experience like?

Confusion of Mental and Physical Events: When Dreams Are Real

Question: Why do young children believe that dreams are real? According to Piaget, the preoperational child has difficulty making distinctions between mental and physical phenomena (Beilin & Pearlman, 1991). For example, children from about the ages of 2 to 4 tend to show a good deal of confusion between symbols and the objects or things that they represent. Egocentrism contributes to the assumption that their thoughts exactly reflect external reality. They do not recognize that words are arbitrary and that people could agree to use different words to refer to things. In *Play, Dreams, and Imitation in Childhood,* Piaget (1946/1962) asks a 4-year-old child, "Could you call this table a cup and that cup a table?" "No," the child responds. "Why not?" "Because," explains the child, "you can't drink out of a table!"

Another example of the preoperational child's confusion of the mental and the physical is the tendency to believe that dreams are real. Dreams are cognitive events that originate within the dreamer, and they seem to be perceived through the dreamer's sensory modalities (eyes, ears, and so on), even though the eyes are closed and the night casts no sound upon the ears. These facts are understood by 7-year-olds. However, many 4-year-olds believe that dreams are real. They think their dreams are visible to others and that dreams come from the outside. It is as though they were watching a movie (Crain, 2000).

animism The attribution of life and intentionality to inanimate objects.

artificialism The belief that environmental features were made by people.

Focus on One Dimension at a Time: Mental Blinders

To gain further insight into preoperational thinking, consider these two problems: Imagine that you pour water from a low, wide glass into a tall, thin glass, as in Figure 9.2. Now, does the tall, thin glass contain more than, less than, or the same

TABLE 9.1 *Examples of Preoperational Thought*

Type of Thought	Sample Questions	Typical Answers
Egocentrism	Why does it get dark out?	So I can go to sleep.
	Why does the sun shine?	To keep me warm.
	Why is there snow?	For me to play in.
	Why is grass green?	Because that's my favorite color.
	What are TV sets for?	To watch my favorite shows and cartoons.
Animism (attributing life and consciousness to physical objects)	Why do trees have leaves?	To keep them warm.
	Why do stars twinkle?	Because they're happy and cheerful.
	Why does the sun move in the sky?	To follow children and hear what they say.
	Where do boats go at night?	They sleep like we do.
Artificialism (assuming that environmental events are human inventions)	What makes it rain?	Someone emptying a watering can.
	Why is the sky blue?	Somebody painted it.
	What is the wind?	A man blowing.
	What causes thunder?	A man grumbling.
	How does a baby get in Mommy's tummy?	Just make it first. (How?) You put some eyes on it, then put on the head.

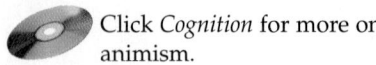

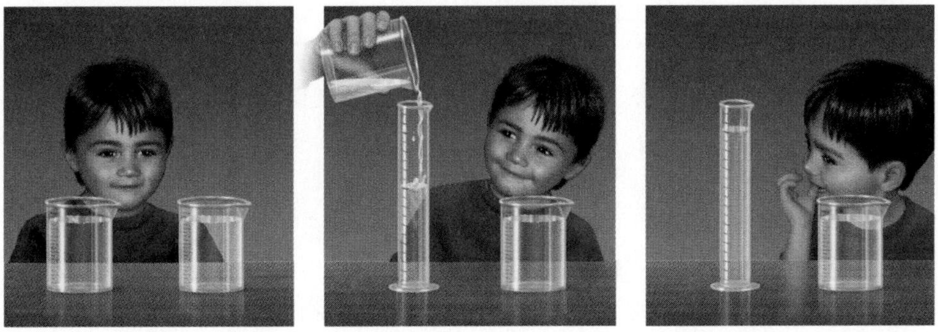

Figure 9.2
Conservation

The boy in this illustration agreed that the amount of water in two identical containers is equal. He then watched as water from one container was poured into a tall, thin container. When asked whether the amounts of water in the two containers are now the same, he says no. Apparently, he is centering on the height of the new container, and, prior to the development of conservation, he focuses on only one dimension of the situation at a time. Therefore, he is not focusing on the fact that the greater width of the lower container compensates for the loss in height.

amount of water as was in the low wide glass? We won't keep you in suspense. If you said *the same* (with possible minor exceptions for spillage and evaporation), you were correct.

Now that you're rolling, here's another problem. If you flatten a ball of clay into a pancake, do you wind up with more, less, or *the same* amount of clay? If you said the same, you are correct once more.

To arrive at the correct answers to these questions, you must understand the law of **conservation.** ***Question: What is conservation (that is, in terms of the cognitive development of the child)?*** The law of conservation holds that properties of substances such as volume, mass, and number remain the same—or are conserved—even if you change their shape or arrangement.

Now, preoperational children are not conservationists. I don't mean that they throw out half-eaten meals (though they do so often enough). I mean that they tend to focus on only one aspect of a problem at a time.

Conservation, as the term is used by cognitive psychologists, requires the ability to focus on two aspects of a situation at once, such as height and width. Conserving the volume, mass, or number of a substance requires recognition that a change in one dimension can compensate for a change in another. But the preoperational boy in Figure 9.2 focuses on just one dimension at a time, a characteristic of thought that Piaget called **centration.** First, the boy is shown two tall, thin glasses of water and agrees that they have the same amount of water. Then, while he watches, water is poured from one tall glass into a squat glass. Asked which glass has more water, he points to the tall glass. Why? When he looks at the glasses, he is "overwhelmed" by the fact that the thinner glass is taller.

conservation In cognitive psychology, the principle that properties of substances such as weight and mass remain the same (are conserved) when superficial characteristics such as their shapes or arrangement are changed.

centration Focusing on one dimension of a situation while ignoring others.

Developing in a World of Diversity

Cross-Cultural Differences in the Origin of Knowledge About Dreams

Do children gradually discover the properties of dreams on their own, as Piaget believed? Or do they learn about dreams from adults? In the United States, a parent comforts a child who has had a bad dream by saying something like "It was only a dream; it didn't really happen." But in some aboriginal cultures, such as the Atayal of Formosa, adults believe that dreams are real. In spite of these adult beliefs, Lawrence Kohlberg (1966) found that Atayal children initially go through the same stages in their understanding of dreams that American and Swiss children do. In other words, they first believe that dreams are real, then realize that they are not. Ultimately, however, they adopt the adult view that dreams are real.

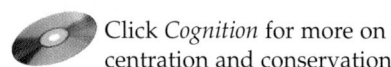

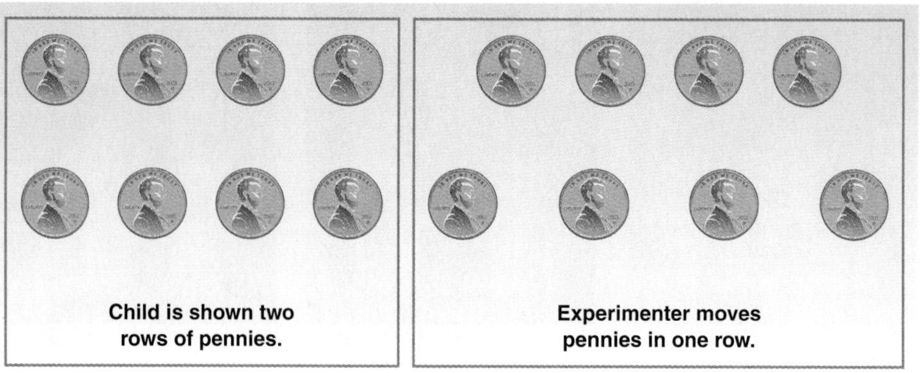
Child is shown two rows of pennies.
Experimenter moves pennies in one row.

Figure 9.3
Conservation of Number

In this demonstration, we begin with two rows of pennies that are spread out equally, as shown in the left-hand part of the drawing. Then one row of pennies is spread out more, as shown in the drawing on the right. We then ask the child, "Do the two rows still have the same number of pennies"? Do you think that a preoperational child will conserve the number of pennies or focus on the length of the longer row in arriving at an answer?

Reflect

Do we as adults sometimes focus on one dimension of a situation at a time? If you injure someone in an accident, should you be held responsible? (Note the two elements: the injury and the fact that it is accidental.) Most people would probably say "An accident is an accident." But: What if you injure eight million people in an accident? Should you be held responsible? (That is, does the enormity of the damage affect responsibility?)

Click *Cognition* for more on centration and conservation.

irreversibility Lack of recognition that actions can be reversed.

class inclusion The principle that one category or class of things can include several subclasses.

The preoperational child focuses on the most apparent dimension of the situation—in this case, the greater height of the thinner glass. He does not realize that the gain in width in the squat glass compensates for the loss in height. If you ask him whether any water has been added or taken away in the pouring process, he will readily reply no. But if you then repeat the question about which glass has more water, he will again point to the taller glass.

The preoperational child's failure to show conservation also comes about because of a characteristic of thought known as **irreversibility.** That is, the child fails to realize that an action such as pouring water from the tall glass to the squat glass can be reversed, thereby restoring things to their original condition.

If all this sounds rather illogical, that is because it is illogical—or, to be precise, preoperational. But if you have any doubts concerning its accuracy, borrow a 3-year-old and try the water experiment for yourself.

After you have tried the experiment with the water, try the following experiment on conservation of number. Make two rows with four pennies in each, about half an inch apart. As the 3-year-old child is watching, move the pennies in the second row to about an inch apart, as in Figure 9.3. Then ask the child which row has more pennies. What do you think the child will say? Why?

Class Inclusion

Now, here we are not referring to whether a class is open to children from diverse backgrounds. We are talking about an aspect of conceptual thinking that you most likely take for granted—including new objects or categories in broader mental classes or categories.

Class inclusion is another task that requires children to focus on two aspects of a situation at once. Class inclusion means that one category or class of things includes several other subclasses. For example, the class "animals" includes the subclasses of dogs, cats, horses (Okay: Horsies. Happy?), and so on.

In one of Piaget's class-inclusion tasks, the child is shown several objects from two subclasses of a larger class (see Figure 9.4). For example, a 4-year-old child is shown pictures of four cats and six dogs. She is asked whether there are more dogs or more animals. Now, this child knows what dogs and cats are. She also knows they are both types of animals. What do you think she will say? You may be surprised to learn that preoperational children typically answer that there are more dogs than animals (Piaget, 1936/1963). In other words, they fail to show class inclusion.

Why do children make this error of logic? According to Piaget, the preoperational child cannot think about the two subclasses and the larger class at the same time and so cannot readily compare them. Put another way, the child views dogs as dogs or as animals, but finds it difficult to see them as both dogs and animals simultaneously (Reyna, 1991). Another view is that young children fail to show class inclusion because their attention is too limited to focus on all aspects of the problem at once (Howe & Rabinowitz, 1991).

Figure 9.4
Class Inclusion

In one of Piaget's class-inclusion tasks, the child is shown several objects from two subclasses of a larger class. For example, a typical 4-year-old child is shown pictures of four cats and six dogs. She is asked whether there are more dogs or more animals. What do you think she will say? Why?

Evaluation of Piaget

Piaget was an astute observer of the cognitive processes of young children. But more recent research questions the accuracy of his age estimates concerning children's failures (or apparent failures) to display certain cognitive skills. As with Piaget's estimates of infant capabilities, the reasons for his underestimation are partly a result of the testing methods used. Let's examine some of the newer testing methods and their results.

Click *Cognition* for more on the contributions and limitations of Piaget's theory.

More Recent Research on Egocentrism

Margaret Donaldson (1979) argues that the difficulty young children have with the three-mountains test may not be due to egocentrism. Instead, she attributes much of their problem to the **demand characteristics** of the three-mountains test—to the demands that this particular experimental approach makes on the young child.

Donaldson believes that the three-mountains test presents a lifeless scene devoid of people and human motives. By contrast, she has found that when children are asked to place a boy doll behind tabletop screens so that it cannot be "seen" by police dolls, $3\frac{1}{2}$-year-olds succeed in doing so most of the time.

Other tasks designed to test the perspective-taking ability of preoperational children similarly reveal that they can, indeed, make inferences about others' views (Newcombe & Huttenlocher, 1992). These tasks typically involve a single object rather than a complex array. Some allow children to move the objects themselves or to use familiar words to label the perspectives of others (Yaniv & Shatz, 1991). In one study, for example, a doll was seated across the table from two empty chairs. A cardboard screen was placed in front of the doll, blocking the doll's view of one of the chairs. When 3-year-olds were asked to put a toy duck on one of the chairs "so that the doll can see it," they correctly picked the chair in the doll's line of view (Yaniv & Shatz, 1988).

Developing language skills may also play a role in tests of children's egocentrism and other aspects of cognitive development. Young children may not quite understand what is being asked of them in the three-mountains test, even though they may proceed to select the (wrong) photograph rather quickly. Let me give you an example. I was interested in knowing whether Allyn, at 2 years 9 months,

demand characteristics The demands that a specific experimental approach or task make on a subject, as opposed to the demands that would be made if the theoretical concepts were tested in a different way.

thought that her mother could see her from another room. "Can Mommy see you now?" I asked. "Sure," said Allyn, "if she wants to." Allyn thought I was asking whether her mother could have permission to see her, not whether her mother had the capacity to see Allyn from behind a wall.

To summarize, children seem able to take on the viewpoints of others earlier than Piaget suggested. One important implication is that they are likely to be concerned about the feelings of others at an earlier age than previously thought.

More Recent Research on Causality

Newer studies indicate that the young child's understanding of causality is somewhat more sophisticated than Piaget believed (Hickling, 2001). Again, much depends on how the task is presented. When 4–7-year-olds are asked the kind of

Developing in a World of Diversity

Cognitive Development and Concepts of Ethnicity and Race

What is the connection between cognitive development and the development of concepts about people from different ethnic and racial backgrounds? When is it most useful to intervene to help children develop open attitudes toward people from different backgrounds?

From interviews of 500 African American, Asian American, Latino and Latina American, and Native American children, psychologist Stephen Quintana (1998; Rabasca, 2000) concluded that children undergo four levels of understanding of ethnicity and race.

Between the ages of 3 and 6, children generally think about racial differences in physical terms. They do not necessarily see race as a fixed or stable attribute. They may think that a person could change his or her race by means of surgery or tanning in the sun.

From the ages of 6 to 10, children generally understand that race is a matter of ancestry that affects not only physical appearance but also one's language, diet, and leisure activities. But understanding at this stage is literal, or concrete. For example, children believe that being Mexican American means that one speaks Spanish and eats Mexican-style food. Interethnic friendships are likely to develop among children of this age group.

From the age of about 10 to 14, children tend to link ethnicity with social class. They become aware of connections between race and income, race, and neighborhood, and race and affirmative action.

During adolescence, many individuals begin to take pride in their ethnic heritage and experience a sense of belonging to their ethnic group. They are less open to intergroup relationships than younger children are.

Quintana's research tells him that middle childhood and early adolescence (the ages 6 to 14) are probably the best times to fend off the development of prejudice by teaching children about peoples from different cultural backgrounds. "That's when [children are] able to go beyond the literal meaning of the words and address their own observations about race and ethnicity," he notes (cited in Rabasca, 2000). Children at these ages also tend to be more open to forming relationships with children from different backgrounds than they are during adolescence.

© Bonnie Kamin/Photoedit

How Stable a Trait Is Ethnicity in the Eyes of Children?

According to research by Quintana, children between the ages of 3 to 6 tend to think about racial differences in physical terms. They do not necessarily see race as a fixed or stable attribute. They may think that people can change their race by means of surgery or sun-tanning.

open-ended questions that Piaget used (for example, "Where did the ocean come from?"), they give artificialistic responses such as "The ocean comes from sinks." But when asked direct questions ("Do you think people made the oceans?"), most will correctly respond that people do not make natural events such as oceans or flowers, but do make such objects as cups and TVs (Gelman & Kremer, 1991).

Another study shows that preoperational children correctly reject artificialistic explanations for certain biological events. Children ages 4 to 7 were asked how dogs, flowers, and cans got their color. The children correctly preferred natural mechanisms for the dogs and flowers. (For example, "While the puppy was still growing inside its mother, the mother gave it some very tiny things which made the puppy turn brown.") But children also recognized that people are responsible for producing the color of manufactured items, such as cans (Springer & Keil, 1991). Even children as young as age 3 reason differently about living organisms and inanimate objects. For example, they realize that young animals increase in size over time but that manufactured items, such as cups and TV sets, do not (Rosengren et al., 1991).

More Recent Research on Conservation

A major criticism of Piaget's tasks is that they require not only knowledge of conservation, but also language and attention skills that are difficult for young children. For instance, young children have difficulty understanding such relational terms as "more," "less," and "the same," which often are used in conservation tasks (Small, 1990).

In addition, certain demand characteristics of the standard conservation task may give a misleading picture of the child's real knowledge of conservation. Recall experiments in which Piaget and other experimenters fill two identical beakers with the same amount of water and then pour the water from one into a beaker of another shape. Before pouring the water from one beaker into another, the experimenter typically does two things. First, he or she asks the child whether both beakers have the same amount of water. Second, the child is instructed to watch the pouring carefully. A variation on this experiment by Susan Rose and Marion Blank (1974) suggests that this approach gives the experiment demand characteristics that push the child toward the wrong answer.

Rose and Blank simply avoided questioning their young subjects as to whether the amounts in the two beakers were the same before the water was poured from one beaker to another. With this approach, 6-year-olds were significantly more likely to state that the differently shaped glasses did contain the same amount of water. The researchers suggest that initially asking children whether the beakers have the same amount of water can prime them to expect a change. The instruction to watch the pouring process closely can then reinforce the expectation of change. And so Piaget and other researchers may have been systematically underestimating the age at which children can conserve quantities of water because of the different demand characteristics of their experimental approach.

Other more recent studies also demonstrate that young children's thought is not as limited as Piaget believed. For example, the development of conservation of number appears to be tied to the development of counting ability in children. One of the key principles underlying counting ability is the cardinal word principle. This principle states that the last number in a count is special because it indicates the total number of items. Studies by Karen Wynn (1990, 1992b) indicate that children appear to learn the **cardinal word principle** at about $3\frac{1}{2}$ years of age, much earlier than Piaget would have predicted. In her 1990 study, $2\frac{1}{2}$–$3\frac{1}{2}$-year-olds were asked to give a puppet one, two, three, five, and six items from a pile. The younger children gave only one or two items and never used counting to solve the task. But the $3\frac{1}{2}$-year-olds counted the items, showing a clear understanding of the cardinal word principle.

cardinal word principle The principle that the last number in a count indicates how many total items there are.

In summary, researchers have taken issue with Piaget's view of the ages at which young children develop certain cognitive skills. As more sensitive tests have been developed, they are revealing that preschoolers have competencies that Piaget believed did not emerge until the school years (Flavell et al., 2002).

Cognitive skills apply to the functioning of the mind. ***Question: What are children's ideas about how the mind works?***

Review

(1) According to Piaget, the __________ stage of cognitive development lasts from about 2 to 7. (2) Preoperational children use __________ to represent objects and relationships among them. (3) The most important symbolic activity is __________. (4) According to Piaget, __________ play is based on the use of symbols. (5) Curran found that in pretend play, one child—the __________—suggests plot ideas. (6) About _____% of preschoolers have imaginary friends. (7) __________ are mental acts in which objects are changed or transformed and can then be returned to their original states. (8) Piaget used the three-mountains test to demonstrate that preoperational children are __________. (9) The type of thinking in which children attribute will to inanimate objects is termed __________ thinking. (10) In __________ reasoning, children reason from one specific event to another. (11) Preoperational children tend to believe that dreams are (false or real?) because they confuse mental events with physical events. (12) The law of __________ holds that properties of substances such as volume, mass, and number remain the same even if their shape or arrangement is changed. (13) Preoperational children focus on (how many?) dimension(s) or aspect(s) of a problem at once.

Pulling It Together: Explain how one-dimensional thinking gives rise to various kinds of mental errors made during early childhood.

A Closer Look

Response Alternation: Another Issue with Research on Conservation

The study by Susan Rose and Marion Blank (1974) described on page 323 indicates that in a standard conservation experiment, children are misled by the repetition of the conservation question. The repeated question is perceived by children as a signal that their previous answer was wrong, and so they change it.

But the failure of young children to stick with their first answer when questioned a second time could also be explained by a simple bias against repeating responses. When children have to choose between two or more alternatives in a guessing task, they tend to alternate responses. So, when children are asked the same question twice in a consecutive task, they may have a tendency to switch their answer the second time. To test this hypothesis, Ed Elbers and his colleagues (1991) tested 4–7-year-olds on a conservation-of-number problem using wooden blocks. One group was tested in the standard way. Both before and after the row of blocks was spread out, they were asked the same question: "Do the two rows have the same number of blocks?" Most children correctly answered "yes" to the first question, but incorrectly switched to "no" the second time.

A second group (the reverse-question group) was first asked "Does one of the rows contain *more* blocks?" After one row was spread out, the group then was asked the standard question ("Do the two rows have the same number of blocks?"). Most children correctly answered "no" to the first question and "yes" to the second. You can see that when the questions are posed in this order, alternating responses results in better performance. So young children's poor performance on Piaget's standard conservation task may be partly due to their tendency to alternate responses and not to a failure to understand the principle of conservation.

Theory of Mind: What Is the Mind? How Does It Work?

Adults appear to have a commonsense understanding of how the mind works. This understanding, known as a **theory of mind,** allows us to explain and predict behavior by referring to mental processes (Flavell, Green, & Flavell, 1993; O'Neill & Gopnik, 1991). For example, we understand that we may acquire knowledge through our senses or through hearsay. We understand the distinction between external and mental events and between how things appear and how they really are. We are able to infer the perceptions, thoughts, and feelings of others. We understand that mental states affect behavior (Flavell et al., 2002; Montgomery, 1992).

At what ages do children begin to develop these different aspects of a "theory of mind"? As we have seen, Piaget would have predicted that preoperational children are too egocentric and too focused on misleading external appearances to have a "theory of mind." But recent research has shown that even preschool-aged children can accurately predict and explain human action and emotion in terms of mental states. They are beginning to understand where knowledge comes from. And they have a rudimentary ability to distinguish appearance from reality (Moses & Chandler, 1992; Wellman, Phillips, & Rodriguez, 2000; Wellman, Cross, & Watson, 2001). Let's examine each of these developments in turn.

Reflect

Why do you think that behaviorists might object to this entire discussion of theory of mind?

False Beliefs: Just Where Are Those Crayons?

One important indication of the young child's understanding that mental states affect behavior is the ability to understand false beliefs. This concept involves children's ability to separate their beliefs from those of another person who has false knowledge of a situation. It is illustrated in a study of 3-year-olds by Louis Moses and John Flavell (1990). The children were shown a videotape in which a girl named Cathy found some crayons in a bag. When Cathy left the room briefly, a clown entered the room. The clown removed the crayons from the bag, hid them in a drawer, and put rocks in the bag instead. When Cathy returned, the children were asked whether Cathy thought there were going to be rocks or crayons in the bag. Most of the 3-year-olds incorrectly answered "rocks," demonstrating their difficulty in understanding that the other person's belief would be different from their own (see Figure 9.5). But by the age of 4 to 5 years, children do not have trouble with this concept and correctly answer "crayons" (Flavell, 1993; Flavell et al., 1990). At this age, they also start to understand that beliefs may be held with differing degrees of certainty (Moore, Pure, & Farrow, 1990). (Really, they can be. All

theory of mind A commonsense understanding of how the mind works.

Figure 9.5
False Beliefs

When are children able to separate their beliefs from those of someone who has false knowledge of a situation? John Flavell and his colleagues showed preschoolers a videotape in which a girl named Cathy found crayons in a bag (a). When Cathy left the room, a clown entered, removed the crayons from the bag, hid them in a drawer (b), and filled the bag with rocks (c). When asked whether Cathy thought there would be rocks or crayons in the bag, most 3-year-olds said "rocks." Most 4-year-olds correctly answered "crayons," showing the ability to separate their own beliefs from someone who has erroneous knowledge of a situation.

is not black and white; there are shades of gray. All right—I'll stop it and get back to the book.)

Another intriguing demonstration of the false belief concept comes from studies of children's ability to deceive others. For example, Beate Sodian and her colleagues (1991) asked children to hide a toy truck driver in one of five cups in a sandbox so that another person could not find it. The child was given the opportunity to deceive the other person by removing real trails in the sand and creating false ones. Once again, 4-year-olds acted in ways that were likely to mislead the other person. Younger children did not.

From the research we have looked at so far, it's tempting to conclude that an understanding of false belief and deception does not emerge until age 4 (Peskin, 1992; Ruffman et al., 1993). But some studies have found that under certain conditions, children at age 3 and even younger may show some knowledge of these concepts (Freeman, Lewis, & Doherty, 1991; Robinson & Mitchell, 1992). One such condition involves asking 3-year-olds a series of very specific questions about their beliefs and those of the other person (Lewis & Osborne, 1990). Even slight changes in experimental procedures or in the way questions are worded can result in 3-year-olds correctly demonstrating knowledge of false beliefs and deceptive strategies (Hala, Chandler, & Fritz, 1991; Siegel & Beattie, 1991; Sullivan & Winner, 1991). Participating in family conversations about feelings and about causality enhances the ability of 3-year-olds to understand other people's beliefs and feelings (Dunn et al., 1991).

Origins of Knowledge: Where Does It Come From?

Another aspect of "theory of mind" is how we acquire knowledge. ***Questions: Do children understand where their knowledge comes from? If so, how early do they show this ability?***

By age 3, most children begin to realize that people gain knowledge about something by looking at it (Pratt & Bryant, 1990). By age 4, children understand that particular senses provide information about only certain qualities of an object—for example, we come to know an object's color through our eyes, but we learn about its weight by feeling it (O'Neill, Astington, & Flavell, 1992; Perner, 1991). In a study by Daniela O'Neill and Alison Gopnik (1991), 3-, 4-, and 5-year-olds learned about the contents of a toy tunnel in three different ways. They either saw the contents, were told about them, or felt them. The children then were asked to state what was in the tunnel and also how they knew what was in the tunnel. While 4- and 5-year-olds had no trouble identifying the sources of their knowledge, the 3-year-olds did. For example, after feeling but not seeing a ball in the tunnel, a number of 3-year-olds told the experimenter that they could tell it was a blue ball. The children apparently did not realize that it was impossible to discover the ball's color just by feeling it.

Reflect

How does this discussion of the origins of knowledge "square" with ethological theory—that is, the notion that some behavior is instinctive? Can both views exist side by side?

The Appearance–Reality Distinction: Appearances Are More Deceiving at Some Ages Than at Others

Questions: Is seeing believing? What do preoperational children have to say about that? One of the most important things children must acquire in developing a theory of mind is a clear understanding of the difference between real events, on the one hand, and mental events, fantasies, and misleading appearances, on the other hand (Flavell, Green, & Flavell, 1993; 2000). This is known as the **appearance–reality distinction.**

appearance–reality distinction The difference between real events on the one hand and mental events, fantasies, and misleading appearances on the other hand.

Piaget's view was that children do not differentiate reality from appearances or mental events until the age of 7 or 8. But more recent studies have found that children's ability to distinguish between the two emerges in the preschool years. Children as young as age 3 can distinguish between pretend actions and real actions, between pictures of objects and the actual objects, and between toy versions of an object and the real object (Woolley & Wellman, 1993). By the age of 4, children make a clear distinction between real items (such as a cup), and imagined items (such as an imagined cup or an imagined monster) (Harris et al., 1991).

Despite these accomplishments, preoperational children still show some difficulties in recognizing the difference between the way things are (reality) and the way they may seem to be (appearance). According to John Flavell and his colleagues (1990, 2000), this is because children of this age still have only a limited understanding of **mental representations.** That is, they have trouble comprehending that a real object or event can take many forms in our minds. This would account for certain problems in distinguishing between appearance and reality. For example, in a recent study by Marjorie Taylor and Barbara Hort (1990), children ages 3 to 5 were shown a variety of objects that had misleading appearances, such as an eraser that looked like a cookie. Children initially reported that the eraser looked like a cookie. But once they learned that it was actually an eraser, they tended to report that it looked like an eraser, ignoring its cookie-like appearance. Apparently, the children could not mentally represent the eraser as both being an eraser and looking like a cookie.

Three-year-olds also have difficulty with other tasks that require them to think of the same object or event in more than one way. For example, children of this age apparently cannot understand changes in their mental states. In one study (Gopnik & Slaughter, 1991), 3-year-olds were shown a crayon box. They consistently said they thought crayons were inside. The box was opened, revealing birthday candles, not crayons. When the children were asked what they had thought was in the box before it was opened, they now said "candles."

Very young children also find it difficult to understand the relationship between a scale model and the larger object or space that it represents (DeLoache, 1991). Perhaps this is because the child cannot conceive that the model can be two things at once: both a representation of something else and an object in its own right.

Review

(14) One's __________ of mind allows one to explain and predict behavior by referring to mental processes. (15) Research shows that preschool-aged children are beginning to understand where knowledge comes from. (16) They also have some ability to distinguish __________ from reality. (17) Moses and Flavell used crayons and a clown to learn whether preschoolers can understand __________ beliefs. (18) By age 3, most children begin to realize that people gain knowledge about a thing through the __________. (19) Children as young as __________ can distinguish between pretend actions and real actions and between toys and the objects they represent.

Pulling It Together: Explain how development in various aspects of the theory of mind come to enable children to understand false beliefs and the distinction between appearances and reality.

Development of Memory: Creating Files and Retrieving Them

Even newborns have some memory skills, and memory improves substantially throughout the first 2 years of life (Kail, 1990). ***Question: What sorts of memory skills do children possess in early childhood?***

mental representations The mental forms that a real object or event can take, which may differ from one another. (Successful problem solving is aided by accurate mental representation of the elements of the problem.)

Click *Cognition* for more on memory skills.

Memory Tasks: Recognition and Recall

Two of the basic tasks used in the study of memory are recognition and recall. Recognition is the easiest type of memory task. For this reason, multiple-choice tests are easier than fill-in-the-blank or essay tests. In a **recognition** test, one simply indicates whether a presented item has been seen before or which of a number of items is paired with a stimulus (as in a multiple-choice test). Children are capable of simple recognition during early infancy, as we have seen. They recognize their mother's nursing pads, her voice, and her face. To test recognition memory in a preschooler, you might show the child some objects and then present those objects along with some new ones. The child is then asked which objects you showed her the first time.

Recall is more difficult than recognition. In a **recall** task, children must reproduce material from memory without any cues. If I ask you to name the capital of Wyoming, that is a test of recall. A recall task for a preschooler might consist of showing her some objects, taking them away, and asking her to name the objects from memory.

When preschoolers are presented lists of objects, pictures, or words to learn, they typically can recognize many more items later on than they can recall (Schneider & Pressley, 1989). In fact, younger preschoolers are almost as good as older ones in recognizing objects they have seen. However, younger preschoolers are not nearly as good as older ones when it comes to recall. In Figure 9.6, compare the ability of 3- and 4½-year-olds to recognize and recall various objects from

Reflect

Would you rather take a multiple-choice test or a fill-in-the-blank test? How does your answer fit in with our discussion of recognition versus recall?

recognition A memory task in which the individual indicates whether presented information has been experienced previously.

recall A memory task in which the individual must reproduce material from memory without any cues.

Developing in the New Millennium

The Mozart Effect—Will Music Provide Children With the Sweet Sounds of Success?

Technological innovations are overleaping themselves in the new millennium. Parents are concerned about what they can do to help their children grasp the new technologies. Whatever environmental factors are found to enhance children's intellectual functioning may well be music to parents' ears. But it may also turn out that music will be spatial reasoning to children's ears.

Research suggests that listening to and studying music may enhance at least one aspect of intellectual functioning—spatial reasoning. In 1993, the research team of Frances Rauscher, Gordon Shaw, and Katherine Ky published an intriguing article in *Nature* on the effects of exposure to Mozart's music. They claimed that listening to 10 minutes of Mozart's Piano Sonata K 448 enhanced college students' scores on spatial-reasoning tasks. For example, they were better able to perceive the design of a "snowflake" after mentally cutting and folding a piece of paper, and they were better able to rotate and compare objects in space (Hershenson, 2000).

These were college students. What about young children? At the 1994 meeting of the American Psychological Association, a research team headed by Rauscher reported the results of a follow-up study with preschoolers in a paper titled "Music and spatial task performance: A causal relationship." They recruited 19

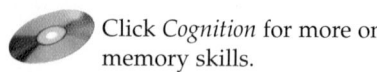

© Bill Bachmann/Index Stock/PictureQuest

The Sweet Sounds of Success?

Some research suggests that training in music enhances children's intellectual functioning, particularly in visual-spatial areas. Perhaps perception of music and spatial relations occupy overlapping neural pathways. However, it should be noted that this field of research is in its infancy and that psychologists disagree as to its implications.

a life-size playhouse (Jones et al., 1988). (We will discuss the "activities" part of this figure later.)

Competence of Memory in Early Childhood

Until a few years ago, most studies of children's memory were done in laboratory settings. The tasks used had little meaning for the children. Results from these studies appeared to show that the memories of young children are deficient relative to those of older children. But parents will often tell you that their children have excellent memories for episodes in their lives. It turns out that they are right. More recently, psychologists have focused their research on children's memory for events and activities that are meaningful to them. These studies show that young children's memories are indeed impressive (K. Nelson, 1990, 1993).

For example, children as young as $11\frac{1}{2}$ months of age can remember organized sequences of events they have just experienced (Bauer & Mandler, 1992). Even after a delay of 6 weeks, 16-month-old children can reenact a sequence of events they experienced only one time, such as placing a ball in a cup, covering it with another cup, and shaking the resulting "rattle" (Bauer & Mandler, 1990). By the age of 4 years, children can remember events that occurred at least $1\frac{1}{2}$ years earlier (Fivush & Hammond, 1990).

Katherine Nelson and her colleagues (1990, 1993) have interviewed children ages 2 to 5 to study their memory for recurring events in their lives, such as having dinner, playing with friends, and going to birthday parties. They found that even 3-year-olds can present coherent, orderly accounts of familiar events. Furthermore, young children seem to form **scripts,** which are abstract, generalized accounts of these repeated events. For example, in describing what happens during a birthday party, a child might say, "You play games, open presents, and eat cake" (Farrar & Goodman, 1990). Details of particular events often are omitted. However, an unusual experience may be remembered in detail for a year or more (K. Nelson, 1989).

scripts Abstract generalized accounts of familiar repeated events.

preschoolers aged from 3 years to 4 years 9 months and gave them 8 months of music lessons, including singing and use of a keyboard. After the lessons, the children's scores on an object-assembly task significantly exceeded those of 15 preschoolers who did not receive the musical training.

Cognitive psychologist Lois Hetland (2000) reports that children given keyboard lessons perform better on spatial-reasoning tests. She also analyzed research with college students and concluded that they scored higher on spatial-reasoning tests after hearing the music of Mozart, Schubert, and Mendelssohn but not the music of Philip Glass (a contemporary composer of classical-style music) or of Pearl Jam and other rock groups. That is, music with complex structure and rhythm apparently had more beneficial cognitive benefits.

How might listening to music or training in music affect spatial reasoning? It may be that neural pathways involved in processing music overlap those involved in other cognitive functions—such as spatial reasoning (Rauscher, 1998). Musical training thus develops the neural firing patterns used in spatial reasoning, which may eventually help children solve geometry problems, design skyscrapers, navigate ships, and perhaps even fit suitcases into the trunk of a car.

The researchers caution that their findings should be considered preliminary. Attempts to replicate the Rauscher studies have met with mixed success (Rauscher & Shaw, 1998). Moreover, it is unclear exactly what aspects of the "treatment" may have influenced students (Nantais & Schellenberg, 1999). Is it the music itself, or could it be related factors like the spatial patterns made by the black and white keys on the keyboard or even a mood change caused by the music (Hershenson, 2000; Steele, 2000; Thompson, Schellenberg, & Husain, 2001)? We don't have the answers (Schellenberg, 2000).

But perhaps the findings are enticing enough to encourage school administrators to maintain music programs, which are often among the first to go when school districts tighten the purse strings. Music, after all, may contribute to the sweet sounds of success.

Search Online With InfoTrac College Edition

For additional information, explore InfoTrac College Edition, your online library. Go to **http://www.infotrac-college.com** and use the passcode from the InfoTrac card that came with your book. Try these search terms: music and cognitive development, Mozart effect, intelligence music, music and reasoning, music physiological aspects.

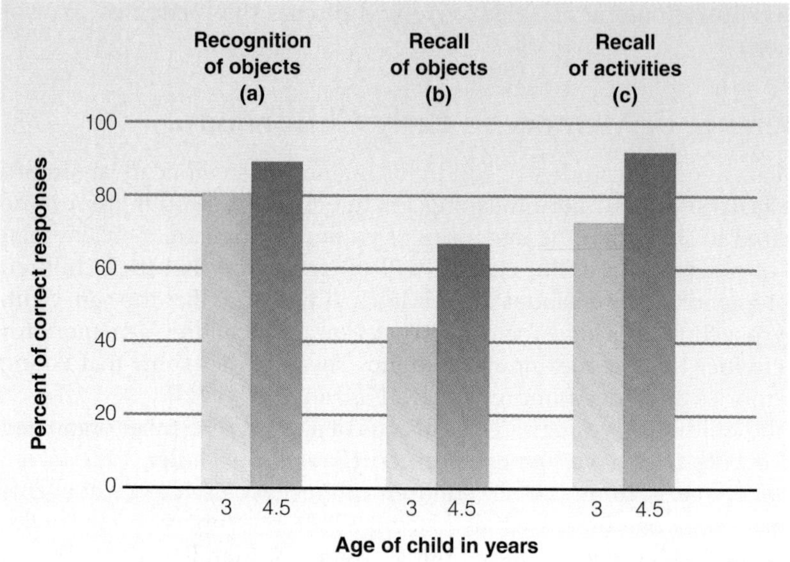

Figure 9.6
Recognition and Recall Memory

Preschoolers can recognize previously seen objects (a) better than they can recall them (b). They also are better at recalling their activities (c) than recalling objects (b). Older preschoolers (green bars) have better memories than younger ones (yellow bars).

Source: D.C. Jones et al., 1988.

© Burke/Triolo Productions/FoodPix/Getty Images

Scripts of Familiar Events

Children in the preschool years form scripts, which are abstract, generalized accounts of repeated events. For example, in describing what happens during a birthday party, a child might say, "You play games, open presents, and eat cake." The script becomes more detailed with repeated experiences.

Young children begin forming scripts after experiencing an event only once. The script becomes more elaborate with repeated experiences. As might be expected, older preschool children form detailed scripts more quickly than younger children (Price & Goodman, 1990; Ratner, Smith, & Padgett, 1990).

Even though children as young as 1 and 2 years of age clearly can remember past events, these memories seldom last into adulthood. Most adults cannot remember significant events in their lives that occurred before the age of 2 or 3 (Howe & Courage, 1993). This memory of specific events—known as **autobiographical memory**—appears to be linked to the development of language skills, as children begin to talk with their parents and others about past events (Farrant & Reese, 2000; Nelson, 1993).

Reflect

Think of some autobiographical memories. What factors determine which ones you remember and how well you remember them? Do these factors also hold in early childhood?

Factors Influencing Memory

Question: What factors affect memory in early childhood? These include what the child is asked to remember, the interest level of the child, the availability of retrieval cues or reminders, and what memory measure we are using. Let's discuss each of these in turn.

Types of Memory

Preschoolers' memories for activities are better than their memories for objects. Return to Figure 9.6 once again. Compare children's accuracy in recalling the activities they engaged in while in the playhouse with their accuracy in recalling the objects they used. You will see that children were much better at recalling their activities (for example, washing a shirt, chopping ice) than they were at recalling specific objects, such as shirts and icepicks (Jones et al., 1988).

Children also find it easier to remember events that follow a logical order than events that do not occur in a particular order. For instance, 3- and 5-year-olds have a better memory for the activities involved in making pretend cookies out of Play-Doh (you put the ingredients in the bowl, then mix the ingredients, then roll out the dough, and so on) than they do for the activities involved in sand play, which can occur in any order (Fivush, Kuebli, & Clubb, 1992).

Click *Cognition* for more on factors influencing memory.

autobiographical memory The memory of specific episodes or events.

Interest Level

There's nothing new about the idea that we pay more attention to the things that interest us. The world is abuzz with signals, and we tend to remember those to which we pay attention. Attention opens the door to memory.

Interest level and motivation also contribute to memory among young children. In one study, for example, 3-year-old boys were more interested in playing with toys like cars and rockets, while 3-year-old girls were more interested in playing with dolls, dishes, and teddy bears. Later, the children showed better recognition and recall for the toys in which they were interested (Renninger, 1990). Even by this age, gender-role expectations may exert their influence on cognitive development.

Reflect

In which courses is it easiest for you to remember the subject matter? Why?

Retrieval Cues

In order to retrieve information (a file) from your computer's storage, you have to remember its name or some part of it. Then you can use a "find" routine. The name is the retrieval cue. In the same way, we need retrieval cues to find things in our own memories.

Although young children can remember a great deal, they depend more than older children on cues provided by adults to help them retrieve their memories. Consider the following interchange between a mother and her 2-year-old child:

Mother: What did we look for in the grass and in the bushes?
Child: Easter bunny.
Mother: Did we hide candy eggs outside in the grass?
Child: (nods)
Mother: Remember looking for them? Who found two? Your brother?
Child: Yes, brother (Hudson, 1990, p. 186).

Young children whose mothers elaborate on the child's experiences and ask questions that encourage the child to contribute information to the narrative remember an episode better than children whose mothers simply provide reminders (K. Nelson, 1990). Parental assistance is more important under some conditions than others. For example, when 4-year-olds were internally motivated to remember items needed to prepare their own sack lunches, they did equally well with or without maternal coaching. But when the task was simply to recall a series of items, they did better with maternal assistance (Rogoff & Mistry, 1990).

Types of Measurement

What we find is in part determined by how we measure it. Children's memory is often measured or assessed by asking them to verbally report what they remember. But verbal reports, especially from very young children, no doubt underestimate how much children actually remember (Mandler, 1990). In one longitudinal study, children's memory for certain events was tested at age $2\frac{1}{2}$ and again at age 4. Most of the information recalled at 4 had not been mentioned at $2\frac{1}{2}$, indicating that when they were younger, the children remembered much more than they reported (Fivush & Hammond, 1990).

Click *Cognition* for more on memory strategies.

What measures might be more accurate than verbal report? One study found that when young children were allowed to use dolls to reenact an event, their recall was much better than when they gave a verbal report of the event (Goodman et al., 1990).

Memory Strategies: Remembering to Remember

Reflect

How do you prepare for a test? How do you remember lists of new vocabulary words, for example? How does a preschooler learn the alphabet?

Question: How do we remember to remember? When adults and older children are trying to remember things, they use strategies to help their memory. One common strategy is mental repetition, or **rehearsal.** If you are trying to remember a new friend's phone number, for example, you might repeat it several times. Another strategy is to organize things to be remembered into

rehearsal Repetition.

© Elizabeth Crews

Helping Young Children Remember

Memory functioning in early childhood—and at other ages—is aided when adults provide cues to help children remember. Adults can help by elaborating on the child's experiences and asking questions that encourage the child to contribute information.

categories. Many students outline textbook chapters to prepare for an exam. This is a way of organizing information in a meaningful way, which makes it easier to learn and remember (Kail, 1990). Similarly, if you are going to buy some things at the grocery store, you might mentally group together items that belong to the same category: dairy items, produce, household cleaners, and so on.

But preschool children generally do not appear to employ memory strategies on their own initiative. The majority of young children do not spontaneously engage in rehearsal until around 5 years of age (Small, 1990). They also rarely group objects into related categories to help them remember (Kail, 1990). By about 5, many children have learned to verbalize information silently to themselves—counting in their heads, for example, instead of aloud. This strategy improves their ability to remember visual information (T. Adler, 1993c).

But even very young children are capable of using some simple and concrete memory aids to help them remember. They engage in behaviors such as looking, pointing, and touching when trying to remember. For example, in a study by Judith DeLoache and her colleagues (1985), 18–24-month-old children observed as the experimenter hid a Big Bird doll under a pillow. They then were given attractive toys to play with and, after a short period of time, were asked to find the hidden object. During the play interval, the children frequently looked or pointed at the hiding place or repeated the name of the hidden object. These behaviors suggest the beginning of the use of strategies to prompt the memory.

Young children also can be taught to successfully use strategies they might not use on their own. For example, 6-year-old children who are trained to rehearse show a marked improvement in their ability to recall items on a memory test (Small, 1990). Similarly, requiring preschoolers to sort objects into categories enhances their memory of the material (Lange & Pierce, 1992; Schneider & Pressley, 1989). Even 3- and 4-year-olds will use rehearsal and labeling strategies if they are explicitly told to try to remember something (Fabricius & Cavalier, 1989; Weissberg & Paris, 1986).

The preschooler's use of memory strategies is not nearly as sophisticated as that of the school-age child. The use of memory strategies and the child's understanding of how memory works advances greatly in middle childhood.

Reflect

What strategies do you use to memorize the subject matter in your courses? What strategies does your textbook author (that's me!) use to help you remember the subject matter in this course?

Review

(20) Two of the basic tasks used in the study of memory are recognition and _________. (21) Children are capable of simple (recognition or recall?) during infancy. (22) Preschoolers have (better or worse?) memory for events and activities when they are meaningful. (23) Young children form _________, which are generalized accounts of repeated events. (24) Memory for episodes in one's life is referred to as _________ memory. (25) Preschoolers' memories for activities are (better or worse?) than their memories for objects. (26) Preschoolers find it (harder or easier?) to remember events that follow a logical order than events that do not occur in a particular order. (27) Interest level is (positively or negatively?) connected with ability to remember. (28) When preschoolers are allowed to use toys to reenact an event, their recall is better than when they give a _________ report. (29) Using mental repetition to remember is termed _________. (30) Preschool children (do or do not?) use memory strategies on their own initiative.

Pulling It Together: How can parents and educators help preschool children improve their memories?

Factors in Cognitive Development: Much of It Is in the HOME

Question: What are some of the factors that influence cognitive development in early childhood? Some of the most important include social and family factors, such as family income; the parents' educational level; family size; parents' mental health; and the presence of stressful family events, such as divorce, job loss, or illness (Bradley et al., 2001). In this section, we examine the role of three key factors in the young child's cognitive development: the home environment provided by the parents, preschool education, and television.

Being at HOME: The Effect of the Home Environment

Bettye Caldwell has developed a measure for evaluating children's home environments labeled, appropriately enough, HOME—an acronym for Home Observation for the Measurement of the Environment. With this method, researchers directly observe parent–child interaction in the home. The HOME inventory contains six subscales, as shown in Table 9.2.

HOME inventory items are better predictors of young children's later IQ scores than social class, mother's IQ, or infant IQ scores (Bradley, 1989; Luster & Dubow, 1992). In a longitudinal study, Caldwell and her colleagues observed children from poor and working-class families over a period of years, starting at 6 months of age. The HOME inventory was used at the early ages, and standard IQ tests were given at ages 3 and 4. The children of mothers who were emotionally and verbally responsive, who were involved with their children, and who provided appropriate play materials and a variety of daily experiences during the early years showed advanced social and language development even at 6 months of age (Parks & Bradley, 1991). These children also attained higher IQ scores at ages 3 and 4 and higher achievement-test scores at age 7 (Bradley, 1989). Other studies support the view that being responsive to preschoolers, stimulating them, and

Reflect

What was your early home environment like? How do you think it would have appeared in terms of the factors described in Table 9.2?

TABLE 9.2 *Scales of the HOME Inventory*

Scales	Sample Items
Emotional and verbal responsiveness of the mother	The mother spontaneously vocalizes to the child during the visit. The mother responds to the child's vocalizations with vocal or other verbal responses.
Avoidance of restriction and punishment	The mother does not shout at the child. The mother does not interfere with the child's actions or restrict the child's movements more than three times during the visit.
Organization of the physical environment	The child's play environment seems to be safe and free from hazards.
Provision of appropriate play materials	The child has a push or a pull toy. The child has one or more toys or pieces of equipment that promote muscle activity. The family provides appropriate equipment to foster learning.
Maternal involvement with child	The mother structures the child's play periods. The mother tends to keep the child within her visual range and looks at the child frequently.
Opportunities for variety in daily stimulation	The child gets out of the house at least four times a week. The mother reads stories to the child at least three times a week.

© Chuck Savage/Corbis Stock Market

The Home Environment
The home environment of the young child is linked to intellectual development and later academic achievement. Key aspects of the home environment include the parents' involvement and encouragement of the child, the availability of toys and learning materials, and the variety of experiences to which the child is exposed.

encouraging independence is connected with higher IQ scores and greater school achievement later on (Molfese, DiLalla, & Bunce, 1997; Steinberg, Brown, & Dornbusch, 1996; Suzuki & Valencia, 1997). Victoria Molfese and her colleagues (1997) found that the home environment was the single most important predictor of scores on IQ tests among children ages 3 to 8.

Click *Cognition* for more on scaffolding and the zone of proximal development.

Scaffolding and the Zone of Proximal Development

Parental responsiveness and interaction with the child is a key ingredient in the child's cognitive development. One component of this social interaction is *scaffolding* (see Chapter 1). A scaffold is a temporary structure used for holding workers during building construction. Similarly, cognitive scaffolding refers to temporary support provided by a parent or teacher to a child who is learning to perform a task. The amount of guidance provided by the adult decreases as the child becomes more skilled and capable of carrying out the task without help (Clarke-Stewart & Beck, 1999; Maccoby, 1992).

Developing in a World of Diversity

Cultural Variations in the Home Environment

Research supports the view that the early environment of the child is linked to IQ scores and academic achievement in a variety of cultures, as well as in various ethnic groups in the United States (Duncan, Brooks-Gunn, & Klebanov, 1993; Moore & Snyder, 1991). For example, Marc Bornstein and Catherine Tamis-LeMonda (1989) studied the responsiveness of Japanese and American mothers toward their babies during the first half of the 1st year. They noted how often mothers responded to their infants' vocalizations or other behaviors by talking, touching, picking up, patting, feeding, and so forth. Maternal responsiveness was positively linked to Japanese children's IQ scores at the ages of $2\frac{1}{2}$ and to American children's scores at age 4.

Similar results were found in a collaborative project involving six different longitudinal studies and three ethnic groups in the United States (Bradley et al., 1989). In this project, three aspects of the home environment during the first 3 years of life were related to higher IQ scores at age 3 for European American, African American, and Mexican American children. These sources of stimulation were the availability of toys and learning materials, the parents' involvement and encouragement of the child, and the variety of experiences to which the child was exposed.

A related concept is Vygotsky's (1978) *zone of proximal development*. The zone refers to the gap between what the child is capable of doing now and what she or he could do with help from others. Adults or older children can best guide the child through this zone by gearing their assistance to the child's capabilities (Flavell et al., 2002).

The concepts of scaffolding and the zone of proximal development are illustrated in a study in which 3- and 5-year-old children were given the task of sorting doll furniture into the rooms in which they belonged (Freund, 1990). Children who were allowed to interact with their mothers performed at a higher level than children who worked alone. Furthermore, mothers adjusted the amount of help they gave to fit the child's level of competence. They gave younger children more detailed, concrete suggestions than they gave older children. When the experimenters made the task more difficult, mothers gave more help to children of both ages.

In another study, K. Alison Clarke-Stewart and Robert Beck (1999) had 31 children who were 5 years old observe a videotaped film segment with their mother, talk about it with her, and then retell the story to an experimenter. They found that the quality of the stories, as retold by the children, was related to the scaffolding strategies the mothers used. Children whose mothers focused the children's attention on the tape, who asked their children to talk about it, and discussed the feelings of the characters told better stories than children whose mothers did not use such scaffolding strategies and children in a control group who did not discuss the story at all. Children's understanding of the characters' emotional states was most strongly connected with the number of questions the mother asked and her correction of the child's misunderstandings of what he or she saw.

In a longitudinal study, Catherine Haden and her colleagues (2001) observed 21 mother–child dyads (pairs) as they engaged in specially constructed tasks when the children were 30, 36, and 42 months of age.[1] They analyzed the children's recall of their performance 1 and 3 days afterward at all three ages. It turned out that the children best recalled those aspects of the tasks they had both worked on and discussed with their mothers. Recall under these circumstances exceeded that of when the activities were (1) handled jointly but talked about only by the mother or (2) handled jointly but not discussed at all.

The Effect of Early Childhood Education: Does It Give Preschoolers a Head Start?

How important are academic experiences in early childhood? Do they facilitate cognitive development? Some educators believe that preschool education enables children to get an early start on school achievement. Others have cautioned against the dangers of academic pressure on children (Rescorla, 1991a). Let's take a closer look at these issues.

Reflect

How do Head Start programs for poorer children compare with nursery school programs for more affluent children?

Would you want your child in a preschool program or at home, "having fun" all day? Explain.

Preschool Education for Economically Disadvantaged Children

Children growing up in poverty generally perform less well on standardized intelligence tests, and they are at greater risk for school failure (Seitz, 1990). As a result, a number of preschool programs were begun in the 1960s and 1970s to enhance the cognitive development and academic skills of poor children to increase their readiness for elementary school. Some, such as the federally funded Head Start program, also provide health care to children and social services to their families (DeParle, 1993). Children in these programs typically are exposed to letters and words, numbers, books, exercises in drawing, pegs and pegboards, puzzles, and toy animals and dolls, along with other materials and activities that

[1]Hey, *dyad* is a technical term. Deal with it.

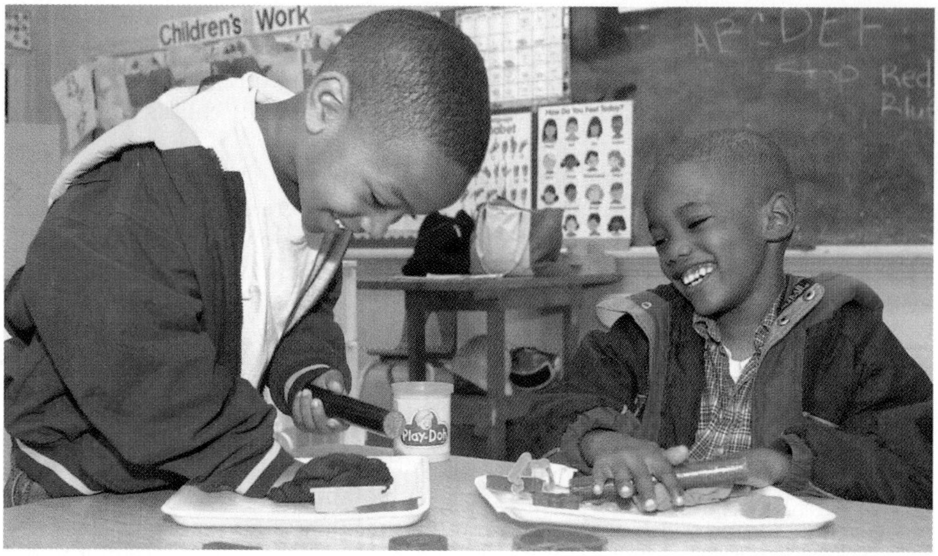

AP/Wide World Photos

Head Start

Preschoolers enrolled in Head Start programs have made dramatic increases in both readiness for elementary school and intelligence test scores. Head Start and other similar programs also can have long-term effects on educational and employment outcomes.

middle-class children can usually take for granted. Many programs encourage parental involvement in the program itself.

Studies of Head Start and other intervention programs provide convincing evidence that environmental enrichment can significantly enhance the cognitive development of economically disadvantaged children (Zigler & Styfco, 2001; Weikart & Schweinhart, 1991). The initial effects often are quite dramatic. In one study, known as the Milwaukee Project, poor children of low-IQ mothers were provided with enriched day care from the age of 6 months. By the late preschool years, their IQ scores averaged about 121, compared with an average of 95 for children from similar backgrounds who did not receive day care (Garber, 1988). In addition to positively influencing IQ scores, Head Start and other programs also lead to gains in school-readiness tests and achievement tests (Haskins, 1989; Lee et al., 1990; Zigler, 1999). Those programs that involve and educate the parents may be particularly beneficial for children (Seitz, 1990; Wasik et al., 1990; Webster-Stratton, Reid, & Hammond, 2001).

One source of concern has been that the gains of the preschoolers tended to evaporate during the elementary school years. By the end of the second or third grade, the performance of children in these programs dropped back to the equivalent of those who had not had early enrichment experiences (Haskins, 1989). However, more recent evaluations of the programs suggest more promising outcomes. For one thing, some of the early results that indicated no lasting effects of early intervention apparently were due to faulty methodology. In some cases, Head Start children were compared to control group children who were from less disadvantaged backgrounds. Such comparisons tend to underestimate the effects of Head Start. When the intellectual competence of Head Start graduates is compared to that of carefully matched control children, the children from Head Start do appear to maintain gains on measures of school success at least through first grade (Lee et al., 1990). Graduates of at least one program, the Carolina Abecedarian Project, continued to show enhanced performance in reading and mathematics through the age of 15 (Campbell & Ramey, 1993).

Furthermore, there is now good evidence that preschool intervention programs can have major long-term effects on important life outcomes for poor children, even if initial IQ gains fade out (Seitz, 1990). During the elementary and high school years, graduates of preschool programs are less likely to have been left back or placed in classes for slow learners. They are more likely to graduate from high school, go on to college, and earn higher incomes. They are less likely to be delinquent, unemployed, or on welfare (Schweinhart & Weikart, 1993; Sigel, 1991; Zigler & Styfco, 2001).

One of the tragic contributors to the perpetuation of the cycle of poverty is the incidence of pregnancy among unwed teenage girls. Pregnancy in these cases usually means that formal education comes to an end, so that the children born to unwed teenagers are destined to be reared by poorly educated mothers. Some researchers have found that girls from preschool education programs are less likely to become unwed mothers (Schweinhart & Weikart, 1993). Others have found that girls who attended preschool intervention programs became pregnant as frequently as matched controls, but were more likely to return to school after giving birth (Haskins, 1989).

Evidence is mounting that the long-term benefits of preschool intervention programs are greatest when the intervention continues into the early elementary school grades (Farran, 1990). One such effort, for example, is the Maryland-based Success for All program, which runs from preschool through third grade. It combines academic tutoring with a family support team that emphasizes parental involvement (Madden et al., 1991). First- through third-graders in the program outperform control children in reading achievement. Similar results have been found for Chicago's Child–Parent Centers, which also enroll children from preschool through at least third grade and employ some of the same methods as Success for All. Children in the program have higher reading scores, are more likely to graduate from high school, and are less likely to be held back a grade than children who have only attended preschool or who have no preschool experience (Chira, 1992b; Reynolds, 1993).

Preschool Education for Middle-Class Children: Too Much Pressure?

According to some educators, academic environments in the preschool years will benefit advantaged as well as disadvantaged children (Rescorla, 1991a). Others argue that formal academic instruction and strong pressures to achieve, especially on the part of middle-class parents, may have a harmful effect on children's learning and social-emotional development (Elkind, 1990, 1991; Sigel, 1991).

A series of studies by Kathy Hirsch-Pasek, Marion Hyson, and Leslie Rescorla examined the effects of strong academic pressures on preschool children. They studied middle-class children attending a variety of preschools, ranging from those with a highly academic orientation (for example, class periods of formal instruction in math, computers, and French) through those that were more child-oriented and less academic (strong free-play emphasis, no direct instruction). Not surprisingly, those mothers who placed a strong value on early academics sent their children to the academically oriented schools (Rescorla, 1991b). They also enrolled their children in music, art, and sports lessons outside of school and were very directive and controlling when interacting with their child (Hyson, 1991). What is the effect on the child of this "hothouse" approach? Maternal academic expectations had a positive but short-lived effect. That is, higher maternal expectations were linked to an increase in academic skills in preschool. However, by kindergarten the other children had caught up. Furthermore, the children of the mothers with high expectations were less creative, showed more anxiety when performing tasks, and tended to think less positively about school (Hirsh-Pasek, 1991; Hirsh-Pasek, Hyson, & Rescorla, 1990).

Television: Window on the World or Prison Within a False World?

How many people do you know who do not have a TV set? American children spend more time watching television than they do in school. By the time they turn 3, the average child already watches between 2 and 3 hours of television a day, and some watch considerably more than this (Huston et al., 1992).

Television has great potential for teaching a variety of cognitive skills, social behaviors, and attitudes. In Chapter 10, we explore the effects of television on children's social behaviors and attitudes (uh oh). Here, we focus on television's

Reflect

How much television did you watch as a child? Can you think of things you learned by watching television? Can you imagine developing in a world without television? Explain.

impact on cognitive development in early childhood. In many ways, television provides children with an important window on the world outside and on the cognitive skills required to succeed in that world.

Educational Television

Sesame Street is clearly the most successful TV program designed to educate children. (*Mr. Rogers' Neighborhood* makes your usually calm author want to hurl, even if he's a nice guy. Sorry, Mr. Rogers.) Begun in 1969, the goal of *Sesame Street* is to promote the intellectual growth of preschoolers, particularly those of lower socioeconomic status (SES). *Sesame Street* is viewed regularly by an estimated 50–60% of all children between the ages of 2 and 3, including large numbers of children from ethnic minority and low-SES[2] households (Comstock & Paik, 1991).

Several large-scale evaluations of the effects of *Sesame Street* have concluded that regular viewing of the program increases children's learning of numbers, letters, and cognitive skills such as sorting and classification (Fisch, Truglio, & Cole, 1999). These effects are found for African American and European American children; girls and boys; and urban, suburban, and rural children.

Longitudinal research by Mabel Rice and her colleagues (1990) shows that viewing *Sesame Street* between the ages of 3 and 5 leads to improved vocabulary at age 5. Viewing animated cartoons, on the other hand, does not benefit vocabulary development.[3] Follow-up studies have found that children learn the most from segments that give them time to respond, clap, or sing along; from segments that are repeated in a show and throughout the season; and from those skits that they find more entertaining (Chira, 1989).

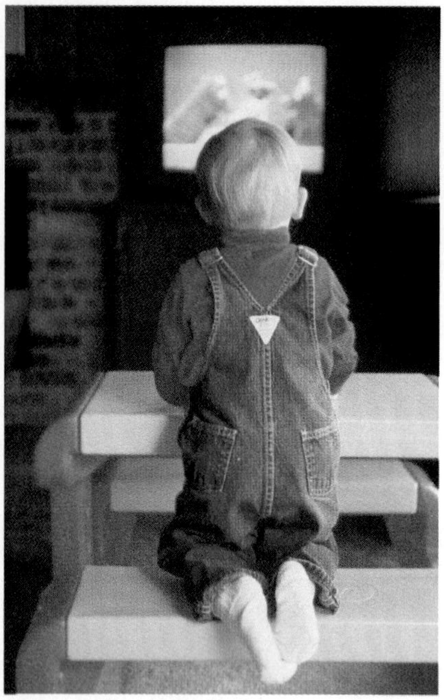

Sesame Street

Sesame Street *is viewed regularly by an estimated 50–60% of children in the United States between 2 and 3 years of age. Research shows that regular viewing of the program improves children's cognitive and language skills.*

What about the effects of television on other aspects of cognitive behavior in the young child? There is some evidence that watching television is connected with impulse control (negatively). One study (Desmond, Singer, & Singer, 1990) found that heavy TV viewing is associated with greater restlessness in children. Other research, however, indicates that exposure to such educational programs as *Sesame Street, Electric Company,* and *Mister Rogers' Neighborhood* may actually increase impulse control and concentration among preschoolers (Comstock & Paik, 1991).

It has been suggested that television may stifle the imagination, but at least among preschoolers, television appears to have little or no effect on children's imaginativeness (Comstock & Paik, 1991). Your author would assume that the type of TV show has something to do with all this. Interested readers (and other readers) may profit from reviewing the suggested guidelines for "Helping Children Use Television Wisely" in the nearby "Developing in the New Millennium" feature. Moreover, this research may not be assessing certain ways in which television affects the child's imagination. Take these conclusions with a grain of salt.

Commercials

Critics are concerned that the cognitive limitations of young children make them particularly susceptible to commercial messages, which can be potentially misleading and even harmful. Children below the age of about 7 or 8 do not understand the selling intent of advertising, and they often are unable to tell the difference between commercials and program content (Freiberg, 1991a; Kutner, 1992c). Exposure to commercials does not make the child a sophisticated consumer. In fact, children who are heavy TV viewers are more likely than light viewers to believe commercial claims (Huston et al., 1992).

Commercials that encourage children to choose nutritionally inadequate foods—such as sugared breakfast cereals, candy, and fast foods—are harmful to

[2]Notice that once I define SES for you, I feel free to use it in all sorts of strange constructions, such as *low-SES household.*

[3]But your author would point out that he learned the phrase "Sufferin' succotash" from watching animated cartoons.

children's nutritional beliefs and diets. Young children do not understand that sugary foods are detrimental to health nor do they understand disclaimers in ads that, for example, sugared cereals should be part of a balanced breakfast (Tinsley, 1992).

Given that television can make both positive and negative contributions to the child's cognitive and social development, what's a parent to do? Simply removing the TV set from the home eliminates the good with the bad. There are a number of things parents can do to help plan their children's TV use, taking advantage of its positive offerings and reducing its negative effects (Antilla, 1993; Huston et al., 1992). The nearby "Developing in the New Millennium" feature provides suggestions.

Review

(31) Caldwell developed a measure for evaluating children's home environments labeled __________. (32) Caldwell and her colleagues found that the children of mothers who are emotionally and verbally __________ show advanced social and

Developing in the New Millennium

Helping Children Use Television Wisely

Overall, television appears to have some very positive effects on cognitive development. But there is more to life than television.* Let me share some ideas as to how parents can help their children reap the benefits of television without allowing it to take over their lives.

General Suggestions

- Encourage children to watch educational programming. Go through the listings with them and help them figure out what is worth looking at.
- Help them choose among cartoon shows. Not all are filled with violence. For example, Nickelodeon's *Hey Arnold!* and *Rugrats* have a good deal of programming that will help foster children's intellectual and social development.
- Encourage your children to sit with you when you are watching some educational programming. (This doesn't have to be classroom stuff. There's good material on Discovery Channel, History Channel, and many others.)
- If your child is spending too much time at the tube, keep a time chart with the child of his or her total activities, including TV viewing, homework, and play with friends. Discuss with the child what to eliminate and what to substitute.
- Set a weekly viewing limit. Have the child select programs from TV schedules at the beginning of the week. Parents can assign points to programs and give the child a point total to spend weekly. Programs that a parent does not want the child to watch can cost more in points.

© Tom & Dee Ann McCarthy/Index Stock/PictureQuest

TV, TV Everywhere—How Do We Teach Children to Stop to Think?

Yes, dear reader, television is in our children's lives, and it appears that television, like "our love," is here to stay. What, then, can we do to at least have a positive impact on our children's cognitive processing of the information they glean from TV programs and commercials? Many things, including pointing out how what they see is not necessarily to be believed. For example, children need to know that TV violence is faked and that commercials are made by companies who wish to profit from them.

Adapted from Huston et al., 1992, pp. 102–103.

*I recognize that this is one of the more controversial comments in this book, and I apologize to people who organize their lives around soap operas, quiz shows, and MTV.

language development. (33) Molfese and her colleagues found that the __________ was the single most important predictor of scores on IQ tests among children. (34) Cognitive __________ refers to temporary support provided by a parent or teacher to a child who is learning to perform a task. (35) Clarke-Stewart and a colleague found that 5-year-olds retell (lower-quality or higher-quality?) stories when their mothers focus their attention on the stories and discuss the feelings of the characters. (36) Head Start programs (can or cannot?) significantly enhance the cognitive development of economically disadvantaged children. (37) During the elementary and high school years, graduates of preschool programs are (more or less?) likely to have been left back or placed in classes for slow learners. (38) American children spend (more or less?) time watching television than they do in school. (39) __________ is the most successful TV program designed to educate children.

Pulling It Together: Why does knowledge of preschoolers' "theory of mind" make it important for parents to explain the purposes of commercials to preschoolers?

Developing in the New Millennium (continued)

- Rule out TV at certain times, such as before breakfast or on school nights.
- Make a list of alternative activities—riding a bicycle, reading a book, working on a hobby. Before watching TV, the child must choose and do something from the list.
- Encourage the entire family to choose a program before turning the TV set on and to turn the set off when the show they planned to watch is over.
- Remember that you set an example for your child. If you watch a lot of television, chances are your child will also.

Coping With Violence

- Watch at least one episode of the programs the child watches to know how violent they are.
- When viewing TV together, discuss the violence with the child. Talk about why the violence happened and how painful it is. Ask the child how conflict can be resolved without violence.
- Explain to the child how violence on TV shows is faked. (Help them make the appearance–reality distinction.)
- Encourage children to watch programs with characters who cooperate, help, and care for each other. These programs have been shown to influence children in a positive way.

Applying TV to Real Life

- Ask children to compare what they see on the screen with people, places, and events they know firsthand, have read about, or have studied in school.
- Encourage children to read newspapers, listen to the radio, talk to adults about their work, or meet people from different ethnic or social backgrounds.
- Tell children what is real and what is make-believe on TV. Explain how TV uses stunt people, camera zooms, dream sequences, and animation to create fantasy.
- Explain to the child your family's values with regard to sex, alcohol, and drugs.

Understanding Advertising

- Explain to children that the purpose of advertising is to sell products to as many viewers as possible.
- Put advertising disclaimers into words children understand; for example, "partial assembly required" means "you have to put it together before you can play with it."
- On shopping trips, let children see the toys that look big, fast, and exciting on the screen, but that look disappointingly small and slow close up.
- Teach the child a few facts about nutrition and then let him or her use them. For example, if the youngster can read package labels, allow the child to choose a breakfast cereal from those in which sugar is not one of the first ingredients listed.

Search Online With InfoTrac College Edition

For additional information, explore InfoTrac College Edition, your online library. Go to http://www.infotrac-college.com and use the passcode from the InfoTrac card that came with your book. Try these search terms: educational programming, educational broadcasting, television and children (influence), television programs for children (evaluation).

Language Development: Why "Daddy Goed Away"

Children's language skills grow enormously during the preschool years. By the 4th year, children are asking adults and each other questions, taking turns talking, and engaging in lengthy conversations. ***Question: What language developments occur during early childhood?*** Some milestones of language development during early childhood are shown in Table 9.3. Let's consider a number of them.

Click *Language* for more on the development of language in early childhood.

Development of Vocabulary: Words, Words, and More Words

The development of vocabulary proceeds at an extraordinary pace during early childhood. Children learn an average of nine new words per day (Rice, 1989). But how can this be possible when each new word has so many potential meanings? Consider the following example. A toddler observes a small black dog running through the park. His older sister points to the animal and says "doggy." The word doggy could mean this particular dog, or all dogs, or all animals. It could refer to one part of the dog (for example, its tail) or to its behavior (running, barking) or to its characteristics (small, black) (Waxman & Kosowski, 1990). Does the child consider all these possibilities before determining what doggy actually means?

TABLE 9.3 *Development of Language Skills in Early Childhood*

Age	Characteristics	Typical Sentences
$2\frac{1}{2}$ years	There is rapid increase in vocabulary, with new additions each day. There is no babbling. Intelligibility is still not very good. Child uses 2–3 words in sentences. Child uses plurals. Child uses possessive. Child uses past tense. Child uses some prepositions.	Two cups. Sarah's car. It broke. Keisha in bed.
3 years	Child has vocabulary of some 1,000 words. Speech nears 100 percent intelligibility. Articulation of *l* and *r* is frequently faulty. Child uses 3–4 words in sentences. Child uses yes–no questions. Child uses *wh* questions. Child uses negatives. Child embeds one sentence within another.	Will I go? Where is the doggy? I not eat yucky peas. That's the book Mommy buyed me.
4 years	Child has vocabulary of 1,500–1,600 words. Speech is fluent. Articulation is good except for *sh, z, ch,* and *j* sounds. Child uses 5–6 words in sentences. Child coordinates two sentences.	I went to Allie's and I had cookies.

Reflect

What are some of the new words you are learning by reading this book? Do the words you chose to list have a single meaning or multiple meanings? (Some examples include conservation, scaffold, *and* mapping.*)*

Studies have generally shown that word learning, in fact, does not occur gradually but is better characterized as a **fast-mapping** process in which the child quickly attaches a new word to its appropriate concept (Behrend, 1990; Waxman, 1990). The key to fast mapping seems to be that children are equipped with early cognitive biases or constraints that lead them to prefer certain meanings over others (Woodward & Markman, 1991).

One bias that children have is assuming that words refer to whole objects and not to their component parts or their characteristics, such as color, size, or texture (Golinkoff, Hirsh-Pasek, Bailey, & Wenger, 1992; Hall, 1991). This inclination is known as the **whole-object assumption.** In the example given at the beginning of the section, this bias would lead the young child to assume that "doggy" refers to the dog rather than to its tail, its color, or its barking.

Children also seem to hold the bias that objects have only one label. Therefore, novel terms must refer to unfamiliar objects and not to familiar objects that already have labels. This is the **contrast assumption,** which is also known as the *mutual exclusivity assumption* (Woodward & Markman, 1991). How might this bias help children figure out the meaning of a new word? Suppose a child is shown two objects, one of which has a known label ("doggy") and one of which is an unknown object. Let us further suppose that an adult now says, "Look at the lemur." If the child assumes that "doggy" and "lemur" each can refer to only one object, the child would correctly figure out that "lemur" refers to the other object and is not just another name for "doggy." Several studies have found evidence of this bias in children, which facilitates their word learning (Au & Glusman, 1990; Merriman & Schuster, 1991; Waxman & Senghas, 1992).

fast mapping A process of quickly determining a word's meaning, which facilitates children's vocabulary development.

whole-object assumption The assumption that words refer to whole objects and not their component parts or characteristics.

contrast assumption The assumption that objects have only one label; also known as the mutual-exclusivity assumption (if a word means one thing, it cannot mean another).

Development of Grammar: Toward More Complex Language

Somewhat like the naming explosion in the 2nd year, during the 3rd year there is a "grammar explosion" (deVilliers & deVilliers, 1992). Children's sentence structure expands to include the words missing in telegraphic speech. During the 3rd year, children usually add to their vocabulary an impressive array of articles (*a, an, the*), conjunctions (*and, but, or*), possessive adjectives (*your, her*), pronouns (*she, him, one*), and prepositions (*in, on, over, around, under,* and *through*). Usually between the ages of 3 and 4, children show knowledge of rules for combining phrases and clauses into complex sentences. An early example of a complex

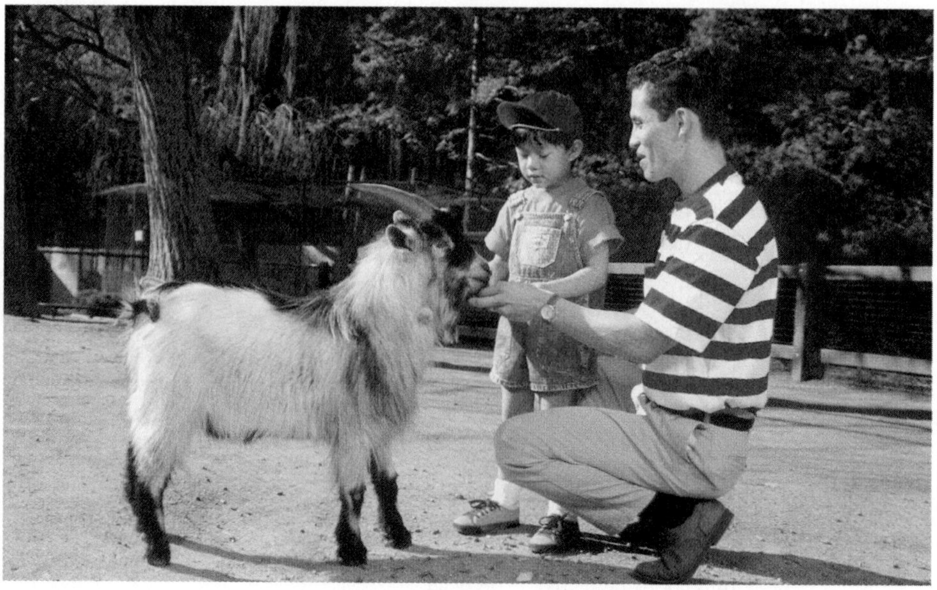
Lawrence Migdale/Stock, Boston

Vocabulary Development

When this adult points to the goat and says "goat," the child assumes that "goat" refers to the whole animal, rather than to its horns, fur, size, or color. This bias, known as the whole-object assumption, *helps children acquire a large vocabulary in a relatively short period of time.*

TABLE 9.4 *Some Examples of Allyn's Speech During the Third Year*

- Objecting to something said to her: "No, that is not a good talk to say. I don't like that."
- Describing her younger sister: "Jordan is very laughy today."
- On the second floor of her home: "This is not home. This is upstairs."
- Objecting to her father's departure: "Stay here for a couple of whiles."
- Directing her father to turn up the stereo: "Make it a big louder, not a small louder."
- Use of the plural number: "I see two policemans."
- Use of the past tense: "I goed on the choo-choo."
- Requesting a nickel: "Give me another money."
- Explaining that she and her mother are finished singing a song: "We singed it all up."
- Requesting an empty cup: "Give me that. I need it to drink nothing."
- Use of the possessive case: "That car is blue, just like us's."
- When she wants her father to hold her: "I want you to pick up me."
- Directing her father to turn on the stereo: "Push the button and make it too loud." (A minute later): "Make it more louder."
- Refusing to answer a question: "I don't want you to ask that to me."
- Confessing what she did with several coins: "I taked those money and put it on the shelf."

sentence is "You goed and Mommy goed, too." Table 9.4 shows some interesting examples of one child's use of language during the 3rd year. (All right! I'm prejudiced. It's my child.)

Overregularization

One of the more intriguing language developments—**overregularization**—is apparently based on the simple fact that children acquire grammatical rules as they learn language. At very young ages they tend to apply these rules rather strictly, even in cases that call for exceptions (Marcus et al., 1992; Stemberger, 1993). Consider the formation of the past tense and plurals in English. We add *d* or *ed* to regular verbs and *s* to regular nouns. Thus, walk becomes walked and doggy becomes doggies. But then there are irregular verbs and irregular nouns. For example, *sit* becomes *sat*, and *go* becomes *went*. Sheep remains sheep (*plural*) and child becomes children.

At first children learn a small number of these irregular constructions by imitating their parents. Two-year-olds tend to form them correctly temporarily. Then they become aware of the syntactic rules for forming the past tense and plurals in English. As a result, they tend to make charming errors (Pinker, 1997). Some 3–5-year-olds, for example, are more likely to say "Mommy sitted down" than "Mommy sat down." They are likely to talk about the "sheeps" they "seed" on the farm and about all the "childs" they ran into at the playground.

Reflect

Can you think of examples of overregularization that you used as a child or that you have heard used by other children? Do any of these examples pertain to languages other than English?

Some parents recognize that their children were forming the past tense of irregular verbs correctly and that they then began to make errors. The thing to remember is that overregularization does represent an advance in the development of syntax. Overregularization reflects accurate knowledge of grammar—not faulty language development. (Really.) In another year or two, "mouses" will be boringly transformed into "mice," and Mommy will no longer have "sitted down." Parents might as well enjoy overregularization while they can.

In a classic experiment designed to show that preschool children are not just clever mimics in their formation of plurals but have actually grasped rules of grammar, Berko (1958) showed children pictures of nonexistent animals (see Figure 9.7). She first showed them a single animal and said, "This is a wug." Then she showed them a picture of two animals and said, "Now there are two of them. There are two __________," asking the children to finish the sentence. Ninety-one percent of the children said "wugs," giving the correct plural of the bogus word.

overregularization The application of regular grammatical rules for forming inflections (for example, past tense and plurals) to irregular verbs and nouns.

This is a wug.
Now there are two of them.
There are two ______.

Figure 9.7
Wugs

Wugs? Why not? Many bright, sophisticated college students have not heard of "wugs." What a pity. Here are several wugs—actually, make-believe animals used in a study to learn whether preschool children can use rules of grammar to form the plurals of unfamiliar nouns.

Asking Questions

Children's first questions are telegraphic and characterized by a rising pitch (which signifies a question mark in English) at the end (Rowland & Pine, 2000). "More milky?" for example, can be translated into "May I have more milk?" "Would you like more milk?" or "Is there more milk?" depending on the context. It is usually toward the latter part of the 3rd year that the *wh* questions appear. Consistent with the child's general cognitive development, certain *wh* questions (*what, who,* and *where*) appear earlier than others (*why, when, which,* and *how*) (Bloom, Merkin, & Wootten, 1982). *Why* is usually too philosophical for the 2-year-old, and *how* too involved. Two-year-olds are also likely to be now-oriented, so that *when,* too, is of less than immediate concern. By the 4th year, most children are spontaneously producing *why, when,* and *how* questions. These *wh* words are initially tacked on to the beginnings of sentences. "Where Mommy go?" can stand for "Where is Mommy going?" "Where did Mommy go?" or "Where will Mommy go?" and its meaning must be derived from context. Later on, the child will add the auxiliary verbs *is, did,* and *will* to indicate whether the question concerns the present, past, or future.

Passive Sentences

Passive sentences, such as "The food is eaten by the dog," are difficult for 2- and 3-year-olds to understand, and so young preschool children almost never produce them. In a fascinating study of children's comprehension (Strohner & Nelson, 1974), 2–5-year-olds used puppets and toys to act out a number of sentences that were read to them. Two- and 3-year-olds in the study made errors in acting out passive sentences (for example, "The car was hit by the truck") 70% of the time. Older children had less difficulty interpreting the meanings of passive sentences correctly. However, most children usually do not produce passive sentences spontaneously even at the ages of 5 and 6.

Pragmatics: Children Can Be Practical

Pragmatics in language development refers to the practical aspects of communication. Children are showing pragmatism when they adjust their speech to fit the social situation. For example, children show greater formality in their choice of words and syntax when they are role-playing high-status figures, such as teachers or physicians, in their games. They also say "please" more often when making requests of high-status people (Owens, 1990). Children also show pragmatism in their adoption of motherese when they are addressing a younger child.

Pragmatism provides another example of the ways in which cognitive and language development are intertwined. As we saw earlier in the chapter, preschoolers tend to be egocentric; that is, they show some difficulty in taking the viewpoints of other people. A 2-year-old telling another child "Gimme my book," without specifying which book, is not just assuming that the other child knows what

pragmatics The practical aspects of communication, such as adaptation of language to fit the social situation.

she herself knows. She is also overestimating the clearness of her communication and how well she is understood (Beal & Flavell, 1983). Once children can perceive the world through the eyes of others, however, they advance in their abilities to make themselves understood to others. Now the child recognizes that the other child will require a description of the book or of its location to carry out the request. Between the ages of 3 and 5, egocentric speech gradually disappears and there is rapid development of pragmatic skills. The child's conversation shows increasing sensitivity to the listener, as, for example, in allowing turn-taking (Baker & Cantwell, 1991).

The Relationship Between Language and Cognition

Language and cognitive development are strongly interwoven. For example, the child gradually gains the capacity to discriminate between animals on the basis of distinct features, such as size, patterns of movement, and the sounds they make. At the same time, the child also is acquiring words that represent broader categories, such as mammal and animal.

But it's chicken-and-egg time. Which comes first? ***Question: What is the relationship between language and cognition?*** Does the child first develop concepts and then acquire the language to describe them? Or does the child's increasing language ability lead to the development of new concepts?

Does Cognitive Development Precede Language Development?

Jean Piaget (1976) believed that cognitive development precedes language development. He argued that children must first understand concepts before they can use words that describe the concepts. Object permanence emerges toward the end of the 1st year. Piaget believed that words that relate to the disappearance and appearance of people and objects (such as *allgone* and *bye-bye*) are used only after the emergence of object permanence.

From Piaget's perspective, children learn words in order to describe classes or categories that they have already created (K. Nelson, 1982). Children can learn the word *doggy* because they have already perceived the characteristics that distinguish dogs from other things.

Some studies support the notion that cognitive concepts may precede language. For example, the vocabulary explosion that occurs at about 18 months of age is related to the child's ability to group a set of objects into two categories, such as "dolls" and "cars" (Gopnik & Meltzoff, 1987, 1992). Both developments may reflect the child's understanding that objects belong in categories. Other studies (Brownell, 1988; Ogura, 1991) show that at the same time children make the transition from one- to two-word sentences, they also begin to string together sequences of play activities (such as placing a doll in bed, covering it with a blanket, and rocking it). These transitions seem to indicate a basic change from "oneness" to "twoness" that is occurring in the child's cognitive development (Bates et al., 1987).

Does Language Development Precede Cognitive Development?

While many theorists argue that cognitive development precedes language development, others reverse the causal relationship and claim that children create cognitive classes in order to understand things that are labeled by words (R. Clark, 1983). When children hear the word *dog,* they try to understand it by searching for characteristics that separate dogs from other things. Research with $4\frac{1}{2}$-year-olds does show that descriptions of events can prompt children to create categories in which to classify occurrences (Nazzi & Gopnik, 2000).

The Interactionist View: An Explanation With Something for Everyone?

Today, most cognitive psychologists find something of value in each of these cognitive views (Gopnik & Choi, 1990; Greenberg & Kuczaj, 1982). In the early stages of language development, concepts often precede words, so that many of the infant's words describe classes that have already developed. Later on, however, language is not merely the servant of thought; language influences thought.

Click *Language* for more on the interactionist view.

Similar ideas were advanced by Lev Vygotsky. Vygotsky believed that during most of the 1st year, vocalizations and thought are separate. But usually during the 2nd year, thought and speech—cognition and language—combine forces. "Speech begins to serve intellect and thoughts begin to be spoken" (Vygotsky, 1962, p. 43). Usually during the 2nd year, children discover that objects have labels. Learning labels becomes more active, more self-directed. At some point, children ask what new words mean. Learning new words clearly fosters the creation of new categories and classes. An interaction develops in which classes are filled with labels for new things, and labels nourish the blossoming of new classes.

Vygotsky's concept of **inner speech** is a key feature of his position. At first, according to Vygotsky, children's thoughts are spoken aloud. You can overhear the 3-year-old giving herself instructions as she plays with toys. At this age her vocalizations may serve to regulate her behavior. But language gradually becomes internalized. What was spoken aloud at 4 and 5 becomes an internal dialogue by 6 or 7. This internal dialogue, or inner speech, is the ultimate binding of language and thought. Inner speech is essential to the development of planning and self-regulation and seems to facilitate children's learning (Bivens & Berk, 1990). Vygotsky's ideas about the self-regulative function of language have inspired psychological treatment approaches for children with self-control problems. For example, hyperactive children can be taught to use self-directed speech to increase self-control (Crain, 2000).

Click *Cognition* for more on Vygotsky's concept of thought and language.

And so language is inextricably bound not only to thought but also to aspects of personality and social behavior in the young child. It is to these areas of development that we turn in Chapter 10.

Review

(40) During early childhood, children learn an average of __________ new words per day. (41) Word learning does not occur gradually but is better characterized as a fast-__________ process. (42) The __________-object assumption refers to the fact that young children assume that words refer to whole objects and not to their component parts or to their characteristics, such as color or texture. (43) Young children also tend to assume that objects have (how many?) label(s). (44) Therefore, they have the __________ assumption, which holds that novel terms must refer to unfamiliar objects and not to familiar objects that already have labels. (45) Young children acquire rules of grammar leading to the __________ of regular verbs and nouns. (46) __________ refers to the practical aspects of communication. (47) Piaget believed that cognitive development (precedes or follows?) language development. (48) Vygotsky believed that during the 2nd year, thought and __________ combine forces. (49) Vygotsky's concept of __________ speech refers to the fact that what was spoken aloud at 4 and 5 becomes an internal dialogue by 6 or 7.

Pulling It Together: What are some of the connections between language development and cognitive development in general?

inner speech Vygotsky's concept of the ultimate binding of language and thought. Inner speech originates in vocalizations that may regulate the child's behavior and become internalized by age 6 or 7.

Recite Recite Recite Recite

1. How do children in the preoperational stage think and behave?	Piaget's preoperational stage lasts from about 2 to 7 and is characterized by the use of symbols to represent objects and the relationships among them, but preoperational logic is in many ways unlike the logic of older children and adults.
2. What is "child's play" like in early childhood?	Symbolic play (also called pretend play) usually begins in the 2nd year, when the child begins to symbolize objects. The ability to engage in pretend play is based on the use and recollection of symbols, or mental representations of things children have encountered or heard about. Children first engage in pretend play about familiar activities such as sleeping , but by 15 to 20 months, they shift their focus to others. By 30 months, children can make believe that other objects take an active role. During the preschool years, pretend play takes on longer, coordinated sequences. The quality of preschoolers' pretend play is connected with children's social and cognitive development. Children may redirect their play according to the suggestions of other children. Imaginary friends are an example of pretend play and are more common among first-born and only children.
3. How do we characterize the logic of the preoperational child?	Mental operations are flexible and reversible mental acts that change or transform objects. Preoperational children cannot yet engage in flexible and reversible mental operations. Preoperational thinking is characterized by egocentrism, immature notions about causality, confusion between mental and physical events, and ability to focus on only one dimension at a time.
4. What is egocentrism?	Egocentrism is the inability to see the world from the perspective of others. Young children often view the world as a stage that is meant to meet their needs. Piaget used the three-mountains test to show that young children literally cannot take the viewpoints of others.
5. What is precausal thinking?	Young children's explanations of cause and effect are likely to have an egocentric, psychological flavor in which they extend will to inanimate objects. For example, they may say it becomes dark outside so that they can go to sleep. Transductive reasoning is an example of precausal thinking in which children reason by going from one specific isolated event to another. A 3-year-old may believe she should not go to sleep because it is light outside. In precausal animistic thinking, they attribute life and intentions to inanimate objects, such as the sun. Artificialism is the belief that environmental features such as rain and thunder have been made by people.
6. Why do young children believe that dreams are real?	Preoperational children have difficulty making distinctions between mental and physical events. Egocentrism contributes to children's beliefs that their thoughts exactly reflect reality.
7. What is conservation?	The law of conservation holds that properties of substances such as volume, mass, and number stay the same (are conserved) even if you change their shape or arrangement. Conservation requires focusing on two aspects of a situation at once, but preoperational children tend to focus on only one aspect of a problem at a time. The preoperational child focuses on the most apparent dimension of a situation. The preoperational child's failure to show conservation also comes about because of "irreversibility"; that is, the child fails to realize that an action can be reversed, restoring things to their original condition. Comprehension of class inclusion—the concept that one class can contain several subclasses—also requires children to focus on two aspects of a situation at once.

Recite Recite Recite Recite

8. What are children's ideas about how the mind works?

One's understanding of how the mind works is one's theory of mind. Children come to understand that we can acquire knowledge through the senses and that there are distinctions between external and mental events and between appearances and realities. Research shows that preschool-aged children can accurately predict and explain human action and emotion in terms of mental states. They also begin to understand the origins of knowledge and have a rudimentary ability to distinguish appearance from reality.

9. Do children understand where their knowledge comes from? If so, how early do they show this ability?

By age 3, most children begin to realize that people gain knowledge through the senses. By age 4, children understand which sense is required to provide information about qualities such as color (vision) and weight (touch).

10. Is seeing believing? What do preoperational children have to say about that?

Although Piaget believed that children do not differentiate reality from appearances or mental events until the age of 7 or 8, research finds that children can do so in the preschool years. Yet preschoolers have only a limited understanding of mental representations; they have trouble understanding that an object or event can take many forms in the mind.

11. What sorts of memory skills do children possess in early childhood?

Recognition and recall are two of the basic tasks used in the study of memory, with recall being the more difficult of the two. Preschoolers can recognize more items than they can recall. Preschoolers' autobiographical memory is linked to their language skills. By the age of 4, children can remember events that occurred $1\frac{1}{2}$ years earlier. Young children seem to form scripts, which are abstract, generalized accounts of these repeated events.

12. What factors affect memory in early childhood?

Factors affecting memory include what the child is asked to remember, interest level and motivation, the availability of retrieval cues, and the memory measure being used. Preschoolers' memories for activities are better than their memories for objects. Young children's memories are enhanced by cues from adults.

13. How do we remember to remember?

Adults and older children use strategies to help them remember. Preschool children generally do not use memory strategies by themselves. But they engage in behaviors such as looking, pointing, and touching when trying to remember. Young children also can be trained to use strategies such as rehearsal and grouping of items that they might not use on their own.

14. What are some of the factors that influence cognitive development in early childhood?

Some of the most important include social and family factors such as family income, parents' educational level, family size, and the presence of stressful family events such as divorce, job loss, or illness. In the measure for evaluating children's home environments called HOME, researchers directly observe parent–child interaction in the home. The children of mothers who are emotionally and verbally responsive, who are involved with their children, and who provide appropriate play materials and various daily experiences show gains in social and language development and, later, IQ scores. Scaffolding supports the child in learning to perform a task. Head Start programs for economically disadvantaged children enhance their cognitive development, academic skills, and readiness for elementary school. But preschool for middle-class children sometimes provides too much pressure. Television teaches cognitive skills, social behaviors, and attitudes. Educational television appears to help children make lasting cognitive gains. Children need to be helped to distinguish between programs and commercials and to understand that commercials are intended to sell products.

Recite Recite Recite Recite

15. What language developments occur during early childhood?

During early childhood, children learn an average of nine new words per day. Word learning often occurs rapidly through fast mapping, in which one meaning is assigned to a word. Children also tend to assume that words refer to entire objects rather than their parts (the whole-object assumption). During the 3rd year, children usually add articles (*a, an, the*), conjunctions (*and, but, or*), possessive adjectives (*your, her*), pronouns (*she, him, one*), and prepositions (*in, on, over, around, under,* and *through*). Between 3 and 4, children gain the ability to combine phrases and clauses into complex sentences. Preschoolers tend to overregularize irregular verbs and noun forms as they acquire rules of grammar. Some *wh* questions (*what, who,* and *where*) appear earlier than others (*why, when, which,* and *how*). Preschoolers develop the ability to show pragmatism—to adjust their speech to fit the social situation.

16. What is the relationship between language and cognition?

Piaget believed that cognitive development precedes language development, that children learn words in order to describe classes or categories that they have already created. Other theorists argue that children create cognitive classes in order to understand things that are labeled by words. Today, most cognitive psychologists believe that concepts often precede words in the early stages of language development, but that later on language influences thought. Vygotsky believed that during most of the 1st year, vocalizations and thought are separate. But usually during the 2nd year, cognition and language combine forces. To Vygotsky, inner speech is the ultimate binding of language and thought.

On the Web

Search Online With InfoTrac College Edition

For additional information, explore InfoTrac College Edition, your online library. Go to **http://www.infotrac-college.com** and use the passcode from the InfoTrac card that came with your book. Try these search terms: Vygotsky, language acquisition analysis, speech development, children as witnesses.

Visit Our Web Site

Go to **http://www.wadsworth.com/psychology** where you will find online resources directly linked to your book.

Child Development CD-ROM

Go to the Wadsworth Child Development CD-ROM for further study of the concepts in this chapter. The CD-ROM also includes quizzes and additional activities to expand your learning experience.

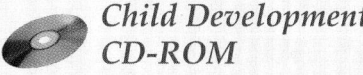

10 Early Childhood: Social and Emotional Development

© Tom Prettyman/PhotoEdit

PowerPreview™

Influences on Development: Parents, Siblings, and Peers

- **Is it good for parents** to be restrictive (strict, that is), or should they be relaxed and permissive?
- **Is there any point** in trying to reason with a child who is 2 to 6 years old?
- **Does encouraging children** to act maturely backfire, or does it—wonder of wonders—result in more mature behavior?
- **First-born children are more** highly motivated to achieve than later-born children. Why? (Do parents "spend" all their good genetic material on the first child?)

Social Behaviors—In the World, Among Others

- **Are children who play** by themselves more likely to develop social problems?
- **Is an aggressive child** likely to develop into an aggressive adult, or does aggression in children just "blow over"?
- **Are children who are physically punished** more likely to behave aggressively themselves?
- **Children who watch 2 to 4 hours of TV** a day will see 8,000 murders and another 100,000 acts of violence by the time they have finished elementary school.
- **Did you know** that virtually all G-rated animated films have scenes of violence and that they last an average of 9 to 10 minutes per film?

Personality and Emotional Development

- **When can children usually** first describe themselves in terms of their usual patterns of behavior and feelings?
- **It is during the preschool years** that children are most likely to have fears that revolve around animals, imaginary creatures, the dark, and personal safety—all those things that "go bump in the night."

Development of Gender Roles and Gender Differences

- **Boys usually grow up** to act like men, and girls usually grow up to act like women. So what does it mean to act "like a man" or "like a woman"?
- **Boys and girls typically think** their own gender is superior.
- **A 2½-year-old may know** that she is a girl but still think that she can grow up to be a daddy.
- **We know why males develop** male reproductive organs and why females develop female reproductive organs (well, almost). Do we know why (many or most) males come to act in stereotypically masculine ways and why (many or most) females come to act in stereotypically feminine ways?

Jeremy and Jessica are both $2^1/_2$ years old. They are standing at the water table in the preschool classroom. Jessica is filling a plastic container with water and spilling it out. She watches the water splash down the drain. Jeremy watches and then goes to get another container. He, too, begins to fill his container with water and spill it out. The two children stand side by side. They both empty and refill their plastic pails; they glance at each other and exchange a few words. They continue playing like this for several minutes until Jessica drops her pail and runs off to ride the tricycle. Soon after, Jeremy, too, loses interest in this activity and finds something else to do.

Meanwhile, the $4^1/_2$-year-olds Melissa and Mike are building in the block corner, making the huge rambling structure that they have decided is a spaceship. They are talking animatedly as they work, discussing who should be the captain of the ship and who should be the space alien. Mike and Melissa take turns adding blocks. They continue to build, working together and talking as they play, engrossed in what they are doing (adapted from Campbell, 1990).

These observations illustrate some of the dramatic changes that occur in social development during early childhood. Toddlers often spend time watching and imitating each other, but they do not interact very much. Older preschoolers are more likely to take turns, work cooperatively toward a goal, and share things. They often engage in fantasy play that involves adopting adult roles.

In this chapter, we examine some of the changes that occur in social and emotional development in early childhood. We consider the important roles that parents, siblings, and peers play in this process. We turn to the social behaviors themselves and examine changes in play, in positive social behaviors such as helping and sharing, and in the negative social behavior of aggression. Then we look at personality and emotional development. We begin with the development of the self-concept, move on to Erikson's stage of initiative and guilt, and explore the changing nature of children's fears. Finally, we discuss the development of gender roles and gender differences in behavior.

Influences on Development: Parents, Siblings, and Peers

Young children usually spend most of their time within the family. Most parents attempt to foster certain behavior patterns in their children. They want their children to develop a sense of responsibility and conform to family routines. They want them to develop into well-adjusted individuals. They want them to acquire a variety of social skills. In other words, they want to ensure healthy social and personality development in their children. How do parents go about trying to achieve these goals? What part do siblings play in this process? And how do a child's peers influence social and personality development? Let's start by examining the influence of parents.

Dimensions of Child Rearing: What Parents Are Like

Parents have different approaches to rearing their children. ***Question: What are the dimensions of child rearing?*** Investigators of parental patterns of child rearing have found it useful to classify them according to two broad dimensions: warmth–coldness and restrictiveness–permissiveness (Baumrind, 1989, 1991a, 1991b). Warm parents can be either restrictive or permissive. So can cold parents.

Warmth–Coldness

Warm parents are affectionate toward their children. They tend to hug and kiss them and to smile at them frequently. Warm parents are caring and supportive of their children. They generally behave in ways that communicate their enjoyment in being with the children. Warm parents are less likely than cold parents to use physical discipline (Wade & Kendler, 2001).

Cold parents may not enjoy being with their children and may have few feelings of affection for them. They are likely to complain about their children's behavior, saying that they are naughty or have "minds of their own." Warm parents may also say that their children have "minds of their own," but they are frequently proud of and entertained by their children's stubborn behavior. Even when they are irked by it, they usually focus on attempting to change it, instead of rejecting the children outright.

It requires no stretch of the imagination to conclude that it is better to be warm than cold toward children (Dix, 1991). The children of parents who are warm and accepting are more likely to develop internalized standards of conduct—a moral sense or conscience (Grusec, Goodnow, & Kuczinski, 2000; Grusec & Lytton, 1988; MacDonald, 1992). Parental warmth also is related to the child's social and emotional well-being (MacDonald, 1992; Miller, McCluskey-Fawcett, & Irving, 1993).

Where does parental warmth come from? Some of it reflects parental beliefs as to how to best rear children, and some reflects parents' tendencies to imitate the behavior of their own parents. But research by E. Mavis Hetherington and her colleagues (Feinberg et al., 2001) suggests that genetic factors may be involved as well.

Reflect

Were your parents warm or cold, restrictive or permissive (or somewhere in the middle)? What were the effects on you? If you are a parent, are you warm or cold, restrictive or permissive? Why?

Restrictiveness–Permissiveness

Parents must generally decide how restrictive they will be toward many of their children's behavior patterns. Consider just a brief list: making excessive noise when other people are sleeping or are trying to converse, playing with dangerous objects, damaging property, keeping their rooms neat, being aggressive, appearing in the nude, and masturbating.

Parents who are highly restrictive tend to impose many rules and to watch their children closely. Parents who are restrictive about one thing also tend to be restrictive about others.

The effects of restrictiveness on children's behavior depend on how "restrictiveness" is defined. If it is defined as consistent control and firm enforcement of rules, it can have positive consequences for the child, particularly when combined with strong support for the child and feelings of affection (Grusec & Lytton, 1988; Putallaz & Heflin, 1990). This parenting style, known as the *authoritative style,* is described in more detail a bit later. But "restrictiveness" defined as physical punishment, interference, or intrusiveness can have negative effects, such as disobedience, lack of compliance, and lower levels of cognitive performance (Olson et al., 1992; Westerman, 1990).

Permissive parents impose few if any rules and supervise their children less closely. They allow their children to do what is "natural"—to make noise, treat the objects in their play spaces carelessly (although they may also extensively child-proof their homes to prevent their children from getting hurt and to protect the furniture), and experiment or play with their own bodies. They may also allow their children to show a good deal of aggression, intervening only when another child appears to be in serious danger—if then. Parents may be permissive for different reasons. Some parents believe that children need the freedom to express their natural urges. Others may be uninterested in their children and uninvolved.

How Parents Enforce Restrictions

Regardless of their general approaches to child rearing, most—if not all—parents are restrictive now and then, even if only when they are teaching their children not to run into the street or to touch the stove. ***Question: What techniques do parents use to restrict their children's behavior?*** In this section we describe the methods of *induction, power assertion,* and *withdrawal of love.*

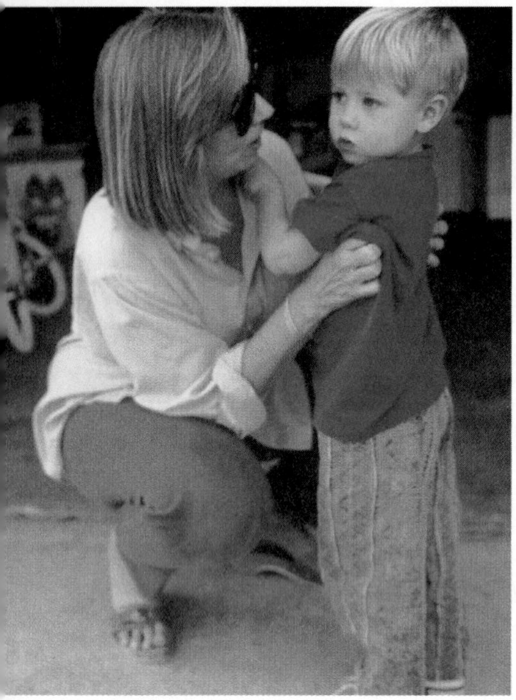
© Joel Gordon Photography

■ **Inductive Reasoning**

Inductive methods for enforcing restrictions attempt to teach children the principles they should use in guiding their own behavior. This mother is using the inductive technique of reasoning.

Inductive Techniques

Inductive methods attempt to provide children with knowledge that will enable them to generate desirable behavior patterns in similar situations. The major inductive technique is "reasoning," or explaining why one sort of behavior is good and another is not. Reasoning with a 1- or 2-year-old can be primitive. "Don't do that—it hurts!" qualifies as reasoning when children are very young. After all, "it hurts!" is an explanation, however brief.

There is some evidence that the inductive approach helps the child develop internalized moral standards of conduct or conscience (Grusec & Lytton, 1988). Induction also appears to promote positive social behaviors such as helping and sharing (Eisenberg & Miller, 1990; Hart et al., 1992).

Power-Assertive Methods

Other parents use power or coercion. Power-assertive methods include physical punishment and deprivation of privileges. Parents who use power assertion often justify physical punishments with sayings such as "Spare the rod, and spoil the child." Power-assertive parents also tend to yell at their children, rather than reason with them.

Reflect

How did your parents enforce restrictions? What were the effects on you? If you are a parent, how do you enforce restrictions? Why?

Power-assertive parents sometimes argue that their approach is necessary precisely because their children are noncompliant. In many cases it is unclear which came first—power-assertive methods or children's noncompliance. Research suggests that the use of power-assertive methods is related not only to the child's temperament and behavior, but also to parents' personalities (Clark, Kochanska, & Ready, 2000). In any event, power assertion and noncompliance can clearly escalate into a (literally) vicious cycle.

For children, parental power assertion is associated with greater defiance (Crockenberg & Litman, 1990), lower acceptance by peers (Hart, Ladd, & Burleson, 1990), poorer academic performance (Wentzel, Feldman, & Weinberger, 1991), and higher rates of antisocial behavior and interpersonal problems (DeBaryshe, Patterson, & Capaldi, 1993; Kochanska, 1992). The more parents use power-assertive techniques, the less children appear to develop internalized standards of moral conduct. The combination of a high use of punishment and rejection is often linked with aggression and delinquency (Grusec & Lytton, 1988; D. O. Lewis, 1991b; Putallaz et al., 1998). Nevertheless, children do not always view parental power-assertion as unwarranted and may actually prefer it to being humiliated in public or—horror of horrors—having parents who treat their siblings better than they treat them (Konstantareas & Desbois, 2001).

As far as the parents are concerned, a Chinese study (Chen et al., 2000) found that parents who choose power-assertive methods are more likely to be authoritarian than authoritative—a distinction we shall pursue in the following pages.

Withdrawal of Love

Still other parents attempt to control their children by threatening them with withdrawal of love. They tend to isolate or ignore their children when they misbehave. Since most children have strong needs for approval and for physical contact with their parents, loss of love can be more threatening than physical punishment. Frequent withdrawal of love seems to facilitate compliance with adult standards, but it also may create feelings of guilt and anxiety (Grusec & Lytton, 1988).

Preschoolers comply more readily with requests to *do* something than with requests to *stop doing* something. Grazyna Kochanska and colleagues (2001) observed 108 children at the ages of 14, 22, 33, and 45 months of age and found that they complied more frequently in doing something that was unpleasant and tedious than in discontinuing behavior that was pleasant and attractive. The message becomes familiar enough to many parents: One way to manage

inductive Characteristic of disciplinary methods, such as reasoning, that attempt to foster an understanding of the principles behind parental demands.

children who are doing something wrong or bad is to involve them in doing something else.

Parenting Styles: How Parents Transmit Values and Standards

Traditional views of the ways in which children acquire values and standards for behavior focus on parenting styles (Grusec et al., 2000). However, many other factors are involved, including the characteristics of a particular child, the child's situation, and other aspects of parental behavior. Psychologist Diana Baumrind (1989, 1991b) has conducted what many consider to be the most important core of research on parenting styles.

Baumrind has focused on the relationship between parenting styles and the development of competent behavior in young children. She uses the two dimensions of child rearing we have just examined: warmth–coldness and restrictiveness–permissiveness. She developed a classification of four parenting styles based on whether parents are high or low on each of the two dimensions, as seen in Table 10.1. ***Question: What are the parenting styles involved in the transmission of values and standards?***

Authoritative Parents

The parents of the most capable children are rated as high on both dimensions of behavior (see Table 10.1). They make strong efforts to control their children (that is, they are highly restrictive) and they make strong demands for maturity. However, they also reason with their children and show them strong support and feelings of love. Baumrind applies the label **authoritative** to these parents in order to suggest that they have a clear vision of what they want their children to do but also respect their children and provide them with warmth.

Compared to other children, the children of authoritative parents tend to show self-reliance and independence, high self-esteem, high levels of activity and exploratory behavior, and social competence. They are highly motivated to achieve and do well in school (Baumrind, 1989, 1991b; Dumas & LaFreniere, 1993; Kaufmann et al., 2000).

Authoritarian Parents

"Because I say so" could well be the motto of parents that Baumrind labels **authoritarian.** These parents tend to look upon obedience as a high virtue. Authoritarian parents believe in strict guidelines for determining what is right and wrong. They demand that their children accept these guidelines without question. Like authoritative parents, they are controlling. Unlike authoritative parents, their enforcement methods rely on coercion. Moreover, authoritarian parents do not communicate well with their children. They do not show respect for their children's viewpoints, and most researchers find them to be generally cold and rejecting. However, among some ethnic groups—such as Egyptians living in Canada—

authoritative A child-rearing style in which parents are restrictive and demanding, yet communicative and warm.

authoritarian A child-rearing style in which parents demand submission and obedience from their children but are not very communicative and warm.

TABLE 10.1 *Baumrind's Patterns of Parenting*

	PARENTAL BEHAVIOR PATTERNS	
Parental Style	**Restrictiveness and Control**	**Warmth and Responsiveness**
Authoritative	High	High
Authoritarian	High	Low
Permissive-Indulgent	Low	High
Rejecting-Neglecting	Low	Low

authoritarianism reflects cultural values, and these authoritarian parents are also warm and reasonably flexible (Rudy & Grusec, 2001).

In Baumrind's research, the sons of authoritarian parents were relatively hostile and defiant, and girls were low in independence and dominance (Baumrind, 1989). Other researchers have found children of authoritarian parents to be less competent socially and academically than children of authoritative parents. Children of authoritarian parents also tend to be conflicted, anxious, and irritable. They are less friendly and spontaneous in their social interactions (DeKovic & Janssens, 1992; Maccoby & Martin, 1983). As adolescents, they may be conforming and obedient but have lower self-reliance and self-esteem (Buri et al., 1988; Lamborn et al., 1991). These findings appear to hold up across cultures and across the years. A Turkish study of 279 students found that students from authoritarian families were less likely to have secure attachment and self-esteem, but more likely to be anxious, than students from authoritative families (Suemer & Guengoer, 1999).

Permissive Parents

Baumrind found two types of parents who are permissive, as opposed to restrictive. One type may be labeled "permissive-indulgent" and the other "rejecting-neglecting." **Permissive-indulgent** parents are rated low in their attempts to control their children and in their demands for mature behavior. They are easygoing and unconventional. Their brand of permissiveness is accompanied by high nurturance (warmth and support).

Reflect

Were your parents authoritative, authoritarian, permissive, or "something else"? Did they have different parenting styles? What are your thoughts on their parenting style(s)?

Rejecting-neglecting parents also are rated low in their demands for mature behavior and their attempts to control their children. But unlike the indulgent parents, they are low in support and responsiveness.

It is perhaps not surprising that the neglectful parenting style is associated with poor outcomes for children. By and large, the children of neglectful parents are the least competent, responsible, and mature and the most prone to problem behaviors. They tend to have low self-esteem, to be insecurely attached to their caregivers, and to be anxious (Suemer & Guengoer, 1999). Children of permissive-indulgent parents, like those of neglectful parents, show less competence in school and more deviant behavior (for example, misconduct and substance abuse) than children of more restrictive, controlling parents. But children from permissive-indulgent homes, unlike those from neglectful homes, are fairly high in social competence and self-confidence (Baumrind, 1991a; Lamborn et al., 1991).

Effects of the Situation and the Child on Parenting Styles

Parenting styles are not just a one-way street, from parent to child. Parenting styles also depend partly on the situation and partly on the characteristics of the child (Grusec et al., 2000). ***Question: How do the situation and the child influence parenting styles?***

As an example of how the situation affects the parenting style, parents are more likely to use power-assertive techniques for dealing with aggressive behavior than social withdrawal behavior (Mills & Rubin, 1990). Parents prefer power-assertive techniques over inductive techniques when they believe that children understand the rules they have violated, are capable of acting more appropriately, and are responsible for their bad behavior (Dix, Ruble, & Zambarino, 1989). Stressful life events, marital discord, and depression in the mother are additional factors that contribute to the mother's use of power-assertive techniques (Campbell et al., 1991).

Children's behaviors and temperamental characteristics also influence adults. In one intriguing experiment (Anderson, Christian, & Luce, 1986), mothers of normal boys and mothers of boys with behavior problems interacted with boys of both types. Both groups of mothers were more negative and controlling when dealing with the boys with conduct disorders. Thus, the child's behavior may elicit certain types of responses from parents.

permissive-indulgent A child-rearing style in which parents are not controlling and restrictive but are warm.

rejecting-neglecting A child-rearing style in which parents are neither restrictive and controlling nor supportive and responsive.

In sum, research by Baumrind and others does not establish that certain child-rearing patterns *cause* the outcomes described. On the other hand, Baumrind's research suggests that we can make an effort to avoid some of the pitfalls of being authoritarian or overly permissive. Some recommended techniques that parents can use to help control and guide their children's behavior are listed in Table 10.2.

Influence of Siblings: Brothers and Sisters Matter

Our neighbor—who will deny this story (but don't believe her)—admits that when she was 5, she would carefully walk her younger sister, then 2, into the middle of the street. And then leave her there! Fortunately, both survived. They are even quite close now. One can say that they literally lived to laugh about it.

Of American families with children, the majority have at least two. In many cases, children spend more time with their siblings in the early years than they spend with their parents (Crouter & McHale, 1989). ***Question: What kinds of influences do siblings have on social and personal development in early childhood?***

Siblings make a unique contribution to one another's social, emotional, and cognitive development (Roberts & Blanton, 2001). They serve many functions, including giving physical care, providing emotional support and nurturance, offering advice and direction, serving as role models, providing social interaction that helps develop social skills, and making demands and imposing restrictions (Roberts & Blanton, 2001). They also advance each other's cognitive development, as shown in research concerning false beliefs and the theory of mind (Cutting & Dunn, 1999; Peterson, 2001; Ruffman, Perner, & Parkin, 1999).

In the early years of childhood, when siblings spend a great deal of time together, their interactions often are emotionally loaded and marked by both positive aspects (cooperation, teaching, nurturance) and negative aspects (conflict, control, competition) (Dunn, Stocker, & Plumin, 1990). By and large, older siblings are more nurturant but also more dominating than younger siblings (Buhrmester, 1992). Younger siblings are more likely to imitate older siblings and to accept their direction.

Reflect

Do you have siblings? How did you get along with them during early childhood? How do you feel about them now? Have your feelings changed over the years?

However, older siblings may also imitate younger siblings, especially when parents remark "how cute" the baby is being in front of the older child. At the age of 2 years 5 months, my daughter Allyn would pretend that she could not talk every once in a while, just like her 5-month-old sister Jordan.

In many cultures (including this one, laments the author's wife), older girls are expected to care for younger siblings (Whiting & Edwards, 1988). Younger siblings frequently turn to older sisters when the mother is unavailable. ("They still do," notes my wife. Her younger siblings are now in their 30s and 40s, which is amazing because my wife is 29.)

Parents often urge their children to stop fighting among themselves, and there are times when these conflicts look deadly (and occasionally they are). It is important to

TABLE 10.2 *Do's and Don'ts for Parents in Guiding Children's Behavior*

Do . . .	Don't . . .
• Reward good behavior with praises, smiles, hugs. • Give clear, simple, realistic rules appropriate to the child's age. • Enforce rules with reasonable consequences. • Ignore annoying behavior such as whining and tantrums. • Child-proof the house, putting dangerous and breakable items out of reach. Then establish limits. • Be consistent.	• Pay attention only to a child's misbehavior. Issue too many rules or enforce them haphazardly. • Try to control behavior solely in the child's domain, such as thumb sucking, which can lead to frustrating power struggles. • Nag, lecture, shame, or induce guilt. • Yell or spank. • Be overly permissive.

Sources: Windell, 1991; Schmitt, 1991.

© Mary Kate Denny/PhotoEdit

Siblings

Siblings make a unique contribution to one another's social, emotional, and cognitive development.

note, however, that garden-variety conflict among siblings can have positive outcomes. (Really.) It appears that conflict between siblings enhances their social competence, their development of self-identity (who they are and what they stand for), and their ability to rear their own children in a healthful manner (Bedford, Volling, & Avioli, 2000). When adults look back upon their childhood conflicts with their siblings, their memories of them are often positive (Bedford et al., 2000).

As siblings move from early childhood through middle childhood and into adolescence, the nature of their relationship changes in at least two important ways (Buhrmester, 1992). First, as siblings grow more competent and their developmental statuses become similar, their relationship becomes more egalitarian. In other words, as later-born siblings grow older and become more self-sufficient, they need and accept less nurturance and direction from older siblings. Second, sibling relationships become less intense as children grow older. The exercise of power and the amount of conflict declines. The extent of warmth and closeness diminishes somewhat as well, although the attachment between siblings remains fairly strong throughout adolescence.

Other factors also affect the development of sibling relationships. For example, there is more conflict between siblings in families in which the parents treat the children differently (Brody, Stoneman, & McCoy, 1992; Brody, Stoneman, McCoy, & Forehand, 1992; Dunn, 1992). Conflict between siblings also is greater when the relationship between the parents or between the parents and children is not

Developing in a World of Diversity

Individualism, Collectivism, and Patterns of Child Rearing

Much of the research on parenting styles has been done with middle-class European American families. But, as Baumrind (1991b) cautions, parenting styles must be viewed within the context of particular cultures. Socialization methods that appear authoritarian or punitive by middle-class standards may be used more frequently among poor families from ethnic minority groups to prepare children to cope with the hazards of daily life. Placing a high value on unquestioned obedience might be considered overly restrictive in a quiet middle-class neighborhood but may be warranted now and then in a more dangerous inner-city environment (Baldwin, Baldwin, & Cole, 1990). Poor families in other countries also tend to use authoritarian child-rearing styles (LeVine, 1974).

What about middle-class families in other parts of the world? How do their parenting styles compare with those of middle-class parents in the United States? An interesting study by Kobayashi-Winata and Power (1989) compared child-rearing practices of middle-class Japanese and American parents whose children ranged in age from 4 to 7. In both groups of families, the most compliant children had parents who provided opportunities for appropriate behavior and who used relatively little punishment. Japanese and American parents did differ, however, in

TABLE 10.3 *Cultural Values and Child-Rearing Techniques—United States and Japan*

Culture	Parental Value	Child-Rearing Practices
United States middle class	• Early socialization • Independence • Individualism	• Expect child to follow more rules • Listen to child's opinion • Use external punishment (e.g., send child to his or her room)
Japanese middle class	• Group harmony • Dependence on others • Conformity	• Make fewer demands • Be more indulgent • Use verbal commands • Use reprimands and explanations

harmonious (Brody, Stoneman, & McCoy, 1992; Brody, Stoneman, McCoy, & Forehand, 1992; Volling & Belsky, 1992). It should also come as no surprise that children who have a difficult temperament have more trouble getting along with their siblings (Dunn, 1993).

Adjusting to the Birth of a Sibling

The birth of a sister or brother is often a source of stress for young children because of changes in family relationships and the environment (Gottlieb & Mendelson, 1990). When a new baby comes into the home, the mother pays relatively more attention to it and spends much less time in playful activities with the older child (Campbell, 1990). No wonder the child may feel displaced and resentful of the affection lavished on the newborn. These feelings are illustrated by the comments of a 3-year-old who worried that his new sister would take all his mother's love and not leave enough for him (Campbell, 1990).

Children show a mixture of negative and positive reactions to the birth of a sibling. These include **regression** to babyish behaviors, such as increased clinging, crying, and toilet accidents. Anger and naughtiness may increase as well. But the same children will often show increased independence and maturity, insisting on feeding or dressing themselves and helping to take care of the baby (Kutner, 1989; Teti, 1992).

What can parents do to help a young child cope with the arrival of a new baby? For one thing, they can prepare the child by explaining in advance what is to come. In one study, preschoolers who attended a sibling preparation class with their mothers showed fewer signs of **sibling rivalry** (Fortier et al., 1991). Parental support is extremely important as well. Children show less distress following the birth of a sibling when the parents give them lots of affection, encouragement, and praise and spend time doing things with them (Gottlieb & Mendelson, 1990).

regression A return to behaviors characteristic of earlier stages of development.

sibling rivalry Jealousy or rivalry among brothers and sisters.

individualist A person who defines herself or himself in terms of personal traits and gives priority to her or his own goals.

collectivist A person who defines herself or himself in terms of relationships to other people and groups and gives priority to group goals.

© Elizabeth Crews

Child-Rearing Techniques in Japan

Japanese parents use more verbal commands, reprimands, and explanations than American parents.

the relative use of various child-rearing practices. American parents were more likely to rely on external punishments such as sending children to their room, whereas Japanese parents more often used verbal commands, reprimands, and explanations (see Table 10.3).

These differences in disciplinary practices apparently reflect differences in cultural values. Cross-cultural research reveals that people in the United States and many northern European nations tend to be individualistic (Ayyash-Abdo, 2001; French et al., 2001). On the other hand, many people from cultures in Africa, Asia, and Central and South America tend to be collectivistic (Abe-Kim, Okazaki, & Goto, 2001; Basic Behavioral Science Task Force, 1996).

Individualists tend to define themselves in terms of their personal identities and to give priority to their personal goals (Triandis, 1995). When asked to complete the statement "I am . . . ," they are likely to respond in terms of their personality traits ("I am outgoing," "I am artistic") or their occupations ("I am a nurse," "I am a systems analyst") (Triandis, 1990). In contrast, **collectivists** tend to define themselves in terms of the groups to which they belong and to give priority to the group's goals (Triandis, 1995). They feel complete in terms of their relationships with others (Markus & Kitayama, 1991; see Figure 10.1). They are more likely than individualists to conform to group norms and judgments (Abe-Kim et al., 2001; Phalet & Schoenpflug, 2001). When asked to complete the statement "I am . . . ," they are more likely to respond in terms of their families, gender, or nation ("I am a father," "I am a Buddhist," "I am Japanese") (Triandis, 1990, 1994).

The seeds of individualism and collectivism are found in the culture in which a person grows up. The capitalist system fosters individualism to some degree. It assumes that individuals are entitled to amass personal fortunes and that the process of doing so creates jobs and wealth for large numbers of people. Children watch TV and films,

Birth Order: Not Just Where in the World, But Also Where in the Family

Let me confess at the beginning of this section that I—your author—am an only child. As I was developing, I experienced what I imagine are most of the rewards and, yes, punishments of being an only child. First and perhaps foremost, I was the little king in my household in The Bronx. A petty tyrant at best, and at worst. I enjoyed all the resources my family had to offer: a relatively good allowance (with which I bought a comic book a day—*Superman* did nothing that escaped my young attention) and lots of parental attention. I never knew that we were poor, because I got most of what I wanted.

On the other hand, for many years I was more comfortable relating to adults than to other children. And there were many times that I was lonely in the home and wished that I had a sister or a brother. But these are the experiences of one person, and it's difficult to know how accurately they are recalled. So let's be more scientific about it. ***Question: What does the research say about the effects of being a first-born or an only child?***

Reflect

Where do you fit into your family of origin? Are you a first-born or only child? Were you born later? How does your own development and personality fit in with the stereotypes discussed in this section?

Many differences in personality and achievement have been observed among first-born and only children as compared with later-born children. On the positive side (from the standpoint of an achievement-oriented author), first-born and only children are more highly motivated to achieve (that's me), perform better academically (that's me), and are more cooperative (not so sure that was me). They are also helpful (not so sure), adult-oriented (that's me), and less aggressive (I guess that was me; not easy to recall) (Braza et al., 2000; Paulhus, Trapnell, & Chen, 1999; Zajonc, 2001). They obtain higher standardized test scores, including

Developing in a World of Diversity (continued)

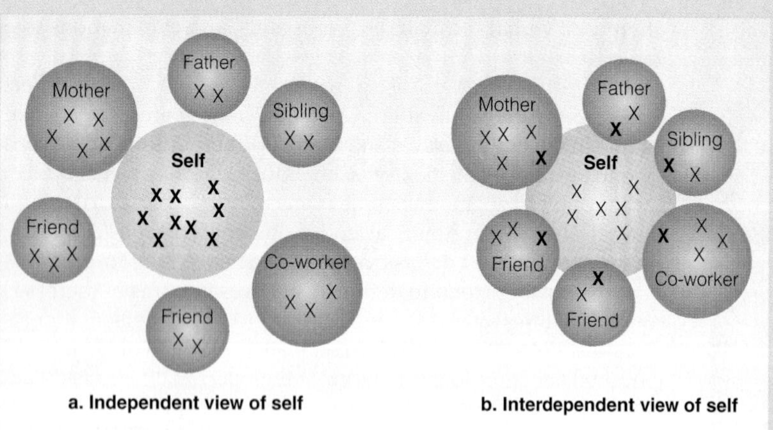

Figure 10.1
The Self in Relation to Others

From the Individualist and Collectivist Perspectives. To an individualist, the self is separate from other people (a). To a collectivist, the self is complete only in terms of relationships to other people (b). (Based on Markus & Kitayama, 1991). Are there differences in the ways in which people in individualist and collectivist cultures rear their children?

and the individualist perspective is found in the self-reliant heroes and antiheroes of Western literature and mass media—from Clint Eastwood's gritty cowboys to Walt Disney's Pocahontas and Mulan. The traditional writings of the East have exalted people who resisted personal temptations in order to do their duty and promote the welfare of the group. Japanese parents tend to be more collectivist than American parents. Japanese parents are more likely to emphasize conformity and acceptance of group goals, whereas American parents are more likely to emphasize independence and individualism. It may be that verbal methods are more effective in ensuring group cooperation.

It must be mentioned, however, that individuals from within the same country can belong to quite different cultures in terms of individualistic and collectivist tendencies. Within the country of Lebanon, for example, Ayyash-Abdo (2001) found that college students who spoke French or English were more likely to be individualistic than students who spoke mainly in Arabic. Moreover, traditional Islamic values were also connected with collectivism.

Other studies reveal additional differences in the child-rearing techniques of American and Japanese parents that appear to foster the American emphasis on early socialization and independence and the Japanese focus on group harmony and dependence on others. For example, in one study, American mothers of preschoolers expected their children to follow more rules but also were more likely to listen to their children's opinions. Japanese mothers, in contrast, made many fewer demands on their children and were more indulgent (Power, Kobayashi-Winata, & Kelley, 1992).

SAT scores (Zajonc & Mullally, 1997). An adoptee study found that first-reared children, regardless of their biological birth order, were more conscientious than later-reared children (Beer & Horn, 2000). As part of their achievement orientation, first-born children also see themselves as being more in control of their successes (Phillips & Phillips, 2000). On the negative side, first-born and only children show greater anxiety (that's me) and are less self-reliant (hmmmmm—I wonder).

Robert Zajonc (2001) and his colleagues support a **confluence model** of development. They suggest that the family structure, including the variables of birth order, family size, and child spacing, flow together ("flowing together" is what's meant by *confluence*) to produce important influences on the intellectual development of children.

First-born children are also more likely than later-born children to have imaginary playmates (Bouldin & Pratt, 1999). It's Allyn, our first-born, who had the imaginary playmate "Loveliness." Our second-born (Jordan) and our third-born (Taylor) were too busy coping with Allyn (and in Taylor's case, both Allyn and Jordan) to have imaginary playmates—or at least imaginary playmates that my wife and I knew about.

Interviews with parents of 478 children ranging in age from 3 to 9 found that children with imaginary playmates were described as being more imaginative than those who did not have them (Bouldin & Pratt, 1999). Of course, one does not have to be a rocket scientist (or a specialist in human development) to recognize that only children (and first-born children are only children at least for a while) are also in greater need of imaginary playmates.

Later-born children frequently learn that they must act aggressively to earn the attention of their parents and older siblings. They also tend to accept—or at least to deal with the fact—that they do not come first (Downey, 2001). Perhaps for that reason, their self-concepts tend to be lower than those of first-born or of only children. The social skills they acquire from dealing with and accommodating to the desires of their older siblings seem to translate into their greater popularity with peers. Research finds that later-born children are considered to be more rebellious, liberal, and agreeable than first-born children (Paulhus et al., 1999; Zweigenhaft & Von Ammon, 2000). These factors—combined—appear to be connected with their relative popularity among peers.

Differences in personality and achievement among first-born and later-born children may be linked to contrasting styles in parenting. First-born children start life with experience as only children. For a year or more, they receive the singular attention of both parents. They are held more, spoken to more, stimulated more. All in all, they spend more time with their parents than later-born children do.

Even after other children come along, parents still tend to relate to the first child more than to later-born children. Parents continue to make demands and to orient their speech toward levels that are appropriate for the first-born child. Parents have greater expectations for first-born children. They impose tougher restrictions on them and make greater demands of them. Parents are more highly involved in their activities. First-born children are often recruited to help teach younger siblings (Zajonc, 2001). As your author can testify, being asked to teach something (often) prompts one to learn something about it.

By and large, parents are more relaxed and flexible with later-born children. Children are quite aware of the greater permissiveness often given to later-born children and may complain about it. (Endlessly.) Why are parents more indulgent with later-born children? They have probably gained some self-confidence in child rearing. They see that the first-born child is turning out just fine (all right, all right: The first-born child *usually* turns out to be just fine, and sometimes "just fine" needs to be qualified as "just fine much of the time"). Parents may interpret the first child's success as a sign of their own competence and may, therefore, assume that later-born children will also turn out, well, just fine. In any event, my wife and I were certainly more "relaxed" with Jordan and with Taylor than we were with Allyn.

There is a more negative interpretation of parents' relative "relaxation" in the rearing of later-born children. Parents have just so many resources, in terms of

confluence model The view that family structure, including factors such as birth order, family size, and child spacing, come together to affect the intellectual development of children.

time, energy, and, yes, financial resources. As new children come along, they "dilute" the existing resources, so that not as much can be devoted to them (Downey, 2001). Put this interpretation in the "sad, but often true" category.

All right, then, siblings hold key places in child development. ***Question: What is the influence of peers on social and personal development in early childhood?***

Peer Relationships

The importance of **peers** in the development of the young child is widely recognized (Putallaz & Dunn, 1990; Rubin & Coplan, 1992). As children move into the preschool years, they spend more time in the company of other children. The peer interactions of children serve many functions. Children learn a variety of social skills in the peer group—sharing, helping, taking turns, dealing with conflict. They learn how to lead and how to follow. Physical and cognitive skills develop through peer interactions. Finally, peers are a source of emotional support (Grusec & Lytton, 1988; Parker & Gottman, 1989). In this section, we look at the development of peer relationships in the preschool years.

Development of Peer Relationships

Infants first show positive interest in one another at about 6 months. If they are placed on the floor facing one another, they will smile, occasionally imitate one another, and often touch one another. Social interaction increases over the next few months, but during the 1st year, contacts between infants tend to be brief (Hartup, 1992b; Howes, 1987). In the 2nd year, children show increased interest in each other and interact by playing with each other's play materials. But they still show relatively little social interaction. By about 2 years of age, however, children are readily imitating one another's play actions and engaging in social games such as follow the leader (Brownell, 1990; Eckerman & Stein, 1990; Hanna & Meltzoff, 1993). Also by the age of 2, children have established preferences for playing with two or three particular playmates (Strayer, 1990).

Friendships

peers Children of the same age. (More generally, people of similar background and social standing.)

The preferences shown by toddlers for certain other children as playmates is an early sign of friendship (Collins & Gunnar, 1990). Friendship goes beyond casual interaction with peers. It is characterized by shared, positive interactions and feel-

Friendship

Friendship takes on different meanings as children develop. Preschoolers focus on sharing toys and activities. Five- to 7-year-olds report that friends are children with whom they have "fun." Sharing confidences becomes important in late childhood and in adolescence.

ings of attachment (Grusec & Lytton, 1988; Park, Kay, & Ramsay, 1993). Even early friendships are fairly stable. Howes (1988) found that 1–6-year-olds tended to maintain their friendships from one year to the next, some for as long as 3 years.

Preschool children behave somewhat differently toward their friends than toward ordinary playmates. Friends, as compared with nonfriends, show higher levels of interaction, helpful behavior, smiling and laughing, and more frequent cooperation and collaboration (Collins & Gunnar, 1990; Costin & Jones, 1992; Rubin & Coplan, 1992). Conflicts between young friends are less intense and are resolved more readily than conflicts between nonfriends (Hartup, 1992a).

What are children's conceptions of friendships? When preschoolers are asked what they like about their friends, they typically mention the play materials and activities that they share (Hartup, 1993). Five- to 7-year-olds usually report that their friends are the children they do things with, the children with whom they have "fun" (Berndt & Perry, 1986). As we shall see in Chapter 13, it is not until late childhood and adolescence that the friends' traits and notions of trust, communication, and intimacy become important aspects of friendship.

Reflect

Do you recall any friendships from early childhood? How would you describe them? If you are a parent, how would you characterize your children's friendships during early childhood?

Review

(1) Investigators of child rearing find it useful to classify parents according to two dimensions: warmth–coldness and ________–permissiveness. (2) ________ methods of enforcing restrictions attempt to give children knowledge that will enable them to generate desirable behavior patterns in similar situations. (3) ________-assertive methods involve physical punishment and deprivation of privileges. (4) Parents who choose power-assertive methods tend to be ________. (5) Parents who use ________ of love tend to isolate or ignore

Developing in a World of Diversity

The Case of the (In)Visible Father

The role of fathers in child development has been relatively invisible when compared with that of mothers (Coley, 2001). During the 17th and 18th centuries, fathers were viewed mainly as breadwinners and teachers of values and religion. They were expected to legitimize their children through marriage and support the family. Over the past two centuries, forces such as urbanization, industrialization, government-funded social welfare programs, and even the women's movement have all contributed to illegitimacy and fathers' abandoning of their families.

Developmentalists today conceptualize responsible fatherhood as providing children with financial support, caregiving (feeding and bathing children, tucking them in, reading to them, spending time with them), emotional support, and legal paternity (Coley, 2001; Doherty, Kouneski, & Erickson, 1996). It's not happening, at least not for a large number of children in the United States today. And the numbers break down into noticeable patterns according to ethnicity and socioeconomic status (level of income) (Coley, 2001). For example, as we entered the new millennium, nearly one third of American children were born to unmarried women. Birth rates outside of marriage were 26% for European Americans, 41% for Latino and Latina Americans, and 69% for African Americans (U.S. Department of Health and Human Services, 1999). Some parental couples do cohabit—that

(In)Visible Fathers?

Developmentalists note that the role of fathers in child development has been relatively invisible when compared with that of mothers. Through much of Western history, fathers have mainly been breadwinners and teachers of values. In the United States today, responsible fathers are seen as providing children with financial support and caregiving as well as legal pater-nity. That's the ideal. It turns out that about one third of American children are born to unmarried women. Even so, many American fathers do share equally, or almost equally, in homemaking, child-rearing, and breadwinning chores with their wives.

children when they misbehave. (6) ________ parents are both warm and restrictive. (7) ________ parents see obedience as a virtue to be pursued for its own sake. (8) ________ parents can be "permissive-indulgent" or "rejecting-neglecting." (9) The children of ________ parents are most competent. (10) Parents tend to become more power-________ when their children are aggressive or when they believe their children understand the rules they have violated. (11) ________-born children are most highly motivated to achieve.

Pulling It Together: How do siblings and peers affect development during early childhood?

Social Behaviors—In the World, Among Others

During the early childhood years, children make tremendous strides in the development of social skills and behavior. Their play activities increasingly involve other children. They learn how to share, cooperate, and comfort others. But young children, like adults, are complex beings. They can be aggressive at times, as well as loving and helpful. We turn now to the development of social behaviors in the early years.

Play—Child's Play, That Is

Question: So what do developmentalists know about child's play?

While children play, developmentalists work to understand just how they do so. They have found that play has many characteristics. It is meaningful, pleasur-

Developing in a World of Diversity *(continued)*

is, live together without being legally married. But all in all, 70% of European American children were living with their biological fathers, as compared with 54% of Latino and Latina American children and 30% of African American children. The group differences cannot be attributed to ethnicity; they are intertwined with level of income. African Americans remain among the poorest Americans, and 33% of American children below the poverty line lived with their biological fathers, as compared with 70% of other children (U.S. Department of Health and Human Services, 1999). For African American families, the legacy of slavery, with family members being bought and sold without regard for family structure, apparently continues to contribute to family instability today (O. L. Patterson, 1998). Many unmarried fathers give lip service to intending to support and care for their children (W. Johnson, 2000), but studies show that the majority drop out as their children go through early childhood (Coley & Chase-Lansdale, 1999).

The other side of the coin is that many fathers are more deeply involved than ever before in the day-to-day lives of their children (Cabrera et al., 2000). They are doing more child care and housework than in the past, even though mothers are usually conceptualized as the primary caregivers and homemakers in the family. This shift, such as it is, is connected with blurring of traditional gender roles and with the fact that the majority of mothers are in the workforce—and often enough, in better-paying positions than their husbands. Moreover, following divorce, a growing number of fathers are obtaining full custody or shared custody of their children.

Note, however, that the absence of the father from the household does not necessarily mean that children are without a father figure. In many cases, stepfathers, maternal partners, relatives, and friends engage in social fathering, especially among low-income families and African Americans (Coley, 2001). Studies of low-income African American families with preschoolers find that one third to one half of the mothers report that father figures are involved with their children (Black, Dubowitz, & Starr, 1999; Jayakody & Kalil, 2000).

Rebekah Levine Coley (2001) notes that none of these statistics, in itself, indicate whether it *matters* whether the father is present or not. She acknowledges that theories of child development generally find significant roles for the father, but argues that a good deal of systematic research is needed to fill in some blanks. For example, what exactly is the father's influence on the child's cognitive development, educational attainment, and social and personal development?

As a father, I am quick to jump on the bandwagon of asserting that fatherhood matters.[1] As a scientist, I must join with Coley (2001) in acknowledging that much needs to be learned as to all the ways in which fatherhood matters.

[1]A father who has been consistent in his failure to do his share of child rearing and housework, notes his wife.

able, voluntary, and internally motivated (Fromberg, 1990). Play is fun! But play also serves many important functions in the life of the young child (Christie & Wardle, 1992; Lewis, 1993; Sutton-Smith, 1993). Play helps children develop motor skills and coordination. It contributes to social development, as children learn to share play materials, take turns, and try on new roles through dramatic play. It supports the development of such cognitive qualities as curiosity, exploration, symbolic thinking, and problem solving. And play may help children learn to deal with conflict and anxiety (Fisher, 1992; J. Johnson 1990).

Parten's Types of Play

In classic research on children's play, Mildred Parten (1932) observed the development of five types of play among 2–5-year-old nursery school children.

First is **solitary play,** in which children play with toys by themselves, independently of the children around them. Solitary players do not appear to be influenced by children around them. They make no effort to approach them.

Second is **onlooker play,** in which children observe other children who are at play. Onlookers frequently talk to the children they are observing and may make suggestions, but they do not overtly join in. Solitary play and onlooker play are both considered types of **nonsocial play**—that is, play in which children do not interact. Nonsocial play occurs more often in 2- and 3-year-olds than in older preschoolers.

Third is **parallel play,** in which children play with toys similar to those of surrounding children. However, they treat the toys as they choose and do not directly interact with other children.

Fourth is **associative play,** in which children interact and share toys. However, they do not seem to share group goals. Although they interact, individuals still treat toys as they choose. The association with the other children appears to be more important than the nature of the activity. They seem to enjoy each other's company.

Fifth is **cooperative play,** in which children interact to achieve common, group goals. The play of each child is subordinated to the purposes of the group. One or two group members direct the activities of others. There is also a division of labor, with different children taking different roles. Children may pretend to be members of a family, animals, space monsters, and all sorts of creatures.

Reflect

What kind of play do you observe among children in early childhood? (You are allowed to visit a playground to help you reflect on this question.)

solitary play Play that is independent from that of nearby children and in which no effort is made to approach other children.

onlooker play Play during which children observe other children at play but do not enter into their play themselves.

nonsocial play Forms of play (solitary play or onlooker play) in which play is not influenced by the play of nearby children.

parallel play Play in which children use toys similar to those of nearby children but approach their toys in their own ways. No effort is made to interact with others.

associative play Play with other children in which toys are shared but there is no common goal or division of labor.

cooperative play Organized play in which children cooperate to meet common goals. There is a division of labor, and children take on specific roles as group members.

Associative Play

Associative play is a form of social play in which children interact and share toys.

Parallel play, associative play, and cooperative play are types of **social play.** In each case children are influenced by other children as they are playing. Parten found that associative and cooperative play become common at age 5. More recent research continues to show that they are more likely to be found among older and more experienced preschoolers (Howes & Matheson, 1992b). Furthermore, girls are somewhat more likely than boys to engage in social play (Zheng & Colombo, 1989).

But there are exceptions to these age trends in social play. Nonsocial play can involve educational activities that foster cognitive development. In fact, many 4- and 5-year-olds spend a good deal of time in parallel constructive play. For instance, they may work on puzzles or build with blocks near other children. Parallel constructive players are frequently perceived by teachers to be socially skillful and are popular with their peers (Coplan et al., 1994; Rubin, 1982). Some toddlers are also more capable of social play than one might expect, given their age. Two-year-olds with older siblings or with a great deal of group experience may engage in advanced forms of social play.

Dramatic Play: "The Play's the Thing"

Children in the 2nd year after birth begin to engage in symbolic or pretend play. From the ages of 2 to 5, pretend play becomes increasingly social, involving recognizable characters such as doctor or teacher and themes such as playing house or cops and robbers. This is a type of cooperative play known as **dramatic play.**

Catherine Garvey (1990) examined the emergence of dramatic play in 3–5-year-olds in a nursery school setting. Even 3-year-olds engaged in dramatic play sequences, but the themes of the older children were more realistic, integrated, and complex. Children assumed a variety of roles in their dramatic play. Of great importance for children of all ages were family roles, such as mommy, daddy, and baby. Older children were more likely than younger ones to adopt character roles such as doctor, nurse, bus driver, or teacher.

Much theorizing has been done about the function of dramatic play. It has been suggested that dramatic play fosters social and emotional development (Nicolopoulou, 1991; Smilansky, 1990). For one thing, social interactions during dramatic play are longer, more positive, and more complex than interactions that occur during nondramatic play (Doyle et al., 1992). For another, dramatic play allows children to experiment with different social roles and obtain feedback from peers. Enacting the roles of other people may help them learn to take the perspective of others and to develop empathy. Finding solutions to make-believe problems may help children find ways to solve problems in the real world. On an emotional level, it has been suggested that dramatic play allows children to express their fears and their fantasies (Singer, 1998).

Gender Differences in Play

Question: Are there boys' toys and girls' toys? It appears that there are. The reasons are a bit harder to pin down.

Lisa Serbin and her colleagues (2001) explored infants' visual preferences for gender-stereotyped toys using the time-honored assumption that infants spend more time looking at objects that are of greater interest. They found that both girls and boys showed significant preferences for gender-stereotyped toys by 18 months of age. Although preferences for gender-typed toys are well developed by the ages of 15 to 36 months, girls are more likely to stray from the stereotypes (Bussey & Bandura, 1999; Frey & Ruble, 1992; Lobel & Menashri, 1993). Girls ask for and play with "boys' toys" such as cars and trucks more often than boys choose dolls and other "girls' toys." These cross-role activities may reflect the greater prestige of "masculine" activities and traits in American culture. Therefore, a boy playing with "girls' toys" might be seen as taking on an inferior role. A girl playing with "boys' toys" might be seen as having an understandable desire for power or esteem.

Girls and boys differ not only in toy preferences but also in their choice of play environments and activities. During the preschool and early elementary school

social play Play in which children interact with and are influenced by the play of others. Examples include parallel play, associative play, and cooperative play.

dramatic play Play in which children enact social roles; made possible by the attainment of symbolic thought. A form of *pretend play.*

years, boys prefer vigorous physical outdoor activities such as climbing, playing with large vehicles, and rough-and-tumble play. In middle childhood, boys spend more time than girls in large play groups of five or more children and spend more time in competitive play (Crombie & Desjardins, 1993; Van Brunschot, Zarbatany, & Strang, 1993). Girls are more likely to engage in arts-and-crafts and domestic play. Their activities are more closely directed and more structured by adults than are boys' activities (Maccoby, 1993b; Pomerleau et al., 1990). Girls spend more time than boys playing with just one other child or with a small group of children (Crombie & Desjardins, 1993; Van Brunschot et al., 1993).

© Philip James Corwin/CORBIS

Girl Enjoying a Game of Baseball

Although preferences for gender-typed toys are well established by the age of 3, girls are more likely to stray from the stereotypes, as in this photograph of a girl playing the masculine-typed game of baseball.

Why do children show these early preferences for gender-stereotyped toys and activities? Although one cannot rule out the possibility of biological factors, such as boys' slightly greater strength and activity levels and girls' slightly greater physical maturity and coordination, note that these differences are just that—slight. On the other hand, parents and other adults treat girls and boys differently from birth onward. They consistently provide gender-stereotyped toys and room furnishings and encourage gender-typing in children's play activities and even household chores (Lytton & Romney, 1991; Pomerleau et al., 1990).

Some studies find that children who "cross the line" by exhibiting an interest in toys or activities considered appropriate for the other gender are often teased, ridiculed, rejected, or ignored by their parents, teachers, other adults, and peers. Boys are more likely to be criticized than girls for such behavior (Fagot & Hagan, 1991; Garvey, 1990). On the other hand, one study of 50 preschoolers—25 girls and 25 boys—found that most children believed that their peers should not be excluded from gender-typed play activities on the basis of gender (Theimer, Killen, & Stangor, 2001). That is, most believed that it was wrong in terms of equality and fairness to prevent girls from playing with trucks and boys from playing with dolls. Perhaps the inconsistency in research findings has something to do with the difference between what preschoolers are observed to do and what they say. (Why should children be more consistent than the rest of us?)

Another well-documented factor involving gender and play is that girls prefer the company of girls, whereas boys prefer to play with boys. This phenomenon is found in a wide variety of cultures and ethnic groups (Whiting & Edwards, 1988), and it appears early in life. Children begin to prefer playmates of the same gender by the age of 2, with girls developing this preference somewhat earlier than boys (Fagot, 1990; Strayer, 1990). The tendency to associate with peers of the same gender becomes even stronger during middle childhood (Bukowski et al., 1993; Crombie & Desjardins, 1993). Perhaps you remember a period during your childhood when you and your friends found members of the other gender absolutely loathsome and wanted nothing to do with them.[2]

Question: Why do children choose to associate with peers of their own gender? Eleanor Maccoby (1990b) believes that two factors are involved. One is that boys' play is more oriented toward dominance, aggression, and rough play. The second is that boys are not very responsive to girls' polite suggestions. Maccoby suggests that girls avoid boys because they want to protect themselves from boys' aggression and because they find it unpleasant to interact with unresponsive people. Additionally, boys may avoid the company of girls because they see girls as being inferior (Caplan & Larkin, 1991).

[2]Your author's wife notes that in her case it is not so certain that this "stage" has passed.

Whom Do You Want to Play With?

During early and middle childhood, children tend to prefer the company of children of their own gender. Why?

Another view is that children simply "like" peers of their own gender more than peers of the other gender (Bukowski et al., 1993). But in the field of psychology, "simple liking" is usually based on similarity in interests. That is, preference for peers of one's own gender is apparently related to preference for toys that are stereotyped as appropriate for one's gender (Etaugh & Liss, 1992). Children who prefer dolls to transportation toys may prefer to associate with children who share their preference.

Prosocial Behavior—It Could Happen, and Does

My wife recalls always trying to help others in early childhood. She remembers sharing her toys, often at her own expense. She had many sad times when toys or favors she gave were not returned or when toys were broken by others. She wishes to add, for any interested readers, that her siblings continue in this pattern until this day. Moreover, now I have been added to the list of takers.

Prosocial behavior, sometimes known as *altruism,* is behavior intended to benefit another without expectation of reward. Prosocial behavior includes helping and comforting others in distress, sharing, and cooperating (Eisenberg, 1992; Eisenberg et al., 1999). ***Question: How does prosocial behavior develop?***

Even in the 1st year, children begin to share. They spontaneously offer food and objects to others (Hay & Murray, 1982). In the 2nd year, children continue to share objects and also begin to comfort distressed companions and help others with tasks and chores (Hay et al., 1991; Zahn-Waxler, Radke-Yarrow, & Wagner, 1992).

By the preschool and early school years, children frequently engage in prosocial behavior. Some types of prosocial behavior occur more often than others. One study observed 4- and 7-year-olds at home and found that helping occurred more often than sharing, affection, and reassuring (Grusec, 1991).

Research suggests that the development of prosocial behavior is linked to the development of other capabilities in the young child, such as empathy and perspective-taking.

Reflect

How do you feel when you see others in pain or in need? Can you recall how far back these feelings go?

Empathy: "I Feel Your Pain"

Empathy is sensitivity to the feelings of others. It is the ability to understand and share another person's feelings and is connected with sharing and cooperation. A study of 60 American and Japanese women aged 25–45 who were mothers of preschoolers found that those from both cultures emphasized social cooperativeness and interpersonal sensitivity as the most desirable behavioral characteristic in young children (Olson, Kashiwagi, & Crystal, 2001). When the mothers were asked to list their primary negative behavioral characteristic, Japanese mothers chose the opposite behavioral pattern: social uncooperativeness and insensitivity. American mothers, possibly living in a more violent society, reported primary concern over aggressive, disruptive behavior.

In terms of empathy, children respond emotionally from a very early age when others are in distress (Caplan & Hay, 1989). During infancy, children frequently begin to cry when they hear other children crying (Eisenberg, 1992). However, this

prosocial behavior Behavior intended to benefit another without expectation of reward.

empathy Ability to share another person's feelings.

early agitated response may be largely reflexive. Crying, like other strong stimuli, can be aversive, and infants generally react to aversive stimulation by crying. Even so, this early unlearned behavior pattern might contribute to the development of empathy.

Empathy appears to promote prosocial behavior and decrease aggressive behavior, and these links are evident by the 2nd year (Eisenberg & Miller, 1990; Hastings et al., 2000; Kalliopuska, 1991). During the 2nd year, many children approach other children and adults who are in distress and attempt to help them. They may try to hug a crying child or tell the child not to cry. Toddlers who are relatively lacking in empathy—and rated as emotionally unresponsive to their caregivers—are more likely to behave aggressively throughout the school years (Olson et al., 2000).

There is some evidence that girls show more empathy than boys and that this difference increases with age (Eisenberg, 1992; Gross & Ballif, 1991). Some research suggests that the difference may arise because girls are socialized to be more attuned to others' emotions than boys are (Eisenberg et al., 1989), but genetic, biological factors may also play a role in the gender difference.

Perspective-Taking: Standing in Someone Else's Shoes

According to Piaget, children in the preoperational stage tend to be egocentric. That is, they tend not to be able to see things from the vantage points of others. It turns out that various cognitive abilities, such as being able to take another person's perspective, are related to knowing when someone is in need or distress (Carlo et al., 1991). Perspective-taking skills improve with age, and so do prosocial skills. Among children of the same age, those with better-developed perspective-taking ability also show more prosocial behavior and less aggressive behavior (Bengtsson & Johnson, 1992; Eisenberg & Miller, 1990; Hastings et al., 2000).

Influences on Prosocial Behavior

Yes, altruistic behavior is usually defined as prosocial behavior that occurs in the absence of rewards or the expectation of rewards. Nevertheless, prosocial behavior is influenced by rewards and punishments.[3] Observations of nursery school children show that the peers of children who are cooperative, friendly, and generous respond more positively to them than they do to children whose behavior is self-centered (Hartup, 1983). Children who are rewarded in this way for acting prosocially are likely to continue these behaviors (Eisenberg, 1992).

Some children at early ages are made responsible for doing household chores and caring for younger siblings. They are taught helping and nurturance skills, and their performances are selectively reinforced by other children and adults. Whiting and Edwards (1988) reported that children given such tasks are more likely to show prosocial behaviors than children who are not.

There is evidence that children can acquire sharing behavior by observing models who help and share. For example, children who watch programs such as *Mister Rogers' Neighborhood* that model prosocial behavior show increased social interaction, sharing behavior, cooperation, and use of positive reinforcement with other children (Comstock & Paik, 1991; Huston et al., 1992). In one experiment in sharing, 29–36-month-olds were more likely to share toys with playmates who first shared toys with them (Levitt et al., 1985). That is, the children appeared to model—and reciprocate—the sharing behavior of their peers.

It also appears that children's prosocial behavior is influenced by the kinds of interactions they have with their parents. For example, prosocial behavior and

[3]It reminds me of these lines from Walt Whitman's "Song of Myself":

> Do I contradict myself?
> Very well then I contradict myself,
> (I am large, I contain multitudes.)

Be tolerant of contradictions. You will find them all around you for the rest of your life.

empathy are enhanced in children who are securely attached to their parents and whose mothers show a high degree of empathy (Clark & Ladd, 2000; Fabes, Eisenberg, & Miller, 1990).

Parenting styles also affect the development of prosocial behavior. Prosocial behavior is fostered when parents use inductive techniques such as explaining how behavior affects others ("You made Josh cry. It's not nice to hit"). Parents of prosocial children are more likely to expect mature behavior from their children. They are less likely to use power-assertive techniques of discipline (Bar-Tal, 1990; Eisenberg, 1992).

Aggression: The Dark Side of Social Interaction

Children, like adults, are complex beings. Not only can they be loving and altruistic, but they can also be aggressive. (More contradictions.) Some children, of course, are more aggressive than others. Aggression refers to behavior intended to cause pain or hurt to another person. ***Question: How does aggression develop?***

Developmental Patterns

Aggressive behaviors, like other social behaviors, seem to follow certain developmental patterns. For one thing, the aggression of preschoolers is frequently instrumental or possession-oriented (Parke & Slaby, 1983). That is, young children tend to use aggression to obtain the toys and things they want, such as a favored seat at the dinner table or in the family car. But older preschoolers are more likely than younger ones to resolve their conflicts over toys by sharing rather than fighting (Caplan et al., 1991). In any event, anger and aggressive behavior in preschoolers most often causes other preschoolers to reject them (Walter & LaFreniere, 2000).

By 6 or 7, aggression becomes hostile and person-oriented. Children taunt and criticize each other and call each other names; they also attack one another physically.

Aggressive behavior appears to be generally stable and predictive of a wide variety of social and emotional difficulties in adulthood (Mesman, Bongers, & Koot, 2001; Nagin & Tremblay, 2001). Boys are more likely than girls to show aggression from childhood through adulthood, a finding that has been well-documented in many cultures (Kupersmidt, Bryant, & Willoughby, 2000; Nagin & Tremblay, 2001).

In longitudinal research, Sheryl Olson and her colleagues (2000) found that toddlers who were perceived as difficult and defiant were more likely to behave aggressively throughout the school years. A longitudinal study of more than 600 children found that aggressive 8-year-olds tended to remain more aggressive than their peers 22 years later, at age 30 (Eron et al., 1991). Aggressive children of both genders were more likely to have criminal convictions as adults, to abuse their spouses, and to drive while drunk.

One longitudinal study by Brame, Nagin, and Tremblay (2001) followed 926 boys from kindergarten through adolescence. Physically aggressive behavior patterns in kindergarten showed some overall tendency to decline over the years. However, the authors point out that very few *new* aggressive tendencies developed over the years. That is, boys who were nonaggressive in kindergarten were not likely to become aggressive later on.

Development of Aggression

Question: What causes aggression in children? What causes some children to be more aggressive than others? Aggression in childhood appears to result from a complex interplay of biological factors and environmental factors such as reinforcement and modeling.

Biological Factors

There is evidence that genetic factors may be involved in aggressive behavior, including criminal and antisocial behavior (Leve et al., 1998; McGuffin et al., 2001; Plomin, 2001a). For example, a classic longitudinal study of more than 14,000 adoptees in Denmark found that biological sons of criminal fathers had elevated crime rates even when adopted at birth and raised by noncriminal parents (Mednick, Moffitt, & Stack, 1987).

If genetics are involved in aggression, genes may do their work at least in part through the male sex hormone testosterone. Testosterone is apparently connected with feelings of self-confidence, high activity levels, and—the negative side—aggressiveness (Dabbs et al., 2001; Pope et al., 2000; Sullivan, 2000). Males are more aggressive than females, and males have higher levels of testosterone than females (Pope et al., 2000). Studies show, for example, that 9–11-year-old boys with conduct disorders are likely to have higher testosterone levels than their less aggressive peers (Chance et al., 2000). Members of "rambunctious" fraternities have higher testosterone levels, on average, than members of more "well-behaved" fraternities (Dabbs, Hargrove, & Heusel, 1996). Testosterone levels also vary with the occasion: The testosterone levels of males tend to be higher when they are "winning"—whether at sports or at games like chess (Bernhardt et al., 1998).

Having noted the apparently pervasive influences of testosterone, let us acknowledge that the effects of testosterone on aggressive behavior in early childhood are not well-understood, or even adequately described, at this point in time. During prenatal development, testosterone is known to stoke the development of male reproductive organs. During adolescence, it is clear that another surge of testosterone is responsible for further development of reproductive organs and, perhaps, at least partially responsible for various traditionally masculine-typed behavior patterns. But the social roles of testosterone during early childhood and middle childhood are presumably less prominent.

Another biologically based factor that may indirectly influence the development of aggression is a child's temperament. Children who are impulsive, uninhibited, and relatively fearless may be more likely to elicit punitive, aggressive reactions from parents (Bates et al., 1991; National Research Council, 1993). In a literally vicious cycle, aggressive parental reactions may contribute to the development of aggression in children.

Still another biological factor that is connected with aggression is traumatic brain injury. One study found that nearly three of five children who experienced severe traumatic brain injury displayed changes in personality (Max, Robertson, & Lansing, 2001). Of the children showing such changes, nearly two in five became more aggressive following the injury. However, it would be erroneous to infer that such injuries can account for a notable fraction of the incidence of aggression among preschoolers. Very few preschoolers actually experience traumatic brain injuries.

Reflect

Do you believe that aggression is "natural"? In his theory of evolution, Charles Darwin noted that more individuals are produced than can find food and survive into adulthood. Therefore, there is a struggle for survival. Individuals who possess characteristics that give them an advantage in this struggle are more likely to mature and contribute their genes to the next generation. In many species, then, whatever genes are linked to aggressive behavior are more likely to be transmitted to new generations.

If aggression is "natural," can we expect children and adults to inhibit aggressive impulses? What do you think?

Cognitive Factors

Person-oriented aggression is apparently connected with cognitive development (Ferguson & Rule, 1980). At 6 or 7 children are more capable of processing information about the motives and intentions of other people. As a result, they are less likely to stand by idly when another child intends to hurt or ridicule them.

Other evidence for the role of information processing is that aggressive boys are more likely than nonaggressive boys to incorrectly interpret the behavior of other children as potentially harmful (Dodge, 1993b; Quiggle et al., 1992). This bias may make the aggressive child quick to respond aggressively in social situations. Research with somewhat older children—781 fourth- and fifth-graders—also found a strong role for cognitive factors (Erdly & Asher, 1998). Children who believed in the legitimacy of aggression were more likely to say they would behave aggressively when they were presented with hypothetical social provocations.

Aggressive children are also often found to be lacking in empathy and the ability to see things from the perspective of other people (Hastings et al., 2000). They fail to conceptualize the experiences of their victims, and so they are less likely to inhibit their aggressive impulses.

Social Learning

Social-cognitive explanations of aggression focus on the role of environmental factors such as reinforcement and observational learning. Children, like adults, are most likely to be aggressive when they are frustrated in their attempts to gain something they want, such as the attention of a parent or a particular toy. Aggressive behavior can be reinforced by removing sources of frustration, especially when the aggressive children are large, strong, or skilled in fighting. When children repeatedly push, shove, and hit in order to grab toys or break into line, other children usually let them have their way (Cole et al., 1991). Children who are thus rewarded for acting aggressively are likely to continue to use aggressive means, especially if they do not have alternative means to achieving their ends.

Aggressive children may also associate with peers who value their aggression and encourage them to be aggressive (Cairns & Cairns, 1991; Perry, Perry, & Boldizar, 1990). These children have often been rejected by their less aggressive peers, a fact that decreases their motivation to please less-aggressive children and reduces their opportunity to learn social skills (Arnold et al., 1999; Walter & LaFreniere, 2000).

Parents as well as peers may encourage aggressive behavior in their children, sometimes quite inadvertently. Gerald Patterson (1982, 1995) and his colleagues have examined families in which parents use coercion as the primary means for controlling their children's behavior. In a typical pattern, parents will threaten, criticize, and punish a "difficult" or "impossible" child. The child will then respond by whining, yelling, and refusing to comply until the parents give in. Parents and children are both relieved when the cycle ends, so when the child misbehaves again, the parents become yet more coercive and the children become yet more defiant, until either the parents or the children give in. A study of 156 children, based on Patterson's observations, found that this cycle of behavior observed in the home at 18 months of age was a predictor of childhood aggression at the age of 5 in both boys and girls, as assessed by teacher ratings (Fagot & Leve, 1998). A more recent study with 407 children who were 5 years old found again that the Patterson model predicts aggressive behavior in both boys and girls (Eddy, Leve, & Fagot, 2001).

Children learn not only from the effects of their own behavior, but also from observing the behavior of others. They may model the aggressive behavior of their peers, their parents, or their communities at large (Linares et al., 2001; Putallaz et al., 1998). Children are more apt to imitate what their parents do than to heed what they say. If adults say they disapprove of aggression, but smash furniture or hit each other when frustrated, children are likely to develop the notion that this is the way to handle frustration.

Children who are physically punished are more likely to behave aggressively themselves (American Psychological Association, 1993; Putallaz et al., 1998; Shields & Cicchetti, 2001; Weiss et al., 1992). Physically aggressive parents serve as models for aggression and also increase their children's anger. Once aggressive patterns of interaction become established, the cycle can be truly vicious.

Reflect

Does violence in the media cause *aggression? Media violence is everywhere—not only in R-rated films, but also in G-rated films, even in children's video games. There are also clear connections between media violence and aggression, but not everyone who witnesses media violence behaves aggressively. So, how do we explain the connection between violence in the media and aggression?*

Media Influences

Real people are not the only models of aggressive behavior in children's lives. A classic study by Bandura, Ross, and Ross (1963) suggests the powerful influence of televised models on children's aggressive behavior. One group of preschool children observed a film of an adult model hitting and kicking an inflated Bobo doll, while a control group saw an aggression-free film. The experimental and control children were then left alone in a room with the same doll, as hidden observers recorded their behavior. The children who had observed the aggressive

Albert Bandura/Dept. of Psychology, Stanford University

Figure 10.2
A Classic Experiment in the Imitation of Aggressive Models

Research by Albert Bandura and his colleagues has shown that children frequently imitate the aggressive behavior they observe. In the top row, an adult model strikes a clown doll. The lower rows show a boy and a girl imitating the aggressive behavior.

model showed significantly more aggressive behavior toward the doll themselves (see Figure 10.2). Many children imitated bizarre attack behaviors devised for the model in this experiment—behaviors that they would not have thought up themselves.

The children exposed to the aggressive model also showed aggressive behavior patterns that had not been modeled. Observing the model, therefore, not only led to imitation of modeled behavior patterns, but also apparently **disinhibited** previously learned aggressive responses. The results were similar whether children observed human or cartoon models on film.

The Bandura study was a setup—an experimental setup, to be sure, but still a setup. It turns out that, for children, television is a major source of informal observational learning. It also turns out that television is a fertile source of aggressive models throughout much of the world (Villani, 2001). Children are routinely exposed to scenes of murder, beating, and sexual assault—just by turning on the TV set (Huesmann & Miller, 1994; Seppa, 1997). If a child watches 2 to 4 hours of TV a day, she or he will have seen 8,000 murders and another 100,000 acts of violence *before finishing elementary school* (Eron, 1993). Are kids less likely to be exposed to violence by going to the movies? No. One study found that virtually all G-rated animated films have scenes of violence, with a mean duration of 9 to 10 minutes per film (Yokota & Thompson, 2000).[4] Other media that contain violence include movies, rock music and music videos, advertising, video games, and the Internet (Villani, 2001).

Violence tends to be glamorized in the media. For example, in one cartoon show, superheroes battle villains who are trying to destroy or take over the world. Violence is often shown to have only temporary or minimal effects. (How often has Wile E. Coyote fallen from a cliff and been pounded into the ground by a boulder,

Click *Learning* in the Child and Adolescent CD-ROM for more on imitation of aggressive models.

disinhibit To stimulate a response that has been suppressed (inhibited) by showing a model engaging in that response without aversive consequences.

[4]Technically speaking, the word *mean* signifies "average" here. However, in this particular case, *mean* could be interpreted as a pun, since violence even in children's films tends to be quite mean.

only to bounce back and pursue the Road Runner once more?) In the great majority of violent TV shows, there is no remorse, criticism, or penalty for violent behavior (Seppa, 1997). Few TV programs show harmful long-term consequences of aggressive behavior. Seeing the perpetrator of the violence go unpunished increases the chances that the child will act aggressively (Krcmar & Cooke, 2001). Children may not even view death as much of a problem. How many times do video-game characters "die"—only to be reborn to fight again because the children have won multiple lives?

Reflect

Would you censor violence in the media? What would be the pluses and the minuses of doing so?

Why all this violence? Simple: Violence sells. But does violence do more than sell? That is, does media violence *cause* real violence? If so, what can parents and educators do to prevent the fictional from spilling over into the real world?

In any event, most organizations of health professionals agree that media violence does contribute to aggression (Holland, 2000; Villani, 2001). This relationship has been found for girls and boys of different ages, social classes, ethnic groups, and cultures. Consider a number of ways in which depictions of violence make such a contribution:

- *Observational learning.* Children learn from observation (Holland, 2000). TV violence supplies *models* of aggressive "skills," which children may acquire. In fact, children are more likely to imitate what their parents do than to heed what they say. If adults say that they disapprove of aggression but smash furniture or slap each other when frustrated, children are likely to develop the notion that aggression is the way to handle frustration. Classic experiments show that children tend to imitate the aggressive behavior they see on the media (Bandura et al., 1963) (see Figure 10.2). Media violence also provides viewers with aggressive *scripts*—that is, ideas about how to behave in situations like those they have observed (Huesmann & Miller, 1994).
- *Disinhibition.* Punishment inhibits behavior. Conversely, media violence may disinhibit aggressive behavior, especially when media characters "get away" with violence or are rewarded for it.
- *Increased arousal.* Media violence and aggressive video games increase viewers' level of arousal. That is, television "works them up." We are more likely to be aggressive under high levels of arousal.
- *Priming of aggressive thoughts and memories.* Media violence "primes" or arouses aggressive ideas and memories (Bushman, 1998).
- *Habituation.* We become "habituated to," or used to, repeated stimuli. Repeated exposure to TV violence may decrease viewers' sensitivity to real violence. If children come to perceive violence as the norm, they may become more tolerant of it and place less value on restraining aggressive urges (Holland, 2000).

A joint statement issued by the American Medical Association, the American Academy of Pediatrics, the American Psychological Association, and the American Academy of Child and Adolescent Psychiatry (Holland, 2000) made some additional points:

- Children who see a lot of violence are more likely to view violence as an effective way of settling conflicts. Children exposed to violence are more likely to assume that violence is acceptable.
- Viewing violence can decrease the likelihood that one will take action on behalf of a victim when violence occurs.
- Viewing violence may lead to real-life violence. Children exposed to violent programming at a young age are more likely to be violent themselves later on in life.

Violent video games are also connected with aggressive behavior. Craig Anderson and Karen Dill (2000) found that playing violent video games increases aggressive thoughts and behavior in the laboratory. It is also connected with a history of juvenile delinquency. However, males are relatively more likely than females to act aggressively after playing violent video games and are more likely to see the world as a hostile place. Students who obtain higher grades are also less likely to behave aggressively following exposure to violent media games. Thus cultural stereotyping of males and females, possible biological gender differences, and moderating variables like academic achievement also come into play when we are talking about the effects of media violence. There is no simple one-to-one connection between media violence and violence in real life.

There seems to be a circular relationship between exposure to media violence and aggressive behavior (Anderson & Dill, 2000; Eron, 1982; Funk et al., 2000). Yes, TV violence and violent video games contribute to aggressive behavior, but aggressive youngsters are also more likely to seek out this kind of "entertainment."

Aggressive children are frequently rejected by their nonaggressive peers—at least in middle-class culture (Eron, 1982; Warman & Cohen, 2000). Aggressive children may watch more television because their peer relationships are less fulfilling and because the high incidence of TV violence tends to confirm their view that aggressive behavior is normal (Eron, 1982). Media violence interacts with other contributors to violence. The family constellation also affects the likelihood that children will imitate the violence they see on TV. Studies find that parental substance abuse, paternal physical punishments, and single motherhood contribute to the likelihood of aggression in early childhood (Brook et al., 2001; Gupta et al., 2001). Parental rejection and use of physical punishment further increase the likelihood of aggression in children (Eron, 1982). These family factors suggest that the parents of aggressive children are absent or unlikely to help their young children understand that the kinds of socially inappropriate behaviors they see in the media are not for them. A harsh home life may also confirm the TV viewer's vision of the world as a violent place and further encourage reliance on television for companionship.

Figure 10.3 illustrates the fact that there is a connection between media violence and aggression. However, it also shows that the nature of the relationship—and causality—remain somewhat clouded.

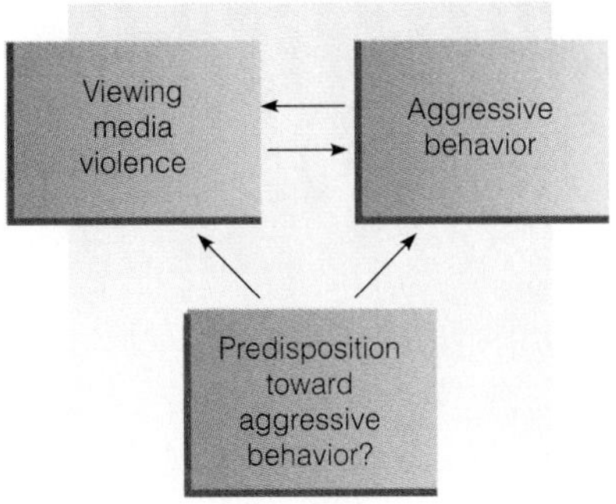

Figure 10.3
What Are the Connections Between Media Violence and Aggressive Behavior?

Does media violence lead to aggression? Does aggressive behavior lead to a preference for viewing violence? Or do other factors, such as viewing violence as an appropriate solution to social problems or parental use of physical punishment, contribute to both?

Developing in the New Millennium

Teaching Children Not *to Imitate Media Violence*

Children are going to be exposed to media violence—if not in Saturday morning cartoon shows, then in evening dramas and in the news. Or they'll hear about violence from friends, watch other children get into fights, or read about violence in the newspapers. If all those sources of violence were somehow hidden from view, they would learn about violence in *Hamlet, Macbeth,* and even the Bible. The notion of preventing children from being exposed to violent models may be impractical.

What, then, should be done? Parents and educators can do many things to tone down the impact of media violence (Broder, 2000; Huesmann et al., 1983). Children who watch violent shows act less aggressively when they are informed that

1. The violent behavior they observe in the media does not represent the behavior of most people.
2. The apparently aggressive behaviors they watch are not real. They reflect camera tricks, special effects, and stunts.
3. Most people resolve conflicts by nonviolent means.
4. The real-life consequences of violence are harmful to the victim and, often, the aggressor.

In observational learning, the emphasis is on the cognitive. If children consider violence to be inappropriate for them, they will probably not act aggressively even if they have acquired aggressive skills.

Search Online With InfoTrac College Edition

For additional information, explore InfoTrac College Edition, your online library. Go to **http://www.infotrac-college.com** and use the passcode from the InfoTrac card that came with your book. Try these search terms: media violence, violence in television, television and family, television and children, violence in mass media.

Review

(12) In ________ play, children play with toys by themselves. (13) In ________ play, children observe other children who are playing. (14) In ________ play, children play with toys similar to those of surrounding children. (15) In ________ play, children interact and share toys. (16) In ________ play, children interact to achieve common, group goals. (17) In ________ play, children include recognizable characters such as a doctor or a teacher. (18) In our society, transportation toys are ________-typed as male, whereas dolls are typed as female. (19) Preschoolers tend to prefer to play with children of the (other or same?) gender. (20) ________ is another term for prosocial behavior. (21) Aggressive behavior appears to be generally (stable or unstable?). (22) Preschoolers tend to (admire or reject?) aggressive peers. (23) Aggressive behavior is linked with the hormone ________. (24) Aggressive boys are more likely than nonaggressive boys to incorrectly interpret the behavior of other children as ________. (25) Social-________ theorists explain aggressive behavior in terms of reinforcement and observational learning. (26) The observation of aggression in the media tends to (inhibit or disinhibit?) aggressive behavior in children. (27) It is most scientifically accurate to say that aggression in the media (is connected with or causes?) aggressive behavior in children.

Pulling It Together: What are the roles of empathy and perspective-taking in altruistic behavior and in aggressive behavior?

Personality and Emotional Development

In the early childhood years, children's personalities start becoming more defined. Their sense of self—who they are and how they feel about themselves—continues to develop and becomes more complex. They begin to acquire a sense of their own abilities and their increasing mastery of the environment. As they move out into the world, they also face new experiences that may cause them to feel fearful and anxious. Let's explore some of these facets of personality and emotional development.

The Self

The sense of self, or the **self-concept,** emerges gradually during infancy. Infants and toddlers visually begin to recognize themselves and differentiate from other individuals such as their parents.

Question: How does the self develop during early childhood? In the preschool years, children continue to develop their sense of self. Almost as soon as they begin to speak, they describe themselves in terms of certain categories, such as age groupings (baby, child, adult) and gender (girl, boy). These self-definitions that refer to concrete external traits have been called the **categorical self** (Damon & Hart, 1992; Lewis & Brooks-Gunn, 1979).

Children as young as age 3 are able to describe themselves in terms of behaviors and internal states that appear to occur frequently and are fairly stable over time (Eder, 1989, 1990). For example, in response to the question "Tell me how you feel when you're scared," young children frequently respond, "Usually like running away" (Eder, 1989). Or, in answer to the question "Tell me how you've usually been with grown-ups?" a typical response might be, "I mostly been good with grown-ups." Thus, even preschoolers seem to understand they have stable characteristics that endure over time.

One aspect of the self-concept is **self-esteem,** the value or worth that people attach to themselves. Children who have a good opinion of themselves during the

self-concept One's impression of one-self; self-awareness.

categorical self Definitions of the self that refer to concrete external traits.

self-esteem The sense of value, or worth, that people attach to themselves.

preschool years show secure attachment and have mothers who are sensitive to their needs (Cassidy, 1988; Mueller & Tingley, 1990). These children also are more likely to engage in prosocial behavior (Cauley & Tyler, 1989).

By the age of 4, children begin to make evaluative judgments about two different aspects of themselves (Harter, 1990a; Harter & Pike, 1984). One is their cognitive and physical competence (for example, being good at puzzles, counting, swinging, tying shoes) and the second is their social acceptance by peers and parents (for example, having lots of friends, being read to by mom). But preschoolers do not yet make a clear distinction between different areas of competence. For example, a child of this age is not likely to report being good in school but poor in physical skills. One is either "good at doing things" or one is not (Harter & Pike, 1984).

During middle childhood, personality traits become increasingly important in children's self-definitions. Children then are also able to make judgments about their self-worth in many different areas of competence, behavioral conduct, appearance, and social relations.

Initiative Versus Guilt

As preschool children continue to develop a separate sense of themselves, they increasingly move out into the world and take the initiative in learning new skills. Erik Erikson refers to these early childhood years as the stage of initiative versus guilt.

Click *Personality* for more on initiative versus guilt.

Children in this stage strive to achieve independence from their parents and master adult behaviors. They are curious, try new things, and test themselves. These qualities are illustrated in the following account of a day in the life of a 5-year-old:

> In a single day, he decided to see how high he could build his blocks, invented a game that consisted of seeing who could jump the highest on his parents' bed, and led the family to a new movie containing a great deal of action and violence. (Crain, 2000)

During these years, children learn that not all of their plans, dreams, and fantasies can be realized. Adults prohibit children from doing certain things, and children begin to internalize these adult rules. Fear of violating the rules may cause the child to feel guilty and may curtail efforts to master new skills. Parents can help children develop and maintain a healthy sense of initiative by encouraging their attempts to learn and explore and by not being unduly critical and punitive.

Fears: The Horrors of Early Childhood

In Erik Erikson's view, fear of violating parental prohibitions can be a powerful force in the life of a young child. ***Question: What sorts of fears do children have in the early years?***

Both the frequency and the content of fears change as children move from infancy into the preschool years. The number of fears seems to peak between $2^{1}/_{2}$ and 4 years and then tapers off (Miller, Boyer, & Rodoletz, 1990).

The preschool period is marked by a decline in fears of loud noises, falling, sudden movement, and strangers. Preschool children are most likely to have fears that revolve around animals, imaginary creatures, the dark, and personal safety (Finch & McIntosh, 1990; Ollendick & King, 1991; Wenar, 1990). The fantasies of young children frequently involve stories they are told, as well as TV and film images. Frightening images of imaginary creatures can persevere. Many young children are reluctant to have the lights turned off at night because of fear that these creatures may harm them in the dark. In a sense, fears of imaginary creatures also involve personal safety.

Reflect

Are there any fears that you remember from early childhood? Have they faded over the years?

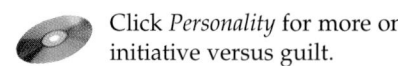

But there are also real objects and situations that cause many children to fear for their personal safety: lightning, thunder and other loud noises, the dark, high places, sharp objects and being cut, blood, people who are unfamiliar or who act strangely, stinging and crawling insects, other animals, and on and on. Some of these objects are also frightening because of their aversiveness, even when they are not direct threats. Children may not expect to be hurt by thunder or worms but may still view them as awful.

During middle childhood, children's fears become more realistic. They become less fearful of imaginary creatures, but fears of bodily harm and injury

A Closer Look

Helping Children Cope With Fears

A number of methods have been developed to help children cope with irrational, debilitating fears. Professionals who work with children today are most likely to use such behavior-modification methods as *counterconditioning, operant conditioning,* and *participant modeling*. Each of them is based on the principles of learning.

Counterconditioning

In the method of counterconditioning, children are exposed gradually to the sources of their fears while they are engaging in behavior that is incompatible with feelings of fear. Fear includes bodily responses such as rapid heart rate and respiration rate. By doing things that reduce the heart and respiration rates, children are doing something that is incompatible with fear.

In a classic study, Mary Cover Jones (1924) used counterconditioning to eliminate a fear of rabbits in a 2-year-old boy named Peter. Jones arranged for a rabbit to be gradually brought closer to Peter while the boy engaged in some of his favorite activities, such as munching merrily away on candy and cookies. Peter, to be sure, cast a wary eye in the rabbit's direction, but he continued to eat. Jones suspected that if she brought the rabbit too close too quickly, the cookies left on Peter's plate and those already eaten might have decorated the walls. But gradually the animal could be brought nearer without upsetting the boy. Eventually, Peter could eat and touch the rabbit at the same time. (No, we don't know how much weight and how many cavities Peter acquired while overcoming his fear of rabbits.)

A favorite counterconditioning technique with adults involves the progressive relaxation of muscle groups throughout the body. This technique has also been used with older children, but other techniques may be more effective with younger children, such as giving the child a treat (as Jones did), playing with a game or favorite toy, or asking the child to talk about a favorite book or TV hero (Vitulano & Tebes, 1991).

In counterconditioning, the parent or helping professional brings the child gradually into closer contact with the feared object or situation, while the child remains relaxed. An excellent way to bring a child into gradual contact with a large mature dog, for instance, is to give the child a puppy. Also, children will frequently do things in the company of their parents that they would be afraid to do alone. Therefore, it may be helpful to help a child adjust to a new situation, such as a day-care center, by initially attending with the child. Then the parent can depart progressively earlier.

Operant-Conditioning Techniques

In operant conditioning, children are guided into desirable behaviors, then reinforced for engaging in them. Reinforcement increases the frequency of desired behavior. Behavior modification in the classroom is an example of the use of operant techniques. In this method, good (desired) behavior is reinforced, and misbehavior is ignored.

Parents and other adults use operant techniques all the time. They may teach children how to draw letters of the alphabet by

Can Chocolate Chip Cookies Countercondition Fears?

Yes, they taste good, but do they have the capacity to countercondition fears? Perhaps they do. In the 1920s, Mary Cover Jones helped a boy overcome his fear of rabbits by having him munch away as the animal was brought closer.

remain fairly common. Children grow more fearful of failure and criticism in school and in social relationships (Finch & McIntosh, 1990; Ollendick & King, 1991; Wenar, 1990).

Girls report more fears and higher levels of anxiety than boys (Ollendick, King, & Frary, 1989; Ollendick, Yule, & Ollier, 1991). Whether these findings reflect actual differences in fears and anxieties or differences in the willingness of girls and boys to report "weaknesses" is a matter of debate (Finch & McIntosh, 1990).

Click *Learning* for more on operant-conditioning techniques.

guiding their hand and saying "Good!" when the desired result is obtained. When children fear touching a dog, parents frequently take their hands and guide them physically in petting the animal. Then they say something reinforcing, such as "Look at that big girl/boy petting that doggy!" or "Isn't the puppy nice and soft?" In one study that demonstrates the effectiveness of operant techniques, two young girls with nighttime fears were successfully treated by praising them for sleeping in their own beds at night (Ollendick, Hagopian, & Huntzinger, 1991).

Participant Modeling

In participant modeling, children first observe models (ideally, children similar in age) engage in the behavior that evokes fear. Then they imitate the behavior of the models. Models may be live or filmed.

Observing models is thought to have a number of positive effects. First, it shows children how to act in the situations that evoke fear. Second, it communicates the idea that the object or situation is not so dreadful. Third, observing others engage in feared activities without negative results may extinguish some of the observer's fear. Fourth, it may motivate children to try the observed behaviors.

In an often-cited experiment on participant modeling, Bandura and his colleagues (1969) found that participant modeling helped people who were afraid of snakes. Figure 10.4 shows children and adults in the Bandura study who imitated models who were unafraid of snakes.

Filmed models can exert a powerful effect on children, and one implication is that television could have significant potential in reducing such commonly occurring fears as going to the dentist, entering school, and so on (Crain, 2000). Some programs, such as *Sesame Street,* have included segments that portray children coping with the potentially stressful experiences of handling animals, making new friends, and going to a new school, among others.

Albert Bandura/Dept. of Psychology, Stanford University

Figure 10.4
Participant Modeling

Participant modeling helps children overcome fears through principles of observational learning. In these photos, children with a fear of snakes observe, then imitate, models who are unafraid. Parents often try to convince children that something tastes good by eating it in front of them and saying "Mmm!"

Review

(28) Self-definitions that refer to concrete external traits are called the ________ self. (29) Children as young as ________ can describe themselves in terms of behaviors and internal states. (30) Self-________ is the value or worth that people attach to themselves. (31) Children who are ________ attached tend to have high self-esteem. (32) By the age of ________, children begin to make evaluative judgments about themselves. (33) Erikson referred to early childhood as the stage of ________ versus guilt. (34) Early childhood fears tend to revolve around personal ________. (35) (Boys or Girls?) report more fears and higher levels of anxiety.

Pulling It Together: How are personality and emotional development intertwined with cognitive development?

Development of Gender Roles and Gender Differences

Two children were treated at Johns Hopkins University Hospital for the same problem. But the treatments and the outcomes were vastly different. Each child was genetically female, and each had the internal sex organs of a female. But because of excessive prenatal exposure to male sex hormones, each had developed external sex organs that resembled a male's (Money & Ehrhardt, 1972).

The problem was identified in one child (let's call her Nora) early. The masculinized sex organs were surgically removed when she was 2. Like many girls, Nora was tomboyish during childhood, but she was feminine in appearance and had a female **gender identity.**

The other child (let's call him Edward) was at first mistaken for a genetic male with stunted external sex organs. The error was discovered at the age of $3^1/_2$. But by then Edward had a firm male gender identity. Surgery further masculinized the appearance of his sex organs. During childhood he preferred typical masculine toys and activities and was accepted as one of the boys.

Nora and Edward both had **androgenital syndrome.** In this hormonal disorder, prenatal exposure to androgens masculinizes the sex organs of genetic females. In the case of Nora, the child was assigned to the female gender and reared as a girl. The other child, Edward, was labeled male and reared as a boy. Each child acquired the gender identity of the assigned gender.

The situation encountered by Nora and Edward is rare. Still, it raises questions about what it means to be a girl or boy in our society. In this section, we explore gender differences and gender-typing. But let us first ask: ***Questions: What are gender roles and stereotypes? How do they develop?***

gender identity Knowledge that one is female or male. Also the name of the first stage in Kohlberg's cognitive-developmental theory of the assumption of gender roles.

androgenital syndrome A disorder in which genetic females become masculinized as a result of prenatal exposure to male hormones.

stereotype A fixed, conventional idea about a group.

Development of Gender Roles and Stereotypes

I am strong
I am invincible
I am woman

These lyrics are from the song "I Am Woman, Hear Me Roar," by Helen Reddy and Ray Burton. They capture the attention because they run counter to the **stereotype** of the woman as being vulnerable and in need of the protection of a man. The stereotype of the "vulnerable woman," like all stereotypes, is a fixed, oversimplified, and often distorted idea about a group of people—in this case, women. The stereotype of the "chivalrous, protective man" is also a stereotype, although a more attractive one.

Cultural stereotypes of males and females involve broad expectations of behavior we call **gender roles.** In our culture, the feminine gender-role stereotype includes such traits as dependence, gentleness, helpfulness, kindness, warmth, emotionality, submissiveness, and home-orientation. The masculine gender-role stereotype includes aggressiveness, self-confidence, independence, competitiveness, and competence in business, math, and science (Rathus et al., 2002).

Reflect

Have gender roles and stereotypes placed any burdens on you or your children? Explain.

Gender-role stereotypes appear to develop through a series of stages. First, children learn to label the genders. Around 2 to $2\frac{1}{2}$ years of age, they become quite accurate in identifying pictures of girls and boys (Fagot & Leinbach, 1993). By age 3, they display knowledge of gender stereotypes for toys, clothing, work, and activities (Fagot, Leinbach, & O'Boyle, 1992; Huston & O'Brien, 1985; Perry, White, & Perry, 1984; Weinraub et al., 1984). For example, children of this age generally agree that boys play with cars and trucks, help their fathers, and tend to hit others. They also agree that girls play with dolls, help their mothers, and don't hit others.

Showing distress apparently becomes gender-typed so that preschoolers judge it to be acceptable for girls. One study found that preschool boys but not girls were rejected by their peers when they showed distress (Walter & LaFreniere, 2000). The same study found that peers rejected preschoolers of both genders when they displayed too much anger.

Children become increasingly traditional in their stereotyping of activities, occupational roles, and personality traits between the ages of 3 and about 9 or 10 (Levy, Sadowsky, & Troseth, 2000; Martin, 1993; Martin, Wood, & Little, 1990; Serbin, Powlishta, & Gulko, 1993). For example, traits such as "cruel" and "repairs broken things" are viewed as masculine, while "often is afraid" and "cooks and bakes" are seen as feminine. A study of 55 middle-class, primarily European American children aged 39–84 months found that they considered men to be more competent in traditionally masculine-typed occupations (such as occupations in science and transportation) and women to be more competent in traditionally feminine-typed occupations (such as nursing and teaching) (Levy et al., 2000). The children equated competence with income: They believed that men earned more money in the masculine-typed jobs, but that women earned more in the feminine-typed jobs.

Stereotyping levels off or declines slightly beyond the preschool years (Biernat, 1991; Ruble, 1988). Older children and adolescents apparently become somewhat more flexible in their perceptions of males and females. They retain the broad stereotypes but also perceive similarities between the genders and recognize that there are individual differences. They are more capable of recognizing the arbitrary aspects of gender categories, and they are more willing to try new behaviors that are typical of the other gender (Katz & Walsh, 1991).

Chauvinism rules. (Huh?) I mean to say that children and adolescents show some chauvinism by perceiving their own gender in a somewhat better light. For example, girls perceive other girls as nicer, harder workers, and less selfish than boys. Boys, on the other hand, think they are nicer, harder workers, and less selfish than girls (Etaugh, Levine, & Mennella, 1984).

Gender Differences

Clearly, females and males are anatomically different. And according to the gender-role stereotypes we have just examined, people believe that they also differ in their behaviors, personality characteristics, and abilities. But, just how different are females and males in terms of cognitive and social and emotional development?

Gender differences in infancy are small and rather inconsistent. In this chapter, we have reviewed gender differences during early childhood. Young girls

gender role A complex cluster of traits and behaviors that are considered stereotypical of females and males.

Reflect

As you are reading, think of the preschool girls and boys you know—or knew—and how well their behavior patterns match these stereotypes.

and boys display some differences in their choices of toys and play activities. Boys engage in more rough-and-tumble play and also are more aggressive. Girls tend to show more empathy and to report more fears. In Chapter 15, we shall see that girls show greater verbal ability than boys, whereas boys show greater visual-spatial ability than girls. Girls excel in certain areas of mathematics, while boys excel in others. ***Question: What are the origins of gender differences in behavior?*** Different theoretical accounts have been proposed. We turn to these now.

Views on the Development of Gender Differences

Like mother, like daughter; like father, like son—at least often, if not always. Why is it that little girls (often) grow up to behave according to the cultural stereotypes of what it means to be female? Why is it that little boys (often) grow up to behave like male stereotypes? Let's have a look at various explanations of the development of gender differences.

Organization of the Brain

Some researchers have looked for the origins of gender differences in the organization of the brain. The organization of the brain would be largely genetically determined, and it would at least in part involve prenatal exposure to sex hormones (Collins et al., 2000; Maccoby, 2000).

The hemispheres of the brain are specialized to perform certain functions. In most people, the left hemisphere is more involved in language skills, whereas the right hemisphere is specialized to carry out visual-spatial tasks.

Both males and females have a left hemisphere and a right hemisphere. They also share other structures in the brain, but the question is whether they use them in quite the same way. Consider the hippocampus, a brain structure that is involved in the formation of memories and the relay of incoming sensory information to other parts of the brain. Matthias Riepe and his colleagues (Grön et al., 2000) have studied the ways in which humans and rats use the hippocampus when they are navigating mazes. Males use the hippocampus in both hemispheres when they are navigating (Riepe, 2000). Women, however, rely on the hippocampus in the right hemisphere in concert with the right prefrontal cortex—an area of the brain that evaluates information and makes plans. Researchers have also found that females tend to rely on landmarks when they are finding their way ("Go a block past Ollie's Noodle Shop, turn left and go to the corner past Café Lalo"). Men rely more on geometry, as in finding one's position in terms of coordinates or on a map ("You're on the corner of Eleventh Avenue and 57th Street, and you want to get to Seventh Avenue and 55th Street,[5] so . . .) (Ritter, 2000). In looking at it from the man's perspective, you'll get less Dim Sum and much less cheesecake, but you'll see the situation from above—at least according to the stereotype. Riepe (2000) speculates that a female's prefrontal activity represents the conscious effort to keep landmarks in mind. The "purer" hippocampal activity in males might represent a more geometric approach.

Some psychological activities, such as the understanding and production of language, are regulated by structures in the left hemisphere—particularly Broca's area and Wernicke's area. But emotional and aesthetic responses, along with some other psychological activities, are more or less regulated in the right hemisphere. Brain-imaging research suggests that the left and right hemispheres of males may be more specialized than those of females (Shaywitz et al., 1995). For example, if you damage the left hemisphere of a man's brain, you may cause greater language difficulties than if you cause similar damage in a woman. The right hemisphere is thought to be relatively more involved in spatial-relations

[5]This is the location of the Carnegie Deli. Cholesterol shmolesterol. You live just once. Go. Enjoy.

© Mug Shots/Corbis Stock Market

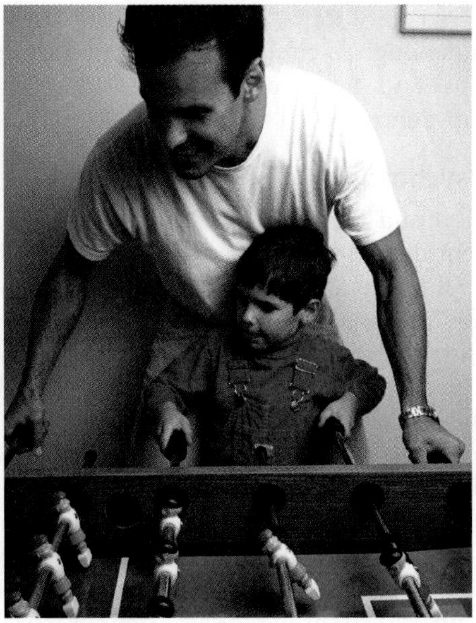

© Pictor International/Pictor Intl., Ltd./PictureQuest

Acquiring Gender Roles

What psychological factors contribute to the acquisition of gender roles? Psychoanalytic theory focuses on the concept of identification. Social-cognitive theory focuses on imitation of the behavior patterns of same-gender adults and reinforcement by parents and peers.

tasks, and damage in this hemisphere is more costly to a male's spatial relations skills than a female's.

If the brain hemispheres of women "get along better" than those of men—that is, if they better share the regulation of various cognitive activities—we may have an explanation of why women frequently outperform men in language tasks that involve some spatial organization, such as spelling, reading, and enunciation. Yet men, with more specialized spatial-relations skills, could be expected to generally outperform women at visualizing objects in space and reading maps.

Sex Hormones

There is no question that sex hormones and other chemical substances stoke the prenatal differentiation of sex organs (Davis, Grattan, & McCarthy, 2000). Toward the end of the embryonic stage, androgens—male sex hormones—are sculpting male genital organs.[6] These chemicals may also "masculinize" or "feminize" the brain; in other words, they may give rise to behavioral tendencies that are consistent with gender-role stereotypes (Collaer & Hines, 1995; Crews, 1994).

Studies with animals have found evidence for a role for sex hormones and other substances (Collaer & Hines, 1995; Crews, 1994). Let's return to navigation. (Got something better to do?) Research shows that male rats generally outperform females in maze-learning, a task that relies on spatial skills. However, if you expose female rats to male sex hormones during prenatal development (as would be the case if they are sharing the uterus with a number of male siblings) or shortly after birth, they will learn maze routes as quickly as males do. They will also exhibit other stereotypical masculine behaviors, including roaming great distances and marking large territories (Vandenbergh, 1993).

Might the greater frequency of aggressive behavior and rough-and-tumble play in boys also be linked to prenatal brain organization? Some researchers theorize that prenatal hormones masculinize or feminize the brain by creating predispositions that are consistent with gender-role stereotypes (Jacklin, 1989; Money, 1987). John Money suggests that predispositions may be created prenatally, but argues that social learning plays a stronger role in the development of gender identity,

[6]How poetic, notes the author's wife. "Men are so full of themselves," she adds.

personality traits, and preferences. He claims that social learning is even powerful enough to counteract many prenatal predispositions.

Let us now consider psychological views of the development of gender differences.

Psychoanalytic Theory

Sigmund Freud, the originator of psychoanalytic theory, believed that children acquire gender roles by means of the defense mechanism of **identification.** Boys could be said to identify with the aggressor—or, according to Freud's theory of the Oedipus complex, to identify with the fantasized aggressor, the father. In psychoanalytic theory, identification is the process of incorporating within ourselves our perceptions of the behaviors, thoughts, and feelings of other people. Given the era in which Freud attended medical school, he could not know of hormonal influences or of the intricacies of the functioning of various brain structures. He thus believed that the child's gender-related behaviors were psychologically based and remained changeable until the resolution of the Oedipus and Electra complexes at about the age of 5 or 6. These complexes are resolved by the child's abandoning incestuous wishes for the parent of the other gender and identifying with the parent of the same gender. Through identification with the same-gender parent, the child develops gender-typed behaviors. But, as we saw earlier in this chapter, children display stereotypical gender-typed behaviors earlier than Freud predicted.

Social-Cognitive Theory

Social-cognitive theorists attempt to straddle the gulf between behaviorism and cognitive perspectives on human development. As such, they pay attention both to the roles of rewards and punishments (reinforcement) in gender-typing and to the ways in which children learn from observing others and then decide what behaviors are appropriate for them. Children learn much about what society considers "masculine" or "feminine" by observing and imitating models of the same gender. These models may be their parents, as well as other adults, children, even TV characters (Jacklin, 1989; Lott & Maluso, 1991).

The importance of observational learning is shown in an experiment conducted by Kay Bussey and Albert Bandura (1984). In this study, children obtained information as to how society categorizes behavior patterns by observing how often they were performed either by men or by women. While children of ages 2 to 5 observed them, female and male adult role models exhibited different behavior patterns, such as choosing a blue or a green hat, marching or walking across a room, and repeating different words. Then the children were given a chance to imitate the models. Girls were twice as likely to imitate the woman's behavior as the man's, and boys were twice as likely to imitate the man's behaviors as the woman's.

Like psychoanalytic theorists, social-cognitive theorists employ the concept of identification. However, whereas psychoanalysts see identification as the more or less swallowing whole of another person's personality, social-cognitive theorists view identification as a broad, continuous learning process in which rewards and punishments influence children to imitate the behavior of adults of the same gender. The parent of the same gender naturally achieves particular prominence. Identification goes beyond imitation in the sense that children strive to become as broadly like the model as they can.

Socialization also plays a role in gender-typing. Parents, teachers, other adults—even other children—provide children with information about the gender-typed behaviors they are expected to display. The provision of information isn't exactly classroom-type stuff. Children are rewarded with smiles and respect and companionship when they display "gender-appropriate" behavior. Children are punished (with frowns and "yucks" and loss of companionship) when they display behavior that is considered inappropriate for their gender. Or perhaps "gender-inappropriate" behavior is extinguished by being ignored. Nor

identification Within social-cognitive theory, a process in which one person becomes like another through broad imitation and incorporation of the other person's personality traits.

is it just trial and error on the part of children. Parents and other people actively encourage them to engage in behavior that they see as being consistent with gender-role stereotypes. When kids do the "wrong" thing, they hear about it, or perhaps Mommy or Daddy looks shocked or chagrined.

Boys are encouraged to be independent, while girls are more likely to be restricted and given assistance. For example, boys are allowed to roam farther from home at an earlier age and are more likely to be left unsupervised after school (Block, 1983). Parents and other adults also have lower expectations for and attach less importance to the academic achievements and accomplishments of girls than of boys (Roggman, Kinnaird, & Carroll, 1991; Ruble, 1988).

Fathers are more likely than mothers to communicate norms for gender-typed behaviors to their children (Lytton & Romney, 1991; Power, 1985). Mothers share fathers' cultural expectations concerning gender-appropriate behavior patterns, but are usually less demanding that children show gender-typed behavior. Fathers tend to encourage their sons to develop instrumental behavior (that is, behavior that gets things done or accomplishes something) and their daughters to develop warm, nurturant, behavior (Block, 1979). Fathers are likely to cuddle their daughters gently. By contrast, they are likely to toss their sons into the air and use hearty language with them, such as "How're yuh doin', Tiger?" and "Hey you, get your keister over here" (Jacklin, DiPietro, & Maccoby, 1984; Power & Parke, 1982). Being a nontraditionalist, your author liked to toss his young daughters into the air, which raised objections from relatives who criticized him for being too rough. This, of course, led him to modify his behavior. He learned to toss his daughters into the air when the relatives were not around.[7]

Siblings also have a powerful impact on gender-typing. Consider a general population study of 527 girls and 582 boys with an older sister, 500 girls and 561 boys with an older brother, and 1,665 singleton girls and 1,707 singleton boys conducted by John Rust and his colleagues (2000). Data from the Pre-School Activities Inventory, which assesses gender-role behaviors, revealed that boys with older brothers and girls with older sisters were significantly more traditionally gender-typed in terms of preschool activities than single children. Moreover, single children were more likely to be traditionally gender-typed than children with an older sibling of the other gender. Having an older brother was connected with more masculine behaviors and fewer feminine behaviors among both boys and girls. Boys with older sisters engaged in more feminine-typed activities than other boys, but they also engaged in masculine-typed activities.

Not all families rear their children alike, of course; nor do they hold identical views regarding gender stereotypes. While many families adhere to traditional gender-role concepts, others are less traditional and make an effort to treat their daughters and sons equally and minimize gender-typing. One study found that in families in which parents actively discouraged gender-typing, preschoolers displayed less stereotyping in their activities and interests, even though they were just as aware of conventional gender roles as children in more traditional families (Weisner & Wilson-Mitchell, 1990). Another study found that elementary school children showed less stereotyping in their activity preferences if their mothers frequently engaged in traditionally "masculine" household and child-care tasks such as doing yard work, washing the car, taking children to ball games, or assembling toys (Serbin et al., 1993).

One change in family life today is that more children are spending part of their childhood in a single-parent home. Children from single-parent homes generally are less traditional in their gender-typing. This may come about for at least two reasons. First, the single parent typically engages in tasks normally carried out by both parents (for example, going to work, doing household repairs, caring for the

[7]Don't think that this admission has escaped my notice, notes the author's wife.

children, cooking, and cleaning) and so provides a less strongly gender-typed model. Second, the absent parent is usually the father, who is often the parent who is more concerned with the gender-typing of the children ("Boys should be boys," "Girls should be girls," yadayada).

Another change in family life today is the increasing participation of mothers in the labor force. More daughters today have mothers who serve as career-minded role models. More boys are exposed to fathers who take a larger role than men used to in child care and household responsibilities. Not surprisingly, many studies show that maternal employment is associated with less stereotyped gender-role concepts for girls and boys (Etaugh, 1993; L. W. Hoffman, 1989). The daughters of employed women also have higher educational and career aspirations than daughters of unemployed women, and they are more likely to choose careers that are nontraditional for women.

Social-cognitive theory has helped outline the ways in which rewards, punishments, and modeling foster gender-typed behavior. But *how* do rewards and punishment influence behavior? Do reinforcers mechanically increase the frequency of behavior, or, as suggested by cognitive theories, do they provide us with concepts that in turn guide our behavior? Let's consider two cognitive approaches to gender-typing that shed light on these matters: cognitive-developmental theory and gender-schema theory.

Cognitive-Developmental Theory

Lawrence Kohlberg (1966) proposed a cognitive-developmental view of gender-typing. According to this perspective, gender-typing is not the product of environmental influences that mechanically stamp in gender-appropriate behavior. Rather, children themselves play an active role. They form concepts about gender and then fit their behavior to their gender concepts. These developments occur in stages and are entwined with general cognitive development.

According to Kohlberg, gender-typing involves the emergence of three concepts: *gender identity, gender stability,* and *gender constancy.* The first step in gender-typing is attaining gender identity. Gender identity is the knowledge that one is male or female. Gender identity appears to originate in gender assignment, that is, the process in which other people label the child a girl or boy. Gender assignment is a response to the child's anatomic sex that usually occurs at birth. Gender assignment is so important to parents that they usually want to know "Is it a girl or a boy?" before they begin to count fingers and toes.

Most children acquire a firm gender identity by the age of 36 months (Money, 1977). At 2 years of age, most children can verbally state whether they are boys or girls. At age $2^1/_2$, they can classify pictures of themselves properly according to gender (Thompson, 1975). By the age of 3, many children also have acquired the capacity to discriminate anatomic gender differences (Bem, 1989).

At around the age of 4 or 5, most children develop the concept of **gender stability,** according to Kohlberg. They recognize that people retain their genders for a lifetime. Girls no longer believe they can grow up to be daddies, and boys no longer think they can become mommies.

By 5 to 7 years of age, Kohlberg believes that most children develop the more sophisticated concept of **gender constancy.** Children with gender constancy recognize that gender does not change, even if people modify their dress or behavior. So, gender remains constant even when appearances change. A woman who cuts her hair short remains a woman. A man who dons an apron and cooks dinner remains a man.

We could relabel gender constancy as "conservation of gender," highlighting the theoretical debt to Jean Piaget. Indeed, researchers have found that the development of gender constancy is related to the general development of conservation (Serbin & Sprafkin, 1986). For this reason, it seems that conservation concepts may lay the cognitive groundwork for gender constancy. More intelligent children also develop gender constancy earlier, further suggestive of its cognitive nature.

gender stability The concept that one's gender is a permanent feature.

gender constancy The concept that one's gender remains the same despite superficial changes in appearance or behavior.

According to cognitive-developmental theory, once children have established concepts of gender stability and constancy, they will be motivated to behave in ways that are consistent with their genders (Bauer, 1993). For example, once girls understand that they will remain female, they will show a preference for "feminine" activities. As shown by the Bussey and Bandura (1984) study described earlier, children do appear to actively seek information about which behavior patterns are "masculine" and which are "feminine." They are then significantly more likely to imitate the "gender-appropriate" patterns.

Interestingly, Ullian (1981) found that 6-year-old children who have developed gender stability but not gender constancy tend to adhere rather rigidly to gender-typed behavior patterns. It is as if they think that behaving in inappropriate ways could actually change their genders. By the age of 8, children are more willing to engage in behaviors associated with the other gender. Perhaps the achievement of gender constancy makes children secure in the knowledge that they will remain as they are (Maccoby, 1990b).

In a similar vein, Smetana and Letourneau (1984) found that girls with gender stability more often chose girl playmates than did girls who had developed gender identity only. The researchers theorize that female companionship helps confirm their female self-concepts prior to the certainty of gender constancy. Once they have attained gender constancy, girls know that playing with boys will not alter their gender. For this reason, they become less rigid in use of gender as a factor in choice of playmates.

Cross-cultural studies in the United States, Samoa, Nepal, Belize, and Kenya (Munroe, Shimmin, & Munroe, 1984) have found that the concepts of gender identity, gender stability, and gender constancy emerge in the order predicted by Kohlberg (Leonard & Archer, 1989; Munroe et al., 1984). Children may achieve gender constancy earlier than Kohlberg stated, however. Many 3- and 4-year-olds show at least some understanding of gender constancy (Bem, 1989; Leonard & Archer, 1989).

Kohlberg's theory also has difficulty accounting for the age at which gender-typed play emerges. Many children prefer gender-typed toys such as cars and dolls by the age of 2 (Caldera et al., 1989). At this age, children are likely to have a sense of gender identity, but gender stability and gender constancy remain at least a year or two away (Ruble, 1988). Therefore, gender identity alone seems to provide a child with sufficient motivation to assume gender-typed behavior patterns (Martin & Little, 1990). Kohlberg's theory also does not explain why the concept of gender plays such a prominent role in children's classification of people and behavior (Bem, 1983; Jacklin & McBride-Chang, 1991). Another cognitive view, gender-schema theory, attempts to address these concerns.

Gender-Schema Theory: An Information-Processing View

Gender-schema theory proposes that children use gender as one way of organizing their perceptions of the world (Bem, 1985; Bigler & Liben, 1992; Signorella et al., 1993). A gender schema is a cluster of mental representations about male and female physical qualities, behaviors, and personality traits. According to gender-schema theory, gender gains prominence as a schema for organizing experience because of society's emphasis on it. As a result, even young children begin to mentally group people of the same gender according to the traits that represent that gender.

As in social-cognitive theory, children learn "appropriate" behavior by observation. Children's cognitive processing of information also contributes to their gender-typing, however.

Consider the dimension of *strength–weakness*. Children learn that strength is linked to the male gender-role stereotype and weakness to the female stereotype. They also learn that some dimensions, such as strength–weakness, are more relevant to one gender than the other—in this case, to males. Bill will learn that the strength he displays in weight training or wrestling affects the way others perceive him. But most girls do not find this trait to be important to others, unless

gender-schema theory The view that one's knowledge of the gender schema in one's society (the behavior patterns that are considered appropriate for men and women) guides one's assumption of gender-typed preferences and behavior patterns.

they are competing in gymnastics, tennis, swimming, or other sports. Even so, boys are expected to compete in these sports and girls are not. Jane is likely to find that her gentleness and neatness are more important in the eyes of others than her strength.

Children thus learn to judge themselves according to the traits that are considered relevant to their genders. When they do so, their self-concepts become blended with the gender schema of society. The gender schema provides standards for comparison. Children whose self-concepts are consistent with their society's gender schema are likely to have higher self-esteem than children whose self-concepts are not (Cramer & Skidd, 1992).

From the viewpoint of gender-schema theory, gender identity is sufficient to inspire "gender appropriate" behavior. Thus, gender-typed behavior is believed to emerge earlier than would be proposed by cognitive-developmental theory. As soon as children understand the labels "girl" and "boy," they actively seek information concerning gender-typed traits and strive to live up to them. Bill may fight back when provoked because boys are expected to do so. Jane may be gentle and kind because that is expected of girls. Bill's and Jane's self-esteem will depend in part on how they measure up to the gender schema.

Studies indicate that children do possess information according to a gender schema. For example, boys show better memory for "masculine" toys, activities, and occupations, while girls show better memory for "feminine" toys, activities, and occupations (Bauer, 1993; Bigler & Liben, 1990; Liben & Signorella, 1993).

In sum, brain organization and sex hormones may contribute to gender-typed behavior. There is also evidence that the effects of social learning may be strong enough to counteract many prenatal biological influences. But social-cognitive theory may pay insufficient attention to children's active roles as seekers of gender-related information. Cognitive-developmental and gender-schema theories integrate the strengths of social-cognitive theory with the ways in which children process information so as to blend their self-concepts with the gender schema of their culture.

Psychological Androgyny

Let's be honest about it. I've made several subtle suggestions about being male and about being female in this chapter. I have acknowledged that there's probably something biological involved in it—including brain organization and baths in bodily fluids that are brimming with sex hormones. But I have probably also suggested that we may put too much stock in what is "masculine" and in what is "feminine" and that we may often do boys and girls more harm than good when we urge them to adhere to strict cultural stereotypes.

Cultural stereotypes tend to polarize females and males; they tend to push females and males to the imagined far ends of a continuum of gender-role traits (Rathus et al., 2002). It is common to label people as being either masculine or feminine. It is also common to assume that the more feminine people are, the less masculine they are, and vice versa. That is, the female U.S. Marines helicopter pilot usually isn't conceptualized as wearing lipstick and letting her hair down on a, yes, date. The tough male business executive isn't usually conceptualized as changing diapers and playing peekaboo. An "emotional" boy who also shows the "feminine" traits of nurturance and tenderness is probably thought of as less masculine than other boys. Outspoken, competitive girls are likely to be seen not only as masculine, but also as unfeminine.

But many psychologists today think of masculinity and femininity as independent personality dimensions. That is, people (male or female) who obtain high scores on measures of masculine traits can also score high on feminine traits (Ward, 2000). ***Question: So what is psychological androgyny?*** People with both stereotypical feminine and masculine traits are termed **psychologically androgynous** (from Greek roots meaning male [*andro*] and woman

psychological androgyny Possession of both stereotypical feminine and masculine traits.

[*gyne*][8]). People high in masculine traits *only* are typed as masculine. People high in feminine traits *only* are typed as feminine. People who show neither strong feminine nor masculine traits are termed "undifferentiated."

Some psychologists suggest that it is worthwhile to promote psychological androgyny in children, because they will then possess both the feminine and masculine traits that are valued in our culture (Hyde et al., 1991). There is a good deal of evidence that androgynous children and adolescents are relatively well adjusted, apparently because they can summon a wider range of traits to meet the challenges in their lives. For example, compared with their masculine, feminine, or undifferentiated peers, androgynous children and adolescents have better social relations and superior adjustment, higher self-esteem, greater creativity (Norlander, Erixon, & Archer, 2000), and more willingness to pursue occupations stereotyped as "belonging" to the other gender (Hebert, 2000).

But some studies have reported little or no differences between androgynous and masculine individuals. Several studies have found that androgynous and masculine individuals are equally high in self-esteem (Williams & D'Alessandro, 1994). It may be the masculine component of androgyny that is most strongly related to the psychosocial well-being of children, adolescents, and adults (Ward, 2000). It is apparently more acceptable for females in our society to adopt masculine traits than for males to adopt feminine traits.

As reviewed by Rathus (remember him?) and his colleagues (2002), some feminist scholars criticize the concept of psychological androgyny, because it is defined in terms of "masculine" and "feminine" personality traits, which tends to lend them reality. Feminists would prefer to see the stereotypes recognized as culturally induced and then dissolved or deemphasized.

The changes in physical, cognitive, social, and emotional development reviewed in the last three chapters lay the groundwork for the next major period in development: the middle childhood years. We will explore those years in the next three chapters, beginning with physical development in Chapter 11.

Reflect

Do you see yourself as being traditionally feminine, traditionally masculine, psychologically androgynous, or "undifferentiated"? How do you feel about your self-concept?

Given prejudices in our culture, do you believe that it is socially "safer" for a girl or a boy to be psychologically androgynous? Explain.

Review

(36) Gender __________ is the sense of being female or being male. (37) Cultural stereotypes of males and females involve broad expectations for behavior that are called gender __________. (38) By the age of __________, children show knowledge of gender stereotypes for toys, clothing, and work. (39) The organization of the brain involves prenatal exposure to __________ hormones. (40) Brain-imaging suggests that the hemispheres of the brain are more specialized in (males or females?). (41) __________ explained the acquisition of gender roles in terms of resolution of the Oedipus and Electra complexes. (42) __________-cognitive theorists explain the development of gender-typed behavior in terms of observational learning, identification, and socialization. (43) (Mothers or Fathers?) are more likely to communicate norms for gender-typed behaviors to children. (44) Kohlberg's cognitive-__________ theory holds that children form concepts about gender and fit their behavior to these concepts. Three key concepts that emerge are gender identity, gender stability, and gender __________. (45) Gender-__________ theory proposes that preschoolers begin to mentally group people of the same gender according to the traits that represent that gender. (46) Children then blend their __________-concepts with the gender schema of their culture.

Pulling It Together: How is the development of gender differences connected with cognitive development?

[8]Let's try a little vocabulary development. How are these Greek roots used in the words *androgen* and *genecology*?

Recite Recite Recite Recite

1. What are the dimensions of child rearing?

Parental approaches to child rearing may be classified according to the independent dimensions of warmth–coldness and restrictiveness–permissiveness. Warm parents are affectionate toward their children. Cold parents are likely to complain about their children. Restrictive parents impose rules and watch their children closely. Consistent control and firm enforcement of rules can have positive consequences for the child. Permissive parents impose few rules and supervise their children less closely.

2. What techniques do parents use to restrict their children's behavior?

Parents tend to use inductive methods, power assertion, and withdrawal of love to enforce rules. Inductive methods use "reasoning," or explaining why one sort of behavior is good and another is not. Power-assertive methods include physical punishment and deprivation of privileges. Withdrawal of love means isolating or ignoring children when they misbehave.

3. What parenting styles are involved in the transmission of values and standards?

The main methods are authoritative, authoritarian, and permissive. Authoritative parents are restrictive but warm and tend to have the most competent and achievement-oriented children. Authoritarian parents are restrictive and cold. They see obedience as a virtue for its own sake. The sons of authoritarian parents tend to be hostile and defiant; daughters are low in independence. Children of authoritarian parents tend to be less socially and academically competent and are also conflicted, anxious, and irritable. Permissive-indulgent parents are warm, whereas rejecting-neglecting parents are cold. Children of neglectful parents show the least competence and maturity.

4. How do the situation and the child influence parenting styles?

Parents tend to prefer power-assertive techniques when they believe that children understand the rules they have violated and are capable of acting appropriately. Stress contributes to the use of power-assertion.

5. What kinds of influences do siblings have on social and personal development in early childhood?

Siblings provide caregiving, emotional support, advice, role models, social interaction, restrictions, and cognitive stimulation. However, they are also sources of conflict, control, and competition. Younger siblings usually imitate older siblings. Children show both negative reactions (because they get less attention from parents) and positive reactions (joy, interest) to the birth of a sibling.

6. What does the research say about the effects of being a first-born or an only child?

First-born and only children are generally more highly motivated to achieve, more cooperative, more helpful, more adult-oriented, and less aggressive. First-born and only children also generally show greater anxiety and are less self-reliant. According to the confluence model, birth order, family size, and child spacing flow together to affect the intellectual development of children. First-born children are more likely than later-born children to have imaginary playmates. Later-born children tend to be more aggressive, have lower self-esteem, and greater social skills with peers. Parents tend to be more relaxed and flexible with later-born children. New children "dilute" existing family resources, so not as much can be devoted to them.

7. What is the influence of peers on social and personal development in early childhood?

Children learn social skills from peers—such as sharing, helping, taking turns, and coping with conflict. Peers foster development of physical and cognitive skills and provide emotional support. By about 2 years of age, children imitate each other's play and engage in social games like follow the leader. Preschoolers' friendships are characterized by shared activities and feelings of attachment.

8. What do developmentalists know about child's play?

Play is meaningful, pleasurable, and internally motivated. Play also develops motor, social, and cognitive skills. It may also help children learn to deal with conflict and

Recite Recite Recite Recite

anxiety. Parten followed the development of five types of play among 2–5-year-olds: solitary play, onlooker play (both are "nonsocial"), parallel play, associative play, and cooperative play (the latter three are "social"). From 2 to 5, pretend play becomes more social and involves characters such as a doctor or teacher—a form of play known as dramatic play.

9. Are there boys' toys and girls' toys?

It seems so. Both girls and boys show preferences for gender-stereotyped toys by 15 to 30 months of age. Boys' toys commonly include transportation toys (cars and trucks) and weapons; girls' toys more often include dolls. Boys in early childhood prefer vigorous outdoor activities and rough-and-tumble play. Girls are more likely to engage in arts and crafts. Preferences for toys may involve the interaction of biological factors and socialization.

10. Why do children choose to associate with peers of their own gender?

Preschool children generally prefer playmates of their own gender, partly because of shared interest in types of activities. Maccoby notes that boys' play is more oriented toward dominance, aggression, and rough play and that boys are not very responsive to girls' suggestions.

11. How does prosocial behavior develop?

Prosocial behavior—altruism—begins to develop in the 1st year, when children begin to share. In the 2nd year, children begin to comfort distressed companions and help others. Among preschoolers, helping is more common than sharing. Development of prosocial behavior is linked to the development of empathy and perspective-taking. Empathy promotes prosocial behavior and decreases aggressive behavior. Girls show more empathy than boys. Prosocial behavior is influenced by rewards and punishments.

12. How does aggression develop?

The aggression of preschoolers is frequently instrumental or possession-oriented. By 6 or 7, aggression becomes hostile and person-oriented. Aggressive behavior appears to be generally stable and predictive of various social and emotional problems in adulthood. Boys are more likely than girls to be aggressive.

13. What causes aggression in children?

Genetic factors may be involved in aggressive behavior. Genes may be expressed at least in part through the male sex hormone testosterone. Aggressiveness is also related to temperament, which is connected with genetics. Impulsive, uninhibited, and relatively fearless children are more likely to be aggressive. Some aggressive preschoolers may have experienced traumatic brain injuries. Aggression is connected with cognitive development in that 6- or 7-year-olds are more capable of understanding other people's motives and thus less likely to accept bullying. Moreover, aggressive boys are more likely than nonaggressive boys to incorrectly assume that other children mean them ill. Social-cognitive theory suggests that children become aggressive as a result of frustration, reinforcement, and observational learning. Aggressive children may associate with peers who value their aggression, but aggressive children are often rejected by less aggressive peers. Children who are physically punished are more likely to behave aggressively themselves, perhaps because parents serve as models for children's behavior. Film-mediated models or televised models—even violent video games—contribute to aggressive behavior in preschoolers, as shown in classic research with Bobo dolls by Bandura, Ross, and Ross. Observing aggressive behavior teaches aggressive skills and disinhibits the child. It increases children's arousal, primes aggressive thoughts and memories, and habituates children to violence. TV violence and violent video games contribute to aggressive behavior, but aggressive youngsters are also more likely to seek out violent "entertainment."

Recite Recite Recite Recite

14. How does the self develop during early childhood?

Preschoolers' self-definitions that refer to concrete external traits have been called the categorical self. Children as young as 3 can describe themselves in terms of characteristic behaviors and internal states. Secure attachment contributes to the development of self-esteem. By the age of 4, children begin to evaluate their abilities, and these are connected with self-esteem. According to Erikson, children in early childhood—the stage of initiative versus guilt—try to achieve independence from parents and master adult behaviors.

15. What sorts of fears do children have in the early years?

Children's fears seem to peak between $2^1/_2$ and 4 and then taper off. Preschoolers are most likely to have fears of animals, imaginary creatures, and the dark; the theme involves threats to personal safety. Other fears include fear of lightning, loud noises, high places, sharp objects, blood, strange people, and insects. Girls report more fears and anxiety than boys.

16. What are gender roles and stereotypes? How do they develop?

A stereotype is a fixed, conventional idea about a group. Females are stereotyped as dependent, gentle, helpful, kind, warm, emotional, submissive, and home-oriented. Males are stereotyped as aggressive, self-confident, independent, and competent in business, math, and science. Our broad expectations of females and males are called gender roles. At 2 to $2^1/_2$, children can identify pictures of girls and boys. By 3, they show knowledge of gender stereotypes. Stereotyping levels off or declines beyond the preschool years.

17. What are the origins of gender differences in behavior?

Brain-imaging research suggests that testosterone may specialize the hemispheres of the brain—more so in males than in females, explaining why females excel in verbal skills that require some spatial organization, such as reading, spelling, and articulation. But males might be better at more specialized spatial-relations tasks. Male sex hormones are connected with greater maze-learning ability in rats and also with aggressiveness. Freud's psychoanalytic theory explains gender-typing in terms of identification as a result of resolution of the Oedipus and Electra complexes at about the age of 5 or 6. But gender-stereotyped behaviors develop earlier than Freud predicted. Social-cognitive theorists explain the development of gender-typed behavior in terms of observational learning, identification, and socialization. According to Kohlberg's cognitive-developmental theory, gender-typing involves the emergence of three concepts: gender identity, gender stability, and gender constancy. Once children have established concepts of gender stability and constancy, they will be motivated to behave in ways that are consistent with their genders. However, gender-typed play emerges much earlier than predicted by Kohlberg. According to gender-schema theory, preschoolers begin to mentally group people of the same gender according to the traits that represent that gender. They then attempt to conform their own behavior to the gender schema of society.

18. What is psychological androgyny?

People with both stereotypical feminine and masculine traits are said to be psychologically androgynous. Theorists differ as to whether it is beneficial to promote psychological androgyny.

On the Web

Search Online With InfoTrac College Edition

For additional information, explore InfoTrac College Edition, your online library. Go to **http://www.infotrac-college.com** and use the passcode from the InfoTrac card that came with your book. Try these search terms: sibling relationships, parenting, birth order, discipline of children, child abuse, emotions in children, emotional problems of children, children play.

Visit Our Web Site

Go to **http://www.wadsworth.com/psychology** where you will find online resources directly linked to your book.

Child Development CD-ROM

Go to the Wadsworth Child Development CD-ROM for further study of the concepts in this chapter. The CD-ROM also includes quizzes and additional activities to expand your learning experience.

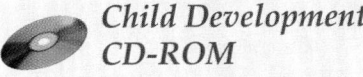

11 Middle Childhood: Physical Development

PowerPreview™

Growth Patterns

- THE AVERAGE MALE is larger than the average female. When do boys begin to surpass girls in height and weight?
- DO CHILDREN TEND TO outgrow "baby fat," or does childhood obesity set a dangerous precedent for adolescent and adult life?
- DO GENETIC FACTORS play a role in obesity, or is it true that "You are what you eat?"
- THE TYPICAL AMERICAN CHILD is exposed to about 10,000 commercials for food each year. (How many? 10,000. Really? Yes.) Do they have a problem with that?

Motor Development

- SO WHO'S ON THE BASEBALL and basketball teams? During the middle childhood years, boys begin to outperform girls in motor activities.
- OKAY—THE FITNESS CRAZE is upon us. People are jogging and swimming, and even Pilates and Tae-Bo classes are in vogue. So are American children fit?

Children With Disabilities

- IS HYPERACTIVITY CAUSED by chemical food additives?
- SINCE STIMULANTS STIMULATE ACTIVITY (that's why they're called stimulants), why are they used to treat hyperactive children?
- SOME CHILDREN WHO ARE INTELLIGENT and provided with stimulating home environments cannot learn how to read or do simple math problems.
- DO DISABLED STUDENTS fare better in classes for students with special needs or in classes that include children with and without disabilities ("mainstreaming")?

Jessica is a 6-year-old attending her first day of school. During recess, she runs to the climbing apparatus in the schoolyard and climbs to the top. As she reaches the top, she announces to the other children, "I'm coming down." She then walks to the parallel bars, goes halfway across, lets go, and tries again.

Steve and Mike are 8-year-olds. They are riding their bikes up and down the street. Steve tries riding with no hands on the handlebars. Mike starts riding fast, standing up on the pedals. Steve shouts, "Boy, you're going to break your neck!" (adapted from Rowen, 1973).

Middle childhood is a time for learning many new motor skills. Success in both gross and fine motor skills reflects children's increasing physical maturity, their opportunities to learn, and personality factors such as their persistence and self-confidence. Competence in motor skills enhances children's self-esteem and their acceptance by their peers.

In this chapter, we will examine physical and motor development during middle childhood. We will also discuss children with certain disabilities.

Growth Patterns

Question: What patterns of growth occur in middle childhood? Gains in height and weight are fairly steady throughout middle childhood. But notable variations in growth patterns also occur from child to child.

Height and Weight

Click *Physical Development* in the Child and Adolescent CD-ROM for more on growth patterns.

Following the growth trends begun in early childhood, boys and girls continue to gain a little over 2 inches in height per year during the middle childhood years. This pattern of gradual gains does not vary significantly until children reach the adolescent **growth spurt** (see Figure 11.1). The average gain in weight between the ages of 6 and 12 is about 5 to 7 pounds a year. During these years, children continue to become less stocky and more slender (Kuczmarski et al., 2000).

Most deviations from these average height and weight figures are quite normal. Individual differences are more marked in middle childhood than they were earlier. For example, most 3-year-olds are within 8 to 10 pounds and 4 inches of each other. But by the age of 10, children's weights may vary by as much as 30 to 35 pounds, and their heights may vary by as much as 6 inches.

Gender and Physical Growth

Figure 11.1 also reveals that boys continue to be slightly heavier and taller than girls through age 9 or 10. Girls then begin their adolescent growth spurt and surpass boys in height and weight until about age 13 or 14. At that time, boys are approaching the peak of their adolescent growth spurt, and they become taller and heavier than girls (Malina, 1991b).

The steady gain in height and weight during middle childhood is paralleled by an increase in muscular strength for both girls and boys (Malina, 1991b). The relative proportion of muscle and fatty tissue is about the same for boys and girls in early middle childhood. But this begins to change at around age 11, as males develop relatively more muscle tissue and females develop more fatty tissue (Michael, 1990).

Reflect

What bodily changes did you experience in middle childhood? How did they contribute to—or detract from—your self-esteem?

Nutrition and Growth

In middle childhood, average body weight doubles. Children also expend a good deal of energy as they engage in physical activity and play. To fuel this growth and activity, children need to eat more than they did in the preschool years. The average 4–6-year-old needs about 1,800 calories per day. But the average 7–10-year-old requires 2,000 calories a day (Ekvall, 1993).

growth spurt A period during which growth advances at a dramatically rapid rate as compared with other periods.

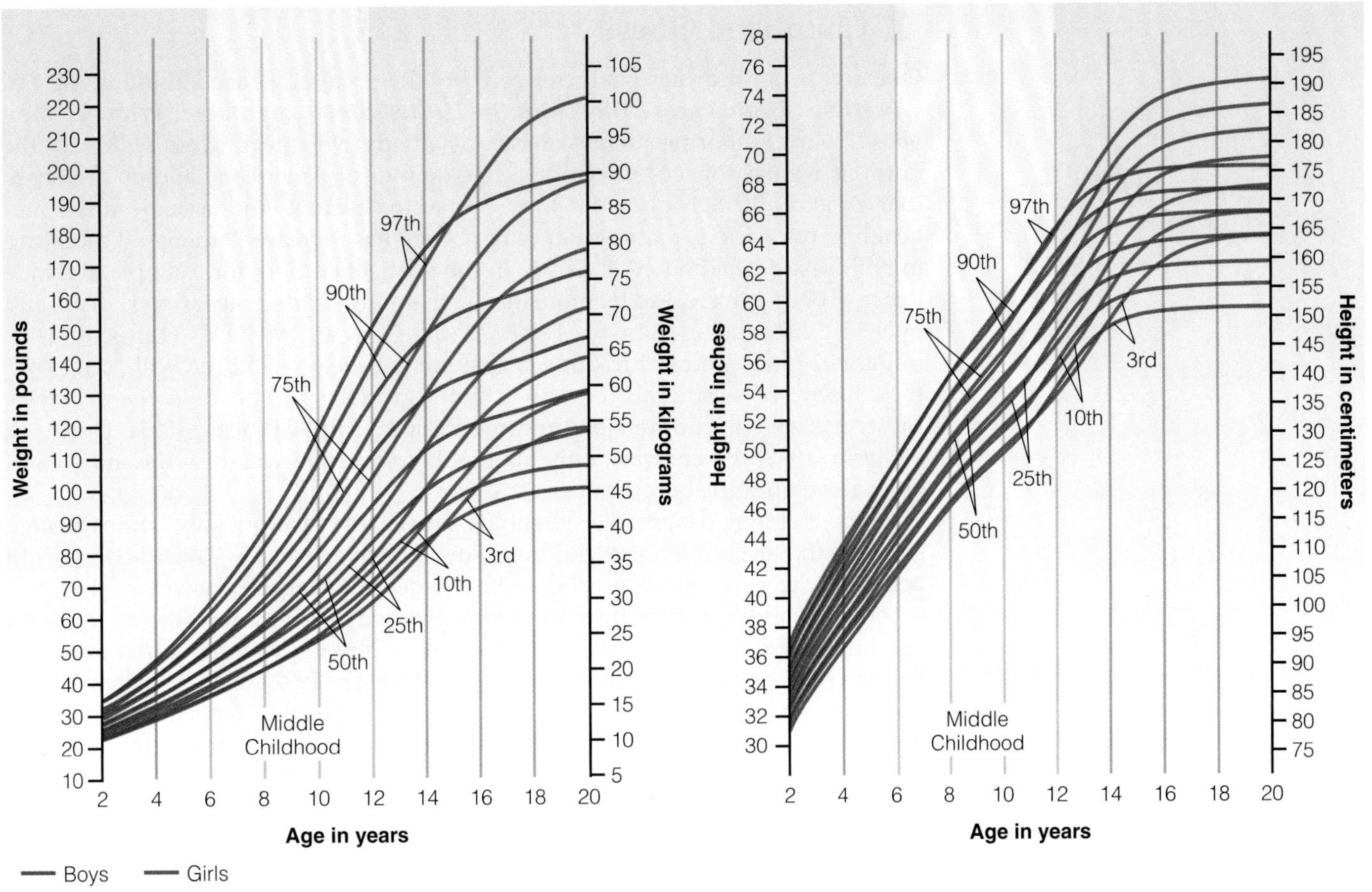

Figure 11.1
Growth Curves for Height and Weight

Gains in height and weight are fairly steady during middle childhood. Boys continue to be slightly heavier and taller than girls through 9 or 10 years of age. Girls then begin their adolescent growth spurt and surpass boys in height and weight until about age 13 or 14.

Source: Kuczmarski, R. J., et al. (2000, December 4). CDC Growth charts: United States. Advance data from vital and health statistics, *no. 314. Hyattsville, MD: National Center for Health Statistics.*

Developing in a World of Diversity

Physical Growth

A number of factors, including nutrition and disease, affect the growth of children. Studies of children in different parts of the world have found that children in urban areas are taller than those living in rural areas and that middle-class children are taller than lower-income children (Meredith, 1978, 1982, 1984; Tanner, 1989). Malnutrition and disease appear to play a large role in these differences in physical growth. By the age of 4, poor Asian and African children are as much as 7 inches shorter and 13 pounds lighter than children of the same age in Europe and the United States. The importance of malnutrition and disease is demonstrated by studies that find only small growth differences among economically advantaged children of different ethnic groups (Hendrick, 1990).

But ethnic origin plays a role as well. For example, Asian children tend to be somewhat shorter than European and African children growing up in comparable environments. In the United States, African American children tend to grow slightly more rapidly than European American children (Eveleth & Tanner, 1990).

Childhood Obesity

Obesity is a disorder characterized by the excessive accumulation of fat. ***Questions: How many children in the United States are obese? Why are they obese?*** Most authorities define obesity as a body weight in excess of 20% of the norm. If we use this criterion, about one quarter of American children are obese (Bar-Or et al., 1998; Meyer, 1997). In spite of the current emphasis on fitness and health in our society, the prevalence of obesity has increased among all races and in both sexes (Mokdad et al., 2000). In the past generation, for example, the incidence of obesity increased by more than half among children ages 6 to 11 years and by nearly 40% among those ages 12 to 17 (Bar-Or et al., 1998; D.V. Harris, 1991).

Parents (and children) frequently assume that heavy children will "outgrow" their "baby fat"—especially once they hit the growth spurt of adolescence. Not so. Most overweight children become overweight adults (Lucas, 1991; Tiwary & Holguin, 1992). By contrast, only about 40% of normal-weight boys and 20% of normal-weight girls become obese adults.

Obese children, despite the stereotype, are usually far from jolly. Some research suggests that even preschool children show negative attitudes toward overweight people (Fritz & Wetherbee, 1982). Other research suggests, however, that preschoolers tend to idealize their own mothers' body weight and shape (Frankova & Chudobova, 2000). Nevertheless, during childhood, heavy children are often rejected by their peers (Bell & Morgan, 2000; Jackson, 1992). They usually perform poorly in sports, which can provide a source of prestige for slimmer children (Smoll & Schultz, 1990). As obese children approach adolescence, they become even less popular, because they are less likely to be found attractive by peers of the other sex. It is no surprise, then, that obese children tend to like their bodies less than children of normal weight (Vander Wal & Thelen, 2000). Moreover, overweight adolescents are more likely to be depressed and anxious than peers who are normal in weight (Brack, Brack, & Orr, 1991; Rosen, Tacy, & Howell, 1990).

Being overweight in adolescence can lead to chronic illness and earlier death in adulthood, even for those teens who later lose weight (Pinhas-Hamiel & Zeitler, 2000). One study reported that overweight boys were more likely than boys of normal weight to die of heart disease, strokes, and cancer before the age of 70 (Must et al., 1992). Women who were overweight as teens had more difficulty with tasks such as climbing stairs, lifting, and walking by the time they became 70.

Reflect

How were obese children treated by their peers in your elementary school? Were you sensitive to these children's feelings, or were you part of the problem?

Causes of Obesity

Obesity runs in families (Baker, Whisman, & Brownell, 2000). Research provides convincing evidence that heredity plays a major role in obesity (Devlin, Yanovski, & Wilson, 2000). One study found that some people inherit a tendency to burn up extra calories, while others inherit a tendency to turn their extra calories into fat (Bouchard et al., 1990). Another study showed that identical twins had the same body weight in adulthood whether they had been reared together or apart (Stunkard et al., 1990). In this study, in other words, childhood experiences appeared to have little effect on adult weight.

Obesity has also been related to the amount of fat cells, or **adipose tissue,** we have, and we may have some tendency to inherit different numbers of fat cells. The hunger drive is connected with the quantity of fat that has accumulated in these cells. The blood-sugar level is relatively high after one has eaten; then it drops as time elapses. As the blood-sugar level declines, the well of fat in fat cells is tapped to nourish the person, and they sort of shrivel up (like the head of a Shar Pei?). Eventually—and in some cases, "eventually" happens sooner than we might like!—the hypothalamus learns of the deficit and stirs the hunger drive (Woods et al., 2000).

Children who have more fat cells than other children have no advantage in our weight-conscious times. Instead, they feel hungry sooner, even if they are the same in weight. Perhaps the possession of more fat cells means that more signals are being transmitted to the hypothalamus in the brain. Children (and adults) who

obesity A disorder characterized by excessive accumulation of fat.

adipose tissue Fat.

Obesity

Like mother, like daughter? Obesity runs in families. Both genetic and environmental factors appear to be involved in the "transmission" of obesity.

are overweight, and those who were once overweight, usually have more fat cells than individuals who have weighed less. This abundance is no blessing. Childhood obesity may cause adolescent or adult dieters to feel persistent hunger, even after they have leveled off at a weight they prefer.

Evidence that genetic and physiological factors are involved in obesity does not necessarily mean that the environment plays no role (Baker et al., 2000). Family, peers, and other environmental factors are likely to influence children's dietary behavior (Weber Cullen et al., 2001). Obese parents, for example, may be models of poor exercise habits, may encourage overeating, and may keep the wrong kinds of food around.

Reflect

Does obesity "run" in your family? If so, what seems to be the reason for it?

Watching television also plays a role in the development of obesity (Bar-Or et al., 1998; T. N. Robinson, 1998). A large-scale longitudinal study showed that children who watched television for 25 or more hours per week during the middle childhood years were more likely to become obese as adolescents (Dietz, 1990; Dietz & Gortmaker, 1985). The influence of TV watching is at least threefold. First, children tend to consume snacks while watching. Second, television bombards children with commercials for fattening foods, such as candy and potato chips (Strasburger, 2001). Here's a question for you: How many food commercials does the "average" child see in a given year? Does the number 10,000 sound about right? It is. Research also shows that the great majority of these commercials—about 90% of them—are *not* for fresh fruits and vegetables and skim milk. Instead, they hawk fast foods (like Burger King and Pizza Hut), highly sweetened cereals, soft drinks, and candy bars (Brownell, 1997; Strasburger, 2001). Third, watching television is a sedentary activity. We burn fewer calories sitting than engaging in strenuous physical activity. Moreover, children who are heavy TV viewers are less physically active overall (Bar-Or et al., 1998; Strasburger, 2001). Overweight children burn even fewer calories than normal-weight children when watching television, which further contributes to their obesity.

Stressors and emotional reactions also play roles in prompting children to eat (Greeno & Wing, 1994). Overeating may occur in response to severe stresses, such as those due to bickering in the home, parental divorce, or the birth of a sibling. Family celebrations and arguments are quite different, but both can lead to overeating or breaking a diet (Drapkin et al., 1995). Efforts to curb food intake may be also hampered by negative feeling states like anxiety and depression (McGuire et al., 1999; Stice et al., 2000). The rule of thumb here seems to be something like this: If life is awful, try chocolate (or french fries, or pizza, or . . . whatever).

For some suggestions on how parents can help their children (and themselves) lose weight, see the nearby feature, "Helping Children Lose Weight."

Review

(1) Gains in height and weight are generally (abrupt or steady?) throughout middle childhood. (2) Children gain a little over ________ inches in height per year during middle childhood. (3) They gain about ________ pounds a year. (4) (Boys or Girls?) are slightly heavier and taller through the age of 9 or 10. (5) Boys begin to become more muscular than girls at about the age of ________ (6) About ________% of American children are obese. (7) Children (do or do not?) tend to outgrow "baby fat." (8) Obesity (does or does not?) run in families.

Pulling It Together: How do genetic and environmental factors interact to foster obesity in children?

Motor Development

Question: What changes in motor development occur in middle childhood? The school years are marked by increases in the child's speed, strength, agility, and balance (Abdelaziz, Harb, & Hisham, 2001; Loovis & Butterfield, 2000). These developments, in turn, lead to more skillful performance of motor activities, such as skipping.

Click *Physical Development* for more on motor development.

A Closer Look

Helping Children Lose Weight

Today's parents not only want to be slimmer themselves, but they are also more aware of the health benefits their children gain by avoiding obesity. However, losing weight is one of the most difficult problems in self-control for children and adults alike. Nevertheless, childhood is the optimal time to prevent or reverse obesity, because it is easiest to promote a lifetime pattern of healthful behaviors during childhood (Nawaz & Katz, 2001).

Long-term, insight-oriented psychotherapy has not been shown to be of much use in helping children lose weight. However, cognitive behavioral methods show promise (Braet, 1999; Epstein et al., 1999, 2000; Robinson, 1999). These methods include: (1) improving nutritional knowledge, (2) reducing calories, (3) exercise, and (4) behavior modification. The behavioral methods involve tracking the child's calorie intake and weight, keeping the child away from temptations, setting a good example, and systematically using praise and other rewards. The most successful weight-loss programs for children combine exercise, decreased caloric intake, behavior modification, and emotional support from parents. Here are some suggestions gleaned from the literature:

- Teach children about their nutritional needs—calories, protein, vitamins, minerals, fiber, food groups, and so on. Indicate which foods may be eaten in nearly unlimited quantities (for example, green vegetables) and which foods should be eaten

Physical Activity, Weight, and Fitness
Get kids away from those TV sets! One way parents can motivate their children to engage in regular physical activity is to find time for family outdoor activities that promote weight control and fitness.

© IT Stock Int'l./Index Stock Imagery

Gross Motor Skills

Throughout middle childhood, children show steady improvement in their ability to perform various gross motor skills (Abdelaziz et al., 2001; Laszlo, 1990). School-age children are usually eager to participate in group games and athletic activities that require the movement of large muscles, such as catching and throwing balls. As seen in Table 11.1, children are hopping, jumping, and climbing by age 6 or so; and by 6 or 7, they are usually capable of pedaling and balancing on a bicycle. By the ages of 8 to 10, children are showing the balance, coordination, and strength that allow them to engage in gymnastics and team sports.

Reflect

When did you become "good at" things like riding a bicycle, skating, or team sports? Did these activities provide an opportunity for fulfillment and social approval or a source of anxiety? Explain.

During these years, the muscles are growing stronger, and the pathways that connect the cerebellum to the cortex are becoming increasingly myelinated. Experience also plays an indispensable role in refining many sensorimotor abilities, especially at championship levels, but there are also individual differences that seem inborn. Some people, for example, have better visual acuity or better depth perception than others. For reasons such as these, they will have an edge in playing the outfield or hitting a golf ball.

One of the most important factors in athletic performance is **reaction time,** or the amount of time required to respond to a stimulus. Reaction time is basic to the child's timing of a swing of the bat to meet the ball. Reaction time is basic to adjusting to a fly ball or hitting a tennis ball. Reaction time is also involved in children's responses to cars and other (sometimes deadly) obstacles when they are riding their bicycles or running down the street.

Reaction time gradually improves (that is, *decreases*) from early childhood to about age 18 (Bard, Hay, & Fleury, 1990; Abdelaziz et al., 2001; Kail, 1991).

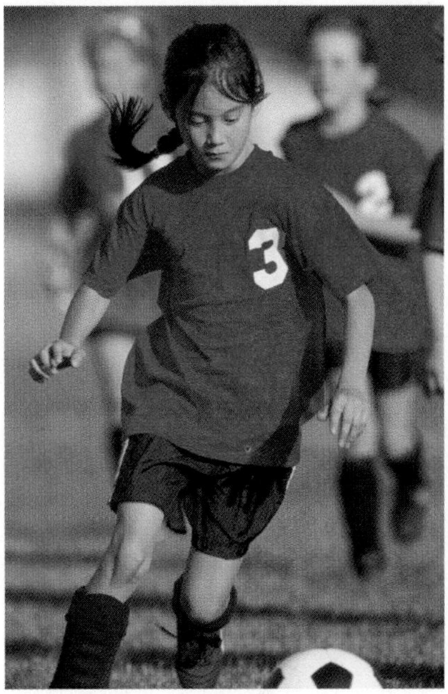

Gross Motor Skills

By the ages of 8 to 10, children are showing the balance, coordination, and strength that allow them to engage in team sports such as soccer. Team sports are an important aspect of life in the United States during middle childhood. Sports are a source of social recognition and self-esteem in some children and a source of embarrassment and misery in others.

only sparingly (cakes, cookies, soft drinks sweetened with sugar, and so on).

- Do not insist that the entire family sit down at the same time for a large meal. Allow your child to eat only when hungry. This will break the tyranny of the clock—the expectation that he or she must be hungry because it's noon or 6 P.M.
- Substitute low-calorie foods for high-calorie foods. There's no way around it: Calories translate into pounds.
- Don't push your child to "finish the plate." Children should be allowed to stop eating when they are no longer hungry. There is no moral or nutritional value to stuffing.
- Prepare low-calorie snacks for your child to eat throughout the day. In this way, children do not become extremely deprived and feel desperate for food. Desperation can prompt binging.
- Do not cook, eat, or display fattening foods when the child is at home. The sight and aroma of tantalizing foods can be more than children can bear.
- Involve the child in more activities. When children are kept busy, they are less likely to think about food. (And physical activity burns calories.)
- Do not take your child food shopping, or, if you do, try to avoid the market aisles with ice cream, cake, and candy. If fattening food is left at the supermarket, it does not wind up in the child's stomach.
- Ask relatives and friends not to offer fattening treats when you visit. Be insistent—think about what you will say to the grandparent who insists that high-calorie foods "can't hurt."
- Don't allow snacking in front of the TV set, while playing, reading, or engaging in any other activity. Allowing children to snack while watching television makes eating a mindless habit.
- Involve the child in calorie-burning exercise. Check with the pediatrician about possible risks, but try to involve the child in activities such as swimming or prolonged bicycle riding. Exercise will burn calories, increase the child's feelings of competence and self-esteem, improve cardiovascular condition, and, possibly, promote lifetime exercise habits.
- Reward the child for taking steps in the right direction, such as eating less or exercising more. Praise and approval are powerful rewards, but children also respond to tangible rewards such as going on a special trip or getting a new toy.
- Don't assume it's a catastrophe if the child slips and goes on a binge. Don't rant and rave. Don't get overly upset. Talk over what triggered the binge with the child so that similar problems may be averted in the future. Remind the child (and yourself) that tomorrow is another day and another start.
- If you and your children are overweight, consider losing weight together. It is more effective for overweight children and their parents to diet and exercise together than for the children to go it alone.

TABLE 11.1 *Development of Gross Motor Skills During Middle Childhood*

Age	Skills
6 years	Hops, jumps, climbs
7 years	Balances on and pedals a bicycle
8 years	Has good body balance
9 years	Engages in vigorous bodily activities, especially team sports such as baseball, football, volleyball, and basketball
10 years	Balances on one foot for 15 seconds; catches a fly ball
12 years	Displays some awkwardness as a result of asynchronous bone and muscle development

However, there are large individual differences (Largo et al., 2001). Reaction time begins to increase again in the adult years. Even so, 75-year-olds still outperform children. Baseball and volleyball may be "child's play," but, everything else being equal, adults will respond to the ball more quickly.

Fine Motor Skills

By 6 to 7 years, children can usually tie their shoelaces and hold their pencils as adults do (see Table 11.2). Their abilities to fasten buttons, zip zippers, brush teeth, wash themselves, and coordinate a knife and fork all develop during the early school years and improve during childhood (Abdelaziz et al., 2001; Cratty, 1986).

Gender and Motor Skills

Question: Are there gender differences in motor skills? Throughout the middle years, boys and girls perform similarly in most motor activities. Boys show slightly greater overall strength and, in particular, more forearm strength, which aids them in swinging a bat or throwing a ball (Butterfield & Loovis, 1993).

TABLE 11.2 *Development of Fine Motor Skills During Middle Childhood*

Age	Skills
6–7 years	Ties shoelaces Throws ball by using wrist and finger release Holds pencil with fingertips Follows simple mazes May be able to hit a ball with a bat
8–9 years	Spaces words when writing Writes and prints accurately and neatly Copies a diamond shape correctly Swings a hammer well Sews and knits Shows good hand–eye coordination

reaction time The amount of time required to respond to a stimulus.

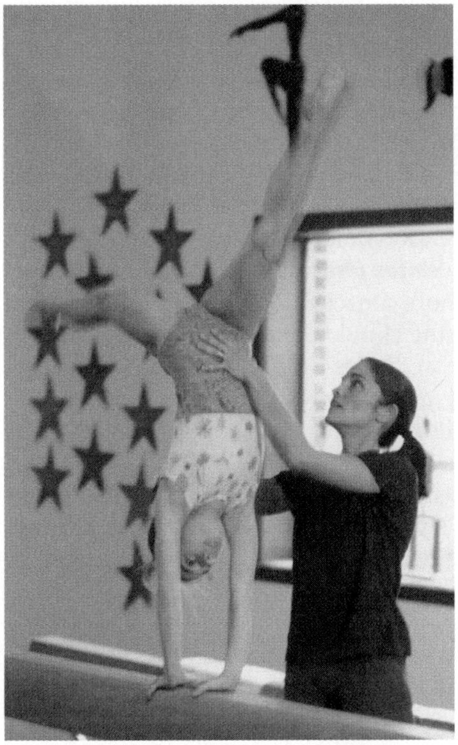

© Steve Prezant/Corbis Stock Market

© David Madison/Stone/Getty Images

Gender and Motor Skills

Girls and boys are similar in their motor abilities in middle childhood. Boys have somewhat greater forearm strength, which helps the young football player throw the ball. Girls, like this gymnast, show somewhat greater coordination of limbs and overall flexibility. Why are so many female gymnasts "washed up" by the time they reach late adolescence?

Girls, on the other hand, show somewhat greater limb coordination and overall flexibility, which is valuable in dancing, balancing, and gymnastics (Abdelaziz et al., 2001; Cratty, 1986). Girls with a certain type of physique seem particularly well-suited to gymnastics. Those who are short, lean, and small boned make the best gymnasts, according to Olympic coaches, because they displace gravity most effectively. This may explain why female gymnasts are considered old for the sport by the time they reach their late teens. By then, they have often grown taller and their body contours have filled out (Adler & Starr, 1992; Press, 1992).

At puberty, gender differences in motor performance favoring boys become progressively greater (Smoll & Schultz, 1990). What factors might account for the development of gender differences in physical performance? In their review of the literature, Thomas and French (1985) concluded that the slight gender differences in motor performance prior to puberty are not large enough to be attributed to biological variables. (The one exception may be throwing, a skill in which boys excel from an early age.) Thomas and French point out that boys are more likely than girls to receive encouragement, support, and opportunities for participation in sports. Even during the preschool years, parents emphasize gross motor behavior in boys more than in girls. By middle childhood, boys are involved in more competitive games than girls and in games of longer duration. They also engage in more vigorous activity than girls (Riddoch et al., 1991; Reynolds et al., 1990).

At puberty, when boys begin to excel in such areas as running, the long jump, sit-ups, and grip strength, boys' greater size and strength confer a certain biological advantage. But some environmental factors that operated in middle childhood may exert even greater importance in puberty. "Tomboy" behavior in girls is less socially accepted in adolescence than it was in middle childhood. Girls may, therefore, become less interested in participating in athletic activities and may be less motivated to do well in the ones in which they do engage (Thomas & French, 1985). By the ages of 12 and 13, girls are less likely than boys to perceive themselves as competent and interested in physical exercise and activity (Ferguson et al., 1989; Whitehead & Corbin, 1991).

Reflect

Were your motor skills "typical" for a girl or boy of your age in the early and middle school years? How did your skills differ from those of the other gender (if they did)?

Exercise and Fitness

The health benefits of exercise for both adults and children are well known. Exercise reduces the risk of heart disease, stroke, diabetes, and certain forms of cancer (Georgiades et al., 2000; Hakim et al., 1998; Hu et al., 2000; Stampfer et al., 2000; Taylor-Tolbert et al., 2000). Exercise confers psychological benefits as well. Physically active adolescents have a better self-image and better coping skills than those who are inactive (Covey & Feltz, 1991; Reynolds et al., 1990).

Questions: Are children in the United States physically fit? If not, why not? Adults in the United States are becoming more conscientious about exercising and staying fit. But curiously, most children in the United States are not physically fit. A study of the fitness of American children in grades 1 through 12 found a decline over a 10-year period in strength, flexibility, and cardiovascular endurance (Brody, 1990c). Nearly two thirds of American children fail to meet the standards set by the President's Council on Physical Fitness (D. V. Harris, 1991).

Reflect

Are you physically fit? If not, why not?

What are some possible reasons for this decline in fitness? Again: one obvious culprit is watching television. High school students who watch relatively little television have less body fat and are more physically fit than those who watch for several hours per day (Armstrong et al., 1998).

Cardiac and muscular fitness, both in childhood and adulthood, is developed by participation in continuous exercise such as running, walking quickly, swimming laps, bicycling, or jumping rope for intervals of several minutes at a time (Michael, 1990). Unfortunately, schools and parents tend to focus on sports such as baseball and football, which are less apt to promote fitness (Brody, 1990c).

As you might expect, children who engage in exercise and are physically fit have more positive attitudes toward physical activity and are more likely to perceive its benefits (Brustad, 1991; Desmond et al., 1990; Ferguson et al., 1989). Children with high levels of physical activity are more likely to have parents who encourage their children to exercise and who actively exercise themselves (Stucky-Ropp & DiLorenzo, 1992). How, then, can more children be motivated to engage in regular physical activity? Here are some suggestions for parents (Bjorklund & Bjorklund, 1989; Brody, 1990b, c):

- Find time for family outdoor activities that promote fitness: walking, swimming, bicycling, skating.
- Reduce the amount of time spent watching television.
- Encourage outdoor play during daylight hours after school.
- Do not assume that your child gets sufficient exercise by participating in a team sport. Many team sports involve long periods of inactivity.

Organized sports for children are enormously popular, but many children lose their enthusiasm and drop out. Participation in sports declines steadily after the age of 10 (Seefeldt, Ewing, & Walk, 1991). Why? Sometimes children are pushed too hard, too early, or too quickly by parents or coaches. Children may thus feel frustrated or inferior, and they are sometimes injured (Brody, 1990b; Kolata, 1992c). Hence, parents are advised not to place excessive demands for performance on their children. Let them progress at their own pace. Encourage them to focus on the fun and health benefits of physical activity and sports, not on winning.

Review

(9) During middle childhood, children show (abrupt or steady?) improvement in gross motor skills. (10) By the age of about __________, children show the balance, coordination, and strength that allows them to engage in gymnastics and team sports. (11) Reaction time gradually (increases or decreases?) from early childhood to about age 18. (12) (Boys or Girls?) tend to show greater overall strength. (13)

(Boys or Girls?) show somewhat greater coordination and flexibility. (14) The majority of children in the United States tend to be physically (fit or unfit?).

Pulling It Together: What are the pluses and minuses of children's participation in sports?

Children With Disabilities

Certain disabilities of childhood are most apt to be noticed in the middle childhood years, when the child enters school. The school setting requires that a child sit still, pay attention, and master a number of academic skills. But some children have difficulty with one or more of these demands. In this section, we focus on children with two types of disabilities: attention-deficit hyperactivity disorder and learning disabilities.

Attention-Deficit Hyperactivity Disorder (ADHD)

Scott, age 7, is extremely restless and distractible in class. Every few minutes, he is out of his seat, exploring something on a bookshelf or looking out the window. When in his seat, he swings his legs back and forth, drums his fingers on the table, shifts around, and keeps up a high level of movement. He speaks rapidly, and his ideas are poorly organized, although his intelligence is normal. During recess, Scott is aggressive and violates many of the playground rules. Scott's behavior at home is similar to his behavior in school. He is unable to concentrate on any activity for more than a few minutes. Scott is suffering from attention-deficit hyperactivity disorder. (Adapted from Halgin & Whitbourne, 1993, p. 335)

Many parents feel that their children do not pay enough attention to them—that they tend to run around as the whim strikes and to do things in their own way. Some inattention, especially at early ages, is to be expected. ***Question: How does run-of-the-mill failure to "listen" to adults differ from attention-deficit hyperactivity disorder?*** In **attention-deficit hyperactivity disorder** (ADHD), the child shows developmentally inappropriate or excessive inattention, impulsivity, and **hyperactivity** (American Psychiatric Association, 2000; Nigg, 2001). A more complete list of problems is shown in Table 11.3. The degree of hyperactive behavior is crucial, since many normal children are labeled overactive and fidgety from time to time. In fact, if talking too much were the sole criterion for ADHD, the label would have applied to many of us.

The onset of ADHD occurs by age 7. The behavior pattern must have persisted for at least 6 months for the diagnosis—a category used by the American Psychiatric Association (2000)—to apply. The hyperactivity and restlessness of children with ADHD impair their ability to function in school. They simply cannot sit still. They also have difficulty getting along with others. Their disruptive, noncompliant behavior often elicits punishment from parents. ADHD is quite common. It is diagnosed in about 1–5% of school-aged children and is one of the most common causes of childhood referrals to mental-health clinics (Ekvall, Ekvall, & Mayes, 1993). ADHD is several times more common in boys than in girls.

Some psychologists and educators note that ADHD tends to be overdiagnosed. That is, many children who do not toe the line in school tend to be diagnosed with ADHD and medicated in order to encourage more acceptable behavior. Research does suggest that those who diagnose children with ADHD tend to be "suggestible." That is, they are more likely to diagnose children with the disorder when they are given other sources of information—for example, from teachers and parents—to the effect that the children do not adequately control their behavior (Simonson & Glenn, 2001).

Reflect

Did you know any hyperactive children in your early school years? (Were you labeled hyperactive?) How were they treated by teachers and other students?

attention-deficit hyperactivity disorder (ADHD) A behavior disorder characterized by excessive inattention, impulsiveness, and hyperactivity.

hyperactivity Excessive restlessness and overactivity. Not to be confused with misbehavior or with normal high activity levels that occur during childhood. One of the primary characteristics of attention-deficit hyperactivity disorder (ADHD).

© Al Cook Photography

A Boy With Attention-Deficit Hyperactivity Disorder

*Hyperactive children are continually on the go, as if their "motors" are constantly running. The psychological disorder we refer to as hyperactivity is not to be confused with the normal high energy levels of children. However, it is sometimes—*sometimes*—difficult to tell where one ends and the other begins.*

Causes of ADHD

Question: What are the causes of ADHD? Because ADHD is in part characterized by excessive motor activity, many theorists focus on possible physical causes. For one thing, ADHD tends to run in families, for both girls and boys with the disorder (Faraone et al., 2000). ADHD is also found to coexist with other psychological disorders and problems, ranging from anxiety and depression to tics (Souza et al., 2001; Spencer et al., 2001). At least some children with ADHD appear to have an inherited defect in the body's thyroid hormone system (Hauser et al., 1993). ADHD also appears to be more prevalent in children who have suffered from encephalitis (Anderson & Cohen, 1991). Recordings of brain waves frequently show abnormalities as well (Hechtman, 1991).

Evidence such as this has led investigators to suggest that children with ADHD suffer from "minimal brain damage" or "minimal brain dysfunction." These labels do not add much to efforts to locate and remedy possible damage. A study by Alan Zametkin and his colleagues (1990) found that individuals with ADHD have reduced activity in areas of the brain that control attention and movement.

It has also been hypothesized that the chemical additives in processed food are largely responsible for hyperactivity. However, experimental studies of the so-called Feingold diet, which removes such additives from children's food, have not supported this hypothesis (Ekvall, Ekvall, & Mayes, 1993; Hynd & Hooper, 1992).

Joel T. Nigg (2001) notes that ADHD is widely thought to be caused by inhibitory processes that do not work efficiently. That is, children with ADHD do not inhibit, or control, impulses that most children are capable of controlling. But he notes that the definition of "inhibition" is defined in somewhat different ways by different theorists. In an article published in *Psychological Bulletin*, Nigg distinguishes between inhibition that is under the executive control of the brain—a sort of cognitive-neurological inhibition—and inhibition that is normally motivated by emotions such as anxiety and fear—for example, anxiety about disappointing a teacher or fear of earning poor grades. Nigg argues that ADHD is unlikely to reflect failure to respond to feelings of anxiety or fear. He believes that the disorder is more likely to be due to a lack of executive control, but admits that the precise nature of this control—for example, specification of possible neurological aspects—remains poorly understood.

TABLE 11.3 *Symptoms of Attention-Deficit Hyperactivity Disorder (ADHD)*

Kind of Problem	Specific Patterns of Behavior
Lack of attention	Fails to attend to details or makes careless errors in schoolwork, etc. Has difficulty sustaining attention in schoolwork or play activities Doesn't appear to pay attention to what is being said Fails to follow through on instructions or to finish work Has trouble organizing work and other activities Avoids work or activities that require sustained attention Loses work tools (e.g., pencils, books, assignments, toys) Becomes readily distracted Forgetful in daily activities
Hyperactivity	Fidgets with hands or feet or squirms in his or her seat Leaves seat in situations such as the classroom in which remaining seated is required Constantly runs around or climbs on things; "running like a motor" Has difficulty playing quietly Shows excessive motor activity when asleep Talks excessively
Impulsivity	Often acts without thinking Shifts from activity to activity Cannot organize tasks or work Requires constant supervision Often "calls out" in class Does not wait his or her turn in line, games, and so on

Note: ADHD begins by the age of 7; significantly impairs academic, social, or occupational functioning; and is characterized by clinical features shown in this table that occur continually in more than one setting, such as in the school and in the home. Source: Adapted from American Psychiatric Association (2000). Diagnostic and statistical manual of mental disorders. DSM–IV–TR. *Washington, DC: Author.*

Treatment and Outcome

The most widespread treatment for ADHD is medical—the use of **stimulants** such as Ritalin and Dexedrine. ***Question: Children with ADHD are often treated with stimulants. Why?*** It may seem ironic that stimulants would be used with children who are already overly active. The rationale is that the activity of the hyperactive child stems from inability of the cerebral cortex to inhibit more primitive areas of the brain (Keating et al., 2001; Nigg, 2001). The drugs block the re-uptake (re-absorption) of two neurotransmitters in the brain: dopamine and noradrenaline. Keeping more of these neurotransmitters active has the effect of stimulating the cerebral cortex and facilitating cortical control of primitive areas of the brain (Keating, McClellan & Jarvis, 2001). This interpretation is supported by evidence that caffeine—the stimulant found in coffee, tea, colas, and chocolate (yes, chocolate)—also helps children control hyperactivity (Leon, 2000; Rezvani & Levin, 2001).

Children with ADHD who are given stimulants show increased attention span, improved cognitive and academic performance (Evans et al., 2001), less activity (Klorman et al., 1994), and a reduction in disruptive, annoying, and aggressive behaviors (Evans et al., 2001). The use of stimulants is controversial, however. Some critics argue that stimulants suppress gains in height and weight, do not contribute to academic gains, and lose effectiveness over time (Henker & Whalen, 1989; Green, 1991). Another concern is that stimulants are overused or misused in

Reflect

Do you believe that children with ADHD are overmedicated? Explain?

stimulants Drugs that increase the activity of the nervous system.

an attempt to control normal high activity levels of children at home or in the classroom. Supporters of stimulant treatment argue that many ADHD children are helped by medication. They counter that the suppression of growth appears to be related to the dosage of the drug and that low doses seem to be about as effective as large doses (Evans et al., 2001).

Another approach that shows some promise in treatment of children with ADHD is cognitive behavioral therapy. This approach attempts to increase the child's self-control and problem-solving abilities through modeling, role playing, and self-instruction. A Spanish study found that it was possible to teach many children with ADHD to "stop and think" before giving in to angry impulses and behaving in an aggressive manner (Miranda & Presentacion, 2000). However, it should be noted that the recent Multimodal Treatment Study, which was sponsored by the National Institute of Mental Health, found that "medical management"—meaning use of stimulant medication—was superior in effectiveness to cognitive behavioral therapy (Greene & Ablon, 2001; Whalen, 2001). Even so, the Multimodal Treatment Study did not match treatments to the needs of the individual child with ADHD (Abikoff, 2001; Whalen, 2001). It is possible that some children will do best with stimulants alone, others with cognitive behavioral therapy, and still others with a combination of the two (Abikoff, 2001; Greene & Ablon, 2001).

Many but not all children appear to "outgrow" ADHD. Some longitudinal studies find that at least two thirds of children with ADHD continue to exhibit one or more of the core symptoms in adolescence and adulthood (Barkley et al., 1991; Gagnon et al., 1993; McGee et al., 1991). Problems in attention, conduct, hyperactivity, and learning frequently continue.

Other studies yield more optimistic results. Consider a study by Salvatore Mannuzza and his colleagues (1998). The researchers interviewed 85 men at an average age of 24.1 years who had been diagnosed with ADHD at an average age of 7.3 years. They compared these men with 73 men who had not been diagnosed with ADHD but who were matched in terms of age and ethnicity (all were European American). They found that men who had been diagnosed with ADHD were significantly more likely to be diagnosed with antisocial personality disorder (12% versus 3%) and substance abuse for drugs other than alcohol (12% versus 4%) as adults. However, there were no significant differences in the prevalence of mood disorders (4% versus 4%) and anxiety disorders (2% versus 7%). Only 4% of the men who had been diagnosed with ADHD as children showed evidence of ADHD as adults. The authors conclude that children diagnosed with ADHD are at significantly greater risk for antisocial and substance-related disorders. But we can view the findings from a more encouraging perspective. First of all, ADHD itself was all but absent among the men who had been diagnosed with the disorder in childhood. Second, even though those who had been diagnosed with ADHD were at greater risk than control subjects of antisocial behavior and substance abuse, the great majority of them (88%, or 7 of 8) did *not* have these problems as adults. But we can also note that the study involved adults who had been diagnosed with ADHD as children. Because there is a tendency to overdiagnose ADHD, especially among children who are aggressive, we can speculate that antisocial behavior in adulthood is frequently preceded by a form of antisocial behavior in childhood rather than being an "outcome" of childhood ADHD. This study may be a shining example of a situation in which statistically significant differences are not all that meaningful. That is, it seems rather "risky" to predict antisocial behavior in adulthood from a childhood diagnosis of ADHD.

dyslexia A reading disorder characterized by problems such as letter reversals, mirror reading, slow reading, and reduced comprehension (from the Greek roots *dys-*, meaning "bad," and *lexikon*, meaning "of words").

learning disabilities A group of disorders characterized by inadequate development of specific academic, language, and speech skills.

Learning Disabilities

Nelson Rockefeller served as vice president of the United States under Gerald Ford. He was intelligent and well educated. Yet despite the best of tutors, he could never master reading. Rockefeller suffered from **dyslexia**.

Question: What are learning disabilities? Dyslexia is one type of **learning disability.** The term *learning disability* refers to a group of disorders characterized by inadequate development of specific academic, language, and speech skills, as shown in Table 11.4. Learning-disabled children may show problems in math, writing, or reading. Some have difficulties in articulating sounds of speech or in understanding spoken language. Others have problems in motor coordination. Children are usually considered to have a learning disability when they are performing below the level expected for their age and level of intelligence and when there is no evidence of other handicaps such as vision or hearing problems, mental retardation, or socioeconomic disadvantage (Shaywitz, 1998). However, some psychologists and educators, such as Frank Vellutino and his colleagues (Vellutino, 2001; Vellutino, Scanlon, & Lyon, 2001) argue that too much emphasis is placed on the discrepancy between intelligence and achievement in reading.

Children with learning disabilities frequently display other problems as well. They are more likely than other children to have attention-deficit hyperactivity disorder (Faraone et al., 2000; Swanson, Mink, & Bocean, 1999). They do not communicate as well with their peers (Lapadat, 1991), have poorer social skills (Vaughn et al., 1990; Wiener & Harris, 1993), show more behavior problems in the classroom (Bender & Smith, 1990), and are more likely to experience emotional problems (Feagans & Haldane, 1991).

For most learning-disabled children, the disorder persists through life (Shaywitz, 1998). But with early recognition and appropriate remediation, many individuals can learn to overcome or compensate for their learning disability (Andrews & Conte, 1993).

To illustrate some of the theoretical and treatment issues involved in learning disabilities, let us consider dyslexia (difficulty in learning to read). As with other learning disabilities, dyslexia is puzzling because there is every indication that the child ought to be able to read. Dyslexic children are usually at least average in intelligence. Their vision and hearing check out as normal. However, problems in developing reading skills persist (American Academy of Pediatrics, 1992; Rack, Snowling, & Olson, 1992).

TABLE 11.4 *Types of Learning Disabilities*

Reading Disability (Dyslexia)	As measured by a standardized test that is given individually, the child's ability to read (accuracy or comprehension) is substantially less than one would expect considering his or her age, level of intelligence, and educational experiences. The reading disorder materially interferes with the child's academic achievement or daily living. If there is also a sensory or perceptual defect, the reading problems are worse than one would expect with it.
Mathematics Disability (Dyscalculia)	As measured by a standardized test that is given individually, the child's mathematical ability is substantially less than one would expect considering his or her age, level of intelligence, and educational experiences. The mathematics disorder materially interferes with the child's academic achievement or daily living. If there is also a sensory or perceptual defect, the problems in mathematics are worse than one would expect with it.
Disorder of Written Expression	As measured by assessment of functioning or by a standardized test that is given individually, the child's writing ability is substantially less than one would expect considering his or her age, level of intelligence, and educational experiences. The problems in writing grammatically correct sentences and organized paragraphs materially interfere with the child's academic achievement or daily living. If there is also a sensory or perceptual defect, the problems in writing are worse than one would expect with it.

Note: The American Psychiatric Association uses the term *learning disorder* rather than *learning disability.* However, educators appear to prefer the term *learning disability. Source:* Adapted from American Psychiatric Association (2000). *Diagnostic and statistical manual of mental disorders. DSM–IV–TR.* Washington, DC: Author.

TABLE 11.5 *Characteristics of Children With Dyslexia*

Usually first recognized during early school years
Omissions and additions of sounds
Reversal or rotation of letters of the alphabet—confusing *b* with *d* and *p* with *q*
Mirror reading and writing—reading and writing words that look normal when viewed in a mirror, such as reading *saw* when presented with the visual stimulus *was*
Slow reading
Poor reading comprehension
Subtle language difficulties, such as problems discriminating sounds, although overall auditory acuity (sharpness of hearing) is normal
At least some impairment in general academic functioning
May be easily distracted or fail to listen or to finish things that he or she has started
May be impulsive, call out in class, find it difficult to wait in lines
More common among twins, preterm children, children of older mothers, and children who have sustained head injuries
May be more common among boys
Reading, speech, and language problems are more common in the family than among the general population
Problem frequently continues into adolescence and adulthood

It has been estimated that dyslexia affects anywhere from 5 to 17.5% of American children (Shaywitz, 1998). Although most studies have shown that dyslexia is much more common in boys than girls, Sally Shaywitz (1998) believes that recent data show that the disorder affects about as many girls as boys. Researchers have identified a number of frequently occurring characteristics of dyslexic children, and these are listed in Table 11.5. Figure 11.2 is a writing sample from a dyslexic child.

In childhood, treatment of dyslexia focuses on remediation (Shaywitz, 1998). Children are given highly structured exercises to help them become aware of how to blend sounds to form words, such as identifying word pairs that rhyme and do not rhyme. Later in life, the focus tends to be on accommodation rather than remediation (Shaywitz, 1998). For example, college students with dyslexia may be

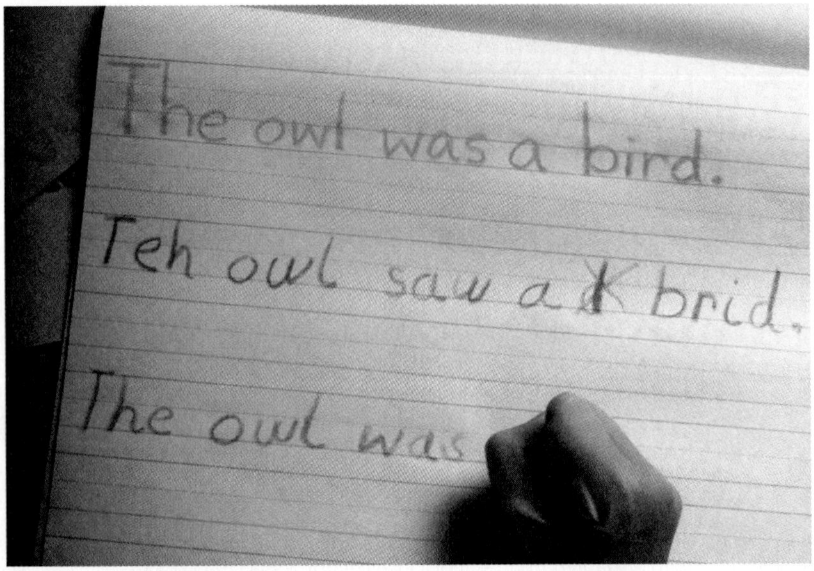

Figure 11.2
Writing Sample of a Dyslexic Child

Dyslexic children have trouble perceiving letters in their correct orientation. They may perceive letters upside down (confusing w *with* m*) or reversed (confusing* b *with* d*). This perceptual difficulty may lead to rotations or reversals in their writing, as shown here.*

given extra time to do the reading involved in taking tests. Interestingly, college students with dyslexia are frequently excellent at word recognition. However, they still show problems in decoding new words.

Origins of Dyslexia

Question: What are the origins of dyslexia? Where does dyslexia come from? When I was a graduate student, I had a course with a professor who was a strict Freudian. His view was that dyslexia stemmed from unconscious sexual conflict. A dyslexic child would have difficulty distinguishing a *b* from a *d*, or a *q* from a *p*, because these letters were phallic-shaped and the child was in conflict about the male sex organs. Other letters, like *o* and *c*—Oh, forget it; psychoanalytically oriented readers will think I am making fun of them, and I do not mean to.

I also heard learning-theory explanations in graduate school. They went something like this. Children develop dyslexia because of faulty and punitive teaching. They become highly anxious when they are trying to read because teachers—or parents or both—have lost patience with them. Under highly anxious conditions, conflicting response tendencies tend to emerge. That is, to coin a phrase, when we are under sufficient stress, we may not know which way to turn. So it becomes more difficult to discriminate *b* from *d*, etc., etc.

Developing in the New Millennium

Back to School—With Methylphenidate

It's fall again in the new millennium. The beaches have been vacated, the air will grow crisper, and millions of children are returning to classrooms amid an increasingly pitched battle over Ritalin and other drugs used to treat behavioral and emotional problems in school. And some of Ritalin's competitors, anxious for market share, are advertising directly to parents, selling the idea that drugs may be the answer to their children's problems in school. At the same time, state legislatures are moving to prevent schools from recommending or requiring that parents put their children on medication.

In 2000, Minnesota became the first state to bar schools and child protection agencies from telling parents they must put their children on drugs to treat disorders like attention-deficit hyperactivity disorder, or ADHD. In 2001, Connecticut went a step further with a new law that prohibits any school staff member from discussing drug treatments with a parent to assure that such talk comes only from doctors. Other states are following the trend.

The legislative push is a reaction to what its advocates call overprescription of the drugs. They say an excessive reliance on Ritalin and several competing drugs is driving parents away from traditional forms of discipline and has created a growing, illegal traffic in what are potent and dangerous speedlike stimulants. In 2000, doctors wrote almost 20 million monthly prescriptions for the stimulants. Most of those prescriptions were written for children, especially boys.

The political concern comes as producers of the drugs have begun an advertising campaign that is unparalleled in spending

Source: Adapted from Kate Zernike & Melody Petersen. (2001, August 19). School's Backing of Behavior Drugs Comes Under Fire. *New York Times* online edition. © 2001 by *The New York Times Co.* Reprinted by permission.

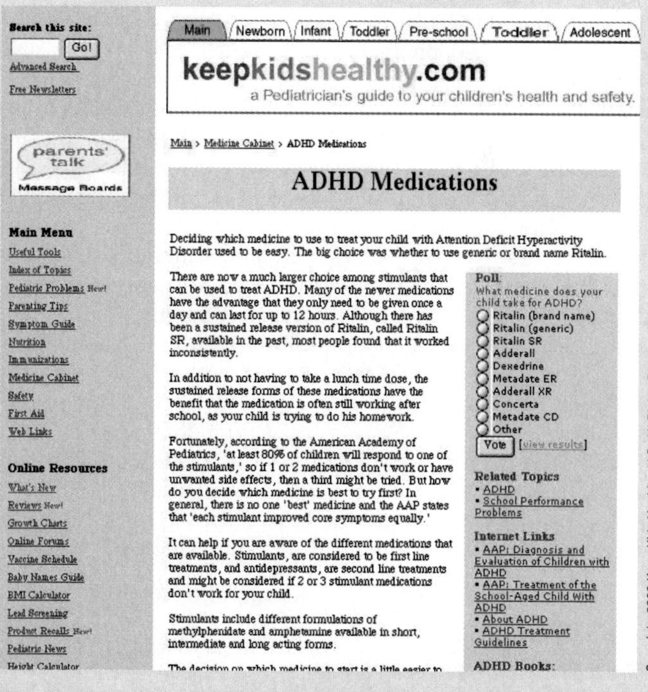
Search this site:
Go!
Advanced Search
Free Newsletters
parents' talk
Message Boards
Main Menu
Useful Tools
Index of Topics
Pediatric Problems New!
Parenting Tips
Symptom Guide
Nutrition
Immunizations
Medicine Cabinet
Safety
First Aid
Web Links
Online Resources
What's New
Reviews New!
Growth Charts
Online Forums
Vaccine Schedule
Baby Names Guide
BMI Calculator
Lead Screening
Product Recalls New!
Pediatric News
Height Calculator

Main | Newborn | Infant | Toddler | Pre-school | Toddler | Adolescent

keepkidshealthy.com
a Pediatrician's guide to your children's health and safety.

Main > Medicine Cabinet > ADHD Medications

ADHD Medications

Deciding which medicine to use to treat your child with Attention Deficit Hyperactivity Disorder used to be easy. The big choice was whether to use generic or brand name Ritalin.

There are now a much larger choice among stimulants that can be used to treat ADHD. Many of the newer medications have the advantage that they only need to be given once a day and can last for up to 12 hours. Although there has been a sustained release version of Ritalin, called Ritalin SR, available in the past, most people found that it worked inconsistently.

In addition to not having to take a lunch time dose, the sustained release forms of these medications have the benefit that the medication is often still working after school, as your child is trying to do his homework.

Fortunately, according to the American Academy of Pediatrics, 'at least 80% of children will respond to one of the stimulants,' so if 1 or 2 medications don't work or have unwanted side effects, then a third might be tried. But how do you decide which medicine is best to try first? In general, there is no one 'best' medicine and the AAP states that 'each stimulant improved core symptoms equally.'

It can help if you are aware of the different medications that are available. Stimulants, are considered to be first line treatments, and antidepressants, are second line treatments and might be considered if 2 or 3 stimulant medications don't work for your child.

Stimulants include different formulations of methylphenidate and amphetamine available in short, intermediate and long acting forms.

Poll:
What medicine does your child take for ADHD?
Ritalin (brand name)
Ritalin (generic)
Ritalin SR
Adderall
Dexedrine
Metadate ER
Adderall XR
Concerta
Metadate CD
Other
Vote [view results]

Related Topics
• ADHD
• School Performance Problems

Internet Links
• AAP: Diagnosis and Evaluation of Children with ADHD
• AAP: Treatment of the School-Aged Child With ADHD
• About ADHD
• ADHD Treatment Guidelines

ADHD Books:

Are Ads Such as These Part of the Solution or Part of the Problem? Or Are They Both?

Many psychologists, educators, and parents are concerned that ADHD medication is prescribed too loosely, yet ads directed at parents tout the benefits of new drugs. Many state legislatures now prevent schools and child protection agencies from telling parents they must put their children on ADHD drugs. Parents want to help their children but wonder if the children are being diagnosed and treated properly. Do they truly "suffer" from ADHD, or is it simply that their behavior is inconvenient for a school system?

Neither of these psychologically oriented explanations of the origins of dyslexia has survived to the present day. Current views of dyslexia generally focus on the ways in which neurological problems may contribute to the perceptual problems we find in dyslexic children (and adults) (Habib, 2000; Nicolson, Fawcett, & Dean, 2001).

A sort of catch-all notion on this topic involves the possibility of "minimal brain damage." Dyslexic children, for example, frequently show a number of behaviors found among children with known brain damage. These include a short attention span and difficulty sitting still. It has therefore been speculated that children with dyslexia may also be brain-damaged, even though the brain damage is so minimal that it cannot be detected by direct means. On the other hand, contemporary methods of imaging the brain are providing new insights into the nature of the brain damage—whether "minimal" or not.

We'll return to the brain in a minute. Let's first note that genetic factors appear to be involved in dyslexia (Plomin, 2001b; Raskind, 2001). In support of this view, it is known that dyslexia runs in families. It has been estimated that about 26–65% of children who have one dyslexic parent are dyslexic themselves (Shaywitz,

Developing in the New Millennium (continued)

and technique. In a fall 2001 back-to-school section of *Ladies' Home Journal*, tucked among the ads for Life cereal, bologna, and Jell-O pudding, were three full-page advertisements for the ADHD treatments. The ads evoked a sense of Rockwellian calm. Children chat happily next to a school bus. A child's hand gently touches the hand of an adult. In one, for Metadate CD, an approving mother embraces her beaming son as the drug itself is named and promoted.

This is a first. Metadate CD, like Ritalin, Adderall, and similar drugs, are known as Schedule II controlled substances, the most addictive substances that are still legal. (Schedule I drugs like heroin and LSD are illegal.) In keeping with a 1971 international treaty, such controlled substances had never been marketed directly to consumers, only to doctors. There was, however, no federal law to prevent drug companies from doing it.

Terry Woodworth, deputy director of the Office of Diversion Control of the Drug Enforcement Administration, said that Celltech, the maker of Metadate CD, "stepped up and beyond everyone else by advertising a drug with a high potential for abuse." He said the campaign could have "diplomatic repercussions" and that Celltech had been asked to stop.

McNeil Consumer Healthcare, which makes a drug called Concerta, and Shire Pharmaceuticals, a British company that makes Adderall, are also advertising directly to consumers, but they are not naming their products. Instead, parents are urged to call a toll-free number to request that brochures be sent to them. That information mentions the drugs by brand name as one treatment option.

Some parents and doctors say they welcome the new drugs and the publicity, which, they believe, helps inform parents of new treatments. Concerta and Metadate CD work longer than Ritalin, the best known of these drugs, so children who take them do not have to see the school nurse at lunch for a booster dose. That avoids embarrassment and reduces the risks associated with drugs being stored at school.

Some physicians who have done research on Ritalin say the state laws are too severe. "To argue that these treatments are inappropriate or ineffective just flies in the face of a scientific knowledge base that is impossible to ignore," said Howard Abikoff, director of research at the Child Study Center at New York University. "You can't close your eyes to this. It's made differences that are monumental in the lives of these kids and their parents." He was one of the principal researchers in a National Institute of Mental Health study of Ritalin that found that medication was more effective than behavioral therapy in treating ADHD. (Actually, the study found that the combination of medication and behavior therapy was more effective than behavior therapy alone [Jensen et al., 2001]. Moreover, the study used a form of behavior therapy referred to as "psychosocial treatment" [Wells et al., 2000] and not what is believed by many social cognitive theorists to be a more effective psychological approach: cognitive behavior therapy [Abikoff, 2001]. There was thus no direct comparison of the effects of medication with cognitive behavior therapy.)

Evelyn Green, a teacher in Chicago and the president of CHADD, Children and Adults with Attention-Deficit/Hyperactivity Disorder, a nonprofit group that represents people with the disorder, said that one of her sons has been taking medication — first Ritalin and now Adderall—for 8 years. Some parents may not be aware of the new longer-acting drugs, Concerta and Metadate CD, which have genuine benefits for many chidren, Ms. Green said. "The danger of the ads," she said, "is that parents could get the message that medication is all there is."

The problems associated with these drugs have escalated. The Drug Enforcement Administration says Ritalin and other stimu-

1998). About 40% of the siblings of children with dyslexia are also dyslexic. Current research is focusing on genes on chromosomes 6 and 15 (Shaywitz, 1998).

The notion of genetic factors can fit quite comfortably with that of brain damage. After all, the brain damage could be inherited. What could that damage be? One possibility is that the damage comprises "faulty wiring" in the left hemisphere of the brain, which is usually involved in language functions. There is some evidence for this view. For one thing, the left hemispheres of people with dyslexia appear to be smaller than those of other people (Hynd & Hooper, 1992). It has also been hypothesized that children with dyslexia learn the alphabet in the "wrong" hemisphere—that is, the right hemisphere rather than the left (Mather, 2001). Fast magnetic resonance imaging (fMRI) finds some support for this hypothesis (Corina et al., 2001).

Let's get more specific. The left hemisphere is usually responsible for language functioning. A part of the brain called the *angular gyrus* lies in the left hemisphere between the visual cortex and Wernicke's area. The angular gyrus "translates" visual information, as when we perceive written words, into auditory information (sounds) and sends it on to Wernicke's area. It appears that problems in the angular gyrus can give rise to reading problems because it becomes difficult for the reader to segment words into sounds (Corina et al., 2001; Shaywitz, 1998).

lants are among the most frequently stolen prescription drugs. Some students are crushing and snorting pills for a speedlike high; in Orem, Utah, an elementary school principal was sentenced to 30 days in jail after he stole his students' Ritalin pills and replaced them with sugar pills. In 2000, the *Journal of the American Medical Association* noted a "disturbing" rise in prescriptions for stimulants and antidepressants for children under 5, most of whom are too young, according to the drugs' labels, to take them.

"Before they came out with these, how did we grow up?" asked Lenny T. Winkler, a nurse and state representative who sponsored Connecticut's new law. "If a child has a problem and it's diagnosed properly, I support that. But I think teachers are far too quick to blame the problem on attention deficit and say to parents, 'This is what needs to be done.'"

Children who take medication for emotional or learning problems in school tend to be labeled "learning disabled" under special education laws and now account for over half of those in special education. The diagnoses for many of the problems have long been controversial, in part because there are no blood or lab tests for attention-deficit disorders or even for schizophrenia or depression.

The Connecticut legislation began with Ms. Winkler's work as an emergency room nurse, where she said she saw more and more children coming in who were on psychotropic drugs, from stimulants to antidepressants and anti-anxiety medications, and requiring metabolic tests and cardiograms. "Why, unless these drugs have some impact on the other body systems, would we have to do these tests?" she said. Then she began receiving calls from constituents who complained that schools had encouraged them to put their children on drugs, even, in some cases, making it a condition of attending class or after-school activities.

In Millbrook, New York, Patricia Weathers said her son's school told her to put him on Ritalin in first grade. By fourth grade, he was showing signs of severe anxiety, she said, chewing his clothes and paper. When Mrs. Weathers took him off the drugs, she said, the school called the state's office of child protective services and accused her of medical neglect. "You have the school psychologist, the teachers, the principal, all bombarding you, saying this is the only way to go," she said. "I fell for it, and I believe most parents fall for it. They want to do what's right for their child, and if the professionals are telling them this is right, you think, 'They must be right.'"

She, like many parents who think Ritalin is overprescribed, complain that there is no scientific basis for the diagnosis of the disorders for which it is prescribed. "You can't tell me they all have this brain disorder during the school year, when during the summer they're fine," said Mrs. Weathers, who now instructs her son at home.

Search Online With InfoTrac College Edition

For additional information, explore InfoTrac College Edition, your online library. Go to **http://www.infotrac-college.com** and use the passcode from the InfoTrac card that came with your book. Try these search terms: Ritalin, ADHD, hyperactive children, behavioral problems children.

Efficient reading requires the ability to process small bits of information (such as the "translation" of written letters and groups of letters into sounds) in rapid succession. That is, we develop habits of seeing, say, an *f* or a *ph* or a *gh* and saying or hearing an *f* sound in our brains. We have to do this rapidly because these letters are followed by vowels or other consonants that also require decoding. We get into the habit of recognizing word-sized groups of letters in an instant or, at least, of rapidly moving from one letter or group of letters to the next. When we look at a second group of letters, we need to retain the perceptual traces of the first; otherwise, we cannot string them together. Thus researchers also suggest that the cluster of psychological and neurological deficits we find in dyslexia prevents children from performing tasks that require the processing of brief stimuli in rapid sequence (Ben-Yehudah et al., 2001; Habib, 2000).

These psychological-neurological problems may be due—in whole or in part—to genetic factors. But some researchers believe that they may stem from excessive prenatal exposure to the male hormone testosterone. Norman Geschwind and Albert Galaburda (1987) propose that a high level of prenatal testosterone slows growth in the left hemisphere. Males normally are exposed to higher levels of testosterone during pregnancy than females, because their testes secrete it. The view that males are more likely than females to be dyslexic was seen to support this hypothesis, but now, as Shaywitz (1998) argues, it may be that girls are about as likely as boys to be dyslexic. Both observations cannot be correct.

In sum, dyslexia would appear to stem from neurological problems in the brain, not from faulty learning or other psychological problems (such as unconscious conflict). The site of the neurological problems appears to involve structures that are involved in translating visual symbols into sounds. The precise origins of these neurological problems is not yet clear, but current methods of imaging are shedding more light—or at least more irradiation—on the functioning of specific areas of the brain every day.

Remediation

Question: What is done to help children with learning disabilities? Just as there are various explanations of the origins of learning disabilities, there are several approaches to helping children with these problems:

The Psychoeducational Approach This approach capitalizes on children's strengths and preferences rather than on aiming to correct assumed, underlying cognitive deficiencies. For example, a child who retains auditory information better than visual information might be taught verbally by means of tape recordings rather than written materials.

The Behavioral Approach The behavioral approach assumes that academic learning is a complex form of behavior that is built on a hierarchy of basic skills, or "enabling behaviors." To read effectively, one must first learn to recognize letters, then attach sounds to letters, then combine letters and sounds into words, and so on. The child is tested to determine where deficiencies lie in the hierarchies of skills. An individualized program of instruction and reinforcement is designed to help the child acquire the skills necessary to perform more complex academic tasks. Typically, parents and schools try to help learning-disabled students by imposing a good deal of structure and rigid rules. But recent research shows that these children may do better in school when teachers and parents provide less control and more reinforcement (Kutner, 1992a).

The Medical Approach This approach assumes that learning disabilities are symptoms of biologically based problems in cognitive processing. Proponents suggest that remediation should be directed at the underlying pathology rather than the learning disability itself. If the child has a visual defect that makes it difficult to follow a line of text, treatment should aim to remediate the visual deficit, perhaps through visual-tracking exercises. Improvement in reading ability ought to follow. One of the more controversial approaches to treating dyslexia involves providing dyslexic individuals with colored lenses that filter out the light of certain wavelengths. Research evidence concerning the use of this technique, developed by Helen Irlen, in improving the reading performance of dyslexic children is mixed (O'Connor et al., 1990; Robinson & Foreman, 1999).

The Neuropsychological Approach This approach assumes that learning disabilities reflect underlying deficits in processing information that involve the cerebral cortex. Remediation involves presentation of instructional material to the more efficient or intact neural systems. Inefficient or damaged parts of the brain are bypassed.

The Linguistic Approach Language deficiencies can give rise to problems in reading, spelling, and verbal expression. Adherents of this approach focus on language deficiencies and instruction in phonics. Language skills are taught sequentially, helping the student to grasp the structure and use of words (Rashotte, MacPhee, & Torgeson, 2001; Torgesen et al., 2001).

The Cognitive Approach This approach focuses on the ways in which children organize their thoughts when they learn academic material. Children are helped to learn by being taught to recognize the nature of the learning tasks, apply effective problem-solving strategies to complete them, and monitor the success of these strategies. Children having problems with arithmetic may be guided to break a math problem down into its component tasks, think through the steps necessary to complete each task, and evaluate performance at each step so that appropriate adjustments can be made. This systematic approach to problem solving can be applied to diverse academic tasks. For example, dyslexic children have trouble breaking words into their constituent sounds. They benefit from tutoring that focuses on this skill (Kolata, 1992d).

In an experiment on instructing children with learning disabilities, Alice Wilder and Joanna Williams (2001) recruited 91 students (59 boys and 32 girls) from special education classrooms in New York City. The New York City Board of Education had certified all the students as being learning-disabled. The authors note that children are usually required to obtain IQ scores of at least 85 so that they can be considered learning-disabled rather than intellectually deficient. They admit that many of the children in this study obtained lower IQ scores. (Guess what? Research methods are sometimes less than perfect.) The study attempted to determine whether special instruction could help the students pick out the themes in stories. A story was read aloud and students were then asked to consider questions such as

Who was the main character?
What was his/her problem?
What did he/she do?
What happened at the end of the story?
Was what happened good or bad?
Why was it good or bad?

Students receiving this form of instruction were more capable of identifying the themes and applying them to everyday life than children who received more traditional instruction. The authors conclude that this sort of "theme identification" program enables children with severe learning disabilities to profit from instruction that is geared toward abstract thinking and understanding. Perhaps we can generalize to note that these results seem to be underscoring the fact that "good teaching helps"—often, if not always. (Why isn't this kind of teaching "traditional instruction"?)

To date, research appears supportive of the linguistic, cognitive, and behavioral approaches to remediation (Koorland, 1986; Wilder & Williams, 2001). It seems that nearly any method that carefully assesses the child's reading skills, identifies deficits, and creates and follows precise plans for remediating these deficits can be of help. Having said that, it seems that no method identified to date provides children with the levels of skills that so many children apply with ease. But reading and other academic skills are important in everyday life in our society, and any advance would appear to be better than none.

Educating Children With Disabilities

Special educational programs have been created to meet the needs of schoolchildren with mild to moderate disabilities. These disabilities include learning disabilities, emotional disturbance, mild mental retardation, and physical disabilities such as blindness, deafness, or paralysis. ***Question: Should children with learning disabilities be placed in regular classrooms (that is, should they be "mainstreamed")?*** Evidence is mixed as to whether placing disabled children in separate classes can also stigmatize them and segregate them from other children. Special-needs classes also negatively influence teacher expectations. Neither the teacher nor the students themselves come to expect very much. This negative expectation becomes a **self-fulfilling prophecy,** and the exceptional students' achievements suffer.

Mainstreaming is intended to counter the negative effects of special-needs classes. In mainstreaming, disabled children are placed in regular classrooms that have been adapted to their needs. The majority of students with mild learning disabilities spend 40% or more of their school day in regular classrooms (Cannon, Idol, & West, 1992).

The mainstreaming of disabled children seems consistent with democratic ideals and the desire to provide every child with an equal opportunity to learn. Mainstreaming also permits disabled and nondisabled children to socialize and interact on a number of levels.

self-fulfilling prophecy An expectation that is confirmed because of the behavior of those who hold the expectation.

mainstreaming Placing disabled children in classrooms with nondisabled children.

©Tony Freeman/PhotoEdit

Mainstreaming

Today, the majority of students with mild disabilities spend at least part of their school day in regular classrooms. The goals of mainstreaming include providing broader educational opportunities for disabled students and fostering interactions with nondisabled children. Mainstreaming often helps, but some disabled children are overwhelmed and even abused in regular classrooms.

The goals of mainstreaming include inspiring disabled students to greater achievements, providing disabled students with better educational opportunities, and fostering normal social interactions between disabled and nondisabled students, so that the disabled will have a better chance of fitting into society as adults.

While the goals of mainstreaming are laudable, observations of the results are mixed. There is some suggestion that disabled children may achieve more when they are mainstreamed (Truesdell & Abramson, 1992). But other studies suggest that many disabled children do not fare well in regular classrooms (Brady et al., 1988; Chira, 1993b). Rather than inspiring them to greater achievements, regular classrooms can be overwhelming for many disabled students. When low-performing students are taught with all students, their failure may become more obvious (Chalfant, 1989). In fact, higher-performing disabled students appear to gain more from regular classes, whereas lower-performing students gain more from segregated classes (Cole et al., 1991).

Nor is it clear that placement in regular classrooms spurs socializing with disabled students. Nondisabled students often choose not to socialize with disabled students in these classes (Honig & McCarron, 1988). Ironically, disabled students sometimes become further isolated and stigmatized. However, efforts to improve the social skills of children with disabilities have met with some success (Hundert & Houghton, 1992; York et al, 1992). These efforts generally appear to be more effective with children who are mainstreamed into regular classes than they are with those who are in special classes (McIntosh, Vaughn, & Zaragora, 1991).

Recent research indicates that structured teaching techniques and appropriate resource support are associated with successful mainstream placement of disabled children (Center, Ward, & Ferguson, 1991). But we need to learn more about what types of teacher training and what types of preparation for nondisabled students will ease the way of the disabled child in the regular classroom. We also need to find out what sorts of supplementary educational experiences are needed to round out the educational and social experiences of mainstreamed children (Murphy & Hicks-Stewart, 1991; Simmons, Fuchs, & Fuchs, 1991). Until we have this information, the results of mainstreaming may remain mixed.

Our examination of educational programs for children with disabilities leads us next into an investigation of cognitive development in middle childhood and the conditions that influence it. We address this topic in Chapter 12.

Review

(15) Children with attention-deficit ________ disorder (ADHD) show developmentally inappropriate or excessive inattention, impulsivity, and hyperactivity. (16) ADHD is more common among (boys or girls?). (17) ADHD (does or does not?) tend to run in families. (18) Nigg notes that ADHD is widely thought to be caused by inefficient (excitatory or inhibitory?) processes. (19) Children with ADHD are likely to be treated with (stimulants or tranquilizers?). (20) Learning ________ are a group of disorders characterized by inadequate development of specific academic, language, and speech skills. (21) Difficulty learning to read is called ________. (22) Current views of dyslexia focus on the ways that ________ problems may contribute to the perceptual problems we find in dyslexic children. (23) Dyslexia (does or does not?) tend to run in families. (24) Children with dyslexia may learn the alphabet in the ________ hemisphere. (25) Research evidence (does or does not?) appear to support the linguistic, cognitive, and behavioral approaches to remediation of dyslexia.

Pulling It Together: What are the pluses and minuses of mainstreaming children with ADHD and learning disabilities?

Recite Recite Recite Recite

1. What patterns of growth occur in middle childhood?

Children tend to gain a little over 2 inches in height and 5 to 7 pounds in weight per year during middle childhood. Children become less stocky and more slender. Boys are slightly heavier and taller than girls through the ages of 9 or 10, when girls begin the adolescent growth spurt and surpass boys in height and weight. At around age 11, boys develop relatively more muscle tissue and females develop more fatty tissue. Children have increasing caloric needs in middle childhood.

2. How many children in the United States are obese? Why are they obese?

About one quarter of American children are obese, and the prevalence of obesity has been increasing. Obese children usually do not "outgrow" "baby fat." During childhood, heavy children are often rejected by their peers. Obesity in adolescence can lead to chronic illness and early death in adulthood. Heredity plays a role in obesity. Children with high numbers of fat cells feel food-deprived sooner than other children. Obese parents may model poor exercise habits, encourage overeating, and keep fattening foods in the home. Sedentary habits, such as extensive watching of television, also foster obesity.

3. What changes in motor development occur in middle childhood?

Middle childhood is marked by increases in the child's speed, strength, agility, and balance. During middle childhood, children show regular improvement in gross motor skills and are often eager to participate in athletic activities, such as ballgames, that require movement of large muscles. Muscles grow stronger and pathways that connect the cerebellum to the cortex become more myelinated. Reaction time gradually decreases from early childhood to adolescence. Fine motor skills also improve, with 6–7-year-olds tying shoelaces and holding pencils as adults do.

4. Are there gender differences in motor skills?

Boys have slightly greater overall strength—especially forearm strength—whereas girls have better coordination and flexibility, which is valuable in dancing, balancing, and gymnastics. Boys generally receive more encouragement than girls to excel in athletics.

5. Are children in the United States physically fit? If not, why not?

Most children in the United States are not physically fit. One reason is the amount of time spent watching television. Schools and parents also tend to focus on sports such as baseball and football, which are not very likely to promote cardiovascular fitness.

6. How does run-of-the-mill failure to "listen" to adults differ from attention-deficit hyperactivity disorder?

Attention-deficit hyperactivity disorder (ADHD) involves developmentally inappropriate or excessive inattention, impulsivity, and hyperactivity. The hyperactivity and restlessness of children with ADHD impair their ability to function in school. ADHD tends to be overdiagnosed and overmedicated.

7. What are the causes of ADHD?

ADHD runs in families and coexists with other psychological disorders and problems. There are often abnormalities in the brain, suggestive of "minimal brain damage" or "minimal brain dysfunction." Children with ADHD do not inhibit, or control, impulses that most children do control, suggesting poor executive control in the brain.

8. Children with ADHD are often treated with stimulants. Why?

Stimulants are used to treat children with ADHD in order to stimulate the cerebral cortex to inhibit more primitive areas of the brain. Stimulants increase the attention span and academic performance of children with ADHD, but there are side effects and the medicines may be used too often. Cognitive behavioral therapy is also of some help in teaching children self-control.

9. What are learning disabilities?

Learning disabilities are disorders characterized by inadequate development of specific academic, language, and speech skills. Children are usually diagnosed with a learning disability when their performance is below that expected for their age and

Recite Recite Recite Recite

level of intelligence and when there are no other apparent handicaps that would cause the disability. Learning disabilities tend to persist through life.

10. What are the origins of dyslexia?

Current views of dyslexia focus on the ways that neurological problems may contribute to perceptual problems. Dyslexic children frequently show behaviors found among children with brain damage, such as short attention span and difficulty sitting still. Genetic factors appear to be involved since dyslexia runs in families. Perhaps inherited brain damage involves "faulty wiring" in the left hemisphere of the brain, which is usually involved in language.

11. What is done to help children with learning disabilities?

There are several approaches to helping children with learning disabilities: psychoeducational, behavioral, medical, neuropsychological, and linguistic.

12. Should children with learning disabilities be placed in regular classrooms (i.e., "mainstreamed")?

Research evidence on this question is mixed. Some studies suggest that disabled children achieve more when they are mainstreamed. Others suggest that many disabled children find regular classrooms to be overwhelming.

On the Web

Search Online With InfoTrac College Edition

For additional information, explore InfoTrac College Edition, your online library. Go to **http://www.infotrac-college.com** and use the passcode from the InfoTrac card that came with your book. Try these search terms: motor ability in children, physical education for children, obesity childhood, disabled students, learning disabled education, dyslexia.

Visit Our Web Site

Go to **http://www.wadsworth.com/psychology** where you will find online resources directly linked to your book.

Child Development CD-ROM

Go to the Wadsworth Child Development CD-ROM for further study of the concepts in this chapter. The CD-ROM also includes quizzes and additional activities to expand your learning experience.

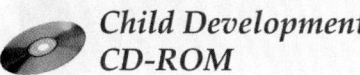

12 Middle Childhood: Cognitive Development

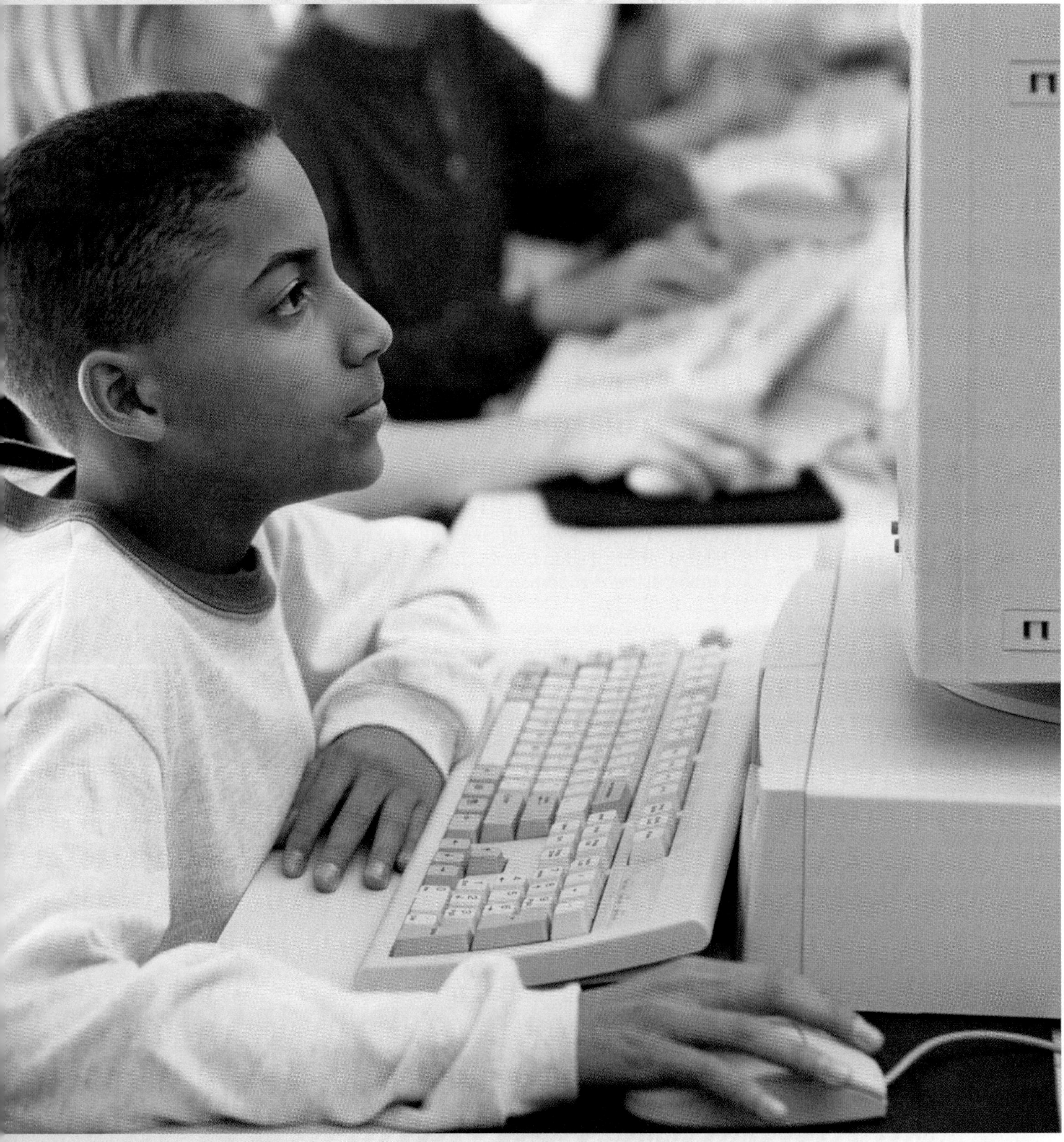

PowerPreview™

Piaget: The Concrete-Operational Stage

- **You have four cats** and six dogs. Do you have more dogs or more animals? (Are you sure?)

Information-Processing Approaches to Cognitive Development

- **Does memorizing the alphabet** require that children keep 26 pieces of information in mind at once?

Theories of Intelligence

- **Madison plays a Bach** piano concerto brilliantly. Does that fact mean that she is intelligent?

Measurement of Intelligence

- **What does the term *IQ*** stand for? Does it mean the same thing as *intelligence*?
- **Two children can answer** exactly the same items on an intelligence test correctly, yet one can be above average in intelligence and the other below average. (Really.)

Intellectual Development

- **Intelligence test scores** taken at the age of 9 correlate very highly with scores at later ages. Does this mean that intellectual development comes to an end at the age of 9?
- **What is meant by mental** retardation? What is meant by giftedness?
- **People from different ethnic** groups tend to obtain different scores on intelligence tests. Why?

Creativity—Flexibility and Fluency in Cognitive Processes

- **What does the word *duck*** mean? What else does it mean? And what else?
- **Are highly intelligent children** creative? (Are highly creative children intelligent?) Just what are the relationships between intelligence and creativity?

The Determinants of Intelligence

- **Do the IQ scores of adopted children** correlate more highly with the IQ scores of their adoptive parents or with the IQ scores of their biological parents? (And why does it matter?)

Language Development

- **Some African American children** can switch back and forth between Ebonics and standard English.
- **Do bilingual children** encounter more academic problems than children who know only one language?

Did you hear the one about the judge who pounded her gavel and yelled, "Order! Order in the court!"? "A hamburger and french fries, Your Honor," responded the defendant.

Or how about this one? "I saw a man-eating lion at the zoo." "Big deal! I saw a man eating snails at a restaurant."

Or how about, "Make me a glass of chocolate milk!"? "Poof! You're a glass of chocolate milk."

These children's jokes are based on ambiguities in the meanings of words and phrases. The joke about order in the court will be found funny by most children when they are about 7 and can recognize that the word *order* has more than one meaning. The jokes about the man-eating lion and chocolate milk will strike most children as funny at about the age of 11, when they can understand ambiguities in grammatical structure.

Children make enormous strides in their cognitive development during the middle childhood years. Their thought processes and language become more logical and more complex.

In this chapter, we follow the course of cognitive development in middle childhood. First, we examine Piaget's cognitive developmental view. We then consider the information-processing approach that has been stimulated by our experience with that high-tech phenomenon, the computer. We next examine the development of intelligence, various ways of measuring it, and the roles of heredity and environment in shaping it. Finally, we turn to the development of language.

Piaget: The Concrete-Operational Stage

Click *Cognition* in the Child and Adolescent CD-ROM for more on the Concrete-Operational stage.

According to Piaget, the typical child is entering the stage of **concrete operations** by the age of 7. ***Question: What is meant by the stage of concrete operations?*** In the stage of concrete operations, which lasts until about the age of 12, children show the beginnings of the capacity for adult logic. However, their thought processes, or operations, generally involve tangible objects rather than abstract ideas. This is why we refer to their thinking as "concrete."

The thinking of the concrete-operational child is characterized by **reversibility** and flexibility. Consider adding the numbers 2 and 3 to get 5. This is an example of an operation. The operation is reversible in that the child can then subtract 2 from 5 to get 3. There is flexibility in that the child can also subtract 3 from 5 to get the number 2. To the concrete-operational child, adding and subtracting are not simply rote activities. The concrete-operational child recognizes that there are certain relationships among numbers—that operations can be carried out according to certain rules. This understanding lends concrete-operational thought flexibility and reversibility.

Reflect

What is the relationship between the concepts of conservation and reversibility?

Concrete-operational children are less *egocentric.* Their abilities to take on the roles of others and view the world, and themselves, from other peoples' perspectives are greatly expanded. They recognize that people see things in different ways due to different situations and different sets of values.

As compared with preoperational children, who can focus on only one dimension of a problem at a time, concrete-operational children can engage in **decentration.** That is, they can focus simultaneously on multiple dimensions or aspects of a problem. Decentration has implications for conservation and other intellectual undertakings.

concrete operations The third stage in Piaget's scheme, characterized by flexible, reversible thought concerning tangible objects and events.

reversibility According to Piaget, recognition that processes can be undone, leaving things as they were before. Reversibility is a factor in conservation of the properties of substances.

decentration Simultaneous focusing (centering) on more than one aspect or dimension of a problem or situation.

Conservation

Concrete-operational children show understanding of the laws of conservation. The 7-year-old girl in Figure 12.1 would say that the flattened ball still has the same amount of clay. If asked why, she might reply, "Because you can roll it up again like the other one." This answer shows reversibility.

Figure 12.1
Conservation of Mass

This girl is in the concrete-operational stage of cognitive development. She has rolled two clay balls. In the photo on the left, she agrees that both have the same amount (mass) of clay. In the photo on the right, she (gleefully) flattens one clay ball. When asked whether the two pieces still have the same amount of clay, she says yes. Since she is in the concrete-operations stage, her thinking is flexible. She recognizes that despite the change in shape, the mass of the clay has been conserved. Moreover, she understands that the flattening of the clay is reversible; it can be rolled up into a ball again.

The concrete-operational girl is also aware of the principle that objects can have several properties or dimensions. Things that are tall can also be heavy or light. Things that are red can also be round or square, or thick or thin. Knowledge of this principle allows her to *decenter* and avoid focusing on only the diameter of the clay pancake. By paying simultaneous attention to both the height and the width of the clay, she recognizes that the loss in height compensates for the gain in width.

Click *Cognition* for more on conservation.

Researchers have found that children do not develop conservation in all kinds of tasks simultaneously (Kreitler & Kreitler, 1989). For example, conservation of mass usually develops first, followed by conservation of weight and conservation of volume. Piaget referred to the sequential development of concrete operations as **horizontal décalage.** As Piaget theorized, the cognitive gains of the concrete-operational stage are so tied to specific events that achievement in one area does not automatically transfer to achievement in another.

Transitivity

We have asked you some tough questions in this book, but here is the real ogre noted in the nearby "Reflect" item: If your parents are older than you are, and you are older than your children, are your parents older than your children? The answer, of course, is yes. But how did you arrive at this answer? If you said yes simply on the basis of knowing that your parents are older than your children (for example, 58 and 56, compared with 5 and 3), your answer was not based on concrete-operational thought. Concrete-operational thought requires awareness of the principle of **transitivity:** If A exceeds B in some property (say age or height), and B exceeds C, then A must also exceed C.

Reflect

Question of the day: If your parents are older than you are, and you are older than your children, are your parents older than your children? (How do you know?)

Seriation is the placing of objects in a series, or order, according to some property or trait, such as lining up one's family members according to age, height, or weight. Seriation is made possible when one has knowledge of transitivity. Let's consider some examples with preoperational and concrete-operational children.

Piaget frequently assessed children's abilities at seriation by asking them to place 10 sticks in order of size. Children at 4–5 years usually place the sticks in a random sequence, or in small groups, as in small, medium, or large. Children at 6–7 years, who are in transition between the preoperational and concrete-operational stages, may arrive at proper sequences. However, they usually do so by trial and error, rearranging their series a number of times. In other words, they are capable of comparing two sticks and deciding that one is longer than the other, but their overall perspective seems limited to the pair they are comparing at the time and does not seem to encompass the entire array.

horizontal décalage The sequential unfolding of the ability to master different kinds of cognitive tasks within the same stage.

transitivity The principle that if A is greater than B in a property, and B is greater than C, then A is greater than C.

seriation Placing objects in an order or series according to a property or trait.

But consider the approach of 7- and 8-year-olds who are capable of concrete operations. They go about the task systematically, usually without error. In the case of the 10 sticks, they look over the array, then select either the longest or shortest and place it at the point from which they will build their series. Then they select the next longest (or shortest) and continue in this fashion until the task is complete.

Knowledge of the principle of transitivity allows concrete-operational children to go about their task unerringly. They realize that if stick A is longer than stick B, and stick B is longer than stick C, then stick A is also longer than stick C. After putting stick C in place, they need not double-check in hope that it will be shorter than stick A; they *know* that it will be.

Concrete-operational children also have the decentration capacity to allow them to seriate in two dimensions at once. Consider a seriation task used by Piaget and his longtime colleague Barbel Inhelder (see Figure 12.2). In this test, children are given 49 leaves and asked to classify them according to size and brightness (from small to large and from dark to light). As the grid is completed from left to right, the leaves become lighter. As it is filled in from top to bottom, the leaves become larger. Preoperational 6-year-olds can usually order the leaves according to size or brightness, but not both simultaneously. But concrete-operational children of age 7 or 8 can work with both dimensions at once and fill in the grid properly.

As with other dimensions of cognitive development, a number of researchers have argued that children develop seriation ability earlier than Piaget believed and that Piaget's results reflected the demand characteristics of his experiments (Blevins-Knabe, 1987; Matlin, 2002). This may be so, but the *sequence* of developments in seriation and transitivity seems to have been captured fairly well by Piaget.

Class Inclusion

Another example of an operation is **class inclusion.** Class inclusion involves the ability to recognize that one class of things (A) includes several other subclasses (B1 and B2). In the example in Chapter 9 (see page 321), a 4-year-old was shown pictures of four cats and six dogs. When asked whether there were more dogs or more animals, she said more dogs. This preoperational child apparently could not focus on the two subclasses (dogs, cats) and the larger subclass (animals) at the same time.

class inclusion The principle that one category or class of things includes several subclasses.

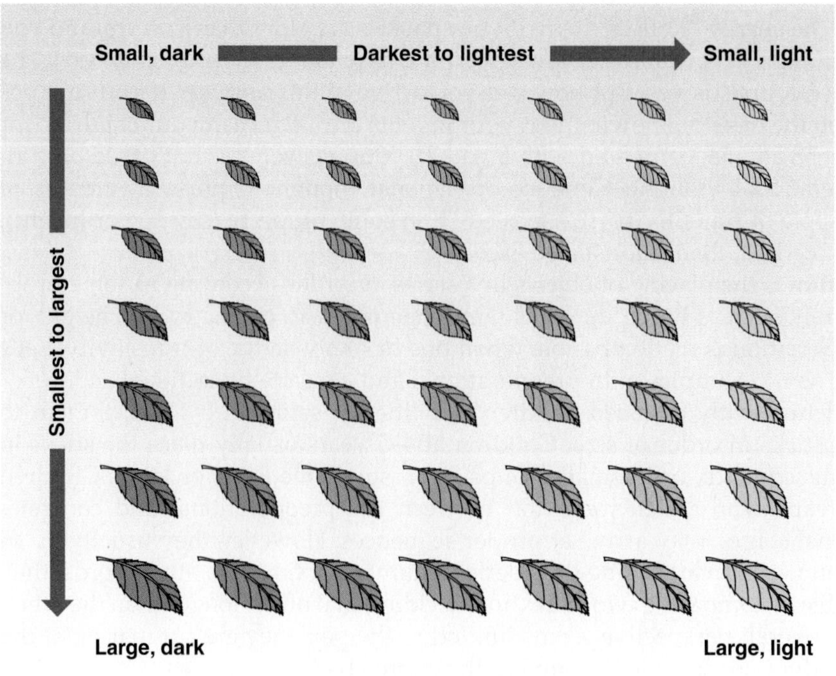

Figure 12.2
A Grid for Demonstrating the Development of Seriation

To classify these 49 leaves, children must be able to focus on two dimensions at once: size and lightness. They must also recognize that if quantity A exceeds quantity B, and quantity B exceeds quantity C, then quantity A must also exceed quantity C. This relationship is called the principle of transitivity.

Concrete-operational children, however, can focus on two dimensions (in this case, classes and subclasses) at the same time. Therefore, they are more likely to answer the question about the dogs and the animals correctly (Chapman & McBride, 1992). But their thought remains concrete in that they will give you the correct answer if you ask them about dogs and animals (or daffodils and flowers), but not if you attempt to phrase the question in terms of abstract symbols, such as *A*, *B1*, and *B2*.

As with other areas of cognitive development, researchers have taken issue with Piaget's views of the ages at which class-inclusion skills develop, and they have argued that language continues to pose hazards for the children being tested. One review of the literature on class inclusion suggests that many children cannot answer standard class-inclusion questions correctly until they are 10 years old or even older (Winer, 1980).

Applications of Piaget's Theory to Education

Question: Can we apply Piaget's theory of cognitive development to educational practices? It seems that we can (Crain, 2000; Davis, 1991). Piaget pointed out some applications himself. First, Piaget felt that learning is a process of active discovery. Therefore, teachers should not simply try to impose knowledge on the child but should find materials to interest and stimulate the child. Second, instruction should be geared to the child's level of development. When teaching a concrete-operational child about fractions, for example, the teacher should not simply lecture but should allow the child to divide concrete objects into parts. Third, Piaget believed that learning to take into account the perspectives of others was a key ingredient in the development of both cognition and morality. Accordingly, he felt that teachers should promote group discussions and interactions among their students.

Recent Views of Piaget's Theory

Although Piaget's theory has led many psychologists to recast their concepts of children, it has also met with criticism on several grounds. Some researchers have shown that Piaget underestimated children's abilities (see Chapters 6 and 9). In regard to egocentricity, researchers who present preschool children with different

Developing in a World of Diversity

Concrete Operations

Piaget's theory stresses the prominence of maturation in cognitive development. In support of Piaget's view, studies have found that children in many different cultures proceed through the stages of cognitive development in the order he predicted (Dasen, 1977; Mwamwenda, 1992). But the rate at which children move through stages, and the level of performance that they ultimately attain, appears to depend on children's experiences within a particular culture. For example, one study gave conservation tasks to rural Mexican children. Half of the children came from families that made pottery for a living, and half came from families that did not (Price-Williams, Gordon, & Ramirez, 1969). The pottery-makers' children, who had extensive experience working with clay, displayed knowledge of conservation earlier than children from families that did not make pottery.

Formal schooling is another experience that shapes performance on cognitive tasks (Cole, 1992; Rogoff, 1990). For example, school experiences give children practice in categorizing objects, memorizing lists of unrelated items, and engaging in logical problem solving (Rogoff, 1990). An extensive review of studies of cognitive development in African children highlights the important role of environmental factors such as formal education and urbanization (Mwamwenda, 1992). The performance of educated children on concrete-operations tasks was found to be superior to that of uneducated children. Educated African children acquired Piagetian concepts at roughly the same chronological age as Western children. Children without formal schooling typically acquired the concepts about 2 years later than educated children. The performance of urban African children was superior to that of rural children. Mwamwenda (1992) suggests that urban areas, with their blend of different cultures, languages, and lifestyles, create an enriched environment that enhances children's cognitive development.

task demands arrive at different impressions of how egocentric they are. Modified task demands suggest that children are capable of conservation and other concrete-operational tasks earlier than Piaget believed.

It may be that cognitive skills develop more independently and continuously than Piaget thought—not in general stages. For example, children's cognitive skills at a given age show *horizontal* inconsistencies. Conservation does not arrive all at once. Children develop conservation for mass, weight, and volume at different ages. The onset of conservation may be more *continuous* than Piaget's theory suggests—seen in terms of the gradual accumulation of problem-solving abilities, instead of in terms of changing cognitive structures (Flavell et al., 2002). If so, research findings may be more consistent with information-processing theory than with Piaget's theory, as we will see in the following pages.

However, the sequences of development—which are at the core of Piaget's theory—continue to appear to be invariant. While the notion of horizontal décalage is inconsistent with some of Piaget's ideas, it may not refute the heart of Piaget's concepts. The sequence of cognitive change—even within horizontal décalage—appears to remain invariant.

Another criticism of Piaget is the extent to which education can accelerate children's cognitive development. Piaget had allowed that some children develop different capacities earlier than others and that training could foster cognitive advances—although in minor and meaningless increments. This is why Piaget paid little attention to what he called the "American question"—that is, how education could be tailored to accelerate cognitive development. But studies have found that children as young as 4 and 5 can develop conservation as a result of demonstrations, instruction, and practice (Gelman & Baillargeon, 1983). The achieving of a stage several years prior to Piaget's expectations is not a "minor" discrepancy. Such a difference creates problems for Piaget's concept of the timing of cognitive development.

In sum, Piaget's theoretical edifice has been rocked, but it has not been dashed to rubble. Although research continues to wear away at his timing and at his views on the futility of attempting to speed up cognitive development, his observations on the sequences of development appear to remain relatively inviolate.

Review

(1) The typical child enters Piaget's stage of _________ operations by the age of 7. (2) Concrete-operational thinking is characterized by _________ and flexibility. (3) Concrete-operational children are (more or less?) egocentric than preoperational children. (4) Piaget termed the sequential development of concrete operations horizontal _________. (5) The principle of _________ holds that if A exceeds B, and B exceeds C, then A must exceed C. (6) Seriation is made possible by knowledge of _________. (7) Class _________ involves the ability to recognize that one class of things (A) can include subclasses (B1 and B2). (8) Piaget felt that learning is a process of active _________.

Pulling It Together: How does ability to focus on various dimensions of a problem at once contribute to the development of concrete-operational thinking?

information processing The view in which cognitive processes are compared to the functions of computers. The theory deals with the input, storage, retrieval, manipulation, and output of information. The focus is on the development of children's strategies for solving problems—their "mental programs."

Information-Processing Approaches to Cognitive Development

Question: What is the difference between Piaget's view of cognitive development and the information-processing approach? Whereas Piaget looked upon children as budding scientists, psychologists who view cognitive development in terms of **information processing** see children (and adults) as akin to computer systems. Sort of. Children, like computers, attain information (input) from the environment, store it, retrieve and manipulate it, then respond to it overtly (output). One goal of the information-processing approach is to learn how children store, retrieve, and manipulate information—how their "mental programs" develop. Information-processing theorists also study the development of children's strategies for processing information (Bjorklund & Rosenblum, 2001; Pickering, 2001).

Although there may be something to be gained from thinking of children in terms of computers, children, of course, are not computers. Children are self-aware and capable of creativity and intuition.

Key elements in information processing include

- Development of selective attention—development of children's abilities to focus on the elements of a problem and find solutions
- Development of capacity for storage and retrieval of information—development of the capacity of memory and of children's understanding of the processes of memory and how to strengthen and use memory
- Development of strategies for processing information—development of ability to solve problems, for example, by finding the correct formula and applying it

Development of Selective Attention

One important cognitive process is the ability to pay attention to relevant features of a task. The ability to focus one's attention and screen out distractions advances steadily through middle childhood (Miller, Birnbaum, & Durbin, 1990). Preoperational children engaged in problem solving tend to focus (or center) their attention on one element of the problem at a time—a major reason that they lack conservation. Concrete-operational children, by contrast, can attend to multiple aspects of the problem at once, permitting them to conserve number, volume, and so on.

Reflect

The world is abuzz with signals. How do you decide what to attend to? How do you decide what it is safe to ignore?

An experiment by Strutt and colleagues (1975) illustrates how selective attention and the ability to ignore distraction develop during middle childhood. The researchers asked children between 6 and 12 years of age to sort a deck of cards as quickly as possible on the basis of the figures depicted on each card (for example, circle versus square). In one condition, only the relevant dimension (that is, form) was shown on each card. In another condition, a dimension not relevant to the sorting also was present (for example, a horizontal or vertical line in the figure). In a third condition, *two* irrelevant dimensions were present (for example, a star above or below the figure, in addition to a horizontal or vertical line in the figure). As seen in Figure 12.3, the irrelevant information interfered with sorting ability for all age groups, but older children were much less affected than younger children.

Developments in the Storage and Retrieval of Information

Click *Cognition* for more on sensory memory.

***Question: What is meant by the term* memory?** Keep in mind that the word **memory** is not a scientific term, even though psychologists and other scientists may use it for sake of convenience. Psychologists usually use the term to refer to the processes of storing and retrieving information. Many but not all psychologists divide memory functioning into three major processes or structures: *sensory memory, short-term memory,* and *long-term memory* (Figure 12.4).

memory The processes by which we store and retrieve information.

Sensory Memory

When we look at an object and then blink our eyes, the visual impression of the object lasts for a fraction of a second in what is called **sensory memory,** or the **sensory register.** Then the "trace" of the stimulus decays.

sensory memory The structure of memory first encountered by sensory input. Information is maintained in sensory memory only for a fraction of a second.

sensory register Another term for sensory memory.

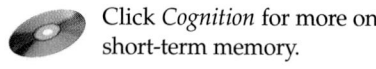

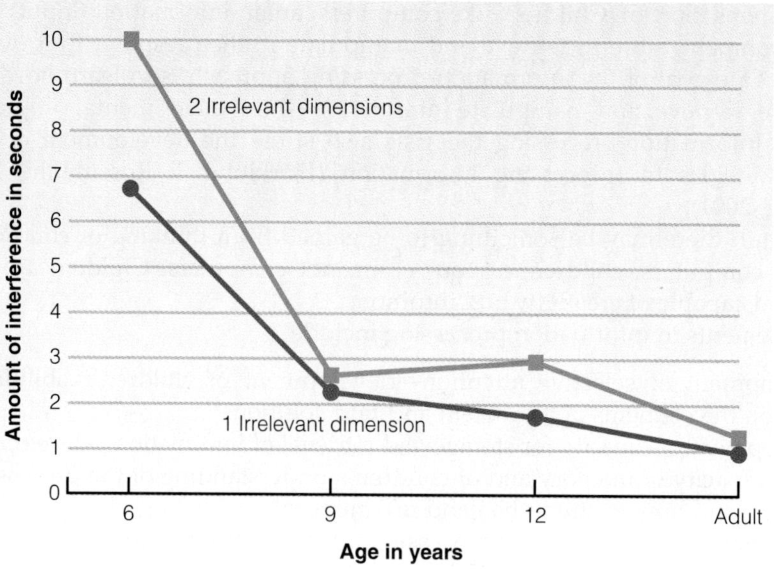

Figure 12.3
Development of the Ability to Ignore Distractions

Strutt and his colleagues (1975) demonstrated how the ability to ignore distraction develops during middle childhood. They asked children to sort a deck of cards as quickly as possible on the basis of figures shown on each card. In one condition, no irrelevant dimension was present. In a second condition, one irrelevant dimension was present; and in a third condition, two irrelevant dimensions were present. The effect of irrelevant dimensions on sorting speed was determined by subtracting the speed of the sort in the no-irrelevant-dimension condition from the speed of the other two conditions. As shown here, irrelevant information interfered with sorting ability for all age groups, but older children were less affected than younger ones.
Source: Strutt et al., 1975.

Short-Term Memory

When children focus their attention on a stimulus in the sensory register, it will tend to be retained in **short-term memory** for up to 30 seconds or so after the trace of the stimulus decays. Ability to maintain information in short-term memory depends on cognitive strategies as well as basic capacity to continue to perceive a vanished stimulus. According to Susan Gathercole (1998), memory function in middle childhood seems largely adult-like in organization and strategies and shows only gradual improvement in a quantitative sense through early adolescence.

Click *Cognition* for more on short-term memory.

Auditory stimuli can be maintained longer in short-term memory than can visual stimuli. For this reason, one strategy for promoting memory is to **encode** visual stimuli as sounds, or auditory stimulation. Then the sounds can be repeated out loud or mentally. That is, the sounds can be **rehearsed.**

Encoding visual material is an example of a cognitive *strategy* that enhances the ability to recall that material. Older children are more successful than younger children at recalling information, both because of improvements in the basic capacities of their short-term memories and because of their sophistication in employing strategies for enhancing memory.

short-term memory The structure of memory that can hold a sensory stimulus for up to 30 seconds after the trace decays.

encode To transform sensory input into a form that is more readily processed.

rehearse Repeat.

Capacity of Short-Term Memory The basic capacity of the short-term memory may be described in terms of the number of "bits" or chunks of information that may be kept in memory at once. To remember a new phone number, for example, one must keep seven chunks of information in short-term memory simultaneously—that is, one must rehearse them consecutively.

Classic research shows that the typical adult can keep about seven chunks of information—plus or minus two—in short-term memory at a time (Miller, 1956).

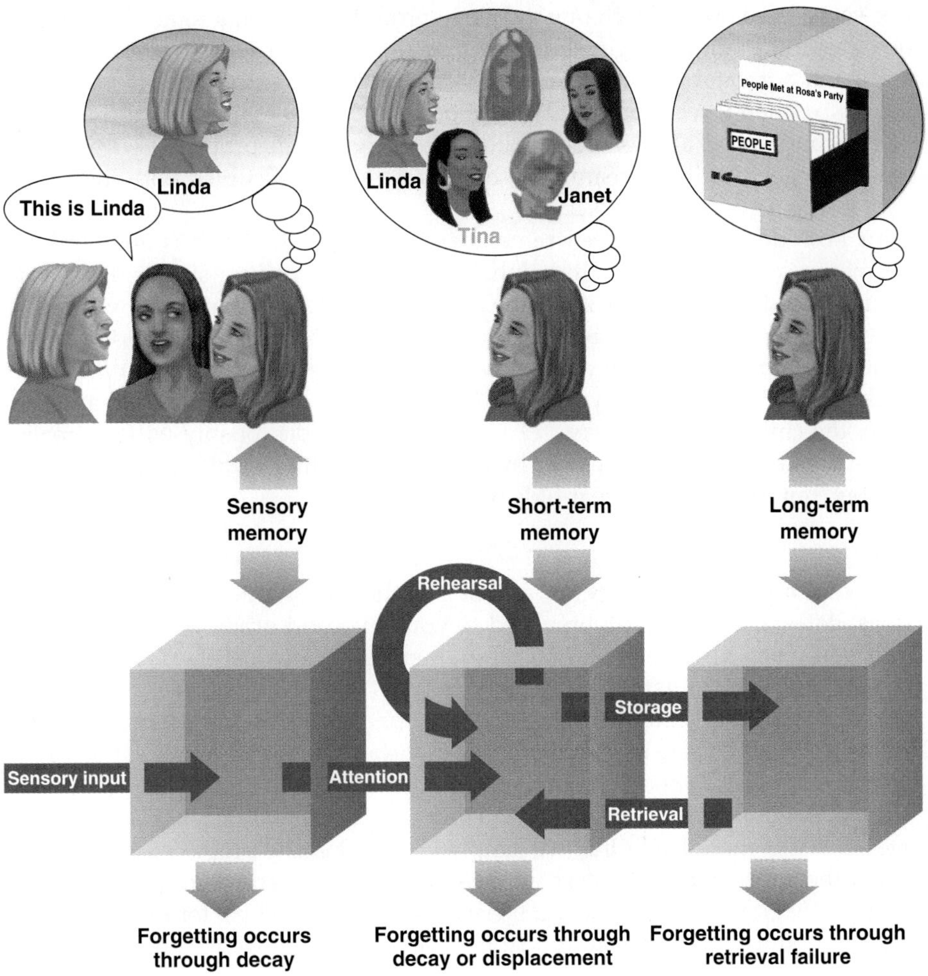

Figure 12.4
The Structure of Memory

Many psychologists divide memory into three processes, or "structures." Sensory information enters the registers of sensory memory, where memory traces are held briefly before decaying. If we attend to the information, much of it is transferred to short-term memory, where it may decay or be displaced if it is not transferred to long-term memory. We usually use rehearsal (repetition) or elaborative strategies to transfer memories to long-term memory. Once in long-term memory, memories may be retrieved through appropriate search strategies. But if information is organized poorly or we cannot find cues to retrieve it, it may be "lost" for all practical purposes.

As measured by the ability to recall digits, the typical 5–6-year-old can work on two chunks of information at a time. The ability to recall series of digits improves throughout middle childhood, and 15-year-olds, like adults, can keep about seven chunks of information in short-term memory at the same time (Cowan et al., 1999, 2000; Pascual-Leone, 1970).

Case's View Robbie Case's information-processing view focuses on children's capacity for memory and their use of cognitive strategies, such as the way in which they focus their attention (Case, 1985, 1992). He notes, for example, that certain Piagetian tasks require several cognitive strategies instead of one and that young children frequently fail at such tasks because they cannot simultaneously hold many pieces of information in their short-term memories. Put another way, preschoolers can solve problems that have only one or two steps, whereas older children can retain information from earlier steps as they proceed to subsequent steps.

Case suggests that older children learn to handle information more quickly, more efficiently, and more automatically. The younger child may have to count three sets of two objects each one by one in order to arrive at a total of six objects. The older child, with a larger short-term memory, familiarity with multiplication tables, and a greater perceptual experience, is likely to automatically arrive at a total of six when three groups of two are perceived. Automaticity in adding, multiplying, and so on allows older children to solve math problems with several steps. Younger children, meanwhile, become lengthily occupied with individual steps, losing sight of the whole.

But how do young children remember the alphabet, which is 26 chunks of information? Children learn the alphabet by **rote learning**—simple associative learning based on repetition. After the alphabet is repeated many, many times, *M* triggers the letter *N*, *N* triggers *O*, and so on. The typical 3-year-old who has learned the alphabet by rote will not be able to answer the question "What letter comes after *N*?" However, if you recite "*H, I, J, K, L, M, N*" with the child and then pause, the child is likely to say, "*O, P.*" The 3-year-old probably will not realize that he or she can find the answer by using the cognitive strategy of reciting the alphabet, but many 5- or 6-year-olds will.

Long-Term Memory

Click *Cognition* for more on long-term memory.

Think of **long-term memory** as a vast storehouse of information containing names, dates, places, what Johnny did to you in second grade, what Alyssa said about you when you were 12. Long-term memories may last days, years, or, for practical purposes, a lifetime.

Questions: How much information can be stored in long-term memory? How is it "filed"? There is no known limit to the amount of information that can be stored in long-term memory. From time to time it may seem that we have forgotten, or lost, a long-term memory, such as the names of elementary or high school classmates. But it is more likely that we simply cannot find the proper cues to help us retrieve the information. It is "lost" in the same way as when we misplace an object but know that it is still in the house. It remains there somewhere for the finding.

How is information transferred from short-term memory to long-term memory? Rehearsal is one method. Older children are more likely than younger children to use rehearsal (Hutton & Towse, 2001; Lehman et al., 2001). But pure rehearsal, with no attempt to make information meaningful by linking it to past learning, is no guarantee the information will be stored permanently.

Reflect

The text asks, "How is information transferred from short-term memory to long-term memory?" How is the process analogous to placing information in a computer's "memory" into a computer's "storage" device? What happens if you forget to "save" information in the computer's memory?

A more effective method than simple rehearsal is to purposefully relate new material to well-known information. Relating new material to well-known material is known as an **elaborative strategy** (Matlin, 2002). English teachers encourage children to use new vocabulary words in sentences to help them remember them. This is an example of an elaborative strategy. In this way, children are building extended **semantic codes** that will help them retrieve their meanings in the future.

Before we proceed to the next section, here's a question for you. Which of the following words is spelled correctly: *retreival* or *retrieval*? The spellings sound alike, so an acoustic code for reconstructing the correct spelling would not be of help. But a semantic code, such as the spelling rule "*i* before *e* except after *c*," would allow you to reconstruct the correct spelling: retr*ie*val. This is why children are taught rules and principles. Of course, whether these rules are retrieved in the appropriate situation is another issue.

Organization in Long-Term Memory

As children's knowledge of concepts advances, the storehouse of their long-term memory becomes gradually organized according to categories. Preschoolers tend to organize their memories by grouping objects that share the same function (Lucariello & Nelson, 1985). "Toast" may be grouped with "peanut butter sandwich," because they are both edible. Only during the early elementary school years are toast and peanut butter likely to be joined into a single category with the term *food* applied to both.

David Bjorklund and Melanie de Marchena (1984) found that as children advanced from the first grade to the seventh grade, they became as likely to

rote learning Learning by repetition.

long-term memory The memory structure capable of relatively permanent storage of information.

elaborative strategy A method for increasing retention of new information by relating it to well-known information.

semantic code A code based on the meaning of information.

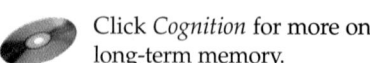

remember the names of animals that are linked categorically (for example, dog and rabbit) as associatively (for example, dog and cat). This finding suggests that the seventh-grade children were more likely to include dogs and rabbits (and cats) in the same category ("animals"), whereas the first-graders were more likely to link dogs and cats just on the basis of their usually going together around the house.

When items are correctly categorized in long-term memory, children and adults are also more likely to recall accurate information about them. For instance, do you "remember" whether whales breathe underwater? If you did not know that whales are mammals, or knew nothing about mammals, a correct answer might depend on some remote instance of rote learning. You might recall some details from a documentary on whales, for example. But if you did know that whales are mammals, you would be able to "remember" (or reconstruct the fact) that whales do not breathe underwater because mammals breathe air.

If children have incorrectly classified whales as fish, they might search their "memories" and construct the incorrect answer that whales do breathe underwater. Correct categorization, in sum, expands children's knowledge and allows them to retrieve information more readily. As they develop, children's knowledge becomes increasingly organized to form complex hierarchies of concepts.

But it has also been shown that when the knowledge of children in a particular area surpasses that of adults, the children show superior capacity to store and retrieve related information. For example, studies have found that chess experts were superior to novice chess players at remembering where chess pieces had been placed on the board (Gobet & Simon, 2000; Saariluoma, 2001). This may not surprise you, until you learn that in these studies, the experts were 8–to-12-year-old children, while the novices were adults. The point is that enhanced knowledge of relationships between concepts improves memory functioning, so that children can outperform adults in those areas in which they have received special training.

Development of Recall Memory

Recall memory involves retrieval of information from memory. As children develop, their capacity for recalling information increases (Matlin, 2002). Their memory improvement appears to be linked to their ability to quickly process (that is, scan and categorize) the stimulus cues (Case, 1985). The functioning of children's memory is a good overall indicator of their general cognitive ability (Hutton & Towse, 2001).

In one experiment on how categorizing information helps children remember, pictures of typical objects that fell into four categories (furniture, clothing, tools, fruit) were placed on a table before second- and fourth-graders (Hasselhorn, 1992). The children were allowed 3 minutes to arrange the pictures as they wished and to remember as many of them as they could. Fourth-graders were more likely to categorize the pictures than second-graders. The tendency to categorize the pictures was directly related to the capacity to recall them.

Click *Cognition* for more on the development of memory strategies.

When the materials to be remembered fall easily into categories, children are more likely to develop effective memory strategies, which they then transfer to other memory tasks that are less well-organized (Best, 1993). These findings suggest that highly structured school settings may induce children to develop task strategies on their own that they can then apply to other less structured materials or settings.

Research also reveals that children are more likely to accurately recall information when they are strongly motivated to do so (Roebers, Moga, & Schneider, 2001). Fear of poor grades can encourage students to recall information more accurately even in middle childhood. The promise of rewards also helps.

Development of Metacognition and Metamemory

metacognition Awareness of and control of one's cognitive abilities, as shown by the intentional use of cognitive strategies in solving problems.

Question: What do children understand about the functioning of their cognitive processes and, more particularly, their memory? Children's awareness and purposeful control of their cognitive abilities is termed **metacognition.** The ability to formulate problems, awareness of the cognitive processes required to solve a problem, the activation of cognitive rules and strategies, keeping one's attention focused on the problem, and checking one's answers—all these are evidence of the emergence of metacognition.

When a sixth-grader decides which homework assignments to do first, memorizes the state capitals for tomorrow's test, and then tests herself to see which ones she needs to study some more, she is engaging in metacognition. Clearly, metacognition has important applications in the field of education. Research suggests that teaching students metacognitive skills improves their performance in reading and other areas (Flavell et al., 2002; Stright et al., 2001).

Click *Cognition* for more on metamemory.

Metamemory is one aspect of metacognition. It more specifically refers to children's awareness of the functioning of their memory processes. Older children show greater insight into how their memories work (Hashimoto, 1991; Kail, 1990). One important reason that older children store and retrieve information more effectively than younger children is the greater sophistication of their metamemory (Kail, 1990; Matlin, 2002).

For example, young elementary school students frequently announce that they have memorized educational materials before they have actually done so. Older elementary school students are more likely to accurately assess the extent of their knowledge (Paris & Winograd, 1990).

Older children also show more knowledge of strategies that can be used to facilitate memory. Preschoolers will usually use rehearsal if someone else suggests that they do, but not until about the ages of 6 or 7 do children use rehearsal without being instructed to do so (Flavell et al., 2002). As elementary school children become older, they also become better at adapting their rehearsal strategies to fit the characteristics of the task at hand (Hutton & Towse, 2001; Lehman et al., 2001; McGilly & Siegler, 1990).

As children develop, they also are more likely to use selective rehearsal to remember important information. That is, they more efficiently exclude the meaningless mass of perceptions milling about them by confining rehearsal to that which they are attempting to remember. This selectivity in rehearsal is found significantly more often among 15- and 18-year-olds than among 11-year-olds (Bray et al., 1985; 1999).

Reflect

What do you do to try to remember names and telephone numbers? What could you do to improve your memory of them?

If you are trying to remember a new phone number, you would know to rehearse it several times or to write it down before setting out to do a series of math problems. However, 5-year-olds, asked whether it would make a difference if they jotted the number down before or after doing the math problems, do not reliably report that doing the problems first would matter. Ten-year-olds, however, are aware that new mental activities (the math problems) can interfere with old ones (trying to remember the telephone number) and usually suggest jotting the number down before attempting the math problems.

Your metamemory is advanced to the point, of course, where you recognize that it would be poor judgment to read this book while watching *General Hospital* or fantasizing about your next vacation, isn't it?

We have seen that children's memory improves throughout middle childhood. But how good is the memory of children for observed or experienced events? For a discussion of this controversial issue, turn to the nearby "A Closer Look."

Review

(9) Psychologists who view cognitive development in terms of ________ processing see children as akin to computer systems. (10) Information-processing theorists study the development of children's ________ for processing information. (11) Ability to screen out distractions (increases or decreases?) through middle childhood. (12) Children (and adults) briefly keep the traces of stimuli in ________ memory. (13) When children focus on stimuli, they can keep them in ________ memory for about 30 seconds. (14) Children can remember visual stimuli longer when they ________ it as sounds. (15) Repetition of sounds or

metamemory Knowledge of the functions and processes involved in one's storage and retrieval of information (memory), as shown by use of cognitive strategies to retain information.

other stimuli is known as __________ learning. (16) __________ rehearsal is the relation of new information to things that are already known. (17) Children can keep about __________ chunks of information in short-term memory. (18) As knowledge advances, children's long-term memory becomes organized in __________. (19) Children's awareness and purposeful control of their cognitive abilities is termed __________. (20) __________ refers to children's awareness of the functioning of their memory processes.

Pulling It Together: How does the development of metacognition help children remember what they have learned in school?

Theories of Intelligence

At an early age, we gain impressions of how intelligent we are as compared with other family members and schoolmates. We think of some people as having more **intelligence** than others. We associate intelligence with academic success, advancement on the job, and appropriate social behavior.

Question: So what is intelligence? Despite our sense of familiarity with the concept of intelligence, intelligence cannot be seen, touched, or measured physically. For this reason, intelligence is subject to various interpretations. Theories about intelligence are some of the most controversial issues in psychology today.

Psychologists generally distinguish between **achievement** and intelligence. Achievement is what a child has learned, the knowledge and skills that have been

intelligence A complex and controversial concept, defined by David Wechsler as the "capacity . . . to understand the world [and the] resourcefulness to cope with its challenges" (from the Latin *inter,* meaning "among," and *legere,* meaning "to choose"). Intelligence implies the capacity to make adaptive choices.

achievement That which is attained by one's efforts and presumed to be made possible by one's abilities.

A Closer Look

Children's Eyewitness Testimony

Jean Piaget, the investigator of children's cognitive development, distinctly remembered an attempt to kidnap him from his baby carriage as he was being wheeled along the Champs Élysées. He recalled the excited throng, the abrasions on the face of the nurse who rescued him, the police officer's white baton, and the flight of the assailant. Although they were graphic, Piaget's memories were false. Years later, the nurse admitted that she had made up the tale.

Children are often called upon to provide legal testimony about events they have seen or experienced. These events often involve instances of alleged child abuse (Koriat et al., 2001). But just how reliable is the eyewitness testimony of children?

Even preschoolers are able to recall and describe personally experienced events, although the account may be somewhat sketchy and lacking in detail (Ceci & Bruck, 1993; McCarthy, 1993). Consequently, the child witness typically is asked questions to provide additional information. Such questions are often leading questions, which suggest an answer to the witness. For example, "What happened at school?" is not a leading question, but "Did your teacher touch you?" is (Kail, 1990).

Are children's recollections susceptible to being distorted by such leading questions? Research suggests that children aged 7–12 can enhance the accuracy of their recollections when they are given the opportunity to reflect and screen out wrong answers (Koriat et al., 2001). It appears that by the age of 10 or 11, children are no more suggestible than adults, but younger children are more likely to be influenced by misleading information (Bruck & Ceci, 1999). Most of this research has studied children's memory for routine or nonstressful stimuli (such as words or pictures). But children in court typically are testifying about stressful and traumatic events, such as molestation. Is a child's memory for such events better or worse than memory for routine occurrences? It is difficult to study this question since it is unethical to deliberately expose children to stressful conditions in experiments. Instead, we have to study children's memory of naturally occurring stressful situations, such as receiving an inoculation or having blood drawn. The results are somewhat mixed. Some research finds that the memory of preschool and school-age children is impaired when they are anxious or frightened (Peters, 1991). Other studies indicate that stress does not affect children's memories (Goodman & Clarke-Stewart, 1991). In fact, very high levels of stress may actually improve children's memory (Goodman et al., 1991).

One hotly debated question is the following: Can children be led into making false reports of abuse? There is no simple answer to this question, as illustrated by a study carried out by Gail gained by experience. Achievement involves specific content areas such as English, history, and math. Educators and psychologists use achievement tests to measure what children have learned in academic areas. The strong relationship between achievement and experience seems obvious. We are not surprised to find that a student who has taken Spanish, but not French, does better on a Spanish achievement test than on a French achievement test.

The meaning of *intelligence* is more difficult to pin down (Neisser et al., 1996). Most psychologists would agree that intelligence somehow provides the cognitive basis for academic achievement. Intelligence is usually perceived as a measure of a child's underlying *competence,* or *learning ability,* whereas achievement involves a child's acquired competencies, or *performance.* Most psychologists also would agree that many of the competencies underlying intelligence manifest themselves during middle childhood, when the child is first exposed to the rigors of formal schooling. Psychologists disagree, however, about the nature and origins of a child's underlying competence or learning ability. Let's consider three approaches to understanding intelligence. Then we shall see how psychologists and educators actually assess intellectual functioning.

Reflect

When did you form an impression of how intelligent you are? Has this impression helped you or hurt you? Explain.

Factor Theories

Many investigators have viewed intelligence as consisting of one or more major mental abilities, or **factors.** ***Question: What are "factor theories" of intelligence?*** For example, Alfred Binet, the Frenchman who developed intelligence testing methods at the turn of the century, believed that intelligence consists of several related factors. Other investigators have argued that intelligence consists of one, two, or hundreds of factors.

In 1904, the British psychologist Charles Spearman suggested that the various behaviors we consider intelligent have a common, underlying factor. He labeled this factor *g,* for "general intelligence." He felt that *g* represented broad reasoning and problem-solving abilities. He supported this view by noting that people who

factor A condition or quality that brings about a result—in this case, "intelligent" behavior. A cluster of related items, such as those found on an intelligence or personality test.

A Closer Look *(continued)*

Goodman and her colleagues (Goodman & Clarke-Stewart, 1991). They interviewed 5- and 7-year-old girls following a routine medical checkup that included genital and anal exams for half of the girls. Most of the children who experienced genital and anal touching failed to mention it when simply asked what happened during the exam. But when asked specific leading questions ("Did the doctor touch you there?"), 31 of 36 girls mentioned the experience. Of the 36 girls who did not have genital and anal exams, none reported any such experience when asked what happened during the exam. When asked the leading questions, three falsely reported being touched in these areas. Goodman and Clarke-Stewart (1991) point out that these results illustrate the dilemma faced by sexual abuse investigators. Their study indicates that children may not reveal genital contact until specifically asked, but that asking may influence some children to give a false report.

Also, research by Stephen Ceci (1993) indicates that repeated questioning over periods of several weeks may lead young children to make up events that never happened to them. In one study, preschoolers were questioned each week for 11 weeks about events that either had or had not happened to them. By the 11th week, 58% of the children reported at least one false event as true.

What are investigators of alleged child abuse to do? Ceci (1993) recommends that interviewers avoid repeated leading or suggestive questions to minimize influencing the child's response.

How Reliable Is Children's Eyewitness Testimony?
This question remains hotly debated. By age 10 or 11, children may be no more suggestible than adults. The findings for younger children are inconsistent, however. Repeated questioning of young children may influence them to give false reports.

excel in one area generally show the capacity to excel in others. But he also noted that even the most capable people seem more capable in some areas—perhaps in music or business or poetry—than in others. For this reason, he also suggested that *s*, or specific capacities, accounts for a number of individual abilities.

This view seems to make sense. Most of us know children who are good at math but poor in English and vice versa. Nonetheless, some link seems to connect different mental abilities, even if it is not so strong as the links among the items that define specific factors. The data still show that the person with excellent reasoning ability is likely to have a larger than average vocabulary and better than average numerical ability. There are few, if any, people who surpass 99% of the population in one mental ability, yet are surpassed by 80% or 90% of the population in others.

The American psychologist Louis Thurstone (1938) used factor analysis with tests of specific abilities and also found only limited evidence for the existence of *g*. Thurstone concluded that Spearman had oversimplified the concept of intelligence. Thurstone's data suggested the presence of nine specific factors, which he termed *primary mental abilities* (see Table 12.1). Thurstone suggested, for example, that we might have high word fluency, enabling us to rapidly develop lists of words that rhyme but not particularly helping us solve math problems.

Reflect

From your own experiences, what seem to be the relationships between general intelligence (g) *and special talents, such as musical or artistic ability? Do you know people who are "good at everything"? Do you know people who are talented in some areas but not in others? In what areas are they talented?*

The Theory of Multiple Intelligences

To psychologist Howard Gardner (1983, 1993), intelligence—or intelligences—reflects much more than logical and problem-solving abilities. ***Question: What is meant by multiple intelligences?*** Gardner refers to each kind of intelligence in his theory as "an intelligence" because they can be so different from one another (see Figure 12.5). He also believes that each kind of intelligence has its neurological base in a different area of the brain.

Three of Gardner's "intelligences" are familiar enough: verbal ability, logical-mathematical reasoning, and spatial intelligence (visual-spatial skills). But Gardner also includes bodily-kinesthetic intelligence (as shown by dancers and

Reflect

Do the talents of dancers, gymnasts, artists, and musicians strike you as various "intelligences"? Why or why not?

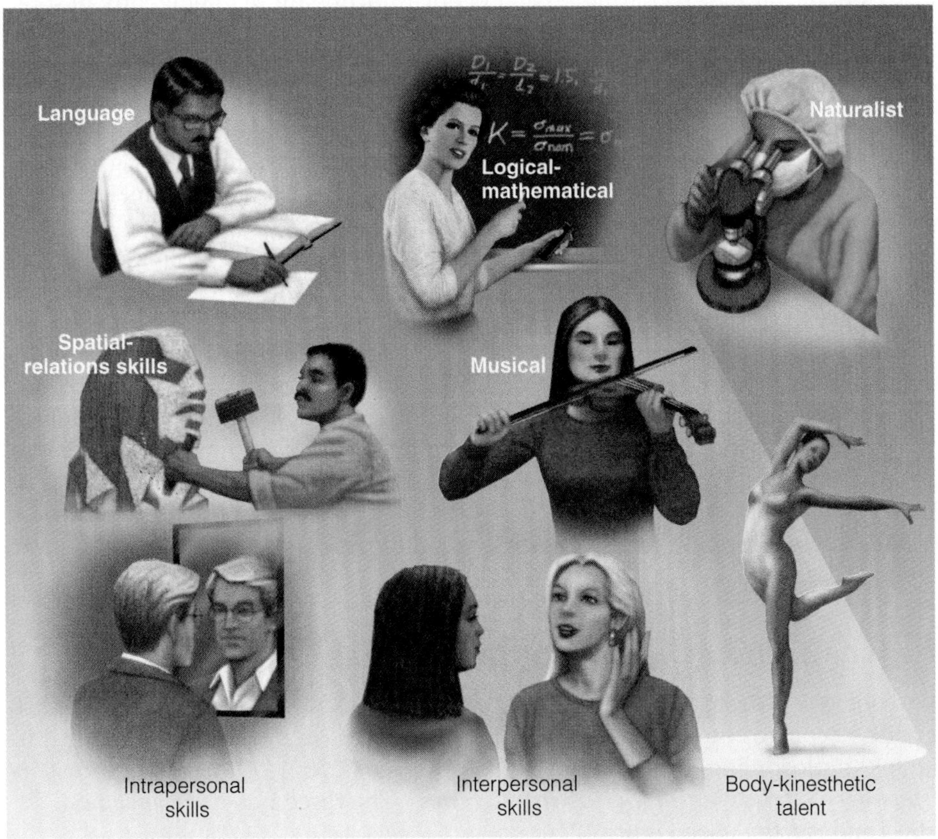

Figure 12.5
Gardner's Theory of Multiple Intelligences

Howard Gardner argues that there are many intelligences, not just one, including bodily talents as expressed through dancing or gymnastics. Each "intelligence" is presumed to have its neurological base in a different part of the brain. Each is an inborn talent that must be developed through educational experiences if it is to be expressed.

TABLE 12.1 *Primary Mental Abilities, According to Thurstone*

Ability	About . . .
Visual and spatial abilities	Visualizing forms and spatial relationships
Perceptual speed	Grasping perceptual details rapidly, perceiving similarities and differences between stimuli
Numerical ability	Computing numbers
Verbal meaning	Knowing the meanings of words
Memory	Recalling information (words, sentences, etc.)
Word fluency	Thinking of words quickly (rhyming, doing crossword puzzles, etc.)
Deductive reasoning	Deriving examples from general rules
Inductive reasoning	Deriving general rules from examples

gymnasts), musical intelligence, interpersonal intelligence (as shown by empathy and ability to relate to others), and personal knowledge (self-insight). Occasionally, individuals show great "intelligence" in one area—as shown by the genius of the young Mozart with the piano, or the island girl who can navigate her small boat to hundreds of islands by observing the changing patterns of the stars—without notable abilities in others. Gardner (2001) has recently added "naturalist intelligence," which refers to the type of scientific insight of a Charles Darwin, and is also considering adding "existential intelligence," which refers to dealing with the larger philosophical issues of life. According to Gardner, one can compose symphonies or advance mathematical theory yet be average in, say, language and personal skills. (Are not some academic "geniuses" foolish in their personal lives?)

Critics of Gardner's view agree that people function more intelligently in some aspects of life than in others. They also agree that many people have special talents, such as bodily-kinesthetic talents, even if their overall intelligence is average. But they question whether such special talents are really "intelligences" or . . . special talents (Neisser et al., 1996). Language skills, reasoning ability, and ability to solve math problems seem to be more closely related than musical or gymnastic talent to what most people mean by intelligence. If people have no musical ability, do we really think of them as *unintelligent?*

Gardner's theory suggests that each kind of intelligence be addressed equally in education to develop a student's capacity to the utmost (Gardner, 1996). In keeping with Gardner's theory, Key School in Indianapolis spends as much time teaching music as teaching the traditional three R's. Children are also placed in small groups to help develop their kinesthetic skills, through dance and athletics, for example, and their spatial and artistic abilities, through drawing and painting, writing and staging plays, and designing puppets and costumes (Murray, 1996). Some educators fear that this approach will undermine the three R's. Others argue that it will enhance performance across subject areas (Ceci, 1996; Krechevsky, 1996). The intellectual effects of such education programs remain to be demonstrated (Fasko, 2001).

The Triarchic Theory of Intelligence

triarchic Governed by three. Descriptive of Sternberg's view that intellectual functioning has three aspects: analytical, creative, and practical.

Psychologist Robert Sternberg (2000) has constructed a three-pronged, or **triarchic,** theory of intelligence, which is reminiscent of a view proposed by the Greek philosopher Aristotle (Tigner & Tigner, 2000). ***Question: What is Sternberg's triarchic model of intelligence?*** The three types are *analytical, creative,* and *practical* (see Figure 12.6).

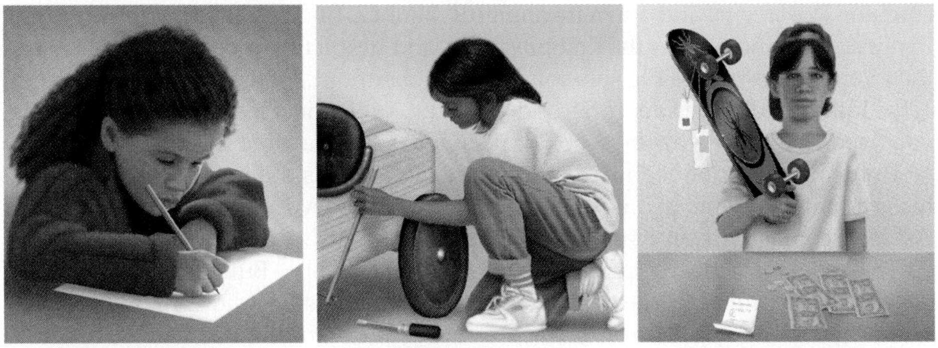

Analytical intelligence
(academic ability)
Abilities to solve problems, compare and contrast, judge, evaluate, and criticize

Creative intelligence
(creativity and insight)
Abilities to invent, discover, suppose, or theorize

Practical intelligence
("street smarts")
Abilities to adapt to the demands of one's environment, apply knowledge in practical situations

Figure 12.6
Sternberg's Triarchic Theory of Intelligence

Robert Sternberg views intelligence as three-pronged—as having analytical, creative, and practical aspects. Analytical intelligence is what we generally consider to be academic ability, which enables us to solve problems and to acquire new knowledge. Creative intelligence is defined by the ability to cope with novel situations and to profit from experience. Practical intelligence enables children to adapt to the demands of their environment.

Analytical Intelligence

Analytical intelligence is similar to Aristotle's "theoretical intelligence" and may be defined as what we generally think of as academic ability. It enables us to solve problems and to acquire new knowledge. Problem-solving skills include encoding information, combining and comparing pieces of information, and generating a solution. Consider Sternberg's analogy problem:

> *Washington* is to *1* as *Lincoln* is to (a) 5, (b) 10, (c) 15, (d) 50?

To solve the analogy, we must first correctly *encode* the elements—*Washington, 1,* and *Lincoln*—by identifying them and comparing them to other information. We must first encode *Washington* and *Lincoln* as the names of presidents[1] and then try to

[1]There are other possibilities. Both are the names of memorials and cities, for example.

A Closer Look

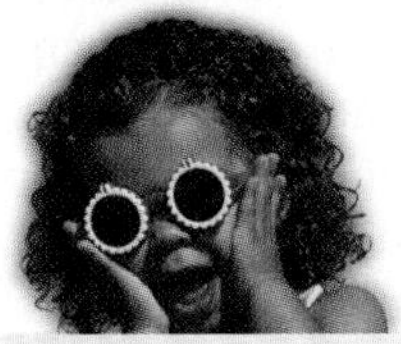

"Emotional Intelligence"

Psychologists Peter Salovey and John Mayer developed the theory of emotional intelligence, which was popularized by *New York Times* writer Daniel Goleman (1995). The theory holds that social and emotional skills are a form of intelligence, just as academic skills are. Emotional intelligence bears more than a little resemblance to two of Gardner's "intelligences"—intrapersonal skills and interpersonal skills.

The theory suggests that self-awareness and social awareness are best learned during childhood. Failure to develop emotional intelligence is connected with childhood depression and aggression. Moreover, childhood experiences may even mold the brain's emotional responses to life's challenges. Therefore, it is useful for schools to teach skills related to emotional intelligence as well as academic ability. "I can foresee a day," wrote Goleman (1995), "when education will routinely include [teaching] essential human competencies such as self-awareness, self-control and empathy, and the arts of listening, resolving conflicts and cooperation."

No one argues that self-awareness, self-control, empathy, and cooperation are unimportant. But critics of the theory of emotional intelligence argue that schools may not have the time (or the competence) to teach these skills and that emotional intelligence may not really be a kind of intelligence at all.

Should emotional intelligence be taught in the schools? Some psychologists believe that "emotional literacy" is as important as literacy (in reading). However, psychologist Robert McCall (1997) echoes the views of other psychologists when he says, "There are so many hours in a day, and one of the characteristics of American schools is we've saddled them with teaching driver's education, sex education, drug education and other skills, to the point that we don't spend as much time on academics as other countries do. There may be consequences for that."

Is emotional intelligence a form of intelligence? Psychologist Ulric Neisser (1997) says that "The skills that Goleman describes . . . are certainly important for determining life outcomes, but nothing is to be gained by calling them forms of intelligence."

combine *Washington* and *1* in a meaningful manner. Two possibilities quickly come to mind. Washington was the first president, and his picture is on the $1 bill. We can then generate two possible solutions and try them out. First, was Lincoln the 5th, 10th, 15th, or 50th president? Second, on what bill is Lincoln's picture found? (Do you need to consult a history book or peek into your wallet at this point?)

To further describe Sternberg's triarchic model, let's follow his examples with his graduate students at Yale. Let's call the first one "Ashley" (*A* is for *analytical*). Ashley scored high on standardized tests such as the Graduate Record Exam (GRE) and had a nearly perfect undergraduate record. But the GRE does not always predict success (Sternberg & Williams, 1997). Ashley did well her first year of graduate school but then dropped in academic standing because of difficulty generating ideas for research.

Creative Intelligence

Creative intelligence is similar to Aristotle's "productive intelligence" and defined by the abilities to cope with novel situations and to profit from experience. The ability to quickly relate novel situations to familiar situations (that is, to perceive similarities and differences) fosters adaptation. Moreover, as a result of experience, we also become able to solve problems more rapidly.

"Carly," another of Sternberg's students (*C* is for *creative*), had obtained excellent letters of recommendation from undergraduate instructors who found her to be highly creative. However, her undergraduate average and her standardized test scores were relatively low when compared to those of other students applying to Yale. Nevertheless, Carly's analytical skills were adequate and, because of her imagination, she surpassed Ashley in performance.

Reflect

Do you know people with "street smarts"? Do street smarts strike you as a kind or form of intelligence? Why or why not?

Practical Intelligence

Aristotle and Sternberg both speak of practical intelligence, or "street smarts." Practical intelligence enables people to adapt to the demands of their environment. For example, keeping a job by adapting one's behavior to the employer's requirements is adaptive. But if the employer is making unreasonable demands, reshaping the environment (by changing the employer's attitudes) or selecting an alternate environment (by finding a more suitable job) is also adaptive (Sternberg, 1997a).

A third graduate student of Sternberg's—"Pam" (*P* is for *practical*)—had the greatest practical intelligence of the three. Pam's test scores and letters of recommendation fell between those of Ashley and Carly. Pam did average-quality graduate work but landed the best job of the three upon graduation—apparently because of her practical intelligence.

There are thus many views of intelligence—what intelligence is and how many types or kinds of intelligence there may be. We do not yet have the final word on the nature of intelligence, but I would like to share with you David Wechsler's definition of intelligence. Wechsler is the originator of the most widely used series of contemporary intelligence tests, and he defined intelligence as the "capacity of an individual to understand the world [and the] resourcefulness to cope with its challenges" (1975, p. 139). To Wechsler, intelligence involves accurate representation of the world and effective problem solving (adapting to one's environment, profiting from experience, selecting the appropriate formulas and strategies, and so on). His definition leaves room for others to continue to consider the kinds of resourcefulness—academic, practical, emotional, even perhaps bodily—that are considered intelligent.

Review

(21) __________ provides the cognitive basis for academic achievement. (22) Spearman suggested that the behaviors we consider intelligent have a common factor which he labeled __________. (23) Thurstone believed that intelligence consisted of nine __________ mental abilities. (24) Gardner argues for the existence of

__________ intelligences, each of which is based in a different area of the brain. (25) Sternberg has constructed a three-pronged theory of intelligence consisting of analytical, creative, and __________ intelligence.

Pulling It Together: What do the various theories of intelligence have in common? How do they differ?

Measurement of Intelligence

There may be disagreements about the nature of intelligence, but thousands of intelligence tests are administered by psychologists and educators every day.

The Stanford-Binet Intelligence Scale (SBIS) and the Wechsler scales for preschool children, school-age children, and adults are the most widely used and well-respected intelligence tests. The SBIS and Wechsler scales yield scores called **intelligence quotients (IQs).** Each of them has been carefully developed and revised over the years. Each of them has been used to make vital decisions about the academic careers of children. In many cases, children whose test scores fall below or above certain scores are placed in special classes for the retarded or the gifted.

It must be noted just as emphatically that each test has been accused of discriminating against ethnic minorities such as African American children and Latino and Latina American children; the foreign-born; and the children of the socially and economically disadvantaged (Okazaki & Sue, 2000). Because of the controversy surrounding IQ tests, probably no single test should be used to make important decisions about a child. Decisions about children should be made only after a battery of tests is given by a qualified psychologist, in consultation with parents and teachers.

Question: What is the Stanford-Binet Intelligence Scale?

Reflect

You have probably taken a number of intelligence tests, most of which were group tests. What were the experiences like? Were you informed as to how well you did on the tests? Do you believe that the test assessed you fairly or arrived at an accurate estimate of your intelligence?

The Stanford-Binet Intelligence Scale (SBIS)

The SBIS originated through the work of Frenchmen Alfred Binet and Theodore Simon about a century ago. The French public school system sought an instrument that could identify children who were unlikely to profit from the regular classroom setting, so that they could receive special attention. The Binet-Simon scale came into use in 1905. Since that time, it has undergone revision and refinement.

Binet believed that intelligence involves a number of factors, including reasoning, comprehension, and judgment. Despite his view that many factors are involved in intellectual functioning, Binet constructed his test to yield a single overall score so that it could be more easily used by the school system.

Binet also assumed that intelligence increased with age. Therefore, older children should get more items right than younger children. Thus, Binet included a series of age-graded questions and he arranged them in order of difficulty, from easier to harder. Items were ordered so that they were answered correctly by about 60% of the children at a given age level. It was also required that they be answered correctly by significantly fewer children who were one year younger and by a significantly greater number of children who were one year older.

The Binet-Simon scale yielded a score called a **mental age (MA).** The MA shows the intellectual level at which a child is functioning. A child with an MA of 6 is functioning, intellectually, like the average child aged 6. In taking the test, children earned months of credit for each correct answer. Their MA was determined by adding the years and months of credit they attained.

Louis Terman adapted the Binet-Simon scale for use with American children. Because Terman carried out his work at Stanford University, he renamed the test the Stanford-Binet Intelligence Scale (SBIS). The first version of the SBIS was published in 1916. The SBIS yielded an intelligence quotient, or IQ, rather than an MA. American educators soon developed interest in learning the IQs of their pupils.

intelligence quotient (IQ) (1) Originally, a ratio obtained by dividing a child's score (or "mental age") on an intelligence test by his or her chronological age. (2) Generally, a score on an intelligence test.

mental age (MA) The accumulated months of credit that a person earns on the Stanford-Binet Intelligence Scale.

The SBIS today may be used with children from the age of 2 onward up to adults. Items at the youngest age levels include placing blocks correctly in a three-holed form board, stating what we do with common objects, naming parts of the body, and repeating a series of two numbers. At older age levels, children are asked to define advanced vocabulary words and are asked questions that require more complex verbal reasoning, as in explaining how objects are alike or different. Table 12.2 shows the kinds of items that define average performance of adults and children in various age groups.

The IQ states the relationship between a child's mental age and actual or **chronological age (CA).** Use of this ratio reflects the fact that the same MA score has different implications for children of different ages. That is, an MA of 8 is an above-average score for a 6-year-old, but an MA of 8 is below average for a 10-year-old.

The IQ is computed by the formula IQ = (Mental Age/Chronological Age) × 100, or

$$IQ = \frac{\text{Mental Age (MA)}}{\text{Chronological Age (CA)}} \times 100$$

According to this formula, you can readily see that a child with an MA of 6 and a CA of 6 would have an IQ of 100. Children who can handle intellectual problems as well as older children will have IQs above 100. For instance, an 8-year-old who does as well on the SBIS as the average 10-year-old will attain an IQ of 125. Children who do not answer as many items correctly as other children of their age

TABLE 12.2 *Items Similar to Those on the Stanford-Binet Intelligence Scale*

Level (Years)	Item
2	1. Children show knowledge of basic vocabulary words by identifying parts of a doll, such as the mouth, ears, and hair.
	2. Children show counting and spatial skills along with visual-motor coordination by building a tower of four blocks to match a model.
4	1. Children show word fluency and categorical thinking by filling in the missing words when they are asked questions such as "Father is a man; mother is a __________?" "Hamburgers are hot; ice cream is __________?"
	2. Children show comprehension by answering correctly when they are asked questions such as "Why do people have automobiles?" "Why do people have medicine?"
9	1. Children can point out verbal absurdities, as in this question: "In an old cemetery, scientists unearthed a skull which they think was that of George Washington when he was only 5 years of age. What is silly about that?"
	2. Children display fluency with words, as shown by answering these questions: "Can you tell me a number that rhymes with snore?" "Can you tell me a color that rhymes with glue?"
Adult	1. Adults show knowledge of the meanings of words and conceptual thinking by correctly explaining the differences between word pairs like "sickness and misery," "house and home," and "integrity and prestige."
	2. Adults show spatial skills by correctly answering questions like: "If a car turned to the right to head north, in what direction was it heading before it turned?"

chronological age (CA) A person's age.

will attain MAs that are lower than their CAs. Consequently, their IQ scores will be below 100.

Today, IQ scores on the SBIS are derived by seeing how children's and adults' performances deviate from those of other people of the same age. People who get more items correct than average attain IQ scores above 100, and people who answer fewer items correctly attain scores below 100.

Question: How do the Wechsler scales differ from the Stanford-Binet?

The Wechsler Scales

David Wechsler (1975) developed a series of scales for use with school-age children (Wechsler Intelligence Scale for Children), younger children (Wechsler Preschool and Primary Scale of Intelligence), and adults (Wechsler Adult Intelligence Scale). These tests, abbreviated WISC, WPPSI, and WAIS, respectively, have been repeatedly revised. The current version of the WISC is referred to as the WISC-III, for example.

The Wechsler scales group test questions into a number of separate subtests (such as those shown in Table 12.3). Each subtest measures a different type of intellectual task. For this reason, the test shows how well a person does on one type of task (such as defining words) as compared with another (such as using blocks to construct geometric designs). In this way, the Wechsler scales help reveal children's relative strengths and weaknesses, as well as provide measures of overall intellectual functioning.

Reflect

What types of items do you believe ought to be on intelligence tests? Do the tests discussed in this section include the types of things that you consider important?

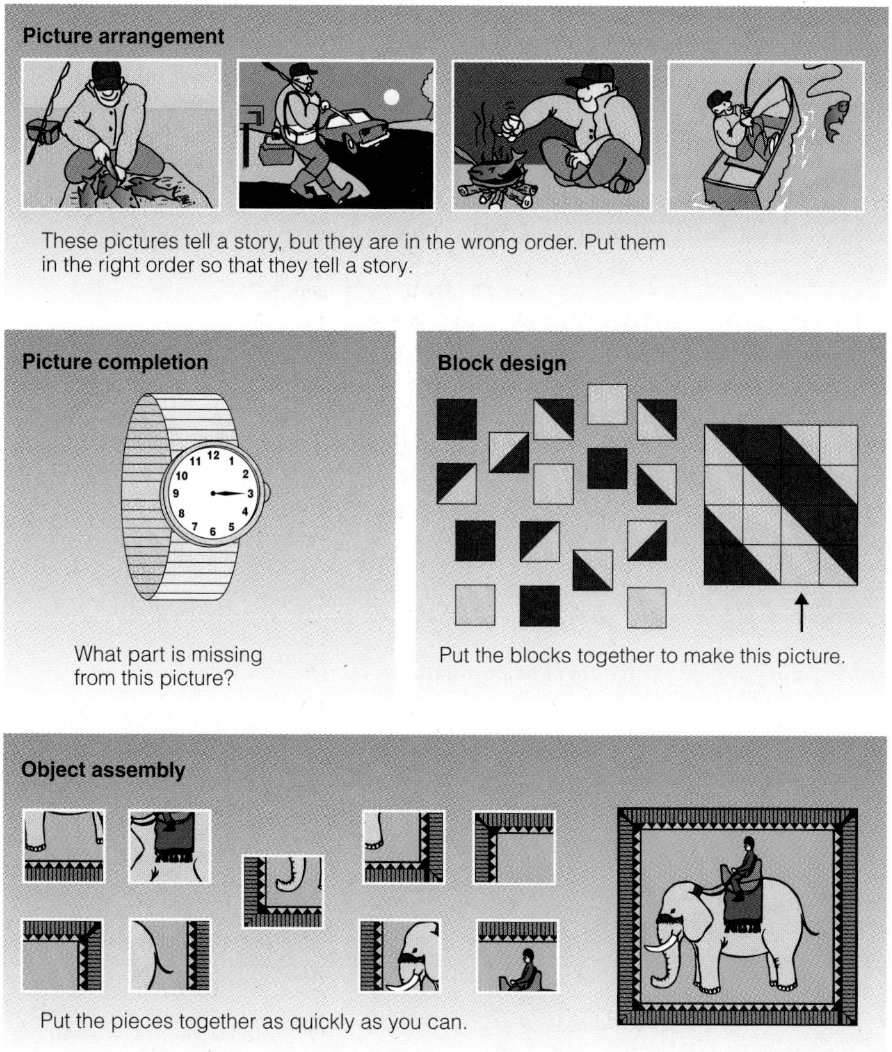

Picture arrangement
These pictures tell a story, but they are in the wrong order. Put them in the right order so that they tell a story.
Picture completion
What part is missing from this picture?
Block design
Put the blocks together to make this picture.
Object assembly
Put the pieces together as quickly as you can.

Figure 12.7 Performance Items on an Intelligence Test

This figure shows a number of items that resemble those found on the Wechsler Intelligence Scales that are used with children.

TABLE 12.3 *Kinds of Items Found on Wechsler Intelligence Scales*

Verbal Items	Nonverbal–Performance Items
Information: "What is the capital of the United States?" "Who was Shakespeare?"	*Picture completion:* Pointing to the missing part of a picture
Comprehension: "Why do we have ZIP codes?" "What does 'A stitch in time saves 9' mean?"	*Picture arrangement:* Arranging cartoon pictures in sequence so that they tell a meaningful story
Arithmetic: "If 3 candy bars cost 25 cents, how much will 18 candy bars cost?"	*Block design:* Copying pictures of geometric designs using multicolored blocks
Similarities: "How are good and bad alike?" "How are peanut butter and jelly alike?"	*Object assembly:* Putting pieces of a puzzle together so that they form a meaningful object
Vocabulary: "What does *canal* mean?"	*Coding:* Rapid scanning and drawing of symbols that are associated with numbers
Digit Span: Repeating a series of numbers, presented by the examiner, forward and backward	*Mazes:* Using a pencil to trace the correct route from a starting point to home

Note: Items for verbal subtests are similar, but not identical, to actual test items on the Wechsler Intelligence Scales.

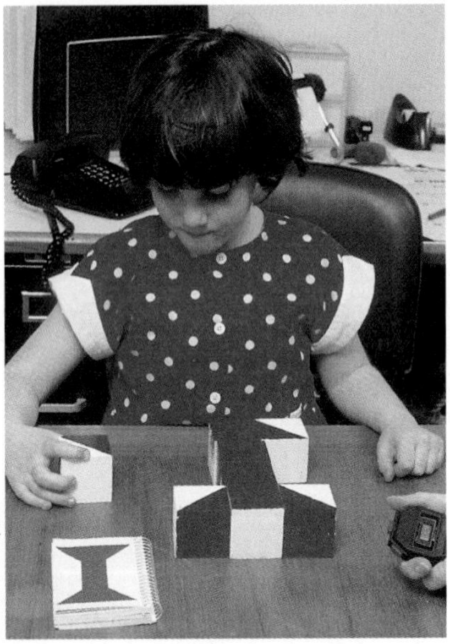

Taking the Wechsler

A number of Wechsler performance subtests, such as the block design subtest shown in this photo, tap spatial relations abilities.

As you can see in Table 12.3, Wechsler described some of his scales as measuring verbal tasks and others as assessing performance tasks. In general, verbal subtests require knowledge of verbal concepts, whereas performance subtests (see Figure 12.7) require familiarity with spatial-relations concepts. Wechsler's scales permit the computation of verbal and performance IQs. It is not unusual for nontechnically oriented college students to attain higher verbal than performance IQs.

Table 12.4 indicates the labels that Wechsler assigned to various IQ scores and the approximate percentages of the population who attain IQ scores at those levels. As you can see, most children's IQ scores cluster around the average. Only about 5% of the population have IQ scores of above 130 or below 70.

Question: Many psychologists and educators consider standard intelligence tests to be culturally biased. What is that controversy about?

The Testing Controversy

I was almost one of the testing casualties. At 15 I earned an IQ test score of 82, three points above the track of the special education class. Based on this score, my counselor suggested that I take up brick-laying because I was "good with my hands." My low IQ, however, did not allow me to see that as desirable. (Williams, 1974, p. 32)

TABLE 12.4 *Variations in IQ Scores*

Range of Scores	Percentage of Population	Interpretation
130 and above	2	Very superior
120–129	7	Superior
110–119	16	Above average
100–109	25	High average
90–99	25	Low average
80–89	16	Dull Normal
70–79	7	Borderline
Below 70	2	Intellectually Deficient

This testimony, offered by African American psychologist Robert Williams, echoes the sentiments of many psychologists. A survey of psychologists and educational specialists found that most consider intelligence tests to be at least somewhat biased against African Americans and members of lower social classes (Snyderman & Rothman, 1990). To fill in a bit more historic background, let's note that during the 1920s intelligence tests were used to prevent many Europeans and others from immigrating to the United States. For example, testing pioneer H. H. Goddard assessed 178 newly arrived immigrants at Ellis Island and claimed that the great majority of Hungarians, Italians, and Russians were "feeble-minded." It was apparently of little concern to Goddard that these immigrants, by and large, did not understand English—the language in which the tests were administered!

The Testing Controversy

Critics of intelligence tests argue that the tests are geared to middle-class European American children who tend to share interests and learning opportunities not available to all children. Some critics recommend that different norms or different tests should be developed for children from different racial and ethnic backgrounds.

Because of a history of abuse of intelligence testing, some states, including California, have outlawed the use of IQ tests as the sole standard for placing children in special education classes (Turkington, 1992).

On the other hand, supporters of standard intelligence tests point out that they accurately measure traits that are required in modern, high-tech societies (Anastasi, 1988). The vocabulary and arithmetic subtests on the Wechsler scales, for example, clearly reflect achievement in language skills and computational ability. It is generally assumed that the broad types of achievement measured by these tests reflect intelligence, but they might also reflect cultural familiarity with the concepts required to answer test questions correctly. In particular, the tests seem to reflect middle-class European American culture in the United States (Allen & Majidi-Ahi, 1991; Okazaki & Sue, 2000).

If scoring well on intelligence tests requires a certain type of cultural experience, the tests are said to have a **cultural bias.** Children reared to speak Ebonics in African American neighborhoods could be at a disadvantage, not because of differences in intelligence, but because of cultural differences (Helms, 1992). For this reason, psychologists have tried to construct **culture-free** or culture-fair intelligence tests.

Some tests do not rely on expressive language at all. For example, Cattell's Culture-Fair Intelligence Test (1949) evaluates reasoning ability through the child's comprehension of the rules that govern a progression of geometric designs, as shown in Figure 12.8.

Unfortunately, culture-free tests have not lived up to their promise. First, middle-class children still outperform lower-class children on them (Anastasi,

cultural bias A factor hypothesized to be present in intelligence tests that provides an advantage for test-takers from certain cultural or ethnic backgrounds, but that does not reflect true intelligence.

culture-free Descriptive of a test in which cultural biases have been removed. On such a test, test-takers from different cultural backgrounds would have an equal opportunity to earn scores that reflect their true abilities.

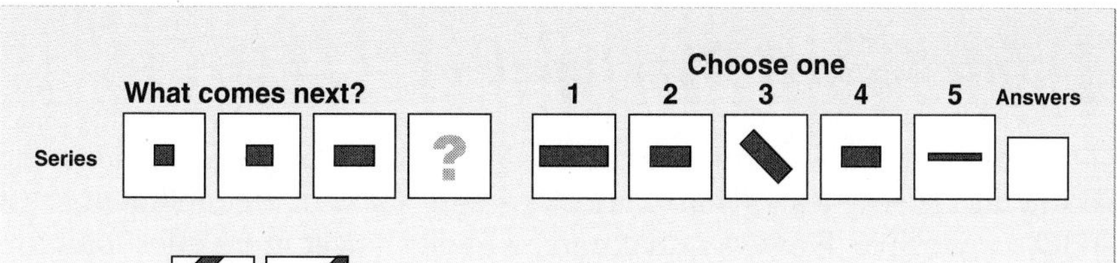

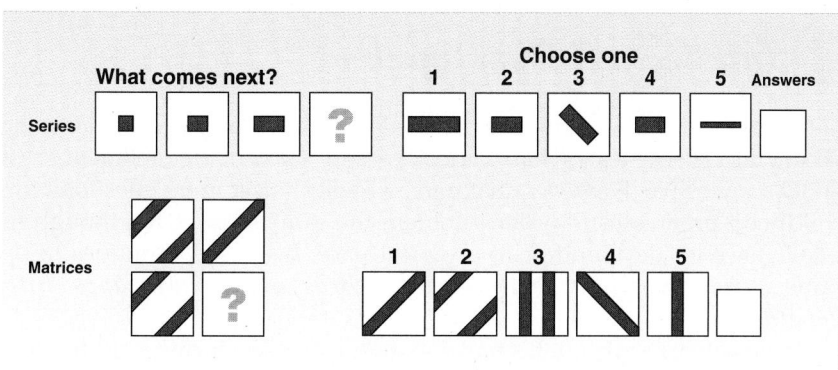

Figure 12.8
Sample Items From Cattell's Culture-Fair Intelligence Test

Culture-fair tests attempt to exclude items that discriminate on the basis of cultural background rather than intelligence.

Reflect

Consider your own ethnic group and the shared experiences of members of your ethnic group. Could you write an "intelligence test" that would provide members of your ethnic group an advantage? What types of items might you include? Would your test be a fair intelligence test, or would it be culturally biased?

1988). Middle-class children, for example, are more likely to have basic familiarity with materials such as blocks and pencils and paper. They are more likely than disadvantaged children to have arranged blocks into various designs (practice relevant to the Cattell test). Second, culture-free tests do not predict academic success as well as other intelligence tests, and scholastic aptitude remains the central concern of educators.

There may really be no such thing as a culture-fair or culture-free intelligence test (Humphreys, 1992). Motivation to do well, for example, might also be a cultural factor. Because of lifestyle differences, children from low-income families in the United States sometimes may not have the same motivation as middle-class children to do well on tests (Zigler & Seitz, 1982). And, as just noted, even basic familiarity with test-relevant materials such as pencils and paper is a cultural factor.

Some of the controversy over using intelligence tests in the public schools might be diffused if they were viewed as broad achievement tests—which, of course, they are—rather than direct measures of intelligence (Elliott, 1988). It would be clearly understood that they measure a child's performance in certain areas on a given day. The focus might be on using follow-up techniques, perhaps behavioral observations or interviews, to more fully outline a child's academic strengths and weaknesses, including factors like motivation and adjustment, and to determine the best strategies to help enhance the child's academic performance (Moses, 1991). Then testing would promote equal opportunity instead of excluding some children from privileges. It is irresponsible to make major decisions about children's lives on the basis of an isolated test score attained in an impersonal group-testing situation.

Review

(26) The Stanford-__________ Intelligence Scale originated through the work of Alfred Binet and Theodore Simon early in the 20th century. (27) The early Binet-Simon scale yielded a score called a __________ age (MA). (28) The IQ states the relationship between a child's mental age and actual or __________ age (CA). (29) The Wechsler scales have subtests that assess __________ tasks and performance tasks. (30) Performance tasks like object assembly and block design assess __________-relations ability. (31) The average IQ score is defined as __________. (32) On the Wechsler scales, about __________% of the population have IQ scores of above 130 or below 70. (33) If scoring well on an IQ test requires a certain type of cultural experience, the tests are said to have a cultural __________. (34) Cattell's Culture-__________ Intelligence Test evaluates reasoning ability through the child's comprehension of the rules that govern a series of geometric designs.

Pulling It Together: Review the kinds of items found on the SBIS and Wechsler scales. How do they reflect middle-class culture in the United States?

Intellectual Development

Sometimes you have to run rapidly to stay in the same place—at least in terms of taking intelligence tests. That is, the "average" taker of an intelligence test obtains an IQ score of 100. However, that person must answer more questions correctly as childhood progresses in order to obtain the same score. Even though his or her intelligence is "developing" at a typical pace, he or she continues to obtain the same score. ***Question: Putting test scores aside, how does intelligence develop?***

Rapid advances in intellectual functioning occur during childhood. Within a few years, children gain the ability to symbolize experiences and manipulate symbols to solve increasingly complex problems. Their vocabularies leap, and their sentences become more complex. Their thought processes become increasingly logical and abstract, and they gain the capacity to focus on two or more aspects of a problem at once.

There seem to be at least two major spurts in intellectual growth. The first occurs at about the age of 6. This spurt coincides with entry into a school system and also with the shift from preoperational to concrete-operational thought. The school experience may begin to help crystallize intellectual functioning at this time. The second spurt occurs at about age 10 or 11, and possible influences are harder to pin down. This spurt may reflect general physical and psychological changes linked to approaching puberty or, perhaps, the shift from concrete-operational thought to the formal operational thought of adolescence (see Chapter 15).

Although there are spurts, once they reach middle childhood, children appear to undergo relatively more stable patterns of gains in intellectual functioning (Schuerger & Witt, 1989; Turkheimer & Gottesman, 1991). As a result, intelligence tests gain greater predictive power at about this time. In a classic study by Marjorie Honzik and associates (1948), intelligence test scores taken at the age of 9 correlated +0.90 with scores at the age of 10 and +0.76 with scores at the age of 18. More recent studies confirm these general findings. This finding does not mean that intellectual development ceases at the age of 9. It *does* mean that the pattern of intellectual development is largely set.

Despite the increased predictive power of intelligence tests during middle childhood, individual differences exist. In the classic Fels Longitudinal Study (see Figure 12.9), two groups of children (1 and 3) made reasonably consistent gains in intelligence-test scores between the ages of 10 and 17, whereas three groups showed declines. Group 4, who had shown the most intellectual promise at age 10, went on to show the most precipitous decline, although they still wound up in the highest 2% to 3% of the population (McCall, Applebaum, & Hogarty, 1973). Many factors can influence changes in intelligence test scores, including changes in the child's home environment, social and economic circumstances, and educational experiences.

Although intelligence-test scores change throughout childhood, many children show reasonably consistent patterns of below-average or above-average performance. In the following section, we discuss children who show consistent patterns of extreme scores—low and high.

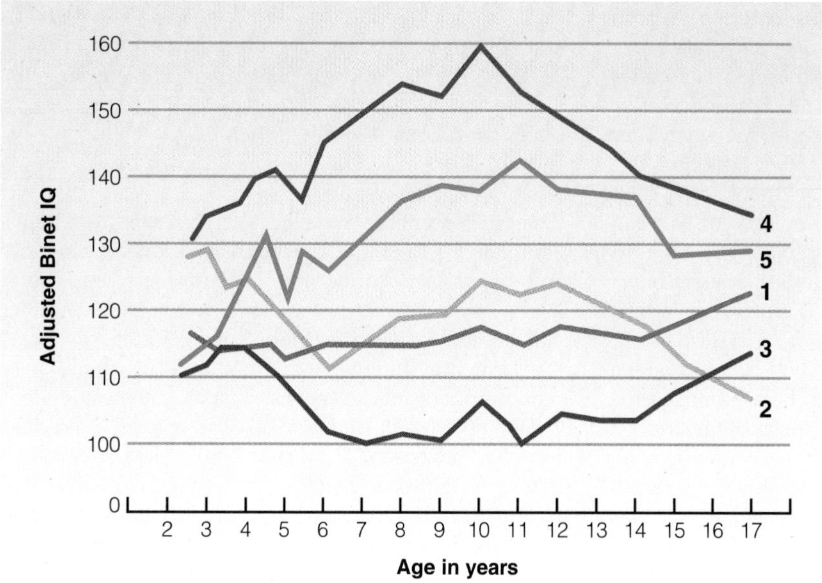

Figure 12.9
Five Patterns of Change in IQ Scores for Children in the Fels Longitudinal Study

In the Fels Longitudinal Study, IQ scores remained stable between the ages of $2^1/_2$ and 17 for only one of five groups—group number 1.
Source: McCall et al., 1973.

Differences in Intellectual Development

The average IQ score in the United States is close to 100. About half of the children in the United States attain IQ scores in the broad average range from 90 to 110 (see Table 12.4). Nearly 95% attain scores between 70 and 130. But what of the other 5%? Children who attain IQ scores below 70 are generally labeled "intellectually deficient" or "mentally retarded." Children who attain scores of 130 or above are usually labeled as "gifted." Both of these labels—these verbal markers of extreme individual differences—lead to certain expectations of children. Both, ironically, can place heavy burdens on children and parents.

Question: What are the socioeconomic and ethnic differences in intelligence? As you can see in the nearby "Developing in a World of Diversity" feature, there are also socioeconomic and ethnic differences in IQ. Individual differences may tax our school systems and create the need for educational innovation, but ethnic and cultural differences have stimulated social and political strife. In this section, we consider mental retardation, gifted and creative children, and social-class and ethnic differences in IQ.

Reflect

Do you know someone who is mentally retarded? What is known about the causes of the retardation? Does he or she have social and other adjustment problems? What kind of educational or training experiences is he or she receiving? Do they seem to be appropriate? Why or why not?

Mental Retardation

Question: What is mental retardation? According to the American Association on Mental Retardation, mental retardation "refers to substantial limitations in present functioning [as] characterized by significantly sub-average intellectual functioning [including an IQ score of no more than 70 to 75], existing concurrently with related limitations in two or more of the following applicable adaptive skill areas: communication, self-care, home living, social skills, community use, self-direction, health and safety, functional academics, leisure and work" (Michaelson, 1993).

Developing in a World of Diversity

Socioeconomic and Ethnic Differences in Intelligence

There is a body of research suggestive of differences in intelligence between socioeconomic and ethnic groups. Lower-class American children obtain IQ scores some 10 to 15 points lower than those obtained by middle- and upper-class children. African American children tend to obtain IQ scores some 15 points lower than those obtained by their European American age-mates (Neisser et al., 1996). Latino and Latina American and Native American children also tend to score below the norms for European American children (Neisser et al., 1996).

Several studies of IQ have confused the factors of social class and ethnicity because disproportionate numbers of African Americans, Latino and Latina Americans, and Native Americans are found among the lower socioeconomic classes (Neisser et al., 1996). When we limit our observations to particular ethnic groups, however, we still find an effect for social class. That is, middle-class European Americans outscore lower-class European Americans. Middle-class African Americans, Latino and Latina Americans, and Native Americans also outscore lower-class members of their own ethnic groups.

Research has also suggested possible cognitive differences between Asians and Caucasians. Asian Americans, for example, frequently outscore European Americans on the math portion of the Scholastic Aptitude Test. Students in China (Taiwan) and Japan also outscore European Americans on standardized achievement tests in math and science (Stevenson, Chen, & Lee, 1993). In the United States, moreover, people of Asian Indian, Korean, Japanese, Filipino, and Chinese descent are more likely to graduate from high school and complete four years of college than European Americans, African Americans, and Latino and Latina Americans (Sue & Okazaki, 1990). Asian Americans are vastly overrepresented in competitive colleges and universities in the United States.

Reflect

What is your own ethnic background? Are there any stereotypes as to how people from your ethnic background perform in school or intelligence tests? If so, what is your reaction to these stereotypes? Why?

There are differences in mathematics ability between high school students in Germany and Japan. Japanese students, who are Asian, outscore their German counterparts, who are Caucasian (Randel, Stevenson, & Witruk, 2000). Most psychologists believe that ethnic differences such as these reflect cultural attitudes toward education rather than inborn racial differences in cognitive ability per se (Neisser et al., 1996). That is, the Asian children may be more motivated to work hard in school. Research shows that Chinese and

Mental retardation is typically assessed through a combination of children's IQ scores and observations of the adaptiveness of their behavior (Michaelson, 1993; Tanguay & Russell, 1991). A number of scales have been developed to assess adaptive behavior. Items from the Vineland Adaptive Behavior Scales are shown in Table 12.5. IQ scores, when used alone, are not highly predictive of how well the child can function.

Most of the children (more than 80%) who are retarded are mildly retarded (see Table 12.6). Mildly retarded children, as the term implies, are the most capable of adjusting to the demands of educational institutions and, eventually, to society at large. Many mildly retarded children are **mainstreamed** in regular classrooms, as opposed to being placed in special-needs classes.

Children with Down syndrome are most likely to fall within the moderately retarded range. Moderately retarded children can learn to speak, dress, feed, and clean themselves, and, eventually, to engage in useful work under supportive conditions, as in the sheltered workshop. However, they usually do not acquire skills in reading and arithmetic. Severely and profoundly retarded children may not acquire speech and self-help skills and remain highly dependent on others for survival throughout their lives.

What causes retardation? Some of the causes of retardation are biological. Retardation, for example, can stem from chromosomal abnormalities, such as Down syndrome; genetic disorders, such as phenylketonuria (PKU); and brain damage (Tanguay & Russell, 1991). Brain damage may have many origins, including accidents during childhood and problems during pregnancy. For example, maternal alcohol abuse, malnutrition, or diseases during pregnancy can lead to retardation in the unborn child.

There is also **cultural-familial retardation,** in which the child is biologically normal but does not develop age-appropriate behaviors at the normal pace because of social isolation of one kind or another. For example, the later-born children of impoverished families may have little opportunity to interact with adults or play with stimulating toys. As a result, they may not develop sophisticated

mainstream To place in educational settings (for example, schools and classrooms) with normal children.

cultural-familial retardation Substandard intellectual performance that is presumed to stem from lack of opportunity to acquire the knowledge and skills considered important within a cultural setting.

Japanese students and their mothers tend to attribute academic successes to hard work (Randel et al., 2000). American mothers, in contrast, are more likely to attribute their children's academic successes to "natural" ability (Basic Behavioral Science Task Force, 1996). That is, Asians are more likely to believe that they can work to make good scores happen, and then they do that work.

Sue and Okazaki (1990) agree. They note that the achievements of Asian and Asian American students reflect their values in the home, the school, or the culture at large. They note that Asian Americans have been discriminated against in blue-collar careers. Therefore, they have come to emphasize the importance of education. In Japan, emphasis on succeeding through hard work is illustrated by the increasing popularity of cram schools, or *juku,* which prepare Japanese children for entrance exams to private schools and colleges (Ruiz & Tanaka, 2001). More than half of all Japanese school children are enrolled in these schools, which meet after the regular school day is over.

Looking to other environmental factors, Steinberg and his colleagues (1996) claim that parental encouragement and supervision in combination with peer support for academic achievement partially explain the superior performances of European Americans and Asian Americans as compared with African Americans and Latino and Latina Americans. Later we will see that other environmental factors, such as stereotype vulnerability, also contribute to these differences.

Who's Smart?

Asian American children frequently outscore other American children on intelligence tests. Can we attribute the difference to genetic factors or to Asian parents' emphasis on acquiring the kinds of cognitive skills that enable children to fare well on such tests and in school?

TABLE 12.5 *Items From the Vineland Adaptive Behavior Scales*

Age Level	Item
1 year 8 months	Removes front-opening coat, sweater, or shirt without assistance
1 year 10 months	Says at least 50 recognizable words
3 years 7 months	Tells popular story, fairy tale, lengthy joke, or plot of television program
4 years 9 months	Ties shoelaces into a bow without assistance
5 years 2 months	Keeps secrets or confidences for more than one day
7 years 7 months	Watches television or listens to radio for information about a particular area of interest
8 years 8 months	Uses the telephone for all kinds of calls without assistance
10 years 2 months	Responds to hints or indirect cues in conversation
12 years 2 months	Looks after own health

Note: Adapted from Vineland Adaptive Behavior Scales, *by S. S. Sparrow, D. A. Ballo, and D. V. Cicchetti, 1984, Circle Pines, MN: American Guidance Service.*

language skills or the motivation to acquire the kinds of knowledge that are valued in a technologically oriented society.

Naturally, we wish to encourage all children to develop to the maximum of their capacities—including retarded children. As a rule of thumb, keep in mind that IQs are scores on tests. They are not perfectly reliable, meaning that they can and do change somewhat from testing to testing. Thus, it is important to focus on children's current levels of achievement in the academic and self-help skills that we wish to impart so that we can try to build these skills gradually and coherently, step by step.

In the case of children with cultural-familial retardation, there is every reason to believe that they can change dramatically when we intervene by providing enriched learning experiences, especially at early ages. Head Start programs, for example, have enabled children at cultural-familial risk to function at above-average levels.

A Musical Prodigy

A gifted child may have outstanding abilities; be capable of high performance in a specific academic area, such as language or mathematics; or show creativity, leadership, distinction in the visual or performing arts, or bodily talents, as in gymnastics and dancing.

Giftedness

Question: What does it mean to be gifted? Giftedness involves more than excellence on the tasks provided by standard intelligence tests. In determining who is gifted, most educators include children who have outstanding abilities, are capable of high performance in a specific academic area, such as language or mathematics, or who show creativity, leadership, distinction in the visual or performing arts, or bodily talents, as in gymnastics and dancing (DeAngelis, 1992; Heller, Monks, & Passow, 1993).

This view of giftedness exceeds the realm of intellectual ability alone and is consistent with Gardner's view that there are multiple intelligences, not one. According to this view, one could compose magnificent symphonies or make advances in mathematical theory while remaining average in, say, language skills.

Much of our knowledge of the progress of children who are gifted in overall intellectual functioning stems from Terman's classic longitudinal studies of genius (Oden, 1968; Janos, 1987). In 1921, Terman began to track the progress of some 1,500 California schoolchild-

TABLE 12.6 *Levels of Retardation, Typical Ranges of IQ Scores, and Types of Adaptive Behaviors*

Range of IQ Scores (Approximate)	Preschool Age (0–5): Maturation and Development	School Age (6–21): Training and Education	21 and Over: Social and Vocational Adequacy
Mild (50–70)	Often not noticed as retarded by casual observer but is slower than most children to walk, feed self, and talk.	Can acquire practical skills and useful reading and arithmetic to a 3rd–6th-grade level with special education. Can be guided toward social conformity.	Can usually achieve social and vocational skills adequate to self-maintenance; may need occasional guidance and support when under unusual social or economic stress.
Moderate (35–49)	Noticeable delays in motor development, especially in speech; responds to training in various self-help activities.	Can learn simple communication, elementary health and safety habits, and simple manual skills; does not progress in functional reading or arithmetic.	Can perform simple tasks under sheltered conditions; participates in simple recreation; travels alone in familiar places; usually incapable of self-maintenance.
Severe (20–34)	Marked delay in motor development; little or no communication skill; may respond to training in elementary self-help—e.g., self-feeding.	Usually walks, barring specific disability; has some understanding of speech and some response; can profit from systematic habit training.	Can conform to daily routines and repetitive activities; needs continuing direction and supervision in protective environment.
Profound (Below 20)	Gross retardation; minimal capacity for functioning in sensorimotor areas; needs nursing care.	Obvious delays in all areas of development; shows basic emotional responses; may respond to skillful training in use of legs, hands, and jaws; needs close supervision.	May walk, need nursing care, have primitive speech; will usually benefit from regular physical activity; incapable of self-maintenance.

ren who had attained IQ scores of 135 or above. The average score was 150, which places these children in a very superior group. As adults, the group members were extremely successful, compared with the general population, in terms of level of education (nearly 10% had earned doctoral degrees), socioeconomic status, and creativity (individuals in the group had published more than 90 books and many more shorter pieces). Boys were much more likely than girls to climb the corporate ladder or distinguish themselves in science, literature, or the arts. But we must keep in mind that the Terman study began in the 1920s, when it was generally agreed that the woman's place was in the home. As a result, more than two thirds of the girls became full-time homemakers or office workers (Rathus et al., 2002). Some of the women later expressed regret that they had not fulfilled their potential. But both the women and men in the study were well-adjusted, with mental illness and suicide rates below the national average. Other, more recent studies are also positive, showing that gifted children tend to be well-adjusted socially and emotionally (Feldhusen, 1989).

Facilitating Development of the Gifted Child Gifted children have more books in their homes and an expanded number of learning opportunities compared with other children. Parents of young gifted children spend more time in reading, play, and stimulating outings with them than do other parents (Fowler et al., 1993; Robinson, 1992). Gifted adults who excel in science, sports, or the arts recall that their parents provided a home environment that was both challenging and nurturing (Tannenbaum, 1992). Responsive, sensitive parenting, but not pushing, appears to facilitate development of the gifted child (Robinson, 1992).

And what of the role of the schools? Educational programs for gifted students typically involve either providing an enriched curriculum or accelerating the student. Acceleration may involve covering all of the normal curriculum but in a shorter period of time (Mills, 1992). The most frequent form of acceleration, however, is skipping a grade.

Some educators are concerned that skipping may cause social and emotional problems (Southern & Jones, 1991). But reviews of the research conclude that skipping and other forms of acceleration are not harmful. In fact, many studies find that acceleration is beneficial to the social and emotional development of gifted children, as well as to their academic progress (Benbow, 1991; Noble, Robinson, & Gunderson, 1992).

Review

(35) Intellectual development during childhood is (rapid or slow?). (36) The first spurt in intellectual growth occurs at about the age of ________. (37) This spurt coincides with entry into a ________ system and with the shift from ________ to concrete-operational thought. (38) Honzik found that intelligence test scores at the age of 9 correlated ________ with scores at the age of 18. (39) Children who attain IQ scores below 70 are generally labeled "intellectually ________." (40) Children who attain scores of 130 or above are usually labeled as "________." (41) Most children who are retarded are (profoundly or mildly?) retarded. (42) In ________-familial retardation, the child is biologically normal but does not develop normally because of social isolation. (43) Classic longitudinal research begun by ________ found that gifted children tend to develop into successful adults. (44) Lower-class children in the United States obtain IQ scores some ________ points lower than those obtained by middle- and upper-class children. (45) ________ American children obtain the highest IQ scores. (46) Many studies of IQ have confused the factors of social ________ and ethnicity.

Pulling It Together: How can we explain the difference in IQ scores among children from various ethnic groups in the United States?

Creativity—Flexibility and Fluency in Cognitive Processes

Question: What is creativity? To illustrate something about the nature of creativity, let me ask you a rather ordinary question: What does the word *duck* mean? Now let me ask you a somewhat more interesting question: How many meanings can you find for the word *duck?* Arriving at a single correct answer to the question might earn you points on an intelligence test. Generating many answers to the question, as we will see, may be a sign of creativity as well as knowledge of the meaning of words.

Creativity is the ability to do things that are novel and useful (Sternberg, 2001). Creative children and adults can solve problems to which there are no preexisting solutions, no tried and tested formulas (Simonton, 2000). Creative children share a number of qualities (Sternberg & Lubart, 1995, 1996):

- They take chances. (They may violate "the rules"—using sentence fragments in essays and coloring outside the lines—when they see that doing so is an effective way of offering new perspective or insight, of saying something in a distinct way.)
- They refuse to accept limitations and try to do the impossible.
- They appreciate art and music (which sometimes leaves them out among their peers).
- They use the materials around them to make unique things.
- They challenge social norms. (Creative children are often independent and nonconformist, but independence and nonconformity do not necessarily make a child creative. Creative children may be at odds with their teachers because

creativity The ability to generate novel solutions to problems. A trait characterized by flexibility, ingenuity, and originality.

of their independent views. Faced with the task of managing large classes, teachers often fall into preferences for quiet, submissive, "good" children.)
- They take unpopular stands (which sometimes gives them the appearance of being oppositional, when they are expressing their genuine ideas and feelings).
- They examine ideas that other people accept at face value. (They come home and say, "__________ said that yadayada. What's that all about?")

Reflect

Do you consider yourself to be creative? Why or why not?

A professor of mine once remarked that there is nothing new under the sun, only new combinations of existing elements. Many psychologists agree. They see creativity as the ability to make unusual, sometimes remote, associations to the elements of a problem to generate new combinations. An essential aspect of a creative response is the leap from the elements of the problem to the novel solution. A predictable solution is not creative, even if it is hard to reach.

Question: What is the relationship between creativity and intelligence? The answer to this question depends to some degree on how one defines intelligence. If one accepts Sternberg's model, creativity is one of three aspects of intelligence (along with analytic thinking and practical intelligence). From this perspective, creativity overlaps with intelligence.

However, given the kinds of tests that are used to measure intelligence and creativity, the relationship between intelligence test scores and measures of creativity are only moderate (Simonton, 2000; Sternberg & Williams, 1997). A Canadian study found that highly intelligent boys and girls aged 9 to 11 were, as a group, more creative than less intelligent children (Kershner & Ledger, 1985). Still, not all of the gifted children were more creative than their less intelligent peers. In terms of Gardner's (1993) theory of multiple intelligences, we can note that some children who have only average intellectual ability in some areas—such as logical analysis—can excel in areas that are considered more creative, such as music or art.

Children mainly use *convergent thinking* to arrive at the correct answers on intelligence tests. In **convergent thinking,** thought is limited to present facts; the problem solver narrows his or her thinking to find the best solution. (A child uses convergent thinking to arrive at the right answer to a multiple-choice question or to a question on an intelligence test.)

Creative thinking tends to be *divergent* rather than convergent. In **divergent thinking,** the child associates freely to the elements of the problem, allowing "leads" to run a nearly limitless course. (Children may use divergent thinking when they are trying to generate ideas to answer an essay question or to find keywords to search on the Internet.) Tests of creativity determine how flexible, fluent, and original a person's thinking is (Simonton, 2000). Here, for example, is an item from a test used by Getzels and Jackson (1962) to measure associative ability, a factor in creativity: "Write as many meanings as you can for each of the following words: (a) duck; (b) sack; (c) pitch; (d) fair." Those who write several meanings for each word, rather than only one, are rated as potentially more creative.

Another measure of creativity might ask children to produce as many words as possible that begin with T and end with N within a minute. Still another item might give people a minute to classify a list of names in as many ways as possible. In how many ways can you classify the following group of names?

MARTHA PAUL JEFFRY SALLY PABLO JOAN

Figure 12.10 presents some other kinds of items from a test of creativity. Sometimes arriving at the right answer involves both divergent and convergent thinking. When presented with a problem, a child may first use divergent thinking to generate many possible solutions to the problem. Convergent thinking may then be used to select likely solutions and reject others.

Intelligence tests like the Stanford Binet and Wechsler scales are not very useful in measuring creativity. They require children to focus in on the single right answer. On intelligence tests, ingenious responses that differ from the designated answers are marked wrong. Tests of creativity, by contrast, are oriented toward determining how flexible and fluent one's thinking can be. Such tests include

convergent thinking A thought process that attempts to narrow in on the single best solution to a problem.

divergent thinking A thought process that attempts to generate multiple solutions to problems. Free and fluent association to the elements of a problem.

One aspect of creativity is the ability to associate freely to all aspects of a problem. Creative people take far-flung ideas and piece them together in novel combinations. Following are items from the Remote Associates Test, which measures ability to find words that are distinctly related to stimulus words. For each set of three words, try to think of a fourth word that is related to all three words. For example, the words *rough*, *resistance*, and *beer* suggest the word *draft* because of the phrases *rough draft*, *draft resistance*, and *draft beer*. The answers are given below.

1.	Charming	Student	Valiant
2.	Food	Catcher	Hot
3.	Hearted	Feet	Bitter
4.	Dark	Shot	Sun
5.	Canadian	Golf	Sandwich
6.	Tug	Gravy	Show
7.	Attorney	Self	Spending
8.	Arm	Coal	Peach
9.	Type	Ghost	Story

Answers: Prince, Dog, Cold, Glasses, Club, Boat, Defense, Pit, Writer

Figure 12.10
The Remote Associates Test
Tests of creativity, such as the Remote Associates Test, typically tap divergent thinking, whereas intelligence tests tend to tap convergent thinking.

items such as suggesting improvements or unusual uses for a familiar toy or object, naming things that belong in the same class, producing words similar in meaning, and writing different endings for a story (Meador, 1992).

Review

(47) _________ is the ability to do things that are novel and useful. (48) Creative children (do or do not?) accept limitations. (49) The relationship between IQ scores and measures of creativity are _________ (weak, moderate, or strong). (50) Children mainly use (convergent or divergent?) thinking to answer questions on intelligence tests. (51) Children tend to use (convergent or divergent) thinking when they are thinking creatively.

Pulling It Together: How are intelligence and creativity connected within Sternberg's triarchic theory?

The Determinants of Intelligence

Questions: What do psychologists know about the determinants of intelligence? What are the roles of nature (heredity) and nurture (environmental influences)? All right, I won't keep you in suspense: After my review of the literature, I conclude that there is ample evidence for both genetic and environmental influences on IQ (Dickens & Flynn, 2001). Moreover, many of the same studies—in particular, kinship studies and studies of adopted children—appear to provide evidence for both genetic and environmental influences.

Consider the problems in attempting to decide whether a child's performance on an intelligence test is mainly influenced by nature or nurture—that is, by genetic or environmental factors. If a superior child has superior parents, do we attribute the superiority to heredity or to the environment provided by these parents? Similarly, if a dull child lives in an impoverished home, do we attribute the dullness to the genetic potential transmitted by the parents or to the lack of intellectual stimulation in the environment?

No research strategy for attempting to ferret out genetic and environmental determinants of IQ is flawless. Still, a number of ingenious approaches have been devised. The total weight of the evidence provided through these approaches may be instructive.

Genetic Influences

Various strategies have been devised for research into genetic factors, including

- Kinship studies: Correlating the IQ scores of twins, other siblings, and parents and children who have lived together and apart. Strong positive correlations between the IQ scores of closely related children, such as monozygotic (identical) twins, who have been reared apart could be taken as evidence of genetic influences.
- Studies of adopted children: Correlating the IQ scores of adopted children with those of their biological and adoptive parents. If the IQ scores of adopted children correlate more highly with those of their biological than their adoptive parents, we have another argument for genetic influences.

Intelligence and Family Relationships (Kinship)

If heredity is involved in human intelligence, closely related people ought to have more similar IQs than distantly related or unrelated people, even when they are reared separately. Figure 12.11 shows the averaged results of more than 100 studies of IQ and heredity in human beings (Bouchard, Lykken, McGue, Segal, & Tellegen, 1990). The IQ scores of identical (MZ) twins are more alike than the scores for any other pairs, even when the twins have been reared apart. The average correlation for MZ twins reared together is +0.85; for those reared apart, it is +0.67.

Reflect

Does your own family seem to be generally similar in overall intellectual functioning? Are there one or more family members who appear to stand out from the others because of intelligence? If so, in what ways? Where do you seem to stand in your family in terms of intellectual functioning?

A Closer Look

The Controversy Over The Bell Curve

When I was in graduate school, a professor remarked that many people think of intelligence as "a knob in the head. Some people have a bigger knob and some people have a smaller one." That is, many people see intelligence as a fixed commodity. From this perspective, some people have more intelligence, some people less, and nothing much can be done about it. The view of intelligence as a knob in the head was expressed forcefully by psychologist Richard Herrnstein and political theorist Charles Murray (1994) in their book *The Bell Curve. The Bell Curve* poured oil onto the fires of controversy over social class, race, and intelligence by making the following assertions:

1. Intelligence tests are valid indicators of intelligence (that is, IQ is an accurate measure of intelligence).
2. A person's intelligence is mainly due to heredity.
3. People with less intelligence (smaller "knobs in the head") are having more children than people with more intelligence ("bigger knobs"), so that the overall intelligence of the population of the United States is declining.
4. The United States is becoming divided in two, with a large lower class of people with low intelligence and a smaller class of wealthier people who are higher in intelligence.
5. Education can do little to affect intelligence (the size of the "knob").

However, intelligence is *not* a knob in the head. Nor is intelligence mainly heritable. They argue that IQ is affected by early learning experiences, academic and vocational motivation, and formal education (Kamin, 1995; Reifman, 2000; Steele, 1994).

In this chapter we see that the argument of *The Bell Curve* that intelligence tests are valid indicators of intelligence begins to fall apart with the nature of the testing situation. By doing nothing more than make testing conditions more optimal for all children, we narrow the IQ gap between European American and African American children. Moreover, there is little reason to believe that IQ tests that are mainly standardized with European American middle-class children are valid measures with children from ethnic minority groups (Okazaki & Sue, 2000). We also see that research findings on the roles of the home environment and educational experiences on intelligence contradict *The Bell Curve*'s argument that little or nothing can be done to enhance intellectual functioning in children. Finally, we see that intellectual functioning appears to reflect the interaction of a complex web of genetic, physical, personal, and sociocultural factors. The views of *The Bell Curve*—that intelligence is largely heritable and that little can be done to affect intellectual functioning—are contradicted by evidence that clearly supports a more balanced view (Reifman, 2000).

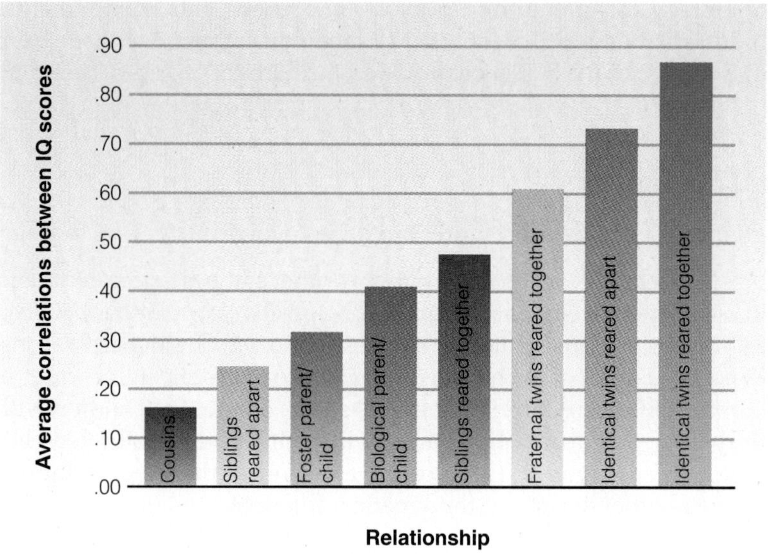

Figure 12.11
Findings of Studies of the Relationship Between IQ Scores and Heredity
The data are a composite of studies summarized in Science *magazine (Bouchard, Lykken, McGue, Segal, & Tellegen, 1990). By and large, correlations grow stronger for persons who are more closely related. Persons reared together or living together have more similar IQ scores than persons reared or living apart. Such findings support both genetic and environmental hypotheses of the origins of intelligence.*

Correlations between the IQ scores of fraternal (DZ) twins, siblings, and parents and children are generally comparable, as is their degree of genetic relationship. The correlations tend to vary from the middle +0.40s to the upper +0.50s. Correlations between the IQ scores of children and their natural parents (+0.48) are higher than those between children and adoptive parents (+0.18).

All in all, studies generally suggest that the **heritability** of intelligence is between 40% and 60% (Bouchard, Lykken, McGue, Segal, & Tellegen, 1990; Neisser et al., 1996). In other words, about half of the variations (the technical term is *variance*) in IQ scores can be accounted for by heredity. This is *not* the same as saying that you inherited about half of your intelligence. The implication of such a statement would be that you "got" the other half of your intelligence somewhere else. It means, rather, that about half of the difference between your IQ score and the IQ scores of other people can be explained in terms of genetic factors.

Let's return to Figure 12.11 for a moment. Note that genetic pairs (like MZ twins) reared together show higher correlations between IQ scores than similar genetic pairs (like other MZ twins) who were reared apart. This finding holds for MZ twins, siblings, parents, children, and unrelated people. *For this reason, the same group of studies that suggests that heredity plays a role in determining IQ scores also suggests that environment plays a role.*

Studies of the Intelligence of Adopted Children

When children are separated from their biological parents at early ages, one can argue that strong relationships between their IQ scores and those of their natural parents reflect genetic influences. Strong relationships between their IQs and those of their adoptive parents, on the other hand, might reflect environmental influences. Several projects involving adopted children in Colorado, Texas, and Minnesota (Coon, Fulker, & DeFries, 1990; Scarr, 1993; Turkheimer, 1991) have found a stronger relationship between the IQ scores of adopted children and those of their biological parents than with the IQ scores of their adoptive parents.

These studies, then, also point to a genetic influence on intelligence. Nonetheless, the environment also has an impact.

Environmental Influences

heritability The degree to which the variations in a trait from one person to another can be attributed to, or explained by, genetic factors.

Studies of environmental influences on IQ employ several research strategies:

- Discovering situational factors that affect IQ scores. If children's motivation to do well, their familiarity with testing materials, their nourishment, and their comfort in the testing situation can be shown to affect IQ scores, environmental influences play a role.

- Exploring children's abilities to rebound from early deprivation. If children who have spent some of their early lives in impoverished circumstances can make dramatic gains in IQ when stimulated later on, it would appear that IQ is subject to environmental influences.
- Exploring the effects of positive early environments. If good parent–child relations, early language stimulation, and preschool programs are linked to gains in IQ, we have more evidence for the role of environmental influences.

Situational Influences on Intelligence

In some cases, we need look no further than the testing situation to explain some of the discrepancy between the IQ scores of middle-class children and those of children from economically disadvantaged backgrounds. In one study (Zigler et al., 1982), the examiner simply made children as comfortable as possible during the test. Rather than being cold and impartial, the examiner was warm and friendly, and care was taken to see that the children understood the directions. As a result, the children's test anxiety was markedly reduced and their IQ scores were six points higher than those for a control group treated in a more indifferent manner. Disadvantaged children made relatively greater gains from the procedure. By doing nothing more than making testing conditions more optimal for all children, we may narrow the IQ gap between low-income and middle-class children.

Rebounding From Early Deprivation

In Chapter 7, we discussed a longitudinal study of retarded orphanage children that provided striking evidence children can recover from early deprivation. In the orphanage these 19-month-old children were placed with surrogate mothers who provided a great deal of intellectual and social stimulation. Four years later, the children had made dramatic gains in IQ scores.

The Effects of Early Home and School Environments

Children whose parents are emotionally and verbally responsive, and who provide appropriate play materials and varied experiences during the early years, attain higher IQ and achievement-test scores (Bradley, Burchinal, & Casey, 2001). Graduates of Head Start and other preschool programs show significant gains in later educational outcomes (Zigler & Styfco, 2001).

Reflect

As you look back on your own childhood, can you point to any kinds of family or educational experiences that seem to have had an impact on your intellectual development? Would you say that your background, overall, was deprived or enriched? In what ways?

Developing in a World of Diversity

Stereotype Vulnerability and IQ

Stereotype vulnerability is another aspect of the testing situation, and it also affects test scores. Psychologist Claude Steele (1996, 1997) suggests that African American students carry an extra burden in performing scholastic tasks: They believe that they risk confirming their group's negative stereotype by doing poorly on such tasks. This concern creates performance anxiety. Performance anxiety distracts them from the tasks, and as a result they perform more poorly than European American students.

In an experiment designed to test this view, Steele and Aronson (1995) gave two groups of African American and European American Stanford undergraduates the most difficult verbal skills test questions from the GRE. One group was told that the researchers were attempting to learn about the "psychological factors involved in solving verbal problems." The other group was told that the items were "a genuine test of your verbal abilities and limitations." African American students who were given the first message performed as well as European American students. African American students who were given the second message—that proof of their abilities was on the line—performed significantly more poorly than the European American students. Apparently the second message triggered their stereotype vulnerability, which led them to self-destruct on the test. Steele's findings are further evidence of the limits of intelligence tests as valid indicators of intelligence.

Back to the Kinship Studies and Studies of Adopted Children

Kinship studies and studies of adoptees suggest that there is a genetic influence on intelligence. But the same studies also suggest a role for environmental influences. For example, an analysis of a large number of twin and kinship studies shows that the older twins and other siblings become, the less alike they are on various measures of intelligence and personality (McCartney, Harris, & Bernjeri, 1990). This appears to be due to increasing exposure to different environments and experiences outside the family.

Studies of adopted children also indicate the importance of environment. African American children who were adopted during the first year by European American parents who were above average in income and education showed IQ scores some 15 to 25 points higher than those attained by African American children reared by their natural parents (Scarr & Weinberg, 1976). The adopted children's average IQ scores, about 106, remained somewhat below those of their adoptive parents' natural children—117 (Scarr & Weinberg, 1977). Even so, the adoptive early environment closed a good deal of the IQ gap.

On the Determinants of Intelligence: A Concluding Note

Many psychologists believe that heredity and environment interact to influence intelligence (Lubinski & Benbow, 2000; Winner, 2000). Experts usually see genetic influences as providing the reaction range for the complex pattern of verbal and reasoning abilities and problem-solving skills that we interpret to be signs of intelligence. An impoverished environment may prevent some children from living up to their potential. An enriched environment may encourage others to realize their potential, minimizing possible differences in heredity.

Perhaps we need not be concerned with how much of a person's IQ is due to heredity and how much is due to environmental influences. Psychology has traditionally supported the dignity of the individual. It might be more appropriate for us to try to identify children of *all* races whose environments place them at high risk for failure and to do what we can to enrich them.

Review

(52) The IQ scores of __________ twins are more alike than the scores for any other pairs. (53) Studies generally suggest that the heritability of intelligence is about __________%. (54) Studies find that there is a stronger relationship between the IQ scores of adopted children and those of their (adoptive or biological?) parents than with the IQ scores of their (adoptive or biological?) parents. (55) Steele found that the intelligence test performance of African American students is impaired by __________ vulnerability. (56) The older twins and other siblings become, the (more or less?) alike they are on measures of intelligence. (57) African American children who are adopted by European American parents obtain IQ scores that are (higher or lower?) than those attained by African American children reared by their natural parents.

Pulling It Together: How is it possible that the same studies can support the roles of nature and of nurture in the development of intelligence?

Language Development

Question: How does language develop in middle childhood? Children's ability to understand and use language becomes increasingly sophisticated in middle childhood. They learn to read as well. Many children are exposed to varieties of linguistic experience other than standard English, and this experience has important ramifications for language development. In this section, we examine each of these topics.

Vocabulary and Grammar

By the age of 6, the child's vocabulary has expanded to 10,000 words, give or take a few thousand. By 7 to 9, most children realize that words can have different meanings, and they become entertained by riddles and jokes that require semantic sophistication. (Remember the jokes at the beginning of the chapter?) By the age of 8 or 9, children are able to form "tag questions," in which the question is tagged on to the end of a declarative sentence (Dennis, Sugar, & Whitaker, 1982). "You want more ice cream, don't you?" and "You're sick, aren't you?" are examples of tag questions.

Children also make subtle advances in articulation and in the capacity to use complex grammar. For example, preschool-age children have difficulty in understanding passive sentences such as "The truck was hit by the car." But children in the middle years have less difficulty interpreting the meanings of passive sentences correctly (Whitehurst, 1982). Children can learn to produce passive sentences in early childhood, but the teaching must be intensive (Tomasello, Brooks, & Stern, 1998); there is also no point to the exercise, except as a method of studying language development.

During these years, children develop the ability to use connectives, as illustrated by the sentence "I'll eat my spinach but I don't want to." They also learn to form indirect object–direct object constructions (for example, "She showed her sister the toy").

Reading Skills

In many ways, reading is a key to unlocking the benefits our society has to offer. Good readers find endless pleasure in literature, reading and rereading favorite poetic passages. Reading makes textbook learning possible. Reading also permits us to identify subway stops, to consider the contents of food packages, to assemble barbecue grills and children's swing sets, and to learn how to use a microcomputer. ***Question: What cognitive skills are involved in reading?***

The Integration of Auditory and Visual Information

Reading is a complex process that depends on perceptual, cognitive, and linguistic processes (Siegel, 1993). It relies on skills in the integration of visual and auditory information. Accurate awareness of the sounds in the child's language is an extremely important factor in subsequent reading achievement (Caravolas & Bruck, 2000; Dufva, Niemi, & Voeten, 2001). Reading also requires the ability to make basic visual discriminations (Cunningham, Perry, & Stanovich, 2001). In reading, for example, children must "mind their *p*'s and *q*'s." That is, in order to recognize letters, children must be able to perceive the visual differences between letters such as *b* and *d*, or *p* and *q*.

During the preschool years, neurological maturation and experience combine to allow most children to make visual discriminations between different letters with relative ease. Those children who can recognize and name the letters of the alphabet by kindergarten age are better readers in the early school grades (Siegler, 1986).

How do children acquire familiarity with their own written languages? More and more today, American children are being exposed to TV programs such as *Sesame Street,* but these are relatively recent educational innovations. Children are also exposed to books, street signs, names of stores and restaurants, and the writing on packages, especially at the supermarket. Some children, of course, have more books in the home than others do. Children from affluent homes where books and other sources of stimulation are plentiful learn to read more readily than children from impoverished homes. But regardless of income level, reading storybooks with

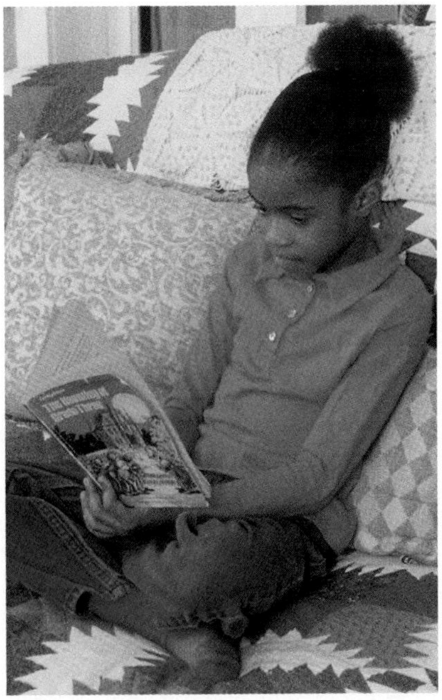

Reading

Children who read at home during the school years show better reading skills in school and more positive attitudes toward reading.

© Tony Freeman/PhotoEdit

Ebonics in the Classroom

Ebonics is spoken by segments of the African American community. The major differences between Ebonics and standard English lie in the use of verbs. Many linguists note that the grammatical rules of Ebonics differ from those of standard English, but Ebonics has consistent rules and allows the expression of thoughts as complex as those permitted by standard English.

parents in the preschool years helps prepare a child for reading (Baker et al., 2001; Clarke-Stewart, 1998). Children who read at home during the school years also show better reading skills in school and more positive attitudes toward reading.

Methods of Teaching Reading

When they read, children integrate visual and auditory information (associate what they see with sounds), whether they are reading by the *word-recognition method* or by the *phonetic method.* If they are using the **word-recognition method,** they must be able to associate visual stimuli such as *cat* and *Robert* with the sound combinations that produce the spoken words "cat" and "Robert." This capacity is usually acquired by *rote learning,* or extensive repetition.

In the **phonetic method,** children first learn to associate written letters and letter combinations (such as *ph* or *sh*) with the sounds they are meant to indicate. Then they sound out words from left to right, decoding them. The phonetic method has the obvious advantage of giving children skills that they can use to decode (read) new words (Bastien-Toniazzo & Jullien, 2001; Dufva et al., 2001). However, some children learn more rapidly at early ages through the word-recognition method. The phonetic method can also slow them down when it comes to familiar words. Most children and adults, in fact, tend to read familiar words by the word-recognition method (regardless of the method of their original training) and to make some effort to sound out new words.

Which method is superior? A controversy rages over the issue and we cannot resolve it here. But let us note that some words in English can be read only by the word-recognition method—consider the words *one* and *two.* This method is useful when it comes to words such as *danger, stop, poison,* and the child's name, for it helps provide children with a basic **sight vocabulary.** But decoding skills must be acquired so that children can read new words on their own.

The Diversity of Children's Linguistic Experiences in the United States

Some children in the United States are exposed to nonstandard English. Others are exposed to English plus a second language. Let's explore their linguistic experiences.

Ebonics

Question: What is Ebonics? The term *Ebonics* is derived from the words *ebony* and *phonics.* It was coined by the African American psychologist Robert Williams (Burnette, 1997). Ebonics was previously called Black English or Black Dialect (Pinker, 1994). Williams explains that a group of African American scholars convened "to name our language, which had always been named by White scholars in the past" (Burnette, 1997, p. 12).

Ebonics has taken hold most strongly in working-class African American neighborhoods. According to linguists, Ebonics is rooted in the remnants of the West African dialects used by slaves. It reflects attempts by the slaves, who were denied formal education, to imitate the speech of the dominant European American culture. Some observers believe that Ebonics uses verbs haphazardly, downgrading standard English. As a result, some school systems react to the concept of Ebonics with contempt—which is hurtful to the child who speaks Ebonics. Other observers say that Ebonics has different grammatical rules than standard English, but that the rules are consistent and allow for complex thought (Pinker, 1994). In 1996, the Oakland, California, school board recognized Ebonics as the primary language of African American students, just as Spanish had been recognized as the primary language of Latino and Latina American students. "I was honored," said Williams. "And truthfully, I was shocked. It was like the truth that had been covered up in the ground for so long just exploded one day" (Burnette, 1997, p. 12).

Reflect

How do you feel when people correct your English? Why?

word-recognition method A method for learning to read in which children come to recognize words through repeated exposure to them.

phonetic method A method for learning to read in which children decode the sounds of words based on their knowledge of the sounds of letters and letter combinations.

sight vocabulary Words that are immediately recognized on the basis of familiarity with their overall shapes, rather than decoded.

"To Be or Not to Be": Use of Verbs in Ebonics There are differences between Ebonics and standard English in the use of verbs. For example, the Ebonics usage "She-ah touch us" corresponds to the standard English "She will touch us." The Ebonics "He be gone" is the equivalent of the standard English "He has been gone for a long while." "He gone" is the same as "He is not here right now" in standard English.

Consider the rules in Ebonics that govern the use of the verb *to be.* In standard English, *be* is part of the infinitive form of the verb and is used to form the future tense, as in "I'll be angry tomorrow." Thus, "I *be* angry" is incorrect. But in Ebonics *be* refers to a continuing state of being. The Ebonics sentence "I be angry" is the same as the standard English "I have been angry for a while" and is grammatically correct.

Ebonics leaves out forms of *to be* in cases in which standard English would use a contraction. For example, the standard "She's the one I'm talking about" could be "*She* the one *I* talking about" in Ebonics. Ebonics also often drops *ed* from the past tense and lacks the possessive *'s.*

"Not to Be or Not to Be Nothing": Negation in Ebonics Consider the sentence "I don't want no trouble," which is, of course, commendable. Middle-class European American children would be corrected for using double negation (do*n't* along with *no*) and would be encouraged to say "I don't want *any* trouble." Yet double negation is acceptable in Ebonics (Pinker, 1994). Nevertheless, many teachers who use standard English have demeaned African American children who speak this way.

Some African American children are bicultural and bilingual. They function competently within the dominant culture in the United States and among groups of people from their own ethnic background. They use standard English in a conference with their teacher or in a job interview, but switch to Ebonics among their friends. Their facility in doing so is a fine example of their use of the pragmatics of speech. Other children cannot switch back and forth. The decision by the Oakland school board was intended in part to help children maintain their self-esteem and stay in school (Ogbu, 1999; Seymour, Abdulkarim, & Johnson, 1999).

Bilingualism: Linguistic Perspectives on the World

Most people throughout the world speak two or more languages. Most countries have minority populations whose languages differ from the national tongue. Nearly all Europeans are taught English and the languages of neighboring nations. Consider the Netherlands. Dutch is the native tongue, but all children are also taught French, German, and English and are expected to become fluent in each of them.

For more than 30 million people in the United States, English is a second language (Barringer, 1993; see Table 12.7). Spanish, French, Chinese, Russian, or Hebrew is spoken in the home and, perhaps, the neighborhood. ***Question: What does research reveal about the advantages and disadvantages of bilingualism?***

A century ago it was widely believed that children reared in **bilingual** homes were retarded in their cognitive and language development. The theory was that cognitive capacity is limited, so people who store two linguistic systems are crowding their mental abilities. It is true that there is some "mixing" of languages by bilingual children (Patterson, 2000), but they can generally separate the two languages from an early age (Mueller & Hulk, 2001). The U.S. Bureau of the Census reports that more than 75% of Americans who first spoke another language in the home also speak English "well" or "very well" (Barringer, 1993). Moreover, a careful analysis of older studies in bilingualism shows that the bilingual children observed often lived in families with low socioeconomic status and little education. Yet these bilingual children were compared to middle-class monolingual children. In addition, achievement and intelligence tests were conducted in the monolingual child's language, which was the second language of the bilingual child (Reynolds, 1991). Lack of education and inadequate testing methods, rather than bilingualism per se, accounted for the apparent differences in achievement and intelligence.

Today most linguists consider it advantageous for children to be bilingual. For one thing, knowledge of more than one language expands children's awareness of

Reflect

Did you grow up speaking a language other than English in the home? If so, what special opportunities and problems were connected with the experience?

bilingual Using or capable of using two languages with nearly equal or equal facility.

TABLE 12.7 *Bilingualism, U.S.A.*

Language Spoken in the Home	Total Number of Speakers, Age 5 and Above 1990	1980	Change (%)
Spanish	17,339,000	11,549,000	50
French[1]	1,703,000	1,572,000	8
German	1,547,000	1,607,000	–4
Italian	1,309,000	1,633,000	–20
Chinese	1,249,000	632,000	98
Tagalog[2]	843,000	452,000	87
Polish	723,000	826,000	–12
Korean	626,000	276,000	127
Vietnamese	507,000	203,000	150
Portuguese	430,000	361,000	19
Japanese	428,000	342,000	25
Greek	388,000	410,000	–5
Arabic	355,000	227,000	57
Hindi, Urdu	331,000	130,000	155
Russian	242,000	175,000	39
Yiddish	213,000	320,000	–34
Thai	206,000	89,000	132
Persian	202,000	109,000	85
French Creole[3]	188,000	25,000	654
Armenian	150,000	102,000	46
Navajo[4]	149,000	123,000	21
Hungarian	148,000	180,000	–18
Hebrew	144,000	99,000	46
Dutch	143,000	146,000	–3
Mon-Khmer[5]	127,000	16,000	676
TOTAL	31,845,000	23,060,00	38%

[1]Spoken commonly in the home in New Hampshire, Maine, and Louisiana.
[2]Main language of the Philippines.
[3]Mainly spoken by Haitians.
[4]Native American language.
[5]Cambodian language.
Source: U.S. Bureau of the Census (1993).

different cultures and broadens their perspectives (Cavaliere, 1996). There is even some evidence that bilingualism contributes to the complexity of the child's cognitive processes (Bialystock, 1999). For example, bilingual children are more likely to understand that the symbols used in language are arbitrary. Monolingual children are more likely to think erroneously that the word *dog* is somehow intertwined with the nature of the beast. Bilingual children therefore have somewhat more cognitive flexibility. Second, learning a second language does not crowd children's available "cognitive space." Instead, learning a second language has been shown to increase children's expertise in their first (native) language. Research evidence reveals that learning French enhances knowledge of the structure of English among Canadian children whose native language is English (Lambert et al., 1991).

Review

(58) By the age of 6, the child's vocabulary is about ________ words. (59) By about ________, most children realize that words can have different meanings. (60) In middle childhood, children (can or cannot?) generally understand passive sentences. (61) Reading relies on skills in the integration of ________ and

Bilingualism

Most people throughout the world speak two or more languages, and most countries have minority populations whose languages differ from the national tongue. It was once thought that children reared in bilingual homes were retarded in their cognitive and language development, but today most linguists consider it advantageous for children to be bilingual. Knowledge of more than one language certainly expands children's awareness of diverse cultures and broadens their perspectives.

Developing in a World of Diversity

Bilingual Education

Many children who speak a different language in the home experience difficulty when learning English in school. A century ago the educational approach to teaching English to non-English-speaking children was simple: sink or swim. Children were taught in English from the outset. They had to catch on as best they could. Most children swam. Some sank.

The sink-or-swim method is also called **total immersion.** Total immersion has a checkered history. There are many successes, but there are also more failures than most educators are willing to tolerate. For this reason, bilingual education has been adopted in many school systems.

Bilingual education legislation requires that non-English-speaking children be given the chance to study in their own language to smooth the transition to life in the United States. The official purpose of federal bilingual programs is to help children who speak foreign languages use their native tongue to learn English rapidly and then switch to a regular school program. Yet the degree of emphasis on English differs from one program to another.

So-called *transitional programs* shoot students into regular English-speaking classrooms as quickly as possible. In a second technique, called the *maintenance method,* rapid mastery of English is still the goal. But students continue to study their own culture and language. A third approach is *two-way immersion.* Two-way immersion encourages native-born American children to achieve fluency in a foreign language at the same time that immigrant children are learning English (Cavaliere, 1996). Students in these programs study half a day in Spanish and half a day in English. Research shows that English-speaking children who are placed in Spanish immersion programs develop vocabularies—English vocabularies, that is—that are superior to children who are not placed in such programs (Cunningham & Graham, 2000). The benefits appear to be largely derived from learning Spanish words that have English *cognates*—that is, words that are similar in both languages and have the same meaning.

Critics of bilingual education contend that it is often more political than educational. For example, children with Spanish surnames may remain segregated long after they have shown that they can handle lessons in English. Also, some children never "graduate" from bilingual classes or high school either (J. Steinberg, 2000). These critics recognize the benefits of cultural pluralism but believe that the key to success in the United States is the ability to communicate in English.

In recent years there has been a backlash against bilingual education, largely because of concern that many children do not seem to profit from it. The research evidence on the issue leaves much to be desired. For example, the state of California assessed children for whom English was a second language two years after they ended bilingual education and returned to the sink-or-swim method. The state found that second-graders increased from the 19th percentile in national rankings for reading to the 28th percentile during that period (J. Steinberg, 2000). It might sound wonderful, but there are limitations, such as the fact that California did not provide for experimental and control groups. It turns out that California reduced the average class size in the elementary grades from in excess of 30 students per class to 20 students per class during the same period. In addition, assessment revealed a great deal of variation in reading scores among school districts: Some gained by double digits and others gained not at all. All in all, it seems clear that the gains were not made *just because* California dropped bilingual education. On the other hand, it makes sense to reduce class sizes where possible and to find out why some school districts do a better job than others. In any event, we do not yet have clear-cut experimental evidence as to the benefits or disadvantages of bilingual education.

auditory information. (62) Reading also requires the ability to make basic __________ discriminations, as in differentiating between *b* and *d*. (63) In using the word-__________ method of reading, children must associate visual stimuli with sound combinations. (64) In using the __________ method of reading, children associate written letters and letter combinations (such as *ph* or *sh*) with the sounds they indicate. (65) The term __________ is derived from the words *ebony* and *phonics*. (66) The rules of Ebonics (are or are not?) consistent and allow for complex thought. (67) Ebonics (does or does not?) permit use of double negation. (68) Bilingual children generally (can or cannot?) separate the two languages at an early age. (69) Today most linguists consider it a(n) (advantage or disadvantage?) to be bilingual.

total immersion A method of language instruction in which a person is placed in an environment in which only the language to be learned is used.

Pulling It Together: How do advances in language reflect the cognitive development of children in middle childhood?

Recite Recite Recite Recite

1. **What is meant by the stage of concrete operations?**

In the stage of concrete operations, children begin to show the capacity for adult logic, but with tangible objects. Concrete-operational thinking is characterized by reversibility, flexibility, and decentration. Concrete-operational children show understanding of the laws of conservation. Piaget termed the sequential development of concrete operations *horizontal décalage.* Concrete-operational children understand the principle of transitivity: If A exceeds B, and B exceeds C, then A exceeds C. Seriation is made possible by knowledge of transitivity. The operation of class inclusion involves ability to recognize that one class of things (A) includes several subclasses (B1 and B2).

2. **Can we apply Piaget's theory of cognitive development to educational practices?**

Yes, to some degree. For example, Piaget believed that learning is a process of active discovery. Thus, teachers should not try to impose knowledge on the child but should find materials to interest and stimulate the child. Instruction should also be geared to the child's level of development.

3. **What is the difference between Piaget's view of cognitive development and the information-processing approach?**

Information-processing theorists aim to learn how children store, retrieve, and manipulate information—how their "mental programs" develop. One key cognitive process is selective attention—attending to the relevant features of a task—which advances steadily through middle childhood.

4. **What is meant by the term *memory*?**

The term *memory* refers to the processes of storing and retrieving information. Many psychologists divide memory functioning into three major processes or structures: sensory memory, short-term memory, and long-term memory. Ability to maintain information in short-term memory depends on cognitive strategies, such as encoding visual stimuli as sounds and rehearsing them. The ability to recall chunks of information improves throughout middle childhood; 15-year-olds, like adults, can keep about seven chunks of information in short-term memory at a time. Robbie Case's view focuses on children's capacity for memory and their use of cognitive strategies; e.g., certain Piagetian tasks require holding several pieces of information in short-term memory. Case notes that older children learn to handle information more quickly, efficiently, and automatically. Children learn the alphabet by rote.

5. **How much information can be stored in long-term memory? How is it "filed"?**

There is no known limit to the capacity of long-term memory. Information is transferred from short-term memory to long-term memory by rehearsal (repetition) and elaboration (relation of new material to well-known information. Relating new material to well-known material is known as an elaborative strategy. As children's knowl-

Recite Recite Recite Recite

edge of concepts advances, the storehouse of their long-term memory becomes organized into categories. Correct categorization expands knowledge and allows for more efficient retrieval of information. As children develop, their capacity for recalling information increases because of their ability to quickly process (scan and categorize) the stimulus cues.

6. What do children understand about the functioning of their cognitive processes and, more particularly, their memory?

Awareness and conscious control of cognitive abilities is termed *metacognition*, as evidenced by ability to formulate problems, awareness of how to solve them, use of rules and strategies, remaining focused, and checking answers. *Metamemory* refers to children's awareness of the workings of their memory—e.g., by 6 or 7 children know to use rehearsal without being instructed to do so.

7. What is intelligence?

Intelligence provides the cognitive basis for academic achievement. Intelligence is a child's underlying competence or learning ability.

8. What are "factor theories" of intelligence?

Spearman suggested that the behaviors we consider intelligent have a common, underlying factor: *g*. But *s*, or specific capacities, accounts for some individual abilities. Thurstone used factor analysis and arrived at the conclusion that there are nine primary mental abilities, including word fluency.

9. What is meant by *multiple intelligences?*

Gardner believes that people have eight or more "intelligences," each of which is based in a different part of the brain. Some of these "intelligences"—verbal ability, logical-mathematical reasoning, and spatial intelligence—are familiar enough. Others—e.g., bodily-kinesthetic intelligence, musical intelligence, interpersonal intelligence, and personal knowledge—strike other psychologists as special talents or other kinds of abilities.

10. What is Sternberg's triarchic model of intelligence?

Sternberg proposes a three-pronged, or *triarchic*, theory of intelligence, including analytical intelligence (academic ability), creative intelligence (ability to cope with novel situations), and practical intelligence ("street smarts").

11. What is the Stanford-Binet Intelligence Scale?

The SBIS assumes that intelligence increases with age, so older children must answer more items correctly than younger children to obtain a comparable score—which Binet referred to as a mental age. A comparison of a child's mental age with his or her chronological age (MA/CA) yields an intelligence quotient (IQ). Items at the youngest age levels include placing blocks in a form board, naming parts of the body, and repeating a series of two numbers. At older age levels, children define advanced vocabulary words and explain how objects are alike or different. The average IQ score is defined as 100.

12. How do the Wechsler scales differ from the Stanford-Binet?

The Wechsler scales group test questions into subtests that measure different types of intellectual tasks. Some tasks are mainly verbal, whereas others rely more on spatial-relations skills. Wechsler innovated a deviation IQ, which is based on how a child's test results differ from those of her or his age-mates.

13. Many psychologists and educators consider standard intelligence tests to be culturally biased. What is that controversy about?

Most psychologists and educational specialists believe that intelligence tests are at least somewhat biased against African Americans and members of lower social classes. In addition to any underlying cognitive competence, they reflect knowledge of the language in which the test is administered and middle-class European American culture. Yet supporters of standard intelligence tests argue that they accurately measure traits that are required in modern, high-tech societies. Culture-free tests have been developed, but they do not appear to be as successful in measuring academic success.

Recite Recite Recite Recite

14. How does intelligence develop?

There are rapid advances in intellectual functioning during childhood. During middle childhood, thought processes become increasingly logical and abstract, and children gain the capacity to focus on two or more aspects of a problem at once. The first intellectual spurt occurs at about the age of 6 and coincides with entry into school. The second spurt occurs at about 10 or 11. Intelligence tests gain greater predictive power during middle childhood.

15. What are the socioeconomic and ethnic differences in intelligence?

Lower-class U.S. children obtain IQ scores some 10 to 15 points lower than those obtained by middle- and upper-class children, and children from most ethnic minority groups tend to obtain IQ scores below those obtained by their European American age-mates. But Asian Americans tend to outscore European Americans, perhaps because of greater belief in the effectiveness of studying and because of hard work in academics. Some studies of IQ have confused the factors of social class and ethnicity.

16. What is mental retardation?

Mental retardation refers to limitations in intellectual functioning that are characterized by an IQ score of no more than 70 to 75 and concurrent limitations in adaptive skills. Most children who are retarded are mildly retarded. Children with Down syndrome are generally moderately retarded. Some of the causes of retardation are biological, but there is also cultural-familial retardation, in which the child does not develop normally because of social isolation.

17. What does it mean to be gifted?

Giftedness involves outstanding abilities, high performance in a specific academic area, such as language or mathematics, or leadership, distinction in the arts, or bodily talents. Terman's classic longitudinal studies of genius find that gifted children tend to be successful as adults.

18. What is creativity?

Creativity is the ability to do things that are novel and useful. Creative children take chances, refuse to accept limitations, and appreciate art and music.

19. What is the relationship between creativity and intelligence?

The relationship between intelligence test scores and measures of creativity are only moderate. Children mainly use *convergent* thinking to arrive at the correct answers on intelligence tests. Creative thinking tends to be *divergent* rather than convergent.

20. What do psychologists know about the determinants of intelligence? What are the roles of nature (heredity) and nurture (environmental influences)?

Various strategies are used to study genetic factors in intelligence, including kinship studies and studies of adopted children. The closer the relationship between people, the more alike their IQ scores, with identical twins having the most similar scores. The heritability of intelligence is estimated as 40% to 60%. The IQ scores of adopted children are more like those of their biological parents than those of their adoptive parents. Studies of environmental influences on IQ consider the situational factors that affect IQ scores—such as motivation, familiarity with testing materials, comfort in the testing situation, and stereotype vulnerability—and the effects of positive early environments.

21. How does language develop in middle childhood?

In middle childhood, language use becomes more sophisticated, including understanding that words can have multiple meanings. There are subtle advances in articulation and use of complex grammar, such as tag questions and passive sentences.

22. What cognitive skills are involved in reading?

Reading relies on skills in the integration of visual and auditory information. During the preschool years, neurological maturation and experience combine to allow most children to make visual discriminations between letters with relative ease. Children read either by the word-recognition method, in which they learn to associate written words with spoken sounds, or by the phonetic method, in which children learn to associate written letters and letter combinations with the sounds they signify.

Recite Recite Recite Recite

23. What is Ebonics?

Ebonics derives from the words *ebony* and *phonics,* and it refers to the English that was previously called Black English or Black Dialect. Ebonics has different grammatical rules than standard English, but the rules are consistent and allow for complex thought. There are key differences between Ebonics and standard English in the use of verbs, and Ebonics permits the use of double negatives.

24. What does research reveal about the advantages and disadvantages of bilingualism?

A century ago it was generally believed that children reared in bilingual homes were retarded in their cognitive development, as shown by mixing of the languages. However, recent research shows that children can generally separate the two languages from an early age and that most Americans who first spoke another language in the home also speak English well. Knowledge of more than one language also expands children's awareness of different cultures and broadens their perspectives.

On the Web

Search Online With InfoTrac College Edition

For additional information, explore InfoTrac College Edition, your online library. Go to **http://www.infotrac-college.com** and use the passcode on the InfoTrac card that came with your book. Try these search terms: intellect—research, intellect—genetic aspects, bilingual education, intelligence tests, mentally disabled children.

Visit Our Web Site

Go to **http://www.wadsworth.com/psychology** where you will find online resources directly linked to your book.

Child Development CD-ROM

Go to the Wadsworth Child Development CD-ROM for further study of the concepts in this chapter. The CD-ROM also includes quizzes and additional activities to expand your learning experience.

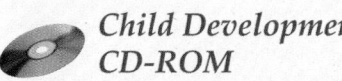

13 Middle Childhood: Social and Emotional Development

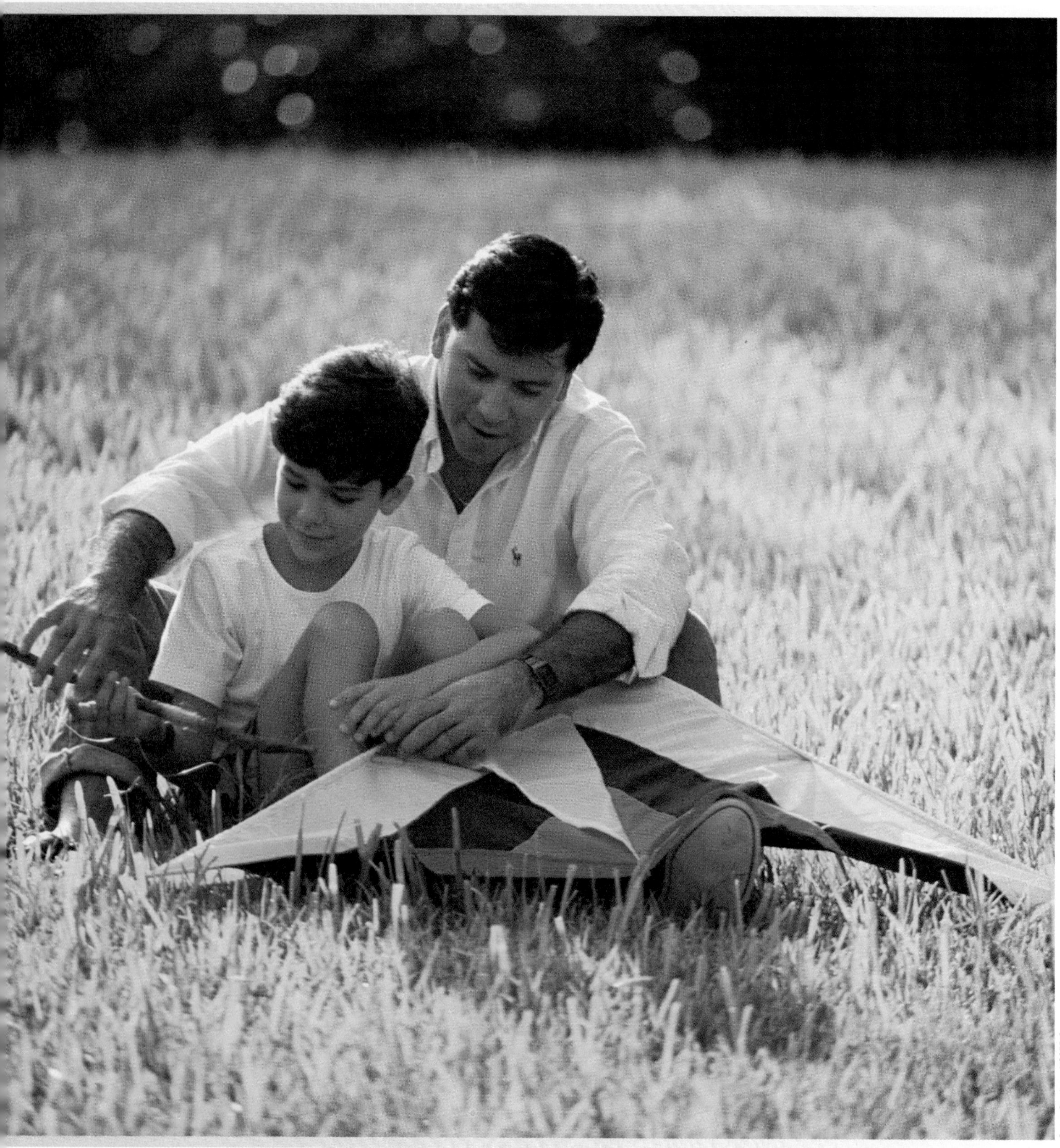

© Joe Gemignani/CORBIS

PowerPreview™

Theories of Social and Emotional Development in Middle Childhood

- **How do children think** of themselves in middle childhood? Do they focus on superficial traits, such as their appearance and activities, or do they include their interests and personality traits?
- **Children's self-esteem** tends to decline in middle childhood. Why?

Peer Relationships

- **How important are** peer influences in middle childhood?
- **What factors contribute** to popularity in middle childhood? Are children in this age group—like adolescents—pressured to conform?

The Family

- **What happens to the power** in the family during middle childhood? Do parents tend to share power with children in middle childhood, or do they tend to become more controlling and restrictive?
- **Should parents who are in conflict** stay together "for the sake of the children," or do children fare better when fighting parents separate?
- **The daughters of employed women** are more achievement-oriented and set themselves higher career goals than the daughters of unemployed women.

The School

- **What kinds of challenges** do children face when they enter school?—"real school," that is, not nursery school.
- **Have you heard of the "Pygmalion effect"?** It seems that teachers who have high expectations of students may elicit greater achievements from them—just as parents with high expectations do.
- **Did you know that teachers** are more likely to accept calling out from boys than from girls? Why?

Social and Emotional Problems

- **What is meant by the term** "conduct disorder"? (Is bad behavior a mental illness?)
- **Some children—like some adults**—blame themselves for all the problems in their lives, whether they deserve the blame or not.
- **Should children with school phobia** be forced to attend school, or is it better for them to remain at home until the origins of the problem are uncovered and resolved?

A college student taking a child development course had the following conversation with a 9-year-old girl named Karen:

Student: Karen, how was school today?
Karen: Oh, it was all right. I don't like it a lot.
Student: How come?
Karen: Sara and Becky won't talk to me. I told Sara I thought her dress was very pretty, and she pushed me out of the way. That made me so mad.
Student: That wasn't nice of them.
Karen: No one is nice except for Amy. At least she talks to me.

Here is part of a conversation between a different college student and her 9-year-old cousin Sue:

Sue: My girl friend Heather in school has the same glasses as you. My girl friend, no, not my girl friend—my friend—my friend picked them up yesterday from the doctor, and she wore them today.
Student: What do you mean—not your girl friend, but your friend? Is there a difference?
Sue: Yeah, my friend. 'Cause Wendy is my girl friend.
Student: But what's the difference between Heather your friend, and Wendy, your girl friend?
Sue: Well, Wendy is my best friend, so she's my girl friend. Heather isn't my best friend, so she's just a friend. (Adapted from Rowen, 1973)

In the years from 6 to 12, the child's social world expands. As illustrated by the remarks of these 9-year-old girls, peers take on greater importance, and friendships become deeper (Hamm, 2000). Entry into school exposes the child to the influence of teachers, as well as to a new peer group. Relationships with parents change as children develop greater independence. Some children will face adjustments resulting from the divorce and remarriage of parents. During these years, major advances occur in children's ability to understand themselves. Their knowledge of social relationships and their skill in developing such relationships increases as well (Collins, 1984a; Davis, 2001). Some children, unfortunately, develop problems during these years, although some are better able than others to cope with life's stresses.

In this chapter, we discuss each of these areas. First we examine major theories of social and emotional development in the middle years. We then examine the development of self-concept and of relationships with peers and parents. Then we turn to the influences of the changing family and the school. Finally, we look at some of the social and emotional problems that may arise in middle childhood.

Theories of Social and Emotional Development in Middle Childhood

Click *Social and Emotional Development* in the Child and Adolescent CD-ROM for more on Freud's view.

Question: What are some features of social and emotional development in middle childhood? The major theories of personality have had less to say about this age group than about the other periods of childhood and adolescence. Nevertheless, common threads emerge. These include the development of skills, the importance of interpersonal relationships, and the expansion of self-understanding.

Psychoanalytic Theory

latency stage In psychoanalytic theory, the fourth stage of psychosexual development; characterized by repression of sexual impulses and development of skills.

According to Freud, children in the middle years are in the **latency stage.** Freud believed that sexual feelings remain repressed (unconscious) during this period. Children use this period to focus on developing intellectual, social, and other culturally valued skills.

Erikson, like Freud, sees the major developmental task of middle childhood as the acquisition of cognitive and social skills. Erikson labels this stage **industry versus inferiority.** To the extent that children are able to master the various tasks and challenges of the middle years, they develop a sense of industry or competence. But if a child has difficulties in school or with peer relationships, a sense of inferiority may result.

Click *Social and Emotional Development* for more on Erikson's view.

Social Cognitive Theory

Social cognitive theory focuses on the continued importance of rewards and modeling in middle childhood. During these years, children depend less on external rewards and punishments and increasingly regulate their own behavior (Crain, 2000).

How do children acquire moral and social standards for judging their own behavior? One mechanism is direct reward and punishment. For example, parents may praise a child when she shares her toys with her younger brother. In time, she incorporates the importance of sharing into her own value system.

Another mechanism for acquiring self-evaluative standards is modeling. Children in the middle years are exposed to an increasing variety of models. Not only parents, but also teachers, other adults, peers, and symbolic models (such as TV characters or the heroine in a story) can serve as influential models (Bandura, 2000).

Reflect

Do you take other people's perspectives in your social relationships? Do you find it annoying when others are "totally into themselves"? Explain.

Cognitive-Developmental Theory and Social Cognition

Cognitive-developmental theory stresses the importance of the child's growing cognitive capacities. According to Piaget, middle childhood coincides with the stage of concrete operations and is partly characterized by a decline in egocentrism and an expansion of the capacity to view the world and oneself from other people's perspectives. This cognitive advance not only enhances the child's intellectual functioning, but also has a major impact on the child's social development.

Question: What is the relationship between social cognition and perspective taking? **Social cognition** refers to the development of children's knowledge about the social world. It focuses on the child's understanding of the relationship between the self and others. A key aspect of the development of social cognition is the ability to assume the role or perspective of another person. Robert Selman and his colleagues (Selman, 1980, 1989; Selman & Schultz, 1989) devised a method to study the development of perspective-taking skills in childhood. They presented children with a social dilemma like the following:

> Holly is an 8-year-old girl who likes to climb trees. She is the best tree climber in the neighborhood. One day while climbing down from a tall tree, she falls off the bottom branch but does not hurt herself. Her father sees her fall. He is upset and asks her to promise not to climb trees any more. Holly promises. Later that day, Holly and her friends meet Sean. Sean's kitten is caught up in a tree and can't get down. Something has to be done right away, or the kitten may fall. Holly is the only one who climbs trees well enough to reach the kitten and get it down, but she remembers her promise to her father. (Selman, 1980, p. 36)

Children then were asked a series of questions designed to test their ability to take the role of another person. (For example, "How will Holly's father feel if he finds out she climbed the tree?") Based on children's responses to these questions, Selman and his colleagues described five levels of perspective-taking skills in childhood (Selman, 1976; see Table 13.1).

industry versus inferiority The fourth stage of psychosocial development in Erikson's theory, occurring in middle childhood. Mastery of tasks leads to a sense of industry, while failure produces feelings of inferiority.

social cognition Development of children's understanding of the relationship between the self and others.

Development of Skills

According to traditional and modern psychoanalytic theories, the major development task of middle childhood is the acquisition of cognitive, social, physical, and other culturally valued skills. Children who develop valued skills tend to have high self-esteem and to be admired by their peers.

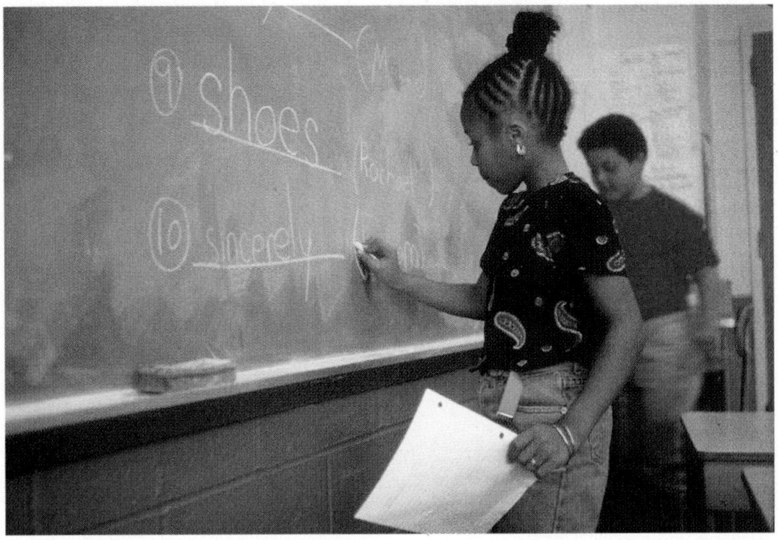

TABLE 13.1 *Levels of Perspective Taking*

Level	Approximate Age	About
0	3–6	Children are still egocentric and do not realize that other people have perspectives different from their own. A child of this age will typically say that Holly will save the kitten because she likes kittens and that her father will be happy because he likes kittens too. The child assumes that everyone feels as she does.
1	5–9*	Children understand that people in different situations or having different information may have different perspectives. But the child still assumes that only one perspective is "right." At this age, a child might say that Holly's father would be angry if he didn't know why she climbed the tree. But if she told him why, he would understand. The child recognizes that the father's perspective may differ from Holly's because of lack of information. But once he has the information, he will assume the "right" (that is, Holly's) perspective.
2	7–12	The child understands that people may think or feel differently because they have different values or ideas. The child also recognizes that others are capable of understanding the child's own perspective. Therefore, the child is better able to anticipate reactions of others. The typical child of this age might say that Holly knows that her father will understand why she climbed the tree and that he therefore won't punish her.
3	10–15	The child finally realizes that she and another person can both consider each other's point of view at the same time. The child may say something like this: Holly's father will think that Holly shouldn't have climbed the tree. But now that he has heard her side of the story, he would feel that she was doing what she thought was right. Holly realizes that her father will consider how she felt.
4	12 and above	The child realizes that mutual perspective taking doesn't always lead to agreement. The perspectives of the larger social group also must be considered. A child of this age might say that society expects children to obey their parents and, therefore, that Holly should realize why her father might punish her.

**Yes, there is overlap between the stages in terms of children's ages. Source: Selman, 1976.*

Research supports Selman's developmental progression in perspective taking (Dixon & Moore, 1990; R. Fox, 1991; Nakkula & Nikitopoulos, 2001). Also, as you might expect, children with better perspective-taking skills tend to be more skilled at peer relations (Strough et al., 2001; Zhang & Lin, 1999).

The Self-Concept

Reflect

How would you describe yourself? What traits or interests seem to be most important? How has your self-concept changed over the years?

Question: How does the self-concept develop during middle childhood? In early childhood, children's self-concepts, or self-definitions, focus on concrete external traits, such as appearance, activities, and living situations. But as children undergo the cognitive developments of middle childhood, their more abstract internal traits, or personality characteristics, begin to play a role in their self-definition. Social relationships and group memberships also take on significance (Damon, 1991; Damon & Hart, 1992).

An investigative method called the Twenty Statements Test bears out this progression and also highlights the relationships between the self-concept and general cognitive development. In this method, children are given a sheet of paper with the question "Who am I?" and 20 spaces in which to write answers. Consider the answers offered by a 9-year-old boy and an 11-year-old girl:

> The nine-year-old boy: My name is Bruce C. I have brown eyes. I have brown hair. I have brown eyebrows. I'm 9 years old. I LOVE? sports. I have 7 people in my family. I have great? eye site. I have lots! of friends. I live on 1923 Pinecrest Drive. I'm going on 10 in September. I'm a boy. I have a uncle that is almost 7 feet tall. My school is Pinecrest. My teacher is Mrs. V. I play hockey! I'm also the smartest boy in the class. I LOVE! food. I love fresh air. I LOVE school.

> The eleven-year-old girl: My name is A. I'm a human being. I'm a girl. I'm a truthful person. I'm not pretty. I do so-so in my studies. I'm a very good cellist. I'm a very good

> pianist. I'm a little bit tall for my age. I like several boys. I like several girls. I'm old fashioned. I play tennis. I am a very good musician. I try to be helpful. I'm always ready to be friends with anybody. Mostly I'm good, but I lose my temper. I'm not well liked by some girls and boys. I don't know if boys like me or not. (Montemayor & Eisen, 1977, pp. 317–318)

Only the 9-year-old lists his age and address, discusses his family, and focuses on physical traits, such as eye color, in his self-definition. The 9-year-old mentions his likes, which may be considered rudimentary psychological traits, but they are tied to the concrete, as would be expected of a concrete-operational child.

The 9- and 11-year-olds both list their competencies. The 11-year-old's struggle to bolster her self-esteem—her insistence on her musical abilities despite her qualms about her attractiveness—shows a greater concern with internal traits, psychological characteristics, and social relationships.

Research also finds that females are somewhat more likely than males to define themselves in terms of the groups to which they belong (Madson & Trafimow, 2001). A Chinese study found that children with siblings are more likely to define themselves in terms of group membership than are only children (Wang, Leichtman, & White, 1998).

Self-Esteem

One of the most critical aspects of self-concept is **self-esteem,** the value or worth that people attach to themselves. A positive self-image is crucial to psychological adjustment in children and adults (Chen, Chen, & Kaspar, 2001; Feinberg et al., 2000). ***Question: How does self-esteem develop during middle childhood?***

As children enter middle childhood, their self-concepts become more differentiated and they are able to evaluate their self-worth in many different areas (Tassi, Schneider, & Richard, 2001). Preschoolers do not generally make a clear distinction between different areas of competence. They are either "good at doing things" or not. At one time, it was assumed that prior to age 8, children could differentiate only between two broad facets of self-concept. One involved general competence and the other, social acceptance (Harter & Pike, 1984). It was also believed that an overall, or general, self-concept did not emerge until the age of 8. But research indicates that even as early as 5 to 7 years of age, children are able to make judgments about their performance in seven different areas: physical ability, physical appearance, peer relationships, parent relationships, reading, mathematics, and general school performance. They also display an overall, or general, self-concept (Eccles, Wigfield, Harold, & Blumenfeld, 1993; Marsh, Craven, & Debus, 1991).

Children's self-esteem declines throughout middle childhood, reaching a low point at about age 12 or 13 and then increasing during middle and late adolescence (Harter, 1990b, 1990c; Pomerantz et al., 1993). What accounts for the decline in self-esteem? Young children are egocentric, as we have seen, and their initial self-concepts may be unrealistic. As children become older, they incorporate more external information into their self-concepts as they compare themselves with other children. For most children, this results in a more realistic and critical self-appraisal and a decline in self-esteem.

Do girls or boys have a more favorable self-image? The answer depends on the area (Quatman & Watson, 2001). Girls tend to have more positive self-concepts regarding reading and general academics than boys do, whereas boys tend to have more positive self-concepts in math, physical ability, and physical appearance (Marsh et al., 1991; Eccles, 1999; Eccles, Wigfield, Harold, & Blumenfeld, 1993). Cross-cultural studies in China (Dai, 2001), Finland (Lepola, Varsus, & Macki, 2000), and Germany (Tiedemann, 2000) also find that girls tend to have higher self-concepts in writing and boys to have higher self-concepts in math.

Why do girls and boys differ in their self-concepts? Socialization and the presence of gender stereotypes appear to have an impact on the way females and males react to their own achievements. For example, girls predict that they will do

self-esteem The sense of value or worth that people attach to themselves.

© Jose Luis Pelaez, Inc./Corbis Stock Market

better on tasks that are labeled "feminine," and boys predict better performance for themselves when tasks are labeled "masculine" (Rathus et al., 2002).

A classic study by Stanley Coopersmith (1967) and more recent research (Baumrind, 1991a, 1991b; Furnham & Cheng, 2000; Hickman, Bartholomae, & McKenry, 2000) suggest that authoritative parenting contributes to high self-esteem in children. In other words, children with a favorable self-image tend to have parents who are strict, involved, and loving. Children with low self-esteem are more likely to have authoritarian or rejecting-neglecting parents.

High self-esteem in children is related to their closeness to their parents, especially as found in father–son and mother–daughter relationships (Dickstein & Posner, 1978; Elrod & Crase, 1980; Fenzel, 2000). Close relationships between the parents themselves also is associated with positive self-concepts in their children (Bagley et al., 2001; Maejima & Oguchi, 2001).

Authoritative Parenting and Self-Esteem

Classic and current research suggest that parental making of demands for mature behavior, imposition of restrictions, and warm encouragement help children develop behavior patterns that are connected with high self-esteem. These behavior patterns do not necessarily include the writing of impossible sentences, as in the case of this caption.

Peers also play an important role in children's self-esteem. Social acceptance by one's peers is related to children's self-perceived competence in a variety of domains—including academic, social, and athletic domains (Cole, 1991b). Parents and classmates have an equally strong impact on children's sense of self-worth in the middle years. Close friends and teachers have somewhat less influence in shaping self-esteem than parents and classmates, although they too play a role (Harter, 1987).

Self-esteem may also have a genetic component, which would contribute to its stability (McGuire et al., 1999). In any event, self-esteem, once established, seems to endure. One longitudinal study, for example, found that children's self-esteem remained stable from the ages of 7 to 11 years (Hoglund & Bell, 1991). Most children will encounter failure, but high self-esteem may contribute to a continuing belief that they can master adversity. Low self-esteem may become a self-fulfilling prophecy: Children with low self-esteem may not carve out much to boast about in life.

Reflect

Are you "responsible" for your own self-esteem, or does your self-esteem pretty much vary with the opinion that others have of you? Why is this an important question?

Learned Helplessness

One outcome of low self-esteem in the academic area is known as **learned helplessness.** ***Question: What is learned helplessness, and how does it develop in middle childhood?*** Learned helplessness refers to an acquired belief that one is unable to obtain the rewards that one seeks. "Helpless" children tend to quit following failure, whereas children who believe in their own ability tend to persist in their efforts or change their strategies (Zimmerman, 2000). One reason for this is that helpless children believe that success is due more to ability than to effort and that they have little ability in a particular area. Consequently, persisting in the face of failure seems futile to them (Bandura et al., 2001; Carr, Borkowski, & Maxwell, 1991). "Helpless" children typically perform more poorly than others in school and on standardized tests of intelligence and achievement (Chapman, Skinner, & Baltes, 1990).

Gender and Learned Helplessness

It is unclear whether girls or boys exhibit more learned helplessness in middle childhood (Boggiano & Barrett, 1991; Valas, 2001). But one area in which a gender difference appears to emerge is mathematics (Stipek & Gralinski, 1991). Jacquelynne Eccles and her colleagues have been carrying out longitudinal studies of elementary- and high-school-aged children (Anderman et al., 2001; Eccles et

learned helplessness An acquired (hence, *learned*) belief that one is unable to control one's environment.

al., 1991). They have found that even when girls are performing as well as boys in math and science, they have less confidence in their aptitude in these areas. Why is this? Parents' expectations that their children will do well (or poorly) in a given area influence both the children's own view of their abilities and their actual performance. Parents tend to hold the stereotyped view that girls have less math ability than boys. This is true regardless of their own daughter's actual mathematical performance. These lowered parental expectations appear to influence girls' estimates of their own abilities. Girls may ultimately shy away from math-related activities and therefore not develop their math skills to the extent that boys do (Eccles et al., 1991). This is an example of the self-fulfilling prophecy.

Review

(1) According to Freud, children in the middle years are in the ________ stage. (2) Erikson labels middle childhood the stage of ________ versus inferiority. (3) According to social cognitive theory, children in middle childhood depend less on external rewards and increasingly ________ their own behavior. (4) According to Piaget, middle childhood coincides with the stage of ________ operations. (5) A key aspect of the development of social cognition is the ability to take the ________ of another person. (6) Selman and his colleagues describe ________ levels of perspective-taking skills in childhood. (7) In middle childhood, children's internal ________ begin to play a role in their self-definition. (8) Children's self-esteem (increases or decreases?) during middle childhood. (9) A classic study by Coopersmith found that ________ parenting contributes to high self-esteem in children. (10) Learned ________ refers to an acquired belief that one is unable to obtain the rewards that one seeks.

Pulling It Together: What contributes to children's self-esteem during middle childhood?

Peer Relationships

Families exert the most powerful influences on a child during his or her first few years. But as children move into middle childhood, their activities and interests become directed farther away from home. ***Question: What is the influence of peers during middle childhood?*** Peers take on increasing importance in middle childhood. Let's explore the ways in which peers socialize one another. Then we examine factors in peer acceptance and rejection. Finally, we see how friendships develop.

Peers as Socialization Influences

Peer relationships are a major part of growing up. Peers exert powerful socialization influences and pressures to conform. As involved and authoritative as they may be, parents can provide their children only with experience in relating to adults. Children also profit from experience in relating to peers. Peers, like adults, have various needs and interests, competencies, and social skills. Not only do they belong to a different generation than parents, but they also differ as individuals. For all these reasons, peer experiences broaden children's lives (Molinari & Corsaro, 2000).

Peers guide children and afford practice in sharing and cooperating, in relating to leaders, and in coping with aggressive impulses, including their own. Peers can be important confidants (Dunn et al., 2001). Peers, like parents, help children learn what types of impulses—affectionate, aggressive, and so on—they can safely express, and with whom. Children who are at odds with their parents can turn to peers as sounding boards. With peers they can compare feelings and experiences they would not bring up in the home. When children share troubling ideas and experiences with peers, they often learn that their friends have similar concerns. They realize that they are normal and not alone (Corsaro & Eder, 1990; Zarbatany, Hartmann, & Rankin, 1990).

Peer Acceptance and Rejection

Acceptance or rejection by peers is of major importance, because problems with peers are a harbinger of later social and emotional maladjustment (Coie & Cillesen, 1993; McCendie & Schneider, 1993). What are the characteristics of popular and rejected children?

On a physical level, popular children tend to be attractive and relatively mature for their age, although physical attractiveness seems to be more important for girls than boys (Jackson, 1992; Langlois et al., 2000). Socially speaking, popular children are friendly, nurturant, cooperative, helpful, and skilled in social interaction (Chen et al., 2001; Newcomb et al., 1993). Popular children tend to be lavish in their dispensing of praise and approval (Landau & Milich, 1990). Popular children have higher self-esteem than other children—something that tends to be related to performance in academics or valued extracurricular activities such as sports (Chen et al., 2001).

Later-born children are more likely to be popular than first-borns, probably because they generally develop superior skills in relating to peers (Hartup, 1983). This trend holds despite the fact that school achievement is a factor in popularity and that first-borns tend to earn higher grades than later-borns.

Children who show behavioral and learning problems, who are aggressive, and who disrupt group activities by bickering or deviant behavior are more likely to be rejected by their peers (Eisenberg et al., 1993; Walter & LaFreniere, 2000). Shy, socially withdrawn children also are likely to be unpopular with their peers

Peer Rejection

Few things are as painful as rejection by one's peers in middle childhood. Children may be rejected if they look unusual or unattractive, if they lack valued skills, or if they are aggressive. Peer rejection in middle childhood can lead to the development of serious social and emotional problems. However, teaching children physical and social skills can enhance their popularity.

(Rubin, 1993; Volling, MacKinnon-Lewis, & Dechman, 1993).

Although pressure to conform to group norms and standards can be powerful indeed, most children who are rejected do not shape up their behavior. Instead, they tend to remain alone, lonely, and on the fringes of the group (Cassidy & Asher, 1992; Crick & Ladd, 1993; Parker & Asher, 1993). In some cases, they join deviant subcultures whose values and goals differ from those of the mainstream. Fortunately, training in social skills seems to have the capacity to increase children's popularity with peers (Cashwell, Skinner, & Smith, 2001; Webster-Stratton, Reid, & Hammond, 2001b).

© Bob Daemmrich/Stock, Boston/PictureQuest

■ Development of Friendships

Question: How do children's concepts of friendship develop? In the early years of middle childhood, friendships are based on geographical closeness or proximity. Friendships are relatively superficial—quickly formed, easily broken. What matters are shared activities and who has the swing set or sandbox. Five- to 7-year-olds usually report that their friends are the children with whom they share activities (Berndt & Perry, 1986; Epstein, 1989). There is little reference to friends' traits.

Between the ages of 8 and 11, children show increased recognition of the importance of friends meeting each other's needs and possessing desirable traits (Zarbatany, McDougall, & Hymel, 2000). Children at these ages are more likely to say that friends are nice to one another and share interests as well as things. During these years, children increasingly pick friends who are similar to themselves in behavior and personality. A sense of loyalty, mutual understanding, and a willingness to disclose personal information characterize friendships in middle childhood and adolescence (Clark & Bittle, 1992; Hamm, 2000; Hartup, 1993). Girls tend to develop more intimate friendships than boys (Zabartany et al., 2000). That is, girls are more likely to seek confidants in friends—girls with whom they can share their inmost feelings.

Robert Selman (1980) has described five stages in children's changing concepts of friendship (see Table 13.2). The stages correspond to the five levels of perspective-taking skills discussed earlier in the chapter.

Friends behave differently with each other than they do with children who are not their friends. School-age friends are more verbal, attentive, expressive, relaxed, and mutually responsive to each other during play than are children who are only acquaintances (Field et al., 1992). Cooperation occurs more readily between friends than between other groupings, as might be expected. But intense competition may also occur among friends, especially among boys (Hartup, 1993). When conflicts occur between friends, they tend to be less intense and are resolved in ways that maintain positive social interaction (Hartup, 1993; Laursen, 1993).

In one study, 696 fourth- and fifth-grade children responded to 30 hypothetical situations involving conflict with a friend (Rose & Asher, 1999). It was found that those children who responded to conflict by seeking revenge were least likely to have friendships or close friendships. Gender differences were also found. Girls were generally more interested in resolving conflicts than boys were.[1]

Children in middle childhood typically will tell you that they have more than one "best" friend (Berndt, Miller, & Park, 1989). One study found that 9-year-

■ Friendship, Friendship . . . A Perfect "Blendship"?

Children's concepts of friendship develop over time. Early on, "friends" are simply those with whom children do things or those who are nearby. In middle childhood, friendship is generally seen in terms of what children do for each other. Later on, in adolescence, children will usually focus on the nature of the relationship itself. These children are at a stage in which they are beginning to value loyalty and intimacy in their friendship.

Reflect

What do you look for in a friend? What "stage" are you in, according to Table 13.2?

[1]"So, what's new?" asks the author's wife.

TABLE 13.2 *Stages in Children's Concepts of Friendship*

Number	Name	Approximate Age	About
0	Momentary physical interaction	3–6	Children remain egocentric and unable to take one another's point of view. Thus, their concept of a friend is one who likes to play with the same things they do and who lives nearby.
1	One-way assistance	5–9	The child realizes that he/she and friends may have different thoughts and feelings but places his/her own desires first. He/she views a friend as someone who does what he/she wants.
2	Fair-weather cooperation	7–12	Friends are viewed as doing things for one another (reciprocity), but the focus remains on each individual's self-interest rather than on the relationship per se.
3	Intimate and mutual sharing	10–15	Now the focus is on the relationship itself, rather than on the individuals separately. The function of friendship is viewed as mutual support over a long period of time, rather than concern about a given activity or self-interest.
4	Autonomous interdependence	12 and above	Children understand that friendships grow and change as people change. They realize that they may need different friends to satisfy different personal and social needs.

Source: Selman, 1980.

olds reported having an average of four best friends (Lewis & Feiring, 1989). Best friends tend to be more similar to each other than other friends (Epstein, 1989).

In middle childhood, girls and boys do not differ in the number of best friends they report (Benenson, 1990; Krappmann et al., 1993). Boys tend to play in larger groups than girls, however. By middle childhood, children's friendships are almost exclusively with others of the same gender, continuing the trend of gender segregation that began in the early years (Hartup, 1993; Krappmann et al., 1993).

During middle childhood, contact with members of the other gender is strongly discouraged by peers. For example, a study of European American, African American, Latino and Latina American, and Native American 10- and 11-year-olds found that those who crossed the "gender boundary" were especially unpopular with their peers (Sroufe et al., 1993). Even so, there are certain circumstances under which contact with the other gender is acceptable, as shown in Table 13.3.

Review

(11) As children move into middle childhood, their activities and interests become directed (closer to or farther away from?) the home. (12) Popular children tend to be attractive and relatively (mature or immature?) for their age. (13) (First-born or Later-born?) children are more likely to be popular. (14) Most children who are rejected by peers (do or do not?) improve their behavior. (15) During middle childhood, children (do or do not?) tend to choose children with similar interests as their friends. (16) During middle childhood, contact with members of the other gender is (encouraged or discouraged?) by peers.

Pulling It Together: How do peers enhance children's development during middle childhood?

TABLE 13.3 *Knowing the Rules: When Is Contact With the Other Gender Permissible? (In Middle Childhood, That Is)*

Rule	Nonverbal–Performance Items
The contact is accidental. ("Well, excuse me.")	You're not looking where you're going, and you bump into someone.
The contact is incidental. ("Hey, they just happened to be there.")	You go to get some lemonade (why not?) and wait in line while two children of the other gender get some. (There should be no conversation.)
The contact is in the guise of some clear and necessary purpose. ("So what else was I supposed to do?")	You may "pass the lemonade" to people of the other gender at the next table. There is no display of interest in them.
An adult compels you to have contact. ("So how else was I supposed to get it?")	"Go get that map from X and Y and bring it to me."
You are accompanied by someone of your own gender. ("I was with Emily, not *them*.")	Two girls may talk to two boys but they must maintain closeness with their own partners and avoid intimacy with the boys.
The interaction or contact is accompanied by disavowal. ("You shoulda seen what I said/did to them!")	You say someone is ugly or hurl some other insult or—more commonly in the case of boys (ugh)—push or throw something at them as you pass by.

Source of useful information about rules and examples: Sroufe, Bennett, Englund, Urban, & Shulman, 1993. Source of unnecessary and annoying parenthetical statements: Your author.

The Family

Question: What kinds of influences are exerted by the family during middle childhood? In middle childhood, the family continues to play a key role in socializing the child, even though peers, teachers, and others outside the family begin to play a greater role than before (Maccoby, 1984a; Peterson, 2001). In this section, we examine developments in parent–child relationships during the middle years. We also look at the effects of living in different types of family environments. We focus on three aspects of family diversity. The first deals with families in different ethnic groups. The second concerns the experience of living in families with varying marital arrangements: original two parents, single parent, stepparent. The third area of family diversity deals with the effects of having a mother who is or is not in the labor force.

Parent–Child Relationships

Parent–child interactions focus on some new concerns during the middle childhood years. These include school-related matters, assignment of chores, and peer activities (DeLuccie & Davis, 1991; Maccoby, 1984a).

During the middle years, parents do less monitoring of children's activities and provide less direct feedback than they did in the preschool years. In middle childhood, children do more monitoring of their own behavior. While the parents still retain control over the child, there is a gradual transfer of control from parent to child, a process known as **coregulation** (Maccoby, 1984b; Wahler, Herring, & Edwards, 2001). Children no longer need to be constantly reminded of do's and don'ts as they begin to internalize the standards of their parents.

Children and parents spend less time together in middle childhood than in the preschool years. But as in the early childhood years, children spend more time

coregulation A gradual transferring of control from parent to child, beginning in middle childhood.

with their mothers than with their fathers (Russell & Russell, 1987). Mothers' interactions with their school-age children continue to revolve around caregiving and household tasks, while fathers are more involved in recreational activities, especially with sons (Collins & Russell, 1991).

In the later years of middle childhood (ages 10 to 12), children evaluate their parents more critically than they do in the early years (Reid et al., 1990). This shift in perception may reflect the child's growing social cognitive capacity to perceive relationships in more complex ways (Selman, 1989). But throughout middle childhood, children rate their parents as their best source of emotional support, rating them even more highly than friends (Reid et al., 1990).

Generation X or Generation EX? What Happens to Children Whose Parents Get Divorced?

To many in the United States, the turn of the millennium was the period of "Generation X." However, it may be more accurate to think of our time at that of "Generation EX"—that is, a generation characterized by ex-wives and ex-husbands. Their children are also a part of Generation EX, which is large and growing continuously. More than 1 million American children each year experience the divorce of their parents (Morrison & Coiro, 1999). Nearly 40% of European American children and 75% of African American children in the United States who are born to married parents will spend at least part of their childhoods in single-parent families resulting from divorce (Amato, 2001). ***Question: What are the effects of divorce on the children?***

Reflect

Have you known children whose families have undergone divorce? What were (or are*) the effects on the children?*

Divorce may be tough on the parents; it can be even tougher on the children (Amato, 2000; Ellis, 2000; Schmidtgall et al., 2000). All the automatic aspects of family life cease being automatic. No longer do children eat with both parents. No longer do they go to ball games, the movies, or to Disneyland with both of them. No longer do they curl up with them on the sofa to watch television. No longer do they kiss both at bedtime. Everything that had occurred automatically now occurs piecemeal or not at all. The parents themselves are now usually supporting two households, resulting in fewer resources for the children (Coleman et al., 1999). Children lose things as well as family life. Sometimes the losses are minor, but many children who live with their mothers scrape by—or fail to scrape by—at the poverty level or below. Some children must move from spacious houses into cramped apartments or from a desirable neighborhood to one where they are afraid to walk the streets. The same mother who was once available may become something of an occasional visitor—spending more time at work and putting the kids in day care for extended periods.

In considering the effects of divorce on family members—both children and adults—Paul Amato (2000) suggests that researchers need to address five questions:

- How do individuals from married and divorced families differ in their well-being? We will see that the children of divorce tend to suffer.
- Are these differences due to divorce or to "selection factors"? For example, are the effects on children due to divorce per se, to marital conflict, to inadequate problem-solving ability on the part of parents, or to changes in financial status (yadayada)?
- Do these differences reflect a temporary crisis to which most children gradually adjust, or are they stressors that persist more or less indefinitely? For example, children are likely to greet news of a divorce with sadness, shock, and disbelief (Burns & Dunlop, 1999). Feelings of relief (at anticipated escape from marital conflict), anger toward the parent they see as responsible for the breakup, and the desire for parental reunion are also common. Three years later, the sadness, shock, disbelief, and desire for parental reunion tend to decline sharply, while feelings of relief may remain. Even 10 years later, children tend to retain anger toward the parent they hold responsible for the family problems.

- What factors mediate the effects of divorce on the adjustment of the child? For example, what happens when divorced parents cooperate in child-rearing strategies and provide as much support as possible?
- What are the moderators (protective factors) that account for individual variability in adjustment to divorce? For example, children aged 8 to 12 who see themselves as being in control of their lives are more likely to adjust to breakup of the family (Sandler, Kim-Bae, & MacKinnon, 2000).

Parents who get divorced are often in conflict about many things, and one of them typically involves how to rear the children. The children usually hear them fighting over how to handle them, and so they may come to blame themselves for the split. Young children, less experienced than adolescents, are more likely to blame themselves for the divorce. Young children also worry more about uncharted territory—in this case, the details of life after the breakup. Adolescents are relatively more independent and have often had the chance to learn that they have some power to control their day-to-day lives.

Most children live with their mothers after a divorce. Some fathers remain fully devoted to their children despite the split, but others tend to spend progressively less time with their children as time goes on (Clingempeel & Repucci, 1982). This pattern is especially common when fathers create other families, such that the children of their new partners are in effect competing for time with their biological children. Not only does the drop off in paternal attention deprive children of various activities and social interactions, but it also saps their self-esteem. "Why doesn't Daddy love me anymore? What's wrong with me?" As part of the pattern, fathers are best about keeping up with child support payments at first, and then the majority fail to make them, contributing to the family's socioeconomic decline.

There is no question that divorce has challenging consequences for the children (Ellis, 2000). The children of divorce are more likely to have psychological problems and conduct disorders, to have lower self-esteem, to abuse drugs and alcohol, and to do more poorly in school (Amato, 2001; Chao, Wang, & He, 2001; O'Connor et al., 2000). There are individual differences in all of this, but by and large, the fallout for children is worst during the 1st year after the breakup, and children tend to rebound after a couple of years or so.

There can be enduring problems. Wallerstein and Blakeslee (1989) engaged in numerous case studies and reported that even a decade years after the split, a sizable minority of children continued to have problems with school, self-esteem, anger, and anxiety. They also found a so-called sleeper effect. That is, even children who appeared to bounce back reported problems later on, especially when it came to the development of their own intimate relationships. For example, many did not believe that their partners' commitments were permanent.

A parental breakup itself apparently turns a child's world topsy-turvy, but is also connected with a disorienting and disruptive decline in the caliber of parenting. A longitudinal study by E. Mavis Hetherington and her colleagues (Hetherington, 1987, 1989; Hetherington, Stanley-Hagan, & Anderson, 1989) tracked the adjustment of children who were 4 years old at the time of the divorce at 2 months, 1 year, 2 years, and 6 years following divorce. They found that the organization of family life tends to deteriorate following divorce. The family is more likely to eat their meals pick-up style, as opposed to sitting down together. Children are less likely to get to school on time or to get to sleep at a regular hour. Divorced mothers have a more difficult time setting limits and enforcing restrictions on sons' behavior. The Hetherington group found that divorced parents, on the whole, are significantly less likely to show the authoritative behaviors that foster instrumental competence. They make fewer demands for mature behavior, show a decline in communication ability, and show less nurturance and warmth. Moreover, their disciplinary methods become inconsistent. And divorced parents who show the poorest parenting skills are more likely to have poorly adjusted children.

Cross-cultural studies show that children of divorce in other cultures experience problems similar to those experienced by children in the United States. For example, one study in China matched 58 children of divorce with 116 children from intact families according to gender, age, and social class. Children of divorce were more likely to make somatic complaints ("My stomach hurts," "I feel nauseous"), demonstrate lower social competence, and behave aggressively than the other children (Liu et al., 2000). Another Chinese study found that the dissolution of a family impairs the quality of parent–child relationships, interferes with parental concern over the children's education, and creates financial distress—all of which hurt the social and emotional well-being of the child (Sun, 2001). A third Chinese study documents the parallel ways in which divorce compromises the academic and social functioning of both Chinese and American children (Zhou et al., 2001).

A study of children and their mothers in Botswana, Africa, has similar findings (Maundeni, 2000). Most of the mothers and children in this study reported that divorce was followed by economic hardship. Economic hardships made some children feel inferior to children who had more resources available. Financial concerns and feelings of resentment and betrayal among the children of divorce led to social and emotional problems. Similar feelings were expressed by the children's mothers.

Back to the United States: Boys seem to have a harder time than girls coping with divorce and they take a longer time to recover (Grych et al., 2000). In the Hetherington study, boys whose parents were divorced showed more conduct problems and more difficulties in peer relations and school achievement than boys whose parents were married. These difficulties sometimes continued up to 6 years following divorce. Girls, on the other hand, tended to be functioning well within 2 years after divorce (Hetherington 1989; Hetherington et al., 1989).

Does a child's age at the time of the divorce make a difference in how well the child adapts? The picture is unclear. Some studies find that preschoolers have the hardest time adjusting, whereas others indicate that children in the elementary and high school years are affected most (Amato, 2001).

A clearer picture emerges for the roles of child temperament and parenting style. Consider three clusters of children identified by Hetherington (1989) 6 years after their parents' divorce: One group, labeled "aggressive and insecure," consisted largely of boys. They were impulsive, aggressive, and socially withdrawn. These children had been temperamentally difficult since early childhood. Their parents tended to use neglecting or authoritarian parenting styles. The other two clusters consisted of competent children who were functioning well. These children had high self-esteem, few behavior problems, got along well with peers and teachers, and did well in school. They had a caring relationship with at least one supportive adult, often a parent but sometimes another relative, teacher, or neighbor. One of the two clusters, called opportunistic-competent, consisted equally of girls and boys. These children were manipulative and opportunistic, often playing one parent against the other. Their families tended to be high in conflict. The caring-competent cluster consisted mostly of girls. They were very prosocial in their behavior and often looked after younger siblings. Their mothers were warm and supportive and encouraged mature independent behavior. In other words, their mothers showed an authoritative parenting style, which, as we have seen, fosters competence in children.

K. Alison Clarke-Stewart and her colleagues (2000) compared the well-being of the children in families headed by a separated or divorced mother with that of about 170 children reared in intact families. The focus of this study was on infancy and early childhood. As a group, the children who were being reared in two-parent families exhibited fewer problematic behaviors, more social skills, and higher scores on tests of intellectual functioning. They were also more securely attached to their mothers. But then the researchers factored in the mother's level of education, her socioeconomic status, and her psychological well-being. Somewhat surprisingly, the differences between the children in the two groups (one-parent versus intact families) decreased to the point where they could represent chance fluctuation. The researchers concluded that at least in this study, it was not the parental breakup per se that caused the problems among the children.

Instead, the difficulties were connected with maternal psychological status, such as feelings of depression, income, and level of education.

It is also possible for the children of divorce to receive psychological help that is appropriate to their age. Many programs include one or both parents. One study of a program that includes the mother assessed its utility with 240 children aged 9 to 12 (Wolchik et al., 2000). The program addressed the quality of the mother–child relationship, ways of disciplining the child, ways of coping with interparental conflict, and the nature of the father–child relationship. Children were also helped to evaluate the way they perceived the stressors in their lives; they were helped to see, for example that the stressors were difficult but not impossible and that they were not to blame for them. This program found significant improvements in the adjustment of the children when the program was completed and at a 6-month follow-up.

© Michael W. Nelson/Stock South/PictureQuest

Generation EX: Ex-Husband, Ex-Wife, Ex-Family, Ex-Security

A good half of marriages today end in divorce, and divorce turns life topsy-turvy for children. Younger children tend to erroneously blame themselves for the dissolution of the family, but children in middle childhood come to see things more accurately. Children of divorce tend to develop academic, behavioral, and emotional problems, many of which fade as time passes. The tendency to remain angry toward the parent they see as responsible for the break-up lingers. Should parents in conflict stay together for the sake of the children? The answer seems to be that the children will not be better off if the parents continue to fight in front of them.

Life in Stepfamilies: His, Hers, Theirs, and . . .

The majority of people who get divorced remarry and usually while the children are still young. More than one in three American children will spend part of his or her childhood in a stepfamily (Coleman, Ganong, & Fine, 2000).

The rule of thumb about the effects of living in stepfamilies is that there is no rule of thumb. Living in a stepfamily may have no measurable psychological effect at all (Coleman et al., 2000). Men can exert positive influences on stepsons, and women can exert positive influences on stepdaughters. Consider a study on the effects of stepparenting on children in middle school. It was found that good stepmother–stepchild relationships were linked with less aggressive behavior in both boys and girls and with higher self-esteem among stepdaughters (Clingempeel & Segal, 1986). In this particular study, frequent visits with a nonresident biological mother appeared to impair relations between stepmothers and stepdaughters. It may be that the natural mothers encouraged their daughters not to get too close to their stepmothers. However, even in these cases, stepmother–stepdaughter relationships showed improvement as time passed.

But not everything comes up roses in stepfamilies. There are some risks. Infanticide (killing infants) is a rarity in the United States, but the crime occurs 60 times as often in stepfamilies as in families with biological kinship (Daly & Wilson, 1998). There is also a significantly higher incidence—by a factor of eight—of sexual abuse by stepparents than by natural parents.

Why do we find these risks in stepfamilies? There are the garden-variety psychosocial explanations. For example, stepfamilies may encounter more economic stress than the intact family, and the individuals in such families are less traditional than those who stick to their marital vows come what may. (On the other hand, strong belief in the traditional family structure is not a prescription for docility.) When it comes to the issue of sexual abuse, we can note that stepparents, like biological parents, are clearly committing a crime when they involve minors in sexual activity. And, again like biological parents, they are breaking their marital vows. However, they are not breaking the incest taboo, and this factor may be involved in the added risk. Evolutionary psychologists also have something to say about the risks of being in stepfamilies. According to evolutionary psychologists, people often behave as if they want their genes to flourish in the next generation. Thus it could be that stepparents are less devoted to rearing the children of other people than their own. They may even see "foreign" children as competitors for resources with their own children; stepfathers in particular may see a woman's possession of children by another man as lessening her capacity to bear and rear their own children (Brody, 1998a). Evolutionary psychologists then often stray into research that describes how dominant males in many species do away with the offspring of females that have been sired by other males. (I'm not going there.)

"All Right, We Fight—Should We Remain Married 'for the Sake of the Children'?"

Question: So what is best for the children? Should parents who bicker remain together for their sake? Let's have it out at once. I am going to address this issue from a psychological perspective only. Many readers will believe—for moral reasons—that marriage and family life are permanent, no matter what. Readers will have to consider the moral issue in the light of their own value systems.

So—from a purely psychological perspective—what should bickering parents do? The answer seems to largely depend on how they behave in the company of the children. Research shows that parental bickering—especially severe fighting—is linked to the same kinds of problems that children experience when their parents get separated or divorced (Amato, 2000; 2001; Davies & Cummings, 1994). Perpetual bickering causes psychological turmoil both in children and adolescents (Furstenberg & Kiernan, 2001). Moreover, when children are exposed to marital conflict, they display elements of an upsetting physiological "alarm reaction": their heart rate, systolic and diastolic blood pressure, and skin conductance response (a measure of perspiration) all rise sharply (El-Sheikh & Harger, 2001). The bodily response is stronger yet when children blame themselves for the marital conflict, which is common among younger children.

Developing in the New Millennium

Online Visitation—A New Wrinkle in Divorce's "Move-Away" Cases

Among divorce lawyers, they are known as move-away cases: the often-bitter disputes that flare when parents with custody of children try to relocate far from ex-spouses with visiting rights. For better or worse, the long-distance prowess of Internet technology is expected to play an expanding role as these cases reach America's courtrooms. The pivotal question: Should the prospect of "virtual visitation"—through e-mail, instant messages, and video-conferencing—make it easier for a custodial parent to get permission to move?

A New Jersey appeals court broached this new legal frontier earlier this year. It ruled that online visiting—along with face-to-face contact—would be a "creative and innovative" way for a father to stay in touch with his 9-year-old daughter if the man's ex-wife moved to California over his objections. The woman later decided against moving, but the ruling intrigued family-law specialists and alarmed fathers-rights advocates.

"This will be another tool for judges to further distance fathers from their children's lives," said Stuart Miller of the American Fathers Coalition, whose group believes family courts are biased in favor of mothers.

Legal experts think it's inevitable that custodial parents seeking to move will propose virtual visitation in hopes of swaying judges.

"From now on, if I have clients who want to move, I'd tell them to offer to buy a (Web) camera and set that up," said Norma Trusch, a family-law attorney from Houston. "It's true that you can't hug a computer," said Trusch, quoting a mantra of virtual visitation opponents. "On the other hand, it's possible with these communication methods to maintain a very close, continual relationship with a child."

Linda Elrod, who chairs the American Bar Association's family law section, said judges won't be able to ignore the new technology as they weigh conflicting pleas from divorced parents. "Move-away cases are balancing acts—one parent's upward mobility versus the other's continuing contact with the child," said Elrod.

Many divorced parents already use virtual visitation—not under court order but because it helps them maintain ties with faraway children. Jim Buie, an Internet consultant from Takoma Park, Md., has published an online journal about his efforts to stay in touch with his son, Matthew—now 17—in the eight years since Matthew and Buie's ex-wife moved to North Carolina. From 500 miles away, Buie has assisted Matthew with homework, helped him create a Web page, e-mailed photographs, and played online chess and Scrabble.

"Virtual parenting is not a panacea. You're still going to have the heartache of not being together," Buie said. "But, alas, it's better than no relationship at all."

Source: Reprinted from David Crary. (2001, May 5). Online visitation new in divorce. New York: Associated Press. Used by permission.

One study analyzed data from 727 children aged 4 to 9 years from intact families and followed them 6 years later, when many of the families had undergone separation or divorce (Morrison & Coiro, 1999). It was found that both separation and divorce were associated with increases in behavior problems in children, regardless of the amount of conflict between the parents. However, in the marriages that remained intact, high levels of marital conflict were associated with even greater increases in children's behavior problems. Message? It seems that separation and divorce are clearly connected with adjustment problems in the children. However, when parents in conflict remain together, the outcomes for the children may be even worse.

The problems caused by parents in conflict are demonstrated in studies that show that many of the psychological problems seen in the children of divorce can be explained by issues in the years prior to the divorce (Kelly, 2000). The children of divorced parents, as a group, have more adjustment problems than the children of intact families. However, these studies question whether the divorce per se is the major cause of these problems because troubled marriages give rise to such problems in the children long before the breakup (Furstenberg & Kiernan, 2001).

Because of the stresses experienced by children caught up in marital conflict, E. Mavis Hetherington suggests that "Divorce is often a positive solution to destructive family functioning" (1989, p. 857). Even so, we still do not know all we need to know about the long-term effects of divorce on children and adolescents. Since many more millions of children are obviously going to be joining the ranks of "Generation EX," this knowledge remains vital to helping us enhance their well-being.

The Effects of Maternal Employment

As we navigate the early years of the third millennium, most people in the United States take the mother's participation in the workforce for granted. Yet in traditionalist societies, such as many in the Middle East and Central Asia, a woman's place is seen as being in the home—and, in some cases, as covering her body from

Reflect

Why is this section labeled "The Effects of Maternal Employment"? Why not parental employment or paternal employment?

Robert Whitfield of Reston, Va., has tried using the Internet to sustain a long-distance relationship with two sons who moved with his ex-wife to New Jersey. He's concerned that court-ordered Web visits could hurt dads in the long run. "Gaining access to their children for most fathers is difficult at best," Whitfield said. "It is likely to become more difficult when a mother says to a judge: 'Johnny can talk to his father on the computer whenever he wants to.'"

Buie's online parenting has been encouraged by his ex-wife, but he suggested that virtual visitation could founder if the divorced parents are hostile. "The custodial parent can sabotage the noncustodial parent's online access to the child, or the noncustodial parent could use bad judgment and introduce the child to things online the child should not be exposed to," Buie said.

No federal laws govern move-aways; they are resolved case by case based on court precedents and state legislation. In recent years, some courts have made it easier for custodial parents to relocate. In California, for example, a parent simply needs to demonstrate that a move is in the child's best interest; in the past, there had to be urgent circumstances. In other states, legislators have tightened move-away criteria, for example requiring longer advance notice before a custodial parent can move.

"We're afraid the Internet will be seen as a trend to make move-aways easier—we want to make them harder," said David Levy, president of Children's Rights Council, which promotes the rights of noncustodial parents.

Richard Crouch, a Virginia lawyer who formerly chaired the ABA's child custody committee, said move-away cases have become "part of the wars of sexual politics," with feminist groups pressing to make relocation more commonplace.

The co-president of the National Women's Law Center, Nancy Duff Campbell, said her Washington-based group believes courts should ease restrictions on move-aways. But ideally, she said, divorced parents could negotiate mutually acceptable arrangements, possibly including Internet visitation. "If there must be separation, it's something that can help the families," she said.

In Philadelphia, one judge already has been encouraging divorced parents to include online technology in their custody and visitation arrangements. "It can be educational for the children, and brings the parents together," said Judge Robert Matthews. "It doesn't replace a hug, but it sure beats not being able to see your kid grow up."

Search Online With InfoTrac College Edition

For additional information, explore InfoTrac College Edition, your online library. Go to **http://www.infotrac-college.com** and use the passcode from the InfoTrac card that came with your book. Try these search terms: visitation rights, joint custody, custody of children, child visitation.

What Are the Effects of Maternal Employment?

Let's be honest here. (Can we talk?) Why doesn't the caption read, "What are the effects of parental employment?" The answer is that the vestiges of sexism continue to run rampant in society. (Don't you hate it when vestiges run rampant?) When things go wrong with children in families where both parents must work—or choose to work—a tendency remains to blame the mother. By and large, research shows that both parents' working is actually connected with few problems with children, but is connected with more egalitarian attitudes. (Go, Mom!)

head to foot when she leaves the home. The past half century has witnessed one of the most dramatic social changes in the history of the United States. Mothers are entering the labor force in record-breaking numbers. A half century ago, most women in the United States also remained in the home. But today, nearly three out of four married mothers of children under age 18 are employed, as are four out of five divorced, separated, or widowed mothers (U.S. Bureau of the Census, 2000). The direction of movement is up, up, up (U.S. Bureau of the Census, 2000). Lifestyles have changed significantly for American families as more women combine maternal and occupational roles. The same social forces that have given rise to women's movement into the workforce have also strengthened the movement toward gender equality (Scarr, 1998).

Yes, women are now in the workforce in droves. ***Question: What are the effects of maternal employment on children?*** Do problems arise when mother is not available for round-the-clock love and attention?

Over the years, many psychologists and educators—as well as lay commentators—have been concerned about the effects of maternal employment on children. Part of the brouhaha has been based on traditionalist, moralistic values which argue that the mother ought to be in the home. But some concern has also been based on research findings by respected professionals which suggest that maternal employment (and its consequence—nonmaternal care) have been demonstrated to have some negative effects on children (Belsky, 2001).

One common belief is that delinquency is one of the consequences of mom's being in the workforce rather than in the home. Using data on 707 adolescents aged 12 to 14 from the National Longitudinal Survey of Youth (NLSY), Vander Ven and colleagues (2001) examined whether the occupational status of a mother actually had an effect on delinquent behavior. They found that maternal employment per se had relatively little or no influence on delinquent behaviors, but there was a slight indirect effect in that deviant behavior was connected somewhat with lack of supervision. The pattern held regardless of whether mothers worked when children were in the preschool years or were currently on the job. The issue, then, would seem to be for the parents to assure that children receive adequate supervision regardless of who—mom or dad—is on the job.

We see right here that the entire issue is gender-biased in the sense that the evidence suggests that paternal employment is as potentially harmful to children as is maternal employment. Yet it would be preposterous to argue that fathers rather than mothers should remain in the home to ward off any problems related to poor supervision. Why? Because the father is the traditional breadwinner and the mother is the traditional homemaker. Tradition often has the effect of exposing today's mothers to a double shift: one in the workforce and another in the home.

Political and moral arguments aside, there is little evidence that maternal employment is significantly detrimental to children (Harvey, 1999; Gottfried, Bathurst, & Gottfried, 1994). Elizabeth Harvey (1999) and other researchers (Han, Waldfogel, & Brooks-Gunn, 2001) have also examined data from the National Longitudinal Survey of Youth on the effects of early parental employment on children. The effects, such as they were, were minimal. Neither the timing nor the continuity of early maternal employment was consistently related to children's development. Harvey did find that working a greater number of hours was linked with slightly lower scores on measures of cognitive development through the age of 9 and with slightly lower academic achievement scores before the age of 7. However, there was no connection between maternal employment and children's behavior problems, compliance, or self-esteem. And now for the pluses: Harvey found that early parental employment was beneficial for single mothers and lower-income families. Why? It brought in cash, and increasing the family income has positive effects on children's development.

Other researchers have found other family benefits for maternal employment. Maternal employment appears to benefit school-age children by fostering greater independence and encouraging responsibility and competence (Hoffman & Yougblade, 1998). Both the sons and daughters of employed women appear to be more flexible in their gender-role stereotypes (Wright & Young, 1998). For example, the sons of working women are more helpful with housework. The daughters of employed women are more achievement-oriented and set themselves higher career goals than the daughters of women who do not work. Adolescent sons and daughters whose mothers are employed show better social and emotional adjustment and have better relationships with family members and schoolmates (Lerner & Hess, 1991). Children with employed mothers also view their mothers as being more competent.

There are other interesting findings on maternal employment. For example, Hoffman and Youngblade (1998) studied a sample of 365 mothers of third- and fourth-graders in an industrialized Midwestern city. They discovered that working-class full-time homemakers were more likely to be depressed than employed mothers. Feelings of depression were related to permissive and authoritarian parenting styles, suggesting that many financially stressed homemakers do not have the emotional resources to give their children the best-possible rearing. Among middle-class mothers, employment was not related to mood or style of parenting. Greater family financial resources apparently lift the mood. (Duh.) So here is another study suggestive of positive rather than negative effects of maternal employment on children.

Employed mothers and their husbands are more egalitarian in their distribution of chores in the home, as well as in the breadwinning role. The fathers spend more time with the children than in single-earner families (Gottfried et al., 1994). When mothers choose to work outside the home and find their work fulfilling, they are happier with their lives (Jackson, 2000; Zaslow, Rabinovich, & Suwalsky, 1991). Perhaps the employed mothers' feelings of competence and high self-esteem transfer into more positive relationships with their children. In any case, mothers who are satisfied with their lives—whether employed or not—have better-adjusted children than mothers who are less satisfied (Scarr, 1998; Wright & Young, 1998).

Review

(17) During the middle years, parents do (more or less?) monitoring of children's activities and provide less direct feedback than they did in the preschool years. (18) Children and parents spend (more or less?) time together in middle childhood than in the preschool years. (19) Children of divorce thus most often experience (upward or downward?) movement in financial status. (20) Ten years after divorce, children still tend to experience _________ toward the parent they hold responsible for the family problems. (21) Most children of divorce live with their (mothers or fathers?). (22) Children of divorced people are likely to earn (higher or lower?) grades than other children. (23) (Boys or Girls?) seem to have a harder time coping with divorce. (24) Clarke-Stewart and her colleagues found evidence that children's well-being is not affected by divorce per se, but rather by the mother's _________. (25) When both parents work, children are (more or less?) likely to engage in delinquent behavior. (26) There is (much or little?) evidence that maternal employment is significantly harmful to children.

Pulling It Together: Should parents in conflict remain together for the sake of the children? Should mothers stay at home rather than join the workforce?

The School

Question: What are the effects of the school on children's social and emotional development? The school exerts a powerful impact on many aspects of the child's development. Schools, like parents, set limits on behavior, make demands for mature behavior, attempt to communicate, and are oriented toward nurturing positive physical, social, and cognitive development. The schools, like parents, have a direct influence on children's IQ scores, achievement motivation, and career aspirations (Sternberg & Williams, 2002; Woolfolk, 2001). Like the family, schools influence social and moral development (Sternberg & Williams, 2002; Woolfolk, 2001).

Schools are also competitive environments, and children who do too well—and students who do not do well enough—can suffer from the resentment or the low opinion of others. An Italian study placed 178 male and 182 female 8–9-year-old elementary school students in competitive situations (Tassi et al., 2001). It was found that when the students were given the task of trying to outperform one another, competition led to social rejection by students' peers. On the other hand, when the students were simply asked to do the best they could, high rates of success led to admiration by one's peers.

In this section, we consider children's transition to school and then examine the effects of the school environment and of teachers.

Entry Into School: Getting to Know You

An increasing number of children attend preschool. About half have had some type of formal prekindergarten experience (Sternberg & Williams, 2002; Woolfolk, 2001). But most children first experience full-time schooling when they enter kindergarten or first grade. Children must master many new tasks when they start school. They will have to meet new academic challenges, learn new school and teacher expectations, and fit into a new peer group. They must learn to accept extended separation from parents and develop increased attention, self-control, and self-help skills.

Reflect

Do you remember what it was like for you to enter school at kindergarten or first grade? Did you experience some adjustment problems? What were they?

What happens to children during the transition from home or preschool to elementary school may be critical for the eventual success or failure of their educational experience. This is particularly true for low-income children. Families of children living in poverty may be less able to supply both the material and emotional supports that help the child adjust successfully to school (Sternberg & Williams, 2002; Woolfolk, 2001).

How well prepared are children to enter school? Discussions of school readiness must consider at least three critical factors:

- The diversity and inequity of children's early life experiences
- Individual differences in young children's development and learning
- The degree to which schools establish reasonable and appropriate expectations of children's capabilities when they enter school

Unfortunately, some children enter school less well prepared than others. In one survey, 7,000 American kindergarten teachers reported that more than one third of their students began school unprepared to learn (Chira, 1991). Nearly half felt that children entered school less ready to learn than had children five years earlier. Most said children often lacked the language skills needed to succeed. This report and others (Sternberg & Williams, 2002; Woolfolk, 2001) conclude that poor health care and nutrition and lack of adequate stimulation and support by parents place many children at risk for academic failure even before they enter school.

A study by the U.S. Department of Education concludes that schools could do a better job of easing the transition to kindergarten (Love et al., 1992). The researchers surveyed schools in 1,003 school districts and also visited eight schools. The average school reported that between 10% and 20% of incoming kindergartners had difficulty adjusting to kindergarten. Adjusting to the academic demands of school was reported to be the area of greatest difficulty. Children whose families were low in socioeconomic status had a more difficult time adjusting than other children, particularly in academics. Sad to say, children who enter school with deficits in language and math skills generally continue to show deficits in these areas during at least the first two years of school (Sternberg & Williams, 2002; Woolfolk, 2001).

Children's adjustment to kindergarten is easier when schools provide transition activities to build continuity between kindergarten and the child's previous experiences at home or in preschool. But most schools do not provide such activities, according to the U.S. Department of Education study. Only 21% of the school districts surveyed reported a wide range of transition activities. About half the schools arranged formal school visits by parents. But only 10% had systematic communication between kindergarten teachers and the child's previous caregivers or teachers.

The School Environment: Setting the Stage for Success, or . . .

Question: What are the characteristics of a good school? Research summaries (Owens, 2001; Snowden & Gorton, 2002; Ubben, Hughes, & Norris, 2001) indicate that an effective school has the following characteristics:

- An active, energetic principal
- An atmosphere that is orderly but not oppressive
- Empowerment of teachers; that is, teachers participating in decision making
- Teachers who have high expectations that children will learn
- A curriculum that emphasizes academics
- Frequent assessment of student performance
- Empowerment of students; that is, students participating in setting goals, making classroom decisions, and engaging in cooperative learning activities with other students

Reflect

Did your elementary school have a "good" environment? How did its environment affect you?

Certain aspects of the school environment are important as well. One key factor is class size. Smaller classes permit students to receive more individual attention and to express their ideas more often (Owens, 2001; Woolfolk, 2001). Smaller classes lead to increased achievement in mathematics and reading in the early primary grades. Smaller classes are particularly useful in teaching the three R's to elementary school students at risk for academic failure (Sternberg & Williams, 2002; Woolfolk, 2001). Small schools have their advantages as well. One study found that students in high schools limited to about 400 students have fewer behavioral problems, better attendance and graduation rates, and, sometimes, higher test scores and grades than students in larger schools (Chira, 1993a).

Teachers: Setting Limits, Making Demands, Communicating Values, and—Oh, Yes—Teaching

The influence of the schools is mainly due to teachers. Teachers, like parents, set limits, make demands, communicate values, and foster development. Teacher–student relationships are more limited than parent–child relationships, but teachers still have

Class Size

Size matters. Smaller classes permit students to receive more individual attention from teachers and to express their ideas more frequently.

the opportunity to serve as powerful role models and dispensers of reinforcement. After all, children spend several hours each weekday in the presence of teachers.

Teacher Influences on Student Performance

Many different aspects of teacher behavior are related to student achievement (Sternberg & Williams, 2002; Woolfolk, 2001). Achievement is enhanced when teachers expect students to master the curriculum, allocate most of the available time to academic activities, and manage the classroom environment effectively. Students learn more in classes when actively instructed or supervised by teachers than when working on their own. The most effective teachers ask a lot of questions, give personalized feedback, and provide ample opportunities for drill and practice, as opposed to straight lecturing.

Student achievement also is linked to the emotional climate of the classroom. Students do not do as well when teachers rely heavily on criticism, ridicule, threats, or punishment. Achievement is high in classrooms with a pleasant, friendly atmosphere, but not in classrooms marked by extreme teacher warmth.

Teacher Expectations

There is a saying that "You find what you're looking for." In Greek mythology, the amorous sculptor Pygmalion breathed life into a beautiful statue he had carved. Similarly, in the musical *My Fair Lady*, which is a reworking of the Pygmalion legend, Henry Higgins fashions a great lady from the working-class Eliza Doolittle.

Teachers also try to bring out positive traits that they believe dwell within their students. A classic experiment by Robert Rosenthal and Lenore Jacobson suggests that teacher expectations can become **self-fulfilling prophecies.** As reported in their book, *Pygmalion in the Classroom*, Rosenthal and Jacobson (1968) first gave students a battery of psychological tests. Then they informed teachers that a handful of the students, although average in performance to date, were late bloomers. The tests clearly suggested that they were about to blossom forth intellectually in the current school year.

Now, the fact is that the tests had indicated nothing in particular about the "chosen" children. These children had been selected at random. The purpose of the experiment was to determine whether modifying teacher expectations could enhance student performance. As it happened, the identified children made significant gains in intelligence-test scores. But in subsequent research, results have been mixed. Some studies have found support for the *Pygmalion effect* (another name for the self-fulfilling prophecy) (Madon et al., 2001). Others have not (Sternberg & Williams, 2002; Woolfolk, 2001). A review of 18 such experiments found that the Pygmalion effect was most pronounced when the procedure for informing teachers of the potential in the target student had greatest credibility (Raudenbusch, 1984). A fair conclusion would seem to be that teacher expectations often, but not always, influence students' motivation to achieve, self-esteem, expectations for success, and actual achievement.

These findings have serious implications for children from ethnic minority and low-income families. There is some indication that teachers expect less academically from children in these groups (Sternberg & Williams, 2002; Woolfolk, 2001). Teachers with lower expectations for certain children may spend less time encouraging and interacting with them.

What are some of the ways that teachers can help motivate *all* students to do their best? Anita Woolfolk (2001) suggests the following:

- Make the classroom and the lesson interesting and inviting.
- Assure that students can fulfill their needs for affiliation and belonging.
- Make the classroom a safe and pleasant place.
- Recognize that students' backgrounds can give rise to diverse patterns of needs.
- Help students take appropriate responsibility for their successes and failures.
- Encourage students to perceive the links between their own efforts and their achievements.
- Help students set attainable, short-term goals.

self-fulfilling prophecy An expectation that is confirmed because of the behavior of those who hold the expectation. In education, often referred to as the *Pygmalion effect*.

Sexism in the Classroom

Although girls were systematically excluded from formal education for centuries, today we might not expect to find **sexism** among teachers. Teachers, after all, are generally well educated. They are also trained to be fair-minded and sensitive to the needs of their young charges in today's changing society.

However, we may not have heard the last of sexism in our schools. According to a review of more than 1,000 publications about girls and education, girls are treated unequally by their teachers, their male peers, the school curriculum, and standardized tests (American Association of University Women, 1992). Among the conclusions of the reviewers were these (Chira, 1992a):

- Teachers pay less attention to girls than boys.
- Girls are subjected to increasing **sexual harassment**—unwelcome verbal or physical conduct of a sexual nature—from male classmates. Many teachers continue to tolerate such behavior.
- School textbooks still stereotype or ignore women. Girls learn almost nothing in school about such pressing problems as discrimination, sexual abuse, and discrimination.
- Some standardized tests, such as the SAT, are biased against girls, hurting their chances of getting into college and getting scholarships.

In one of the most widely cited studies mentioned in the review, Myra and David Sadker (1985; 1994) observed students in fourth-, sixth-, and eighth-grade classes in four states and in the District of Columbia. Teachers and students were European American and African American, urban, suburban, and rural. In almost all cases, findings were depressingly similar. Boys generally dominated classroom communication, whether the subject was math (a traditionally "masculine" area) or language arts (a traditionally "feminine" area). Boys, in fact, were eight times more likely than girls to call out answers without raising their hands. So far, it could be said, we have evidence of a gender difference, but not of sexism. However, teachers were less than impartial in responding to boys and girls when they called out. Teachers, male and female, were significantly more likely to accept calling out from boys. Girls were significantly more likely, as the song goes, to receive "teachers' dirty looks"—or to be reminded that they should raise their hands and wait to be called upon. Boys, it appears, are expected to be impetuous, but girls are reprimanded for "unladylike behavior." Sad to say, teachers generally were unaware, until they saw tapes of themselves, that they were treating girls and boys differently.

Other studies show that elementary and secondary teachers give more active teaching attention to boys than to girls. They call on boys more often, ask them more questions, talk to and listen to them more, give them lengthier directions, and praise and criticize them more often (Snowden & Gorton, 2002; Sternberg & Williams, 2002; Woolfolk, 2001).

The irony is that our educational system has been responsible for lifting many generations of the downtrodden into the mainstream of American life. Unfortunately, the system may be doing more to encourage development of academic skills in boys than girls.

Reflect

Did you experience or witness sexism in the classroom in elementary school? What did you do about it? (What will you do about it in the future?)

Review

(27) (How many?) American children have some type of formal prekindergarten experience. (28) A study by the U.S. Department of Education found that about ________ % of incoming kindergartners had difficulty adjusting to kindergarten. (29) Children whose families are (high or low?) in socioeconomic status have a more difficult time adjusting to school. (30) (Smaller or Larger?) classes facilitate learning during middle childhood. (31) An experiment by Rosenthal and Jacobson suggests that teacher expectations can become ________ prophecies.

sexism Discrimination or bias against people based on their gender.

sexual harassment Unwelcome verbal or physical conduct of a sexual nature.

(32) The self-fulfilling prophecy has also been called the ________ effect. (33) (Boys or Girls?) tend to be victimized more often by sexism in the classroom.

Pulling It Together: How can school systems help children make the transition to full-time education?

Social and Emotional Problems

Reflect

Have you known children with conduct disorders, depression, or separation anxiety disorder (or school phobia)? Do you have thoughts as to the origins of the problems? Were the problems treated? What happened to the children?

Millions of children in the United States suffer from emotional or behavioral problems that would seem to require professional treatment. But the majority of them are unlikely to receive the help they need. What are some of the more common psychological problems of middle childhood? In previous chapters, we examined ADHD and learning disabilities. Now we focus on conduct disorders, depression, and separation anxiety disorder. In doing so, we refer to the terminology in the Diagnostic and Statistical Manual (DSM) of the American Psychiatric Association (2000), because it is the most widely used compilation of psychological problems and disorders.

Conduct Disorders

David is a 16-year-old high school dropout. He has just been arrested for the third time in 2 years for stealing video equipment and computers from people's homes. Acting alone, David was caught in each case when he tried to sell the stolen items. In describing his actions in each crime, David expressed defiance and showed a lack of remorse. In fact, he bragged about how often he had gotten away with similar crimes. (Adapted from Halgin & Whitbourne, 1993, p. 335)

David has a **conduct disorder.** ***Questions: What are conduct disorders? What can we do about them?*** Children with conduct disorders, like David, persistently break rules or violate the rights of others. They exhibit behaviors such as lying, stealing, fire setting, truancy, cruelty to animals, and fighting (American Psychiatric Association, 2000). To receive this diagnosis, children must have engaged in the troublesome behavior pattern for at least 6 months. Conduct disorders typically emerge by 8 years of age and are much more prevalent among boys than girls.

Children with conduct disorders are often involved in sexual activity prior to puberty and often engage in smoking, drinking, and the abuse of various other substances (American Psychiatric Association, 2000). They typically have a low tolerance for frustration and may have temper flare-ups. They usually blame other people for the scrapes they get into. They believe that they are misperceived and treated unfairly. Their academic accomplishments are usually below grade level, but their intelligence usually does not fall below the average range. Many children with conduct disorders also are diagnosed with ADHD (Decker et al., 2001; Hudziak, 2001).

Conduct disorders show a good deal of stability. One longitudinal study found that children who show conduct disorders in kindergarten through third grade have more contacts with police through adolescence (Spivack, Maraes, & Swift, 1986). Longitudinal data from the Berkeley Guidance study show that children who had temper tantrums at ages 8 to 10 were more likely than others to have erratic work lives and get divorced as adults (Caspi, Elder, & Bem, 1987). Children with conduct disorders also are more likely to display antisocial behavior and substance abuse as adults (Ihle et al., 2000).

Origins of Conduct Disorders

There may be a genetic component in conduct disorders (Hudziak, 2001). They are more likely to be found among the biological parents than the adoptive parents of adopted children with such problems (Langbehn & Cadoret, 2001). But sociopathic models in the family, deviant peers, inconsistent discipline, parents' insensitivity to the child's behavior, corporal punishment, and family stress can

conduct disorders Disorders marked by persistent breaking of the rules and violations of the rights of others.

also contribute to antisocial behavior (Eddy & Chamberlain, 2000; Kilgore, Snyder, & Lentz, 2000; Straus, 2000). Conduct disorders in children also sometimes appear to reflect parents' marital problems (Curtner-Smith, 2000).

A study with 123 African American boys and girls pointed toward the relationship among parental discipline, parental monitoring, and the development of early conduct problems (Kilgore et al., 2000). The researchers found that coercive parental discipline and poor parental monitoring at the age of 4½ were reliable predictors of conduct problems for both boys and girls at the age of 6. The families were poor, and the parents had no choice but to send the children to schools with many peers with conduct disorders. However, once socioeconomic status and school choice were taken into account, parental discipline and monitoring were the strongest predictors of conduct disorders. The findings are consistent with research on European American, more advantaged, boys, which suggests that family processes are stronger predictors of conduct disorders than the child's gender or ethnicity.

Conduct Disorders

Children with conduct disorders continually break the rules or violate the rights of others. They may lie, steal, set fires, be truant, torture animals, and get into fights. Unfortunately, conduct disorders are rather stable. Children with these disorders often become antisocial adolescents and adults.

Treatment of Conduct Disorders

The treatment of conduct disorders is challenging and less than satisfactory. No one approach has been shown to be completely effective, although it would now seem that cognitive-behavioral techniques that involve parent training hold promise (Cavell, 2001; Kazdin, 2000; Kazdin & Wassell, 2000; O'Reilly & Dillenburger, 2000). It appears that children with conduct disorders profit from interventions in which their behavior is monitored closely, there are consequences such as time out for unacceptable behavior, corporal punishment is avoided, and positive social behaviors are rewarded. That is, rather than targeting noncompliant behavior alone, it is also important to pay attention to children when they are behaving properly and to reward them for doing so (Cavell, 2001).

Other approaches include teaching aggressive children various methods for coping with feelings of anger that will not violate the rights of others. One promising cognitive behavioral method teaches children social skills and how to use problem solving to manage interpersonal conflicts (Webster-Stratton et al., 2001b). Desirable social skills include asking other children to stop annoying behavior rather than hitting them. Children are also taught to "stop and think" before engaging in aggressive behavior. They are encouraged to think about the possible outcomes of unacceptable behavior and to find acceptable ways to achieve their goals.

Childhood Depression

> Kristin, an 11-year-old, feels that "nothing is working out for me." For the past year, she has been failing in school, although she previously had been a B student. She has trouble sleeping, feels tired all the time, and has started refusing to go to school. She cries easily and thinks her peers are making fun of her because she is "ugly and stupid." Her mother recently found a note written by Kristin that said she wanted to jump in front of a car "to end my misery." (Adapted from Weller & Weller, 1991, p. 655)

Childhood is the happiest time of life, correct? Not necessarily. This stereotype is true enough for many children, who are protected by their parents and are unencumbered by adult responsibilities. From the perspective of aging adults, their bodies seem made of rubber and free of aches. Their energy is apparently boundless.

Yet many children (and adults) like Kristin are depressed. ***Questions: What is depression? What can we do about it?*** Depressed children may feel sad, blue, and down in the dumps. They may complain of or demonstrate poor appetite,

© Jean Claude Le Jeune/Stock, Boston/PictureQuest

Childhood Depression

Depressed children may feel sad and blue. They may complain of poor appetite, insomnia, lack of energy, difficulty concentrating, loss of interest in other people and activities they used to like, and feelings of worthlessness. But many depressed children do not recognize feelings of sadness. In some cases, childhood depression is "masked" by behaviors such as physical complaints, academic problems, and anxiety—even conduct disorders.

insomnia, lack of energy and inactivity, loss of self-esteem, difficulty concentrating, loss of interest in other people and activities they usually enjoy, crying, feelings of hopelessness and helplessness, and thoughts of suicide (American Psychiatric Association, 2000).

But many depressed children do not report, and are not aware of, feelings of sadness. Part of the problem is cognitive-developmental. Children do not usually recognize depression in themselves until the age of 7 or so. The capacity for concrete operations apparently contributes to children's abilities to perceive internal feeling states (Glasberg & Aboud, 1982).

When children cannot report their feelings, depression is inferred from behavior. Depressed children in middle childhood engage in less social activity and have poorer social skills than peers who are not depressed (American Psychiatric Association, 2000). In some cases, childhood depression is "masked" by apparently unrelated behaviors. Conduct disorders, physical complaints, academic problems, and anxiety are sometimes associated with depression. But the causal connections between depression and these other problems are not always clear.

Nor is it clear how many children are depressed, although it has been estimated that between 5% and 9% of children are likely to be seriously depressed within a given year (American Psychiatric Association, 2000; Petersen et al., 1993). While depression occurs equally often in girls and boys during childhood, higher rates are found in females starting in adolescence (Petersen et al., 1993). Depressed children frequently continue to have depressive episodes as adults.

Origins of Depression

The origins of depression are complex and varied. Both psychological and biological explanations have been proposed. Psychoanalysts, for example, have suggested that depressed children have typically been severely threatened with loss of parental love for their shortcomings. They tend to repress rather than express feelings of anger. The net result is that they turn their anger inward upon themselves, experiencing it as misery and self-hatred (Weller & Weller, 1991).

Some social cognitive theorists focus on relationships between competencies (knowledge and skills) and feelings of self-esteem in explaining depression. Children who gain academic, social, and other competencies also usually have high feelings of self-esteem. Perceived low levels of competence are linked to helplessness, low self-esteem, and depression in children and adolescents. A 4-year longitudinal study of 631 elementary school children found that problems in five developmentally important domains predicted the development of feelings of depression: academic competence, social acceptance, physical appearance, behavioral conduct, and sports competence (Cole, Jacquez, & Maschman, 2001). Conversely, it was also found that self-perceived competence in these areas was negatively related to levels of self-reported depressive symptoms 4 years later (Cole et al., 2001). That is, self-perceived competence appears to "protect" children from feelings of depression.

Children who have not developed competencies because of lack of training opportunities, inconsistent parental reinforcement, and so on may develop feelings of helplessness and hopelessness. Similarly, a study by Reinecke and DuBois (2001) found that stressful life events, daily hassles, poor problem-solving ability, and low self-esteem gave rise to ideas of helplessness and hopelessness. These ideas, in turn, triggered feelings of depression. On the other hand, support and belief in one's ability to succeed tend to "protect" children from depression (Reinecke & DuBois, 2001). A study of more than 1,000 fifth- and sixth-graders found that recent stresses such as family disruption gave rise to feelings of helplessness and loss of control which, as in the study by Reinecke and DuBois, evoked feelings of depression (Rudolph, Kurlakowsky, & Conley, 2001). Some children who do have competencies might not credit themselves because of excessive parental expectations. Or children may be perfectionistic themselves. In any event perfectionistic children are frequently depressed because they cannot meet their own high standards.

Children in elementary school are likely to be depressed as a result of situational stresses, such as family problems. Middle schoolers, however, who have advanced cognitive abilities, are also likely to turn these abilities against themselves. There are cognitive factors in depression, and they are powerful. For example, a study of 582 Chinese children from Hong Kong secondary schools found that cognitive distortions, such as minimizing accomplishments and blowing failures and shortcomings out of proportion, were associated with feelings of depression (Leung & Poon, 2001). A European study found that ruminating about problems (going over them again and again—and again), blaming oneself for things that are not one's fault, and blowing problems out of proportion are linked with depression (Garnefski, Kraaij, & Spinhoven, 2001).

The last study found that blaming others rather than oneself for one's problems tends to protect children from feelings of depression (Garnefski et al., 2001). Of course, it is "appropriate" to be accurate in attributing the source of the blame for one's problems.[2] In any event, a tendency to blame oneself (an *internal* attribution) or others or even chance (an *external* attribution) is one aspect of the way in which children's **attributional styles** contribute to helplessness and hopelessness, and hence depression. Research has shown that children and adolescents who are depressed are more likely to attribute the causes of their failures to *internal, stable,* and *global* factors—factors that they are relatively helpless to change (Lewinsohn, Rohde, Seeley, Klein, & Gotlib, 2000). Helplessness then triggers feelings of depression. Consider the case of two children who do poorly on a math test. John thinks, "I'm a jerk! I'm just no good in math! I'll never learn." Jim thinks, "That test was tougher than I thought it would be. I'll have to work harder next time." John is perceiving the problem as *global* (he's "a jerk") and *stable* (he'll "never learn"). Jim perceives the problem as *specific* rather than global (related to the type of math test the teacher makes up) and as *unstable* rather than stable (he can change the results by working harder). In effect, John thinks "It's me" (an internal attribution). By contrast, John thinks "It's the test" (an external attribution). Depressed children tend to explain negative events in terms of internal, stable, and global causes. As a result, they, like John, are more likely than Jim to be depressed.

There is also evidence for genetic factors in depression (Nurnberger et al., 2001; Sullivan, Neale, & Kendler, 2000). For example, the children of depressed parents are at greater risk for depression and other disorders (Dodge, 1990; Hudziak, 2001). The concordance rate for depression is about 75% for identical twins compared with only 19% for fraternal twins (Weller & Weller, 1991). On a neurological level, there is evidence that depressed children (and adults) underutilize the neurotransmitter **serotonin** (Yatham et al., 2000). Learned helplessness is linked to lower serotonin levels in the brains of humans and rats (Wu et al., 1999). Depressed children often respond to drugs that increase the effects of serotonin.

Treatment of Depression

Parents and teachers can do a good deal to alleviate relatively mild feelings of depression among children. They can involve children in enjoyable activities, encourage the step-by-step development of instrumental competencies, offer praise when appropriate, and point out when children are being too hard on themselves. But if feelings of depression persist, treatment is called for.

An approach that combines both biological and psychological intervention often is used (Skaer et al., 2000). Such an approach includes individual or family psychotherapy, social skills training, and medical management. Psychotherapy for depression tends to be mainly cognitive-behavioral these days, and it is often quite straightforward and confrontational. That is, children (and adolescents) are made aware of their tendencies to minimize their accomplishments, catastrophize their problems, and blame themselves for too many of the shortcomings that affect their lives (Ellis & Dryden, 1996).

The literature is quite mixed in its assessment of the usefulness of antidepressant medication with childhood depression. First of all, the "older" generation of

[2]Don't blame me if you are experiencing problems in this course. I just wrote the book. But don't blame your instructor either. After all, he or she decided to use my book (great judgment).

attributional style The way in which one is disposed toward interpreting outcomes (successes or failures), as in tending to place blame or responsibility on oneself or external factors.

serotonin A neurotransmitter that is implicated in depression.

antidepressants—called "tricyclics"—has not been shown to be effective in the treatment of childhood depression (Skaer et al., 2000; Wagner & Ambrosini, 2001). The newer generation of antidepressants consists of *selective serotonin reuptake inhibitors (SSRIs)*. The category includes popular drugs like Luvox, Prozac, and Zoloft, and they work by increasing the action of serotonin in the brain. Studies of their effectiveness in the treatment of childhood depression yield a somewhat mixed review, ranging from something like "not sure" to "somewhat effective" (Emslie et al., 1999; Wagner & Ambrosini, 2001). It is something of an irony that so-called antidepressant drugs are more effective in the treatment of childhood anxiety disorders than depression, as we see in the next section (Walkup et al., 2001).

Separation Anxiety Disorder (SAD)

It is normal for children to show anxiety when they are separated from their caregivers. Separation anxiety is a normal feature of the child–caregiver relationship and begins during the 1st year. But the sense of security that is usually provided by bonds of attachment encourages children to explore their environments and become progressively independent of caregivers. ***Question: What, then, is separation anxiety disorder?***

separation anxiety disorder An extreme form of otherwise normal separation anxiety that is characterized by anxiety about separating from parents and often takes the form of refusal to go to school.

Separation anxiety disorder (SAD) is diagnosed when separation anxiety is persistent and excessive, when it is inappropriate for the child's developmental level, and when it interferes with the child's daily activities or development tasks—most

Developing in the New Millennium

Talking to Children About Terrorism

Terrorism, once a problem found mainly in foreign countries, is a reality within the United States in the new millennium. The terrorist attacks in New York and Washington, DC, in 2001 did not spare the children of the nation, noted the director of the Federal Emergency Management Agency (FEMA). Children saw the terrible television pictures and heard the adults in their lives discussing the tragic events. Yet many adults don't know how to talk to children about this disaster and others like it, or they don't know how to recognize that their children are feeling distress.

FEMA for Kids, the part of the FEMA Web site devoted to children, offers advice on how parents can discuss terrorism with their children. The site also includes general guidelines about dealing with disasters' impact on children and an opportunity for schools to submit artwork children have done in an effort to share their feelings. The address for the site is **http://www.fema.gov/kids.**

"Children affected by disasters may suddenly act younger than they are or may appear stoic—not crying or expressing concern," said Holly Harrington, the FEMA for Kids manager. "Parents can help their children by talking to them, keeping them close, and even spoiling them for a little while. We also advise

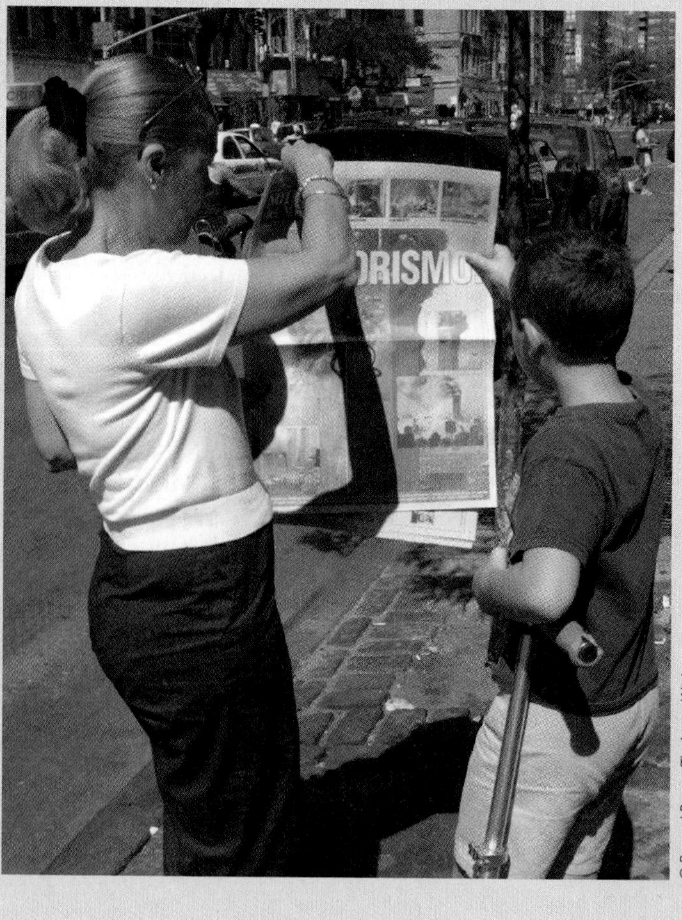

© Rommel Pescon/The Image Works

How Do You Explain the Attacks of September 11, 2001, and Other Acts of Terrorism to a Child?

It's difficult, but the Federal Emergency Management Agency has some helpful ideas that are presented here.

importantly, attending school. Six-year-olds ought to be able to enter first grade without anxiety-related nausea and vomiting and without persistent dread that they or their parents will come to harm because of separation. Children with SAD tend to cling to their parents and follow them around the house. They may voice concerns about death and dying and insist that someone stay with them while they are falling asleep. They may complain of nightmares, stomachaches, and nausea and vomiting on school days. They may plead with their parents not to leave the house, or they may throw tantrums when their parents are about to depart.

SAD may occur prior to middle childhood. Some children do not adjust well to day care or nursery school because of separation anxiety. In adolescence, refusal to attend school is often connected with academic and social problems, in which cases the label of SAD would not apply. SAD becomes a significant problem in middle childhood, because that is the period during which children are expected to adjust to life in school. Children with the disorder may refuse to attend school for fear that something will happen to their parents while they are away. The disorder may persist into adulthood, leading to an exaggerated concern about the well-being of one's children and spouse and difficulty tolerating any separation from them.

SAD frequently develops after a stressful life event, such as illness, the death of a relative or pet, or a change of schools or homes. Alison's problems followed the death of her grandmother:

> Alison's grandmother died when Alison was 7 years old. Her parents decided to permit her request to view her grandmother in the open coffin. Alison took a tentative glance from her father's arms across the room, then asked to be taken out of the room. Her 5-year-old sister took a leisurely close-up look, with no apparent distress.
>
> Alison had been concerned about death for 2 or 3 years by this time, but her grandmother's passing brought on a new flurry of questions: "Will I die?" "Does everybody die?" and so on. Her parents tried to reassure her by saying, "Grandma was

that children not be overexposed to the news coverage of the terrorist events."

Talking to children about terrorism can be particularly problematic since providing them with safety guidelines to protect themselves from terrorism is difficult. According to psychologists, questions about terrorism are teaching opportunities. Adults should answer questions about terrorism by providing understandable information and realistic reassurance. And children don't need to be overwhelmed with information, so less is better than more in terms of details.

After a disaster, children may:

- Change from being quiet, obedient, and caring to loud, noisy, and aggressive or may change from being outgoing to shy and afraid
- Develop nighttime fears, have nightmares or bad dreams
- Be afraid the event will reoccur
- Become easily upset, crying and whining
- Lose trust in adults—after all, their adults were not able to control the disaster
- Revert to younger behavior such as bed-wetting and thumb sucking
- Not want parents out of their sight and refuse to go to school or child care
- Have symptoms of physical illness, such as headaches, vomiting or fever
- Worry about where they and their family will live

Source: "FEMA Offers Advice on How to Talk to Children About Terrorist Attacks." (2001, September 12). Washington, DC: Federal Emergency Management Agency. **http://www.fema.gov/nwz01_99.htm.**

What to Do

- Talk with the children about how they are feeling and listen without judgment.
- Let the children take their time to figure things out. Don't rush them.
- Help them learn to use words that express their feelings, such as *happy, sad, angry,* or *mad.*
- Assure children that you will be there to take care of them. Reassure them often.
- Stay together as a family as much as possible.
- Let them have some control, such as choosing what outfit to wear or what meal to have for dinner.
- Encourage the children to give or send pictures they have drawn or things they have written.
- Help children regain faith in the future by helping them develop plans for activities that will take place later—next week, next month.
- Allow the children to grieve for their losses.

Search Online With InfoTrac College Edition

For additional information, explore InfoTrac College Edition, your online library. Go to **http://www.infotrac-college.com** and use the passcode from the InfoTrac card that came with your book. Try these search terms: crisis intervention, children trauma, crisis children, cope tragedy, post-traumatic stress disorder children.

very, very old, and she also had a heart condition. You are very young and in perfect health. You have many, many years before you have to start thinking about death."

Alison also could not be alone in any room in her house. She pulled one of her parents or her sister along with her everywhere she went. She also reported nightmares about her grandmother and, within a couple of days, insisted on sleeping in the same room with her parents. Fortunately, Alison's fears did not extend to school. Her teacher reported that Alison spent some time talking about her grandmother, but her academic performance was apparently unimpaired.

Alison's parents decided to allow Alison time to "get over" the loss. Alison gradually talked less and less about death, and by the time 3 months had passed, she was able to go into any room in her house by herself. She wanted to continue to sleep in her parents' bedroom, however. So her parents "made a deal" with her. They would put off the return to her own bedroom until the school year had ended (a month away), if Alison would agree to return to her own bed at that time. As a further incentive, a parent would remain with her until she fell asleep for the first month. Alison overcame the anxiety problem in this fashion with no additional delays. (The author's files)

Separation Anxiety Disorder, School Phobia, and School Refusal

Question: What are the connections between separation anxiety disorder, school phobia, and school refusal? SAD is similar to but not exactly the same as *school phobia*. Separation anxiety disorder is an extreme form of otherwise normal separation anxiety. It is characterized by anxiety about separating from parents and often takes the form of **school phobia**—which translates as *fear* of school—or of refusal to go to school (which can be based on fear of school or other factors). Separation anxiety—fear—does not appear to be behind all instances of school refusal. Some children refuse school because they perceive it as an unpleasant, unsatisfying, or hostile environment. For example, some children are concerned about doing poorly in school or being asked to answer questions in class (in which case, they might be suffering from the social phobia of stage fright). High parental

school phobia Fear of attending school, marked by extreme anxiety at leaving parents.

Developing in a World of Diversity

Got No Money? Show Me the . . . Resilience

Perhaps all children experience some stresses in their lives. But some children are exposed to a minimal amount of stress, whereas others face a heavier burden. The cumulative effect of such events and conditions as parental discord and/or divorce, a parent's loss of job, poverty, abuse or neglect, or a parent with psychiatric problems places children at high risk for emotional and behavioral maladjustment (Davies & Windle, 2001).

But some children are more resilient than others. That is, they adapt successfully and thrive in the face of the most stressful life events (Masten, 2001). Consider, for example, the results of a longitudinal study of a multiracial group of children born on the island of Kauai, Hawaii, in 1955 (Werner, 1990). One third of the infants were considered at risk because they had experienced stressful births and were reared in poverty conditions in a family marked either by marital discord and divorce or by parental mental illness or alcoholism. While two out of three of these high-risk children later developed behavioral or emotional problems, one third overcame their stressful childhoods to become competent, confident, and caring young adults.

How are these resilient children different from those who are more vulnerable to stress? Two key factors appear to be the child's personality and the availability of social support.

Personality Characteristics

At 1 year of age, resilient children are securely attached to their mothers. At the age of 2, they are independent and easygoing, with a high tolerance for frustration, even when they are being abused or neglected. By age 3½, these children are cheerful, persistent, flexible, and good at seeking out help from adults. In middle childhood, they are able to distance themselves from turmoil and are confident and independent. They have high self-esteem that is connected with *self-efficacy*—that is, with confidence in their ability to exercise control over their environment and to succeed (Griffin et al., 2001; Sandler, 2001). They tend to be temperamentally easy going rather than difficult. Not only is the easygoing child less likely to be the target of negative behavior from parents, but he or she is also better able to cope with problems when they arise (Rutter, 1990).

expectation to perform may contribute to their concerns. Other children refuse to attend school because of unpleasant and difficult relationships with classmates.

There is a strong but incomplete overlap between SAD and school refusal. First of all, epidemiological studies indicate that SAD affects about 4%–5% of children and young adolescents and that it occurs more frequently among girls (American Psychiatric Association, 2000; Masi et al., 2001). School refusal is reported in about 75% of children with SAD, and SAD is reported to occur in as many as 80% of those children who refuse to go to school. ***Question: What can we do about school phobia or school refusal?***

Treatment of School Phobia or School Refusal

The first rule is this: Get the child back into school. The second rule is, Get the child back into school. The third rule . . .

When health professionals and educators treat children who refuse to go to school, the primary goal is to get the child back in school as soon as possible. That means *now*. Even without investigating the "meanings" of the child's refusal to attend school, many of the "symptoms" of the disorder disappear once the child is back in school on a regular basis.

Put it this way. There's nothing wrong with trying to understand why a child refuses to attend school. Knowledge of the reasons for refusal can help parents and educators devise strategies for assisting the child to adjust. But should such understanding *precede* insistence that the child return to school? Perhaps not.

Here are some things parents can do to get a child back into school (Brody, 1991):

- Don't give in to the child's demands to stay home. If the child complains of being tired or being ill, tell the child that he or she will feel better once he or she gets to school and that he or she can rest there if he or she needs to.
- Discuss the problem with the child's teacher, principal, and school nurse.
- If there is a specific school-related problem, such as a strict teacher, help the child find ways of handling the situation. But finding ways to handle such problems can be accomplished while the child is attending school. It is not necessarily the case that parents should wait until all such problems are ironed out before insisting that the child return to school.

Social Support

Support from others—parents, grandparents, siblings, peers, or teachers—improves the ability of children (and adults) to cope with life's stresses (Davies & Windle, 2001; LeTourneau et al., 2001). E. Mavis Hetherington's longitudinal study of divorce and remarriage provides an example. A key characteristic of children who adjusted well following their parents' divorce was a relationship with a caring adult, whether a parent, other relative, teacher, or neighbor (Hetherington, 1989).

Social support systems are particularly important for children who live in poverty and who therefore are at greater risk for adverse developmental outcomes. Children from ethnic minority groups and from families headed by single mothers are especially likely to be poor. The poverty rate in 2000, the last year for which we have statistics, was at 11.3%. About 31.1 million people were poor in 2000, and most of them were children. African Americans and Latino and Latina Americans were "overrepresented" in the statistics, with 22.1% of African Americans and 21.2% of Latino and Latina Americans living in poverty. By contrast, only 7.5% of European Americans and 10.8% of Asian Americans lived in poverty. But here's a startler: 24.7% of households headed by single women were living in poverty, as compared with only 4.7% of households headed by a married couple.

Yet many poor children from ethnic minority groups have extended families that include grandparents and other relatives who either live with them or nearby. Members of extended families provide considerable economic, social, and emotional support for children in the family (Murry et al., 2001). Grandmothers, in particular, play a key role in the parenting of children. In the words of one resident of a low-income African American community, "If it wasn't for grandmom, the kids wouldn't survive. . . . If it wasn't for a lot of the grandmothers, a whole lot of kids wouldn't be able to eat or sleep neither" (Anderson, 1990, p. 90). The involvement of the grandmother and other extended-family members in one-parent families has been shown to facilitate the mother's participation in self-improvement activities, increase the quality of child care, and reduce negative effects of single parenting (Cebello & Olson, 1993; Oyserman, Radin, & Benn, 1993; Tolson & Wilson, 1990). One study of African American adolescents and their single mothers found that emotional support from family members reduced mother–adolescent conflict and increased the self-esteem of the youngster (Wadsworth & McLoyd, 1993).

The message is that many, many children do well despite adversity. In fact, Ann Masten (2001) characterizes such an outcome as somewhat "ordinary." Hey, kids: Just do it!

© Sean Cayton/The Image Works

■ **Separation Anxiety**

School phobia is often a form of separation anxiety. This boy is afraid to be separated from his mother. He imagines that something terrible will happen to her (or to him) when they are apart. Many mornings he complains of a tummy-ache or of being too tired to go to school. School phobias may have many meanings that are worth exploring with helping professionals, but the most important task may be to get the child back into school. Today, now. (Yesterday, if possible.) Getting the child back into school shows the child that he—and the world around him—will survive and also . . . gets the child back into school.

- Reward the child for attending school. (Yes, yes, I know that parents shouldn't "have to" reward a child for doing the things that are normally expected of a child, but do you want the child to be in school or not?)

What if these measures don't work? How do professionals help? A variety of therapeutic approaches have been tried, and it would appear that cognitive-behavioral approaches are the most effective (Masi et al., 2001; Short et al., 2001). One cognitive-behavioral method is counterconditioning to reduce the child's fear. (As noted in Chapter 10, Mary Cover Jones used this method to reduce Peter's fear of rabbits.) Others are operant-conditioning approaches, such as rewarding the child for attending school.

Comprehensive treatment programs involving a cluster of cognitive-behavioral techniques are advised. In one study, the cognitive-behavioral methods of systematic desensitization, modeling, cognitive restructuring, and the shaping and rewarding of school-attending behaviors were used to treat SAD in seven children (Kearney & Silverman, 1990). Six of the seven children were attending school full-time after treatment and when followed up 6 months later.

When possible, the children's parents are brought into treatment to learn how to consistently apply cognitive-behavioral methods. One study assessed the effectiveness of so-called family-based group cognitive-behavioral treatment (FGCBT) for anxious children (Shortt et al., 2001). It included 71 children between the ages of 6 to 10 who were diagnosed with either SAD, generalized anxiety disorder (continuous feelings of anxiety), or social phobia (for example, stage fright). (Many such studies include children with various kinds of anxiety disorders.) The children and their families were assigned at random to FGCBT or to a 10-week wait-list ("We'll get to you in 10 weeks") control group. The effectiveness of the treatment was evaluated right after treatment and at a 12-month follow-up. The researchers found that 69% of the children who had completed FGCBT were no longer diagnosable with anxiety disorders, as compared with 6% of the children who had been placed on the wait-list. Even at the 12-month follow-up, 68% of children remained diagnosis-free.

Antidepressant medication has been used—often in conjunction with cognitive behavioral methods—with a good deal of success (Murphy et al., 2000; Pine et al., 2001). Antidepressants can have side effects, however, such as abdominal discomfort (Burke & Baker, 2001). Because drugs have side effects and do not in themselves teach children how to cope with situations, many health professionals suggest that they—in this case, antidepressants—are best used only when psychological treatments have proven to be ineffective (Masi et al., 2001).

Daniel Pine and his colleagues (2001) reported a study on the treatment of 128 anxious children aged 6 to 17 years. Like those in the Shortt study, they were diagnosed with either social phobia (e.g., stage fright), SAD, or generalized anxiety disorder (continuous feelings of anxiety). All the children had received psychological treatment for 3 weeks but had not shown improvement. Thus they became eligible for drug therapy. The children were assigned at random to receive either an antidepressant medication (fluvoxamine) or a placebo (a "sugar pill") for 8 weeks. Neither the children, their parents, their teachers, nor the researchers knew which child had received what.[3] The children's degrees of anxiety and impairment were then evaluated. On one evaluation instrument, referred to as the Clinical Global Impressions–Improvement scale in this study, 48 of 63 children (76%) who had received the antidepressant improved significantly, as compared with 19 of 65 children (29%) who had received the placebo.

[3]Yes, a numerical code was used so that it could be determined who had taken what after all assessments were completed. No magic or guesswork here.

It seems unfortunate to be leaving our chronicle of middle childhood with a discussion of the effects of drugs. But these are "good" drugs. That is, they are prescribed by helping professionals for positive purposes. One of the topics in the next chapter, which addresses aspects of physical development in adolescence, will be not-so-good drugs. These are the drugs—alcohol, marijuana, cocaine, and so on—that many adolescents "prescribe" for themselves or for other adolescents, even though they have been shown to be harmful. Yet, as we will see, most adolescents do very well indeed, as do most children between the ages of 6 to 12.

Review

(34) Children with ________ disorders persistently break rules or violate the rights of others. (35) Many children with conduct disorders also are diagnosed with ________. (36) Conduct disorders are more likely to be found among the (biological or adoptive?) parents of adopted children with such problems. (37) Cognitive-________ techniques that include parent training hold promise for treatment of conduct disorders. (38) Depressed children may complain of poor appetite, insomnia, and (high or low?) energy levels, self-esteem, and interest in people and activities they usually enjoy. (39) Childhood depression is sometimes ________ by conduct disorders, physical complaints, and academic problems. (40) Self-perceived competence appears to (protect children from, or make children vulnerable to) feelings of depression. (41) Depressed children tend to (underutilize or overutilize?) the neurotransmitter serotonin in the brain. (42) Separation ________ disorder is similar to but not exactly the same as *school phobia*. (43) Separation anxiety (is or is not?) behind all instances of school refusal. (44) The most important aspect of treatment of school refusal is to (get the child back into school, or understand the reasons for the school refusal?).

Pulling It Together: Argue for or against the view that childhood is the happiest time of life.

Recite Recite Recite Recite

1. **What are some features of social and emotional development in middle childhood?**

Social development in middle childhood involves the development of skills, changes in interpersonal relationships, and the expansion of self-understanding. Freud viewed the period as the latency stage, and Erikson saw it as the stage of industry versus inferiority. Social cognitive theorists note that during these years, children depend less on external rewards and punishments and increasingly regulate their own behavior. Cognitive-developmental theory notes that concrete operations enhance the child's social development.

2. **What is the relationship between social cognition and perspective taking?**

In middle childhood, children become more capable of taking the role or perspective of another person. Selman and his colleagues theorize that children undergo five stages of development from egocentricity to being able to see the world through the eyes of others.

3. **How does the self-concept develop during middle childhood?**

In early childhood, children's self-concepts focus on concrete external traits. In middle childhood, children begin to include abstract internal traits. Social relationships and group memberships take on importance.

4. **How does self-esteem develop during middle childhood?**

In middle childhood, children's self-concepts become more differentiated. Competence and social acceptance contribute to self-esteem, but self-esteem tends to decline

Recite Recite Recite Recite

during middle childhood, perhaps because the self-concept becomes more realistic. Research suggests that authoritative parenting and closeness to parents contribute to children's self-esteem.

5. What is learned helplessness, and how does it develop in middle childhood?

Learned helplessness is the acquired belief that one cannot obtain desired rewards. "Helpless" children tend not to persist in the face of failure. Girls tend to feel more helpless in math than boys do, largely because of societal gender-role expectations.

6. What is the influence of peers during middle childhood?

Peers take on increasing importance in middle childhood. Peers exert pressure to conform. Peer experiences broaden children. Peers afford practice in sharing and cooperation, relating to leaders, and coping with aggressive impulses. Popular children tend to be attractive and mature for their age. Popular children are friendly and skilled in social interaction.

7. How do children's concepts of friendship develop?

Early in middle childhood, friendships are based on proximity. Between the ages of 8 and 11, children become more aware of the value of friends as meeting each other's needs and having traits such as loyalty. Friends come to share inmost feelings. During middle childhood, peers tend to discourage contact with members of the other gender.

8. What kinds of influences are exerted by the family during middle childhood?

In middle childhood, the family continues to play a key role in socialization. Parent–child interactions now focus on school-related issues, chores, and peers. Parents do less monitoring of children's activities, and coregulation develops.

9. What are the effects of divorce on the children?

Divorce disrupts children's lives and usually lowers the family's financial status. Children are likely to greet divorce with sadness, shock, and disbelief; these feelings tend to fade, while anger toward the parent who is responsible for the break-up tends to persist. Children of divorce fare better when the parents cooperate on child rearing. Children's adjustment to divorce appears to be closely related to the mother's coping ability.

10. Should parents who bicker remain together for the sake of the children?

In terms of the child's psychological adjustment, the answer seems to be "Not necessarily." Children appear to suffer as much from marital conflict as from divorce per se.

11. What are the effects of maternal employment on children?

Having both parents in the workforce appears to have some negative effects on children. The effects seem to be related to relative lack of supervision. However, there is little evidence that maternal employment is significantly detrimental to children. Moreover, maternal employment appears to benefit school-age children by fostering greater independence and flexibility in gender-role stereotypes among children.

12. What are the effects of the school on children's social and emotional development?

Schools make demands for mature behavior and nurture positive physical, social, and cognitive development. Children must master new social and academic challenges when they start school. Readiness for school is related to the diversity and inequity of children's early life experiences, individual differences in children's development and learning, and the schools' establishment of appropriate expectations of children.

13. What are the characteristics of a good school?

An effective school has an energetic principal, an orderly atmosphere, empowerment of teachers and students, high expectations of children, and emphasis on academics. Teacher's expectations can become self-fulfilling prophecies, as we see in the so-called Pygmalion effect. Many students—especially girls—suffer from sexism and sexual harassment in the school, even in middle childhood. Math and science are generally stereotyped as male "domains," whereas language arts is stereotyped as a female "domain."

Recite Recite Recite Recite

14. What are conduct disorders? What can we do about them?

Children with conduct disorders persistently break rules or violate the rights of others. There may be a genetic component in conduct disorders, but the presence of sociopathic models in the family, deviant peers, and inconsistent discipline all seem to make contributions. Cognitive-behavioral techniques that involve parent training seem to hold promise for treating conduct disorders.

15. What is depression? What can we do about it?

Depressed children feel sad and tend to complain of poor appetite, insomnia, lack of energy, and feelings of worthlessness. Social cognitive theorists focus on relationships between competencies (knowledge and skills) and feelings of self-esteem in explaining depression. Depressed children also tend to blame themselves excessively for shortcomings. Parents and teachers can alleviate depression by involving children in enjoyable activities and encouraging the development of competencies. Psychotherapy tends to make children aware of their tendencies to minimize their accomplishments and blame themselves for too many of their shortcomings. The newer generation of antidepressants—*selective serotonin reuptake inhibitors (SSRIs)*—is sometimes helpful.

16. What is separation anxiety disorder?

Separation anxiety disorder (SAD) is diagnosed when separation anxiety is persistent and excessive and interferes with daily life. Children with SAD tend to cling to parents and may refuse to attend school.

17. What are the connections between separation anxiety disorder, school phobia, and school refusal?

SAD is an extreme form of otherwise normal separation anxiety and sometimes, but not always, takes the form of school phobia, which is a severe fear of school. But children can refuse to attend school for reasons other than fear; some perceive school to be unpleasant, unsatisfying, or hostile.

18. What can we do about school phobia or school refusal?

The most important aspect of treatment is to place the child back in school by refusing to accede to the child's demands to remain at home. Attempts can also be made to understand and iron out possible social or academic problems in the school. Cognitive-behavioral therapy methods and antidepressant medications have also been shown to be of help.

On the Web

Search Online With InfoTrac College Edition

For additional information, explore InfoTrac College Edition, your online library. Go to **http://www.infotrac-college.com** and use the passcode from the InfoTrac card that came with your book. Try these search terms: children of abused women, children of divorced parents, childhood friendships, parenting childhood, conduct disorder.

Visit Our Web Site

Go to **http://www.wadsworth.com/psychology** where you will find online resources directly linked to your book.

Child Development CD-ROM

Go to the Wadsworth Child Development CD-ROM for further study of the concepts in this chapter. The CD-ROM also includes quizzes and additional activities to expand your learning experience.

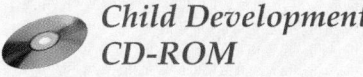

14 Adolescence: Physical Development

PowerPreview™

Views of Adolescent Development

- **Adolescence has been** referred to as a time of "storm and stress." Is it?

Puberty: The Biological Eruption

- **Are American adolescents** growing taller than their parents?
- **Do nocturnal emissions** in boys accompany "wet dreams"? (And what are *wet dreams*?)
- **Are girls capable of becoming** pregnant after they have their first menstrual periods?
- **Do boys and girls** who mature early have higher self-esteem than those who mature late?

Health in Adolescence

- **What is the leading cause** of death among male adolescents in the United States? (Hint: It isn't illness.)

Nutrition—An Abundance of Food and an Abundance of Eating Disorders

- **Someone once said,** "You can never be too skinny or too rich." Is it true?
- **Some college women** control their weight by going on cycles of binge eating followed by self-induced vomiting.

Substance Abuse and Dependence—Where Does It Begin? Where Does It End?

- **Is substance use and abuse** on the rise among high school students?
- **Are European American or African American** 12th-graders more likely to use illicit drugs?

Sexually Transmitted Infections

- **Do adolescents who are not gay** and who do not shoot up drugs need to be concerned about contracting HIV/AIDS?
- **Some public school districts provide** students with condoms to help prevent the spread of HIV/AIDS.

"Why is my chest getting bumpy?"

"Why is my voice acting so funny?"

"Why do I get pimples?"

"Why am I getting hairy?"

"Why is mine not like his?"

"What's happening to me?"

(Adapted from Mayle, 1975)

Psychologists and educators view adolescence as a unique period because of the many changes that occur during this time. Biological change is greater than at any other time except infancy. Height and weight increase markedly, body shape changes, and the capacity to reproduce emerges. The development of abstract thinking ability leads to changes in the self-concept and in conceptions of morality. Partly as a result of these cognitive advances, relationships with peers and parents undergo changes as well.

Question: So what is adolescence? Adolescence is a transitional period between childhood and adulthood, a coming of age. A century ago, most children in the United States assumed adult responsibilities early. Adolescence as a distinct stage of development between childhood and adulthood began to emerge when the demands of an increasingly complex society required a longer period of education and delayed entry into the labor force. It is no longer easy for American adolescents to know when they have made the transition to adulthood. In many preindustrial societies, the transition is marked by clear rites of passage, such as circumcision for boys or special ceremonies surrounding the first menstrual period for girls. But Western societies do not provide such clear rites of passage into adulthood, with the exception of the Jewish tradition of the bar mitzvah for boys and the bat mitzvah for girls. One legally becomes an adult at different ages, depending on whether one is buying a drink, driving a car, voting, or getting married.

In this chapter, we focus on the biological and physical changes of adolescence. We start by looking at some theoretical views of adolescence. Next we examine the many changes that occur during puberty. Finally, we look at the health and health problems of adolescents.

Views of Adolescent Development

It is often heard that adolescence is characterized by wildly fluctuating, unpredictable mood swings and by serious conflicts and rebellion against parents. Although many parents and many adolescents might endorse this view, it stereotypes adolescents and, in some ways, trivializes them. The real picture is more complex, as we will see.

Is Adolescence a Period of Storm and Stress?

The idea that adolescence is an important and separate developmental stage was first proposed by G. Stanley Hall (1904), an early American psychologist. Hall believed that adolescence is marked by intense turmoil. He used the German term *sturm und drang* ("storm and stress") to refer to the conflicts and stresses experienced during this stage. According to Hall, adolescents swing back and forth between happiness and sadness, overconfidence and self-doubt, dependence and independence. Hall believed that adolescent mood swings and conflicts with parents are a necessary part of growing up. He felt that children have to rebel against their parents and their parents' values in order to make the transition to adulthood.

Psychoanalytic Views

Sigmund Freud (1933/1964) placed relatively little emphasis on adolescence, since he believed that the first 5 years of life are the most critical. According to Freud, we enter the **genital stage** of psychosexual development at puberty. Hormonal changes trigger the reemergence of sexual urges, which were repressed during the latency stage. Sexual feelings initially are aimed toward the parent of the other gender, as they were during the phallic stage, but they become transferred, or displaced, onto other adults or adolescents of the other gender.

Anna Freud (1969), Sigmund's daughter, saw adolescence as a turbulent period resulting from an increase in the sex drive. (We now know that the hormonal stoking of puberty is a key ingredient of the sex drive.) These sexual feelings are assumed to cause anxiety and uncertainty. Conflict arises as the ego and superego try to keep these surging sexual impulses in check and redirect them from the parents to more acceptable outlets. The result is unpredictable behavior, defiance of parents, confusion, and mood swings. Anna Freud, like G. Stanley Hall, believed that adolescent turmoil not only is common but also is actually necessary for normal development.

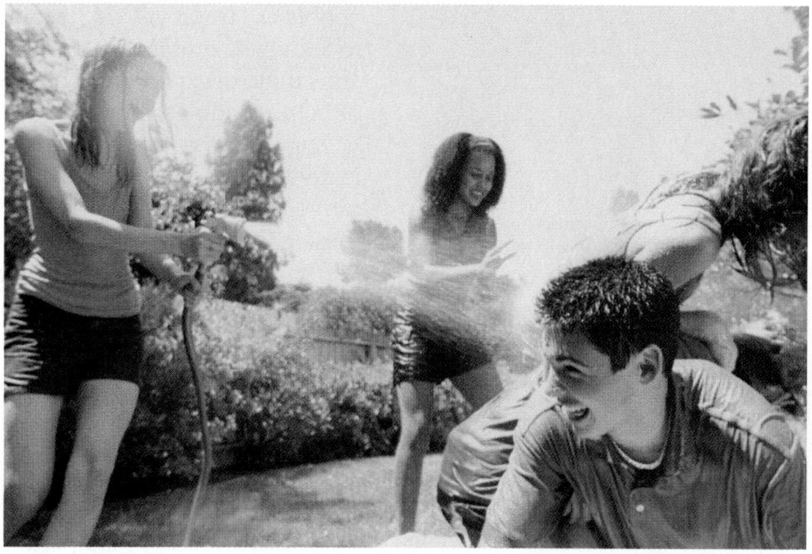

Is Adolescence a Period of Storm and Stress?

Research challenges the view that "storm and stress" is either normal or beneficial for adolescents. Neither violent mood swings nor deep-rooted parental conflicts appear to be inevitable, and most teenagers report feeling happy with their lives. Critics suggest that the storm-and-stress stereotype marginalizes adolescents.

Current Views

More current views challenge the traditional assumption that "storm and stress" is either normal or beneficial for adolescents (Buchanan, Eccles, & Becker, 1992; Griffin, 2001). Jeffrey Arnett (1999) outlines three areas of assumptions about storm and stress: conflict with parents, mood disruptions, and risky behavior. He argues that a review of the research suggests that we need a "modified storm-and-stress view" that takes individual differences and cultural variations into consideration. He notes that not all adolescents experience storm and stress, but admits that for those who do, storm and stress is more likely during adolescence than at other ages. Adolescent storm and stress tends to be lower in traditional, collectivist cultures than in the West but may increase as globalization increases because of an increase in individualism. In collectivist societies, adolescents tend to define themselves in terms of their group memberships—for example, their religion and their geographic location. But in individualistic societies, adolescents are more likely to define themselves in terms of their individual traits, skills, interests, and views—setting the stage for an identity crisis.

One study investigated whether adolescence is a time of greater emotionality in urban middle-class Indian youth (Verma & Larson, 1999). One hundred eighth-graders (mean age 13.2 years) and their parents provided more than 13,000 reports on their activities and emotions when signaled randomly by alarm watches over a period of 1 week. The data showed that the adolescents reported significantly more negative states and extreme positive states than their parents. However, the negative emotional states of the adolescents seemed to be preceded by stresses in school and problems with family and peers. Thus, the negative emotional states of the adolescents didn't "just happen." Teenagers who encounter several life changes at the same time, such as starting puberty, changing schools, breaking up with a boyfriend or girlfriend, and so on, are more likely than other teens to experience emotional distress.

Some theorists suggest that the concept of adolescence as a period of storm and stress has the effect of marginalizing adolescents (Griffin, 2001). Seeing young

Reflect

Was your own adolescence a period of "storm and stress"? Explain.

genital stage In psychoanalytic theory, the fifth and final stage of psychosexual development in which gratification is attained through sexual intercourse with an individual of the other gender.

people as "troubled" or "troubling" encourages adults to eye them warily and not to take their problems seriously. It is better to try to understand the kinds of problems that are experienced by many adolescents in our society and to develop ways of helping adolescents cope with them.

Regardless of whether adolescence is a period of "storm and stress," all adolescents are faced with the challenge of adapting to the numerous biological, cognitive, and social and emotional changes in their lives. Let us now begin to explore these changes, starting with the biological changes of puberty. ***Questions: What is puberty? What happens during puberty?***

Review

(1) ________ is a transitional period between childhood and adulthood. (2) G. Stanley Hall proposed that adolescence is a period of storm and ________. (3) According to Freud, people enter the ________ stage of psychosexual development at puberty.

Pulling It Together: How might the view of adolescence as a period of storm and stress have the effect of marginalizing adolescents?

Click *Physical Development* in the Child and Adolescent CD-ROM for more on puberty.

Puberty: The Biological Eruption

Puberty is defined as a stage of development characterized by reaching sexual maturity and the ability to reproduce. The onset of adolescence coincides with the advent of puberty. Puberty, however, is a biological concept, whereas adolescence is a psychosocial concept with biological correlates.

Puberty is controlled by a complex **feedback loop** involving the **hypothalamus, pituitary gland,** gonads—ovaries in females and testes in males—and hormones. The hypothalamus sends signals to the pituitary gland, which, in turn, releases hormones that control physical growth and the functioning of the gonads. The gonads respond to pituitary hormones by increasing their production of sex hormones (androgens and estrogens). The sex hormones further stimulate the hypothalamus, thus perpetuating the feedback loop.

The sex hormones also trigger the development of both the primary and secondary sex characteristics. The **primary sex characteristics** are the structures that make reproduction possible. In girls, these structures are the ovaries, vagina, uterus, and Fallopian tubes. In boys, they are the penis, testes, prostate gland, and seminal vesicles. The **secondary sex characteristics** are physical indicators of sexual maturation that do not involve the reproductive structures; these include breast development, deepening of the voice, and the appearance of facial, pubic, and underarm hair. Let's now explore the physical changes of puberty, starting with the growth spurt and then examining other pubertal changes in boys and girls involving the primary and secondary sex characteristics. ***Question: What happens during the adolescent growth spurt?***

puberty The biological stage of development characterized by changes that lead to reproductive capacity. Puberty signals the beginning of adolescence.

feedback loop A system in which the hypothalamus, pituitary gland, and gonads regulate each other's functioning through a series of hormonal messages.

hypothalamus A pea-sized structure that is located above the pituitary gland in the brain and is involved in the regulation of body temperature, motivation (for example, hunger, thirst, sex), and emotion.

pituitary gland The body's "master gland," which is located in the lower central part of the brain and secretes many hormones essential to development, such as oxytocin, prolactin, and growth hormone.

primary sex characteristics The structures that make reproduction possible.

secondary sex characteristics Physical indicators of sexual maturation—such as changes to the voice and growth of bodily hair—that do not directly involve the reproductive structures.

The Adolescent Growth Spurt: Changed Forever

When will it happen? How tall will I be?

The stable growth patterns in height and weight that characterize early and middle childhood come to an abrupt end with the adolescent growth spurt. Girls start to spurt in height sooner than boys, at an average age of a little over 10. Boys start to spurt about 2 years later, at an average age of about 12. Girls and boys reach their periods of peak growth in height about 2 years after the growth spurt begins, at about 12 and 14 years, respectively (see Figure 14.1). The spurt in height

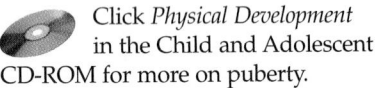

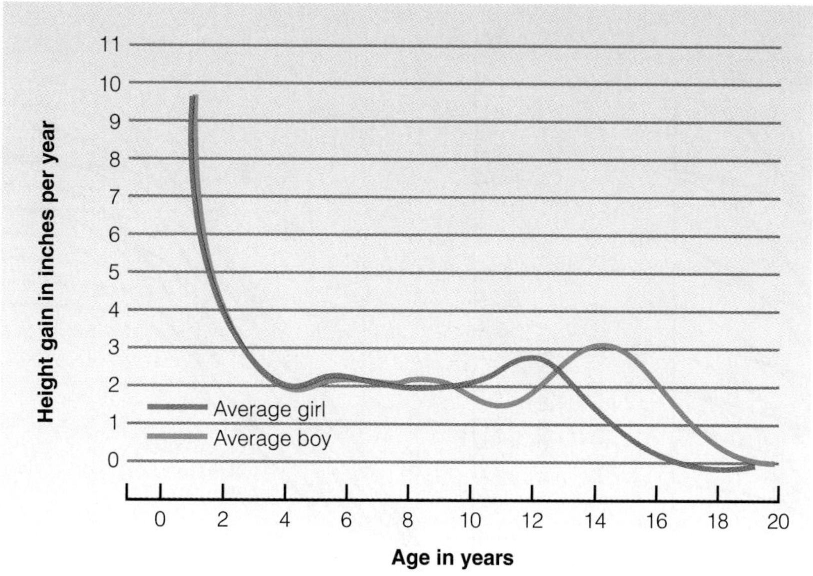

Figure 14.1
Spurts in Growth

Girls begin the adolescent growth spurt about 2 years earlier than boys. Girls and boys reach their periods of peak growth about 2 years after the spurt begins—at about 12 and 14 years, respectively.

for both girls and boys continues for about another 2 years at a gradually declining pace. Boys grow more than girls do during their spurt, averaging nearly 4 inches per year during the fastest year of the spurt compared with slightly over 3 inches per year for girls. Overall, boys add an average of $14^1/_2$ inches to their height during the spurt, and girls add a little over 13 inches (Tanner, 1991a).

Adolescents begin to spurt in weight about half a year after they begin to spurt in height. The period of peak growth in weight occurs about a year and a half after the onset of the spurt. As is the case with height, the growth spurt in weight then continues for a little more than 2 years for both girls and boys. As you can see in Figure 14.2, girls are taller and heavier than boys from about ages 9 or 10 until about age 13 or 14 since their growth spurt occurs earlier. Once boys begin their growth spurt, they catch up with girls and eventually become taller and heavier.

Since the spurt in weight lags behind the spurt in height, many adolescents are relatively slender as compared with their preadolescent and postadolescent stature. However, adolescents tend to eat enormous quantities of food to fuel their growth spurts. Active 14- and 15-year-old boys may consume 5,000 to 6,000 calories a day without becoming obese. If they were to eat this much 20 years later, they might gain upwards of 100 pounds per year. Little wonder that adults fighting the dismal battle of the bulge stare at adolescents in amazement as they inhale pizza for lunch and go out later for burgers and fries!

Girls' and boys' body shapes begin to differ in adolescence. For one thing, boys' shoulders become broader than those of girls, while the hip dimensions of both genders do not differ much. So, girls have relatively broader hips compared with their shoulders, whereas the opposite is true for boys. You've also noticed that a girl's body shape is more rounded than that of a boy. This is due to the fact that during puberty, girls gain almost twice as much fatty tissue as boys do, while boys gain twice as much muscle tissue as girls. Thus, a larger proportion of a male's body weight is composed of his muscle mass, whereas a relatively larger part of a female's body weight is composed of fatty tissue.

Reflect

What were your experiences of puberty and the adolescent growth spurt like? Do you recall a gawky period? Were you anxious about the way everything would turn out? Did you just "sail through"? Explain.

Individual Differences in the Growth Spurt

The figures given above are averages. Few of us begin or end our growth spurts right on the mark. Children who spurt earlier are also likely to wind up with somewhat shorter legs and longer torsos, while children who spurt late are somewhat longer-legged. However, there are no significant differences between early and late spurters in the total height attained at maturity (Tanner, 1991a).

Click *Physical Development* for more on the adolescent growth spurt.

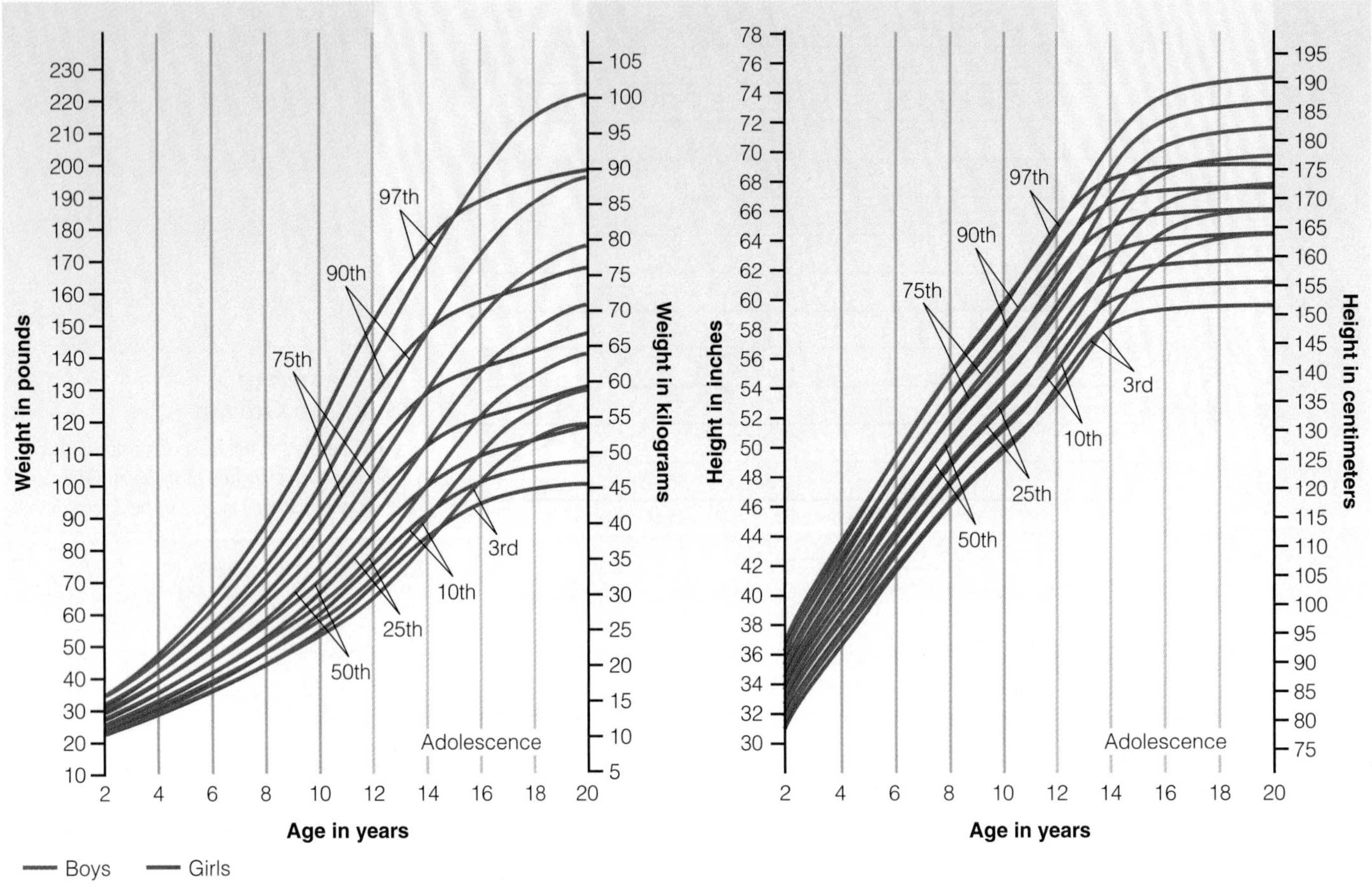

Figure 14.2
Growth Curves for Height and Weight

Girls are taller and heavier than boys from about age 9 or 10 until about age 13 since their growth spurt occurs earlier. Once boys begin their growth spurt, they catch up with girls and eventually become taller and heavier.

Source: Figures 9–12, Kuczmarski, R. J., et al. (2000, December 4). CDC Growth charts: United States. Advance data from vital and health statistics, *no. 314. Hyattsville, MD: National Center for Health Statistics.*

Regardless of the age at which the growth spurt begins, there is a moderate-to-high correlation between a child's height at the onset of adolescence and at maturity (Tanner, 1989). Are there exceptions? Of course. However, everything else being equal, a tall child has a reasonable expectation of becoming a tall adult, and vice versa.

Asynchronous Growth: On Being Gawky

Adolescents are often referred to as awkward and gawky. A major reason for this is **asynchronous growth**—different parts of the body grow at different rates. In an exception to the principle of proximodistal growth, the hands and feet mature before the arms and legs do. As a consequence, adolescent girls and boys may complain of big hands or feet. And, in an apparent reversal of the cephalocaudal growth trend, legs reach their peak growth before the shoulders and chest. This means that boys stop growing out of their pants about a year before they stop growing out of their jackets (Tanner, 1989).

The Secular Trend in Growth

During the past century, children in the Western world have grown dramatically more rapidly and wound up taller than children from earlier times. This historical trend toward increasing adult height, which also has been accompanied by an earlier onset of puberty, is known as the **secular trend.** Figure 14.3 shows that Swedish boys and girls grew more rapidly in 1938 and 1968 than they did in 1883 and ended up several centimeters taller. At the age of 15, the boys were more than 6 inches taller and the girls were more than 3 inches taller, on the average, than their counterparts from the previous century (Tanner, 1989). The occurrence of a secular trend in height and also in weight has been documented in nearly all European countries and the United States.

asynchronous growth Imbalanced growth, such as that which occurs during the early part of adolescence and causes many adolescents to appear gawky.

secular trend A historical trend toward increasing adult height and earlier puberty.

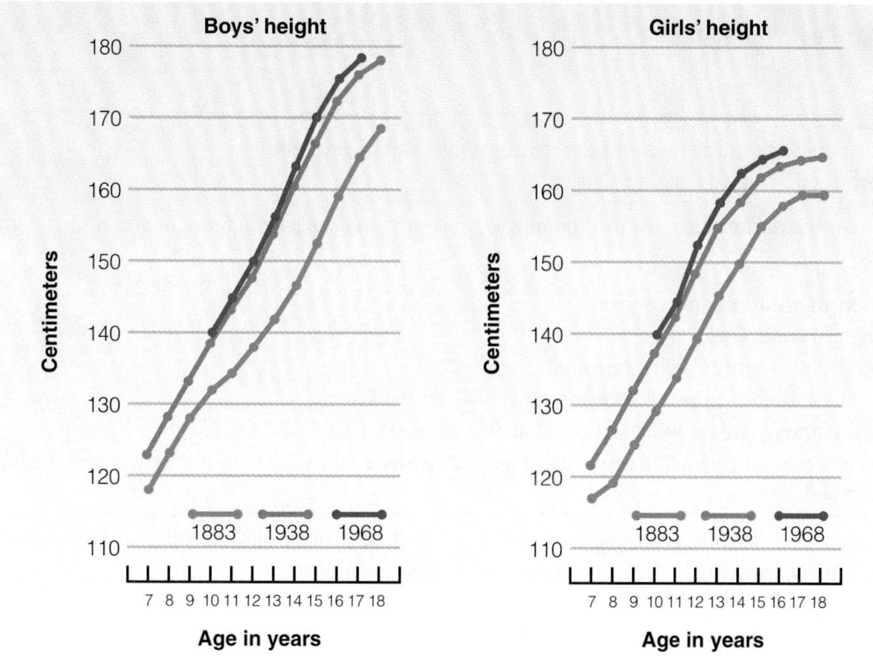

Figure 14.3
Are We Still Growing Taller Than Our Parents?

Twentieth-century children grew more rapidly and grew taller than children in preceding centuries. However, it seems that children from affluent families are no longer growing taller than their parents. But children from the lower part of the socioeconomic spectrum are still doing so.
Source: Tanner, 1989.

However, it turns out that children from middle- and upper-class families in industrialized countries have now stopped growing taller, whereas their poorer counterparts continue to make gains in height from generation to generation (Tanner, 1989). Why?

Nutrition apparently plays an important role in the rate of growth and size at maturity. U.S. government surveys have shown that children from middle- and upper-class families are taller and heavier than their age-mates from lower-class families. This in and of itself would not be very convincing. It could, for example, be argued that genetic factors provide advantages that increase the chances for financial gain as well as for greater height and weight. But remember that children from the middle- and upper-class portion of the socioeconomic spectrum are no longer growing taller. Perhaps Americans who have had nutritional and medical advantages have simply reached their full genetic potential in height. Continued gains among families of lower socioeconomic status suggest that poorer children are still benefiting from gradual improvements in nutrition.

We now examine some of the other changes that occur during puberty. These are summarized in Table 14.1. You will notice that there are wide individual differences in the timing of the events of puberty. In a group of teenagers of the same age and gender, you may well find some who have completed puberty, others who haven't even started, and others who are somewhere in between.

Pubertal Changes in Boys—Bigger, Stronger

At puberty, the pituitary gland stimulates the testes to increase their output of testosterone, leading to further development of the male genitals. The first visible sign of puberty is accelerated growth of the testes, which begins at an average age of about $11^1/_2$, although a range of ages of plus or minus 2 years is considered perfectly normal. Testicular growth further accelerates testosterone production and other pubertal changes. The penis begins a spurt of accelerated growth about a year later, and still later pubic hair begins a growth spurt.

Click *Physical Development* for more on pubertal changes in boys.

Underarm hair appears at about age 15. Facial hair is at first a fuzz on the upper lip. An actual beard does not develop for another 2 to 3 years—only half of American boys shave (of necessity) by 17. The beard and chest hair continue to develop past the age of 20.

TABLE 14.1 *Stages of Pubertal Development*

In Females	
Beginning sometime between ages 8 and 11	Pituitary hormones stimulate ovaries to increase production of estrogen. Internal reproductive organs begin to grow.
Beginning sometime between ages 9 and 15	First the areola (the darker area around the nipple) and then the breasts increase in size and become more rounded. Pubic hair becomes darker and coarser. Growth in height continues. Body fat continues to round body contours. A normal vaginal discharge becomes noticeable. Sweat and oil glands increase in activity, and acne may appear. Internal and external reproductive organs and genitals grow, making the vagina longer and the labia more pronounced.
Beginning sometime between ages 10 and 16	Areola and nipples grow, often forming a second mound sticking out from the rounded breast mound. Pubic hair begins to grow in a triangular shape and to cover the center of the mons. Underarm hair appears. Menarche occurs. Internal reproductive organs continue to develop. Ovaries may begin to release mature eggs capable of being fertilized. Growth in height slows.
Beginning sometime between ages 12 and 19	Breasts near adult size and shape. Pubic hair fully covers the mons and spreads to the top of the thighs. The voice may deepen slightly (but not as much as in males). Menstrual cycles gradually become more regular. Some further changes in body shape may occur into the young woman's early 20s.

Note: This table is a general guideline. Changes may appear sooner or later than shown and do not always appear in the indicated sequence.
Source: Copyright © 1990 by the Kinsey Institute for Research in Sex, Gender, and Reproduction. From The Kinsey Institute New Report on Sex. *Reprinted by permission of the publisher.*

At 14 or 15, the voice deepens because of growth of the "voice box," or **larynx,** and the lengthening of the vocal cords. The developmental process is gradual, and adolescent boys sometimes encounter an embarrassing cracking of the voice. Because women were not allowed to sing in the opera during most of pre-19th-century Europe, many boys with promising voices were *castrated* so they could assume women's roles later on. So-called *castrati* were used in the pope's choir until early in the last century. At that time nothing was known of hormones, so it was not understood that castration prevented the appearance of secondary sex characteristics in boys by depriving them of testosterone.

Testosterone also triggers the development of acne, which afflicts between 75% and 90% of adolescents (Lowrey, 1986). Severe acne is manifested by multiple pimples and blackheads on the face, chest, and back. Although boys are more prone to acne than girls, we cannot say that girls suffer less from it. In our society, a smooth complexion has a higher value for girls than boys, and girls with cases of acne that boys would consider mild may suffer terribly.

Males are capable of producing erections in early infancy (and some male babies are born with erections), but the phenomenon is not a frequent one until age 13 or 14. Many middle school boys worry that they will be caught with erections when walking between classes or when asked to stand before the class. The organs that produce **semen** grow rapidly, and boys typically ejaculate seminal fluid by age 13 or 14—about $1^1/_2$ years after the penis begins its growth spurt—although here, too, there is much individual variation. About a year later they begin to have **nocturnal emissions,** also called "wet dreams" because of the myth that emissions accompany erotic dreams. However, nocturnal emissions and erotic dreams need not

larynx The part of the throat that contains the vocal cords.

semen The fluid that contains sperm and substances that nourish and help transport sperm.

nocturnal emission Emission of seminal fluid while asleep.

TABLE 14.1 *(continued)*

In Males	
Beginning sometime between ages 9 and 15	The testicles begin to grow. The skin of the scrotum becomes redder and coarser. A few straight pubic hairs appear at the base of the penis. Muscle mass develops, and the boy begins to grow taller. The areola grows larger and darker.
Beginning sometime between ages 11 and 16	The penis begins to grow longer. The testicles and scrotum continue to grow. Pubic hair becomes coarser and more curled and spreads to cover the area between the legs. The body gains in height. The shoulders broaden. The hips narrow. The larynx enlarges, resulting in a deepening of the voice. Sparse facial and underarm hair appears.
Beginning sometime between ages 11 and 17	The penis begins to increase in circumference as well as in length (though more slowly). The testicles continue to increase in size. The texture of the pubic hair is more like an adult's. Growth of facial and underarm hair increases. Shaving may begin. First ejaculation occurs. In nearly half of all boys, gynecomastia (breast enlargement) occurs, which then decreases in a year or two. Increased skin oils may produce acne.
Beginning sometime between ages 14 and 18	The body nears final adult height, and the genitals achieve adult shape and size, with pubic hair spreading to the thighs and slightly upward toward the belly. Chest hair appears. Facial hair reaches full growth. Shaving becomes more frequent. For some young men, further increases in height, body hair, and muscle growth and strength continue into their early 20s.

coincide at all. Mature sperm are found in ejaculatory emissions by about the age of 15. And so ejaculation is not adequate evidence of reproductive capacity. Ejaculatory ability in boys usually precedes the presence of mature sperm by at least a year. Girls also typically menstruate before they can reproduce.

Nearly half of all boys experience temporary enlargement of the breasts, or **gynecomastia.** This condition probably stems from the small amount of female sex hormones secreted by the testes.

At 20 or 21, men stop growing taller because testosterone causes **epiphyseal closure,** preventing the long bones from making further gains in length. And so, puberty draws to a close.

Pubertal Changes in Girls—On Becoming a Well-Rounded Person

In girls, the pituitary gland signals the ovaries to vastly increase estrogen production at puberty. Estrogen may stimulate the growth of breast tissue ("breast buds") as early as the ages of 8 or 9, but the breasts usually begin to enlarge during the 10th year. The development of fatty tissue and ducts elevates the areas of the breasts surrounding the nipples and causes the nipples themselves to protrude. The breasts typically reach full size in about 3 years, but the **mammary glands** do not mature fully until childbirth.

gynecomastia Temporary enlargement of the breasts in adolescent males.

epiphyseal closure The process by which the cartilage that separates the long end (epiphysis) of a bone from the main part of the bone turns to bone.

mammary glands Glands that secrete milk.

Click *Physical Development* for more on pubertal changes in girls.

Estrogen also promotes the growth of the fatty and supporting tissue in the hips and buttocks, which, along with the widening of the pelvis, causes the hips to become rounded. Growth of fatty deposits and connective tissue varies considerably. For this reason, some girls develop pronounced breasts, whereas others may have relatively large hips.

Small amounts of androgens produced by girls' adrenal glands, along with estrogen, stimulate the growth of pubic and underarm hair, beginning at about the age of 11. Excessive androgen production can darken or increase the amount of facial hair.

While estrogen causes the **labia,** vagina, and uterus to develop during puberty, androgens cause the **clitoris** to develop. The vaginal lining varies in thickness according to the amount of estrogen in the bloodstream.

Estrogen typically brakes the female growth spurt some years before testosterone brakes that of males. Girls deficient in estrogen during their late teens may grow quite tall, but most girls reach their heights because of normal, genetically determined variations.

Reflect

For women only: What did menarche mean to you? Did your sociocultural background influence your reaction? Explain.

Menarche: The Transition to Womanhood?

Question: What is menarche? **Menarche** (first menstruation) commonly occurs between the ages of 11 and 14. But it is quite normal for menarche to occur as early as age 9 or as late as age 16 (Golub, 1992). In the middle 1800s, European girls first menstruated at about the age of 16, as shown in Figure 14.4. But during the past century and a half, the processes of puberty have occurred at progressively earlier ages in Western nations, an example of the secular trend in development. By the 1960s, the average age of menarche in the United States had plummeted to its current figure of $12^1/_2$ (Frisch, 1991; Tanner, 1991b).

What accounts for the earlier age of puberty? The **critical fat hypothesis** suggests that girls must reach a certain body weight to trigger pubertal changes such as menarche. Body fat would trigger the changes because fat cells secrete the protein leptin. Leptin would then signal the brain to secrete a cascade of hormones that result in higher levels of estrogen in the body. It is known that menarche comes later to girls who have a lower percentage of body fat, such as athletes (Frisch, 1997). Injections of leptin also cause laboratory animals to reach sexual

labia The major and minor lips of the female genitalia.

clitoris A female sex organ that is highly sensitive to sexual stimulation but not directly involved in reproduction.

menarche The onset of menstruation.

critical fat hypothesis The view that a critical body weight triggers menarche because fat cells signal the brain to release a cascade of hormones that raise estrogen levels in girls.

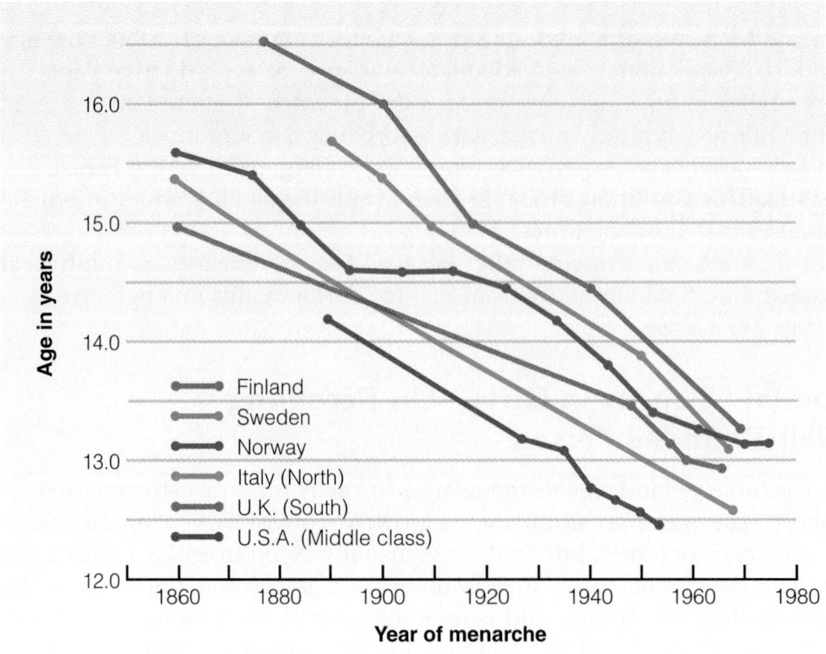

Figure 14.4
The Decline in Age at Menarche

The age at menarche has been declining since the mid-1800s among girls in Western nations, apparently because of improved nutrition and health care. Menarche may be triggered by the accumulation of a critical percentage of body fat.
Source: Tanner, 1989.

maturity early (Angier, 1997). The average body weight for triggering menarche depends on one's height. For females ranging from 5 feet to $5^1/_2$ feet tall, the average triggering weight is between 97 and 114 pounds (Frisch, 1991).

Today's children are larger than those of the early part of the century probably because of improved nutrition and health care. But the age limits for reaching menarche may have been reached, because the average age has leveled off in recent years.

No single theory of the onset of puberty has found wide acceptance. In any event, the average age of the advent of puberty for girls and boys appears to have leveled off in recent years. The precipitous drop suggested in Figure 14.4 seems to have come to an end.

Hormonal Regulation of the Menstrual Cycle

While testosterone levels remain fairly stable in boys, estrogen and progesterone levels vary markedly and regulate the menstrual cycle. Following menstruation—the sloughing off of the endometrium—estrogen levels increase, leading once more to the growth of endometrial tissue. Once girls have begun to ovulate, which usually occurs about 12 to 18 months after menarche, the surge of estrogen also causes an ovum to ripen. The ripe ovum is released by the ovary when estrogen reaches peak blood levels. Then the inner lining of the uterus thickens in response to the secretion of progesterone. In this way, it gains the capacity to support an embryo if fertilization should occur. If the ovum is not fertilized, estrogen and progesterone levels drop suddenly, triggering menstruation once again.

The average menstrual cycle is 28 days, but variation between girls and in the same girl is common. Girls' cycles are often irregular for a few years after menarche but later tend to assume patterns that are reasonably regular. The majority of menstrual cycles during the first 2 years or so after menarche occur without ovulation having taken place. But keep in mind that in any given individual cycle, an ovum may be produced, making pregnancy possible. So it is possible to become pregnant shortly after the onset of menarche.

The Psychological Impact of Menarche

In different times, in different places, menarche has had different meanings. The Manus of New Guinea greet menarche with elaborate ceremony (Golub, 1992). The other girls of the village sleep in the menstruating girl's hut. They feast and have parties.

In the West, menstruation has historically received a mixed response (Golub, 1992). The menstrual flow itself has generally been seen, erroneously, as polluting, and menstruating women have been stereotyped as irrational. Menarche itself has generally been perceived as the event in which a girl suddenly develops into a woman, but because of taboos and the unjustified prejudice against menstruating women, girls usually matured in ignorance of menarche.

Things are changing. In the United States, most of the negative stereotypes about menstruation are diminishing, but some people still do not consider menstruation an appropriate topic for "polite conversation." In one study, a minority of 9–12-year-old girls in suburban Midwest schools still clung to certain "taboos" and negative feelings: 36% of them believed that menstruating women should not go swimming; 16% believed that strenuous sports should be avoided; and 10% still saw menstruation as dirty or unclean (Williams, 1983). On the positive side, 64% of the 9–12-year-old girls in the Williams (1983) study agreed that "Menstruation is exciting because it means a girl is growing up" (p. 146). Also, most premenarcheal girls hope that they will "get their periods" when their agemates do (Petersen, 1983), just as they hope that their breasts will develop at the same time.

Most girls receive advance information about menstruation, usually from their mothers, sisters, and girlfriends. Early information about menstruation appears to foster more positive feelings toward it (Brooks-Gunn, 1991b; Golub, 1992).

Early and Late Maturers: Does It Matter When You Arrive, as Long as You Do?

I remember Al from my high school days. When Al entered the ninth grade, he was all of 14, but he was also about 6 feet 3 inches tall, with broad shoulders and arms thick with muscle. His face was cut from rock, and his beard was already dark. Al paraded down the hallways with an entourage of male and female admirers. When there were shrieks of anticipation, you could bet that Al was coming around the corner. Al was given a wide berth in the boys' room. He would have to lean back when he combed his waxed hair up and back—otherwise, his head would be too high for the mirror. At that age, my friends and I liked to tell ourselves that Al was not all that bright. (This stereotype is unfounded, as we shall see.) Nevertheless, my friends and I were extremely envious of Al.

Al had arrived.

Al had matured early, and he had experienced the positive aspects of maturing early. What causes some children to mature earlier or later than others? Genetic, dietary, and health factors all seem to influence the timing of puberty. And one controversial new theory suggests that childhood stress may trigger early puberty in girls. ***Question: What are the effects of early or late maturation on adolescents?***

Reflect

Did you mature relatively early or late? What were the effects of the timing of maturation on your social and emotional development?

Click *Physical Development* for more on early and late maturation.

Early and Late Maturation in Boys

Studies are somewhat mixed in their findings about boys who mature early, but the weight of the evidence suggests that the effects of early maturation are generally positive (Alsaker, 1992). Late-maturing boys may feel conspicuous because they are among the last of their peers to lose their childhood appearance. Remember that almost all the girls and most of the boys will already have begun the physical changes of puberty (Nottelmann et al., 1990).

Classic research on a cohort of children who participated in the Berkeley Growth Study found that early-maturing boys are more popular than their late-maturing peers and are more likely to be leaders in school (Jones, 1957; Mussen & Jones, 1957). Early-maturing boys are also more poised, relaxed, and good-natured. Their edge in sports and the admiration of their peers heightens their sense of self-worth. Some studies have suggested that the stereotype of the mature, tough-looking boy as dumb is just that—a stereotype. Early-maturing boys may actually be somewhat ahead of their peers intellectually (Tanner, 1982). However, these differences are slight, and, where they exist, they tend to evaporate by adulthood (Jones, 1957).

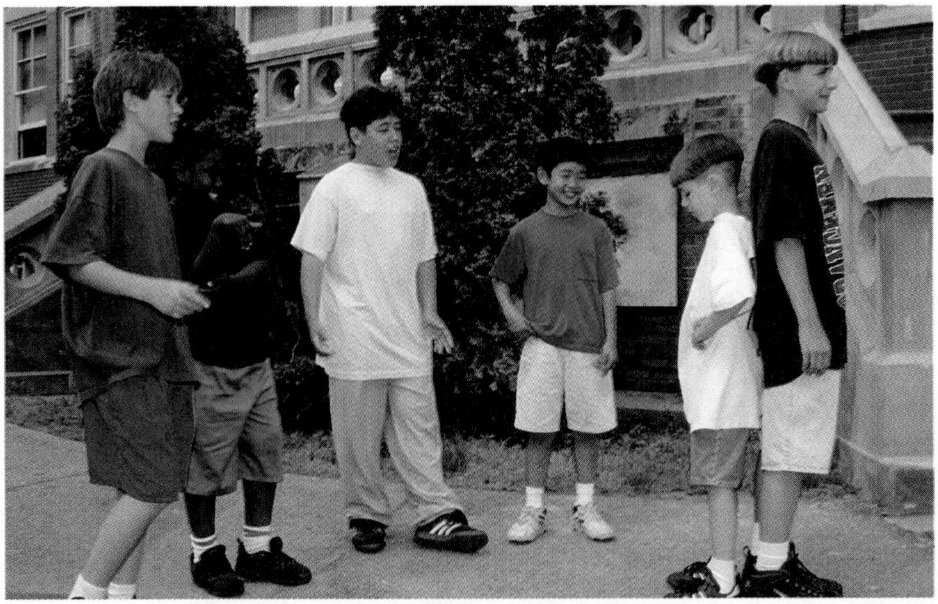

© Ellen Senisi/The Image Works

Early and Late Maturation in Boys

The effects of early maturation in boys are generally positive. Late-maturing boys may feel conspicuous because they are among the last of their peers to lose their childhood appearance. By then, almost all of the girls and most of the boys will have begun the physical changes of puberty.

On the negative side, early maturation may hit some boys before they are psychologically prepared to live up to the expectations of those who admire their new bodies. Coaches may expect too much of them in sports, and peers may want them to fight their battles for them (Ge, Conger, & Elder, 2001a; O'Sullivan, Meyer-Bahlberg, & Watkins, 2000). Sexual opportunities may create demands before they know how to respond to them. Some early maturers may therefore worry about living up to the expectations of others.

Late maturers have the advantage of avoiding this early pressure. They are not rushed into maturity. On the other hand, late-maturing boys often feel dominated by early-maturing boys. They have been found to be more dependent and insecure. Although they are smaller and weaker than early maturers, they may be more rebellious and more likely to get into fights—perhaps in an effort to prove themselves to be adult (Ge, Conger, & Elder, 2001a; O'Sullivan et al., 2001).

But there are many individual differences. While some late maturers appear to fight their physical status and get into trouble, others adjust to their physical development status and find acceptance through academic achievement, music, clubs, and other nonathletic extracurricular activities. Late-maturing boys also show more flexibility and social sensitivity and a greater sense of humor than their early-maturing counterparts. The benefits of early maturation appear to be greatest among lower-income adolescents, because physical prowess is valued more highly among these youngsters than among middle- or upper-income adolescents. Middle- and upper-income adolescents also are likely to place more value on the types of achievements—academic and so on—available to late-maturing boys (Rutter, 1980).

Early and Late Maturation in Girls

The situation is somewhat reversed for girls. Whereas early maturation poses distinct advantages for boys, the picture is mixed for girls. Adolescents tend to be concerned if they are different from their peers. So early-maturing girls may feel awkward, because they are among the first of their peers to begin the physical changes of puberty. They outgrow not only their late-maturing female counterparts, but also their male age-mates. With their tallness and their developing breasts, they quickly become conspicuous. Boys of their age may tease them about their breasts and their height. Tall girls of dating age frequently find that shorter boys are reluctant to approach them or be seen with them. Occasionally, tall girls walk with a slight hunch, as if trying to minimize their height.

Girls who mature early feel less positive about their puberty and have a poorer body image than those who mature later (Williams & Currie, 2000). These negative feelings are more pronounced for girls who are still in elementary school, where they are more conspicuous, and are less pronounced if they are in high school, where others are catching up.

Adolescent girls are quite concerned about their body shapes. Early maturers who are taller and heavier than other girls their age do not conform to the current cultural emphasis on thinness. Thus, they have more negative feelings about their bodies. Early maturation in girls is associated with a variety of other problems. Early-maturing girls obtain lower grades in school, have more conduct problems, and have a higher incidence of emotional disturbance, including depression, than other girls (Ge, Conger, & Elder, 2001b; Stice, Presnall, & Bearman, 2001). They are more vulnerable to deviant peer pressure (Ge, Conger, & Elder, 1996). They are likely to be involved in violations of societal norms: ignoring parents' prohibitions, staying out late without permission, being truant from school, smoking, drinking, and shoplifting (Stice, Hayward, Cameron, Killen, & Taylor, 2000). They engage in sexual intercourse at an earlier age (Magnusson, 2001; Rosenthal, Smith, & deVisser, 1999). Sexual activity is connected with association with older peers and interest from older boys. Their concern about their body shape also appears to heighten the risk of developing eating disorders (Kaltiala-Heino et al., 2001; Striegel-Moore et al., 2001).

The parents of early-maturing girls may increase their vigilance and restrictiveness. Increased restrictiveness can lead to new child–parent conflicts. A study of 302 African American adolescent–mother pairs found that mothers of early

Body Image

Adolescent females in our society are much more preoccupied with body weight and slimness than are adolescent males. Why?

maturing daughters had more heated discussions with them than with later-maturing daughters (Sagrestano et al., 1999). Sad to say, girls who mature early are also more likely to experience child sexual abuse (Kaltiala-Heino et al., 2001; Romans et al., 2001). The early-maturing girl can thus be a target of inappropriate parental attention and develop severe conflicts about her body, which may well be related to this "attention."

Yet not all early-maturing girls develop difficulties. Rather, early maturation appears to accentuate problems among girls who already had difficulty adjusting earlier in childhood (Caspi & Moffitt, 1991).

Although early-maturing girls are less poised, sociable, and expressive than their late-maturing counterparts during the latter part of middle childhood (Jones, 1958), they appear to adjust by the time they reach high school. Once in high school, they do not stand out so much, and their size may earn them admiration rather than curiosity. At this time, early-maturing girls may also take on the roles of cosmetic and sexual advisers to later-maturing age-mates. Perhaps the task of coping with the problems posed by early maturation also helps them develop coping mechanisms that they use to their advantage in later years.

Body Image

Reflect

How do you feel about your body? How important are these feelings in your daily life?

Our *body image* refers to how physically attractive we perceive ourselves to be and to how we feel about our body. Adolescents are quite concerned about their physical appearance, particularly in early adolescence when the rapid physical changes of puberty are occurring (Striegel-Moore et al., 2001; Williams & Currie, 2000).

Question: How do adolescents feel about their bodies? By the age of 18, girls and boys are more satisfied with their bodies than they were in the earlier teen years. In a 5-year longitudinal study, Holsen and colleagues (2001) investigated the relationship between body image and depressed mood in 645 adolescents at ages 13, 15, and 18. On average, girls reported having a more negative body image and feeling more depressed about their bodies at all three ages. Yet dissatisfaction with body image led to feelings of depression among both girls and boys (Holsen, Kraft, & Roysamb, 2001). Adolescent females in our society tend to

Click *Physical Development* for more on body image concerns.

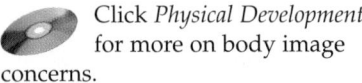

Competition for the Average American Adolescent Female?

Stiff competition indeed. One of my female students saw this picture and exclaimed, "This is what makes us (meaning: average women) suicidal!" The typical model is a good deal taller and slimmer than the average American female. Yet adolescents tend to compare their own body images with the images of "perfection" they see in the media. Males tend to be more self-forgiving or—should we say—somewhat less aware of their own bodies in relation to those found among models in the media. In any event, current standards of feminine beauty have pushed the majority of females in our society to be on a diet at one time or another—or, in some cases, perpetually.

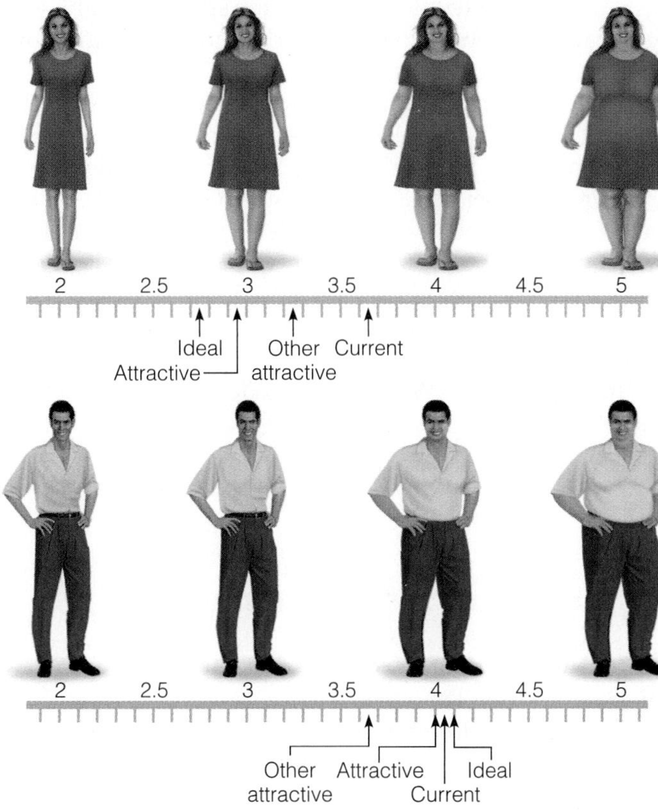

Figure 14.5
Can You Ever Be Too Thin?
For many adolescent females in our society, the answer is a resounding no. And this answer has given rise to hundreds of thousands of women with eating disorders. Research suggests that most adolescent females believe that their current weight is higher than their ideal weight ("Ideal"), the weight that would be attractive for them ("Attractive"), and the weight that males would find to be attractive ("Other attractive"). Adolescent males, by contrast (by stark *contrast!), generally consider their current weights to be about the same as their ideal weights and the weights that they believe are attractive. However, adolescent females ("Other attractive") would actually prefer the males to be slimmer than they are. Adolescents of both genders err in their assumptions as to what members of the other gender find to be attractive—but in opposite directions.*

be more preoccupied with body weight and slimness than adolescent males (McCabe & Ricciardelli, 2001). Compared with females, however, many adolescent males want to put weight *on* and build their muscle mass (McCabe & Ricciardelli, 2001; Vartanian, Giant, & Passino, 2001). Compared with adolescent boys, adolescent girls have a less positive body image and are more dissatisfied with their weight; the majority are likely to diet—either to have dieted or to be on a diet currently (Holsen et al., 2001; Stice & Bearman, 2001). And girls are more likely to suffer from the eating disorders of *anorexia nervosa* and *bulimia nervosa*.

College women generally see themselves as significantly heavier than the figure they believe is most attractive to males and females and heavier still than the "ideal" female figure (Rozin & Fallon, 1988; see Figure 14.5). College men actually prefer an average-size female body to a thin one. It appears that a thin ideal of female body attractiveness is held by females but not by males.

Adolescents who have a more positive body image have higher self-esteem (Vartanian et al., 2001). Girls' feelings about themselves are even more closely linked to their physical appearance than is the case for boys (Williams, 1992). For example, girls who are concerned about their weight tend to have lower self-esteem than girls who do not have this concern. But concern about weight is not related to self-esteem in boys.

Review

(4) ________ is a stage of development that is characterized by reaching sexual maturity. (5) Puberty is controlled by a ________ loop involving hormones. (6) The ________ signals the pituitary gland, which, in turn, releases hormones that control growth and the gonads. (7) The gonads produce ________ hormones (androgens and estrogens). (8) Sex hormones trigger the development of ________ and secondary sex characteristics. (9) Girls begin their ________ spurt in height at about 10, and boys spurt about 2 years later. (10) Adolescents spurt in

_________ about half a year after they spurt in height. (11) There (are or are not?) significant differences between early and late spurters in the height attained at maturity. (12) Adolescents may be gawky due to _________ growth. (13) The tendency to grow more rapidly and become taller than one's parents is called the _________ trend. (14) Development of acne is caused by _________. (15) Sperm is contained in a fluid called _________. (16) Males stop growing taller because testosterone causes _________ closure. (17) _________ brakes the female growth spurt. (18) First menstruation is called _________. (19) The menstrual cycle is governed by _________. (20) (Boys or Girls?) are more likely to benefit from early maturation. (21) (Boys or Girls?) are more likely to have a positive body image.

Pulling It Together: What kinds of effects do hormones have on the development of adolescents?

Health in Adolescence

Adolescents are young and growing. Most seem sturdy. Injuries tend to heal quickly. ***Question: How healthy are American adolescents?*** The good news is that most American adolescents are healthy. Few are chronically ill or miss school. However, about one out of five of the nation's adolescents has at least one serious health problem (USDHHS, 2001). American teenagers may be less healthy than their parents were at the same age. The reason is not an increase in the incidence of infectious diseases or other physical illnesses. Rather, the causes are external and rooted in lifestyle and risky behavior: excessive drinking, substance abuse, reckless driving, violence, disordered eating behavior, and unprotected sexual activity leading to sexually transmitted infections and pregnancy (CDC, 2000c). While risk taking sometimes is viewed as a normal part of adolescent development, risk-taking behaviors can be detrimental to the adolescent's health and well-being (USDHHS, 2001). Let us look at some of the health risks of adolescence. We will start by examining causes of death in adolescence. We then turn to three major health problems faced by teens: eating disorders, substance abuse, and sexually transmitted infections.

Causes of Death

Although adolescents are healthy as a group, a number of them die. ***Questions: How many adolescents die? What are the causes of death among adolescents?*** Death rates are low in adolescence, although they are higher for older adolescents than for younger ones. For example, each year about twice as many 15–17-year-olds as 12–14-year-olds die (USDHHS, 2001). Death rates are nearly twice as great for male adolescents as for female adolescents (USDHHS, 2001). A major reason for this is that males are more likely to take risks that end in death due to accidents, suicide, or homicide (USDHHS, 2001). These three causes of death account for 75% of all adolescent deaths.

Sixty percent of adolescent deaths are due to accidents, and most of these involve motor vehicles (USDHHS, 2001). Alcohol often is involved in accidental deaths. Alcohol-related motor vehicle accidents are the leading cause of death for 15–24-year-olds. Alcohol frequently is implicated in other causes of accidental death or injury, including drowning and falling (Bonomo et al., 2001; Denscombe, 2001).

Adolescents who are poor and who live in urban areas of high population density have the greatest risk of death by homicide (USDHHS, 2001). African American adolescents are more likely than European American adolescents to fit this description. Therefore, it is not surprising that the homicide rate is greater among African American adolescents.

Reflect

Are you surprised to learn of the main causes of death among adolescents? Explain.

Accidental Death

The majority of adolescent deaths are due to accidents, most of them involving motor vehicles. Alcohol often is involved in accidental deaths.

Homicide is the leading cause of death in 15–19-year-old African American males, whereas accidents are the major cause of death for European American teens ("Influence of homicide," 2001; USDHHS, 2000). African American adolescents aged 15 and 19 are nearly 10 times as likely as their European American age-mates to be murdered. Females are not exempt from this pattern. African American females aged 15 to 19 are more than five times as likely as their European American counterparts to be victims of homicide. The figures for Latino and Latina American adolescents are lower than those for African American youth but higher than those for European Americans (USDHHS, 2000).

The suicide rate for teenagers has increased dramatically in recent years (USDHHS, 2001). It is the second leading cause of death for European American adolescents and the third leading cause for African American adolescents. We take a closer look at suicide in Chapter 16.

Review

(22) The (majority or minority?) of American adolescents are healthy. (23) Death rates are greater for (male or female?) adolescents. (24) Most adolescent deaths are due to ________. (25) ________ is the second leading cause of death for European American adolescent, and the third leading cause for African American adolescents.

Pulling It Together: Why can we say that the majority of deaths among adolescents are self-inflicted?

Nutrition—An Abundance of Food and an Abundance of Eating Disorders

Physical growth occurs more rapidly in the adolescent years than at any other time after birth, with the exception of the 1st year of life (McCoy & Kenney, 1991). ***Questions: What are the nutritional needs of adolescents? What do they actually eat?*** To fuel this growth, the average girl needs to consume about 2,200 calories per day, while the average boy needs about 3,000 calories (Ekvall, 1993b). The nutritional needs of adolescents vary according to their stage of pubertal development. For example, at the peak of their growth spurt, adolescents use twice as much calcium, iron, zinc, magnesium, and nitrogen as they do during the other years of adolescence (Rockett et al., 2001). Calcium intake is particularly important for females to build up their bone density and help prevent a serious condition known as **osteoporosis** later in life. Osteoporosis, a progressive loss of bone, affects millions of women, particularly after **menopause.** But most teenagers—both girls and boys—do not consume enough calcium. Adolescents also are likely to obtain less vitamin A, thiamin, and iron and more fat, sugar, protein, and sodium than recommended (Rockett et al., 2001).

One reason for adolescents' nutritional deficiencies is their often irregular eating patterns. Breakfast frequently is skipped, especially by females who are

Reflect

Do you ensure that you take in the vitamins, minerals, and other food substances you need for good health? If not, why not?

osteoporosis A condition involving progressive loss of bone tissue.

menopause The cessation of menstruation, typically occurring between ages 48 and 52.

"watching their weight." Teenagers are more likely to miss meals or eat away from home than they were in the childhood years. They may consume large amounts of fast food and junk food, which is high in fat and calories but not very nutritious (Monge-Rojas, 2001; Pate et al., 2000; Piper et al., 2000).

Eating Disorders: When Dieting Turns Deadly

The American ideal has slimmed down to where the majority of American females of "average" weight (we're not talking here about those who are overweight!) are dissatisfied with the size and shape of their bodies (McLaren, 2002). The wealthier your family, the more unhappy you're likely to be with your body (McLaren, 2002). Perhaps, then, it is no surprise that dieting has become the normal way of eating for more than half of American women (Kassirer & Angell, 1998)! Plumpness has been valued in many preliterate societies, and Western paintings of former centuries suggest that there was a time when (literally) well-rounded women were the ideal. But in contemporary Western culture, slenderness is in, especially for females (Peresmitre, 1999).

Adolescents are highly concerned about their bodies. Puberty brings rapid changes, and adolescents wonder what they will look like once the flood of hormones has ebbed. In the next chapter we see that adolescents also tend to think that others are paying a great deal of attention to their appearance.[1] Because of cultural emphasis on slimness and the psychology of the adolescent, adolescents—especially female adolescents—are highly vulnerable to eating disorders. ***Question: What are eating disorders?*** The eating disorders of *anorexia nervosa* and *bulimia nervosa* are characterized by gross disturbances in patterns of eating.

Anorexia Nervosa

So more adolescent girls are on a diet than not. What's wrong with that? After all, as Barbara "Babe" Paley once said, "You can never be too skinny or too rich." Most people make no objection to having a fat bank account, but the fact is that one can most certainly be too skinny, as in the case of **anorexia nervosa.** Anorexia nervosa is a life-threatening eating disorder characterized by extreme fear of being too heavy, dramatic weight loss, a distorted body image, and resistance to eating enough to reach or maintain a healthful weight, as we see in the case of Karen:

> I wanted to be a runner. Runners were thin and I attributed this to dieting, not training. So I began restricting my diet: No butter, red meat, pork, dessert, candy, or snacking. If I ate any of the forbidden items I obsessed about it and felt guilty for days.
>
> As a high school freshman, I wanted to run with the fastest girls so I trained hard, really hard and ate less. Lunch was lettuce sandwiches, carrots, and an apple. By my senior year, I was number three on the team and lunch was a bagel and an orange.
>
> I maintained a rigid schedule—running cross country and track, having a seat on student council, volunteering, and maintaining a 3.9 GPA throughout high school—while starving myself (1,000 calories per day), trying to attain the impossible perfection I thought couldn't be far away if I only slimmed down a little bit more.
>
> Several teammates were concerned, but I shrugged them off saying family members were tall and slender; I was a health nut, I didn't like fatty foods; I was a vegetarian; I didn't like sweets; I wasn't hungry; I wasn't starving.
>
> A psychiatrist didn't help at all. I went in, sat on the couch, and told her what she wanted to hear: I would eat more, run less, stop restricting myself, and quit obsessing about being thin. I was very good at knowing exactly what to tell others.
>
> I dropped 10 pounds my freshman year—from 125 to 115 pounds. I was five feet, eight inches tall and wore a size five. I hated my body so I starved myself and ran like a mad woman.
>
> In quiet moments, I was sad and worried about what might be going on inside me. I was already taking birth control to regain my menstrual cycle; my weight was 15

anorexia nervosa An eating disorder characterized by irrational fear of weight gain, distorted body image, and severe weight loss.

[1] See the discussion of Piaget's concept of the *imaginary audience* in Chapter 15.

percent below what was recommended for my height; I was always cold; I had chest pains and an irregular heartbeat; my hair was limp and broke off; my skin was colorless.

It wasn't until I came to the University of Iowa and joined the varsity women's cross country team that I began to see what I was doing to myself. A teammate had an eating problem. Every time I saw her, I felt sick to my stomach.

She had sunken cheeks, eyes so big they swallowed her face. She was an excellent student and a college-level varsity athlete. Many people wondered at her determination, but I understood. She used the same excuses I did.

For one sick instant, I wondered if I would be happier if I were that thin. That is when I started to realize I was slowly killing myself.

At the urging of my coach, I saw the team nutritionist who recommended a psychiatrist who felt no pity for me and made me take a brutally honest look at who I was and why I was starving myself. She didn't accept any of my excuses. She helped me realize that there are other things to think about besides food and body image. About this time I decided to quit the cross country team. The pressure I felt to be thin and competition at the college level were too much when I needed to focus on getting well.

After two months of therapy, my weight had dropped again. I'm not sure how far because I refused to step on a scale, but my size five pants were falling off. My psychiatrist required weekly weigh-ins.

I wasn't putting into practice any of the things my nutritionist and counselor suggested. They told me that if I wanted to have children someday I needed to eat. They warned me of osteoporosis at age 30. Then my psychiatrist scared me to death. She told me I needed to start eating more or I would be checked into the hospital and hooked up to an IV. That would put me on the same level as my Iowa teammate. I had looked at her with such horror and never realized that I was in the same position.

My psychiatrist asked how my family would feel if they had to visit me in the hospital because I refused to eat. It was enough to make me think hard the next time I went through the food service lines.

Of course, I didn't get better the next day. But it was a step in the right direction. It's taken me three years to get where I am now. At five foot, eight and three-fourth inches (I even grew as I got healthier) and 145 pounds, I look and feel healthier, have better eating and exercise habits, and I don't obsess about food as much as I used to. On rare occasions, I think about controlling my food intake. My eating disorder will haunt me for the rest of my life. If I'm not careful, it could creep back. (Ballweg, 2001)

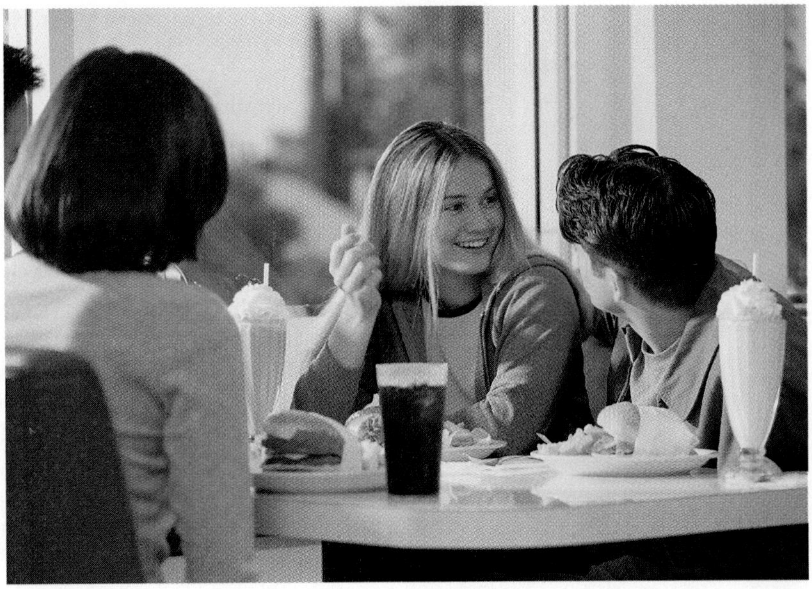
© RNT Productions/CORBIS

Nutritional Needs—or Should We Say *Habits*—of Adolescents

Teenagers require lots of calories to fuel the adolescent growth spurt. They may consume large amounts of fast food and junk food, which is high in calories and fat but not always very nutritious.

Karen, like other people with anorexia nervosa, weighed less than 85% of her desirable body weight, and "desirable" body weights are already too slender for many individuals. Anorexia nervosa afflicts males as well as females, but females with eating disorders outnumber males by more than six to one (Goode, 2000). By and large, anorexia nervosa afflicts women during adolescence and young adulthood (Heatherton et al., 1997; Winzelberg et al., 2000). The typical person with anorexia is a young European American female of higher socioeconomic status (McLaren, 2002). Affluent females have greater access to fitness centers and health clubs and are more likely to read the magazines that idealize slender bodies and shop in the boutiques that cater to females with svelte figures. All in all, they are regularly confronted with unrealistically high standards of slimness that make them extremely unhappy with their own physiques (McLaren, 2002). We know that the incidences of anorexia nervosa and bulimia nervosa have increased markedly in recent years. Women with these disorders greatly outnumber the men who have them, but we lack precise data on their prevalence (Striegel-Moore & Cachelin, 2001).

Reflect

Are you happy with your body shape? Do you feel pressure to be thinner (or heavier) than you are? Explain.

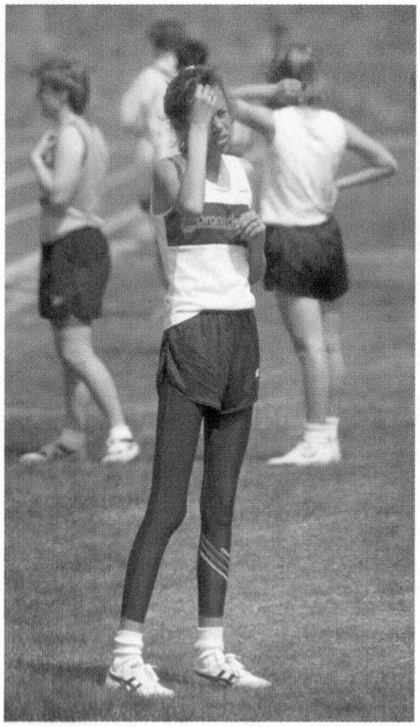

Anorexia Nervosa

Anorexia nervosa is a life-threatening eating disorder in which an individual—most often, an adolescent or young adult female—has a distorted body image and consequently refuses to eat. She may lose 25% of her body weight in a year and impair the health of nearly all of her bodily systems, including the cardiovascular, respiratory, and skeletal systems. Why are the typical eating habits of the average American female characterized by dieting?

Females with anorexia may lose 25% or more of their body weight in a year. Severe weight loss triggers abnormalities in the endocrine system (that is, with hormones) that stop ovulation (Treasure & Serpell, 2001). General health deteriorates. Nearly every system in the body is affected. There are problems with the respiratory system (Key, Lacey, & Nussey, 2001) and with the cardiovascular system (Eidem et al., 2001). Females with anorexia are also at risk for premature development of osteoporosis, a condition characterized by loss of bone density that usually afflicts people in late adulthood (Geiser et al., 2001; Treasure & Serpell, 2001). Given all these problems, it is not surprising that the mortality rate for girls and women with anorexia nervosa is estimated to be 4–5%.

In one common pattern, a girl sees that she has gained some weight after menarche and decides that she must lose it. But even after the weight is gone, she maintains her pattern of dieting and, in many cases, exercise at a fever pitch. Both diet and exercise continue as she plunges toward her desirable weight—according to weight charts—and even after those who care about her tell her that she is becoming all skin and bones. Denial is a huge part of anorexia nervosa. Girls with the disorder deny that they are losing too much weight. They deny any health problems, pointing to their feverish exercise routines as evidence of their strength. Distortion of the body image is a major feature of the disorder (Winzelberg et al., 2000). In one study, researchers recruited women who weighed an average of 31% below their desirable weight according to Metropolitan Life Insurance Company charts (Penner et al., 1991). They found that the women overestimated the size of their bodies by exactly 31%! Friends, co-workers, and families see females with anorexia nervosa as skin and bones. Meanwhile, the women fix their gaze into the mirror and believe that they are looking at a body shape that is too heavy.

Ironically, individuals with anorexia do not literally distance themselves from food. They may become as preoccupied with food as they are with their own body shape. They may devour cookbooks (rather than food), shop for their families, and prepare gourmet feasts—for other people, that is.

Bulimia Nervosa

Bulimia nervosa is sort of a companion disorder to anorexia nervosa, as we see in the case of Nicole:

> Nicole awakens in her cold dark room and already wishes it was time to go back to bed. She dreads the thought of going through this day, which will be like so many others in her recent past. She asks herself the question every morning, "Will I be able to make it through the day without being totally obsessed by thoughts of food, or will I blow it again and spend the day [binge eating]"? She tells herself that today she will begin a new life, today she will start to live like a normal human being. However, she is not at all convinced that the choice is hers. (Boskind-White & White, 1983, p. 29)

So, does Nicole begin a new life today? No. Despite her pledge to herself, Nicole begins the day with eggs and toast—butter included. Then she downs cookies; bagels smothered with cream cheese, butter, and jelly; doughnuts; candy bars; bowlfuls of cereal and milk—all in less than an hour. When her body cries "No more!" she turns to the next step: purging. Purging also is a routine. In the bathroom, she ties back her hair. She runs the shower to mask any noise, drinks some water, and makes herself throw everything up. Afterward she makes another pledge to herself: "Starting tomorrow, I'm going to change." Will she change? In truth, she doubts it.

bulimia nervosa An eating disorder characterized by cycles of binge eating and vomiting as a means of controlling weight gain.

Bulimia nervosa, Nicole's eating disorder, is symptomized by recurrent cycles of binge eating and purging. Binge eating often follows on the heels of food restriction—as in dieting (Lowe et al., 1996). There are various methods of purging. Nicole vomited. Other avenues include strict dieting or fasting, laxatives, and demanding, prolonged exercise regimes. Individuals with eating disorders, like

Karen and Nicole, tend to be perfectionistic about their bodies. They will not settle for less than their idealized body shape and weight (Halmi et al., 2001; Santonastaso, Friederici, & Favaro, 2001). Bulimia, like anorexia, is also connected with endocrine problems: One study found that nearly half of the females with bulimia nervosa have irregular menstrual cycles (Gendall et al., 2000).

Bulimia nervosa, like anorexia nervosa, tends to afflict women during adolescence and young adulthood (Lewinsohn, Rohde, Seeley, Klein, & Gotlib, 2000; Winzelberg et al., 2000). Eating disorders are upsetting and dangerous in themselves, of course, but they are also connected with deep depression (Stice, Hayward, Cameron, Killen, & Taylor, 2000). However, it seems that depression is more likely to co-occur with eating disorders than to be caused by them (Wade et al., 2000). ***Question: What are the origins of the eating disorders?***

Reflect

Are you happy with your body shape? Do you feel pressure to be thinner (or heavier) than you are? Explain.

Perspectives on the Eating Disorders

Health professionals have done a great deal of research into the origins of the eating disorders. Yet they will be the first to admit that many questions about these disorders remain unanswered (Striegel-Moore & Cachelin, 2001).

According to some psychoanalysts, anorexia nervosa may symbolize a young woman's efforts to cope with sexual fears, especially the possibility of becoming pregnant. Keep in mind that anorexia is connected with *amenorrhea* (lack of menstruation). Some psychoanalysts interpret the behavior pattern as a female's attempt to regress to her lifestyle prior to puberty. Anorexia nervosa prevents some adolescents from separating from their families and assuming adult responsibilities. Their breasts and hips flatten once more due to the loss of fatty tissue. In the adolescent's fantasies, perhaps, she remains a sexually undifferentiated child.

Many parents are obsessed with encouraging their children—especially their infants—to eat adequately. Thus some psychoanalysts suggest that children now and then refuse to eat as a way of engaging in warfare with their parents. ("You have to eat something!" "I'm not hungry!") It often seems that warfare does occur in the families of adolescents with eating disorders. Parents in such families are often unhappy with the family's functioning. They frequently have issues with eating and dieting themselves. They also "act out" against their daughters—letting them know that they consider them unattractive, and, prior to the development of the eating disorder, letting them know that they think they should lose weight (Baker, Whisman, & Brownell, 2000; Cooper, Galbraith, & Drinkwater, 2001; Fairburn et al., 1998). The family environment, in other words, is negative, negative, negative.

Carl Rogers teaches us that self-acceptance and self-esteem are related to how well we are accepted by others, particularly our parents. Studies such as a Polish study of 12–20-year-old females find that females with anorexia nervosa have lower levels of self-acceptance than do females without the disorder (Talarczyk & Rajewski, 2001).

A particularly disturbing risk factor for eating disorders in adolescent females is a history of child abuse, particularly sexual abuse (Fairburn et al., 1998). One study found a history of childhood sexual abuse in about half of women with bulimia nervosa, as opposed to a rate of about 7% among women without the disorder (Deep et al., 1999). Another study compared 45 pairs of sisters, one of whom was diagnosed with anorexia nervosa (Karwautz et al., 2001). Those with anorexia were significantly more likely to be exposed to high parental expectations *and* to sexual abuse.

Some social-cognitive theorists believe that weight loss acquires strong reinforcement value through its provision of feelings of personal perfectibility (Vitousek & Manke, 1994). But "perfection" is obviously an unreachable goal for most individuals. When you check out *Cosmopolitan*, *Glamour*, or the *Victoria's Secret* catalogue, you are looking at models who, on average, are 9% taller and 16% thinner than the typical female (Williams, 1992). Yet they set the standard.

Also consider the sociocultural features of eating disorders. Miss America, the annually renewed American role model, has also been slenderizing herself across the years. The pageant began in 1922. Over the past 80 years, the winner has added only 2% in height but has lost 12 pounds in weight. In the early days of the 1920s, Miss America's weight relative to her height yielded a Body Mass Index (BMI)[2] of 20–25, which is considered normal by the World Health Organization (WHO). WHO labels people as malnourished when their BMIs are lower than 18.5. However, recent Miss Americas come in at a BMI near 17 (Rubinstein & Caballero, 2000). So Miss America adds to the woes of "normal" young women and even to those of young women who hover near the WHO "malnourished" borderline. As the cultural ideal slenderizes, women with desirable body weights according to the health charts feel overweight, and overweight women feel gargantuan (Winzelberg et al., 2000).

Many individuals with eating disorders, like Karen, are involved in activities that demand weight limits, such as dancing, acting, and modeling. Male wrestlers also feel the pressure to stay within an "acceptable" weight range (Goode, 2000). Men, like women, experience pressure to create an ideal body, one with power in the upper torso and a trim abdomen (Goode, 2000).

Now and then, a case of anorexia nervosa represents a failed effort to stay healthy. Eating fats and cholesterol are risk factors for heart disease. One 15-year-old male adolescent developed anorexia nervosa after his grandfather—an overweight man who gorged on steak and french fries—had a lethal heart attack while he and his grandson were playing checkers (Markel, 2000).

Eating disorders tend to run in families (Strober et al., 2000), which raises the possibility of the involvement of genetic factors. Genetic factors would not directly cause eating disorders, but appear to involve obsessionistic and perfectionistic personality traits (Bellodi et al., 2001; Halmi et al., 2000; Kaye et al., 2000; Speranza et al., 2001). In a society in which so much attention is focused on the ideal of the slender body, these personality traits then encourage dietary restriction (Wade et al., 2000). Anorexia also often co-occurs with depression (Lewinsohn, Rohde, Seeley, Klein, & Gotlib, 2000; Wade et al., 2000). We can note that perfectionistic people are likely to be disappointed in themselves, giving rise to feelings of depression. But it may also be that both disorders share genetic factors. Genetically inspired perfectionism, cultural emphasis on slimness, self-absorption, and family conflict may create a perfect recipe for development of eating disorders (Baker et al., 2000).

Treatment and Prevention

Treatment of the eating disorders—particularly anorexia nervosa—is a great challenge (Stein et al., 2001). The disorders are connected with serious health problems, and the low weight of individuals with anorexia is often life-threatening. Many children and adolescent girls are admitted to the hospital for treatment against their will (Watson, Bowers, & Anderson, 2000). Denial is a feature of anorexia nervosa, and many girls do not recognize—or do not admit—that they have a problem. When the individual with anorexia does not—or cannot—eat adequately through the mouth, measures such as nasogastric (tube) feeding may be used. Nasogastric feeding can be unpleasant, but some children and adolescents actually understand and appreciate its value (Niederman et al., 2001).

What are the outcomes of hospitalization? They vary, and they are not always good. A British study attempted to contact 84 women who had been hospitalized 21 years earlier for anorexia (Zipfel et al., 2000). The researchers found that about half of the women had achieved complete recovery; nearly 16% had died from causes related to anorexia, such as weakness or imbalances in body chemistry; about 10% were still anorexic; and the remaining 23% could not be contacted or

[2]You can calculate your Body Mass Index as follows. Write down your weight in pounds. Multiply it by 703. Divide the product by your height in inches squared. For example, if you weigh 160 lbs and are 5'8" tall, your BMI is $(160 \times 703)/68^2$, or 24.33. A BMI of more than 25 is defined as overweight.

had outcomes that were unclear. These outcomes seem rather severe, but they resulted only from women who had been hospitalized for anorexia. Women with less serious cases may not require hospitalization.

Medication, especially antidepressants, is frequently used in the treatment of eating disorders. Eating disorders are frequently accompanied by depression, and it may be that the common culprit in the eating and mood disorders is a lower-than-normal level of the neurotransmitter serotonin. Antidepressants such as Prozac and Zoloft enhance the activity of serotonin in the brain, often increasing food intake in anorexic individuals and decreasing binge eating in bulimic people. In one study, 10 or 11 anorexic patients showed significant weight gain after 14 weeks of treatment with an antidepressant, and they maintained the gain at a 64-week follow-up (Santonastaso et al., 2001). They were also evaluated as being significantly less depressed and perfectionistic (obsessive) than they had been.

Because family problems are commonly connected with eating disorders, family therapy is often used to treat these disorders (Diamond & Siqueland, 2001; Lock & Le Grange, 2001). Family therapy has positive outcomes in many cases, but is not an appropriate setting for dealing with childhood sexual abuse.

Cognitive-behavioral therapy has been used to help anorexic and bulimic individuals challenge their perfectionism and their attitudes toward their bodies. It has also been used to systematically reinforce appropriate eating behavior. But let's remember that all of this is connected with cultural attitudes that idealize excessive thinness. "Prevention" will have to address cultural values as well as potential problems in individual adolescents.

Review

(26) Although adolescents may consume many calories, they may be malnourished because of eating _________ foods. (27) _________ nervosa is a life-threatening eating disorder characterized by intense fear of being overweight, a distorted body image, and refusal to eat. (28) _________ nervosa is characterized by recurrent cycles of binge eating followed by dramatic measures to purge the food. (29) Females with eating disorders are (more or less?) likely than other females to have experienced child sexual abuse. (30) Anorexia nervosa and bulimia nervosa (do or do not?) tend to run in families. (31) Medication in the form of _________ is frequently used to treat eating disorders.

Pulling It Together: Why are females more likely than males to develop eating disorders?

Substance Abuse and Dependence—Where Does It Begin? Where Does It End?

Think of the United States as a cafeteria with brightly colored drugs glimmering on the shelves and in the trays. In almost any high school in any part of the country, adolescents will tell you that drugs are available. In fact, so will many middle schoolers. And so will some elementary school children. Credit adolescents who do not use drugs. They generally refuse them as a matter of choice, not because of lack of supply. The drugs are there, and some of the most harmful drugs are perfectly legal, at least for adults.

Children and adolescents use drugs not only to cope with medical problems, but also to deal with daily tensions, run-of-the-mill depression, even boredom. Drugs are used properly when they are required to maintain or restore health, but drugs are used for many other reasons. Many children and adolescents use drugs for the same reasons that adults do. But they also use drugs because they are imitating their friends, and sometimes they use drugs as a way of rebelling against parents who implore them not to use them. They use drugs to experience pleasure, to deaden pain, and to earn prestige among their peers.

Adolescents frequently get involved with drugs that cripple their ability to attend school or to pay attention when they do attend (Basen-Engquist, Edmundson, & Parcel, 1996). Alcohol and other drugs are also linked with reckless, sometimes deadly, behavior (CDC, 2000c). Alcohol is the BDOC—that is, the Big Drug on Campus. It is the most widely used substance in high schools and on college campuses (Johnston, O'Malley, & Bachman, 2001). Marijuana is no slacker either. More than two college students in five have tried it; 1 student in 6 or 7 has smoked it in the last 30 days (Johnston et al., 2001).

© Michael Siluk/The Image Works

Substance Use and Abuse

It is important to distinguish between the use and abuse of substances. Many adolescents occasionally experiment with substances such as alcohol and marijuana. But where does substance use end and substance abuse begin?

Where does the use of a drug or substance end and substance abuse begin? ***Questions: What is substance abuse? What is substance dependence?*** According to the American Psychiatric Association (2000), **substance abuse** is the ongoing use of a substance despite the social, occupational, psychological, or physical problems it causes. When children or adolescents miss school or fail to complete assignments because they are intoxicated or "sleeping it off," they are abusing alcohol. The amount they drink is not the issue; the problem is the role that the substance plays in their lives.

Substance dependence is more serious than substance abuse. An adolescent who is dependent on a substance loses control over using it and may organize his or her life around obtaining the substance and using it. Substance dependence is also known by the ways in which it changes the body. Having the substance in one's body becomes the norm so that the adolescent may experience tolerance of the substance, withdrawal symptoms in its absence, or both. **Tolerance** develops as the body becomes habituated to the substance; as a result, the adolescent has to use progressively higher doses to achieve the same effects. A number of substances are physically addictive, so that when the addicted adolescent stops using it, or lowers the dosage, there are characteristic withdrawal symptoms that are also known as **abstinence syndrome.** When addicted individuals lower their intake of alcohol, they may experience symptoms such as tremors (shakes), high blood pressure, rapid heart and pulse rate, anxiety, restlessness, and weakness. Many adolescents who begin to use substances such as alcohol for pleasure wind up using them to escape the withdrawal symptoms of the abstinence syndrome.

Reflect

Do you know an adolescent who abuses a substance or is dependent on it? Does the adolescent admit there is a problem or deny it? Do you have any thoughts as to how to help the adolescent?

substance abuse A persistent pattern of use of a substance characterized by frequent intoxication and impairment of physical, social, or emotional well-being.

substance dependence A persistent pattern of use of a substance that is accompanied by physiological addiction.

tolerance Habituation to a drug such that increasingly higher doses are needed to achieve similar effects.

abstinence syndrome A characteristic cluster of symptoms that results from sudden decreases in the level of usage of a substance.

sedatives Drugs that soothe or quiet restlessness or agitation.

Effects of Various Substances

Why, you might wonder, are psychologists and educators so concerned about substance abuse? It's not just a moral issue. Drugs are not "bad" simply because they are illegal. Children and adolescents are not advised to avoid them simply because they are under age. Drugs can have serious harmful effects on health. Consider the effects of some depressants, stimulants, and hallucinogenics.

Depressants

Question: What are the effects of depressants? All depressants slow the activity of the nervous system. Beyond that, they have somewhat different cognitive and biological effects. Depressants include alcohol, narcotics derived from the opium poppy (heroin, morphine, and the like), and **sedatives** (such as barbiturates and methaqualone).

Research with people and rats shows that alcohol lessens inhibitions, meaning that adolescents may do things when they are drinking that they would otherwise resist (deWit et al., 2000; Feola, deWit, & Richards, 2000). Ingesting five or more drinks in a row—that is, *binge drinking*—is connected with bad grades and risky behavior, including risky (unprotected, promiscuous) sex, acts of aggression, and injurious and deadly accidents (MacDonald et al., 2000; Vik et al., 2000). Small amounts of alcohol can be stimulating, but high doses have a sedative effect. It is the latter effect that causes alcohol to be labeled a depressant drug. Alcohol is relaxing and relieves minor aches and pains. It is also an intoxicant. In other words, alcohol distorts perceptions, impairs intellectual functioning, hinders coordination, and slurs the speech. The media seem to pay more attention to deaths due to heroin and cocaine overdoses, but the fact is that hundreds of college students die each year from causes related to drinking, including accidents and alcohol overdoses (Li et al., 2001). (Yes, a person can die from drinking too much at one sitting.)

Reflect

Do you believe that adolescents are responsible for the things they do when they have been drinking? Explain.

Adolescent drinking is connected with bad grades and other problems (Wills et al., 2000). This is a two-way street. Yes, drinking compromises grades, but some adolescents drink to alleviate stressors, whether they be academic, social, or other stressors.

Regular drinking can lead to dependence. Addicted adolescents drink just to avoid withdrawal symptoms. Adolescent drinking often leads to drinking as an adult, and chronic drinking can lead to serious physical disorders such as cirrhosis or cancer of the liver. Chronic heavy drinking has been linked to cardiovascular disorders. Heavy drinking increases a woman's risk of breast cancer and may harm the embryo, if she is pregnant.

Heroin is a depressant that is derived from the opium poppy. Like morphine and other opioids, its major medical use is relief from pain. But it can also provide a euphoric "rush," which is why many experimenters are tempted to use it regularly. Heroin is addictive, and regular users develop tolerance, but high doses distort perception of the passage of time, cause drowsiness and stupor, and hinder judgment. Withdrawal from heroin can also be quite disturbing, especially when the individual has become used to high doses. Withdrawal symptoms can include flulike symptoms (runny nose, chills alternating with sweating, and so on), tremors (shakes), digestive problems (cramps, diarrhea, and vomiting), rapid heart rate, high blood pressure, and insomnia. Once the adolescent is dependent on heroin, it can be difficult to stop using it.

Barbiturates are also depressants with various legitimate medical uses, such as relief from pain, alleviation of anxiety and tension, and treatment of insomnia, high blood pressure, and epilepsy. But people can become rapidly dependent on barbiturates and a similar sedative, methaqualone. These drugs are popular among adolescents because of their relaxing sedative effects and their ability to produce a mild euphoria. But as with other depressants, high doses cause drowsiness and stupor, hinder coordination, slur the speech, impair judgment, and make people irritable. (Not a good formula for driving an automobile.) People who are strongly addicted can experience convulsions and die if they are withdrawn abruptly from high doses of barbiturates. Depressants have additive effects; therefore, mixing barbiturates and other depressants is extremely risky.

Stimulants

Question: What are the effects of stimulants? Using stimulants is like stepping on the body's accelerator pedal. They speed up the heartbeat and other bodily functions. They can also keep people awake and alert, but at the expense of some wear and tear. We consider the stimulants nicotine, cocaine, and amphetamines.

The stimulant nicotine is found in cigars, cigarettes, and chewing tobacco—also in nicotine gums, skin patches, and the like. Nicotine causes the adrenal glands to release the hormone adrenaline. It also stimulates the release of a number of neurotransmitters, including acetylcholine (connected with muscle contractions and the formation of memories) and dopamine (which is involved in voluntary movements, learning and memory, and emotional arousal). Adrenaline ramps up the autonomic nervous system, accelerating the heart, disrupting the rhythm of the heart, and causing the liver to pour sugar into the blood (Wang et al., 2000).

Because acetylcholine is involved in the formation of memories, some students believe that smoking helps them study. Nicotine does appear to improve memory and attention and to enhance performance on some simple kinds of tasks (Kinnunen et al., 1996; O'Brien, 1996). It also appears to elevate the mood. Although nicotine is a stimulant, it also appears to help people relax (O'Brien, 1996). Nicotine, like other stimulants, also raises the rate at which the body burns calories and lowers the appetite, so it is not surprising that some adolescents smoke as a means of weight control (Jeffery et al., 2000). All this might make nicotine seem like a wonder drug, and in some ways it may be—but we will see that the vehicles which deliver nicotine, such as cigarettes and cigars, are lethal.

Nicotine is the chemical that addicts people to tobacco (F. Baker et al., 2000; American Lung Association, 2000). The abstinence syndrome from nicotine includes symptoms such as drowsiness and loss of energy (the stimulant is gone, after all), palpitations of the heart (irregular heartbeats), sweating, tremors, lightheadedness and dizziness, insomnia, headaches, and digestive problems (irregular bowel movements and cramps).

Cigarette packs carry warnings such as "Warning: The Surgeon General Has Determined That Cigarette Smoking Is Dangerous to Your Health." Cigarette advertising is not allowed on radio and television. More than 400,000 Americans die from smoking-related problems each year (American Lung Association, 2000). The number is higher than that of all the American soldiers lost in World War II. It exceeds the number of people who die from other risk-related behaviors—auto accidents, abuse of all other substances, homicide, suicide, and AIDS *combined*. Cigarette smoke contains carbon monoxide, which compromises the ability of the blood to carry oxygen and thus causes shortness of breath. Smoke also contains hydrocarbons ("tars") that are responsible for nearly seven of every eight cases of lung cancer (American Lung Association, 2000). Cigarette smoke also causes various other lung and respiratory diseases; it worsens heart disease. Smoking reduces bone density in women, heightening the risk of hip fractures. Pregnant smokers increase the risk of miscarriage, stillbirths, preterm births, and low-birthweight babies (American Lung Association, 2000).

Passive smoking—that is, being in the room or house with a smoker—also leads to respiratory problems like asthma and other disorders. Extensive childhood exposure to tobacco smoke in the house increases the risk of lung cancer in adulthood (American Lung Association, 2000).

The stimulant cocaine produces feelings of euphoria, relieves pain, boosts the self-confidence, and reduces the appetite. Some adolescents brew cocaine from coca leaves as a sort of "tea." Others "snort" cocaine as a powder. Still others inject it as a liquid. Snorting constricts blood vessels in the nose, such that regular use can dry the skin, expose cartilage, and pierce the nasal septum. "Crack" and "bazooka" are unrefined and less expensive cocaine derivatives. Cocaine has biological as well as psychological effects: It accelerates the heart rate, spurs sudden spikes in blood pressure, constricts the arteries of the heart, and thickens the blood—a complex of dangerous events that can cause cardiovascular and respiratory collapse (Moliterno et al., 1994). Use of cocaine has caused the deaths of several athletes, who were likely to be more resistant to these effects than the average adolescent. Because cocaine is a stimulant, overdoses can cause restlessness, insomnia, and tremors. It also causes headaches, nausea, and convulsions and psychotic hallucinations and delusions (persistent erroneous beliefs, such as the idea that one is being followed). Use of crack—powerful and unrefined—has caused strokes.

During World War II, the group of stimulants known as amphetamines was used by soldiers to keep them awake throughout the night. Truck drivers use them to drive through the night. Amphetamines are widely known to students as enablers of all-night cram sessions. Many dieters rely on them to reduce their appetites. On the street, amphetamines are called *speed*, *uppers*, *bennies* (for Benzedrine), and *dexies* (Dexedrine). In high doses, they can produce a euphoric "rush." Adolescents who have been on extended amphetamine highs can "crash," or come down suddenly into severe depression or deep sleep.

Tolerance for amphetamines develops rapidly, and adolescents can become dependent on them, especially when they use them to self-medicate for depression. Regular use of the powerful amphetamine called methamphetamine may well be physically addictive (Volkow et al., 2001a, 2001b), but the extent to which amphetamines cause physical addiction has been a subject of controversy. High doses of amphetamines, like high doses of cocaine, can cause restlessness and insomnia, irritability, and loss of appetite. Heavy users risk an "amphetamine psychosis," in which they experience hallucinations and delusions.

Hallucinogenics

Question: What are the effects of hallucinogenics? **Hallucinogenics** give rise to perceptual distortions called hallucinations. The hallucinator may believe that the hallucination cannot be real; yet it assaults the senses so strongly that it is confused with reality. Marijuana, LSD, and PCP are examples of hallucinogenic drugs.

Marijuana is derived from the *Cannabis sativa* plant, which is why it is also referred to as *cannabis*. Marijuana is usually produced from the branches and leaves of the plant. The more powerful *hashish*, or "hash," is obtained from the resin. Marijuana is typically smoked, although it can be eaten.

Many adolescents report that marijuana helps them relax and elevates their mood. Some report that marijuana helps them get by in social situations. Adolescents who use marijuana report effects including greater sensory awareness, self-insight, creativity, and empathy for other people's feelings. Smokers become highly attuned to bodily sensations, especially their heartbeat, which tends to be accelerated. They experience visual hallucinations, frequently in the form of perceptual distortions. For example, the passage of time generally seems to slow down so that a song might seem to go on indefinitely. But strong intoxication can disorient smokers. Some smokers enjoy disorientation, but others fear getting "lost" and feeling that their heart will "run away" with them.

Marijuana carries a number of health risks. For example, it impairs the perceptual-motor coordination used in driving and operating machines. It impairs short-term memory and slows learning (Ashton, 2001). Although it causes positive mood changes in many people, there are also disturbing instances of anxiety and confusion and occasional reports of psychotic reactions (Johns, 2001). Marijuana apparently affects the functioning of the brain, the immune system, and the cardiovascular and reproductive systems (Nahas, Sutin, & Bennett, 2000). For example, it has been known that marijuana use impairs learning and memory, but it was assumed by many that marijuana simply distracted people from learning tasks. Now, however, laboratory research suggests that marijuana also reduces the release of neurotransmitters involved in the consolidation of learning (J. M. Sullivan, 2000). MRI and PET scan studies suggest that marijuana may have little or no effect on the size or makeup of the brain of adults (Block et al., 2000). However, males who began using marijuana before the age of 17 may have smaller brains and less gray matter than other males (Wilson et al., 2000). Both males and females who started using marijuana early may be generally smaller in height and weight than other people. William Wilson and his colleagues (2000) suggest that these differences may reflect the effect of marijuana on pituitary and sex hormones.

Marijuana smoke also contains more hydrocarbons than tobacco smoke—a risk factor in cancer. Smokers of marijuana often admit that they know that marijuana smoke can be harmful, but they counter that compared with cigarette smokers, they smoke very few "joints" per day. Yet marijuana also elevates the heart rate and, in some people, the blood pressure. This higher demand on the heart and circulation poses a threat to people with hypertension and cardiovascular disorders. This is more of a threat to older users, but perhaps it is not to be ignored by adolescents—especially adolescents who are not in the best of health.

There is no question that adolescents can become psychologically dependent on marijuana. However, recent research also suggests that regular users may experience tolerance and an abstinence syndrome, which are signs of physical addiction (American Psychiatric Association, 2000; Johns, 2001).

hallucinogenics Drugs that give rise to hallucinations.

LSD is the acronym for lysergic acid diethylamide, more commonly simply referred to as "acid." LSD is a humanmade hallucinogenic drug. Users report that LSD "expands consciousness." They say that it opens new worlds. LSD is a potent hallucinogenic drug that brings on vivid hallucinations. There are other hallucinogenic drugs. Mescaline is derived from the peyote cactus. Phencyclidine (PCP) was developed as an anesthetic and goes by the street names "angel dust," "ozone," "wack," and "rocket fuel." The street terms "killer joints"and "crystal supergrass" refer to PCP that is combined with marijuana. "Ecstasy," or MDMA (the abbreviation of 3, 4-Methylenedioxymethamphetamine), is a synthetic drug that possesses the properties of stimulant and hallucinogenic drugs. MDMA possesses chemical variations of the stimulant amphetamine or methamphetamine and a hallucinogen, most often mescaline.

Regular use of hallucinogenics can cause psychological dependence and tolerance, but people are not known to become physically addicted to them. High doses can impair coordination and judgment (driving on hallucinogenic drugs poses grave risks), change the mood, and cause psychotic symptoms, including frightening hallucinations and paranoid delusions (belief that one is in danger or being observed or followed).

Various kinds of drugs and their effects are summarized in Table 14.2.

TABLE 14.2 *Common Drugs and Their Effects*

Drug	Type	How Taken	Desired Effects	Tolerance	Abstinence Syndrome	Side Effects
Alcohol	Depressant[1]	By mouth	Relaxation, euphoria, lowered inhibitions	Yes	Yes	Impaired coordination, poor judgment, hangover*
Heroin	Depressant	Injected, smoked, by mouth	Relaxation, euphoria, relief from anxiety and pain	Yes	Yes	Impaired coordination and mental functioning, drowsiness, lethargy*
Barbiturates and Methaqualone	Depressants	By mouth, injected	Relaxation, sleep, euphoria, lowered inhibitions	Yes	Yes	Impaired coordination and mental functioning, drowsiness, lethargy*
Amphetamines	Stimulants[2]	By mouth, injected	Alertness, euphoria	Yes	?	Restlessness, loss of appetite, psychotic symptoms
Cocaine	Stimulant	By mouth, snorted, injected	Euphoria, self-confidence	Yes	Yes	Restlessness, loss of appetite, convulsions, strokes, psychotic symptoms
Nicotine (cigarettes)	Stimulant	By tobacco (smoked, chewed, or sniffed)	Relaxation, stimulation, weight control	Yes	Yes	Cancer, heart disease, lung and respiratory diseases
Marijuana	Hallucinogenic[3]	Smoked, by mouth	Relaxation, perceptual distortions, enhancement of experience	?	?	Impaired coordination, learning, respiratory problems, panic
LSD, PCP	Hallucinogenics	By mouth	Perceptual distortions, vivid hallucinations	Yes	No	Impaired coordination, psychotic symptoms, panic

*Overdose can result in death.
[1]Depressant drugs slow the activity of the central nervous system. There are also effects that are specific to each depressant drug.
[2]Stimulants increase the activity of the nervous system. Their other effects vary somewhat, and some contribute to feelings of euphoria and self-confidence.
[3]Hallucinogenic drugs produce hallucinations—that is, sensations and perceptions in the absence of external stimulation. But hallucinogenic drugs may also have additional effects such as relaxation, euphoria, or, in some cases, panic.

Prevalence of Substance Abuse

Ongoing surveys of high school students by the University of Michigan find that use of illicit drugs has increased over the past decade (Johnston et al., 2001). ***Question: How widespread is substance abuse among adolescents?*** Table 14.3

Reflect

How widespread was substance abuse in your own high school? Which substances were most widely used? Why?

TABLE 14.3 *Trends in Lifetime Prevalence of Use of Various Drugs for 8th-, 10th-, and 12th-Graders*

		Year 1991 (%)	Year 2000 (%)
Any illicit drug	8th grade	18.7	26.8
	10th grade	30.6	45.6
	12th grade	44.1	54.0
Marijuana	8th grade	10.2	20.3
	10th grade	23.4	40.3
	12th grade	36.7	48.8
Inhalants	8th grade	17.6	17.9
	10th grade	15.7	16.6
	12th grade	17.6	14.2
LSD	8th grade	2.7	3.9
	10th grade	5.6	7.6
	12th grade	8.8	11.1
PCP	8th grade	—	—
	10th grade	—	—
	12th grade	—	3.4
MDMA (Ecstasy)	8th grade	—	4.3
	10th grade	—	7.3
	12th grade	—	11.0
Cocaine	8th grade	2.3	4.5
	10th grade	4.1	6.9
	12th grade	7.8	7.7
Crack	8th grade	1.3	3.1
	10th grade	1.7	3.7
	12th grade	3.1	3.9
Heroin	8th grade	1.2	1.9
	10th grade	1.2	2.2
	12th grade	0.9	2.4
Amphetamines	8th grade	10.5	9.9
	10th grade	13.2	15.7
	12th grade	15.4	15.6
Barbiturates	8th grade	—	—
	10th grade	—	—
	12th grade	6.2	9.2
Alcohol	8th grade	58.0*	51.7
	10th grade	75.0*	71.4
	12th grade	81.0*	80.3
Cigarettes	8th grade	44.0	40.5
	10th grade	55.1	55.1
	12th grade	63.1	62.5
Steroids	8th grade	1.9	3.0
	10th grade	1.8	3.5
	12th grade	2.1	2.5

**Estimate. Source: Johnston, L. D., O'Malley, P. M., & Bachman, J. G. (2001).* Monitoring the Future: national survey results on drug use, 1975–2000. Volume I: Secondary school students *(NIH Publication No. 01-4924). Bethesda, MD: National Institute on Drug Abuse, Table 2-1.*

shows that the self-reported lifetime use of illicit drugs among eighth-graders increased from 18.7% to 26.8% between the years 1991 and 2000.[3] The increase among twelfth-graders during the same period was from 44.1% to 54%. The table suggests that much of the increase can be accounted for by patterns of smoking marijuana. The lifetime prevalence of use of marijuana doubled among eighth-graders from 10.2% to 20.3%. It increased among twelfth-graders from 36.7% to 48.8%. By contrast, the lifetime prevalence of use of cigarettes appears to have remained stable throughout the 10-year period for eighth-, tenth-, and twelfth-graders. Self-reported cocaine use doubled among eighth-graders in the same period, from about 2.3% to 4.5%. Perhaps adolescents are starting to use cocaine earlier, but the overall number of individuals who wind up using it is not rising noticeably. Again, students seem to be starting to experiment with alcohol a bit earlier, but by twelfth grade it would appear that the overall rate of experience with alcohol remains at about 80%. However, drinking in early adolescence is a risk factor for alcohol abuse later on (de Wit et al., 2000).

The widespread occurrence of binge drinking, in which five or more drinks in a row are consumed, is of particular concern. Binge drinking is connected with occasional deaths from alcohol overdose and with a variety of reckless behaviors, such as engaging in unprotected sex.[4] According to the University of Michigan survey, about 30% of high school seniors have engaged in binge drinking. The survey also found binge drinking among 10–20% of eighth-graders (Johnston et al., 2001; Table 4-9).

Use of stimulants other than cocaine (such as amphetamines) has remained rather steady over the past decade. Fewer than one student in six appears to have experimented with amphetamines, but I have heard anecdotes to the effect that some parents in highly competitive secondary schools encourage their children to use amphetamines so that they can study longer and perform better on tests. In the year 2000, about 9% of twelfth-graders report having used the sedatives known as barbiturates. About 11% of seniors have used the hallucinogenic drug LSD.

About 3% of high school students have used steroids. Steroids, which build muscle mass, are typically used by high school males in an effort to improve athletic performance, although some users also want to improve their physical appearance.

The other commonly used licit drug is tobacco. In the year 2000, nearly five of eight high school seniors had smoked a cigarette at one time or another, and so had two out of five eighth-graders. These numbers have hardly budged over the past decade, despite all the publicity about the harmful effects of smoking.

Students' Attitudes Toward Drugs

The University of Michigan researchers have also tracked the extent to which high school students *disapprove* of drug use over the past generation. ***Question: How many adolescents disapprove of use of drugs?*** Table 14.4 shows the percentage of high school seniors who disapproved of various kinds of drug use in the year 1975, and again in the year 2000. In most cases the table compares the disapproval rating for drugs that are used experimentally ("once or twice") or regularly. Generally speaking, students of both eras are more likely to disapprove of regular drug use than experimental drug use. For example, about half of students disapprove of use of marijuana on an experimental basis (47% in 1975 and 53% in 2000), but the disapproval rate for regular smoking of marijuana rises to 72% in 1975 and 80% in 2000. The discrepancy between disapproval for experimental and

Reflect

Check out the categories of drug use in Table 14.4 and indicate whether you approve or disapprove of these uses. How do your views compare with those of the majority of high school seniors?

[3]"Lifetime use" refers to whether the individual ever used the drug. Individuals who report experimenting with the drug even once would fall into this category. The University of Michigan group uses "30-day prevalence"—that is, whether the individual has used the drug within the past month—to arrive at estimates of more regular usage.

[4]That is, sexual activity without use of a condom, thus increasing the probability of unwanted pregnancy and the spread of sexually transmitted infections (STIs).

regular use of alcohol is most noticeable. Only one out of four or five high school seniors (22% in 1975 and 25% in 2000) disapproved of trying a drink or two. However, the great majority of seniors in both eras disapproved of daily drinking and of weekend binge drinking. As you study Table 14.4, you will find that except in the case of LSD, disapproval ratings are somewhat higher in year 2000 than in 1975. It is possible that anti-drug-abuse messages have been having some effect. And in the case of LSD, we can note that the disapproval rating was high even back in 1975. Similarly, the percentage of students who disapproved of experimenting with heroin or taking it regularly was extremely high in both eras. This high disapproval rating is connected with the very low rate of usage you see in Table 14.3. All in all, high school seniors are least likely to be concerned about trying a drink or two and most likely to disapprove of regular use of LSD, cocaine, crack, heroin, amphetamines, and barbiturates. About 7 in 10 disapproved of smoking in 1975 and, again, today. Students are clearly more concerned about illicit drugs than they are about smoking cigarettes and occasional light drinking. Laurie Chassin and her colleagues (2001) note that prevention programs still need to break through adolescents' resistance to the fact that cigarette smoking is harmful to their health.

TABLE 14.4 *Long-Term Trends in Disapproval of Drug Use by Twelfth Graders*

Do you disapprove of people (who are 18 or older) doing each of the following?	Percentage disapproving —Class of 1975	Percentage disapproving —Class of 2000
Try marijuana once or twice	47	53
Smoke marijuana regularly	72	80
Try LSD once or twice	83	82
Take LSD regularly	94	94
Try MDMA (Ecstasy) once or twice	—	81
Try cocaine once or twice	81	88
Take cocaine regularly	93	96
Try crack once or twice	—	88
Take crack regularly	—	93
Try heroin once or twice	92	93
Take heroin regularly	97	97
Try amphetamines once or twice	75	82
Take amphetamines regularly	92	94
Try barbiturates once or twice	78	86
Take barbiturates regularly	93	95
Try one or two drinks of an alcoholic beverage (beer, wine, liquor)	22	25
Take one or two drinks nearly every day	68	70
Take four or five drinks nearly every day	89	88
Have five or more drinks once or twice each weekend	60	65
Smoke one or more packs of cigarettes per day	68	70
Take steroids	—	89

Source of data: Johnston, L. D., O'Malley, P. M., & Bachman, J. G. (2001). Monitoring the Future: national survey results on drug use, 1975–2000. Volume I: Secondary school students *(NIH Publication No. 01-4924). Bethesda, MD: National Institute on Drug Abuse, Table 8-4.*

Developing in a World of Diversity

Sociocultural Factors and Substance Abuse

There are fascinating sociocultural differences in the prevalence of substance abuse among adolescents. In order to obtain a measure of regular drug use, rather than experimental use, a University of Michigan survey asked high school seniors whether they had used a substance within the past 30 days. One analysis of results is shown in Table 14.5. One finding is that male seniors were more likely than female seniors to have used all but two of the substances within the past 30 days. The exceptions were MDMA (Ecstasy), where the results were tied at 3.1%, and amphetamines, where the results were not statistically significant (4.9% of males as compared with 5.0% of females).

One can interpret the finding in various ways. First, one can note that the differences are not all that substantial for any drug grouping. For example, overall, 27.5% of males were likely to have used an illicit drug within the past 30 days; but so were 24.9% of the females. Heavily used substances—alcohol, cigarettes, marijuana—were heavily used by both boys and girls. Rarely used drugs—e.g., PCP, crack, heroin, methaqualone, steroids—were used rarely by both boys and girls. Past surveys showed greater discrepancies in drug use between boys and girls, and it may be that "once upon a time," much tighter social constraints were placed on females. The movement toward equality is apparently accompanied by similar usage of drugs.

It is perhaps of more interest that adolescents' plans for their future seem to have an effect on their prevalence of substance abuse. Adolescents who planned to continue their education and obtain 4-year college degrees were less likely to abuse substances than those who expected not to attend college or to attend college for less than 4 years. Perhaps substance abuse does not fit with plans for a future that involves achievement motivation and self-control?

The survey also found differences in prevalence of substance abuse among students whose parents had achieved different levels of education. Table 14.5 compares results for students whose parents had not finished high school with those whose parents had graduated from college. The overall difference in prevalence of use of illicit drugs is not remarkable: 25.4% for those whose parents had little education as compared with 24.7% of those whose parents were college graduates. But note that the children of college

TABLE 14.5 *Thirty-Day Prevalence of Use of Various Drug by Subgroups— Twelfth Graders, Year 2000 (Percentages)*

		Gender		College Plans		Parental Education	
Drug	Total	Male	Female	None or under 4 Years	Complete 4 Years	Did Not Graduate High School	College Graduate
Any illicit drug	24.9	27.5	22.1	29.2	23.0	25.4	24.7
Marijuana	21.6	24.7	18.3	26.0	19.6	21.5	21.3
Inhalants	2.2	2.9	1.7	3.2	1.8	2.5	3.3
LSD	1.6	2.1	0.9	2.0	1.5	2.0	2.1
PCP	0.9	1.6	0.3	2.0	0.7	5.8	0.2
MDMA (Ecstasy)	3.6	3.1	3.1	3.8	3.4	5.9	4.1
Cocaine	2.1	2.7	1.6	3.1	1.8	3.7	1.7
Crack	1.1	1.4	0.7	2.1	0.7	1.8	0.7
Heroin	0.7	0.9	0.6	0.7	0.6	1.9	0.6
Amphetamines	5.0	4.9	5.0	6.7	4.6	5.5	5.3
Barbiturates	3.0	3.3	2.6	3.4	2.8	2.6	2.3
Methaqualone	0.2	0.3	0.1	0.1	0.1	0.0	0.4
Alcohol	50.0	54.0	46.1	54.3	48.3	43.4	54.0
Cigarettes	31.4	32.8	29.7	43.6	27.3	31.3	27.4
Steroids	0.8	1.0	0.6	1.1	0.8	0.7	1.6

Source: Johnston, L. D., O'Malley, P. M., & Bachman, J. G. (2001). Monitoring the Future: National survey results on drug use, 1975–2000. Volume I: Secondary school students *(NIH Publication No. 01-4924). Bethesda, MD: National Institute on Drug Abuse, Table 4-7.*

graduates were more likely to drink (54%) than the children of those who had not completed high school (43.4%). Yet the children of those with less education were a bit more likely to smoke than the children of college graduates. Perhaps the inference is that alcohol has a place in "learned" society, whereas cigarette smoking is a hazard that better-educated people take pains to prevent.

Patterns of adolescent drug use also vary among different racial and ethnic groups. Native Americans exhibit the greatest overall rate of substance use, and Asian Americans have the lowest rate (Johnston et al., 2001). What about African Americans, Latino and Latina Americans, and European Americans? Different studies give different answers. National surveys of older adolescents tend to suggest that African Americans and Latino and Latina Americans have equal or higher rates of substance abuse than European Americans. Poverty, unemployment, discrimination, deviant role models, and escape from the harsh realities of life in the inner city or on the reservation have been offered as explanations for the higher incidence of drug use among ethnic minorities, particularly among those who are economically and socially disadvantaged.

Yet the University of Michigan annual survey of high school seniors presents a very different picture, as you see in Table 14.6. Whether we are talking about the lifetime or 30-day prevalence of use of illicit or licit drugs, it is clear that the African American adolescents have significantly lower rates of substance abuse than European Americans and Latino and Latina Americans. How do we account for the disparity in findings of the national surveys of adolescents and the University of Michigan survey of high school seniors?

The fact is that high school seniors do not adequately represent the population of people of their age. High school seniors have remained in school for more than 11 years, whereas others have dropped out. People of different ethnic backgrounds drop out at different rates, and substance abuse is higher among high school dropouts. Latino and Latina Americans and African Americans have higher dropout rates than European Americans. Those African American and Latino and Latina American youth who are involved with drugs will be more likely to drop out and so will not be included in a survey of high school seniors. This point was illustrated in a study (Chavez & Swain, 1992) that compared drug-use rates of Mexican American and European American 8th- and 12th-graders. Mexican American 8th-graders had higher use rates than their European American age-mates, but the pattern was reversed among 12th-grade students. The results appear to reflect the higher dropout rate of Mexican American youth who use drugs.

TABLE 14.6 *Ethnic Comparisons of Lifetime and 30-Day Prevalence of Use of Various Drugs Among Twelfth-Graders, Years 1999 & 2000 (Percentages)*

	Ever Use Drug?			Use Drug in Past 30 Days?		
Drug	European American	African American	Latino/Latina American	European American	African American	Latino/Latina American
Any illicit drug	54.8%	48.7%	60.0%	25.9%	20.3%	27.4%
Marijuana	49.4	45.7	55.5	22.7	19.0	24.6
Inhalants	16.7	4.6	15.4	2.1	1.3	3.1
LSD	13.2	1.7	13.1	2.3	0.8	2.4
MDMA (Ecstasy)	10.5	1.6	13.3	3.3	0.9	4.5
Cocaine	9.9	1.9	13.3	2.5	0.8	3.6
Crack	4.4	0.8	6.3	1.0	0.4	2.1
Heroin	0.9	0.4	2.6	0.5	0.2	1.2
Amphetamines	18.2	4.9	15.1	5.3	1.2	4.5
Barbiturates	10.3	2.4	8.1	3.2	0.8	2.2
Methaqualone	1.1	0.3	0.4	0.2	0.1	0.0
Alcohol	82.0	70.3	84.3	55.1	30.0	51.2
Cigarettes	67.2	45.5	66.1	37.9	14.3	27.7
Steroids	2.8	1.3	3.4	0.8	0.4	1.5

Source: Johnston, L. D., O'Malley, P. M., & Bachman, J. G. (2001). Monitoring the Future: National survey results on drug use, 1975–2000. Volume I: Secondary school students *(NIH Publication No. 01-4924). Bethesda, MD: National Institute on Drug Abuse, Table 4-9.*

Factors in Substance Abuse and Dependence

Question: What factors are associated with substance abuse and dependence? Adolescents often become involved with substance abuse and dependence through experimental use (Chassin et al., 2000; Lewinsohn, Brown, Seeley, & Ramsey, 2000). Why do children and adolescents experiment with alcohol and other drugs? There are any number of reasons (Chassin et al., 2000; Finn et al., 2000; Wills et al., 2000). Some are conforming to peer pressure; acceptance by peers means doing what the peers do. Some are rebelling against moral or social constraints. Others are in it for the experience. Of these, some are simply curious; they want to see what effects the drugs will have. Others are trying to escape from boredom or from the pressures of academic life or "the 'hood." Some, of course, are looking for pleasure or excitement. Some youngsters are imitating what they see their own parents doing. Some parents, in fact, intentionally introduce their children to illicit drugs (Leinwand, 2000).

Psychological Factors

From the traditional psychoanalytic perspective, excessive drinking and other forms of substance abuse are oral activities, suggestive of too little or too much gratification in the oral stage of psychosexual development. To be frank, we no longer find much research into this hypothesis, and most authors ignore it.

Social cognitive theorists suggest that children and adolescents usually try drugs because someone has recommended them or because they have observed someone else using them. But whether or not they continue to use the drug depends on factors such as whether use is reinforced by peer approval. The drug can also be reinforcing by enhancing the user's mood or by reducing unpleasant emotions such as anxiety and tension. For individuals who are addicted, the prevention of the abstinence syndrome is reinforcing. Carrying the substance and obtaining a "rainy-day" supply are reinforcing because the child or adolescent doesn't have to worry about being caught short.

Why, you may wonder, do children and adolescents use drugs when their health-education courses inform them that they are harmful? Don't they believe their teachers? Some do; some don't. But the reinforcement value of the substances occurs *now, today*. The harmful effects are frequently long-term or theoretical.

Parents who use licit or illicit drugs increase their children's awareness of them. Many children grow up in a house filled with drugs of one kind or another, and they assume that people simply drink or pop pills as a part of life. Parents in such households are also "educating" their children—for example, demonstrating that alcohol can be used to handle tension or facilitate social interactions (Stacy & Newcomb, 1999).

Biological Factors

Biological factors are apparently involved in determining which experimenters will continue to use a drug and which will not. Children may inherit genetic predispositions toward abuse of specific substances, including depressants (alcohol and opioids) and stimulants (nicotine and cocaine) Ellenbroek, Sluyter, & Cools, 2000; Finn et al., 2000; Kendler et al., 2000; Kendler, Thornton, & Pederson, 2000). Consider the findings of some adoptee studies. It turns out that the natural children of alcoholics who are reared by adoptive parents are more likely to abuse alcohol than are the biological children of the adoptive parents. What would a "genetic predisposition" toward alcohol abuse entail? It might have two or more components: One could be higher sensitivity to alcohol (which allows for greater enjoyment of alcohol), and the second could be greater tolerance for alcohol (which allows the individual to drink more and consequently develop physiological dependence) (Pihl, Peterson, & Finn, 1990). College students with alcoholic parents do appear to be more tolerant of alcohol; they show better coordination and muscle control when they are given alcohol than do

Smoking

The "Monitoring the Future" survey finds that about 70% of 12th-graders disapprove of smoking a pack or more of cigarettes a day, yet about 31% of students have smoked a cigarette within the past 30 days. Students who plan to go to college are somewhat less likely to smoke than students who do not. Why do young people smoke when they know that smoking is harmful?

students whose parents do not abuse alcohol. These students also feel less intoxicated (Pihl et al., 1990).

Peers

Associating with peers who use drugs and who tolerate drug use is one of the strongest predictors of adolescent drug use and abuse (Chassin et al., 2000, 2001). Children are highly vulnerable to peer pressure in the early teen years. If children of this age group are closely involved with a group that uses drugs, they may experience enormous pressure to do so themselves. Adolescents who are extensively involved with their peers, especially to the exclusion of their families, are at greater risk for drug use.

Family

Children whose parents use drugs such as alcohol, tobacco, tranquilizers, and stimulants are more likely to turn to drugs themselves (Chassin et al., 2000; Finn et al., 2000). Modeling increases children's awareness of drugs and conveys the unfortunate message that use of drugs is appropriate to relieve the stresses and strains of daily life. Adolescents whose parents and siblings have more tolerant attitudes toward deviant, unconventional, and non-law-abiding behaviors also are more likely to use drugs (Leinwand, 2000). Poor parent–child relationships and family discord are contributing factors as well.

Parenting style also plays a role. Having open lines of communication with a parent helps to inhibit drug use. More generally, the authoritative pattern of child rearing appears to protect children from substance abuse (Baumrind, 1991b). This style of parenting is characterized by high parental involvement, the setting of strict limits, demands for mature behavior, democratic discussion of values and goals, and warmth and encouragement. Heavy drug use is most likely to occur in families with either permissive or neglecting-rejecting parenting styles.

It is becoming increasingly apparent that to understand the nature of family influences on adolescent substance abuse, we must also consider how the behaviors of children influence parental behaviors. Childhood problem behaviors, such as hyperactivity, aggression, and refusing adult requests, cause mothers to feel more distress. Mothers who are more distressed show less effective parental coping behaviors, which, in turn, can lead to increased levels of adolescent problem behaviors such as marijuana use, alcohol problems, and delinquency (DeLucia, Belz, & Chassin, 2001).

Other Factors

Adolescent drug users often experience school problems. They do poorly in school, and their academic motivation is low (Wills et al., 2000). Certain psychological characteristics are associated with drug use. These include impulsiveness, rebelliousness, and low self-esteem (Moeller et al., 2001). Adolescent drug users are more likely to suffer from depression and anxiety (Beitchman et al., 2001; Dierker et al., 2001). Problem behaviors such as aggression, delinquency, early sexual behavior, and premarital pregnancy also are associated with teenage drug involvement. A number of female adolescent substance abusers also have problems with eating disorders (Stice et al., 2001).

Frequent drug users often show signs of maladjustment in childhood. Many of them are anxious or depressed, or both. Some engage in antisocial behavior (Altindag, Oezkan, & Oto, 2001; Beitchman et al., 2001; Hallman, Persson, & Klinteberg, 2001). They have problems getting along with other children; they are insecure and undependable and show many indications of emotional distress. Boys who later become alcoholics show a variety of interpersonal deficits, including being less considerate and more indifferent to mothers and siblings. The fact that these signs of maladjustment often emerge before the beginning of drug abuse alerts us to the difficulty of separating cause and effect when we examine factors associated with adolescent drug use (Beitchman et al., 2001; Gray & Nye, 2001). Does drug use cause school failure, or does failing in school cause a youngster to turn to drugs? Does substance abuse lead to depression and anxiety, or do individuals take up drugs to deal with these painful emotional states?

All right, substance abuse can mess up a life. ***Question: How can we treat and prevent substance abuse?***

Treatment and Prevention

Health professionals, educators, police departments, and laypeople have devised many approaches to the prevention and treatment of substance abuse and dependence among adolescents. However, treatment has been a frustrating endeavor, and it is not clear which approaches are most effective (Deas & Thomas, 2001). In many cases, adolescents with drug dependence really do not want to discontinue the substances they are abusing. Many are referred to treatment by parents or school systems, but deny the negative impact of drugs on their lives. They may belong to a peer group that frowns on prevention or treatment programs. When addicted adolescents come for treatment, helping them through a withdrawal syndrome may be straightforward enough. But once their bodies no longer require the substance to feel "normal," they may return to the social milieu that fosters substance abuse and be unable to find strong reasons for living a life without drugs. The problem of returning to abuse and dependence following treatment—that is, the problem of *relapse*—can thus be more troublesome than the problems involved in initial treatment (Kaminer, 2001; Tripathi et al., 2001).

Many adolescents with substance abuse problems also have psychological disorders or serious family problems. When treatment programs focus only on substance abuse and do little to treat the psychological disorder or relationships in the family, the outcome of treatment tends to suffer (Beitchman et al., 2001; Rohde et al., 2001).

Reflect

Why is substance abuse so difficult to treat and prevent?

Biological Approaches

For adolescents with chemical dependencies, biological treatment typically begins with *detoxification*—that is, helping them through the withdrawal period from the addictive substance. Simply discontinuing some substances, such as alcohol and barbiturates, can be dangerous and lead to convulsions. Detoxification to such substances is often carried out in a hospital setting to provide the support needed to help the adolescent withdraw safely. Tranquilizers such as Librium and Valium may help block more severe withdrawal symptoms.

The drug disulfiram (brand name Antabuse) discourages alcohol consumption because the combination of the two produces a strong aversive reaction consisting of nausea, sweating, flushing, and rapid heart rate. The effectiveness of disulfiram is limited because many who want to continue drinking simply stop using it. Antidepressant drugs have shown some promise in reducing cravings for cocaine following withdrawal from the drug. Antidepressants may help by stimulating neural processes that underlie feelings of pleasure in everyday experiences. However, antidepressants have not yet produced consistent results in reducing relapse rates for cocaine dependence (O'Brien, 1996).

Nicotine replacement therapy is a promising development in the treatment of cigarette smoking (Killen et al., 2001; Solberg et al., 2001; Sweeney et al., 2001). Adolescents (and anyone else!) can use gums, skin patches, or nasal sprays laced with nicotine to reduce the craving for the nicotine in cigarettes. Once they have managed to go without cigarettes for a few weeks, ex-smokers can gradually wean themselves from the nicotine replacement. A combination of nicotine replacement therapy and counseling appears to be more effective than nicotine replacement alone, because the counseling can help adolescents learn how to resist temptations to return to smoking.

Individuals addicted to heroin are often treated by replacing the heroin with the human-made drug methadone. Methadone is chemically similar to heroin. It satisfies cravings for heroin without producing the intense "high" of heroin. But methadone is also addictive, and adolescents who are treated with methadone are in effect playing "musical drugs"; that is, they are swapping dependence on one drug for dependence on another (Fiellin et al., 2001).

Psychological and Educational Approaches

Despite the complexity of the factors contributing to substance abuse and dependence, these problems are often handled by laypeople or nonprofessionals. Such people are often recovering from the same problem with substance abuse. For example, self-help group meetings are sponsored by organizations like Alcoholics Anonymous (AA), Narcotics Anonymous, and Cocaine Anonymous. These groups promote abstinence and provide members an opportunity to discuss their feelings and experiences in a supportive group setting. Al-Anon is a spinoff of AA that supports the families of people with alcoholism. Another spinoff of AA, Alateen, supports adolescents whose parents have problems with alcohol. Despite their popularity, there is very little controlled research on the effectiveness of these programs (Deas & Thomas, 2001).

The peer education approach to prevention is based on the assumptions that peers have more credibility than adults among adolescents and that peer pressure is a key factor in substance abuse. Peer education has been shown to be helpful in increasing knowledge about drugs and may help reduce substance abuse or prevent it (Mellanby, Rees, & Tripp, 2000).

Hospitalization or residential treatment is often recommended when substance abusers cannot exercise self-control in their usual environments, cannot tolerate withdrawal symptoms, or demonstrate behavior that is self-destructive or dangerous to others. Some residential therapeutic communities have professional staffs. Others are run by laypeople. Residents are required to assume responsibility for their own behavior so that they will accept that they are in charge of their use of drugs and so that they can decide what they will do to make their lives more productive. Residents in such programs may begin by assuming responsibility for their personal hygiene, beds, and rooms, but eventually work toward contributing to community life in the residence. Lapses are confronted in group sessions. Residents are also confronted about their excuses for failing to take responsibility for themselves and about their denial of the damage being done by their abuse. There is little controlled research into the long-term effectiveness of residential programs.

Cognitive-behavioral approaches to substance abuse and dependence focus on modifying abusive and dependent ideas and behavior patterns (Waldron et al.,

2001). They teach abusers either to avoid temptation or to change their behavior when they are faced with temptation. The method of self-control training helps abusers develop skills they can use to change their abusive behavior. For example, adolescents can learn to avoid socializing with others with substance abuse problems (Latimer et al., 2000). They can avoid situations linked to abuse—bars, the street, bowling alleys, and so on. They can learn to frequent substance-free environments such as gyms, museums, evening classes. They can learn to use competing responses when they are tempted—taking a bath or shower, walking the dog, walking around the block, taking a drive, calling a friend, or exercising. The cognitive-behavioral method of social skills training helps adolescents develop effective interpersonal responses in social situations that prompt substance abuse (Blake et al., 2001). They may teach adolescents how to fend off social pressures to drink or have a cigarette. The adolescent learns to "just say no" without picking a fight or having to leave the situation.

A major problem, however, is that most adolescents who abuse substances have no contact with treatment programs or self-help organizations. In many cases, they also need help in handling family problems and other psychological problems (Grella et al., 2001; Rohde et al., 2001). In the case of inner-city youth who have become trapped within a milieu of street drugs and hopelessness, job-training opportunities may be required to help them assume more productive social roles.

The development of ways to help adolescents recognize the negative effects of substances and forgo the powerful and immediate reinforcements they provide remains a major challenge. Prevention programs, which rely mainly on education about the harmful effects of drugs, have had some impact on the prevalence of substance abuse (Johnston et al., 2001; Mellanby, Rees, & Tripp, 2000), but many adolescents also need something better to look forward to.

Review

(32) Substance abuse is the repeated use of a substance despite the fact that it is causing or compounding social, occupational, psychological, or physical problems. (33) Substance dependence is characterized by loss of control over the substance, tolerances, and an ________ syndrome. (34) ________ slow the activity of the nervous system. (35) Alcohol ________ cognitive functioning. (36) ________ speed up the heartbeat and other bodily functions. (37) ________ is the agent that creates physiological dependence on tobacco. (38) ________ give rise to perceptual distortions called hallucinations. (39) ________ distorts perception of the passage of time. (40) High school seniors are more likely to disapprove of (experimental or regular?) drug use. (41) Substance abuse and dependence usually begin with ________ use.

Pulling It Together: Why is it so difficult to treat and prevent substance abuse and dependence?

Sexually Transmitted Infections

> A boyfriend of mine got very angry with me when he wanted to have sex without a condom and I wouldn't let him. He was quite promiscuous, and how should I know how clean those other girls were? We both wanted to be tested for AIDS, but we didn't because we were too scared. If one of us did have AIDS, we really wouldn't know what to do.
>
> —Maureen, 19, Florida
> (Rathus & Boughn, 1993)

Given a "new" body that is sexually mature, a flood of sex hormones that stokes the sex drive, vulnerability to peer pressure, and limited experience in handling temptation, teenagers are at particularly high risk for sexually transmitted infections (STIs). Sexually active adolescents have higher rates of STIs than any other age group. Each year, an estimated 3 million adolescents—one of every six—contracts a sexually transmitted infection (CDC, 2001e). ***Question: What kinds of sexually transmitted infections are there?*** Chlamydia (a bacterial infection of the vagina or urinary tract that may result in sterility) is the most commonly occurring STI in adolescents, followed by gonorrhea, genital warts, genital herpes, syphilis, and **HIV/AIDS.** Because of its lethality, HIV/AIDS tends to capture most of the headlines. However, other STIs are more widespread, and some of them can also be deadly.

Nearly 4 million new chlamydia infections occur each year (CDC, 2001e). The incidence of chlamydia infections is especially high among teenagers and college students (CDC, 2001e). Chlamydia is a major cause of pelvic inflammatory disease (PID), which often leads to infertility.

There are about 1 million new HPV (*human papilloma virus*) infections each year in the United States. It is estimated that more than half of the sexually active adolescent women in some cities in the United States are infected with HPV. Though the warts may appear in visible areas of the skin, in perhaps 7 of 10 cases they appear in areas that cannot be seen, such as on the cervix in women or in the urethra in men. Within a few months following infection, the warts are usually found in the genital and anal regions. Women are more susceptible to HPV infection because cells in the cervix divide swiftly, facilitating the multiplication of HPV. Women who initiate coitus prior to the age of 18 and who have many sex partners are particularly susceptible to infection.

A survey of first-year college students found a great deal of ignorance about HPV and genital warts (Baer, Allen, & Braun, 2000). The findings were ironic: Although nearly all (96% of the males and 95% of the females) had heard of genital warts, only 4% of the males and 12% of the females knew that HPV caused them. Moreover, the students were generally ignorant of the modes of transmission of both genital warts and HPV. Ignorance in this case may be danger rather than bliss because HPV infection is linked to cervical cancer (Cannistra & Niloff, 1996; Josefsson et al., 2000).

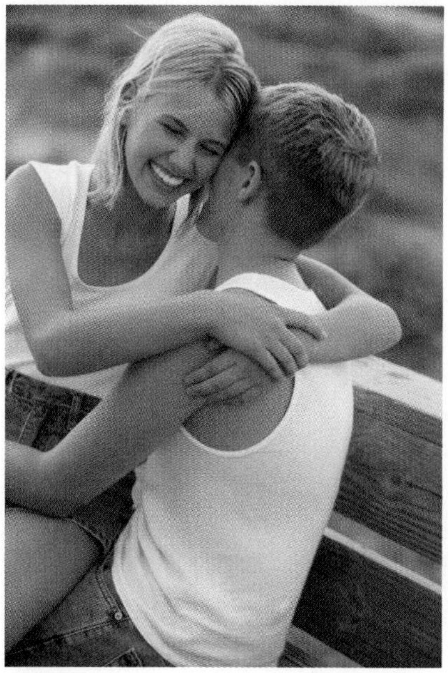

© Steve Thornton/CORBIS

What Is the Risk of Their Contracting a Sexually Transmitted Infection?

Young people generally know of the risks of HIV/AIDS, but knowledge of risks does not always translate into behavior. Young people have heard of chlamydia and of genital warts, but they tend to underestimate the effects of these STIs.

Risk Factors

Adolescents often take risks with harmful consequences for their health and well-being. ***Question: What factors place adolescents at risk for contracting STIs?***

First, and perhaps most obvious, is sexual activity itself. Someone who doesn't engage in sexual intercourse is not likely to contract a sexually transmitted infection. Over the past 30 years, the age at first sexual experience has been dropping. The average age of first sexual intercourse is 16, but in some inner-city areas, it is 12. By the age of 19, between 70% and 90% of adolescents have initiated sexual intercourse (Dailard, 2001; Santelli et al., 2000).

A second high-risk behavior for contracting STIs is having sex with multiple partners. Increasing numbers of teenage girls have multiple sex partners. Currently, about one in five high school students engages in sex with four or more different partners (Dailard, 2001).

A third factor that increases the chance of contracting STIs is failure to use condoms. In two recent surveys, two thirds of sexually active adolescents reported not using condoms or using them only inconsistently. About one quarter to one third do not use any contraceptives at all (Dailard, 2001).

A fourth factor is substance abuse (United Nations Special Session on AIDS, 2001). Adolescents who abuse drugs are also more likely to engage in other risky behaviors, such as engaging in sexual activity without condoms (Santelli et al., 2001).

HIV/AIDS and other STIs are described in Table 14.7 (p. 545).

Reflect

Why is knowledge of the threat of STIs often insufficient to cause people to take adequate precautions against becoming infected?

HIV/AIDS HIV stands for *human immunodeficiency virus*, the virus that causes AIDS. AIDS stands for *acquired immunodeficiency syndrome*, a condition that cripples the body's immune system, rendering the individual susceptible to diseases that would not otherwise be threatening or as threatening.

HIV/AIDS

HIV/AIDS is the most devastating of STIs; if left untreated, it is lethal. (And the long-term prospects of those who do receive treatment remain unknown.) First identified in 1981, HIV—the virus that causes AIDS—is spreading rapidly around the world and had infected about 40 million people worldwide by the turn of the millennium (United Nations Special Session on AIDS, 2001). Perhaps 1 million Americans are infected with HIV. This may not sound like a lot. But more than 20% of all Americans with AIDS are in their 20s (CDC, 2001e). Since HIV has a long incubation period, up to a decade and longer, it is likely that many of these young adults became infected when they were teenagers.

Young gay males and homeless and runaway youths have elevated risk for HIV/AIDS. Anal intercourse is a likely route of transmission of HIV and is often practiced by gay males (Valleroy et al., 2000). However, some males pressure female adolescents into anal intercourse (Friedman et al., 2001). Homeless and runaway adolescents are likely to engage in unprotected sex with several partners. Injecting drugs is another risk factor for HIV/AIDS because sharing needles with infected individuals can transmit HIV. Sex partners of people who inject drugs are vulnerable as well (CDC, 2001d). Hemophiliacs and other individuals who receive blood from transfusions are unlikely to be infected with HIV today because donors and donated blood are screened for the presence of HIV.

Women account for a minority of cases of HIV/AIDS in the United States but are more likely than males to be infected with HIV in many places around the world. A United Nations study in Europe, Africa, and Southeast Asia has found

A Closer Look

Adolescence, Ethnicity, and HIV/AIDS

"I was young and stupid. I wasn't scared of anything. It was just about having fun. I didn't listen to older people. I thought they didn't know what they were talking about."

—Shernika, 16

"I was scared. I was like, 'I shouldn't have done this.' But he didn't look like nothing was wrong with him."

—George, 14

"Everybody I've been with, I knew a long time, since childhood. I didn't think they'd have something like that."

—Dicki, 16

They heard endless warnings about the dangers of intravenous drug use, about the wisdom of using condoms. Many even knew older relatives, neighbors, and friends who had died because of AIDS.

But somehow, it didn't add up. Not me, they said. Couldn't happen to me.

And so a 16-year-old girl became infected with HIV because she had unprotected sex with a friend. A 14-year-old boy never took his condom out of its wrapper, and now he is HIV-positive. A 16-year-old girl trusted her boyfriend, a drug user. She shouldn't have.

The experiences of African American teenagers are far from unique. African American youths have become the new face of HIV, making up about two thirds of the new cases among people under 25, according to studies by the CDC (2000a, 2001d).

"The disease is disappearing from the mainstream and becoming a disease of kids who are disenfranchised anyway," said Lawrence D'Angelo, who runs the Burgess Clinic for HIV-infected adolescents at Children's Hospital in Washington.

Risky sexual behavior is nothing new among young people. But medical professionals find it disturbing that the risk taking continues, despite extensive educational campaigns, and that African American youths are paying an especially high price. That is a major change from the early 1980s, when gay European American men made up the majority of young people infected with HIV.

"For many of our kids, HIV has become just one of the many problems in their lives, like are they going to get a good meal, who are they going to live with, are they going to school?" D'Angelo said.

D'Angelo and Ligia Peralta, who treats HIV-infected adolescents in Baltimore, began to notice the change in the 1990s when growing numbers of young African American women, most of them poor, began entering their programs.

"Theoretically, they do understand the risks," said Peralta, who runs Star Track, an HIV and AIDS clinic for adolescents at the University of Maryland Medical Center in Baltimore. "However, from there to recognizing that my partner, the person that I choose, may be infected with HIV, there's the major disconnect."

The disease is spread casually among young people, the doctors have found in the course of conducting a long-term HIV that sexually active teenage girls have higher rates of HIV infection than older women or young men (Glynn et al., 2001). A number of erroneous assumptions about HIV/AIDS have had a disproportionately negative impact on women. They include the notions that HIV/AIDS is primarily a disease of gay men and people who inject drugs and that it is difficult to contract HIV/AIDS through male–female intercourse. However, the primary mode of HIV transmission worldwide is male–female intercourse. Larger numbers of Americans also are being infected by male–female intercourse. Among American women, male–female intercourse is the major source of infection by HIV.

Studies regarding knowledge, attitudes, and beliefs about HIV/AIDS find that even children in the early school years are aware of HIV/AIDS. General knowledge of HIV/AIDS is even greater among adolescents. Nearly all high school students know that HIV/AIDS is transmitted by sexual intercourse, but about half do not modify their sexual practices as a result of fear of the disease (Santelli et al., 2000). Adolescents often deny the threat of HIV/AIDS to them. As one high school girl says, "I can't believe that anyone I would have sex with would be infected." Guess what: Some are. Given the threat of HIV/AIDS and other STIs, ***Question: What can be done to prevent STIs?***

Prevention

Prevention and education strategies are the primary weapons against STIs.

What should be the goals of a school-based program designed to prevent STIs? Increasing knowledge certainly is important (United Nations Special Session on AIDS, 2001). Adolescents need to learn about the transmission, symptoms, and consequences of STIs. They need to learn about "safer sex" techniques, including abstinence, and, if they are sexually active, the use of condoms. Educating young people to use condoms is associated with lower levels of infection around the

study. Once infected youths discover that they have HIV, many are unwilling to admit it to sexual partners. D'Angelo said that only about half tell their regular partners that they are HIV-positive, and almost none bothers to tell an occasional partner.

And with a stigma still attached to homosexuality in some communities, young African American men who have sex with other men tend to be less likely than their European American peers to identify themselves as gay, possibly causing them to ignore HIV-prevention messages aimed at gay men, said Helene Gayle, director of the CDC's National Center for HIV, STI and TB Prevention. "I think it means we have to make sure our prevention messages are keeping pace with the times and keeping pace with the population at risk," Gayle said.

The Personal Fable and Exposure to HIV

Some say yet another factor—the sense that young people have that they can live forever—also is at work. "All youth—rich, poor, black, white—have this sense of invincibility, invulnerability," says Ronald King (2000), executive director of the HIV Community Coalition of Metropolitan Washington, explaining why many adolescents who know the risks still expose themselves to HIV infection.

The developmental psychologist Jean Piaget noted that adolescents appear to believe in a *personal fable.* The fable is that their feelings and ideas are special, even unique, and that they are invulnerable. The personal fable is apparently connected with adolescent behavior patterns such as showing off and taking risks. Many adolescents have an "It can't happen to me" attitude; they assume they can smoke without risk of cancer or engage in sexual activity without risk of STIs or pregnancy.

Peralta and D'Angelo have found that adolescent girls in all groups are especially vulnerable to sexually transmitted infections, such as HIV, because the cervix at their age is not fully mature and is more susceptible to infection. Also, many of the young men and women in both programs were sexually abused as children and became sexually active at a young age. Most of the women also were infected by men 10 to 20 years older.

While some national studies show that condom use has increased among young people in recent years and that they are delaying sex until their mid-teens, a recent survey of 4,500 patients at Children's Hospital showed that the average age when boys begin having sex is 12; for girls, the average age is 13.

Search Online With InfoTrac College Edition

For additional information, explore InfoTrac College Edition, your online library. Go to http://www.infotrac-college.com and use the passcode from the InfoTrac card that came with your book. Try these search terms: HIV adolescents, sexual ethics for youth, teenage boys sexual behavior, teenage girls sexual behavior, sexually transmitted diseases.

Source: Much of this feature is adapted from L. Frazier (2000, July 16). The new face of HIV is young, black. Washington Post, *p. C01.*

globe (Ford et al., 2000; Fylkesnes et al., 2001). (See the nearby "Developing in the New Millennium" feature for a discussion of safer sex and other techniques for preventing HIV/AIDS and other STIs.)

But knowledge may not be enough to change behavior (Parsons et al., 2000). For example, many female adolescents lack power in their relationships. Males are likely to pressure females into unwanted sexual relations or to pressure them into unprotected sexual relations (Friedman et al., 2001; Garcia-Moreno & Watts, 2000). Other goals of educational programs should include enhancing the adolescent's sense of control over the prevention of AIDS and modifying sexual and drug behaviors associated with acquiring the disease. As with programs designed to prevent substance abuse, the development of effective decision-making and social skills may be critical in programs designed to prevent STIs. In many cases, that is, prevention involves the empowerment of adolescent females (United Nations Special Session on AIDS, 2001).

Developing in the New Millennium

Preventing HIV/AIDS and Other STIs: It's More Than Safe(r) Sex

How does one protect oneself from being infected with a sexually transmitted infection (STI)? Doing so can be awkward. It can be difficult. But it's also extremely important. Consider the comments of one young woman:

> It's one thing to talk about "being responsible about [STIs]" and a much harder thing to do it at the very moment. It's hard to imagine murmuring into someone's ear at a time of passion, "Would you mind slipping on this condom or using this cream just in case one of us has [an STI]?" Yet it seems awkward to bring it up beforehand, if it's not yet clear between us that we want to make love with one another. (Boston Women's Health Book Collective, 1992, pp. 311–312)

Because discussing STIs with a partner can be a daunting task, some people wing it. They admit that they just hope for the best. But even if they do bring up the topic, they need to recognize that many people—perhaps most people—do not know whether they are infected with an STI, especially the organisms that cause chlamydia, gonorrhea, and AIDS (Turner et al., 2002). In any event, putting blinders on is not the answer to STIs. What can we do to prevent HIV/AIDS and other STIs? A number of things.

1. *Use sex education in the school.* An overwhelming 98% of American parents believe that the schools should make children and adolescents aware of the dangers of HIV/AIDS and other STIs (Schemo, 2000).
2. *Refuse to deny the prevalence and harmful nature of AIDS.* Many young people—and many older people—try not to think about the threats posed by HIV/AIDS and other STIs. The first, and perhaps most important, step in protecting oneself against AIDS is thus psychological: keeping it in mind—refusing to play the dangerous game that involves pretending (at least for the moment) that it does not exist. The other measures involve modifying behavior.
3. *Just Say No—that is, remain abstinent.* One way of curtailing the transmission of HIV and other pathogens is abstinence. But what does *abstinence* mean? The term can be limited to avoiding engaging in sexual intercourse with another person. Hugging, light kissing (without exchanging saliva), and petting (without contacting semen or vaginal fluids) are usually safe, although readers may argue about whether these behaviors are consistent with the definition of abstinence.
4. *Limit yourself to a monogamous relationship with a partner who is not infected.* It is safe to engage in sexual intercourse in a monogamous relationship with a person who does not have an STI. The issue is how one can be certain that one's partner is free of STIs and faithful.

Adolescents who are unwilling to abstain from sexual intercourse or to limit themselves to one partner can still do things to make sex safer—that's saf*er*, not absolutely safe:

5. *Be picky.* Limit sexual activity to people you know well. Ask yourself whether these individuals are likely to have done things that could infect them with HIV or other disease organisms.
6. *Check out one's partner's genitals.* Examine one's partner's genitals for unpleasant odors, discharges, blisters, rashes, warts, and lice while engaged in foreplay. These are all possible symptoms of STIs.
7. *Wash the genitals.* Washing oneself beforehand helps protect one's partner. Washing with soap and water afterward may kill or remove some pathogens. Urinating afterward might be of some help, particularly to men, since the acidity of urine can kill some pathogens in the urethra.
8. *Use latex condoms.* Latex condoms protect both partners from exchanging infected bodily fluids. Condoms are particularly effective in preventing transmission of gonorrhea, syphilis, and HIV.
9. *Talk to a doctor.* Use of antibiotics after unprotected sex can guard against bacterial and viral infections, even HIV. Adolescents should check with a doctor immediately if they think they may have been exposed to STIs.
10. *Have regular medical checkups.* These include blood tests. In this way, one can learn about and treat a number of disorders—particularly chlamydia and gonorrhea—whose symptoms had gone unnoticed.

TABLE 14.7 *Overview of Sexually Transmitted Infections (STIs)*

Acquired Immune Deficiency Syndrome (AIDS)

AIDS is caused by the human immunodeficiency virus (HIV). HIV is transmitted by sexual intercourse, injection of contaminated blood, and breast-feeding. Infected children, adolescents, and adults may not show symptoms for months or years, although children usually succumb more quickly than older people. AIDS is symptomized by weight loss, fever, fatigue, diarrhea, and other disorders that take advantage of the weakened immune system, such as particular types of pneumonia, Kaposi's sarcoma, and cancer of the cervix. HIV infection is normally diagnosed by detection of HIV antibodies in blood, saliva, or urine. There is no vaccine for HIV/AIDS. A "cocktail" of antiviral drugs, including protease inhibitors, usually reduces the amount of HIV in the bloodstream, sometimes to undetectable levels.

Bacterial Vaginosis

Bacterial vaginosis is caused by the *Gardnerella vaginalis* bacterium and others. This disorder can be transmitted sexually but also arises naturally by overgrowth of bacteria in the vagina. The disorder can occur without symptoms, but is often symptomized in females by a thin, foul-smelling vaginal discharge, and by irritation of genitals and discomfort when urinating. In males the disorder is symptomized by inflammation of the penis, painful urination, and cystitis. The disorder is diagnosed by culture and examination of bacteria and is usually treated with metronidazole, taken orally.

Candidiasis (moniliasis, thrush, "yeast infection")

Candidiasis is caused by the yeastlike fungus *Candida albicans.* The fungus can be transmitted sexually, but also arises by overgrowth of the fungus in the vagina and even by sharing a washcloth with an infected person. It is symptomized in females by vulval itching; a white, cheesy, foul-smelling discharge; and by soreness or swelling of vaginal and vulval tissues. In males it is symptomized by painful urination or inflammation of the penis. The disorder is usually diagnosed on the basis of the presence of the symptoms. It is usually treated by vaginal suppositories, creams, or tablets that contain miconazole, clotrimazole, or teraconazole. The infected region should be kept dry, and changes in the use of other medicines and chemical agents is often recommended.

Chlamydia and Nongonococcal Urethritis (NGU)

Chlamydia is caused by the *Chlamydia trachomatis* bacterium. In males NGU may also be caused by the *Ureaplasma urealyticum* bacterium and other germs. The pathogens can be transmitted by vaginal, oral, or anal sexual activity; by touching the eyes after touching the genitals of an infected partner; and by passing through the birth canal of an infected mother. It is symptomized in females by frequent and painful urination, abdominal discomfort, and a vaginal discharge, but most females are symptom-free. In males the symptoms include burning or painful urination and a slight discharge, but some males are also symptom-free. Chlamydia is diagnosed by examination of a cervical smear in females and treated with antibiotics.

Genital Herpes

Genital herpes is caused by the Herpes simplex virus–type 2 (HSV-2). It is almost always transmitted by vaginal, oral, or anal sexual activity and is most contagious during active outbreaks. It is symptomized by painful, reddish bumps around the genitals, thigh, or buttocks; in females, these bumps are also found in the vagina or on the cervix. The bumps turn into blisters or sores that fill with pus and break, shedding viral particles. Other symptoms can include burning urination, fever, aches and pains, swollen glands, and, in females, a vaginal discharge. The disorder is diagnosed by inspection of the sores and by culture and examination of fluid drawn from the base of a sore. Antiviral drugs such as acyclovir may provide relief and prompt healing of sores, but they do not cure herpes.

Genital Warts

Genital warts are caused by the Human papilloma virus (HPV). They can be transmitted by sexual and other contacts, such as contact with infected towels or clothing. Females—especially those with multiple sex partners—are particularly vulnerable. Symptoms include painless warts on the penis, foreskin, scrotum, or urethra in males, and on the vulva, labia, vaginal wall, or cervix in females. They may also be found around the anus and in the rectum. HPV is also connected with cervical cancer. The warts are diagnosed by clinical inspection and usually removed surgically, frozen, burned, or treated with podophyllin.

Gonorrhea ("clap," "drip")

Gonorrhea is caused by the gonococcus bacterium (*Neisseria gonorrhoeae*). The bacterium is transmitted by vaginal, oral, or anal sexual activity or from mother to baby during delivery. Although most females do not show early symptoms, males develop a thick yellow discharge and experience burning urination. Females develop burning urination, a vaginal discharge, and irregular menstrual bleeding. The disorder is diagnosed by clinical examination or by culture of the discharge. It is treated with antibiotics.

Pubic Lice ("crabs")

Pubic lice are technically known as *Phthirus pubis,* which, despite the slang term for the disorder, is an insect and not a crab. The lice are transmitted by sexual contact or by contact with an infested sheet, towel, or toilet seat. They cause intense itching in the pubic area and other hairy areas to which the lice can attach themselves. They are treated by prescription drugs or by over-the-counter medications that contain pyrethrins or piperonal butoxide, such as NIX, A200, RID, and Triple X.

Syphilis

Syphilis is caused by the *Treponema pallidum* bacterium. It is transmitted by vaginal, oral, or anal sexual activity, or by touching an infectious sore, called a chancre. In the primary stage, syphilis is symptomized by a hard, round painless chancre or sore that appears at the site of infection within 2 to 4 weeks. The disorder can progress through secondary, latent, and tertiary stages if it is not treated. The disorder is diagnosed by clinical examination or by examination of fluid drawn from a chancre. It can also be diagnosed by a blood test called a VDRL. It is treated with antibiotics.

Trichomoniasis ("trich")

Trichomoniasis is caused by the *Trichomonas vaginalis* protozoan, which is a one-celled animal, and is almost always transmitted sexually. Although many females are symptom-free, others show a foamy, yellow, odorous, vaginal discharge, and itching or burning in the vulva. Males are usually symptom-free, but may develop mild inflammation of the urethra, which can cause burning urination. It is diagnosed by examination of a smear of vaginal discharge and treated with metronidazole.

In an effort to prevent AIDS, as well as teenage pregnancy, some school districts now distribute condoms to students. This practice has aroused considerable controversy. Some oppose giving contraceptives on religious and moral grounds. Opponents also argue that providing condoms encourages teenagers to become sexually active. Advocates of condom distribution programs argue that while abstinence may be desirable, the fact remains that many teens are sexually active. Given this reality, they contend, the schools should help protect sexually active teens from AIDS and unwanted pregnancies. What is your opinion on this issue?

But even the best school-based programs, unless started early enough, will not reach the 25% or so of students who drop out during the high school years. These students often are already at high risk for developing AIDS and other STIs because of involvement in sexual activity and substance abuse. Broader, community-based efforts are needed to reach these youth.

The ability of teenagers to deal with the physical changes of adolescence and to engage in health-promoting behaviors depends in part on their growing cognitive abilities. We examine development in that area in Chapter 15.

Review

(42) __________ is the most commonly occurring sexually transmitted infection in adolescents. (43) Infection by __________ is linked to development of cancer of the cervix. (44) The virus that causes __________ had infected about 40 million people worldwide by the turn of the millennium. (45) Injecting drugs is another risk factor for __________.

Pulling It Together: Why do many adolescents who know of the risks of sexually transmitted infections nevertheless fail to prevent their transmission?

Recite Recite Recite Recite

1. What is adolescence?

Adolescence is a transitional period between childhood and adulthood. G. Stanley Hall believed that adolescence is marked by "storm and stress," that adolescent mood swings and conflicts with parents are a necessary part of growing up. According to Freud, adolescence begins with the genital stage of psychosexual development. Current views challenge the assumption that "storm and stress" is either normal or beneficial for adolescents. Some theorists suggest that the concept of adolescence as a period of storm and stress marginalizes adolescents.

2. What is puberty? What happens during puberty?

Puberty is a stage of development that is characterized by reaching sexual maturity. Puberty is controlled by a feedback loop involving the hypothalamus, pituitary gland, and the gonads. Sex hormones trigger the development of primary and secondary sex characteristics.

3. What happens during the adolescent growth spurt?

Girls start to spurt sooner than boys. Boys tend to spurt up to 4 inches per year, and girls, up to 3 inches per year. Girls are larger than boys from about 9 or 10 until about 13 or 14, but during their spurts, boys catch up with girls and become taller and heavier. Boys' shoulders become broader than those of girls, while girls develop relatively broader and rounder hips. More of a male's body weight is composed of muscle. Adolescents may look awkward and gawky because of asynchronous growth. During the past century, children in the Western world have grown dramatically more rapidly and wound up taller than children from earlier times. Boys typically ejaculate seminal fluid by age 13 or 14. First menstruation is called menarche and is seen by many

Recite Recite Recite Recite

as signaling a woman's coming of age. It may be that girls need to attain a certain body weight to trigger menarche. Female sex hormones regulate the menstrual cycle, with surges of estrogen causing ova to ripen.

4. What are the effects of early or late maturation on adolescents?

The effects of early maturation are generally positive for boys and negative for girls. Early-maturing boys tend to be more popular, leaders in school, are poised, and to have an edge in sports. Yet some boys, like many early-maturing girls, may develop before they are psychologically prepared to live up to the expectations of others. With their tallness and their developing breasts, early-maturing girls become conspicuous, leading to a negative body image.

5. How do adolescents feel about their bodies?

By age 18, adolescents are more satisfied with their bodies than they were earlier. Girls are generally more dissatisfied with their bodies than boys are. Adolescent females tend to want to be slimmer, whereas adolescent males often want to add weight and build muscle. Adolescents with a more positive body image have higher self-esteem.

6. How healthy are American adolescents?

Most American adolescents are healthy, but about one in five has a serious health problem. Most adolescent health problems stem from their lifestyle or risky behavior.

7. How many adolescents die? What are the causes of death among adolescents?

Death rates are greater for older adolescents and for male adolescents. Accidents, suicide, and homicide account for about three in four deaths among adolescents.

8. What are the nutritional needs of adolescents? What do they actually eat?

The average girl needs about 2,200 calories per day, and the average boy needs about 3,000 calories. Adolescents need high quantities of elements such as calcium, iron, zinc, magnesium, and nitrogen. Adolescents usually need more vitamins than they take in but less sugar, fat, protein, and sodium.

9. What are eating disorders?

The eating disorders include anorexia nervosa and bulimia nervosa. Anorexia nervosa is a life-threatening eating disorder characterized by fear of being overweight, a distorted body image, and refusal to eat. Bulimia nervosa is characterized by recurrent cycles of binge eating followed by dramatic measures to purge the food. Eating disorders mainly afflict women during adolescence and young adulthood.

10. What are the origins of the eating disorders?

Some psychoanalysts suggest that anorexia represents an unconscious effort to cope with sexual fears, particularly fear of pregnancy. Perhaps refusal to eat is a weapon against parents; parents of adolescents with eating disorders tend to have family conflict, to think that their daughters should lose weight, and to consider their daughters unattractive. One risk factor for eating disorders in adolescent females is a history of child abuse, particularly sexual abuse. Other psychologists connect eating disorders with fear of gaining weight due to cultural idealization of the slim female. Eating disorders tend to run in families, and there may be genetic factors that connect them with obsessionistic and perfectionistic personality styles. Even so, cultural influences could explain why perfectionism becomes associated with the desire to be thin. Anorexia is also frequently found together with depression, suggesting that both problems share genetic factors. Medication with antidepressants is often used to treat eating disorders, but cognitive behavioral therapy may help anorexic and bulimic individuals challenge their distorted body images and their perfectionism.

11. What is substance abuse? What is substance dependence?

Substance abuse is repeated use of a substance despite the social, occupational, psychological, or physical problems it causes. Substance dependence is characterized by loss of control over the substance. Biologically, dependence is typified by tolerance and withdrawal symptoms.

Recite Recite Recite Recite

12. What are the effects of depressants?

Depressants slow the activity of the nervous system. Alcohol lowers inhibitions, relaxes, and intoxicates—impairing cognitive functioning. Heroin can provide a strong euphoric "rush," although high doses can cause drowsiness and stupor. Barbiturates relieve anxiety and tension but lead rapidly to dependence.

13. What are the effects of stimulants?

Stimulants accelerate the heartbeat and other bodily functions. Nicotine is the stimulant in tobacco. Nicotine depresses the appetite and raises the metabolic rate, which is why some adolescents smoke to control their weight. The hydrocarbons ("tars") in cigarette smoke lead to lung cancer. The stimulant cocaine produces euphoria, reduces hunger, and bolsters self-confidence, but it also stimulates sudden rises in blood pressure, constricts coronary arteries, and thickens the blood—a combination that can result in respiratory and cardiovascular collapse. Students use amphetamines to remain awake for all-night cram sessions and to reduce hunger (that is, to diet).

14. What are the effects of hallucinogenics?

Hallucinogenics give rise to perceptual distortions called hallucinations. Marijuana helps some adolescents relax and elevates the mood, but strong intoxication can cause disorientation. Marijuana impairs perceptual-motor coordination and short-term memory. LSD—"acid"—produces vivid and colorful hallucinations. High doses may cause frightening hallucinations and paranoid delusions.

15. How widespread is substance abuse among adolescents?

About half of high school seniors have tried illicit drugs. Marijuana use seems to be on the rise. The majority of students have tried alcohol, and many use it regularly. About 30% of high school seniors have engaged in binge drinking.

16. How many adolescents disapprove of use of drugs?

Adolescents are more likely to disapprove of regular drug use than experimental drug use. Few disapprove of trying a drink or two, but most disapprove of daily drinking or binge drinking. Most seniors disapprove of regular use of LSD, cocaine, crack, heroin, amphetamines, and barbiturates. About 7 in 10 disapprove of smoking.

17. What factors are associated with substance abuse and dependence?

Substance abuse and dependence usually begin with experimental use in adolescence. Adolescents may experiment due to curiosity, conformity to peer pressure, parental use, rebelliousness, and a desire to escape from boredom or pressure and to seek excitement or pleasure. Adolescents who are dependent may use a substance to avoid withdrawal symptoms. Certain individuals may also have a genetic predisposition toward physiological dependence on various substances. Personality characteristics such as impulsiveness, rebelliousness, and low self-esteem also place adolescents at risk for substance abuse.

18. How can we treat and prevent substance abuse?

Treatment is difficult, and it is not clear which approaches are most effective. It may be relatively simple to help an adolescent through an abstinence syndrome (the process is called detoxification); it is more difficult to prevent relapse. Antidepressant drugs have shown some promise in reducing cravings for cocaine. Nicotine replacement therapy helps many quit smoking. Individuals addicted to heroin are often treated by replacing the heroin with methadone, which satisfies cravings for heroin without producing a "high." Treatment is often handled by laypeople or nonprofessionals, as in Alcoholics Anonymous (AA). Peer education increases adolescents' knowledge about drugs and often discourages abuse. Cognitive-behavioral approaches focus on modifying abusive and dependent ideas and behavior patterns. For example, they teach abusers to avoid temptation or to change their behavior when they experience temptation.

19. What kinds of sexually transmitted infections are there?

These include bacterial infections such as chlamydia, gonorrhea, and syphilis; viral infections such as HIV/AIDS, HPV, and genital herpes; and some others. There are

Recite Recite Recite Recite

nearly 4 million new chlamydia infections each year, and 1 million new HPV infections each year in the United States. The incidence of HIV/AIDS is lower, but HIV/AIDS is more deadly.

20. What factors place adolescents at risk for contracting STIs?

These include sexual activity itself, especially with multiple partners; failure to use condoms; and substance abuse. Sharing needles with an infected person can transmit HIV, and substance abuse is connected with other risky behaviors, such as unprotected sexual activity.

21. What can be done to prevent STIs?

Prevention involves education about the nature, modes of transmission, and risks of various STIs, along with advice concerning abstinence or "safer sex."

On the Web

Search Online With InfoTrac College Edition

For additional information, explore InfoTrac College Edition, your online library. Go to **http://www.infotrac-college.com** and use the passcode from the InfoTrac card that came with your book. Try these search terms: obesity in adolescence, puberty timing, eating disorders, drug abuse adolescence, depression in adolescence.

Visit Our Web Site

Go to **http://www.wadsworth.com/psychology** where you will find online resources directly linked to your book.

Child Development CD-ROM

Go to the Wadsworth Child Development CD-ROM for further study of the concepts in this chapter. The CD-ROM also includes quizzes and additional activities to expand your learning experience.

15 Adolescence: Cognitive Development

PowerPreview™

The Adolescent in Thought: My, My, How "Formal"

- **Piaget had some ideas** about why so many adolescents are obsessed with their privacy.
- **Many adolescents must think** of themselves as action heroes. They act as if they're made of steel. Can that be normal?
- **Are adolescent males** or females smarter? (At what? Are you sure?)

The Adolescent in Judgment: Moral Development

- **Don't try the "Yes, but"** defense with a 5-year-old. If you did it, you're guilty, even if it was an accident.
- **Which is more important?** "Whodunit" or "Why did he/she do it?"
- **According to one theorist**, people who have arrived at the highest level of moral development follow their own ethical principles and may choose to disobey the laws of the land.
- **What are the most important moral** principles to you—Freedom? Equality? Justice? Tolerance? How about absolute obedience to tradition?
- **Do girls or boys reach** a higher level of moral development? Many psychologists and educators have grave reservations about the views of one popular theorist.

The Adolescent in School: Dropping In, Dropping Out

- **Is the transition to high school** more difficult for boys or girls?
- **How many adolescents** drop out of high school? Why do they do it?

The Adolescent at Work: Career Development and Work Experience

- **A feminist remarked**, "I have yet to hear a man ask for advice on how to combine marriage and a career." What did she mean?
- **How many adolescents** work after school? Why do they do it?

I am a college student of extremely modest means. Some crazy psychologist interested in something called "formal operational thought" has just promised to pay me $20 if I can make a coherent logical argument for the proposition that the federal government should under no circumstances ever give or lend more to needy college students. Now what could people who believe *that* possibly say by way of supporting that argument? Well, I suppose they *could* offer this line of reasoning . . .

—Flavell et al., 2002

This "college student of extremely modest means" is thinking like an adolescent, quite differently from an elementary school child and differently from most middle schoolers. Children in the concrete-operational stage are bound by the facts as they are. They are not given to hypothetical thinking, to speculation about what might be. They are mainly stuck in what *is*. But the adolescent, like the adult, can ponder abstract ideas and see the world *as it could be*. Our "college student of extremely modest means" recognizes that a person can find arguments for causes in which he or she does not believe (Flavell et al., 2002).

In this chapter, we examine cognitive development in adolescence. We focus first on aspects of intellectual development, including Piaget's stage of formal operations, adolescent egocentrism, and gender differences. We then turn to an exploration of moral development, focusing on the views of Piaget, Kohlberg, and Gilligan. We conclude with a look at some areas that are strongly tied to cognitive development: school, vocational development, and work experience.

The Adolescent in Thought: My, My, How "Formal"

The growing intellectual capabilities of adolescents change the way they approach the world. The cognitive changes of adolescence influence how adolescents view themselves and their families and friends, as well as how they deal with broader social and moral questions. ***Question: What is cognitive development during adolescence like, according to Piaget's stage of formal operations?***

Piaget's Stage of Formal Operations

Click *Cognitive Development* in the Child and Adolescent CD-ROM for more on formal operations.

The stage of **formal operations** is the top level in Piaget's theory. Children or adolescents in this stage have reached cognitive maturity, even if some rough edges remain. Yet it can begin quite early—at about the time of puberty, 11 or 12 years—for many children in developed nations. But some reach this stage somewhat later, and some not at all.

Reflect

Do you engage in formal-operational thought? How so?

Piaget describes the accomplishments of the stage of formal operations in terms of the individual's increased ability to classify objects and ideas, engage in logical thought, and hypothesize—as researchers make hypotheses in their investigations. The adolescent in the stage of formal operations can think about abstract ideas as well as concrete objects. The adolescent can group and classify symbols, statements, even theories—just as we classify certain views of child development as psychoanalytic theories, learning theories, or sociocultural theories, even if they differ quite a bit in their particulars. Formal operations are flexible and reversible. Adolescents are thus capable of following and formulating arguments from their premises to their conclusions and back once more, even if they do not believe in them. Hypothetical thinking, the use of symbols to represent other symbols, and deductive reasoning allow the adolescent to more fully comprehend the real world and to play with the world that dwells within the mind alone.

formal operations The fourth stage in Piaget's cognitive-developmental theory, characterized by the capacity for flexible, reversible operations concerning abstract ideas and concepts, such as symbols, statements, and theories.

Hypothetical Thinking

In formal-operational thought, children—or, should we say, adolescents?—discover the concept of "what might be" rather than "what is." Adolescents can project themselves into situations that transcend their immediate experience; and,

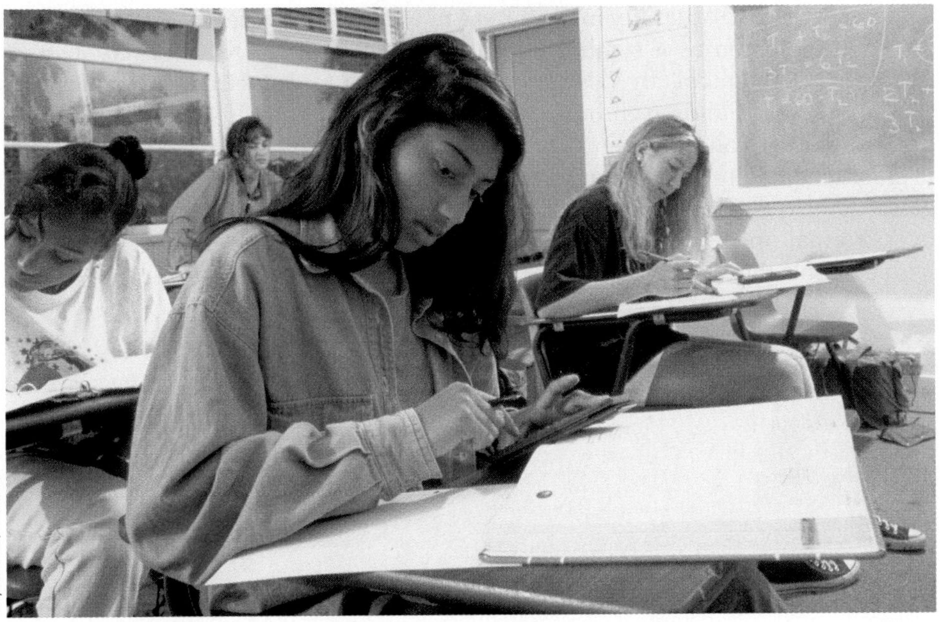

Tony Freeman/PhotoEdit

Formal Operations

The ability to deal with the abstract and the hypothetical and the capacity to engage in deductive reasoning are the key features of formal-operational thought. Formal-operational thinking allows adolescents to engage in scientific reasoning.

for this reason, they may become wrapped up in lengthy fantasies. Many adolescents can explore endless corridors of the mind, perceiving what would happen as one decision leads to another point where a choice presents itself—and then still another decision is made. Adolescents become aware that situations can have different outcomes. They can think ahead, systematically trying out various possibilities in their minds.

You may think of scientists as people in white laboratory coats, with advanced degrees and devotion to exploring uncharted territory. And some are like that, of course. But many more wear blue jeans and experiment with their hair and ways of relating to people they find attractive. Many adolescents in the stage of formal operations consider themselves to be uninterested in science, yet they conduct research daily to see whether their hypotheses about themselves and their friends and teachers are correct. These are not laboratory experiments that involve calipers or Bunsen burners. It is more common for adolescents to explore uncharted territory by trying on different clothes and "attitudes" to see which work best for them. When I was in my teens, I experimented with my hair (buzz cut, parting it on the side, or a John Travolta–"Grease" pompadour), my "attitude" (whether I should be emotional or "cool"—cool, it turned out, wasn't the real me), and whether I would increase my attractiveness to girls by acting interested in them or indifferent to them (indifferent wasn't me either).

Adolescents, who can look ahead to multiple outcomes, may also see varieties of possibilities for themselves. Some become acutely aware that they have the capacity, to a large extent, to create or fashion themselves according to their own images of what they are capable of becoming. In terms of career decisions, the wealth of possible directions leads some adolescents to experience anxiety about whether they will pick the one career that really *is* them and to experience a sense of loss about the fact that they probably will have the opportunity to choose only one.

This capacity to look ahead, to fashion futures, also frequently leads to **utopian** thinking. Just as adolescents can foresee many possibilities for themselves, they can also imagine different outcomes for suffering humanity. "What if" thinking enables adolescents to fashion schemes for putting an end to hunger, disease, and international strife.

Sophisticated Use of Symbols

Children in elementary school can understand what is meant by abstract symbols such as 1 and 2. They can also perform operations in which numbers are manipulated—added, subtracted, and so on. But now consider X, that unknown (and

utopian Referring to an ideal vision of society.

sometimes evasive) quantity in algebra. *X* may be a familiar letter of the alphabet, but its designation as a symbol for an unknown quantity is a formal abstract operation. One symbol (an *X*) is being made to stand for something just as abstract (the unknown). Children through the age of 11 or 12 or so usually cannot fully understand this concept, even if they can be taught the mechanics of solving for *X* in simple equations. But older, formal-operational children show a sophisticated grasp of the nature of symbols that allows them to grasp intuitively what is meant by *X*. Formal-operational children, or adolescents, can perform mental operations with symbols that stand for nothing in their own experience.

A Closer Look

The Puzzle and the Pendulum

If you hang a weight from a string and set it swinging back and forth, you have a pendulum. Bärbel Inhelder and Jean Piaget (1959) used a pendulum to explore ways in which children of different ages go about solving problems.

The researchers showed children several pendulums, with different lengths of string and with different weights at their ends, as in Figure 15.1. They attached the strings to rods and sent the weights swinging. They dropped the weights from various heights and pushed them with different amounts of force. The question they posed—the puzzle—was, What determines how fast the pendulum will swing back and forth?

The researchers had varied four factors:

1. the amount of weight
2. the length of the string
3. the height from which the weight was released
4. the force with which the weight was pushed

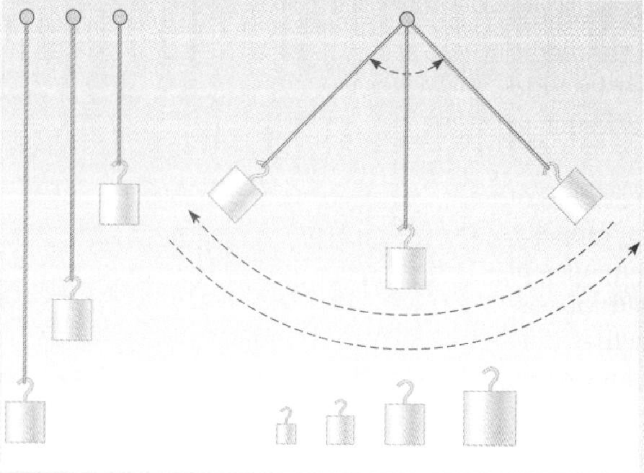

Figure 15.1
The Pendulum Problem

What determines how fast the pendulum will swing back and forth? The amount of weight? The length of the string? The height from which the weight is released? The force with which the weight is pushed? Or a combination of the above? Formal-operational children attempt to exclude each factor systematically.

The answer lies in either one of these factors or in some combination of them. That is, one factor, two factors, three factors, or all four factors could determine the speed of the pendulum. The answer could be expressed as 1, 2, 3, or 4; or 1 and 2, 1 and 3, 1 and 4; 2 and 3, and so on.

One could try to solve this problem by deduction based on principles of physics, and experienced physicists might prefer a deductive, mathematical approach. However, one can also arrive at a solution by trying out each possible combination of factors and observing the results. This is an empirical approach. Since children (and most adults) are not physicists, they will usually take the empirical approach.

Of the children observed by Inhelder and Piaget, those between the ages of 8 and 13 could not arrive at the correct answer. The fault lay largely in their approach, which was only partly systematic. They made some effort to account for the various factors but did not control carefully for every single possibility. For example, one child compared a pendulum with a light weight and a short string to a pendulum with a heavy weight and a long string. They swung at different speeds, and so the child concluded that both factors, weight and length, were involved. After narrowing the problem to the two factors, the child did not attempt to control for weight by switching weights while holding the length constant.

The 14- and 15-year-olds generally sat back and reflected for a while before doing anything. Then, in contrast to the younger children, who haphazardly varied multiple factors at the same time, the older children attempted to exclude each factor systematically. You could say that they used the "process of elimination," as we often do with multiple-choice tests. Not all of the 14–15-year-olds solved the problem; but as a group, their approach was more advanced and more likely to succeed.

According to Inhelder and Piaget, the approach of the 14- and 15-year-olds was characteristic of formal-operational thought. The approach of the 8–13-year-olds was characteristic of concrete-operational thought. As with many other aspects of Piaget's views and methods, we have to be flexible about Piaget's age estimates for ability to solve the problem. Robert Siegler and his associates (1973), for example, were able to train 10-year-olds to approach the problem systematically and isolate the correct answer (drum roll!): the length of the string. Thus education and training can influence the development of cognitive skills.

These symbols include the symbols found in geometry. Adolescents work with points that have no dimensions, lines that have no width and are infinite in length, and circles that are perfectly round, even though they may never find them in nature. The ability they obtain to manipulate these symbols will eventually permit them to do work in theoretical physics or math or to obtain jobs in engineering or architecture. They learn to apply symbols to the world of tangible objects and materials.

Formal-operational individuals can also understand, appreciate, and sometimes produce metaphors. Metaphors are figures of speech in which words or phrases that ordinarily signify one thing are applied to another. We find endless examples of metaphor in literature, but consider for a moment how everyday figures of speech enhance and transform our experience: *squeezing* out a living, *basking in the sunshine* of fame or glory, *hanging by a thread, jumping* to conclusions, and so on.

Consider the sentence "The ship plowed through the water." A plow is an instrument that furrows the soil. Portraying a ship as plowing through water suggests a comparison between the ship and the plow and creates an image of cutting through and turning up water, as the plow does to the soil. Metaphors play with words as symbols. Words are poetically assimilated to new schemes (as plowing is assimilated to our understanding of the movements of ships). But accommodation also occurs as the schemes are transformed in the process; the plowing metaphor transforms our image of the ship. The adaptation of words as metaphors requires the mental flexibility to associate words with situations that are perceived as having some property in common (for example, the common movements of the ship and plow).

Deductive Reasoning

Formal-operational individuals can reason deductively. Consider this frequently cited **syllogism:** "All people are mortal. Socrates is a person. Therefore, Socrates is mortal." Formal-operational people can follow the logical process in this syllogism. First, a statement is made about a class or group of objects ("All people are mortal"). Second, a particular object or event (in this case, Socrates) is assigned to that class—that is, "Socrates is a person." Finally, it is concluded, or deduced,[1] that what is true for the class (people) is also true for the particular object or event (Socrates)—that is, "Socrates is mortal."

The moral judgments of many adolescents and adults are based on formal-operational thought. That is, they derive their judgments about what is right and wrong in specific situations by reasoning deductively from general moral principles. Their capacity for decentration also allows them to take a broad view of the situation. That is, they can focus on many aspects of a situation at once in arriving at their judgments and solving moral dilemmas.

The enhanced cognitive abilities can backfire when they lead adolescents to adamantly advance their religious, political, and social ideas without recognition of the subtleties and practical issues that may give pause to adults. Following the attack of September 11, 2001, on the World Trade Center, in which 15 of the 19 terrorists were Saudi Arabians, I heard many adolescents saying things like "Let's just nuke them!" or "Let's nuke 'em all!" When I asked them what they meant, some said they meant to vaporize all of Saudi Arabia, others referred to the Arab world in general, and still others to all Muslims. The deductive logic was clear yet oversimplified: "It is wrong to kill people. They (Saudi Arabians, Arabs, Muslims) killed Americans. They are wrong and must be punished." The nature of the punishment was based on the Golden Rule: "Do unto them as . . ." Many adolescents with whom I spoke were not interested in distinguishing between the terrorists and Saudi Arabians, Arabs, or Muslims in general. Nor were they thinking about the complex political problems and moral questions that were raised by their urges. Some adolescents were not even particularly interested in distinguishing among men, women, and children, or among nations and regimes and terrorists.

[1]Look, this is a college textbook, so I'm required to use technical terms like these.

syllogism A type of reasoning in which two statements or premises are set forth and a logical conclusion is drawn from them.

Adolescents' new intellectual powers often present them with what seem to be crystal-clear solutions to the world's problems, and they may become intolerant of the relative stodginess of their parents. Their own brilliant images of how to reform the world cause them to be unsympathetic to their parents' earthbound pursuit of a livelihood and other mundane matters.

Reevaluation of Piaget's Theory

Piaget's account of formal operations has received quite a bit of support. There appears to be little question that unique changes do occur in the nature of reasoning between preadolescence and adolescence (Mueller, Sokol, & Overton, 1999; Mueller, Overton, & Reese, 2001). For example, research strongly supports Piaget's view that the capacity to reason deductively does not emerge until adolescence (Mueller, Sokol, & Overton, 1999; Mueller, Overton, & Reese, 2001).

But critics have pointed out some limitations in Piaget's views about formal operations (Keating, 1991; Kuhn, 1991). For one thing, formal-operational thought does not appear to be a universal step in cognitive development. The ability to solve abstract problems, such as those found in algebra and the pendulum problem, is much more likely to be developed in technologically oriented Western societies or in major cities than in rural areas or less-well-developed nations (Keating & Clark, 1980; Super, 1980). Moreover, formal-operational thought may occur later than Piaget thought, if at all. For example, many early adolescents (ages 13 to 16) still perform better on concrete problems than on abstract ones (Markovitz & Vachon, 1990). And reviews of the literature (Keating, 1991; Leadbeater, 1991) suggest that formal-operational thought is found only among 40–60% of first-year college students. Also, the same individual may do well on one type of formal-operational task and poorly on another. We are more likely to use formal-operational thought in the academic areas on which we focus. Some of us are formal operational in math or science, but not in the study of literature, and vice versa. Piaget (1972) himself admitted that although formal reasoning is within the grasp of adolescents, they may not always demonstrate it because they lack familiarity with a particular task.

Adolescent Egocentrism

Did you think that egocentrism was limited to the thought of preschool children, who show difficulty taking the perspective of other people in the three-mountains test? Wrong. Yes, teenagers are capable of hypothetical thinking, and they can argue for causes in which they do not believe (if you pay them enough to do so). However, there are also a number of ways in which they show a somewhat different brand of egocentrism (Elkind, 1967, 1985). Adolescents comprehend the ideas of other people but have difficulty sorting out those things that concern other people from the things that concern themselves. ***Question: How is adolescent egocentrism shown in the imaginary audience and in the personal fable?***

Reflect

Did you have a strong need for privacy when you were an adolescent? If so, why?

Click *Cognitive Development* for more on the imaginary audience.

The Imaginary Audience

Many adolescents fantasize about becoming rock stars or movie stars who are adored by millions. The concept of the **imaginary audience** achieves part of that fantasy—sort of. It places the adolescent on stage—surrounded by critics, however, more than by admirers. Adolescents assume that other people are concerned with their appearance and behavior, much more so than they really are (Milstead et al., 1993; Vartanian, 2001). So adolescents feel on stage, with countless eyes on them.

The intense desire for privacy that often emerges during adolescence may be a by-product of the concept of the imaginary audience. The concept helps explain why teenagers are so preoccupied with their appearance. It helps explain why the mirror is the constant companion of the teenager, who grooms endlessly, searches out every facial blemish, and agonizes over every zit. This preoccupation with the mirror seems to peak sometime during the eighth grade and decline over the remainder of the course of adolescence. Girls tend to be relatively more caught up in their appear-

imaginary audience The belief that others around us are as concerned with our thoughts and behaviors as we are; one aspect of adolescent egocentrism.

ance than boys are, perhaps because society places more emphasis on a girl's complexion and other aspects of her appearance (Elkind & Bowen, 1979; Vartanian, 2001).

Michael Newman/PhotoEdit

■ **The Imaginary Audience**

Adolescents tend to feel that other people are continuously scrutinizing their appearance and behavior. This may explain why so many adolescents worry about every facial blemish and spend long hours grooming.

The Personal Fable

Wesley Snipes and Lara Croft, stand aside! Due to the **personal fable,** many adolescents become action heroes, at least in their own minds. If the imaginary audience puts adolescents on stage, the personal fable justifies their being there. The personal fable, another aspect of adolescent egocentrism, is the belief that one's thoughts and emotions are special and unique. It also refers to the common adolescent belief in immortality—that one is invulnerable, like Superman or Superwoman. The personal fable is connected with behaviors such as showing off and risk taking (Arnett, 1992; Lapsley, 1990, 1991; Milstead et al., 1993). Many adolescents assume that they can smoke with impunity. Cancer? "It can't happen to me." They drive recklessly. They engage in spontaneous unprotected sexual activity, assuming that sexually transmitted infections (STIs) and unwanted pregnancies happen to other people, not to them. Ronald King (2000) of the HIV Community Coalition of Washington, DC, puts it this way: "All youth—rich, poor, black, white—have this sense of invincibility, invulnerability." Adolescents are much more likely than their parents to minimize the risk of an activity (Adler, 1993b).

The specialness and uniqueness of the adolescent experience? Many adolescents believe that their parents and other adults—even their age-mates—could never feel what they are feeling or even know what they feel: the depth of their experiences, their passions. "You just don't understand me!" claims the adolescent. But, at least often enough, we do.

Reflect

Did you ever believe that you were unique or invulnerable during adolescence? You are unique, of course, but did a belief in invulnerability ever have a harmful effect on your behavior?

Click *Cognitive Development* for more on personal fable.

■ Gender Differences in Cognitive Abilities

Although females and males do not differ in overall intelligence, gender differences do appear in certain cognitive abilities starting in childhood (Halpern & LaMay, 2000). ***Question: What are the gender differences in cognitive abilities?*** Females are somewhat superior to males in verbal ability. Males, on the other hand, seem somewhat superior in visual-spatial ability. The picture for mathematics ability is more complex, with females excelling in some areas and males excelling in others (Anderman et al., 2001). Let's take a closer look at these gender differences.

Verbal Ability

Verbal abilities include a large number of language skills, such as reading, spelling, grammar, oral comprehension, and word fluency. As a group, females surpass males in verbal ability (Halpern & LaMay, 2000). These differences show up early. Girls seem to acquire language faster than boys. They make more prelinguistic vocalizations, utter their first word sooner, and develop larger vocabularies. Later in childhood, the differences are smaller and more inconsistent (Hyde & Linn, 1988). Boys in the United States are more likely than girls to be dyslexic (Halpern & LaMay, 2000). They also are more likely to have other reading problems, such as reading below grade level. In high school, girls continue to perform better than boys in reading and writing skills (Mullis et al., 1991).

Why do females excel in verbal abilities? For one thing, parents talk more to their infant daughters than to their infant sons (see Chapter 7). This encouragement of verbal interaction may be connected with girls' relative verbal precocity. Because

personal fable The belief that our feelings and ideas are special and unique and that we are invulnerable; one aspect of adolescent egocentrism.

of this early language advantage, girls may rely more on verbal skills to interact with people, thus furthering their abilities in this area (Halpern & LaMay, 2000). How do we account for gender differences in reading? Biological factors such as the organization of the brain may play a role, but do not discount cultural factors. One issue is whether a culture stamps reading as a gender-neutral, masculine, or feminine activity (Matlin, 2002). Consider Nigeria and England. Reading is looked upon as a masculine activity in these nations, and boys traditionally surpass girls in reading (and other academic) skills in Nigeria and England. In the United States and Canada, however, reading tends to be stereotyped as feminine, and girls tend to excel in reading in these nations. People of all ages and all cultures tend to apply themselves more diligently to pursuits that they believe are "meant" for them—whether it be the life of the nomad, ballet, ice hockey, or reading.

Visual-Spatial Ability

Visual-spatial ability refers to the ability to visualize objects or shapes and to mentally manipulate and rotate them. As you can imagine, this ability is important in such fields as art, architecture, and engineering. Boys begin to outperform girls on many types of visual-spatial tasks starting at age 8 or 9, and the difference persists into adulthood (Cai & Chen, 2000; Halpern & LaMay, 2000; Loranger et al., 2000). The gender difference is greatest on **mental rotation** tasks (see Figure 15.2), which require imagining how objects will look if rotated in space (Scali, Brownlow, & Hicks, 2000). Somewhat smaller differences are found on tests of spatial perception, which may involve the ability to identify the horizontal or vertical in spite of distracting information (Liben, 1991). For example, individuals may be shown a partially filled glass and asked to anticipate the position of the water when the glass is tilted at various positions (see Figure 15.2).

What is the basis for the gender difference in visual-spatial skills? A number of biological and environmental explanations have been offered. One biological theory that has received some attention is that visual-spatial ability is influenced by sex-linked recessive genes on the X sex chromosome. But this theory has not been supported by research (Halpern & LaMay, 2000).

There also are some interesting suggestions that the timing of puberty is linked to development of visual-spatial skills. Researchers have found that late maturers, whether boys or girls, perform better than early maturers on tests of visual-spatial ability (Dubas, 1991). And so late maturation would seem to favor development of visual-spatial skills. Boys usually mature later than girls do (see Chapter 14), a timing factor that could account for their (common but far from universal) superiority in visual-spatial skills.

Other research links sex hormone levels to visual-spatial performance (Hines, 1990; Kimura, 1992). For example, high levels of prenatal androgens have been linked to better performance on visual-spatial and arithmetic tasks among 4- and 6-year-old girls (Finegan, Niccols, & Sitarenios, 1992; Jacklin et al., 1988). One study (Kimura & Hampson, 1992) found that women performed better on visual-spatial tasks when their estrogen levels were low than when estrogen levels were high. (By contrast, they were better on tasks involving verbal skills or motor coordination when estrogen levels were high than when they were low.)

A number of environmental theories also have been proposed to account for the gender difference in visual-spatial skills. One theory is based on the assumption that just as reading is considered feminine in our culture, visual-spatial activities are stereotyped as masculine. (Just think of such visual-spatial activities as throwing a football, basketball, or baseball or building model planes and cars.) If we further assume that individuals perform better on cognitive tasks that match their self-image, then females and males with more masculine self-concepts should perform better on visual-spatial tasks (Halpern & LaMay, 2000). There is some support for this view (Krasnoff, Walker, & Howard, 1989; Newcombe & Dubas, 1992). For example, college women and men whose self-descriptions include many stereotypical masculine traits or few stereotypical feminine traits perform better on visual-spatial tasks (Signorella &

mental rotation Imagining how objects will look if they are rotated in space.

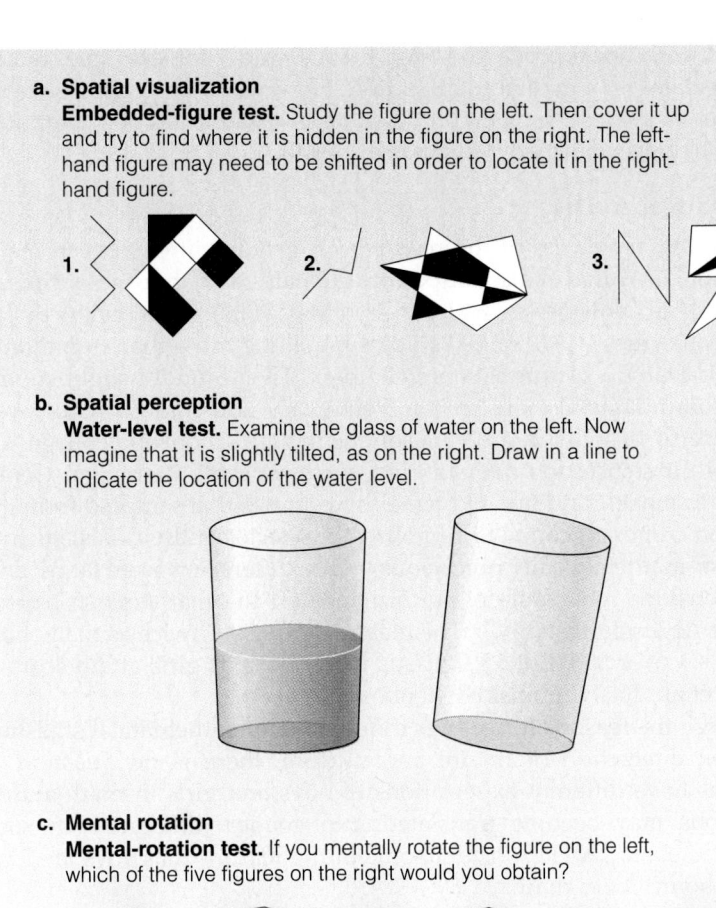

a. Spatial visualization

Embedded-figure test. Study the figure on the left. Then cover it up and try to find where it is hidden in the figure on the right. The left-hand figure may need to be shifted in order to locate it in the right-hand figure.

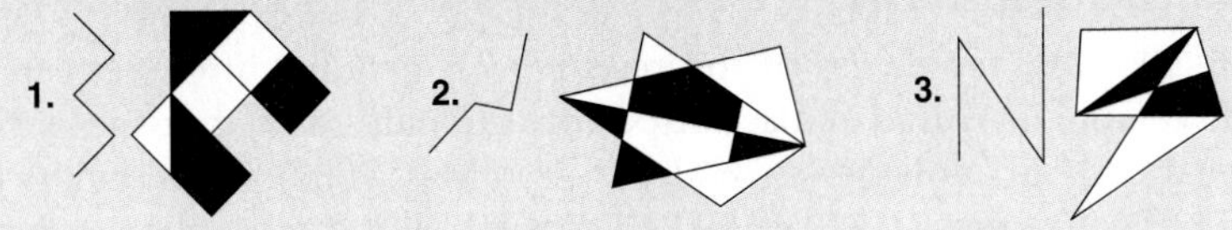

b. Spatial perception

Water-level test. Examine the glass of water on the left. Now imagine that it is slightly tilted, as on the right. Draw in a line to indicate the location of the water level.

c. Mental rotation

Mental-rotation test. If you mentally rotate the figure on the left, which of the five figures on the right would you obtain?

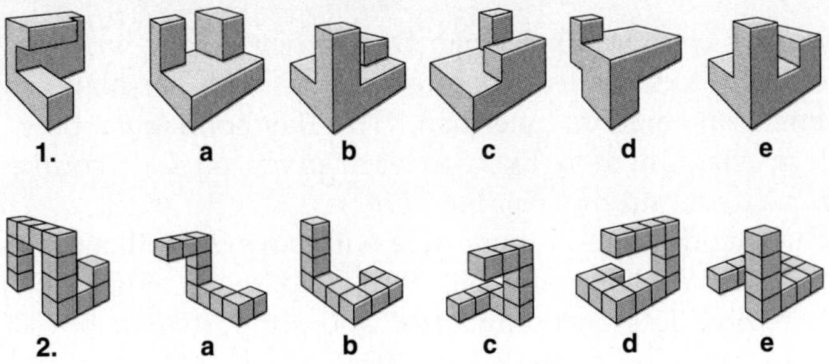

The answers to these three tests appear below.

Answers: a. 1: Orient the pattern as if it were a tilted capital M, with the left portion along the top of the white triangle. 2: This pattern fits along the right sides of the two black triangles on the left. 3: Rotate this figure about 100° to the right, so that it forms a Z, with the top line coinciding with the top line of the top white triangle. **b.** The line should be horizontal, not tilted. **c.** 1: c; 2: d.

Figure 15.2
Examples of Tests Used to Measure Visual-Spatial Ability

No gender differences are found on spatial visualization tasks (A). Boys do somewhat better than girls on tasks measuring spatial perception (B). The gender difference is greatest on mental rotation tasks (C). What are some possible reasons for these differences?

Source: Matlin, 2002.

Frieze, 1989). (Yes, yes, I hear you saying that this data is correlational and not experimental. Therefore, whatever influences lead to seeing oneself as having masculine or feminine traits could also lead to differential performance on visual-spatial tasks.)

Another related environmental theory is that gender stereotypes also influence the amount and type of spatial experiences children obtain. Gender-stereotyped "boys' toys," such as blocks, Legos, and Erector sets, provide more practice with spatial skills than gender-stereotyped "girls' toys." Boys also are more likely to engage in sports, which involve moving balls and other objects through space. Boys are also allowed to travel farther from home than girls are, providing greater opportunities for exploration (Halpern & LaMay, 2000). Several studies have found that participation in spatially related activities is associated with better performance on visual-spatial tasks (Newcombe & Dubas, 1992; Voyer, Nolan, & Voyer, 2000). Further evidence of the importance of experience in developing visual-spatial skills comes from studies showing that visual-spatial ability can be improved with appropriate training. In one study, for example, males outperformed females on a mental rotation task. However, both groups were then given 15 minutes of training in mental rotation tasks with the aid of a computer, and the gender difference vanished (Larson et al., 1999).

Mathematical Ability

Until recently, reviewers of the research on gender differences in mathematical ability concluded that males outperform females and that these differences first appear early in adolescence (Halpern & LaMay, 2000). But a review by Janet Hyde and her colleagues (1990) of 100 studies involving more than 3 million individuals reveals that the picture is more complex. They found a slight superiority for girls in computational skills in the elementary and middle school years. Boys began to perform better in problem solving in high school and college. There were no gender differences in understanding math concepts at any age. Gender differences were smallest and favored females in studies that sampled from the general population. Among groups of more highly selected individuals, such as college students or mathematically precocious youth, differences were larger and favored males. Consider, for example, performance on the mathematics portion of the Scholastic Aptitude Test (SAT). The mean score is 500. Twice as many boys as girls attain scores over 500. But 13 times as many boys as girls attain scores over 700 (Benbow et al., 2000; Lubinski & Benbow, 1992).

Although the reasons for gender differences in mathematical skills may reflect a complex interaction of nature and nurture, there is no question that most Americans have different expectations of boys and girls in math and that these expectations may become translated into gender differences in socialization (Anderman et al., 2001). Consider some of the reasons that boys are likely to feel more "at home" with math:

- Mom may be more likely than Dad to help Missy write an essay, but Dad is more likely to be called upon to help her with her homework with fractions, decimals, and algebra (Sherman, 1983; Raymond & Benbow, 1986).
- Male teachers are more likely to teach advanced math courses—algebra, geometry, calculus, and the like (Fox, 1982).
- Teachers tend to spend more time with boys in math and to expect more from them (AAUW, 1992; Fennema, 1990; Halpern & LaMay, 2000).
- Girls receive less encouragement and support than boys from parents and peers for studying math (Eccles, 1993).

Is Math in the "Male Domain"?

Despite egalitarian trends, teachers and parents still sometimes convey the message that math is not for girls. For example, math teachers still tend to spend more time instructing and interacting with boys than with girls. Has the day arrived to end all this? How can we do it? (The "we" in the last sentence = You + Me. I'm writing this book and identifying the problem. What is your role?)

- As early as first grade, parents in the United States, China, and Japan believe that boys are better at math than girls (Lummis & Stevenson, 1990).
- Parents are more likely to buy math and science books for boys than for girls (Eccles, 1993).

Given these typical experiences with math, we should not be surprised that

- By middle school, boys see themselves as being better in math than girls, even when their mastery and grades are identical (Watt & Bornholt, 2000).
- By middle school, students perceive math as being part of the male domain (Correll, 2001; Watt & Bornholt, 2000).
- By middle school boys are more likely to perceive math as playing a useful role in their lives (Meece et al., 1982).
- Whereas boys are likely to have a positive self-concept in terms of math, girls are more likely to experience anxiety about math (Osborne, 2001).
- High school and college women take fewer math courses than males do and are less likely to pursue careers in math or related fields, even when they excel in them (Chipman et al., 1992; Watt & Bornholt, 2000).

A Cautionary Note

In sum, it does appear that within our culture, girls show greater verbal ability than boys do, whereas boys show greater visual-spatial ability than girls. Girls excel in certain areas of mathematics, whereas boys excel in others. However, two factors should caution us not to attach too much importance to these gender differences. First, in most cases they are very small (Caplan & Caplan, 1994; Halpern & LaMay, 2000). Boys and girls are much more similar in their cognitive abilities than they are different. In recent years, the size of the gender difference in verbal, visual-spatial, and mathematical abilities has become even smaller (Barnett & Hyde, 2001; Feingold, 1993).

Second, gender differences in cognitive skills are *group differences*, not individual differences. That is, the difference in, say, reading skills between a male who reads well and a male who is dyslexic is much greater than the group average distance between males and females in reading ability. Moreover, despite group differences, millions of females exceed the average American male in math and in visual-spatial skills. Similarly, despite group differences, millions of males exceed the average American female in writing and spelling. Hundreds of thousands of American women are performing excellently in domains that had once been considered masculine, such as medicine and law (Glater, 2001).

Review

(1) The stage of ________ operations is the final one in Piaget's scheme. (2) The flexibility and reversibility of ________ allow adolescents to follow arguments from premises to conclusions and back again. (3) Adolescents may become wrapped up in ________ because they can project themselves into situations that transcend their immediate experience. (4) Formal-operational thinking is found in the mathematical disciplines of ________ and geometry and in the use of metaphor. (5) Formal-operational individuals can reason ________, as in the case of the syllogism. (6) Adolescent egocentrism is connected with the concepts of the imaginary audience and the personal ________. (7) Females are somewhat (superior or inferior?) to males in verbal ability. (8) Males are somewhat (superior or inferior?) in visual-spatial ability. (9) Research links levels of ________ hormone levels to visual-spatial performance.

Pulling It Together: What types of academic activities are considered to be in the masculine or feminine "domain"? How might this stereotyping affect adolescents' performance in these activities?

The Adolescent in Judgment: Moral Development

Moral development in childhood and adolescence is a complex issue, with both cognitive and behavioral aspects. On a cognitive level, moral development concerns whether children and adolescents can deduce judgments of right and wrong from social principles. In this section, we examine the contributions of Jean Piaget and Lawrence Kohlberg to our understanding of the cognitive aspects of moral development.

Piaget and Kohlberg argued that moral reasoning undergoes a universal and invariant cognitive-developmental pattern. The moral considerations that children weigh at a given age are likely to reflect the values of the social and cultural settings in which they are being reared. However, moral reasoning is also theorized to reflect the orderly unfolding of cognitive processes (Navaez et al., 1999). Patterns of moral reasoning are related to the individual's overall cognitive development. ***Question: How does Piaget view the development of moral reasoning?***

Piaget's Theory of Moral Development

Click *Select Theorist* for more on Piaget's theory of moral development.

In a sense, child morality throws light on adult morality. If we want to form men and women, nothing will fit us so well for the task as to study the laws that govern their formation (Piaget, 1932, p. 9).

For years, Piaget observed children playing games like marbles and making judgments on the seriousness of the wrongdoing of characters in stories. On the basis of these observations, he concluded that children's moral judgments develop in two major overlapping stages: the stages of moral realism and autonomous morality (1932).

Reflect

Why is moral development discussed in the chapter on cognitive development rather than in the chapter on social and emotional development?

The Stage of Moral Realism

The earlier stage is usually referred to as the stage of **moral realism,** or of **objective morality.** During this stage, which emerges at about the age of 5, children consider behavior to be correct when it conforms to authority or to the rules of the game. When asked why something should be done in a certain way, the 5-year-old may answer "Because that's the way to do it" or "Because my Mommy says so." [2]

At the age of 5 or so, children perceive rules as somehow embedded in the structure of the universe. Rules, to them, reflect ultimate reality. Hence, the term *moral realism*. Rules and right and wrong are seen as unchanging and absolute. They are not seen as deriving from people to meet group needs. Realism may reflect the egocentrism of the preoperational child, who frequently assumes that thoughts and mental representations are exact equivalents of external reality.

Another consequence of viewing rules as embedded in the fabric of the world is **immanent justice,** or automatic retribution. Punishment is perceived as structurally connected to wrongdoing. Therefore, punishment is inevitable. Five- or 6-year-old children who lie or steal usually believe that they will be found out or at least punished for their acts. If they become ill or trip and scrape their knees, they may assume that this outcome represents punishment for a recent transgression.

Preoperational children also tend to focus on only one dimension at a time. They judge the wrongness of an act only in terms of the amount of damage done, not in terms of the intentions of the wrongdoer. Children in the stage of moral realism are tough jurors indeed. They do not excuse the person who harms by accident. As an illustration, consider children's response to Piaget's story about the broken cups. Piaget told children a story in which one child breaks 15 cups accidentally and

moral realism According to Piaget, the stage during which children judge acts as moral when they conform to authority or to the rules of the game. Morality at this stage is perceived as embedded in the structure of the universe.

objective morality The perception of morality as objective—that is, as existing outside the cognitive functioning of people; a characteristic of Piaget's stage of moral realism.

immanent justice The view that retribution for wrongdoing is a direct consequence of the wrongdoing, reflective of the belief that morality is embedded within the structure of the universe.

[2]The author's wife wishes to go on record as supporting the view that "Because Mommy says so" is the rule in the author's house and has been shown, over time, to be the wisest reason for doing something or believing something. The author wishes to go on record as saying that . . . in order to avert domestic disaster, he will not take issue with his wife's remarks.

another child breaks 1 cup deliberately. Which child is naughtiest? Which should be punished most? Children in the stage of moral realism typically say that the child who did the most damage is the naughtiest and should be punished most. The amount of damage is more important than the child's intentions (Piaget, 1932).

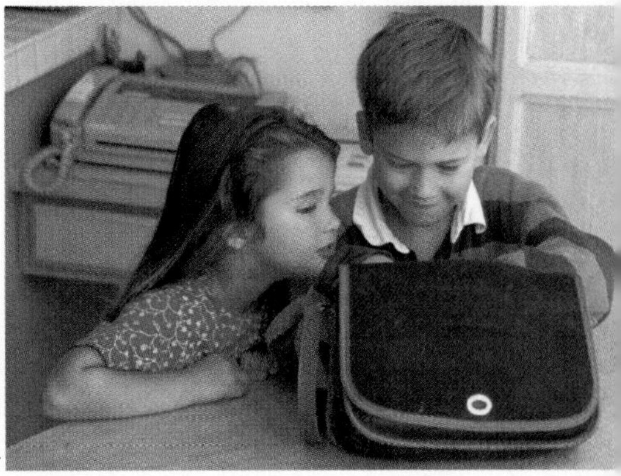

Spencer Grant/PhotoEdit

Moral Realism

It looks bad, but Mom asked them to find her car keys. Mom wasn't thinking of having them go through her purse, however. If they break things or drop them on the floor in the effort, are the children being "bad"? Children in the stage of moral realism would say "yes" because they focus on the amount of damage done, not on the intentions of the wrongdoer.

The Stage of Autonomous Morality

Piaget found that when children reach the ages of 9 to 11, they begin to show **autonomous morality.** Their moral judgments tend to become more *autonomous*, or self-governed. The tendency to strictly interpret social rules declines. Children come to view these rules as arbitrary agreements that can be changed. Children no longer automatically view obedience to authority figures as right. They realize that circumstances can require breaking the rules.

Children who show autonomous morality are capable of flexible operational thought. They show decentration in their ability to focus simultaneously on multiple dimensions. And so they consider not only social rules, but also the motives of the wrongdoer and the demands of the situation.

Children in this stage also show a greater capacity to take the point of view of others, to empathize with them. Decentration and increased empathy prompt children to weigh the intentions of the wrongdoer more heavily than the amount of damage done. The child who broke 1 cup deliberately may be seen as deserving of more punishment than the child who broke 15 cups accidentally. Children now become capable of considering mitigating circumstances. Accidents are less likely to be considered crimes.

Piaget assumed that autonomous morality usually develops as a result of cooperative peer relationships. But he also believed that parents help foster autonomous morality when they attempt to establish more egalitarian relationships with their children and explain the rationales for social rules.

Evaluation of Piaget's Theory of Moral Development

Many researchers agree that children's moral development proceeds from a stage of moral realism to one of autonomous morality (Hoffman, 1988; Karniol, 1980; Shultz, 1980). A number have found that very young children do make moral judgments on the basis of the consequences of an act, rather than on the intentions of the wrongdoer (Brandt & Strattner-Gregory, 1980).

Still, there are some problems with Piaget's views. One is that many more issues than the amount of damage done and the intentions of the transgressor influence children's moral judgments (Rest, 1983; Smetana, 1985). These include the ultimate outcomes of the acts, whether the object of wrongdoing was an object or a person, whether the effects of the act were physical or psychological, and so on.

Another criticism centers on Piaget's age estimates and on the demand characteristics of his research methods. A number of studies suggest, for example, that most children show autonomous morality prior to the age of 9. Piaget's experimental stories, such as the story of the cups, require that children remember the intentions of two people and the outcomes of two acts. Young children cannot process all this information simultaneously. But when the situations are described one at a time or when intentions are more clearly outlined, many 5- and 6-year-olds consider the intentions of the wrongdoer in passing their moral judgments (Feldman et al., 1976; S. A. Nelson, 1980; Surber, 1977).

One study asked children of ages 5, 8, 9, and 11 to judge the wrongness of lies. All age groups considered both the amount of damage done by the lie and the intentions of the liar (Peterson, Peterson, & Seeto, 1983). Lies that did no harm were judged less serious than harmful lies, but selfishly motivated lies were judged as worse than unintended lies and lies that were intended to please the listener. However, the 11-year-olds explained the wrongness of lying in terms of violation of trust and fairness in relationships. Younger children referred to the likelihood of being caught and punished. So, in this study there were clear cognitive developments. Younger children judged social behavior in terms of rewards and punishments, and older children relied on abstract ethical principles that govern

Reflect

"Accidents happen," and when they do, we adults do not blame the perpetrator—or do we? For example, are the effects of some accidents so enormous that we blame the perpetrator? Explain.

Click *Select Theorist* for more on evaluating Piaget's theory of moral develpoment.

autonomous morality The second stage in Piaget's cognitive-developmental theory of moral development. In this stage, children base moral judgments on the intentions of the wrongdoer, as well as on the amount of damage done. Social rules are viewed as agreements that can be changed.

social relationships. But these developmental changes were not reflected in a clear transition from moral realism to autonomous morality.

Kohlberg's Theory of Moral Development

Click *Select Theorist* for more on Kohlberg's theory of moral development.

Question: What is Kohlberg's theory of moral development? Lawrence Kohlberg (1981, 1985) advanced the cognitive-developmental theory of moral development by elaborating on the kinds of information children use, as well as on the complexities of moral reasoning. Before we discuss Kohlberg's views, read the tale that Kohlberg used in his research, and answer the questions that follow.

> In Europe a woman was near death from a special kind of cancer. There was one drug that the doctors thought might save her. It was a form of radium that a druggist in the same town had recently discovered. The drug was expensive to make, but the druggist was charging 10 times what the drug cost him to make. He paid $200 for the radium and charged $2,000 for a small dose of the drug. The sick woman's husband, Heinz, went to everyone he knew to borrow the money, but he could only get together about $1,000 which was half of what it cost. He told the druggist that his wife was dying and asked him to sell it cheaper or let him pay later. But the druggist said: "No, I discovered the drug and I'm going to make money from it." So Heinz got desperate and broke into the man's store to steal the drug for his wife. (Kohlberg, 1969)

Reflect

What's your view? Should Heinz steal the drug? Why or why not?

Kohlberg emphasized the importance of being able to view the moral world from the perspective of another person (Carpendale, 2000). Look at this situation from Heinz's perspective. What do you think? Should Heinz have tried to steal the drug? Was he right or wrong? As you can see from Table 15.1, the issue is more complicated than a simple yes or no. Heinz is caught up in a moral dilemma in which a legal or social rule (in this case, laws against stealing) is pitted against a strong human need (Heinz's desire to save his wife). According to Kohlberg's theory, children and adults arrive at yes or no answers for different reasons. These reasons can be classified according to the level of moral development they reflect.

Children (and adults) are faced with many moral dilemmas. Consider two issues concerning cheating that children frequently face in school. When children fear failing a test, they may be tempted to cheat. Different children may decide not to cheat for

A Closer Look

Lawrence Kohlberg

His car was found parked beside Boston Harbor. Three months later his body washed up onto the shore. He had discussed the moral dilemma posed by suicide with a friend, and perhaps Lawrence Kohlberg (1927–1987) had taken his own life. He was suffering from a painful parasitic intestinal disease that he had acquired 40 years earlier while smuggling Jewish refugees from Europe past the British blockade into Palestine (now Israel). There had also been recent disappointments in his work. Nevertheless, Carol Gilligan wrote that he had "almost single-handedly established moral development as a central concern of developmental psychology" (Hunt, 1993, p. 381).

Kohlberg was born into a wealthy family in suburban New York. He graduated from Phillips Academy as World War II came to an end. Rather than go on immediately to college, he became a merchant mariner and helped save people who had been displaced by the war. He was captured and imprisoned on the Mediterranean island of Cyprus. He soon escaped, but not before acquiring the disease that would bring him a lifetime of pain. Between high school and college, Kohlberg had already decided that one must attend more to one's own conscience than to law and authority figures in determining what was right and wrong.

Robert Williams

Lawrence Kohlberg

very different reasons. One child may simply fear getting caught. A second child may decide that it is more important to live up to her moral principles than to get the highest possible grade. In each case, the child's decision is not to cheat. However, the cognitive processes behind each decision reflect different levels of reasoning.

Other children may observe a classmate cheating and decide to inform the teacher—again, for different reasons. A child with a grudge against the cheater may tell the teacher so that the cheater will be punished. A second child may tell the teacher to prevent the cheater from getting a high grade and making other students' grades—including the informant's—look bad by comparison. A third may tell the teacher because she believes that reporting cheating is the normal thing to do. A fourth may hate the idea of squealing, but may still inform on the cheater because of concern that the social system could break down if cheating is tolerated by peers.

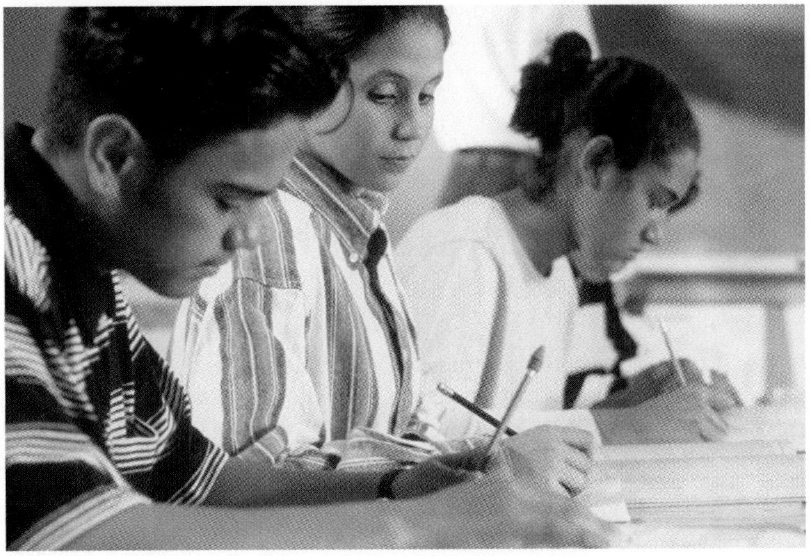

Cheating

When adolescents fear failing a test, they may be tempted to cheat. Different adolescents may decide to cheat—or not to cheat—for a variety of reasons that reflect their individual level of moral development.

As a stage theorist, Kohlberg argued that the developmental stages of moral reasoning follow an invariant sequence. Children progress at different rates, and not all children (or adults) reach the highest stage. But children must experience stage 1 before they enter stage 2, and so on. According to Kohlberg, there are three levels of moral development and two stages within each level.

Let's return to Heinz and see how responses to the questions we have posed can reflect different levels and stages of moral development.

The Preconventional Level

In the **preconventional level,** children base their moral judgments on the consequences of their behavior. For instance, stage 1 is oriented toward obedience and punishment. Good behavior is obedient and allows one to avoid punishment. According to stage 1 reasoning, Heinz could be urged to steal the drug because he did ask to pay for it first. But he could also be urged not to steal the drug so that he will not be sent to jail (see Table 15.1).

In stage 2, good behavior allows people to satisfy their own needs and, perhaps, the needs of others. A stage 2 reason for stealing the drug is that Heinz's wife needs it. Therefore, stealing the drug—the only way of attaining it—is not wrong. A stage 2 reason for not stealing the drug would be that Heinz's wife might die even if he does so. Thus, he might wind up in jail needlessly.

In a study of American children aged 7 through 16, Kohlberg (1963) found that stage 1 and 2 types of moral judgments were offered most frequently by 7- and 10-year-olds. There was a steep falling off of stage 1 and 2 judgments after age 10.

The Conventional Level

In the **conventional level** of moral reasoning, right and wrong are judged by conformity to conventional (family, religious, societal) standards of right and wrong. According to the stage 3 "good-boy/good-girl orientation," it is good to meet the needs and expectations of others. Moral behavior is what is "normal"—what the majority does. From the stage 3 perspective, Heinz should steal the drug, because that is what a "good husband" would do. It is "natural" or "normal" to try to help one's wife. Or Heinz should not steal the drug because "good people do not steal." Stage 3 judgments also focus on the role of sympathy—on the importance of doing what will make someone else feel good or better.

In stage 4, moral judgments are based on rules that maintain the social order. Showing respect for authority and duty is valued highly. From this perspective, one could argue that Heinz must steal the drug, because it is his duty to save his wife. He would pay the druggist when he could. Or one could argue that Heinz

preconventional level According to Kohlberg, a period during which moral judgments are based largely on expectations of rewards or punishments.

conventional level According to Kohlberg, a period during which moral judgments largely reflect social rules and conventions.

TABLE 15.1 *Kohlberg's Levels and Stages of Moral Development*

Stage of Development	Examples of Moral Reasoning That Support Heinz's Stealing the Drug	Examples of Moral Reasoning That Oppose Heinz's Stealing the Drug
	Level I: Preconventional	
STAGE 1: Judgments guided by obedience and the prospect of punishment (the consequences of the behavior)	It isn't wrong to take the drug. Heinz did try to pay the druggist for it, and it's only worth $200, not $2,000.	Taking things without paying is wrong because it's against the law. Heinz will get caught and go to jail.
STAGE 2: Naively egoistic, instrumental orientation (Things are right when they satisfy people's needs.)	Heinz ought to take the drug because his wife really needs it. He can always pay the druggist back.	Heinz shouldn't take the drug. If he gets caught and winds up in jail, it won't do his wife any good.
	Level II: Conventional	
STAGE 3: Good-boy orientation (Moral behavior helps others and is socially approved.)	Stealing is a crime, so it's bad, but Heinz should take the drug to save his wife or else people would blame him for letting her die.	Stealing is a crime. Heinz shouldn't just take the drug because his family will be dishonored and they will blame him.
STAGE 4: Law-and-order orientation (Moral behavior is doing one's duty and showing respect for authority.)	Heinz must take the drug to do his duty to save his wife. Eventually, he has to pay the druggist for it, however.	If we all took the law into our own hands, civilization would fall apart, so Heinz shouldn't steal the drug.
	Level III: Postconventional	
STAGE 5: Contractual, legalistic orientation (One must weigh pressing human needs against society's need to maintain social order.)	This thing is complicated because society has a right to maintain law and order, but Heinz has to take the drug to save his wife.	I can see why Heinz feels he has to take the drug, but laws exist for the benefit of society as a whole and can't simply be cast aside.
STAGE 6: Universal ethical principles orientation (People must follow universal ethical principles and their own conscience, even if it means breaking the law.)	In this case, the law comes into conflict with the principle of the sanctity of human life. Heinz must take the drug because his wife's life is more important than the law.	If Heinz truly believes that stealing the drug is worse than letting his wife die, he should not take it. People have to make sacrifices to do what they think is right.

should not steal the drug, because he would be breaking the law. He might also be contributing to the breakdown of the social order. Many people do not develop beyond the conventional level.

Kohlberg (1963) found that stage 3 and 4 types of judgments are all but absent among 7-year-olds. However, they are reported by about 20% of 10-year-olds and higher percentages of 13- and 16-year-olds. Stage 3 and 4 moral judgments are the types of judgments made most frequently by 13- and 16-year-olds.

Reviews of the research show that juvenile delinquents are less advanced in their moral reasoning than their nondelinquent age-mates (Nelson, Smith, & Dodd, 1990; Smetana, 1990). Higher percentages of juvenile delinquents engage in stage 2 moral reasoning than do their nondelinquent counterparts. Adolescents who are not delinquents are more likely to show moral reasoning typical of stages 3 and 4. Stage 2 reasoning (viewing what is right and wrong in terms of satisfying personal needs) is also characteristic of offenders who engage in crimes such as robbery (Thornton & Reid, 1982).

The Postconventional Level

In the **postconventional level,** moral reasoning is based on the person's own moral standards. In each instance, moral judgments are derived from personal values, not from conventional standards or authority figures. In the contractual, legalistic orientation of stage 5, it is recognized that laws stem from agreed-upon procedures and that many rights have great value and should not be violated. But

postconventional level According to Kohlberg, a period during which moral judgments are derived from moral principles and people look to themselves to set moral standards.

under exceptional circumstances, laws cannot bind the individual. A stage 5 reason for stealing the drug might be that it is the right thing to do, even though it is illegal. Conversely, it could be argued that if everyone in need broke the law, the legal system and the social contract would be destroyed.

Stage 6 thinking relies on supposed universal ethical principles such as those of human life, individual dignity, justice, and **reciprocity.** Behavior that is consistent with these principles is considered right. If a law is seen as unjust or contradicts the right of the individual, it is wrong to obey it. Postconventional people look to their consciences as the highest moral authority. This point has created confusion. To some it suggests that it is right to break the law when it is convenient. But Kohlberg meant that postconventional people feel obligated to do what they believe is right, even if it counters social rules or laws or requires personal sacrifice.

Consider examples from recent history of large-scale moral dilemmas that required personal sacrifice. During the 1960s, many people in the United States broke local laws in their civil rights demonstrations. In most cases these local laws were later overturned by the Supreme Court as discriminatory. During the 1960s and 1970s, many young men who believed that American military involvement in Vietnam was wrong were faced with a dilemma when they were drafted into the armed forces. If they allowed themselves to be inducted, they would be supporting what they saw as an immoral cause. But by refusing induction, they were breaking the law. In the 1980s, other people in the United States broke the law in their efforts to prevent the construction of plants for generating nuclear energy. However, they also believed that it would be wrong for them to stand idly by while the country—from their perspective—was building machines that could lead to its own destruction. For these citizens, belief in their cause compelled them to break laws, even though they risked losing their families, careers, social status, and freedom. In recent years, environmental issues and globalization have emerged as major concerns. Individuals have engaged in demonstrations—sometimes illegally—to protest such activities as deforestation, wildlife extinction, and air pollution. Others have demonstrated against international trade agreements.

Of course, it can be argued, and correctly, that not all of the demonstrators and law breakers in the civil rights, anti–Vietnam War, antinuclear, and environmental crusades have acted from a principled perspective. Some demonstrators broke the law to avoid the disapproval of their own peer groups. Some college students have admitted to participating in demonstrations to find dates. And a few young men refused induction into the armed forces to avoid exposure to the dangers of Vietnam, despite claims of higher moral concerns. Nevertheless, many did break the law because of their interpretation of moral principles and were operating at Kohlberg's stage 6. College students at the postconventional level were more likely than peers at the conventional level of morality to participate in the campus demonstrations and civil disobedience of the 1960s (Haan, Smith, & Block, 1968).

Return to the case of Heinz. It could be argued from the perspective of stage 6 that the principle of preserving life takes precedence over laws prohibiting stealing. Therefore, it is morally necessary for Heinz to steal the drug, even if he must go to jail. Note that it could also be asserted, from the principled orientation, that if Heinz finds the social contract or the law to be the highest principle, he must remain within the law, despite the consequences.

Stage 5 and 6 moral judgments were virtually absent among the 7- and 10-year-olds in Kohlberg's (1963) sample of American children. They increased in frequency during the early and middle teens. By age 16, stage 5 reasoning was shown by about 20% and stage 6 reasoning by about 5% of adolescents. However, stage 3 and 4 judgments were made more frequently at all ages, 7 through 16, studied by Kohlberg and other investigators (Colby et al., 1983; Rest, 1983; see Figure 15.3.)

Situational Influences on Moral Development

People who are capable of a certain level of moral reasoning do not always use it. Situational factors apparently play an important role in whether moral judgments will be based on conventional or postconventional principles. A study by Tapp

Reflect

What is your stage of moral development, according to Kohlberg? How do you know? How do you feel about it?

reciprocity The principle that actions have mutual effects and that people depend upon one another to treat each other morally.

Figure 15.3
Age and Type of Moral Judgment

The incidence of preconventional (premoral) reasoning declines from greater than 90% of moral statements at age 7 to under 20% of moral statements at age 16. Conventional moral statements increase with age between 7 and 13, but then level off to account for 50–60% of moral statements at ages 13 to 16. Postconventional (principled) moral statements are all but absent at ages 7 to 10, but account for about 20–25% of moral statements at ages 13 to 16.
Source: Kohlberg, 1963.

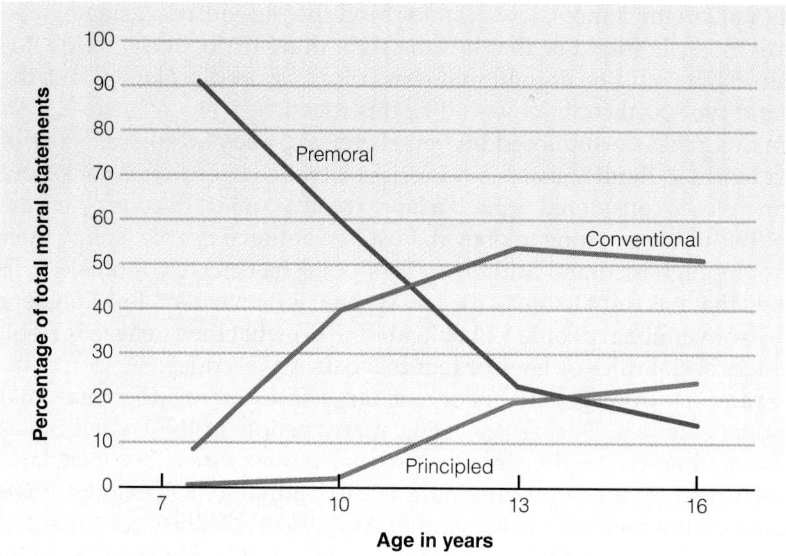

and Levine (1972), for example, suggests that it is easier to talk about higher levels of moral development in theoretical discussions than it is to apply them to one's own life. The investigators asked children and adolescents two questions: (1) "Why should people follow rules?" and (2) "Why do *you* follow rules?" Answers to the first were more advanced. For example, children were more likely to say that people should follow rules to maintain the social order than they were to offer this reason for their own behavior. In their own lives, they admitted

Developing in a World of Diversity

Cross-Cultural and Gender Differences in Moral Development

Cultural background is a powerful shaper of moral reasoning. Kohlberg found postconventional thinking among a minority of American adolescents, but it was all but absent among adolescents in villages in Mexico, Taiwan, Turkey (Kohlberg, 1969), and the Bahamas (White et al., 1978). A review of 45 studies of moral development carried out in 27 countries concluded that postconventional reasoning is more likely to be found in urban cultural groups and middle-class populations, but is rarely seen in traditional folk cultures (Snarey, 1985).

Another cross-cultural study indicates that the moral reasoning of children from Western industrialized countries such as Germany, Poland, and Italy is similar to that of American children from urban areas (Boehnke et al., 1989). On the other hand, the moral reasoning of American children and Israeli city children is more self-oriented and less oriented to the needs of others than the reasoning of Israeli kibbutz children (Eisenberg, Hertz-Lazarowitz, & Fuchs, 1990). These differences are consistent with the differences in the children's social environments. The kibbutz is a collective farm community that emphasizes cooperative relationships and a communal philosophy.

A similar pattern has been found in comparisons of middle-class American and Hindu Indian children and adults. Hindu Indians are more likely to show a caring orientation in making moral judgments, whereas Americans more often demonstrate a justice orientation. These findings are consistent with the greater emphasis Hindu Indian culture puts on the importance of taking responsibility for others (Miller, 1994; Miller & Bersoff, 1992).

Gender Differences in Moral Development

One of the more controversial notions in the history of child development is that males show higher levels of moral development than females. From his psychoanalytic perspective, Freud assumed that males would have stronger superegos than females because of the wrenching Oedipus complex, the fear of castration, and the male's consequent identification with authority figures and social codes. But Freud's views on the Oedipus complex were speculative, and his views on women reflected the ignorance and prejudice of his times.

However, in more recent years, some cognitively oriented researchers have claimed to find that males reason at higher levels of moral development than females in terms of responses to Heinz's dilemma. For example, Kohlberg and Kramer (1969) reported that the average stage of moral development for men was stage 4, which emphasizes justice, law, and order. The average stage for women was reported to be stage 3, which emphasizes caring and concern for others.

that their behavior was more likely to be governed by expectations of reward or punishment.

Similar results were obtained in a study in which teenagers and their parents told how they had handled recent real-life moral dilemmas (Krebs et al., 1991). They also responded to Kohlberg's standard moral dilemmas. Both the adolescents and their parents scored an average of one stage lower on the real-life conflicts than they did on Kohlberg's tests.

A study by Sobesky (1983) also suggests the power of situational influences. High school and college students who were told it was certain Heinz would go to prison for stealing the drug were significantly less likely to use principled thinking and suggest that Heinz should help his wife. Once the consequences were made so clear and certain, many of these students seemed compelled by the situation into making stage 1 moral judgments that were controlled by fear of punishment. Other students, who were told that the drug would definitely save Heinz's wife, were significantly more likely to suggest that Heinz steal the drug and to justify their decision with principled reasoning.

Moral Behavior and Moral Reasoning: Is There a Relationship?

Is there a relationship between moral cognitive development and moral behavior? Are children whose moral development is more mature less likely to commit immoral acts? Is there a correspondence between children's behavior and their moral judgments? The answer seems to be yes, for many studies have found positive relationships between the child's level of moral development and moral behavior (Cheung et al., 2001; Palmer & Hollin, 2000).

Preadolescents whose moral reasoning is at stage 2 cheat and engage in other conduct problems in the classroom more frequently than age-mates whose moral reasoning is at higher stages (Bear, 1989; Richards et al., 1992). Among adolescents, those with higher levels of moral reasoning are more likely to exhibit moral behavior, including altruism and other prosocial behaviors (Eisenberg et al., 1991).

Click *Select Theorist* for more on Gilligan and gender differences in moral development.

Carol Gilligan (1977, 1982; Gilligan & Attanucci, 1988) argues that this gender difference reflects different patterns of socialization for boys and girls. Gilligan makes her point through two examples of responses to Heinz's dilemma. Eleven-year-old Jake views the dilemma as a math problem. He sets up an equation showing that life has greater value than property. Heinz is thus obligated to steal the drug. Eleven-year-old Amy, on the other hand, notes that stealing the drug and letting Heinz's wife die would both be wrong. Amy searches for alternatives, such as getting a loan, stating that it would profit Heinz's wife little if he went to jail and were no longer around to help her.

But Gilligan sees Amy's pattern of reasoning as being as sophisticated as Jake's. (With Kohlberg, it's the complexity of reasoning that's important, not necessarily the direction of the conclusion.) Still, Amy would be rated as showing a lower level of moral development. Gilligan asserts that Amy, like other girls, has been socialized into focusing on the needs of others and foregoing simplistic judgments of right and wrong. As a consequence, Amy is more likely to appear to show stage 3 reasoning, which focuses in part on empathy for others and caring (Gilligan, 1977). Jake, by contrast, has been socialized into making judgments based on logic. To him, clear-cut conclusions are to be derived from a set of premises. Amy was aware of the logical considerations that struck Jake, of course. However, she processed them as one source of information—not as the sole acceptable source. It is ironic that Amy's empathy, a trait that has "defined the 'goodness' of women," marks Amy "as deficient in moral development" (Gilligan, 1982, p. 18).* Prior to his death in 1987, Kohlberg (1985) had begun efforts to correct the sexism in his scoring system.

For all their differences, both Kohlberg and Gilligan agree that in making moral judgments, females are more likely to show a caring orientation, whereas males are more likely to assume a justice orientation. But other researchers disagree with this notion. Most studies, in fact, find that concerns with caring and justice coexist in the judgments of both genders and find that girls do not reason at lower levels than boys (Clopton & Sorell, 1993; Galotti, Kozberg, & Farmer, 1991; Garrod, Beal, & Shin, 1991; Kahn, 1992; Smetana, Killen, & Turiel, 1991a). Two extensive reviews of the literature comparing moral reasoning of females and males (Walker, 1984, 1991) revealed no gender differences. Another review (Thoma, 1986) found a tendency for adolescent girls to obtain slightly higher moral reasoning scores than adolescent boys.

In his review of the literature on gender differences in moral reasoning, Lawrence Walker (1991) concludes that the apparent gender differences found in a few studies could be attributed to gender differences in educational and occupational achievement—at least among adult subjects. That is, subjects who showed the highest levels of moral reasoning had had more education and higher levels of occupational attainment.

*Look: My wife is female (no surprise), my children are female, my grandchildren are female, and even the family dog is female. If you think that I'm going to allow any suggestion that males are superior, think again. (And Phoebe, the dog, is watching over me as I write this.)

Experiments also have been conducted in the hope of advancing moral reasoning as a way of decreasing immoral behavior. A number of studies have found that group discussion of moral dilemmas elevates delinquents' level of moral reasoning (Smetana, 1990). Is moral behavior affected as well? In one study, discussions of moral dilemmas improved moral reasoning and reduced incidents such as school tardiness, behavior referrals, and police/court contacts among adolescents with behavioral problems (Arbuthnot & Gordon, 1988).

Evaluation of Kohlberg's Theory of Moral Development

Click *Select Theorist* for more on evaluating Kohlberg's theory of moral development.

Evidence supports Kohlberg's view that the moral judgments of children develop toward higher stages in sequence (Boom, Brugman, & van der Heijden, 2001; Walker & Taylor, 1991a), even though most children do not reach postconventional thought. Postconventional thought, when it is found, first occurs during adolescence.

Why doesn't postconventional moral reasoning appear until age 13 or so? A number of studies (Tomlinson-Keasey & Keasey, 1974; Kuhn et al., 1977) suggest that formal-operational thinking is a prerequisite condition. That is, postconventional reasoning appears to require the capacities to understand abstract moral principles and to empathize with the attitudes and emotional responses of other people. However, the appearance of formal-operational thought does not guarantee that postconventional moral judgments will follow.

Consistent with Kohlberg's theory, children do not appear to skip stages as they progress (Kohlberg & Kramer, 1969; Kuhn, 1976; White, Bushnell, & Regnemer, 1978). Children exposed to examples of moral reasoning above and below that of their own stage generally prefer the higher level of reasoning (Rest, 1983). Thus, the thrust of moral development is from lower to higher stages, even if children can be sidetracked by social influences.

One longitudinal study did find that one's level of moral reasoning can slip backward in response to changed circumstances. James Rest and his colleagues (Rest & Narvaez, 1991) observed young adults who went on to college after high school. They showed increasingly higher levels of moral development over the course of the next 10 years. However, high school graduates who did not attend college showed increases in moral development over the next 2 years, and then their development tended to fall back to levels similar to those at the time of graduation. Rest suggests a number of explanations for the advances of the college students, including socialization into the (more principled) values likely to be held by college students, the study of moral philosophies, and general intellectual stimulation. The educational thrust of high school may have fueled the development of young people who did not go on to college for another 2 years or so. But then, perhaps, they were socialized into groups with more of a law-and-order orientation. Or, perhaps, less intellectual stimulation stemmed the incentive to examine moral issues.

Kohlberg believed that the stages of moral development are universal, following the unfolding of innate sequences. However, he seems to have underestimated the influence of social, cultural, and educational institutions (Tappan & Packer, 1991). Educators have designed programs to enhance the moral development of schoolchildren. The programs involve discussion of moral dilemmas and inspire students to get in touch with their own values and those of others (Battistich, Watson, Solomon, Schaps, & Solomon, 1991a; Lickona, 1991). Typically, about half the students in a class show some advancement in moral reasoning as a result of participating in these programs (Lickona, 1991).

Kohlberg also appears to have underestimated the parental role in children's moral development (Walker, Hennig, & Krettenauer, 2000). One study, for example, found that the moral development of children and adolescents was enhanced when parents engaged in a higher level of moral reasoning themselves and when parents discussed moral dilemmas with the children intensely (Walker & Taylor, 1991b). The use of inductive disciplinary methods, including discussions of the feelings of others, also advances moral reasoning (Hoffman, 1984, 1988; Palmer & Hollin, 2001). Mothers seem to be particularly influential in fostering advanced

Parents Influence Their Children's Moral Development

Parents help advance their children's moral development when they discuss moral dilemmas with them. And believe it or not, most adolescents tend to respect their parents' views.

moral reasoning; mothers are more likely than fathers to look into children's motives and encourage empathy with the feelings of victims (Hoffman, 1982). (Are there any who still view women's moral development as inferior to men's?)

There is also cross-cultural evidence concerning the importance of the **macrosystem.** The fact that postconventional thinking is all but absent in developing societies—and infrequent even in the United States—suggests that postconventional reasoning may reflect Kohlberg's personal ideals and not a natural, universal stage of development. Stage 6 reasoning is based on the acceptance of supposedly universal ethical principles. The principles of freedom, justice, equality, tolerance, integrity, and reverence for human life have high appeal for most American adolescents. But Americans are reared in a culture that idealizes these principles and elevates them to a higher moral status than tradition and conventions such as dress codes and food rituals (Damon, 1988).

As we look around the world—and at many of the horrors of the new millennium—we find that abstract principles like freedom and tolerance of difference are not universally revered. They are more reflective of Western cultural influences than of the cognitive development of the child. In some cultures, for instance, violation of the dominant religious tradition is a capital offense and freedom to worship—or the freedom not to worship—is unheard of. In his later years, Kohlberg (1985) dropped stage 6 reasoning from his theory in recognition of these problems.

Review

(10) Piaget and Kohlberg argued that moral reasoning undergoes a (culture-specific or universal?) and invariant cognitive-developmental pattern. (11) Piaget believed that children's moral judgments develop in two stages: moral realism and ________ morality. (12) Moral realism is also known as ________ morality. (13) Preoperational children judge the wrongness of an act in terms of (the amount of damage done or the intentions of the wrongdoer?). (14) Kohlberg emphasized the importance of being able to view the moral world from the ________ of another person. (15) According to Kohlberg, there are ________levels of moral development and two stages within each level. (16) In Kohlberg's ________ level, children base their moral judgments on the consequences of their behavior.

macrosystem In ecological theory, the basic institutions and ideologies that influence the child, such as the American ideals of freedom of expression and equality under the law.

(17) In the ________ level, right and wrong are judged by conformity to conventional (family, religious, societal) standards of right and wrong. (18) In the ________ level, moral reasoning is based on the person's own moral standards. (19) Many studies have found (positive or negative?) relationships between the child's level of moral development and moral behavior.

Pulling It Together: Should Heinz have taken the drug without paying? What does your reasoning suggest about your level of moral development?

The Adolescent in School: Dropping In, Dropping Out

How can we emphasize the importance of the school to the development of the adolescent? Adolescents are highly influenced by the opinions of their peers and their teachers. Their self-esteem rises or falls consistently with the pillars of their skills. ***Question: How do adolescents make the transition from elementary school to middle or high school?***

Making the Transition From Elementary School

Students make at least one and sometimes two transitions to a new school before they complete high school. Think back to your own school days. Did you spend the years from kindergarten to eighth grade in one building and then move on to high school? Did you instead attend elementary school through sixth grade and then go to middle school for grades 7–9 before starting high school? Or did you complete grades K through 4 or 5 in one school, then attend a middle school for grades 5 or 6 to 8, and then move on to high school for grades 9–12? (This has become the most common pattern in recent years.)

Reflect

Do you recall your own transition from elementary school to middle school or high school? What did you experience?

The transition to middle or high school generally involves a shift from a smaller, neighborhood elementary school with self-contained classrooms to a larger, more impersonal setting with many more students and with different teachers for different classes (Fenzel, 2000). These changes may not fit very well with the developmental needs of early adolescents. For example, adolescents express a desire for increased autonomy, yet teachers in middle school typically allow less student input and exert more behavioral control than teachers in elementary school (Eccles, 1991b; Eccles et al., 1993). Moreover, in the shift to the new school, students move from being the "top dog" (that is, the oldest and most experienced students) to being the "bottom dog." These changes aren't the only ones facing the early adolescent. Many youngsters also are going through the early stages of pubertal development at about the same time they move to a new school.

How well do students adjust to the transition to a new school? Much of the research has examined children's experiences as they move from elementary school to middle school. The transition to the new school setting often is accompanied by a decline in grades and in participation in school activities. Students may also experience a drop in self-esteem and an increase in psychological distress (Rudolph, Lambert, Clark, & Kurlakowsky, 2001; Seidman et al., 1994, 1996).

Girls appear to be more vulnerable to the middle school transition than boys. In one study, for example, girls who switched to a middle school for seventh grade showed a decrease in self-esteem, whereas girls who stayed in their kindergarten through eighth-grade school did not. Boys' self-esteem did not change when they switched to middle school (Simmons & Blyth, 1987). Why are girls more vulnerable than boys to the transition to middle school? Children who experience several life changes at the same time find it more difficult to adjust to a new school

(Flanagan & Eccles, 1993; Simmons & Blyth, 1987). Remember that girls start puberty sooner than boys, on average, and start dating sooner. Both of these life changes often coincide with the girl's entry into middle school. Boys will not experience those changes until later. This may explain why the shift to middle school is more problematic for girls.

But the transition to a new school need not be stressful. Students who are in greater control of their lives tend to do better with the transition (Rudolph, Lambert, Clark, & Kurlakowsky, 2001). Elementary and middle schools can also help ease the transition to high school. For example, one longitudinal study followed the progress of students who received a 2-year social decision-making and problem-solving program in elementary school. When followed up in high school 4 to 6 years later, these students showed higher levels of prosocial behavior and lower levels of antisocial, self-destructive, and socially disordered behavior than did students who had not been exposed to this program (Elias et al., 1991). Some middle schools have tried to create a more intimate, caring atmosphere. West Baltimore Middle School, for instance, has created smaller schools within the school building, housing each grade in a separate wing. It has also scheduled regular advisory periods when students can talk with a teacher or counselor (Celis, 1992). Other school districts have created bridge programs to carry students through the summer between middle school and high school by introducing them to the new school culture and new style of learning and strengthening their academic skills (Suro, 1992).

The Transition From Elementary School

The transition to middle or high school is not always easy. They go from being "top dog" at their former school to "bottom dog" in the new school. The transition coincides with the biological forces of puberty and concerns about how one will turn out—physically, that is. It is not surprising that some children experience a decline in grades and self-esteem. "Sensitive" school-based programs can help ease the transition.

Dropping Out of School

School is a key path to success in our society, but not all adolescents complete high school (Eccles, 1991a). ***Questions: What are the consequences of dropping out of school? Why do adolescents drop out?***

Completing high school is one of the most critical developmental tasks facing adolescents. The consequences of dropping out can be grim indeed. High school dropouts are more likely to be unemployed (McWhirter et al., 1993). They make lower salaries. Research suggests that each year of education, from grade school through graduate school, adds about 16% to an individual's lifetime earnings (Passell, 1992). (This is a good incentive for you not only to complete college, but also to think about graduate work!) Dropouts also are more likely to show a variety of problem behaviors, including delinquency, criminal behavior, and substance abuse (Ellickson, Tucker, & Klein, 2001; Lane & Cherek, 2001). However, it is sometimes difficult to disentangle the consequences of dropping out from its causes. A pattern of delinquent behavior, for example, often precedes as well as follows dropping out.

Reflect

Do you know people who dropped out of high school? Why did they drop out? What were the consequences?

Students Who Drop Out

It is difficult to estimate accurately the magnitude of the school dropout problem, since states use different reporting systems, and most do not keep track of those who quit after eighth grade. Overall, about 15% of males aged 18 to 24 and 12% of females in the same age group have dropped out of high school (National Center for Education Statistics [NCES], 2002). Table 15.2 contains data from the *Local Education Agency Universe Survey* of the National Center for Education Statistics in 13 sample states (NCES, 2002). Note that more males than females in each state drop out and that the percentages show remarkable consistency: About 58% of dropouts overall are male. The percentage of dropouts who belong to ethnic minority groups varies considerably from state to state, however, with California, Texas, and New York having the highest percentages of dropouts who belong to ethnic minority groups.

However, the dropout rates vary considerably from ethnic group to ethnic group in the United States. For example, about one in three Latino and Latina Americans, one in seven African Americans, and one in ten European Americans has dropped out (NCES, 1992, 2002). The higher dropout rates for children from African American and Latino and Latina American minority groups are linked to the lower socioeconomic status of their families. Children from lower-income households have higher dropout rates. On average, families from these minority groups have lower income levels than European American families. When income levels are held constant, ethnic differences in school dropout rates are greatly reduced (NCES, 1992, 2002). And when African American and European American students with similar test scores and high school grades are compared, African Americans are actually somewhat more likely than European Americans to finish high school, go to college, and complete a college degree (Entwisle, 1990).

Beyond demographics, who is most at risk for dropping out? Excessive school absence and reading below grade level are two of the earliest and strongest predictors of later school dropout (Weitzman & Siegel, 1992). Other risk factors include low academic achievement, poor problem-solving ability, low self-esteem,

A Closer Look

Beyond the Classroom: Why Can't Johnny Read Julius Caesar

Some adolescents profit more from education than others. Why do some adolescents perform better than others in the classroom? Certainly intelligence plays a role. So does the adequacy of the school and the teachers. Surveys of high school students suggest that the behavior and attitudes of parents and teenagers play key roles as well (Bacete & Remirez, 2001; Steinberg, 1996). One study, by psychologist Laurence Steinberg and his colleagues, cut across the ethnic spectrum. It included 20,000 African American, Asian American, Latino and Latina American, and European American students from California and Wisconsin and is recounted in Steinberg's 1996 book *Beyond the Classroom.*

One problem that is connected with poor school performance is that many parents, according to Steinberg, are "disconnected" from their children's lives. Note some of his findings:

- Half the students said it would not upset their parents if they brought home grades of C or worse.
- Forty percent of students said their parents never attended school functions.
- One third of the students said their parents did not even know how they were doing in school.
- One third said that they primarily spent the day "goofing off" with their friends.
- Only one third of students said that they had daily conversations with their parents.

Steinberg and his co-researchers, Bradford Brown and Sanford Dornbusch, also looked at the situation from the parents' point of view. Many parents say they would like to be involved in their children's school and leisure activities, but they are just too busy. By the time the children enter high school, many parents admit looking upon education as the school's job, not theirs. In fact, half of the parents surveyed admitted that they did not know who their children's friends were or where their children went (and what they did) after school.

Steinberg makes some recommendations. First and foremost, parents need to be more involved with their teenagers. For example, parents can

- Communicate regularly with their teenagers about school and personal matters
- Use consistent discipline (as opposed to being dictatorial or too permissive)
- Regularly attend school functions
- Consult with their children's teachers and follow through on their suggestions

And What of Peers?

The researchers found that some teenagers encourage others to do well in school. However, by and large, peers have a harmful effect on grades. For example, over half the students surveyed said that they did not talk about schoolwork with their friends. In fact, nearly one in five said that he or she did not do as well as possible for fear of earning the disapproval of peers!

difficulty getting along with teachers, dissatisfaction with school, substance abuse, being too old for grade level, and being male (Gelinas et al., 2000). Adolescents who adopt adult roles early, especially marrying at a young age or becoming a teenage parent, also are more likely to drop out (Jimerson et al., 2000). Demographic factors play a role as well. Students from low-income households, large urban areas, and the West and South are at greater risk (NCES, 1992, 2002). But not all dropouts come from low-income families. Middle-class youth who feel bored with school, alienated, or strongly pressured to succeed also are at risk (Battin-Pearson, 2000).

Michael Newman/PhotoEdit

Are These Adolescents on the Path to Dropping Out of School?

The consequences of dropping out of school can be harsh. High school dropouts earn less and are more likely to be unemployed. A variety of programs have been developed to help prevent school dropouts, but first potential dropouts must be identified.

Preventing Dropping Out of School

Many programs have been developed to prevent school dropout. Some of the more successful programs have certain common characteristics (Sternberg & Williams, 2002; Woolfolk, 2001):

- Early preschool intervention. Examples are early childhood compensatory education, such as Head Start.
- Identification and monitoring of high-risk students throughout the school years
- Small class size, individualized instruction, and counseling (you know, the same kind of stuff that helps any kid at any age[3])
- Strong vocational components that link learning and community work experiences
- Involvement of adults from families or community organizations
- Positive school climate, which makes students feel like part of a community
- Clear and reasonable educational goals (if you don't know where you're going, how you get there isn't very important), student accountability for behavior, and motivational systems that involve penalties and rewards

These intervention efforts (with the exception of the early preschool intervention programs) usually are not employed until students are on the verge of dropping out. And few programs are designed to handle students who have already dropped out. More needs to be done to identify and help students at an early age who are at risk of dropping out (Sternberg & Williams, 2002; Woolfolk, 2001).

TABLE 15.2 *Percentage of School Dropouts From Several States Who Are Male and Who Belong to Ethnic Minority Groups*

	Male	Belong to Ethnic Minority Groups
Alabama	58	41
California	56	74
Indiana	59	21
Massachusetts	58	38
Minnesota	57	33
Montana	57	19
Nevada	55	44
New York	56	64
Ohio	60	43
Oregon	56	24
Pennsylvania	58	43
South Carolina	62	51
Texas	54	71

Source: National Center for Education Statistics. (2002, January 16). Common core of data, Local Education Agency Universe Survey. *Washington, DC: Office of Educational Research & Improvement, U.S. Department of Education.* http://nces.ed.gov/

[3]It might have even helped me graduate from collge in 4 years. Instead, it took me 6 years.

Review

(20) Teachers in middle school typically exert (more or less?) behavioral control than teachers in elementary school. (21) Students undergoing the transition are more likely to experience a (rise or drop?) in self-esteem. (22) (Boys or Girls?) appear to be more vulnerable to the middle school transition. (23) High school dropouts are (more or less?) likely to be unemployed. (24) (Boys or Girls?) are more likely to drop out of high school. (25) The higher dropout rates for children from African American and Latino and Latina American minority groups are linked to their lower _________ status.

Pulling It Together: How do programs that prevent students from dropping out of school attack the causes of dropping out?

The Adolescent at Work: Career Development and Work Experience

Deciding what job or career we will pursue after completion of school is one of the most important choices we make. ***Questions: How do adolescents make career choices? Does gender affect career choice?***

Career Development

Reflect

When you were little, what did you want to be when you grew up? Were your early desires connected with what you are doing now? If so, how? If not, why not?

When I was a child, I wanted to be an astronaut or an explorer. I became a psychologist and author. My daughter Allyn wanted to be a rock star. Now in college, she is a musical theatre major and hasn't given up on the possibility of becoming a rock star.

My course of career development is more typical than Allyn's—or at least it is as of today. Children's career aspirations may not be practical at first. They become increasingly realistic—and often duller—as children mature and gain experience. In adolescence, ideas about the kind of work one wants to do tend to become more firmly established, or crystallized, but a particular occupation may not be chosen until the college years or afterward (Super, 1984, 1985).

Many factors influence choice of a career, including one's abilities and personality traits (Holland, 1996; Osipow, 1990). Consider two individuals: Michelle and Mark. Michelle has excellent mathematical and mechanical abilities. She is practical and somewhat materialistic. Mark has excellent artistic ability. He is expressive and creative. Which one do you think is more likely to choose a career in computer engineering? Which one is more likely to become a graphic designer? Life experiences, job opportunities, parental expectations, and economic factors play roles as well. Perhaps Michelle's family owns a small business, and she works there on weekends and vacations throughout high school and college. Her parents make it clear that when they retire, they would like Michelle to take over the business. Perhaps she will choose to follow in their footsteps rather than become a computer engineer. Mark would like to become a graphic designer, but perhaps his family does not have the resources to send him to college. Perhaps his girlfriend becomes pregnant. Mark may take the best job he can find given his background—a sales position in a discount store—to help support his new family. Like many others, Mark didn't make a career decision at all (Hardin, Leong, & Osipow, 2001). He sort of fell into his job because it was there when he needed it.

Holland's Career Typology

Psychologists have devised approaches to matching personality traits with careers to predict adjustment in a given career. John Holland's (1997) method matches six personality types to various kinds of careers: realistic, investigative, artistic, social, enterprising, and conventional (see Figure 15.4). Note that within each "kind" of career, some are more sophisticated than others and require more education and training.

Realistic people, according to Holland, are concrete in thinking. They are mechanically oriented. They tend to be best-adjusted in occupations that involve motor activity. Examples of such occupations include unskilled labor, such as

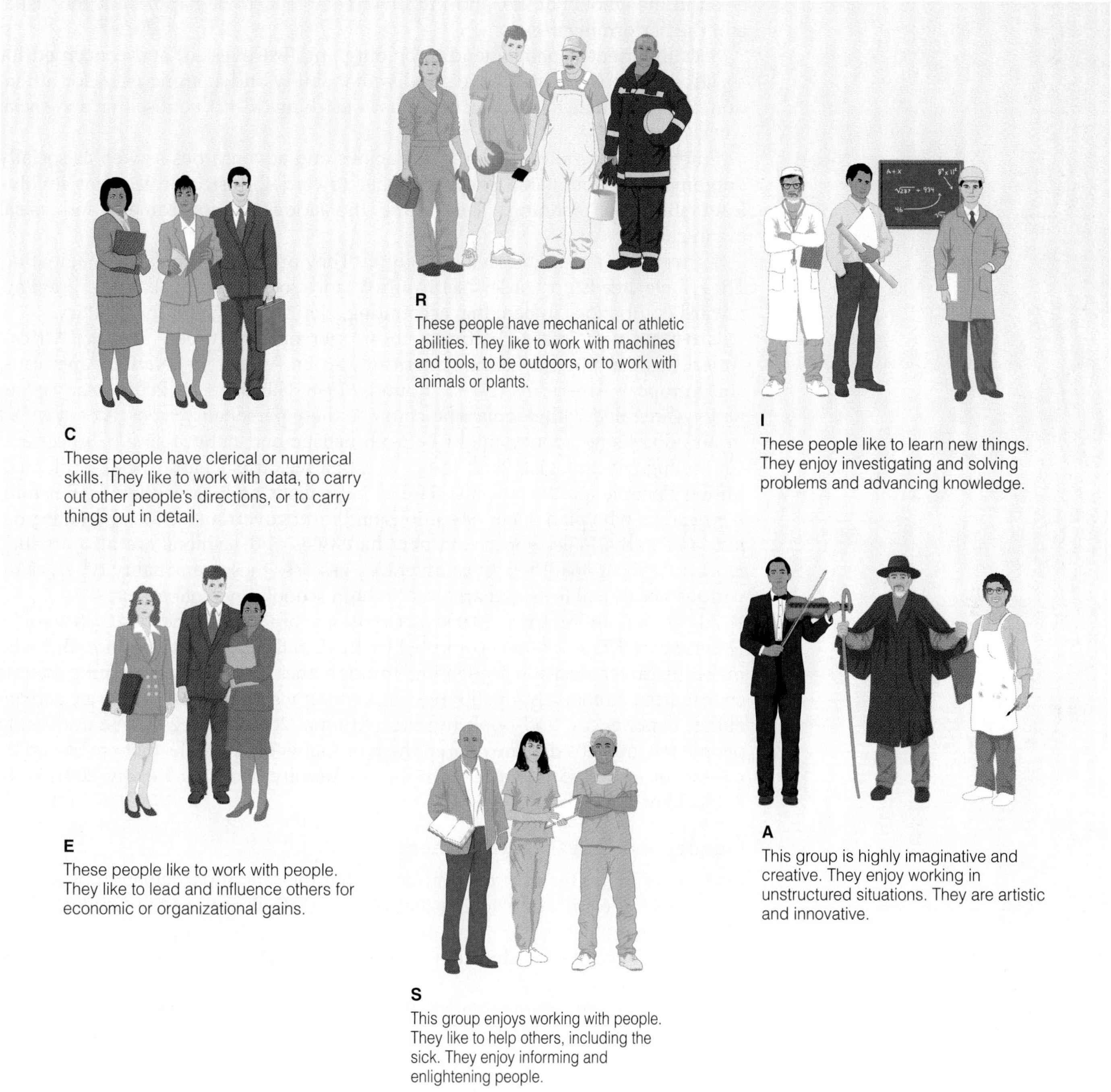

R
These people have mechanical or athletic abilities. They like to work with machines and tools, to be outdoors, or to work with animals or plants.
C
These people have clerical or numerical skills. They like to work with data, to carry out other people's directions, or to carry things out in detail.
I
These people like to learn new things. They enjoy investigating and solving problems and advancing knowledge.
E
These people like to work with people. They like to lead and influence others for economic or organizational gains.
A
This group is highly imaginative and creative. They enjoy working in unstructured situations. They are artistic and innovative.
S
This group enjoys working with people. They like to help others, including the sick. They enjoy informing and enlightening people.

Figure 15.4
Assessing an Adolescent's Career Type by Attending a "Job Fair"

Adolescents can be given insight into where they might fit in the career world by picturing themselves at a job fair like the one pictured here. Students and potential employers have an opportunity to chat at such fairs. As time passes, they discover mutual interests and begin to collect in groups accordingly. Adolescents can consider the types of people in the six groups by reading the descriptions for each. Then they can ask themselves, "Which group would I most like to join?" What does their answer suggest about the career choices that might be of greatest interest to them?

attending gas stations; farming; and the skilled trades, such as auto repairs, electrical work, plumbing, or construction work.

Investigative people are abstract in their thinking. They are often creative and tend to be introverted. They tend to do well in college and university teaching and in research positions.

Artistic people also tend to be creative. As a group, they are emotional, interested in the emotional life, and intuitive. They tend to be happiest in the visual and the performing arts.

Socially oriented people tend to be outgoing (extroverted) and concerned for social welfare. They often have good verbal ability and a strong need for affiliation. They gravitate toward occupations in teaching (K–12), counseling, and social work.

Enterprising people tend to be audacious and adventurous as well as socially outgoing and dominant. They gravitate toward industrial roles that involve leadership and planning. They climb the ladder in government and social organizations.

Conventional people thrive on routine. They are not particularly imaginative. They have needs for order, self-control, and social approval. They gravitate toward occupations in banking, accounting, clerical work, and the military.

Cross-cultural research finds these personality types among African Americans, Latino and Latina Americans, Asian Americans, Native Americans, and European Americans (Day & Rounds, 1998; Hardin et al., 2001). Many occupations are filled with people who combine these personality types. A copywriter in an advertising agency might be both artistic and enterprising. Clinical and counseling psychologists tend to be investigative, artistic, and socially oriented. Military people and beauticians tend to be realistic and conventional. (But military leaders who plan major operations and form governments are also enterprising; and individuals who create new hairstyles and fashions are also artistic.) Holland's Vocational Preference Inventory assesses these personality types, as do various vocational tests that are used in high schools and colleges.

All in all, more than 20,000 occupations are found in the *Dictionary of Occupational Titles*, which is compiled by the U.S. Department of Labor. But who makes a career decision by leafing through these pages? Most young people choose from a relatively small range of occupations that is based on their personalities, experiences, and opportunities (Arbona, 2000; Herr, 2001). Many young people fall into jobs that are offered them or follow career paths that are blazed by parents or respected role models in the community (Nauta & Kokaly, 2001; Wahl & Blackhurst, 2000).

Gender and Career Development

One fact of life in the new millennium is that the rate of participation of women in the labor force is approaching that of men (U.S. Bureau of the Census, 2000). Most young women expect to be employed following the completion of their education. And the more education a woman has, the more likely she is to be employed.

To some degree, women and men still choose different types of careers, and these career choices are influenced by traditional gender-role stereotypes (Correll, 2001). Because of the complex interaction of tradition, personal preference, biology, and opportunity, women still make up the majority of K–12 teachers and nurses, but a relatively small percentage of truck drivers and upper-level management (Becker, 2002). On a more encouraging note, the numbers of women in medical and law schools now rival those of men (Glater, 2001). It will still take time for large numbers of these women to rise to positions of leadership, but they appear to be on their way. Nonetheless, the fields of math, science, and engineering continue to look very much like male domains—so much so that I was recently driven to circulate among my friends the fact that a woman astronomer was being profiled in the *New York Times*.

Yet young children remain given to **occupational gender-typing.** That is, they retain some tendency to divide the workplace into "women's jobs" and "men's jobs." A study of children aged 39 to 84 months found that they clearly considered some kinds of jobs appropriate for women and others as appropriate for men (Levy, Sadosky, & Troseth, 2000). Moreover, they assumed that men would be more successful in "masculine" occupations and women would be more successful in "feminine" occupations. They also had more positive feelings about entering occupations that were traditionally consistent with their gender identity.

A study of children aged 8, 12, and 16 years found that younger children were relatively more likely to want to enter occupations that were traditionally consistent with their gender identity (Miller & Budd, 1999). This study and others (Jessell & Beymer, 1992) find that boys are more likely than girls to engage in occupational gender-typing. Other studies find that girls engage in more complex reasoning about the types of careers they will pursue (Segal et al., 2001). In a sense, they have to reason deeply if they are going to forge ahead, because social expectations remain stacked in favor of males.

Research by Albert Bandura and his colleagues (2001) suggests that girls who have more confidence in their ability to function in the business world—that is, higher self-efficacy expectations—are more likely to choose to select nontraditional careers. Other research finds that intellectually gifted girls are more likely than their less gifted peers to break out of the shackles of traditional career expectations (Mendez, 2000).

Cross-cultural research involving Italian, American, and Bulgarian children suggests that Italian children are most likely to engage in occupational gender-typing, and Bulgarian children are least likely to engage in occupational gender-typing (Trice, 2000). Children in the United States fall in the middle. Italian society, then, appears to remain more traditional than American society. Contemporary Bulgarian society may reflect decades of Communist influence, which held that all people—females and males—are equal.

© Dan McCoy/Rainbow

A Female Architectural Engineer

More women today are pursuing careers traditionally dominated by males. The number of men pursuing traditionally female-dominated careers also has increased but not to the same extent. What might account for the discrepancy in shifts to "nontraditional" careers by women and men?

Mixing Careers and Family Life

> I have yet to hear a man ask for advice on how to combine marriage and a career.
>
> —Gloria Steinem

Question: What do adolescent girls look forward to when they consider being in the workplace? Women, like men, find many rewards in work: financial, personal, and social. Unless you have inherited a fortune, work is the path to financial independence. Many people achieve much of their identity through their work; for example, they think and say "I am a nurse," "I am an architect," or "I am a lawyer," not "I nurse sick people," "I design buildings," or "I write contracts." Work provides an arena for social interaction, and a sense of achievement combined with a positive response from other people works wonders for the self-esteem. Yet preparing for and entering the workplace can mean delaying marriage and a family. It can mean role overload, since about 90% of women in the workforce continue to bear the primary responsibility for rearing the children (Lewin, 1995; Senecal, Vallerand, & Guay, 2001). Most developed countries give families allowances for children and pay for maternity leave (Gauthier, 1999), but American companies are less likely to provide such assistance. It can mean sexism in the rating of one's performance on the job since many male supervisors give male workers better evaluations (Bowen et al., 2000). And it usually means an earnings gap with male workers.

Working women typically work both the day shift and the night shift; they serve their companies and their supervisors; they serve their husbands and their children. Women are twice as likely to stay home with sick kids (Wasserman, 1993). Working women are still likely to shop, cook, and clean. There is a saying that "A woman's work is never done." Sure it is. It's just that with commuting, working, caring for the kids, and cleaning the house, American women in the workforce put in about 15 hours a day (Klein et al., 1998). Where's the union?

Reflect

Do you know any working mothers who are experiencing role overload? What do you think can be done to help?

occupational gender-typing
Judgments that certain occupations are more appropriate for one gender than the other.

Adolescents in the Workforce

> Kimberly, age 16, has a job at a fast-food restaurant located in the suburb of a Midwestern city. She has already saved $1,000 toward a car and a stereo by working at the restaurant after school and on weekends. Kimberly is worried because her state legislature is considering regulations that would cut back the number of hours she is allowed to work.

Life experiences help shape vocational development. One life experience that is common among American teenagers is holding a job. ***Questions: How many American adolescents hold jobs? What are the pros and cons of adolescents' working?***

Prevalence of Adolescent Employment

About half of all high school sophomores, two thirds of juniors, and almost three quarters of seniors have a job during the school year (Freiberg, 1991b). Girls and boys are equally likely to be employed, but boys work more hours. The average male high school senior, for example, works about 21 hours a week, whereas the average female senior works 18 hours (Mortimer, 1991).

Reflect

When you were in high school, did you have a job after school or on weekends? What were effects of working on your grades, your social life, and your social maturation?

At least 4 million adolescents between the ages of 14 to 18 are legally employed. But perhaps another 2 million are working illegally. Some of these teenagers are paid in cash so their employers can avoid paying taxes or minimum wages. Others work too many hours, work late hours on school nights, or work at hazardous jobs. Some are under 14 and are too young to be legally employed except on farms (Kolata, 1992b).

Part-time employment among teenagers is much more common in the United States than in other industrialized countries (Mortimer, 1991). For example, it is estimated that only about 20% of European and Japanese adolescents work during the school year (Freiberg, 1991b; Waldman & Springen, 1992).

Within the United States, there are both ethnic and social-class differences in adolescent employment rates. European American teenagers are twice as likely to be employed as teenagers from ethnic minority groups, for example. In past years, teenagers from poorer households were more likely to work in order to help support the family. Nowadays, adolescent employment is more common among middle-class youth. This change may be partly related to the fact that middle-class families are more likely to live near locations, such as suburban shopping malls, that are a fertile source of jobs for teenagers. Lower-income adolescents who are employed work longer hours than middle-class teens, however (Fine, Mortimer, & Roberts, 1990; Mortimer, 1991).

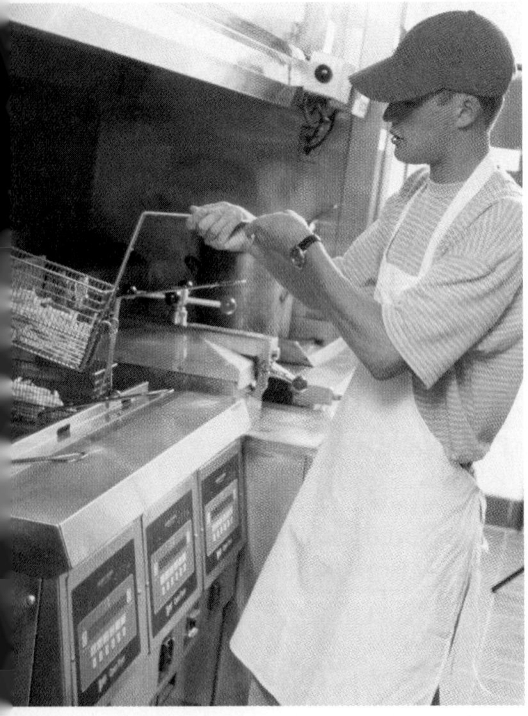

© Ariel Skelley/Corbis Stock Market

Teenagers and Work
Part-time employment during adolescence has its pros and cons. What are they?

Pros and Cons of Adolescent Employment

The potential benefits of adolescent employment include developing a sense of responsibility, self-reliance, and discipline; learning to appreciate the value of money and education; acquiring positive work habits and values; and enhancing occupational aspirations. On the other hand, the meaning of work for adolescents—at least for middle-class adolescents—seems to have changed. Although adolescents of lower socioeconomic status work mainly to supplement the family income (Leventhal, Graber, & Brooks-Gunn, 2001), middle-class adolescents do not necessarily work to help support their families. Instead, most use their income for personal purchases, such as clothing, CDs and DVDs, sports equipment, stereos, TVs, and car payments (Bachman & Schulenberg, 1993; Fine et al., 1990). The proportion of earnings devoted to future college expenses or family expenses is small.

In addition, most employed adolescents are in service and retail jobs that have low pay, high turnover, little authority, and little chance for advancement. They typically perform simple, repetitive tasks requiring no special skills, minimal supervision, and little interdependence with other workers (Mortimer, 1991). Some question the benefits of such jobs.

Furthermore, research indicates that the effects of teenage employment may be detrimental, particularly for those students who work long hours. Longitudinal research into the effects of school-year jobs in ethnically and socioeconomically diverse samples of adolescents find that compared with classmates who do not work or who work only a few hours each week, students who work lengthy hours—more than 11 to 13 hours per week—also report lower grades, higher rates of drug and alcohol use, more delinquent behavior, lower self-esteem, and higher levels of psychological problems (Quirk, Keith, & Quirk, 2001; Steinberg & Dornbusch, 1991). Grades and time spent on homework drop sharply for students who work more than 20 hours a week. But drug and alcohol use increases once a student exceeds only 10 hours of weekly employment. Adolescents who work longer hours also spend less time in family activities, are monitored less by their parents, and are granted more autonomy over day-to-day decisions. The negative effects of employment generally cut across all ethnic, socioeconomic, and age groups.

A cautionary note is in order in interpreting these findings. It is possible that the link between long hours of employment and reduced student achievement could come about because students who are less academically able or interested in school may choose to work longer hours (Fine et al., 1990). And those who already use drugs and alcohol may be more likely to work long hours in order to earn extra money to buy these substances. Two studies have examined these issues (Bachman & Schulenberg, 1993; Steinberg, Fegley, & Dornbusch, 1993). Both found evidence that high school students who work—particularly those who work more than 20 hours a week—are poorer students to begin with. Their grades are lower; they have been held back at least once in school; and they do not plan to complete college. One of the studies (Bachman & Schulenberg, 1993) also found that adolescents who work were more involved than their peers in alcohol, cigarette, and illicit drug use *before* they entered the workforce.

But the studies also showed that working long hours produced even further disengagement from school and contributed to increased drug use, delinquent behavior, aggression, and arguments with parents. Students who were employed for many hours also had less sleep, were less likely to eat breakfast or exercise, and had less leisure time.

Probably the most prudent course of action at this point is for parents, educators, and policymakers to continue monitoring the number of hours adolescents work. Some states already have begun to tighten their regulations on the number of hours teenagers can work during the school year.

Throughout this chapter, we have seen that the intellectual, moral, and vocational development of adolescents is influenced by parents and peers. Adolescents' relationships with family and friends, along with other aspects of their social and emotional development, are the topic of the final chapter.

Review

(26) Children's career aspirations become increasingly ________ as they mature and gain experience. (27) Factors that influence the choice of a career include one's ________ and personality traits. (28) The rate of participation of women in the American labor force is (about half that of men or approaching that of men?). (29) Career choices of males and females are still to some degree determined by traditional ________-role stereotypes. (30) (Boys or Girls?) are more likely to engage in occupational gender-typing. (31) Research shows that many male raters of job performance are biased toward giving (female or male?) workers more favorable evaluations. (32) Working (women or men?) usually work two shifts, one in the workplace and one at home. (33) The (majority or minority?) of high school students have a job during the school year.

Pulling It Together: What are the pros and cons of adolescent employment while in high school?

Recite Recite Recite Recite

1. What is cognitive development during adolescence like, according to Piaget's stage of formal operations?

In Western societies, formal-operational thought begins at about the time of puberty. The major achievements of the stage involve classification, logical thought (deductive reasoning), and the ability to hypothesize. Adolescents can project themselves into situations that transcend their experience and become wrapped up in fantasies. Formal-operational children can perform mental operations with symbols that stand for nothing in their own experience. They can also understand metaphors.

2. How is adolescent egocentrism shown in the imaginary audience and in the personal fable?

Adolescent thought also is marked by a kind of egocentrism or inability to take another's point of view, giving rise to the imaginary audience and the personal fable. The imaginary audience concept is the belief that others around us are as concerned with our thoughts and behaviors as we are, giving rise to the adolescent's intense desire for privacy. The personal fable is the belief that our feelings and ideas are special and unique and that we are invulnerable, which may underlie adolescent showing off and risk taking.

3. What are the gender differences in cognitive abilities?

Females are somewhat superior to males in verbal ability. Males are somewhat superior in visual-spatial ability. The picture for math ability is more complex, with females excelling in some areas and males excelling in others. Girls seem to acquire language faster than boys. Boys are more likely than girls to have reading problems. Boys begin to outperform girls in visual-spatial tasks at about 8 or 9 and the difference persists into adulthood. The gender difference in visual-spatial skills has been linked to genes, the timing of puberty, and sex hormones. Gender stereotypes also influence the amount and type of spatial experiences children obtain. Girls are slightly superior to boys in computational skills in the elementary and middle school years. Boys begin to perform better in problem solving in high school and college.

4. How does Piaget view the development of moral reasoning?

Piaget theorized that children's moral judgments develop in two stages: moral realism (or objective morality) and autonomous morality. The earlier stage emerges at about the age of 5 and looks upon behavior as correct when it conforms to authority. Five-year-olds see rules as embedded in the structure of the universe, and thus they believe in immanent justice, or automatic retribution. Preoperational children focus on one dimension at a time—in this case, the amount of damage done and not the intentions of the wrongdoer. Children begin to show autonomous morality at 9 to 11. Now they view social rules as arbitrary agreements that can be changed.

5. What is Kohlberg's theory of moral development?

Kohlberg elaborated on the kinds of information children use, as well as on the complexities of moral reasoning. He also emphasized the importance of being able to view the moral world from the perspective of another person. As a stage theorist, Kohlberg argued that the developmental stages of moral reasoning follow an invariant sequence. He believed there are three levels of moral development and two stages within each level. In the preconventional level, children base their moral judgments on the consequences of their behavior. In the conventional level, right and wrong are judged by conformity to conventional (family, religious, societal) standards of right and wrong. In the postconventional level, moral reasoning is based on the person's own moral standards.

6. How do adolescents make the transition from elementary school to middle or high school?

The transition to middle or high school generally involves a shift from a smaller, neighborhood elementary school to a larger, more impersonal setting. In the shift to the new school, students move from being the "top dog" to the "bottom dog." The transition to the new school setting often is accompanied by a decline in grades and a drop in self-esteem. Students who are in greater control of their lives tend to do better with the transition.

Recite Recite Recite Recite

7. What are the consequences of dropping out of school? Why do adolescents drop out?	High school dropouts are more likely to be unemployed and earn lower salaries. Dropouts are more likely to show a variety of problem behaviors, including delinquency, criminal behavior, and substance abuse. About 58% of dropouts overall are male. Higher dropout rates for children from African American and Latino and Latina American minority groups are linked to the lower socioeconomic status of their families. Excessive school absence and reading below grade level are strong predictors of school dropout.
8. How do adolescents make career choices? Does gender affect career choice?	Children's career aspirations are often not practical at first but become increasingly realistic as children mature and gain experience. Factors that influence choice of a career include abilities and personality traits. Most of us make career choices based on our experiences, personalities, and opportunities. To some degree, women and men still choose different types of careers, and these career choices are still to some degree influenced by traditional gender-role stereotypes.
9. What do adolescent girls look forward to when they consider being in the workplace?	Adolescents girls expect that work will bring them financial independence, self-esteem, the opportunity for social interaction, and a strong self-identity. But work may also mean delaying a family and role overload. Working women usually work two shifts, one in the workplace and one at home.
10. How many American adolescents hold jobs? What are the pros and cons of adolescents' working?	About half of high school sophomores, two thirds of juniors, and almost three quarters of seniors have a job during the school year. Girls and boys are equally likely to work, but boys usually work longer hours. European American teenagers are twice as likely to be employed as teenagers from ethnic minority groups. The potential benefits of adolescent employment include developing a sense of responsibility, self-reliance, and discipline, and learning to appreciate the value of money and education. Students who work lengthy hours report lower grades, higher rates of drug and alcohol use, lower self-esteem, and more psychological problems.

On the Web

Search Online With InfoTrac College Edition

For additional information, explore InfoTrac College Edition, your online library. Go to **http://www.infotrac-college.com** and use the passcode from the InfoTrac card that came with your book. Try these search terms: teenagers education, teenagers moral, teenagers employment, teenagers vocational guidance, dropouts, high school dropout.

Visit Our Web Site

Go to **http://www.wadsworth.com/psychology** where you will find online resources directly linked to your book.

Child Development CD-ROM

Go to the Wadsworth Child Development CD-ROM for further study of the concepts in this chapter. The CD-ROM also includes quizzes and additional activities to expand your learning experience.

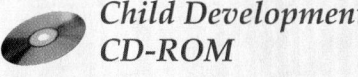

16 Adolescence: Social and Emotional Development

© Mary Kate Denny/Photo Edit

PowerPreview™

Identity and Self-Concept: "Who Am I?" (And Who Else?)

- **Adolescent see, adolescent do?** It is common for adolescents to slavishly imitate their peers' clothing, speech, hairstyles, and ideals.
- **Are adolescent males more** concerned about occupational choices than adolescent females are?
- **What happens to children's** self-esteem as they enter adolescence?
- **Do adolescents from** ethnic minority groups in the United States have lower self-concepts than European American adolescents?

Relationships With Parents and Peers

- **"Storm and Stress" time:** Are adolescents in a constant state of rebellion against their parents?
- **Do adolescents have fewer friends** or more friends than younger children do?
- **Are most adolescents' friends** "bad influences"? Or let's rephrase the question: Do parents and peers tend to exert conflicting influences on adolescents?

Sexuality—When? What? (How?) Who? Where? and Why?—Not to Mention, "Should I?"

- **Kellogg's Corn Flakes** were created in an effort to prevent adolescents from masturbating. (Would I kid you?)
- **Adolescents who have a close** relationship with their parents are less likely to initiate sexual activity at an early age.
- **About 800,000 American teenagers** become pregnant each year. Why? (No wisecracks allowed.)

Juvenile Delinquency

- **Do only a minority of American adolescents** engage in acts of juvenile delinquency? (Or is "everyone" doing it?)

Suicide: When the Adolescent Has Everything to Lose

- **Why would an adolescent** who has "everything to live for" commit suicide? How many actually do so?

Epilogue: Emerging Adulthood—Bridging Adolescence and the Life Beyond

- **How do we determine** when someone has become an adult? Marriage? Self-support? Making one's own life decisions? Is the answer none, some, or all of the above?
- **Are you an adolescent**, an emerging adult, or have you fully emerged? (And how do you know?)

What am I like as a person? Complicated! I'm sensitive, friendly and outgoing, though I can also be shy, self-conscious, and even obnoxious. I'd *like* to be friendly and tolerant all of the time. That's the kind of person I want to be, and I'm disappointed when I'm not. I'm responsible, even studious every now and then, but on the other hand I'm a goof-off too, because if you're too studious, you won't be popular. I'm a pretty cheerful person, especially with my friends, where I can even get rowdy. But I'm usually pretty stressed-out at home, or sarcastic, since my parents are always on my case. They expect me to get all A's. It's not fair! I worry about how I probably *should* get better grades. But I'd be mortified in the eyes of my friends. Sometimes I feel phony, especially around boys. Say I think some guy might be interested in asking me out. I try to act different, like Madonna. I'll be flirtatious and fun-loving. And then everybody else is looking at me like they think I'm totally weird! Then I get self-conscious and embarrassed and become radically introverted, and I don't know who I really am! But I don't really care what they think anyway. I just want to know what my close friends think. I can be my true self with my close friends. I can't be my real self with my parents. They don't understand me. They treat me like I'm still a kid. That gets confusing, though. I mean, which am I, a kid or an adult? It's scary, too, because I don't have any idea what I want to be when I grow up. I mean, I have lots of *ideas*. My friend Sheryl and I talk about whether we'll be teachers, or lawyers, veterinarians, maybe mothers. I know I *don't* want to be a waitress or a secretary. But how do you decide all of this? I mean, I think about it a lot, but I can't resolve it. (Adapted from Harter, 1990c, pp. 352–353)

This self-description of a 15-year-old girl illustrates a key aspect of the adolescent years: the search for an answer to the question "Who am I?" She is struggling to reconcile her seemingly contradictory traits and behaviors to determine the "real me." She is preoccupied not only with her present self, but also with what she wants to become. What were *your* concerns at this age?

In this chapter, we explore social and emotional development in adolescence. We begin with the formation of identity and related changes in self-concept and self-esteem. We consider adolescents' relationships with their parents and their peers. We consider the emergence of sexual behaviors and attitudes and focus on the issue of teenage pregnancy. We address the problems of juvenile delinquency and suicide. Then, as we bring our present voyage to a close, we explore what some developmentalists think of as a new stage in human development: emerging adulthood.

Identity and Self-Concept: "Who Am I?" (And Who Else?)

Adolescence is a key period in the lifelong process of defining just who we are—and who we are not. In this section, we examine Erik Erikson's influential theory of identity development in adolescence. We then turn to James Marcia's expansion of Erikson's theory and explore his four identity statuses. Next, we consider gender and cultural perspectives on identity development. Finally, we look at the development of self-concept and self-esteem during adolescence.

Erikson's View of Identity Development

Question: What does Erikson have to say about the development of identity during adolescence? Erikson's fifth stage of psychosocial development is called identity versus identity diffusion. The primary task of this stage is for adolescents to develop **ego identity:** a sense of who they are and what they stand for. Individuals are faced with making choices about their future occupation, their ideological view of the world (including political and religious beliefs), their sexual orientation, and their gender-role behaviors. The ability to engage in formal-operational thinking helps adolescents make these choices. Since thought is no

ego identity According to Erikson, one's sense of who one is and what one stands for.

Jeff Greenberg/PhotoEdit

Are These Adolescents in the Throes of an Identity Crisis?

According to Erik Erikson, the development of identity—or ego identity*—is a key task of adolescence. In their search for identity, adolescents may join "in" groups, imitating their peers' clothing, speech, hairstyles, and ideals. Until adolescents develop a firm sense of who they are and what they stand for—and some never do—they are highly subject to the influences of others.*

longer tied to concrete experience, adolescents can weigh the options available to them even though they may not have directly experienced any of them (Kahlbaugh & Haviland, 1991; Schwartz, 2001).

An important aspect of identity development is what Erikson (1968) referred to as a **psychological moratorium.** This may be described as a time-out period during which adolescents experiment with different roles, values, beliefs, and relationships. During this moratorium period, adolescents often experience an **identity crisis.** Erikson defined the identity crisis as a turning point in development during which one examines one's values and makes decisions about life roles. Which college should I choose? Which career? Should I become sexually active or not? If so, with whom? Adolescents may feel overwhelmed by the many options before them and by the need to make choices that inevitably will reduce their future alternatives (Crain, 2000).

In their search for identity, adolescents may join "in" groups, slavishly imitating their peers' clothing, speech, hairstyles, and ideals. They may become intolerant of others outside the group (Erikson, 1963). Those who successfully resolve their identity crisis develop a strong sense of who they are and what they stand for. Those who fail to resolve the crisis may continue to be intolerant of people who are different and may continue to *blindly* follow people who adhere to conventional ways.

psychological moratorium A time-out period when adolescents experiment with different roles, values, beliefs, and relationships.

identity crisis A turning point in development during which one examines one's values and makes decisions about life roles.

"Identity Statuses"—Searching for the Self, Making a Commitment

Building upon Erikson's approach, James Marcia (1991; Marcia et al., 1993) has identified four identity statuses. ***Question: What are Marcia's "identity statuses"?*** These represent the four possible combinations of the dimensions of *exploration* and *commitment* that Erikson believed were critical for the development of identity (Schwartz, 2001; see Table 16.1). **Exploration** involves active questioning and searching among alternatives in the quest to establish goals, values, or beliefs. **Commitment** is a stable investment in one's goals, values, or beliefs.

Identity diffusion is the least developmentally advanced status. This category includes individuals who do not have commitments and who are not in the process of trying to form them (Patterson, Sochting, & Marcia, 1992). This stage often is characteristic of children before they reach high school and in the early high school years. Older adolescents who remain diffused may drift through life

exploration Active questioning and searching among alternatives in the quest to establish goals, values, or beliefs.

commitment A stable investment in one's goals, values, or beliefs.

identity diffusion An identity status that characterizes those who have no commitments and who are not in the process of exploring alternatives.

TABLE 16.1 *The Four Identity Statuses of James Marcia*

		Exploration: Yes	Exploration: No
Commitment	Yes	Identity Achievement	Foreclosure
	No	Moratorium	Diffusion

in a carefree, uninvolved way or may be unhappy and lonely. Some individuals in the diffusion status are apathetic and adopt an "I don't care" attitude. Others are angry, alienated, and rebellious and may reject socially approved goals, values, and beliefs (Archer & Waterman, 1990; Marcia, 1991; Marcia et al., 1993).

In the **foreclosure** status, individuals have made commitments without ever seriously considering alternatives. These commitments usually are established early in life and often are based on identification with parents, teachers, or other authority figures who have made a strong impression on the child. For example, a college student may unquestioningly prepare for a career that has been chosen for him by his parents. In other cases, the adolescent may uncritically adopt the lifestyle of a religious cult or extremist political group (Waterman & Archer, 1990). Foreclosed individuals tend to be more authoritarian and inflexible than individuals in other identity statuses (Berzonsky, Kuk, & Storer, 1993; Marcia, 1991).

The **moratorium** identity status refers to a person who is actively exploring alternatives in an attempt to make choices with regard to occupation, ideological beliefs, and so on (Patterson et al., 1992). Individuals in the moratorium status often are anxious and intense and have ambivalent feelings toward their parents as they struggle to work toward commitment (Kroger, 1989, 2000).

The **identity achievement** status includes those who have experienced a period of exploration and have developed relatively firm commitments. Individuals who have achieved a clear sense of identity show a number of strengths. They have a sense of personal well-being in the form of high self-esteem and self-acceptance. They are cognitively flexible and show high levels of moral reasoning. They are able to set goals and work toward achieving them (Berzonsky et al., 1993; Waterman, 1992, 1999).

Reflect

In which of Marcia's "identity statuses" would you place yourself on, for example, career matters and religious beliefs?

foreclosure An identity status that characterizes those who have made commitments without considering alternatives.

moratorium An identity status that characterizes those who are actively exploring alternatives in an attempt to form an identity.

identity achievement An identity status that characterizes those who have explored alternatives and have developed commitments.

Development of Identity Statuses

Before the high school years, children show little interest in questions related to identity. Most of them are either in the identity diffusion or foreclosure statuses. During the high school and college years, adolescents increasingly move from the diffusion and foreclosure statuses to the moratorium and achievement statuses (Kroger, 1989, 2000; Waterman & Archer, 1990). The greatest gains in identity formation occur during the college years (Waterman, 1985, 1999). In college, individuals are exposed to a broad spectrum of lifestyles, belief systems, and career choices. These experiences can serve as a catalyst for consideration of a variety of identity issues. Are you one of the many college students who have changed majors once or twice (or more)? If so, you have most likely experienced the moratorium identity status, which is quite common among college students. You should be comforted by the results of numerous studies that show that college seniors have a stronger sense of personal identity than first-year students. Furthermore, the identity commitments of seniors are more likely to result from successfully resolving the identity crises experienced during the moratorium phase (Waterman & Archer, 1990).

Ethnicity, Gender, and Identity

The question "Who am I?" had a special significance for journalist Don Terry as he was growing up:

> When I was a kid growing up in Chicago, I used to do anything I could to put off going to bed. One of my favorite delaying tactics was to engage my mother in a discussion about the important questions of the day, questions my friends and I had debated in the backyards of our neighborhood that afternoon—like Who did God root for, the Cubs or the White Sox? (The correct answer was, and still is, the White Sox.)
>
> Then one night I remember asking my mother something I had been wondering for a long time. "Mom," I asked, "What am I?"
>
> "You're my darling Donny," she said.
>
> "I know. But what else am I?"
>
> "You're a precious little boy who someday will grow up to be a wonderful, handsome man."
>
> "What I mean is, you're white and Dad's black, so what does that make me?"
>
> "Oh, I see," she said. "Well, you're half-black and you're half-white, so you're the best of both worlds."
>
> The next day, I told my friends that I was neither black nor white. "I'm the best of both worlds," I announced proudly.
>
> "Man, you're crazy," one of the backyard boys said. "You're not even the best of your family. Your sister is. That girl is fine."
>
> For much of my life, I've tried to believe my mother. Having grown up in a family of blacks and whites, I'd long thought I saw race more clearly than most people. I appreciated being able to get close to both worlds, something few ever do. It was like having a secret knowledge.
>
> And yet I've also known from an early age that things were more complicated than my mother made them out to be. Our country, from its very beginnings, has been obsessed with determining who is white and who is black. Our history has been shaped by that disheartening question. To be both black and white, then, is to do nothing less than confound national consciousness.
>
> —Don Terry (© 2000 by the New York Times Co. Reprinted by Permission.)

To be both black and white—African American and European American—can also confound or confuse the consciousness of the individual. Don Terry's mother had been married earlier to a European American, and he had European American brothers. His experiences of the next several years reveal his efforts to come to grips with a nation that saw him as African American, not half and half. He chronicles his experiences with prejudice, even within his own family, and how he eventually:

> "embraced blackness—as a shield and a cause." I signed up for a course on black nationalism. The decision was one of the most important developments of my life. Black studies saved me. It gave me a sense of discovery both academically and personally. Black studies helped me find an identity. As important, it helped me for the first time to understand my father's anger.

Question: How do sociocultural factors such as ethnicity and gender relate to one's self-identity? Being African American, Asian American, European American, Latino or Latina American, Native American, or a combination of these is part of the self-identity of the individual. So is one's gender—being male or being female. So is one's religion, whether it is Christianity, Hinduism, Judaism, or any of the hundreds of other religions we find in the United States.

Ethnicity and Development of Identity

The development of self-identity is a key task for all American adolescents. The task is more complex for adolescents who are members of ethnic minority groups (Phinney, 2000). Adolescents who belong to the dominant culture—in this country, European Americans of Christian, especially Protestant, heritage—are usually faced with assimilating one set of cultural values into their identities. However,

Reflect

Does your ethnic background play an important role in your own identity? Explain.

adolescents who belong to ethnic minority groups, such as African Americans and Jewish Americans, confront two sets of cultural values—the values of the dominant culture and those of their particular ethnic group (Phinney et al., 2000; Spencer et al., 2000). If the cultural values conflict, the adolescent needs to sort out the values that are most meaningful to him or her and incorporate them into his or her identity. Some adolescents do it cafeteria style; they take a little bit of this and a little bit of that. For example, a young Catholic woman may decide to use artificial means of birth control even though doing so conflicts with her religious teachings. Methods of birth control are well-publicized in the culture at large, and the woman may decide to use them, although she may not tell her priest, or her family.

Another problem in forging a sense of identity is that adolescents from ethnic minority groups often experience prejudice and discrimination. Furthermore, their cultural heroes may be ignored. A relative scarcity of successful role models can also be a problem, particularly for youth who live in poverty (Spencer et al., 2000). Identifying too strongly with the dominant culture may lead to rejection by the minority group. On the other hand, rejecting the dominant culture's values for those of the minority group may limit opportunities for advancement in the larger society (Phinney & Rosenthal, 1992). Biracial adolescents—those with parents from two different racial or ethnic groups—wrestle not only with these issues but also with issues relating to their dual cultural heritage (Gibbs & Hines, 1992; Spencer et al., 2000).

Many adolescents from ethnic minority groups have fewer educational and career opportunities than those from the dominant culture. If one cannot foresee a viable future, why explore one's options in any depth (Shorter-Gooden, 1992)? Some studies have found that adolescents from ethnic minority groups—Latino and Latina Americans, Asian Americans, African Americans, and Native Americans—tend to foreclose earlier on identity issues than do their European American peers (Streitmatter, 1988). Other studies find that many minority teenagers are actively engaged in the search for identity (Watson & Protinsky, 1991). Adolescents from ethnic minority groups may develop strategies for handling conflicting cultural demands such as those we find in the following comment:

> Being invited to someone's house, I have to change my ways of how I act at home, because of culture differences. I would have to follow what they do . . . I am used to it now, switching off between the two. It is not difficult. (Phinney & Rosenthal, 1992)

Question: Are there stages in developing an ethnic identity—that is, a sense of belonging to an ethnic group? According to Jean Phinney, the answer is yes. Phinney (1989) has proposed a three-stage model of the development of **ethnic identity.** The first stage is one of **unexamined ethnic identity.** It is similar to Marcia's ego-identity statuses of diffusion or foreclosure. In some cases, the early adolescent simply hasn't given much thought to ethnic identity issues (diffusion). In other instances, the young adolescent may have adopted an identity either with the dominant group or with the minority group based on societal or parental values, but without exploring or thinking about the issues involved. This represents a foreclosed status. In the second stage, the adolescent embarks upon an **ethnic identity search.** This stage, similar to Marcia's moratorium stage, may be based on a significant experience or incident that makes the adolescent aware of her ethnicity. During this stage, the adolescent may explore her ethnic culture, intensely participating in cultural events, reading, and talking to others. In the third stage, individuals have an **achieved ethnic identity.** This involves a clear, confident acceptance of oneself as a member of one's ethnic group.

As minority youth move through adolescence, they are increasingly likely to explore their own ethnicity and to acquire an achieved ethnic identity status. For example, only about one third of African American 8th-graders were found to show evidence of ethnic identity search, as compared with half of African American 10th-graders (Phinney, 1989; Phinney & Tarver, 1988). A longitudinal study (Phinney & Chavira, 1992) found movement from lower to higher stages of

Reflect

In which of Phinney's "identity statuses" is your ethnic identity? Are you satisfied with that status? Explain.

ethnic identity A sense of belonging to an ethnic group.

unexamined ethnic identity The first stage of ethnic identity development; similar to the diffusion or foreclosure identity statuses.

ethnic identity search The second stage of ethnic identity development; similar to the moratorium identity status.

achieved ethnic identity The final stage of ethnic identity development; similar to the identity achievement status.

ethnic identity between 16 and 19 years of age. And college undergraduates show higher levels of ethnic identity achievement than 11th- or 12th-graders (Phinney, 1992).

One way parents can facilitate adolescent ethnic identity is to be sensitive to cultural diversity. A study found that Asian American, African American, and Latino and Latina American adolescents who scored high on a measure of ethnic identity had parents who were more likely to state that they had tried to prepare their child for living in a culturally diverse society (Phinney & Nakayama, 1991).

Bill Aron/PhotoEdit

How Does Ethnic Identity Develop?

According to Jean Phinney, adolescents undergo a three-stage process of the development of ethnic identity: unexamined ethnic identity, ethnic identity search, and achieved ethnic identity. Adolescents from ethnic minority groups are typically faced with two sets of cultural values: those of their own ethnic group and those of the dominant culture. The values of the two cultures may conflict, presenting the adolescent from the minority group with the challenging task of reconciling and incorporating elements of both into his or her self-identity.

Gender and Development of Identity

And what of gender? Is the development of identity comparable for adolescent girls and boys? Erikson believed that there were important differences, and it seems that these differences reflected the times in which he wrote, more than a generation ago. Erikson wrote that the development of ego identity involves the development of a general outlook on life and the making of a commitment to an occupation or career. Individuals develop intimate relationships involving deep emotional attachment and sexual love in the following stage, that of intimacy versus isolation. Erikson himself admitted that this sequence more accurately described the traditional development of males. He suggested that the development of identity in females differed from that of males (Erikson, 1968, 1975).

Question: Does the development of ego identity differ in males and females? According to Erikson, the answer was yes. Erikson compared the importance of interpersonal relationships, careers, and philosophies of life to males and females. He concluded that relationships were more important to women's development of identity, whereas occupational and ideological matters were relatively more important to men's. He believed that a young woman's identity was intimately bound up with her roles as wife and mother. Erikson, like most thinkers of his day, saw a woman's primary roles as related to her home life. In sum, it was normal for men to develop their identities before they developed (meaningful) intimate relationships. Women, on the other hand, might well develop their identities simultaneously with the development of their intimate relationships (Patterson et al., 1992).

But is the development of identity in women and men as different as Erikson supposed? The evidence from numerous studies suggests that females approach identity formation in a manner that is comparable to, and sometimes more sophisticated than, that of males (Archer, 1992; Murray, 1998). In other words, as in so many other areas, the similarities between females and males apparently exceed the differences. In one study, both men and women claimed that the interpersonal area was the most important to them (Bilsker, Schiedel, & Marcia, 1988). Other studies (Archer, 1985, 1992) have found that adolescent females and males are equally concerned about occupational choices. Females, however, are more likely to integrate occupational and family plans than males are. For example, Sally Archer (1985) asked high school students questions regarding their vocational plans and their family plans. The vast majority of boys saw no relationship or potential conflict between their vocational choices and their plans to marry and have children. But the majority of girls saw interconnections between their career and family goals and expressed a desire to integrate both into their daily lives. This gender difference apparently exists because females continue to assume primary responsibility for child rearing, even though the majority of women now are

Reflect

Did your own development of ego identity follow either the "masculine" or "feminine" pattern described by Erikson? Explain.

employed outside the home. Archer poses the question: If society begins to hold males as accountable as females for family responsibilities, will males also begin to integrate their vocational and family goals?

What about the timing of identity development in women and men? Both begin the process of identity formation during adolescence. Those women who have uninterrupted careers tend to complete the task of identity achievement in late adolescence. Women who are full-time homemakers or who defer employment until their children are in school are more likely to develop a strong sense of personal identity after their children reach school age (Patterson et al., 1992).

Finally, men appear to develop identity before intimacy, as Erickson suggested. Some women also develop identity before intimacy, whereas others achieve intimacy before identity or achieve them concurrently (Schiedel & Marcia, 1985).

Development of the Self-Concept in Adolescence

The adolescent preoccupation with developing a sense of identity is part of a broader process of redefining the way adolescents view themselves. ***Question: How does the self-concept develop during adolescence?*** Prior to adolescence, children describe themselves primarily in terms of their physical characteristics and their actions. As they approach adolescence, children begin to incorporate psychological characteristics and social relationships into their self-descriptions. Young adolescents frequently describe themselves as having distinct and enduring personality traits (Damon, 1991).

The self-concept also becomes more differentiated; adolescents add more categories to their self-description. Also, self-descriptions begin to vary according to adolescents' social roles. Like the 15-year-old at the beginning of the chapter, adolescents may describe themselves as anxious or sarcastic with parents, but as caring, talkative, and cheerful with friends. Such contradictions and conflicts in self-description reach their peak at about age 14 and then begin to decline in later adolescence (Harter & Monsour, 1992). The more advanced formal-operational skills of the older adolescent allow her to integrate the many apparently contradictory elements of the self. For example, the older adolescent might say "I'm very adaptable. When I'm around my friends, who think that what I say is important, I'm very talkative; but around my family, I'm quiet because they're not interested enough to really listen to me" (Damon, 1991, p. 988).

Self-Esteem in Adolescence—Bottoming? Rising?

Reflect

What was your self-esteem like during early adolescence (about 12–14)? How did it differ during your late teen years? How do you explain the changes?

Question: What happens to self-esteem during adolescence? **Self-esteem** is often at a low ebb in early adolescence, at about age 12 or 13 (Harter, 1990a). That is, self-esteem tends to decline as the child progresses from middle childhood into early adolescence. What might account for this drop in self-esteem? The growing cognitive maturity of young adolescents makes them increasingly and painfully aware of the disparity between their ideal self and their real self. The sense of discrepancy between the real and ideal self is especially great in the area of physical appearance (Damon, 1991). Physical appearance contributes more to the development of self-esteem during adolescence than any other characteristic (Harter, 1990b, 1990c).

After hitting a low point at around age 12 or 13, self-esteem gradually improves throughout adolescence (Mullis, Mullis, & Normandin, 1992). It may be that adolescents adjust their notions of the ideal self to better reflect reality. Also, as adolescents increasingly develop competence in areas of importance to themselves, their parents, and their peers, they may gradually become less critical of themselves (Harter, 1990b, 1990c).

For most adolescents, low self-esteem produces a temporary sense of emotional discomfort (Damon, 1991). For others, low self-esteem has serious psychological and behavioral consequences. For example, low self-esteem is often found in teenagers who are depressed or suicidal (Bongar, 2002; Harter & Marold, 1991; Patton, 1991).

self-esteem The sense of value or worth that people attach to themselves.

Emotional support from parents and peers is important in the development of self-esteem during adolescence. Adolescents who feel that they are highly regarded by family and friends are more likely to have positive feelings about themselves than are those who feel they are lacking such support (Harter, 1990b; Roberts et al., 2000). In early adolescence, support from parents is equally as important as support from peers. By late adolescence, peer support carries more weight (Damon, 1991).

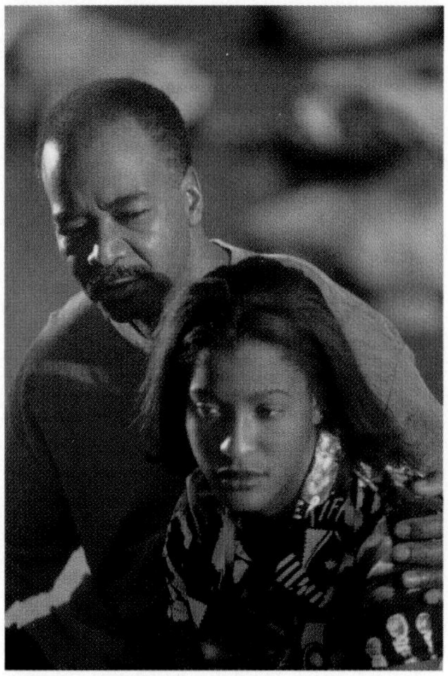

©SW Productions/Index Stock/PictureQuest

The Development of Self-Esteem During Adolescence

Self-esteem tends to dip during early adolescence as young people face the discrepancy between their selves and their self-ideals. Self-esteem then seems to rise as adolescence progresses and the adolescent develops competencies. During this critical period, emotional support from parents and peers can help the adolescent maintain and enhance self-esteem.

Ethnicity and Self-Esteem During Adolescence

Question: Are there ethnic differences in the development of self-esteem during adolescence? Erik Erikson (1968) believed that minority adolescents are likely to form poor self-concepts because they internalize society's negative views of minority groups. But research has consistently found that the self-concepts and self-esteem of minority youth are as positive as or more positive than those of European American youth (Gibbs & Hines, 1992). One study, for example, examined the self-concepts of African American, Latino and Latina American, and European American eighth-graders. Eleven different aspects of self-concept were measured. These included four academic aspects (including verbal and mathematical self-concepts) and seven nonacademic aspects (including physical ability, physical appearance, and relationships with parents and with members of the same and the other sex). African American students had higher self-concept ratings than did European American and Latino and Latina American students on all four academically related self-concept scales, as well as on six of the seven nonacademic scales (Widaman et al., 1992).

Other research has examined the relationship between self-esteem and the stages of developing ethnic identity. Jean Phinney and her colleagues interviewed Latino and Latina American, Asian American, African American, and European American students attending high school and college. Those who showed higher stages of ethnic identity also had higher self-esteem (Phinney, 1989; Phinney & Alipuria, 1990; Phinney et al., 1992). The association between self-esteem and ethnic identity was stronger for the minority youth than for the European American students. These studies and others suggest that having a positive self-concept is related to the extent to which adolescents have learned to understand and accept their ethnicity (Phinney & Rosenthal, 1992).

Gender and Self-Esteem During Adolescence

Question: Are there gender differences in self-esteem during adolescence? Girls generally show lower self-esteem than boys during adolescence (Block & Robins, 1993; Harper & Marshall, 1991). A national survey of 3,000 children in grades 4–10 indicates that the gender gap in self-esteem increases between the grade school and high school years (American Association of University Women, 1991). At 8 and 9 years of age, 60% of the girls and 67% of the boys were confident, assertive, and happy with themselves. But by the ages of 16 and 17, only 29% of girls, compared with 46% of boys, retained their positive self-esteem. More African American girls maintained high self-esteem than European American or Latina American girls.

Why is the drop in self-esteem greater for girls? One factor may be the physical changes of adolescence, which are central to the development of self-esteem in adolescence. Although physical appearance is a concern for both girls and boys, it is relatively more important for girls.

Others attribute the drop in girls' self-esteem to the negative messages that girls receive in school. In the words of one report, "Students sit in classes that day in and day out deliver the message that women's lives count far less than men's" (American Association of University Women, 1992, p. 67).

Carol Gilligan and her colleagues (Brown & Gilligan, 1992; Gilligan, Lyons, & Hammer, 1990) offer a related explanation, based on their interviews of girls as they make the transition from the elementary grades into middle school and high school. They report that as girls move into adolescence, they become aware of the conflict between the positive way they see themselves and society's view of females. Many

Reflect

How would you describe the roles played by your ethnicity and gender in your self-esteem during adolescence?

girls respond by "losing their voices"—that is, by submerging their own feelings and accepting the negative view of women conveyed by adult authorities.

Why are African American girls more likely to maintain their confidence in high school than other girls? One factor, researchers suggest, is that African American girls are surrounded by strong women they admire. Another factor may be that African American parents often teach their children that there is nothing wrong with them, only with the way the world treats them (Daley, 1991).

Review

(1) Erikson's fifth (adolescent) stage of psychosocial development is called ________ versus identity diffusion. (2) Erikson defined a psychological ________ as a time-out period during which adolescents experiment with different roles, values, beliefs, and relationships. (3) During the moratorium, adolescents often experience an identity ________. (4) Marcia identified four identity statuses representing the four possible combinations of the dimensions of exploration and ________. (5) In the ________ status, adolescents make commitments without seriously considering alternatives. (6) Identity ________ refers to adolescents who have experienced a period of exploration and developed relatively firm commitments. (7) The greatest gains in identity formation occur during the (high school or college?) years. (8) Phinney proposed a ________-stage model of the development of ethnic identity, beginning with unexamined ethnic identity and concluding with an achieved ethnic identity. (9) Erikson proposed that the development of interpersonal relationships is more important to (men's or women's) identity than are occupational and ideological issues. (10) Research shows that females approach identity formation in a manner that is (comparable to or different from?) that of males. (11) Men appear to develop identity (after or before?) intimacy. (12) During adolescence, the self-concept becomes (more or less?) differentiated. (13) Self-esteem is often (high or low?) in early adolescence. (14) Girls generally show (higher or lower?) self-esteem than boys during adolescence.

Pulling It Together: What are the connections between self-identity and self-esteem among adolescents from ethnic minority groups?

Relationships With Parents and Peers

Adolescents coping with the task of establishing a sense of identity and direction in their lives are heavily influenced by both their parents and peers. ***Question: How do relationships with one's parents and peers change during the course of the teenage years?***

Viewing adolescence as a period of "storm and stress" suggests that adolescents are in continuous rebellion against their parents. This picture is far from accurate. Adolescence is a time of transition in the relationship between parents and teenagers, but the changes need not be negative. Many, in fact, are quite positive (Collins, 1990; Steinberg, 1991).

During adolescence, children spend much less time with their parents than they did during childhood. In one study, for example, children ranging in age from 9 to 15 years carried electronic pagers for 1 week and reported what they were doing each time they were signaled by the pagers (Larson & Richards, 1991). There was a dramatic decline in the amount of time spent with family as children got older. The 15-year-olds spent half as much time with their families as the 9-year-olds. For older boys, the time with family was replaced by time spent alone, whereas older girls spent more time alone and with friends.

Adolescents continue to interact more with their mothers than with their fathers, continuing the pattern begun in childhood. Teenagers engage in more conflicts with their mothers, but they also view their mothers as being more supportive, as knowing them better, and as being more likely to accept the teenager's opinions (Collins & Russell, 1991; Noller & Callan, 1990). No wonder that teenagers are more likely to seek and follow advice from their mothers than their fathers (Greene & Grimsley, 1990).

The decrease in time spent with family may reflect the adolescent's striving to become more independent from parents. A certain degree of distancing from parents may be adaptive for adolescents as they engage in the tasks of forming relationships outside the family and entering adulthood (Galambos, 1992). But greater independence does not mean that adolescents become emotionally detached from their mothers and fathers. Adolescents continue to maintain a great deal of love, loyalty, and respect for their parents (Montemayor & Flannery, 1991). And adolescents who feel close to their parents are more likely to show greater self-reliance and independence, higher self-esteem, better school performance, and fewer psychological and social problems (Davey, 1993; Forehand et al., 1991; Papini & Roggman, 1992; Steinberg, 1996).

Reflect

How did your relationships with family members change during adolescence? Did you make the changes or simply respond to them? Were the changes for the better or for the worse? Explain.

The relationship between parents and teens is not always rosy, of course. Early adolescence, in particular, is a period characterized by an increase in bickering and disagreements and by a decrease in shared activities and in expressions of affection (Montemayor, Eberly, & Flannery, 1993; Smetana, Yau, Restrepo, & Braeges, 1991).

Conflict is greatest during the changes of puberty; conflict declines in later adolescence (Collins & Russell, 1991). Conflicts typically center on the everyday details of family life such as chores, homework, curfews, personal appearance, finances, and dating (Galambos & Almeida, 1992; Smetana, Yau, Restrepo, & Braeges, 1991; Steinberg, 1990a). Conflicts may arise in these areas because adolescents believe that personal issues—such as choice of clothes and friends—that were previously controlled by parents should now come under the control of the adolescent (Smetana, Yau, Restrepo, & Braeges, 1991). But parents, especially mothers, continue to believe that they should retain control in most areas. And so conflicts arise. On the other hand, many studies have confirmed that parents and adolescents are quite similar in their values and beliefs regarding basic social, political, religious, and economic issues (Paikoff & Collins, 1991). Disagreements in these areas are relatively few. Even though the notion of a generation gap between adolescents and their parents may persist as a popular stereotype, there is little evidence to support it.

And so it appears that adolescence is a time when teenagers and their parents establish a balance between adolescent independence and continued family connectedness. While some conflict is inevitable, it usually is not severe (Montemayor & Flannery, 1991). Although parent–child relationships change during the transition from childhood to adolescence, the change is gradual and is not marked by feelings of alienation. Most adolescents feel that they are close to and get along well with their parents (Galambos, 1992). Adolescents do not reject their parents' values, although they develop a less idealized view of their parents (Silverberg, Tennenbaum, & Jacob, 1992). A very small proportion of families—perhaps 5 to 10%—do suffer severe strains during a child's adolescence (Steinberg, 1991). But this is not normal, and professional help should be sought in these instances.

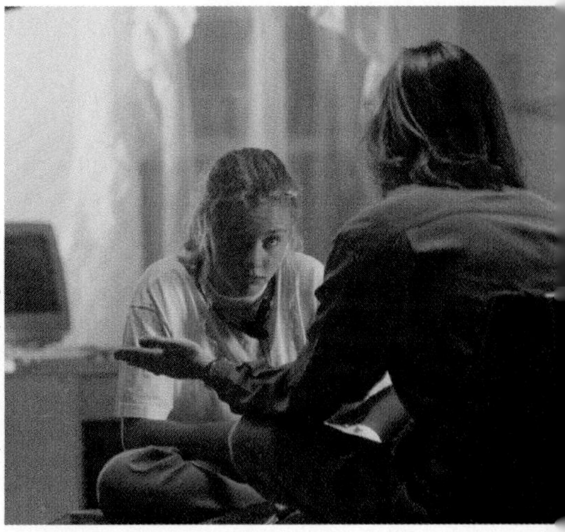

What Happens to Relationships With Parents During Adolescence?

Parent–adolescent relationships become redefined to some degree during adolescence, as most adolescents engage in normal striving for independence. There are often conflicts about choice of friends and clothing and how and where the adolescent spends his or her time. But most parent–adolescent relationships remain reasonably warm; and, despite conflict, the majority of adolescents continue to love and respect their parents.

Parenting Styles

Children's development is affected by the degree to which their parents show warmth and set limits on the child's behavior. Differences in parenting styles continue to influence the development of adolescents as well (Baumrind, 1991a, 1991b; Lamborn et al., 1991). Authoritative parents are warm and permit their adolescents to express their opinions, and yet they also set limits on their behavior. Adolescents from authoritative homes show more competent behavior than any other group of teenagers. They are more self-reliant, do better in school, have better mental health, and show the lowest incidence of psychological problems and misconduct, including drug use. Permissive parents are high in warmth but low in control. Their adolescents are nearly as competent and well-adjusted as those from authoritative homes, but they are more likely to show deviant behavior such as school misconduct and drug use. Authoritarian parents are high in restrictiveness and control but low in warmth. Their adolescents do reasonably well in school, and they show a low incidence of deviant behavior. But they are more likely to be withdrawn, anxious, and depressed and to have low self-confidence. Neglecting–rejecting parents, who are low in both control and warmth, have adolescents who are the least competent and have the most problems in all areas.

Relationships With Peers

The transition from childhood to adolescence is accompanied by a shift in the relative importance of parents and peers. Although relationships with parents generally remain positive in adolescence, the role of peers as a source of activities, influence, and support increases markedly during the teen years. For example, parents are perceived as the most frequent providers of social and emotional support by fourth-graders. But by seventh grade, friends of the same gender are seen to be as supportive as parents. And by tenth grade, same-gender friends are viewed as providing more support than parents (Furman & Buhrmester, 1992). Let's examine more closely the role of friends and the peer group during adolescence.

Friendships in Adolescence

Friendships occupy an increasingly important place in the lives of adolescents. Adolescents have more friends than younger children do (Feiring & Lewis, 1991). Most adolescents have one or two "best friends" and several good friends. Teenagers see their friends frequently, usually several hours a day (Hartup, 1993). And when teenagers are not with their friends, you can often find them talking with each other on the phone. In fact, I frequently warned my children that I would take them in for major surgery—telephonectomy—unless they got the phones out of their ears by themselves. The warning went unheard (because the children were on the phone). I therefore solved the problem by having a separate line installed for the children and investing heavily in the local telephone company.

The Development of Friendship in Adolescence

Adolescents tend to spend more time with their friends than with their families. They look for one or more close friends with whom they can share their inmost thoughts and feelings. Adolescents also tend to belong to groups that are referred to as cliques *and* crowds. *All serve somewhat different but overlapping functions in the adolescent's life.*

Friendships in adolescence differ in important ways from the friendships of childhood. For one thing, adolescents are much more likely to stress the importance of intimate self-disclosure and mutual understanding in their friendships. For example, one eighth-grade girl described her best friend this way: "I can tell her things and she helps me talk. And she doesn't laugh at me if I do something weird—she accepts me for who I am" (Berndt & Perry, 1990, p. 269). Second, adolescents stress loyalty and faithfulness as important aspects of friendship more than younger children do. For example, they may say that a friend will "stick up for you in a fight" and won't "talk about you behind your back" (Berndt & Perry, 1990). Finally, adolescents are more likely than younger children to share equally with friends and to compete less with them.

Adolescents and their friends are similar in many respects. They typically are the same age and the same race. They almost always are the same gender. Even though romantic attachments increase during the teen years, most adolescents still choose members of their own gender as best friends (Hartup, 1993). Friends are likely to share certain behavioral similarities. They often are alike in their school attitudes, educational aspirations, and school achievement. Friends also tend to have similar attitudes about drinking, drug use, and sexual activity (Hartup, 1993; Youniss & Haynie, 1992).

Why are friends similar? Two possibilities exist (Hartup, 1993). First, individuals who are alike to begin with may choose each other as friends. Second, friends become more similar over time as they influence each other and share common experiences. Both factors may be at work.

Friendship is important in developing a positive self-concept and good psychological adjustment. Adolescents who have a close friend have higher self-esteem than adolescents who do not. Teenagers who have intimate friendships also are more likely to show advanced stages of identity development and have better psychological and social adjustment (Berndt, 1992; Bukowski, Hoza, & Boirin, 1993). These relationships have been found for both European American and African American youth (Savin-Williams & Berndt, 1990).

Ethnicity, Gender, and Adolescent Friendships

> I always notice one thing when I walk through the commons at my high school: The whites are on one side of the room, and the blacks are on the other. When I have to walk through the "black" side to get to class, the black students just quietly ignore me and look in the other direction, and I do the same. But there's one who sometimes catches my eye, and I can't help feel awkward when I see him. He was a close friend from childhood. Ten years ago, we played catch in our backyards, went bike riding, and slept over at one another's houses. By the fifth grade, we went to movies and amusement parks and bunked together at summer camp. We're both juniors now at the same high school. We usually don't say anything when we see each other, except maybe a polite "Hi." Since entering high school, we haven't shared a single class or sport. It's as if fate has kept us apart, though, more likely, it's peer pressure. (Adapted from Jarvis, 1993, p. 14)

Children are more likely to choose friends from their own ethnic group than from other ethnic groups (Hamm, 2000). This pattern strengthens in adolescence (Hartup, 1993). Adolescents from ethnic minority groups become aware of the differences between their culture and the dominant culture. Peers from their own ethnic group provide a sense of sisterhood or brotherhood that reduces the pain of feeling isolated from the dominant culture (Spencer et al., 1990).

One study compared friendship patterns of African American and European American adolescents attending an integrated middle school (DuBois & Hirsch, 1990). More than 80% of the students of both ethnic groups reported having a school friend of the other ethnicity, but only 28% of the students saw such a friend frequently outside of school. African American youths were almost twice as likely as European American youths to see a friend of another ethnicity outside of school. Children who lived in integrated as opposed to segregated neighborhoods were more likely to see a friend of another ethnicity outside the school setting.

Gender differences relating to peer intimacy and support were found for European American students but not for African American students. European American girls reported talking more with friends about personal problems and reported that their friends were more available for help than did European American boys. These findings are consistent with the gender differences discussed earlier in this chapter (Hartup, 1993; Youniss & Haynie, 1992). But African American girls and boys reported the same degree of intimacy and support in their friendships. How can these differences be explained? The researchers suggest that the African American students may have faced a number of ethnicity-related stressors in their school, which was integrated but predominantly European American. To cope more effectively, both girls and boys may have relied heavily on the support of their peers.

Intimacy and closeness appear to be more central to the friendships of girls than boys both in childhood and in adolescence (Berndt & Perry, 1990; Clark-Lempers, Lempers, & Ho, 1991; Manke, 1993). Both female and male adolescents describe girls'

Developing in the New Millennium

Teenage Lingo: The Case of "Hooking Up"

"Only yesterday," notes the copywriter for the Farrar, Straus & Giroux fall catalog, "boys and girls spoke of embracing and kissing (necking) as getting to first base. Second base was deep kissing, plus groping and fondling this and that." No longer; first base is today deep kissing, also known as *tonsil hockey*. The writer then speeds up to date in orally touching second and rounding third base, which is now "going all the way," and slides home with a surprise twist of the old sex-as-baseball metaphor: "Home plate is being introduced by name."

The occasion for this recollection and updating of antediluvian teenage lingo is the promotion of a new book of essays and short fiction by Tom Wolfe titled "Hooking Up." "How rarely our *hooked-up* boys and girls are introduced by name!" laments the promotion copy, which goes on to promise a chronicle of "everything from the sexual manners and mores of teenagers to fundamental changes in the way human beings now regard themselves, thanks to the new fields of genetics and neuroscience."

Wolfe has a sensitivity to *le mot juste** in describing social phenomena. The title of his "Right Stuff," a book about the early astronauts, has now become part of the language, as is his popularization of the mathematicians' *pushing the envelope*. In selecting *hooking up* as his title, he is again on the cusp of usage.

When we hear a sultry seductress say to an aging Lothario, "We'll *hook up* one of these days," what does her promise mean? (A *Lothario* is a male deceiver, from a character in Nicholas Rowe's 1703 play, "The Fair Penitent."

The compound noun *hook-up* (which *The New York Times* no longer hyphenates) was born in a political context in 1903, as "a *hook-up* with the reform bunch," and meant a general linkage. In 1930, the term became specific, as "a national *hook-up*" came to denote a radio network.

*French phrase meaning "the right or proper word."

© Tom & Dee Ann McCarthy/Corbis Stock Market

Is a Kiss by Any Other Name a Kiss?
Are these adolescents kissing? *Playing* tonsil hockey? Getting to first base? Hooking up? *Would you prefer to say that they are engaging in* tongue sushi? *Or if Japanese food isn't your cup of tea (huh?), perhaps it occurs to you that they may be* sucking face, messing around, mashing, macking, *or* mugging? *If all of that is too obscure, why don't we simply agree to say that they have their* linguae engaged in lubricious osculation? *Certainly, no one could argue with that. (Oh, go ahead: argue.)*

Source: Reprinted with permission from William Safire. (2000, June 18). Hooking up. The New York Times Magazine *online.*

friendships as more intimate than boys' friendships (Hartup, 1993). Girls spend more time with their friends than do boys (Wong & Csikszentmihalyi, 1991). Adolescent girls view close friendships as more important than adolescent boys do, and they report putting more effort into improving the depth and quality of the relationship (Moore & Boldero, 1991). Adolescent and adult females also are more likely than males to disclose secrets, personal problems, thoughts, and feelings to their friends (Dolgin, Meyer, & Schwartz, 1991; Papini et al., 1990; Dindia & Allen, 1992).

Friendship networks among girls are smaller and more exclusive than friendship networks among boys (Crombie & Desjardins, 1993). That is, girls tend to have one or two close friends, whereas boys tend to congregate in larger, less intimate groups. The activities of girls' and boys' friendship networks differ as well. Girls are more likely to engage in unstructured activities such as talking and listening to music. Boys, on the other hand, are more likely to engage in organized group activities, games, and sports (Youniss & Haynie, 1992).

Peer Groups

In addition to forming close friendships, most adolescents also belong to one or more larger peer groups. ***Question: What kinds of adolescent peer groups are there?*** Brown (1990) has identified two types of adolescent peer groups: *cliques*

As a verb, to *hook-up* has for a century also meant "to marry," a synonym of "to get hitched," as a horse is to a wagon. But not until the 1980's did the meaning change to a less formal sexual involvement. It was first defined as "to pick someone up at a party" and then progressed to "become sexually involved with; to make out."

The swinging sense mainstreamed in 1995. "A few women insist," wrote *USA Today*, "they never go out with the intention of '*hooking up*' or having sex," while a CNN commentator noted, "The kids see shacking up and *hooking up* as the equivalent of marriage." In 1997, *The Cleveland Plain Dealer* quoted a Brown University student as saying, "In a normal Brown relationship, you meet, get drunk, *hook-up* and then either avoid eye contact the next day or find yourself in a relationship." The scholarly reporter noted, "Depending on the context, a *hook-up* can mean anything from 20 minutes of strenuous kissing to spending the night together fully clothed to sexual intercourse."

To be *hooked*, taken from the fishing vocabulary, is to be addicted to drugs; however, with the addition of *up* to make the compound, the term has no sinister narcotics meaning. In current usage, which may not last long and is probably already fading, it most often means "have a sexual relationship." Nor is the "linking" verb limited to American English. An exasperated Liz Jones, editor of *Marie Claire*, wrote in the *Sunday Times* of London this year about men who are habitual sexual deceivers (*Lotharios*), "Are all men like this or is it just the ones I *hook-up* with?"

Linguae Engaged in Lubricious Osculation (Say That Again?)

Let's go back to first base. *Tonsil hockey*, as used at Farrar, Straus & Giroux to mean "deep kissing," is at least a decade old, having replaced *tonsil boxing*. A more recent variation is *tongue sushi*, which shows some metaphoric imagination: the Japanese *sushi*—cold rice rolled up with bits of raw fish and vegetables—is evoked to describe the mutual rolling-up of teenage linguae engaged in lubricious osculation[†].

Tonsil hockey goalies have, in a spasm of good taste, rejected the phrase, popular in the 80's, "to suck face." That undeniably vivid but odious locution seems to have been replaced in some localities with the almost euphemistic *mess around.* Its variants include *mashing*, *macking* (from *smack*, the sound of a kiss) and *mugging*, the senses of which run the semantic gamut from "flirting" to "foreplay with no intention of intercourse." Those familiar with Old Slang would call it "taking a long lead off first base."

Though *hooking up* seems a mediumistic metaphor for what used to be euphemized as "sleeping together," it is more romantic than the phrase in current use on college campuses: *parallel parking*.

Search Online With InfoTrac College Edition

For additional information, explore InfoTrac College Edition, your online library. Go to **http://www.infotrac-college.com** and use the passcode from the InfoTrac card that came with your book. Try these search terms: teenagers sexual behavior, hooking up, youth language.

[†]Tongue kissing, that is.

and *crowds.* **Cliques** are groups of 5 to 10 individuals who hang around together and who share activities and confidences. **Crowds** are larger groups of individuals who may or may not spend much time together and who are identified by the particular activities or attitudes of the group. Crowds are usually given labels by other adolescents. Think back on your high school days. Different groups of individuals are commonly given labels such as "jocks," "brains," "druggies," "nerds," and so on. The most negatively labeled groups ("druggies," "rejects," and so on) show higher levels of alcohol and drug use, delinquency, and depression than other groups (Downs & Rose, 1991).

Reflect

Did you belong to a clique or a crowd when you were in high school? What were the defining characteristics of the group?

Adolescent peer groups differ from childhood peer groups in a number of ways. For one thing, the time spent with peers increases. In the United States, teenagers spend an average of 20 hours per week with peers, compared with the two to three hours reported in Japan and Russia (Savin-Williams & Berndt, 1990). High school students spend more than half of their time with peers and only about 15% of their time with parents or other adults (Csikszentmihalyi & Larson, 1984).

A second difference between adolescent and childhood peer groups is that adolescent peer groups function with less adult guidance or control (Brown, 1990). Childhood peer groups stay closer to home, under the watchful eye of parents. Adolescent peer groups are more likely to congregate away from home in settings with less adult supervision (the school, for example) or with no supervision at all (shopping malls, for example).

A third change in adolescent peer groups is the addition of peers of the other gender. This sharply contrasts with the gender segregation of childhood peer groups (Brown, 1990). Association with peers of the other gender leads in some cases to dating and romantic relationships.

Dating and Romantic Relationships

Question: When do romantic relationships develop? Romantic relationships begin to appear during early and middle adolescence, and the majority of adolescents start dating by the time they graduate from high school (Savin-Williams & Berndt, 1990). The development of dating typically takes the following sequence: putting oneself in situations where peers of the other gender probably will be present (for example, hanging out in the mall), going to group activities where peers of the other gender definitely will be present (for example, school dances), participating in group dating (for example, joining a mixed-gender group at the movies), and finally, traditional two-person dating (Padgham & Blyth, 1991).

Dating serves a number of important functions. First and foremost, people date to have fun. High school students rate time spent with a person of the other gender as the time when they are happiest (Csikszentmihalyi & Larson, 1984). Dating, especially in early adolescence, also serves to enhance prestige with one's peers. Dating gives adolescents additional experiences in learning to relate positively to different people. Finally, dating provides preparation for adult courtship activities (Padgham & Blyth, 1991).

Dating relationships tend to be casual and short-lived in early adolescence. In late adolescence, relationships tend to become more stable and committed (Connolly, Furman, & Konarski, 2000). It is therefore not surprising that 18-year-olds are more likely than 15-year-olds to mention love, trust, and commitment when describing their romantic relationships (Feiring, 1993).

Peer Influence

Parents often worry that their teenage children will fall in with the wrong crowd and be persuaded by their peers to engage in behaviors that are self-destructive or go against the parents' wishes (Brown et al., 1993). How much influence do peers have on each other? Does peer pressure cause adolescents to adopt behaviors and attitudes of which their parents disapprove? Peer pressure actually is fairly weak in early adolescence. It peaks during mid-adolescence and declines in late adolescence, after about age 17 (Brown et al., 1993; Youniss & Haynie, 1992).

clique A group of 5 to 10 individuals who hang around together and who share activities and confidences.

crowd A large, loosely organized group of people who may or may not spend much time together and who are identified by the activities of the group.

Why do peers increase in influence during adolescence? One suggestion is that peers provide a standard by which adolescents measure their behavior as they begin to develop independence from the family (Foster-Clark & Blyth, 1991). Another reason is that peers provide social, emotional, and practical support in times of trouble (Kirchler, Pomberi, & Palmonari, 1991; Pombeni, Kirchler, & Palmonari, 1990).

It was once the conventional wisdom that peer influence and parental influence were in conflict, with peers exerting pressure on adolescents to engage in negative behaviors such as alcohol and drug use. Research paints a more complex picture. For one thing, we have seen that adolescents often maintain close and warm relationships with their parents. Parents and peers usually are complementary rather than competing influences on teenagers (Brown et al., 1993; Youniss & Haynie, 1992).

Parents and peers also seem to exert influence in somewhat different domains. Adolescents are more likely to conform to peer standards in matters pertaining to style and taste, such as clothing, hairstyles, speech patterns, and music (Camarena, 1991). They are much more likely to agree with their parents on many serious issues, such as moral principles and future educational and career goals (Savin-Williams & Berndt, 1990).

Adolescents influence each other both positively and negatively. Brown and his colleagues found that peer pressure to finish high school and achieve academically were stronger than pressures to engage in areas of misconduct, such as drug use, sexual activity, and minor delinquency (Brown et al., 1993). Moreover, teenagers were much less inclined to follow peer pressure to engage in antisocial activity than in neutral activity.

On the other hand, a 10-year study of 20,000 9th- through 12th-graders did find that some adolescents encourage one another to do well in school (Steinberg, 1996). Yet more often than not, adolescents discouraged one another from doing well or from doing too well. One in five reported not trying to perform as well as possible for fear of earning the disapproval of peers. Then, too, half reported that they never discussed schoolwork and grades with their friends.

It is true that adolescents who smoke, drink, use drugs, and engage in sexual activity often have friends who also engage in these behaviors. But we must keep in mind that adolescents tend to choose friends and peers who are similar to them to begin with. Peers reinforce behavior patterns and predispositions that may have existed before the individual joined the group. This is true for positive behaviors, such as academic achievement, as well as for negative behaviors, such as drug use (Brown, 1990).

A number of other factors affect the susceptibility of adolescents to peer influence. One of these is gender. Girls appear to be slightly more concerned with peer acceptance than boys, but boys are more likely than girls to conform to pressures to engage in misconduct (Camarena, 1991; Foster-Clark & Blyth, 1991). Parenting style also is related to susceptibility to peer pressure. Authoritative parenting appears to discourage negative peer influence, while authoritarian and permissive parenting seems to encourage it (Fuligni & Eccles, 1993; Foster-Clark & Blyth, 1991).

Review

(15) During adolescence, children spend (more or less?) time with their parents than they did during childhood. (16) Adolescents interact more with their (mothers or fathers?). (17) Adolescents generally (do or do not?) love and respect their parents. (18) Parent–adolescent conflict is greatest during the changes of ________. (19) In terms of parenting styles, adolescents from ________ homes show more competent behavior than any other group of teenagers. (20) The role of peers (increases or decreases?) markedly during the teen years. (21) Adolescents are likely to stress the importance of intimate self-________and mutual understanding in their friendships. (22) Children are more likely to choose friends

from (their own or other?) ethnic groups. (23) Brown has identified two types of adolescent peer groups: cliques and ________. (24) Peer pressure peaks during (early, middle, or late) adolescence.

Pulling It Together: What are the effects of peers on the development of the adolescent?

Sexuality—When? What? (How?) Who? Where? and Why?—Not to Mention, "Should I?"

> My first sexual experience occurred in a car after the high school junior prom. We were both virgins, very uncertain but very much in love. We had been going together since eighth grade. The experience was somewhat painful. I remember wondering if I would look different to my mother the next day. I guess I didn't because nothing was said. (Adapted from Morrison et al., 1980, p. 108)

In an episode of the TV series *Growing Pains,* an adolescent was referred to as a "hormone with feet." Yes, it's fair to say that many or most adolescents are preoccupied with sexual concerns to some degree and that these concerns are fueled by a powerful sex drive. And many or most adolescents are not quite sure about what to do with these pressing urges. Should they masturbate? Should they pet? Should they engage in sexual intercourse? Parents and sex educators often say no, or wait. Yet it can seem that "Everyone's doing it." Teenagers today are bombarded with sexual messages in the media, including those offered by scantily clad, hip grinding, crotch-grabbing pop stars; print ads for barely-there underwear; and countless articles on "How to tell if your boyfriend has been (whatever)" and "The ten things that will drive your girlfriend wild" (Rathus et al., 2002). Teenagers are strongly motivated to follow the crowd; yet, they are also influenced by the views of their parents and teachers. So what is a teen to do? What *do* American teens do? ***Questions: What are some patterns of sexual behavior in adolescence? What are some of the factors that influence these behaviors?***

Sexual activity in adolescence can take many forms. In this section, we consider masturbation, homosexuality, heterosexuality, and use of contraceptives.

Masturbation

Masturbation, or sexual self-stimulation, is the most common sexual outlet in adolescents. Even before children conceive of sexual experiences with others, they may learn that touching their own genitals can produce pleasure. But pleasure is not the only reason that adolescents masturbate. Table 16.2 lists reasons for masturbation, according to a survey taken in the 1990s. The survey was taken with people aged 18–59, so the actual percentages may not be all that accurate for adolescents. But it is worth noting that respondents report that the main reasons for masturbation are to relieve sexual tension, to obtain physical pleasure, and to fill in for the unavailability of sex partners. Many also masturbate to relieve general tension—that is, to relax.

However, most adolescents in the United States come from the Judeo-Christian tradition; and within that tradition, masturbation has been condemned as sinful (Allen, 2000). Early Judeo-Christian attitudes toward masturbation reflected the censure that was applied toward nonprocreative sexual acts. Historians suspect that ancient Jews and Christians condemned sexual practices that did not lead to pregnancy because of the need for an increase in their numbers. The need for children is also linked to the widespread view that marital sex is the only morally acceptable avenue of sexual expression. Throughout most of history, medical "experts" jumped aboard the bandwagon of condemnation. The 18th-century

masturbation Sexual self-stimulation.

TABLE 16.2 *Reasons for Masturbation (in Percentages of Respondents Who Report Reason)*

Reasons for Masturbation	Males	Females
To relax	26	32
To relieve sexual tension	73	63
Partners are unavailable	32	32
Partner does not want to engage in sexual activity	16	6
Boredom	11	5
To obtain physical pleasure	40	42
To help get to sleep	16	12
Fear of AIDS and other STIs	7	5
Other reasons	5	5

Source: Adapted with permission from Laumann, E. O., Gagnon, J. H., Michael, R. T., & Michaels, S. (1994). The social organization of sexuality: Sexual practices in the United States. *Chicago: University of Chicago Press, Table 3.3, p. 86.*

physicians S. A. D. Tissot and Benjamin Rush (a signer of the Declaration of Independence) believed that masturbation caused tuberculosis, "nervous diseases," poor eyesight ("going blind"), loss of memory, and epilepsy. In the 19th century, the Reverend Sylvester Graham was persuaded that certain foods stimulated the sex organs. He recommended grain products to help people control their sexual impulses and invented the "graham cracker." One Dr. J. H. Kellogg (1852–1943) identified 39 signs of masturbation, including acne, paleness, heart palpitations, rounded shoulders, weak backs, and convulsions. Also an advocate of grain products for impulse control, he originated the Kellogg cereals we find in supermarkets around the world. Now you are an expert on the history of cornflakes.

Despite this history, there is no scientific evidence that masturbation causes insanity, grows hair on the hands, or causes warts or the other psychological and physical ills once ascribed to it. Of course, adolescents who consider masturbation to be wrong, harmful, or sinful may experience anxiety or guilt if they masturbate or want to masturbate (Coles & Stokes, 1985; Laumann et al., 1994). Only about one in three (31%) of the adolescents surveyed by Coles and Stokes (1985) reported feeling completely free of guilt over masturbation.

Despite the widespread condemnation of masturbation in our society, surveys indicate that most adolescents masturbate at some time. The well-known Kinsey studies, published in the mid-20th century (Kinsey et al., 1948, 1953), suggested that masturbation was nearly universal among male adolescents, giving rise to the quip that "There are those who do it and those who lie about it." He found the incidence to be lower among adolescent females. The gender difference is found in nearly every survey that has been done on masturbation (Baumeister, Catanese, & Vohs, 2001; Coles & Stokes, 1985; Laumann et al., 1994; Leitenberg et al., 1993; Schwartz, 1999). Some researchers attribute the gender difference in masturbation to a stronger sex drive for males, due to higher amounts of testosterone (Baumeister et al., 2001). Some support for this view is found in research that shows that women—even older women—with higher levels of testosterone are more likely to masturbate (Shifren et al., 2000). Others attribute the gender difference to the greater social constraints that are often placed on females. Adolescents in the Coles and Stokes survey reported they started to masturbate at an average age of 11 years 8 months.

Table 16.3 shows the frequency of masturbation during the past 12 months among 18–24-year-olds, broken down according to level of education, religion, and ethnicity. These data conflict with a survey of high school students that suggests that Asian Americans are the ethnic group that is least likely to masturbate (Schuster et al., 1998).

Reflect

If someone asked you to participate in a survey on sexual behavior, would you do so? How do people who agree to participate differ from people who refuse? Can a survey be accurate when it excludes findings from people who refuse to participate?

TABLE 16.3 *Sociocultural Factors and Frequency of Masturbation for 18–24-Year-Olds During Past 12 Months*

	Frequency of Masturbation (%)			
	Not at all		At least once a week	
Sociocultural Characteristics	**Men**	**Women**	**Men**	**Women**
Frequency	**41.2**	**64.4**	**29.2**	**9.4**
Education (All age groups)†				
Less than high school	54.8	75.1	19.2	7.6
High school graduate	45.1	68.4	20.0	5.6
Some college	33.2	51.3	30.8	6.9
College graduate	24.2	47.7	33.2	10.2
Advanced degree	18.6	41.2	33.6	13.7
Religion (All age groups)				
None	32.6	41.4	37.6	13.8
Liberal, moderate Protestant	28.9	55.1	28.2	7.4
Conservative Protestant	48.4	67.3	19.5	5.8
Catholic	34.0	57.3	24.9	6.6
Ethnicity (All age groups)				
European American	33.4	55.7	28.3	7.3
African American	60.3	67.8	16.9	10.7
Latino and Latina American	33.1	65.5	24.4	4.7
Asian American	38.7	-----*	31.3	-----*
Native American	-----*	-----*	-----*	-----*

*Sample sizes too small to report findings. †Ages 18–59.

Source: Adapted with permission from Laumann, E. O., Gagnon, J. H., Michael, R. T., & Michaels, S. (1994). The social organization of sexuality: Sexual practices in the United States. *Chicago: University of Chicago Press, Table 3.1, p. 82.*

Such surveys are riddled with inaccuracies. One large issue is the extent to which the samples selected represent the population of the United States. Then there is the issue of the accuracy of the self-reports of the respondents. One study found, for example, that adolescents are less willing to admit that they are masturbating at the time than when they are asked to look back some years later (Halpern et al., 2000). Perhaps they feel less guilty in retrospect.

Education is a liberating influence on masturbation. For both genders, people with more education reported more frequent masturbation. Perhaps better-educated people are less likely to believe the old horror stories about masturbation or to be subject to traditional social restrictions. Conservative religious beliefs appear to constrain masturbation. Conservative Protestants are less likely to masturbate than liberal and moderate Protestants.

Given these discrepancies, what can we conclude? First, most adolescents have masturbated. Masturbation is a common outlet for sexual tensions during adolescence. Second, more boys than girls masturbate. Third, we do not have accurate figures on the incidence of masturbation. Fourth, although many adolescents believe that masturbation is harmful or wrong, education is a liberating influence on masturbation.

Sexual Orientation

The great majority of people, including the great majority of adolescents, have a *heterosexual* orientation. That is, they are sexually attracted to and interested in forming romantic relationships with people of the other gender. However, some people have a **homosexual** orientation. That is, they are attracted to and

homosexuality An erotic orientation toward members of one's own gender.

interested in forming romantic relationships with people of their own gender. Males with a homosexual orientation are referred to as *gay males*. Females with a homosexual orientation are referred to as *lesbians*. However, males and females with a homosexual orientation are sometimes categorized together as "gay people," or "gays." *Bisexual* people are attracted to both females and males.

The concept of *sexual orientation* is not to be confused with *sexual activity*. For example, engaging in sexual activity with people of one's own gender does not necessarily mean that one has a homosexual orientation. Sexual activity between males sometimes reflects limited sexual opportunities. Adolescent males may manually stimulate one another while fantasizing about girls. Male Sambian adolescents in New Guinea engage in oral sex with older males, since it is believed that they must drink "men's milk" to achieve the fierce manhood of the headhunter (Rathus et al., 2002). Once they reach marrying age, however, they engage in sexual activity with females only.

Coming Out

Gay and lesbian adolescents often face special problems. The process of "coming out"—that is, accepting one's homosexual orientation and declaring it to others—may be a long and painful struggle (Bagley & D'Augelli, 2000; Crockett & Silbereisen, 2000). Gay adolescents may be ostracized and rejected by family and friends. Depression and suicide rates are higher among gay youth than among heterosexual adolescents:

> Sexual orientation emerges strongly during early adolescence. Youths with emerging identities that are gay, lesbian, or bisexual, living in generally hostile climates, face particular dilemmas. They are well aware that in many secondary schools the words "fag" and "dyke" are terms of denigration and that anyone who is openly gay, lesbian, or bisexual is open to social exclusion and psychological and physical persecution. Some of their families too will express negative feelings about people who are gay, lesbian, or bisexual; youths in such families may be victimized if they disclose that they are not heterosexual. (Bagley & D'Augelli, 2000)

It has been estimated that as many as one gay, lesbian, or bisexual adolescent in three has attempted suicide (Hershberger & D'Augelli, 2000). They often engage in substance abuse, run away from home, and do poorly in school (Kilpatrick et al., 2000). These factors also heighten the risk of suicide among gay, lesbian, and bisexual adolescents (Goldfried, 2001; Hershberger & D'Augelli, 2000). And males who engage in anal intercourse without condoms are at greater risk of being infected with HIV.

Recognition of a gay sexual orientation—that is, "coming out to oneself"— may be only the first step in a lifelong process of sexual identity formation. Acceptance of being gay becomes part of one's self-definition. The term *gay, or homosexual, identity* refers to the subjective sense of being gay.

"Coming out to others" sometimes means an open declaration to the world. More often an adolescent feels more comfortable telling a couple of close friends than his or her parents. Gay adolescents often anticipate negative reactions from informing family members, including denial, anger, and rejection (Bagley & D'Augelli, 2000). Yet some families are more accepting. Perhaps they had suspicions and prepared themselves for the news. Then, too, many families are initially rejecting but often eventually come to at least grudging acceptance that an adolescent is gay.

■ Development of Gay Male or Lesbian Sexual Orientation

Students at Stratford, Connecticut high school get together weekly after classes to talk about sexuality and antigay bigotry. Many gay males and lesbians become aware of their sexual orientations during adolescence. Because much of society continues to condemn a homosexual orientation, many or most fear "coming out" to other people. Some do not even admit their sexual orientations to themselves—that is, "come out to themselves." Families differ in their willingness to accept a gay or lesbian family member, so many gay males and lesbians can only turn to one another for support. In any event, sexual orientation is one more factor that individuals incorporate into their overall self-identities.

Reflect

What are the attitudes of people from your sociocultural group toward gay males and lesbians? Do you share these attitudes? Why, or why not?

The Origins of Sexual Orientation

Surveys find that about 3% of the males and 2% of the females in the United States identify themselves as being gay (Laumann et al., 1994). Theories of the origins of sexual orientation look both at nature and nurture—the biological makeup of the individual and environmental influences. Several theories bridge the two. ***Question: What do we know about the origins of gay male and lesbian sexual orientations?***

Let's begin our search for the psychological roots of sexual orientation with psychodynamic theory, largely because of its historic importance. Freudian theory attributes the individual's sexual orientation to his or her identification with either male or female figures, particularly his or her father or mother. Identification with males or females has to do with the outcome of the Oedipus or Electra complex (Downey & Friedman, 1998). Freud believed that homosexuality represented an abnormal resolution of these complexes. Traditionally speaking, many psychoanalysts have attributed faulty resolution of the Oedipus complex to a "classic pattern" of family life that involves a "close-binding" mother and a "detached–hostile" father. In such a setting, boys are more likely to identify with their mothers than their fathers. Evidence for this view is sketchy, however, relying on a number of case studies. Also, many gay males have good relationships with both parents. Besides, many heterosexuals develop in homes that could be described as fitting the "classic pattern."

Reflect

Have you heard the term sexual preference? *The term implies that people choose their sexual orientation. Do you believe that people decide whether to be heterosexual or gay? Did* you?

Learning theorists look for the roles of factors such as reinforcement and observational learning. From this perspective, reinforcement of sexual behavior with members of one's own gender—as in reaching orgasm with them when members of the other gender are unavailable—might affect one's sexual orientation. Similarly, childhood sexual abuse by someone of the same gender could lead to fantasies about sex with people of one's own gender and affect sexual orientation. Observation of others engaged in enjoyable male–male or female–female sexual encounters could also affect the development of sexual orientation. But critics point out that most individuals become aware of their sexual orientation before they experience sexual contacts with other people of either gender (Laumann et al., 1994). Moreover, in a society that generally condemns homosexuality, young people are unlikely to believe that male–male or female–female contacts they observe or hear about in others will have positive effects for them.

Although gay people are less likely than heterosexual people to reproduce, sexual orientation nevertheless tends to run in families. There is some evidence for genetic factors in sexual orientation (Bailey et al., 2000; Dawood et al., 2000; Kendler, Thornton, Gilman, & Kessler, 2000). One study found that 22% of the brothers of 51 gay men were gay or bisexual, although one would expect to find only 3% of the brothers to also be gay if the relationship were just coincidental (Pillard & Weinrich, 1986). Twin studies support a role for genes. About 52% of identical (monozygotic) twin pairs are "concordant" (in agreement) for a gay male sexual orientation, as compared with 22% for fraternal (dizygotic) twins (Bailey & Pillard, 1991). Monozygotic (MZ) twins fully share their genetic heritage, whereas dizygotic (DZ) twins, like other pairs of siblings, have a 50% overlap.

Reflect

Why are people who believe that the origins of sexual orientation are biological generally more accepting of gay male and lesbian sexual orientations?

Sex hormones promote the development of male and female sex organs and regulate the menstrual cycle. They also have both activating and organizing effects on sexual behavior. That is, they fuel the sex drive and affect *whom* one will find to be sexually attractive. Sex hormones are thus likely candidates for influencing the development of sexual orientation (Lalumière, Blanchard, & Zucker, 2000).

In many species, there is little room for thinking about sex and deciding whether an individual will pursue sexual relationships with males or females. Sexual behavior comes under the almost complete governance of sex hormones (Crews, 1994). And much sexual behavior is determined by whether the brains and sex organs of fetuses are bathed in large doses of testosterone in the uterus. In male fetuses, testosterone is normally produced by the developing testes. Yet female fetuses may also be exposed to testosterone. They can be flooded with testosterone naturally if they share the uterus with many male siblings. Researchers can also inject male sex hormones into the uterus. When they do, the sex organs of females become masculinized in appearance and their brains become organized in the male direction, creating a tendency toward female–female mating efforts and other masculine-typed behavior patterns at maturity (Crews, 1994). Among rodents with such prenatal experience, girls will be boys—although infertile boys.

And in other experiments with laboratory animals, boys will be girls. In a typical study, pregnant rats were injected with drugs that block the effects of testosterone. When the drugs were injected during the sexual differentiation of the embryo's brains, male offspring were likely to exhibit feminine mating patterns at maturity (Ellis & Ames, 1987). That is, they made no attempt to mount females and became receptive to the advances of other males.

All right: It has been demonstrated repeatedly that sex hormones predispose lower animals toward stereotypical masculine or feminine mating patterns. Does this research suggest that gay males and lesbians differ from heterosexuals in their levels of sex hormones? Among gay male and lesbian adolescents and adults, the answer is apparently not. Sexual orientation has not been reliably connected with adolescent or adult levels of sex hormones (Friedman & Downey, 1994).

But do sex hormones influence the developing human embryo and fetus in the way that they affect rodents? The evidence is somewhat mixed and this possibility is continuing to receive intensive study (Dessens et al., 1999; Ellis, 1990). And if prenatal hormone levels affect the sexual orientation of the fetus, what causes the fluctuation in hormone levels? The answer may be that hormone levels in utero are affects by genetic factors, maternal stress, and a host of other factors—some suspected, many completely unknown. How does maternal stress fit into the equation? Stressful experiences can trigger the release of stress hormones including *adrenaline* and *cortisol*. Athletes sometimes use steroids to pump up their muscle mass (and aggressiveness). Cortisol is a steroid produced by the cortex of the adrenal gland, and it is chemically similar to testosterone. Cortisol could thus affect the prenatal development of the brain, especially if the mother is under continuous stress. It is possible that the brains of some gay males were feminized in utero and that the brains of some lesbians were masculinized in utero (Collaer & Hines, 1995; Friedman & Downey, 1994).

We have to conclude by confessing that much about the development of sexual orientation remains speculative. There are possible roles for prenatal exposure to certain hormones. Exposure to these hormones, in turn, may be related to genetic factors, use of drugs (prescribed and illicit), even maternal stress. Moreover, the possibility that childhood experiences play a role has not been ruled out. But the interactions among these factors largely remain a mystery. Nor is there any reason to believe that the development of sexual orientation will follow precisely the same pattern for all individuals.

Male–Female Sexual Behavior

Since the sexual revolution of the 1960s, adolescents have become sexually active in greater numbers and at younger ages (Gardner & Wilcox, 1993). Males tend to become sexually active at younger ages than females, and African American youth become active earlier than European Americans and Latino and Latina Americans (Dryfoos, 1990). By age 15, about 20% of all boys and 5% of all girls report having had intercourse. Among African American males and females, the figures are higher: 40% and 10%, respectively. By age 17, two thirds of European American and Latino American males are sexually active, compared with nearly 90% of African American males. By age 19, nearly 85% of European American and Latino American males and almost all African American males report sexual experience. Among 17-year-old females, 40% of European Americans and Latino and Latina Americans and 60% of African Americans are sexually active. By 19 years of age, 70% of European American and Latina American females and 85% of African American females have initiated sexual activity.

Use of Contraceptives

Despite the fact that more teenagers are engaging in sexual activity, many of them do not use birth control. More than half of all adolescents do not use contraceptives the first time they have sexual relations (Mundy, 2000). A substantial number of teenagers use contraceptives only sporadically or not at all.

Question: Which adolescents are most likely to use contraceptives regularly? The older teenagers are when they begin sexual activity, the more likely they are to use contraceptives (Treboux & Busch-Rossnagel, 1991). Other factors associated with contraceptive use include being in a committed relationship, having high educational achievement and aspirations, having knowledge about sex and contraception, having good communication and a supportive relationship with parents, and having high self-esteem and feelings of control over one's life (Mundy, 2000).

Determinants of Early Sexual Behavior

Most teenagers do not plan their first sexual experience. Rather, it is something that they perceive as simply happening to them (Brooks-Gunn & Furstenberg, 1989). ***Question: Why do some teenagers initiate sexual activity at an early age, while others wait until later?*** Let's consider some of the determinants of early sexual behavior.

Reflect

How important a part of your adolescence (or that of your peers) was sexuality? Did any of your peers experience problems related to their sexuality during adolescence? Did they resolve these problems? If so, how?

Effects of Puberty

The hormonal changes of puberty probably are partly responsible for the onset of sexual activity. In boys, levels of testosterone are associated with sexual behavior. In girls, however, testosterone levels are linked to sexual interests but not sexual behavior. Social factors may therefore play a greater role in regulating sexual behavior in girls than in boys (Brooks-Gunn & Furstenberg, 1989).

The physical changes associated with puberty also may serve as a trigger for the onset of sexual activity. For example, the development of secondary sex characteristics such as breasts in girls and muscles and deep voices in boys may make them more sexually attractive. Early-maturing girls are more likely to have older friends, which may draw them into early sexual relationships.

Parental Influences

Teenagers who have close relationships with their parents are less likely to initiate sexual activity at an early age (Meschke et al., 2000). Adolescents who communicate well with their parents also delay the onset of sexual activity (Brooks-Gunn & Furstenberg, 1989; Meschke et al., 2000). If these youngsters do have sexual intercourse, they are more likely to use birth control and to have fewer sexual partners. Among African American males, parental strictness also is associated with more consistent use of condoms and fewer sexual partners (Jemmott & Jemmott, 1992).

The double standard of sexuality in our society—that premarital sexual activity is acceptable for boys but not for girls—seems to influence the way in which parental communication affects sexual behavior in teenagers. In one study, for example, discussing sexual topics with parents was linked with delayed sexual activity in high school girls but with earlier sexual activity and with contraceptive use in boys (Meschke et al., 2000; Treboux & Busch-Rossnagel, 1990). The message for daughters appears to be "Don't do it," whereas the message for sons is "It's okay to do it as long as you take precautions."

Peer Influences

Peers also play an important role in determining the sexual behavior of adolescents. One of the most powerful predictors of sexual activity for both female and male adolescents is the sexual activity of their best friends (DiBlasio & Benda, 1992; Meschke et al., 2000).

When 1,000 teenagers were asked why they had not waited to have sexual intercourse until they were older, the top reason given was usually peer pressure (Dickson et al., 1998). Peers, especially those of the same gender, also serve as the primary source of sex education for adolescents. According to an ABC News *Nightline* poll (1995), 53% of American adults learned about sex from their friends. Thirty percent learned from their parents. When asked where teenagers today learn about sex, five of six (83%) said they learned from friends.

Developing in the New Millennium

Youth and Online Sexual Solicitation

"There are so many great things about the Internet," said Dr. Kimberly Mitchell in an interview (ABCNEWS.com, 2001). "It is definitely something that parents should encourage children to use, but we also think that parents should be aware of what is going on."

What was "going on" was online sexual solicitation. This means that children were being approached sexually by strangers online.

A preliminary study reported in the *Journal of the American Medical Association* (Mitchell, Finkelhor, & Wolak, 2001) found that nearly one in five (19%) youths who used the Internet regularly reported receiving some kind of sexual query or invitation from a stranger. According to this study, "Some of the unwanted behavior included simple requests like 'What do you look like?' to 'What is your bra size?'" The telephone survey of 1,501 randomly selected youth aged 10–17 also found that 25% of the youth who were solicited were highly upset by the experience.

Certain background information and behavior tended to put some children at greater risk of being solicited than others. The risk of being solicited was greater for girls than boys and for older teens than for preteens. The risk was higher for youth who had experienced a death in the family, had moved to a new home, whose parents were separated or divorced or recently unemployed. The risk was also higher for youth who participated in chat rooms, posted personal information, made rude or nasty comments, chatted about sex with strangers, or visited adult Web sites.

Mitchell further reported that only about one third of the youth's parents used any kind of filtering device to protect their children from unwanted solicitations—or to prevent them from visiting sex-oriented Web sites. Mitchell suggests that many parents do not use such devices because of "the ambiguity in them"; that is, their purposes and methodology are unclear to many parents.

What to Do

Parents can do several things to protect their children from online solicitation:

- Warn children not to give out personal information such as telephone numbers, addresses, or names online.
- Warn children not to give out their present location, such as the name of their school, their favorite haunts, and so on.
- Set the home computer in an open area like the living room or kitchen, rather than hiding it away in a bedroom or basement area.
- Report solicitations and questionable behavior to the police or to the Internet service provider.

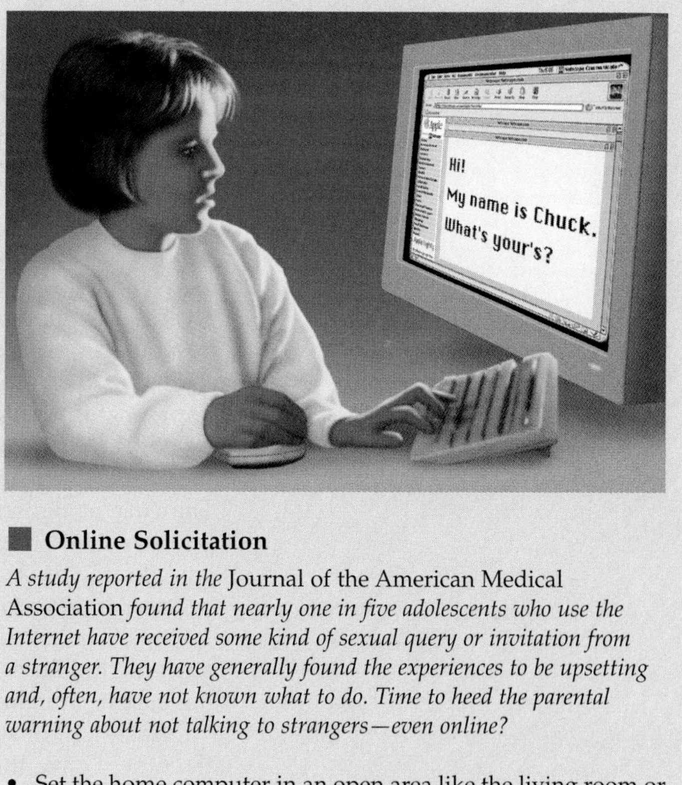

Online Solicitation

A study reported in the Journal of the American Medical Association *found that nearly one in five adolescents who use the Internet have received some kind of sexual query or invitation from a stranger. They have generally found the experiences to be upsetting and, often, have not known what to do. Time to heed the parental warning about not talking to strangers—even online?*

Search Online With InfoTrac College Edition

For additional information, explore InfoTrac College Edition, your online library. Go to **http://www.infotrac-college.com** and use the passcode from the InfoTrac card that came with your book. Try these search terms: chat rooms social aspects, chat rooms sexual behavior, chat rooms analysis, online sex, child sexual abusers.

Teenage Pregnancy

The title of this section is "loaded." It suggests that there is a problem with teenage pregnancy. So let's throw in a couple of caveats right at the beginning. First, throughout most of history, even most of the history of the United States, girls were first becoming pregnant during their teenage years. Second, throughout most cultures in the world today, girls are first becoming pregnant during their teenage years. Why, then, do we bother with a section on this topic? The answer is that in the United States today, most adolescents who become pregnant are unmarried. Moreover, most teenage pregnancies are unwanted. Most adolescents in the United States and many other developed nations choose to defer pregnancy until after they have completed part or all of their education. Some people defer pregnancy until they are well into their careers—in their late 20s, their 30s, even their 40s. So it is in our place and time that we have a topic called "Teenage Pregnancy," carrying the implication that it is something most people in the United States would rather not see.

Question: In this cultural setting, why do teenage girls become pregnant? There are many, many reasons. For one thing, adolescent girls typically get little advice in school or at home on how to deal with boys' sexual overtures or advances. Most adolescent girls do not have ready access to contraceptive devices. Among those who do have access, fewer than half use contraceptives reliably (CDC, 2000c). A number of teenage girls purposefully get pregnant in an effort to force their partners into making a commitment to them. There are those who are rebelling against their parents or the moral standards of their communities. Most girls are impregnated, however, because they know less than they think they know or their math is wrong. That is, they don't know as much about reproduction and contraception as they think they do, or they miscalculate the odds of getting pregnant. Even those who have been to all the sex-ed classes and who have access to family-planning clinics slip up now and then, especially if their boyfriends push them or don't want to use condoms.

For all these reasons, about 800,000 teenage girls in the United States are impregnated each year. The pregnancies result in about half a million births (CDC, 2000d; Ventura et al., 2001). It may surprise you that there is some "good news" in this; ten to twenty years ago, about 1 million girls were getting pregnant each year. The current figures, while large enough to make your head turn, represent an improvement. There has been a decline in the teenage pregnancy rate over the past decade or so because sexual activity among teenagers has leveled off and because more adolescents are, in fact, using contraception consistently (CDC, 2000c, 2000d). Researchers at the Centers for Disease Control and Prevention attribute the drop-off in careless sex to concerted educational efforts by schools, the media, churches, and communities.

Nearly half of all pregnant teenagers will get an abortion. The great majority of the others have their babies out of wedlock. Pregnancy rates are higher among adolescents of lower socioeconomic status and among those from ethnic minority groups (CDC, 2000d).

Consequences of Teenage Pregnancy

Question: What are the consequences of teenage pregnancy? Again, some caveats: The outcome of teenage pregnancies for young women who want their babies and have the resources to nurture them are generally good (Rathus et al., 2002). Females tend to be healthy in late adolescence, and again—historically speaking—people might wonder why we raise this issue at all.

We raise it because the medical, social, and economic costs of *unplanned* or *unwanted* pregnancies among adolescents are enormous both to the mothers and to the children. The problems begin with the pregnancy itself. Adolescent mothers are more likely to experience medical complications during the months of pregnancy, and their labor is likely to be prolonged. The babies are at greater risk of being premature and of low birthweight. These medical problems are not necessarily due to the age of the mother, but rather to the fact that teenage mothers—especially those who dwell at the lower end of the socioeconomic spectrum—are less likely to have access to prenatal care or to obtain adequate nutrition (Fraser, Brockert, & Ward, 1995).

The education of the teenage mother also suffers. She is less likely than her peers to graduate high school or move on to college (CDC, 2000c). Her deficit in education means that she earns less and is in greater need of public assistance (Desmond, 1994). Few teenage mothers obtain reliable assistance—financial or emotional—from the babies' fathers. The fathers typically cannot support themselves, much less a family. Their marriages—if they are married—are more likely to be unstable, and they often have more children than they intended (CDC, 2000c).

While the most attention has been directed toward teenage mothers, young fathers bear an equal responsibility for teenage pregnancies. The consequences of parenthood for adolescent fathers are similar to those for adolescent mothers. Teenage fathers tend to have lower grades in school than their peers, and they enter the workforce at an earlier age (Neville & Parke, 1991).

Children born to teenage mothers also are at a disadvantage. As early as the preschool years, they show lower levels of cognitive functioning and more behavioral and emotional problems. Boys appear to be more affected than girls. By adolescence, offspring of teenage mothers are doing more poorly in school, and they are more likely to become teenage parents themselves (Coley & Chase-Lansdale, 1998).

Again, these problems seem to result not from the mother's age but from the socially and economically deprived environments in which teen mothers and

Developing in a World of Diversity

Teen Births—Great Britain, Sweden, France, Canada, and USA

Does the United States stand to learn a lesson in sex education from other Western nations? A similar number of American adolescents are sexually active, but the birthrate among American teenagers is twice that of Great Britain and Canada and exceeds that of Sweden and France by five times. A study by the Alan Guttmacher Institute (2001), funded by the Ford Foundation and the Henry J. Kaiser Family Foundation, acknowledged that the birthrate among American adolescents has dropped by more than 20% in the past decade. Nevertheless, it remains a good deal higher than the rates in these four other Western nations.

© LWA–Stephen Welstead/Corbis Stock Market

What Did She Know, and When Did She Know It—About Birth Control, That Is?

American adolescents are no more likely to engage in sexual activity than adolescents in France, Great Britain, Canada, and Sweden, but they are much more likely to become pregnant. Why? Some social critics argue that the reason is that sex education in the United States often translates simply into "Don't do it." The other nations are more "realistic" about adolescent sexual activity and more willing to provide adolescents with information and contraceptives. Other social critics support the just-don't-do-it approach and attribute teenage pregnancy to the "breakdown in moral standards." What's your view?

their children often live. Teenage mothers also may be less knowledgeable about child rearing than older mothers and may provide their babies with fewer opportunities for stimulation (Coley & Chase-Lansdale, 1998).

Some teenage mothers and their children fare better than others. A study of teenage mothers in Baltimore who were followed over a 20-year period found that many of these women returned to school, left public assistance, and found stable employment (Furstenberg, Hughes, & Brooks-Gunn, 1992). Such positive changes in the lives of teenage mothers are associated with more favorable development in their children (Dubow & Luster, 1990).

Support for Pregnant Teenagers

A number of programs have been designed to promote positive social, economic, health, and developmental outcomes for pregnant teenagers and their children (Paikoff & Brooks-Gunn, 1991b). Programs for pregnant teenagers often include prenatal care services. Teen mothers who receive prenatal care during pregnancy are more likely to have healthy babies than those who do not have such care (Fraser et al., 1995).

Supportive services for teenage parents include family planning services, child-care services, and education about parenting skills, work skills, and life options. Some of these programs have been moderately successful in improving the lives of adolescent parents. Teenagers who participate in such programs have fewer children in the long run. They are less likely to drop out of high school and more likely to become economically self-sufficient. Their babies develop better as well (Coley & Chase-Lansdale, 1998). In one study by Tiffany Field and her colleagues (Field, 1991a), 80 low-income teenage mothers received training in stimulating and caring for their infants. In addition, half of these mothers were trained and employed as teachers' aides in an infant nursery. Compared with a control group,

Developing in a World of Diversity *(continued)*

In the year 2000, the birthrate among American adolescents aged 15–19 was 49 per 1,000. The birthrate for the same age group in Sweden, the lowest of the five countries, was 7 per 1,000 in 1999. Yet about the same percentage of American and Swedish adolescents are sexually active: 49% of American teenagers have initiated sexual intercourse by the age of 18, as compared with 53% of Swedish 18-year-olds. A similar percentage of adolescents was sexually active in each of the five nations, but Americans were somewhat more likely to become sexually active at below the age of 15. But this difference was too small to explain the discrepancy in birthrates.

Birthrates among adolescents are as high as they are in the United States because American teenagers are significantly less likely to use contraceptives, especially the birth control pill or related hormonal methods, according to the Guttmacher Institute. As a matter of fact, one in five American adolescents who was sexually active reported using no birth control method at all, as compared with 4% of English adolescents, 7% of Swedish adolescents, 12% of French adolescents, and 13% of Canadian adolescents. Whereas the majority of the sexually active adolescent girls in the other countries used birth control pills, only about one in three sexually active American girls did so.

There were some other differences in sexual behavior among adolescents in the five nations. For example, American adolescents reported engaging in sexual activity less regularly and with more partners than adolescents in the other nations. This pattern contributed not only to the higher birthrate but also to a higher rate of sexually transmitted infections. And although pregnant American girls were somewhat less likely to choose to have an abortion than girls in the other nations, American girls had more abortions overall because their pregnancy rate was much higher.

According to the researchers, cultural differences explain the discrepancy in birthrates. Great Britain, Sweden, France, and Canada are more accepting of the idea that adolescents will be sexually active. As a result, they provide adolescents with easier access to contraceptives and other reproductive health services and expect that adolescents who engage in sexual activity will do so responsibly. By contrast, many American teenagers do not have access to contraceptives, especially birth control pills.

In the United States, much of the emphasis in sex education is on promoting abstinence rather than responsible sexual behavior. As Leslee Unruh (2001), president of the National Abstinence Clearinghouse, says, the cultural approaches in the other Western nations are not "lessons we want to have instilled in our young people—more birth control pills, more condoms and a higher rate of abortion."

Yet Surgeon General David Satcher (2001) argued that schools in the United States should teach about contraception as well as abstinence. The Guttmacher Institute notes that the United States is the only Western country with a national policy that focuses on promoting abstinence only. Here the message seems to be "Don't do it—end of story." Other Western nations seem to accept the idea that many adolescents will be engaging in sexual activity and need help from adults to prevent unwanted pregnancies and sexually transmitted infections.

the babies of the mothers who received training showed superior growth and motor development during the first 2 years of life. The mothers themselves were more likely to return to school or work and were less likely to become pregnant again. This was especially true for the mothers who were trained as teachers' aides. Sad to say, the positive effects on both infants and mothers were short-lived and were no longer apparent by the time the children had reached grade school.

Preventing Teenage Pregnancy

The past several decades have seen a dramatic increase in programs to help prevent teenage pregnancies. The prevention efforts include educating teenagers about sexuality and contraception and providing contraceptive and family planning services. An overwhelming majority of American parents want their children to have sex education in the public schools. The nearby "A Closer Look" feature specifies what parents would like to see covered in sex education.

How successful are sex education programs? The better programs increase students' knowledge about sexuality. Despite fears that sex education will increase sexual activity in teenagers, that concern appears to be unfounded. In fact, some programs seem to delay the onset of sexual activity (Kolbe, 1998). Among teenagers who already are sexually active, sex education is associated with the increased use of effective contraception (Kolbe, 1998). And some sex education programs appear to reduce teen pregnancy rates.

School-based clinics that distribute contraceptives and contraceptive information to students have been established in some school districts—and not without controversy (Levy, 1993; "Where the Norplant Debate," 1993). In high schools that have such clinics, birthrates often drop significantly. In one such program in St. Paul, MN, not only did the birthrate drop, but contraceptive use also continued to be high over a 2-year period. One of the best-known programs is in Baltimore, where pregnancy rates dropped 30% in inner-city high schools that distributed contraceptives and contraceptive information but rose nearly 60% in schools that did not (Lewin, 1991).

The Washington, DC, Campaign to Prevent Teen Pregnancy is working to cut the rate of teenage pregnancy by encouraging parents and other adults to discuss the issues involved with teenagers (Donovan, 2000). The Web site of the campaign has links to information and resources on teen pregnancy. For more information, go to **http://www.teenpregnancydc.org**.

Review

(25) ________ is the most common sexual outlet in adolescents. (26) Within the Judeo-Christian tradition, masturbation has been seen as ________. (27) There (is or is not?) scientific evidence that masturbation causes physical or psychological problems. (28) A ________ orientation is defined as being attracted to and interested in forming romantic relationships with people of one's own gender. (29) The process of accepting a homosexual orientation and declaring it to others is called "________ out." (30) It is believed that prenatal exposure to sex ________ may play a key role in sexual orientation. (31) Adolescents who have (high or low?) educational achievement and aspirations are more likely to use contraceptives when they engage in sexual activity. (32) Teenagers who have close relationships with their parents are (more or less?) likely to initiate sexual activity at an early age. (33) The top reason usually given by adolescents as to why they did not wait to have sexual intercourse is ________ pressure. (34) Each year in the United States, about ________ teenage girls get pregnant. (35) Teenage mothers are (more or less?) likely to graduate from high school or attend college than other girls their age.

Pulling It Together: What suggestions do you have for preventing teenage pregnancy? What kinds of values underlie your suggestions?

A Closer Look

What Parents Want From Sex Education Courses

As a mother and librarian at a suburban high school outside Washington, Susan Madden holds few illusions about the sexual innocence of teenagers. She has overheard girls chattering in the corridors about condoms, shuddered at the scantily dressed stars on music videos and come across students' notes that read like intrepid dispatches from between the sheets.

"Now, it's everywhere, in your face," she said. None too pleased, Ms. Madden, a mother of three, turns to public schools for help. "There's so much bad information out there, and learning it from their friends is even worse."

While clashes over sex education often focus on parents who fear schools have been too permissive in teaching about sexuality, a recent survey suggests that the overwhelming majority of parents want schools to provide more, not less, sex education once children reach their teenage years. And they want discussions to cover a wide array of topics: abstinence, avoiding pregnancy, sexually transmitted infections, abortion, even sexual orientation.

The consensus found in the survey by the Henry J. Kaiser Family Foundation, a health research organization, appeared largely consistent throughout the country, and cut across socioeconomic groups.

It also blurred the lines of a polarized debate between advocates of a conservative approach that frames marriage as the only acceptable venue for sexual relations and a more liberal one that says teenagers should receive comprehensive information about sex, delivered without value judgments.

Instead, parents said schools should borrow from both sides, discussing abstinence, but also advising students about how to use condoms, discuss birth control with a partner and get tested for AIDS.

"Parents want it all," said Steve Rabin, a senior vice president at the Kaiser Family Foundation.

The Kaiser report polled 1,501 sets of parents and students, as well as teachers and principals, from February to May 1999, with a margin of error of three percentage points for parents, teachers and students, and a margin of error of six percentage points for principals.

The survey uncovered a gap between what parents say they want and what schools deliver. Nearly two-thirds of parents said sex education should last half a semester or more, and 54% said boys and girls should be taught in separate classes. The typical class, though, includes boys and girls and consumes just one or two periods of a more general course in health education. Almost all classes teach children about the dangers of contracting AIDS and other sexually transmitted diseases, along with the basics of reproduction and some discussion of abstinence.

But most parents want sex education to cover much more. Some 84% want sex education to explain how to obtain and use birth control. Even more parents want schools to teach children how to be tested for HIV or AIDS, how to respond to pressure to have sex, discuss birth control with a partner and deal with the emotional consequences of sex. They want schools to tell students what to do if they are raped. Four out of five parents want teachers to discuss abortion with their children, and three out of four want their children to learn about homosexuality and sexual orientation in the classroom.

Benita Garcia, a 40-year-old homemaker and mother of three in suburban Maryland, said she believed teenagers needed to learn about sex in school. "They're living a crazy life," she said. "Sometimes they don't listen to what the parents have to say. They think we're antiquated." With a 13-year-old daughter, though, she is worried that talking about sex with students too early could "open their mentality when they're not ready for it."

Heather E. Cirmo, a spokeswoman for the Family Research Council, a conservative research group in Washington, said the report's findings would not change her organization's position favoring abstinence until marriage, with no instructions about obtaining birth control or using condoms to prevent diseases.

"We believe that the parents who are participating in the study have been duped into believing that comprehensive-based sex education is what's best for their children," Ms. Cirmo said. "If you have a standards-based approach to sex that says abstinence is what we expect from you, teens will live up to that."

Source: Reprinted from Diana Jean Schemo. (2000, October 4). Survey finds parents favor more detailed sex education. New York Times, *pp. A1, A27.*

©Jonathan Nourok/PhotoEdit

What Parents Want in Sex Education Courses

American parents overwhelmingly favor sex education, according to recent surveys. One survey found that 98% of American parents want these courses to educate about sexually transmitted infections, and 79% believe that they should cover abortion. Three parents in four also wanted the courses to cover sexual orientation.

The Kaiser foundation's findings confirmed earlier, if less thorough, polls tracking parental attitudes toward sex education. Various polls have found steadily increasing support since the 1970's for teaching about birth control in sex education courses. Now, as the generation that matured during the sexual revolution is watching its own children come of age, support for frank discussions of sexuality with them has become nearly universal. Many parents say the threat of AIDS lends particular urgency to such talks.

A 1981 survey done by the Gallup Organization, on behalf of the Phi Delta Kappa association of professional educators, showed 70% of Americans believed young people should learn about sex in high school. Of them, 84% believed high schools should teach about sexually transmitted diseases, a figure that was up to 98% of all parents in the Kaiser report. Some 54% of those favoring sex education in 1981 believed it should cover abortion, a sentiment now shared by 79% of all parents. And 45% of those who favored teaching about sex in high schools in 1981 wanted courses to include some discussion of homosexuality. Today, 76% of parents want teachers to discuss sexual orientation with their teenagers.

"Parents want lots of messages, protective messages, coming at their kids," said Mary McKay, an associate professor of sociology at the Columbia University School of Social Work. "And as kids get older, they want it coming from a variety of sources."

Ramon C. Cortines, chancellor of the New York City school system from 1993 to 1995, said the survey showed that schools should "teach what students need to know, not to please the politicians or parents who scream the loudest." He added, "More, not less, sex education should be taught in the classrooms."

TABLE 16.4 *What to Teach About Sex*

Percentage of Parents Who Say Sex Education Should Cover . . .	
HIV/AIDS and other sexually transmitted infections	98
Abstinence; what to do in cases of rape or sexual assault; how to talk with parents about sex	97
How to deal with pressure to have sex and the emotional consequences of sex	94
How to be tested for HIV and other sexually transmitted infections	92
The basics of reproduction and birth control	90
How to talk with a partner about birth control and sexually transmitted infections	88
How to use condoms	85
How to use and where to get other birth control	84
Abortion	79
Sexual orientation and homosexuality	76

Source: Kaiser Family Foundation; reported in Diana Jean Schemo. (2000, October 4). Survey finds parents favor more detailed sex education. The New York Times, *pp. A1, A27.*

Educators around the country said they were not surprised by the broad support for ample information surrounding sex, though several described blocking of sex education by parents who view sex education as contributing to a breakdown in morality. In part, that is because parents who favor more thorough approaches to sex education nevertheless do not consider it a priority. [See Table 16.4.]

"I think the opponents are more vocal and more organized," said Arlene Zielke, a consultant to the Illinois Parent Teacher Association, of which she is a past president. "We're the largest parent organization in the state. Among our membership, we don't get the response back that this is the No. 1 priority, or 2, 3, 4 or 5."

Jan Wilkerson, chairwoman of the health concerns committee of the Texas Parent Teacher Association, served on a committee to update the health education curriculum of her state's public schools four years ago. But when it came to sex education, she found it impossible to overcome a well-organized opposition that insisted that only parents should discuss sex with their children.

"At that time in Texas, we had a 24-year-old grandfather," said Ms. Wilkerson, who lives in Diboll, in rural East Texas. "We had a 29-year-old grandmother in my town. I said, 'These people have families. But do those families have the ability to teach their children? Apparently not.'"

The Kaiser report found a disparity, however, between what teachers say they are teaching and what students say they are learning. A third of the teachers surveyed said they taught that "young people should only have sex when they are married," but only 18% of the students surveyed described that as the main message of their sex education.

The survey also suggested that the battle lines drawn by the camps that fight over sex education obscured, rather than described, the views of parents. Among the one-third of all parents who say schools should teach abstinence until marriage, for example, a substantial number also want schools to arm their children in case they do become sexually active, providing information about obtaining and using condoms, birth control and abortion.

Carol Callaway, a health and physical education teacher at Wakefield High School in Arlington, Va., said that her school district's policy was to teach teenagers to forswear sex until marriage, but that questions from students could take discussions elsewhere. "We might say until marriage, but what we're really trying to do is delay," she said.

Susan Soule, who teaches health education at Montgomery Blair High School in Silver Spring, Md., said teenagers from 76 nations and a variety of cultures filled her classroom. Many come from homes where their parents never married.

She could not insist that sex outside marriage is wrong, she said, adding, "I'm dealing with a population where marriage might not be the norm for them." Her school, more liberal than most, offers an elective course in sex education, and its roster of student organizations includes one devoted to gay pride.

Ms. Madden, an employee at Montgomery Blair whose children attended the school, said teachers often had more credibility than parents with adolescents, who seemed hardened these days by images of violence and nudity. "They're not allowed to be kids anymore," she said, and shook her head. "Teens have that invincible attitude, with drinking, driving, and sex, too."

© Chuck Savage/Corbis Stock Market

Shoplifting

Shoplifting is one form of juvenile delinquency. Male juvenile delinquents are more likely than females to commit crimes of violence. Females are more likely to commit "status offenses" such as truancy or running away. Overall, males are many times more likely than females to commit serious offenses.

Juvenile Delinquency

Did you ever commit a delinquent act in your teen years? If you said yes, then you are like most adolescents. In one large-scale study, for example, four out of five 11–17-year-olds reported that they had at some time engaged in a delinquent behavior (Dryfoos, 1990).

Question: What is juvenile delinquency? The term **juvenile delinquency** covers a broad range of illegal activities committed by a child or adolescent. At the most extreme end, it includes serious behaviors such as homicide, rape, and robbery, which are considered criminal acts regardless of the age of the offender. Other less serious offenses, such as truancy, underage drinking, running away from home, and sexual promiscuity, are considered illegal only when performed by minors. Hence, these are known as **status offenses** (Senna & Siegel, 2002).

Antisocial and criminal behaviors show a dramatic increase in many societies during adolescence and then taper off during adulthood. For example, about 4 in 10 serious crimes in the United States are committed by individuals under the age of 21, and about 3 in 10 are committed by adolescents under the age of 18 (Siegel, 2002).

Many delinquent acts do not result in arrest or conviction. And when adolescents are arrested, their cases may be disposed of informally, such as by referral to a mental health agency, without the juvenile's being formally declared delinquent in a juvenile court (Senna & Siegel, 2002). One thing is clear: Prior to the age of 40, the mortality rate for delinquents is twice that for other people (Laub & Vaillant, 2000). The "excess" deaths are generally due to accidents, violence, and substance abuse.

Ethnicity and Juvenile Delinquency

African American adolescents are more likely to be arrested than European American adolescents. For example, African American youths constitute about 13% of the adolescent population in the United States but about one quarter of the juvenile arrests and about one half of those arrested for violent crimes (Dryfoos, 1990). Yet self-reports of delinquent behavior are not much different for African American and European American youth (Siegel, 2002). How can this discrepancy be explained?

Several researchers have suggested that the overrepresentation of African American youth in the juvenile justice system is a product of racial bias. One study, for example, found that African American teens who were serious offenders were twice as likely to be arrested as European American serious offenders. And African American adolescents who had committed nonserious offenses were seven times more likely to be arrested than European American nonserious offenders (Siegel, 2002).

Economic factors also may help explain higher delinquency rates among youth from ethnic minority groups. Low family income, poor housing, and other socioeconomic deprivations increase the risk of delinquency for all adolescents (Campbell et al., 2001; Siegel, 2002). But since adolescents from ethnic minority groups are more likely than European American adolescents to live in depressed social and economic circumstances, they are at higher risk for delinquency (Gibbs & Hines, 1992).

Reflect

Were there any juvenile delinquents in your high school? What behavior patterns led to the label?

Gender and Juvenile Delinquency: What's Saucy for the Gander Isn't Necessarily Saucy for the Goose

Question: What are the gender differences in delinquent behavior? Boys are much more likely than girls to engage in most delinquent behaviors. About four boys are arrested for every girl, but the gender difference is as much as 8 to 1 for serious crimes (Siegel, 2002). Boys are more apt to commit crimes of violence, whereas girls are more likely to commit status offenses such as truancy or running

juvenile delinquency Conduct in a child or adolescent characterized by illegal activities.

status offenses Offenses considered illegal only when performed by minors, such as truancy and underage drinking.

away (Siegel, 2002). Some social scientists believe that the gender difference in the commission of violent crimes reflects the pressure of evolutionary forces. This view holds that females have inherited a "lower threshold for fear" because they are the ones who become mothers, and maternal survival is necessary for reproductive success (Campbell et al., 2001).

Even though the delinquent behavior of female adolescents is less frequent and severe than that of males, girls are more likely than boys to be arrested for being runaways. One obvious explanation for this fact is that girls may actually be more likely than boys to run away from home. Another possibility is that the juvenile justice system has a double standard in this area, viewing female running away as a more serious problem than male running away, and thus treating female offenders more harshly (Senna & Siegel, 2002).

Who Are the Delinquents? What Are They Like?

Question: Who is most likely to engage in delinquent behavior? Many risk factors are associated with juvenile delinquency. No one variable stands out as being most critical. Most likely, a combination of several factors increases the odds of a child's showing delinquent behavior (Lynam et al., 2000; Vander Ven et al., 2001). The direction and timing of these factors isn't always clear-cut. For example, poor school performance is related to delinquency. But does school failure lead to delinquency, or is delinquency the cause of the school failure (Dryfoos, 1990)?

Even if the causal paths are less than clear, a number of factors are associated with delinquency. Children who show aggressive, antisocial, and hyperactive behavior at an early age are more likely to show delinquent behavior in adolescence (Loeber et al., 1999). Delinquency also is associated with having a lower verbal IQ, immature moral reasoning, low self-esteem, feelings of alienation, and impulsivity (Lynam et al., 2000). Other personal factors include poor school performance, little interest in school or religion, early substance abuse, early sexuality, and delinquent friends (Ge, Donellan, & Wenk, 2001; Junger, Stroebe, & Van Der Laan, 2001; Laub & Vaillant, 2000). On a cognitive level, aggressive delinquents tend to approve of violence as a way of dealing with social provocations and to misinterpret other people's intentions as hostile when they are not (Shahinfar, Kupersmidt, & Matza, 2001).

Family factors also are powerful predictors of delinquent behavior. The families of juvenile delinquents often are characterized by lax and ineffective discipline; low levels of affection; and high levels of family conflict, physical abuse, severe parental punishment, and neglect (Dryfoos, 1990; Siegel, 2002; Widom, 1991). The parents and siblings of juvenile delinquents frequently have engaged in antisocial, deviant, or criminal behavior themselves (Mednick, Baker, & Carothers, 1990; Rowe, Rodgers, & Meseck-Bushey, 1992). For example, one nationwide study found that more than half of all juvenile delinquents imprisoned in state institutions had immediate family members who also had been incarcerated (Butterfield, 1992). This finding has sparked a lively debate about the possible role of genetic factors in criminal behavior. One point of view is that while most factors that increase the risk of delinquency are environmental, some children may be genetically more vulnerable than others. For example, hyperactivity, one of the risk factors for delinquency, may have a genetic basis (Zigler, Taussig, & Black, 1992). But most observers believe that delinquency and criminality are largely the outcome of a long and complex chain of psychological and social events and that genetic factors play at most a limited and indirect role (Goleman, 1992a).

Prevention and Treatment of Delinquency

Many approaches have been tried to prevent delinquent behavior or to deal with it early (Clark, 2001; Siegel, 2002). What are some of these approaches, and how effective are they?

Developing in the New Millennium

Keeping Teenagers in Line Online

A divorced mother of two teenagers in Livingston, N.J., finally realized that her 14-year-old son's online habits called for drastic steps. For months he had been glued to the family computer at all hours, getting into online quarrels. His grades were sinking, and letters from America Online were piling up, citing violations of its policy against vulgar language in its forums.

His mother tried parental-control software, but he circumvented it within minutes. She tried closing the family's America Online account several times; feigning her voice, he had it reopened. She installed hardware requiring a password to be entered to start the computer; he reconfigured the circuitry to get back in. One night, in desperation, she slept with the power cord under her pillow.

Then she took the computer away. For 7 months she hid the computer tower in the trunk of her car, covered with blankets. Finally, she said "he got it back, with the explicit understanding that I have the passwords to all his screen names." Since then she has been vigilant in inspecting the cache of Web sites he has visited, checking the Recycle Bin for signs of trouble.

"He certainly improved my computer skills," she said.

Teenagers, the moment you have been dreading has arrived: Parents are starting to get a clue about the Internet, and they are more and more determined to gain control of where you go, what you read, whom you talk to, and how you behave online. The Internet age is ushering in a new mode of parental oversight, one in which Mom and Dad draw Web-based boundaries, issue computer curfews, and worry about whether their hack-happy youngsters are making trouble.

Granted, many parents would still not know a motherboard from Mother Hubbard, but that doesn't mean they are not trying. In a survey by the Pew Internet and American Life Project, a nonprofit research center, more than 60% of parents reported that they checked to see which Web sites their teenagers had visited. About 60% of the 754 parents surveyed also said that they had set time limits for Internet use. In a survey of 774 parents conducted for Disney Online, 71% said they had set rules about what kinds of content their children could see online, and 88% said they had forbidden Internet access in the bedroom (a rule that the mother in Livingston swears by).

Some parents say they have no qualms about reading their children's e-mail by logging in under their screen names. Others report that they have learned to distinguish between the pause-laden typing patterns that signal that their children are doing homework and the frenetic tap-tap-tap of instant messaging. It is the modern equivalent of listening furtively at the bathroom door after the teenager drags the phone in there for a private conversation.

Roni Murillo, a mother in Syosset, N.Y., said she has "sneak-in times" when she tries to read the instant messages sent and received by her 15-year-old son, who once received a citation from AOL for posting a note containing profanity in a professional-wrestling forum. "I have to do it," she said, though abashedly. "I've seen other kids answer him with all these curses. There is no way to monitor that unless you are right there."

The snooping, needless to say, does not sit well with those snooped upon. Checking e-mail In boxes is considered the most flagrant privacy violation. "That's just wrong," said Freddie Alvarez, a 16-year-old from Islip, N.Y., who said he bought his own computer so he can use it whenever he wants. Other teenagers liken the e-mail box to a diary in arguing for their right to privacy.

Jen Albanese, 16, from Bergenfield, N.J., uses command keys to minimize her instant-messaging screen whenever her mother walks into the room. "She'll be like over my shoulder, saying: 'Jen what are you doing? Why did you put that screen down?'" she said.

The primary threats driving them to set rules, many parents say, are online pornography and child predators. But 45% of the parents surveyed by Pew said they also worried that their children might be the instigators of misbehavior like online threats or hacking. Many parents report that boys seem more inclined than girls to get into trouble. Surveys may validate their concerns. In an online poll conducted by Scholastic News Zone, an educational Web site, almost half of the 47,235 respondents, in grades one through eight, said they did not consider hacking a crime, even though unauthorized entry into computer networks is illegal. In Pew's study, about 9% of boys ages 15 to 17 reported that they had sent prank e-mail or an "e-mail bomb," which clogs people's e-mail In boxes with dozens or hundreds of copies of the same message.

Source: Adapted from Lisa Guernsey. (2001, July 19). Looking for Clues in Junior's Keystrokes. *New York Times*, pp. G1, G9. © 2000 by the New York Times Co. Reprinted by permission.

A Battle for Control

Parents' Tactics

- Enforcing time limits by installing software like TooMuchPC (**http://www.blairsoft.com**) and PC TimeCop (**http://www.parental-control-software.com**).
- Recording the keystrokes their children have typed in by using software like ChildSafe (**http://www.webroot.com/childsafe1.htm**).
- Using AOL's parental controls or installing filtering software.
- Setting up parent-only passwords that must be entered to log on.
- Checking for misbehavior by searching temporary Internet files or the Web browser history log or rooting through the desktop Recycle Bin.

Teenagers' Tactics

- Switching screens or minimizing windows when Mom enters the room.
- Forgoing the family's America Online account in favor of free e-mail sources like Hotmail.
- Arguing that their schoolwork requires more time online.
- Complaining that filtering software blocks too many educational sites.
- Clearing out the temporary Internet files, clearing the Web browser History log and emptying the Recycle Bin before logging off, to erase traces of where they have been.

■ Just Where Is He Going Today? Maybe "Nowhere" in the Physical World, but Too Far in Cyberspace?

In the "old days," parents might have been concerned that their adolescents were sharing Playboy *magazines or attending an R-rated movie. Today, however, adolescents may be surfing the Net for sex. What to do?*

Even when their teenagers seem to have no inclination toward computer mischief, parents have another concern: the sheer amount of time the children spend online. Robert and Marilyn Pohn of Chicago require their 15-year-old daughter and 12-year-old son to seek permission before going online and constantly check to ensure that they are using the computer only for schoolwork. Lauren, their daughter, seems resigned to the restrictions, remarking that the situation could be worse: "I have a friend who has an hour on Fridays. That's it. She's not happy."

David Blair, a software programmer and father of two teenagers in Fairfield, Iowa, decided that rules were not enough. He designed a shareware program called TooMuchPC that enables parents to set an automated timer that shuts down the computer at specific times or after a specified number of hours. In his house, where the computer is in the family office, a little window pops up on the screen when one of his children has been on the machine for an hour, to signal that it is the sibling's turn. His daughter, he said, "is addicted to ICQ," the instant-messaging tool, and used to fight over the computer with her brother, who wanted to play Soldier of Fortune. Now harmony reigns. "It is great," he said. "It eliminated all those arguments."

Addiction to instant messaging may not seem serious, of course, given the stories about teenagers' getting into far worse trouble. A wave of attacks that crippled access to some of the Internet's busiest sites in 2000, including CNN.com, Yahoo!, Amazon, and eBay, turned out to be the handiwork of a 15-year-old from Montreal who called himself Mafiaboy. As a minor, he faces up to two years in detention.

Dennis Moran, an 18-year-old in New Hampshire who went by the online name coolio, is serving 9 months in jail for defacing DARE, an antidrug Web site, with pro-drug slogans and images. In April, a 15-year-old in Connecticut was charged with hacking into government computer systems that track the movements of Air Force planes.

The image of the teenage hacker hunched over his bedroom computer has existed for some 20 years now. The difference today is that not only are vast numbers of children online, but many parents also are heavy Internet users themselves, both at work and at home, and are therefore at least aware of what their children might be doing. Chris Goggans, a founding member of a 1980's hacking group called Legion of Doom, said he was the only person in his family to have a computer back then—"I got mine from mowing lawns," he said—and his parents never used one. Eventually federal agents learned of Mr. Goggans's online snooping and obtained a warrant to search his computer. (He was never charged with a crime, he said.) His parents had until then been largely oblivious to his online activity.

"They knew something interesting was going on," said Mr. Goggans, 32, who is now an independent security consultant in northern Virginia. "They got phone calls from people who were obviously long-distance, people I'd met in bulletin boards. But as long as I was on the computer and not on the streets knocking over mailboxes, there were no indicators that there was anything negative in what was going on."

Some parents today are still oblivious—either to the online activities of their children or to the implications of those activities. Sarah Gordon, a senior research fellow at Symantec, has talked with several parents in analyzing the behavior of people who write computer viruses. She said she was dismayed to hear fathers saying that their sons' activities were "cool."

As a result, Ms. Gordon counts herself among a handful of security experts, including Mr. Goggans, who are trying to get parents to think beyond time limits, Internet filters, and computer confiscation. They hope to persuade parents and schools to teach children about the repercussions of their actions online.

One of the leaders of that crusade is Winn Schwartau, author of "Internet and Computer Ethics for Kids (and Parents and Teachers Who Haven't Got a Clue)." Mr. Schwartau said the book's aim was to get parents to ask themselves this question: "It's 3:30 p.m.—do you know where your children are in cyberspace?" He said he started working on the book years ago when he realized that his daughter, who is now 16, might not understand the hazards of hacking. Then last summer he discovered that his son, Adam, then 9, had stolen a friend's AOL password to read her e-mail. "I blew a minor gasket," he said.

In an interview, Adam still sounded surprised that his actions —which had begun with his secretly writing his friend Holly's password on a piece of paper as she used the computer—caused such consternation. "I was just bored, it was summer," he said. When Holly found out, he said, "she kind of kicked me."

Some parents are convinced that online discipline, combined with some poking around for verification, is the only strategy that will keep their teenagers in line online. Ms. Murillo, the mother of the 15-year-old in Syosset, said her next challenge would be the new computer that her son will be getting before school starts. "God knows what will happen then," she said. "But I'll be watching. God knows I'll be watching."

Search Online With InfoTrac College Edition

For additional information, explore InfoTrac College Edition, your online library. Go to http://www.infotrac-college.com and use the passcode from the InfoTrac card that came with your book. Try these search terms: internet filtering software usage, internet filtering software evaluation, parents internet children, chat rooms safety and security measures.

One type of approach focuses on the individual adolescent offender. Such programs may provide training in moral reasoning, social skills, problem-solving skills, or a combination of these. In some cases, these programs have the positive effect of reducing subsequent antisocial or delinquent behavior during short-term follow-ups of 6 months to a year. But long-term outcomes are not as promising (Guerra & Slaby, 1990). A problem with such approaches is that they focus on individual offenders rather than on the larger social systems in which juvenile delinquents are embedded.

Another approach tries to deal with various social systems, such as the family, peer groups, school, or community (Chamberlain & Reid, 1998; Perkins-Dock, 2001). Examples of such interventions are family therapy approaches; school-based strategies involving teams of students, parents, teachers, and staff; and various community and neighborhood-based programs. These broader, multisystem approaches appear to be more successful in reducing problem behaviors and improving family relations of delinquent adolescents (American Psychological Association, 1993; Dryfoos, 1990).

One other promising approach starts with the very young child and is aimed at promoting a host of positive child outcomes, not just delinquency prevention. This approach consists of the early childhood intervention programs, such as Head Start. The preschoolers who participated in several of these programs have been tracked longitudinally through adolescence. These follow-ups show several encouraging outcomes, including reductions in aggressive and delinquent behavior (Dryfoos, 1990; Zigler et al., 1992).

Review

(36) About __________ out of five 11–17-year-olds report engaging in a delinquent behavior at some time. (37) Offenses that are illegal only when performed by minors are called __________ offenses. (38) Boys are (more or less?) likely than girls to engage in most delinquent behaviors. (39) Children who show aggressive, antisocial, and hyperactive behavior at an early age are (more or less?) likely to show delinquent behavior in adolescence.

Pulling It Together: What are the risk factors for juvenile delinquency? What can be done to prevent juvenile delinquency?

Suicide: When the Adolescent Has Everything to Lose

In January 2002, 15-year-old Charles Bishop flew his small airplane into the side of a bank building in Tampa, Florida. It was no accident. He left a suicide note expressing sympathy for what terrorists had done 4 months earlier, flying passenger jets into the towers of the World Trade Center in New York and the Pentagon, outside Washington, DC. His teachers and friends expressed shock and dismay.

Terrorist examples and politics aside, his teachers and friends were trying to understand how Charles could have intentionally flown into the side of an—in this case—extremely unforgiving skyscraper. After all, he, like so many children and teenagers, had "so much to live for." Didn't he? Apparently Charles didn't think so. Neither do the other thousands of American teenagers who take their own lives each year.

Questions: How many adolescents commit suicide? Why do they do so? Suicide is the third or fourth leading cause of death among older teenagers

(National Center for Health Statistics, 2002). Since 1960, the suicide rate has more than tripled for young people ages 5 to 19. About 1 to 2 American adolescents in 10,000 commit suicide each year. About 1 in 10 has attempted suicide at least once. What prompts young people to take their own lives? Who is most at risk of attempting or committing suicide?

Risk Factors in Suicide

Most suicides among adolescents and adults are linked to feelings of depression and hopelessness (Sampaio et al., 2001). Jill Rathus—who has presented your author with grandchildren and research articles—and her colleagues (Miller at al., 2000; Velting, Rathus, & Miller, 2000) have found that suicidal adolescents experience four areas of psychological problems: (1) confusion about the self, (2) impulsiveness, (3) emotional instability, and (4) interpersonal problems. Some suicidal teenagers are highly achieving, rigid perfectionists who have set impossibly high expectations for themselves (Miller et al., 2000; Wu et al., 2001). Many teenagers throw themselves into feelings of depression and hopelessness by comparing themselves negatively with others, even when the comparisons are inappropriate (Barber, 2001). ("Yes, you didn't get into Harvard, but you did get into the University of California at Irvine, and it's a great school.")

Adolescent suicide attempts are more common following stressful life events, especially "exit events." Exit events entail loss of social support—as in the death of a parent or friend, breaking up with a boyfriend or girlfriend, or a family member's leaving home—and result in what Shneidman (1998) refers to as psychological pain, or "psychache." Other contributors to suicidal behavior include concerns over sexuality, pressures to achieve in school, problems at home, and substance abuse (Miller et al., 2000; Wu et al., 2001). It is not always a stressful event itself that precipitates suicide but the adolescent's anxiety or fear of being "found out" about something, such as failing a course or getting arrested (Marttunen, 1998). Problem-solving ability—or lack of it—is connected with suicide. Adolescents who consider suicide are apparently less capable of solving problems, especially their social problems, than other adolescents (Miller et al., 2000). Young people contemplating suicide are thus less likely to find productive ways of changing the stressful situation. They have borne the "psychache"; now they want a magical solution to problems that require work, or else a quick way out (Shneidman, 1998).

There is a tendency for suicide to run in families (Bongar, 2002). Many suicide attempters have family members with serious psychological problems, and about 25% have family members who have taken their lives (Sorensen & Rutter, 1991; Wilson, 1991). How do we account for the correlation? Do genetic factors play a role, possibly leading to psychological disorders, like depression, that are connected with suicide? Could it be that a socially impoverished family environment infuses several family members with feelings of hopelessness? Or does the suicide of one family member simply give others the idea that suicide is the way in which one manages problems? Perhaps these possibilities and others—such as poor problem-solving ability—form a complex web of contributing factors.

Ethnicity, Gender, and Suicide

Rates of suicide and suicide attempts vary among different ethnic groups. One in every six Native American teenagers (17%) has attempted suicide—a rate higher than that of other American teenagers (Blum et al., 1992). About one in eight Latino and Latina American high school students has attempted suicide and three in ten have considered it (National Center for Health Statistics, 2002). European Americans are next, with 8% attempting and 28% contemplating suicide. African American teens are least likely to attempt suicide (6.5%) or to think about it (20%). The actual suicide rates for African Americans are only about two thirds of those for European Americans at all ages, despite the fact that African Americans are more likely to live in poverty and suffer from discrimination (see Table 16.5). How can we explain this "disconnect" between hope for the future and suicide rates? One possibility is that some suicidal African American males may engage in risk-taking behaviors that lead to early death by homicide or accident. Another possibility is that cultural factors such as the support offered by extended families and the important role of religion may have a protective effect. Yet another possibility is that when African Americans are feeling low, they tend to blame social circumstances, including discrimination. Many European American adolescents, on the other hand, may feel that there is no one to blame but themselves.

About three times as many adolescent females as males attempt suicide, but about five times as many males succeed (National Center for Health Statistics, 2002; see Table 16.5). In part, males are more likely to "succeed" in their suicide attempts because of the methods they choose. The methods preferred by males are more deadly and more rapid: Males are more likely to shoot or hang themselves; females more often use drugs, such as overdoses of tranquilizers or sleeping pills, or poisons. Females often do not take enough of these chemicals. It also takes a while for them to work, giving people the opportunity to find them and intervene.

While the risk factors for suicide are similar for males and females, the relative importance of these factors differs. Thus, the likelihood of a teenage girl committing suicide is greatest if she suffers from major depression. But the best predictor of suicide for teenage boys is a prior suicide attempt (Pfeffer, 1991). The nearby "A Closer Look" feature describes some of the warning signs of suicide and some things you can do if you notice them in a friend or family member.

Review

(40) Suicide is a (rare or common?) cause of death among older teenagers. (41) Most suicides among adolescents and adults are linked to feelings of ________. (42) Suicide (does or does not?) tend to run in families.

Pulling It Together: How do we explain the different suicide rates among adolescent boys and girls and among adolescents from different ethnic groups?

TABLE 16.5 *Suicide Rates Among European Americans and African Americans—Rank of Suicide as a Leading Cause of Death and Number of Deaths by Suicide per 100,000 Population*

	All Races Combined		European Americans		African Americans	
	Male	**Female**	**Male**	**Female**	**Male**	**Female**
All Ages	8th leading cause of death 18.6/100,000	Not in top 10 causes of death*	8th leading cause of death 20.3/100,000	Not in top 10 causes of death	Not in top 10 causes of death	Not in top 10 causes of death
Ages 5–14	4th leading cause of death 1.2/100,000	6th leading cause of death 0.4/100,000	3rd leading cause of death 1.3/100,000	6th leading cause of death 0.5/100,000	7th leading cause of death	Not in top 10 causes of death
Ages 15–24	3rd leading cause of death 18.5/100,000	4th leading cause of death 3.3/100,000	2nd leading cause of death 19.3/100,000	3rd leading cause of death 3.5/100,000	3rd leading cause of death 15.0/100,000	6th leading cause of death 2.2/100,000

*Number per 100,000 unavailable in cases in which suicide is not among top 10 leading causes of death.
Source: National Center for Health Statistics. (2002, January 8). Abstracted from suicide statistics by age, race, and sex. Monthly Vital Statistics Report, 48 *(11). Atlanta: Centers for Disease Control and Prevention.* **http://www.cdc.gov/nchs/fastats/suicide.htm**

Epilogue: Emerging Adulthood—Bridging Adolescence and the Life Beyond

> When our mothers were our age, they were engaged. They at least had some idea what they were going to do with their lives. I, on the other hand, will have a dual degree in majors that are ambiguous at best and impractical at worst (English and political science), no ring on my finger and no idea who I am, much less what I want to do. Under duress, I will admit that this is a pretty exciting time. Sometimes, when I look out across the wide expanse that is my future, I can see beyond the void. I realize that having nothing ahead to count on means I now have to count on myself; that having no direction means forging one of my own.
>
> —Kristen, Age 22 (Page, 1999, pp. 18, 20)

Well, Kristen has some work to do: She needs to forge her own direction. Just think: What if Kristen had been born into the caste system of old England or India, into a traditional Islamic society, or into the United States of the 1950s, where the TV sitcom *Father Knows Best* was perennially in the top ten? Kristen would have had a sense of direction, that's certain. But, of course, it would have been the sense of direction society or tradition created for her, not her own.

But Kristen wasn't born into any of these societies. She was born into the open and challenging United States of the current generation. She has the freedom to become whatever the interaction of her genetic heritage and her educational and social opportunities will enable her to become—and the opportunities are many.

A Closer Look

Warning Signs of Suicide

The great majority of young people who commit suicide send out a variety of signals about their impending act (Bongar, 2002; Hendin et al., 2001). Sad to say, these signals often are overlooked, sometimes because parents and other people do not recognize them, sometimes because parents and other people in the adolescents' lives do not have adequate access to health care (MacDonald, 1999; Wu et al., 2001). Sometime adolescents do not receive help until they actually attempt suicide, and sometimes not even then (Gili-Planas et al., 2001; Wu et al., 2001). Here are some clues that a teenager may be at risk of committing suicide (Hendin et al., 2001; Maine, Shute, & Martin, 2001):

- Changes in eating and sleeping patterns
- Difficulty concentrating on school work
- A sharp decline in school performance and attendance
- Loss of interest in previously enjoyed activities
- Giving away prized possessions
- Complaints about physical problems when no organic basis can be found
- Withdrawal from social relationships
- Personality or mood changes
- Talking or writing about death or dying
- Abuse of drugs or alcohol
- An attempted suicide
- Availability of a handgun
- A precipitating event such as an argument with parents, a broken romantic relationship, academic difficulties, loss of a friend, or trouble with the law
- Knowing or hearing about another teenager who has committed suicide (which can lead to so-called "cluster" suicides)
- Threatening to commit suicide

Here are some things you can do if you notice one or more of these warning signs (Omer & Elitzur, 2001; Shneidman, 1998):

- Make an immediate appointment for the adolescent with a helping professional, and make sure the appointment is kept. Or suggest that the adolescent go *with* you to obtain professional help *now.* The emergency room of a general hospital, the campus counseling center or infirmary, or the campus or local police will do. Some campuses have suicide hotlines you can call. Some cities have suicide prevention centers with hotlines that people can use anonymously.
- Draw the adolescent out. Edwin Shneidman (1998), cofounder of the Los Angeles Suicide Prevention Center, suggests asking questions such as "What's going on?" "Where do you hurt?" "What would you like to see happen?" Questions such as these may encourage people to express frustrated psychological needs and provide some relief. They also give you time to assess the danger and think.

With freedom comes the need to make choices. When we need to make choices, we profit from information. Kristen is in the process of accumulating information about herself and about the world outside. According to psychologist Jeffrey Arnett (2000a), she is in *emerging adulthood*. In earlier days, adolescents made a transition, for better or worse, directly into adulthood. Now many of them—especially those in affluent nations with abundant opportunities—spend time in what some theorists think of as a new period of development.

***Question: So how do we define* adulthood?** There's a question. Legally speaking, adulthood has many ages, depending on what you want to do. The age of consent to marriage varies from state to state, but generally permits marriage in the teens. The age for drinking legally is 21. The age for driving varies. By and large, however, adulthood is usually defined in terms of what people do rather than how old they are. Over the years, marriage has been a key criterion for people who write about human development (Schlegel, 1998). Other criteria in use today include holding a full-time job and living independently (not with one's parents). Today, the transition to adulthood is mainly marked by adjustment issues such as deciding on one's values and beliefs, accepting self-responsibility, becoming financially independent, and establishing an equal relationship with one's parents (Arnett, 2001). Regardless of the continuing popularity of marriage, it is no longer necessarily a crucial marker for entering adulthood (Arnett, 1998a).

Adulthood itself has been divided into stages, and the first of these, young adulthood, has been largely seen as the period of life when people focus on establishing their careers or pathways in life. It has been acknowledged that the transition to adulthood could be slow or piecemeal, with many individuals in their late teens and early twenties remaining dependent on their parents and reluctant or unable to make enduring commitments, either in terms of identity formation or

A Closer Look *(continued)*

- Be empathetic. Show that you understand how upset the adolescent is. Do not say, "Don't be silly" or "You're crazy." Do *not* insist on contact with specific people, such as parents or a teacher. Conflict with these people may have led to the suicidal thinking.
- Suggest that measures other than suicide might be found to solve the problem, even if they are not evident at the time. Shneidman suggests that suicidal people can typically see only two solutions to their problems—either death or a magical resolution of their problems. Therapists thus attempt to remove the mental blinders of suicidal people.
- Ask how the adolescent intends to commit suicide. Adolescents with concrete plans and a weapon at hand are at greater risk. Ask if you might hold on to the weapon for a while. Sometimes the adolescent says yes.
- Extract a promise that the adolescent will not commit suicide before seeing you again. Arrange a concrete time and place to meet. Get professional help as soon as you are apart.

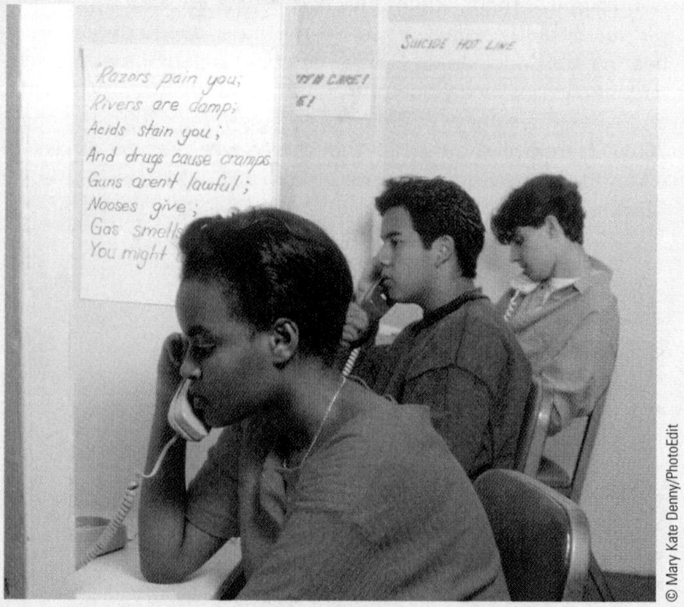

© Mary Kate Denny/PhotoEdit

Adolescents May Have "So Much to Live for"—But . . .

Suicide is a key cause of death for adolescents. Adolescents experience many conflicts and also dips in self-esteem. When they have failed at something—social or academic—when they feel they will be found out for something, when they are experiencing a "psychache," their thoughts may turn to suicide. How can you determine whether an adolescent is considering suicide? What can you do about it?

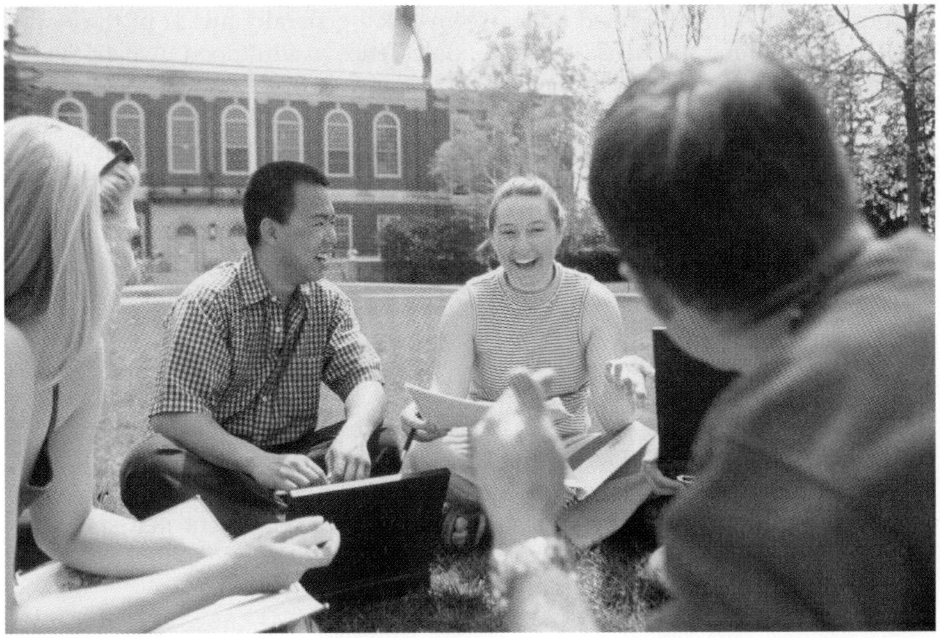

© Tom Stewart/Corbis Stock Market

"Emerging Adulthood"— A New Stage of Human Development?

Some researchers suggest that affluent societies like our own have spawned a new stage of development, emerging adulthood, which bridges adolescence and the full assumption of adult responsibilities. Emerging adulthood would be largely defined by an extended period of self-exploration, during which one has not yet become financially independent.

the development of intimate relationships. The question is whether we can speak of the existence of another stage of development, one that bridges adolescence and young adulthood. A number of developmental theorists, including Arnett (2000a), argue that we can. ***Question: What is "emerging adulthood"?***

Emerging adulthood is theorized to be a distinct period of development that straddles the ages of 18 through 25; it is found only in societies that allow young people an extended opportunity to explore their roles in life. These are affluent societies, such as we find in developed nations, our own among them. Parents in the United States are often affluent enough to continue to support their children throughout college and in graduate school. When parents cannot do the job, the government often steps in to help, through student loans, for example. These supports allow young people the luxury of sorting out identity issues and creating meaningful life plans—even if some still don't know where they are going after they graduate from college. Should they know who they are and what they are doing by the age of 21 or 22? Are they spoiled? These are value judgments that may or may not be on the mark. But let's note that many adults change their careers several times partially because they did not sort out who they were and where they were going at an early age. On the other hand, even in the United States, many people cannot obtain the supports necessary for sojourning in emerging adulthood.

Reflect

Do you know people who can be characterized as being in emerging adulthood? What about you?

Erik Erikson (1968) did not use the term *emerging adulthood*, but he did recognize that developed nations tend to elongate the period of adolescence. Erikson used the term *moratorium* to describe the extended quest for identity among people who dwell in adolescence. Erikson and other theorists also believed that it was more meaningful for the individual to take the voyage to identity rather than foreclose it by adopting the viewpoints of other people. While there are pluses to taking time to formulate one's identity, there are downsides. For example, remaining dependent on parents can compromise an individual's self-esteem. Taking out loans for graduate school means that there is more to pay back; many individuals mortgage their own lives as they invest in their futures. Women who focus on their educations and their careers may marry later and bear children later. Although many people appreciate children more when they bear them later in life, they also become less fertile as the years wend their way, and they may find themselves in a race with the "biological clock."

Young people in the United States seem to be generally aware of the issues involved in defining the transition from adolescence to adulthood. Arnett (2000a) reports what individuals in in their late teens and early 20s say when they are asked whether they think they have become adults. About three in five say something like, "in some respects yes and in other respects no." Many feel that they have developed beyond the conflicts and exploratory voyages of adolescence, but they may not yet have obtained the ability to assume the financial and interpersonal responsibilities they associate with adulthood.

And then, of course, there are those who remain adolescents forever.

Review

(43) Historically speaking, _________ has been an important standard in determining whether or not one has reached adulthood. (44) Today, the criteria of holding a full-time _________ and a separate residence are also applied. (45) _________ adulthood is a hypothesized period of development that spans the ages of 18 through 25 and exists in societies that permit young people extended periods of independent role exploration.

Pulling It Together: Are you an adolescent, an emerging adult, or an adult? What standards are you using in defining yourself?

Recite Recite Recite Recite

1. **What does Erikson have to say about the development of identity during adolescence?**

Erikson's adolescent stage of psychosocial development is identity versus identity diffusion. The primary task of this stage is for adolescents to develop a sense of who they are and what they stand for. An important aspect of identity development is the psychological moratorium—a "time-out," often a crisis, during which adolescents experiment with different roles, values, beliefs, and relationships.

2. **What are Marcia's "identity statuses"?**

These represent the four possible combinations of the dimensions of exploration and commitment. Exploration involves active questioning and searching; commitment is a stable investment in goals, values, or beliefs. Identity diffusion includes adolescents who do not have commitments and are not searching. In the foreclosure status, adolescents have made commitments without considering alternatives. Moratorium refers to active exploration of alternatives. Identity achievement refers to stable commitment following a period of exploration.

3. **How do sociocultural factors such as ethnicity and gender relate to one's self-identity?**

Development of identity is more complicated for adolescents who belong to ethnic minority groups. Youth from minority groups are faced with two sets of cultural values and may need to reconcile and incorporate elements of both. A scarcity of successful role models can be a problem, particularly for youth who live in poverty.

4. **Are there stages in developing an ethnic identity—that is, a sense of belonging to an ethnic group?**

Phinney proposes a three-stage model of the development of ethnic identity: unexamined ethnic identity, an ethnic identity search, and an achieved ethnic identity. As minority youth move through adolescence, they are increasingly likely to explore their ethnicity and to acquire an achieved ethnic identity status.

Recite Recite Recite Recite

5. Does the development of ego identity differ in males and females?

Erikson proposed that the development of interpersonal relationships is more important to women's identity than are occupational and ideological issues, but research suggests that adolescent females and males are equally concerned about occupational choices. However, females are more likely to integrate occupational and family plans. Men appear to develop identity before intimacy, as Erikson suggested.

6. How does the self-concept develop during adolescence?

Adolescents incorporate psychological characteristics and social relationships into their self-descriptions. Adolescents add more categories to their self-description.

7. What happens to self-esteem during adolescence?

Self-esteem tends to decline as the child progresses from middle childhood into early adolescence, perhaps because of increasing recognition of the disparity between the ideal self and the real self. But self-esteem gradually improves throughout adolescence, as adolescents develop competence in areas of importance to themselves, their parents, and their peers.

8. Are there ethnic differences in the development of self-esteem during adolescence?

Research suggests that the self-concepts and self-esteem of adolescents from ethnic minority groups are as positive as or more positive than those of European Americans. Latino and Latina American, Asian American, African American, and European American adolescents who show higher stages of ethnic identity also have higher self-esteem.

9. Are there gender differences in self-esteem during adolescence?

Girls generally have lower self-esteem than boys during adolescence. African American girls maintain higher self-esteem than European American or Latina American girls. The physical changes of adolescence may be connected with adolescent girls' self-esteem. Gilligan reports that as girls move into adolescence, they become aware of the conflict between the positive way they see themselves and society's view of females as second-class citizens.

10. How do relationships with one's parents and peers change during the course of the teenage years?

During adolescence, children spend much less time with their parents than they did during childhood. They tend to interact more with their mothers than with their fathers, as before. They may have more conflicts with their mothers, but they also view their mothers as being more supportive and knowing them better. Although adolescents become more independent of their parents, they generally continue to love and respect them. The role of peers as a source of activities, influence, and support increases markedly during the teen years. Friendships become increasingly important, and adolescents are more likely than younger children to stress the importance of intimate self-disclosure and mutual understanding in their friendships. Adolescents and their friends tend to be similar in age and race.

11. What kinds of adolescent peer groups are there?

The two major types of peer groups are cliques and crowds. In the United States, teenagers spend more than half of their time with peers and only about 15% of their time with parents or other adults. Adolescent peer groups function with less adult guidance or control than child peer groups. Adolescent peer groups also include peers of the other gender.

12. When do romantic relationships develop?

Romantic relationships begin to appear during early and middle adolescence. Most adolescents start dating by the time they graduate from high school. Dating is a source of fun, it enhances prestige, and it provides experience in relating to different people. Dating is also a preparation for adult courtship.

Recite Recite Recite Recite

13. What are some patterns of sexual behavior in adolescence? What are some of the factors that influence these behaviors?

Masturbation is the most common sexual outlet in adolescents. Adolescents masturbate to relieve sexual tension, to obtain physical pleasure, and to fill in for the unavailability of sex partners. However, many adolescents believe that masturbation is wrong. There is no scientific evidence that masturbation causes physical or psychological problems. Education is a liberating influence on masturbation. Some adolescents have a homosexual orientation. The process of "coming out"—that is, accepting one's homosexual orientation and declaring it to others—may be a long and painful struggle for many adolescents.

14. What do we know about the origins of gay male and lesbian sexual orientations?

Psychodynamic theory ties sexual orientation to identification with male or female figures, depending on the outcome of the Oedipus and Electra complexes. From a learning theory point of view, early reinforcement of sexual behavior influences sexual orientation. Researchers have found evidence for possible genetic factors in sexual orientation, and sex hormones may also play a role in sexual orientation, particularly during prenatal development.

15. Which adolescents are most likely to use contraceptives regularly?

More than half of adolescents do not use contraceptives when they initiate sexual activity. Adolescents are more likely to use contraceptives when they are in a committed relationship, have high educational aspirations, know about contraception, have a supportive relationship with parents, and have a sense of control over their lives.

16. Why do some teenagers initiate sexual activity at an early age, while others wait until later?

In boys, levels of testosterone are associated with sexual behavior, but hormone levels play a lesser role in girls' sexual behavior. Early onset of puberty is connected with earlier sexual activity. Adolescents who have close relationships with parents are less likely to initiate sexual activity early. A powerful predictor of sexual activity is the sexual activity of adolescents' best friends. The most common reason given for initiating sexual activity is peer pressure.

17. In this cultural setting, why do teenage girls become pregnant?

Many girls who become pregnant receive little advice at home or in school about how to resist sexual advances. Most of them do not have ready access to contraception. Some teenage girls become pregnant as a way of obtaining a commitment from their partner or rebelling against their parents. But most misunderstand reproduction or miscalculate the odds of conception.

18. What are the consequences of teenage pregnancy?

Teenage mothers are more likely to have medical complications during pregnancy and birth, largely due to inadequate medical care rather than age-related reasons per se. The babies are more likely to be premature and low in birthweight. Teenage mothers are less likely to graduate from high school and thus have a lower standard of living and a greater need for public assistance. Children born to teenage mothers have more academic and emotional problems.

19. What is juvenile delinquency?

Juvenile delinquency refers to illegal activities committed by a child or adolescent. Behaviors, such as drinking, that are considered illegal when performed by minors are called status offenses. Prior to the age of 40, the mortality rate for delinquents is twice that for other people, due mainly to accidents, violence, and substance abuse.

20. What are the gender differences in delinquent behavior?

Boys are more likely than girls to engage in most delinquent behaviors. Boys are more apt to commit crimes of violence, whereas girls are more likely to commit status offenses such as truancy or running away. Girls are more likely than boys to be arrested for being runaways.

Recite Recite Recite Recite

21. Who is most likely to engage in delinquent behavior?

Risk factors associated with juvenile delinquency include poor school performance, delinquent friends, early aggressive or hyperactive behavior, substance abuse, low verbal IQ, low self-esteem, impulsivity, and immature moral reasoning. The parents of delinquents often are characterized by ineffective discipline, low levels of affection, and high levels of family conflict, abuse, and neglect. The parents and siblings of delinquents frequently have engaged in antisocial behavior themselves.

22. How many adolescents commit suicide? Why do they do so?

Suicide is the third or fourth leading cause of death among older teenagers, and 1 to 2 American adolescents in 10,000 commit suicide each year. Most suicides among adolescents and adults are linked to feelings of depression, identity problems, impulsivity, and social problems. Adolescent suicide attempts are more common following stressful life events, especially "exit events." Girls are more likely to attempt suicide, whereas boys—who use deadlier means—are more likely to "succeed" at it.

23. How do we define *adulthood*?

Historically, marriage has been an important criterion in defining *adulthood*. Today the focus is more on holding a full-time occupation and maintaining a separate residence.

24. What is "emerging adulthood"?

Emerging adulthood is a period of development spanning the ages of 18–25, in which young people engage in extended role exploration. Emerging adulthood can occur in affluent societies, societies that can grant young people the luxury of developing their unique identities and their individual life plans.

On the Web

Search Online With InfoTrac College Edition

For additional information, explore InfoTrac College Edition, your online library. Go to http://www.infotrac-college.com and use the passcode from the InfoTrac card that came with your book. Try these search terms: teenagers family, stress in adolescence, juvenile delinquency, self-perception in adolescence, African American teenagers, minority teenagers, sexual ethics for youth.

Visit Our Web Site

Go to http://www.wadsworth.com/psychology where you will find online resources directly linked to your book.

Child Development CD-ROM

Go to the Wadsworth Child Development CD-ROM for further study of the concepts in this chapter. The CD-ROM also includes quizzes and additional activities to expand your learning experience.

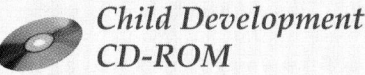

Glossary

Abstinence syndrome A characteristic cluster of symptoms that results from sudden decreases in the level of usage of a substance.

Accommodation According to Piaget, the modification of existing schemes in order to incorporate new events or knowledge.

Achieved ethnic identity The final stage of ethnic identity development; similar to the identity achievement status.

Achievement That which is attained by one's efforts and presumed to be made possible by one's abilities.

Adaptation According to Piaget, the interaction between the organism and the environment. It consists of two processes: assimilation and accommodation.

Adipose tissue Fat.

Adolescence The stage bounded by the advent of puberty at the lower end and the taking on of adult responsibilities at the upper end. Puberty is a biological concept, while adolescence is a psychological concept.

Adrenaline A hormone that generally arouses the body, increasing the heart and respiration rates.

AIDS Acronym for *acquired immune deficiency syndrome.* A fatal, usually sexually transmitted infection (STI) that is caused by a virus (HIV) and cripples the body's immune system, making the person vulnerable to opportunistic diseases.

Allele A member of a pair of genes.

Alpha-fetoprotein (AFP) assay A blood test that assesses the mother's blood level of alpha-fetoprotein, a substance that is linked with fetal neural-tube defects.

Ambivalent/resistant attachment A type of insecure attachment characterized by severe distress at the leave-takings of, and ambivalent behavior at reunions with, an attachment figure.

American Sign Language (ASL) The communication of meaning through the use of symbols that are formed by moving the hands and arms. The language used by some deaf people.

Amniocentesis (AM-nee-oh-sen-TEE-sis) A procedure for drawing and examining fetal cells sloughed off into amniotic fluid to determine the presence of various disorders.

Amniotic fluid Fluid within the amniotic sac that suspends and protects the fetus.

Amniotic sac The sac containing the fetus.

Amplitude Height. The higher the amplitude of sound waves, the louder they are.

Anal stage The second stage of psychosexual development, when gratification is attained through anal activities such as eliminating wastes.

Androgenital syndrome A disorder in which genetic females become masculinized as a result of prenatal exposure to male hormones.

Androgens Male sex hormones (from roots meaning "giving birth to men").

Anesthetics Agents that produce partial or total loss of the sense of pain (from Greek roots meaning "without feeling").

Animism The attribution of life and intentionality to inanimate objects.

Anorexia nervosa An eating disorder characterized by irrational fear of weight gain, distorted body image, and severe weight loss.

Anoxia A condition characterized by lack of oxygen.

Apgar scale A measure of a newborn's health that assesses appearance, pulse, grimace, activity level, and respiratory effort.

Aphasia A disruption in the ability to understand or produce language.

Apnea (AP-knee-uh) Temporary suspension of breathing (from the Greek *a-*, meaning "without," and *pnoie,* meaning "wind").

Appearance-reality distinction The difference between real events on the one hand and mental events, fantasies, and misleading appearances on the other hand.

Artificial insemination Injection of sperm into the uterus to fertilize an ovum.

Artificialism The belief that environmental features were made by people.

Assimilation According to Piaget, the incorporation of new events or knowledge into existing schemes.

Associative play Play with other children in which toys are shared but there is no common goal or division of labor.

Asynchronous growth Imbalanced growth, such as that which occurs during the early part of adolescence and causes many adolescents to appear gawky.

Attachment An affectional bond between individuals characterized by a seeking of closeness or contact and a show of distress upon separation.

Attachment-in-the-making phase The second phase in the development of attachment, occurring at 3 or 4 months of age and characterized by preference for familiar figures.

Attention-deficit hyperactivity disorder (ADHD) A behavior disorder characterized by excessive inattention, impulsiveness, and hyperactivity.

Attributional style The way in which one is disposed toward interpreting outcomes (successes or failures), as in tending to place blame or responsibility on oneself or external factors.

Authoritarian A child-rearing style in which parents demand submission and obedience from their children but are not very communicative and warm.

Authoritative A child-rearing style in which parents are restrictive and demanding, yet communicative and warm.

Autism A developmental disorder characterized by failure to relate to others, communication problems, intolerance of change, and ritualistic behavior.

Autobiographical memory The memory of specific episodes or events.

Autonomous morality The second stage in Piaget's cognitive-developmental theory of moral development. In this stage, children base moral judgments on the intentions of the wrongdoer, as well as on the amount of damage done. Social rules are viewed as agreements that can be changed.

Autonomy versus shame and doubt Erikson's second stage of psychosocial development, during which the child develops (or does not develop) the capacity to exercise self-control and independence.

Autosome Either member of a pair of chromosomes (with the exception of sex chromosomes).

Autostimulation theory The view that REM sleep in infants fosters the development of the brain by stimulating neural activity.

Avoidant attachment A type of insecure attachment characterized by apparent indifference to the leave-takings of, and reunions with, an attachment figure.

Axon A long, thin part of a neuron that transmits impulses to other neurons through small branching structures called axon terminals.

Babbling The child's first vocalizations that have the sounds of speech.

Babinski reflex A reflex in which infants fan their toes when the undersides of their feet are stroked.

Bed-wetting Failure to control the bladder during the night. (Frequently used interchangeably with *enuresis,* although bed-wetting refers to the behavior itself and *enuresis* is a diagnostic category, related to the age of the child.)

Behaviorism John B. Watson's view that a science or theory of development must study observable behavior only and investigate relationships between stimuli and responses.

Behavior modification The systematic application of principles of learning to change problem behaviors or encourage desired behaviors.

Bilingual Using or capable of using two languages with nearly equal or equal facility.

Blastocyst A stage within the germinal period of prenatal development in which the zygote has the form of a sphere of cells surrounding a cavity of fluid.

Bonding The process of forming bonds of attachment between parent and child.

Braxton-Hicks contractions The first, usually painless, contractions of childbirth.

Brazelton Neonatal Behavioral Assessment Scale A measure of a newborn's motor behavior, response to stress, adaptive behavior, and control over physiological state.

Broca's aphasia A form of aphasia caused by damage to Broca's area and characterized by slow, laborious speech.

Bulimia nervosa An eating disorder characterized by cycles of binge eating and vomiting as a means of controlling weight gain.

Canalization The tendency of growth rates to return to genetically determined patterns after undergoing environmentally induced change.

Cardinal word principle The principle that the last number in a count indicates how many total items there are.

Carrier A person who carries and transmits characteristics but does not exhibit them.

Case study A carefully drawn biography of the life of an individual.

Categorical self Definitions of the self that refer to concrete external traits.

Centration Focusing on one dimension of a situation while ignoring others.

Cephalocaudal (SEFF-uh-low-CAW-d'l) From top to bottom; from head to tail.

Cerebellum (sera-BELL-um) The part of the hindbrain involved in muscle coordination and balance.

Cerebrum (sir-REE-brum) The large mass of the forebrain, which consists of two hemispheres.

Cesarean section A method of childbirth in which the neonate is delivered through a surgical incision in the abdomen. (Also spelled Caesarean.)

Child A person undergoing the period of development from infancy through puberty.

Chorionic villus sampling (CORE-ee-ON-ick Vill-iss) A method for the prenatal detection of genetic abnormalities that samples the membrane enveloping the amniotic sac and fetus.

Chromosomes Rod-shaped structures, composed of genes, that are found within the nuclei of cells.

Chronological age (CA) A person's age.

Classical conditioning A simple form of learning in which one stimulus comes to bring forth the response usually brought forth by a second stimulus by being paired repeatedly with the second stimulus.

Class inclusion The principle that one category or class of things can include several subclasses.

Clear-cut-attachment phase The third phase in the development of attachment, occurring at 6 or 7 months of age and characterized by intensified dependence on the primary caregiver.

Clique A group of 5 to 10 individuals who hang around together and who share activities and confidences.

Clitoris A female sex organ that is highly sensitive to sexual stimulation but not directly involved in reproduction.

Cognitive-developmental theory The stage theory that holds that the child's abilities to mentally represent the world and solve problems unfold as a result of the interaction of experience and the maturation of neurological structures.

Cohort effect Similarities in behavior among a group of peers that stem from the fact that group members are approximately of the same age (a possible source of misleading information in cross-sectional research).

Collectivist A person who defines herself or himself in terms of relationships to other people and groups and gives priority to group goals.

Commitment A stable investment in one's goals, values, or beliefs.

Conception The union of a sperm cell and an ovum, which occurs when the chromosomes of each of these cells combine to form 23 new pairs; the process of becoming pregnant.

Concordance Agreement.

Concrete operations The third stage in Piaget's scheme, characterized by flexible, reversible thought concerning tangible objects and events.

Conditioned response (CR) A learned response to a previously neutral stimulus.

Conditioned stimulus (CS) A previously neutral stimulus that elicits a response, because it has been paired repeatedly with a stimulus that already elicited that response.

Conduct disorders Disorders marked by persistent breaking of the rules and violations of the rights of others.

Cones Cone-shaped receptors of light that transmit sensations of color.

Confluence model The view that family structure, including factors such as birth order, family size, and child spacing, come together to affect the intellectual development of children.

Congenital Present at birth; resulting from the prenatal environment.

Conservation In cognitive psychology, the principle that properties of substances such as weight and mass remain the same (are conserved) when superficial characteristics such as their shapes or arrangement are changed.

Contact comfort The pleasure derived from physical contact with another; a hypothesized need or drive for physical contact with another.

Contrast assumption The assumption that objects have only one label; also known as the mutual-exclusivity assumption (if a word means one thing, it cannot mean another).

Control subjects Participants in an experiment who do not receive the treatment but for whom all other conditions are held comparable to those of experimental subjects.

Conventional level According to Kohlberg, a period during which moral judgments largely reflect social rules and conventions.

Convergence The inward movement of the eyes as they focus on an object that is drawing nearer.

Convergent thinking A thought process that attempts to narrow in on the single best solution to a problem.

Cooing Prelinguistic, articulated vowel-like sounds that appear to reflect feelings of positive excitement.

Cooperative play Organized play in which children cooperate to meet common goals. There is a division of labor, and children take on specific roles as group members.

Coregulation A gradual transferring of control from parent to child, beginning in middle childhood.

Corpus callosum The thick bundle of nerve fibers that connects the left and right hemispheres of the brain.

Correlational method A method in which researchers determine whether one behavior or trait being studied is related to, or correlated with, another.

Correlation coefficient A number ranging from +1.00 to −1.00 that expresses the direction (positive or negative) and strength of the relationship between two variables.

Creativity The ability to generate novel solutions to problems. A trait characterized by flexibility, ingenuity, and originality.

Critical period A period of development during which a releasing stimulus can elicit a fixed action pattern (FAP), or instinctive response; also a period during which an embryo is particularly vulnerable to a certain teratogen.

Cross-modal transfer The ability to recognize that an object experienced in one sensory modality is the same as an identical object experienced in a different modality.

Cross-sectional research The study of developmental processes by taking measures of children of different age groups at the same time.

Cross-sequential research An approach that combines the longitudinal and cross-sectional methods by following individuals of different ages for abbreviated periods of time.

Crowd A large, loosely organized group of people who may or may not spend much time together and who are identified by the activities of the group.

Cultural bias A factor hypothesized to be present in intelligence tests that provides an advantage for test-takers from certain cultural or ethnic backgrounds, but that does not reflect true intelligence.

Cultural-familial retardation Substandard intellectual performance that is presumed to stem from lack of opportunity to acquire the knowledge and skills considered important within a cultural setting.

Culture-free Descriptive of a test in which cultural biases have been removed. On such a test, test-takers from different cultural backgrounds would have an equal opportunity to earn scores that reflect their true abilities.

Cystic fibrosis A fatal genetic disorder in which mucus obstructs the lungs and pancreas.

Decentration Simultaneous focusing (centering) on more than one aspect or dimension of a problem or situation.

Deep structure The underlying meaning of a sentence.

Deferred imitation The imitation of people and events that occurred hours, days, or weeks in the past.

Demand characteristics The demands that a specific experimental approach or task make on a subject, as opposed to the demands that would be made if the theoretical concepts were tested in a different way.

Dendrite A rootlike part of a neuron that receives impulses from other neurons (from the Greek *dendron,* meaning "tree," and referring to the branching appearance of dendrites).

Deoxyribonucleic acid (DNA) Genetic material that takes the form of a double helix composed of phosphates, sugars, and bases.

Dependent variable A measure of an assumed effect of an independent variable.

DES Abbreviation for *diethylstilbestrol,* a powerful estrogen that has been linked to cancer in the reproductive organs of children whose mothers used the hormone when pregnant.

Design stage A stage in drawing in which children begin to combine shapes.

Development The processes by which organisms unfold features and traits, grow, and become more complex and specialized in structure and function.

Differentiation The processes by which behaviors and physical structures become more specialized.

Dilate To make wider or larger.

Disinhibit To stimulate a response that has been suppressed (inhibited) by showing a model engaging in that response without aversive consequences.

Disorganized-disoriented attachment A type of insecure attachment characterized by dazed and contradictory behaviors toward an attachment figure.

Divergent thinking A thought process that attempts to generate multiple solutions to problems. Free and fluent association to the elements of a problem.

Dizygotic (DZ) twins Twins that derive from two zygotes; fraternal twins.

Dominant trait A trait that is expressed.

Donor IVF The transfer of a donor's ovum, fertilized in a laboratory dish, to the uterus of another woman.

Down syndrome A chromosomal abnormality characterized by mental retardation and caused by an extra chromosome in the 21st pair.

Dramatic play Play in which children enact social roles; made possible by the attainment of symbolic thought. A form of *pretend play.*

Dyslexia A reading disorder characterized by problems such as letter reversals, mirror reading, slow reading, and reduced comprehension (from the Greek roots *dys-,* meaning "bad," and *lexikon,* meaning "of words").

Echolalia The automatic repetition of sounds or words.

Ecological systems theory The view that explains child development in terms of the reciprocal influences between children and the settings that make up their environment.

Ecology The branch of biology that deals with the relationships between living organisms and their environment.

Ectoderm The outermost cell layer of the newly formed embryo, from which the skin and nervous system develop.

Efface To rub out or wipe out; to become thin.

Ego (EE-go) The second element of personality to develop, characterized by self-awareness, planning, and the delay of gratification (a Latin word meaning "I").

Egocentrism Putting oneself at the center of things such that one is unable to perceive the world from another person's point of view. Egocentrism is normal in early childhood but a matter of choice, and rather intolerable, in adults.

Ego identity According to Erikson, one's sense of who one is and what one stands for.

Elaborative strategy A method for increasing retention of new information by relating it to well-known information.

Electra complex A conflict of the phallic stage in which the girl longs for her father and resents her mother.

Electroencephalograph (EEG) An instrument that measures electrical activity of the brain.

Embryonic disk The platelike inner part of the blastocyst that differentiates into the ectoderm, mesoderm, and endoderm of the embryo.

Embryonic stage The stage of prenatal development that lasts from implantation through the 8th week and is characterized by the development of the major organ systems.

Embryonic transplant The transfer of an embryo from the uterus of one woman to that of another.

Emotion A state of feeling that has physiological, situational, and cognitive components.

Emotional regulation Techniques for controlling one's emotional states.

Empathy The ability to share another person's feelings or emotions.

Empirical Based on observation and experimentation.

Empiricism The view that experience determines the ways in which children perceive the world.

Encode To transform sensory input into a form that is more readily processed.

Encopresis Failure to control the bowels once the normal age for bowel control has been reached. Also called *soiling*.

Endoderm The inner layer of the embryo, from which the lungs and digestive system develop.

Endometriosis Inflammation of endometrial tissue sloughed off into the abdominal cavity rather than out of the body during menstruation and characterized by abdominal pain and, sometimes, infertility.

Endometrium The inner lining of the uterus.

Enuresis (en-you-REE-sis) Failure to control the bladder (urination) once the normal age for control has been reached.

Epiphyseal closure The process by which the cartilage that separates the long end (epiphysis) of a bone from the main part of the bone turns to bone.

Episiotomy (ep-pee-zee-OTT-to-me) A surgical incision in the perineum that widens the vaginal opening, preventing random tearing during childbirth.

Equilibration The creation of an equilibrium, or balance, between assimilation and accommodation as a way of incorporating new events or knowledge.

Ethnic groups Groups of people distinguished by cultural heritage, race, language, and common history.

Ethnic identity A sense of belonging to an ethnic group.

Ethnic identity search The second stage of ethnic identity development, similar to the moratorium identity status.

Ethologist A scientist who studies the behavior patterns that are characteristic of various species.

Ethology The study of behavior patterns that are characteristic of various species.

Exosystem Community institutions and settings that indirectly influence the child, such as the school board and the parents' workplaces (from the Greek *exo-*, meaning "outside").

Experiment A method of scientific investigation that seeks to discover cause-and-effect relationships by introducing independent variables and observing their effects on dependent variables.

Experimental subjects Participants who receive a treatment in an experiment.

Exploration Active questioning and searching among alternatives in the quest to establish goals, values, or beliefs.

Expressive language style Use of language primarily as a means for engaging in social interaction.

Expressive vocabulary The sum total of the words that one can use in the production of language.

Extinction The decreased appearance and eventual disappearance of a response in the absence of reinforcement.

Factor A condition or quality that brings about a result; a cluster of related items, such as those found on an intelligence or personality test.

Failure to thrive (FTT) A disorder of impaired growth in infancy and early childhood, characterized by failure to gain weight within normal limits.

Fallopian tube A tube through which ova travel from an ovary to the uterus.

Fast mapping A process of quickly determining a word's meaning, which facilitates children's vocabulary development.

Feedback loop A system in which the hypothalamus, pituitary gland, and gonads regulate each other's functioning through a series of hormonal messages.

Fetal alcohol effect (FAE) A cluster of symptoms less severe than those of FAS shown by children of women who drink moderately during pregnancy.

Fetal alcohol syndrome (FAS) A cluster of symptoms shown by children of women who drink heavily during pregnancy, including characteristic facial features and mental retardation.

Fetal monitoring The use of instruments to track the heart rate and oxygen levels of the fetus during childbirth.

Fetal stage The stage of development that lasts from the beginning of the 9th week of pregnancy through birth and is characterized by gains in size and weight and maturation of the organ systems.

Fetoscopy (fee-TOSS-co-pea) Surgical insertion of a narrow tube into the uterus in order to examine the fetus.

Fine motor skills Skills employing the small muscles used in manipulation, such as those in the fingers.

Fixation In psychoanalytic theory, arrested development; attachment to objects of an earlier stage.

Fixed action pattern (FAP) Instinct; a stereotyped behavior pattern that is characteristic of a species and is triggered by a releasing stimulus; abbreviated FAP.

Forceps A curved instrument that fits around the head of the baby and permits it to be pulled through the birth canal.

Foreclosure An identity status that characterizes those who have made commitments without considering alternatives.

Formal handling Activities used by parents in Africa and in cultures of African origin to stimulate sitting and walking in their infants.

Formal operations The fourth stage in Piaget's cognitive-developmental theory, characterized by the capacity for flexible, reversible operations concerning abstract ideas and concepts, such as symbols, statements, and theories.

Gender The state of being female or male.

Gender constancy The concept that one's gender remains the same despite superficial changes in appearance or behavior.

Gender identity Knowledge that one is female or male. Also the name of the first stage in Kohlberg's cognitive-developmental theory of the assumption of gender roles.

Gender role A complex cluster of traits and behaviors that are considered stereotypical of females and males.

Gender-schema theory The view that one's knowledge of the gender schema in one's society (the behavior patterns that are considered appropriate for men and women) guides one's assumption of gender-typed preferences and behavior patterns.

Gender stability The concept that one's gender is a permanent feature.

Gene The basic unit of heredity. Genes are composed of deoxyribonucleic acid (DNA).

General anesthesia The process of eliminating pain by putting the person to sleep.

Genetic counseling Advice concerning the probabilities that a couple's children will show genetic abnormalities.

Genetics The branch of biology that studies heredity.

Genital stage In psychoanalytic theory, the fifth and final stage of psychosexual development in which gratification is attained through sexual intercourse with an individual of the other gender.

Genotype The genetic form or constitution of a person as determined by heredity.

Germinal stage The period of development between conception and the implantation of the embryo in the uterine wall.

Goodness of fit Agreement between the parents' expectations of or demands on the child and the child's temperamental characteristics.

Grasping reflex A reflex in which infants grasp objects that cause pressure against the palms.

Gross motor skills Skills employing the large muscles used in locomotion.

Growth The processes by which organisms increase in size, weight, strength, and other traits as they develop.

Growth spurt A period during which growth advances at a dramatically rapid rate as compared with other periods.

Gynecomastia Temporary enlargement of the breasts in adolescent males.

Habituate To show a decline in interest as a repeated stimulus becomes familiar.

Habituation A process in which one becomes used to and therefore pays less attention to a repeated stimulus.

Hallucinogenics Drugs that give rise to hallucinations.

Handedness The tendency to prefer using the left or right hand in writing and other activities.

Hemophilia A genetic disorder in which blood does not clot properly.

Heredity The transmission of traits and characteristics from parent to child by means of genes.

Heritability The degree to which the variations in a trait from one person to another can be attributed to, or explained by, genetic factors.

Heterozygous Having two different alleles.

HIV/AIDS HIV stands for *human immunodeficiency virus,* the virus that causes AIDS. AIDS stands for *acquired immunodeficiency syndrome,* a condition that cripples the body's immune system, rendering the individual susceptible to diseases that would not otherwise be threatening or as threatening.

Holophrase A single word that is used to express complex meanings.

Homosexuality An erotic orientation toward members of one's own gender.

Homozygous Having two identical alleles.

Horizontal décalage The sequential unfolding of the ability to master different kinds of cognitive tasks within the same stage.

Hue Color.

Huntington's disease A fatal genetic neurologic disorder with onset in middle age.

Hyaluronidase An enzyme that briefly thins the zona pellucida, enabling a single sperm cell to penetrate (from roots referring to a "substance that breaks down a glasslike fluid").

Hyperactivity Excessive restlessness and overactivity. Not to be confused with misbehavior or with normal high activity levels that occur during childhood. One of the primary characteristics of attention-deficit hyperactivity disorder (ADHD).

Hypothalamus A pea-sized structure that is located above the pituitary gland in the brain and is involved in the regulation of body temperature, motivation (for example, hunger, thirst, sex), and emotion.

Hypothesis (high-POTH-uh-sis) A Greek word meaning "groundwork" or "foundation" that has come to mean a specific statement about behavior that is tested by research.

Hypoxia A condition characterized by less oxygen than is required.

Id An element of personality that is present at birth, represents physiological drives, and is fully unconscious (a Latin word meaning "it").

Identification Within social-cognitive theory, a process in which one person becomes like another through broad imitation and incorporation of the other person's personality traits.

Identity achievement An identity status that characterizes those who have explored alternatives and have developed commitments.

Identity crisis According to Erikson, turning point in development, a period of inner conflict during which one examines one's values and makes decisions about one's life roles.

Identity diffusion An identity status that characterizes those who have no commitments and who are not in the process of exploring alternatives.

Identity versus identity diffusion Erikson's fifth stage of psychosocial development, during which adolescents develop (or fail to develop) a sense of who they are and what they stand for.

Imaginary audience The belief that others around us are as concerned with our thoughts and behaviors as we are; one aspect of adolescent egocentrism.

Immanent justice The view that retribution for wrongdoing is a direct consequence of the wrongdoing, reflective of the belief that morality is embedded within the structure of the universe.

Imprinting The process by which some animals exhibit the fixed action pattern (FAP) of attachment in response to a releasing stimulus. The FAP occurs during a critical period and is difficult to modify.

Incubator A heated, protective container in which premature infants are kept.

Independent variable A condition in a scientific study that is manipulated (changed) so that its effects may be observed.

Indiscriminate attachment The display of attachment behaviors toward any person.

Individualist A person who defines herself or himself in terms of personal traits and gives priority to her or his own goals.

Inductive Characteristic of disciplinary methods, such as reasoning, that attempt to foster an understanding of the principles behind parental demands.

Industry versus inferiority The fourth stage of psychosocial development in Erikson's theory, occurring in middle childhood. Mastery of tasks leads to a sense of industry, while failure produces feelings of inferiority.

Infancy The period of very early childhood, characterized by lack of complex speech; the first 2 years after birth.

Information processing The view in which cognitive processes are compared to the functions of computers. The theory deals with the input, storage, retrieval, manipulation, and output of information. The focus is on the development of children's strategies for solving problems, their "mental programs."

Initial-preattachment phase The first phase in the formation of bonds of attachment, lasting from birth to about 3 months of age and characterized by indiscriminate attachment.

Initiative versus guilt Erikson's third stage of psychosocial development, during which the child initiates new activities. Punishment of the child's activities may produce feelings of guilt.

Inner speech Vygotsky's concept of the ultimate binding of language and thought. Inner speech originates in vocalizations that may regulate the child's behavior and become internalized by age 6 or 7.

Insomnia One or more of a number of sleep problems including difficulty falling asleep, difficulty remaining asleep during the night, and waking early.

Intelligence A complex and controversial concept, defined by David Wechsler as the "capacity . . . to understand the world [and the] resourcefulness to cope with its challenges" (from the Latin *inter,* meaning "among," and *legere,* meaning "to choose"). Intelligence implies the capacity to make adaptive choices.

Intelligence quotient (IQ) (1) Originally, a ratio obtained by dividing a child's score (or "mental age") on an intelligence test by his or her chronological age. (2) Generally, a score on an intelligence test.

Intensity Brightness.

Intonation The use of pitches of varying levels to help communicate meaning.

In vitro fertilization (VEE-tro) Fertilization of an ovum in a laboratory dish.

Irreversibility Lack of recognition that actions can be reversed.

Juvenile delinquency Conduct in a child or adolescent characterized by illegal activities.

Kibbutz An Israeli farming community in which children are reared in group settings.

Klinefelter's syndrome A chromosomal disorder found among males that is caused by an extra X sex chromosome and characterized by infertility and mild mental retardation.

Labia The major and minor lips of the female genitalia.

Lamaze method A childbirth method in which women are educated about childbirth, learn to relax and breathe in patterns that conserve energy and lessen pain, and have a coach (usually the father) present during childbirth. Also termed *prepared childbirth.*

Language acquisition device (LAD) In psycholinguistic theory, neural "pre-wiring" that facilitates the child's learning of grammar.

Lanugo (lan-OO-go) Fine, downy hair that covers much of the body of the neonate, especially preterm babies.

Larynx The part of the throat that contains the vocal cords.

Latency stage In psychoanalytic theory, the fourth stage of psychosexual development, characterized by repression of sexual impulses and development of skills.

Learned helplessness An acquired (hence, *learned*) belief that one is unable to control one's environment.

Learning disabilities A group of disorders characterized by inadequate development of specific academic, language, and speech skills.

Life crisis An internal conflict that attends each stage of psychosocial development. Positive resolution of early life crises sets the stage for positive resolution of subsequent life crises.

Local anesthetic A method that reduces pain in an area of the body.

Locomotion Movement from one place to another.

Longitudinal research The study of developmental processes by taking repeated measures of the same group of children at various stages of development.

Long-term memory The memory structure capable of relatively permanent storage of information.

Macrosystem In ecological theory, the basic institutions and ideologies that influence the child, such as the American ideals of freedom of expression and equality under the law (from the Greek *makros,* meaning "long" or "enlarged").

Mainstreaming Placing disabled children in classrooms with nondisabled children.

Mammary glands Glands that secrete milk.

Masturbation Sexual self-stimulation.

Maturation The unfolding of genetically determined traits, structures, and functions.

Maturational theory Arnold Gesell's view that development is self-regulated by the unfolding of natural plans (that is, heredity) and processes.

Mean length of utterance (MLU) The average number of morphemes used in an utterance.

Medulla (meh-DULL-ah) An oblong-shaped area of the hindbrain involved in heartbeat and respiration.

Meiosis The form of cell division in which each pair of chromosomes splits, so that one member of each pair moves to the new cell. As a result, each new cell has 23 chromosomes.

Memory The processes by which we store and retrieve information.

Menarche The onset of menstruation.

Menopause The cessation of menstruation, typically occurring between ages 48 and 52.

Mental age (MA) The accumulated months of credit that a person earns on the Stanford-Binet Intelligence Scale.

Mental representations The mental forms that a real object or event can take, which may differ from one another. (Successful problem solving is aided by accurate mental representation of the elements of the problem.)

Mental rotation Imagining how objects will look if they are rotated in space.

Mesoderm The central layer of the embryo, from which the bones and muscles develop.

Mesosystem The interlocking settings that influence the child, such as the interaction of the school and the larger community when children are taken on field trips (from the Greek *mesos,* meaning "middle").

Metacognition Awareness of and control of one's cognitive abilities, as shown by the intentional use of cognitive strategies in solving problems.

Metamemory Knowledge of the functions and processes involved in one's storage and retrieval of information (memory), as shown by use of cognitive strategies to retain information.

Microsystem The immediate settings with which the child interacts, such as the home, the school, and one's peers (from the Greek *mikros,* meaning "small").

Midwife An individual who helps women in childbirth (from Old English roots meaning "with woman").

Mitosis The form of cell division in which each chromosome splits lengthwise to double in number. Half of each chromosome combines with chemicals to retake its original form and then moves to the new cell.

Models In learning theory, those whose behaviors are imitated by others.

Monozygotic (MZ) twins Twins that derive from a single zygote that has split into two; identical twins. Each MZ twin carries the same genetic code.

Moral realism According to Piaget, the stage during which children judge acts as moral when they conform to authority or to the rules of the game. Morality at this stage is perceived as embedded in the structure of the universe.

Moratorium An identity status that characterizes those who are actively exploring alternatives in an attempt to form an identity.

Moro reflex A reflex in which infants arch their back, fling out their arms and legs, and draw them back toward the chest in response to a sudden change in position.

Morpheme The smallest unit of meaning in a language.

Motility Self-propulsion.

Motor development The development of the capacity for movement, particularly that made possible by changes in the nervous system and the muscles.

Multifactorial problems Problems that stem from the interaction of heredity and environmental factors.

Multiple sclerosis A disorder in which myelin is replaced by hard fibrous tissue that impedes neural transmission.

Multipotent stem cells More specialized stem cells, capable of giving rise to a specific group of cells, such as blood cells or skin cells.

Muscular dystrophy (DISS-tro-fee) A chronic disease characterized by a progressive wasting away of the muscles.

Mutation A sudden variation in an inheritable characteristic, as by an accident that affects the composition of genes.

Mutism Inability or refusal to speak.

Myelination The process by which axons are coated with myelin.

Myelin sheath (MY-uh-lin) A fatty, whitish substance that encases and insulates neurons, permitting more rapid transmission of neural impulses.

Nativism The view that children are born with predispositions to perceive the world in certain ways.

Natural childbirth A method of childbirth in which women use no anesthesia and are educated about childbirth and strategies for coping with discomfort.

Naturalistic observation A method of scientific observation in which children (and others) are observed in their natural environments.

Nature The processes within an organism that guide that organism to develop according to its genetic code.

Negative correlation A relationship between two variables in which one variable increases as the other variable decreases.

Negative reinforcer A reinforcer that, when removed, increases the frequency of a response.

Neonate A newborn child (from the Greek *neos,* meaning "new," and the Latin *natus,* meaning "born").

Nerves Bundles of axons from many neurons.

Neural Referring to the nervous system.

Neural tube A hollowed-out area in the blastocyst from which the nervous system develops.

Neurons Nerve cells; cells found in the nervous system that transmit messages.

Neuroticism A personality trait characterized by anxiety and emotional instability.

Neurotransmitter A chemical substance that enables the transmission of neural impulses from one neuron to another.

Nightmares Frightening dreams that occur during REM sleep, often in the morning hours.

Nocturnal emission Emission of seminal fluid while asleep.

Non-rapid-eye-movement (NREM) sleep Periods of sleep during which we are unlikely to dream.

Nonsocial play Forms of play (solitary play or onlooker play) in which play is not influenced by the play of nearby children.

Nurture The processes external to an organism that nourish it as it develops according to its genetic code or cause it to swerve from its genetically programmed course. Environ-mental factors that influence development.

Obesity A disorder characterized by excessive accumulation of fat.

Objective morality The perception of morality as objective, that is, as existing outside the cognitive functioning of people; a characteristic of Piaget's stage of moral realism.

Object permanence Recognition that objects continue to exist even when they are not seen.

Observational learning The acquisition of expectations and skills by means of observing others. In observational learning, skills can be acquired without being emitted and reinforced.

Occupational gender-typing Judgments that certain occupations are more appropriate for one gender than the other.

Oedipus complex (ED-uh-puss) A conflict of the phallic stage in which the boy wishes to possess his mother sexually and perceives his father as a rival in love.

Onlooker play Play during which children observe other children at play but do not enter into their play themselves.

Operant conditioning A simple form of learning in which an organism learns to engage in behavior that is reinforced.

Operations Flexible, reversible mental manipulations of objects, in which objects can be mentally transformed and then returned to their original states.

Oral rehydration therapy A treatment involving administration of a salt and sugar solution to a child who is dehydrated from diarrhea.

Oral stage The first stage of psychosexual development, during which gratification is attained primarily through oral activities such as sucking and biting.

Osteoporosis A condition involving progressive loss of bone tissue.

Ovary A female reproductive organ, located in the abdomen, that produces female reproductive cells (ova).

Overextension Use of words in situations in which their meanings become extended, or inappropriate.

Overregularization The application of regular grammatical rules for forming inflections (for example, past tense and plurals) to irregular verbs and nouns.

Ovulation The release of an ovum from an ovary.

Ovum A female reproductive cell.

Oxytocin (ox-see-TOE-sin) A pituitary hormone that stimulates labor contractions (from the Greek *oxys,* meaning "quick," and *tokos,* meaning "birth").

Pacifier An artificial nipple, teething ring, or similar device that soothes babies.

Parallel play Play in which children use toys similar to those of nearby children but approach their toys in their own ways. No effort is made to interact with others.

Peers Children of the same age. (More generally, people of similar background and social standing.)

Pelvic inflammatory disease (PID) An infection of the abdominal region that may have various causes and impair fertility.

Perceptual constancy The tendency to perceive objects as the same although sensations produced by them may differ when, for example, they differ in position or distance.

Perineum The area between the female's genital region and the anus.

Permissive-indulgent A child-rearing style in which parents are not controlling and restrictive but are warm.

Personal fable The belief that our feelings and ideas are special and unique and that we are invulnerable; one aspect of adolescent egocentrism.

Personality An individual's distinctive ways of responding to people and events.

Phallic stage The third stage of psychosexual development, characterized by a shift of libido to the phallic region (from the Greek *phallos,* meaning "image of the penis").

Phenotype The actual form or constitution of a person as determined by heredity and environmental factors.

Phenylketonuria (PKU) (fee-nill-key-tone-NEW-ree-uh) A genetic abnormality in which phenylalanine builds up and causes mental retardation.

Phonetic method A method for learning to read in which children decode the sounds of words based on their knowledge of the sounds of letters and letter combinations.

Pictorial stage A stage in drawing attained between ages 4 and 5 in which designs begin to resemble recognizable objects.

Pincer grasp The use of the opposing thumb to grasp objects between the thumb and other fingers.

Pitch The highness or lowness of a sound, as determined by the frequency of sound waves.

Pituitary gland The body's "master gland," which is located in the lower central part of the brain and secretes many hormones essential to development, such as oxytocin, prolactin, and growth hormone.

PKU Phenylketonuria. A genetic abnormality in which a child cannot metabolize phenylalanine, an amino acid, which consequently builds up in the body and causes mental retardation. If treated with a special diet, retardation is prevented.

Placement stage An early stage in drawing, usually found among 2-year-olds, in which children place their scribbles in various locations on the page (such as in the middle or near a border).

Placenta (pluh-SENT-uh) An organ connected to the uterine wall and to the fetus by the umbilical cord. The placenta serves as a relay station between mother and fetus for exchange of nutrients and wastes.

Plasticity The tendency of new parts of the brain to take up the functions of injured parts.

Pluripotent stem cells Stem cells that are capable of giving rise to most tissues of an organism, but not the placenta. Thus they cannot form an embryo.

Polygenic Refers to characteristic that results from many genes.

Positive correlation A relationship between two variables in which one variable increases as the other variable increases.

Positive reinforcer A reinforcer that, when applied, increases the frequency of a response.

Postconventional level According to Kohlberg, a period during which moral judgments are derived from moral principles and people look to themselves to set moral standards.

Postpartum depression (PPD) More severe, prolonged depression that afflicts 10–20% of women after delivery and is characterized by sadness, apathy, and feelings of worthlessness.

Postpartum period The period that immediately follows childbirth.

Post-traumatic stress disorder (PTSD) A disorder that follows a psychologically distressing event that is outside the range of normal human experience. It is characterized by symptoms such as intense fear, avoidance of stimuli associated with the event, and reliving of the event.

Pragmatics The practical aspects of communication, such as adaptation of language to fit the social situation.

Precausal A type of thought in which natural cause-and-effect relationships are attributed to will and other preoperational concepts. (For example, the sun sets because it's tired.)

Preconscious In psychoanalytic theory, refers to a state where something is not in awareness but capable of being brought into awareness by focusing of attention.

Preconventional level According to Kohlberg, a period during which moral judgments are based largely on expectations of rewards or punishments.

Prelinguistic Referring to vocalizations made by the infant prior to the development of language. (In language, words symbolize objects and events.)

Premature Born before the full term of gestation (also referred to as *preterm*).

Prenatal Refers to period before birth.

Prenatal period The period of development from conception to birth (from roots meaning "prior to birth").

Preoperational stage The second stage in Piaget's scheme, characterized by inflexible and irreversible mental manipulation of symbols.

Preterm Born at or prior to completion of 37 weeks of gestation.

Primary circular reactions The repetition of actions that first occurred by chance and that focus on the infant's own body.

Primary sex characteristics The structures that make reproduction possible.

Progestin A hormone used to maintain pregnancy that can cause masculinization of the fetus.

Prosocial behavior Behavior intended to benefit another without expectation of reward.

Prostaglandins (pross-tuh-GLAND-ins) Hormones that stimulate uterine contractions.

Proximodistal From near to far; from the central axis of the body outward to the periphery.

Psycholinguistic theory The view that language learning involves an interaction between environmental influences and an inborn tendency to acquire language. The emphasis is on the inborn tendency.

Psychological androgyny Possession of both stereotypical feminine and masculine traits.

Psychological moratorium A time-out period when adolescents experiment with different roles, values, beliefs, and relationships.

Psychosexual development In psychoanalytic theory, the process by which libidinal energy is expressed through different erogenous zones during different stages of development.

Psychosocial development Erikson's theory, which emphasizes the importance of social relationships and conscious choice throughout the eight stages of development.

Puberty (PEW-burr-tee) The biological stage of development characterized by changes that lead to reproductive capacity. Puberty signals the beginning of adolescence.

Punishment An unpleasant stimulus that suppresses behavior.

Rapid-eye-movement (REM) sleep A period of sleep during which we are likely to dream, as indicated by rapid eye movements.

Reaction range The variability in the expression of inherited traits as they are influenced by environmental factors.

Reaction time The amount of time required to respond to a stimulus.

Recall A memory task in which the individual must reproduce material from memory without any cues.

Receptive vocabulary The sum total of the words whose meanings one understands.

Recessive trait A trait that is not expressed when the gene or genes involved have been paired with dominant genes. Recessive traits are transmitted to future generations and expressed if they are paired with other recessive genes.

Reciprocal determinism Mutual interplay of the child's behavior, cognitive characteristics, and environment.

Reciprocity The principle that actions have mutual effects and that people depend upon one another to treat each other morally.

Recognition A memory task in which the individual indicates whether presented information has been experienced previously.

Referential language style Use of language primarily as a means for labeling objects.

Reflex An unlearned, stereotypical response to a stimulus.

Regression A return to behaviors characteristic of earlier stages of development.

Rehearsal Repetition; to rehearse is to repeat.

Reinforcement The process of providing stimuli following a response, which has the effect of increasing the frequency of the response.

Rejecting-neglecting A child-rearing style in which parents are neither restrictive and controlling nor supportive and responsive.

Releasing stimulus In ethology, a stimulus that elicits an instinctive response (FAP).

Respiratory distress syndrome A cluster of breathing problems, including weak and irregular breathing, to which preterm babies are particularly prone.

Retrolental fibroplasia A form of blindness that stems from excessive oxygen, such as may be found in an incubator.

Reversibility According to Piaget, recognition that processes can be undone, leaving things as they were before. Reversibility is a factor in conservation of the properties of substances.

Rh incompatibility A condition in which antibodies produced by the mother are transmitted to the child and may cause brain damage or death.

Risk factors Variables such as ethnicity and social class that are associated with the likelihood of problems but do not directly cause problems.

Rods Rod-shaped receptors of light that are sensitive to intensity only. Rods permit black-and-white vision.

Rooting reflex A reflex in which infants turn their mouths and heads in the direction of a stroking of the cheek or the corner of the mouth.

Rote learning Learning by repetition.

Rough-and-tumble play Play-fighting and chasing.

Rubella A viral infection that can cause retardation and heart disease in the embryo. Also called *German measles.*

Saturation Richness or purity of a color.

Scaffolding Vygotsky's term for temporary cognitive structures or methods of solving problems that help the child as he or she learns to function independently.

Scheme According to Piaget, an action pattern (such as a reflex) or mental structure that is involved in the acquisition or organization of knowledge.

Schizophrenia A severe psychological disorder that is characterized by disturbances in thought and language, perception and attention, motor activity, and mood and by withdrawal and absorption in daydreams or fantasy.

School phobia Fear of attending school, marked by extreme anxiety at leaving parents.

Scripts Abstract generalized accounts of familiar repeated events.

Secondary circular reactions The repetition of actions that produce an effect on the environment.

Secondary sex characteristics Physical indicators of sexual maturation such as changes to the voice and growth of bodily hair that do not directly involve the reproductive structures.

Secular trend A historical trend toward increasing adult height and earlier puberty.

Secure attachment A type of attachment characterized by mild distress at leave-takings, seeking nearness to an attachment figure, and being readily soothed by the figure.

Sedatives Drugs that soothe or quiet restlessness or agitation.

Self-concept One's impression of one-self; self-awareness.

Self-esteem The sense of value, or worth, that people attach to themselves.

Self-fulfilling prophecy An expectation that is confirmed because of the behavior of those who hold the expectation. In education, often referred to as the Pygmalion effect.

Semantic code A code based on the meaning of information.

Semen The fluid that contains sperm and substances that nourish and help transport sperm.

Sensitive period In linguistic theory, the period from about 18 months to puberty when the brain is thought to be especially capable of learning language because of plasticity of the brain.

Sensory memory The structure of memory first encountered by sensory input. Information is maintained in sensory memory only for a fraction of a second.

Sensory register Another term for sensory memory.

Separation anxiety Fear of being separated from a target of attachment usually a primary caregiver.

Separation-anxiety disorder An extreme form of otherwise normal separation anxiety that is characterized by anxiety about separating from parents and often takes the form of refusal to go to school.

Separation-individuation The child's increasing sense of becoming separate from and independent of the mother.

Seriation Placing objects in an order or series according to a property or trait.

Serotonin A neurotransmitter that is implicated in depression.

Sex chromosome A chromosome in the shape of a Y (male) or X (female) that determines the sex of the child.

Sexism Discrimination or bias against people based on their gender.

Sex-linked genetic abnormalities Abnormalities due to genes that are found on the X sex chromosome. They are more likely to be shown by male offspring (who do not have an opposing gene from a second X chromosome) than by female offspring.

Sexual harassment Unwelcome verbal or physical conduct of a sexual nature.

Shape constancy The tendency to perceive objects as being the same shape although the shapes of their retinal images may differ when the objects are viewed from different positions.

Shape stage A stage in drawing, attained by age 3, in which children draw basic shapes such as circles, squares, triangles, crosses, and odd shapes.

Shaping In learning theory, the gradual building of complex behavior patterns through reinforcement of successive approximations of the target behavior.

Short-term memory The structure of memory that can hold a sensory stimulus for up to 30 seconds after the trace decays.

Sibling rivalry Jealousy or rivalry among brothers and sisters.

Sickle-cell anemia A genetic disorder that decreases the blood's capacity to carry oxygen.

SIDS Sudden infant death syndrome (discussed in Chapter 5).

Sight vocabulary Words that are immediately recognized on the basis of familiarity with their overall shapes, rather than decoded.

Size constancy The tendency to perceive objects as being the same size although the sizes of their retinal images may differ as a result of distance.

Sleep terrors Frightening, dreamlike experiences that occur during the deepest stage of NREM sleep, shortly after the child has gone to sleep.

Small for dates Descriptive of neonates who are unusually small for their age.

Social cognition Development of children's understanding of the relationship between the self and others.

Social cognitive theory A cognitively oriented learning theory that emphasizes observational learning in the determining of behavior.

Socialization The systematic exposure of children to rewards and punishments and to role models who guide them into socially acceptable behavior patterns.

Social play Play in which children interact with and are influenced by the play of others. Examples include parallel play, associative play, and cooperative play.

Social referencing Using another person's reaction to a situation to form one's own assessment of it.

Social smile A smile that occurs in response to a human voice or face.

Solitary play Play that is independent from that of nearby children and in which no effort is made to approach other children.

Somnambulism Sleepwalking (from the Latin *somnus,* meaning "sleep," and *ambulare,* meaning "to walk").

Sonogram A procedure for using ultrasonic sound waves to create a picture of an embryo or fetus.

Spina bifida A neural-tube defect that causes abnormalities of the brain and spine.

Spontaneous abortion Unplanned, accidental abortion (*miscarriage* is the popular term).

Stage theory A theory of development characterized by hypothesizing the existence of distinct periods of life. Stages follow one another in an orderly sequence.

Standardized test A test of some ability or trait in which an individual's score is compared to the scores of a group of similar individuals.

Status offenses Offenses considered illegal only when performed by minors, such as truancy and underage drinking.

Stem cells Cells that have the ability to divide for indefinite periods in culture and to give rise to specialized cells.

Stepping reflex A reflex in which infants take steps when held under the arms and leaned forward so that the feet press against the ground.

Stereotype A fixed, conventional idea about a group.

Stillbirth The birth of a dead fetus.

Stimulants Drugs that increase the activity of the nervous system.

Stimulus A change in the environment that leads to a change in behavior.

Stranger anxiety A fear of unfamiliar people that emerges between 6 and 9 months of age. Also called *fear of strangers.*

Substance abuse A persistent pattern of use of a substance characterized by frequent intoxication and impairment of physical, social, or emotional well-being.

Substance dependence A persistent pattern of use of a substance that is accompanied by physiological addiction.

Sudden infant death syndrome (SIDS) The death, while sleeping, of apparently healthy babies who stop breathing for unknown medical reasons. Also called *crib death.*

Superego The third element of personality, which functions as a moral guardian and sets forth high standards for behavior.

Surface structure The superficial grammatical construction of a sentence.

Surfactants Substances that lubricate the walls of the air sacs in the lungs.

Surrogate mother A woman who is artificially inseminated and carries to term a child who is then given to another woman, typically the spouse of the sperm donor.

Syllogism A type of reasoning in which two statements or premises are set forth and a logical conclusion is drawn from them.

Symbolic play Play in which children make believe that objects and toys are other than what they are. Also termed *pretend play.*

Syntax The rules in a language for placing words in proper order to form meaningful sentences (from the Latin syntaxis, meaning "joining together").

Syphilis A sexually transmitted infection (STI) that, in advanced stages, can attack major organ systems.

Tay-Sachs disease A fatal genetic neurological disorder.

Telegraphic speech Type of speech in which only the essential words are used, as in a telegram.

Temperament Individual differences in styles of reaction that are present very early in life.

Teratogens Environmental influences or agents that can damage the embryo or fetus (from the Greek *teras,* meaning "monster").

Term A set period of time.

Tertiary circular reactions The purposeful adaptation of established schemes to new situations.

Testosterone A male sex hormone a steroid that is produced by the testes and promotes growth of male sexual characteristics and sperm.

Thalidomide A sedative used in the 1960s that has been linked to birth defects, especially deformed or absent limbs.

Theory A formulation of relationships underlying observed events. A theory involves assumptions and logically derived explanations and predictions.

Theory of mind A commonsense understanding of how the mind works.

Time lag The study of developmental processes by taking measures of children of the same age group at different times.

Time out A behavior-modification technique in which a child who misbehaves is temporarily placed in a drab, restrictive environment in which reinforcement is unavailable.

Toddler A child who walks with short, uncertain steps. Toddlerhood lasts from about 18 to 30 months of age, thereby bridging infancy and early childhood.

Tolerance Habituation to a drug such that increasingly higher doses are needed to achieve similar effects.

Tonic-neck reflex A reflex in which infants turn their head to one side, extend the arm and leg on that side, and flex the limbs on the opposite side. Also known as the "fencing position."

Total immersion A method of language instruction in which a person is placed in an environment in which only the language to be learned is used.

Totipotent stem cells Stem cells that have total potential, or unlimited capability. Totipotent stem cells have the capacity to specialize into the embryo and supportive tissues and organs, such as the placenta.

Toxemia A life-threatening disease that can afflict pregnant women and is characterized by high blood pressure.

Track To follow.

Tranquilizer A drug that reduces feelings of anxiety and tension.

Transductive reasoning Reasoning from the specific to the specific. (In deductive reasoning, one reasons from the general to the specific; in inductive reasoning, one reasons from the specific to the general.)

Transition The initial movement of the head of the fetus into the birth canal.

Transitional object A soft, cuddly object often carried to bed by a child to ease the separation from parents.

Transitivity The principle that if A is greater than B in a property, and B is greater than C, then A is greater than C.

Treatment In an experiment, a condition received by participants so that its effects may be observed.

Triarchic Governed by three. Descriptive of Sternberg's view that intellectual functioning has three aspects: analytical, creative, and practical.

Trophoblast The outer part of the blastocyst, from which the amniotic sac, placenta, and umbilical cord develop.

Trust versus mistrust The first of Erikson's stages of psychosocial development, during which the child comes to (or comes not to) develop a basic sense of trust in others.

Turner's syndrome A chromosomal disorder found among females that is caused by having a single X sex chromosome and characterized by infertility.

Ulnar grasp A method of grasping objects in which the fingers close somewhat clumsily against the palm.

Ultrasound Sound waves too high in pitch to be sensed by the human ear.

Umbilical cord A tube that connects the fetus to the placenta.

Unconditioned response (UCR) An unlearned response. A response to an unconditioned stimulus.

Unconditioned stimulus (UCS) A stimulus that elicits a response from an organism without learning.

Unconscious In psychoanalytic theory, refers to a state where something is not available to awareness by simple focusing of attention.

Unexamined ethnic identity The first stage of ethnic identity development; similar to the diffusion or foreclosure identity status.

Uterus The hollow organ within females in which the embryo and fetus develop.

Utopian Referring to an ideal vision of society.

Vacuum extraction tube An instrument that uses suction to pull the baby through the birth canal.

Variable Quantity that can vary from child to child, or from occasion to occasion, such as height, weight, intelligence, and attention span.

Vernix An oily, white substance that coats the skin of the neonate, especially preterm babies.

Visual accommodation The automatic adjustments made by the lenses of the eyes to bring objects into focus.

Visual acuity Keenness or sharpness of vision.

Visual recognition memory The kind of memory shown in an infant's ability to discriminate previously seen objects from novel objects.

Voluntarily Intentionally.

Wernicke's aphasia A form of aphasia caused by damage to Wernicke's area and characterized by impaired comprehension of speech and difficulty in attempting to produce the right word.

Whole-object assumption The assumption that words refer to whole objects and not their component parts or characteristics.

Womb simulator An artificial environment that mimics some of the features of the womb, particularly temperature, sounds, and rocking movements.

Word-recognition method A method for learning to read in which children come to recognize words through repeated exposure to them.

Zona pellucida A gelatinous layer that surrounds an ovum (from roots referring to a "zone through which light can shine").

Zone of proximal development (ZPD) Vygotsky's term for the situation in which a child carries out tasks with the help of someone who is more skilled, frequently an adult who represents the culture in which the child develops.

Zygote A fertilized ovum.

References

AAP Media Alert on Breastfeeding. (1999, February 11). **http://www.aap.org/visit/brmdalt.htm**

Abbott, S. (1992). Holding on and pushing away: Comparative perspectives on an Eastern Kentucky child-rearing practice. *Ethos, 20,* 33–65.

ABCNEWS.com. (2001, June 19). Study: One in five kids solicited online.

ABC News *Nightline* Poll. (1995, February 17). Most favor sex ed in schools, believing it changes behavior.

Abdelaziz, Y. E., Harb, A. H., & Hisham, N. (2001). *Textbook of Clinical Pediatrics.* Philadelphia: Lippincott Williams & Wilkins.

Abe-Kim, J., Okazaki, S., & Goto, S. G. (2001). Unidimensional versus multidimensional approaches to the assessment of acculturation for Asian American populations. *Cultural Diversity & Ethnic Minority Psychology,* 7(3), 232–246.

Abikoff, H. (2001). Tailored psychosocial treatments for ADHD: The search for a good fit. *Journal of Clinical Child Psychology, 30*(1), 122–125.

Abravanel, E., & DeYong, N. G. (1991). Does object modeling elicit imitative-like gestures from young infants? *Journal of Experimental Child Psychology,* 52, 22–40.

Acebo, C., & Thomas, E. B. (1992). Crying as social behavior. Infant *Mental Health Journal, 13,* 67–82.

Achenbach, T. M., Howell, C. T., Aoki, M. F., & Rauh, V. A. (1993). Nine-year outcome of the Vermont intervention program for low birth weight infants. *Pediatrics, 91,* 45–55.

Achenbach, T. M., Phares, V., Howell, C. T., Rauh, V. A., & Nurcombe, B. (1990). Seven-year outcome of the Vermont intervention program for low-birth-weight infants. *Child Development, 61,* 1672–1681.

Adams, D. M., Overholser, J. C., & Spirito, A. (1992, August). *Life stress related to adolescent suicide attempts.* Paper presented at the meeting of the American Psychological Association, Washington, DC.

Adcock, A. G., Nagy, S., & Simpson, J. A. (1991). Selected risk factors in adolescent suicide attempts. *Adolescence, 104,* 817–827.

Adler, J., et al. (1992, February 17). Hey, I'm terrific! *Newsweek,* pp. 46–51.

Adler, J., & Starr, M. (1992, August 10). Flying high now. *Newsweek,* pp. 20–21.

Adler, T. (1993a, January). EEGs differ widely for those with different temperaments. *APA Monitor,* p. 7.

Adler, T. (1993b, April). Sense of invulnerability doesn't drive teen risks. *APA Monitor,* p. 15.

Adler, T. (1993c, June). Kids' memory improves if they talk to themselves. *APA Monitor,* p. 8.

Adnams, C. M., et al. (2001). Patterns of cognitive-motor development in children with fetal alcohol syndrome from a community in South Africa. *Alcoholism: Clinical & Experimental Research, 25*(4), 557–562.

Adolph, K. E. (2000). Specificity of learning: Why infants fall over a veritable cliff. *Psychological Science, 11*(4), 290–295.

Affonso, D. D., De, A. K., Horowitz, J. A., & Mayberry, L. J. (2000). An international study exploring levels of postpartum depressive symptomatology. *Journal of Psychosomatic Research, 49*(3), 207–216.

After years of decline, Caesareans on the rise again. (2000, August 29). The Associated Press online.

Agence France-Presse. (2001, May 6). India cracks down on sex tests for fetuses. *The New York Times,* p. L4.

Aguiar, A., & Baillargeon, R. (1998). Eight-and-a-half-month-old infants' reasoning about containment events. *Child Development, 69*(3), 636–653.

Aguiar, A., & Baillargeon, R. (1999). 2.5-month-old infants' reasoning about when objects should and should not be occluded. *Cognitive Psychology, 39*(2), 116–157.

Ahluwalia, I. B., Merritt, R., Beck, L. F., & Rogers, M. (2001). Multiple lifestyle and psychosocial risks and delivery of small for gestational age infants. *Obstetrics & Gynecology, 97*(5), 649–656.

Ainsworth, M. D. S. (1967). *Infancy in Uganda: Infant care and the growth of love.* Baltimore: Johns Hopkins University Press.

Ainsworth, M. D. S. (1989). Attachments beyond infancy. *American Psychologist, 44,* 709–716.

Ainsworth, M. D. S., Blehar, M. C., Waters, E., & Wall, S. (1978). *Patterns of attachment: A psychological study of the Strange Situation.* Hillsdale, NJ: Erlbaum.

Ainsworth, M. D. S., & Bowlby, J. (1991). An ethological approach to personality development. *American Psychologist, 46,* 331–341.

Akhtar, N., Dunham, F., & Dunham, P. J. (1991). Directive interactions and early vocabulary development: The role of joint attentional focus. *Journal of Child Language, 18,* 41–49.

Alan Guttmacher Institute. (1991). *Facts in brief.* New York: Author.

Alan Guttmacher Institute. (2001). *Teen-age sexual and reproductive behavior in developed countries: Can more progress be made?* New York: Alan Guttmacher Institute.

Alcazar, A. I. R., Rodriguez, J. O., & Sanchez Meca, J. (1999). Meta-analisis de las intervenciones conductuales de la enuresis en España. *Anales de Psicologia, 15*(2), 157–167.

Alessandri, S. M., Bendersky, M., & Lewis, M. (1998). Cognitive functioning in 8- to 18-month-old drug-exposed infants. *Developmental Psychology, 34*(3), 565–573.

Al-Krenawi, A., Slonim-Nevo, V., Maymon, Y., & Al-Krenawi, S. (2001). Psychological responses to blood vengeance among Arab adolescents. *Child Abuse & Neglect, 25*(4), 457–472.

Allen, L., & Majidi-Ahi, S. (1991). Black American children. In J. T. Gibbs, L. N. Huang & Associates (Eds). *Children of color: Psychological interventions with minority youth.* San Francisco: Jossey-Bass.

Allen, M. C., & Alexander, G. R. (1990). Gross motor milestones in preterm infants: Correction for degree of prematurity. *Journal of Pediatrics, 116,* 955–959.

Allen, M. N., Donohue, P. K., & Dusman, A. E. (1993). The limit of viability—Neonatal outcome of infants born at 22 to 25 weeks' gestation. *The New England Journal of Medicine online, 329*(22).

Allen, P. L. (2000). *The wages of sin: Sex and disease, past and present.* Chicago: University of Chicago Press.

Alsaker, F. D. (1992). Pubertal timing, overweight, and psychological adjustment. *Journal of Early Adolescence, 12,* 396–419.

Altepeter, T. S., & Walker, C. E. (1992). Prevention of physical abuse of children through parent training. In D. J. Willis, E. W. Holden, & M. Rosenberg (Eds.), *Prevention of child maltreatment.* New York: Wiley.

Altindag, A., Oezkan, M., & Oto, R. (2001). Inhalanla Iliskili bozukluklar. *Klinik Psikofarmakoloji Buelteni, 11*(2), 143–148.

Aman, M. G., Arnold, L. E., & Armstrong, S. C. (1999). Review of serotonergic agents and perseverative behavior in patients with developmental disabilities. *Mental Retardation & Developmental Disabilities Research Reviews, 5*(4), 279–289.

Amato, P. R. (2000). The consequences of divorce for adults and children. *Journal of Marriage & the Family, 62*(4), 1269–1287.

Amato, P. R. (2001) Children of divorce in the 1990s: An update of the Amato and Keith (1991) meta-analysis. *Journal of Family Psychology, 15*(3), 355–370.

Ambrosio, E., Martin, S., Garcia-Lecumberri, C., Crespo, J. A. (1999). The neurobiology of cannabinoid dependence: Sex differences and potential interactions between cannabinoid and opioid systems. *Life Sciences, 65*(6–7), 687–694.

American Academy of Pediatrics. (1992). Learning disabilities, dyslexia, and vision. *Pediatrics, 90,* 124–126.

American Academy of Pediatrics. (2002, February 7). *A woman's guide to breastfeeding.* **http://www.aap.org/family/brstguid.htm**

American Association of University Women. (1991). *Shortchanging girls, shortchanging America.* Washington, DC: AAUW Educational Foundation.

American Association of University Women. (1992). *How schools shortchange women: The AAUW report.* Washington, DC: AAUW Educational Foundation.

American Association of University Women. (1993). *Hostile hallways.* Washington, DC: AAUW Educational Foundation.

American College of Obstetricians and Gynecologists (2001, March 31.) Pregnancy-related mortality from preeclampsia and eclampsia. ACOG Press; **http://www.acog.com/**

American Lung Association (2000). Smoking fact sheet, URL **http:/www.lungusa.org**

American Psychiatric Association (2000). *Diagnostic and statistical manual of mental disorders. DSM-IV-TR.* Washington, DC: Author.

American Psychological Association. (1992). Ethical principles of psychologists and code of conduct. *American Psychologist, 47,* 1597–1611.

American Psychological Association. (1993). *Violence and youth.* Washington, DC: Author.

Anastasi, A. (1988). *Psychological testing* (6th ed). New York: Macmillan.

Anderman, E. M., Eccles, J. S., Yoon, K. S., Roeser, R., Wigfield, A., & Blumenfeld, P. (2001). Learning to value mathematics and reading: Relations to mastery and performance-oriented instructional practices. *Contemporary Educational Psychology, 26*(1), 76–95.

Anders, T. F., Halpern, L. F., & Hua, J. (1992). Sleeping through the night: A developmental perspective. *Pediatrics, 90,* 554–560.

Anderson, C. A., & Dill, K. E. (2000). Video games and aggressive thoughts, feelings, and behavior in the laboratory and in life. *Journal of Personality and Social Psychology, 78*(4), 772–790.

Anderson, E. (1990). *Streetwise: Race, class, and change in an urban community.* Chicago: University of Chicago Press.

Anderson, G. M., & Cohen, D. J. (1991). The neurology of childhood neuropsychiatric disorders. In M., Lewis (Ed.), *Child and adolescent psychiatry: A comprehensive textbook.* Baltimore: Williams & Wilkins.

Anderson, S. R., Christian, W. P., & Luce, S. C. (1986). Transitional residential programming for autistic individuals. *Behavior Therapist, 9,* 205–211.

Andersson, B. (1992). Effects of day-care on cognitive and socioemotional competence of thirteen-year-old Swedish schoolchildren. *Child Development, 63,* 20–36.

Andrews, J., & Conte, R. (1993, March). *Enhancing the social cognition of learning disabled children through a cognitive strategies approach.* Paper presented at the meeting of the Society for Research in Child Development, New Orleans, LA.

Andrews, J. A., & Lewinsohn, P. M. (1992). Suicidal attempts among older adolescents: Prevalence and co-occurrence with psychiatric disorders. *Journal of American Academy of Child and Adolescent Psychiatry, 31,* 655–662.

Angier, N. (1997). Chemical tied to fat control could help trigger puberty. *The New York Times,* pp. C1, C3.

Anisfeld, E., Casper, V., Kozyce, M., & Cunningham, N. (1990). Does infant carrying promote attachment? An experimental study of the effects of increased physical contact on the development of attachment. *Child Development, 61,* 1617–1627.

Anisfeld, M. (1991). Review: Neonatal imitation. *Developmental Review, 11,* 60–97.

Annas, G. J. (1993, Spring). Who's afraid of the human genome? *National Forum,* pp. 35–37.

Antilla, S. (1993, January 10). Bringing up a TV-wise child. *The New York Times,* pp. A4, 34–35.

Antonio, M. T., & Leret, M. L. (2000). Study of the neurochemical alterations produced in discrete brain areas by perinatal low-level exposure. *Life Sciences, 67*(6), 635–642.

Apgar, V. (1953). A proposal for a new method of evaluation in the newborn infant. *Anesthesia and Analgesia, 52,* 260–267.

Arbona, C. (2000). Practice and research in career counseling and development. *Career Development Quarterly, 49*(2), 98–134.

Arbuthnot, J., & Gordon, D. A. (1988). Crime and cognition: Community applications of sociomoral reasoning development. *Criminal Justice & Behavior, 15*(3), 379–393.

Archer, S. L. (1985). Career and/or family: The identity process for adolescent girls. *Youth and Society, 16,* 289–314.

Archer, S. L. (1991). Gender differences in identity development. In R. M. Lerner, A. C. Petersen, & J. Brooks-Gunn (Eds.), *Encyclopedia of adolescence.* New York: Garland.

Archer, S. L. (1992). A feminist's approach to identity research. In G. R. Adams, T. P. Gullotta, & R. Montemayor (Eds.), *Adolescent identity formation.* Newbury Park, CA: Sage.

Archer, S. L. & Waterman, A. S. (1990). Varieties of identity diffusions and foreclosures: An exploration of subcategories of the identity statuses. *Journal of Adolescent Research, 5,* 96–111.

Aries, P. (1962). *Centuries of childhood.* New York: Knopf.

Armstrong, C. A., et al. (1998). Children's television viewing, body fat, and physical fitness. *American Journal of Health Promotion, 12*(6), 363–368.

Arnett, J. J. (1992). Reckless behavior in adolescence: A developmental perspective. *Developmental Review, 12,* 339–373.

Arnett, J. J. (1998a). Learning to stand alone: The contemporary American transition to adulthood in cultural and historical context. *Human Development, 41*(5–6), 295–315.

Arnett, J. J. (1998b). Risk behavior and family role transitions during the twenties. *Journal of Youth & Adolescence, 27*(3), 301–320.

Arnett, J. J. (1999). Adolescent storm and stress, reconsidered. *American Psychologist, 54*(5), 317–326.

Arnett, J. J. (2000a). Emerging adulthood. *American Psychologist, 55*(5), 469–480.

Arnett, J. J. (2000b). High hopes in a grim world: Emerging adults' view of their futures and "Generation X." *Youth & Society, 31*(3), 267–286.

Arnett, J. J. (2001). Conceptions of the transition to adulthood: Perspectives from adolescence through midlife. *Journal of Adult Development, 8*(2), 133–143.

Arnold, D. H., Homrok, S., Ortiz, C., & Stowe, R. M. (1999). Direct observation of peer rejection acts and their temporal relation with aggressive acts. *Early Childhood Research Quarterly, 14*(2), 183–196.

Arnold, D. H., Lonigan, C. J., Whitehurst, G. J., & Epstein, J. N. (1994). Accelerating language development through picture book reading. *Journal of Educational Psychology, 86,* 235–243.

Arthur, B. I., Jr., et al. (1998). Sexual behaviour in *Drosophila* is irreversibly programmed during critical period. *Current Biology, 8*(21), 1187–1190.

Asendorpf, J. B. (1993). Beyond temperament: A two-factorial coping model of the development of inhibition during childhood. In K. H. Rubin & J. B. Asendorpf (Eds.), *Social withdrawal, inhibition, and shyness in childhood.* Hillsdale, NJ: Erlbaum.

Asendorpf, J. B., & Baudonniere, P. (1993). Self-awareness and other-awareness: Mirror self-recognition and synchronic imitation among unfamiliar peers. *Developmental Psychology, 29,* 88–95.

Ashton, A. K., et al. (2000). Antidepressant-induced sexual dysfunction and ginkgo biloba. *American Journal of Psychiatry, 157,* 836–837.

Aslin, R. N. (1987). Visual and auditory development in infancy. In J. D. Osofsky (Ed.), *Handbook of infant development* (2nd ed.). New York: Wiley.

Aslin, R. N., Pisoni, D. B., & Juscyk, P. W. (1983). Auditory development and speech perception in infancy. In P. H. Mussen (Ed.), *Handbook of child psychology: Vol. 2. Infancy and experimental psychobiology.* New York: Wiley.

Astley, S. J., & Clarren, S. K. (2001). Measuring the facial phenotype of individuals with prenatal alcohol exposure: Correlations with brain dysfunction. *Alcohol & Alcoholism, 36*(2), 147–159.

Astley, S. J., Clarren, S. K., Little, R. E., Sampson, P. D., & Daling, J. R. (1992). Analysis of facial shape in children gestationally exposed to marijuana, alcohol, and/or cocaine. *Pediatrics, 89,* 67–77.

Au, T. K., & Glusman, M. (1990). The principle of mutual exclusivity in word learning: To honor or not to honor? *Child Development, 61,* 1474–1490.

Autti-Raemoe, I. (2000). Twelve-year follow-up of children exposed to alcohol in utero. *Developmental Medicine & Child Neurology, 42*(6), 406–411.

Avis, J., & Harris, P. L. (1991). Belief-desire reasoning among Baka children: Evidence for a universal conception of mind. *Child Development, 62,* 460–467.

Ayyash-Abdo, H. (2001). Individualism and collectivism: The case of Lebanon. *Social Behavior & Personality, 29*(5), 503–518.

Azar, B. (1997). It may cause anxiety, but day care can benefit kids. *APA Monitor, 28*(6), 13.

Azar, B. (1998). What predicts which foods we eat? A genetic disposition for certain tastes may affect people's food preferences. *APA Monitor, 29,* 1.

Bacete, F. G., & Remirez, J. R. (2001). Family and personal correlates of academic achievement. *Psychological Reports, 88*(2), 533–547.

Bachman, J. G. (1991). School dropouts. In R. M. Lerner, A. C. Petersen, & J. Brooks-Gunn (Eds.), *Encyclopedia of adolescence.* New York: Garland.

Bachman, J. G., & Schulenberg, J. (1993). How part-time work intensity relates to drug use, problem behavior, time use, and satisfaction among high school seniors: Are these consequences or merely correlates? *Developmental Psychology, 29,* 220–235.

Baer, H., Allen, S., & Braun, L. (2002). Knowledge of human papillomavirus infection among young adult men and women: Implications for health education and research. *Journal of Community Health: The Publication for Health Promotion & Disease Prevention, 25*(1), 67–78.

Bagley, C., Bertrand, L., Bolitho, F., & Mallick, K. (2001). Discrepant parent–adolescent views on family functioning: Predictors of poorer self-esteem and problems of emotion and behaviour in British and Canadian adolescents. *Journal of Comparative Family Studies, 32*(3), 393–403.

Bagley, C., & D'Augelli, A. R. (2000). Suicidal behaviour in gay, lesbian, and bisexual youth. *British Medical Journal, 320,* 1617–1618.

Bailey, J. M., Dunne, M. P., & Martin, N. G. (2000). Genetic and environmental influences on sexual orientation and its correlates in an Australian twin sample. *Journal of Personality and Social Psychology, 78*(3), 524–536.

Bailey, J. M., & Pillard, R. C. (1991). A genetic study of male sexual orientation. *Archives of General Psychiatry, 48,* 1089–1096.

Bailey, J. M., Pillard, R. C., Neale, M. C., & Agyei, Y. (1993). Heritable factors influence sexual orientation in women. *Archives of General Psychiatry, 50,* 217–223.

Baillargeon, R. (1987). Object permanence in 3½- and 4½-month-old infants. *Developmental Psychology, 23,* 655–664.

Baillargeon, R. (1991). Reasoning about the height and location of a hidden object in 4½- and 6½-month-old infants. *Cognition, 38,* 13–42.

Baillargeon, R., Graber, M., DeVos, J., & Black, J. (1990). Why do young infants fail to search for hidden objects? *Cognition, 36,* 255–284.

Bakan, P. (1990). Nonright-handedness and the continuum of reproductive casualty. In S. Coren (Ed.), *Left-handedness: Behavior implications and anomalies.* Amsterdam: North-Holland.

Baker, C. W., Whisman, M. A., & Brownell, K. D. (2000). Studying intergenerational transmission of eating attitudes and behaviors: Methodological and conceptual questions. *Health Psychology, 19*(4), 376–381.

Baker, F., et al. (2000). Health risks associated with cigar smoking. *Journal of the American Medical Association, 284*(6), 735–740.

Baker, L., & Cantwell, D. P. (1991). The development of speech and language. In M. Lewis (Ed.), *Child and adolescent psychiatry: A comprehensive textbook.* Baltimore: Williams & Wilkins.

Baker, L., Mackler, K., Sonnenschein, S., & Serpell, R. (2001). Parents' interactions with their first-grade children during storybook reading and relations with subsequent home reading activity and reading achievement. *Journal of School Psychology, 39*(5), 415–438.

Baldwin, A. L., Baldwin, C., & Cole, R. E. (1990). Stress-resistant families and stress-resistant children. In J. Rolf, A. Masten, D. Cicchetti, K. Nuechterlein & S. Weintraub (Eds.)., *Risk and protective factors in the development of psychopathology.* Cambridge: Cambridge University Press.

Balluz, L. S., et al. (2000). Vitamin and mineral supplement use in the United States: Results from the Third National Health and Nutrition Examination Survey. *Archives of Family Medicine, 9,* 258.

Ballweg, Rachel. 2001 Can you be too rich or too thin? *Well and Good,* no. 3. Retreived from **http://www.uihealthcare.com/news/wellandgood/2001issue3/eatingdisorders.html**

Bamford, F. N., et al. (1990). Sleep in the first year of life. *Developmental Medicine and Child Neurology, 32,* 718–724.

Bandura, A. (1989). Social cognitive theory. In R. Vasta (Ed.), *Annals of child development* (Vol. 6). Greenwich, CT: JAI Press.

Bandura, A. (1991). Human agency: The rhetoric and the reality. *American Psychologist, 46,* 157–162.

Bandura, A. (2000). Social cognitive theory: An agentic perspective. *Annual Review of Psychology, 52,* 1–26.

Bandura, A., Barbaranelli, C., Vittorio Caprara, G., & Pastorelli, C. (2001). Self-efficacy beliefs as shapers of children's aspirations and career trajectories. *Child Development, 72*(1), 187–206.

Bandura, A., Blanchard, E. B., & Ritter, B. (1969). The relative efficacy of desensitization and modeling approaches for inducing behavioral, affective, and cognitive changes. *Journal of Personality and Social Psychology, 13,* 173–199.

Bandura, A., Ross, S. A., & Ross, D. (1963). Imitation of film-mediated aggressive models. *Journal of Abnormal and Social Psychology, 66,* 3–11.

Banks, M. S., & Salapatek, P. (1983). Infant visual perception. In P. H. Mussen (Ed.), *Handbook of child psychology: Vol. 2. Infancy and experimental psychobiology.* New York: Wiley.

Banks, M. S., & Shannon, E. (1993). Spatial and chromatic visual efficiency in human neonates. In C. E. Granrud (Ed.), *Visual perception and cognition in infancy.* Hillsdale, NJ: Erlbaum.

Barabas, G. (1990). Physical disorders. In M. Lewis & S. M. Miller (Eds.), *Handbook of developmental pathology.* New York: Plenum.

Barbarin, O. A., Richter, L., & deWet, T. (2001). Exposure to violence, coping resources, and psychological adjustment of South African children. *American Journal of Orthopsychiatry, 71*(1), 16–25.

Barber, J. G. (2001). Relative misery and youth suicide. *Australian & New Zealand Journal of Psychiatry, 35*(1), 49–57.

Bard, C., Hay, L., & Fleury, M. (1990). Timing and accuracy of visually directed movements in children: Control of direction and amplitude components. *Journal of Experimental Child Psychology, 50,* 102–118.

Bard, K. A., Coles, C. D., Platzman, K. A., & Lynch, M. E. (2000). The effects of prenatal drug exposure, term status, and caregiving on arousal and arousal modulation in 8-week-old infants. *Developmental Psychobiology, 36*(3), 194–212.

Barkley, R. A., Anastopoulos, A. D., Guevremont, D. C., & Fletcher, K. E. (1991). Adolescents with ADHD: Patterns of behavioral adjustment, academic functioning and treatment utilization. *Journal of the American Academy of Child and Adolescent Psychiatry, 30,* 752–761.

Barnard, K. E., & Bee, H. L. (1983). The impact of temporally patterned stimulation on the development of preterm infants. *Child Development, 54,* 1156–1167.

Barnett, R. C., & Hyde, J. S. (2001). Women, men, work, and family: An expansionist theory. *American Psychologist, 56*(10), 781–796.

Bar-Or, O., et al. (1998). Physical activity, genetic, and nutritional considerations in childhood weight management. *Medicine & Science in Sports & Exercise, 30*(1), 2–10.

Barr, H. M., & Streissguth, A. P. (2001). Identifying maternal self-reported alcohol use associated with fetal alcohol spectrum disorders. *Alcoholism: Clinical & Experimental Research, 25*(2) 283–287.

Barr, H. M., Streissguth, A. P., Darby, B. L., & Sampson, P. D. (1990). Prenatal exposure to alcohol, caffeine, tobacco, and aspirin: Effects on fine and gross motor performance in 4-year-old children. *Developmental Psychology, 26,* 339–348.

Barr, R. G., Rotman, A., Yaremko, J., Leduc, D., & Francoeur, T. E. (1992). The crying of infants with colic: A controlled empirical description. *Pediatrics, 90,* 14–21.

Barratt, M. S., Negayama, K., & Minami, T. (1993). The social environments of early infancy in Japan and the United States. *Early Development and Parenting, 2,* 51–64.

Barrett, D. E., Radke-Yarrow, M., & Klein, R. E. (1982). Chronic malnutrition and child behavior: Effects of early caloric supplementation on social and emotional functioning at school age. *Developmental Psychology, 18,* 541–556.

Barrett, M., Harris, M., & Chasin, J. (1991). Early lexical development and maternal speech: A comparison of children's initial and subsequent uses of words. *Journal of Child Language, 18,* 21–40.

Barrile, M., Armstrong, E. S., & Bower, T. G. R. (1999). Novelty and frequency as determinants of newborn preference. *Developmental Science, 2*(1), 47–52.

Barringer, F. (1993, April 28). Immigration in 80's made English a foreign language for millions. *The New York Times,* pp. A1, 10.

Barros, F. C., Huttly, S. R. A., Victora, C. G., Kirkwood, B. R., & Vaughan, J. P. (1992). Comparison of the causes and consequences of prematurity and intrauterine growth retardation: A longitudinal study in Southern Brazil. *Pediatrics, 90,* 238–244.

Bar-Tal, D. (1990). Prosocial behavior. In R. M. Thomas (Ed.), *The encyclopedia of human development and education: Theory, research, and studies.* Oxford: Pergamon.

Bartko, W. T., & McHale, S. M. (1991). The household labor of children from dual- versus single-earner families. In S. V. Lerner & N. L. Galambos (Eds.), *Employed mothers and their children.* New York: Garland.

Basen-Engquist, K., Edmundson, E. W., & Parcel, G. S. (1996). Structure of health risk behavior among high school students. *Journal of Consulting and Clinical Psychology, 64,* 764–775.

Basic Behavioral Science Task Force of the National Advisory Mental Health Council. (1996). Basic behavioral science research for mental health: Sociocultural and environmental practices. *American Psychologist, 51,* 722–731.

Bastien-Toniazzo, M., & Jullien, S. (2001). Nature and importance of the logographic phase in learning to read. *Reading & Writing, 14*(1–2), 119–143.

Bates, E., O'Connell, B., & Shore, C. (1987). Language and communication in infancy. In J. D. Osofsky (Ed.), *Handbook of infant development* (2nd ed.). New York: Wiley.

Bates, E., Thal, D., & Janowsky, J. S. (1992). Early language development and its neural correlates. *Handbook of Neuropsychology, 7,* 69–110.

Bates, J. E., Bayles, K., Bennett, D. S., Ridge, B., & Brown, M. M. (1991). Origins of externalizing behavior problems at eight years of age. In D. J. Pepler & K. H. Rubin (Eds.), *The development and treatment of childhood aggression.* Hillsdale, NJ: Erlbaum.

Battin-Pearson, S., et al. (2000). Predictors of early high school dropout: A test of five theories. *Journal of Educational Psychology, 92*(3), 568–582.

Battistich, V., Watson, M., Solomon, D., Schaps, E., & Solomon, J. (1991a). The Child Development Project: A comprehensive program for the development of prosocial character. In W. M. Kurtines & J. L. Gewirtz (Eds.), *Handbook of moral behavior and development* (Vol. 3). Hillsdale, NJ: Erlbaum.

Battistich, V., Schaps, E., Solomon, D., & Watson, M. (1991b). The role of the school in prosocial development. In H. E. Fitzgerald, B. M. Lester, & M. W. Yogman (Eds.), *Theory and research in behavioral pediatrics* (Vol. 5). New York: Plenum.

Bauer, P. J. (1993). Memory for gender-consistent and gender-inconsistent event sequences by twenty-five-month-old children. *Child Development, 64,* 285–297.

Bauer, P. J., & Mandler, J. M. (1990). Remembering what happened next: Very young children's recall of event sequences. In R. Fivush & J. A. Hudson (Eds.), *Knowing and remembering in young children.* Cambridge: Cambridge University Press.

Bauer, P. J., & Mandler, J. M. (1992). Putting the horse before the cart: The use of temporal order in recall of events by one-year-old children. *Developmental Psychology, 28,* 441–452.

Bauer, W. D., & Twentyman, C. T. (1985). Abusing, neglectful, and comparison mothers' responses to child-related and non-child-related stressors. *Journal of Consulting and Clinical Psychology, 53,* 335–343.

Bauerfeld, S. L., & Lachenmeyer, J. R. (1992). Prenatal nutritional status and intellectual development. In B. B. Lahey & A. E. Kazdin (Eds.), *Advances in clinical child psychology* (Vol. 14). New York: Plenum.

Baumeister, R. F., Catanese, K. R., & Vohs, K. D. (2001). Is there a gender difference in strength of sex drive? Theoretical views, conceptual distinctions, and a review of relevant evidence. *Personality & Social Psychology Review, 5*(3), 242–273.

Baumrind, D. (1989). Rearing competent children. In W. Damon (Ed.), *Child development today and tomorrow.* San Francisco: Jossey-Bass.

Baumrind, D. (1991a). The influence of parenting style on adolescent competence and substance use. *Journal of Early Adolescence, 11,* 56–95.

Baumrind, D. (1991b). Parenting styles and adolescent development. In J. Brooks-Gunn, R. Lerner, & A. C. Petersen (Eds.), *Encyclopedia of adolescence.* New York: Garland.

Baydar, N., & Brooks-Gunn, J. (1991). Effects of maternal employment and child-care arrangements on preschoolers' cognitive and behavioral outcomes: Evidence from the Children of the National Longitudinal Survey of Youth. *Developmental Psychology, 27,* 932–945.

Bayley, N. (1993). *Bayley Scales of Infant Development.* New York: The Psychological Corporation.

Beal, C. R., & Flavell, J. H. (1983). Young speakers' evaluation of their listeners' comprehensions in a referential communication task. *Child Development, 54,* 148–153.

Bear, G. G. (1989). Sociomoral reasoning and antisocial behaviors among normal sixth graders. *Merrill-Palmer Quarterly, 35,* 181–196.

Becker, E. (2002, January 24). Study finds a growing gap between managerial salaries for men and women. *The New York Times,* p. A24.

Bedford, V. H., Volling, B. L., & Avioli, P. S. (2000). Positive consequences of sibling conflict in childhood and adulthood. *International Journal of Aging & Human Development, 51*(1), 53–69.

Beer, J. M., & Horn, J. M. (2000). The influence of rearing order on personality development within two adoption cohorts. *Journal of Personality, 68*(4), 789–819.

Behrend, D. A. (1990). The development of verb concepts: Children's use of verbs to label familiar and novel events. *Child Development, 61,* 681–696.

Behrman, R. E., Kliegman, R. M., & Jenson, H. B. (2000). *Nelson review of pediatrics* (2nd ed.). Philadelphia: W. B. Saunders.

Beilin, H., & Pearlman, E. G. (1991). Children's iconic realism: Object versus property realism. In H. W. Reese (Ed.), *Advances in child development and behavior* (Vol. 23). San Diego, CA: Academic Press.

Beitchman, J. H., et al. (2001). Comorbidity of psychiatric and substance use disorders in late adolescence: A cluster analytic approach. *American Journal of Drug & Alcohol Abuse, 27*(3), 421–440.

Belkin, L. (1992, March 25). Births beyond hospitals fill an urban need. *The New York Times,* pp. A1, 15.

Bell, S. K., & Morgan, S. B. (2000). Children's attitudes and behavioral intentions toward a peer presented as obese: Does a medical explanation for the obesity make a difference? *Journal of Pediatric Psychology, 25*(3), 137–145.

Bellinger, D., et al. (1991). Low-level lead exposure and children's cognitive function in the preschool years. *Pediatrics, 87,* 219–227.

Bellinger, D., Leviton, A., Waternaux, C., Needleman, H. L., & Rabinowitz, M. (1987). Longitudinal analysis of prenatal and postnatal lead exposure and early cognitive development. *New England Journal of Medicine, 316,* 1037–1043.

Bellinger, D. C., Stiles, K. M., & Needleman, H. L. (1992). Low-level lead exposure, intelligence and academic achievement: A long-term follow-up study. *Pediatrics, 90,* 855–861.

Bellodi, L., et al. (2001). Morbidity risk for obsessive-compulsive spectrum disorders in first-degree relatives of patients with eating disorders. *American Journal of Psychiatry, 158,* 563–569.

Belsky, J. (1990a). Developmental risks associated with infant day care: Attachment insecurity, noncompliance and aggression? In S. Cherazi (Ed.), *Psychosocial issues in day care.* New York: American Psychiatric Press.

Belsky, J. (1990b). The "effects" of infant day care reconsidered. In N. Fox & G. G. Fein (Eds.), *Infant day care: The current debate.* Norwood, NJ: Ablex.

Belsky, J. (2001). Emanuel Miller Lecture: Developmental risks (still) associated with early child care. *Journal of Child Psychology & Psychiatry & Allied Disciplines, 42*(7), 845–859.

Belsky, J., & Eggebeen, D. (1991). Early and extensive maternal employment and young children's socioemotional development: Children of the National Longitudinal Survey of Youth. *Journal of Marriage and the Family, 53,* 1083–1098.

Belsky, J., & Rovine, M. (1988). Nonmaternal care in the first year of life and infant–parent attachment security. *Child Development, 59,* 157–167.

Belsky, J., Rovine, M., & Fish, M. (1989). The developing family system. In M. R. Gunnar & E. Thelen (Eds.), *Systems and development* (Vol. 22). Hillsdale, NJ: Erlbaum.

Belsky, J., Steinberg, L., & Draper, P. (1991a). Childhood experience, interpersonal development, and reproductive strategy: An evolutionary theory of socialization. *Child Development, 62,* 647–670.

Belsky, J., Steinberg, L., & Draper, P. (1991b). Further reflections on an evolutionary theory of socialization. *Child Development, 62,* 682–685.

Belsky, J., Weinraub, M., Owen, M., & Kelly, J. (2001, April). Quantity of child care and problem behavior. In J. Belsky (Chair), *Early childcare and children's development prior to school entry.* Symposium conducted at the 2001 Biennial Meetings of the Society for Research in Child Development, Minneapolis, MN.

Bem, S. L. (1983). Gender schema theory and its implications for child development: Raising gender-aschematic children in a gender-schematic society. *Signs, 8,* 598–616.

Bem, S. L. (1985). Androgyny and gender schema theory: A conceptual and empirical integration. In T. B. Sonderegger (Ed.), *Nebraska symposium on motivation, 1984: Psychology and gender.* Lincoln: University of Nebraska Press.

Bem, S. L. (1989). Genital knowledge and gender constancy in preschool children. *Child Development, 60,* 649–662.

Benagiano, G., & Bianchi, P. (1999). Sex preselection: An aid to couples or a threat to humanity? *Human Reproduction, 14,* 868–870.

Benbow, C. P. (1991). Meeting the needs of gifted students through use of acceleration. In M. C. Wang, M. C. Reynolds, & H. J. Walberg (Eds.), *Handbook of special education: Research and practice.* Oxford: Pergamon.

Benbow, C. P., & Arjmond, O. (1990). Predictors of high academic achievement in mathematics and science by mathematically talented students: A longitudinal study. *Journal of Educational Psychology, 82,* 430–441.

Benbow, C. P., Lubinski, D., Shea, D., & Eftekhari-Sanjani, H. (2000). Sex differences in mathematical reasoning ability at age 13: Their status 20 years later. *Psychological Science, 11*(6), 474–480.

Bender, W. N., & Smith, J. K. (1990). Classroom behavior of children and adolescents with learning disabilities: A meta-analysis. *Journal of Learning Disabilities, 23,* 298–305.

Benenson, J. F. (1990). Gender differences in social networks. *Journal of Early Adolescence, 10,* 472–495.

Bengtsson, H., & Johnson, L. (1992). Perspective taking, empathy, and prosocial behavior in late childhood. *Child Study Journal, 22,* 11–22.

Bennett, N. G. (1998, September 16). Who should decide the sex of a baby? *The New York Times,* p. A28.

Ben-Yehudah, G., Sackett, E., Malchi-Ginzberg, L., & Ahissar, M. (2001). Impaired temporal contrast sensitivity in dyslexics is specific to retain-and-compare paradigms. *Brain, 124*(7), 1381–1395.

Berg, W. K., & Berg, K. M. (1987). Psychophysiological development in infancy: State, startle, and attention. In J. D. Osofsky (Ed.), *Handbook of infant development* (2nd ed.). New York: Wiley.

Bergeson, T. R., & Trehub, S. E. (1999). Mothers' singing to infants and preschool children. *Infant Behavior & Development, 22*(1), 51–64.

Berglund, E., Eriksson, M., & Johansson, I. (2001). Parental reports of spoken language skills in children with Down syndrome. *Journal of Speech, Language, & Hearing Research, 44*(1), 179–191.

Berko, J. (1958). The child's learning of English morphology. *Word, 14,* 150–177.

Berkowitz, G. S., Skovron, M. L., Lapinski, R. H., & Berkowitz, R. L. (1990). Delayed childbearing and the outcome of pregnancy. *New England Journal of Medicine, 322,* 659–664.

Berman, B. D., Winkleby, M., Chesterman, E., & Boyce, W. T. (1992). After-school child care and self-esteem in school-age children. *Pediatrics, 89,* 654–659.

Berndt, T. J. (1992). Friendship and friends' influence in adolescence. *Current Directions in Psychological Science, 1,* 156–159.

Berndt, T. J., Cheung, P. C., Lau, S., Hau, K., & Lew, W. J. F. (1993). Perceptions of parenting in mainland China, Taiwan, and Hong Kong: Sex differences and societal differences. *Developmental Psychology, 29,* 156–164.

Berndt, T. J., Miller, K. E., & Park, K. E. (1989). Adolescents' perceptions of friends and parents' influence on aspects of their school adjustment. *Journal of Early Adolescence, 9,* 419–435.

Berndt, T. J., & Perry, T. B. (1986). Children's perceptions of friendships as supportive relationships. *Developmental Psychology,* 640–648.

Berndt, T. J., & Perry, T. B. (1990). Distinctive features and effects of early adolescent friendships. In R. Montemayor, G. R. Adams, & T. P. Gullotta (Eds.), *From childhood to adolescence: A transitional period?* Newbury Park, CA: Sage.

Bernhardt, P. C., Dabbs, J. M., Jr., Fielden, J. A., & Lutter, C. D. (1998). Testosterone changes during vicarious experiences of winning and losing among fans at sporting events. *Physiology & Behavior, 65*(1) 59–62.

Bertenthal, B. I., & Campos, J. J. (1990). A systems approach to the organizing effects of self-produced locomotion during infancy. In C. Rovee-Collier & L. Lipsitt (Eds.), *Advances in infancy research* (Vol. 6). Norwood, NJ: Ablex.

Berzonsky, M. C., Kuk, L. S., & Storer, C. J. (1993, March). *Identity development, autonomy, and personal effectiveness.* Paper presented at the meeting of the Society for Research in Child Development, New Orleans, LA.

Best, D. L. (1993). Inducing children to generate mnemonic organizational strategies: An examination of long-term retention and materials. *Developmental Psychology, 29,* 324–336.

Betancourt, H., & Lopez, S. R. (1993). The study of culture, ethnicity, and race in American psychology. *American Psychologist, 48,* 629–637.

Bialystock, E. (1999). Cognitive complexity and attentional control in the bilingual mind. *Child Development, 70*(3), 636–644.

Biernat, M. (1991). A multicomponent, developmental analysis of sex typing. *Sex Roles, 24,* 567–586.

Biesecker, B. (2001). Prenatal diagnoses of sex chromosome conditions. *British Medical Journal, 322,* 441–442.

Bigelow, B. J. (2001). Relational scaffolding of school motivation: Developmental continuities in students' and parents' ratings of the importance of school goals. *Journal of Genetic Psychology, 162*(1), 75–92.

Bigler, R. S., & Liben, L. S. (1990). The role of attitudes and interventions in gender-schematic processing. *Child Development, 61,* 1440–1452.

Bigler, R. S., & Liben, L. S. (1992). Cognitive mechanisms in children's gender stereotyping: Theoretical and educational implications of a cognitive-based intervention. *Child Development, 63,* 1351–1363.

Bilsker, D., Schiedel, D., & Marcia, J. E. (1988). Sex differences in identity status. *Sex Roles, 18,* 231–236.

Birch, L. L. (1990). Development of food acceptance patterns. *Developmental Psychology, 26,* 515–519.

Birch, L. L., Gunder, L., Grimm-Thomas, K., & Laing, D. G. (1998). Infants' consumption of a new food enhances acceptance of similar foods. *Appetite, 30*(3), 283–295.

Bivens, J. A., & Berk, L. E. (1990). A longitudinal study of the development of elementary school children's private speech. *Merrill-Palmer Quarterly, 36,* 443–463.

Bjorklund, D. F., & Bjorklund, B. R. (1989, June). Physically fit families. *Parents' Magazine,* p. 215.

Bjorklund, D. F., & de Marchena, M. R. (1984). Developmental shifts in the basis of organization in memory: The role of associative versus categorical relatedness in children's free recall. *Child Development, 55,* 952–962.

Bjorklund, D. F., & Rosenblum, K. E. (2001). Children's use of multiple and variable addition strategies in a game context. *Developmental Science, 4*(2), 184–194.

Black, M. M., Dubowitz, H., & Starr, R. H., Jr. (1999). African American fathers in low-income, urban families: Development, behavior, and home environments of their 3-year-old children. *Child Development, 70,* 967–978.

Blake, S. M., Amaro, H., Schwartz, P. M., & Flinchbaugh, L. J. (2001). A review of substance abuse prevention interventions for young adolescent girls. *Journal of Early Adolescence, 21*(3), 294–324.

Blakeslee, S. (1998, August 4). Re-evaluating significance of baby's bond with mother. *The New York Times,* pp. F1, F2.

Blanchette, N., Smith, M. L., Fernandes-Penney, A., King, S., & Read, S. (2001). Cognitive and motor development in children with vertically transmitted HIV infection. *Brain & Cognition, 46*(1–2), 50–53.

Blass, E. M., & Smith, B. A. (1992). Differential effects of sucrose, fructose, glucose, and lactose on crying in 1- to 3-day-old human infants: Qualitative and quantitative considerations. *Developmental Psychology, 28,* 804–810.

Blevins-Knabe, B. (1987). Development of the ability to insert into a series. *Journal of Genetic Psychology, 148,* 427–441.

Block, J., & Robins, R. W. (1993). A longitudinal study of consistency and change in self-esteem from early adolescence to early adulthood. *Child Development, 64,* 909–923.

Block, J. H. (1979, August). *Personality development in males and females: The influence of differential socialization.* Paper presented at the meeting of the American Psychological Association, New York.

Block, J. H. (1983). Differential premises arising from differential socialization of the sexes: Some conjectures. *Child Development, 54,* 1335–1354.

Block, R. I., et al. (2000). Effects of frequent marijuana use on brain tissue volume and composition. *Neuroreport: For Rapid Communication of Neuroscience Research, 11*(3), 491–496.

Bloom, L. (1993, Winter). Word learning. *SRCD Newsletter,* pp. 1, 9, 13.

Bloom, L., Merkin, S., & Wootten, J. (1982). *Wh*-questions: Linguistic factors that contribute to the sequence of acquisition. *Child Development, 53,* 1084–1092.

Blum, R. W., Harmon, B., Harris, L., Bergeisen, L., & Resnick, M. D. (1992). American Indian–Alaska native youth health. *Journal of the American Medical Association, 267,* 1637–1644.

Boccia, M., & Campos, J. J. (1989). Maternal emotional signals, social referencing, and infants' reactions to strangers. In N. Eisenberg (Ed.), *New directions for child development: No. 44. Empathy and related emotional responses.* San Francisco: Jossey-Bass.

Boddy, J., Skuse, D., & Andrews, B. (2000). The developmental sequelae of nonorganic failure to thrive. *Journal of Child Psychology & Psychiatry & Allied Disciplines, 41*(8), 1003–1014.

Boehnke, K., Silbreisen, R. K., Eisenberg, N., Reykowski, J., & Palmonari, A. (1989). The development of prosocial motivation: A cross-national study. *Journal of Cross-Cultural Psychology, 20,* 219–243.

Boggiano, A. K., & Barrett, M. (1991). Strategies to motivate helpless and mastery-oriented children: The effect of gender-based expectancies. *Sex Roles, 25,* 487–510.

Bohannon, J. N., III, & Stanowicz, L. (1988). The issue of negative evidence: Adult responses to children's language errors. *Developmental Psychology, 24,* 684–689.

Boismier, J. D. (1977). Visual stimulation and wake-sleep behavior in human neonates. *Developmental Psychology, 10,* 219–227.

Bongar, B. (2002). *The suicidal patient: Clinical and legal standards of care* (2nd ed.). Washington, DC: American Psychological Association.

Bonomo, Y., et al. (2001). Adverse outcomes of alcohol use in adolescents. *Addiction, 96*(10), 1485–1496.

Boom, J., Brugman, D., & van der Heijden, P. G. M. (2001). Hierarchical structure of moral stages assessed by a sorting task. *Child Development, 72*(2), 535–548.

Booth, J. R., & Burman, D. D. (2001). Development and disorders of neurocognitive systems for oral language and reading. *Learning Disability Quarterly, 24*(3), 205–215.

Borden, M. C., & Ollendick, T. H. (1992). The development and differentiation of social subtypes in autism. In B. B. Lahey & A. E. Kazdin (Eds.), *Advances in clinical child psychology* (Vol. 14). New York: Plenum.

Bornstein, M. H. (1992). Perceptual development in infancy, childhood, and old age. In M. H. Bornstein & M. E. Lamb (Eds.), *Developmental psychology: An advanced textbook* (3rd ed.). Hillsdale, NJ: Erlbaum.

Bornstein, M. H., et al. (1992a). Functional analysis of the contents of maternal speech to infants of 5 and 13 months in four cultures: Argentina, France, Japan, and the United States. *Developmental Psychology, 28,* 593–603.

Bornstein, M. H., et al. (1992b). Maternal responsiveness to infants in three societies: The United States, France, and Japan. *Child Development, 63,* 808–821.

Bornstein, M. H., & Lamb, M. E. (1992). *Development in infancy: An introduction* (3rd ed.). New York: McGraw-Hill.

Bornstein, M. H., & Tamis-LeMonda, C. S. (1989). Maternal responsiveness and cognitive development in children. In M. H. Bornstein (Ed.), *New directions for child development: No. 43. Maternal responsiveness: Characteristics and consequences.* San Francisco: Jossey-Bass.

Borst, S. R., Noarn, G. G., & Bartok, J. A. (1991). Adolescent suicidality: A clinical-developmental approach. *Journal of the American Academy of Child and Adolescent Psychiatry, 30,* 796–803.

Boskind-White, M., & White, W.C. (1983). *Bulimarexia: The binge/purge cycle.* New York: Norton.

Boston Women's Health Book Collective (1992). *The new our bodies, ourselves.* New York: Simon & Schuster.

Bouchard, C., et al. (1990). The response to long-term overfeeding in identical twins. *New England Journal of Medicine, 322,* 1477–1482.

Bouchard, T. J., Jr., Lykken, D. T., McGue, M., Segal, N. L., & Tellegen, A. (1990). Sources of human psychological differences: The Minnesota study of twins reared apart. *Science, 250,* 223–228.

Bouldin, P., & Pratt, C. (1999). Characteristics of preschool and school-age children with imaginary companions. *Journal of Genetic Psychology, 160*(4), 397–410.

Bouma, A. (2001). Hersenkronkels in neuropsychologisch perspectief. *Psycholoog, 36*(2), 50–55.

Bowen, Chieh-Chen, Swim, J. K., & Jacobs, R. R. (2000). Evaluating gender biases on actual job performance of real people: A meta-analysis. *Journal of Applied Social Psychology, 30*(10), 2194–2215.

Bower, T. G. R. (1974). *Development in infancy.* San Francisco: W. H. Freeman.

Bowlby, J. (1988). *A secure base.* New York: Basic Books.

Brack, C. J., Brack, G., & Orr, D. P. (1991, August). *Relationships between behaviors, emotions and health behaviors in early adolescents.* Paper presented at the meeting of the American Psychological Association, San Francisco.

Brackbill, Y., McManus, K., & Woodward, L. (1985). *Medication in maternity: Infant exposure and maternal information.* Ann Arbor: University of Michigan Press.

Bradley, B. S., & Gobbart, S. K. (1989). Determinants of gender-typed play in toddlers. *Journal of Genetic Psychology, 150,* 453–455.

Bradley, R. H. (1989). HOME measurement of maternal responsiveness. In M. H. Bornstein (Ed.), *New directions for child development: No 43. Maternal responsiveness: Characteristics and consequences.* San Francisco: Jossey-Bass.

Bradley, R. H., Burchinal, M. R., & Casey, P. H. (2001). Early intervention: The moderating role of the home environment. *Applied Developmental Science, 5*(1), 2–8.

Bradley, R. H., et al. (1989). Home environment and cognitive development in the first 3 years of life: A collaborative study involving six sites and three ethnic groups in North America. *Developmental Psychology, 25,* 217–235.

Brady, M. P., Swank, P. R., Taylor, R. D., & Freiberg, H. J. (1988). Teacher-student interactions in middle school mainstreamed classes: Differences with special and regular students. *Journal of Educational Research, 81,* 332–340.

Braet, C. (1999). Treatment of obese children: A new rationale. *Clinical Child Psychology & Psychiatry, 4*(4), 579–591.

Braine, M. D. S. (1976). Children's first word combinations. *Monographs of the Society for Research in Child Development, 41* (1, Serial No. 164).

Brame, B., Nagin, D. S., & Tremblay, R. E. (2001). Developmental trajectories of physical aggression from school entry to late adolescence. *Journal of Child Psychology & Psychiatry & Allied Disciplines, 42*(4), 503–512.

Brandt, M. M., & Strattner-Gregory, M. J. (1980). Effect of highlighting intention on intentionality and restitutive justice. *Developmental Psychology, 16,* 147–148.

Braungart, J. M., Plomin, R., DeFries, J. C., & Fulker, D. W. (1992). Genetic influence on tester-rated infant temperament as assessed by Bayley's infant behavior record: Nonadoptive and adoptive siblings and twins. *Developmental Psychology, 28,* 40–47.

Bray, N. W., Hersh, R. E., & Turner, L. A. (1985). Selective remembering during adolescence. *Developmental Psychology, 21,* 290–294.

Bray, N. W., Huffman, L. F., & Fletcher, K. L. (1999). Developmental and intellectual differences in self-report and strategy use. *Developmental Psychology, 35*(5), 1223–1236.

Braza, F., et al. (2000). Efecto de los hermanos en la flexibilidad de comportamiento de niños preescolares. *Revista Mexicana de Psicologia, 17*(2), 181–190.

Brazelton, T. B. (1990a). Forward: Observations of the neonate. In C. Rovee-Collier & L. P. Lipsitt (Eds.), *Advances in infancy research* (Vol. 6). Norwood, NJ: Ablex.

Brazelton, T. B. (1990b). Saving the bathwater. *Child Development, 61,* 1661–1671.

Brazelton, T. B., Nugent, J. K., & Lester, B. M. (1987). Neonatal behavior assessment scale. In J. D. Osofsky (Ed.), *Handbook of infant development* (2nd ed.). New York: Wiley.

Brentlinger, P. E., et al. (1999). Childhood malnutrition and postwar reconstruction in rural El Salvador: A community-based survey. *Journal of the American Medical Association, 281,* 184.

Bretherton, I., Golby, B., & Halvorsen, C. (1993, March). *Fathers as attachment and caregiving figures.* Paper presented at the meeting of the Society for Research in Child Development, New Orleans, LA.

Bretherton, I., Stolberg, U., & Kreye, M. (1981). Engaging strangers in proximal interaction: Infants' social initiative. *Developmental Psychology, 17,* 746–755.

Brice-Heath, S. (1988). Language socialization. In D. T. Slaughter (Ed.), *New directions for child development, No. 42. Black children and poverty: A developmental perspective.* San Francisco: Jossey-Bass.

Bridges, K. (1932). Emotional development in early infancy. *Child Development, 3,* 324–341.

Brieger, P., Sommer, S., Bloeink, R., & Marneros, A. (2001). What becomes of children hospitalized for enuresis? Results of a catch-up study. *European Psychiatry, 16*(1), 27–32.

British study finds leukemia risk in children of A-plant workers (1990, February 18). *The New York Times,* p. A27.

Broberg, A. G. (1993). Inhibition and children's experiences of out-of-home care. In K. H. Rubin & J. B. Asendorpf (Eds.), *Social withdrawal, inhibition, and shyness in childhood.* Hillsdale, NJ: Erlbaum.

Broberg, A. G., Wessels, H., Lamb, M. E., & Hwang, C. P. (1997). Effects of day care on the development of cognitive abilities in 8-year-olds: A longitudinal study. *Developmental Psychology, 33*(1), 62–69.

Broder, S. (2000, July 29). Fighting media violence! **http://www.FamilyEducation.com**

Brody, G. H., Stoneman, Z., & McCoy, J. K. (1992). Associations of maternal and paternal direct and differential behavior with sibling relationships: Contemporaneous and longitudinal analyses. *Child Development, 63,* 82–92.

Brody, G. H., Stoneman, Z., McCoy, J. K., & Forehand, R. (1992). Contemporaneous and longitudinal associations of sibling conflict with family relationship assessments and family discussions about sibling problems. *Child Development, 63,* 391–400.

Brody, J. E. (1990a, February 22). Bulimia and anorexia, insidious eating disorders thast are best treated when detected early. *The New York Times,* p. B9.

Brody, J. E. (1990b, May 31). Children in sports: Tailoring activities to their abilities and needs will avoid pitfalls. *The New York Times,* p. B8.

Brody, J. E. (1990c, May 24). Preventing children from joining yet another unfit generation. *The New York Times,* p. B14.

Brody, J. E. (1991, September 4). Averting a crisis when the offspring show symptoms of school phobia. *The New York Times,* p. B7.

Brody, J. E. (1998a, February 10). Genetic ties may be factor in violence in stepfamilies. *The New York Times,* pp. F1, F4.

Brody, J. E. (1998b, November 3). Keeping clinical depression out of the aging formula. *The New York Times,* p. F7.

Brody, L. R., Zelazo, P. R., & Chaika, H. (1984). Habituation–dishabituation to speech in the neonate. *Developmental Psychology, 20,* 114–119.

Bronfenbrenner, U. (1973). The dream of the kibbutz. In *Readings in human development.* Guilford, CT: Dushkin.

Bronfenbrenner, U. (1977). Toward an experimental ecology of human development. *American Psychologist, 32,* 513–531.

Bronfenbrenner, U. (1979). *The ecology of human development: Experiments by nature and design.* Cambridge, MA: Harvard University Press.

Bronfenbrenner, U. (1989). Ecological systems theory. In R. Vasta (Ed.), *Annals of child development* (Vol. 6). Greenwich, CT: JAI Press.

Bronfenbrenner, U., & Evans, G. W. (2000). Developmental science in the 21st century: Emerging questions, theoretical models, research designs and empirical findings. *Social Development, 9*(1) 115–125.

Bronson, G. W. (1990). Changes in infants' visual scanning across the 2- to 14-week age period. *Journal of Experimental Child Psychology, 49,* 101–125.

Bronson, G. W. (1991). Infant differences in rate of visual encoding. *Child Development, 62,* 44–54.

Bronson, G. W. (1997). The growth of visual capacity: Evidence from infant scanning patterns. *Advances in Infancy Research, 11,* 109–141.

Brook, J. S., Zheng, L., Whiteman, M., & Brook, D. W. (2001). Aggression in toddlers: Associations with parenting and marital relations. *Journal of Genetic Psychology, 162*(2), 228–241.

Brooks-Gunn, J. (1991a). Antecedents of maturational timing variations in adolescent girls. In R. M. Lerner, A. C. Petersen, & J. Brooks-Gunn (Eds.), *Encyclopedia of adolescence.* New York: Garland.

Brooks-Gunn, J. (1991b). How stressful is the transition to adolescence for girls? In M. E. Colten & S. Gore (Eds.), *Adolescent stress: Causes and consequences.* New York: Aldine deGruyter.

Brooks-Gunn, J., & Chase-Lansdale, P. L. (1991). Adolescent childbearing: Effects on children. In R. M. Lerner, A. C. Petersen, & J. Brooks-Gunn (Eds.), *Encyclopedia of adolescence.* New York: Garland.

Brooks-Gunn, J., & Furstenberg, F. F. (1989). Adolescent sexual behavior, *American Psyhologist, 44,* 249–257.

Brooks-Gunn, J., Klebanov, P. K., Liaw, F., & Spiker, D. (1993). Enhancing the development of low-birthweight, premature infants: Changes in cognition and behavior over the first three years. *Child Development, 64,* 736–768.

Brooks-Gunn, J., & Ruble, D. N. (1983). The experience of menarche from a developmental perspective. In J. Brooks-Gunn & A. C. Petersen (Eds.), *Girls at puberty.* New York: Plenum.

Brophy, J. (1986). Teacher influences on student achievement. *American Psychologist, 41,* 1069–1077.

Brophy, J. E. (1983). Research on the self-fulfilling prophecy and teacher expectations. *Journal of Educational Psychology, 75,* 631–661.

Brown, A. M. (1990). Development of visual sensitivity to light and color vision in human infants: A critical review. *Vision Research, 30,* 1159–1188.

Brown, B. B., Mounts, N., Lamborn, S. D., & Steinberg, L. (1993). Parenting practices and peer group affiliation in adolescence. *Child Development, 64,* 467–482.

Brown, L. M., & Gilligan, C. (1992). *Meeting at the crossroads: Women's psychology and girls' development.* Cambridge, MA: Harvard University Press.

Brown, R. (1973). *A first language: The early stages.* Cambridge, MA: Harvard University Press.

Brown, R. (1977). Introduction. In C. A. Snow & C. Ferguson (Eds.), *Talking to children.* New York: Cambridge University Press.

Brown, S. A., & Grimes, D. E. (1993). *Nurse practitioners and certified midwives: A meta-analysis of studies on nurses in primary care roles.* Washington, DC: American Nurses Publishing.

Browne, C. A., Colditz, P. B., & Dunster, K. R. (2000). Infant autonomic function is altered by maternal smoking during pregnancy. *Early Human Development, 59*(3), 209–218.

Brownell, C. A. (1988). Combinatorial skills: Converging developments over the second year. *Child Development, 59,* 675–685.

Brownell, C. A. (1990). Peer social skills in toddlers: Competencies and constraints illustrated by same-age and mixed-age interaction. *Child Development, 61,* 838–848.

Brownell, C. A., & Carriger, M. S. (1990). Changes in cooperation and self–other differentiation during the second year. *Child Development, 61,* 1164–1174.

Brownell, K. D. (1997). We must be more militant about food. *APA Monitor, 28*(3), 48.

Bruch, H. (1978). *The golden cage: The enigma of anorexia nervosa.* Cambridge, MA: Harvard University Press.

Bruck, M., & Ceci, S. J. (1999). The suggestibility of children's memory. *Annual Review of Psychology, 50,* 419–439.

Brunswick, A. F. (1999). Structural strain: An ecological paradigm for studying African American drug use. *Drugs & Society, 14*(1–2), 5–19.

Brustad, R. J. (1991). Children's perspectives on exercise and physical activity: Measurement issues and concerns. *Journal of School Health, 61,* 228–230.

Buchanan, C. M., Eccles, J. S., & Becker, J. B. (1992). Are adolescents the victims of raging hormones? Evidence for activational effects of hormones on moods and behavior at adolescence. *Psychological Bulletin, 111,* 62–107.

Buchanan, L., Pavlovic, J., & Rovet, J. (1998). The contribution of visuospatial working memory to impairments in facial processing and arithmetic in Turner syndrome. *Brain & Cognition, 37*(1), 72–75.

Bugental, D. B., Blue, J., & Cruzcosa, M. (1989). Perceived control over caregiving outcomes: Implications for child abuse. *Developmental Psychology, 25,* 532–539.

Bugental, D. B., Blue, J., & Lewis, J. (1990). Caregiver beliefs and dysphoric affect directed to difficult children. *Developmental Psychology, 26,* 631–638.

Buhrmester, D. (1992). The developmental courses of sibling and peer relationships. In F. Boar & J. Dunn (Eds.), *Children's sibling relationships: Developmental and clinical issues.* Hillsdale, NJ: Erlbaum.

Bukowski, W. M., Gauze, C., Hoza, B., & Newcomb, A. F. (1993). Differences and consistency between same-sex and other-sex peer relationships during early adolescence. *Developmental Psychology, 29,* 255–263.

Bukowski, W. M., Hoza, B., & Boivin, M. (1993). Popularity, friendship and emotional adjustment during early adolescence. In B. Laursen (Ed.), *New directions in child development: No. 60. Close friendships in adolescence.* San Francisco: Jossey-Bass.

Bullock, M., & Lutkenhaus, P. (1990). Who am I? Self-understanding in toddlers. *Merrill-Palmer Quarterly, 36,* 217–238.

Buri, J. R., Louiselle, P. A., Misukanis, T. M., & Mueller, R. A. (1988). Effects of parental authoritarianism and authoritativeness of self-esteem. *Personality and Social Psychology Bulletin, 14,* 271–282.

Burke, J. M., & Baker, R. C. (2001). Is fluvoxamine safe and effective for treating anxiety disorders in children? *Journal of Family Practice, 50*(8), 719.

Burnette, E. (1997). "Father of Ebonics" continues his crusade. *APA Monitor, 28*(4), 12.

Burns, A., & Dunlop, R. (1999). "How did you feel about it?" Children's feelings about their parents' divorce at the time and three and ten years later. *Journal of Divorce & Remarriage, 31*(3–4), 19–35.

Bushman, B. J. (1998). Priming effects of media violence on the accessibility of aggressive constructs in memory. *Personality & Social Psychology Bulletin, 24*(5), 537–545.

Bushman, B. J., & Anderson, C. A. (2001). Media violence and the American public. *American Psychologist, 56*(6/7), 477–489.

Bushnell, E. W. (1993, June). *A dual-processing approach to cross-modal matching: Implications for development.* Paper presented at the Society for Research in Child Development, New Orleans, LA.

Bushnell, I. W. R. (2001). Mother's face recognition in newborn infants: Learning and memory. *Infant & Child Development, 10*(1–2), 67–74.

Buss, D. M. (2000). The evolution of happiness. *American Psychologist, 55,* 15–23.

Bussey, K., & Bandura, A. (1984). Influence of gender constancy and social power on sex-linked modeling. *Journal of Personality and Social Psychology, 47,* 1292–1302.

Bussey, K., & Bandura, A. (1999). Social cognitive theory of gender development and differentiation. *Psychological Review, 106*(4), 676–713.

Butterfield, F. (1992, January 1). Studies find a family link to criminality. *The New York Times,* pp. A1, 8.

Butterfield, S. A., & Loovis, E. M. (1993). Influence of age, sex, balance, and sport participation on development of throwing by children in grades K-8. *Perceptual and Motor Skills, 76,* 459–464.

Butterworth, G. (1990). Self-perception in infancy. In D. Cicchetti & M. Beeghly (Eds.), *The self in transition.* Chicago: University of Chicago Press.

Butterworth, G., Verweij, E., & Hopkins, B. (1997). The development of prehension in infants: Halverson revisited. *British Journal of Developmental Psychology, 15*(2), 223–236.

Byrd, V. (2001, April 23). Passages. *People,* p. 87.

Byrne, J., Ellsworth, C., Bowering, E., & Vincer, M. (1993). Language development in low birth weight infants: The first two years of life. *Developmental and Behavioral Pediatrics, 14,* 21–27.

Cabrera, N. J., Tamis-LeMonda, C. S., Bradley, R. H., Hofferth, S., & Lamb, M. E. (2000). Fatherhood in the twenty-first century. *Child Development, 71,* 127–136.

Cai, H., & Chen, C. (2000). The development of mental rotation ability and its correlationship with intelligence. *Psychological Science (China), 23*(3), 363–365.

Caine, D., & Watson, J. D. G. (2000). Neuropsychological and neuropathological sequelae of cerebral anoxia: A critical review. *Journal of the International Neuropsychological Society, 6*(1), 86–99.

Cairns, R. B., & Cairns, B. D. (1991). Social cognition and social networks: A developmental perspective. In D. J. Pepler & K. H. Rubin (Eds.), *The development and treatment of childhood aggression.* Hillsdale, NJ: Erlbaum.

Caldera, Y. M., Huston, A. C., & O'Brien, M. (1989). Social interactions and play patterns of parents and toddlers with feminine, masculine, and neutral toys. *Child Development, 60,* 70–76.

Call, J. (2001). Object permanence in orangutans *(Pongo pygmaeus),* chimpanzees *(Pan troglodytes),* and children *(Homo sapiens). Journal of Comparative Psychology, 115*(2), 159–171.

Camarena, P. M. (1991). Conformity in adolescence. In R. M. Lerner, A. C. Petersen, & J. Brooks-Gunn (Eds.), *Encyclopedia of adolescence.* New York: Garland.

Campbell, A., Muncer, S., & Bibel, D. (2001). Women and crime: An evolutionary approach. *Aggression & Violent Behavior, 6*(5), 481–497.

Campbell, D. W., & Eaton, W. O. (1999). Sex differences in the activity level of infants. *Infant & Child Development, 8*(1), 1–17.

Campbell, F. A., & Bryant, D. M. (1993, March). *Growing into a wider world: Transition from Head Start to kindergarten in Chapel Hill-Carrboro.* Paper presented at the meeting of the Society for Research in Child Development, New Orleans, LA.

Campbell, F. A., & Ramey, C. T. (1993, March). *Mid-adolescent outcomes for high-risk students: An examination of the continuing effects of early intervention.* Paper presented at the meeting of the Society for Research in Child Development, New Orleans, LA.

Campbell, J. O., Bliven, T. D., Silver, M. M., Snyder, K. J., & Spear, L. P. (2000). Effects of prenatal cocaine on behavioral adaptation to chronic stress in adult rats. *Neurotoxicology & Teratology, 22*(6), 845–850.

Campbell, S. B. (1990). *Behavior problems in preschool children: Clinical and developmental issues.* New York: Guilford.

Campbell, S. B., Pierce, E. W., March, C. L., & Ewing, L. J. (1991). Noncompliant behavior, overactivity, and family stress as predictors of negative maternal control with preschool children. *Development and Psychopathology, 3,* 175–190.

Campos, J. J., Hiatt, S., Ramsey, D., Henderson, C., & Svejda, M. (1978). The emergence of fear on the visual cliff. In M. Lewis & L. Rosenblum (Eds.), *The origins of affect.* New York: Plenum.

Campos, J. J., Langer, A., & Krowitz, A. (1970). Cardiac responses on the visual cliff in prelocomotor human infants. *Science, 170,* 196–197.

Camras, L. A., Campos, J. J., Oster, H., Miyake, K., & Bradshaw, D. (1992). Japanese and American infants' responses to arm restraint. *Developmental Psychology, 28,* 578–583.

Camras, L. A., & Sachs, V. B. (1991). Social referencing and caretaker expressive behavior in a day care setting. *Infant Behavior and Development, 14,* 27–36.

Camras, L. A., Sullivan, J., & Michel, G. (1993, Fall). Do infants express discrete emotions?: Adult judgments of facial, vocal, and body actions. *Journal of Nonverbal Behavior, 17,* 171–186.

Cannistra, S.A., & Niloff, J. M. (1996). Cancer of the uterine cervix. *New England Journal of Medicine, 334,* 1030–1038.

Cannon, G. S., Idol, L., & West, J. F. (1992). Educating students with mild handicaps in general classrooms: Essential teaching practices for general and special educators. *Journal of Learning Disabilities, 25,* 300–317.

Capirci, O., Iverson, J. M., Pizzuto, E., & Volterra, V. (1996). Gestures and words during the transition to two-word speech. *Journal of Child Language, 23*(3), 645–673.

Caplan, M., & Hay, D. F. (1989). Preschoolers' responses to peers' distress and beliefs about bystander intervention. *Journal of Child Psychology and Psychiatry, 30,* 231–242.

Caplan, M., Vespo, J., Pedersen, J., & Hale, D. F. (1991). Conflict and its resolution in small groups of one- and two-year-olds. *Child Development, 62,* 1513–1524.

Caplan, P. J., & Caplan, J. B. (1994). *Thinking critically about research on sex and gender.* New York: HarperCollins.

Caplan, P. J., & Larkin, J. (1991). The anatomy of dominance and self-protection. *American Psychologist, 46,* 536.

Capone, G. T. (2001). Down syndrome: Advances in molecular biology and the neurosciences. *Journal of Developmental & Behavioral Pediatrics, 22*(1), 40–59.

Capute, A. J., Shapiro, B. K., Palmer, F. B., Ross, A., & Wachtel, R. C. (1985). Normal gross motor development: The influences of race, sex, and socioeconomic status. *Developmental Medicine and Child Neurology, 27,* 635–643.

Caravolas, M., & Bruck, M. (2000). Vowel categorization skill and its relationship to early literacy skills among first-grade Quebec-French children. *Journal of Experimental Child Psychology, 76*(3), 190–221.

Carey, G., & DiLalla, D. L. (1994). Personality and psychopathology: Genetic perspectives. *Journal of Abnormal Psychology, 103,* 32–43.

Carlo, G., Knight, G. P., Eisenberg, N., & Rotenberg, K. (1991). Cognitive processes and prosocial behaviors among children: The role of affective attributions and reconciliations. *Developmental Psychology, 27,* 456–461.

Carlson, D. (2001, July 14). Update on diagnosis and impact of the most common congenital abnormalities. Segment of a course, Practical Obstetric-Gynecologic Ultrasonography, presented to the meeting of the American College of Obstetricians and Gynecologists, San Francisco.

Caron, A. J., Caron, R. F., & Carlson, V. R. (1979). Infant perception of the invariant shape of objects varying in slant. *Child Development, 50,* 716–721.

Carpendale, J. I. M. (2000). Kohlberg and Piaget on stages and moral reasoning. *Developmental Review, 20*(2), 181–205.

Carpenter, C. C. J., et al. (2000). Antiretroviral therapy in adults: Updated recommendations of the International AIDS Society–USA Panel. *Journal of the American Medical Association, 283,* 381–390.

Carr, M., Borkowski, J. G., & Maxwell, S. E. (1991). Motivational components of underachievement. *Developmental Psychology, 27,* 108–118.

Carroll, L. (2000). Childbirth advice keystrokes away: How to find the best Web sites. MSNBC online.

Carson, J., Burks, V., & Parke, R. D. (1993). Parent–child physical play: Determinants and consequences. In K. MacDonald (Ed.), *Parent–child play: Descriptions and implications.* Albany, NY: SUNY Press.

Carter, J. E., & Schuchman, E. H. (2001). Gene therapy for neurodegenerative diseases: Fact or fiction? *British Journal of Psychiatry, 178,* 392–394.

Carvalho, N., et al. (2001). Severe malnutrition among young children—Georgia, January 1997–June 1999. *Morbidity and Mortality Weekly Report, 50,* 224–227.

Casaer, P. (1993). Old and new facts about perinatal brain development. *Journal of Child Psychology and Psychiatry, 34,* 101–109.

Case, R. (1985). *Intellectual development: Birth to adulthood.* New York: Academic Press.

Case, R. (1992). *The mind's staircase: Exploring the conceptual underpinnings of children's thought and knowledge.* Hillsdale, NJ: Erlbaum.

Cashwell, T. H., Skinner, C. H., & Smith, E. S. (2001). Increasing second-grade students' reports of peers' prosocial behaviors via direct instruction, group reinforcement, and progress feedback: A replication and extension. *Education & Treatment of Children, 24*(2), 161–175.

Caspi, A., Elder, G. H., Jr., & Bem, D. J. (1987). Moving against the world: Life-course patterns of explosive children. *Developmental Psychology, 23,* 308–313.

Caspi, A., & Moffitt, T. E. (1991). Individual differences are accentuated during periods of social change: The sample case of girls at puberty. *Journal of Personality and Social Psychology, 61,* 157–168.

Cassia, V. M., Simion, F., & Umilta, C. (2001). Face preference at birth: The role of an orienting mechanism. *Developmental Science, 4*(1), 101–108.

Cassidy, J. (1988). Child–mother attachment and the self in six-year-olds. *Child Development, 59,* 121–134.

Cassidy, J., & Asher, S. R. (1992). Loneliness and peer relations in young children. *Child Development, 63,* 350–365.

Cattell, R. B. (1949). *The culture-free intelligence test.* Champaign, IL: Institute for Personality and Ability Testing.

Caughy, M. O., DiPietro, J. A., & Strobino, D. M. (1994). Day-care participation as a protective factor in the cognitive development of low-income children. *Child Development, 65*(2), 457–471.

Cauley, K., & Tyler, B. (1989). The relationship of self-concept to prosocial behavior in children. *Early Childhood Research Quarterly, 4,* 51–60.

Caulfield, R. (2000). Beneficial effects of tactile stimulation on early development. *Early Childhood Education Journal, 27*(4), 255–257.

Cavaliere, F. (1996). Bilingual schools face big political challenges. *APA Monitor, 27*(2), 36.

Cavell, T. A. (2001). Updating our approach to parent training. I: The case against targeting noncompliance. *Clinical Psychology: Science & Practice, 8*(3), 299–318.

CDC. (See Centers for Disease Control).

Cebello, R., & Olson, S. L. (1993, March). *The role of alternative caregivers in the lives of children from poor, single-parent families.* Paper presented at the meeting of the Society for Research in Child Development, New Orleans, LA.

Ceci, S. J. (1991). How much does schooling influence general intelligence and its cognitive components? A reassessment of the evidence. *Developmental Psychology, 21,* 703–722.

Ceci, S. J. (1993, August). *Cognitive and social factors in children's testimony.* Master lecture presented at the meeting of the American Psychological Association, Toronto.

Ceci, S. J. (1996). Cited in Murray, B. (1996). Students stretch beyond the "three Rs." *APA Monitor, 26*(4), 46.

Ceci, S. J., & Bruck, M. (1993). Suggestibility of the child witness: A historical review and synthesis. *Psychological Bulletin, 113,* 403–439.

Celis, W. (1992, June 10). Educators focus on the forgotten years: The middle grades. *The New York Times,* p. B8.

Center, Y., Ward, J., & Ferguson, C. (1991). Towards an index to evaluate the integration of children with disabilities into regular classes. *Educational Psychology, 11,* 77–95.

Centers for Disease Control. (1991). Attempted suicide among high school students—United States, 1990. *Morbidity and Mortality Weekly Report, 40,* 633–635.

Centers for Disease Control. (1993). Infant mortality—United States, 1990. *Morbidity and Mortality Weekly Report, 42,* 161–165.

Centers for Disease Control and Prevention (1998, October 7). Assessment of infant sleeping position—Selected states, 1996. *National Vital Statistics Reports, 47*(4).

Centers for Disease Control and Prevention. (1999, October.) National Center for HIV, STD and TB Prevention. Division of Sexually Transmitted Diseases. **http://www.cdc.gov**

Centers for Disease Control and Prevention. (2000a). *HIV/AIDS surveillance report: U.S. HIV and AIDS cases reported through December 1999, 11*(2).

Centers for Disease Control and Prevention. (2000b). Health, United States, 2000. National Center for Health Statistics and National Immunization Program: the National Immunization Survey.

Centers for Disease Control and Prevention. (2000c, June 9). Youth risk behavior surveillance—United States, 1999. *Morbidity and Mortality Weekly Report, 49*(SS05); 1–96.

Centers for Disease Control and Prevention. (2000d). National and state-specific pregnancy rates among adolescents—United States, 1995–1997. *Morbidity and Mortality Weekly Report, 49*(27).

Centers for Disease Control and Prevention. (2001a, May 12). TABLE III. Provisional cases of selected notifiable diseases preventable by vaccination, United States week ending May 12, 2001. *Morbidity and Mortality Weekly Report* Tables (Morbidity).

Centers for Disease Control and Prevention. (2001b, June 8). Racial disparities in median age at death of persons with Down syndrome—United States, 1968–1997. *Morbidity and Mortality Weekly Report, 50*(22).

Centers for Disease Control and Prevention. (2001c). 10 Things you need to know about immunizations. **http://www.cdc.gov/nip/publications/fs/gen/shouldknow.htm**

Centers for Disease Control and Prevention. (2001d). *HIV/AIDS surveillance report: U.S. HIV and AIDS cases reported through December 2000, 12*(2).

Centers for Disease Control and Prevention. (2001e, December 3). Sexually transmitted disease surveillance 2000. Atlanta, GA: Division of STD Prevention, National Center for HIV, STD and TB Prevention.

Cernoch, J., & Porter, R. (1985). Recognition of maternal axillary odors by infants. *Child Development, 56,* 1593–1598.

Chalfant, J. C. (1989). Learning disabilities: Policy issues and promising approaches. *American Psychologist, 44,* 392–398.

Chamberlain, P., & Reid, J. B. (1998). Comparison of two community alternatives to incarceration for chronic juvenile offenders. *Journal of Consulting & Clinical Psychology, 66*(4), 624–633.

Chance, S. E., Brown, R. T., Dabbs, J. M., Jr., & Casey, R. (2000). Testosterone, intelligence and behavior disorders in young boys. *Personality & Individual Differences, 28*(3) 437–445.

Chao, Q., Wang, P., & He, N. (2001). Comparative research on self-concept of middle school students from complete and divorced families. *Chinese Journal of Clinical Psychology, 9*(2), 143.

Chapman, J. K. (2000a). Developmental outcomes in two groups of infants and toddlers: Prenatally cocaine exposed and noncocaine exposed: Part 1. *Infant–Toddler Intervention, 10*(1), 19–36.

Chapman, J. K. (2000b). Developmental outcomes in two groups of young children: Prenatally cocaine exposed and noncocaine exposed: Part 2. *Infant-Toddler Intervention, 10*(2), 81–96.

Chapman, M., & McBride, M. C. (1992). Beyond competence and performance: Children's class inclusion strategies, superordinate class cues, and verbal justifications. *Developmental Psychology, 28,* 319–327.

Chapman, M., Skinner, E. A., & Baltes, P. B. (1990). Interpreting correlations between children's perceived control and cognitive performance: Control, agency, or means–ends beliefs? *Developmental Psychology, 26,* 246–253.

Chassin, L., Presson, C. C., Pitts, S. C., & Sherman, S. J. (2000). The natural history of cigarette smoking from adolescence to adulthood in a Midwestern community sample: Multiple trajectories and their psychological correlates. *Health Psychology, 19,* 223–231.

Chassin, L., Presson, C. C., Rose, J. S., & Sherman, S. J. (2001). From adolescence to adulthood: Age-related changes in beliefs about cigarette smoking in a Midwestern community sample. *Health Psychology, 20*(5), 377–386.

Chavez, E. L., & Swain, R. C. (1992). An epidemiological comparison of Mexican-American and white non-Hispanic 8th- and 12th-grade students' substance use. *American Journal of Public Health, 82,* 445–447.

Chen, X., et al. (2000). Maternal authoritative and authoritarian attitudes and mother–child interactions and relationships in urban China. *International Journal of Behavioral Development, 24*(1), 119–126.

Chen, X., Chen, H., & Kaspar, V. (2001). Group social functioning and individual socioemotional and school adjustment in Chinese children. *Merrill-Palmer Quarterly, 47*(2), 264–299.

Chess, S., & Thomas, A. (1984). *Origins and evolution of behavior disorders: From infancy to early adult life.* New York: Brunner/Mazel.

Chess, S., & Thomas, A. (1991). Temperament. In M. Lewis (Ed.), *Child and adolescent psychiatry: A comprehensive textbook.* Baltimore: Williams & Wilkins.

Cheung, C., Chan, W., Lee, T., Liu, S., & Leung, K. (2001). Structure of moral consciousness and moral intentions among youth in Hong Kong. *International Journal of Adolescence & Youth, 9*(2–3), 83–116.

Child safety seats. (1992, January). *Consumer Reports,* pp. 16–20.

Chilmonczyk, B. A., et al. (1993). Association between exposure to environmental tobacco smoke and exacerbations of asthma in children. *The New England Journal of Medicine, 328,* 1665–1669.

Chipman, S. F., Krantz, D. H., & Silver, R. (1992). Mathematics anxiety and science careers among able college women. *Psychological Science, 3,* 292–295.

Chira, S., (1989, November 15). "Sesame Street" at 20: Taking stock of learning. *The New York Times,* p. B13.

Chira, S. (1991, December 8). Report says too many aren't ready for school. *The New York Times,* p. B18.

Chira, S. (1992a, February 12). Bias against girls is found rife in schools, with lasting damage. *The New York Times,* pp. A1, B6.

Chira, S. (1992b, March 4). New Head Start studies raise question on help: Should fewer get more? *The New York Times,* p. B9.

Chira, S. (1993a, July 14). Is small better? Educators now say yes for high school. *The New York Times,* pp. A1, 10.

Chira, S. (1993b, May 19). When disabled students enter regular classrooms. *The New York Times,* pp. A1, B8.

Chisholm, J. S. (1983). *Navajo infancy.* New York: Aldine deGruyter.

Chomsky, N. (1988). *Language and problems of knowledge.* Cambridge, MA: MIT Press.

Chomsky, N. (1990). On the nature, use, and acquisition of language. In W. G. Lycan (Ed.), *Mind and cognition.* Oxford: Blackwell.

Christie, J. F., & Wardle, F. (1992, March). How much time is needed for play? *Young Children,* 28–32.

Christophersen, E. R. (1989). Injury control. *American Psychologist, 44,* 237–241.

Clark, E. V. (1973). What's in a word? On the child's acquisition of semantics in his first language. In E. Moore (Ed.), *Cognitive development and the acquisition of language.* New York: Academic Press.

Clark, E. V. (1975). Knowledge, context, and strategy in the acquisition of meaning. In D. P. Date (Ed.), *Georgetown University roundtable on language and linguistics.* Washington, DC: Georgetown University Press.

Clark, K. E., & Ladd, G. W. (2000). Connectedness and autonomy support in parent–child relationships: Links to children's socioemotional orientation and peer relationships. *Developmental Psychology, 36*(4), 485–498.

Clark, L. A., Kochanska, G., & Ready, R. (2000). Mothers' personality and its interaction with child temperament as predictors of parenting behavior. *Journal of Personality & Social Psychology, 79*(2), 274–285.

Clark, M. D. (2001). Influencing positive behavior change: Increasing the therapeutic approach of juvenile courts. *Federal Probation, 65*(1), 18–27.

Clark, M. L., & Bittle, M. L. (1992). Friendship expectations and the evaluation of present friendships in middle childhood and early adolescence. *Child Study Journal, 22,* 115–135.

Clark, R. (1983). *Family life and school achievement: Why poor black children succeed or fail.* Chicago: University of Chicago Press.

Clark-Lempers, D. S., Lempers, J. D., & Ho, C. (1991). Early, middle, and late adolescents' perceptions of their relationships with significant others. *Journal of Adolescent Research, 6,* 296–315.

Clarke-Stewart, K. A. (1989). Infant day care: Maligned or malignant? *American Psychologist, 44,* 266–273.

Clarke-Stewart, K. A. (1990). The "effects" of infant day care reconsidered: Risks for parents, children, and researchers. In N. Fox & G. G. Fein (Eds.), *Infant day care: The current debate.* Norwood, NJ: Ablex.

Clarke-Stewart, K. A. (1991). A home is not a school: The effects of child care on children's development. *Journal of Social Issues, 47,* 105–123.

Clarke-Stewart, K. A. (1998). Reading with children. *Journal of Applied Developmental Psychology, 19*(1), 1–14.

Clarke-Stewart, K. A., & Beck, R. J. (1999). Maternal scaffolding and children's narrative retelling of a movie story. *Early Childhood Research Quarterly, 14*(3), 409–434.

Clarke-Stewart, K. A., Goossens, F. A., & Allhusen, V. D. (2001). Measuring infant–mother attachment: Is the Strange Situation enough? *Social Development, 10*(2), 143–169.

Clarke-Stewart, K. A., Vandell, D. L., McCartney, K., Owen, M. T., & Booth, C. (2000). Effects of parental separation and divorce on very young children. *Journal of Family Psychology, 14*(2), 304–326.

Clay, R. A. (1996a). Beating the "biological clock" with zest. *APA Monitor, 27*(2), 37.

Clay, R. A. (1996b). Older men are more involved fathers, studies show. *APA Monitor, 27*(2), 37.

Clingempeel, W. G., & Repucci, N. D. (1982). Joint custody after divorce: Major issues and goals for research. *Psychological Bulletin, 91,* 102–127.

Clingempeel, W. G., & Segal, S. (1986). Stepparent–stepchild relationships and the psychological adjustment of children in stepmother and stepfather families. *Child Development, 57,* 474–484.

Clopton, N. A., & Sorell, G. T. (1993). Gender differences in moral reasoning. *Psychology of Women Quarterly, 17,* 85–101.

Cnattingius, S., et al. (2000). Caffeine intake and the risk of first-trimester spontaneous abortion. *The New England Journal of Medicine, 343*(25), 1839–1845.

Cnattingius, S., Forman, M. R., Berendes, H. W., & Isotalo, L. (1992). Delayed childbearing and risk of adverse perinatal outcome. *Journal of the American Medical Association, 268,* 886–890.

Cnattingius, S., Bergstrom, R., Lipworth, L., & Kramer, M. S. (1998). Prepregnancy weight and the risk of adverse pregnancy outcomes. *New England Journal of Medicine, 338,* 147–152.

Coates, D. C., & Van Widenfelt, B. (1991). Pregnancy in adolescence. In R. M. Lerner, A. C. Petersen, & J. Brooks-Gunn (Eds.), *Encyclopedia of adolescence.* New York: Garland.

Cohen, L. B., DeLoache, J. S., & Strauss, M. S. (1979). Infant visual perception. In J. D. Osofsky (Ed.), *Handbook of infant development.* New York: Wiley.

Cohen, R. (1996). Cited in Clay, R. A. (1996). Beating the "biological clock" with zest. *APA Monitor, 27*(2), 37.

Coie, J.D., & Cillessen, A. H. N. (1993). Peer rejection: Origins and effects on children's development. *Current Directions in Psychological Science, 2,* 89–92.

Coie, J. D., Dodge, K. A., Terry, R., & Wright, V. (1991). The role of aggression in peer relations: An analysis of aggression episodes in boys' play groups. *Child Development, 62,* 812–826.

Colby, A., Kohlberg, L. Gibbs, J., & Lieberman, M. (1983). A longitudinal study of moral judgment. *Monographs of the Society for Research in Child Development, 48*(4, Serial No. 200).

Cole, D. A. (1991a). Adolescent suicide. In R. M. Lerner, A. C. Petersen, & J. Brooks-Gunn (Eds.), *Encyclopedia of adolescence.* New York: Garland.

Cole, D. A. (1991b). Change in self-perceived competence as a function of peer and teacher evaluation. *Developmental Psychology, 27,* 682–688.

Cole, D. A., Jacquez, F. M., & Maschman, T. L. (2001). Social origins of depressive cognitions: A longitudinal study of self-perceived competence in children. *Cognitive Therapy & Research, 25*(4) 377–395.

Cole, K. N., Mills, P. E., Dale, P. S., & Jenkins, J. R. (1991). Effects of preschool integration for children with disabilities. *Exceptional Children, 58,* 36–45.

Cole, M. (1992). Culture in development. In M. H. Bornstein & M. E. Lamb (Eds.), *Developmental psychology: An advanced textbook* (3rd ed.). Hillsdale, NJ: Erlbaum.

Coleman, M., Ganong, L. H., & Fine, M. (2000). Reinvestigating remarriage: Another decade of progress. *Journal of Marriage & the Family, 62*(4) 1288–1307.

Coleman, M., Ganong, L. H., Killian, T., & McDaniel, A. K. (1999). Child support obligations: Attitudes and rationale. *Journal of Family Issues, 20*(1), 46–68.

Coles, C. D., Platzman, K. A., Smith, I. E., James, M. E., & Falek, A. (1992). Effects of cocaine and alcohol use in pregnancy on neonatal growth and neurobehavioral status. *Neurotoxicology and Teratology, 14,* 23–33.

Coles, R., & Stokes, G. (1985). *Sex and the American teenager.* New York: Harper & Row.

Coley, J. D. (1993, March). *Parental feedback to child labeling as input to conceptual development.* Paper presented at the meeting of the Society for Research in Child Development, New Orleans, LA.

Coley, R. L. (2001). (In)visible men: Emerging research on low-income, unmarried, and minority fathers. *American Psychologist, 56*(9), 743–753.

Coley, R. L., & Chase-Lansdale, P. L. (1998). Adolescent pregnancy and parenthood: Recent evidence and future directions. *American Psychologist, 53*(2), 152–166.

Coley, R. L., & Chase-Lansdale, P. L. (1999). Stability and change in paternal involvement among urban African American fathers. *Journal of Family Psychology, 13,* 1–20.

Collaer, M. L., & Hines, M. (1995). Human behavioral sex differences: A role for gonadal hormones during early development? *Psychological Bulletin, 118,* 55–107.

Collier, G. (1994). *Social origins of mental ability.* New York: Wiley.

Collins, W. A. (1984a). Conclusion: The status of basic research on middle childhood. In W. A. Collins (Ed.), *Development during middle childhood: The years from six to twelve.* Washington, DC: National Academy Press.

Collins, W. A. (1984b). Introduction. In W. A. Collins (Ed.), *Development during middle childhood: The years from six to twelve.* Washington, DC: National Academy Press.

Collins, W. A. (1990). Parent–child relationships in the transition to adolescence: Continuity and change in interaction, affect, and cognition. In R. Montemayor, G. R. Adams, & T. P. Gullotta (Eds.), *From childhood to adolescence: A transitional period.* Newbury Park, CA: Sage.

Collins, W. A., & Gunnar, M. R. (1990). Social and personality development. *Annual Review of Psychology, 41,* 387–416.

Collins, W. A., Maccoby, E. E., Steinberg, L., Hetherington, E. M., & Bornstein, M. H. (2000). Contemporary research on parenting: The case for nature and nurture. *American Psychologist, 55*(2), 218–232.

Collins, W. A., & Russell, G. (1991). Mother–child and father–child relationships in middle childhood and adolescence: A developmental analysis. *Developmental Review, 11,* 99–136.

Colombo, J. (1993). *Infant cognition.* Newbury Park, CA: Sage.

Colombo, J., Moss, M., & Horowitz, F. D. (1989). Neonatal state profiles: Reliability and short-term predictions of neurobehavioral status. *Child Development, 60,* 1102–1110.

Colyar, D. E. (1991). Residential care and treatment of youths with conduct disorders: Conclusions of a conference of childcare workers. *Child and Youth Care Forum, 20,* 195–204.

Comstock, G., & Paik, H. (1991). *Television and the American child.* San Diego: Academic Press.

Conde-Agudelo, A., & Belizán, J. M. (2000). Maternal morbidity and mortality associated with interpregnancy interval: Cross sectional study. *British Medical Journal, 321,* 1255–1259.

Condon, W. S., & Sander, L. W. (1974). Synchrony demonstrated between movements of the neonate and adult speech. *Child Development, 45,* 456–462.

Conel, J. L. (1959). *The postnatal development of the human cerebral cortex.* Cambridge, MA: Harvard University Press.

Conger, R. D., et al. (1993). Family economic stress and adjustment of early adolescent girls. *Developmental Psychology, 29,* 206–219.

Connolly, J., Furman, W., & Konarski, R. (2000). The role of peers in the emergence of heterosexual romantic relationships in adolescence. *Child Development, 71*(5), 1395–1408.

Connor, E. M., et al. (1994). Reduction of maternal-infant transmission of human immunodeficiency virus type 1 with zidovudine treatment. *New England Journal of Medicine, 331,* 1173–1180.

Coon, H., Carey, G., Corley, R., & Fulker, D. W. (1992). Identifying children in the Colorado adoption project at risk for conduct disorder. *Journal of the American Academy of Child and Adolescent Psychiatry, 31,* 503–511.

Coon, H., Fulker, D. W., & DeFries, J. C. (1990). Home environment and cognitive ability of 7-year-old children in the Colorado adoption project: Genetic and environmental etiologies. *Developmental Psychology, 26,* 459–468.

Coons, S., & Guilleminault, C. (1982). Development of sleep-wake patterns and non-rapid-eye-movement sleep stages during the first six months of life in normal infants. *Pediatrics, 69,* 793–798.

Cooper, M., Galbraith, M., & Drinkwater, J. (2001). Assumptions and beliefs in adolescents with anorexia nervosa and their mothers. *Eating Disorders: The Journal of Treatment & Prevention, 9*(3), 217–223.

Cooper, P. J., et al. (1999). Post-partum depression and the mother–infant relationship in a South African peri-urban settlement. *British Journal of Psychiatry, 175,* 554–558.

Cooper, R. P., & Aslin, R. N. (1990). Preference for infant-directed speech in the first month after birth. *Child Development, 61,* 1584–1595.

Coopersmith, S. (1967). *The antecedents of self-esteem.* San Francisco: W. H. Freeman.

Coplan, R. J., Rubin, K. H., Fox, N. A., Calkins, S. D., & Stewart, S. L. (1994). Being alone, playing alone, and acting alone: Distinguishing among reticence, and passive-, and active-solitude in young children. *Child Development, 65,* 129–137.

Corcoran, J. (2000). Ecological factors associated with adolescent sexual activity. *Social Work in Health Care, 30*(4), 93–111.

Corcoran, J. (2001). Multi-systemic influences on the family functioning of teens attending pregnancy prevention programs. *Child & Adolescent Social Work Journal, 18*(1), 37–49.

Coren, S. (1990). (Ed.). *Left-handedness: Behavioral implications and anomalies.* Amsterdam: North-Holland.

Coren, S. (1992). *The left-hander syndrome.* New York: Free Press.

Coren, S., & Searleman, A. (1990). Birth stress and left-handedness: The rare trait marker model. In S. Coren (Ed.), *Left-handedness: Behavior implications and anomalies.* Amsterdam: North-Holland.

Corina, D. P., et al. (2001). fMRI auditory language differences between dyslexic and able reading children. *Neuroreport: For Rapid Communication of Neuroscience Research, 12*(6), 1195–1201.

Correll, S. J. (2001). Gender and the career choice process: The role of biased self-assessments. *American Journal of Sociology, 106*(6), 1691–1730.

Corsaro, W. A., & Eder, D. (1990). Children's peer cultures. *Annual Review of Sociology, 16,* 197–220.

Cossette, L., Malcuit, G., & Pomerleau, A. (1991). Sex differences in motor activity during early infancy. *Infant Behavior and Development, 14,* 175–186.

Costin, S. E., & Jones, D. C. (1992). Friendship as a facilitator of emotional responsiveness and prosocial interventions among young children. *Developmental Psychology, 28,* 941–947.

Courage, M. L., & Adams, R. J. (1993, March). *Infant peripheral vision: The development of spatial resolution in the early months of life.* Paper presented at the meeting of the Society for Research in Child Development, New Orleans, LA.

Covey, L. A., & Feltz, D. L. (1991). Physical activity and adolescent female psychological development. *Journal of Youth and Adolescence, 20,* 463–474.

Cowan, C. P. (1992). *When partners become parents.* New York: Basic Books.

Cowan, N., Nugent, L. D., Elliott, E. M., Ponomarev, I., & Saults, J. S. (1999). The role of attention in the development of short-term memory: Age differences in the verbal span of apprehension. *Child Development, 70*(5), 1082–1097.

Cowan, N., Nugent, L. D., Elliott, E. M., & Saults, J. S. (2000). Persistence of memory for ignored lists of digits: Areas of developmental constancy and change. *Journal of Experimental Child Psychology, 76*(2), 151–172.

Cowan, P. A. (1978). *Piaget with feeling.* New York: Holt, Rinehart and Winston.

Cox, D. J., Borowitz, S., Kovatchev, B., & Ling, W. (1998). Contribution of behavior therapy and biofeedback to laxative therapy in the treatment of pediatric encopresis. *Annals of Behavioral Medicine, 20*(2), 70–76.

Cox, M. J., Owen, M. T., Henderson, V. K., & Margand, N. A. (1992). Prediction of infant–father and infant–mother attachment. *Developmental Psychology, 28,* 474–483.

Crain, W. C. (2000). *Theories of development: Concepts and applications* (4th ed.). Englewood Cliffs, NJ: Prentice Hall.

Cramer, J., & Oshima, T. C. (1992). Do gifted females attribute their math performance differently than other students? *Journal for the Education of the Gifted, 16,* 18–35.

Cramer, P., & Skidd, J. E. (1992). Correlates of self-worth in preschoolers: The role of gender-stereotyped styles of behavior. *Sex Roles, 26,* 369–390.

Cratty, B. (1986). *Perceptual and motor development in infants and children* (3rd ed.). Englewood Cliffs, NJ: Prentice Hall.

Crews, D. (1994). Animal sexuality. *Scientific American, 270*(1), 108–114.

Crick, N. R., & Ladd, G. W. (1993). Children's perceptions of their peer experiences: Attributions, loneliness, social, anxiety, and social avoidance. *Developmental Psychology, 29,* 244–254.

Crittenden, P. M., & Ainsworth, M. D. S. (1989). Child maltreatment and attachment theory. In D. Cicchetti & V. Carlson (Eds.), *Child maltreatment: Theory and research on the causes and consequences of child abuse and neglect.* Cambridge: Cambridge University Press.

Crnic, K. A., Ragozin, A. S., Greenberg, M. T., Robinson, M. N., & Basham, R. B. (1983). Social interaction and developmental competence of preterm and full-term infants during the first year of life. *Child Development, 54, 1199–1210.*

Crockenberg, S., & Litman, C. (1990). Autonomy as competence in 2-year-olds: Maternal correlates of child defiance, compliance, and self-assertion. *Developmental Psychology, 26,* 961–971.

Crockett, L. J., & Silbereisen, R. K. (Eds.) (2000). *Negotiating adolescence in times of social change.* Cambridge: Cambridge University Press.

Crombie, G., & Desjardins, M. J. (1993, March). *Predictors of gender: The relative importance of children's play, games, and personality characteristics.* Paper presented at the meeting of the Society for Research in Child Development, New Orleans, LA.

Crook, C. K., & Lipsitt, L. P. (1976). Neonatal nutritive sucking: Effects of taste stimulation upon sucking rhythm and heart rate. *Child Development, 47,* 518–522.

Crossette, B. (2000, August 29). Researchers raise fresh issues in breast-feeding debate. *The New York Times online.*

Crouch, J. L., & Behl, L. E. (2001). Relationships among parental beliefs in corporal punishment, reported stress, and physical child abuse potential. *Child Abuse & Neglect, 25*(3) 413–419.

Crouter, A., & McHale, S. (1989, April). *Childrearing in dual- and single-earner families: Implications for the development of school-age children.* Paper presented at the meeting of the Society for Research in Child Development, Kansas City, MO.

Crowe, H. P., & Zeskind, P. S. (1992). Psychophysiological and perceptual response to infant cries varying in pitch: Comparison of adults with low and high scores on the child abuse potential inventory. *Child Abuse and Neglect, 16,* 19–29.

Crowell, J. A., & Waters, E. (1990). Separation anxiety. In M. Lewis and S. M. Miller (Eds.), *Handbook of developmental psychopathology.* New York: Plenum.

Csikszentmihalyi, M., & Larson, R. (1984). *Being adolescent.* New York: Basic Books.

Cummings, M. R. (1991). *Human heredity: Principles and issues* (2nd ed.). St. Paul, MN: West.

Cunningham, A. E., Perry, K. E., & Stanovich, K. E. (2001). Converging evidence for the concept of orthographic processing. *Reading & Writing, 14*(5–6), 549–568.

Cunningham, T. H., & Graham, C. R. (2000). Increasing Native English vocabulary recognition through Spanish immersion: Cognate transfer from foreign to first language. *Journal of Educational Psychology, 92*(1), 37–49.

Curran, J. M. (1999). Constraints of pretend play: Explicit and implicit rules. *Journal of Research in Childhood Education, 14*(1), 47–55.

Curtiss, S. (1997). Genie: A psycholinguistic study of a modern-day "wild child." New York: Academic Press.

Curtner-Smith, M. E. (2000). Mechanisms by which family processes contribute to school-age boy's bullying. *Child Study Journal, 30*(3), 169–186.

Cutting, A. L., & Dunn, J. (1999). Theory of mind, emotion understanding, language, and family background: Individual differences and interrelations. *Child Development, 70*(4), 853–865.

Cutts, D. B., Pheley, A. M., & Geppert, J. S. (1998). Hunger in Midwestern inner-city young children. *Archives of Pediatric and Adolescent Medicine, 152,* 489–493.

Cystic Fibrosis Foundation. (2001, May 15). **http://www.cff.org/**

Dabbs, J. M., Jr., Bernieri, F. J., Strong, R. K., Campo, R., & Milun, R. (2001). Going on stage: Testosterone in greetings and meetings. *Journal of Research in Personality, 35*(1) 27–40.

Dabbs, J. M., Jr., Hargrove, M. F., & Heusel, C. (1996). Testosterone differences among college fraternities: Well-behaved vs rambunctious. *Personality & Individual Differences, 20*(2), 157–161.

Dahl, R. E., Scher, M. S., Williamson, D. E., Robles, N., & Day, N. (1995). A longitudinal study of prenatal marijuana use: Effects on sleep and arousal at age 3 years. *Archives of Pediatric and Adolescent Medicine, 149,* 145–150.

Dai, D. Y. (2001). A comparison of gender differences in academic self-concept and motivation between high-ability and average Chinese adolescents. *Journal of Secondary Gifted Education, 13*(1), 22–32.

Dailard, C. (2001, February). Sex education: Politicians, parents, teachers and teens. *The Guttmacher Report on Public Policy.* New York: The Alan Guttmacher Institute.

Daley, S. (1991, January 19). Girls' self-esteem is lost on way to adolescence, new study finds. *The New York Times,* pp. B1, 6.

Daly, M., & Wilson, M. (1998). Cited in Brody, J. E. (1998, February 10). Genetic ties may be factor in violence in stepfamilies. *The New York Times,* pp. F1, F4.

Damon, W. (1988). *The moral child.* New York: The Free Press.

Damon, W. (1991). Adolescent self-concept. In R. M. Lerner, A. C. Petersen, & J. Brooks-Gunn (Eds.), *Encyclopedia of adolescence.* New York: Garland.

Damon, W., & Hart, D. (1992). Self-understanding and its role in social and moral development. In M. H. Bornstein & M. E. Lamb (Eds.), *Developmental psychology: An advanced textbook.* Hillsdale, NJ: Erlbaum.

Danner, F., Noland, F., McFadden, M., Dewalt, K., & Kotchen, J. M. (1991). Description of the physical activity of young children using movement sensor and observation methods. *Pediatric Exercise Science, 3,* 11–20.

Dasen, P. R. (Ed.). (1977). *Piagetian psychology: Cross-cultural contributions.* New York: Gardner.

Davey, L. F. (1993, March). *Developmental implications of shared and divergent perceptions in the parent–adolescent relationship.* Paper presented at the meeting of the Society for Research in Child Development, New Orleans, LA.

Davies, P. T., & Cummings, E. M. (1994). Marital conflict and child adjustment. *Psychological Bulletin, 116,* 387–411.

Davies, P. T., & Windle, M. (2001). Interparental discord and adolescent adjustment trajectories: The potentiating and protective role of intrapersonal attributes. *Child Development, 72*(4), 1163–1178.

Davis, A. (1991). Piaget, teachers and education: Into the 1990's. In P. Light, S. Sheldon, & M. Woodhead (Eds.), *Learning to think.* New York: Rutledge.

Davis, A. M., Grattan, D. R., & McCarthy, M. M. (2000). Decreasing GAD neonatally attenuates steroid-induced sexual differentiation of the rat brain. *Behavioral Neuroscience, 114*(5) 923–933.

Davis, H. A. (2001). The quality and impact of relationships between elementary school students and teachers. *Contemporary Educational Psychology, 26*(4), 431–453.

Dawood, K., Pillard, R. C., Horvath, C., Revelle, W., & Bailey, J. M. (2000). Familial aspects of male homosexuality. *Archives of Sexual Behavior, 29*(2), 155–163.

Day, S. X., & Rounds, J. (1998). Universality of vocational interest structure among racial and ethnic minorities. *American Psychologist, 53,* 728–736.

DeAngelis, T. (1992, April). Conference explores issues of giftedness. *APA Monitor,* pp. 42–43.

DeAngelis, T. (1993, July). Science meets practice on PKU studies' findings. *APA Monitor,* pp. 16–17.

DeAngelis, T. (1997). Abused children have more conflicts with friends. *APA Monitor, 28*(6), 32.

Deas, D., & Thomas, S. E. (2001). An overview of controlled studies of adolescent substance abuse treatment. *American Journal on Addictions, 10*(2), 178–189.

DeBaryshe, B. D., Patterson, G. R., & Capaldi, D. M. (1993). A performance model for academic achievement in early adolescent boys. *Developmental Psychology, 29,* 795–804.

de Boysson-Bardies, B., Halle, P., Sogart, L., & Durand, C. (1989). A crosslinguistic investigation of vowel formants in babbling. *Journal of Child Language, 16,* 1–17.

DeCasper, A. J., & Fifer, W. P. (1980). Of human bonding: Newborns prefer their mothers' voices. *Science, 208,* 1174–1176.

DeCasper, A. J., & Prescott, P. A. (1984). Human newborns' perception of male voices: Preference, discrimination, and reinforcing value. *Developmental Psychobiology, 17,* 481–491.

DeCasper, A. J., & Spence, M. J. (1986). Prenatal maternal speech influences newborns' perception of speech sounds. *Infant Behavior and Development, 9,* 133–150.

DeCasper, A. J., & Spence, M. J. (1991). Auditorially mediated behavior during the perinatal period: A cognitive view. In M. J. Weiss & P. R. Zelazo (Eds.), *Infant attention,* 142–176. Norwood, NJ: Ablex.

Decker, S. L., McIntosh, D. E., Kelly, A. M., Nicholls, S. K., & Dean, R. S. (2001). Comorbidity among individuals classified with attention disorders. *International Journal of Neuroscience, 110*(1–2), 43–54.

Declercq, E. R. (1992). The transformation of American midwifery: 1975 to 1988. *American Journal of Public Health, 82,* 680–684.

de Cubas, M. M., & Field, T. (1993). Children of methadone-dependent women: *Developmental outcomes. American Journal of Orthopsychiatry, 63,* 266–276.

Deep, A. L., et al. (1999). Sexual abuse in eating disorder subtypes and control women: The role of comorbid substance dependence in bulimia nervosa. *International Journal of Eating Disorders, 25*(1), 1–10.

De Guerrero, M. C. M., & Villamil, O. S. (2000). Activating the ZPD: Mutual scaffolding in L2 peer revision. *Modern Language Journal, 84*(1), 51–68.

DeKovic, M., & Janssens, J. (1992). Parents' child-rearing style and child's sociometric status. *Developmental Psychology, 28,* 925–932.

Delaney-Black, V., et al. (2000). Expressive language development of children exposed to cocaine prenatally: Literature review and report of a prospective cohort study. *Journal of Communication Disorders, 33*(6), 463–481.

DeLoache, J. S. (1991). Symbolic functioning in very young children: Understanding of pictures and models. *Child Development, 62,* 736–752.

DeLoache, J. S., Cassidy, D. J., & Brown, A. L. (1985). Precursors of mnemonic strategies in very young children's memory. *Child Development, 56,* 125–137.

DeLong, G. R. (1999). Autism: New data suggest a new hypothesis. *Neurology,* 52(5), 911–916.

DeLuccie, M. F., & Davis, A. J. (1991). Father–child relationships from the preschool years through mid-adolescence. *Journal of Genetic Psychology, 152,* 225–238.

DeLucia, C., Belz, A., & Chassin, L. (2001). Do adolescent symptomatology and family environment vary over time with fluctuations in paternal alcohol impairment? *Developmental Psychology, 37*(2), 207–216.

DeMulder, E. K., & Radke-Yarrow, M. (1991). Attachment with affectively ill and well mothers: Concurrent behavioral correlates. *Development and Psychopathology, 3,* 227–242.

Denmark, F., Russo, N. F., Frieze, I. H., & Sechzer, J. A. (1988). Guidelines for avoiding sexism in psychological research. *American Psychologist, 43,* 582–585.

Dennis, M., Sugar, J., & Whitaker, H. A. (1982). The acquisition of tag questions. *Child Development, 53,* 1254–1257.

Dennis, W. (1960). Causes of retardation among institutional children: Iran. *Journal of Genetic Psychology, 96,* 47–59.

Dennis, W., & Dennis, M. G. (1940). The effect of cradling practices upon the onset of walking in Hopi children. *Journal of Genetic Psychology, 56,* 77–86.

Dennis, W., & Sayegh, Y. (1965). The effect of supplementary experiences upon the behavioral development of infants in institutions. *Child Development, 36,* 81–90.

Denscombe, M. (2001). Critical incidents and the perception of health risks: The experiences of young people in relation to their use of alcohol and tobacco. *Health, Risk & Society, 3*(3), 293–306.

de Oliveira, F. S., Viana, M. R., Antoniolli, A. R., & Marchioro, M. (2001). Differential effects of lead and zinc on inhibitory avoidance learning in mice. *Brazilian Journal of Medical and Biological Research, 34*(1), 117–120.

DeParle, J. (1993, March 19). Sharp criticism for Head Start, even by friends. *The New York Times*, pp. A1, 11.

Desmond, A. M. (1994). Adolescent pregnancy in the United States: Not a minority issue. *Health Care for Women International, 15*(4), 325–331.

Desmond, R. J., Singer, J. L., & Singer, D. G. (1990). Family mediation: Parental communication patterns and the influences of television on children. In J. Bryant (Ed.), *Television and the American family*. Hillsdale, NJ: Erlbaum.

Dessens, A. B., et al. (1999). Prenatal exposure to anticonvulsants and psychosexual development. *Archives of Sexual Behavior, 28*(1) 31–44.

Dessureau, B. K., Kurowski, C. O., & Thompson, N. S. (1998). A reassessment of the role of pitch and duration in adults' responses to infant crying. *Infant Behavior & Development, 21*(2), 367–371.

deVilliers, P. A., & deVilliers, J. G. (1992). Language development. In M. H. Bornstein & M. E. Lamb (Eds.), *Developmental psychology: An advanced textbook* (3rd ed.). Hillsdale, NJ: Erlbaum.

Devlin, M. J., Yanovski, S. Z., & Wilson, G. T. (2000). Obesity: What mental health professionals need to know. *American Journal of Psychiatry, 157*(6), 854–866.

DeVries, R. (2000). Vygotsky, Piaget, and education: A reciprocal assimilation of theories and educational practices. *New Ideas in Psychology, 18*(2–3), 187–213.

de Wit, H., Crean, J., & Richards, J. B. (2000). Effects of *d*-amphetamine and ethanol on a measure of behavioral inhibition in humans. *Behavioral Neuroscience, 114*(4), 830–837.

Dezube, B. J. (2000). AIDS-Related Kaposi sarcoma: The role of local therapy for a systemic disease. *Archives of Dermatology, 136,* 1554.

Diamond, G., & Siqueland, L. (2001). Current status of family intervention science. *Child & Adolescent Psychiatric Clinics of North America, 10*(3), 641–661.

Diamond, J. M., Kataria, S., & Messer, S. C. (1989). Latchkey children: A pilot study investigating behavior and academic achievement. *Child and Youth Care Quarterly, 18,* 131–140.

DiBlasio, F. A., & Benda, B. B. (1992). Gender differences in theories of adolescent sexual activity. *Sex Roles, 27,* 221–239.

Dickens, W. T., & Flynn, J. R. (2001). Heritability estimates versus large environmental effects: The IQ paradox resolved. *Psychological Review, 108*(2), 346–369.

Dick-Read, G. (1944). *Childbirth without fear: The principles and practices of natural childbirth.* New York: Harper & Bros.

Dickson, N., Paul, C., Herbison, P., & Silva, P. (1998). First sexual intercourse: Age, coercion, and later regrets reported by a birth cohort. *British Medical Journal, 316,* 29–33.

Dickstein, E., & Posner, J. M. (1978). Self-esteem and relationship with parents. *Journal of Genetic Psychology, 133,* 273–276.

Dickstein, S., & Parke, R. D. (1988). Social referencing in infancy: A glance at fathers and marriage. *Child Development, 59,* 506–511.

Didden, R., et al. (2001). Use of a modified Azrin-Foxx toilet training procedure with individuals with Angelman-Syndrome. *Journal of Applied Research in Intellectual Disabilities, 14*(1), 64–70.

Dierker, L. C., et al. (2001). Association between psychiatric disorders and the progression of tobacco use behaviors. *Journal of the American Academy of Child & Adolescent Psychiatry, 40*(10), 1159–1167.

Dietz, W. H. (1990). You are what you eat—what you eat is what you are. *Journal of Adolescent Health Care, 11,* 76–81.

Dietz, W. H., Jr., & Gortmaker, S. L. (1985). Do we fatten our children at the television set? Obesity and television viewing in children and adolescents. *Pediatrics, 75,* 807–812.

DiLalla, D. L., Carey, G., Gottesman, I. I., & Bouchard, T. J., Jr. (1996). Heritability of MMPI personality indicators of psychopathology in twins reared apart. *Journal of Abnormal Psychology, 105,* 491–499.

DiLalla, D. L., Gottesman, I. I.; Carey, G., & Bouchard, T. J., Jr. (1999). Heritability of MMPI Harris-Lingoes and Subtle-Obvious subscales in twins reared apart. *Assessment, 6*(4), 353–366.

DiMatteo, M. R., et al. (1996). Cesarean childbirth and psychosocial outcomes: A meta-analysis. *Health Psychology, 15,* 303–314.

Dindia, K., & Allen, M. (1992). Sex differences in self-disclosure: A meta-analysis. *Psychological Bulletin, 112,* 106–124.

Division of Reproductive Health, National Center for Chronic Disease Prevention and Health Promotion; Division of Applied Public Health Training, Epidemiology Program Office; Division of Vital Statistics, National Center for Health Statistics; and an EIS Officer, CDC. (2000). Contribution of assisted reproduction technology and ovulation-inducing drugs to triplet and higher-order multiple births, United States, 1980–1997. *Morbidity and Mortality Weekly Report, 49,* 535–538.

Division of Reproductive Health, National Center for Chronic Disease Prevention and Health Promotion; and an EIS Officer, CDC. (2001, May 11). Pregnancy-related deaths among Hispanic, Asian/Pacific Islander, and American Indian/Alaska Native Women—United States, 1991–1997. *Morbidity and Mortality Weekly Report, 50*(18), 361–364.

Dix, T. (1991). The affective organization of parenting: Adaptive and maladaptive processes. *Psychological Bulletin, 110,* 3–25.

Dix, T., Ruble, D. N., & Zambarino, R. J. (1989). Mother's implicit theories of discipline: Child effects, parental effects and the attribution process. *Child Development, 60,* 1373–1392.

Dixon, J. A., & Moore, C. F. (1990). The development of perspective taking: Understanding differences in information and weighting. *Child Development, 61,* 1502–1513.

Dodge, K. A. (1990). Developmental psychopathology in children of depressed mothers. *Developmental Psychology, 26,* 3–6.

Dodge, K.A. (1993a, March). *Effects of intervention on children at high risk for conduct problems.* Paper presented at the meeting of the Society for Research in Child Development, New Orleans, L.A.

Dodge, K.A. (1993b, March). *Social information processing and peer rejection factors in the development of behavior problems in children.* Paper presented at the meeting of the Society for Research in Child Development, New Orleans, LA.

Dodwell, P. C., Humphrey, G. K., & Muir, D. W. (1987). Shape and pattern perception. In P. Salapatek & L. Cohen (Eds.), *Handbook of infant perception: Vol. 2. From perception to cognition.* Orlando, FL: Academic Press.

Doherty, W. J., Kouneski, E. F., & Erickson, M. F. (1996). *Responsible fathering: An overview and conceptual framework.* Washington, DC: U.S. Department of Health and Human Services. Retrieved June 7, 2001, from the World Wide Web: **http://fatherhood.hhs.gov/concept.htm**

Doherty, W. J., & Needle, R. H. (1991). Psychological adjustment and substance use among adolescents before and after a parental divorce. *Child Development, 62,* 328–337.

Dolgin, K. G., Meyer, L., & Schwartz, J. (1991). Effects of gender, target's gender, topic, and self-esteem on disclosure to best and middling friends. *Sex Roles, 25,* 311–329.

Dombrowski, M. A. S., et al. (2000). Kangaroo skin-to-skin care for premature twins and their adolescent parents. *American Journal of Maternal/Child Nursing, 25*(2), 92–94.

Donaldson, M. (1979). *Children's minds.* New York: Norton.

Donovan, C. (2000, May 30). *Confronting teen pregnancy. The Washington Post,* p. Z17.

Dornbusch, S. M., Ritter, P. L., Leiderman, P. H., Roberts, D. F., & Fraleigh, M. J. (1987). The relation of parenting style to adolescent school performance. *Child Development, 58,* 1244–1257.

Downey, D. B. (2001). Number of siblings and intellectual development: The resource dilution explanation. *American Psychologist, 56*(6/7).

Downey, J. I., & Friedman, R. C. (1998). Female homosexuality: Classical psychoanalytic theory reconsidered. *Journal of the American Psychoanalytic Association, 46*(2), 471–506.

Downs, W. R., & Rose, S. R. (1991). The relationship of adolescent peer groups to the incidence of psychosocial problems. *Adolescence, 26,* 473–492.

Doyle, A., Ceschin, F., Tessier, O., & Doehring, P. (1991). The relation of age and social class factors in children's social pretend play to cognitive and symbolic ability. *International Journal of Behavioral Development, 14,* 395–410.

Doyle, A. B., Doehring, P., Tessier, O., & De Lorimier, S. (1992). Transitions in children's play: A sequential analysis of states preceding and following social pretense. *Developmental Psychology, 28,* 137–144.

Draper, W. (1990). Father's role in development. In R. M. Thomas (Ed.), *The encyclopedia of human development and education: Theory, research and studies.* Oxford: Pergamon.

Drapkin, R. G., Wing, R. R., & Shiffman, S. (1995). Responses to hypothetical high risk situations. *Health Psychology, 14,* 427–434.

Drasgow, E., Halle, J. W., & Phillips, B. (2001). Effects of different social partners on the discriminated requesting of a young child with autism and severe language delays. *Research in Developmental Disabilities, 22*(2), 125–139.

Drewett, R., Wolke, D., Asefa, M., Kaba, M., & Tessema, F. (2001). Malnutrition and mental development: Is there a sensitive period? A nested case-control study. *Journal of Child Psychology & Psychiatry & Allied Disciplines, 42*(2). 181–187.

Drews, C. D., et al. (1996, April). *Pediatrics.* Cited in "Smokers more likely to bear retarded babies, study says." (1996, April 10). *The New York Times,* p. B7.

Dubas, J. S. (1991). Cognitive abilities and physical maturation. In R. M. Lerner, A. C. Petersen, & J. Brooks-Gunn (Eds.), *Encyclopedia of adolescence.* New York: Garland.

DuBois, D. L., & Hirsch, B. J. (1990). School and neighborhood friendship patterns of blacks and whites in early adolescence. *Child Development, 61,* 524–536.

Dubow, E. F., & Luster, T. (1990). Adjustment of children born to teenage mothers: The contribution of risk and protective factors, *Journal of Marriage and the Family, 52,* 393–404.

Dufva, M., Niemi, P., & Voeten, M. J. M. (2001). The role of phonological memory, word recognition, and comprehension skills in reading development: From preschool to grade 2. *Reading & Writing, 14*(1–2), 91–117.

Dugger, C. W. (2001a, April 22). Abortion in India is tipping scales sharply against girls. *The New York Times online.*

Dugger, C. W. (2001b, May 6). Modern Asia's anomaly: The girls who don't get born. *The New York Times,* p. WK4.

Dumas, J. E., & La Freniere, P. J. (1993). Mother–child relationships as sources of support or stress: A comparison of competent, average, aggressive, and anxious dyads. *Child Development, 64,* 1732–1754.

Dumtschin, J. U. (1988, March). Recognize language development and delay in early childhood. *Young Children,* 16–24.

Duncan, G. J., Brooks-Gunn, J., & Klebanov, P. K. (1993, March). *Economic deprivation and early-childhood development.* Paper presented at the meeting of the Society for Research in Child Development, New Orleans, LA.

Duncan, S. (1991). Convention and conflict in the child's interaction with others. *Developmental Review, 11,* 337–366.

Dunham, P., & Dunham, F. (1992). Lexical development during middle infancy: A mutually driven infant–caregiver process. *Developmental Psychology, 28,* 414–420.

Dunn, J. (1992). Siblings and development. *Current Directions in Psychological Science, 1,* 6–9. Hillsdale, NJ: Erlbaum.

Dunn, J. (1993). *Young children's close relationships: Beyond attachment.* Newbury Park, CA: Sage.

Dunn, J., Brown, J., Slomkowski, C., Tesla, C., & Youngblade, L. (1991). Young children's understanding of other people's feelings and beliefs: Individual differences and their antecedents. *Child Development, 62,* 1352–1366.

Dunn, J., Davies, L. C., O'Connor, T. G., & Sturgess, W. (2001). Family lives and friendships: The perspectives of children in step-, single-parent, and nonstep families. *Journal of Family Psychology, 15*(2), 272–287.

Dunn, J., & Hughes, C. (2001). "I got some swords and you're dead!": Violent fantasy, antisocial behavior, friendship, and moral sensibility in young children. *Child Development, 72*(2), 491–505.

Dunn, J., Stocker, C. & Plomin, R. (1990). Assessing the relationship between young siblings: A research note. *Journal of Child Psychology and Psychiatry, 31,* 983–991.

Dunning, J. (1997, July 16). Pursuing perfection: Dancing with death. *The New York Times,* p. C11.

Durand, A. M. (1992). The safety of home birth: The farm study. *American Journal of Public Health, 82,* 450–453.

Durik, A. M., Hyde, J. S., & Clark, R. (2000). Sequelae of cesarean and vaginal deliveries: Psychosocial outcomes for mothers and infants. *Developmental Psychology, 36,* 2, 251–260.

Dyer, C. A. (1999). Pathophysiology of phenylketonuria. *Mental Retardation & Developmental Disabilities Research Reviews, 5*(2), 104–112.

Dykman, R. A., Casey, P. H., Ackerman, P. T., & McPherson, W. B. (2001). Behavioral and cognitive status in school-aged children with a history of failure to thrive during early childhood. *Clinical Pediatrics, 40*(2), 63–70.

Earned degrees. (1993, June 2). *The Chronicle of Higher Education,* pp. A25, 26.

Eason, E., & Feldman, P. (2000). Much ado about a little cut: Is episiotomy worthwhile? *Obstetrics & Gynecology, 95*(4), 616–618.

Eason, E., Labrecque, M., Wells, G., & Feldman, P. (2000). Preventing perineal trauma during childbirth: A systematic review. *Obstetrics & Gynecology, 95,* 464–471.

East, P. L., et al. (1992). Early adolescent-peer group fit, peer relations, and psychosocial competence: A short-term longitudinal study. *Journal of Early Adolescence, 12,* 132–152.

Easterbrook, M. A., & Goldberg, W. A. (1984). Toddler development in the family: Impact of father involvement and parenting characteristics. *Child Development, 55,* 740–752.

Easterbrook, M. A., Kisilevsky, B. S., Hains, S. M. J., & Muir, D. W. (1999). Faceness or complexity: Evidence from newborn visual tracking of facelike stimuli. *Infant Behavior & Development, 22*(1), 17–35.

Easterbrook, M. A., Kisilevsky, B. S., Muir, D. W., & Laplante, D. P. (1999). Newborns discriminate schematic faces from scrambled faces. *Canadian Journal of Experimental Psychology, 53*(3), 231–241.

Eaton, W. O., McKeen, N. A., & Campbell, D. W. (2001). The waxing and waning of movement: Implications for psychological development. *Developmental Review, 21*(2), 205–223.

Eaton, W. O., & Saudino, K. J. (1992). Prenatal activity level as a temperament dimension? Individual differences and developmental functions in fetal movement. *Infant Behavior and Development,* 15, 57–70.

Eaton, W. O., & Yu, A. P. (1989). Are sex differences in child motor activity a function of sex differences in maturational status? *Child Development, 60,* 1005–1011.

Eberhardy, F. (1967). The view from "the couch." *Journal of Child Psychological Psychiatry, 8,* 257–263.

Eccles, J. S. (1985). Sex differences in achievement patterns. In T. Sonderegger (Ed.), *Nebraska symposium on motivation.* Lincoln: University of Nebraska Press.

Eccles, J. S. (1991a). Academic achievement. In R. M. Lerner, A. C. Petersen, & J. Brooks-Gunn (Eds.), *Encyclopedia of adolescence.* New York: Garland.

Eccles, J. S. (1991b). Changes in motivation and self-perceptions. In R. M. Lerner, A. C. Petersen, & J. Brooks-Gunn (Eds.), *Encyclopedia of adolescence.* New York: Garland.

Eccles, J. S. (1993, March). *Parents as gender-role socializers during middle childhood and adolescence.* Paper presented at the meeting of the Society for Research on Child Development, New Orleans, LA.

Eccles, J. S. (1999). The development of children ages 6 to 14. *Future of Children, 9*(2), 30–44.

Eccles, J. S., et al. (1991, August). *Expectancy effects are alive and well on the home front: Influences on, and consequences of, parents' beliefs regarding their daughters' and sons' abilities and interests.* Paper presented at the meeting of the American Psychological Association, San Francisco.

Eccles, J. S., et al. (1993). Development during adolescence. *American Psychologist, 48,* 90–101.

Eccles, J. S., Wigfield, A., Harold, R. D., & Blumenfeld, P. (1993). Age and gender differences in children's self- and task perceptions during elementary school. *Child Development, 64,* 830–847.

Eckenrode, J., Laird, M., & Doris, J. (1993b). School performance and disciplinary problems among abused and neglected children. *Developmental Psychology, 29,* 53–62.

Eckerman, C. O., Hsu, H-C, Molitor, A., Leung, E. H. L., & Goldstein, R. F. (1999). Infant arousal in an en-face exchange with a new partner: Effects of prematurity and perinatal biological risk. *Developmental Psychology, 35*(1) 282–293.

Eckerman, C. O., & Oehler, J. M. (1992). Very-low-birthweight newborns and parents as early social partners. In S. L. Friedman & M. D. Sigman (Eds.), *The psychological development of low birthweight infants.* Norwood, NJ: Ablex.

Eckerman, C. O., & Stein, M. R. (1990). How imitation begets imitation and toddlers' generation of games. *Developmental Psychology, 26,* 370–378.

Eder, R. A. (1989). The emergent personologist: The structure and content of 3½-, 5½-, and 7½-year-olds' concepts of themselves and other persons. *Child Development, 60,* 1218–1228.

Eder, R. A. (1990). Uncovering young children's psychological selves: Individual and developmental differences. *Child Development, 61,* 849–863.

Eddy, J. M., & Chamberlain, P. (2000). Family management and deviant peer association as mediators of the impact of treatment condition on youth antisocial behavior. *Journal of Consulting & Clinical Psychology, 68*(5), 857–863.

Eddy, J. M., Leve, L. D., & Fagot, B. I. (2001). Coercive family processes: A replication and extension of Patterson's Coercion Model. *Aggressive Behavior, 27*(1), 14–25.

Egeland, B., & Farber, E. A. (1984). Infant–mother attachment: Factors related to its development and changes over time. *Child Development, 55,* 753–771.

Egeland, B., Jacobvitz, D., & Sroufe, L. A. (1988). Breaking the cycle of abuse. *Child Development, 59,* 1080–1088.

Egeland, B., & Sroufe, L. A. (1981). Attachment and early maltreatment. *Child Development, 52,* 44–52.

Eidem, B. W., et al. (2001). Early detection of cardiac dysfunction: Use of the myocardial performance index in patients with anorexia nervosa. *Journal of Adolescent Health, 29*(4), 267–270.

Eiden, R. D. (1999). Exposure to violence and behavior problems during early childhood. *Journal of Interpersonal Violence, 14*(12), 1299–1313.

Eil, C. (1991). Gynecomastia. In R. M. Lerner, A. C. Petersen, & J. Brooks-Gunn (Eds.), *Encyclopedia of adolescence.* New York: Garland.

Eimas, P. D., Sigueland, E. R., Juscyk, P., & Vigorito, J. (1971). Speech perception in infants. *Science, 171,* 303–306.

Eisenberg, N., et al. (1993). The relations of emotionality and regulation to preschoolers' social skills and sociometric status. *Child Development, 64,* 1418–1438.

Eisenberg, N., et al. (1999). Consistency and development of prosocial dispositions: A longitudinal study. *Child Development, 70*(6), 1360–1372.

Eisenberg, N., Fabes, R. A., Schaller, M., & Miller, P. A. (1989). Sympathy and personal distress: Development, gender differences, and interrelations of indexes. In N. Eisenberg (Ed.), *New directions for child development: No. 44. Empathy and related emotional responses.* San Francisco: Jossey-Bass.

Eisenberg, N., Hertz-Lazarowitz, R., & Fuchs, I. (1990). Prosocial moral judgment in Israeli kibbutz and city children: A longitudinal study. *Merrill-Palmer Quarterly, 36,* 273–285.

Eisenberg, N., & Miller, P. (1990). The development of prosocial behavior versus nonprosocial behavior in children. In M. Lewis & S. M. Miller (Eds.), *Handbook of developmental psychopathology.* New York: Plenum.

Eisenberg, N., Miller, P. A., Shell, R., McNalley, S., & Shea, C. (1991). Prosocial development in adolescence: A longitudinal study. *Developmental Psychology, 27,* 849–857.

Eisner, E. W. (1990). The role of art and play in children's cognitive development. In E. Klugman & S. Smilansky (Eds.), *Children's play and learning: Perspectives and policy implications.* New York: Teachers College Press.

Ekvall, S. W. (1993a). Nutritional assessment and early intervention. In S. W. Ekvall (Ed.), *Pediatric nutrition in chronic diseases and developmental disorders: Prevention, assessment, and treatment.* New York: Oxford.

Ekvall, S. W. (Ed.). (1993b). *Pediatric nutrition in chronic diseases and developmental disorders: Prevention, assessment, and treatment.* New York: Oxford.

Ekvall, S. W. (1993c). Prenatal growth in pregnancy. In S. W. Ekvall (Ed.), *Pediatric nutrition in chronic diseases and developmental disorders: Prevention, assessment, and treatment.* New York: Oxford.

Ekvall, S. W., Ekvall, V., & Mayes, S. D. (1993). Attention deficit hyperactivity disorder. In S. W. Ekvall (Ed.), *Pediatric nutrition in chronic diseases and developmental disorders: Prevention, assessment, and treatment.* New York: Oxford.

Elbers, E., Wiegersma, S., Brand, N., & Vroon, P. A. (1991). Response alternation as an artifact in conservation research. *Journal of Genetic Psychology, 152,* 47–56.

Elias, L. J., Saucier, D. M., & Guylee, M. J. (2001). Handedness and depression in university students: A sex by handedness interaction. *Brain & Cognition, 46*(1–2), 125–129.

Elias, M. J., Gara, M. A., Schuyler, T. F., Brandon-Muller, L. R., & Sayette, M. A. (1991). The promotion of social competence: Longitudinal study of a preventative school-based program. *American Journal of Orthopsychiatry, 61,* 409–417.

Elkind, D. (1967). Egocentrism in adolescence. *Child Development, 38,* 1025–1034.

Elkind, D. (1985). Egocentrism redux. *Developmental Review, 5,* 218–226.

Elkind, D. (1990). Academic pressures—too much, too soon: The demise of play. In E. Klugman & S. Smilansky (Eds.), *Children's play and learning: Perspectives and policy.* New York: Teachers College Press.

Elkind, D. (1991). Early childhood education. In M. Lewis (Ed.), *Child and adolescent psychiatry: A comprehensive textbook.* Baltimore: Williams & Wilkins.

Elkind, D., & Bowen, R. (1979). Imaginary audience behavior in children and adolescents. *Developmental Psychology, 15,* 38–44.

Ellenbroek, B. A., Sluyter, F., & Cools, A. R. (2000). The role of genetic and early environmental factors in determining apomorphine susceptibility. *Psychopharmacology, 148*(2), 124–131.

Ellickson, P. L., Tucker, J. S., & Klein, D. J. (2001). High-risk behaviors associated with early smoking: Results from a 5-year follow-up. *Journal of Adolescent Health, 28*(6), 465–473.

Elliott, R. (1988). Tests, abilities, race, and conflict. *Intelligence, 12,* 333–350.

Ellis, A., & Dryden, W. (1996). *The practice of rational emotive behavior therapy.* New York: Springer.

Ellis, E. M. (2000). *Divorce wars: Interventions with families in conflict.* Washington, D.C.: American Psychological Association.

Ellis, L. (1990). Prenatal stress may affect sex-typical behaviors of a child. Brown University *Child Behavior and Development Letter, 6*(1)1–3.

Ellis, L., & Ames, M. A. (1987). Neurohormonal functioning and sexual orientation: A theory of homosexuality–heterosexuality. *Psychological Bulletin, 101,* 233–258.

Elrod, M. M., & Crase, S. J. (1980). Sex differences in self-esteem and parental behavior. *Psychological Reports, 46,* 719–727.

El-Sheikh, M., & Harger, J. (2001). Appraisals of marital conflict and children's adjustment, health, and physiological reactivity. *Developmental Psychology, 37*(6), 875–885.

Emde, R. N., Gaensbauer, T. J., & Harmon, R. J. (1976). *Emotional expression in infancy: A biobehavioral study.* New York: International Universities Press.

Emde, R. N., Harmon, R. J., Metcalf, D., Koenig, K. L., & Wagonfeld, S. (1971). Stress and neonatal sleep. *Psychosomatic Medicine, 33,* 491–497.

Emde, R. N., Plomin, R., Robinson, J., Corley, R., DeFries, J., Fulker, D. W. Reznick, J. S., Campos, J., Kagan, J., & Zahn-Waxler, C. (1992). Temperament, emotion, and cognition at fourteen months: The MacArthur Longitudinal Twin Study. *Child Development, 63,* 1437–1455.

Emslie, G. J., Walkup, J. T., Pliszka, S. R., & Ernst, M. (1999). Nontricyclic antidepressants: Current trends in children and adolescents. *Journal of the American Academy of Child & Adolescent Psychiatry, 38*(5), 517–528.

Entwisle, D. R. (1990). Schools and the adolescent. In S. S. Feldman & G. R. Elliott (Eds.), *At the threshold: The developing adolescent.* Cambridge, MA: Harvard University Press.

Epstein, J. L. (1989). The selection of friends: Changes across the grades and in different school environments. In T. J. Berndt & G. W. Ladd (Eds.), *Peer relationships in child development.* New York: Wiley.

Epstein, L. H., et al. (2000). Problem solving in the treatment of childhood obesity. *Journal of Consulting & Clinical Psychology, 68*(4), 717–721.

Epstein, L. H., Kilanowski, C. K., Consalvi, A. R., & Paluch, R. A. (1999). Reinforcing value of physical activity as a determinant of child activity level. *Health Psychology, 18*(6), 599–603.

Erdley, C. A., & Asher, S. R. (1998). Linkages between children's beliefs about the legitimacy of aggression and their behavior. *Social Development, 7*(3), 321–339.

Erel, O., & Burman, B. (1995). Interrelatedness of marital relations and parent–child relations: A meta-analytic review. *Psychological Bulletin, 118,* 108–132.

Erel, O., Oberman, Y., & Yirmiya, N. (2000). Maternal versus nonmaternal care and seven domains of children's development. *Psychological Bulletin, 126*(5), 727–747.

Erikson, E. H. (1963). *Childhood and society.* New York: Norton.

Erikson, E. H. (1968). *Identity: Youth and crisis.* New York: Norton.

Erikson, E. H. (1975). *Life history and the historical moment.* New York: Norton.

Eron, L. D. (1982). Parent–child interaction, television violence, and aggression of children. *American Psychologist, 37,* 197–211.

Eron, L. D. (1993). Cited in DeAngelis, T. (1993). It's baaack: TV violence, concern for kid viewers. *APA Monitor, 24*(8), 16.

Eron, L. D., Huesmann, L. R., & Zelli, A. (1991). The role of parental variables in the learning of aggression. In D. J. Pepler & K. H. Rubin (Eds.), *The development and treatment of childhood aggression.* Hillsdale, NJ: Erlbaum.

Ertem, I. O., Leventhal, J. M., & Dobbs, S. (2000). Intergenerational continuity of child physical abuse: how good is the evidence? *Lancet, 356,* 814–819.

Escobar, G. J., Littenberg, B., & Petitti, D. B. (1991). Outcome among surviving very low birthweight infants: A meta-analysis. *Archives of Disease in Childhood, 66,* 204–211.

Espinosa, M. P., Sigman, M. D., Neumann, C. G., Bwibo, N. O., & McDonald, M. A. (1992). Playground behaviors of school-age children in relation to nutrition, schooling, and family characteristics. *Developmental Psychology, 28,* 1188–1195.

Etaugh, C. (1983). Introduction: The influence of environmental factors on sex differences in children's play. In M. B. Liss (Ed.), *Social and cognitive skills: Sex roles and children's play.* New York: Academic Press.

Etaugh, C., Levine, D., & Mennella, A. (1984). Development of sex biases in children: 40 years later. *Sex Roles, 10,* 911–922.

Etaugh, C., & Liss, M. B. (1992). Home, school, and playroom: Training grounds for adult gender roles. *Sex Roles, 26,* 129–147.

Ethics Committee of the American Society of Reproductive Medicine. (2000, June 7). Sex selection and preimplantation genetic diagnosis. *Webtrack.*

Evans, S. W., et al. (2001). Dose–response effects of methylphenidate on ecologically valid measures of academic performance and classroom behavior in adolescents with ADHD. *Experimental & Clinical Psychopharmacology, 9*(2), 163–175.

Eveleth, P. B., & Tanner, J. M. (1990). *Worldwide variation in human growth* (2nd ed.). Cambridge: Cambridge University Press.

Eyer, D. E. (1993). *Mother–infant bonding: A scientific fiction.* New Haven, CT: Yale University Press.

Fabes, R. A., Eisenberg, N., & Miller, P. A. (1990). Maternal correlates of children's vicarious emotional responsiveness. *Developmental Psychology, 26,* 639–648.

Fabricius, W. V., & Cavalier, L. (1989). The role of causal theories about memory in young children's memory strategy choice. *Child Development, 60,* 298–308.

Fagan, J. F., & Detterman, D. K. (1992). The Fagan test of infant intelligence: A technical summary. *Journal of Applied Developmental Psychology, 13,* 173–193.

Fagot, B. I. (1990). A longitudinal study of gender segregation: Infancy to preschool. In F. F. Strayer (Ed.), *Social interaction and behavioral development during early childhood.* Montreal: La Maison D'Ethologie de Montreal.

Fagot, B. I., & Hagan, R. (1991). Observations of parent reactions to sex-stereotyped behaviors: Age and sex effects. *Child Development, 62,* 617–628.

Fagot, B. I., & Kavanagh, K. (1993). Parenting during the second year: Effects of children's age, sex, and attachment classification. *Child Development, 64,* 258–271.

Fagot, B. I., & Leinbach, M. D. (1993). Gender-role development in young children: From discrimination to labeling. *Developmental Review, 13,* 205–224.

Fagot, B. I., Leinbach, M. D., & O'Boyle, M. D. (1992). Gender labeling, gender stereotyping, and parenting behaviors. *Developmental Psychology, 28,* 225–230.

Fagot, B. I., & Leve, L. D. (1998). Teacher ratings of externalizing behavior at school entry for boys and girls: Similar early predictors and different correlates. *Journal of Child Psychology & Psychiatry & Allied Disciplines, 39*(4), 555–566.

Fairburn, C. G., et al. (1998). Risk factors for binge eating disorder: A community-based, case-control study. *Archives of General Psychiatry, 55*(5), 425–432.

Famularo, R., Kinscherff, R., & Fenton, T. (1992). Parental substance abuse and the nature of child maltreatment. *Child Abuse and Neglect, 16,* 475–483.

Fantz, R. L. (1961). The origin of form perception. *Scientific American, 204,* 66–72.

Fantz, R. L., Fagan, J. F., III, & Miranda, S. B. (1975). Early visual selectivity. In L. B. Cohen & P. Salapatek (Eds.), *Infant perception: From sensation to cognition* (Vol. 1). New York: Academic Press.

Faraone, S. V., et al. (2000). Family study of girls with attention deficit hyperactivity disorder. *American Journal of Psychiatry, 157*(7), 1077–1083.

Farran, D. C. (1990). Effects of intervention with disadvantaged and disabled children: A decade review. In S. J. Meisels & J. P. Shonkoff (Eds.), *Handbook of early childhood intervention.* Cambridge: Cambridge University Press.

Farrant, K., & Reese, E. (2000). Maternal style and children's participation in reminiscing: Stepping stones in children's autobiographical memory development. *Journal of Cognition & Development, 1*(2), 193–225.

Farrar, M. J., & Goodman, G. S. (1990). Developmental differences in the relation between scripts and episodic memory: Do they exist? In R. Fivush & J. A. Hudson (Eds.), *Knowing and remembering in young children.* Cambridge: Cambridge University Press.

Farver, J. A. M., Kim, Y. K., & Lee-Shin, Y. (2000). Within cultural differences: Examining individual differences in Korean American and European American preschoolers' social pretend play. *Journal of Cross-Cultural Psychology, 31*(5), 583–602.

Fasko, D., Jr. (2001). An analysis of multiple intelligences theory and its use with the gifted and talented. *Roeper Review, 23*(3), 126–130.

Feagans, L. V., & Haldane, D. (1991). Adolescents with learning disabilities. In R. M. Lerner, A. C. Petersen, & J. Brooks-Gunn (Eds.), *Encyclopedia of adolescence.* New York: Garland.

Feinberg, M. E., Neiderhiser, J. M., Howe, G., & Hetherington, E. M. (2001). Adolescent, parent, and observer perceptions of parenting: Genetic and environmental influences on shared and distinct perceptions. *Child Development, 72*(4), 1266–1284.

Feinberg, M. E., Neiderhiser, J. M., Simmens, S., Reiss, D., & Hetherington, E. M. (2000). Sibling comparison of differential parental treatment in adolescence: Gender, self-esteem, and emotionality as mediators of the parenting–adjustment association. *Child Development, 71*(6), 1611–1628.

Feingold, A. (1993). Cognitive gender differences: A developmental perspective. *Sex Roles, 29,* 91–112.

Feingold, S. (1997). Cited in DeAngelis, T. (1997). There's new hope for women with postpartum blues. *APA Monitor, 28*(9), 22–23.

Feinman, S., & Lewis, M. (1983). Social referencing at 10 months: A second-order effect on infants' responses to strangers. *Child Development, 54,* 878–887.

Feiring, C. (1993, March). *Developing concepts of romance from 15 to 18 years.* Paper presented at the meeting of the Society for Research in Child Development, New Orleans, LA.

Feiring, C., & Lewis, M. (1991). The transition from middle to early adolescence: Sex differences in the social network and perceived self-competence. *Sex Roles, 24,* 489–509.

Feldhusen, J. F. (1989, March). Synthesis of research on gifted youth. *Educational Leadership,* pp. 6–11.

Feldman, N. S., Klosson, E. C., Parsons, J. E., Rholes, W. S., & Ruble, D. N. (1976). Order of information presentation and children's moral judgments. *Child Development, 47,* 556–559.

FEMA. (2001, September 12). FEMA offers advice on how to talk to children about terrorist attacks. Washington, D.C. **http://www.fema.gov/nwz01/nwz01_99.htm**

Female valedictorians stymied by multiple roles. (1988, Winter). *On Campus With Women, 17*(3), pp. 8–9.

Fennema, E. (1990). Teachers' beliefs and gender differences in mathematics. In E. Fennema & G. C. Leder (Eds.), *Mathematics and gender.* New York: Teachers College Press.

Fenzel, L. M. (2000). Prospective study of changes in global self-worth and strain during the transition to middle school. *Journal of Early Adolescence, 20*(1), 93–116.

Feola, T. W., de Wit, H., & Richards, J. B. (2000). Effects of *d*-amphetamine and alcohol on a measure of behavioral inhibition in rats. *Behavioral Neuroscience, 114*(4), 838–848.

Ferguson, K. J., Yesalis, C. E., Pomrehn, P. R., & Kirkpatrick, M. B. (1989). Attitudes, knowledge, and beliefs as predictions of exercise intent and behavior in schoolchildren. *Journal of School Health, 59,* 112–115.

Ferguson, T. J., & Rule, B. G. (1980). Effects of inferential sex, outcome severity, and basis of responsibility on children's evaluations of aggressive acts. *Developmental Psychology, 16,* 141–146.

Fernald, A. (1991). Prosody in speech to children: Prelinguistic and linguistic functions. In R. Vasta (Ed.), *Annals of child development* (Vol. 8). London: Kingsley.

Fernald, A. (1992). Meaningful melodies in mother's speech to infants. In H. Papousek, U. Jurgens, & M. Papousek (Eds.), *Nonverbal vocal communication: Comparative and developmental aspects.* Cambridge: Cambridge University Press.

Fernald, A., & Mazzie, C. (1991). Prosody and focus in speech to infants and adults. *Developmental Psychology, 27,* 209–221.

Fernald, A., & Morikawa, H. (1993). Common themes and cultural variations in Japanese and American mothers' speech to infants. *Child Development, 64,* 637–656.

Field, T. M. (1980). Interactions of high risk infants: Quantitative and qualitative differences. In D. B. Sawin, R. C. Hawkins, L. P. Walker, & J. H. Penticuff (Eds.), *Exceptional infant: Vol. 4. Psychosocial risks in infant environmental transactions.* New York: Brunner/Mazel.

Field, T. M. (1990). *Infancy: The developing child.* Cambridge, MA: Harvard University Press.

Field, T. M. (1991a). Adolescent mothers and their young children. In R. M. Lerner, A. C. Petersen, & J. Brooks-Gunn (Eds.), *Encyclopedia of adolescence.* New York: Garland.

Field, T. M. (1991b). Quality infant day-care and grade school behavior and performance. *Child Development, 62,* 863–870.

Field, T. M. (1991c). Young children's adaptations to repeated separations from their mothers. *Child Development, 62,* 539–547.

Field, T. M. (1992). Interventions in early infancy. *Infant Mental Health Journal, 13*(4), 329–336.

Field, T. M., et al. (1992). Behavior state matching during interactions of preadolescent friends versus acquaintances. *Developmental Psychology, 28,* 242–250.

Field, T. M., Gewirtz, J. L., Cohen, D., Garcia, R., Greenberg, R., & Collins, K. (1984). Leave-takings and reunions of infants, toddlers, preschoolers, and their parents. *Child Development, 55,* 628–635.

Fielder, A. R., Dobson, V., Mazel, M. J., & Mayer, D. L. (1992). Preferential looking—clinical lessons. *Ophthalmic Paediatrics and Genetics, 13,* 101–110.

Fiellin, D. A., et al. (2001). Methadone maintenance in primary care: A randomized controlled trial. *Journal of the American Medical Association, 286*(14), 1724–1731.

Finch, A. J., & McIntosh, J. A. (1990). Assessment of anxieties and fears in children. In A. LaGreca (Ed.), *Through the eyes of a child.* Boston: Allyn & Bacon.

Finch, B. K., Vega, W. A., & Kolody, B. (2001). Substance use during pregnancy in the state of California, USA. *Social Science & Medicine, 52*(4), 571–583.

Fine, G., Mortimer, J., & Roberts, D. (1990). Leisure, work, and mass media. In S. Feldman & G. Elliot (Eds.), *At the threshold: The developing adolescent.* Cambridge, MA: Harvard University Press.

Finegan, J. K., Niccols, G. A., & Sitarenios, G. (1992). Relations between prenatal testosterone levels and cognitive abilities at 4 years. *Developmental Psychology, 28,* 1075–1089.

Finkelhor, D., & Dziuba-Leatherman, J. (1994). Victimization of children. *American Psychologist, 49,* 173–183.

Finn, J. D., & Achilles, C. M. (1990). Answers and questions about class size: A statewide experience. *American Educational Research Journal, 27,* 557–577.

Finn, P. R., Sharkansky, E. J., Brandt, K. M., & Turcotte, N. (2000). The effects of familial risk, personality, and expectancies on alcohol use and abuse. *Journal of Abnormal Psychology, 109*(1), 122–133.

Fisch, S., Truglio, R. T., & Cole, C. F. (1999). The impact of *Sesame Street* on preschool children: A review and synthesis of 30 years' research. *Media Psychology, 1*(2), 165–190.

Fisher, E. P. (1992). The impact of play on development: A meta-analysis. *Play and Culture, 5,* 159–181.

Fitzgerald, H. E., & Brackbill, Y. (1976). Classical conditioning in infancy: Development and constraints. *Psychological Bulletin, 83,* 353–376.

Fitzgerald, H. E., et al. (1991). The organization of lateralized behavior during infancy. In H. E. Fitzgerald, B. M. Lester, & M. W. Yogman (Eds.), *Theory and research in behavioral pediatrics.* New York: Plenum.

Fivush, R. (1993). Emotional content of parent–child conversations about the past. In C. A. Nelson (Ed.), *Minnesota symposia on child psychology: Vol. 26. Memory and affect in development.* Hillsdale, NJ: Erlbaum.

Fivush, R., & Hammond, N. R. (1990). Autobiographical memory across the preschool years: Toward reconceptualizing childhood amnesia. In R. Fivush & J. A. Hudson (Eds.), *Knowing and remembering in young children.* Cambridge: Cambridge University Press.

Fivush, R., Kuebli, J., & Clubb, P. A. (1992). The structure of events and event representations: A developmental analysis. *Child Development, 63,* 188–201.

Flanagan, C. A., & Eccles, J. S. (1993). Changes in parents' work status and adolescents' adjustment at school. *Child Development, 64,* 246–257.

Flavell, J. H. (1993). Young children's understanding of thinking and consciousness. *Current Directions in Psychological Science, 2,* 40–43.

Flavell, J. H., Flavell, E. R., Green, F. L., & Moses, L. J. (1990). Young children's understanding of fact beliefs versus value beliefs. *Child Development, 61,* 915–928.

Flavell, J. H., Green, F. L., & Flavell, E. R. (1993). Children's understanding of the stream of consciousness. *Child Development, 64,* 387–398.

Flavell, J. H., Green, F. L., & Flavell, E. R. (2000). Development of children's awareness of their own thoughts. *Journal of Cognition & Development, 1*(1), 97–112.

Flavell, J. H., Miller, P. H., & Miller, S. A. (2002). *Cognitive development* (4th ed.). Upper Saddle River, NJ: Prentice-Hall.

Fleming, A. S. (1989, Spring). Maternal responsiveness in human and animal mothers. In M. H. Bornstein (Ed.), *New directions for child development: No. 43. Maternal responsiveness: Characteristics and consequences.* San Francisco: Jossey-Bass.

Food and Drug Administration. (1997, September 11). Thalidomide: Important patient information. DHHS Publication No.(FDA) 96-3222. **http://www.fda.gov/cder/news/thalidomide.htm**

Ford, K., Wirawan, D. N., Reed, B. D., Muliawan, P., & Sutarga, M. (2000). AIDS and STD knowledge, condom use, and HIV/STD infection among female sex workers in Bali, Indonesia. *AIDS Care, 12*(5), 523–534.

Forehand, R., et al. (1991). The role of family stressors and parent relationships on adolescent functioning. *Journal of the American Academy of Child and Adolescent Psychiatry, 30,* 316–322.

Forrest, J. D. (1990). Cultural influences on adolescents' reproductive behavior. In J. Bancroft & J. M. Reinisch (Eds.), *Adolescence and puberty.* New York: Oxford.

Fortier, J. C., Carson, V. B., Will, S., & Shubkagel, B. L. (1991). Adjustment to a newborn: Sibling preparation makes a difference. *Journal of Obstetric, Gynecologic, and Neonatal Nursing, 20,* 73–79.

Foster, H. W., et al. (2000). Intergenerational effects of high socioeconomic status on low birthweight and preterm birth in African Americans. *Journal of the National Medical Association, 92*(5), 213–221.

Foster-Clark, F. S., & Blyth, D. A. (1991). Peer relations and influences. In R. M. Lerner, A. C. Petersen, & J. Brooks-Gunn (Eds.), *Encyclopedia of adolescence.* New York: Garland.

Fowler, W., Ogston, K., Roberts-Fiati, G., & Swenson, A. (1993, February). *The long term development of giftedness and high competencies in children enriched in language during infancy.* Paper presented at the Esther Katz Rosen Symposium on the Psychological Development of Gifted Children, University of Kansas.

Fox, L. H. (1982). *Sex differences among the mathematically gifted.* Paper presented at the meeting of the American Association for the Advancement of Science, Washington, DC.

Fox, L. H., Brody, L., & Tobin, D. (1985). The impact of early intervention programs upon course-taking and attitudes in high school. In S. F. Chipman, L. R. Brush, & D. M. Wilson (Eds.), *Women and mathematics: Balancing the equation.* London: Erlbaum.

Fox, N. A. (1991). If it's not left, it's right. *American Psychologist, 46,* 863–872.

Fox, N. A. (1992). The role of temperament in attachment in normal and high-risk infants. In C. W. Greenbaum & J. G. Auerbach (Eds.), *Longitudinal studies of children at psychological risk: Cross-national perspectives.* Norwood, NJ: Ablex.

Fox, N. A., Kimmerly, N. L., & Schafer, W. D. (1991). Attachment to mother/attachment to father: A meta-analysis. *Child Development, 62,* 210–225.

Fox, R. (1991). Developing awareness of mind reflected in children's narrative writing. *British Journal of Developmental Psychology, 9,* 281–298.

Foxx, R. M., & Azrin, N. H. (1973). *Toilet training the retarded: A rapid program for day and night time independent toileting.* Champaign, IL: Research Press.

Frank, D. A., Augustyn, M., Knight, W. G., Pell, T., Zuckerman, B. (2001). Growth, development, and behavior in early childhood following prenatal cocaine exposure: A systematic review. *Journal of the American Medical Association, 285*(12), 1613–1625.

Frank, R. G., Bouman, D. E., Cain, K., & Watts, C. (1992). Primary prevention of catastrophic injury. *American Psychologist, 47,* 1045–1049.

Frankel, K. A., & Bates, J. E. (1990). Mother-toddler problem solving: Antecedents in attachment, home behavior, and temperament. *Child Development, 61,* 810–819.

Frankenburg, W. K., Dodds, J., Archer, P., Shapiro, H., & Bresnick, B. (1992). The Denver II: A major revision and restandardization of the Denver Developmental Screening Test. *Pediatrics, 89,* 91–97.

Frankova, S., & Chudobova, P. (2000). Development of body image in preschool girls. *Homeostasis in Health & Disease, 40*(5), 161–169.

Fraser, A. M., Brockert, J. E., & Ward, R. H. (1995). Association of young maternal age with adverse reproductive outcomes. *New England Journal of Medicine, 332,* 1113–1117.

Freeman, M. S., Spence, M. J., and Oliphant, C. M. (1993, June). *Newborns prefer their mothers' low-pass filtered voices over other female filtered voices.* Paper presented at the meeting of the American Psychological Society, Chicago.

Freeman, N. H., Lewis, C., & Doherty, M. J. (1991). Preschoolers' grasp of a desire for knowledge in false-belief prediction: Practical intelligence and verbal report. *British Journal of Developmental Psychology, 9,* 139–157.

Freiberg, P. (1991a, January). Bills aiding children passed by Congress. *APA Monitor,* p. 22.

Freiberg, P. (1991b, June). Teens' long work hours detrimental, study says. *APA Monitor,* pp. 19–20.

Freiberg, P. (1991c, June). More long-term problems seen for abused kids. *APA Monitor,* pp. 18–19.

French, D. C., Rianasari, M., Pidada, S., Nelwan, P., & Buhrmester, D. (2001). Social support of Indonesian and U.S. children and adolescents by family members and friends. *Merrill-Palmer Quarterly, 47*(3), 377–394.

Freud, A. (1969). Adolescence as a developmental disturbance. In G. Kaplan & S. Leborici (Eds.), *Adolescence: Psychosocial perspectives.* New York: Basic Books.

Freud, S. (1964). New introductory lectures. In *Standard edition of the complete psychological works of Sigmund Freud* (Vol. 22). London: Hogarth. (Original work published 1933).

Freund, C. S. (1990). Maternal regulation of children's problem-solving behavior and its impact on children's performance. *Child Development, 61,* 113–126.

Frey, K. S., & Ruble, D. N. (1992). Gender constancy and the "cost" of sex-typed behavior: A test of the conflict hypothesis. *Developmental Psychology, 28,* 714–721.

Frick, P. J., et al. (1991). Oppositional defiant disorder and conduct disorder in boys: Patterns of behavioral covariation. *Journal of Clinical Child Psychology, 20,* 202–208.

Fried, P. A., O'Connell, C. M., & Watkinson, B. (1992, December). 60- and 72-month follow-up of children prenatally exposed to marijuana, cigarettes, and alcohol: Cognitive and language assessment. *Journal of Developmental and Behavioral Pediatrics, 13,* 383–391.

Fried, P. A., & Smith, A. M. (2001) A literature review of the consequences of prenatal marihuana exposure: An emerging theme of a deficiency in aspects of executive function. *Neurotoxicology & Teratology, 23*(1), 1–11.

Friedman, R. C., & Downey, J. I. (1994). Homosexuality. *New England Journal of Medicine, 331,* 923–930.

Friedman, S. R., et al. (2001). Correlates of anal sex with men among young adult women in an inner city minority neighborhood. *AIDS, 15*(15), 2057–2060.

Frisch, R. E. (1991). Puberty and body fat. In R. M. Lerner, A. C. Petersen, & J. Brooks-Gunn (Eds.), *Encyclopedia of adolescence.* New York: Garland.

Frisch, R. (1997). Cited in Angier, N. (1997). Chemical tied to fat control could help trigger puberty. *The New York Times,* pp. C1, C3.

Fritz, J., & Wetherbee, S. (1982). Preschoolers' beliefs regarding the obese individual. *Canadian Home Economics Journal, 33,* 193–196.

Frodi, A. M. (1985). When empathy fails: Infant crying and child abuse. In B. M. Lester & C. F. Z. Boukydis (Eds.), *Infant crying.* New York: Plenum.

Frodi, A., & Senchak, M. (1990). Verbal and behavioral responsiveness to the cries of atypical infants. *Child Development, 61,* 76–84.

Fromberg, D. (1990). Play issues in early childhood education. In C. Seefeldt (Ed.), *Continuing issues in early childhood education.* Columbus, OH: Merrill.

Fugger, E. F., et al. (1998, September 9). *Human Reproduction.* Cited in Kolata, G. (1998, September 9). Researchers report success in method to pick baby's sex. *The New York Times* online.

Fuligni, A. J., & Eccles, J. S. (1993). Perceived parent–child relationships and early adolescents' orientation toward peers. *Developmental Psychology, 29,* 622–632.

Funk, J. B., Buchman, D., Myers, M., Jenks, J. (2000, August 7). Asking the right question in research on violent electronic games. Paper presented to the annual meeting of the American Psychological Association, Washington, D.C.

Furman, W., & Buhrmester, D. (1992). Age and sex differences in perceptions of networks of personal relationships. *Child Development, 63,* 103–115.

Furman, W., Rahe, D., & Hartup, W. W. (1979). Social rehabilitation of low-interactive preschool children by peer intervention. *Child Development, 50,* 915–922.

Furnham, A., & Cheng, H. (2000). Perceived parental behaviour, self-esteem, and happiness. *Social Psychiatry & Psychiatric Epidemiology, 35*(10), 463–470.

Furstenberg, F. F., Jr., & Cherlin, A. J. (1991). *Divided families: What happens to children when parents part?* Cambridge, MA: Harvard University Press.

Furstenberg, F. F., Hughes, M. E., & Brooks-Gunn, J. (1992). The next generation: The children of teenage mothers grow up. In M. K. Rosenheim & M. F. Testa (Eds.), *Early parenthood and coming of age in the 1990s.* New Brunswick, NJ: Rutgers University Press.

Furstenberg, F. F., & Kiernan, K. E. (2001). Delayed parental divorce: How much do children benefit? *Journal of Marriage & the Family, 63*(2), 446–457.

Fylkesnes, K., et al. (2001). Declining HIV prevalence and risk behaviours in Zambia: Evidence from surveillance and population-based surveys. *AIDS, 15*(7), 907–916.

Gagnon, C., Tremblay, R. E., Craig, W., & Zhou, R. M. (1993, March). *Kindergarten predictors of boys' stable disruptive behavior at the end of elementary school.* Paper presented at the meeting of the Society for Research in Child Development, New Orleans, LA.

Galambos, N. L. (1992). Parent–adolescent relations. *Current Directions in Psychological Science, 1,* 146–149.

Galambos, N. L., & Almeida, D. M. (1992). Does parent–adolescent conflict increase in early adolescence? *Journal of Marriage and the Family, 54,* 737–747.

Galler, J. A. (1989). A follow-up study of the influence of early malnutrition on development: Behavior at home and at school. *Journal of the American Academy of Child and Adolescent Psychiatry, 28,* 254–261.

Galler, J. R., Ramsey, F. C., Morley, D. S., Archer, E., & Salt, P. (1990). The long-term effects of early kwashiorkor compared with marasmus IV. Performance on the national high school entrance examination. *Pediatric Research, 28,* 235–239.

Galotti, K. M., Kozberg, S. F., & Farmer, M. C. (1991). Gender and developmental differences in adolescents' conception of moral reasoning. *Journal of Youth and Adolescence, 20,* 13–30.

Gan, L. (1998). Left-handed children in Singapore. *Early Child Development & Care, 144,* 113–117.

Ganchrow, J. R., Steiner, J. E., & Daher, M. (1983). Neonatal facial expressions in response to different qualities and intensities of gustatory stimuli. *Infant Behavior and Development, 6,* 189–200.

Gao, F., Levine, S. C., & Huttenlocher, J. (2000). What do infants know about continuous quantity? *Journal of Experimental Child Psychology, 77*(1), 20–29.

Garbarino, J. (1982). *Children and families in the social environment.* New York: Aldine deGruyter.

Garbarino, J. (1992). *Children in danger: Coping with the consequences of community violence.* San Francisco: Jossey-Bass.

Garbarino, J. (2001). An ecological perspective on the effects of violence on children. *Journal of Community Psychology, 29*(3), 361–378.

Garbarino, J., Dubrow, N., & Kostelny, K. (1991). *No place to be a child: Growing up in a war zone.* Lexington, MA: Lexington Books.

Garber, H. L. (1988). *The Milwaukee Project: Preventing mental retardation in children at risk.* Washington, DC: American Association on Mental Retardation.

Garcia-Coll, C. T. (1990). Developmental outcome of minority infants: A process-oriented look into our beginnings. *Child Development, 61,* 270–289.

Garcia-Coll, C. T., Halpern, L. F., Vohr, B. R., Seifer, R., & Oh, W. (1992). Stability and correlates of change of early temperament in preterm and full-term infants. *Infant Behavior and Development, 15,* 137–153.

Garcia-Moreno, C., & Watts, C. (2000). Violence against women: Its importance for HIV/AIDS. *AIDS, 14*(Suppl3), S253–S265.

Gardner, H. (1982). *Art, mind, and brain: A cognitive approach to creativity.* New York: Basic Books.

Gardner, H. (1983). *Frames of mind: The theory of multiple intelligences.* New York: Basic Books.

Gardner, H. (1993). *Multiple intelligences.* New York: Basic Books.

Gardner, H. (1996). Cited in Murray, B. (1996). Students stretch beyond the "three Rs." *APA Monitor, 26*(4), 46.

Gardner, H. (2001, April 5). Multiple intelligence. *The New York Times,* p. A20.

Gardner, J. M. M., Grantham-McGregor, S. M., Chang, S. M., Himes, J. H., & Powell, C. A. (1995). Activity and behavioral development in stunted and nonstunted children and response to nutritional supplementation. *Child Development, 66*(6), 1785–1797.

Garling, A., & Garling, T. (1993). Mothers' supervision and perception of young children's risk of unintentional injury in the home. *Journal of Pediatric Psychology, 18,* 105–114.

Garnefski, N., Kraaij, V., & Spinhoven, P. (2001). De relatie tussen cognitieve copingstrategieen en symptomen van depressie, angst en suiecidaliteit. *Gedrag & Gezondheid: Tijdschrift voor Psychologie & Gezondheid, 29*(3), 148–158.

Garner, P. W., & Landry, S. H. (1992). Preterm infants' affective responses in independent versus toy-centered play with their mothers. *Infant Mental Health Journal, 13,* 219–230.

Garrod, A., Beal, C., & Shin, P. (1991). The development of moral orientation in elementary school children. *Sex Roles, 22,* 13–27.

Garvey, C. (1990). *Developing child.* Cambridge, MA: Harvard University Press.

Gathercole, S. E. (1998). The development of memory. *Journal of Child Psychology & Psychiatry & Allied Disciplines, 39*(1), 3–27.

Gauthier, A. H. (1999). Historical trends in state support for families in Europe (post-1945). *Children & Youth Services Review, 21*(11–12), 937–965.

Gazzaniga, M. S. (1995). Consciousness and the cerebral hemispheres. In M. S. Gazzaniga (Ed.), *The cognitive neurosciences.* Cambridge, MA: MIT Press.

Ge, X., Conger, R. D., & Elder, Jr., G. H. (1996). Coming of age too early: Pubertal influences on girls' vulnerability to psychological distress. *Child Development, 67,* 3386–3400.

Ge, X., Conger, R. D., & Elder, G. H., Jr. (2001a). The relation between puberty and psychological distress in adolescent boys. *Journal of Research on Adolescence, 11*(1), 49–70.

Ge, X., Conger, R. D., & Elder, G. H., Jr. (2001b). Pubertal transition, stressful life events, and the emergence of gender differences in adolescent depressive symptoms. *Developmental Psychology, 37*(3), 404–417.

Ge, X., Donnellan, M. B., & Wenk, E. (2001). The development of persistent criminal offending in males. *Criminal Justice & Behavior, 26*(5), 731–755.

Geiser, F., et al. (2001). Magnetic resonance spectroscopic and relaxometric determination of bone marrow changes in anorexia nervosa. *Psychosomatic Medicine, 63*(4), 631–647.

Gelinas, I., et al. (2000). Etude des liens entre le risque d'abandon scolaire, les strategies d'adaptation, le rendement scolaire et les habiletes scolaires. *Revue Canadienne de Psycho-Education, 29*(2), 223–240.

Gelman, R. (1978). Cognitive development. *Annual Review of Psychology, 29,* 297–332.

Gelman, R., & Baillargeon, R. (1983). A review of some Piagetian concepts. In P. H. Mussen (Ed.), *Handbook of child psychology: Vol. 3. Cognitive development.* New York: Wiley.

Gelman, S. A., & Kremer, K. E. (1991). Understanding natural cause: Children's explanations of how objects and their properties originate. *Child Development, 62,* 396–414.

Gendall, K. A., Bulik, C. M., Joyce, P. R., McIntosh, V. V., & Carter, F. A. (2000). Menstrual cycle irregularity in bulimia nervosa: Associated factors and changes with treatment. *Journal of Psychosomatic Research, 49*(6), 409–415.

Georgiades, A., et al. (2000). Effects of exercise and weight loss on mental stress-induced cardiovascular responses in individuals with high blood pressure. *Hypertension, 36,* 171–176.

Gerbner, G. (1993). *Violence in cable-originated television programs: A report to the National Cable Television Association.* University Park: University of Pennsylvania, Annenberg School for Communication.

Gerstner, L. V., Jr. (1994, May 27). Our schools are failing. Do we care? *The New York Times,* p. A27.

Geschwind, D. H. (2000) Cited in Rosenbaum, D. E. (2000, May 16). On left-handedness, its causes and costs. *The New York Times,* pp. F1, F6.

Geschwind, N., & Galaburda, A. M. (1987). *Cerebral lateralization: Biological mechanisms, associations, and pathology.* Cambridge, MA: MIT Press.

Gesell, A. (1928). *Infancy and human growth.* New York: Macmillan.

Gesell, A. (1929). Maturation and infant behavior patterns. *Psychological Review, 36,* 307–319.

Gesell, A. (1972). *The embryology of behavior.* Westport, CT: Greenwood. Getzels, J. W., & Jackson, P. W. (1962). *Creativity and intelligence.* New York: Wiley.

Getzels, J. W., & Jackson, P. W. (1962). *Creativity and intelligence.* New York: Wiley.

Gewirtz, J. L., & Pelaez-Nogueras, M. (1992). B. F. Skinner's legacy to human infant behavior and development. *American Psychologist, 47,* 1411–1422.

Gibbs, J. T. (1991). Toward an integration of Kohlberg's and Hoffman's theories of morality. In W. M. Kurtines & J. L. Gewirtz (Eds.), *Handbook of moral behavior and development* (Vol. 1). Hillsdale, NJ: Erlbaum.

Gibbs, J. T., & Hines, A. M. (1992). Negotiating ethnic identity: Issues for black–white biracial adolescents. In M. P. P. Root (Ed.), *Racially mixed people in America.* Newbury Park, CA: Sage.

Gibran, K. (1970). *The prophet.* New York: Knopf.

Gibson, E. J. (1969). *Principles of perceptual learning and development.* New York: Appleton-Century-Crofts.

Gibson, E. J. (1991). *An odyssey in learning and perception.* Cambridge, MA: MIT Press.

Gibson, E. J., & Walk, R. D. (1960). The visual cliff. *Scientific American, 202,* 64–71.

Gil, K. M., et al. (2001). Daily coping practice predicts treatment effects in children with sickle cell disease. *Journal of Pediatric Psychology, 26*(3), 163–173.

Gili-Planas, M., Roca-Bennasar, M., Ferrer-Perez, V., & Bernardo-Arroyo, M. (2001). Suicidal ideation, psychiatric disorder, and medical illness in a community epidemiological study. *Suicide & Life-Threatening Behavior, 31*(2), 207–213.

Gilligan, C. (1977). In a different voice: Women's conceptions of self and morality. *Harvard Educational Review, 47,* 481–517.

Gilligan, C. (1982). *In a different voice.* Cambridge, MA: Harvard University Press.

Gilligan, C., & Attanucci, J. (1988). Two moral orientations: Gender differences and similarities. *Merrill-Palmer Quarterly, 34,* 223–237.

Gilligan, C., Lyons, P., & Hanmer, T. J. (Eds.). (1990). *Making connections: The relational worlds of adolescent girls at Emma Willard School.* Cambridge, MA: Harvard University Press.

Gillio, R. G. (1999). Bitter pills: Inside the hazardous world of legal drugs. *Journal of the American Medical Association, 281,* 469.

Ginsberg, E. (1972). Toward a theory of occupational choice: A restatement. *Vocational Guidance Quarterly, 20,* 169–176.

Glasberg, R., & Aboud, F. (1982). Keeping one's distance from sadness: Children's self-reports of emotional experience. *Developmental Psychology, 18,* 287–293.

Glater, J. D. (2001, March 16). Women are close to being majority of law students. *The New York Times,* pp. A1, A16.

Gleason, T., Sebanc, A., & Hartup, W. W. (2000). Imaginary companions of preschool children. *Developmental Psychology, 36*(4), 419–428.

Glik, D. C., Greaves, P. E., Kronenfeld, J. J., & Jackson, K. L. (1993). Safety hazards in households with young children. *Journal of Pediatric Psychology, 18,* 115–131.

Glynn, J. R., et al. (2001). Why do young women have a much higher prevalence of HIV than young men? A study of Kisumu, Kenya, and Ndola Zambia. *AIDS, 15*(Suppl4), S51–S60.

Gobet, F., & Simon, H. A. (2000). Five seconds or sixty? Presentation time in expert memory. *Cognitive Science, 24*(4), 651–682.

Goetz, M. J., Johnstone, E. C., & Ratcliffe, S. G. (1999). Criminality and antisocial behaviour in unselected men with sex chromosomes abnormalities. *Psychological Medicine, 29*(4), 953–962.

Gogate, L. J., Bahrick, L. E., & Watson, J. D. (2000). A study of multimodal motherese: The role of temporal synchrony between verbal labels and gestures. *Child Development, 71*(4), 878–894.

Goldberg, S. (1983). Parent–infant bonding: Another look. *Child Development, 54,* 1355–1382.

Goldfield, B. A., & Reznick, J. S. (1990). Early lexical acquisition: Rate, content and the vocabulary spurt. *Journal of Child Language, 17,* 171–183.

Goldfried, M. R. (2001). Integrating gay, lesbian, and bisexual issues into mainstream psychology. *American Psychologist, 56*(11), 977–988.

Goldschmidt, L., Day, N. L., & Richardson, G. A. (2000). Effects of prenatal marijuana exposure on child behavior problems at age 10. *Neurotoxicology & Teratology, 22*(3), 325–336.

Goldson, E. (1992). The longitudinal study of very low birthweight infants and its implications for interdisciplinary research and public policy. In C. W. Greenbaum & J. G. Auerbach (Eds.), *Longitudinal studies of children at psychological risk: Cross-national perspectives.* Norwood, NJ: Ablex.

Goleman, D. (1991, July 30). Theory links early puberty to childhood stress. *The New York Times,* pp. B5, 6.

Goleman, D. (1992a, September 15). New storm brews on whether crime has roots in genes. *The New York Times,* pp. B5, B8.

Goleman, D. (1992b, December 6). Attending to the children of all the world's war zones. *The New York Times,* p. E7.

Goleman, D. (1993, July 13). New treatments for autism arouse hope and skepticism. *The New York Times,* pp. B5, 7.

Goleman, D. J. (1995). *Emotional intelligence.* New York: Bantam Books.

Golinkoff, R., Hirsh-Pasek, K., Bailey, L., & Wenger, N. (1992). Young children and adults use lexical principles to learn new nouns. *Developmental Psychology, 28,* 99–108.

Golub, S. (1992). *Periods: From menarche to menopause.* Newbury Park, CA: Sage.

Goode, E. (2000, June 25). Thinner: The male battle with anorexia. *The New York Times,* p. MH8.

Goodman, G. S., & Clarke-Stewart, A. (1991). Suggestibility in children's testimony: Implications for sexual abuse investigations. In J. Doris (Ed.), *The suggestibility of children's recollections.* Washington, DC: American Psychological Association.

Goodman, G. S., Hirschman, J. E., Hepps, D., & Rudy, L. (1991). Children's memory for stressful events. *Merrill-Palmer Quarterly, 37,* 109–157.

Goodman, G. S., Rudy, L., Bottoms, B. L., & Aman, C. (1990). Children's concerns and memory: Issues of ecological validity in the study of children's eyewitness testimony. In R. Fivush & J. A. Hudson (Eds.), *Knowing and remembering in young children.* Cambridge: Cambridge University Press.

Goodsitt, J. V., Morse, P. A., Ver Hoeve, J. N., & Cowan, N. (1984). Infant speech recognition in multisyllabic contexts. *Child Development, 55,* 903–910.

Gopnik, A., & Choi, S. (1990). Do linguistic differences lead to cognitive differences? A cross-linguistic study of semantic and cognitive development. *First Language, 10,* 199–215.

Gopnik, A., & Meltzoff, A. N. (1987). The development of categorization in the second year and its relation to other cognitive and linguistic developments. *Child Development, 58,* 1523–1531.

Gopnik, A., & Meltzoff, A. N. (1992). Categorization and naming: Basic-level sorting in eighteen-month-olds and its relation to language. *Child Development, 63,* 1091–1103.

Gopnik, A., & Slaughter, V. (1991). Young children's understanding of changes in their mental states. *Child Development, 62,* 98–110.

Gordon, D. E. (1990). Formal operational thinking: The role of cognitive-developmental processes in adolescent decision-making about pregnancy and contraception. *American Journal of Orthopsychiatry, 60,* 346–356.

Gormally, S., et al. (2001). Contact and nutrient caregiving effects on newborn infant pain responses. *Developmental Medicine & Child Neurology, 43*(1), 28–38.

Gottfried, A. E., Bathurst, K., & Gottfried, A. W. (1994). Role of maternal and dual-earner employment in children's development: A longitudinal study. In A. E. Gottfried & A. W. Gottfried (Eds.), *Redefining families: Implications for children's development.* New York: Plenum.

Gottlieb, G. (1991). The experimental canalization of behavioral development: Theory. *Developmental Psychology, 27,* 4–13.

Gottlieb, L. N., & Mendelson, M. J. (1990). Parental support and firstborn girls' adaptation to the birth of a sibling. *Journal of Applied Developmental Psychology, 11,* 29–48.

Granot, D., & Mayseless, O. (2001). Attachment security and adjustment to school in middle childhood. *International Journal of Behavioral Development, 25*(6), 530–541.

Granrud, C. E. (1987). Size constancy in newborn human infants. *Investigative Ophthalmology and Visual Science, 28*(Suppl.), 5.

Grant, J. P. (1994). *The state of the world's children.* New York: UNICEF and Oxford University Press.

Gray, N., & Nye. P. S. (2001). American Indian and Alaska Native substance abuse: Co-morbidity and cultural issues. *American Indian & Alaska Native Mental Health Research, 10*(2) 67–84.

Grazioli, R., & Terry, D. J. (2000). The role of cognitive vulnerability and stress in the prediction of postpartum depressive symptomatology. *British Journal of Clinical Psychology, 39*(4), 329–347.

Greco, C., Rovee-Collier, C., Hayne, H., Griesler, P., & Early, L. (1986). Ontogeny of early event memory: II. Encoding and retrieval by 2-and 3-month-olds. *Infant Behavior and Development, 9,* 461–472.

Green, J. A., Gustafson, G. E., & McGhie, A. C. (1998). Changes in infants' cries as a function of time in a cry bout. *Child Development, 69*(2), 271–279.

Green, J. A., Jones, L. E., & Gustafson, G.E. (1987). Perception of cries by parents and nonparents: Relation to cry acoustics. *Developmental Psychology, 23,* 370–382.

Green, W. H. (1991). Principles of psychopharmacotherapy and specific drug treatments. In M. Lewis (Ed.), *Child and adolescent psychiatry: A comprehensive textbook.* Baltimore: Williams & Wilkins.

Greenberg, J., & Kuczaj, S. A., II. (1982). Towards a theory of substantive word-meaning acquisition. In S. A. Kuczaj, II (Ed.), *Language development: Vol. 1. Syntax and semantics.* Hillsdale, NJ: Erlbaum.

Greene, A. L., & Grimsley, M. D. (1990). Age and gender differences in adolescents' preferences for parental advice: Mum's the word. *Journal of Adolescent Research, 5,* 396–413.

Greene, R. W., & Ablon, J. S. (2001). What does the MTA study tell us about effective psychosocial treatment for ADHD? *Journal of Clinical Child Psychology, 30*(1), 114–121.

Greenfield, P. M., & Cocking, R. R. (Eds.). (1994). *Cross-cultural roots of minority children development.* Hillsdale, NJ: Erlbaum.

Greeno, C. G., & Wing, R. R. (1994). Stress-induced eating. *Psychological Bulletin, 115,* 444–464.

Greenough, B. S. (1993, April 5). Breaking the genetic code. *Newsweek,* pp. 10–11.

Greenough, W. T. (1991). Experience as a component of normal development: Evolutionary considerations. *Developmental Psychology, 27,* 14–17.

Greenough, W. T., Black, J. E., & Wallace, C. S. (1987). Experience and brain development. *Child Development, 58,* 539–559.

Greenwood, C. R., et al. (1992). Out of the laboratory and into the community. *American Psychologist, 47,* 1464–1474.

Grella, C. E., Hser, Y-I., Joshi, V., & Rounds-Bryant, J. (2001). Drug treatment outcomes for adolescents with comorbid mental and substance use disorders. *Journal of Nervous & Mental Disease, 189*(6), 384–392.

Griffin, C. (2001). Imagining new narratives of youth: Youth research, the "new Europe" and global youth culture. *Childhood: A Global Journal of Child Research, 8*(2), 147–166.

Griffin, K. W., Scheier, L. M., Botvin, G. J., Diaz, T. (2001). Protective role of personal competence skills in adolescent substance use: Psychological well-being as a mediating factor. *Psychology of Addictive Behaviors, 15*(3), 194–203.

Grimshaw, G. M., Bryden, M. P., & Finegan, J. K. (1995). Relations between prenatal testosterone and cerebral lateralization in children. *Neuropsychology, 9*(1), 68–79.

Grodin, M. A., & Laurie, G. T. (2000). Susceptibility genes and neurological disorders: Learning the right lessons from the Human Genome Project. *Archives of Neurology, 57*(11), 1569–1574.

Grön, G., Wunderlich, A. P., Spitzer, M., Tomczak, R. & Riepe, M. W. (2000). Brain activation during human navigation: Gender-different neural networks as substrate of performance. *Nature Neuroscience, 3*(4), 404–408.

Gross, A. L., & Ballif, B. (1991). Children's understanding of emotion from facial expressions and situations: A review. *Developmental Review, 11,* 368–398.

Grossmann, K., & Grossmann, K. E. (1991). Newborn behavior, the quality of early parenting, and later toddler–parent relationships in a group of German infants. In J. K. Nugent, B. M. Lester, & T. B. Brazelton (Eds.), *The cultural context of infancy* (Vol. 2). Norwood, NJ: Ablex.

Groves, B. M., Zuckerman, B., Marans, S., & Cohen, D. J. (1993, January 13). Silent victims: Children who witness violence. *Journal of the American Medical Association, 269,* 262–264.

Grusec, J. E. (1991). Socializing concern for others in the home. *Developmental Psychology, 27,* 338–342.

Grusec, J. E. (1992). Social learning theory and developmental psychology: The legacies of Robert Sears and Albert Bandura. *Developmental Psychology, 28,* 776–786.

Grusec, J. E., Goodnow, J. J., & Kuczynski, L. (2000). New directions in analyses of parenting contributions to children's acquisition of values. *Child Development, 71*(1), 205–211.

Grusec, J. E., & Lytton, H. (1988). *Social development: History, theory and research.* New York: Springer-Verlag.

Gruson, L. (1993, February 16). A mother's gift: Bearing her grandchild. *The New York Times,* pp. B1, 4.

Grych, J. H., Fincham, F. D., Jouriles, E. N., & McDonald, R. (2000). Interparental conflict and child adjustment: Testing the mediational role of appraisals in the cognitive-contextual framework. *Child Development, 71*(6), 1648–1661.

Guelseren, L. (1999). Dogum sonrasi depresyon: Bir goezden gecirme. *Turk Psikiyatri Dergisi, 10*(1), 58–67.

Guerin, D. W., Gottfried, A. W., & Thomas, C. W. (1997). Difficult temperament and behaviour problems: A longitudinal study from 1.5 to 12 years. *International Journal of Behavioral Development, 21*(1), 71–90.

Guerra, A. L., & Braungart-Rieker, J. M. (1999). Predicting career indecision in college students: The roles of identity formation and parental relationship factors. *Career Development Quarterly, 47*(3), 255–266.

Guerra, N. G., & Slaby, R. G. (1990). Cognitive mediators of aggression in adolescent offenders: Intervention. *Developmental Psychology, 26,* 269–277.

Guilford, J. P. (1959). Traits of creativity. In H. H. Anderson (Ed.), *Creativity and its cultivation.* New York: Harper & Row.

Gupta, V. B., Nwosa, N. M., Nadel, T. A., & Inamdar, S. (2001). Externalizing behaviors and television viewing in children of low-income minority parents. *Clinical Pediatrics, 40*(6), 337–341.

Gustafson, G. E., Green, J. A., & Cleland, J. W. (1994). Robustness of individual identity in the cries of human infants. *Developmental Psychobiology, 27*(1), 1–9.

Gustafson, G. E., & Harris, K. L. (1990). Women's responses to young infants' cries. *Developmental Psychology, 26*(1), 144–152.

Gutknecht, L. (2001). Full-genome scans with autistic disorder: A review. *Behavior Genetics, 31*(1), 113–123.

Guttman, N., & Zimmerman, D. R. (2000). Low-income mothers' views on breastfeeding. *Social Science & Medicine, 50*(10), 1457–1473.

Haan, N., Smith, M. B., & Block, J. (1968). Moral reasoning of young adults: Political-social behavior, family background, and personality correlates. *Journal of Personality and Social Psychology, 10,* 183–201.

Habib, M. (2000). The neurological basis of developmental dyslexia: An overview and working hypothesis. *Brain, 123*(12), 2373–2399.

Habib, M., Touze, F., & Galaburda, A. M. (1990). Intrauterine factors in sinistrality: A review. In S. Coren (Ed.), *Left-handedness: Behavior implications and anomalies.* Amsterdam: North-Holland.

Hack, M., Breslau, N., & Aram, D. (1992). The effect of very low birth weight and social risk on neurocognitive abilities at school age. *Journal of Developmental & Behavioral Pediatrics, 13,* 412–420.

Haden, C. A., Ornstein, P. A., Eckerman, C. O., & Didow, S. M. (2001). Mother-child conversational interactions as events unfold: Linkages to subsequent remembering. *Child Development, 72*(4), 1016–1031.

Haenen, J. (2001). Outlining the teaching–learning process: Piotr Gal'perin's contribution. *Learning & Instruction, 11*(2), 157–170.

Hainline, L., & Abramov, I. (1992). Assessing visual development: Is infant vision good enough? In C. Rovee-Collier & L. P. Lipsitt (Eds.), *Advances in infancy research* (Vol. 7). Norwood, NJ: Ablex.

Haith, M. M. (1966). The response of the human newborn to visual movement. *Journal of Experimental Child Psychology, 3,* 235–243.

Haith, M. M. (1979). Visual cognition in early infancy. In R. B. Kearsly & I. E. Sigel (Eds.), *Infants at risk: Assessment of cognitive functioning.* Hillsdale, NJ: Erlbaum.

Haith, M. M. (1986). Sensory and perceptual processes in early infancy. *Journal of Pediatrics, 109,* 158–171.

Haith, M. M. (1990). Progress in the understanding of sensory and perceptual processes in early infancy. *Merrill-Palmer Quarterly, 36,* 1–26.

Haith, M. M. (1998). Who put the cog in infant cognition? Is rich interpretation too costly? *Infant Behavior & Development, 21*(2), 167–179.

Hakim, A. A., et al. (1998). Effects of walking on mortality among nonsmoking retired men. *New England Journal of Medicine, 338,* 94–99.

Hala, S., Chandler, M., & Fritz, A. S. (1991). Fledgling theories of mind: Deception as a marker of three-year-olds' understanding of false belief. *Child Development, 62,* 83–97.

Hale, C., & Windecker, E. (1993, March). *Influence of parent–child interaction during reading on preschoolers' cognitive abilities.* Paper presented at the meeting of the Society on Research in Child Development, New Orleans, LA.

Halgin, R. P., & Whitbourne, S. K. (1993). *Abnormal psychology.* Fort Worth, TX: Harcourt Brace Jovanovich.

Hall, D. G. (1991). Acquiring proper nouns for familiar and unfamiliar animate objects: Two-year-olds' word-learning biases. *Child Development, 62,* 1142–1154.

Hall, G. S. (1904). *Adolescence: Its psychology and its relation to physiology, anthropology, sociology, sex, crime, religion, and education.* Englewood Cliffs, NJ: Prentice-Hall.

Hall, J. A., Herzberger, S. D., & Skowronski, K. J. (1998). Outcome expectancies and outcome values as predictors of children's aggression. *Aggressive Behavior, 24*(6), 439–454.

Hallman, J., Persson, M., & Klinteberg, B. (2001). Female alcoholism: Differences between female alcoholics with and without a history of additional substance misuse. *Alcohol & Alcoholism, 36*(6), 564–571.

Halmi, K. A., et al. (2000). Perfectionism in anorexia nervosa: Variation by clinical subtype, obsessionality, and pathological eating behavior. *American Journal of Psychiatry, 157,* 1799–1805.

Halpern, C. J. T., Udry, J. R., Suchindran, C., & Campbell, B. (2000). Adolescent males' willingness to report masturbation. *Journal of Sex Research, 37*(4), 327–332.

Halpern, D. F., & LaMay, M. L. (2000). The smarter sex: A critical review of sex differences in intelligence. *Educational Psychology Review, 12*(2), 229–246.

Hamm, J. V. (2000). Do birds of a feather flock together? The variable bases for African American, Asian American, and European American Adolescents' selection of similar friends. *Developmental Psychology, 36*(2), 209–219.

Hampson, J. (1989, April). *Elements of style: Maternal and child contributions to expressive and referential styles of language acquisition.* Paper presented at the meeting of the Society for Research in Child Development, Kansas City, MO.

Han, W., Waldfogel, J., & Brooks-Gunn, J. (2001). The effects of early maternal employment on later cognitive and behavioral outcomes. *Journal of Marriage & the Family, 63*(2), 336–354.

Handford, H. A., Mattison, R. E., & Kales, A.(1991). Sleep disturbances and disorders. In M. Lewis (Ed.), *Child and adolescent psychiatry: A comprehensive textbook.* Baltimore: Williams & Wilkins.

Handyside, A. H., et al. (1992). Birth of a normal girl after in vitro fertilization and preimplantation diagnostic testing for cystic fibrosis. *New England Journal of Medicine, 327,* 905–909.

Hanna, E. (1993, March). *Sex differences in play and imitation in toddlers.* Paper presented at the meeting of the Society for Research in Child Development, New Orleans, LA.

Hanna, E., & Meltzoff, A. N. (1993). Peer imitation by toddlers in laboratory, home, and day care contexts: Implications for social learning and memory. *Developmental Psychology, 29,* 701–710.

Hannon, P. R., Willis, S. K., Bishop-Townsend, V., Martinez, I. M., & Scrimshaw, S. C. (2000). African-American and Latina adolescent mothers' infant feeding decisions and breastfeeding practices: A qualitative study. *Journal of Adolescent Health, 26*(6), 399–407.

Hans, S. L., Henson, L. C., & Jeremy, R. J. (1992). The development of infants exposed in utero to opioid drugs. In C. W. Greenbaum & J. G. Auerbach (Eds.), *Longitudinal studies of children at psychological risk: Cross-national perspectives.* Norwood, NJ: Ablex.

Hardin, E. E., Leong, F. T. L., & Osipow, S. H. (2001). Cultural relativity in the conceptualization of career maturity. *Journal of Vocational Behavior, 58*(1), 36–52.

Harlow, H. F., & Harlow, M. K. (1966). Learning to love. *American Scientist, 54,* 244–272.

Harlow, H. F., Harlow, M. K., & Suomi, S. J. (1971). From thought to therapy: Lessons from a primate laboratory. *American Scientist, 59,* 538–549.

Harold, G. T., Fincham, F. D., Osborne, L. N., & Conger, R. D. (1997). Mom and Dad are at it again: Adolescent perceptions of marital conflict and adolescent psychological distress. *Developmental Psychology, 33,* 333–350.

Harper, J. F., & Marshall, E. (1991). Adolescents' problems and their relationship to self-esteem. *Adolescence, 26,* 799–807.

Harris, D. L., Brown, E., Marriott, C., Whittall, S., & Harmer, S. (1991). Monsters, ghosts and witches: Testing the limits of the fantasy–reality distinction in young children. *British Journal of Developmental Psychology, 9,* 105–123.

Harris, D. V. (1991). Exercise and fitness during adolescence. In R. M. Lerner, A. C. Petersen, & J. Brooks-Gunn (Eds.), *Encyclopedia of adolescence.* New York: Garland.

Harris, J. (1990). *Early language development.* New York: Routledge.

Harris, L. J. (1990). Cultural influences on handedness: Historical and contemporary theory and evidence. In S. Coren (Ed.), *Left-handedness: Behavior implications and anomalies.* Amsterdam: North-Holland.

Harris, L. J. (1991). The human infant in studies of lateralization of function: A historical perspective. In H. E. Fitzgerald, B. M. Lester, & M. W. Yogman (Eds.), *Theory and research in behavioral pediatrics.* New York: Plenum.

Harris, P. L. (1987). The development of search. In P. Salapatek & L. Cohen (Eds.), *Handbook of infant perception: Vol. 2. From perception to cognition.* New York: Academic Press.

Harris, P. L., & Kavanaugh, R. D. (1993). Young children's understanding of pretense. *Monographs of the Society for Research in Child Development, 58*(1, Serial No. 231).

Hart, B. (1991). Input frequency and children's first words. *First Language, 11,* 289–300.

Hart, C. H., DeWolf, D. M., Wozniak, P., & Burts, D. C. (1992). Maternal and paternal disciplinary styles: Relations with preschoolers' playground behavioral orientations and peer status. *Child Development, 63,* 879–892.

Hart, C. H., Ladd, G. W., & Burleson, B. R. (1990). Children's expectations of the outcomes of social strategies: Relations with sociometric status and maternal disciplinary styles. *Child Development, 61,* 127–138.

Harter, S. (1987). The determinants and mediational role of global self-worth in children. In N. Eisenberg (Ed.), *Contemporary topics in developmental psychology.* New York: Wiley.

Harter, S. (1990a). Issues in the assessment of the self-concept of children and adolescents. In A. LaGreca (Ed.), *Through the eyes of a child.* Boston: Allyn & Bacon.

Harter, S. (1990b). Processes underlying adolescent self-concept formation. In R. Montemayor, G. R. Adams, T. P. Gullotta (Eds.), *From childhood to adolescence: A transitional period?* Newbury Park, CA: Sage.

Harter, S. (1990c). Self and identity development. In S. S. Feldman & G. R. Elliott (Eds.), *At the threshold: The developing adolescent.* Cambridge, MA: Harvard University Press.

Harter, S., & Marold, D. B. (1991). A model of the determinants and mediational role of self-worth: Implications for adolescent depression and suicidal ideation. In J. Strauss & G. R. Goethals (Eds.), *The self: Interdisciplinary approaches.* New York: Springer-Verlag.

Harter, S., & Monsour, A. (1992). Developmental analysis of conflict caused by opposing attributes in the adolescent self-portrait. *Developmental Psychology, 28,* 251–260.

Harter, S., & Pike, R. (1984). The pictorial scale of perceived competence and social acceptance for young children. *Child Development, 55,* 1969–1982.

Hartup, W. W. (1983). The peer system. In P. H. Mussen (Ed.), *Handbook of child psychology: Vol. 4. Socialization, personality, and social development.* New York: Wiley.

Hartup, W. W. (1992a). Conflict and friendship relations. In C. U. Shantz & W. W. Hartup (Eds.), *Conflict in child and adolescent development.* Cambridge, MA: Cambridge University Press.

Hartup, W. W. (1992b). Friendships and their developmental significance. In H. McGurk (Ed.), *Childhood social development.* Hove, United Kingdom: Erlbaum.

Hartup, W. W. (1993). Adolescents and their friends. In B. Laursen (Ed.), *New directions in child development: No. 60. Close friendships in adolescence.* San Francisco: Jossey-Bass.

Harvey, C. (2000, September 4). Where to go for help. *The Los Angeles Times online.*

Harvey, E. (1999). Short-term and long-term effects of early parental employment on children of the National Longitudinal Survey of Youth. *Developmental Psychology, 35*(2), 445–459.

Hashimoto, N. (1991). Memory development in early childhood: Encoding process in a spatial task. *Journal of Genetic Psychology, 152,* 101–117.

Haskins, R. (1989). Beyond metaphor: The efficacy of early childhood education. *American Psychologist, 44,* 274–282.

Haslam, C., & Draper, E. S. (2001). A qualitative study of smoking during pregnancy. *Psychology, Health & Medicine, 6*(1), 95–99.

Hasselhorn, M. (1992). Task dependency and the role of typicality and metamemory in the development of an organizational strategy. *Child Development, 63,* 202–214.

Hastings, P. D., Zahn-Waxler, C., Robinson, J., Usher, B., & Bridges, D. (2000). The development of concern for others in children with behavior problems. *Developmental Psychology, 36*(5), 531–546.

Hatch, E. E., et al. (1998). Cancer risk in women exposed to diethylstilbestrol in utero. *Journal of the American Medical Association, 280*(7), 630–634.

Hatcher, R. A., et al. (1998). *Contraceptive technology* (17th rev. ed.). New York: Ardent Media.

Haugaard, J. J. (2000). The challenge of defining child sexual abuse. *American Psychologist, 55*(9), 1036–1039.

Hauser, P., et al. (1993). Attention deficit-hyperactivity disorder in people with generalized resistance to thyroid hormone. *New England Journal of Medicine, 328,* 997–1001.

Havard, J. (1991). The role of legislation. In M. Manciaux & C. J. Romer (Eds.), *Accidents in childhood and adolescence.* Geneva: World Health Organization.

Hawkins, C., & Williams, T. I. (1992). Nightmares, life events, and behaviour problems in preschool children. *Child: Care, Health, and Development, 18,* 117–128.

Hay, D. F., Caplan, M., Castle, J., & Stimson, C. A. (1991). Does sharing become increasingly "rational" in the second year of life? *Developmental Psychology, 27,* 987–993.

Hay, D. F., & Murray, P. (1982). Giving and requesting: Social facilitation of infants' offers to adults. *Infant Behavior and Development, 5,* 301–310.

Haznedar, M. M., et al. (1997). Anterior cingulate gyrus volume and glucose metabolism in autistic disorder. *American Journal of Psychiatry, 154,* 1047–1050.

Healthy People 2000: National health promotion and disease prevention objectives and healthy schools. (1991). *Journal of School Health, 61,* 298–311.

Heath, A. C., Kessler, R. C., Neale, M. C., Eaves, L. J., & Kendler, K. S. (1992). Evidence for genetic influences on personality from self-reports and informant ratings. *Journal of Personality and Social Psychology, 63,* 85–96.

Heatherton, T. F., Mahamedi, F., Striepe, M., Field, A. E., & Keel, P. (1997). A 10-year longitudinal study of body weight, dieting, and eating disorder symptoms. *Journal of Abnormal Psychology, 106,* 117–125.

Hebert, T. P. (2000). Gifted males pursuing careers in elementary education: Factors that influence a belief in self. *Journal for the Education of the Gifted, 24*(1), 7–45.

Hechtman, L. (1991). Developmental, neurobiological, and psychosocial aspects of hyperactivity, impulsivity, and inattention. In M. Lewis (Ed.), *Child and adolescent psychiatry: A comprehensive textbook.* Baltimore: Williams & Wilkins.

Heim, C., et al. (2000). Pituitary-adrenal and autonomic responses to stress in women after sexual and physical abuse in childhood. *Journal of the American Medical Association, 284,* 592–597.

Heller, D. A., de Faire, U., Pedersen, N. L., Dahlén, G., & McClearn, G. E. (1993). Genetic and environmental influences on serum lipid levels in twins. *New England Journal of Medicine, 328,* 1150–1156.

Heller, K. A., Monks, F. J., & Passow, A. H. (Eds.) (1993). *International handbook of research and development of giftedness and talent.* New York: Pergamon.

Hellings, J. A. (1999). Psychopharmacology of mood disorders in persons with mental retardation and autism. *Mental Retardation & Developmental Disabilities Research Reviews, 5*(4) 270–278.

Helms, J. E. (1992, September). Why is there no study of cultural equivalence in standardized cognitive ability testing? *American Psychologist, 47,* 1083–1101.

Hendin, H., Maltsberger, J. T., Lipschitz, A., Pollinger H., & Kyle, J. (2001). Recognizing and responding to a suicide crisis. *Suicide & Life-Threatening Behavior, 31*(2), 115–128.

Hendrick, J. B. (1990). Early childhood. In R. M. Thomas (Ed.), *The encyclopedia of human development and education: Theory, research, and studies.* Oxford: Pergamon.

Hendricks, K., et al. (2000). Neural tube defect surveillance and folic acid intervention—Texas–Mexico Border, 1993–1998. *Morbidity and Mortality Weekly Report, 49,* 1–4.

Henker, B., & Whalen, C. K. (1989). Hyperactivity and attention deficits. *American Psychologist, 44,* 216–223.

Hepper, P. G., Shahidullah, S., & White, R. (1990, October 4). Origins of fetal handedness. *Nature, 347,* 431.

Hergenhahn, B. R. (2000). *An introduction to the history of psychology,* 4th ed. Pacific Grove, CA: Brooks/Cole.

Herman-Giddens, M. E., Brown, G., Verbiest, S., Carlson, P. J., Hooten, E. G., Howell, H., & Butts, J. D. (1999). Underascertainment of child abuse mortality in the United States. *Journal of the American Medical Association, 282,* 463.

Herr, E. L. (2001). Career development and its practice: A historical perspective. *Career Development Quarterly, 49*(3). 196–211.

Herrnstein, R. J., & Murray, C. (1994). *The bell curve: Intelligence and class structure in American life.* New York: Free Press.

Hershberger, S. L., & D'Augelli, A. R. (2000). Issues in counseling lesbian, gay, and bisexual adolescents. In R. M. Perez, K. A. DeBord, & K. J. Bieschke (Eds.), *Handbook of counseling and psychotherapy with lesbian, gay, and bisexual clients* (pp. 225–247). Washington, DC: American Psychological Association.

Hershenson, R. (2000, August 6). Debating the Mozart theory. *The New York Times Magazine online.*

Hespos, S. J., & Baillargeon, R. (2001a). Infants' knowledge about occlusion and containment events: A surprising discrepancy. *Psychological Science, 121*(2), 141–147.

Hespos, S. J., & Baillargeon, R. (2001b). Reasoning about containment events in very young infants. *Cognition, 78*(3), 207–245.

Hetherington, E. M. (1979). Divorce: A child's perspective. *American Psychologist, 34,* 851–858.

Hetherington, E. M. (1987). Family relations six years after divorce. In K. Pasley & M. Ihinger-Tallman (Eds.), *Remarriage and stepparenting: Current theory and research.* New York: Guilford.

Hetherington, E. M. (1989). Coping with family transition: Winners, losers, and survivors. *Child Development, 60,* 1–14.

Hetherington, E. M., Anderson, E. R., & Hagan, M. S. (1991). Divorce: Effects on adolescents. In R. M. Lerner, A. C. Petersen, & J. Brooks-Gunn (Eds.), *Encyclopedia of adolescence.* New York: Garland.

Hetherington, E. M., et al. (1992). Coping with marital transitions. *Monographs of the Society for Research in Child Development, 57*(2–3, Serial No. 227).

Hetherington, E. M., Stanley-Hagan, M., & Anderson, E. R. (1989). Marital transitions: A child's perspective. *American Psychologist, 44,* 303–312.

Hetland, L. (2000). Cited in Hershenson, R. (2000, August 6). Debating the Mozart theory. *The New York Times Magazine online.*

Hickling, A. K. (2001). The emergence of children's causal explanations and theories: Evidence from everyday conversation. *Developmental Psychology, 37*(5), 668–683.

Hickman, G. P., Bartholomae, S., & McKenry, P. C. (2000). Influence of parenting style on the adjustment and academic achievement of traditional college freshmen. *Journal of College Student Development, 41*(1), 41–54.

Higgins, A. T., & Turnure, J. E. (1984). Distractibility and concentration of attention in children's development. *Child Development, 55,* 1799–1810.

High school dropout rates down. (1993, June 21). *Higher Education and National Affairs, 42*(12), p. 3.

Higley, J. D., Lande, J. S., & Suomi, S. J. (1989). Day care and the promotion of emotional development: Lessons from a monkey laboratory. In J. S. Lande, S. Scarr, & N. Gunzenhauser (Eds.), *Caring for children: Challenge to America.* Hillsdale, NJ: Erlbaum.

Hinde, R. A. (1991). When is an evolutionary approach useful? *Child Development, 62,* 671–675.

Hindley, C. B., Filliozat, A. M., Klackenberg, G., Nicolet-Neister, D., & Sand, E. A. (1966). Differences in age of walking for five European longitudinal samples. *Human Biology, 38,* 364–379.

Hindmarsh, G. J., O'Callaghan, M. J., Mohay, H. A., & Rogers, Y. M. (2000). Gender differences in cognitive abilities at 2 years in ELBW infants. *Early Human Development, 60*(2), 115–122.

Hines, M. (1990). Gonadal hormones and human cognitive development. In J. Balthazart (Ed.), *Hormones, brain and behavior in vertebrates: Vol. 1. Sexual differentiation, neuroanatomical aspects, neurotransmitters, and neuropeptides.* Basel: Karger.

Hirshberg, L. M., & Svejda, M. (1990). When infants look to their parents: I. Infants' social referencing of mothers compared to fathers. *Child Development, 61,* 1175–1186.

Hirsh-Pasek, K. (1991). Pressure or challenge in preschool? How academic environments affect children. In L. Rescorla, M. C. Hyson, & K. Hirsh-Pasek (Eds.), *New directions in child development: No. 53. Academic instruction in early childhood: Challenge or pressure?* San Francisco: Jossey-Bass.

Hirsh-Pasek, K., Hyson, M. C., & Rescorla, L. (1990). Academic environments in preschool: Do they pressure or challenge young children? *Early Education and Development, 1,* 401–423.

Hodges, J., & Tizard, B. (1989). Social and family relationships of ex-institutional adolescents. *Journal of Child Psychology and Psychiatry, 30,* 77–97.

Hoff-Ginsberg, E. (1986). Function and structure in maternal speech: Their relation to the child's development of syntax. *Developmental Psychology, 22,* 155–163.

Hoff-Ginsberg, E. (1990). Maternal speech and the child's development of syntax: A further look. *Journal of Child Language, 17,* 85–99.

Hoff-Ginsberg, E. (1991). Mother-child conversation in different social classes and communicative settings. *Child Development, 62,* 782–796.

Hoff-Ginsberg, E. (1998). The relation of birth order and socioeconomic status to children's language experience and language development. *Applied Psycholinguistics, 19*(4) 603–629.

Hoffman, L. W., & Youngblade, L. M. (1998). Maternal employment, morale, and parenting style: Social class comparisons. *Journal of Applied Developmental Psychology, 19*(3), 389–413.

Hoffman, M. L. (1982). The role of the father in internal moralization. In M. E. Lamb (Ed.), *The role of the father in child development.* New York: Wiley.

Hoffman, M. L. (1984). Empathy, its limitations, and its role in a comprehensive moral theory. In W. M. Kurtines & J. L. Gewirtz (Eds.), *Morality, moral behavior, and moral development.* New York: Wiley.

Hoffman, M. L. (1988). Moral development. In M. H. Bernstein & M. E. Lamb (Eds.), *Developmental psychology: An advanced textbook* (2nd ed.). Hillsdale, NJ: Erlbaum.

Hoglund, C. L., & Bell, T. S. (1991, August). *Longitudinal study of self-esteem in children from 7–11 years.* Paper presented at the meeting of the American Psychological Association, San Francisco.

Holland, J. J. (2000, July 25). Groups link media to child violence. The Associated Press online.

Holland, J. L. (1996). Exploring careers with a typology. *American Psychologist, 51,* 397–406.

Holland, J. L. (1997). Making vocational choices: *A theory of vocational personalities and work environments* (3rd ed.). Odessa, FL: Psychological Assessment Resources.

Hollenbeck, A. R., Gewirtz, J. K., & Sebris, S. L. (1984). Labor and delivery medication influences parent–infant interaction in the first postpartum month. *Infant Behavior and Development, 7,* 201–209.

Holmes-Farley, S. R. (1998, September 16). Who should decide the sex of a baby? *The New York Times,* p. A28.

Holsen, I., Kraft, P., & Roysamb, E. (2001). The relationship between body image and depressed mood in adolescence: A 5-year longitudinal panel study. *Journal of Health Psychology, 6*(6), 613–627.

Honein, M. A., Paulozzi, L. J., Mathews, T. J., Erickson, J. D., & Wong, L. C. (2001). Impact of folic acid fortification of the U.S. food supply on the occurrence of neural tube defects. *Journal of the American Medical Association, 285*(23), 2981–2986.

Honig, A. S., & McCarron, P. A. (1988). Prosocial behaviors of handicapped and typical peers in an integrated preschool. *Early Child Development and Care, 33,* 113–125.

Honig, A. S., & Park, K. (1993, March). *Preschool aggression and cognition: Effects of infant care.* Paper presented at the meeting of the Society for Research in Child Development, New Orleans, LA.

Honzik, M. P., Macfarlane, J. W., & Allen, L. (1948). The stability of mental test performance between two and eighteen years. *Journal of Experimental Education, 17,* 309–324.

Hood, K. E. (1991). Menstrual cycle. In R. M. Lerner, A. C. Petersen, & J. Brooks-Gunn (Eds.), *Encyclopedia of adolescence.* New York: Garland.

Hoosain, R. (1991). Cerebral lateralization of bilingual functions after handedness switch in childhood. *Journal of Genetic Psychology, 152,* 263–268.

Hopkins, B. (1991). Facilitating early motor development: An intracultural study of West Indian mothers and their infants living in Britain. In J. K. Nugent, B. M. Lester, & T. B. Brazelton (Eds.), *The cultural context of infancy* (Vol. 2). Norwood, NJ: Ablex.

Hopkins, B., & Westra, T. (1990). Motor development, maternal expectations, and the role of handling. *Infant Behavior and Development, 13,* 117–122.

Hopkins, E. (1992, March 15). Tales from the baby factory. *The New York Times Magazine,* pp. 40–41, 78, 80, 82, 84, 90.

Hopkins, W. D., Dahl, J. F., & Pilcher, D. (2001). Genetic influence on the expression of hand preferences in chimpanzees (*Pan troglodytes*): Evidence in support of the right-shift theory and developmental instability. *Psychological Science, 12*(4), 299–303.

Horne, R. S. C., et al. (2001). Apnoea of prematurity and arousal from sleep. *Early Human Development, 61*(2), 119–133.

Horney, K. (1967). *Feminine psychology.* New York: Norton.

Horowitz, F. D. (1992). John B. Watson's legacy: Learning and environment. *Developmental Psychology, 28,* 360–367.

Hossain, Z., Field, T., Pickens, J., Malphurs, J., & Del Valle, C. (1997). Fathers' caregiving in low-income African-American and Hispanic-American families. *Early Development & Parenting, 6*(2), 73–82.

Hossain, Z., & Roopnarine, J. L. (1993). Division of household labor and child care in dual-earner African-American families with infants. *Sex Roles, 29*(9–10), 571–583.

Hossain, Z., & Roopnarine, J. L. (1994). African-American fathers' involvement with infants: Relationship to their functioning style, support, education, and income. *Infant Behavior & Development, 17*(2), 175–184.

Howard, M., & McCabe, J. B. (1990). Helping teenagers postpone sexual involvement. *Family Planning Perspectives, 22,* 21–26.

Howards, S. S. (1995). Current concepts: Treatment of male infertility. *New England Journal of Medicine, 332,* 312–317.

Howe, M. L., & Courage, M. L. (1993). On resolving the enigma of infantile amnesia. *Psychological Bulletin, 113,* 305–326.

Howe, M. L., & Rabinowitz, F. M. (1991). Gist another panacea? Or just the illusion of inclusion. *Developmental Review, 11,* 305–316.

Howes, C. (1987). Social competence with peers in young children: Developmental sequences. *Developmental Review, 7,* 252–272.

Howes, C. (1988). Peer interaction of young children. *Monographs of the Society for Research in Child Development, 53*(1, Serial No. 217).

Howes, C., & Matheson, C. C. (1992a). Contextual constraints on the concordance of mother–child and teacher–child relationships. In R. C. Pianta (Ed.), *New directions for child development: No. 57. Beyond the parent: The role of other adults in children's lives.* San Francisco, Jossey-Bass.

Howes, C., & Matheson, C. C. (1992b). Sequences in the development of competent play with peers: Social and social pretend play. *Developmental Psychology, 28,* 961–974.

Howes, C., Phillips, D. A., & Whitebook, M. (1992). Thresholds of quality: Implications for the social development of children in center-based child care. *Child Development, 63,* 449–460.

Hoy, E. A., & McClure, B. G. (2000). Preschool experience: A facilitator of very low birthweight infants' development? *Infant Mental Health Journal, 21*(6), 481–494.

Hu, F. B., et al. (2000). Physical activity and risk of stroke in women. *Journal of the American Medical Association, 283,* 2961–2967.

Huber, J., Darling, S., Park, K., & Soliman, K. F. A. (2001). Altered responsiveness to stress and NMDA following prenatal exposure to cocaine. *Physiology & Behavior, 72*(1–2) 181–188.

Hudson, J. A. (1990). The emergence of autobiographical memory in mother–child conversation. In R. Fivush & J. A. Hudson (Eds.), *Knowing and remembering in young children.* Cambridge: Cambridge University Press.

Hudziak, J. J. (2001). Latent class analysis of ADHD and comorbid symptoms in a population sample of adolescent female twins. *Journal of Child Psychology & Psychiatry & Allied Disciplines, 42*(7), 933–942.

Huesmann, L. R., Eron, L. D., Klein, R., Brice, P., & Fischer, P. (1983). Mitigating the imitation of aggressive behaviors by changing children's attitudes about media violence. *Journal of Personality and Social Psychology, 44,* 899–910.

Huesmann, L. R., & Guerra, N. G. (1997). Children's normative beliefs about aggression and aggressive behavior. *Journal of Personality & Social Psychology, 72*(2), 408–419.

Huesmann, L. R., & Miller, L. S. (1994). Long-term effects of repeated exposure to media violence in childhood. In L. R. Huesmann (Ed.), *Aggressive behavior.* New York: Plenum.

Humphreys, L. G. (1992). Commentary: What both critics and users of ability tests need to know. *Psychological Science, 3,* 271–274.

Hundert, J., & Houghton, A. (1992). Promoting social interaction of children with disabilities in integrated preschools: A failure to generalize. *Exceptional Children, 58,* 311–398.

Hunt, M. (1993). *The story of psychology.* New York: Anchor Books.

Hunt, M., & Berry, H. (1993). Phenylketonuria. In S. W. Ekvall (Ed.), *Pediatric nutrition in chronic diseases and developmental disorders: Prevention, assessment, and treatment.* New York: Oxford.

Huntington, L., Hans, S. L., & Zeskind, P. S. (1990). The relations among cry characteristics, demographic variables, and developmental test scores in infants prenatally exposed to methadone. *Infant Behavior and Development, 13,* 535–538.

Huston, A. C., et al. (1992). *Big world, small screen: The role of television in American society.* Lincoln: University of Nebraska Press.

Huston, A. C., & O'Brien, M. (1985). Activity level and sex-stereotyped toy choice in toddler boys and girls. *Journal of Genetic Psychology, 146,* 527–533.

Hutcheson, J. J., et al. (1997). Risk status and home intervention among children with failure-to-thrive: Follow-up at age 4. *Journal of Pediatric Psychology, 22*(5), 651–668.

Hutt, C. (1978). Biological bases of psychological sex differences. *American Journal of Diseases of Children, 132,* 170–177.

Huttenlocher, J., Haight, W., Bryk, A., Seltzer, M., & Lyons, T. (1991). Early vocabulary growth: Relation to language input and gender. *Developmental Psychology, 27,* 236–248.

Hutton, U. M. Z., & Towse, J. N. (2001). Short-term memory and working memory as indices of children's cognitive skills. *Memory, 9*(4–6), 383–394.

Hyde, J. S., Fennema, E., & Lamon, S. J. (1990). Gender differences in mathematics performance: A meta-analysis. *Psychological Bulletin, 107,* 139–155.

Hyde, J. S., Krajnik, M., & Skuldt-Niederberger, K. (1991). Androgyny across the life span: A replication and longitudinal follow-up. *Developmental Psychology, 27,* 516–519.

Hyde, J. S., & Linn, M. C. (1988). Gender differences in verbal ability: A meta-analysis. *Psychological Bulletin, 104,* 53–69.

Hynd, G. W., & Hooper, S. R. (1992). *Neurological basis of childhood psychopathology.* Newbury Park, CA: Sage.

Hyson, M. C. (1991). Building the hothouse: How mothers construct academic environments. In L. Rescorla, M.C. Hyson, & K. Hirsh-Pasek (Eds.), *New directions in child development: No. 53. Academic instruction in early childhood: Challenge or pressure?* New York: Jossey-Bass.

Ihle, W., Esser, G., Schmidt, M. H., & Blanz, B. (2000). Praevalenz, Komorbiditaet und Geschlechtsunterschiede psychischer Stoerungen vom Grundschul-bis ins fruehe Erwachsenenalter. *Zeitschrift fuer Klinische Psychologie und Psychotherapie: Forschung und Praxis, 29*(4), 263–275.

Ike, N. (2000). Current thinking on XYY syndrome. *Psychiatric Annals, 30*(2), 91–95.

Influence of homicide on racial disparity in life expectancy, United States, 1998. (2001). *Morbidity and Mortality Weekly Report, 50,* 780–783.

Inhelder, B., & Piaget, J. (1959). *The early growth of logic in the child: Classification and seriation.* New York: Harper & Row.

Insel, T. R. (2000). Toward a neurobiology of attachment. *Review of General Psychology, 4*(2), 176–185.

Insel, T. R., O'Brien, D. J., & Leckman, J. F. (1999). Oxytocin, vasopressin, and autism: Is there a connection? *Biological Psychiatry, 45*(2), 145–157.

International Human Genome Sequencing Consortium. (2001). Initial sequencing and analysis of the human genome. *Nature, 409,* 860–921.

Isabella, R. A. (1993). Origins of attachment: Maternal interactive behavior across the first year. *Child Development, 64,* 605–621.

Isik, U., Oezek, E., Bilgen, H., & Cebeci, D. (2000). Comparison of oral glucose and sucrose solutions on pain response in neonates. *Journal of Pain, 1*(4), 275–278.

Iverson, J. M., Capirci, O., Longobardi, E., & Caselli, M. C. (1999). Gesturing in mother–child interactions. *Cognitive Development, 14*(1), 57–75.

Izard, C. E. (1983). *Maximally discriminative facial movement scoring system.* Newark, DE: University of Delaware Instructional Resources Center.

Izard, C. E. (1991). *The psychology of emotions.* New York: Plenum.

Izard, C. E. (1992). Basic emotions, relations among emotions, and emotion–cognition relations. *Psychological Review, 99,* 561–565.

Izard, C. E., Haynes, O. M., Chisholm, G., & Baak, K. (1991). Emotional determinants of infant–mother attachment. *Child Development, 62,* 906–917.

Izard, C. E., Hembree, E. A., & Huebner, R. R. (1987). Infants' emotion expressions to acute pain: Developmental change and stability of individual differences. *Developmental Psychology, 23,* 105–113.

Izard, C. E., & Malatesta, C. Z. (1987). Perspectives on emotional development. I. Differential emotions theory of early emotional development. In J. D. Osofsky (Ed.), *Handbook of infant development* (2nd ed.). New York: Wiley.

Jacklin, C. N. (1989). Female and male: Issues of gender. *American Psychologist, 44,* 127–133.

Jacklin, C. N., DiPietro, J. A., & Maccoby, E. E. (1984). Sex-typing behavior and sex-typing pressure in child–parent interaction. *Sex Roles, 13,* 413–425.

Jacklin, C. N., & McBride-Chang, C. (1991). The effects of feminist scholarship on developmental psychology. *Psychology of Women Quarterly, 15,* 549–556.

Jacklin, C. N., Wilcox, K. T., & Maccoby, E. E. (1988). Neonatal sex-steroid hormones and cognitive abilities at six years. *Developmental Psychobiology, 21,* 567–574.

Jackson, A. P. (2000). Maternal self-efficacy and children's influence on stress and parenting among single black mothers in poverty. *Journal of Family Issues, 21*(1), 3–16.

Jackson, L. A. (1992). *Physical appearance and gender: Sociobiological and sociocultural perspectives.* Albany, NY: SUNY Press.

Jacobson, J. L., & Jacobson, S. W. (1990). Methodological issues in human behavioral teratology. In C. Rovee-Collier & L. P. Lipsitt (Eds.), *Advances in infancy research* (Vol. 6). Norwood, NJ: Ablex.

Jacobson, J. L., Jacobson, S. W., Padgett, R. J., Brumitt, G.A., & Billings, R. L. (1992). Effects of prenatal PCB exposure on cognitive processing efficiency and sustained attention. *Developmental Psychology, 28,* 297–306.

Jacobson, S. W. (1979). Matching behavior in the young infant. *Child Development, 50,* 425–430.

Jacobson, S. W., & Frye, K. F. (1991). Effect of maternal social support on attachment: Experimental evidence. *Child Development, 62,* 572–582.

James, W. (1890). *The principles of psychology.* New York: Holt.

Jamieson, S., & Marshall, W. L. (2000). Attachment styles and violence in child molesters. *Journal of Sexual Aggression, 5*(2), 88–98.

Jancin, B. (1988). Prenatal gender selection appears to be gaining acceptance. *Obstetrical and Gynecological News, 23,* 30.

Janos, P. M. (1987). A fifty-year follow-up of Terman's youngest college students and IQ-matched agemates. *Gifted Child Quarterly, 31,* 55–58.

Jarvis, B. (1993, May 3). Against the great divide. *Newsweek,* p. 14.

Jayakody, R., & Kalil, A. (2000). Social fathering in low-income, African American families with preschool children. Unpublished manuscript, referenced in Coley, R. L. (2001). (In)visible men: Emerging research on low-income, unmarried, and minority fathers. *American Psychologist, 56*(9), 743–753.

Jeffery, R. W., Hennrikus, D. J., Lando, H. A., Murray, D. M., & Liu, J. W. (2000). Reconciling conflicting findings regarding postcessation weight concerns and success in smoking cessation. *Health Psychology, 19,* 242–246.

Jemmott, L. S., & Jemmott, J. B., III. (1992). Family structure, parental strictness, and sexual behavior among inner-city black male adolescents. *Journal of Adolescent Research, 7,* 192–207.

Jeng, S-F, Yau, K-I T., Liao, H-F, Chen, L-C, & Chen, P-S. (2000). Prognostic factors for walking attainment in very low-birthweight preterm infants. *Early Human Development, 59*(3), 159–173.

Jensen, J. K., & Neff, D. L. (1993). Development of basic auditory discrimination in preschool children. *Psychological Science, 4,* 104–107.

Jensen, P. S., et al. (2001). Findings from the NIMH Multimodal Treatment Study of ADHD (MTA): Implications and applications for primary care providers. *Journal of Developmental & Behavioral Pediatrics, 22*(1), 60–73.

Jessell, J. C., & Beymer, L. (1992). The effects of job title vs. job description on occupational sex typing. *Sex Roles, 27,* 73–83.

Jimerson, S. R., Egeland, B., Sroufe, L. A., & Carlson, B. (2000). A prospective longitudinal study of high school dropouts: Examining multiple predictors across development. *Journal of School Psychology, 38*(6), 525–549.

Johanson, R. (2000). Perineal massage for prevention of perineal trauma in childbirth. *The Lancet, 355*(9200), 250–251.

Johns, A. (2001). Psychiatric effects of cannabis. *The British Journal of Psychiatry, 178,* 116–122.

Johnson, C. M. (1991). Infant and toddler sleep: A telephone survey of parents in one community. *Developmental and Behavioral Pediatrics, 12,* 108–114.

Johnson, J. (1990). The role of play in cognitive development. In E. Klugman & S. Smilansky (Eds.), *Children's play and learning.* New York: Teachers College Press.

Johnson, M. H., Dziurawiec, S., Bartrip, J., & Morton, J. (1992). The effects of movement of internal features on infants' preferences for face-like stimuli. *Infant Behavior and Development, 15,* 129–136.

Johnson, T. D., & Moely, B. E. (1993, March). *The psychosocial impact of encopresis on children and their families.* Paper presented at the meeting of the Society for Research in Child Development, New Orleans, LA.

Johnson, W. (2000). Work preparation and labor market behavior among urban, poor, nonresident fathers. In S. Danziger & A. C. Lin (Eds.), *Coping with poverty: The social contexts of neighborhood, work, and family in the African American community.* Ann Arbor: University of Michigan Press.

Johnson, W., Emde, R. N., Pannabecker, B., Stenberg, C., & Davis, M. (1982). Maternal perception of infant emotion from birth to 18 months. *Infant Behavior and Development, 5,* 313–322.

Johnston, L. D., O'Malley, P. M., & Bachman, J. G. (2000, December). *Cigarette use and smokeless tobacco use decline substantially among teens.* University of Michigan News and Information Services online: Ann Arbor, MI. **http://www.monitoringthefuture.org**

Johnston, L. D., O'Malley, P. M., & Bachman, J. G. (2001). *Monitoring the Future national survey results on drug use, 1975–2000. Volume I: Secondary school students* (NIH Publication No. 01–4924). Bethesda, MD: National Institute on Drug Abuse.

Johnstone, S. J., et al. (2001). Obstetric risk factors for postnatal depression in urban and rural community samples. *Australian & New Zealand Journal of Psychiatry, 35*(1), 69–74.

Jones, D. C., Swift, D. J., & Johnson, M. A. (1988). Nondeliberate memory for a novel event among preschoolers. *Developmental Psychology, 24,* 641–645.

Jones, J. (1991). Psychological models of race: What have they been and what should they be? In J. Goodchilds (Ed.), *Psychological perspectives on human diversity in America.* Washington, DC: American Psychological Association.

Jones, M. C. (1924). Elimination of children's fears. *Journal of Experimental Psychology, 7,* 381–390.

Jones, M. C. (1957). The late careers of boys who were early- or late-maturing. *Child Development, 28,* 115–128.

Jones, M. C. (1958). The study of socialization patterns at the high school level. *Journal of Genetic Psychology, 93,* 87–111.

Jones, T. A., & Greenough, W. T. (1996). Ultrastructural evidence for increased contact between astrocytes and synapses in rats reared in a complex environment. *Neurobiology of Learning & Memory, 65*(1), 48–56.

Jones, T. A., Klintsova, A. Y., Kilman, V. L., Sirevaag, A. M., & Greenough, W. T. (1997). Induction of multiple synapses by experience in the visual cortex of adult rats. *Neurobiology of Learning & Memory, 68*(1), 13–20.

Joos, S. K., Pollitt, K. E. Mueller, W. H., & Albright, D. L. (1983). The Bacon Chow study: Maternal nutritional supplementation and infant behavioral development. *Child Development, 54,* 669–676.

Josefsson, A. M., et al. (2000). Viral load of human papilloma virus 16 as a determinant for development of cervical carcinoma in situ: a nested case-control study. *The Lancet, 355,* 2189–2193.

Junger, M., Stroebe, W., & Van Der Laan, A. M. (2001). Delinquency, health behaviour and health. *British Journal of Health Psychology, 6*(2), 103–120.

Jussim, L. (1989). Teacher expectations: Self-fulfilling prophecies, perceptual biases and accuracy. *Journal of Personality and Social Psychology, 87,* 469–480.

Jussim, L. (1991). Social perception and social reality: A reflection-construction model. *Psychological Review, 98,* 54–73.

Kaemingk, K. L., & Halverson, P. T. (2000). Spatial memory following prenatal alcohol exposure: More than a material specific memory deficit. *Child Neuropsychology, 6*(2), 115–128.

Kafka, R. R., & Linden, P. (1991). Communication in relationships and adolescent substance use: The influence of parents and friends. *Adolescence, 26,* 587–598.

Kagan, J. (1992). Yesterday's premises, tomorrow's promises. *Developmental Psychology, 28,* 990–997.

Kagan, J., & Klein, R. E. (1973). Cross-cultural perspectives on early development. *American Psychologist, 28,* 947–961.

Kagan, J., & Snidman, N. (1991). Temperamental factors in human development. *American Psychologist, 46,* 856–862.

Kagan, J., Snidman, N., & Arcus, D. (1993). On the temperamental categories of inhibited and uninhibited children. In K. H. Rubin & J. B. Asendorpf (Eds.), *Social withdrawal, inhibition, and shyness in childhood.* Hillsdale, NJ: Erlbaum.

Kagan, S. L. (1990). Children's play: The journey from theory to practice. In E. Klugman & S. Smilansky (Eds.), *Children's play and learning: Perspectives and policy implications.* New York: Teachers College Press.

Kagay, M. R. (1993, June 8). Poll finds knowledge about AIDS increasing. *The New York Times,* p. B9.

Kahlbaugh, P., & Haviland, J. M. (1991). Formal operational thinking and identity. In R. M. Lerner, A. C. Petersen, & J. Brooks-Gunn (Eds.), *Encyclopedia of adolescence.* New York: Garland.

Kahn, P. H. (1992). Children's obligatory and discretionary moral judgments. *Child Development, 63,* 416–430.

Kail, R. (1990). *The development of memory in children* (3rd ed.). New York: W. H. Freeman.

Kail, R. (1991). Processing time declines exponentially during childhood and adolescence. *Developmental Psychology, 27,* 259–266.

Kakita, A., et al. (2000). Intrauterine methylmercury intoxication: Consequence of the inherent brain lesions and cognitive dysfunction in maturity. *Brain Research, 877*(2), 322–330.

Kalliopuska, M. (1991). Study on the empathy and prosocial behavior of children in three day-care centres. *Psychological Reports, 68,* 375–378.

Kaltiala-Heino, R., Rimpelae, M., Rissanen, A., & Rantanen, P. (2001). Early puberty and early sexual activity are associated with bulimic-type eating pathology in middle adolescence. *Journal of Adolescent Health, 28*(4), 346–352.

Kamin, L. J. (1995). Behind the curve [Review of *The Bell Curve: Intelligence and Class Structure in American Life*]. *Scientific American, 272,* 99–103.

Kaminer, Y. (2001). Adolescent substance abuse treatment: Where do we go from here? *Psychiatric Services, 52*(2), 147–149.

Kanefield, L. (1999). The reparative motive in surrogate mothers. *Adoption Quarterly, 2*(4), 5–19.

Kano, K., & Arisaka, O. (2000). Fluvoxamine and enuresis. *Journal of the American Academy of Child & Adolescent Psychiatry, 39*(12), 1464–1465.

Kaplan, S. J. (1991). Physical abuse and neglect. In M. Lewis (Ed.), *Child and adolescent psychiatry: A comprehensive textbook.* Baltimore: Williams & Wilkins.

Karapetsas, A., & Kantas, A. (1991). Visuomotor organization in the child: A neuropsychological approach. *Perceptual and Motor Skills, 72,* 211–217.

Karniol, R. (1980). A conceptual analysis of immanent justice response in children. *Child Development, 51,* 118–130.

Karwautz, A., et al. (2001). Individual-specific risk factors for anorexia nervosa: A pilot study using a discordant sister-pair design. *Psychological Medicine, 31*(2), 317–329.

Kassirer, J. P., & Angell, M. (1998). Losing weight—An ill-fated New Year's resolution. *New England Journal of Medicine, 338,* 52–54.

Katchadourian, H. (1990). Sexuality. In S. S. Feldman & G. R. Elliott (Eds.), *At the threshold: The developing adolescent.* Cambridge, MA: Harvard University Press.

Katz, P. A., & Walsh, P. V. (1991). Modification of children's gender-stereotyped behavior. *Child Development, 62,* 338–351.

Kaufman, J., & Zigler, E. (1992). The prevention of child maltreatment: Programming, research, and policy. In D. J. Willis, E. W. Holden, & M. Rosenberg (Eds.), *Prevention of child maltreatment: Developmental and ecological perspectives.* New York: Wiley.

Kaufmann, D., et al. (2000). The relationship between parenting style and children's adjustment: The parents' perspective. *Journal of Child & Family Studies, 9*(2), 231–245.

Kaye, W. H., Klump, K. L., Frank, G. K. W., & Strober, M. (2000). Anorexia and bulimia nervosa. *Annual Review of Medicine, 51,* 200–313.

Kazdin, A. E. (1990). Assessment of childhood depression. In A. M. LaGreca (Ed.), *Through the eyes of a child.* Boston: Allyn and Bacon.

Kazdin, A. E. (1993a). Adolescent mental health. *American Psychologist, 48,* 127–141.

Kazdin, A. E. (1993b). Psychotherapy for children and adolescents. *American Psychologist, 48,* 644–657.

Kazdin, A. E. (2000). Treatments for aggressive and antisocial children. *Child & Adolescent Psychiatric Clinics of North America, 9*(4), 841–858.

Kazdin, A. E., & Wassell, G. (2000). Therapeutic changes in children, parents, and families resulting from treatment of children with conduct problems. *Journal of the American Academy of Child & Adolescent Psychiatry, 39*(4), 414–420.

Kazui, M., Endo, T., Tanaka, A., Sakagami, H., & Suganuma, M. (2000). Intergenerational transmission of attachment: Japanese mother–child dyads. *Japanese Journal of Educational Psychology, 48*(3), 323–332.

Kearney, C. A., & Silverman, W. K. (1990). A preliminary analysis of a functional model of assessment and treatment for school refusal behavior. *Behavior Modification, 14,* 340–366.

Keating, D. P. (1991). Adolescent cognition. In R. M. Lerner, A. C. Petersen, & J. Brooks-Gunn (Eds.), *Encyclopedia of adolescence.* New York: Garland.

Keating, D. P., & Clark, L. V. (1980). Development of physical and social reasoning in adolescents. *Developmental Psychology, 16,* 23–30.

Keating, G. M., McClellan, K., & Jarvis, B. (2001). Methylphenidate (OROS(R) formulation). *CNS Drugs, 15*(6), 495–500.

Kellman, P. J., & von Hofsten, C. (1992). The world of the moving infant: Perception of motion, stability, and space. In C. Rovee-Collier & L. P. Lipsitt (Eds.), *Advances in infancy research* (Vol. 7). Norwood, NJ: Ablex.

Kellogg, R. (1970). Understanding children's art. In P. Cramer (Ed.), *Readings in developmental psychology today.* Del Mar, CA: CRM.

Kelly, A. (1988). Gender differences in teacher-pupil interactions: A meta-analytic review. *Research in Education, 39,* 1–23.

Kelly, J. B. (2000). Children's adjustment in conflicted marriage and divorce: A decade review of research. *Journal of the American Academy of Child & Adolescent Psychiatry, 39*(8), 963–973.

Kempe, A., et al. (1992). Clinical determinants of the racial disparity in very low birth weight. *The New England Journal of Medicine, 327,* 969–973.

Kendall-Tackett, K. A., Williams, L. M., & Finkelhor, D. (1993). Impact of sexual abuse on children: A review and synthesis of recent empirical studies. *Psychological Bulletin, 113,* 164–180.

Kendler, K .S., et al. (1997). Resemblance of psychotic symptoms and syndromes in affected sibling pairs from the Irish study of high-density schizophrenia families: Evidence for possible etiologic heterogeneity. *American Journal of Psychiatry, 154,* 191–198.

Kendler, K. S., et al. (2000). Illicit psychoactive substance use, heavy use, abuse, and dependence in a US population-based sample of male twins. *Archives of General Psychiatry, 57,* 261–269.

Kendler, K. S., Myers, J. M., Neale, M. C. (2000). A multidimensional twin study of mental health in women. *American Journal of Psychiatry, 157,* 506–513.

Kendler, K. S., Thornton, L. M., Gilman, S. E., & Kessler, R. C. (2000). Sexual orientation in a U.S. national sample of twin and nontwin sibling pairs. *American Journal of Psychiatry, 157,* 1843–1846.

Kendler, K. S., Thornton, L. M., & Pedersen, N. L. (2000). Tobacco consumption in Swedish twins reared apart and reared together. *Archives of General Psychiatry, 57,* 886–892.

Kennell, J. H., & Klaus, M. H. (1984). Mother–infant bonding: Weighing the evidence. *Developmental Review, 4,* 275–282.

Kennell, J. H., Klaus, M. H., McGrath, S., Robertson, S., & Hinkley, C. (1991). Continuous emotional support during labor in a U.S. hospital: A randomized clinical trial. *Journal of the American Medical Association, 265,* 2197–2201.

Kennell, J. H., & McGrath, S. (1993, March). *Perinatal effects of labor support.* Paper presented at the meeting of the Society for Research in Child Development, New Orleans, LA.

Kershner, J. R., & Ledger, G. (1985). Effect of sex, intelligence, and style of thinking on creativity: A comparison of gifted and average IQ children. *Journal of Personality and Social Psychology, 48,* 1033–1040.

Kessen, W., Leutzendoff, A. M., & Stoutsenberger, K. (1967). Age, food deprivation, non-nutritive sucking and movement in the human newborn. *Journal of Comparative and Physiological Psychology, 63,* 82–86.

Key, A., Lacey, J. H., & Nussey, S. (2001). Do starvation diets lead to irreversible lung changes? *European Eating Disorders Review, 9*(5), 348–353.

Kilgore, K., Snyder, J., & Lentz, C. (2000). The contribution of parental discipline, parental monitoring, and school risk to early-onset conduct problems in African American boys and girls. *Developmental Psychology, 36*(6), 835–845.

Killen, J. D., et al. (2001). Do adolescent smokers experience withdrawal effects when deprived of nicotine? *Experimental & Clinical Psychopharmacology, 9*(2), 176–182.

Kilpatrick, D. G., et al. (2000). Risk factors for adolescent substance abuse and dependence: Data from a national sample. *Journal of Consulting and Clinical Psychology, 68,* 19–30.

Kilshaw, D., & Annett, M. (1983). Right- and left-hand skill: Effects of age, sex, and hand preferences showing superior in left-handers. *British Journal of Psychology, 74,* 253–268.

Kimball, M. M. (1989). A new perspective on women's math achievement. *Psychological Bulletin, 105,* 198–214.

Kimura, D. (1992). Cognitive function: Sex differences and hormonal influences. *Neuroscience year: Supplement 2 to the Encyclopedia of neuroscience.* Boston: Birkhauser.

Kimura, D., & Hampson, E. (1992). Neural and hormonal mechanisms mediating sex differences in cognition. In P. A. Vernon (Ed.), *Biological approaches to the study of human intelligence.* Norwood, NJ: Ablex.

King, C. A., Raskin, A., Gdowski, C. L., Butkus, M., & Opipari, L. (1990). Psychosocial factors associated with urban adolescent female suicide attempts. *Journal of the American Academy of Child and Adolescent Psychiatry, 29,* 289–294.

King, L. A., Scollon, C. K., Ramsey, C., & Williams, T. (2000). Stories of life transition: Subjective well-being and ego development in parents of children with Down Syndrome. *Journal of Research in Personality, 34*(4), 509–536.

King, R. (2000). Cited in Frazier, L. (2000, July 16). The new face of HIV is young, black. *The Washington Post,* p. C01.

King, R. A., Pfeffer, C., Gammon, G. D., & Cohen, D. J. (1992). Suicidality of childhood and adolescence. In B. B. Lahey & A. E. Kazdin (Eds.), *Advances in clinical child psychology* (Vol. 14). New York: Plenum.

Kinnunen, T., Doherty, K., Militello, F. S., & Garvey, A. J. (1996). Depression and smoking cessation. *Journal of Consulting and Clinical Psychology, 64,* 791–798.

Kinsey, A. C., Pomeroy, W. B., & Martin, C. E. (1948). *Sexual behavior in the human male.* Philadelphia: W. B. Saunders.

Kinsey, A. C., Pomeroy, W. B., Martin, C. E., & Gebhard, P. H. (1953). *Sexual behavior in the human female.* Philadelphia: W. B. Saunders.

Kirchler, E., Pombeni, M. L., & Palmonari, A. (1991). Sweet sixteen . . . Adolescents' problems and the peer group as source of support. *European Journal of Psychology of Education, 6,* 393–410.

Kirsh, S. J., Crnic, K. A., & Greenberg, M. T. (1995). Relations between parent–child affect and synchrony and cognitive outcome at 5 years of age. *Personal Relationships, 2*(3) 187–198.

Klahr, D. (1992). Information-processing approaches to cognitive development. In M. H. Bornstein & M. E. Lamb (Eds.), *Developmental psychology: An advanced textbook* (3rd ed.). Hillsdale, NJ: Erlbaum.

Klaus, M., & Kennell, J. (1976). *Maternal-infant bonding.* St. Louis: C. V. Mosby.

Klaus, M. H., & Kennell, J. H. (1978). Parent-to-infant attachment. In J. H. Stevens, Jr., & M. Mathews (Eds.), *Mother/child, father/child relationships.* Washington, DC: National Association for the Education of Young Children.

Klebanoff, M. A., Levine, R. J., DerSimonian, R., Clemens, J. D., & Wilkins, D. G. (1999). Maternal serum paraxanthine, a caffeine metabolite, and the risk of spontaneous abortion. *The New England Journal of Medicine, 341*(22), 1639–1644.

Klein, H. G. (2000). Will blood transfusion ever be safe enough? *Journal of the American Medical Association online, 284*(2).

Klein, J. (1993, June 21). Make the daddies pay. *Newsweek,* p. 33.

Klein, M. H., Hyde, J. S., Essex, M. J., & Clark, R. (1998). Maternity leave, role quality, work involvement, and mental health one year after delivery. *Psychology of Women Quarterly, 22*(2), 239–266.

Klein, P. J., & Meltzoff, A. N. (1999). Long-term memory, forgetting and deferred imitation in 12–month-old infants. *Developmental Science, 2*(1), 102–113.

Klimes-Dougan, B. (1993, March). *The emergence of negotiation.* Paper presented at the meeting of the Society for Research in Child Development, New Orleans, LA.

Klingberg, T., Vaidya, C. J., Gabrieli, J. D. E., Moseley, M. E., & Hedehus, M. (1999). Myelination and organization of the frontal white matter in children: A diffusion tensor MRI study. *Neuroreport: For Rapid Communication of Neuroscience Research, 10*(13), 2817–2821.

Klinnert, M. C., Emde, R. N., & Butterfield, P. (1986). Social referencing: The infant's use of emotional signals from a friendly adult with mother present. *Developmental Psychology, 22,* 427–432.

Klintsova, A. Y., & Greenough, W. T. (1999). Synaptic plasticity in cortical systems. *Current Opinion in Neurobiology, 9*(2), 203–208.

Klorman, R., Brumaghim, J. T., Fitzpatrick, P. A., Borgstedt, A. D., & Strauss, J. (1994). Clinical and cognitive effects of methylphenidate on children with attention deficit disorder as a function of aggression/oppositionality and age. *Journal of Abnormal Psychology, 103,* 206–221.

Kobayashi-Winata, H., & Power, T. G. (1989). Childrearing and compliance: Japanese and American families in Houston. *Journal of Cross-Cultural Psychology, 20,* 333–356.

Kochanska, G. (1992). Children's interpersonal influence with mothers and peers. *Developmental Psychology, 28,* 491–499.

Kochanska, G. (2001). Emotional development in children with different attachment histories: The first three years. *Child Development, 72*(2), 474–490.

Kochanska, G., Coy, K. C., Murray, K. T. (2001). The development of self-regulation in the first four years of life. *Child Development, 72*(4), 1091–1111.

Kochanska, G., & Radke-Yarrow, M. (1992). Inhibition in toddlerhood and the dynamics of the child's interaction with an unfamiliar peer at age five. *Child Development, 63,* 325–335.

Kogan, M. D., et al. (2000). Trends in twin birth outcomes and prenatal care utilization in the United States, 1981–1997. *Journal of the American Medical Association, 284*(3), 335.

Kohlberg, L. (1963). Moral development and identification. In H. W., Stevenson (Ed.), *Child psychology: 62nd yearbook of the National Society for the Study of Education.* Chicago: University of Chicago Press.

Kohlberg, L. (1966). Cognitive stages and preschool education. *Human Development, 9,* 5–17.

Kohlberg, L. (1969). Stage and sequence: The cognitive-developmental approach to socialization. In D. A. Goslin (Ed.), *Handbook of socialization theory and research.* Chicago: Rand McNally.

Kohlberg, L. (1981). *The meaning and measurement of moral development.* Worcester, MA: Clark University Press.

Kohlberg, L. (1985). *The psychology of moral development.* San Francisco: Harper & Row.

Kohlberg, L., & Kramer, R. (1969). Continuities and discontinuities in childhood and adult moral development. *Human Development, 12,* 93–120.

Kolata, G. (1991, November 10). Young women offer to sell their eggs to infertile couples, *The New York Times,* pp. A1, 16.

Kolata, G. (1992a, July 15). As fears about a fetal test grow, many doctors are advising against it. *The New York Times,* p. B7.

Kolata, G. (1992b, June 21). More children are employed, often perilously. *The New York Times,* pp. 1, 22.

Kolata, G. (1992c, April 26). A parents' guide to kids' sports. *The New York Times Magazine,* pp. 12–15, 40, 44–46.

Kolata, G. (1992d, January 16). Study reports dyslexia isn't always permanent. *The New York Times,* p. A13.

Kolata, G. (1997, February 24). With cloning of a sheep, the ethical ground shifts. *The New York Times,* pp. A1, B8.

Kolata, G. (1998, January 5). Infertile foreigners see opportunity in the U.S. *The New York Times.*

Kolata, G. (1998, September 9). Researchers report success in method to pick baby's sex. *The New York Times* online.

Kolb, B., Gibb, R., & Gorny, G. (2001). Cortical plasticity and the development of behavior after early frontal cortical injury. *Developmental Neuropsychology, 18*(3), 423–444.

Kolbe, L. (1998). Cited in Poll shows decline in sex by high school students. (1998, September 18). *The New York Times,* p. A26.

Konner, M. J. (1977). Infancy among the Kalahari San. In P. H. Leiderman, S. R. Tulkin, & A. Rosenfeld (Eds.), *Culture and infancy: Variations in the human experience.* New York: Academic Press.

Konstantareas, M. M., & Desbois, N. (2001). Preschoolers perceptions of the unfairness of maternal disciplinary practices. *Child Abuse & Neglect, 25*(4), 473–488.

Kontos, S. (1993, March). *The ecology of family day care.* Paper presented at the meeting of the Society for Research in Child Development, New Orleans, LA.

Koop, C. E. (1988). *Understanding AIDS* (HHS Publication No. [CDC] HHS-88–8404). Washington, DC: U.S. Government Printing Office.

Koorland, M. A. (1986). Applied behavior analysis and the correction of learning disabilities. In J. K. Togesen, & B. Y. L. Wong (Eds.), *Psychological and educational perspectives on learning disabilities.* Orlando, FL: Academic Press.

Kopp, C. B. (1989). Regulation of distress and negative emotions: A developmental view. *Developmental Psychology, 25,* 343–354.

Kopp, C. B. (1992, Spring). Emotional distress and control in young children. In N. Eisenberg & R. A. Fabes (Eds.), *New directions for child development: No. 55. Emotion and its regulation in early development.* San Francisco: Jossey-Bass.

Koriat, A., Goldsmith, M., Schneider, W., & Nakash-Dura, M. (2001). The credibility of children's testimony: Can children control the accuracy of their memory reports? *Journal of Experimental Child Psychology, 79*(4), 405–437.

Korner, A. F. (1987). Preventive intervention with high-risk newborns: Theoretical, conceptual, and methodological perspectives. In J. D. Osofsky (Ed.), *Handbook of infant development* (2nd ed). New York: Wiley.

Kramer, M. S. et al., for the PROBIT Study Group. (2001). Promotion of Breastfeeding Intervention Trial (PROBIT): A randomized trial in the Republic of Belarus. *Journal of the American Medical Association, 285,* 413–420.

Krappmann, L., Oswald, H., Weiss, K., & Uhlendorff, H. (1993, March). *Peer relationships of children in middle childhood.* Paper presented at the meeting of the Society for Research in Child Development, New Orleans, LA.

Krasnoff, A. G., Walker, J. T., & Howard, M. (1989). Early sex-linked activities and interests related to spatial abilities. *Personality and Individual Differences, 10,* 81–85.

Krcmar, M., & Cooke, M. C. (2001). Children's moral reasoning and their perceptions of television violence. *Journal of Communication, 51*(2), 300–316.

Krebs, D. L., Vermeulen, S. C. A., Carpendale, J. I., & Denton, K. (1991). In W. M. Kurtines & J. L. Gewirtz (Eds.), *Handbook of moral behavior and development* (Vol. 2). Hillsdale, NJ: Erlbaum.

Krechevsky, M. (1996). Cited in Murray, B. (1996). Students stretch beyond the "three Rs." *APA Monitor, 26*(4), 46.

Kreitler, S., & Kreitler, H. (1989). Horizontal decalage: A problem and its solution. *Cognitive Development, 4,* 89–119.

Kroger, J. (1989). *Identity in adolescence.* New York: Routledge.

Kroger, J. (2000). Ego identity status research in the new millennium. *International Journal of Behavioral Development, 24*(2), 145–148.

Kuczaj, S. A., II (1982). On the nature of syntactic development. In S. A. Kuczaj, II (Ed.), *Language development: Vol. 1. Syntax and semantics.* Hillsdale, NJ: Erlbaum.

Kuczmarski, R. J., et al. (2000, December 4). CDC Growth charts: United States. Advance data from vital and health statistics; no. 314. Hyattsville, MD: National Center for Health Statistics.

Kuczynski, L., & Kochanska, G. (1990). Development of children's noncompliance strategies from toddlerhood to age 5. *Developmental Psychology, 26,* 398–408.

Kuhl, P. K. (1987). Perception of speech and sound in early infancy. In P. Salapatek & L. Cohen (Eds.), *Handbook of infant perception: Vol. 2. From perception to cognition.* Orlando, FL: Academic Press.

Kuhl, P. K., Williams, K. A., Lacerda, F., Stevens, K. N., & Lindblom, B. (1992). Linguistic experience alters phonetic perception in infants by 6 months of age. *Science, 255,* 606–608.

Kuhn, D. (1976). Short-term longitudinal evidence for the sequentiality of Kohlberg's early stages of moral development. *Developmental Psychology, 2,* 162–166.

Kuhn, D. (1991). Higher-order reasoning in adolescence. In R. M. Lerner, A. C. Petersen, & J. Brooks-Gunn (Eds.), *Encyclopedia of adolescence.* New York: Garland.

Kuhn, D., Kohlberg, L., Langer, J., & Hanna, N. (1977). The development of formal operations in logical and moral judgment. *Genetic Psychology Monographs, 95,* 97–188.

Kunugi, H., Nanko, S., & Murray, R. M. (2001). Obstetric complications and schizophrenia: Prenatal underdevelopment and subsequent neurodevelopmental impairment. *British Journal of Psychiatry, 178*(Suppl40), S25–S29.

Kupersmidt, J. B., Bryant, D., & Willoughby, M. T. (2000). Prevalence of aggressive behaviors among preschoolers in Head Start and community child care programs. *Behavioral Disorders, 26*(1), 42–52.

Kuther, T. L. (1999). A developmental-contextual perspective on youth covictimization by community violence. *Adolescence, 34*(136), 699–714.

Kutner, L. (1989, May 30). Helping a child adapt to the new baby in the family. *The New York Times,* p. C2.

Kutner, L. (1992a, February 27). Encouragement rather than control is often best in helping children with learning disabilities. *The New York Times,* p. B6.

Kutner, L. (1992b, March 12). The more subtle shades of body dissatisfaction are just as insidious as anorexia and bulimia. *The New York Times,* p. B2.

Kutner, L. (1992c, May 17). When young children watch television, they usually believe everything they see. *The New York Times,* p. B4.

Kutner, L. (1993, May 6). No no no no lima beans: Picky eaters may just be responding to biology. *The New York Times,* p. B5.

Ladd, G. W., & Price, J. M. (1987). Predicting children's social and school adjustment following the transition from preschool to kindergarten. *Child Development, 58,* 1168–1189.

La Freniere, P. J., Dumas, J. E., Capuano, F., & Dubeau, D. (1992). Development and validation of the preschool socioaffective profile. *Psychological Assessment, 4,* 442–450.

Lai, T. J., Guo, Y. I., Guo, N-W., & Hsu, C. C. (2001). Effect of prenatal exposure to polychlorinated biphenyls on cognitive development in children: A longitudinal study in Taiwan. *British Journal of Psychiatry, 178*(Suppl40), S49–S52.

Lalumière, M. L., Blanchard, R., & Zucker, K. J. (2000). Sexual orientation and handedness in men and women: A meta-analysis. *Psychological Bulletin, 126*(4), 575–592.

Lamaze, F. (1981). *Painless childbirth.* New York: Simon & Schuster.

Lamb, M. (1987). Predictive implications of individual differences in attachment. *Journal of Consulting and Clinical Psychology, 55,* 817–824.

Lamb, M. E. (1981). The development of father–infant relationships. In M. E. Lamb (Ed.), *The role of the father in child development.* New York: Wiley.

Lamb, M. E., Ketterlinus, R. D., & Fracasso, M. P. (1992). Parent–child relationships. In M. H. Bornstein & M. E. Lamb (Eds.), *Developmental psychology: An advanced textbook* (3rd ed.). Hillsdale, NJ: Lawrence Erlbaum.

Lamb, M. E., & Oppenheim, D. (1989). Fatherhood and father–child relationships. In S. H. Cath, A. Gurwitt, & L. Gunsberg (Eds.), *Fathers and their families.* Hillsdale, NJ: Analytic Press.

Lamb, M. E., Sternberg, K. J., & Ketterlinus, R. D. (1992). Child care in the United States: The modern era. In M. E. Lamb, K. J. Sternberg, C. Hwang, & A. G. Broberg (Eds.), *Child care in context.* Hillsdale, NJ: Erlbaum.

Lamb, M. E., Sternberg, K. J., & Prodromidis, M. (1992). Nonmaternal care and the security of infant–mother attachment: A reanalysis of the data. *Infant Behavior and Development, 15,* 71–83.

Lamb, M. E., & Teti, D. M. (1991). Adolescent childbirth and marriage: Associations with long-term marital instability. In R. M. Lerner, A. C. Petersen, & J. Brooks-Gunn (Eds.), *Encyclopedia of adolescence.* New York: Garland.

Lambert, W. E., Genesee, F., Holobow, N., & Chartrand, L. (1991). *Bilingual education for majority English-speaking children.* Montreal: McGill University.

Lamborn, S. D., Mounts, N. S., Steinberg, L., & Dornbusch, S. M. (1991). Patterns of competence and adjustment among adolescents from authoritative, authoritarian, indulgent and neglectful families. *Child Development, 62,* 1049–1065.

Lampl, M., Veldhuis, J. D., & Johnson, M. L. (1992). Saltation and stasis: A model of human growth. *Science, 258,* 801–803.

Landau, S., & Milich, R., (1990). Assessment of children's social status and peer relations. In A. M. LaGreca (Ed.), *Through the eyes of a child.* Boston: Allyn and Bacon.

Landesman, S. (1990). Institutionalization revisited: Expanding views on early and cumulative life experiences. In M. Lewis & S. M. Miller (Eds.), *Handbook of developmental psychopathology.* New York: Plenum.

Lane, S. D., & Cherek, D. R. (2001). Risk taking by adolescents with maladaptive behavior histories. *Experimental & Clinical Psychopharmacology, 9*(1), 74–82.

Lang, P. J., & Melamed, B. B. (1969). Case report: Avoidance conditioning therapy of an infant with chronic ruminative vomiting. *Journal of Abnormal Psychology, 74,* 1–8.

Langbehn, D. R., & Cadoret, R. J. (2001). The adult antisocial syndrome with and without antecedent conduct disorder: Comparisons from an adoption study. *Comprehensive Psychiatry, 42*(4), 272–282.

Lange, G., & Pierce, S. H. (1992). Memory-strategy learning and maintenance in preschool children. *Developmental Psychology, 28,* 453–462.

Langlois, J. H., et al. (2000). Maxims or myths of beauty? A meta-analytic and theoretical review. *Psychological Bulletin, 126*(3), 390–423.

Langlois, J. H., Ritter, J. M., Roggman, L. A., & Vaughn, L. S. (1991). Facial diversity and infant preferences for attractive faces. *Developmental Psychology, 26,* 153–159.

Langlois, J. H., Roggman, L. A., & Rieser-Danner, L. A. (1990). Infants' differential social responses to attractive and unattractive faces. *Developmental Psychology, 26,* 153–159.

Laor, N., Wolmer, L., & Cohen, D. J. (2001). Mothers' functioning and children's symptoms 5 years after a SCUD missile attack. *American Journal of Psychiatry, 158*(7), 1020–1026.

Lapadat, J. C. (1991). Pragmatic language skills of students with language and/or learning disabilities: A quantitative synthesis. *Journal of Learning Disabilities, 24,* 147–157.

Lapsley, D. K. (1990). Continuity and discontinuity in adolescent social cognitive development. In R. Montemayor, G. R. Adams, & T. P. Guillotta (Eds.), *From childhood to adolescence: A transitional period?* Newbury Park, CA: Sage.

Lapsley, D. K. (1991). Egocentrism theory and the "new look" at the imaginary audience and personal fable in adolescence. In R. M. Lerner, A. C. Petersen, & J. Brooks-Gunn (Eds.), *Encyclopedia of adolescence.* New York: Garland.

Largie, S., Field, T., Hernandez-Reif, M., Sanders, C. E., & Diego, M. (2001). Employment during adolescence is associated with depression, inferior relationships, lower grades, and smoking. *Adolescence, 36*(142), 395–401.

Largo, R. H., et al. (2001). Neuromotor development from 5 to 18 years. Part 1: Timed performance. *Developmental Medicine & Child Neurology, 43*(7), 436–443.

Larson, P., et al. (1999). Gender issues in the use of virtual environments. *CyberPsychology & Behavior, 2*(2), 113–123.

Larson, R., & Richards, M. H. (1991). Daily companionship in late childhood and early adolescence: Changing developmental contexts. *Child Development, 62,* 284–300.

Laszlo, J. I. (1990). Child perceptive-motor development: Normal and abnormal development of skilled behavior. In C. A. Hauert (Ed.), *Developmental psychology: Cognitive, perceptive-motor, and neuropsychological perspectives.* Amsterdam: North-Holland.

Latimer, W. W., Winters, K. C., Stinchfield, R., & Traver, R. E. (2000). Demographic, individual, and interpersonal predictors of adolescent alcohol and marijuana use following treatment. *Psychology of Addictive Behaviors, 14*(2), 162–173.

Laub, J. H., & Vaillant, G. E. (2000). Delinquency and mortality: A 50-year follow-up study of 1,000 delinquent and nondelinquent boys. *American Journal of Psychiatry, 157*(1), 96–102.

Laumann, E. O., Gagnon, J. H., Michael, R. T., & Michaels, S. (1994). *The social organization of sexuality.* Chicago: University of Chicago Press.

Laurendeau, M., & Pinard, A. (1970). *The development of the concept of space in the child.* New York: International Universities Press.

Laursen, B. (1993). Conflict management among close peers. In B. Laursen (Ed.), *New directions in child development: No. 60. Close friendships in adolescence.* San Francisco: Jossey-Bass.

Laveman, L. (2000). The Harmonium Project: A macrosystemic approach to empowering adolescents. *Journal of Mental Health Counseling, 22*(1), 17–31.

Law, J. (2000). The politics of breastfeeding: Assessing risk, dividing labor. *Signs, 25*(2), 407–450.

Lawrence, R. A. (2001). Breastfeeding in Belarus. *Journal of the American Medical Association online, 285*(4).

Leadbeater, B. (1991). Relativistic thinking in adolescence. In R. M. Lerner, A. C. Petersen, & J. Brooks-Gunn (Eds.), *Encyclopedia of adolescence.* New York: Garland.

Leary, W. E. (1992, November 4). For some adults, bed-wetting is far from a distant memory. *The New York Times,* p. A19.

Lecanuet, J. P., Graniere-Deferre, C., Jacquet, A.-Y., & DeCasper, A. J. (2000). Fetal discrimination of low-pitched musical notes. *Developmental Psychobiology, 36*(1), 29–39.

Lederberg, A. R., & Mobley, C. E. (1990). The effect of hearing impairment on the quality of attachment and mother–toddler interaction. *Child Development, 61,* 1596–1604.

Lee, D. T. S., et al. (2001). A psychiatric epidemiological study of postpartum Chinese women. *American Journal of Psychiatry, 158*(2), 220–226.

Lee, N. E., Brooks-Gunn, J., Schnur, E., & Liaw, F. R. (1990). Are Head Start effects sustained? A longitudinal follow-up comparison of disadvantaged children attending Head Start, no preschool, and other preschool programs. *Child Development, 61,* 495–507.

Lehman, E. B., McKinley-Pace, M., Leonard, A. M., Thompson, D., & Johns, K. (2001). Item-cued directed forgetting of related words and pictures in children and adults: Selective rehearsal versus cognitive inhibition. *Journal of General Psychology, 128*(1), 81–97.

Leinwand, D. (2000, August 24). 20% say they used drugs with their mom or dad, Among reasons: Boomer culture and misguided attempts to bond. *USA Today online.*

Leitenberg, H., Ditzer, M. J., & Srebnik, D. (1993). Gender differences in masturbation and the relation of masturbation experience in preadolescence and/or early adolescence to sexual behavior and sexual adjustment in young adulthood. *Archives of Sexual Behavior, 22,* 87–98.

Lenneberg, E. H. (1967). *Biological foundations of language.* New York: Wiley.

Leon, M. R. (2000). Effects of caffeine on cognitive, psychomotor, and affective performance of children with attention-deficit/hyperactivity disorder. *Journal of Attention Disorders, 4*(1) 27–47.

Leonard, S. P., & Archer, J. (1989). A naturalistic investigation of gender constancy in three- to four-year-old children. *British Journal of Developmental Psychology, 7,* 341–346.

Lepola, J., Vaurus, M., & Maeki, H. (2000). Gender differences in the development of academic self-concept of attainment from the 2nd to the 6th grade: Relations with achievement and perceived motivational orientation. *Psychology: The Journal of the Hellenic Psychological Society, 7*(3), 290–308.

Lerner, G. (1993). *The creation of feminist consciousness.* New York: Oxford University Press.

Lerner, J. V., Hertzog, C., Hooker, K. A., Hassibi, M., & Thomas, A. (1988). A longitudinal study of negative emotional states and adjustment from early childhood through adolescence. *Child Development, 59,* 356–366.

Lerner, J. V., & Hess, L. E. (1991). Maternal employment influences on adolescent development. In R. M. Lerner, A. C. Petersen, & J. Brooks-Gunn (Eds.), *Encyclopedia of adolescence.* New York: Garland.

Lerner, R. M. (1991). Changing organism-context relations as the basic process of development: A developmental contextual perspective. *Developmental Psychology, 27,* 27–32.

Lester, B. M., Als, H., & Brazelton, T. B. (1982). Regional obstetric anesthesia and newborn behavior: A reanalysis toward synergistic effects. *Child Development, 53,* 687–692.

Lester, B. M., Boukydis, C. F. Z., Garcia-Coll, C. T., Hole, W., & Peucker, M. (1992). Infantile colic: Acoustic cry characteristics, maternal perception of cry, and temperament. *Infant Behavior and Development, 15,* 15–26.

LeTourneau, N., et al. (2001). Supporting parents: Can intervention improve parent–child relationships? *Journal of Family Nursing, 7*(2), 159–187.

Leung, P. W. L., & Poon, M. W. L. (2001). Dysfunctional schemas and cognitive distortions in psychopathology: A test of the specificity hypothesis. *Journal of Child Psychology & Psychiatry & Allied Disciplines, 42*(6), 755–765.

Leve, L. D., Winebarger, A. A., Fagot, B. I., Reid, J. B., & Goldsmith, H. H. (1998). Environmental and genetic variance in children's observed and reported maladaptive behavior. *Child Development, 69*(5), 1286–1298.

Leventhal, E. A., Leventhal, H., Shacham, S., & Easterling, D. V. (1989). Active coping reduces reports of pain from childbirth. *Journal of Consulting & Clinical Psychology, 57*(3), 365–371.

Leventhal, T., Graber, J. A., & Brooks-Gunn, J. (2001). Adolescent transitions to young adulthood: Antecedents, correlates, and consequences of adolescent employment. *Journal of Research on Adolescence, 11*(3), 297–323.

LeVine, R. A. (1974). Parental goals: A cross-cultural view. In H. J. Leichter (Ed.), *The family as educator.* New York: Teachers College Press.

Levitt, M. J., Weber, R. A., Clark, M. C., & McDonnell, P. (1985). Reciprocity of exchange in toddler sharing behavior. *Developmental Psychology, 21,* 122–123.

Levy, G. D., Sadovsky, A. L., & Troseth, G. L. (2000). Aspects of young children's perceptions of gender-typed occupations. *Sex Roles, 42*(11–12), 993–1006.

Lewin, T. (1991, February 8). Studies on teen-age sex cloud condom debate. *The New York Times,* p. A10.

Lewin, T. (1995). Women are becoming equal providers. *The New York Times,* p. A27.

Lewinsohn, P. M., Brown, R. A., Seeley, J. R., & Ramsey, S. E. (2000a). Psychological correlates of cigarette smoking abstinence, experimentation, persistence, and frequency during adolescence. *Nicotine & Tobacco Research, 2*(2), 121–131.

Lewinsohn, P. M., Rohde, P., Seeley, J. R., Klein, D. N., & Gotlib, I. H. (2000). Natural course of adolescent major depressive disorder in a community sample: Predictors of recurrence in young adults. *American Journal of Psychiatry, 157,* 1584–1591.

Lewis, C., & Osborne, A. (1990). Three-year-olds' problems with false belief: Conceptual deficit or linguistic artifact? *Child Development, 61,* 1514–1519.

Lewis, D. O. (1991a). Conduct disorder. In M. Lewis (Ed.), *Child and adolescent psychiatry: A comprehensive textbook.* Baltimore: Williams & Wilkins.

Lewis, D. O. (1991b). The development of the symptom of violence. In M. Lewis (Ed.), *Child and adolescent psychiatry.* Baltimore: Williams & Wilkins.

Lewis, J. M. (1993). Childhood play in normality, pathology, and therapy. *American Journal of Orthopsychiatry, 63,* 6–15.

Lewis, M. (1990). Social knowledge and social development. *Merrill-Palmer Quarterly, 36,* 93–116.

Lewis, M. (1991). Ways of knowing: Objective self-awareness or consciousness. *Developmental Review, 11,* 231–243.

Lewis, M. (1997). *Altering fate—Why the past does not predict the future.* New York: Guilford Press.

Lewis, M. (1998). Cited in Blakeslee, S. (1998, August 4). Re-evaluating significance of baby's bond with mother. *The New York Times,* pp. F1, F2.

Lewis, M., & Brooks-Gunn, J. (1979). *Social cognition and the acquisition of self.* New York: Plenum.

Lewis, M., & Feiring, C. (1989). Early predictors of childhood friendship. In T. J. Berndt & G. W. Ladd (Eds.), *Peer relationships in child development.* New York: Wiley.

Lewis, M., Worobey, J., Ramsay, D. S., & McCormack, M. K. (1992). Prenatal exposure to heavy metals: Effect on childhood cognitive skills and health status. *Pediatrics, 89,* 1010–1015.

Li, G., Baker, S. P., Smialek, J. E., & Soderstrom, C. A. (2001). Use of alcohol as a risk factor for bicycling injury. *Journal of the American Medical Association, 284,* 893–896.

Liben, L. S. (1991). The Piagetian water-level task: Looking below the surface. In R. Vasta (Ed.), *Annals of child development* (Vol. 8). London: Kingsley.

Liben, L. S., & Signorella, M. L. (1993). Gender-schematic processing in children: The role of initial interpretations of stimuli. *Developmental Psychology, 29,* 141–149.

Lickliter, R. (2001). The dynamics of language development: From perception to comprehension. *Developmental Science, 4*(1), 21–23.

Lickona, T. (1991). Moral development in the elementary school classroom. In W. M. Kurtines & J. L. Gewirtz (Eds.), *Handbook of moral behavior and development* (Vol. 3). Hillsdale, NJ: Erlbaum.

Liebert, R. M., & Fischel, J. E. (1990). The elimination disorders: Enuresis and encopresis. In M. Lewis & S. M. Miller (Eds.), *Handbook of developmental pathology.* New York: Plenum.

Linares, L. O., et al. (2001). A mediational model for the impact of exposure to community violence on early child behavior problems. *Child Development, 72*(2), 639–652.

Linn, S., et al. (1988). Adverse outcomes of pregnancy in women exposed to diethylstilbestrol in pregnancy. *Journal of Reproductive Medicine, 33,* 3–7.

Linney, J. A., & Seidman, E. (1989). The future of schooling. *American Psychologist, 44,* 336–340.

Lipper, G. M., et al. (2000). Recent therapeutic advances in dermatology. *Journal of the American Medical Association, 283,* 175.

Lipsitt, L. P. (1990a). Learning and memory in infants. *Merrill-Palmer Quarterly, 36,* 53–66.

Lipsitt, L. P. (1990b). Learning process in the human newborn. In A. Diamond (Ed.), *The development and neutral bases of higher cognitive functions.* New York: New York Academy of Sciences.

Little, A. H., Lipsitt, L. P., & Rovee-Collier, C. (1984). Classical conditioning and retention of the infants' eyelid response: Effects of age and interstimulus interval. *Journal of Experimental Child Psychology, 37,* 512–524.

Liu, X., et al. (2000). Behavioral and emotional problems in Chinese children of divorced parents. *Journal of the American Academy of Child & Adolescent Psychiatry, 39*(7), 896–903.

Liu, X., Sun, Z., Uchiyama, M., Li, Y., & Okawa, M. (2000). Attaining nocturnal urinary control, nocturnal enuresis, and behavioral problems in Chinese children aged 6 through 16 years. *Journal of the American Academy of Child & Adolescent Psychiatry, 39*(12), 1557–1564.

Liu, Y., Curtis, J. T., & Wang, Z. (2001). Vasopressin in the lateral septum regulates pair bond formation in male prairie voles *(Microtus ochrogaster). Behavioral Neuroscience, 115*(4), 910–919.

Lobel, M., Dunkel-Schetter, C., & Scrimshaw, S. C. M. (1992). Prenatal maternal stress and prematurity: A prospective study of socioeconomically disadvantaged women. *Health Psychology, 11,* 32–40.

Lobel, T. E., & Menashri, J. (1993). Relations of conceptions of gender-role transgressions and gender constancy to gender-typed toy preferences. *Developmental Psychology, 29,* 150–155.

Lock, J., & Le Grange, D. (2001). Can family based treatment of anorexia nervosa be manualized? *Journal of Psychotherapy Practice & Research, 10*(4). 253–261.

Loeber, R., Wei, E., Stouthamer-Loeber, M., Huizanga, D., & Thornberry, T. P. (1999). Behavioral antecedents to serious and violent offending: Joint analyses from the Denver Youth Survey, Pittsburgh Youth Study and the Rochester Youth Development Study. *Studies on Crime & Crime Prevention, 8*(2), 245–263.

Loehlin, J. C. (1992). *Genes and environment in personality development.* Newbury Park, CA: Sage.

Loovis, E. M., & Butterfield, S. A. (2000). Influence of age, sex, and balance on mature skipping by children in grades K–8. *Perceptual & Motor Skills, 90*(3), 974–978.

Loranger, M., Pepin, M., Cote, M., Boisvert, J., & Blais, M. (2000). Differences entre adolescents et adolescentes a quatre taches de visualisation spatiale. *Canadian Psychology, 41*(1), 61–68.

Lorenz, K. (1962). *King Solomon's ring.* London: Methuen.

Lorenz, K. (1981). *The foundations of ethology.* New York: Springer-Verlag.

Lott, B., & Maluso, D. (1991, August). *The social learning of gender: A feminist review.* Paper presented at the meeting of the American Psychological Association, San Francisco.

Lovaas, O. I. (1977). *The autistic child: Language development through behavior modification.* New York: Halstead Press.

Lovaas, O. I., Smith, T., & McEachin, J. J. (1989). Clarifying comments on the young autism study: Reply to Schapler, Short, and Mesibov. *Journal of Consulting and Clinical Psychology, 57,* 165–167.

Love, J. M., Logue, M. E., Trudeau, J. V., & Thayer, K. (1992). *Transitions to kindergarten in American schools.* Portsmouth, N. H.: RMC Research Corp.

Lowe, M. R., et al. (1996). Restraint, dieting, and the continuum model of bulimia nervosa. *Journal of Abnormal Psychology, 105,* 508–517.

Lowrey, G. H. (1986). *Growth and development of children.* Chicago: Year Book Medical Publishers.

Lubinski, D., & Benbow, C. P. (1992). Gender differences in abilities and preferences among the gifted: Implications for the math–science pipeline. *Current Directions in Psychological Science, 1,* 61–66.

Lubinski, D., & Benbow, C. P. (2000). States of excellence. *American Psychologist, 55,* 137–150.

Lucariello, J., & Nelson, K. (1985). Slotfiller categories as memory organizers for young children. *Developmental Psychology, 21,* 272–282.

Lucas, A. R. (1991). Eating disorders. In M. Lewis (Ed.), *Child and adolescent psychiatry: A comprehensive textbook.* Baltimore: Williams & Wilkins.

Ludman, E. J., et al. (2000). Stress, depressive symptoms, and smoking cessation among pregnant women. *Health Psychology, 19*(1), 21–27.

Lukas, W. D., & Campbell, B. C. (2000). Evolutionary and ecological aspects of early brain malnutrition in humans. *Human Nature, 11*(1), 1–26.

Lummis, M., & Stevenson, H. W. (1990). Gender differences in beliefs and achievement: A cross-cultural study. *Developmental Psychology, 26,* 254–263.

Luster, T., & Dubow, E. (1992). Home environment and maternal intelligence as predictors of verbal intelligence: A comparison of preschool and school-age children. *Merrill-Palmer Quarterly, 38,* 151–173.

Lydon-Rochelle, M., Holt, V. L., Easterling, T. R., & Martin, D. P. (2001). Risk of uterine rupture during labor among women with a prior cesarean delivery. *The New England Journal of Medicine, 345*(1), 3–8.

Lykken, D. T., McGue, M., Tellegen, A., & Bouchard, T. J., Jr. (1992). Emergenesis: Genetic traits that may not run in families. *American Psychologist, 47,* 1565–1577.

Lykken, D., & Tellegen, A. (1996). Happiness is a stochastic phenomenon. *Psychological Science, 7*(3), 186–189.

Lynam, D. R., et al. (2000). The interaction between impulsivity and neighborhood context on offending: The effects of impulsivity are stronger in poorer neighborhoods. *Journal of Abnormal Psychology, 109*(4), 563–574.

Lyons-Ruth, K., Alpern, L., & Repacholi, B. (1993). Disorganized infant attachment classification and maternal psychosocial problems as predictors of hostile-aggressive behavior in the preschool classroom. *Child Development, 64,* 572–585.

Lyons-Ruth, K., Connell, D. B., Grunebaum, H. U., & Botein, S. (1990). Infants at social risk: Maternal depression and family support services as mediators of infant development and security of attachment. *Child Development, 61,* 85–98.

Lytton, H. (1990a). Child and parent effects in boys' conduct disorder: A reinterpretation. *Developmental Psychology, 26,* 683–697.

Lytton, H. (1990b). Child effects—still un-welcome? Response to Dodge and Wahler. *Developmental Psychology, 26,* 702–704.

Lytton, H., & Romney, D. M. (1991). Parents' differential socialization of boys and girls: A meta-analysis. *Psychological Bulletin, 109,* 267–296.

Maccoby, E. E. (1984a). Middle childhood in the context of the family. In A. Collins (Ed.), *Development during the middle years: The years from six to twelve.* Washington, DC: National Academy of Sciences Press.

Maccoby, E. E. (1984b). Socialization and developmental change. *Child Development, 55,* 317–328.

Maccoby, E. E. (1990a). Gender and relationships: A developmental account. *American Psychologist, 45,* 513–520.

Maccoby, E. E. (1990b). The role of gender identity and gender constancy in sex-differentiated development. In D. Schrader (Ed.), *New directions for child development: No. 47. The legacy of Lawrence Kohlberg.* San Francisco: Jossey-Bass.

Maccoby, E. E. (1991a). Different reproductive strategies in males and females. *Child Development, 62,* 676–681.

Maccoby, E. E. (1991b). Gender and relationships: A reprise. *American Psychologist, 46,* 538–539.

Maccoby, E. E. (1992). The role of parents in the socialization of children: An historical overview. *Developmental Psychology, 28,* 1006–1017.

Maccoby, E. E. (1993, March). *Trends and issues in the study of gender role development.* Paper presented at the meeting of the Society for Research in Child Development, New Orleans, LA.

Maccoby, E. E. (2000). Perspectives on gender development. *International Journal of Behavioral Development, 24*(4), 398–406.

Maccoby, E. E., & Feldman, S. (1972). Mother-attachment and stranger reactions in the third year of life. *Monographs of the Society for Research in Child Development, 37*(1, Serial No. 146).

Maccoby, E. E., & Jacklin, C. N. (1974). *The psychology of sex differences.* Stanford, CA: Stanford University Press.

Maccoby, E. E., & Jacklin, C. N. (1987). Gender segregation in childhood. In H. W. Reese (Ed.), *Advances in child development and behavior* (Vol. 20). Orlando, FL: Academic Press.

Maccoby E. E., & Martin, J. A. (1983). Socialization in the context of the family: parent–child interaction. In P. Mussen (Ed.), *Handbook of child psychology: Vol. 4. Socialization, personality, and social development.* New York: Wiley.

MacDonald, K. (1992). Warmth as a developmental construct: An evolutionary analysis. *Child Development, 63,* 753–773.

MacDonald, M. G. (1999). Suicide-intervention trainees' perceptions of awareness for warning signs of suicide. *Psychological Reports, 85*(3, Pt 2 [Spec Issue]), 1195–1198.

MacDonald, T. K., MacDonald, G., Zanna, M. P., & Fong, G. T. (2000). Alcohol, sexual arousal, and intentions to use condoms in young men: Applying alcohol myopia theory to risky sexual behavior. *Health Psychology, 19,* 290–298.

Macey, T. J., Harmon, R. J., & Easterbrooks, M. A. (1987). Impact of premature birth on the development of the infant in the family. *Journal of Consulting and Clinical Psychology, 55,* 846–852.

Macfarlane, A. (1977). *The psychology of childbirth.* Cambridge, MA: Harvard University Press.

Macfarlane, A., Harris, P., & Barnes, I. (1976). Central and peripheral vision in early infancy. *Journal of Experimental Child Psychology, 21,* 532–538.

Macfarlane, A. (1975). Olfaction in the development of social preferences in the human neonate. In M. A. Hofer (Ed.), *Parent–infant interaction.* Amsterdam: Elsevier.

MacKay, A. P., Berg, C. J., & Atrash, H. K. (2001). Pregnancy-related mortality from preeclampsia and eclampsia. *Obstetrics & Gynecology, 97*(4), 533–538.

Mackey, M. C. (1990). Women's preparation for the childbirth experience. *Maternal-Child Nursing Journal, 19*(2), 143–173.

Mackey, M. C. (1995). Women's evaluation of their childbirth performance. *Maternal-Child Nursing Journal, 23*(2), 57–72.

Madden, N. A., Slavin, R. E., Karweit, N. L., Dolan, L., & Wasik, B. A. (1991, April). Success for all. *Phi Delta Kappan,* pp. 593–599.

Madon, S., et al. (2001). Am I as you see me or do you see me as I am? Self-fulfilling prophecies and self-verification. *Personality & Social Psychology Bulletin, 27*(9), 1214–1224.

Madson, L., & Trafimow, D. (2001). Gender comparisons in the private, collective, and allocentric selves. *Journal of Social Psychology, 141*(4), 551–559.

Maejima, K., & Oguchi, T. (2001). The effect of marital discord on children's self-esteem, emotionality, and aggression. *Japanese Journal of Family Psychology, 15*(1), 45–56.

Magnusson, Chris (2001). Adolescent girls' sexual attitudes and opposite-sex relation in 1970 and in 1996. *Journal of Adolescent Health, 28*(3), 242–252.

Mahler, M. S., Pine, F., & Bergman, A. (1975). *The psychological birth of the human infant: Symbiosis and individuation.* New York: Basic Books.

Mahoney, M. C., & James, D. M. (2000). Predictors of anticipated breastfeeding in an urban, low-income setting. *Journal of Family Practice, 49*(6), 529–533.

Main, M., & Cassidy, J. (1988). Categories of responses to reunion with the parent at age 6: Predictable from infant attachment classifications and stable over a 1–month period. *Developmental Psychology, 24,* 415–426.

Main, M., & Hesse, E. (1990). Parents' unresolved traumatic experiences related to infant disorganized attachment status: Is frightened and/or frightening parental behavior the linking mechanism? In M. T. Greenberg, D. Cicchetti, & E. M. Cummings (Eds.), *Attachment in the preschool years.* Chicago: University of Chicago Press.

Main, M., & Weston, D. R. (1981). The quality of the toddler's relationship to mother and to father: Related to conflict behavior and the readiness to establish new relationships. *Child Development, 52,* 932–940.

Maine, S., Shute, R., & Martin, G. (2001). Educating parents about youth suicide: Knowledge, response to suicidal statements, attitudes, and intention to help. *Suicide & Life-Threatening Behavior, 31*(3), 320–332.

Malatesta, G. Z., Culver, C., Tesman, J. R., & Shepard, B. (1989). The development of emotion expression during the first two years of life. *Monographs of the Society for Research in Child Development, 54*(1–2, Serial No. 219).

Malinosky-Rummell, R., & Hansen, D. H. (1993). Long-term consequences of childhood physical abuse. *Psychological Bulletin, 114,* 68–79.

Mandler, J. M. (1990). Recall and its verbal expression. In R. Fivush & J. A. Hudson (Eds.), *Knowing and remembering in young children.* Cambridge: Cambridge University Press.

Mangelsdorf, S. C. (1992). Developmental changes in infant–stranger interaction. *Infant Behavior and Development, 15,* 191–208.

Mangelsdorf, S., Gunnar, M., Kestenbaum, R., Lang, S., & Andreas, D. (1990). Infant proneness-to-distress temperament, maternal personality, and mother–infant attachment: Associations and goodness of fit. *Child Development, 61,* 820–831.

Manke, B. (1993, March). *Dimensions of intimacy during adolescence: Correlates and antecedents.* Paper presented at the Society for Research in Child Development, New Orleans, LA.

Mannuzza, S., Klein, R. G., Bessler, A., Malloy, P., & LaPadula, M. (1998). Adult psychiatric status of hyperactive boys grown up. *American Journal of Psychiatry, 155*(4), 493–498.

Marcia, J. E. (1991). Identity and self-development. In R. M. Lerner, A. C. Petersen, & J. Brooks-Gunn (Eds.), *Encyclopedia of adolescence.* New York: Garland.

Marcia, J. E., Waterman, A. S., Matteson, D. R., Archer, S. L., & Orlofsky, J. L. (1993). *Ego identity: A handbook for psychosocial research.* New York: Springer-Verlag.

Marcus, G. F., et al. (1992). Overregularization in language acquisition. *Monographs of the Society for Research in Child Development, 57*(4, Serial No. 228).

Marean, G. C., Werner, L. A., & Kuhl, P. K. (1992). Vowel categorization by very young infants. *Developmental Psychology, 28,* 396–405.

Markel, H. (2000, July 25). Anorexia can strike boys, too. *The New York Times online.*

Markovitz, H., & Vachon, R. (1990). Conditional reasoning, representation, and level of abstraction. *Developmental Psychology, 26,* 942–951.

Marks, I. M. (1987). The development of normal fear: A review. *Journal of Child Psychology and Psychiatry, 28,* 667–697.

Markus, H., & Kitayama, S. (1991). Culture and the self. *Psychological Review, 98*(2), 224–253.

Marsh, H. W., Craven, R. G., & Debus, R. (1991). Self-concepts of young children 5 to 8 years of age: Measurement and multidimensional structure. *Journal of Educational Psychology, 83,* 377–392.

Martin, B., & Hoffman, J. A. (1990). Conduct disorders. In M. Lewis & S. M. Miller (Eds.), *Handbook of developmental psychopathology.* New York: Plenum.

Martin, C. L. (1990). Attitudes and expectations about children with nontraditional and traditional gender roles. *Sex Roles, 22,* 151–165.

Martin, C. L. (1993). New directions for investigating children's gender knowledge. *Developmental Review, 13,* 184–204.

Martin, C. L., & Little, J. K. (1990). The relation of gender understanding to children's sex-typed preferences and gender stereotypes. *Child Development, 61,* 1427–1439.

Martin, C. L., Wood, C. H., & Little, J. K. (1990). The development of gender stereotype components. *Child Development, 61,* 1891–1904.

Martinez, F. D., Cline, M., & Burrows, B. (1992). Increased incidence of asthma in children of smoking mothers. *Pediatrics, 89,* 21–26.

Marttunen, M. J., et al. (1998). Completed suicide among adolescents with no diagnosable psychiatric disorder. *Adolescence, 33*(131), 669–681.

Masataka, N. (1998). Perception of motherese in Japanese sign language by 6-month-old hearing infants. *Developmental Psychology, 34*(2), 241–246.

Masi, G., Mucci, M., & Millepiedi, S. (2001). Separation anxiety disorder in children and adolescents: Epidemiology, diagnosis, and management. *CNS Drugs, 15*(2), 93–104.

Masten, A. S. (2001). Ordinary magic: Resilience processes in development. *American Psychologist, 56*(3), 227–238.

Mather, D. S. (2001). Does dyslexia develop from learning the alphabet in the wrong hemisphere? A cognitive neuroscience analysis. *Brain & Language, 76*(3), 282–316.

Matlin, M. (1999). *The psychology of women* (4th ed.). Fort Worth: Harcourt Brace.

Matlin, M. (2002). *Cognitive psychology* (5th ed.). Fort Worth: Harcourt.

Matthews, J. (1990). Drawing and individual development. In R. M. Thomas (Ed.), *The encyclopedia of human development and education: Theory, research and studies.* Oxford: Pergamon.

Matus, I. (1996.) Cited in Clay, R. A. (1996a). Beating the "biological clock" with zest. *APA Monitor, 27*(2), 37.

Maundeni, T. (2000). The consequences of parental separation and divorce for the economic, social, and emotional circumstances of children in Botswana. *Childhood: A Global Journal of Child Research, 7*(2), 213–223.

Maurer, D. M., Lewis, T, L., Brent, H. P., & Levin, A. V. (1999). Rapid improvement in the acuity of infants after visual input. *Science, 286*(5437), 108–110.

Maurer, D. M., & Maurer, C. E. (1976, October). Newborn babies see better than you think. *Psychology Today,* pp. 85–88.

Max, J. E., Robertson, B. A. M., & Lansing, A. E. (2001). The phenomenology of personality change due to traumatic brain injury in children and adolescents. *Journal of Neuropsychiatry & Clinical Neurosciences, 13*(2), 161–170.

Maxson, S. C. (1998). Homologous genes, aggression, and animal models. *Developmental Neuropsychology, 14*(1), 143–156.

Mayes, L. C. (1991). Infant assessment. In M. L. Lewis (Ed.), *Child and adolescent psychiatry: A comprehensive textbook.* Baltimore: Williams & Wilkins.

Mayes, L. C., & Zigler, E. (1992). An observational study of the affective concomitants of mastery in infants. *Journal of Child Psychology & Psychiatry, 33,* 659–667.

McAdoo, J. L. (1993). The roles of African American fathers: An ecological perspective. *Journal of Contemporary Human Services, 74,* 28–34.

McCabe, M. P., & Ricciardelli, L. A. (2001). Parent, peer, and media influences on body image and strategies to both increase and decrease body size among adolescent boys and girls. *Adolescence, 36*(142), 225–240.

McCall, R. B. (1991). Underachievers and dropouts. In R. M. Lerner, A. C. Petersen, & J. Brooks-Gunn (Eds.), *Encyclopedia of adolescence.* New York: Garland.

McCall, R. B. (1997). Cited in Sleek, S. (1997). Can "emotional intelligence" be taught in today's schools? *APA Monitor, 28*(6), 25.

McCall, R. B., Applebaum, M. I., & Hogarty, P. S. (1973). Developmental changes in mental performance. *Monographs of the Society for Research in Child Development, 38*(3, Serial No. 150).

McCall, R. B., & Carriger, M. S. (1993). A meta-analysis of infant habituation and recognition memory performance as predictors of later IQ. *Child Development, 64,* 57–79.

McCarthy, K. (1993, July). Kids' eyewitness recall is focus for conference. *APA Monitor,* pp. 1, 28–29.

McCartney, K., Harris, M. J., & Bernjeri, F. (1990). Growing up and growing apart: A developmental meta-analysis of twin studies. *Psychological Bulletin, 107,* 226–237.

McCendie, R., & Schneider, B. (1993, March). *Problematic peer relations in childhood and adult maladjustment: A quantitative synthesis.* Paper presented at the meeting of the Society for Research in Child Development, New Orleans, LA.

McCourt, K., et al. (1999). Authoritarianism revisited: Genetic and environmental influences examined in twins reared apart and together. *Personality & Individual Differences, 27*(5), 985–1014.

McCoy, J. H., & Kenney, M. A. (1991). Nutrient intake of female adolescents. In R. M. Lerner, A. C. Petersen, & J. Brooks-Gunn (Eds.), *Encyclopedia of adolescence.* New York: Garland.

McCrae, R. R., et al. (2000). Nature over nurture: Temperament, personality, and life span development. *Journal of Personality & Social Psychology, 78*(1), 173–186.

McCune, L. (1993). The development of play as the development of consciousness. In M. H. Bornstein & A. W. O'Reilly (Eds.), *New directions for child development: No 59. The role of play in the development of thought.* San Francisco: Jossey-Bass.

McDevitt, T. M., & Ormrod, J. E. (2002). *Child development and education.* Upper Saddle River, NJ: Prentice-Hall.

McDonald, A. D., Armstrong, B. G., & Sloan, M. (1992a). Cigarette, alcohol, and coffee consumption and congenital defects. *American Journal of Public Health, 82,* 91–93.

McDonald, A. D., Armstrong, B. G., & Sloan, M. (1992b). Cigarette, alcohol, and coffee consumption and prematurity. *American Journal of Public Health, 82,* 87–90.

McEachin, J. J., Smith, T., & Lovaas, O. I. (1993). Long-term outcome for children with autism who received early intensive behavioral treatment. *Journal of Mental Retardation, 97,* 359–372.

McEwan, M. H., Dihoff, R. E., & Brosvic, G. M. (1991). Early infant crawling experience is reflected in later motor skill development. *Perceptual and Motor Skills, 72,* 75–79.

McGee, R., Partridge, F., Williams, S., & Silva, P. (1991). A twelve-year follow-up of preschool hyperactive children. *Journal of the American Academy of Child and Adolescent Psychiatry, 30,* 224–232.

McGilly, K., & Ziegler, R. S. (1990). The influence of encoding and strategic knowledge on children's choices among serial recall strategies. *Developmental Psychology, 26,* 931–941.

McGinty, D. J., & Drucker-Colin, R. (1982). Sleep mechanisms: Biology and control of REM sleep. *International Review of Neurobiology, 23,* 391–436.

McGlaughlin, A., & Grayson, A. (2001). Crying in the first year of infancy: Patterns and prevalence. *Journal of Reproductive & Infant Psychology, 19*(1), 47–59.

McGovern, T. V., Furumoto, L., Halpern, D. F., Kimble, G. A., & McKeachie, W. J. (1991). Liberal education, study in depth, and the arts and sciences major-psychology. *American Psychologist, 46,* 598–605.

McGrath, M. L., Mellon, M. W., & Murphy, L. (2000). Empirically supported treatments in pediatric psychology: Constipation and encopresis. *Journal of Pediatric Psychology, 25*(4), 225–254.

McGue, M., Pickens, R. W., & Svikis, D. S. (1992). Sex and age effects on the inheritance of alcohol problems: A twin study. *Journal of Abnormal Psychology, 101,* 3–17.

McGuffin, P., Riley, B., & Plomin, R. (2001). Toward behavioral genomics. *Science, 291*(5507), 1232–1249.

McGuinness, D. (1990). Behavioral tempo in preschool boys and girls. *Learning and Individual Differences, 2,* 315–325.

McGuire, M. T., Wing, R. R., Klem, M. L., Lang, W., & Hill, J. O. (1999). What predicts weight regain in a group of successful weight losers? *Journal of Consulting & Clinical Psychology, 67*(2), 177–185.

McGuire, S., Manke, B., Saudino, K. J., Reiss, D., Hetherington, E. M., & Plomin, R. (1999). Perceived competence and self-worth during adolescence: A longitudinal behavioral genetic study. *Child Development, 70*(6), 1283–1296.

McIntosh, R., Vaughn, J., & Zaragora, N. (1991). A review of social interventions for students with learning disabilities. *Journal of Learning Disabilities, 24,* 451–458.

McKusick, V. A. (1992). *Mendelian inheritance in man: Catalog of autosomal dominant, autosomal recessive, and X-linked phenotypes* (10th ed.). Baltimore: Johns Hopkins University Press.

McLaren, L. (2002). Cited in Wealthy women most troubled by poor image. (2002, February 11). Reuters online.

McLaughlin, F. J., et al. (1992). Randomized trial of comprehensive prenatal care for low-income women: Effect on infant birth weight. *Pediatrics, 89,* 128–132.

McLoyd, V. C. (1990). The impact of economic hardship on black families and children: Psychological distress, parenting, and socioemotional development. *Child Development, 61,* 311–346.

McMahon, M. J., et al. (1996). Comparison of a trial of labor with an elective second cesarean section. *The New England Journal of Medicine, 335,* 689–695.

McManus, I. C., & Bryden, M. P. (1991). Geschwind's theory of cerebral lateralization: Developing a formal, causal model. *Psychological Bulletin, 110,* 237–253.

McManus, I. C., et al. (1988). The development of handedness in children. *British Journal of Developmental Psychology, 6,* 257–273.

McWhirter, J. J., McWhirter, A. M., & McWhirter, E. H. (1993). *At-risk youth: A comprehensive response.* Pacific Grove, CA: Brooks/Cole.

Meador, K. S. (1992). Emerging rainbows: A review of the literature on creativity in preschoolers. *Journal for the Education of the Gifted, 15,* 163–181.

Mednick, B. R., Baker, R. L., & Carothers, L. E. (1990). Patterns of family instability and crime: The association of timing of the family's disruption with subsequent adolescent and young adult criminality. *Journal of Youth and Adolescence, 19,* 201–220.

Mednick, S. A., Moffitt, T. E., & Stack, S. (1987). *The causes of crime: New biological approaches.* Cambridge: Cambridge University Press.

Meece, J. L., Parsons, J. E., Kaczala, C. M., Goff, S. B., & Futterman, R. (1982). Sex differences in math achievement: Toward a model of academic choice. *Psychological Bulletin, 91,* 324–348.

Mehregany, D. V. (1991, Winter). The relation of temperament and behavior disorders in a preschool clinical sample. *Child Psychiatry and Human Development, 22,* 129–136.

Meijer, J., & Elshout, J. J. (2001). The predictive and discriminant validity of the zone of proximal development. *British Journal of Educational Psychology, 71*(1), 93–113.

Mellanby, A. R., Rees, J. B., & Tripp, J. H. (2000). Peer-led and adult-led school health education: A critical review of available comparative research. *Health Education Research, 15*(5), 533–545.

Mellon, M. W., & McGrath, M. L. (2000). Empirically supported treatments in pediatric psychology: Nocturnal enuresis. *Journal of Pediatric Psychology, 25*(4), 193–214.

Meltzoff, A. N. (1988). Infant imitation and memory: Nine-month-olds in immediate and deferred tests. *Child Development, 59,* 217–225.

Meltzoff, A. N. (1990). Towards a developmental cognitive science. In A. Diamond (Ed.), *The development and neural bases of higher cognitive functions.* New York: New York Academy of Sciences.

Meltzoff, A. N. (1997). Cited in Azar, B. (1997). New theory on development could usurp Piagetian beliefs. *APA Monitor, 28*(6), 9.

Meltzoff, A. N., & Moore, M. K. (1992). Early imitation within a functional framework: The importance of person identity, movement, and development. *Infant Behavior and Development, 15,* 479–505.

Meltzoff, A. N., & Moore, M. K. (1998). Object representation, identity, and the paradox of early permanence: Steps toward a new framework. *Infant Behavior & Development, 21*(2), 201–235.

Mendelsohn, A. L., et al. (1999). Low-level lead exposure and cognitive development in early childhood. *Journal of Developmental & Behavioral Pediatrics, 20*(6), 425–431.

Mendez, L. M. R. (2000). Gender roles and achievement-related choices: A comparison of early adolescent girls in gifted and general education programs. *Journal for the Education of the Gifted, 24*(2), 149–169.

Mennella, J. A. (2001). Regulation of milk intake after exposure to alcohol in mothers' milk. *Alcoholism: Clinical & Experimental Research, 25*(4), 590–593.

Mennella, J. A., & Garcia, P. L. (2000). Children's hedonic response to the smell of alcohol: Effects of parental drinking habits. *Alcoholism: Clinical & Experimental Research, 24*(8), 1167–1171.

Meredith, H. V. (1978). Research between 1960 and 1970 on the standing height of young children in different parts of the world. In H. W. Reese & L. P. Lipsitt (Eds.), *Advances in child development and behavior* (Vol. 12). New York: Academic Press.

Meredith, H. V. (1982). Research between 1950 and 1980 on urban-rural differences in body size and growth rate of children and youths. In H. W. Reese (Ed.), *Advances in child development and behavior* (Vol. 17). New York: Academic Press.

Meredith, H. V. (1984). Body size of infants and children around the world in relation to socioeconomic status. In H. W. Reese (Ed.), *Advances in child development and behavior* (Vol. 18). New York: Academic Press.

Merewood, A. (1991, April). Sperm under siege: More than we ever guessed, having a healthy baby may depend on dad. *Health,* pp. 53–57, 76–77.

Merriman, W. E., & Schuster, J. M. (1991). Young children's disambiguation of object name reference. *Child Development, 62,* 1288–1301.

Meschede, D., et al., (2000). Clustering of male infertility in the families of couples treated with intracytoplasmic sperm injection. *Human Reproduction, 15,* 1604–1608.

Meschke, L. L., Zweig, J. M., Barber, B. L., & Eccles, J. S. (2000). Demographic, biological, psychological, and social predictors of the timing of first intercourse. *Journal of Research on Adolescence, 10*(3), 315–338.

Mesman, J., Bongers, I. L., & Koot, H. M. (2001). Preschool developmental pathways to preadolescent internalizing and externalizing problems. *Journal of Child Psychology & Psychiatry & Allied Disciplines, 42*(5), 679–689.

Meyer, S. L., Murphy, C. M., Cascardi, M., & Birns, B. (1991). Gender and relationships: Beyond the peer group. *American Psychologist, 46,* 537.

Meyer, T. (1997). Americans are getting fatter. *The National Health and Nutrition Examination Survey.* Associated Press.

Meyer, T. (1998, February 18). AZT short treatment works. The Associated Press online.

Michael, E. D. (1990). Physical development and fitness. In R. M. Thomas (Ed.), *The encyclopedia of human development and education: Theory, research, and studies.* Oxford: Pergamon.

Michaelson, R. (1993, May). Tug-of-war is developing over defining retardation. *APA Monitor,* pp. 34–35.

Michel, C. (1989). Radiation embryology. *Experientia, 45,* 69–77.

Mikkelsen, E. J. (1991). Modern approaches to enuresis and encopresis. In M. Lewis (Ed.), *Child and adolescent psychiatry: A comprehensive textbook.* Baltimore: Williams & Wilkins.

Mikulincer, M., Hirschberger, G., Nachmias, O., & Gillath, O. (2001). The affective component of the secure base schema: Affective priming with representations of attachment security. *Journal of Personality & Social Psychology, 81*(2), 305–321.

Mikulincer, M., & Shaver, P. R. (2001). Attachment theory and intergroup bias: Evidence that priming the secure base schema attenuates negative reactions to out-groups. *Journal of Personality & Social Psychology, 81*(1), 97–115.

Millar, W. S. (1972). A study of operant conditioning under delayed reinforcement in early infancy. *Monographs of the Society for Research in Child Development, 37*(2, Serial No. 147).

Millar, W. S. (1990). Span of integration for delayed-reward contingency learning in 6- to 8-month-old infants. In A. Diamond (Ed.), *The development and neural bases of higher cognitive functions.* New York: New York Academy of Sciences.

Miller, A. L., Wyman, S. E., Huppert, J. D., Glassman, S. L., & Rathus, J. H. (2000). Analysis of behavioral skills utilized by suicidal adolescents receiving dialectical behavior therapy. *Cognitive & Behavioral Practice, 7*(2), 183–187.

Miller, D. A. F., McCluskey-Fawcett, K., & Irving, L. M. (1993). The relationship between childhood sexual abuse and subsequent onset of bulimia nervosa. *Child Abuse and Neglect, 17,* 305–314.

Miller, G. A. (1956). The magical number seven, plus or minus two: Some limits on our capacity to process information. *Psychological Review, 63,* 81–97.

Miller, J. G. (1994). Cultural diversity in the morality of caring: Individually-oriented versus duty-based interpersonal moral codes. *Cross-Cultural Research, 28,* 3–39.

Miller, J. G., & Bersoff, D. M. (1992). Culture and moral judgment: How are conflicts between justice and interpersonal responsibilities resolved? *Journal of Personality and Social Psychology, 62,* 541–554.

Miller, L., & Budd, J. (1999). The development of occupational sex-role stereotypes, occupational preferences, and academic subject preferences in children at ages 8, 12, and 16. *Educational Psychology, 19*(1), 17–35.

Miller, N. B., Cowan, P. A., Cowan, C. P., Hetherington, E. M., & Clingempeel, W. G. (1993). Externalizing in preschoolers and early adolescents: A cross-study replication of a family model. *Developmental Psychology, 29,* 3–18.

Miller, S. M., Birnbaum, A., & Durbin, D. (1990). Etiologic perspectives on depression in childhood. In M. Lewis & S. M. Miller (Eds.), *Handbook of developmental psychopathology.* New York: Plenum.

Miller, S. M., Boyer, B.A., & Rodoletz, M. (1990). Anxiety in children: Nature and development. In M. Lewis & S. M. Miller (Eds.), *Handbook of developmental psychopathology.* New York: Plenum.

Mills, C. J. (1992). Academically talented children: The case for early identification and nurturance. *Pediatrics, 89,* 156–157.

Mills, J. L., et al. (1993). Moderate caffeine use and the risk of spontaneous abortion and intrauterine growth retardation. *Journal of the American Medical Association, 269,* 593–597.

Mills, J. L., Graubard, B. I., Harley, E. E., Rhoads, G. G., & Berendes, H. W. (1984). Maternal alcohol consumption and birth weight: How much drinking is safe during pregnancy? *Journal of the American Medical Association, 252,* 1875–1879.

Mills, R. S. L., & Rubin, K. H. (1990). Parental beliefs about problematic social behaviors in early childhood. *Child Development, 61*, 138–152.

Milstead, M., Lapsley, D., & Hale, C. (1993, March). *A new look at imaginary audience and personal fable.* Paper presented at the meeting of the Society for Research in Child Development, New Orleans, LA.

Miranda, A., & Presentacion, M. J. (2000). Efectos de un tratamiento cognitivo-conductual en niños con trastorno por deficit de atencion con hiperactividad, agresivos y no agresivos. Cambio clinicamente significativo. *Infancia y Aprendizaje, 92*, 51–70.

Mitchell, K. J., Finkelhor, D., & Wolak, J. (2001). Risk factors for and impact of online sexual solicitation of youth. *Journal of the American Medical Association, 285*(23), 3011–3014.

Mitchell, P. R., & Kent, R. D. (1990). Phonetic variation in multisyllable babbling. *Journal of Child Language, 17*, 247–265.

Moeller, F. G., et al. (2001). Psychiatric aspects of impulsivity. *American Journal of Psychiatry, 158*(11), 1783–1793.

Mofenson, L. M. (2000). Perinatal exposure to zidovudine—Benefits and risks. *The New England Journal of Medicine online, 343*(11).

Moffitt, T. E., Caspi, A., Belsky, J., & Silvis, P. A. (1992). Childhood experience and the onset of menarche: A test of a sociobiological model. *Child Development, 63*, 47–58.

Mokdad, A. H., et al. (2000). The continuing epidemic of obesity in the United States. *Journal of the American Medical Association online, 284*(13).

Molfese, D. L., Burger-Judisch, L. M., & Hans, L. L. (1991). Consonant discrimination by newborn infants: Electrophysiological differences. *Developmental Neuropsychology, 7*, 177–195.

Molfese, V. J., DiLalla, L. F., & Bunce, D. (1997). Prediction of the intelligence test scores of 3- to 8-year-old children by home environment, socioeconomic status, and biomedical risks. *Merrill-Palmer Quarterly, 43*(2) 219–234.

Molinari, L., & Corsaro, W. A. (2000). Le relazioni amicali nella scuola dell'infanzia e nella scuola elementare: Uno studio longitudinale. *Eta evolutiva, 67*, 40–51.

Moliterno, D. J., et al. (1994). Coronary-artery vasoconstriction induced by cocaine, cigarette smoking, or both. *New England Journal of Medicine, 330*, 454–459.

Moller, L. C., Hymel, S., & Rubin, K. H. (1992). Sex typing in play and popularity in middle childhood. *Sex Roles, 26*, 331–353.

Money, J. (1977). Human hermaphroditism. In F. A. Beach (Ed.), *Human sexuality in four perspectives.* Baltimore: Johns Hopkins University Press.

Money, J. (1987). Sin, sickness, or status? Homosexual gender identity and psychoneuroendocrinology. *American Psychologist, 42*, 384–399.

Money, J., & Ehrhardt, A. A. (1972). *Man and woman, boy and girl: The differentiation and dimorphism of gender identity from conception to maturity.* Baltimore: Johns Hopkins University Press.

Monge-Rojas, R. (2001). Dietary intake as a cardiovascular risk factor in Costa Rican adolescents. *Journal of Adolescent Health, 28*(4), 328–337.

Montemayor, R., Adams, G. R., & Gullotta, T. P. (1990). Introduction. In R. Montemayor, G. R. Adams, & T. P. Gullottla (Eds.), *From childhood to adolescence: A transitional period?* Newbury Park, CA: Sage.

Montemayor, R., Eberly, M., & Flannery, D. J. (1993). Effects of pubertal status and conversation topic on parent and adolescent affective expression. *Journal of Early Adolescence, 13*, 431–447.

Montemayor, R., & Eisen, M. (1977). The development of self-conceptions from childhood to adolescence. *Developmental Psychology, 13*, 314–319.

Montemayor, R., & Flannery, D. J. (1991). Parent–adolescent relations in middle and late adolescence. In R. M. Lerner, A. C. Petersen, & J. Brooks-Gunn (Eds.), *Encyclopedia of adolescence.* New York: Garland.

Montgomery, D. E. (1992). Review: Young children's theory of knowing: The development of a folk epistemology. *Developmental Review, 12*, 410–430.

Moore, C., Pure, K., & Furrow, O. (1990). Children's understanding of the model expression of speaker certainty and uncertainty and its relation to the development of a representational theory of mind. *Child Development, 61*, 722–730.

Moore, K. A., & Snyder, N. O. (1991). Cognitive attainment among firstborn children of adolescent mothers. *American Sociological Review, 56*, 612–624.

Moore, L. L., et al. (1991). Influence of parents' physical activity levels on activity levels of young children. *Journal of Pediatrics, 118*, 215–219.

Moore, S., & Boldero, J. (1991). Psychosocial development and friendship functions in adolescence. *Sex Roles, 25*, 521–536.

Morelli, G. A., Oppenheim, D., Rogoff, B., & Goldsmith, D. (1992). Cultural variation in infants' sleeping arrangements: Questions of independence. *Developmental Psychology, 28*, 604–613.

Moro, C., & Rodriguez, C. (2000). La creation des representations chez l'enfant au travers des processus de semiosis. *Enfance, 52*(3), 287–294.

Morris, L. B. (2000, June 25). For the partum blues, a question of whether to medicate. *The New York Times online.*

Morrison, D. R., & Coiro, M. J. (1999). Parental conflict and marital disruption: Do children benefit when high-conflict marriages are dissolved? *Journal of Marriage & the Family, 61*(3), 626–637.

Morrison, E. S., Starks, K., Hyndman, C., & Ronzio, N. (1980). *Growing up sexual.* New York: Van Nostrand Reinhold.

Morrison, F. J., Griffith, E. M., & Williamson, G. L. (1993, March). *Two strikes from the start: Individual differences in early literacy.* Paper presented at meeting of the Society for Research in Child Development, New Orleans, LA.

Morrongiello, B. A., & Clifton, R. K. (1984). Effects of sound frequency on behavioral and cardiac orienting in newborn and 5-month-old infants. *Journal of Experimental Child Psychology, 38*, 429–446.

Morrongiello, R. A., Fenwick, K. D., & Chance, G. (1990). Sound localization acuity in very young infants: An observer-based testing procedure. *Developmental Psychology, 26*, 75–84.

Mortimer, J. T. (1991). Employment. In R. M. Lerner, A. C. Petersen, & J. Brooks-Gunn (Eds.), *Encyclopedia of adolescence.* New York: Garland.

Morton, J., & Johnson, M. H. (1991). CONSPEC and CONLERN: A two-process theory of infant face recognition. *Psychological Review, 98*, 164–181.

Moses, L. J., & Chandler, M. J. (1992). Traveler's guide to children's theories of mind. *Psychological Inquiry, 3*, 286–301.

Moses, L. J., & Flavell, J. H. (1990). Inferring false beliefs from actions and reactions. *Child Development, 61*, 929–945.

Moses, S. (1991, December). Special-ed assessment plans opposed. *APA Monitor*, pp. 36–37.

Moss, E., & St-Laurent, D. (2001). Attachment at school age and academic performance. *Developmental Psychology, 37*(6), 863–874.

Mroczek, D., & Kolarz, C. (1998). *Journal of Personality and Social Psychology, 74.* Cited in Goode, E. (1998, October 27). Happiness may grow with aging, study finds. *The New York Times;* America Online.

Mueller, E., & Tingley, E. (1990). The Bear's Picnic: Children's representations of themselves and their families. In I. Bretherton & M. W. Watson (Eds.), *New directions for child development: No. 48. Children's perspectives on the family.* San Francisco: Jossey-Bass.

Mueller, N., & Hulk, A. (2001). Crosslinguistic influence in bilingual language acquisition: Italian and French as recipient languages. *Bilingualism: Language & Cognition, 4*(1), 1–21.

Mueller, R., Pierce, K., Ambrose, J. B., Allen, G., & Courchesne, E. (2001). Atypical patterns of cerebral motor activation in autism: A functional magnetic resonance study. *Biological Psychiatry, 49*(8) 665–676.

Mueller, U., Overton, W. F., & Reene, K. (2001). Development of conditional reasoning: A longitudinal study. *Journal of Cognition & Development, 2*(1), 27–49.

Mueller, U., Sokol, B., & Overton, W. F. (1999). Developmental sequences in class reasoning and propositional reasoning. *Journal of Experimental Child Psychology, 74*(2), 69–106.

Muir, D. W., & Hains, S. M. J. (1993). Infant sensitivity to perturbations in adult facial, vocal, tactile, and contingent stimulation during face-to-face interactions. In de Boysson-Bardies, B., de Schonen, S., Jusczyk, P. W., MacNeilage, P. F., & Morton, J. (Eds.), *Changes in speech and face processing in infancy: A glimpse at developmental mechanisms of cognition.* Dordrecht, The Netherlands: Klumer Academic Publishers.

Muir, G. D. (2000). Early ontogeny of locomotor behaviour: A comparison between altricial and precocial animals. *Brain Research Bulletin, 53*(5), 719–726.

Mullis, A. K., Mullis, R. L., & Normandin, D. (1992). Cross-sectional and longitudinal comparisons of adolescent self-esteem. *Adolescence, 27*, 51–61.

Mullis, I. V. S., Dossey, J. A., Foertsch, M. A., Jones, L. R., & Gentile, C. A. (1991). *Trends in academic progress* (Report No. 21–T-01). Washington DC: National Center for Educational Statistics.

Mumme, D. L., Fernald, A., & Herrera, C. (1996). Infants' responses to facial and vocal emotional signals in a social referencing paradigm. *Child Development, 67*(6), 3219–3237.

Mundy, L. (2000, July 16). Sex and sensibility. *The Washington Post online.*

Munroe, R. H., Shimmin, H. S., & Munroe, R. L. (1984). Gender role understanding and sex role preference in four cultures. *Developmental Psychology, 20*, 673–682.

Murphy, L. B. (1983). Issues in the development of emotion in infancy. In R. Plutchik & H. Kellerman (Eds.), *Emotion: Theory, research, and experimentation.* New York: Academic Press.

Murphy, T. K., Bengtson, M. A., Tan, J. Y., Carbonell, E., & Levin, G. M. (2000). Selective serotonin reuptake inhibitors in the treatment of paediatric anxiety disorders: A review. *International Clinical Psychopharmacology, 15*(Suppl2), S47–S63.

Murphy, V., & Hicks-Stewart, K. (1991). Learning disabilities and attention deficit-hyperactivity disorder: An interactional perspective. *Journal of Learning Disabilities, 24*, 386–388.

Murray, A. D., Johnson, J., & Peters, J. (1990). Fine-tuning of utterance length to preverbal infants: Effects on later language development. *Journal of Child Language, 17,* 511–525.

Murray, B. (1996). Students stretch beyond the "three Rs." *APA Monitor, 26*(4), 46.

Murray, B. (1998). Survey reveals concerns of today's girls. *APA Monitor, 29*(10).

Murry, V. M., Bynum, M. S., Brody, G. H., Willert, A., & Stephens, D. (2001) African American single mothers and children in context: A review of studies on risk and resilience. *Clinical Child & Family Psychology Review, 4*(2), 133–155.

Mussen, P. H., & Jones, M. C. (1957). Self-conceptions, motivations, and interpersonal attitudes of late- and early-maturing boys. *Child Development, 28,* 243–256.

Must, A., Jacques, P. F., Dallal, G. E., Bajema, C. J., & Dietz, W. (1992). Long-term morbidity and mortality of overweight adolescents. *New England Journal of Medicine, 327,* 1350–1354.

Mwamwenda, T. S. (1992). Cognitive development in African children. *Genetic, Social, and General Psychology Monographs, 118*(1), 7–72.

Myers, C. E., Hopkins, R. O., Kesner, R. P., Monti, L., & Gluck, M. A. (2000). Conditional spatial discrimination in humans with hypoxic brain injury. *Psychobiology, 28*(3), 275–282.

Myers, K., et al. (1991). Risks for suicidality in major depressive disorder. *Journal of the American Academy of Child and Adolescent Psychology, 30,* 86–94.

Myers, M. M., et al. (1998). Effects of sleeping position and time after feeding on the organization of sleep/wake states in prematurely born infants. *Sleep, 21*(4), 343–349.

Nagin, D. S., & Tremblay, R. E. (2001). Parental and early childhood predictors of persistent physical aggression in boys from kindergarten to high school. *Archives of General Psychiatry, 58*(4), 389–394.

Nahas, G., Sutin, K., & Bennett, W. M. (2000). Review of "Marihuana and Medicine." *The New England Journal of Medicine online, 343*(7).

Nakkula, M. J., & Nikitopoulos, C. E. (2001). Negotiation training and interpersonal development: An exploratory study of early adolescents in Argentina. *Adolescence, 36*(141), 1–20.

Nano, S. (2001, July 4). Study: Labor risky after caesarean. *The Associated Press Online.*

Nantais, K. M., & Schellenberg, E. G. (1999). The Mozart effect: An artifact of preference. *Psychological Science, 10*(4), 370–373.

Narvaez, D., Getz, I., Rest, J. R., & Thoma, S. J. (1999). Individual moral judgment and cultural ideologies. *Developmental Psychology, 35*(2), 478–488.

Nation, J. R., & Gleaves, D. H. (2001). Low-level lead exposure and intelligence in children. *Archives of Clinical Neuropsychology, 16*(4), 375–388.

National Association for the Education of Young Children. (1990, November). NAEYC position statement on school readiness. *Young Children, 46,* 21–23.

National Center for Biotechnology Information (NCBI). (2000, March 30). National Institute of Health. **http://www.ncbi.nlm.nih.gov/disease/SRY.html**

National Center for Children in Poverty. (2001). **http://cpmcnet.columbia.edu/dept/nccp/**

National Center for Education Statistics. (1992). *Dropout rates in the United States: 1991.* Washington, DC: U.S. Government Printing Office.

National Center for Education Statistics. (2002, January 16). *Common core of data, Local Education Agency Universe Survey.* Washington, DC: Office of Educational Research & Improvement, U.S. Department of Education. **http://nces.ed.gov/**

National Center for Health Statistics. (2002, January 8). Suicide statistics by age, race, and sex. Atlanta: Centers for Disease Control and Prevention. **http://www.cdc.gov/nchs/fastats/suicide.htm**

National Institute of Child Health & Human Development (2001, July 6). America's children: Key national indicators of well-being. **http://156.40.88.3/publications/pubs/report2001.pdf**

National Library of Medicine. (1997, August 28). Thalidomide: Potential benefits and risks. **http://www.nlm.nih.gov/pubs/cbm/thalidomide.html**

Natsopoulos, D., Kiosseoglou, G., & Xeromeritou, A. (1992). Handedness and spatial ability in children: Further support for Geschwind's hypothesis of "pathology of superiority" and for Annett's theory of intelligence. *Genetic, Social, and General Psychology Monographs, 118*(1) 103–126.

Nauta, M. M., & Kokaly, M. L. (2001). Assessing role model influences on students' academic and vocational decisions. *Journal of Career Assessment, 9*(1), 81–99.

Navarro, M., & Rodriguez de Fonseca, F. (1998). Early cannabinoid exposure as a source of vulnerability to opiate addiction: A model in laboratory rodents. *Spanish Journal of Psychology, 1*(1), 39–58.

Nawaz, H., & Katz, D. (2001). American College of Preventive Medicine practice policy statement: Weight management counseling of overweight adults. *American Journal of Preventive Medicine, 21*(1), 73–78.

Nazzi, T., & Gopnik, A. (2000). A shift in children's use of perceptual and causal cues to categorization. *Developmental Science, 3*(4), 389–396.

NCES. (See National Center for Education Statistics.)

Nduati, R., et al. (2000). Effect of breastfeeding and formula feeding on transmission of HIV-1. *Journal of the American Medical Association, 283,* 1167–1174.

Needleman, H. L., & Bellinger, D. (2001). Studies of lead exposure and the developing central nervous system. *Archives of Clinical Neuropsychology, 16*(4), 359–374.

Needlman, R. (2000). What you can do about bed-wetting. America Online: AOL Parenting.

Needlman, R. (2001). Understanding encopresis (fecal soiling). America Online: AOL Parenting.

Neiderman, M., Farley, A., Richardson, J., & Lask, B. (2001). Nasogastric feeding in children and adolescents with eating disorders: Toward good practice. *International Journal of Eating Disorders, 29*(4) 441–448.

Neisser, U. (1997). Cited in Sleek, S. (1997). Can "emotional intelligence" be taught in today's schools? *APA Monitor, 28*(6), 25.

Neisser, U., et al. (1996). Intelligence: Knowns and unknowns. *American Psychologist, 51,* 77–101.

Nelson, C. A., et al. (2000). Neurocognitive sequelae of infants of diabetic mothers. *Behavioral Neuroscience, 114*(5), 950–956.

Nelson, C. A., & Ludemann, P. M. (1989). Past, current and future trends in infant face perception research. *Canadian Journal of Psychology, 43,* 183–198.

Nelson, J. R., Smith, D. J., & Dodd, J. (1990). The moral reasoning of juvenile delinquents: A meta-analysis. *Journal of Abnormal Child Psychology, 18,* 231–239.

Nelson, K. (1973). Structure and strategy in learning to talk. *Monographs for the Society for Research in Child Development, 38*(1–2, Serial No. 149).

Nelson, K. (1981). Individual differences in language development: Implications for development of language. *Developmental Psychology, 17,* 170–187.

Nelson, K. (1982). The syntagmatics and paradigmatics of conceptual development. In S. A. Kuczaj, II (Ed.), *Language development: Vol. 2. Language, thought, and culture.* Hillsdale, NJ: Erlbaum.

Nelson, K. (1989). Remembering: A functional developmental perspective. In P. R. Solomon, G. R. Goetheys, C. M. Kelley, & B. R. Stephens (Eds.), *Memory: An interdisciplinary approach.* New York: Springer-Verlag.

Nelson, K. (1990). Remembering, forgetting, and childhood amnesia. In R. Fivush & J. A. Hudson (Eds.), *Knowing and remembering in young children.* Cambridge: Cambridge University Press.

Nelson, K. (1993). Events, narratives, memory: What develops? In C. A. Nelson (Ed.), *Minnesota symposia on child psychology: Vol. 26. Memory and affect in development.* Hillsdale, NJ: Erlbaum.

Nelson, S. A. (1980). Factors influencing young children's use of motives and outcomes as moral criteria. *Child Development, 51,* 823–829.

Nevid, J. S., Rathus, S. A., & Greene, B. A. (2000). *Abnormal psychology in a changing world* (4th ed.). Englewood Cliffs, NJ: Prentice-Hall.

Neville, B., & Parke, R. D. (1991). Adolescent fathers. In R. M. Lerner, A. C. Petersen, & J. Brooks-Gunn (Eds.), *Encyclopedia of adolescence.* New York: Garland.

Newacheck, P. W., & Taylor, W. R. (1992). Childhood chronic illness: Prevalence, severity, and impact. *American Journal of Public Health, 82,* 364–371.

Newcomb, A. F., Bukowski, W. M., & Pattee, L. (1993). Children's peer relations: A meta-analytic review of popular, rejected, neglected controversial, and average sociometric status. *Psychological Bulletin, 113,* 99–128.

Newcombe, N., & Dubas, J. S. (1992). A longitudinal study of predictors of spatial ability in adolescent females. *Child Development, 63,* 37–46.

Newcombe, N., & Huttenlocher, J. (1992). Children's early ability to solve perspective-taking problems. *Developmental Psychology, 28,* 635–643.

Newnham, J. P., et al. (1993). Effects of frequent ultrasound during pregnancy: A randomized controlled trial. *The Lancet, 342,* 887–891.

Newport, E. L. (1992, June). *Critical periods and creolization: Effects of maturational state and input on the acquisition of language.* Paper presented at the meeting of American Psychological Society, San Diego, CA.

Newport, E. L. (1998). Cited in Azar, B. (1998). Acquiring sign language may be more innate than learned. *APA Monitor, 29*(4), 12.

Nicely, P., Tamis-LeMonda, C. S., & Bornstein, M. H. (1999). Mothers' attuned responses to infant affect expressivity promote earlier achievement of language milestones. *Infant Behavior & Development, 22*(4), 557–568.

Nichols, S., & Stich, S. (2000). A cognitive theory of pretense. *Cognition, 74*(2), 115–147.

Nicolopoulou, A. (1991). Play, cognitive development, and the social world. In B. Scales, M. Almy, A. Nicolopoulou, & S. Ervin-Tripp (Eds.), *Play and the social context of development in early care and education.* New York: Teachers College Press.

Nicolson, R. I., Fawcett, A. J., Dean, P. (2001). Dyslexia, development and the cerebellum. *Trends in Neurosciences, 24*(9), 515–516.

Niedbala, B., & Tsang, R. (1993). The small for gestational age infant. In S. W. Ekvall (Ed.), *Pediatric nutrition in chronic diseases and developmental disorders: Prevention, assessment, and treatment.* New York: Oxford.

Nielsen, M., & Dissanayake, C. (2000). An investigation of pretend play, mental state terms, and false belief understanding: In search of a metarepresentational link. *British Journal of Developmental Psychology, 18*(4), 609–624.

Nigg, J. T. (2001). Is ADHD a disinhibitory disorder? *Psychological Bulletin, 127*(5), 571–598.

Nijhuis-van der Sanden, R. W. G., Smits-Engelsman, B. C. M., & Eling, P. A. T. M. (2000). Motor performance in girls with Turner syndrome. *Developmental Medicine & Child Neurology, 42*(10), 685–690.

Ninio, A., & Rinotti, N. (1988). Fathers' involvement in the care of their infants and their attributions of cognitive competence in infants. *Child Development, 59,* 652–663.

Noble, K. D., Robinson, N. M., & Gunderson, S. A. (1992). All rivers lead to the sea: A follow-up study of gifted young adults. *Roeper Review, 15,* 124–130.

Noll, J. G., Trickett, P. K., & Putnam, F. W. (2000). Social network constellation and sexuality of sexually abused and comparison girls in childhood and adolescence. *Child Maltreatment: Journal of the American Professional Society on the Abuse of Children, 5*(4), 323–337.

Noll, R. B., et al. (2001). Neuropsychological functioning of youths with sickle cell disease: Comparison with non-chronically ill peers. *Journal of Pediatric Psychology, 26*(2), 69–78.

Noller, P., & Callan, V. J. (1990). Adolescents' perceptions of the nature of their communication with parents. *Journal of Youth and Adolescence, 19,* 349–362.

Noppe, I. C., Noppe, L. D., & Hughes, F. P. (1991). Stress as a predictor of the quality of parent–infant interactions. *Journal of Genetic Psychology, 152,* 17–28.

Nordqvist, K., & Lovell-Badge, R. (1994). Setbacks on the road to sexual fulfillment. *Nature Genetics, 7,* 7–9.

Norlander, T., Erixon, A., & Archer, T. (2000). Psychological androgyny and creativity: Dynamics of gender-role and personality trait. *Social Behavior & Personality, 28*(5), 423–435.

Nottelmann, E. D., Inoff-Germain, G., Susman, E. J., & Chrousos, G. P. (1990). Hormones and behavior at puberty. In J. Bancroft & J. M. Reinisch (Eds.), *Adolescence and puberty.* New York: Oxford.

Nsamenang, A. B. (1992). *Human development in cultural context.* Newbury Park, CA: Sage.

Nugent, J. K., Lester, B. M., & Brazelton, T. B. (Eds.). (1991). *The cultural context of infancy* (Vol. 2). Norwood, NJ: Ablex.

Nurnberger, J. I., Jr., et al. (2001). Evidence for a locus on chromosome 1 that influences vulnerability to alcoholism and affective disorder. *American Journal of Psychiatry, 158,* 718–724.

Obesity is linked to birth defects. (1996, April 10). *The New York Times,* p. C10.

O'Boyle, M. W., & Benbow, C. P. (1990). Handedness and its relationship to ability and talent. In S. Coren (Ed.), *Left-handedness: Behavior implications and anomalies.* Amsterdam: North-Holland.

O'Brien, C. P. (1996). Recent developments in the pharmacotherapy of substance abuse. *Journal of Consulting and Clinical Psychology, 64,* 677–686.

O'Connor, J., Fitzgerald, M., & Hoey, H. (2000). The relationship between karyotype and cognitive functioning in Turner syndrome. *Irish Journal of Psychological Medicine, 17*(3), 82–85.

O'Connor, P. D., Sufo, F., Kendall, L., & Olsen, G. (1990). Reading disabilities and the effects of colored filters. *Journal of Learning Disabilities, 23,* 597–603.

O'Connor, T. (1989). Cultural voices and strategies for multicultural education. *Journal of Education, 171,* 57–74.

O'Connor, T. G., Caspi, A., DeFries, J. C., & Plomin, R. (2000). Are associations between parental divorce and children's adjustment genetically mediated? An adoption study. *Developmental Psychology, 36*(4), 429–437.

O'Dell, K. M. C., & Kaiser, K. (1997). Sexual behaviour: Secrets and flies. *Current Biology, 7*(6), R345–R347.

Oden, M. H. (1968). The fulfillment of promise: 40-year follow-up of the Terman gifted group. *Genetic Psychology Monographs, 77,* 3–93.

Oeztuerk, C., et al. (1999). Hand and eye preference in normal preschool children. *Clinical Pediatrics, 38*(11), 677–680.

Offer, D., & Church, R. B. (1991). Generation gap. In R. M. Lerner, A. C. Petersen, & J. Brooks-Gunn (Eds.), *Encyclopedia of adolescence.* New York: Garland.

Ogbu, J. U. (1999). Beyond language: Ebonics, proper English, and identity in a Black-American speech community. *American Educational Research Journal, 36*(2), 147–184.

Ogura, T. (1991). A longitudinal study of the relationship between early language development and play development. *Journal of Child Language, 18,* 273–294.

Ohnishi, T., et al. (2000). Abnormal regional cerebral blood flow in childhood autism. *Brain, 123*(9), 1838–1844.

Okazaki, S., & Sue, S. (2000). Implications of test revisions for assessment with Asian Americans. *Psychological Assessment, 12*(3), 272–280.

O'Leary, D. S. (1990). Neuropsychological development in the child and adolescent: Functional maturation of the central nervous system. In C. A. Hauert (Ed.), *Developmental psychology: Cognitive, perceptuo-motor, and neuropsychological perspectives.* Amsterdam: North-Holland.

Ollendick, T. H., Hagopian, L. P., & Huntzinger, R. M. (1991). Cognitive-behavior therapy with nighttime fearful children. *Journal of Behavioral Therapy and Experimental Psychiatry, 22,* 113–121.

Ollendick, T. H., & King, N. J. (1991). Origins of childhood fears: An evaluation of Rachman's theory of teen-acquisition. *Behavior Research and Therapy, 29,* 117–123.

Ollendick, T. H., King, N. J., & Frary, R. B. (1989). Fears in children and adolescents: Reliability and generalizability across gender, age, and nationality. *Behavior Research and Therapy, 27,* 19–26.

Ollendick, T. H., Yule, W., & Ollier, K. (1991). Fears in British children and their relationship to manifest anxiety and depression. *Journal of Child Psychology and Psychiatry, 32,* 321–331.

Oller, D. K. (1981). Infant vocalizations: Exploration and reflectivity. In R. E. Stark (Ed.), *Language behavior in infancy and early childhood.* New York: Elsevier.

Oller, D. K., & Eilers, R. E. (1988). The role of audition in infant babbling. *Child Development, 59,* 441–449.

Olofsson, M. (2000). Born med medfodte alkoholskader. *Psykologisk Paedagogisk Radgivning, 37*(3) 269–280.

Olson, H. C., Sampson, P. D., Barr, H., Streissguth, A. P., & Bookstein, F. L. (1992). Prenatal exposure to alcohol and school problems in late childhood: A longitudinal prospective study. *Development and Psychopathology, 4,* 341–359.

Olson, S. L. (1992). Development of conduct problems and peer rejection in preschool children: A social systems analysis. *Journal of Abnormal Child Psychology, 20,* 327–350.

Olson, S. L., Bates, J. E., & Bayles, K. (1990). Early antecedents of childhood impulsivity: The role of parent–child interaction, cognitive competence, and temperament. *Journal of Abnormal Child Psychology, 18,* 317–334.

Olson, S. L., Bates, J. E., Sandy, J. M., & Lanthier, R. (2000). Early developmental precursors of externalizing behavior in middle childhood and adolescence. *Journal of Abnormal Child Psychology, 28*(2), 119–133.

Olson, S. L., Kashiwagi, K., & Crystal, D. (2001). Concepts of adaptive and maladaptive child behavior: A comparison of U.S. and Japanese mothers of preschool-age children. *Journal of Cross-Cultural Psychology, 32*(1), 43–57.

Omer, H., & Elitzur, A. C. (2001). What would you say to the person on the roof? A suicide prevention text. *Suicide & Life-Threatening Behavior, 31*(2), 129–139.

O'Neill, D. K., Astington, J. W., & Flavell, J. H. (1992). Young children's understanding of the role that sensory experiences play in knowledge acquisition. *Child Development, 63,* 474–490.

O'Neill, D. K., & Gopnik, A. (1991). Young children's ability to identify the sources of their beliefs. *Developmental Psychology, 27,* 390–397.

Oram, J., & Oshima-Takane, Y. (1993, March). *Parental language functions and attentional types: Relationship to child language.* Paper presented at the meeting of the Society for Research in Child Development, New Orleans, LA.

O'Reilly, D., & Dillenburger, K. (2000). The development of a high-intensity parent training program for the treatment of moderate to severe child conduct problems. *Research on Social Work Practice, 10*(6), 759–786.

Osberg, J. S., & DiScala, C. (1992, March). Morbidity among pediatric motor vehicle crash victims: The effectiveness of seat belts. *American Journal of Public Health, 82,* 422–425.

Osborne, J. W. (2001). Testing stereotype threat: Does anxiety explain race and sex differences in achievement? *Contemporary Educational Psychology, 26*(3), 291–310.

Osipow, S. (1990). Convergence in theories of career choice and development: Review and prospect. *Journal of Vocational Behavior, 39,* 122–131.

Oster, H., Hegley, D., & Nagel, L. (1992). Adult judgments and fine-grained analysis of infant facial expressions: Testing the validity of a priori coding formulas. *Developmental Psychology, 28,* 1115–1131.

O'Sullivan, L. F., Meyer-Bahlburg, H. F. L., & Watkins, B. X. (2000). Social cognitions associated with pubertal development in a sample of urban, low-income, African-American and Latina girls and mothers. *Journal of Adolescent Health, 27*(4), 227–235.

Ottinger, C., & Sikula, R. (1993). *Women in higher education: Where do we stand?* Washington, DC: American Council on Education.

Overbeek, P. (1999). Cited in Philipkoski, K. (1999, October 28). Why men are that way. *Wired Digital.*

Overpeck, M. D., Hoffman, H. J., & Prager, K. (1992). The lowest-birth-weight infants and the U.S. infant mortality rate: NCHS 1983 linked birth/infant death data. *American Journal of Public Health, 82,* 441–444.

Overstreet, D. H., et al. (2000). Enduring effects of prenatal cocaine administration on emotional behavior in rats. *Physiology & Behavior, 70*(1–2), 149–156.

Owens, R. E. (1990). Development of communication, language, and speech. In G. Shames & E. Wiig (Eds.), *Human communication disorders* (3rd ed.). Columbus, OH: Merrill.

Owens, R. G. (2001). *Organizational behavior in education: Instructional leadership and school reform* (7th ed.). Boston: Allyn & Bacon.

Oyserman, D., Radin, N., & Benn, R. (1993). Dynamics in a three-generational family: Teens, grandparents, and babies. *Developmental Psychology, 29,* 564–572.

Padgham, J. J., & Blyth, D. A. (1991). Dating during adolescence. In R. M. Lerner, A. C. Petersen, & J. Brooks-Gunn (Eds.), *Encyclopedia of adolescence.* New York: Garland.

Padilla, A. M., & Lindholm, K. J. (1992, August). *What do we know about culturally diverse children?* Paper presented at the meeting of the American Psychological Association, Washington, DC.

Page, K. (1999, May 16). The graduate. *Washington Post Magazine, 152,* 18, 20.

Paikoff, R. L., & Brooks-Gunn, J. (1991a). Do parent–child relationships change during puberty? *Psychological Bulletin, 110,* 47–66.

Paikoff, R. L., & Brooks-Gunn, J. (1991b). Interventions to prevent pregnancy. In R. M. Lerner, A. C. Petersen, & J. Brooks-Gunn (Eds.), *Encyclopedia of adolescence.* New York: Garland.

Paikoff, R. L., Buchanan, C. M., & Brooks-Gunn, J. (1991). Methodological issues in the study of hormone-behavior links at puberty. In R. M. Lerner, A. C. Petersen, & J. Brooks-Gunn (Eds.), *Encyclopedia of adolescence.* New York: Garland.

Paikoff, R. L., & Collins, A. C. (1991). Editors' notes: Shared views in the family during adolescence. In R. L. Paikoff (Ed.), *New directions for child development: No. 51. Shared views in the family during adolescence.* San Francisco: Jossey-Bass.

Palkovitz, R. (1984). Parental attitudes and fathers' interactions with their 5-month-old infants. *Developmental Psychology, 20,* 1054–1060.

Palmer, E. J., & Hollin, C. R. (2000). The interrelations of socio-moral-reasoning, perceptions of own parenting and attributions of intent with self-reported delinquency. *Legal & Criminological Psychology, 5*(Part2), 201–218.

Palmer, E. J., & Hollin, C. R. (2001). Sociomoral reasoning, perceptions of parenting and self-reported delinquency in adolescents. *Applied Cognitive Psychology, 15*(1), 85–100.

Papini, D. R., Farmer, F. F., Clark, S. M., Micka, J. C., & Barnett, J. K. (1990). Early adolescent age and gender differences in patterns of emotional self-disclosure to parents and friends. *Adolescence, 25,* 959–976.

Papini, D. R., & Roggman, L. A. (1992). Adolescent perceived attachment to parents in relation to competence, depression, and anxiety: A longitudinal study. *Journal of Early Adolescence, 12,* 420–440.

Papousek, M., Papousek, H., & Symmes, D. (1991). The meanings of melodies in motherese in tone and stress languages. *Infant Behavior and Development, 14,* 415–440.

Papousek, M., & von Hofacker, N. (1998). Persistent crying in early infancy: A non-trivial condition of risk for the developing mother–infant relationship. *Child: Care, Health & Development, 24*(5), 395–424.

Parazzini, F., et al. (1998). Coffee consumption and risk of hospitalized miscarriage before 12 weeks of gestation. *Human Reproduction, 13,* 2286–2291.

Parent, S., Normandeau, S., & Larivee, S. (2000). A quest for the Holy Grail in the new millennium: In search of a unified theory of cognitive development. *Child Development, 71*(4), 860–861.

Paris, S. G., & Winograd, P. (1990). How metacognition can promote academic learning and instruction. In B. F. Jones & L. Idol (Eds.), *Dimensions of thinking and cognitive instruction.* Hillsdale, NJ: Erlbaum.

Park, K. A., Lay, K., & Ramsay, L. (1993). Individual differences and developmental changes in preschoolers' friendships. *Developmental Psychology, 29,* 264–270.

Parke, R. D., & Slaby, R. G. (1983). The development of aggression. In P. H. Mussen (Ed.), *Handbook of child psychology: Vol. 4. Socialization, personality and social development.* New York: Wiley.

Parke, R. D., & Tinsley, B. J. (1987). Family interaction in infancy. In J. D. Osofsky (Ed.), *Handbook of infant development.* New York: Wiley.

Parker, J. G., & Asher, S. R. (1993). Friendship and friendship quality in middle childhood: Links with peer group acceptance and feelings of loneliness and social dissatisfaction. *Developmental Psychology, 29,* 611–621.

Parker, J. G., & Gottman, J. M. (1989). Social and emotional development in a rational context. In T. J. Berndt & G. W. Ladd (Eds.), *Peer relationships in child development.* New York: Wiley.

Parker, J. G., & Herrera, C. (1996). Interpersonal processes in friendship: A comparison of abused and nonabused children's experience. *Developmental Psychology, 32,* 1025–1038.

Parker, K. J., & Lee, T. M. (2001). Central vasopressin administration regulates the onset of facultative paternal behavior in *Microtus pennsylvanicus* (meadow voles). *Hormones & Behavior, 39*(4), 285–294.

Parker, S. J., Zahr, L. K., Cole, J. G., & Brecht, M. (1992). Outcome after developmental intervention in the neonatal intensive care unit for mothers of preterm infants with low socioeconomic status. *Journal of Pediatrics, 120,* 780–785.

Parks, P., & Bradley, R. (1991). The interaction of home environment features and their relation to infant competence. *Infant Mental Health Journal, 12,* 3–16.

Parsons, J. T., Halkitis, P. N., Bimbi, D., & Borkowski, T. (2000). Perceptions of the benefits and costs associated with condom use and unprotected sex among late adolescent college students. *Journal of Adolescence, 23*(4), 377–391.

Parten, M. B. (1932). Social participation among preschool children. *Journal of Abnormal and Social Psychology, 27,* 243–269.

Pascual-Leone, J. (1970). Mathematical model for the transition rule in Piaget's developmental stages. *Acta Psychologica, 63,* 301–345.

Pascual-Leone, J. (2000a). Is the French connection Neo-Piagetian? Not nearly enough! *Child Development, 71*(4), 843–845.

Pascual-Leone, J. (2000b). Reflections on working memory: Are the two models complementary? *Journal of Experimental Child Psychology, 77*(2), 138–154.

Passell, P. (1992, August 9). Twins study shows school is a sound investment. *The New York Times,* p. A14.

Pate, R. R., et al. (2000). Community interventions to promote proper nutrition and physical activity among youth. *Preventive Medicine: An International Journal Devoted to Practice & Theory, 31*(2, Pt. 2), S138–S149.

Patterson, G. R. (1982). *Coercive family processes.* Eugene, OR: Castilia Press.

Patterson, G. R. (1995). Coercion—A basis for early age of onset for arrest. In J. McCord (Ed.), *Coercion and punishment in long-term perspective* (pp. 81–105). New York: Cambridge University Press.

Patterson, J. L. (2000). Observed and reported expressive vocabulary and word combinations in bilingual toddlers. *Journal of Speech, Language, & Hearing Research, 43*(1), 121–128.

Patterson, O. (1998). *Rituals of blood: Consequences of slavery in two American centuries.* Washington, DC: Civitas Counterpoint.

Patterson, S. J., Sochting, I., & Marcia, J. E. (1992). The inner space and beyond: Women and identity. In G. R. Adams, T. P. Gullotta, & R. Montemayor (Eds.), *Adolescent identity formation.* Newbury Park, CA: Sage.

Patton, W. (1991). Relationship between self-image and depression in adolescents. *Psychological Reports, 68,* 867–870.

Paul, R. H. (1996). Toward fewer cesarean sections—The role of a trial of labor. *The New England Journal of Medicine, 335,* 735–736.

Paulhus, D. L., Trapnell, P. D., & Chen, D. (1999). Birth order effects on personality and achievement within families. *Psychological Science, 10*(6), 482–488.

Paus, T., et al. (1999). Structural maturation of neural pathways in children and adolescents: In vivo study. *Science, 283*(5409), 1908–1911.

Paxton, S. J., et al. (1991). Body image satisfaction, dieting beliefs, and weight loss behaviors in adolescent girls and boys. *Journal of Youth and Adolescence, 20,* 361–379.

Pear, R. (1992, September 13). U.S. orders testing of poor children for lead poisoning. *The New York Times,* pp. 1, 18.

Pear, R. (1993, August 16). U.S. to guarantee free immunization for poor children. *The New York Times,* p. A1, 9.

Pederson, D. R., & Moran, G. (1993, March). *A categorial description of infant–mother relationships in the home and its relation to Q-sort measures of infant attachment security and maternal sensitivity.* Paper presented at the meeting of the Society for Research in Child Development, New Orleans, LA.

Pellegrini, A. D. (1990). Elementary school children's playground behavior: Implications for children's social-cognitive development. *Children's Environments Quarterly, 7,* 8–16.

Pellegrini, A. D., & Perlmutter, J. C. (1988, January). Rough-and-tumble play on the elementary school playground. *Young Children,* pp. 14–17.

Pemberton, E. F. (1990). Systematic errors in children's drawings. *Cognitive Development, 5,* 395–404.

Penner, L. A., Thompson, J. K., & Coovert, D. L. (1991). Size overestimation among anorexics: Much ado about very little? *Journal of Abnormal Psychology, 100,* 90–93.

Penner, S. G. (1987). Parental responses to grammatical and ungrammatical child utterances. *Child Development, 58,* 376–384.

Peresmitre, G. G. (1999). Preadolescentes Mexicanas y la cultura de la delgadez: Figura ideal anorectica y preocupacion excesiva por el peso corporal. *Revista Mexicana de Psicologia, 16*(1), 153–165.

Perkins-Dock, Robin E. (2001). Family interventions with incarcerated youth: A review of the literature. *International Journal of Offender Therapy & Comparative Criminology, 45*(5), 606–625.

Perner, J. (1991). *Understanding the representational mind.* Cambridge, MA: MIT Press.

Perry, C. L. (1991). Programs for smoking prevention with early adolescents. In R. M. Lerner, A. C. Petersen, & J. Brooks-Gunn (Eds.), *Encyclopedia of adolescence.* New York: Garland.

Perry, D. G., Perry, L. C., & Boldizar, J. P. (1990). Learning of aggression. In M. Lewis & S. M. Miller (Eds.), *Handbook of developmental psychopathology.* New York: Plenum.

Perry, D. G., White, A. S., & Perry, L. C. (1984). Does early sex typing result from children's attempts to match their behavior to sex role stereotypes? *Child Development, 55,* 2114–2121.

Perry, E. K., et al. (2001). Cholinergic activity in autism: Abnormalities in the cerebral cortex and basal forebrain. *American Journal of Psychiatry, 158*(7), 1058–1066.

Peskin, J. (1992, January). Ruse and representations: On children's ability to conceal information. *Developmental Psychology, 28,* 84–89.

Peters, D. P. (1991). The influence of stress and arousal on the child witness. In J. Doris (Ed.), *The suggestibility of children's recollections.* Washington, DC: American Psychological Association.

Peters, M. (1990). Phenotype in normal left-handers: An understanding of phenotype is the basis for understanding mechanism and inheritance of handedness. In S. Coren (Ed.), *Left-handedness: Behavior implications and anomalies.* Amsterdam: North-Holland.

Petersen, A. C. (1983). Menarche: Meaning of measures and measuring meaning. In S. Golub (Ed.), *Menarche.* Lexington, MA: Lexington Books.

Petersen, A. C., Compas, B. E., Brooks-Gunn, J., Stemmler, M., Ey, S., & Grant, K. E. (1993). Depression in adolescence. *American Psychologist, 48,* 155–168.

Peterson, C. C. (2001). Influence of siblings' perspectives on theory of mind. *Cognitive Development, 15*(4), 435–455.

Peterson, C. C., Peterson, J. L., & Seeto, D. (1983). Developmental changes in ideas about lying. *Child Development, 54,* 1529–1535.

Peterson, L., & Roberts, M. C. (1992). Complacency, misdirection, and effective prevention of children's injuries. *American Psychologist, 47,* 1040–1044.

Petittio, L. A., & Marentette, P. F. (1991). Babbling in the manual mode: Evidence for the ontogeny of language. *Science, 251,* 1493–1496.

Pfeffer, C. R. (1991). Attempted suicide in children and adolescents: Causes and management. In M. Lewis (Ed.), *Child and adolescent psychiatry: A comprehensive textbook.* Baltimore: Williams & Wilkins.

Phalet, K., & Schoenpflug, U. (2001). Intergenerational transmission of collectivism and achievement values in two acculturation contexts: The case of Turkish families in Germany and Turkish and Moroccan families in the Netherlands. *Journal of Cross-Cultural Psychology, 32*(2), 186–201.

Pharoah, P. (2001). Genetics and public health in the 21st century: Using genetic information to improve health and prevent disease. *British Medical Journal, 322,* 1068.

Phillips, A. S., & Phillips, C. R. (2000). Birth-order differences in self-attributions for achievement. *Journal of Individual Psychology, 56*(4), 474–480.

Phinney, J. S. (1989). Stages of ethnic identity in minority group adolescents. *Journal of Early Adolescence, 9,* 34–49.

Phinney, J. S. (1992). The multigroup ethnic identity measure: A new scale for use with adolescents and young adults with diverse groups. *Journal of Adolescent Research, 12,* 156–176.

Phinney, J. S. (2000). Identity formation across cultures: The interaction of personal, societal, and historical change. *Human Development, 43*(1), 27–31.

Phinney, J. S., & Alipuria, L. (1990). Ethnic identity in older adolescents from four ethnic groups. *Journal of Adolescence, 13,* 171–183.

Phinney, J. S., & Chavira, P. (1992). Ethnic identity and self-esteem: An exploratory longitudinal study. *Journal of Adolescence, 15,* 1–11.

Phinney, J. S., DuPont, S., Espinosa, C., Onwughalu, M., Revill, J., & Sanders, K. (1992, March). *Group identity among minority adolescents: Ethnic, American, or bicultural?* Paper presented at the meeting of the Society for Research on Adolescence, Washington, DC.

Phinney, J. S., & Nakayama, S. (1991, April). *Parental influence on ethnic identity formation in minority adolescents.* Paper presented at the meeting of the Society for Research in Child Development, Seattle.

Phinney, J. S., Ong, A., & Madden, T. (2000). Cultural values and intergenerational value discrepancies in immigrant and non-immigrant families. *Child Development, 71*(2), 528–539.

Phinney, J. S., & Rosenthal, D. A. (1992). Ethnic identity in adolescence: Process, context, and outcome. In G. R. Adams, T. P. Gullotta, & R. Montemayor (Eds.), *Adolescent identity formation.* Newbury Park, CA: Sage.

Phinney, J. S., & Tarver, S. (1988). Ethnic identity search and commitment in black and white eighth graders. *Journal of Early Adolescence, 8,* 265–277.

Piaget, J. (1932). *The moral judgment of the child.* London: Kegan Paul.

Piaget, J. (1962). *Play, dreams, and imitation in childhood.* New York: Norton. (Original work published 1946).

Piaget, J. (1963). *The origins of intelligence in children.* New York: Norton. (Original work published 1936).

Piaget, J. (1967). In D. Elkind (Ed.), *Six psychological studies.* New York: Random House. (Original work published 1964).

Piaget, J. (1972). Intellectual evolution from adolescence to adulthood. *Human Development, 15,* 1–12.

Piaget, J. (1976). *The grasp of consciousness: Action and concept in the young child.* Cambridge, MA: Harvard University Press.

Piaget, J., & Inhelder, B. (1969). *Psychology of the child.* New York: Basic Books.

Piaget, J., & Smith, L. (Trans). (2000). Commentary on Vygotsky's criticisms of language and thought of the child and judgment and reasoning in the child. *New Ideas in Psychology, 18*(2–3), 241–259.

Pianta, R. C., & Steinberg, M. (1992). Teacher–child relationships and the process of adjusting to school. In R. C. Pianta (Ed.), *New directions for child development: No. 57. Beyond the parent: The role of other adults in children's lives.* San Francisco: Jossey-Bass.

Pick, A. D. (1991). Perception. In R. M. Thomas (Ed.), *The encyclopedia of human development and education: Theory, research, and studies.* Oxford: Pergamon.

Pickering, S. J. (2001). The development of visuo-spatial working memory. *Memory, 9*(4–6), 423–432.

Pickles, A., et al. (2000). Variable expression of the autism broader phenotype: Findings from extended pedigrees. *Journal of Child Psychology & Psychiatry & Allied Disciplines, 41*(4), 491–502.

Pihl, R. O., & Peterson, J. B. (1991). Attention-deficit hyperactivity disorder, childhood conduct disorder, and alcoholism. *Alcohol Health and Research World, 15,* 25–31.

Pihl, R. O., Peterson, J. B., & Finn, P. (1990). Inherited predisposition to alcoholism. *Journal of Abnormal Psychology, 99,* 291–301.

Pike, K. M., & Rodin, J. (1991). Mothers, daughters, and disordered eating. *Journal of Abnormal Psychology, 100,* 198–204.

Pillard, R. C., & Weinrich, J. D. (1986). Evidence of familial nature of male homosexuality. *Archives of Sexual Behavior, 43,* 808–812.

Pine, D. S., et al. (2001). Fluvoxamine for the treatment of anxiety disorders in children and adolescents. *New England Journal of Medicine, 344*(17), 1279–1285.

Pinhas-Hamiel, O., & Zeitler, P. (2000). "Who is the wise man?—the one who foresees consequences": Childhood obesity, new associated comorbidity, and prevention. P*reventive Medicine: An International Journal Devoted to Practice & Theory, 31*(6), 702–705.

Pinker, S. (1994). *The language instinct.* New York: William Morrow.

Pinker, S. (1997). Words and rules in the human brain. *Nature, 387*(6633), 547–548.

Piper, D. L., Moberg, D. P., & King, M. J. (2000). The Healthy for Life project: Behavioral outcomes. *Journal of Primary Prevention, 21*(1), 47–73.

Piven, J. (1999). Genetic liability for autism: The behavioural expression in relatives. *International Review of Psychiatry, 11*(4), 299–308.

Piven, J., et al. (1995). An MRI study of brain size in autism. *American Journal of Psychiatry, 152,* 1145–1149.

Piven, J., et al. (1997). An MRI study of the corpus callosum in autism. *American Journal of Psychiatry, 154,* 1051–1056.

Plomin, R. (2000). Behavioural genetics in the 21st century. *International Journal of Behavioral Development, 24*(1), 30–34.

Plomin, R. (2001a). Genetics and behaviour. *Psychologist, 14*(3), 134–139.

Plomin, R. (2001b). Genetic factors contributing to learning and language delays and disabilities. *Child & Adolescent Psychiatric Clinics of North America, 10*(2), 259–277.

Plomin, R., Owen, M. J., & McGuffin, P. (1994). The genetic basis of complex human behaviors. *Science, 264,* 1733–1739.

Poest, C. A., Williams, J. R., Witt, D., & Atwood, M. E. (1989). Physical activity patterns of preschool children. *Early Childhood Research Quarterly, 4,* 367–376.

Polan, H. J., et al. (1991). Psychopathology in mothers of children with failure to thrive. *Infant Mental Health Journal, 12,* 55–64.

Polan, H. J., & Ward, M. J. (1994). Role of the mother's touch in failure to thrive: A preliminary investigation. *Journal of the American Academy of Child & Adolescent Psychiatry, 33*(8), 1098–1105.

Pollack, W. S. (1996). Cited in Clay, R. A. (1996). Older men are more involved fathers, studies show. *APA Monitor, 27*(2), 37.

Pollitt, E., Gorman, K. S., Engle, P., Martorell, R., & Rivera, J. (1993). Early supplementary feeding and cognition: Effect over two decades. *Monographs of the Society for Research in Child Development, 58,* (7, Serial No. 235).

Pollock, B., Prior, H., & Güntürkün, O. (2000). Development of object permanence in food-storing magpies *(Pica pica). Journal of Comparative Psychology, 114*(2), 148–157.

Pombeni, M. L., Kirchler, E., & Palmonari, A. (1990). Identification with peers as a strategy to muddle through the troubles of the adolescent years. *Journal of Adolescence, 13,* 351–369.

Pomerantz, E. M., Frey, K., Greulich, F., & Ruble, D. N. (1993, March). *Explaining the decrease in perceived competence: Grade and gender differences in perceptions of ability as stable.* Paper presented at the meeting of the Society for Research in Child Development. New Orleans, LA.

Pomerleau, A., Bolduc, D., Malcuit, G., & Cossette, L. (1990). Pink or blue: Environmental gender stereotypes in the first two years of life. *Sex Roles, 22,* 359–367.

Ponnappa, B. C., & Rubin, E. (2000). Modeling alcohol's effects on organs in animal models. *Alcohol Research & Health, 24*(2), 93–104.

Pope, H.G., Kouri, E. M., & Hudson, J. I. (2000). Effects of supraphysiologic doses of testosterone on mood and aggression in normal men: A randomized controlled trial. *Archives of General Psychiatry, 57,* 133–140.

Porac, C., & Buller, T. (1990). Overt attempts to change hand preference: A study of group and individual characteristics. *Canadian Journal of Psychology, 44,* 512–521.

Porter, R. H., Makin, J. W., Davis, L. B., & Christensen, K. M. (1992). Breast-fed infants respond to olfactory cues from their own mother and unfamiliar lactating females. *Infant Behavior and Development, 15,* 85–93.

Power, T. G. (1985). Mother- and father-infant play: A developmental analysis. *Child Development, 56,* 1514–1524.

Power, T. G., Gershenhorn, S., & Stafford, D. (1990). Maternal perceptions of infant difficulties: The influence of maternal attitudes and attributions. *Infant Behavior and Development, 13,* 421–437.

Power, T. G., Kobayashi-Winata, H., & Kelley, M. L. (1992). Childrearing patterns in Japan and the United States: A cluster analytic study. *International Journal of Behavioral Development, 15,* 185–205.

Power, T. G., & Parke, R. D. (1982). Play as a context for early learning: Lab and home analysis. In L. M. Laosa & I. E. Sigel (Eds.), *The family as a learning environment.* New York: Plenum.

Pratt, C., & Bryant, P. (1990). Young children understand that looking leads to knowing (so long as they are looking into a single barrel). *Child Development, 61,* 973–982.

Press, A. (1992, August 10). Old too soon, wise too late? *Newsweek,* pp. 22–25.

Price, D. W. W., & Goodman, G. S. (1990). Visiting the wizard: Children's memory for a recurring event. *Child Development, 61,* 664–680.

Price, R. H. (1992). Psychosocial impact of job loss on individuals and families. *Current Directions in Psychological Science, 1,* 9–11.

Price-Williams, D. R., Gordon, W., & Ramirez, M. (1969). Skill and conservation. *Developmental Psychology, 1,* 769.

Prior, S. M., & Welling, K. A. (2001). "Read in your head": A Vygotskian analysis of the transition from oral to silent reading. *Reading Psychology, 22*(1), 1–15.

Provence, S., & Lipton, R. C. (1962). *Infants in institutions.* New York: International Universities Press.

Pryce, C. R., Bettschen, D., Bahr, N. I., & Feldon, J. (2001). Comparison of the effects of infant handling, isolation, and nonhandling on acoustic startle, prepulse inhibition, locomotion, and HPA activity in the adult rat. *Behavioral Neuroscience, 115*(1), 71–83.

Pugh, K. R., et al., (2000). The angular gyrus in developmental dyslexia: Task-specific differences in functional connectivity within posterior cortex. *Psychological Science, 11*(1), 51–56.

Purvis, A. (1990, November 26). The sins of the fathers. *Time,* pp. 90, 92.

Putallaz, M., Costanzo, P. R., Grimes, C. L., & Sherman, D. M. (1998). Intergenerational continuities and their influences on children's social development. *Social Development, 7*(3), 389–427.

Putallaz, M., & Dunn, S. E. (1990). The importance of peer relations. In M. Lewis & S. M. Miller (Eds.), *Handbook of developmental psychopathology.* New York: Plenum.

Putallaz, M., & Heflin, A. H. (1990). Parent–child interaction. In S. R. Asher & J. D. Coie (Eds.), *Peer rejection in childhood.* Cambridge: Cambridge University Press.

Quatman, T., & Watson, C. M. (2001). Gender differences in adolescent self-esteem: An exploration of domains. *Journal of Genetic Psychology, 162*(1), 93–117.

Quiggle, N. L., Garber, J., Panak, W. F., & Dodge, K. A. (1992). Social information processing in aggressive and depressed children. *Child Development, 63,* 1305–1320.

Quintana, S. M. (1998). Children's developmental understanding of ethnicity and race. *Applied & Preventive Psychology, 7*(1), 27–45.

Quirk, K. J., Keith, T. Z., & Quirk, J. T. (2001). Employment during high school and student achievement: Longitudinal analysis of national data. *Journal of Educational Research, 95*(1), 4–10.

Rabasca, L. (2000). Pre-empting racism. *Monitor on Psychology, 31*(11), 60.

Rack, J. P., Snowling, M. J., & Olson, R. K. (1992). The nonword reading deficit in developmental dyslexia: A review. *Reading Research Quarterly, 27,* 29–53.

Rakic, P. (1991). Plasticity of cortical development. In S. E. Brauth, W. S. Hall, & R. J. Dooling (Eds.), *Plasticity of development.* Cambridge, MA: MIT Press.

Ramey, C. T., et al. (1992). Infant health and development program for low birth weight, premature infants: Program elements, family participation, and child intelligence. *Pediatrics, 89,* 454–465.

Ramey, C. T., Campbell, F. A., & Ramey, S. L. (1999). Early intervention: Successful pathways to improving intellectual development. *Developmental Neuropsychology, 16*(3) 385–392.

Randel, B., Stevenson, H. W., & Witruk, E. (2000). Attitudes, beliefs, and mathematics achievement of German and Japanese high school students. *International Journal of Behavioral Development, 24*(2), 190–198.

Rapin, I. (1997). Autism. *The New England Journal of Medicine, 337,* 97–104.

Raschka, L. B. (2000). Paternal age and schizophrenia in dizygotic twins. *British Journal of Psychiatry, 176,* 400–401.

Rashotte, C. A., MacPhee, K., & Torgesen, J. K. (2001). The effectiveness of a group reading instruction program with poor readers in multiple grades. *Learning Disability Quarterly, 24*(2), 119–134.

Raskind, W. H. (2001). Current understanding of the genetic basis of reading and spelling disability. *Learning Disability Quarterly, 24*(3), 141–157.

Rathus, S. A. (1988). *Understanding child development.* New York: Holt, Rinehart and Winston.

Rathus, S. A. (2002). *Psychology in the new millennium* (8th ed.). Fort Worth: Harcourt.

Rathus, S. A., & Boughn, S. (1993). *AIDS—What every student needs to know.* Fort Worth, TX: Harcourt Brace Jovanovich.

Rathus, S. A., Nevid, J. S., & Fichner-Rathus, L. (2002). *Human sexuality in a world of diversity* (5th ed.). Boston: Allyn & Bacon.

Ratner, H. H., Smith, B. S., & Padgett, R. J. (1990). Children's organization of events and event memories. In R. Fivush & J. A. Hudson (Eds.), *Knowing and remembering in young children.* Cambridge: Cambridge University Press.

Raudenbusch, S. W. (1984). Magnitude of teacher expectancy effects on pupil IQ as a function of credibility of expectancy induction: A synthesis from 18 experiments. *Journal of Experimental Psychology, 76,* 85–97.

Rauh, V. A., Achenbach, T. M., Nurcombe, B., Howell, C. T., & Teti, D. M. (1988). Minimizing adverse effect of low birthweight: Four-year results of an early intervention program. *Child Development, 59,* 544–553.

Rauscher, F. H. (1998). Response to Katie Overy's paper, "Can music really 'improve' the mind?" *Psychology of Music, 26*(2), 197–199.

Rauscher, F. H., & Shaw, G. L. (1998). Key components of the Mozart effect. *Perceptual & Motor Skills, 86*(3), 835–841.

Rawlins, R. (1998). Cited in Kolata, G. (1998, September 9). Researchers report success in method to pick baby's sex. *The New York Times* online.

Raymond, C. L., & Benbow, C. P. (1986). Gender differences in mathematics: A function of parental support and student sex typing? *Developmental Psychology, 22,* 808–819.

Rayner, K. (1993). Reading symposium: An introduction. *Psychological Science, 4,* 280–282.

Raz, S., et al. (1998). The effects of perinatal hypoxic risk on developmental outcome in early and middle childhood: A twin study. *Neuropsychology, 12*(3), 459–467.

Rebok, G. W. (1987). *Life-span cognitive development.* New York: Holt, Rinehart and Winston.

Reid, M., Ramey, S. L., & Burchinal, M. (1990). Dialogues with children about their families. In I. Bretherton & M. Watson (Eds.), *New directions for child development: No. 48. Children's perspectives on their families.* San Francisco: Jossey-Bass.

Reifman, A. (2000). Revisiting *The Bell Curve. Psycoloquy, 11,* np. **http://www.cogsci.soton.ac.uk/cgi/psyc/newpsy?11.099**

Reiger, K. (2000). Reconceiving citizenship: The challenge of mothers as political activists. *Feminist Theory, 1*(3), 309–327.

Reinecke, M. A., DuBois, D. L. (2001). Socioenvironmental and cognitive risk and resources: Relations to mood and suicidality among inpatient adolescents. *Journal of Cognitive Psychotherapy, 15*(3), 195–222.

Reinisch, J. M., Ziemba-Davis, M., & Sanders, S. A. (1991). Hormonal contributions to sexually dimorphic behavioral development in humans. *Psychoneuroendocrinology, 16*(1–3), 213–278.

Reisman, J. E. (1987). Touch, motion, and proprioception. In P. Salapatek & L. Cohen (Eds.), *Handbook of infant perception: Vol. 1. From sensation to perception.* Orlando, FL: Academic Press.

Reissland, N. (1988). Neonatal imitation in the first hour of life: Observations in rural Nepal. *Developmental Psychology, 24,* 464–469.

Renninger, K. A. (1990). Children's play interests, representation, and activity, In R. Fivush & J. A. Hudson (Eds.), *Knowing and remembering in young children.* Cambridge: Cambridge University Press.

Rescorla, L. (1991a). Early academics: Introduction to the debate. In L. Rescorla, M. C. Hyson, & K. Hirsh-Pasek (Eds.), *New directions in child development: No. 53. Academic instruction in early childhood: Challenge or pressure?* San Francisco: Jossey-Bass.

Rescorla, L. (1991b). Parent and teacher attitudes about early academics. In L. Rescorla, M. C. Hyson, & K. Hirsh-Pasek (Eds.), *New directions in child development: No. 53. Academic instruction in early childhood: Challenge or pressure?* San Francisco: Jossey-Bass.

Rest, J. R. (1983). Morality. In P. H. Mussen (Ed.), *Handbook of child psychology: Vol. 3. Cognitive development.* New York: Wiley.

Rest, J. R., & Narvaez, D. (1991). The college experience and moral development. In W. M. Kurtines & J. L. Gewirtz (Eds.), *Handbook of moral behavior and development* (Vol. 2). Hillsdale, NJ: Erlbaum.

Rest, J. R., & Thoma, S. J. (1985). Relation of moral judgment development to formal education. *Developmental Psychology, 21,* 709–714.

Reyna, V. F. (1991). Class inclusion, the conjunction fallacy, and other cognitive illusions. *Developmental Review, 11,* 317–336.

Reynolds, A. G. (1991). The cognitive consequences of bilingualism. In A. G. Reynolds (Ed.), *Bilingualism, multiculturalism, and second language learning.* Hillsdale, NJ: Erlbaum.

Reynolds, A. J. (1993, March). *Effects of a preschool plus follow-on intervention program for children at risk.* Paper presented at the meeting of the Society for Research in Child Development, New Orleans, LA.

Reynolds, K. D., et al. (1990). Psychological predictors of physical activity in adolescents. *Preventive Medicine, 19,* 541–551.

Reznick, J. S., & Goldfield, B. A. (1992). Rapid change in lexical development in comprehension and production. *Developmental Psychology, 28,* 406–413.

Rezvani, A. H., & Levin, E. D. (2001). Cognitive effects of nicotine. *Biological Psychiatry, 49*(3), 258–267.

Rheingold, H. L., & Cook, K. V. (1975). The contents of boys' and girls' rooms as an index of parents' behavior. *Child Development, 46,* 459–463.

Rheingold, H. L., Gewirtz, J. L., & Ross, H. W. (1959). Social conditioning of vocalizations in the infant. *Journal of Comparative and Physiological Psychology, 52,* 68–73.

Ricci, E., Parazzini, F, & Pardi, G. (2000). Caesarean section and antiretroviral treatment. *The Lancet, 355*(9202), 496–502.

Ricciuti, H. N. (1993). Nutrition and mental development. *Current Directions in Psychological Science, 2,* 43–46.

Rice, M. L. (1989). Children's language acquisition. *American Psychologist, 44,* 149–156.

Rice, M. L., Huston, A. C., Truglio, R., & Wright, J. (1990). Words from "Sesame Street": Learning vocabulary while viewing. *Developmental Psychology, 26,* 421–428.

Richards, H. C., Bear, G. G., Stewart, A. L., & Norman, A. D. (1992). Moral reasoning and classroom conduct: Evidence of a curvilinear relationship. *Merrill-Palmer Quarterly, 38,* 176–190.

Richards, M. H., & Duckett, E. (1991). Maternal employment and adolescents. In S. V. Lerner & N. L. Galambos (Eds.), *Employed mothers and their children.* New York: Garland.

Richards, T. W., & Nelson, V. L. (1938). Studies in mental development: 2. Analyses of abilities tested at six months by the Gesell schedule. *Journal of Genetic Psychology, 52,* 327–331.

Riddoch, C., Mahoney, C., Murphy, N., Boreham, C., & Cran, G. (1991). The physical activity patterns of Northern Irish schoolchildren ages 11–16 years. *Pediatric Exercise Science, 3,* 300–309.

Riepe, M. (2000). Cited in Ritter, M. (2000, March 21). Brains differ in navigation skills. The Associated Press online.

Ritter, C., Hobfoll, S. E., Lavin, J., Cameron, R. P., & Hulsizer, M. R. (2000). Stress, psychosocial resources, and depressive symptomatology during pregnancy in low-income, inner-city women. *Health Psychology, 19*(6) 576–585.

Ritter, M. (2000, March 21). Brains differ in navigation skills. *The Associated Press online.*

Ritvo, E. R., Freeman, B. J., Mason-Brothers, A., Mo, A., & Ritvo, A. M. (1985). Concordance for the syndrome of autism in 40 pairs of afflicted twins. *American Journal of Psychiatry, 142,* 74–77.

Robbins, C., & Ehri, L. C. (1994). Reading storybooks to kindergartners helps them learn new vocabulary words. *Journal of Educational Psychology, 86,* 54–64.

Roberts, A., et al. (2000). Perceived family and peer transactions and self-esteem among urban early adolescents. *Journal of Early Adolescence, 20*(1), 68–92.

Roberts, J. M. (2000). Recent advances: Obstetrics. *British Medical Journal, 321*(7252), 33–35.

Roberts, K. B. (2000). *Manual of clinical problems in pediatrics* (5th ed). Philadelphia: Lippincott Williams & Wilkins.

Roberts, L. C., & Blanton, P. W. (2001). "I always knew mom and dad loved me best": Experiences of only children. *Journal of Individual Psychology, 57*(2), 125–140.

Roberts, R. N., Wasik, B. H., Casto, G., & Ramey, C. T. (1991). Family support in the home: Programs, policy, and social change. *American Psychologist, 46,* 131–137.

Robins, L. N. (1991). Conduct disorder. *Journal of Child Psychology and Psychiatry, 32,* 193–212.

Robinson, E. J., & Mitchell, P. (1992). Children's interpretation of messages from a speaker with a false belief. *Child Development, 62,* 639–652.

Robinson, G. E., & Wittebols, J. H. (1986). Class size research: *A related cluster analysis for decision making.* Arlington, VA: Educational Research Service.

Robinson, G. L., & Foreman, P. J. (1999). Scotopic sensitivity/Irlen syndrome and the use of coloured filters: A long-term placebo-controlled study of reading strategies using analysis of miscue. *Perceptual & Motor Skills, 88*(1), 35–52.

Robinson, J. N., Norwitz, E. R., Cohen, A. P., & Lieberman, E. (2000). Predictors of episiotomy use at first spontaneous vaginal delivery. *Obstetrics & Gynecology, 96*(2), 214–218.

Robinson, J. R., Drotar, D., & Boutry, M. (2001). Problem-solving abilities among mothers of infants with failure to thrive. *Journal of Pediatric Psychology, 26*(1), 21–32.

Robinson, N. M. (1992, August). *Development and variation: The challenge of nurturing gifted young children.* Paper presented at the meeting of the American Psychological Association, Washington, DC.

Robinson, T. N. (1998). Does television cause childhood obesity? *Journal of the American Medical Association, 279,* 959.

Robinson, T. N. (1999). Reducing children's television viewing to prevent obesity: A randomized controlled trial. *Journal of the American Medical Association online, 282*(16).

Rockett, H. R. H., Berkey, C. S., Field, A. E., & Colditz, G. A. (2001). Cross-sectional measurement of nutrient intake among adolescents in 1996. *Preventive Medicine: An International Journal Devoted to Practice & Theory, 33*(1), 27–37.

Rodning, C., Beckwith, L., & Howard, J. (1991). Quality of attachment and home environments in children prenatally exposed to PCP and cocaine. *Development and Psychopathology, 3,* 351–366.

Rodriguez, A., Bohlin, G., & Lindmark, G. (2000). Psychosocial predictors of smoking and exercise during pregnancy. *Journal of Reproductive & Infant Psychology, 18*(3), 203–223.

Roebers, C. M., Moga, N., & Schneider, W. (2001). The role of accuracy motivation on children's and adults' event recall. *Journal of Experimental Child Psychology, 78*(4), 313–329.

Roffwarg, H. P., Muzio, J. N., & Dement, W. C. (1966). Ontogenetic development of the human sleep-dream cycle. *Science, 152,* 604–619.

Roggman, L. A., Kinnaird, J. V., & Carroll, K. A. (1991, August). *Physical attractiveness, sex, and clothing effects on adults' expectations of children.* Paper presented at the meeting of the American Psychological Association, San Francisco.

Rogoff, B. (1990). *Apprenticeship in thinking.* Oxford: Oxford University Press.

Rogoff, B., & Mistry, J. (1990). The social and functional context of children's remembering. In R. Fivush & J. A. Hudson (Eds.), *Knowing and remembering in young children.* Cambridge: Cambridge University Press.

Rogoff, B., & Morelli, G. (1989). Perspectives on children's devel-opment from cultural psychology. *American Psychologist, 44,* 343–348.

Rohde, P., Clarke, G. N., Lewinsohn, P. M., Seeley , J. R., & Kaufman, N. K. (2001). Impact of comorbidity on a cognitive-behavioral group treatment for adolescent depression. *Journal of the American Academy of Child & Adolescent Psychiatry, 40*(7), 795–802.

Romans, S. E., Gendall, K. A., Martin, J. L., & Mullen, P. E. (2001). Child sexual abuse and later disordered eating: A New Zealand epidemiological study. *International Journal of Eating Disorders, 29*(4), 380–392.

Roncesvalles, M. N. C., Woollacott, M. H., & Jensen, J. L. (2001). Development of lower extremity kinetics for balance control in infants and young children. *Journal of Motor Behavior, 33*(2), 180–192.

Roopnarine, J. L., Talukder, E., Jain, D., Joshi, P., & Srivastav, P. (1990). Characteristics of holding, patterns of play, and social behaviors between parents and infants in New Delhi, India. *Developmental Psychology, 26,* 667–673.

Rose, A. J., & Asher, S. R. (1999). Children's goals and strategies in response to conflicts within a friendship. *Developmental Psychology, 35*(1), 69–79.

Rose, S. A., & Blank, M. (1974). The potency of context in children's cognition: An illustration through conservation. *Child Development, 45,* 499–502.

Rose, S. A., Feldman, J. F., & Jankowski, J. J. (2001). Visual short-term memory in the first year of life: Capacity and recency effects. *Developmental Psychology, 37*(4), 539–549.

Rose, S. A., Feldman, J. F., Rose, S. L., Wallace, I. F., & McCarton, C. (1992). Behavior problems at 3 and 6 years: Prevalence and continuity in full-terms and preterms. *Development and Psychopathology, 4,* 361–374.

Rose, S. A., Feldman, J. F., & Wallace, I. F. (1992). Infant information processing in relation to six-year cognitive outcomes. *Child Development, 63,* 1126–1141.

Rose, S. A., & Orlian, E. K. (1991). Asymmetries in infant cross-model transfer. *Child Development, 62,* 706–718.

Rose, S. A., & Ruff, M. A. (1987). Cross-modal abilities in human infants. In J. Osofky (Ed.), *Handbook of infant development* (2nd ed.). New York: Wiley.

Rosen, H. J., Ojemann, J. G., Ollinger, J. M., & Petersen, S. E. (2000). Comparison of brain activation during word retrieval done silently and aloud using fMRI. *Brain & Cognition, 42*(2), 201–217.

Rosen, J. C., Tacy, B., & Howell, D. (1990). Life stress, psychological symptoms, and weight reducing behavior in adolescent girls: A prospective analysis. *International Journal of Eating Disorders, 9,* 17–26.

Rosen, K., & Rothbaum, F. (1993). Quality of parental caregiving and security of attachment. *Developmental Psychology, 29,* 358–367.

Rosen, W. D., Adamson, L. B., & Bakeman, R. (1992). An experimental investigation of infant social referencing: Mothers' messages and gender differences. *Developmental Psychology, 28,* 1172–1178.

Rosenbaum, D. E. (2000, May 16). On left-handedness, its causes and costs. *The New York Times,* pp. F1, F6.

Rosenberg, M. S. (1987). New directions for research on the psychological maltreatment of children. *American Psychologist, 42,* 166–171.

Rosengren, K. S., Gelman, S. A., Kalish, C. W., & McCormick, M. (1991). As time goes by: Children's early understanding of growth in animals. *Child Development, 62,* 1302–1320.

Rosenstein, D., & Oster, H. (1988). Differential facial responses to four basic tastes. *Child Development, 59,* 1555–1568.

Rosenthal, D. A., Smith, A. M. A., & de Visser, R. (1999). Personal and social factors influencing age at first sexual intercourse. *Archives of Sexual Behavior, 28*(4), 319–333.

Rosenthal, E. (1990a, January 4). New insights on why some children are fat offer clues on weight loss. *The New York Times*, p. B7.

Rosenthal, E. (1990b, February 4). When a pregnant woman drinks. *The New York Times Magazine,* pp. 30, 49, 61.

Rosenthal, E. (1991, July 10). Technique for early prenatal test comes under question in studies. *The New York Times,* p. B6.

Rosenthal, R., & Jacobson, L. (1968). *Pygmalion in the classroom.* New York: Holt, Rinehart and Winston.

Ross, G., Kagan, J., Zelazo, P., & Kotelchuck, M. (1975). Separation protest in infants in home and laboratory. *Developmental Psychology, 11,* 256–257.

Ross, J. L., Roeltgen, D., Feuillan, P., Kushner, H., & Cutler, G. B. (2000). Use of estrogen in young girls with Turner syndrome: Effects on memory. *Neurology, 54*(1), 164–170.

Ross, J. L., Zinn, A., & McCauley, E. (2000). Neurodevelopmental and psychosocial aspects of Turner syndrome. *Mental Retardation & Developmental Disabilities Research Reviews, 6*(2), 135–141.

Rossetti, L. M. (1990). *Infant–toddler assessment: An interdisciplinary approach.* Boston: College Hill Press.

Rosso, I. M., et al. (2000). Obstetric risk factors for early-onset schizophrenia in a Finnish birth cohort. *American Journal of Psychiatry, 157*(5), 801–807.

Rothbart, M. K., & Ahadi, S. A. (1994). Temperament and the development of personality. *Journal of Abnormal Psychology, 103,* 55–66.

Rothbart, M. K., Ziaie, H., & O'Boyle, C. G. (1992). Self-regulation and emotion in infancy. In N. Eisenberg & R. A. Fabes (Eds.), *New directions for child development: No. 55. Emotion and its regulation in early development.* San Francisco, CA: Jossey-Bass.

Rotheram-Borus, M. J., Trautman, P. D., Dopkins, S. C., & Shrout, P. E. (1990). Cognitive style and pleasant activities among female adolescent suicide attempters. *Journal of Consulting and Clinical Psychology, 58,* 554–561.

Roussounis, S. H., Hubley, P. A., & Dear, P. R. (1993). Five-year follow-up of very low birthweight infants: Neurological and psychological outcome. *Health and Development, 19,* 45–59.

Routh, D. K. (1990). Taxonomy in developmental psychopathology: Consider the source. In M. Lewis & S. M. Miller (Eds.), *Handbook of developmental psychopathology.* New York: Plenum.

Rovee-Collier, C. (1993). The capacity for long-term memory in infancy. *Current Directions in Psychological Science, 2,* 130–135.

Rovee-Collier, C., & Shyi, G. (1992). A functional and cognitive analysis of infant long-term retention. In M. L. Howe, C. J. Brainerd, & V. F. Reyna (Eds.), *Development of long-term retention.* New York: Springer-Verlag.

Rovet, J. F. (1993). The psychoeducational characteristics of children with Turner syndrome. *Journal of Learning Disabilities, 26,* 333–341.

Rowe, D. C., Rodgers, J. L., & Meseck-Bushey, S. (1992). Sibling delinquency and the family environment: Shared and unshared influences. *Child Development, 63,* 59–67.

Rowen, B. (1973). *The children we see.* New York: Holt, Rinehart & Winston.

Rowland, C. F., & Pine, J. M. (2000). Subject-auxiliary inversion errors and *wh*-question acquisition: "What children do know?" *Journal of Child Language, 27*(1), 157–181.

Rozin, P. (1990). Development in the food domain. *Developmental Psychology, 26,* 555–562.

Rozin, P., & Fallon, A. (1988). Body image, attitudes to weight, and misperceptions of figure preferences of the opposite sex: A comparison of men and women in two generations. *Journal of Abnormal Psychology, 97,* 342–345.

Rubenstein, A. J., Kalakanis, L., & Langlois, J. H. (1999). Infant preferences for attractive faces: A cognitive explanation. *Developmental Psychology, 35*(3), 848–855.

Rubin, K. H. (1982). Nonsocial play in preschoolers: Necessary evil. *Child Development, 53,* 651–657.

Rubin, K. H. (1993). The Waterloo Longitudinal Project: Correlates and consequences of social withdrawal from childhood to adolescence. In K. H. Rubin & J. B. Asendorpf (Eds.), *Social withdrawal, inhibition, and shyness,* Hillsdale, NJ: Erlbaum.

Rubin, K. H., & Coplan, R. J. (1992). Peer relationships in childhood. In M. H. Bornstein & M. E. Lamb (Eds.), *Developmental psychology: An advanced textbook* (3rd ed.). Hillsdale, NJ: Erlbaum.

Rubin, R. T. (1990). Mood changes during adolescence. In J. Bancroft & J. M. Reinisch (Eds.), *Adolescence and puberty.* New York: Oxford.

Rubinstein, S., & Caballero, B. (2000). Is Miss America an undernourished role model? *Journal of the American Medical Association, 283*(12), 1569.

Ruble, D. N. (1988). Sex role development. In M. H. Bornstein & M. E. Lamb (Eds.), *Developmental psychology: An advanced textbook* (2nd ed.). Hillsdale, NJ: Erlbaum.

Rudolph, K. D., Kurlakowsky, K. D., & Conley, C. S. (2001). Developmental and social-contextual origins of depressive control-related beliefs and behavior. *Cognitive Therapy & Research, 25*(4), 447–475.

Rudolph, K. D., Lambert, S. F., Clark, A. G., & Kurlakowsky, K. D. (2001). Negotiating the transition to middle school: The role of self-regulatory processes. *Child Development, 72*(3), 929–946.

Rudy, D., & Grusec, J. E. (2001). Correlates of authoritarian parenting in individualist and collectivist cultures and implications for understanding the transmission of values. *Journal of Cross-Cultural Psychology, 32*(2), 202–212.

Ruff, H. A., & Lawson, K. R. (1990). Development of sustained, focused attention in young children during free play. *Developmental Psychology, 26,* 85–93.

Ruffman, T., Olson, D. R., Ash, T., & Keenan, T. (1993). The ABCs of deception: Do young children understand deception in the same way as adults? *Developmental Psychology, 29,* 74–87.

Ruffman, T., Perner, J., & Parkin, L. (1999). How parenting style affects false belief understanding. *Social Development, 8*(3), 395–411.

Ruiz, F., & Tanaka, K. (2001). The ijime phenomenon and Japan: Overarching considerations for cross-cultural studies. *Psychologia: An International Journal of Psychology in the Orient, 44*(2), 128–138.

Russell, G., & Russell, A. (1987). Mother–child and father–child relationships in middle childhood. *Child Development, 58,* 1573–1585.

Rust, J., et al. (2000). The role of brothers and sisters in the gender development of preschool children. *Journal of Experimental Child Psychology, 77*(4), 292–303.

Rutter, M. (1980). *Changing youth in a changing society: Patterns of adolescent development and disorder.* Cambridge, MA: Harvard University Press.

Rutter, M. (1981). *Maternal deprivation reassessed* (2nd ed.). Middlesex, England: Penguin Books.

Rutter, M. (1990). Psychosocial resilience and protective mechanisms. In J. Rolf, A. S. Masten, D. Chicchetti, K. H. Nuechterlein, & S. Weintraub, (Eds.), *Risk and protective factors in the development of psychopathology.* New York: Cambridge University Press.

Rymer, R. (1993). *Genie: An abused child's flight from silence.* New York: HarperCollins.

Saariluoma, P. (2001). Chess and content-oriented psychology of thinking. *Psicologica, 22*(1), 143–164.

Sadker, M., & Sadker, D. (1985, March). Sexism in the schoolroom of the '80s. *Psychology Today,* pp. 54–57.

Sadker, M., & Sadker, D. (1994). *Failing at fairness: How America's schools cheat girls.* New York: Scribners.

Sagi, A., Van IJzendoorn, M. H., & Koren-Karie, N. (1991). Primary appraisal of the Strange Situation: A cross-cultural analysis of preseparation episodes. *Developmental Psychology, 27,* 587–596.

Sagrestano, L. M., McCormick, S. H., Paikoff, R. L., & Holmbeck, G. N. (1999). Pubertal development and parent–child conflict in low-income, urban, African American adolescents. *Journal of Research on Adolescence 9*(1), 85–107.

Sahler, O. J. Z., & McAnarney, E. R. (1981). *The child from three to eighteen.* St. Louis, MO: Mosby.

Salapatek, P. (1975). Pattern perception in early infancy. In L. B. Cohen & P. Salapatek (Eds.), *Infant perception: From sensation to cognition.* New York: Academic Press.

Sampaio, D., et al. (2000). Representacoes sociais do suicidio em estudantes do ensino secundario. *Analise Psicologica, 18*(2), 139–155.

Sandler, I. (2001). Quality and ecology of adversity as common mechanisms of risk and resilience. *American Journal of Community Psychology, 29*(1), 19–61.

Sandler, I., Kim-Bae, L. S., & MacKinnon, D. (2000). Coping and negative appraisal as mediators between control beliefs and psychological symptoms in children of divorce. *Journal of Clinical Child Psychology, 29*(3), 336–347.

Santelli, J. S., Lindberg, J. D., Abma, J., McNeely, C. S., & Resnick, M. (2000). Adolescent sexual behavior: Estimates and trends from four nationally representative surveys. *Family Planning Perspectives, 32*(4), 156–165, 194.

Santelli, J. S., Robin, L., Brener, N. D., & Lowry, R. (2001). Timing of alcohol and other drug use and sexual risk behaviors among unmarried adolescents and young adults. *Family Planning Perspectives online, 33*(5).

Santonastaso, P., Friederici, S., & Favaro, A. (2001). Sertraline in the treatment of restricting anorexia nervosa: An open controlled trial. *Journal of Child & Adolescent Psychopharmacology, 11*(2), 143–150.

Santos, D. C. C., Gabbard, C., & Goncalves, V. M. G. (2000). Motor development during the first 6 months: The case of Brazilian infants. *Infant & Child Development, 9*(3), 161–166.

Satcher, D. (2001). Cited in J. Sommerfeld. (2001, November 29). U.S. lags behind in cutting teen births. MSNBC online.

Saudino, K. J., & Eaton, W. O. (1993, March). *Genetic influences on activity level: II. An analysis of continuity and change from infancy to early childhood.* Paper presented at the meeting of the Society for Research in Child Development, New Orleans, LA.

Savin-Williams, R. C., & Berndt, T. (1990). Friendship and peer relations. In S. S. Feldman & G. R. Elliott (Eds.), *At the threshold: The developing adolescent.* Cambridge, MA: Harvard University Press.

Savulescu, J., & Dahl, E. (2000). Sex selection and preimplantation diagnosis: A response to the Ethics Committee of the American Society of Reproductive Medicine. *Human Reproduction, 15,* 1879–1880.

Saywitz, K. J., Mannarino, A. P., Berliner, L., & Cohen, J. A. (2000). Treatment for sexually abused children and adolescents. *American Psychologist, 55*(9), 1040–1049.

Scali, R. M., Brownlow, S., & Hicks, J. L. (2000). Gender differences in spatial task performance as a function of speed or accuracy orientation. *Sex Roles, 43*(5–6), 359–376.

Scarborough, H. S. (1993, March). *Fostering literacy through shared parent–child reading: Past results and current direction.* Paper presented at the meeting of the Society for Research in Child Development, New Orleans, LA.

Scarr, S. (1993, March). *IQ correlations among members of transracial adoptive families.* Paper presented at the meeting of the Society for Research in Child Development, New Orleans, LA.

Scarr, S. (1998). American child care today. *American Psychologist, 53*(2), 95–108.

Scarr, S., & Kidd, K. K. (1983). Developmental behavior genetics. In M. Haith & J. J. Campos (Eds.), *Handbook of child psychology.* New York: Wiley.

Scarr, S., & Weinberg, R. A. (1976). IQ test performance of black children adopted by white families. *American Psychologist, 31,* 726–739.

Scarr, S., & Weinburg, R. A. (1977). Intellectual similarities within families of both adopted and biological children. *Intelligence, 1,* 170–191.

Schaffer, H. R. (Ed.). (1971). *The origins of human social relations.* New York: Academic Press.

Schaffer, H. R., & Emerson, P. E. (1964). The development of social attachments in infancy. *Monographs of the Society for Research in Child Development, 29*(Whole No. 94).

Schatz, J., Brown, R. T., Pascual, J. M., Hsu, L., & DeBaun, M. R. (2001). Poor school and cognitive functioning with silent cerebral infarcts and sickle cell disease. *Neurology, 56*(8), 1109–1111.

Schellenberg, E. G. (2000). Cited in Hershenson, R. (2000, August 6). Debating the Mozart theory. *The New York Times Magazine online.*

Schemo, D. J. (2000, October 4). Survey finds parents favor more detailed sex education. *The New York Times,* pp. A1, A27.

Schiedel, D. G., & Marcia, J. E. (1985). Ego identity, intimacy, sex-role orientation, and gender. *Developmental Psychology, 21,* 149–160.

Schlegel, A. (1998). The social criteria of adulthood. *Human Development, 41*(5–6), 323–325.

Schmidtgall, K., King, A., Zarski, J. J., & Cooper, J. E. (2000). The effects of parental conflict on later child development. *Journal of Divorce & Remarriage, 33*(1–2), 149–157.

Schmitt, B. D. (1991). *Your child's health.* New York: Bantam.

Schneider, W., & Bjorklund, D. (1992, April). Expertise, aptitude, and strategic remembering. *Child Development, 63,* 461–473.

Schneider, W., & Pressley, M. (1989). *Memory development between 2 and 20.* New York: Springer-Verlag.

Schneider-Rosen, K., & Cicchetti, D. (1991). Early self-knowledge and emotional development: Visual self-recognition and affective reactions to mirror self-images in maltreated and non-maltreated toddlers. *Developmental Psychology, 27,* 471–478.

Scholl, T. O., Hediger, M. L., Khoo, C., Healey, M. F., & Rawson, N. L. (1991). Maternal weight gain, diet, and infant birth weight: Correlations during adolescent pregnancy. *Journal of Clinical Epidemiology, 44,* 423–428.

Schonfeld, A. M., et al. (2001). Verbal and nonverbal fluency in children with heavy prenatal alcohol exposure. *Journal of Studies on Alcohol, 62*(2), 239–246.

Schotte, D. E., Cools, J., & Payvar, S. (1990). Problem-solving deficits in suicidal patients: Trait vulnerability or state phenomenon? *Journal of Consulting and Clinical Psychology, 58,* 562–564.

Schuerger, J. M., & Witt, A. C. (1989). The temporal stability of individually tested intelligence. *Journal of Clinical Psychology, 45,* 294–302.

Schultz, S. R. (1990). Nutrition and human development. In R. M. Thomas (Ed.), *The encyclopedia of human development and education: Theory, research, and studies.* Oxford: Pergamon.

Schulz, R., & Heckhausen, J. (1996). A life span model of successful aging. *American Psychologist, 51,* 702–714.

Schuster, M. A., Bell, R. M., Nakajima, G. A., & Kanouse, D. E. (1998). The sexual practices of Asian and Pacific Islander high school students. *Journal of Adolescent Health, 23*(4), 221–231.

Schwartz, I. M. (1999). Sexual activity prior to coital interaction: A comparison between males and females. *Archives of Sexual Behavior, 28*(1), 63–69.

Schwartz, M. (1990). Left-handedness and prenatal complications. In S. Coren (Ed.), *Left-handedness: Behavior implications and anomalies.* Amsterdam: North-Holland.

Schwartz, S. J. (2001). The evolution of Eriksonian and neo-Eriksonian identity theory and research: A review and integration. *Identity, 1*(1), 7–58.

Schwartz, T. H., Haglund, M. M., Lettich, E., & Ojemann, G. A. (2000). Asymmetry of neuronal activity during extracellular microelectrode recording from left and right human temporal lobe neocortex during rhyming and line-matching. *Journal of Cognitive Neuroscience, 12*(5), 803–812.

Schweinhart, L. J., & Weikart, D. P. (Eds.) (1993). *Significant benefits: The High/Scope Perry Preschool Study Through Age 27.* Ypsilanti, MI: High/Scope Press.

Sciarra, J. J., et al. (2000). *Gynecology and obstetrics.* Philadelphia: Lippincott Williams & Wilkins.

Scott, J. R., DiSaia, P. J., Hammond, C. B., & Spellacy, W. N. (Eds.). (1999). *Danforth's obstetrics and gynecology* (8th ed.). Philadelphia: Lippincott.

Seefeldt, C. (1990). Assessing young children. In C. Seefeldt (Ed.), *Continuing issues in early childhood education.* Columbus, OH: Merrill.

Seefeldt, V., Ewing, M., & Walk, S. (1991). *An overview of youth sports programs in the United States.* Washington, DC: Carnegie Council on Adolescent Development.

Segal, H. G., DeMeis, D. K., Wood, G. A., & Smith, H. L. (2001). Assessing future possible selves by gender and socioeconomic status using the Anticipated Life History measure. *Journal of Personality, 69*(1) 57–87.

Seidman, E., Aber, J. L., Allen, L., & French, S, E. (1996). The impact of the transition to high school on the self-esteem and perceived social context of poor urban youth. *American Journal of Community Psychology, 24*(4) 489–515.

Seidman, E., Allen, L., Aber, J. L., Mitchell, C., & Feinman, J. (1994). The impact of school transitions in early adolescence on the self-system and perceived social context of poor urban youth. *Child Development, 65*(2), 507–522.

Seitz, V. (1990). Intervention programs for impoverished children: A comparison of educational and family support models. *Annals of Child Development, 7,* 73–103.

Seitz, V., & Apfel, N. H. (1993, March). *Long-term effects of a school for pregnant students: Repeated childbearing through six years postpartum.* Paper presented at the meeting of the Society for Research in Child Development, New Orleans, LA.

Selman, R. L. (1976). Social-cognitive understanding. In T. Lickona (Ed.), *Moral development and behavior: Theory, research, and social issues.* New York: Holt, Rinehart & Winston.

Selman, R. (1980). *The growth of interpersonal understanding: Developmental and clinical analysis.* New York: Academic Press.

Selman, R. L. (1989). Fostering intimacy and autonomy. In W. Damon (Ed.), *Child development today and tomorrow.* San Francisco: Jossey-Bass.

Selman, R. L., & Schultz, L. H. (1989). Children's strategies for interpersonal negotiation with peers: An interpretive/empirical approach to the study of social development. In T. J. Berndt & G. W. Ladd (Eds.), *Peer relationships in child development.* New York: Wiley.

Senecal, C., Vallerand, R. J., & Guay, F. (2001). Antecedents and outcomes of work–family conflict: Toward a motivational model. *Personality & Social Psychology Bulletin, 27*(2), 176–186.

Senna, J. J., & Siegel, L. J. (2002). *Introduction to criminal justice* (9th ed.). Belmont, CA: Wadsworth.

Sepkoski, C. M., et al. (1993, March). *Predicting developmental delay from cry analysis in preterm infants.* Paper presented at the meeting of the Society for Research in Child Development, New Orleans, LA.

Sepkoski, C. M., Lester, B. M., & Brazelton, T. B. (1994). Berry Neonatal effects of maternal epidurals. *Developmental Medicine & Child Neurology, 36*(4), 375–376.

Sepkoski, C. M., Lester, B. M., Ostheimer, G. W., & Brazelton, T. B. (1992). The effects of maternal epidural anesthesia on neonatal behavior during the first month. *Developmental Medicine & Child Neurology, 34*(12), 1072–1080.

Seppa, N. (1997). Children's TV remains steeped in violence. *APA Monitor, 28*(6), 36.

Serbin, L. A., Poulin-Dubois, D., Colburne, K. A., Sen, M. G., & Eichstedt, J. A. (2001). Gender stereotyping in infancy: Visual preferences for and knowledge of gender-stereotyped toys in the second year. *International Journal of Behavioral Development, 25*(1), 7–15.

Serbin, L. A., Powlishta, K. K., & Gulko, J. (1993). The development of sex typing in middle childhood, *Monographs of the Society for Research in Child Development, 58*(2, Serial No. 232).

Serbin, L. A., & Sprafkin, C. (1986). The salience of gender and the process of sex typing in three- to seven-year-old children. *Child Development, 57,* 1188–1199.

Seymour, H. N., Abdulkarim, L., & Johnson, V. (1999). The Ebonics controversy: An educational and clinical dilemma. *Topics in Language Disorders, 19*(4), 66–77.

Shahinfar, A., Kupersmidt, J. B., & Matza, L. S. (2001). The relation between exposure to violence and social information processing among incarcerated adolescents. *Journal of Abnormal Psychology, 110*(1), 136–141.

Shakin, M., Shakin, D., & Sternglanz, S. H. (1985). Infant clothing: Sex labeling for strangers. *Sex Roles, 12,* 955–964.

Shakoor, B., & Chalmers, D. (1991). Co-victimization of African-American children who witness violence: Effects on cognitive, emotional, and behavioral development. *Journal of the National Medical Association, 83,* 233–237.

Shaw, J., Claridge, G., & Clark, K. (2001). Schizotypy and the shift from dextrality: A study of handedness in a large non-clinical sample. *Schizophrenia Research, 50*(3), 181–189.

Shaywitz, B. A., et al. (1995). Sex differences in the functional organization of the brain for language. *Nature, 373,* 607–609.

Shaywitz, S. E. (1998). Dyslexia. *The New England Journal of Medicine, 338,* 307–312.

Shea, S., Stein, A. D., Basch, C. E., Contento, I. R., & Zybert, P. (1992). Variability and self-regulation of energy intake in young children in their everyday environment. *Pediatrics, 90,* 542–546.

Sheeber, L. B., & Johnson, J. H. (1992). Child temperament, maternal adjustment, and changes in family life style. *American Journal of Orthopsychiatry, 62,* 178–185.

Sherman, J. A. (1983). Factors predicting girls' and boys' enrollment in college preparatory mathematics. *Psychology of Women Quarterly, 7,* 272–281.

Shettles, L. (1982, June). Predetermining children's sex. *Medical Aspects of Human Sexuality,* p. 172.

Shields, A., & Cicchetti, D. (2001). Parental maltreatment and emotion dysregulation as risk factors for bullying and victimization in middle childhood. *Journal of Clinical Child Psychology, 30*(3), 349–363.

Shields, A., Ryan, R., M., & Cicchetti, D. (2001). Narrative representations of caregivers and emotion dysregulation as predictors of maltreated children's rejection by peers. *Developmental Psychology, 37*(3), 321–337.

Shifren, J. L., et al. (2000). Transdermal testosterone treatment in women with impaired sexual function after oophorectomy. *The New England Journal of Medicine, 343*(10), 682–688.

Shneidman, E. S. (1998). Perspectives on suicidology: Further reflections on suicide and psychache. *Suicide & Life-Threatening Behavior, 28*(3), 245–250.

Shonk, S. M., & Cicchetti, D. (2001). Maltreatment, competency deficits, and risk for academic and behavioral maladjustment. *Developmental Psychology, 37*(1), 3–17.

Shorter-Gooden, K. (1992, February). *Identity development in African-American female adolescents.* Paper presented at the meeting of the Association of Women in Psychology, Long Beach, CA.

Shortt, A. L., Barrett, P. M., & Fox, T. L. (2001). Evaluating the FRIENDS Program: A cognitive-behavioral group treatment for anxious children and their parents. *Journal of Clinical Child Psychology, 30*(4), 525–535.

Shott, S. R. (2000). Down syndrome: Common pediatric ear, nose, and throat problems. *Down Syndrome Quarterly, 5*(2), 1–6.

Shu, M., Jia, S., & Zhang, F. (2001). Clinical features and brain image of children with autism. *Chinese Mental Health Journal, 15*(1), 39–41.

Shucard, J. L., & Shucard, D. W. (1990). Auditory evoked potentials and hand preference in 6-month-old infants: Possible gender-related differences in cerebral organization. *Developmental Psychology, 26,* 923–930.

Shultz, T. (1980). Development of the concept of intention. In W. A. Collins (Ed.), *Minnesota symposia on child psychology* (Vol. 13). Hillsdale, NJ: Erlbaum.

Shuster, S. M., & Sassaman, C. (1997). Genetic interaction between male mating strategy and sex ratio in a marine isopod. *Nature, 388*(6640), 373–377.

Shute, B., & Wheldall, K. (1999). Fundamental frequency and temporal modifications in the speech of British fathers to their children. *Educational Psychology, 19*(2), 221–233.

SIDS Network (2001, May 14). **http://www.sids-network.org/**

Siegel, L. J. (2002). *Juvenile delinquency: The core.* Belmont, CA: Wadsworth.

Siegel, L. S. (1992). Infant motor, cognitive, and language behaviors as predictors of achievement at school age. In C. Rovee-Collier & L. P. Lipsitt (Eds.), *Advances in infancy research* (Vol. 7). Norwood, NJ: Ablex.

Siegel, L. S. (1993). The development of reading. In H. W. Reese (Ed.), *Advances in child development and behavior* (Vol. 24). Orlando, FL: Academic Press.

Siegel, M. (1987). Are sons and daughters treated more differently by fathers than by mothers? *Developmental Review, 7,* 183–209.

Siegel, M., & Beattie, K. (1991). Where to look first for children's knowledge of false beliefs. *Cognition, 38,* 1–12.

Siegler, R. S. (1986). *Children's thinking.* Englewood Cliffs, NJ: Prentice-Hall.

Siegler, R. S., Liebert, D. E., & Liebert, R. M. (1973). Inhelder and Piaget's pendulum problem: Teaching pre-adolescents to act as scientists. *Developmental Psychology, 9,* 97–101.

Sigel, I. E. (1991). Preschool education: For whom and why? In L. Rescorla, M. C. Hyson, & K. Hirsh-Pasek (Eds.), *New directions in child development: No. 53. Academic instruction in early childhood: Challenge or pressure?* San Francisco: Jossey-Bass.

Sigelman, C., Didjurgis, T., Marshall, B., Vargas, F., & Stewart, A. (1992). Views of problem drinking among Native American, Hispanic, and Anglo children. *Child Psychiatry and Human Development, 22,* 265–276.

Sigelman, C., Maddock, A., Epstein, J., & Carpenter, W. (1993). Age differences in understandings of disease causality: AIDS, colds, and cancer. *Child Development, 64,* 272–284.

Sigman, M., & Sena, R. (1993, March). Pretend play in high-risk and developmentally delayed children. In M. H. Bornstein & A. W. O'Reilly (Eds.), *New directions for human development: No. 59. The role of play in the development of thought.* San Francisco: Jossey-Bass.

Signorella, M. L., Bigler, R. S., & Liben, L. S. (1993). Developmental differences in children's gender schemata about others: A meta-analytic review. *Developmental Review, 13,* 147–183.

Signorella, M. L., & Frieze, I. H. (1989). Gender schemas in college students. *Psychology: A Journal of Human Behavior, 26,* 16–23.

Silverberg, S. B., Tennenbaum, D. L., & Jacob, T. (1992). Adolescence and family interaction. In V. B. VanHasselt and M. Hersen (Eds.), *Handbook of social development.* New York: Plenum.

Simion, F., Cassia, V. M., Turati, C., & Valenza, E. (2001). The origins of face perception: Specific versus non-specific mechanisms. *Infant & Child Development, 10*(1–2), 59–65.

Simmons, D. C., Fuchs, D., & Fuchs, L. S. (1991). Instructional and curricular requisites of mainstreamed students with learning disabilities. *Journal of Learning Disabilities, 24,* 354–360.

Simmons, R. G., & Blyth, D. A. (1987). *Moving into adolescence: The impact of pubertal change and school context.* Hawthorne, NY: Aldine deGruyter.

Simons, R. L., Lorenz, F. O., Wu, C., & Conqer, R. D. (1993). Social network and marital support as mediators and moderators of the impact of stress and depression on parental behavior. *Developmental Psychology, 29,* 368–381.

Simonson, B. M., & Glenn, S. (2001). The effects of suggestions on ratings of attention deficit hyperactivity disorder. *Psychology & Education: An Interdisciplinary Journal, 38*(2), 42–47.

Simonton, D. K. (2000). Creativity: Cognitive, personal, developmental, and social aspects. *American Psychologist, 55,* 151–158.

Simpson, J. L. (2000, June 1). Invasive diagnostic procedures for prenatal genetic diagnosis. *Journal Watch Women's Health.*

Simpson, J. L., & Carson, S. A. (1999). The reproductive option of sex selection. *Human Reproduction, 14,* 870–872.

Simpson, J. M. (2001). Stress and sleep deprivation as an aetiological basis for the sudden infant death syndrome. *Early Human Development, 61*(1), 1–43.

Singer, J. L. (1998). Imaginative play in early childhood: A foundation for adaptive emotional and cognitive development. *International Medical Journal, 5*(2), 93–100.

Singer, L. T., Arendt, R., Minnes, S., Farkas, K., & Salvator, A. (2000). Neurobehavioral outcomes of cocaine-exposed infants. *Neurotoxicology & Teratology, 22*(5), 653–666.

Singer, L. T., Song, L. Y., Hill, B. P., & Jaffee, A. C. (1990). Stress and depression in mothers of failure-to-thrive children. *Journal of Pediatric Psychology, 15,* 711–720.

Singh, G. K., & Yu, S. M. (1995, July 10). Cited in Pear, R. Infant mortality rate drops but racial disparity grows. *The New York Times,* p. B9.

Singh, M., Manjary, M., & Dellatolas, G. (2001). Lateral preferences among Indian school children. *Cortex, 37*(2), 231–241.

Skaer, T. L., Robison, L. M., Sclar, D. A., & Galin, R. S. (2000). Treatment of depressive illness among children and adolescents in the United States. *Current Therapeutic Research, 61*(10), 692–705.

Skeels, H. M. (1966). Adult status of children with contrasting early life experiences: A follow-up study. *Monographs of the Society for Research in Child Development, 31*(3, Serial No. 105).

Skinner, B. F. (1957). *Verbal behavior.* New York: Appleton.

Skinner, B. F. (1983). *A matter of consequences.* New York: Knopf.

Slater, A., Mattock, A., & Brown, E. (1990). Size constancy at birth: Newborn infants' responses to retinal and real size. *Journal of Experimental Child Psychology, 49,* 314–322.

Slavin, R. E. (1989). Achievement effects of substantial reductions in class size. In R. E. Slavin (Ed.), *School and classroom organization.* Hillsdale, NJ: Erlbaum.

Slobin, D. I. (1972, July). Children and language: They learn the same way all around the world. *Psychology Today,* pp. 71–74ff.

Slobin, D. I. (1973). Cognitive prerequisites for the development of grammar. In C. A. Ferguson & D. I. Slobin (Eds.), *Studies of child development.* New York: Holt, Rinehart and Winston.

Slobin, D. I. (1983, April). *Crosslinguistic evidence for basic child grammar.* Paper presented at the meeting of the Society for Research in Child Development, Detroit.

Slobin, D. I. (1988). From the garden of Eden to the tower of Babel. In F. S. Kessel (Ed.), *The development of language and language researchers.* Hillsdale, NJ: Erlbaum.

Small, M. Y. (1990). *Cognitive development.* San Diego, CA: Harcourt Brace Jovanovich.

Smetana, J. G. (1985). Children's impressions of moral and conventional transgressors. *Developmental Psychology, 21,* 715–724.

Smetana, J. G. (1990). Morality and conduct disorders. In M. Lewis & S. M. Miller (Eds.), *Handbook of developmental psychopathology.* New York: Plenum.

Smetana, J. G., Killen, M., & Turiel, E. (1991). Children's reasoning about interpersonal and moral conflicts. *Child Development, 62,* 629–644.

Smetana, J. G., & Letourneau, K. J. (1984). Development of gender constancy and children's sex-typed free play behavior. *Developmental Psychology, 20,* 691–696.

Smetana, J. G., Yau, J., Restrepo, A., & Braeges, J. L. (1991b). Conflict and adaptation in adolescence: Adolescent–parent conflict. In M. E. Colten & S. Gore (Eds.), *Adolescent stress: Causes and consequences.* New York: Aldine deGruyter.

Smilansky, S. (1990). Sociodramatic play: Its relevance to behavior and achievement in school. In E. Klugman & S. Smilansky (Eds.), *Children's play and learning.* New York: Teachers College Press.

Smith, B. A., Fillion, T. J., & Blass, E. M. (1990). Orally mediated sources of calming in 1- to 3- day-old human infants. *Developmental Psychology, 26,* 731–737.

Smith, K. E., et al. (1999). Is severity of respiratory disease associated with differences in neurodevelopmental patterns in preterm infants? *Developmental Neuropsychology, 16*(1) 59–77.

Smith, P. K. (1979). The ontogeny of fear in children. In W. Sluckin (Ed.), *Fears in animals and man.* London: Van Nostrand Reinhold.

Smoll, F. L., & Schultz, R. W. (1990). Quantifying gender differences in physical performance: A developmental perspective. *Developmental Psychology, 26,* 360–369.

Smyth, C. M., & Bremner, W. J. (1998). Klinefelter syndrome. *Archives of Internal Medicine, 158*(12), 1309–1314.

Snarey, J. R. (1985). Cross-cultural universality of social-moral development: A critical review of Kohlbergian research. *Psychological Bulletin 97,* 202–232.

Snowden, P. E., & Gorton, R. A. (2002). *School leadership and administration (6th ed.).* New York: McGraw-Hill.

Snyderman, M., & Rothman, S. (1990). *The I.Q. controversy.* New Brunswick, NJ: Transaction.

Sobesky, W. E. (1983). The effects of situational factors on moral judgments. *Child Development, 54,* 575–584.

Sodian, B., Taylor, C., Harris, P. L., & Perner, J. (1991). Early deception and the child's theory of mind: False trails and genuine markers. *Child Development, 62,* 468–483.

Solberg, L. I., et al. (2001). Aids to quitting tobacco use: How important are they outside controlled trials? *Preventive Medicine: An International Journal Devoted to Practice & Theory, 33*(1), 53–58.

Sommer, K., Whitman, T. L., Borkowski, J. G., Schellenbach, C., Maxwell, S., & Keogh, D. (1993). Cognitive readiness and adolescent parenting. *Developmental Psychology, 29,* 389–398.

Sondik, E. (2001, June 16.) Healthy People 2000: Violent and abusive behavior progress review. Hyattsville, MD: U.S. Department of Health and Human Services: National Center for Health Statistics.

Sontag, L. W. (1966). Implications of fetal behavior and environment for adult personality. *Annals of the New York Academy of Science, 134,* 782–786.

Sontag, L. W., & Richards, T. W. (1938). Studies in fetal behavior: Fetal heart rate as a behavioral indicator. *Child Development Monographs, 3*(4).

Sorce, J. F., Emde, R. N., Campos, J. J., & Klinnert, M. D. (1985). Maternal emotional signaling: Its effect on the visual cliff behavior of 1-year-olds. *Developmental Psychology, 21,* 195–200.

Sorenson, S. B., & Rutter, C. M. (1991). Transgenerational patterns of suicide attempt. *Journal of Consulting and Clinical Psychology, 59,* 861–866.

Southern, T., & Jones, E. D. (1991). *The academic acceleration of gifted children.* New York: Teachers College Press.

Souza, I., Serra, M. A., Mattos, P., & Franco, V. A. (2001). Comorbidade em criancas e adolescentes com transtorno do deficit de atencao: Resultados preliminares. *Arquivos de Neuro-Psiquiatria, 59*(2), 401–406.

Spangler, G. (1990). Mother, child, and situational correlates of toddler's social competence. *Infant Behavior and Development, 13,* 405–419.

Spelke, E. S., & Owsley, C. (1979). Intermodal exploration and knowledge in infancy. *Infant Behavior and Development, 2,* 13–27.

Spencer, M. B., Dornbusch, S. M., & Mont-Reynaud, R. (1990). Challenges in studying minority youth. In S. S. Feldman & G. R. Elliott (Eds.), *At the threshold: The developing adolescent.* Cambridge, MA: Harvard University Press.

Spencer, M. S., Icard, L. D., Harachi, T. W., Catalano, R. F., & Oxford, M. (2000). Ethnic identity among monoracial and multiracial early adolescents. *Journal of Early Adolescence, 20*(4), 365–387.

Spencer, T. J., et al. (2001). Impact of tic disorders on ADHD outcome across the life cycle: Findings from a large group of adults with and without ADHD. *American Journal of Psychiatry, 158*(4), 611–617.

Speranza, M., et al. (2001). Obsessive compulsive disorders in eating disorders. *Eating Behaviors, 2*(3), 193–207.

Spitz, R. A. (1965). *The first year of life: A psychoanalytic study of normal and deviant object relations.* New York: International Universities Press.

Spivack, G., Marcus, J., & Swift, M. (1986). Early classroom behaviors and later misconduct. *Developmental Psychology, 22,* 124–131.

Spohr, H. L., Willms, J., & Steinhausen, H. C. (1993). Prenatal alcohol exposure and long-term developmental consequences. *Lancet, 341,* 907–910.

Springer, K., & Keil, F. C. (1991). Early differentiation of causal mechanisms appropriate to biological and nonbiological kinds. *Child Development, 62,* 767–781.

Sroufe, L. A. (1979). Socioemotional development. In J. Osofsky (Ed.), *Handbook of infant development.* New York: Wiley.

Sroufe, L. A. (1998). Cited in Blakeslee, S. (1998, August 4). Re-evaluating significance of baby's bond with mother. *The New York Times,* pp. F1, F2.

Sroufe, L. A., Bennett, C., Englund, M., Urban, J., & Shulman, S. (1993). The significance of gender boundaries in preadolescence: Contemporary correlates and antecedents of boundary violation and maintenance. *Child Development, 64,* 455–466.

Sroufe, L. A., Waters, E., & Matas, L. (1974). Contextual determinants of infant affectional response. In M. Lewis & L. Rosenblum (Eds.), *The origins of fear.* New York: Wiley.

Stacy, A. W., & Newcomb, M. D. (1999). Adolescent drug use and adult drug problems in women: Direct, interactive, and mediational effects. *Experimental & Clinical Psychopharmacology, 7*(2), 160–173.

Stagnitti, K., Unsworth, C., & Rodger, S. (2000). Development of an assessment to identify play behaviours that discriminate between the play of typical preschoolers and preschoolers with pre-academic problems. *Canadian Journal of Occupational Therapy, 67*(5), 291–303.

Stampfer, M. J., Hu, F. B., Manson, J. E., Rimm, E. B., & Willett, W. C. (2000). Primary prevention of coronary heart disease in women through diet and lifestyle. *New England Journal of Medicine, 343*(1), 16–22.

Stanwood, G. D., et al. (2001). Prenatal cocaine exposure as a risk factor for later developmental outcomes. *Journal of the American Medical Association, 286*(1), 45.

Stanwood, G. D., Washington, R. A., & Levitt, P. (2001). Identification of a sensitive period of prenatal cocaine exposure that alters the development of the anterior cingulate cortex. *Cerebral Cortex, 11*(5), 430–440.

Stark, L. J., Owens-Stively, J., Spirito, A., Lewis, A., & Guevremont, D. (1991). Group behavioral treatment of retentive encopresis. *Journal of Pediatric Psychology, 15,* 659–671.

Steele, C. M. (1994, October 31). Bizarre black IQ claims abetted by media. *San Francisco Chronicle,* editorial page.

Steele, C. M. (1996), August). The role of stereotypes in shaping intellectual identity. Master lecture presented to the meeting of the American Psychological Association, Toronto.

Steele, C. M. (1997). A threat in the air: How stereotypes shape intellectual identity and performance. *American Psychologist, 52,* 613–629.

Steele, C. M., & Aronson, J. (1995). Stereotype threat and the intellectual test performance of African Americans. *Journal of Personality and Social Psychology, 69,* 797–811.

Steele, K. M. (2000). Arousal and mood factors in the "Mozart effect." *Perceptual & Motor Skills, 91*(1), 188–190.

Stein, R. I., et al. (2001). Treatment of eating disorders in women. *Counseling Psychologist, 29*(5), 695–732.

Steinberg, J. (2000, August 21). Increase in test scores counters dire forecasts for bilingual ban. *The New York Times,* pp. 1, 22.

Steinberg, L. (1988). Reciprocal relation between parent–child distance and pubertal maturation. *Developmental Psychology, 24,* 122–128.

Steinberg, L. (1989). Pubertal maturation and parent–adolescent distance: An evolutionary perspective. In G. Adams, R. Montemayor, & T. Gullotta (Eds.), *Advances in adolescent development* (Vol. 1). Beverly Hills, CA: Sage.

Steinberg, L. (1990a). Autonomy, conflict, and harmony in the family relationship. In S. S. Feldman & G. R. Elliott (Eds.), *At the threshold: The developing adolescent.* Cambridge, MA: Harvard University Press.

Steinberg, L. (1990b). Psychological well-being of parents with early adolescent children. *Developmental Psychology, 26,* 658–666.

Steinberg, L. (1991). Parent–adolescent relations. In R. M. Lerner, A. C. Petersen, & J. Brooks-Gunn (Eds.), *Encyclopedia of adolescence.* New York: Garland.

Steinberg, L. (1996). *Beyond the classroom: Why school reform has failed and what parents need to do.* New York: Simon & Schuster.

Steinberg, L., Brown, B. B., & Dornbusch, S. M. (1996). Ethnicity and adolescent achievement. *American Educator, 20*(2), 28–35.

Steinberg, L., & Dornbusch, S. M. (1991). Negative correlates of part-time employment during adolescence: Replication and elaboration. *Developmental Psychology, 27,* 304–313.

Steinberg, L., Fegley, S., & Dornbusch, S. M. (1993). Negative impact of part-time work on adolescent adjustment: Evidence from a longitudinal study. *Developmental Psychology, 29,* 171–180.

Steinberg, L., Lamborn, S. D., Dornbusch, S. M., & Darling, N. (1992). Impact of parenting practices on adolescent achievement: Authoritative parenting, school involvement, and encouragement to succeed. *Child Development, 63,* 1266–1281.

Steiner, J. E. (1979). Facial expressions in response to taste and smell discrimination. In H. W. Reese & L. P. Lipsitt (Eds.), *Advances in child development and behavior* (Vol. 13). New York: Academic Press.

Stemberger, J. P. (1993). Vowel dominance in overregularizations. *Journal of Child Language, 20,* 503–522.

Stern, M., & Karraker, K. H. (1989). Sex stereotyping of infants: A review of gender labeling studies. *Sex Roles, 20,* 501–521.

Sternberg, R. J. (1997a). The concept of intelligence and its role in lifelong learning and success. *American Psychologist, 52,* 1030–1037.

Sternberg, R. J. (1997b). What does it mean to be smart? *Educational Leadership, 54,* 20–24.

Sternberg, R. J. (2000). In search of the zipperump-a-zoo. *Psychologist, 13*(5), 250–255.

Sternberg, R. J. (2001). What is the common thread of creativity? *American Psychologist, 56*(4), 360–362.

Sternberg, R. J., & Lubart, T. I. (1995). *Defying the crowd: Cultivating creativity in a culture of conformity.* New York: Free Press.

Sternberg, R. J., & Lubart, T. I. (1996). Investing in creativity. *American Psychologist, 51,* 677–688.

Sternberg, R. J., & Williams, W. M. (1997). Does the Graduate Record Examination predict meaningful success in the graduate training of psychologists? *American Psychologist, 52,* 630–641.

Sternberg, R. J., & Williams, W. M. (2002). *Educational psychology.* Boston: Allyn & Bacon.

Stevens, C. P., Raz, S., & Sander, C. J. (1999). Peripartum hypoxic risk and cognitive outcome: A study of term and preterm birth children at early school age. *Neuropsychology, 13*(4), 598–608.

Stevenson, H. W., Chen, C., & Lee, S. (1993). Mathematics achievement of Chinese, Japanese, and American children: Ten years later. *Science, 259,* 53–58.

Stevenson, J. (1992). Evidence for a genetic etiology in hyperactivity in children. *Behavior Genetics, 22,* 337–344.

Steward, D. K. (2001). Behavioral characteristics of infants with nonorganic failure to thrive during a play interaction. *American Journal of Maternal/Child Nursing, 26*(2), 79–85.

Stice, E., Akutagawa, D., Gaggar, A., & Agras, W. S. (2000). Negative affect moderates the relation between dieting and binge eating. *International Journal of Eating Disorders, 27*(2), 218–229.

Stice, E., & Bearman, S. K. (2001). Body-image and eating disturbances prospectively predict increases in depressive symptoms in adolescent girls: A growth curve analysis. *Developmental Psychology, 37*(5), 597–607.

Stice, E., Hayward, C., Cameron, R. P., Killen, J. D., & Taylor, C. B. (2000). Body-image and eating disturbances predict onset of depression among female adolescents: A longitudinal study. *Journal of Abnormal Psychology, 109*(3), 438–444.

Stice, E., Presnell, K., & Bearman, S. K. (2001). Relation of early menarche to depression, eating disorders, substance abuse, and comorbid psychopathology among adolescent girls. *Developmental Psychology, 37*(5), 608–619.

Stiles, J. (2001). Neural plasticity and cognitive development. *Developmental Neuropsychology, 18*(2), 237–272.

Stipek, D. (1992). The child at school. In M. H. Bornstein & M. E. Lamb (Eds.), *Developmental psychology: An advanced textbook* (3rd ed.). Hillsdale, NJ: Erlbaum.

Stipek, D. J., & Gralinski, J. H. (1991). Gender differences in children's achievement-related beliefs and emotional responses to success and failure in mathematics. *Journal of Educational Psychology, 83,* 361–371.

Stipek, D. J., Gralinski, J. H., & Kopp, C. B. (1990). Self-concept development in the toddler years. *Developmental Psychology, 26,* 972–977.

Stipek, D., Recchia, S., & McClintic, S. (1992). Self-evaluation in young children. *Monographs of the Society for Research in Child Development, 57*(1, Serial No. 226).

Stockhammer, T. F., Salzinger, S., Feldman, R. S., Mojica, E., & Primavera, L. H. (2001). Assessment of the effect of physical child abuse within an ecological framework: Measurement issues. *Journal of Community Psychology, 29*(3) 319–344.

Stockman, I. J., & Vaughn-Cooke, F. (1992). Lexical elaboration in children's locative action expression. *Child Development, 63,* 1104–1125.

Stolberg, S. G. (1998, March 9). U.S. awakes to epidemic of sexual diseases. *The New York Times,* pp. A1, A14.

Stone, W. L., & Caro-Martinez, L. M. (1990). Naturalistic observations of spontaneous communication in autistic children. *Journal of Autism and Developmental Disorders, 20,* 437–453.

Stone, W. L., & Lemanek, K. L. (1990). Parental report of social behaviors in autistic preschoolers. *Journal of Autism and Developmental Disorders, 20,* 513–522.

Storfer, M. D. (1990). *Intelligence and giftedness: The contributions of heredity and early environment.* San Francisco: Jossey-Bass.

Strasburger, V. C. (2001). Children and TV advertising: Nowhere to run, nowhere to hide. *Journal of Developmental & Behavioral Pediatrics, 22*(3), 185–187.

Straus, M. A. (1995). Cited in Collins, C. (1995, May 11). Spanking is becoming the new don't. *The New York Times,* p. C8.

Straus, M. A. (2000). Corporal punishment and primary prevention of physical abuse. *Child Abuse & Neglect, 24*(9), 1109–1114.

Straus, M. A., & Gelles, R. J. (1990). Societal change and change in family violence from 1975 to 1985 as revealed by two national surveys. In M. A. Straus & R. J. Gelles (Eds.), *Physical violence in American families.* New Brunswick, NJ: Transaction.

Straus, M. A., & Smith, C. (1990). Family patterns and child abuse. In M. A. Straus & R. J. Gelles (Eds.), *Physical violence in American families.* New Brunswick, NJ: Transaction.

Straus, M. A., & Stewart, J. H. (1999). Corporal punishment by American parents: National data on prevalence, chronicity, severity, and duration, in relation to child and family characteristics. *Clinical Child & Family Psychology Review, 2*(2), 55–70.

Strayer, F. F. (1990). The social ecology of toddler play groups and the origins of gender discrimination. In F. F. Strayer (Ed.), *Social interaction and behavioral development during early childhood.* Montreal: La Maison D'Ethologie de Montreal.

Streissguth, A. P., Aase, J. M., Clarren, S. K., Randels, S. P., LaDue, R. A., & Smith, D. F. (1991). Fetal alcohol syndrome in adolescents and adults. *Journal of the American Medical Association, 265,* 1961–1967.

Streissguth, A. P., Barr, H. M., & Sampson, P. D. (1992). Alcohol use during pregnancy and child development: A longitudinal, prospective study of human behavioral teratology. In C. W. Greenbaum & J. G. Auerbach (Eds.), *Longitudinal studies of children at psychological risk: Cross-national perspectives.* Norwood, NJ: Ablex.

Streitmatter, J. L. (1988). Ethnicity as a mediating variable of early adolescent identity development. *Journal of Adolescence, 11,* 335–346.

Striegel-Moore, R. H., & Cachelin, F. M. (2001). Etiology of eating disorders in women. *Counseling Psychologist, 29*(5), 635–661.

Striegel-Moore, R. H., et al. (2001). Exploring the relationship between timing of menarche and eating disorder symptoms in black and white adolescent girls. *International Journal of Eating Disorders, 30*(4), 421–433.

Stright, A. D., Neitzel, C., Sears, K. G., & Hoke-Sinex, L. (2001). Instruction begins in the home: Relations between parental instruction and children's self-regulation in the classroom. *Journal of Educational Psychology, 93*(3), 456–466.

Strober, M., Freeman, R., Lampert, C., Diamond, J., & Kaye, W. (2000). Controlled family study of anorexia nervosa and bulimia nervosa: Evidence of shared liability and transmission of partial syndromes. *American Journal of Psychiatry, 157,* 393–401.

Strohner, H., & Nelson, K. E. (1974). The young child's development of sentence comprehension: Influence of event probability, nonverbal context, syntactic form, and strategies. *Child Development, 45,* 567–576.

Strong, S. M., Williamson, D. A., Netemeyer, R. G., & Geer, J. H. (2000). Eating disorder symptoms and concerns about body differ as a function of gender and sexual orientation. *Journal of Social & Clinical Psychology, 19*(2), 240–255.

Strough, J., Berg, C. A., & Meegan, S. P. (2001). Friendship and gender differences in task and social interpretations of peer collaborative problem solving. *Social Development, 10*(1), 1–22.

Strutt, G. F., Anderson, D. R., & Well, A. D. (1975). A developmental study of the effects of irrelevant information on speeded classification. *Journal of Experimental Child Psychology, 20,* 127–135.

Stucky-Ropp, R. C., & DiLorenzo, T. M. (1992, August). *Determinants of exercise in children.* Paper presented at the meeting of the American Psychological Association, Washington, DC.

Study finds risk to infant in early prenatal test. (1994, March 12). *The New York Times,* p. 6.

Stunkard, A. J., Harris, J. R., Pedersen, N. I., & McClearn, G. E. (1990). The body-mass index of twins who have been reared apart. *New England Journal of Medicine, 322,* 1483–1487.

Sue, S. (1991). Ethnicity and culture in psychological research and practice. In J. D. Goodchilds (Ed.), *Psychological perspectives on human diversity in America.* Washington, DC : American Psychological Association.

Sue, S., & Okazaki, S. (1990). Asian-American educational achievements. *American Psychologist, 45,* 913–920.

Suemer, N., & Guengoer, D. (1999). Cocuk yetistirme stillerinin baglanma stilleri, benlik degerlendirmeleri ve yakin iliskiler uezerindeki etkisi. *Turk Psikoloji Dergisi, 14*(44), 35–58.

Suess, G. J., Grossmann, K. E., & Sroufe, L. A. (1992). Effects of infant attachment to mother and father on quality of adaptation in preschool: From dyadic to individual organisation of self. *International Journal of Behavioral Development, 15,* 43–65.

Sullivan, A. (2000, April 2). The He hormone. *The New York Times Magazine,* pp. 46–51ff.

Sullivan, J. M. (2000) Cellular and molecular mechanisms underlying learning and memory impairments produced by cannabinoids. *Learning & Memory, 7*(3), 132–139.

Sullivan, K., & Winner, E. (1991). When 3–year-olds understand ignorance, false belief, and representational change. *British Journal of Developmental Psychology, 9,* 159–171.

Sullivan, P. F., Neale, M. C., & Kendler, K. S. (2000). Genetic epidemiology of major depression: Review and meta-analysis. *American Journal of Psychiatry, 157,* 1552–1562.

Sullivan, S. A., & Birch, L. L. (1990). Pass the sugar, pass the salt: Experience dictates preference. *Developmental Psychology, 26,* 546–551.

Sun, Y. (2001). Family environment and adolescents' well-being before and after parents' marital disruption: A longitudinal analysis. *Journal of Marriage & Family, 63*(3), 697–713.

Suomi, S. J., Harlow, H. F., & McKinney, W. T. (1972). Monkey psychiatrists. *American Journal of Psychiatry, 128,* 927–932.

Super, C. M. (1980). Cognitive development: Looking across at growing up. In C. M. Super & S. Harkness (Eds.), *New directions for child development: No. 8. Anthropological perspectives on child development.* San Francisco: Jossey-Bass.

Super, C. M., & Harkness, S. (1981). Figure, ground and gestalt: The cultural context of the active individual. In R. M. Lerner & N. A. Busch-Rossnagel (Eds.), *Individuals as producers of their development.* New York: Academic Press.

Super, C. M., Herrena, M. G., & Mora, J. O. (1990). Long-term effects of food supplementation and psychosocial intervention on the physical growth of Colombian infants at risk of malnutrition. *Child Development, 61,* 29–49.

Super, D. E. (1984). Career and life development. In D. Brown & L. Brooks (Eds.), *Career choice and development.* San Francisco: Jossey-Bass.

Super, D. E. (1985). Coming of age in Middletown: Careers in the making. *American Psychologist, 40,* 405–414.

Surber, C. F (1977). Developmental processes in social inference: Averaging of intentions and consequences in moral judgment. *Developmental Psychology, 13,* 654–665.

Surbey, M. (1990). Family composition, stress, and human menarche. In F. Bercovitch & T. Zeigler (Eds.), *The socioendocrinology of primate reproduction.* New York: Liss.

Sureau, C. (1999). Gender selection: A crime against humanity or the exercise of a fundamental right? *Human Reproduction, 14,* 867–868.

Suro, R. (1992, August 2). Bridging a gap. *The New York Times,* Special Report: Education, p. 20.

Sutton-Smith, B. (1993). Dilemmas in adult play with children. In K. MacDonald (Ed.), *Parent–child play: Descriptions and implications.* Albany, NY: SUNY Press.

Suzuki, L. A., & Valencia, R. R. (1997). Race-ethnicity and measured intelligence: Educational implications. *American Psychologist, 52,* 1103–1114.

Swanson, H. L., Mink, J., & Bocian, K. M. (1999). Cognitive processing deficits in poor readers with symptoms of reading disabilities and ADHD: More alike than different? *Journal of Educational Psychology, 91*(2), 321–333.

Sweeney, C. T., et al. (2001). Combination nicotine replacement therapy for smoking cessation: Rationale, efficacy, and tolerability. *CNS Drugs, 15*(6), 453–467.

Swinford, S. P., DeMaris, A., Cernkovich, S. A., & Giordano, P. C. (2000). Harsh physical discipline in childhood and violence in later romantic involvements: The mediating role of problem behaviors. *Journal of Marriage & the Family, 62*(2), 508–519.

Szapocznik, J., & Kurtines, W. M. (1993). Family psychology and cultural diversity. *American Psychologist, 48,* 400–407.

Tabor, M. B. W. (1996, August 7). Comprehensive study finds parents and peers are most crucial influences on students. *The New York Times,* p. A15.

Takahashi, K. (1990). Are the key assumptions of the "Strange Situation" procedure universal? A view from Japanese research. *Human Development, 33,* 23–30.

Talarczyk, M., & Rajewski, A. (2001). Poziom samoakceptacji u chorych z jadlowstretem psychicznym. *Psychiatria Polska, 35*(3), 389–398.

Tallandini, M. A., & Valentini, P. (1991). Symbolic prototypes in children's drawings of schools. *Journal of Genetic Psychology, 152,* 179–190.

Tamis-LeMonda, C. S., & Bornstein, M. H. (1991). Individual variation, correspondence, stability, and change in mother and toddler play. *Infant Behavior and Development, 14,* 143–162.

Tamis-LeMonda, C. S., Bornstein, M. H., & Baumwell, L. (2001). Maternal responsiveness and children's achievement of language milestones. *Child Development, 72*(3), 748–767.

Tamis-LeMonda, C. S., Bornstein, M. H., Cyphers, L., Toda, S., & Ogino, M. (1992). Language and play at one year: A comparison of toddlers and mothers in the United States and Japan. *International Journal of Behavioral Development, 15,* 19–42.

Tan, G. (1999). Perceptions of multiculturalism and intent to stay in school among Mexican American students. *Journal of Research & Development in Education, 33*(1), 1–14.

Tanguay, P. E., & Russell, A. T. (1991). Mental retardation. In M. Lewis (Ed.), *Child and adolescent psychiatry: A comprehensive textbook.* Baltimore: Williams & Wilkins.

Tannenbaum, A. (1992). Early signs of giftedness: Research and commentary. In P. Klein and A. Tannenbaum (Eds.), *To be young and gifted.* Norwood, NJ: Ablex.

Tanner, J. M. (1982). *Growth at adolescence* (2nd ed.). Oxford: Scientific Publications.

Tanner, J. M. (1989). *Fetus into man: Physical growth from conception to maturity.* Cambridge, MA: Harvard University Press.

Tanner, J. M. (1991a). Adolescent growth spurt, I. In R. M. Lerner, A. C. Petersen, & J. Brooks-Gunn (Eds.), *Encyclopedia of adolescence.* New York: Garland.

Tanner, J. M. (1991b). Secular trend in age of menarche. In R. M. Lerner, A. C. Petersen, & J. Brooks-Gunn (Eds.), *Encyclopedia of adolescence.* New York: Garland.

Tapp, J. L., & Levine, F. J. (1972). Compliance from kindergarten to college: A speculative research note. *Journal of Adolescence and Youth, 1,* 233–249.

Tappan, M. B., & Packer, M. (1991). Editors' notes. In M. B. Tappan & M. Packer (Eds.), *New directions for child development: No. 54. Narrative and story telling: Implication for understanding moral development.* San Francisco: Jossey-Bass.

Tassi, F., Schneider, B. H., & Richard, J. F. (2001). Competitive behavior at school in relation to social competence and incompetence in middle childhood. *Revue Internationale de Psychologie Sociale, 14*(2), 165–184.

Taylor, H. G., Klein, N., Minich, N. M., & Hack, M. (2000). Middle-school-age outcomes in children with very low birthweight. *Child Development, 71*(6), 1495–1511.

Taylor, M., Cartwright, B. S., & Carlson, S. M. (1993). A developmental investigation of children's imaginary companions. *Developmental Psychology, 29,* 276–285.

Taylor, M., & Hort, B. (1990). Can children be trained in making the distinction between appearances and reality? *Cognitive Development, 5,* 89–99.

Taylor, S. E., et al. (2000). Biobehavioral responses to stress in females: Tend-and-befriend, not fight-or-flight. *Psychological Review, 107*(3), 411–429.

Taylor-Tolbert, N. S., et al. (2000). Exercise reduces blood pressure in heavy older hypertensive men. *American Journal of Hypertension, 13,* 44–51.

Teller, D. Y., & Lindsey, D. T. (1993). Motion nulling techniques and infant color vision. In C. E. Granrud (Ed.), *Visual perception and cognition in infancy.* Hillsdale, NJ: Erlbaum.

Terry, D. (2000, July 16). Getting under my skin. *The New York Times online.*

Terry, D. J., Mayocchi, L., & Hynes, G. J. (1996). Depressive symptomology in new mothers: A stress and coping perspective. *Journal of Abnormal Psychology, 105,* 220–231.

Testa, M. F. (1992). Introduction. In M. K. Rosenheim & M. F. Testa (Eds.), *Early parenthood and coming of age in the 1990s.* New Brunswick, NJ: Rutgers University Press.

Teti, D. M. (1992). Sibling interaction. In V. B. VanHasselt & M. Hersen (Eds.), *Handbook of social development.* New York: Plenum.

Teti, D. M., Gelfand, D. M., & Messinger, D. S. (1992, August). *Attachment security & mothering: Does depression make a difference?* Paper presented at the meeting of the American Psychological Association, Washington, D.C.

te Velde, E. R., & Cohlen, B. J. (1999). The management of infertility. *The New England Journal of Medicine, 340*(3), 224.

Thal, D., & Bates, E. (1990). Continuity and variation in early language development. In J. Colombo & J. Fagen (Eds.), *Individual differences in infancy: Reliability, stability, and prediction.* Hillsdale, NJ: Erlbaum.

Theimer, C. E., Killen, M., & Stangor, C. (2001). Young children's evaluations of exclusion in gender-stereotypic peer contexts. *Developmental Psychology, 37*(1), 18–27.

Thelen, E. (1990). Dynamical systems and the generation of individual differences. In J. Colombo & J. W. Fagen (Eds.), *Individual differences in infancy: Reliability, stability, and prediction.* Hillsdale, NJ: Erlbaum.

Thelen, E. (2000). Motor development as foundation and future of developmental psychology. *International Journal of Behavioral Development, 24*(4), 385–397.

Thelen, E., & Adolph, K. E. (1992). Arnold L. Gesell: The paradox of nature and nurture. *Developmental Psychology, 28,* 368–380.

Thelen, E., & Ulrich, B. D. (1991). Hidden skills. *Monographs of the Society for Research in Child Development, 56*(1, Serial No. 223).

Thoma, S. J. (1986). Estimating gender differences in the comprehension and preference of moral issues. *Developmental Review, 6,* 165–180.

Thoman, E. B. (1993). Obligation and option in the premature nursery. *Developmental Review, 13,* 1–30.

Thomas, A., & Chess, S. (1989). Temperament and personality. In G. A. Kohnstamm, J. E. Bates, & M. K. Rothbart (Eds.), *Temperament in childhood.* Chichester, England: Wiley.

Thomas, J. R., & French, K. E. (1985). Gender differences across age in motor performance: A meta-analysis. *Psychological Bulletin, 98,* 260–282.

Thomas, R. M. (1990). Motor development. In R. M. Thomas (Ed.), *The encyclopedia of human development and education: Theory, research, and studies.* Oxford: Pergamon.

Thomas, R. M. (1992). *Comparing theories of child development* (3rd ed.). Belmont, CA: Wadsworth.

Thompson, L. A., Fagan, J. F., & Fulker, D. W. (1991). Longitudinal prediction of specific cognitive abilities from infant novelty preference. *Child Development, 62,* 530–538.

Thompson, R. A. (1991a). Attachment theory and research. In M. Lewis (Ed.), *Child and adolescent psychiatry: A comprehensive textbook.* Baltimore: Williams & Wilkins.

Thompson, R. A. (1991b). Infant daycare: Concerns, controversies, choices. In J. V. Lerner & N. L. Galambos (Eds.), *Employed mothers and their children.* New York: Garland.

Thompson, R. A., Lamb, M. E., & Estes, D. (1982). Stability of infant-mother attachment and its relationship to changing life circumstances in an unselected middle-class sample. *Child Development, 53,* 144–148.

Thompson, R. A., & Limber, S. P. (1990). "Social anxiety" in infancy: Stranger and separation reactions. In H. Leitenberg (Ed.), *Handbook of social and evaluation anxiety.* New York: Plenum.

Thompson, S. K. (1975). Gender labels and early sex role development. *Child Development, 46,* 339–347.

Thompson, W. F., Schellenberg, E. G., & Husain, G. (2001). Arousal, mood, and the Mozart effect. *Psychological Science, 12*(3), 248–251.

Thomson, M. E., & Kramer, M. S. (1984). Methodologic standards for controlled clinical trials of early contact and maternal-infant behavior. *Pediatrics, 73,* 294–300.

Thorkildsen, T. A. (1993, March). *Morality in the sphere of school.* Paper presented at the meeting of the Society for Research in Child Development, New Orleans, LA.

Thorndike, R. L., Hagan, E. P., & Sattler, J. M. (1985). *The Stanford-Binet Intelligence Scale* (4th ed.). Chicago: Riverside.

Thornton, D., & Reid, R. L. (1982). Moral reasoning and type of criminal offense. *British Journal of Social Psychology, 21,* 231–238.

Thorpe, L., et al. (2000). Folic acid and the prevention of neural tube defects. *British Medical Journal, 321,* 176.

Thurstone, L. L. (1938). Primary mental abilities. *Psychometric Monographs, 1.*

Thurstone, L. L., & Thurstone, T. G. (1963). *SRA primary abilities.* Chicago: SRA.

Tideman, E. (2000). Longitudinal follow-up of children born preterm: Cognitive development at age 19. *Early Human Development, 58*(2), 81–90.

Tiedemann, J. (2000). Parents' gender stereotypes and teachers' beliefs as predictors of children's concept of their mathematical ability in elementary school. *Journal of Educational Psychology, 92*(1), 144–151.

Tigner, R. B., & Tigner, S. S. (2000). Triarchic theories of intelligence: Aristotle and Sternberg. *History of Psychology, 3*(2), 168–176.

Timler, G. R., & Olswang, L. B. (2001). Variable structure/variable performance: Parent and teacher perspectives on a school-age child with FAS. *Journal of Positive Behavior Interventions, 3*(1), 48–56.

Tinsley, B. J. (1992). Multiple influences on the acquisition and socialization of children's health attitudes and behavior: An integrative review. *Child Development, 63,* 1043–1069.

Tiwary, C., & Holguin, A. H. (1992). Prevalence of obesity among children of military dependents at two major medical centers. *American Journal of Public Health, 82,* 354–357.

Tizabi, Y., et al. (2000). Prenatal nicotine exposure: Effects on locomotor activity and central[-sup-1-sup-2-sup-5I]alpha-BT binding in rats. *Pharmacology, Biochemistry & Behavior, 66*(3) 495–500.

Tizard, B., Philips, J., & Plewis, I. (1976). Play in preschool centres. *Journal of Child Psychology and Psychiatry, 17,* 265–274.

Tocci, C. M., & Engelhard, G. (1991). Achievement, parental support, and gender differences in attitudes toward mathematics. *Journal of Education Research, 84,* 280–286.

Tolson, T. F. J., & Wilson, M. N. (1990). The impact of two- and three-generational black family structure on perceived family climate. *Child Development, 61,* 416–428.

Tomasello, M., Brooks, P. J, & Stern, E. (1998). Learning to produce passive utterances through discourse. *First Language, 18*(53), 223–237.

Tombs, D. A. (1991). Child psychiatric emergencies. In M. Lewis (Ed.), *Child and adolescent psychiatry: A comprehensive textbook.* Baltimore: Williams & Wilkins.

Tomlinson-Keasey, C., & Keasey, C. B. (1974). The mediating role of cognitive development in moral judgment. *Child Development, 45,* 291–298.

Toren, P., et al. (2001). Fluvoxamine is ineffective in the treatment of enuresis in children and adolescents: An open-label pilot study. *Human Psychopharmacology Clinical & Experimental, 16*(4), 327–332.

Torgesen, J. K., et al. (2001). Intensive remedial instruction for children with severe reading disabilities: Immediate and long-term outcomes from two instructional approaches. *Journal of Learning Disabilities, 34*(1), 33–58.

Toth, S. L., Manly, J. T., & Cicchetti, D. (1992). Child maltreatment and vulnerability to depression. *Development and Psychopathology, 4,* 97–112.

Treasure, J., & Serpell, L. (2001). Osteoporosis in young people: Research and treatment in eating disorders. *Psychiatric Clinics of North America, 24*(2), 359–370.

Treboux, D., & Busch-Rossnagel, N A. (1990). Social network influences on adolescent sexual attitudes and behaviors. *Journal of Adolescent Research, 5*(2), 175–189.

Treboux, D. A., & Busch-Rossnagel, N. A. (1991). Age differences in adolescent sexual behavior, sexual attitudes and contraceptive use. In R. M. Lerner, A. C. Petersen, & J. Brooks-Gunn (Eds.), *Encyclopedia of adolescence.* New York: Garland.

Trehub, S. E., Schneider, B. A., Thorpe, L. A., & Judge, P. (1991). Observational measures of auditory sensitivity in early infancy. *Developmental Psychology, 27,* 40–49.

Trehub, S. E., Trainor, L. J., & Unyk, A. M. (1993). Music and speech processing in the first year of life. In H. W. Reese (Ed.), *Advances in child development and behavior* (Vol. 24). San Diego, CA: Academic Press.

Triandis, H. C. (1990). Cross-cultural studies of individualism and collectivism. In J. J. Berman (Ed.), *Nebraska Symposium on Motivation, 1989. Cross-cultural perspectives.* Lincoln: University of Nebraska Press.

Triandis, H. C. (1994). *Culture and social behavior.* New York: McGraw-Hill.

Triandis, H. C. (1995). *Individualism and collectivism.* Boulder, CO: Westview Press.

Trice, A. D. (2000). Italian, Bulgarian, and U.S. children's perceptions of gender-appropriateness of occupations. *Journal of Social Psychology, 140*(5), 661–663.

Trickett, P. K., Aber, J. L., Carlson, V., & Cicchetti, D. (1991). Relationship of socioeconomic status to the etiology and developmental sequelae of physical child abuse. *Developmental Psychology, 27,* 148–158.

Trickett, P. K., & Kuczynski, L. (1986). Children's misbehaviors and parental discipline strategies in abusive and nonabusive families. *Developmental Psychology, 22,* 115–123.

Trickett, P. K., & Putnam, F. W. (1993). Impact of child sexual abuse on females: Toward a developmental, psychobiological integration. *Psychological Science, 4,* 81–87.

Tripathi, B. M., Lal, R., & Kumar, N. (2001). Substance abuse in children and adolescents: An overview. *Journal of Personality & Clinical Studies, 17*(2), 67–74.

Tronick, E. Z. (1989). Emotions and emotional communication in infants. *American Psychologist, 44,* 112–119.

Truesdell, L. A., & Abramson, T. (1992). Academic behavior and grades of mainstreamed students with mild disabilities. *Exceptional Children, 58,* 392–398.

Tsuneishi, S., & Casaer, P. (2000). Effects of preterm extraunterine visual experience on the development of the human visual system: A flash VEP study. *Developmental Medicine & Child Neurology, 42*(10), 663–668.

Tubman, J. G., Lerner, R. M., Lerner, J. V., & von Eye, A. (1992). Temperament and adjustment in young adulthood: A 15-year longitudinal analysis. *American Journal of Orthopsychiatry, 62,* 564–574.

Tuma, J. M. (1989). Mental health services for children. *American Psychologist, 44,* 188–199.

Turkheimer, E. (1991). Individual and group differences in adoption studies of IQ. *Psychological Bulletin, 110,* 392–405.

Turkheimer, E., & Gottesman, I. I. (1991). Individual differences and the canalization of human behavior. *Developmental Psychology, 27,* 18–22.

Turkington, C. (1992, December). Ruling opens door—a crack—to IQ-testing some black kids. *APA Monitor,* pp. 28–29.

Turner, J. S., & Helms, D. B. (1983). *Lifespan development* (2nd ed.). New York: Holt, Rinehart & Winston.

Ubben, G. C., Hughes, L. W., & Norris, C. J. (2001). *The principal: Creative leadership for effective schools* (4th ed.). (2001). Boston: Allyn & Bacon.

Ullian, D. Z. (1981). The child's construction of gender: Anatomy as destiny. In E. K. Shapiro & E. Weber (Eds.), *Cognitive and affective growth.* Hillsdale, NJ: Erlbaum.

United Nations Special Session on AIDS. (2001, June 25–27). Preventing HIV/AIDS among young people. New York: United Nations.

Unruh, L. (2001). Cited in J. Sommerfeld. (2001, November 29). U.S. lags behind in cutting teen births. MSNBC online.

USBC (See U.S. Bureau of the Census.)

U.S. Bureau of the Census. (1993). *Statistical abstract of the United States: 1993* (113th ed.). Washington, DC: U.S. Government Printing Office.

U.S. Bureau of the Census. (1998). *Statistical abstract of the United States* (118th ed.). Washington, DC: U.S. Government Printing Office.

U.S. Bureau of the Census. (2000). *Statistical abstract of the United States* (120th ed.). Washington, DC: U.S. Government Printing Office.

U.S. Bureau of the Census. (2001, revised September 25). *March 2001 supplement to the Current Population Survey* (CPS). Washington, DC: U.S. Government Printing Office.

U.S. Department of Agriculture. (2000). *Dietary guidelines for Americans, 5th Edition.* http://www.nal.usda.gov/fnic/dga/

USDHHS (See U. S. Department of Health and Human Services.)

U.S. Department of Health and Human Services. (1999). *Trends in the well-being of America's children and youth: 1999.* Hyattsville, MD: Author.

U.S. Department of Health and Human Services. (2000) *Youth violence: A report of the Surgeon General.* Rockville, Maryland: U.S. Department of Health and Human Services, CDC, National Center for Injury Prevention and Control; Substance Abuse and Mental Health Services Administration, Center for Mental Health Services; and National Institutes of Health, National Institute of Mental Health.

U.S. Department of Health and Human Services, National Center for Health Statistics. (2001). Vital statistics mortality data, underlying cause death, 1998. Hyattsville, Maryland: U.S. Department of Health and Human Services, CDC, National Center for Health Statistics.

U.S. Environmental Protection Agency. (1993). *Respiratory health effects of passive smoking: Lung cancer and other disorders.* Washington, DC: Author.

Valas, H. (2001). Learned helplessness and psychological adjustment: Effects of age, gender, and academic achievement. *Scandinavian Journal of Educational Research, 45*(1), 71–90.

Valleroy, L. A., et al. (2000). HIV prevalence and associated risks in young men who have sex with men. *Journal of the American Medical Association, 284*(2), 198–204.

Van Brunschot, M., Zarbatany, L., & Strang, K. (1993, March). *Ecological contributions to gender differences in intimacy among peers.* Paper presented at the meeting of the Society for Research in Child Development, New Orleans, LA.

van de Grift, W. (1990). Educational leadership and academic achievement in elementary education. *School Effectiveness and School Improvement, 1,* 26–40.

Vandell, D. L. (1990). Development in twins. In R. Vasta (Ed.), *Annals of child development* (Vol. 7). London: Kingsley.

Vandell, D. L., & Ramanan, J. (1991). Children of the national longitudinal survey of youth: Choices in after-school care and child development. *Developmental Psychology, 27,* 637–643.

Vandell, D. L., & Ramanan, J. (1992). Effects of early and recent maternal employment on children from low-income families. *Child Development, 63,* 938–949.

Van den Bergh, B. R. H. (1990). The influence of maternal emotions during pregnancy on fetal and neonatal behavior. *Pre- and Peri-Natal Psychology, 5,* 119–130.

Vandenbergh, J. G. (1993). Cited in Angier, N. (1993, August 24). Female gerbil born with males is found to be begetter of sons. *The New York Times,* p. C4.

Vander Ven, T. M., Cullen, F. T., Carrozza, M. A., & Wright, J. P. (2001). Home alone: The impact of maternal employment on delinquency. *Social Problems, 48*(2), 236–257.

Vander Wal, J. S., & Thelen, M. H. (2000). Eating and body image concerns among obese and average-weight children. *Addictive Behaviors, 25*(5), 775–778.

Van IJzendoorn, M. H., & Hubbard, F. O. A. (2000). Are infant crying and maternal responsiveness during the first year related to infant-mother attachment at 15 months? *Attachment & Human Development, 2*(3), 371–391.

van IJzendoorn, M. H., & Kroonenberg, P. M. (1988). Cross-cultural patterns of attachment: A meta-analysis of the Strange Situation. *Child Development, 59,* 147–156.

van IJzendoorn, M. H., Moran, G., Belsky, J., Pederson, D., Bakermans-Kranenburg, M. J., & Kneppers, K. (2000). The similarity of siblings' attachments to their mother. *Child Development, 71*(4), 1086–1098.

van IJzendoorn, M. H., Sagi, A., & Lambermon, M. W. E. (1992). The multiple caretaker paradox: Data from Holland and Israel. In R. C. Pianta (Ed.), *New directions for child development: No. 57. Beyond the parent: The role of other adults in children's lives.* San Francisco: Jossey-Bass.

Van Kammen, W. B., Loeber, R., & Stouthamer-Lober, M. (1991). Substance use and its relationship to conduct problems and delinquency in young boys. *Journal of Youth and Adolescence, 20,* 399–413.

Van Riper, M. (2000). Family variables associated with well-being in siblings of children with Down syndrome. *Journal of Family Nursing, 6*(3), 267–286.

Vartanian, L. R. (2001). Adolescents' reactions to hypothetical peer group conversations: Evidence for an imaginary audience. *Adolescence, 36*(142), 347–380.

Vartanian, L. R., Giant, C. L., & Passino, R. M. (2001). "Ally McBeal vs. Arnold Schwarzenegger": Comparing mass media, interpersonal feedback, and gender as predictors of satisfaction with body thinness and muscularity. *Social Behavior & Personality, 29*(7), 711–723.

Vaughn, B. E., et al. (1992). Attachment security and temperament in infancy and early childhood: Some conceptual clarifications. *Developmental Psychology, 28,* 463–473.

Vaughn, S., Hogan, A., Kouzekanani, K., & Shapiro, S. (1990). Peer acceptance, self-perceptions, and social skills of learning disabled students prior to identification. *Journal of Educational Psychology, 82,* 101–106.

Veijola, J., et al. (2000–2001). Early associations of schizophrenia in the 1966 North Finland general population birth cohort. *International Journal of Mental Health, 29*(4), 84–90.

Velez de la Calle, J. F., et al. (2001). Male infertility risk factors in a French military population. *Human Reproduction, 16,* 481–486.

Vellutino, F. R. (2001). Further analysis of the relationship between reading achievement and intelligence. *Journal of Learning Disabilities, 34*(4), 306–310.

Vellutino, F. R., Scanlon, D. M., & Lyon, G. R. (2000). Differentiating between difficult-to-remediate and readily remediated poor readers: More evidence against the IQ-achievement discrepancy definition of reading disability. *Journal of Learning Disabilities, 33*(3), 223–238.

Velting, D. M., Rathus, J. H., & Miller, A. L. (2000). MACI personality scale profiles of depressed adolescent suicide attempters: A pilot study. *Journal of Clinical Psychology, 56*(10), 1381–1385.

Ventura, S. J., et al. (2001). Trends in pregnancy rates for the United States, 1976–97: An update. *National Vital Statistics Reports, 49*(4). Atlanta: Centers for Disease Control and Prevention.

Verma, S., & Larson, R. (1999). Are adolescents more emotional? A study of the daily emotions of middle class Indian adolescents. *Psychology & Developing Societies, 11*(2), 179–194.

Vetter, B. (1992, Fall). Ferment: yes progress: maybe change: slow. *Mosaic, 23*(3), 34–41.

Vik, P. W., Carrello, P., Tate, S. R., & Field, C. (2000). Progression of consequences among heavy-drinking college students. *Psychology of Addictive Behaviors, 14*(2), 91–101.

Vilain, E. (2000). Genetics of sexual development. *Annual Review of Sex Research, 11,* 1–25.

Villani, S. (2001). Impact of media on children and adolescents: A 10–year review of the research. *Journal of the American Academy of Child & Adolescent Psychiatry, 40*(4), 392–401.

Violato, C., & Grossi, V. (1991, August). *Adolescent suicide and early loss: A stepwise discriminant analysis.* Paper presented at the meeting of the American Psychological Association, San Francisco.

Vitulano, L. A., & Tebes, J. K. (1991). Child and adolescent behavior therapy. In M. Lewis (Ed.), *Child and adolescent psychiatry.* Baltimore: Williams & Wilkins.

Vitousek, K., & Manke, F. (1994). Personality variables and disorders in anorexia nervosa and bulimia nervosa. *Journal of Abnormal Psychology, 103,* 137–147.

Vogel, D. A., Lake, M. A., Evans, S., & Karraker, K. H. (1991). Children's and adult's sex-stereotyped perceptions of infants. *Sex Roles, 24,* 605–616.

Volden, J., & Lord, C. (1991). Neologisms and idiosyncratic language in autistic speakers. *Journal of Autism and Developmental Disorders, 21,* 109–130.

Volkmar, F. R. (1991). Autism and the pervasive developmental disorders. In M. Lewis (Ed.), *Child and adolescent psychiatry.* Baltimore: Williams & Wilkins.

Volkmar, F. R. (2001). Pharmacological interventions in autism: Theoretical and practical issues. *Journal of Clinical Child Psychology, 30*(1), 80–87.

Volkow, N. D., et al. (2001a). Association of dopamine transporter reduction with psychomotor impairment in methamphetamine abusers. *American Journal of Psychiatry, 158,* 377–382.

Volkow, N. D., et al. (2001b). Higher cortical and lower subcortical metabolism in detoxified methamphetamine abusers. *American Journal of Psychiatry, 158,* 383–389.

Volling, B. L. (2001). Early attachment relationships as predictors of preschool children's emotion regulation with a distressed sibling. *Early Education & Development, 12*(2), 185–207.

Volling, B. L., & Belsky, J. (1992). The contribution of mother–child and father–child relationships to the quality of sibling interaction: A longitudinal study. *Child Development, 63,* 1209–1222.

Volling, B. L., MacKinnon-Lewis, C., & Dechman, K. (1993). *The family correlates of peer rejection and social withdrawal.* Paper presented at the meeting of the Society for Research in Child Development, New Orleans, LA.

Vorhees, C. V., & Mollnow, E. (1987). Behavioral teratogenesis long-term influences on behavior from early exposure to environmental agents. In J. D. Osofsky (Ed.), *Handbook of infant development* (2nd ed.). New York: Wiley.

Voyer, D., Nolan, C., & Voyer, S. (2000). The relation between experience and spatial performance in men and women. *Sex Roles, 43*(11–12), 891–915.

Vuchinich, S., Bank, L., & Patterson, G. R. (1992). Parenting, peers, and the stability of antisocial behavior in preadolescent boys. *Developmental Psychology, 28,* 510–521.

Vurpillot, E. (1968). The development of scanning strategies and their relation to visual differention. *Journal of Experimental Child Psychology, 6,* 632–650.

Vygotsky, L. S. (1962). *Thought and language.* Cambridge, MA: MIT Press.

Vygotsky, L. (1978). *Mind in society: The development of higher psychological processes.* Cambridge, MA: Harvard University Press.

Wachs, T. D. (1993). Multidimensional correlates of individual variability in play and exploration. In M. H. Bornstein & A. W. O'Reilly (Eds.), *New directions for child development: No. 59. The role of play in the development of thought.* San Francisco: Jossey-Bass.

Wade, T. D., Bulik, C. M., Neale, M., & Kendler, K. S. (2000). Anorexia nervosa and major depression: Shared genetic and environmental risk factors. *American Journal of Psychiatry, 157,* 469–471.

Wade, T. D., & Kendler, K. S. (2001). Parent, child, and social correlates of parental discipline style: A retrospective, multi-informant investigation with female twins. *Social Psychiatry & Psychiatric Epidemiology, 36*(4), 177–185.

Wadsworth, K. W., & McLoyd, V. C. (1993, March). *The impact of mother–adolescent self-esteem: Effects of social support.* Paper presented at the meeting of the Society for Research in Child Development, New Orleans, LA.

Wagner, K. D., & Ambrosini, P. J. (2001). Childhood depression: Pharmacological therapy/treatment (pharmacotherapy of childhood depression). *Journal of Clinical Child Psychology, 30*(1), 88–97.

Wagner, R. K. (1997). Intelligence, training, and employment. (1997). *American Psychologist, 52,* 1059–1069.

Wahl, K. H., & Blackhurst, A. (2000). Factors affecting the occupational and educational aspirations of children and adolescents. *Professional School Counseling, 3*(5), 367–374.

Wahler, R. G., Herring, M., & Edwards, M. (2001). Coregulation of balance between children's prosocial approaches and acts of compliance: A pathway to mother–child cooperation? *Journal of Clinical Child Psychology, 30*(4), 473–478.

Walden, T. A., & Baxter, A. (1989). The effect of context and age on social referencing. *Child Development, 60,* 1511–1518.

Waldman, S., & Springen, K. (1992, November 16). Too old, too fast? *Newsweek,* pp. 80–88.

Waldron, H. B., Slesnick, N., Brody, J. L., & Peterson, T. R. (2001). Treatment outcomes for adolescent substance abuse at 4- and 7-month assessments. *Journal of Consulting & Clinical Psychology, 69*(5), 802–813.

Walker, L. J. (1982). The sequentiality of Kohlberg's stages of moral development. *Child Development, 53,* 1330–1336.

Walker, L. J. (1984). Sex differences in the development of moral reasoning: A critical review. *Child Development, 55,* 677–691.

Walker, L. J. (1991). Sex differences in moral reasoning. In W. M. Kurtines & J. L. Gewirtz (Eds.), *Handbook of moral behavior and development* (Vol. 2). Hillsdale, NJ: Erlbaum.

Walker, L. J., Hennig, K. H., & Krettenauer, T. (2000). Parent and peer contexts for children's moral reasoning development. *Child Development, 71*(4), 1033–1048.

Walker, L. J., & Taylor, J. H. (1991a). Family interactions and the development of moral reasoning. *Child Development, 62,* 264–283.

Walker, L. J., & Taylor, J. H. (1991b). Stage transitions in moral reasoning: A longitudinal study of development processes. *Developmental Psychology, 27,* 330–337.

Walker, N. C., & O'Brien, B. (1999). The relationship between method of pain management during labor and birth outcomes. *Clinical Nursing Research, 8*(2), 119–134.

Walkup, J. T., et al. (2001). Fluvoxamine for the treatment of anxiety disorders in children and adolescents. *New England Journal of Medicine, 344*(17), 1279–1285.

Wallerstein, J. S., & Blakeslee, S. (1989). *Second chances: Women and children a decade after divorce.* New York: Ticknor & Fields.

Walter, J. L., & LaFreniere, P. J. (2000). A naturalistic study of affective expression, social competence, and sociometric status in preschoolers. *Early Education & Development, 11*(1), 109–122.

Walther, F. J., den Ouden, A. L., & Verloove-Vanhorick, S. P. (2000). Looking back in time: Outcome of a national cohort of very preterm infants born in The Netherlands in 1983. *Early Human Development, 59*(3), 175–191.

Wang, H., et al. (2000). Nicotine as a potent blocker of the cardiac A-type K^+ channels: Effects on cloned Kv4.3 channels and native transient outward current. *Circulation, 102,* 1165–1171.

Wang, M. C., Haertel, G. D., & Walberg, H. J. (1990). What influences learning? A content analysis of review literature. *Journal of Educational Research, 84,* 30–43.

Wang, M. C., Haertel, G. D., & Walberg, H. J. (1993). Toward a knowledge base for school learning. *Review of Educational Research, 63,* 249–294.

Wang, Q., Leichtman, M. D., & White, S. H. (1998). Childhood memory and self-description in young Chinese adults: The impact of growing up an only child. *Cognition, 69*(1), 73–103.

Ward, C. A. (2000). Models and measurements of psychological androgyny: A cross-cultural extension of theory and research. *Sex Roles, 43*(7–8), 529–552.

Ward, M. J., Lee, S. S., & Lipper, E. G. (2000). Failure-to-thrive is associated with disorganized infant–mother attachment and unresolved maternal attachment. *Infant Mental Health Journal, 21*(6), 428–442.

Warman, D. M., & Cohen, R. (2000). Stability of aggressive behaviors and children's peer relationships. *Aggressive Behavior, 26*(4), 277–290.

Wasik, B. H., Ramey, C. T., Bryant, D. M., & Sparling, J. J. (1990). A longitudinal study of two early intervention strategies: Project CARE. *Child Development, 61,* 1682–1696.

Wasserman, G. A., et al. (2000). Yugoslavia Prospective Lead Study: Contributions of prenatal and postnatal lead exposure to early intelligence. *Neurotoxicology & Teratology, 22*(6), 811–818.

Wasserman, G. A., Liu, X., Pine, D. S., & Graziano, J. H. (2001). Contribution of maternal smoking during pregnancy and lead exposure to early child behavior problems. *Neurotoxicology & Teratology, 23*(1), 13–21.

Wasserman, J. (1993, September 3). It's still women's work. *Daily News,* p. 7.

Waterman, A. S. (1985). Identity in the context of adolescent psychology. In A. S. Waterman (Ed.), *Identity in adolescence: Processes and contents.* San Francisco: Jossey-Bass.

Waterman, A. S. (1992). Identity as an aspect of optimal psychological functioning. In G. R. Adams, T. P. Gullotta, & R. Montemayor (Eds.), *Adolescent identity formation.* Newbury Park, CA: Sage.

Waterman, A. S. (1999). Issues of identity formation revisited: United States and The Netherlands. *Developmental Review, 19*(4), 462–479.

Waterman, A. S., & Archer, S. L. (1990). A life-span perspective on identity formation: Developments in form, function, and process. In P. B. Baltes, D. L. Featherman, & R. M. Lerner (Eds.), *Life-span development and behavior* (Vol. 10). Hillsdale, NJ: Erlbaum.

Watkins, B., & Bentovim, A. (1992). The sexual abuse of male children and adolescents: A review of current research. *Journal of Child Psychology and Psychiatry, 33,* 197–248.

Watson, J. B. (1924). *Behaviorism.* New York: Norton.

Watson, J. D., & Crick, F. H. C. (1958). Molecular structure of nucleic acids: A structure for deoxyribose nucleic acid. *Nature, 171,* 737–738.

Watson, M. F., & Protinsky, H. (1991, Winter). Identity status of black adolescents: An empirical investigation. *Adolescence, 26,* 963–966.

Watson, M. W., & Getz, K. (1990). Developmental shifts in Oedipal behaviors related to family role understanding. In I. Bretherton & M. W. Watson (Eds.), *New directions for child development: No. 48. Children's perspectives on the family.* San Francisco: Jossey-Bass.

Watson, T. L., Bowers, W. A., & Andersen, A. E. (2000). Involuntary treatment of eating disorders. *American Journal of Psychiatry, 157,* 1806–1810.

Watt, H. M. G., & Bornholt, L. J. (2000). Social categories and student perceptions in high school mathematics. *Journal of Applied Social Psychology, 30*(7), 1492–1503.

Waxman, S. R. (1990). Linguistic biases and the establishment of conceptual hierarchies: Evidence from preschool children. *Cognitive Development, 5,* 123–150.

Waxman, S. R., & Kosowski, T. D. (1990). Nouns mark category relations: Toddlers' and preschoolers' word-learning biases. *Child Development, 61,* 1461–1473.

Waxman, S. R., & Senghas, A. (1992). Relations among word meaning in early lexical development. *Developmental Psychology, 28,* 862–873.

Weber Cullen, K., et al. (2001). Child-reported family and peer influences on fruit, juice, and vegetable consumption: Reliability and validity of measures. H*ealth Education Research, 16*(2), 187–200.

Webster-Stratton, C., Reid, M. J., & Hammond, M. (2001a). Preventing conduct problems, promoting social competence: A parent and teacher training partnership in Head Start. *Journal of Clinical Child Psychology, 30*(3), 283–302.

Webster-Stratton, C., Reid, J., & Hammond, M. (2001b). Social skills and problem-solving training for children with early-onset conduct problems: Who benefits? *Journal of Child Psychology & Psychiatry & Allied Disciplines, 42*(7), 943–952.

Wechsler, D. (1975). Intelligence defined and undefined: A relativistic appraisal. *American Psychologist, 30,* 135–139.

Weikart, D. P., & Schweinhart, L. J. (1991). Disadvantaged children and curriculum effects. In L. Rescorla, M. C. Hyson, & K. Hirsh-Pasek (Eds.), *New directions in child development: No. 53. Academic instruction in early childhood: Challenge or pressure?* San Francisco: Jossey-Bass.

Weiner, T. S., & Adolph, K. E. (1993, March). *Toddler's perception of slant vs. slope height for descending slopes.* Paper presented at the meeting of the Society for Research in Child Development, New Orleans, LA.

Weinraub, M., et al. (1984). The development of sex role stereotypes in the third year: Relationships to gender labeling, gender identity, sex-typed toy preference, and family characteristics, *Child Development, 55,* 1493–1503.

Weisner, T. S., & Wilson-Mitchell, J. E. (1990). Nonconventional family lifestyles and sex typing. *Child Development, 61,* 1915–1933.

Weiss, B., Dodge, K. A., Bates, J. E., & Pettit, G. S. (1992). Some consequences of early harsh discipline: Child aggression and a maladaptive social information processing style. *Child Development, 63,* 1321–1335.

Weissberg, J. A., & Paris, S. G. (1986). Young children's remembering in different contexts: A reinterpretation of Istomine's study. *Child Development, 57,* 1123–1129.

Weitzman, M., Gortmaker, S., & Sobol, A. (1992). Maternal smoking and behavior problems of children. *Pediatrics, 90,* 342–348.

Weitzman, M., & Siegel, D. M. (1992). What we have not learned from what we know about excessive school absence and school dropout. *Developmental and Behavioral Pediatrics, 13,* 55–58.

Weller, E. B., & Weller, R. A. (1991). Mood disorders. In M. Lewis (Ed.), *Child and adolescent psychiatry: A comprehensive textbook.* Baltimore: Williams & Wilkins.

Wellman, H. M., Cross, D., & Bartsch, K. (1986). Infant search and object permanence: A meta-analysis of the A-not-B error. *Monographs of the Society for Research in Child Development, 5*(3, Serial No. 214).

Wellman, H. M., Cross, D., & Watson, J. (2001). Meta-analysis of theory-of-mind development: The truth about false belief. *Child Development, 72*(3), 655–684.

Wellman, H. M., Phillips, A. T., Rodriguez, T. (2000). Young children's understanding of perception, desire, and emotion. *Child Development, 71*(4), 895–912.

Wells, K. C., et al. (2000). Psychosocial treatment strategies in the MTA study: Rationale, methods, and critical issues in design and implementation. *Journal of Abnormal Child Psychology, 28*(6), 483–505.

Wenar, C. (1990). Childhood fears and phobias. In M. Lewis & S. M. Miller (Eds.), *Handbook of developmental psychopathology.* New York: Plenum.

Wentworth, N., Benson, J. B., & Haith, M. M. (2000). The development of infants' reaches for stationary and moving targets. *Child Development, 71*(3), 576–601.

Wentzel, K. R., Feldman, S. S., & Weinberger, D. A. (1991). Parental child rearing and academic achievement in boys: The mediational role of social-emotional adjustment. *Journal of Early Adolescence, 11,* 321–339.

Werker, J. (1989). Becoming a native listener. *American Scientist, 77,* 54–59.

Werner, E. E. (1988). A cross-cultural perspective on infancy. *Journal of Cross-Cultural Psychology, 19,* 96–113.

Werner, E. E. (1990). Protective factors and individual resilience. In S. J. Meisels & J. P. Shonkoff (Eds.), *Handbook of early childhood intervention.* Cambridge: Cambridge University Press.

Werner, L. A., & Bargones, J. Y. (1992). Psychoacoustic development of human infants. In C. Rovee-Collier & L. P. Lipsitt (Eds.), *Advances in infancy research* (Vol. 7). Norwood, NJ: Ablex.

Werner, L. A., & Gillenwater, J. M. (1990). Pure-tone sensitivity of 2- to 5- week-old infants. *Infant Behavior and Development, 13,* 355–375.

Werry, J. S. (1991). Brain and behavior. In M. Lewis (Ed.), *Child and adolescent psychiatry: A comprehensive textbook.* Baltimore: Williams & Wilkins.

Westerman, M. A. (1990). Coordination of maternal directives with preschoolers' behavior in compliance-problem and healthy dyads. *Developmental Psychology, 26,* 621–630.

Wexler, N. (1993, Spring). Presymptomatic testing for Huntington's disease. *National Forum,* pp. 22–26.

Whalen, C. K. (2001). ADHD treatment in the 21st Century: Pushing the envelope. *Journal of Clinical Child Psychology, 30*(1), 136–140.

Where the Norplant debate hits home. (1993, March 7). *The New York Times,* p. 17.

Whitall, J. (1991). The developmental effect of concurrent cognitive and locomotor skills: Time-sharing from a dynamical perspective. *Journal of Experimental Child Psychology, 51,* 245–266.

White, C. B., Bushnell, N., & Regnemer, J. L. (1978). Moral development in Bahamian school children: A three-year examination of Kohlberg's stages of moral development. *Developmental Psychology, 14,* 58–65.

White, K. S., Bruce, S. E., Farrell, A. D., & Kliewer, W. (1998). Impact of exposure to community violence on anxiety: A longitudinal study of family social support as a protective factor for urban children. *Journal of Child & Family Studies, l7*(2), 187–203.

White, R. W. (1959). Motivation reconsidered: The concept of competence. *Psychological Review, 66,* 297–333.

White, S. D., & DeBlassie, R. R. (1992). Adolescent sexual behavior. *Adolescence, 27,* 183–191.

Whitehead, J. R., & Corbin, C. B. (1991). Effects of fitness test type, teacher, and gender on exercise intrinsic motivation and physical self-worth. *Journal of School Health, 61,* 11–16.

Whitehurst, G. J. (1982). Language development. In B. B. Wolman (Ed.), *Handbook of developmental psychology.* Englewood Cliffs, NJ: Prentice-Hall.

Whitehurst, G. J., et al. (1993). *A picture book reading intervention in daycare and home for children from low-income families.* Paper presented at the meeting of the Society for Research in Child Development, New Orleans, LA.

Whitehurst, G. J., & Valdez-Menchaca, M. C. (1988). What is the role of reinforcement in early language acquisition? *Child Development, 59,* 430–440.

Whiting, B. B., & Edwards, C. P. (1988). *Children of different worlds.* Cambridge, MA: Harvard University Press.

Widaman, J. F., MacMillan, D. L., Hemsley, R. E., Little, T. D., & Balow, I. H. (1992). Differences in adolescents' self-concept as a function of academic level, ethnicity, and gender. *American Journal on Mental Retardation, 96,* 387–404.

Widom, C. S. (1991). Childhood victimization: Risk factor for delinquency. In M. E. Colten & S. Gore (Eds.), *Adolescent stress: Causes and consequences.* New York: Aldine deGruyter.

Wiener, J., & Harris, P. J. (1993). *Social interaction of children with and without learning disabilities in dyads and small groups.* Paper presented at the meeting of the Society for Research in Child Development, New Orleans, LA.

Wigfield, A., & Eccles, J. S. (1992). The development of achievement task values: A theoretical analysis. *Developmental Review, 12,* 265–310.

Wilcox, A. J., et al. (1995). Timing of sexual intercourse in relation to ovulation: Effects on the probability of conception, survival of the pregnancy, and sex of the baby. *New England Journal of Medicine, 333,* 1517–1521.

Wilder, A. A., & Williams, J. P. (2001). Students with severe learning disabilities can learn higher order comprehension skills. *Journal of Educational Psychology, 93*(2), 268–278.

Willer, B., & Bredekamp, S. (1990, July). Redefining readiness: An essential requisite for educational reform. *Young Children,* 22–24.

Williams, D. E., & D'Alessandro, J. D. (1994) A comparison of three measures of androgyny and their relationship to psychological adjustment. *Journal of Social Behavior and Personality, 9*(3) 469–480.

Williams, H. (1983). *Perceptual and motor development.* Englewood Cliffs, NJ: Prentice-Hall.

Williams, J. M., & Currie, C. (2000). Self-esteem and physical development in early adolescence: Pubertal timing and body image. *Journal of Early Adolescence, 20*(2), 129–149.

Williams, L. (1992, February 6). Woman's image in a mirror: Who defines what she sees? Girl's self-image is mother of the woman. *The New York Times,* pp. A1, B7.

Williams, R. L. (1974, May). Scientific racism and IQ: The silent mugging of the black community. *Psychology Today,* p. 32.

Willinger, M., Ko, C-W., Hoffman, H. J., Kessler, R. C., & Corwin, M. J. (2000). Factors associated with caregivers' choice of infant sleep position, 1994–1998: The National Infant Sleep Position Study. *Journal of the American Medical Association, 283*(16), 2135–2142.

Wills, T. A., Gibbons, F. X., Gerrard, M., & Brody, G. H. (2000). Protection and vulnerability processes relevant for early onset of substance use: A test among African American children. *Health Psychology, 19,* 253–263.

Wilson, C., Nettelbeck, T., Turnbull, C., & Young, R. (1992). IT, IQ, and age: A comparison of developmental functions. *British Journal of Developmental Psychology, 10,* 179–188.

Wilson, G. L. (1991). Comment: Transgenerational patterns of suicide attempt. *Journal of Consulting and Clinical Psychology, 59,* 869–873.

Wilson, W., et al. (2000). Brain morphological changes and early marijuana use: A magnetic resonance and positron emission tomography study. *Journal of Addictive Diseases, 19*(1), 1–22.

Windell, J. (1991). *Discipline: A sourcebook of 50 failsafe techniques for parents.* Indialantic, FL: Collier Books.

Winer, G. A. (1980). Class-inclusion reasoning in children: A review of the empirical literature. *Child Development, 51,* 309–328.

Winner, E. (1989). Development in the visual arts. In W. Damon (Ed.), *Child development today and tomorrow.* San Francisco: Jossey-Bass.

Winner, E. (2000). The origins and ends of giftedness. *American Psychologist, 55,* 159–169.

Winzelberg, A. J., et al. (2000). Effectiveness of an Internet-based program for reducing risk factors for eating disorders. *Journal of Consulting and Clinical Psychology, 68,* 346–350.

Wolchik, S. A., et al. (2000). An experimental evaluation of theory-based mother and mother–child programs for children of divorce. *Journal of Consulting & Clinical Psychology, 68*(5), 843–856.

Wolf, A., & Lozoff, B. (1989). Object attachment, thumbsucking, and the passage to sleep. *Journal of the American Academy of Child and Adolescent Psychiatry, 28,* 287–292.

Wong, M. M., & Csikzentmihalyi, M. (1991). Affiliation motivation and daily experience: Some issues on gender differences. *Journal of Personality and Social Psychology, 60,* 154–164.

Wood, E., et al. (2000). Extent to which low-level use of antiretroviral treatment could curb the AIDS epidemic in sub-Saharan Africa. *The Lancet, 355,* 2095–2100.

Wood, N. S., et al. (2000). Neurologic and developmental disability after extremely preterm birth. *The New England Journal of Medicine, 343*(6), 378–384.

Woodard, J. L., & Fine, M. A. (1991). Long-term effects of self-supervised and adult-supervised child care arrangements on personality traits, emotional adjustment, and cognitive development. *Journal of Applied Developmental Psychology,* 12, 73–85.

Woods, N. S., Eyler, F. D., Behnke, M., & Conlon, M. (1993). Cocaine use during pregnancy: Maternal depressive symptoms and infant neurobehavior over the first month. *Infant Behavior and Development,* 16, 83–98.

Woods, S. C., Schwartz, M. W., Baskin, D. G., & Seeley, R. J. (2000). Food intake and the regulation of body weight. *Annual Review of Psychology, 51,* 255–277.

Woodward, A. L., & Markman, E. M. (1991). Constraints on learning as default assumptions: Comments on Merriman and Bowman's "The mutuality exclusivity bias in children's word learning." *Developmental Review, 11,* 137–163.

Woolfolk, A. E. (2001). *Educational psychology* (8th ed.). Boston: Allyn & Bacon.

Woolley, J. D., & Wellman, H. M. (1993). Origin and truth: Young children's understanding of imaginary mental representations. *Child Development, 64,* 1–17.

Worell, J. (1990). Images of women in psychology. In M. Paludi & G. A. Steuernagel (Eds.), *Foundations for a feminist restructuring of the academic disciplines.* New York: Harrington Park.

Worell, J., Stilwell, D., Oakley, D., & Robinson, D. (1999). Educating about women and gender: Cognitive, personal and professional outcomes. *Psychology of Women Quarterly, 23*(4), 797–811.

World Health Organization. (2001, August 17). Children's environmental health—An issue of great concern. http://www.who.int

Wright, C., & Birks, E. (2000). Risk factors for failure to thrive: A population-based survey. *Child: Care, Health & Development, 26*(1), 5–16.

Wright, D. W., & Young, R. (1998). The effects of family structure and maternal employment on the development of gender-related attitudes among men and women. *Journal of Family Issues, 19*(3), 300–314.

Wu, J., et al. (1999). Serotonin and learned helplessness: A regional study of 5–HT-sub(1A), 5–HT-sub(2A) receptors and the serotonin transport site in rat brain. *Journal of Psychiatric Research, 33*(1), 17–22.

Wu, P., et al. (2001). Factors associated with use of mental health services for depression by children and adolescents. *Psychiatric Services, 52*(2), 189–195.

Wulff, K., & Siegmund, R. (2001). Circadian and ultradian time patterns in human behaviour: Part 1: Activity monitoring of families from prepartum to postpartum. *Biological Rhythm Research, 31*(5), 581–602.

Wynn, K. (1990). Children's understanding of counting. *Cognition, 36,* 155–193.

Wynn, K. (1992a, August 27). Addition and subtraction by human infants. *Nature, 358,* pp. 749–750.

Wynn, K. (1992b). Children's acquisition of the number words and the counting system. *Cognitive Psychology, 24,* 220–251.

Yamada, H., et al. (2000). A milestone for normal development of the infantile brain detected by functional MRI. *Neurology, 55*(2), 218–223.

Yamazaki, J. N., & Schull, W. J. (1990). Perinatal loss and neurological abnormalities among children of the atomic bomb. *Journal of the American Medical Association, 264,* 605–609.

Yang, O. S. (2000). Guiding children's verbal plan and evaluation during free play: An application of Vygotsky's genetic epistemology to the early childhood classroom. *Early Childhood Education Journal, 28*(1), 3–10.

Yaniv, I., & Shatz, M. (1988). Children's understanding of perceptibility. In J. W. Astinton, P. L. Harris, & D. R. Olson (Eds.), *Developing theories of mind.* London: Cambridge University Press.

Yaniv, I., & Shatz, M. (1991). Heuristics of reasoning and analogy in children's visual perspective taking. *Child Development, 61,* 1491–1501.

Yarrow, L. J., & Goodwin, M. S. (1973). The immediate impact of separation: Reactions of infants to a change in mother figures. In L. J. Stone, H. T. Smith, & L. B. Murphy (Eds.), *The competent infant: Research and commentary.* New York: Basic Books.

Yarrow, L. J., Goodwin, M. S., Manheimer, H., & Milowe, I. D. (1971, March). *Infant experiences and cognitive and personality development at ten years.* Paper presented at the meeting of the American Orthopsychiatric Association, Washington, DC.

Yates, T. (1991). Theories of cognitive development. In M. Lewis (Ed.), *Child and adolescent psychiatry: A comprehensive textbook.* Baltimore: Williams & Williams.

Yatham, L. N., et al. (2000). Brain serotonin$_2$ receptors in major depression: A positron emission tomography study. *Archives of General Psychiatry, 57,* 850–858.

Yirmiya, N., Sigman, M. D., Kasari, C., & Mundy, P. (1992). Empathy and cognition in high-functioning children with autism. *Child Development, 63,* 150–160.

Yokota, F., & Thompson, K. M. (2000). Violence in G-rated animated films. *Journal of the American Medical Association, 283,* 2716–2720.

York, J., Vandercook, T., MacDonald, C., Heise-Neff, C., & Caughey, E. (1992). Feedback about integrating middle-school students with severe disabilities in general education classes. *Exceptional Children, 58,* 244–258.

Young, G., & Gagnon, M. (1990). Neonatal laterality, birth stress, familial sinistrality, and left-brain inhibition. *Developmental Neuropsychology, 6,* 127–150.

Youngblade, L. M., & Belsky, J. (1992). Parent–child antecedents of 5–year-olds' close friendships: A longitudinal analysis. *Developmental Psychology, 28,* 700–713.

Youngstrom, N. (1991, September). Drug exposure in home elicits worst behaviors. *APA Monitor,* p. 23.

Youniss, J., & Haynie, D. L. (1992). Friendship in adolescence. *Developmental and Behavioral Pediatrics, 13,* 59–66.

Zabin, L. S. (1991). Early sexual onset. In R. M. Lerner, A. C. Petersen, & J. Brooks-Gunn (Eds.), *Encyclopedia of adolescence.* New York: Garland.

Zahn-Waxler, C., Radke-Yarrow, M., & Wagner, E. (1992). Development of concern for others. *Developmental Psychology, 28,* 126–136.

Zahr, L. K., Parker, S., & Cole, J. (1992). Comparing the effects of neonatal intensive care unit intervention on premature infants at different weights. *Developmental and Behavioral Pediatrics, 13,* 165–172.

Zajonc, R. B. (2001). The family dynamics of intellectual development. *American Psychologist, 56*(6/7).

Zajonc, R. B., & Mullally, P. R. (1997). Birth order: Reconciling conflicting effects. *American Psychologist, 52*(7), 685–699.

Zametkin, A. J., Nordahl, T. E., Gross, M., King, A. C., Semple, W. E., Rumsey, J., Hamburger, S., & Cohen, R. M. (1990). Cerebral glucose metabolism in adults with hyperactivity of childhood onset. *The New England Journal of Medicine, 323,* 1361–1366.

Zarbatany, L., Hartmann, D. P., & Rankin, D. B. (1990). The psychological function of pre-adolescent peer activities. *Child Development, 61,* 1067–1080.

Zarbatany, L., McDougall, P., & Hymel, S. (2000). Gender-differentiated experience in the peer culture: Links to intimacy in preadolescence. *Social Development, 9*(1), 62–79.

Zaslow, M. J., Rabinovich, B. A., & Suwalsky, J. T. D. (1991). From maternal employment to child outcomes: Pre-existing group differences and moderating variables. In S. V. Lerner & N. L. Galambos (Eds.), *Employed mothers and their children.* New York: Garland.

Zelazo, N. A., Zelazo, P. R., Cohen, K. M., & Zelazo, P. D. (1993). Specificity of practice effects on elementary neuromotor patterns. *Developmental Psychology, 29,* 686–691.

Zelazo, P. R. (1998). McGraw and the development of unaided walking. *Developmental Review, 18*(4), 449–471.

Zelkowitz, P., & Milet, T. H. (1996). Postpartum psychiatric disorders: Their relationship to psychological adjustment and marital satisfaction in the spouses. *Journal of Abnormal Psychology, 105,* 281–285.

Zeskind, P. S., & Shingler, L. (1991). Child abusers' perceptual responses to newborn infant cries varying in pitch. *Infant Behavior and Development, 14,* 335–347.

Zhang, W., & Lin, C. (1999). The development of children's social perspective-taking and its relation to their peer interaction. *Acta Psychologica Sinica, 31*(4), 418–427.

Zheng, S., & Colombo, J. (1989). Sibling configuration and gender differences in preschool social participation. *Journal of Genetic Psychology, 150,* 45–50.

Zhou, Z., Bray, M. A., Kehle, T. J., & Xin, T. (2001). Similarity of deleterious effects of divorce on Chinese and American children. *School Psychology International, 22*(3), 357–363.

Zigler, E. (1999). Head Start is not child care. *American Psychologist, 54*(2), 142.

Zigler, E., Abelson, W. D., Trickett, P. K., & Seitz, V. (1982). Is an intervention program necessary in order to improve economically disadvantaged children's IQ scores? *Child Development, 53,* 340–348.

Zigler, E., & Seitz, V. (1982). Social policy and intelligence. In R. Sternberg (Ed.), *Handbook of human intelligence.* New York: Cambridge University Press.

Zigler, E., & Styfco, S. J. (2001). Extended childhood intervention prepares children for school and beyond. *Journal of the American Medical Association, 285*(18), 2378–2380.

Zigler, E. Taussig, C., & Black, K. (1992, August). Early childhood intervention: A promising preventive for juvenile delinquency. *American Psychologist, 47,* 997–1006.

Zimmerman, B. J. (2000). Self-efficacy: An essential motive to learn. *Contemporary Educational Psychology, 25*(1), 82–91.

Zimmermann, P., Maier, M. A., Winter, M., & Grossmann, K. E. (2001). Attachment and adolescents' emotion regulation during a joint problem-solving task with a friend. *International Journal of Behavioral Development, 25*(4), 331–343.

Zipfel, S., et al. (2000). Long-term prognosis in anorexia nervosa: Lessons from a 21-year follow-up study. *The Lancet, 355*(9205), 721–722.

Zuckerman, B., & Frank, D. A. (1992, February). "Crack kids": Not broken. *Pediatrics, 89,* 337–339.

Zweigenhaft, R. L., & Von Ammon, J. (2000). Birth order and civil disobedience: A test of Sulloway's "born to rebel" hypothesis. *Journal of Social Psychology, 140*(5), 624–627.

Name Index

Subject Index